FINANCIAL ACCOUNTING AND MANAGERIAL CONTROL FOR NONPROFIT ORGANIZATIONS

Regina E. Herzlinger
Professor/Harvard University

Denise Nitterhouse
Associate Professor/DePaul University

COLLEGE DIVISION South-Western Publishing Co.

Cincinnati Ohio

Publisher: Mark R. Hubble
Sponsoring Editor: David L. Shaut
Developmental Editor: Sara E. Bates
Production Editor: Rebecca Roby
Production House: Sheridan Publications Services
Cover Designer: AbneyHuninghake Design
Interior Designer: The Book Company
Marketing Manager: Martin W. Lewis

AK60AA

ISBN: 0-538-81602-3

1 2 3 4 5 6 7 8 9 Dl 1 0 9 8 7 6 5 4 3

Printed in the United States of America

Library of Congress Cataloging-in-Publication Data

Herzlinger, Regina E.
    Financial accounting and managerial control for nonprofit
organizations / Regina E. Herzlinger and Denise Nitterhouse.
        p.   cm.
    Includes bibliographical references and index.
    ISBN 0-538-81602-3
    1. Corporations, Nonprofit--United States--Accounting.
2. Corporations, Nonprofit--United States--Finance.
I. Nitterhouse, Denise,   II. Title.
HF5686.N56H47   1994
657'.98--dc20   91-17144
                                                                 CIP

 This book is printed on acid-free paper that meets Environmental Protection Agency standards for recycled paper.

I(T)P South-Western is a subsidiary of ITP (International Thomson Publishing). The trademark ITP is used under license.

Foreword

DURING THE PAST TWENTY YEARS, WE had the great good fortune to teach financial management to tens of thousands of students, executives, and board members of nonprofit organizations. They shared many characteristics. In addition to their devotion to nonprofits, they were lively, intelligent, and accomplished. They generally shared one other characteristic—an inability to comprehend the financial activities of their organizations. Able, energetic students of public and nonprofit administration could not interpret financial statements; shrewd, tough police chiefs could not evaluate the cities' financial management of their hard-earned pension funds; articulate public broadcasting executives could not develop a financial strategy to secure their organizations' futures; and accomplished business executives and professionals on the boards of large hospitals and colleges could not assess their organizations' financial status.

This condition was vividly illustrated by the experience of a businessman sitting on the board of a world-famous museum. He was recruited by the board because of the great success of the entrepreneurial firm he created. His financial acumen was particularly noted. But he was frustrated by his inability to comprehend the museum's financial condition. He sat through meeting after meeting in a daze. During financial presentations, strange words and concepts floated past his ears; he had never heard them before. Finally, he stopped one of the presentations:

Help me understand the fundamental terms you use. What is a fund? A transfer? Then tell me what our financial status is now and how the accounting statements help me to understand it. Last, since we are now contemplating doubling the square feet of the museum—a very important change—help me understand the pros and cons of the financial considerations. And do it in English. It is the only language I speak.

A stunned silence greeted his outburst. The presenter recovered first, saying:

> Forgive me. I have been so caught up with the intricacies of my work I never thought about how difficult it is to communicate. You are right. I was speaking a different language. From now on, I will check myself to ensure that I speak English.

Many others share this businessman's experience. No matter how intelligent and energetic, they cannot comprehend the financial management of their nonprofit organizations because they never learned to speak the language. And the nonprofit financial language is different from that of business organizations because nonprofit organizations differ in important ways from business organizations. The language difference is not pedantic; it reflects the differences in the basic missions of the organizations and their sources and uses of money.

The purpose of this book is to teach the nonprofit financial language so that our readers can participate actively and intelligently in the financial management of nonprofit organizations. It differs from other books that bear similar titles. We are interested in teaching present and potential managers and board members, not accountants or financial managers. Our focus is managerial rather than technical. Accounting terminology and financial procedures are discussed because they are the language in which financial management is conducted, and for no other reason. When technical subjects are addressed, they are discussed as they relate to management, rather than as ends in themselves.

Our managerial focus manifests itself in the tone and content of this book. As in this foreword, our tone is personal and informal. We use many real-life examples. And we try to write in English, avoiding buzzwords, arcane accounting terms, and tautological definitions (e.g., a fund is a fund). When we use technical terms, we ensure that we have clearly defined them and that they are relevant for managerial purposes. For this reason, the order of presentation of the material is different from that of other books. We place the chapters that discuss techniques, like those of accounting or discounting, after the chapters that describe their purpose, to underscore that our goal is to impart managerial, not solely technical, knowledge. The content of this book is managerial too. It addresses the key topics of nonprofit financial management and how managers implement them. The book is studded with case studies drawn from real-life managerial decisions and issues, to buttress our managerial orientation.

The book is divided into three parts. The first discusses the language of financial management and how to use the financial statements written in this language. Sedulous readers of this section will, at its end, be able to interpret nonprofit financial statements and assess the nonprofit organization's financial status. The second part discusses the internal managerial activities that translate strategic dreams into financial reality: planning and budgeting processes that appropriately reflect the financial steps needed to implement a strategic vision; managerial control systems that delineate managerial responsibilities, measure their attainments, and motivate and reward managers; and the decision-making techniques that assist in allocating limited resources. Readers of this part will become familiar with the range of managerial activities available for careful, productive financial management of nonprofit organizations. The third part applies the lessons of the first two to the four major sectors of nonprofit organizations: colleges and universities, hospitals, governments, and voluntary health and welfare and other nonprofit organizations. It enables readers who specialize in one of these types of nonprofits to focus on its unique accounting and financial management issues.

We do not mean to imply that the resulting book makes for light reading. *Financial Accounting and Managerial Control for Nonprofit Organizations* is a difficult book because the underlying concepts are complicated and implementing them is at least as hard. We have not sacrificed depth for breadth. This book is not a mile wide and an inch deep; its scope is comprehensive and every topic is discussed in depth. Rather, we have tried to make the learning process as easy and relevant as possible, on the basis of our many years in teaching, consulting, and participating on the boards of nonprofit organizations.

Because this book addresses many audiences, ranging from beginning students of nonprofit management to seasoned nonprofit board members, you may find some of its parts not suited to your interests or experiences. For example, executives and board members may not find the questions that end each chapter of interest while new students of administration may find some of the case studies overwhelmingly detailed. You may also find some sections repetitious. This too is by design. The repetition is based on our observation that most people learn this subject best with repeated discussions of the topics. If you think that you know the issue being discussed well enough or that a particular section is not relevant to your needs, please feel free to skip that part of the book.

This book is inevitably shaped by our experiences and interests. Both of us derive great satisfaction from teaching. Because our teaching style is interactive, we have benefited from the feedback of our many students. Both of us are involved with the Harvard Business School, an institution whose managerial, real-life focus we, and this book, reflect. And both of us are fundamentally interested in financial management, a topic to which we have devoted much of our professional lives.

Although we jointly reviewed each part of the book, our contributions, and those of others to it, are, nevertheless, separable. Professor Herzlinger was the sole author of Part Two, the Instructor's Guide, and the end-of-chapter material. She also authored all but three of the case studies in the book and was the primary author of Part One. She developed and analyzed the Everdash College and Wabash cases and analyzed the hospital case which are discussed in separate chapters of Part Three. Professor Nitterhouse provided the detailed analyses of Everdash and the hospital case, was otherwise the primary author of the text in Part Three, and contributed significantly to Chapters 3, 4, and 6 in Part One. We are grateful to Professor David Sherman, who developed the example of financial statement preparation of Chapter 15 and prepared the Pepys College discussion in Chapter 6; Professor Nancy Kane, who developed the hospital case study in Chapter 17; and the late Graeme Taylor, as represented by Charles Greene, Professor Robert Howell, and Professor Claudine Malone for permitting the use of their case studies in this book. Professor Herzlinger is also grateful for the support of the president of the college, which she renamed Everdash, of the municipal officials of the town she renamed Wabash, and the Lyndhurst Foundation of Chattanooga, Tennessee.

We are very grateful to the many people who helped us with this book. We will acknowledge them separately:

I, Professor Herzlinger, owe foremost thanks to my students at the Harvard Schools of Business Administration, Education, Public Administration, and Public Health, and the University of Chicago's School of Social Service. I am also grateful to the executives in the professional education courses I conducted for the National Association of Educational Broadcasting and the Girl Scouts of the USA, and Harvard University's Institute for Educational Management and Program for Health Systems Management. I am greatly indebted to the executives of nonprofit organizations who so willingly shared their wisdom with me—foremost among them are the brilliant Frances Hesselbein and Harold Richmond—and to Peter Ferro and now Professors David Sherman and Nancy Kane, who served so ably as my research assistants. Robert Culver, Joel Myerson, and Robert Forrester were very helpful. Professor Robert Anthony, who inspired my work in this field, has my greatest regard. I am also grateful to the late Jon Cook of Support Centers of America for his careful reading of this text.

A special thanks to Diana Gaeta for pulling it all together, to Aimee Hamel for her word processing skills, to Sarah Eriksen for assisting with my research, and to the anonymous organizations that helped me with the Everdash and Wabash cases and analyses.

I, Professor Nitterhouse, owe thanks to my students at the Harvard University Graduate School of Public Administration, the University of Illinois, DePaul University, and the Center for Enterprise Development. I am also grateful to the many nonprofit managers and board members who have been so generous with their penetrating insights and questions. Thanks to Lynn E. Martino for her thorough editing and to Morgan McCurdy for assistance with assembling and processing cases.

We are also grateful to the South-Western Publishing team, particularly to Mark Hubble, James Sitlington, Sara Bates, Rebecca Roby, and David Shaut.

We both wish to thank the following people for assisting us in the development of this book by providing us with timely, informative reviews:

Kent John Chabotar (Vice President for Finance and Administration and Treasurer, Bowdoin College)

Florence Corsello (Controller, Girl Scouts of the United States of America)

Mark Covaleski (Professor, University of Wisconsin)

Robert Culver (Senior Vice President/Treasurer, Northeastern University)

Allan Drebin (Professor, Northwestern University)

Eshan H. Feroz (Associate Professor, University of Minnesota—Duluth)

J. Richard Gaintner (President and CEO, New England Deaconess Hospital)

Jesse Hughes (Associate Professor, Old Dominion University)

Nancy Kane (Professor, Harvard School of Public Health)

Ronald Kovener (Director, Policy and Government Relations, Healthcare Financial Management Association)

Jay Pieper (Senior Vice President and CFO, Brigham and Women's Hospital)

Benjamin N. Pyne (Graduate Student, Harvard University)

Kris K. Raman (Professor, University of North Texas)

Carol Raphael (CEO, Visiting Nurse Service of New York)

Ann Laura Ryan (Senior Associate, Prudential Investment Corporation)

Robert Scott (Vice President for Finance, Harvard University)

Mary Alice Seville (Associate Professor, Oregon State University)

David Sherman (Professor, Northeastern University)

Richard Siegrist (Adjunct Lecturer, Harvard School of Public Health)

Russy D. Sumariwalla (Vice President and Senior Fellow, United Way Strategic Institute, United Way of America)

Ann Thornburg (Partner/Northeast Region for Healthcare, Coopers and Lybrand)

Of course, none of these people are responsible for any errors that remain in the book.

Regina E. Herzlinger, Belmont, Massachusetts
Denise Nitterhouse, Chicago, Illinois
June 1993

Contents in Brief

Contents

Chapter 12 Motivating and Rewarding Performance 417

Chapter 13 The Framework for Financial Decision-Making in Nonprofit Organizations 449

Chapter 14 Techniques for Financial Decision-Making 491

Chapter 18 Governmental Entities 797

1   A View from the Top

NONPROFIT ORGANIZATIONS FULFILL THE NOBLEST PURPOSES of our society. They educate us, nourish our souls with music and art, feed our poor, and protect the helpless among us. They are the caretakers of the national conscience, pushing and prodding our system of government to uphold the tenets of democracy. They employ people of extraordinary courage and altruism, who risk their lives in raging fires and festering slums for the greater good of humanity. They uphold the highest values of civilization: knowledge, beauty, charity, and freedom.

The nonprofit sector is a surprisingly large part of the American economy, as well as a major force in shaping its society. Its largest part, the government, consists of more than 80,000 federal, state, and local governmental units, with expenditures of $1,696 billion in 1986.[1] The size of the private nonprofit sector has been pegged at 970,000 nonprofit organizations, with 7.4 million employees and contributions of $104 billion annually.[2] More than 40 million Americans served as volunteers to these organizations in 1989.[3] A sector of this size and importance deserves the very best available management techniques and practices.

WHAT IS A NONPROFIT ORGANIZATION?

Nonprofit organizations comprise a very diverse set. Under our nonprofit umbrella, we include any organization that is exempted from payment of taxes and whose primary purpose is to benefit society. Our definition thus includes federal, state, and local government, hospitals, museums, associations,

---

[1]Bureau of the Census, *Statistical Abstract of the United States: 1989*, 109th ed. (Washington, DC: 1989), Tables No. 445-446.
[2]John A. Byrne, ''Profiting from the Nonprofits,'' *Business Week* (March 26, 1990): 68.
[3]''One in Five Americans Volunteer Some Time,'' *The Wall Street Journal*, 31 May 1990, p. B1.

foundations, cultural institutions, national service organizations, religious groups, community-based welfare, and similar organizations.

Others provide different definitions. Some define them as "nonbusinesses," arguing that nonprofit organizations are unlike businesses because they do not exist to earn a profit. This negative definition of a positive organization is not ours. While we concur that nonprofit organizations do not exist to earn a profit, they should be defined positively, by their immense contributions to a civilized way of life, rather than negatively, by the absence of a profit-seeking motive.

Others seek to define them legally. The benefits nonprofit organizations provide are so highly valued by our culture that they are exempted from paying income and other taxes, and complex legal strictures have been created to define precisely the types of organizations that qualify for these valuable tax exemptions. But we reject these legalisms as adequate definitions for nonprofit organizations. Their judicial basis deflates the essentially spiritual concept of these organizations with the pinpricks of its legal details.

Defining the nature of nonprofit organizations is no mere academic quibble—it is fundamental to their success. An organization defined by legal or financial requirements cannot serve as the keeper of civilization's heart, mind, and soul. And that is ultimately the purpose of nonprofit organizations—our great colleges and universities, museums, symphonies, charities, governments, and public interest groups.

THE ROLE OF MANAGEMENT IN NONPROFIT ORGANIZATIONS

Our definition of purpose imposes extraordinary demands on the managers of nonprofit organizations. Maintaining financial and organizational stability or growth is not sufficient for successful exercise of their responsibilities, as it would be in a business. In nonprofit organizations, their foremost mandate is a spiritual one. Attaining a balance between sober financial management and the creation of enlightening services is far from easy. The difficulty is amplified by two characteristics of these organizations. First, they are staffed by dedicated, articulate service providers, who rarely value prudent financial management. Few educators, curators, physicians, musicians, social workers, mayors, or public-interest lawyers will ever concede that their activities are adequately funded or that managerial review of their work is appropriate. For example, after Professor Herzlinger's presentation of her analysis of the managerial strengths and weaknesses of the Costa Rican health care system, one listener responded: "That's all very well and good. But, why are we discussing management? Is not our largest and foremost obligation to provide health care services to the poor?" To him, as to many other professionals, management concerns must always take a back seat.

Second, nonprofit organizations lack the signals of success or failure generated for businesses by the working of the marketplace. When General Motors' sales are down, the market provides it with a clear signal: we prefer other cars to yours. But when patrons fail to throng an *avant-garde* museum exhibition, the signal is not nearly so clear. After all, it is the museum's purpose to shape and guide our artistic taste and, in its initial phase, cultural leadership is almost inevitably unpopular. Another important market message also is absent in nonprofit organizations. When General Motors' financial performance is weak, its stock takes a pounding. In this way, the millions of people involved in the stock market send the company a clear message of their assessment of its management. But no stock exchange exists for nonprofit organizations. They lack the unambiguous evaluation of managerial success or failure it provides.

Managers of nonprofit organizations must balance the passionate advocacy of their professional employees with signals of organizational effectiveness devined from an ambiguous external environment. Although it is not our purpose here to help managers best fulfill the service mandates of their nonprofit organizations, we hope to help nonprofit managers and their boards with the latter skill—we can help them to measure their managerial effectiveness and, if it is found wanting, to improve it. We label this measurement process *financial analysis* and the process of improvement as *managerial control*. In the first part of this book, we discuss how to simulate the workings of the marketplace in analyzing the financial performance of a nonprofit. In the second, we discuss the use of various managerial control techniques to improve its financial performance.

This book is thus about two key activities: evaluating performance and using the results of the evaluation for positive end results. Because organizations conduct many of these crucial activities in financial terms, we devote considerable space to discussing the financial language of accounting and financial techniques. But do not be misled by the number of pages these discussions require. It is our purpose to help nonprofit organization conduct effective financial analysis and management. We view mastery of accounting and financial techniques merely as a tool for achieving that goal, not as an end in itself.

FINANCIAL ANALYSIS AND MANAGERIAL CONTROL

Frances Hesselbein exemplifies the dazzling organizational results that can be achieved through financial analysis and managerial control. When Mrs. Hesselbein was appointed the national executive director of the Girl Scouts of the USA (GSUSA) in 1976, she found a somewhat dispirited organization. Some of the members feared that the days of its former glory were long gone. Both adult and girl memberships were waning and revenues were dropping. When she resigned in 1990, the GSUSA was completely turned around: membership at an all-time high, positive staff morale, and stable finances.

Achieving this reversal of fortunes was akin to turning a battleship around in a lake. For one thing, GSUSA is a massive organization, with 3.2 million girl members and 751,000 adult volunteers. For another, it is an affiliation of local councils, each directed by an autonomous board of directors, rather than an hierarchical organization. While Mrs. Hesselbein could inspire, prod, and cajole local councils, she could not hire or fire their officers, determine their salaries, or in any other way directly supervise their work. Last, GSUSA was rich in history—some would say mired in it. The organization had a strong sense of its heritage, one it was reluctant to change.

An Example of Financial Analysis

When she took office, Mrs. Hesselbein evaluated the organization's status. She found many positives as well as negatives. On the positive side were the dedicated volunteers, board members, and career employees (each council employs staff members). Then too, many young girls increasingly required GSUSA's services—the friendship of other girls, the familiarity with nature, and the mastery of the outdoors that are the hallmarks of the scouting experience. Selling the famous Girl Scout cookies could also be an important part of their development: making a sale, delivering the cookies, and collecting the money increased young girls' sense of competence and self-confidence. And the organization was virtually debt free.

But there were negatives as well. Girl and adult membership was decreasing. Those who could most benefit from the services, the inner-city girls who were far removed from the Girl Scouts' camping properties, were not sufficiently represented. There seemed to be far too many camps—some were barely used and others were in bad physical shape. And Mrs. Hesselbein was concerned about the magnitude of the revenues generated by the cookie sale. They were accounting for an increasingly larger fraction of total revenues. Were means and ends being inverted? Were cookies sold for the revenues they generated rather than for their role in the Scouts' development? Many councils were surprised by their year-end financial results. If they were negative—and bad news was becoming more frequent—the staff understandably became depressed. Morale was plummeting.

Let us restate Mrs. Hesselbein's analysis in financial terms. She performed four fundamental analyses:

(1) *Match between financial resources and goals.* This analysis evaluates whether the organizations's financial resources are being generated and used in a manner consistent with its mission.

(2) *Intergenerational equity.* This analysis assesses whether the present generation is using no more and no less than its fair share of organizational resources (the amount it contributed).

(3) *Match between sources and uses of resources.* This analysis examines whether assets are matched with appropriate sources of funds.

(4) *Sustainability of financial resources.* This analysis assesses the stability of revenues, expenses, assets, and liabilities.

The terms of financial analyses might seem far removed from GSUSA and nonprofit organizations. We will illustrate their relevance below, fitting Mrs. Hesselbein's observations to them.

(1) *Match between financial resources and goals.* When Mrs. Hesselbein observed the possibility of "too many camps," she was questioning whether the quantity of Girl Scouts resources invested in camping activities was appropriately matched with the importance of camping as a goal. Almost all of the assets of some councils and nearly 60 percent of their expenses were used for camping; but only about 20 percent of their girl members attended the camps. Her concern about the fraction of revenues generated by the sale of cookies focused on yet another potential mismatch between goals and financial resources: the possible subversion of the goal of developing girls' character for the achievement of financial resources. Finally, the absence of liabilities was a mixed blessing. Perhaps the councils with substantial real estate were unwittingly tying up resources that could otherwise produce services. A loan secured by some of the council's substantial property holdings, or their sale, would free up this money for use in service delivery, particularly to poorer girls.

(2) *Intergenerational Equity.* Another appropriate match is between revenues and expenses. Revenues should generally exceed expenses by a reasonable margin, even in a nonprofit organization. With this "profit margin," the organization can maintain its physical plant and provide a cushion against adverse financial events. But if revenues are less than expenses, the organization consumes past resources to provide current services. Organizations with a continual pattern of losses cannot survive. They deplete the past and rob the future to finance the present. Mrs. Hesselbein's concern with "losses" reflected a deeper concern with GSUSA's ability to perpetuate itself.

(3) *Match between sources and uses of resources.* Capital sources and uses should have similar lifetimes. When we buy a house, a long-lived asset, we usually finance it with a long-lived loan. Expensive long-lived assets generally cannot be purchased over a short period of time. Similarly, long-lived expenses should be matched with revenue sources that are likely to last for a similar period. For example, the costs of maintaining a building should be financed with a long-term source of revenue, such as the income

earned from invested capital. But in the Girl Scout councils, the cost of the camps, a long-term expense, was paid primarily from short-term cookie sale revenues.

(4) *Sustainability of financial resources.* Revenues earned from only one or two sources are riskier than revenues earned from many sources because the loss of these few sources has much more serious impact on the organization. Mrs. Hesselbein's concern about the large fraction of revenues generated by the sale of cookies and her recommendation for development of other sources of money proved prescient. Her wisdom was borne out a few years later when reports of glass shards found in the cookies caused sales to plummet. (The reports were false.) The councils that heeded her advice and diversified their revenue sources were much less affected by the decline in cookie sales.

Just as dispersion of sources is a hallmark of sustainable revenues, flexibility and controllability are desired characteristics of expenses. Fixed costs—for example, those of a tenured faculty or long-term employees—are virtually impossible to change even if demand declines. They thus impose a heavy burden on an organization. Provision of a camping program entails considerable fixed costs in staff and facilities.

Assets should be as dispersed and stable as revenues. Excessive concentration of resources in any one asset increases the organization's vulnerability to changes in the usefulness, cost, or market value of that asset. Organizations whose assets are invested primarily in a computer risk its obsolescence. Girl Scout councils whose assets were invested primarily in camps experienced the unhappy consequences of the sizeable decline in their use.

Ratio Analysis

Financial ratio analysis formalizes and quantifies the financial data used in these four analyses. The most frequent financial ratios and their relationship to each of the four analyses are described in Table 1-1.

Like Mrs. Hesselbein, we should use accounting information to evaluate the financial health of the organization. Is it in excellent health? Does it have a cold? The flu? Or is it time to put out the RIP sign? The diagnostic dimensions of liquidity, solvency, asset management, return on invested capital, profitability, and revenue and expense composition presented in Table 1-1 are like medical diagnostics such as temperature, blood pressure, cholesterol count, heart rate, and reflexes. Each is designed to detect a certain type of symptom; a collection of symptoms, in turn, reflects the underlying state of health and suggests an appropriate treatment plan.

TABLE 1-1 **Financial Ratios Used in Financial Analysis**

Ratio	Role in Financial Analysis
Asset turnover	Matches assets and goals. Slow turnover assets require considerable investment and reduce flexibility.
Profitability and return on invested capital	Analyzes intergenerational equity and the match between sources and uses of money. Neither excessive profits nor losses are desirable.
Liquidity and solvency	Matches sources and uses of financial resources. Is the organization flirting with bankruptcy in the short-term? In the long-term?
Percentage of revenues, by source	Analyzes quality of revenues and relation to mission. Is the organization excessively dependent on a few revenue sources? Are revenue sources consistent with the organization's mission?
Percentage of expenses, by type	Analyzes quality of expenses and relation to mission. A large percentage of fixed expenses decreases the organization's flexibility. Are expenses consistent with the organization's mission?

An Example of Managerial Control

Having noted these problems and opportunities, Mrs. Hesselbein undertook a program to correct the problems by building on the base of the organization's considerable strengths. Her purpose also was to instill greater confidence in council employees and to celebrate their contributions to American society. "I want you to see yourselves life-size," she would say at annual conventions.

Her methods for accomplishing these goals were many, but primary among them was a "corporate management" process. Councils were urged to use the techniques of business—indeed, to think of themselves as businesses, for managerial purposes. The process was depicted in a series of manuals on each of the following topics: Planning, Budgeting, Pricing, Reporting, and Control. These are the cornerstones of managerial control, and are discussed in Part Two.

The corporate management process was wildly successful. Not only did overall membership soar, but minority membership also increased from 5 percent in 1979 to 15 percent in 1989. Financial resources became more consistent with the Girl Scout mission and of higher quality. And staff morale levels zoomed. The corporate management process gave them dignity and strength. They were no longer surprised by year-end financial results. Instead, they planned the results and, because they were superlative managers, they caused their plans to materialize.

None of this was easy. Ten years and enormous effort were required. But the turnaround was accomplished. And financial analysis and management were key to its success.

THE CURRENT STATUS OF FINANCIAL ACCOUNTING AND MANAGERIAL CONTROL IN NONPROFIT ORGANIZATIONS

Despite their importance, financial analysis and managerial control remain among the most difficult areas for managers and directors of nonprofit organizations to conquer. The inherently difficult basic subjects are shrouded in a mysterious veil of technical jargon, guarded by the high priests of the accounting world. Moreover, these subjects are relatively foreign to nonprofit cultures based in "people skills" and "social concerns." There is simply no good way to acquire and polish such financial analysis and management skills in most nonprofit organizations. Historically, there has been little support or reward for doing so: no well-developed body of knowledge, no set of curricula, and no pool of trained personnel from which to draw. Finally, the accounting and management information systems required of nonprofit organizations are much more complex than those required of business organizations of comparable size. Although the requirement that nonprofits be accountable to their many constituencies is entirely appropriate, it is onerous because nonprofits have so many more constituencies than profit-oriented organizations. They must track not only financial resource generation and consumption but also outputs that cannot be measured in financial terms, and may be very difficult to measure in any quantifiable terms.[4]

Nevertheless, effective accounting and managerial control practices are at least as important to nonprofits as to for-profit organizations. American cities that teeter on the brink of bankruptcy have found this out the hard way. The U.S. government's financial problems are substantial and unfortunately there is no higher power the public can look to for a bail-out. Several educational institutions have already closed their doors and a number of hospitals are following suit. And the financial scandals of nonprofit organizations that abuse the public trust are all too frequent. Among the latest of these is the tragic misuse of funds in the United Way, a multi-billion dollar U.S. charity.

---

[4]See Regina E. Herzlinger, "Managing the Finances of Nonprofit Organizations," *California Management Review* (Spring 1979) and "Why Data Systems in Nonprofit Organizations Fail," *Harvard Business Review* (January 1977) for further discussion.

Role of Accounting

We all speak a common language to communicate. Although accounting has been called the language of business, it is really the language of management. The accounting language helps to frame the way we view our organizations and the things on which we focus.

Speaking the language of accounting is complicated by the existence of accounting practices in different nonprofit organizations that are more diverse than their substantive organizational and mission-related differences would lead one to predict. Different types of organizations may follow different accounting rules, and similar types of events may be accounted for differently within the same organization. The absence of uniform accounting standards enabled the development of a variety of practices, each with its proponents and detractors.

The rigid structure of double-entry bookkeeping mechanics may mask the essentially interpretive nature of accounting. Accounting rules and procedures consist of social conventions rather than physical-science principles; they are negotiated and invented more than they are discovered. Many otherwise savvy managers are astonished at the difficulty and the lack of guidance in recognizing certain types of accounting events. There is seldom a single, hard and fast, right answer; there are often many ways of viewing, and thus of accounting for, a given event. And even when accounting rules are clear, it may still be appropriate to develop supplementary information based on different accounting procedures for certain tasks.

Current Status of
Nonprofit Financial Management

Evidence of past financial mismanagement abounds. Taxes are skyrocketing today because for many years politicians have made unfulfillable commitments for future pension benefits. They knew they were safe; accounting did not require their promises to be reflected as current costs and financial management did not require current cash outlays. Nor did accounting reflect the deterioration of our infrastructure as politicians delayed much-needed maintenance of our roads, bridges, water systems, and buildings. Unfortunately, we continue to engage in the same kind of legerdemain today. The federal government's bailout of bankrupt savings and loan companies will cost hundreds of billions of dollars; yet it is, somehow, magically being done "off budget" and ostensibly cost free. Those chickens will come home to roost in the form of future generation tax increases.

Poor accounting conventions and managerial control permit and sustain these fiascos. As a dramatic example of this problem, consider the

U.S. comptroller general's assessment of the federal government's financial status:[5]

> (Although) the official word is that the budget crisis is on the way to being solved...the deficit is just as large today as when the Gramm-Rudman-Hollings deficit reduction process was begun in 1986. We can, indeed, solve the budget crisis, but to do so, we must recognize that it is a delusion to believe that the problem is already...solved.
>
> ...The U.S. government does not currently have the internal control systems necessary to effectively operate its programs and safeguard its assets. The problem is systemic. ...Scandals like HUD's [mismanagement of its low-income housing program] make big news. But what makes them possible is a situation less "newsworthy" but more far-reaching than any particular case of wrong-doing or mismanagement. Weak internal controls and second-rate accounting systems allow these incidents to happen.

The federal government is not alone. Its problems appear to dwarf those of other nonprofit organizations only because their dollar values are so much greater.

WHY THIS BOOK?

We have argued strongly for the importance and difficulty of sound financial management of nonprofit organizations. Our mission in writing this book is to bring the tools of financial analysis and managerial control, as practiced in successful for-profit and nonprofit organizations, to a broad audience of nonprofit managers. It is not a goal we can attain alone. As authors, we must ensure sufficient breadth and depth in our discussion of these complex subjects and a presentation that is accessible and appealing, not hopelessly mired in technical jargon. But, you, the readers, must work toward clearing the hurdles created by the intrinsic difficulty of the subjects to achieve their mastery. At the end of this book, we hope you will conclude that all of us have accomplished our missions.

DISCUSSION QUESTIONS

1. What distinguishes nonprofit organizations from for-profit organizations?
2. What is the purpose of financial analysis and managerial control in a nonprofit organization?

[5]Charles A. Bowsher, *Facing Facts*, Comptroller General's 1989 Annual Report (Washington, DC: United States General Accounting Office, 1989), pp. 3 and 11.

3. What financial questions should be asked of a nonprofit organization, and what sorts of financial data should be examined to learn the answers?

4. Why is accounting important in the financial management of nonprofit organizations?

Case

CASE STUDY

The University of Trent case study describes the financial condition and managerial control activities of a large nonprofit organization. The case study, like most of the others in this book, describes a real organization. It depicts the complex data and activities of real-life managers. If you are not familiar with such data, you may find the case study excessively detailed, especially after reading only one chapter of this book. Come back and review it after you have finished Part One of the book. If you are familiar with such data, you will find this an interesting and provocative example of how a middle-level manager tried to improve the managerial control of what he perceived as sluggish and unresponsive organization and a challenging setting for financial analysis.

CASE 1.1 University of Trent

I started working here six months ago, in July 19X6, for the vice president of administration. On September 15, my boss, Carl Johnson, received a letter from the director of financial planning and budgets, Harrison Fielding, about the $1,000,000 overrun in our budget.

The letter said: ". . . Carl, we are very concerned. It is awfully late in the year to still have uncertainties of this size in our operations." Harry was right. I felt I had to do something about it.

Now, here I am, six months later. My salary has nearly doubled. My data systems are off and running. And we seem to have our expenses under better control, but there are still many things left to do.

I don't know if I want to be, or even can be, the person to do them.

This case was prepared by Professor Regina E. Herzlinger.

Copyright ©1977 by the President and Fellows of Harvard College. Harvard Business School case 9-177-245. Revised January 1993.

Chip Wise was talking intensely, in his slow southern drawl, about his experiences while working at the University of Trent. He was in his early 30s, an ex-Navy supply officer, and an MBA degree holder. He had chosen his job carefully and deliberately:

> I always wanted a public sector career. And I know I have a lot to contribute. Not only my experience in the Navy and my training, but more importantly, the kind of person I am. I want to do a good job. I expect other people to do the same. If they don't, I deal with that issue. I'm not afraid to be tough. I don't expect everybody to love me.
>
> Mainly, I want to do a good job here and to have a good life. I got my B.A. at this school. It was one of the greatest periods of my life, being a student here. And I'd like to show my thanks now. But I don't know if I can stay, there are so many problems.

THE BUDGET SITUATION

> The university has had a deficit in three of the past five years (see **Exhibit 1**). And although revenues have grown, the expenses have grown even faster. The university is going on a big fund drive, but it also has to control expenses to show donors their funds will be well spent.
>
> My own area has not helped the problem much. We have a budget of about $24 million, and, as you can tell from the letter from Fielding, we've had trouble in controlling it.
>
> Under the vice president of administration are separate units for the Bookstore, Dining Services, Construction, Personnel, Real Estate, Physical Plant, and Security. And on top of them we have an additional $12 million utility budget. Altogether, we employ 600 people. And Carl Johnson and I, as well as one administrative assistant and a secretary, are sitting on top of this big budget.
>
> When Harry Fielding's letter first arrived I started looking at the activities of each of these different units and managed to effect significant changes in the operations of the Bookstore, the Dining Services, and the Physical Plant. Let me tell you what I did in each of these areas.

The Auxiliary Enterprises

> The Bookstore and the Dining Service are two auxiliary enterprises. They are supposed to break even, but they hadn't done so in quite a while. (See **Exhibit 1**.) Although the Bookstore appeared to have a surplus in 19X6, that was because it had a large amount of obsolete inventory (cameras, clothes, out-of-date textbooks) which weren't being written off. A discount bookstore had opened just down the street from our main store and it had a much larger paperback collection and had managed to sign a contract with the University of Trent Press to buy all its seconds. Well, the seconds were in pretty good shape, they were being sold at a very low price, and our store was taking a beating. I told them to hold an inventory sale. It was a big success. And I carefully monitored their expenses and lopped off some odds and ends. We have them budgeted for $50,000 profit next year. But that's not the long-run solution. We have to spin them off, set them up as a separate corporation, and free them of any kind of subsidy. Maybe I can convince somebody to do it.

The Dining Services are a much more complicated problem. First of all, a couple of years ago we built a big dining hall and we also built apartment-style dormitories with a kitchen on every floor. And the dean of students put all freshmen on a voluntary meal plan. Simultaneously, the total costs of the dining service went sky-high. And so a contract was signed with Chuckwagon Services, a big food-service outfit, to provide food services. But the food service was still losing money hand over fist.

I looked into the situation and found we didn't have the volume to cover rapidly accelerating costs. The contract with Chuckwagon was something else—a guaranteed management fee and no provision for loss-sharing, only a provision for profit-sharing. Chuckwagon was making quite a profit; it sold us food at market price (not at their cost), and it charged us full cost every time one of their staff visited us. The profit-sharing agreement couldn't have meant all that much to them.

So, I got rid of them and put in our own management. But the employees are all unionized. And the contract is one-sided—everybody gets paid for a full eight-hour shift, despite the fact that actual working hours are much lower. And the wages are very high. When the school closes for vacation, they all go on unemployment insurance which, in this state, gets charged to the university. Nobody has ever thought of turning down their claims.

Anyway, by getting rid of Chuckwagon, I saved a few hundred thousand, but we're still losing money. I appointed a sharp guy as head of Dining Services. And he's doing good things. He put in a salad bar, they've got natural cereals for breakfast, and there's a make-your-own sundae line. And he's got a good catering business going. Our revenues are picking up, but with the voluntary plan and our big fixed costs, it's hard to make ends meet. Next year they're still budgeted to lose money. Of course, we keep raising our fees.

I don't know what we can do about this situation. Unless I can convince the dean to change his voluntary meal plan or to close some of the dining halls or some of the kitchens in the dormitories, I don't know what else to do. Also, I have to live with the results of those past union negotiations.

The Physical Plant

The Physical Plant office is a big operation. My boss personally inspects the work on a frequent basis. He's got a fine sense for the beauty of our historical campus and a good perspective of the importance of maintaining it in top-notch condition.

The Physical Plant unit was at the heart of our problem. They accounted for $700,000 out of our $1.0 million dollar overrun. In looking into the situation, I found out why. Although they hadn't hired more people, the overtime, vacations, sick leave, etc., in this unit were way over budget.

I did two things. First, I filled the vacant position of head of the office of Physical Plant with a guy who had worked his way up through the ranks. They used to hire engineers for this job but I thought an insider would be better. Second, I put in an automated system that on the Monday after the end of the week prints out exactly how much overtime, vacation time, sick leave, etc., each person has put in for in the week and cumulatively for the month and year-to-date.

We cut costs by reducing overtime and by laying off the temporary employees we normally used. Some of the things I found by reading the reports were amazing; for example, one person took his full sick leave allowance just before his employment anniversary date, took his next year's sick leave allowance just after the date, and then went on vacation. We had a little talk with him.

When I first put in this system, I used to go over every name with the head of the office. Now I just spend twenty minutes on it. I pick out the unusual cases and I call him about them. The system is really working. As you can see (**Exhibit 2**), the numbers are beginning to look a lot better.

Of course, there's still a lot left to do with this unit. I don't know how big the job backlog is for repairs and maintenance, nor how the jobs are scheduled. I want to make sure that they've always got a number of useful projects on hand.

Buildings

Because a big part of our budget is linked to the amount of space in the university, I looked into consolidation of the buildings. One particular building looked like a good candidate for closing. It was built for the university by the state. Its classrooms and lecture halls were in use only 50 percent of the time. If the buildings were closed, more than $100,000 a year could be saved. And we had classroom space elsewhere.

But a study committee looked into it and decided the building couldn't be closed. It would be embarrassing to tell the state we didn't need their building when we asked for more capital funds. And no one was willing to deal with the faculty who were the primary users of the building to tell them they would have to walk further from their offices to teach class. Anyhow, nothing got done about it.

Response to the 19X6 Budget Crisis

While the work I did with the auxiliary enterprises and the physical plant cut back on our overrun, two other things enabled me to balance the budget:

(1)   The energy crisis of the 1970s had led the budget unit to increase our utilities budget by 8 percent every year, but the real increases are never that much. Harry Fielding budgets by last year's budgets, not by last year's actual expenses. So, we had a positive variance from our utilities budget to help balance the overrun in other areas.

(2)   We have an account for special work that different users might want done. They pay us for it. We cut it back.

The 19X7 Budget

In preparation for the 19X7 budget, Harry Fielding sent around a memo explaining zero-base budgeting (ZBB) and urging us to apply it in our own areas. It described ZBB as having two basic steps: developing decision packages and ranking them. A decision package is a discrete activity or function that is to be compared to other activities.

The decision package was to include the purpose of the activity, the consequences of not performing the activity, the measures of performance, alternative courses of action, and costs and benefits. The alternative courses of action were to include analyses of different ways of performing the activity as well as analyses of different levels of effort in doing so. These decision packages were to be evaluated and ranked in order of importance through benefit/cost analyses or other evaluation techniques.

I was intrigued with this method of budgeting and used it in three of our offices. (See **Exhibit 3** for the analysis of one unit.) I did the analyses by talking to the managers of these different offices and expressing their ideas in ZBB terminology. I sent the analyses to Harry and Carl, but I haven't gotten any feedback from them.

THE BUDGETING PROCESS

The process normally starts with very detailed budget estimates coming down from Harry's shop, based on guidelines he gets from the budget committee—things like the allowable increase in student fees, the desired bottom line, etc. He then figures out what expenses ought to look like in order to meet the guidelines.

In the past year, his budget involved a decrease in our real budget (after adjusting for inflationary increases). He tells us what our total budget is going to be and leaves it to us to allocate across different line items. I've put in a program budgeting system to help me in this process and I did the ZBB. But I got little feedback on it.

I guess that's part of my problem—no feedback. Carl is a great guy and well-respected in the community. Everybody likes him. And Harry is an economist; he used to be on the faculty. He's got a staff of only four people and they tell us what our budget is going to be. Both Harry and Carl report to Larry Richman, our president—a world-famous classics scholar. Larry is very busy with our big capital drive and will be for the next two years, since it's a three-year drive. All the administrative people have been here for a long time.

The other administrative functions are straightforward: the comptroller accounts, the treasurer finances, the personnel office negotiates contracts and benefits packages and so on. Some administrative functions, such as running the residence halls, are under the provost's wing—as in many other educational organizations.

Our board of trustees has some of the most powerful and inspiring members of the business community on it. They devote a lot of their time to the school, but they don't seem to get involved with our administrative issues. They raise money and study programs. I can't imagine that any of them would have let the kind of labor contracts we have get by in their own firms.

So, I'm kind of in a bind. I get large financial rewards, but it's not enough, it's not why I'm working here. And I guess I'll have to leave.

ASSIGNMENT

a. Do your best to analyze the financial position of the University of Trent using the data in **Exhibit 1-A** and **1-B**. (We will discuss how to analyze such statements in detail in subsequent chapters.)

b. Evaluate Chip's performance in terms of the technical quality of the changes he made and the methods he used to implement them.

c. Do you think Chip's overall performance is helpful to the University of Trent? Why? If you think his performance is less than perfect, specify how he should change it.

EXHIBIT 1-A **A Five-Year Review (years ended June 30; thousands of dollars)**

	19X2	19X3	19X4	19X5[a]	19X6
Revenues (by source)					
Student tuition and fees	$ 30,295	$ 34,696	$ 38,211	$ 44,154	$ 51,810
State appropriations	13,131	13,826	14,468	15,060	15,991
U.S. government contracts and grants	31,749	34,195	37,430	43,668	49,539
Investment income	11,760	13,570	10,535	11,130	10,449
Gifts and private grants	8,069	7,496	9,930	11,598	10,780
Sales and service of:					
Alexander Hospital	29,015	29,555	34,656	43,272	53,193
Other educational and medical activities	4,599	5,657	7,820	12,963	16,979
Other sources	5,250	5,836	6,950	5,636	7,046
Auxiliary enterprises:					
Bookstore	3,087	3,003	3,257	3,578	3,853
Dining service	1,837	1,600	2,122	2,565	2,726
Other	9,107	8,465	9,269	9,949	11,463
	$147,899	$157,899	$174,648	$203,573	$233,829
Expenditures (by function)					
Instruction	$ 39,420	$ 43,979	$ 47,575	$ 48,661	$ 54,412
Research	24,600	25,184	27,187	32,648	36,864
Libraries	3,946	4,326	4,872	5,252	5,583
Other educational and medical activities	7,991	8,771	9,661	17,002	22,209
Student aid	2,470	2,612	2,836	4,406	7,066
Student services	3,888	3,789	3,905	4,476	4,474
Alexander Hospital	30,245	31,492	37,589	47,589	55,620
Operation and maintenance	7,457	8,361	10,011	12,077	12,252
General expense	6,161	7,748	9,106	11,571	8,514
General administration	4,726	5,741	6,293	6,411	6,311
Auxiliary enterprises:					
Bookstore	3,127	3,164	3,327	3,790	3,839
Dining services	2,874	2,242	2,533	2,898	3,009
Other	10,906	11,111	11,949	12,507	13,203
	$147,811	$158,520	$176,844	$209,288	$233,356

[a]Restated and reclassified to conform to 19X6 presentation.

EXHIBIT 1-B **Balance Sheet (June 30, 19X6, with comparative totals as of June 30, 19X5; thousands of dollars)**

	June 30, 19X5ᵃ	June 30, 19X6							
	Totals	Totals	Unrestricted	Restricted	Loan Funds	Endowment and Similar Funds	Unexpended Building	Investment in Plant	Agency Funds
Assets:									
Cash	$ 1,866	$ 2,803	$ 2,803	$ -	$ -	$ -	$ -	$ -	$ -
Accounts receivable, net of allowance for doubtful accounts of $3,977	25,017	26,062	17,085	7,984	-	873	120	-	-
Loans receivable, net of allowance for doubtful loans of $570	30,584	34,570	3,114	-	31,456	-	-	-	-
Inventories, at cost	2,851	3,219	3,219	-	-	-	-	-	-
Prepaid expenses and deferred charges	6,220	7,266	7,225	-	-	41	-	-	-
Investments:									
Stocks and bonds	102,113	130,340	-	4,097	-	100,984	25,020	-	239
Real estate, mortgages, etc.	11,598	12,551	138	1,189	29	10,928	265	-	2
Invested in plant	282,545	296,290	-	-	-	564	-	295,726	-
Interfund balances:									
Advances for plant	-	-	10,401	127	1,722	2,301	12,800	(12,829)	694
Other	-	-	(38,818)	14,783	-	8,819	-	-	-
	$462,794	$513,101	$ 5,167	$28,180	$33,207	$124,510	$38,205	$282,897	$935
Liabilities and Fund Balances:									
Accounts payable and accrued expenses	$ 5,863	$ 11,662	$10,351	$ -	$ -	$ -	$ 1,311	$ -	$ -
Student deposits	1,295	1,342	1,342	-	-	-	-	-	-
Notes payable, principally banks	19,993	5,780	2,000	-	2,443	-	1,337	-	-
Long-term debt	63,013	94,717	-	-	-	-	16,622	78,095	-
Advances on research contracts	3,759	4,365	-	4,154	-	-	211	-	-
Deferred income	2,796	2,929	2,874	-	-	-	55	-	-
Agency funds	739	935	-	-	-	-	-	-	935
Reserves	1,524	2,228	1,065	-	-	-	1,163	-	-
Fund balances	363,812	389,143	(12,465)	24,026	30,764	124,510	18,843	203,465	-
	$462,794	$513,101	$ 5,167	$28,180	$33,207	$124,510	$38,205	$282,897	$935

ᵃRestated and reclassified to conform to 19X6 presentation.

EXHIBIT 2 **Monthly Analysis of Salaries – Shops Only**

	Yearly Budget	July and Aug.	Sept.	Oct.	Nov.	Dec.	Jan.	Feb.	Mar.
Number of Weeks in Period	(52)	(9)	(5)	(4)	(4)	(4)	(5)	(4)	(5)
Regular time	$4,332	$ 713	$432	$359	$353	$303	$342	$330	$407
Overtime:									
Time-and-a-half	334	111	77	30	14	13	21	15	16
Double time	-	13	19	7	1	2	1	1	4
Shift differential	-	11	5	6	3	5	5	7	4
Subtotal	334	135	101	43	18	20	27	23	24
Other paid time:									
Vacation	397	167	43	11	12	14	16	8	7
Sick leave	221	38	28	33	28	23	41	29	41
Personal days	178	10	7	5	3	6	6	5	5
Holidays	57	17	17	2	-	37	74	1	3
Union business	6	2	1	-	1	-	-	1	2
Other	-	6	6	-	1	-	-	(1)	(3)
Subtotal	859	240	102	51	44	80	137	43	55
Training	14	23	-	-	-	-	-	(3)	(6)
Total payroll	5,539	1,111	635	453	415	403	506	393	480
Employee benefits	1,108	226	124	90	81	79	99	79	98
Total compensation	$6,647	$1,337	$ 759	$543	$496	$482	$605	$472	$578
Budget at average week		1,150	639	511	511	511	639	511	639
Deviation from average		$ (187)	$(120)	$ (32)	$ 15	$ 29	$ 34	$ 39	$ 61

EXHIBIT 3 **Zero-Base Budget Analysis of Construction Division**

Identification:	**CON**
Purpose/Function:	1. Provide coordination, inspection, and liaison on all major construction projects.
	2. Provide engineering service to facilitate repairs and additions to mechanical and electrical systems.
	3. Provide estimates for all construction projects of $100,000 or less; including both contracted and Physical Plant work.
	4. Provide architectural, mechanical, and electrical design support for engineering services.
Benefits:	Office required to assure compliance with specifications in construction contracts; to ensure repairs or additions to mechanical and electrical systems are compatible and appropriate; facilitates hundreds of minor construction jobs each year that require estimates.
Improvements:	1. Reduction of one ($16,000) mechanical designer from FY 19X7 proposed in CON (6 of 6)[c]
	2. Reduction of one ($18,000) electrical designer from FY 19X7 proposed in CON (6 of 6)[b]
	3. Reduction of one ($15,000) estimator from FY 19X7 proposed in CON (5 of 6)[b]
Consequences:	1. Mechanical design staff will be reduced 50 percent so that development program work cannot be adequately done in-house, nor can existing Physical Plant minor construction projects be properly supported.
	2. Electrical design for development program and in-house Physical Plant projects cannot be accomplished.
	3. Requests for estimates will be delayed an additional 7-14 days by 33 percent reduction (from 3 to 2); inspection of minor construction projects will become less frequent.
Alternatives/Consequences:	Eliminate office—Increased costs from inadequate coordination, inspection, and liaison of major construction projects; inadequate planning and improper additions to major university systems that will be costly to correct.

EXHIBIT 3 (Continued)

> *CON (1 of 6)*—Keep central office staff only; could not provide construction, engineering, estimating, or design service in-house.

> *CON (2 of 6)*—Add accounting function for transfer and control of funds.

> *CON (3 of 6)*—Provide construction coordination and inspection of major projects over $100,000.

> *CON (4 of 6)*—Provide engineering services for repairs and additions to mechanical and electrical systems.

> *CON (5 of 6)*—Provide estimator/inspector for minor contract and physical plant projects.

> *CON (6 of 6)*—Provide in-house architectural, electrical, and mechanical design work for minor construction projects and in-house work.

Rank	Package	FY 19X7 Gross	FY 19X8 Gross	Cumulative Gross	Cumulative % of FY 19X8 Gross
1	CON (1 of 6)	$44,483	$44,483	$ 44,483	15%
2	CON (2 of 6)	16,506	16,506	60,989	21
3	CON (3 of 6)	57,110	57,110	118,099	40
4	CON (4 of 6)	55,346	55,346	173,445	59
5	CON (5 of 6)	34,509	34,509	207,954	71
6	CON (6 of 6)	35,437	35,437	243,391	83
7	CON (5 of 6)[b]	15,000	15,000	258,391	88
8	CON (6 of 6)[b]	18,000	18,000	276,391	95
9	CON (6 of 6)[c]	16,000	16,000	292,391	100

Part One

Financial Accounting and Analysis in Nonprofit Organizations

2   Principles of Accounting

ACCOUNTING IS THE PROCESS OF MEASURING economic events. It is the language in which all financial management is conducted. The long history of accounting dates back to Sumerian and Egyptian societies in which traders used accounting to measure their economic performance. First formalized in the fifteenth century by an Italian mathematician and monk, Fr. Pacioli, to enable measurement of the substantial economic activity then taking place in the Mediterranean region, it has survived since that time to inform and bewilder students of the subject.

Accounting is shaped by many conventions. We hope we do not offend with the name we have given—we call them accountingese. Because of its importance, we will devote the next four chapters to discussing the many aspects of accounting. Chapters 2, 3, and 4 discuss the separate components of the financial statements, and Chapter 5 explains their analysis. At their end you will speak and read and even be able to conduct financial analysis with the language of accounting.

In Chapter 6 we discuss the aspects of accounting that are unique to nonprofit organizations. We conclude Part One with an explanation of accounting mechanics. Although most books on this subject begin with accounting mechanics, we chose to discuss them in an optional later chapter. Our choice reflects our focus on financial analysis, rather than the mechanical aspects of accounting.

THE NATURE AND PURPOSE OF ACCOUNTING

Accounting supports the management of nonprofit organizations in several ways. For one, the accounting system and the financial statements it produces provide a historic record of the financial activities and status of an organization. These can be used to assess the organization's *stewardship* of the resources entrusted to it. (Stewardship is the responsibility for using resources in the ways intended by their donor.) For example, the accounting statements should enable a donor of monies to provide meals for the homeless to ensure that the donated funds are used in the intended manner.

Accounting also provides the basis for the diagnostic tests and measurements known collectively as *financial analysis*. They can help assess the financial health of the organization, just as doctors use the results of medical diagnostic tests and measurements to assess physical health. The purpose of financial analysis is to detect signs of failing fiscal health and to highlight the appropriate corrective action.

Accounting also aids *managerial control*. Managers and board members use it to make decisions about the level of fees to be charged for services, whether to make or buy a product or service, whether to invest in equipment, and how to allocate resources among alternative programs. Regulators also use financial information to help them decide if organizations are abiding by the rules that govern them or whether to grant a requested rate increase. Donors, too, use financial information to help them evaluate whether to contribute to the organization.

Types of Accounting

Accounting is typically classified as either financial or managerial. *Financial accounting* refers to the process of preparing financial statements for people who are external to the organization, such as donors or other sources of capital and regulators. They use the statements to make decisions about the types and extent of the interactions they choose to have with the organization. Financial accounting statements primarily reflect transactions between the organization and its external environment. They are referred to as *general purpose financial statements* because they are intended to serve the needs of many different types of users who are unable to demand specific types of information. To enhance the credibility of these statements to the outside users, financial statements are frequently audited by certified public accountants (CPAs), using well-documented and accepted auditing techniques in a process called a *financial audit*.

Managerial accounting, in contrast, provides detailed financial and operating data about the organization's internal activities. It is used primarily by managers and others internal to the organization to help manage its operations. Pricing, investment, cost control, and resource allocation decisions are but a few of the typical decisions supported by managerial accounting. Because it is meant for internal purposes, managerial accounting is audited, if at all, by internal auditors. Financial auditing techniques are much more documented and standardized than internal auditing techniques.

Chapters 2 through 7 discuss the nature and mechanics of the financial accounting systems and reports that support financial analysis. The managerial control techniques of planning, budgeting and control, cost accounting, variance analysis, relevant factor and sensitivity analysis, and discounting that support financial management are covered in Chapters 8 through 14.

Basis of Accounting

All financial accounting and many managerial accounting data are *historical*, reflecting what has happened in the past. Accounting information about the past provides useful feedback on the success or failure of past actions. As George Santayana noted , ''Those who cannot remember the past are condemned to repeat it.'' Historical accounting information also is usually the best starting point from which to predict the likely effects of changes from the past on the future. Many sophisticated analytical and statistical techniques can be applied to accounting information to help make these predictions.

INTRODUCTION TO
FINANCIAL ACCOUNTING STATEMENTS

Accounting is a natural process for measuring the economic state and activity of any entity. We use it instinctively for valuing our personal economic situation. For example, think about what you want to know about your own financial status. You likely want to know what you are worth financially. You might also want to understand the reasons for the changes in your financial worth from one period of time to the next and the changes in the amount of cash you have.

Accountants present this information in three financial statements. The *Balance Sheet* is the statement of your financial position at any given time. The combined *Operating Statement and Statement of Changes in Net Worth* traces changes in your worth over time, usually for the past year. Last, the *Statement of Cash Flows* analyzes the changes in your cash balance over time.

These statements are computed in a straightforward manner. Even people untrained in accounting can prepare simple ones. For example, to prepare a personal Balance Sheet, you would list all the valuable resources you own and all the financial obligations you owe. The things of value you own are *assets* such as cash, stocks or bonds, your car, real estate, and other things with economic value. You would then list all the amounts you owe, your *liabilities*. These include the debt you incurred to buy your assets and any other amounts you owe. The difference between the value of your assets and your liabilities is your *net worth*.

In nonprofit organizations, these statements carry different names from their business counterparts. In a nonprofit, the Operating Statement is called the *Statement of Revenues and Expenses and Changes in Fund Balances*, and net worth is called *fund balance*. In for-profit organizations and individual reporting, they are titled an *Income Statement* and *owners equity* or *retained earnings,* respectively. The alternative terminology proposed for nonprofits labels the operating statement the *Statement of Changes in Net Assets* and net worth, *net assets.* (You may wonder why we bother to include for-profit terminology. We do so because nonprofit managers must understand equivalent for-profit terminology in order to communicate with bankers, board members, and others from the business community. Knowledge of equivalent terminology also facilitates comparison of for-profit and nonprofit organizations that compete in the same markets, such as overnight mail and health care delivery.)

The Balance Sheet

For our first example of a financial statement, we will construct a Balance Sheet. Suppose you have $5,000 in the bank, own other valuable assets, such as stocks that cost $2,000, and own a $12,000 car that you just bought with a $10,000 loan. Your net worth would be $9,000, the sum of the things you own ($19,000) less the amount you owe (the outstanding loan of $10,000). An accountant would present this information in a Balance Sheet. Assets would be listed on the left-hand side and all the sources of financing for the assets (liabilities and net worth, sometimes referred to collectively as *capital*) would be listed on the right-hand side. The Balance Sheet would look something like the one shown in Table 2-1.

The Balance Sheet describes your financial position at a certain date: the right-hand side lists all the sources of capital, the left-hand side shows how the capital is invested. The Balance Sheet is valid only for that particular date; if you sell your stocks the next day for $2,000 cash, your assets would change to a cash balance of $7,000 and a stock value of $0.

Combined Income Statement and Statement of Changes in Net Worth

You might want to track the changes in your net worth—the cumulative amount of all the money you earned or were given less all the money you

TABLE 2-1 **A Personal Balance Sheet, Year 1**

Balance Sheet			
As of the End of Year 1 For Mr. or Ms. X			
Cash	$ 5,000	Car loan	$10,000
Stocks	2,000	Net worth	9,000
Car	12,000		
Total assets	$19,000	Total capital	$19,000

spent for things you consumed. Changes in net worth are typically accounted for a year at a time, although shorter or longer periods can also be used.

For example, if you earned $15,000 during the year and spent $14,000 for living expenses, the addition to your net worth for the year is the difference between the two, $1,000. It is also your *net income* for the year. Income is the difference between revenues and expenses. Note that the $14,000 of expenses account only for items you consumed, or used up, during the year; they do not include money you spent to acquire assets that were not consumed. Money spent to buy assets does not change your net worth, it merely changes the type of assets you own. But money consumed for living expenses reduces your net worth. For example, if you use cash to buy an asset such as a car, it still has value at the end of the year. But if you spend the same amount of money on taxi fares, at the end of the year you have no assets to show for your expenditures. Taxi fares are thus an expense, while a car purchase is the exchange of one asset, cash, for another, a car.

Accountants present the net income calculation of an individual or for-profit organization in an *Income Statement*, as shown in Table 2-2. The equivalent statement for a nonprofit organization is called a *Statement of Revenues and Expenses*, or some variation of this basic title. It lists all the resources (revenues) you earned during a time period and deducts from them the resources (expenses) you used up during the same period. The Income Statement is similar to a video in that it records activity during a period of time, while the Balance Sheet is a snapshot of your position at a particular point in time. If you had more than one type of revenues and expenses, their details would also normally be shown on this statement. For example, if you earned $10,000 and won a $5,000 prize, the statement would show revenues of $10,000 from salary and $5,000 from the prize.

Accountants typically summarize how net worth changed during the year, as shown in Table 2-3. In a for-profit organization, this might be called a *Statement of Changes in Retained Earnings*. In a nonprofit organization, it is called a *Statement of Changes in Fund Balance*. For an individual, it can be called a *Statement of Changes in Net Worth*.

TABLE 2-2 **Personal Income Statement, Year 2**

Income Statement		
From Beginning to End of Year 2		
for Mr. or Ms. X		
	Revenues	$15,000
Less:	Expenses	14,000
	Income	$ 1,000

TABLE 2-3 **A Personal Statement of Changes in Net Worth, Year 2**

Statement of Changes in Net Worth From Beginning to End of Year 2 for Mr. or Ms. X		
	Net worth, end of Year 1	$ 9,000
Plus:	Income of the year	1,000
	Net worth, end of Year 2	$10,000

To test your understanding of the concepts introduced thus far, consider the following situation. You started Year 2 with the Balance Sheet shown in Table 2-1, and increased your net worth by $1,000 during Year 2, as shown in Table 2-2 and Table 2-3. You also sold your stock for $2,000, and used cash to pay off $7,000 of your car loan. What would your end-of-year Balance Sheet look like? Check your answer against Table 2-4.

Calculating three of the items in Table 2-4 is relatively straightforward. Your net worth at the end of Year 2 is as calculated in Table 2-3. The loan decreased from $10,000 to $3,000 because you paid off $7,000. You no longer have stocks because you sold them for $2,000 of cash. Calculating the ending cash balance is more complex and provides valuable information that is presented in a separate Statement of Cash Flows.

Statement of Cash Flows

Why did the cash decrease by $4,000 during the year? The cash balance started at $5,000, was increased by $2,000 from the sale of the stocks, was decreased by $7,000 for the loan repayment, and increased yet another $1,000 by your net income for the year. Because cash is very important, and because it is affected by many different types of activities, a *Statement of Cash Flows* is used to show how the change in cash from $5,000 to $1,000 came about. It lists the sources of cash (net income of $1,000 and the stock sale of $2,000) and the uses of cash (to pay off $7,000 of the car loan). The cash balance decreased because the total uses of cash ($7,000) exceeded the total sources of cash ($3,000) by $4,000 ($3,000 − $7,000). An accountant would show this in a statement similar to the one in Table 2-5.

This statement is sometimes called a *Statement of Changes in Financial Position Prepared on a Cash Basis*. A similar statement is sometimes used to explain the changes in assets other than cash. If so, it is given the more general title of *Statement of Changes in Financial Position*, and describes the other assets whose changed value it explains.

We have just prepared simple examples of the three fundamental financial statements. The *Balance Sheet* measures the assets owned and the

TABLE 2-4 **A Personal Balance Sheet, Year 2**

Balance Sheet
As of End of Year 2
for Mr. or Ms. X

Cash	$ 1,000	Car loan	$ 3,000
Car	12,000	Net worth	10,000
Total assets	$13,000	Total capital	$13,000

liabilities and net worth used to finance those assets. The *Statement of Revenues and Expenses* accounts for the resources received and used up during a period of time. The *Statement of Changes in Financial Position* traces the sources of some specific asset, usually cash, and how it was used over a period of time. Review these statements until you feel comfortable with this discussion. Although the financial statements of real organizations are more complex than these and may follow different formats, these simple statements distill the essence of the financial information on which financial analysis and management are built.

More complex statements and the rules governing their preparation are covered in Chapters 3 through 7. Before moving to that level of detail and complexity, however, it is important to discuss the major conventions used in preparing financial accounting reports.

TABLE 2-5 **A Personal Statement of Cash Flows, Year 2**

Statement of Cash Flows
From the Start to the End of Year 2
for Mr. or Ms. X

Sources of cash:	
Income	$1,000
Sale of stock	2,000
Total sources	$3,000
Uses of cash:	
Repayment of loan	(7,000)*
Sources less uses	$(4,000)*
+ Beginning cash balance, Year 2	5,000
Ending cash balance, Year 2	$1,000

*In a financial statement, parentheses around financial data indicate a negative number.

CONVENTIONS OF ACCOUNTING

Most organizations, large and small, for-profit and nonprofit, use financial statements to report the economic results of their activities over a certain period of time. Certain concepts or principles guide the preparation of these statements. In accountingese, they are called conventions. Understanding these principles is crucial to understanding the statements.

(1) The *entity* concept requires that only resources owned by the organization and activities of the organization are reported by the financial accounting system. This defines the boundary of what is included. When you prepare your personal financial statements, you are the entity; your friends' resources would not be included because you do not own them, even though your friends might allow you to use them.

(2) The *money measurement* concept further restricts the resources included in the financial statements to those that can be objectively measured in monetary terms. Thus, an organization's excellent reputation is not included in the statements because that reputation does not have an objectively determinable monetary value. In practice, objective measures usually refer to the costs of the resources when they were purchased.

(3) The *going concern* concept means that an organization's activities and resources are measured on the assumption that it will continue operations for the foreseeable future; it will not close its doors or go bankrupt. Therefore, most things are measured on the basis of what they *cost* the organization, rather than on the basis of their market value. Market values are relevant only if the organization were about to sell its resources and stop operating.[1]

(4) A related principle holds that resources are measured in a *conservative* manner. In practice, this means that revenues and assets are valued at the lower end of their actual likely value and that liabilities and expenses are valued at the higher end of their actual likely value.

(5) Measurement and financial reporting are required only for *material* events or activities that would cause the user of the information to make a different decision from that made without it. For example, a small inventory of inexpensive pens or paper need not be considered as part of your net worth because it is negligible, or immaterial, in value.

(6) The *accrual* concept requires that financial resource inflows are measured when the entity is legally entitled to them (which may be

---

[1]Marketable securities are the exception to this rule and nonprofit organizations usually have the option of valuing them at either cost or market.

before or after cash is received) and that resource outflows are measured when the entity uses up the resources in operations (which may be before or after cash is paid for the resources).

These principles are key for understanding financial statements. For example, some people believe that the value of the total assets listed on the Balance Sheet is the market value of the organization's assets. These people do not understand that the cost concept causes assets to be valued at their cost. Others believe that all the organization's assets are listed on the Balance Sheet. They do not understand that many important and valuable assets, such as the organization's reputation, are not included because of the money measurement concept.

Many nonprofit organizations use cash basis accounting because it is simpler than accrual accounting. Unfortunately, this simplicity exacts a price; the reported data may not accurately reflect the resource flows of the organization. If the difference between the results of operations under the cash and accrual bases of accounting is not significant, it may be appropriate to keep the accounting records on a cash basis and adjust the financial statements to an accrual basis only annually or quarterly. However, financial statements should be prepared on an accrual basis at least annually.

RECOGNIZING FINANCIAL STATES AND EVENTS

In this section, we will discuss how assets, liabilities, revenues, and expenses are measured. In accountingese, our term for the conventions of accounting, this measurement process is called *recognition*.

Recognizing Assets and Liabilities

Assets must have all three of the following properties:

(1) They must be owned by the organization.

(2) They must have monetary value.

(3) The monetary value must be objectively measured.

To illustrate how these criteria are applied, consider how the following types of asset are valued:

- Equipment owned by the organization and used in operations, with an objectively determinable value, will be recognized as an asset. However, if the equipment is obsolete, is no longer being used in operations, and cannot be sold, it should not be recorded as an asset because it has no value to the organization.

- Patents and trademarks frequently are not recognized because their value cannot be objectively determined and, therefore, they do not

meet the third criterion for asset recognition. But if a patent, trademark, or goodwill is purchased from another organization, its value
is recognized at the price for which it was acquired.

- An organization's good reputation and its valuable human resources
  are generally not recognized in the financial statements as assets
  because they are not owned and they cannot be objectively valued.

Cash, inventories, and real estate are the most common assets. However,
many items that do not have physical substance are also recognized as assets
under accrual accounting. For example, amounts due from clients or customers for services rendered or products sold are recognized as assets called
accounts receivable, because they meet the three criteria for asset valuation.
Similarly, if the organization buys a three-year insurance policy, accrual
accounting recognizes an asset called *prepaid insurance* because the policy
is owned by the organization and has an objectively measurable, clearly determinable value.

Liabilities are amounts of money owed by the entity. They are recognized
if they meet the following criteria:

(1) They are owed and will have to be paid at some future point;

(2) The amount of repayment can be objectively measured.

Items such as salaries and wages owed to employees and money owed
to suppliers meet these criteria and are recognized as liabilities called *salaries
and wages payable* and *accounts payable*. Other liabilities are more formal forms
of indebtedness and have signed documents indicating the existence and the
amount of debt, such as mortgages, loans, and bonds. Because of the accrual
principle, the value of some liabilities, such as pension and other post-
retirement benefits, is estimated and recorded even though it cannot be
precisely measured. For them, the liability is the amount of money that must
be available at the time of the accounting to meet all the future obligations
for benefits. It can only be estimated because the exact amount of money
that will be paid out in the future is not known exactly at the present time.
For example, the pension holders may live longer than currently expected.

Recognizing Resource Inflows

There are two types of resource inflows in nonprofit organizations:
revenues and support. Revenues measure the amount of resources earned
by selling goods and services or by investing assets. Resource inflows that
are not earned, *per se*, such as contributions and grants, are sometimes called
support rather than revenue.

Revenues are recognized when all three of the following events occur:

(1) Goods or services are delivered, thus effectively and legally earning
the right to the resource inflow.

(2) There is reasonable certainty that the monetary value of those goods or services can be measured objectively.

(3) There is reasonable certainty of the ability to collect that value.

In service-producing organizations these events occur either at the point of service delivery or when a bill is sent for the service. Many organizations recognize revenues at the point of billing because it is the earliest point at which all three conditions are met. However, when objective evidence exists of the value of a service and there is reasonable assurance that the payment will be collectible before billing, revenues may be recognized at the point of service delivery. For example, when home health agencies in California were paid at a predetermined rate per visit from the state government, they recognized revenues when the service was delivered. Organizations that sell products, rather than services, recognize revenues when the products are delivered and a bill is sent or when a cash transaction takes place. Thus, the gift shop in a hospital earns revenues equal to its cash sales plus its credit sales during a period of time.

If cash is received before the goods or services are delivered, it is recorded as a liability called *deferred revenue*. It is a liability because the cash is owed to the customer until the revenue is earned by delivering the goods or services. When the goods or services are delivered, the amount of the liability is reduced and a corresponding amount of revenue is recognized.

For example, assume a reputable foundation awards a nonprofit organization an operating grant of $100,000 at the beginning of the year. If the grant has no restrictions it will be recognized as revenues as soon as the organization is officially notified of the award. However, if the award does not specify the amount of the grant or if there is doubt about the ability to collect the money awarded, revenue will not be recognized until both of the first two conditions are met. When a grant is contingent on accomplishing certain objectives or is restricted in some other way, the revenue should not be recognized until the terms of the grant have been fulfilled.

Support inflows are recognized under accrual accounting when all three of the following occur:

(1) There is objective evidence of their monetary value.

(2) There is reasonable certainty that the value is collectible.

(3) Any conditions for receiving the support have been met.

If cash is received before the conditions have been met, it should be recorded as a liability called *deferred support* until those conditions are fulfilled. It is a liability because the recipient organization owes the money that has not been spent for the designated purposes to the granting agency.

In cash basis accounting, resource inflows are recognized only when cash is collected, and are properly referred to as *cash receipts* instead of revenues. In accrual accounting, revenues are generally recognized at the earlier point

FIGURE 2-1 **Differences in Timing of Recognition of Resource Inflow Under Cash and Accrual Accounting**

Period	1	2	3
Activity	Delivery of Good or Service	Billing	Collection of Cash
Accrual Accounting	* or	*	
Cash Accounting			*

(Stars indicate inflow recognition in the accounting statements.)

of billing or delivery of goods or services. Figure 2-1 illustrates these differences in the timing of the recognition of revenues under accrual and cash accounting for a service-delivery organization.

Recognizing Resource Outflows

Resource outflows are recognized under accrual accounting as either expenses or expenditures. *Expenditures* recognize the acquisition of a product or service with a loan, cash payments, or in exchange for other assets. Accrual accounting recognizes an expenditure when a product or service is acquired, whether or not there is a cash payment. Many resources, such as inventory and equipment, are acquired before being used up in operations. *Expenses* represent the value of the resources consumed in the process of operating the organization. Many items, such as labor, are typically used in operations before they are paid for in cash. When goods or services are used in operations, accrual accounting recognizes an expense to record their consumption. Cash accounting recognizes an expenditure and expense simultaneously, only when a cash payment is made; no record is made of the asset's use except when a cash transaction takes place. Figure 2-2 illustrates the differences between cash and accrual accounting in recognizing an expenditure and an expense, with the acquisition and use of a piece of equipment as an example. As indicated, accrual accounting recognizes more events and recognizes them earlier than does cash basis accounting.

Differences Between Accrual and Cash Accounting

Accrual accounting generally recognizes economic events earlier than does cash accounting and recognizes more types of events. It is useful because

FIGURE 2-2 **Differences in Timing of Recognition of Resource Outflow Under Cash and Accrual Accounting**

Activity	Receipt of Equipment Purchased on Credit Terms	Payment for the Equipment	Use of the Equipment
Accrual Accounting	*Expenditure	*Expenditure	*Expense
Cash Accounting		*Expenditure or Expense	

(Stars indicate outflow recognition in the accounting statements.)

it more accurately reflects economic reality. For example, if you work for a month and are owed wages of $1,500, is your net worth increased by $1,500, or not? Most of us would say we are $1,500 richer, even though we have not yet received the cash. Accrual accounting recognizes the $1,500 as *revenue* and the related asset of $1,500 of *accounts receivable*, while cash accounting would not recognize anything until you are paid. Conversely, if you owe someone who worked for you $1,000, accrual accounting will recognize the $1,000 as *expense* and a related liability, of *salary payable*, whereas cash basis accounting would not recognize anything until the payment is made.

Figure 2-3 summarizes the differences between these two methods of accounting in recognizing expenses and expenditures and related assets and liabilities. Similar differences exist between the two methods of accounting in the recognition of revenues, as illustrated in Figure 2-4.

Most people agree that accrual accounting paints a more accurate picture of an organization's financial activities and status. For this reason, accrual accounting is almost universally used in for-profit organizations as the method for measuring and reporting economic events. But many nonprofit organizations continue to use cash accounting.

ACCOUNTING INFORMATION SYSTEMS AND INFORMATION TECHNOLOGY

Manual accounting systems are being replaced by computerized systems. Whether the replacement is breathtakingly rapid or painfully slow, there is general agreement that it is inexorable. Unfortunately, good computerized nonprofit accounting systems are still not generally available at reasonable

FIGURE 2-3 **Differences in Measuring Asset Purchase and Use Under Accrual and Cash Accounting**

Period	1	2	3
Activity	Asset Purchased on Credit	Asset Used in Operations	Asset Paid for in Cash
Accrual Accounting	Recognize Asset and Liability	Recognize Expense and Decrease Asset Value	Decrease Liability and Decrease Cash
Cash Accounting	No entry	No entry	Decrease Cash and Recognize Asset

FIGURE 2-4 **Differences in Revenue Recognition Under Accrual and Cash Accounting**

Period	1	2	3
Activity	Service Delivered	Bill Sent	Payment of Bill in Cash
Accrual Accounting	Generally No Entry	Recognize Revenue and Accounts Receivable	Decrease Accounts Receivable and Increase Cash
Cash Accounting	No Entry	No Entry	Increase Cash and Recognize Revenue

prices. Many nonprofit organizations also continue to be plagued by a lack of technical expertise about information technology, much as they have traditionally lacked accounting expertise comparable to that of for-profit organizations.

A computer is not a panacea, and it can be dangerous. The havoc wrought by weeks of a poor manual system can be replicated by a computer in a matter of hours. Large amounts of time can be spent trying to figure out the computer system or recovering from data losses caused by inadequately protected data. Perhaps the most insidious problem with computer systems is the assumption that computer generated data must be right. Users of such data may ask fewer and less penetrating questions. While the accurate depiction of computer systems is "Garbage in, garbage out," too often people believe "Garbage in, gospel out."

Inadequate training also contributes to many nonprofit information systems problems. Ironically, many nonprofit organizations that devoted substantial effort to acquiring computer hardware and software are loath to pay for the training they require.

Despite these many pitfalls, computers can provide nonprofit organizations with much needed information processing capabilities. The transaction processing and reporting requirements of a nonprofit organization are much greater than those of a comparably sized for-profit organization, whether measured by revenue, number of employees, or assets. When used well, information technology can contribute positively to nonprofit accounting and financial management. When used poorly, it can be very dangerous.

THE SOCIAL STRUCTURE OF ACCOUNTING

As with any language, accounting is a social phenomenon, developed to support communication among individuals and organizations. Because managerial accounting is a private language, used only within a given organization, managerial accounting systems vary widely among organizations. Financial accounting, however, is the language the organization must use to communicate with the outside world. Effective financial accounting communication requires all organizations to use the same rules of the language. This section describes how these rules are set.

Sources of Authority for Accounting Principles

Financial accounting and reporting rules are called *generally accepted accounting principles* (GAAP). These rules govern the events that must be accounted for, acceptable valuation methods and processes of accounting, the disclosure required in the financial statements, and the form of the disclosure. Several institutions are involved in the process of developing GAAP. Foremost among these are the Financial Accounting Standards Board (FASB), the Governmental Accounting Standards Board (GASB), the American Institute of Certified Public Accountants (AICPA), and for nonprofit organizations, various organizations representing the accounting interests of different parts of the nonprofit sector. The reporting requirements and other standards of the Internal Revenue Service (IRS), Securities and Exchange Commission (SEC), General Accounting Office (GAO), Office of Management and Budget (OMB), and various state and local government certifying and regulating bureaus may also affect financial reporting standards, although they are not considered part of GAAP.

GAAP are documented primarily in the *Statements* issued by the FASB and GASB, and the *Statements of Position, Audit Guides,* and *Technical Pronouncements* issued by the AICPA. FASB and GASB perform parallel standard setting functions for nongovernmental and governmental organizations, respectively. The Securities and Exchange Acts of the early 1930s empowered the SEC to establish the accounting principles to be used in preparing the financial statements of companies and the standards to be used in auditing those financial statements. The SEC grants the accounting profession a major role in promulgating accounting principles and auditing standards. (FASB and GASB are pronounced as "fazbee" and "gazbee," whereas the other accounting groups are identified by their initials.)

FASB was formed in 1973 by the accounting profession as an independent organization with the power to develop generally accepted accounting principles. It supplanted its predecessor organization, the Accounting Principles Board (APB) because of concerns about APB's independence. FASB issues statements that specify standards for particular accounting issues. The statements are based on extensive research and are available for public comments for a period of at least 60 days before they are issued in final form. FASB tries to respond to the diverse interests of its constituencies by modifying its statements from their draft form to reflect these interests. It also periodically issues interpretations of existing statements and sponsors research in particular areas of interest.

Several aspects of nonprofit GAAP are inconsistent with for-profit GAAP and are inconsistent among different types of nonprofits. How a FASB statement applies to nonprofit organizations is explicitly discussed in each statement. Several task forces and committees have addressed the issue of nonprofit accounting standards.

In 1978, FASB sponsored Robert N. Anthony's study of "Financial Accounting in Nonbusiness Institutions: An Exploratory Study of Conceptual Issues" (Stamford, Connecticut: FASB, 1978). It explored the objectives and concepts underlying financial accounting and reporting for all organizations other than business enterprises.[2] The study also discussed the boundaries that distinguish nonprofit from for-profit organizations and whether a single set of concepts can be used for all nonprofit organizations. It provided the foundation for much of the work that has followed.

The 1980 FASB Statement of Financial Accounting Concepts (SFAC) No. 4, *Objectives of Financial Reporting by Nonbusiness Organizations,* established the objectives of general purpose external financial reporting by nonbusiness

---

[2]He identified four broad categories of information: financial viability, fiscal compliance, management performance, and cost of services provided. Several important and difficult issues were addressed: aggregation of financial statements, measurement of nonrevenue operating inflows and earnings, recording of depreciation and donated services, and accounting for pension costs.

organizations. Although it emphatically states that external financial reporting for both business and nonprofit organizations is based on a single integrated conceptual framework, it also explicitly addressed the differences between the two types of organizations:

> The major distinguishing characteristics of nonbusiness organizations include: (a) receipts of significant amounts of resources from resource providers who do not expect to receive either repayment or economic benefits proportionate to resources provided, (b) operating purposes that are primarily other than to provide goods or services at a profit or profit equivalent, and (c) absence of defined ownership interests that can be sold, transferred or redeemed or that convey entitlement to a share of a residual distribution of resources in the event of liquidation of the organization.

> These characteristics result in certain types of transactions that are infrequent in business enterprises such as contributions and grants, and in the absence of transactions with owners.[3]

The 1985 FASB SFAC No. 6, *Elements of Financial Statements,* expanded application of SFAC No. 2, *Qualitative Characteristics of Accounting Information,* to both nonprofit and profit-oriented organizations. The elements of financial statements set forth in SFAC 6 are essentially the same for both business and nonprofit organizations, except for the portion we have thus far called net worth.[4] This statement introduced the term *net assets* for the fund balance or net worth of nonprofit organizations as a substitute for the more common term, *fund balance.* For the foreseeable future, both fund balance and net assets are likely to be used interchangeably. These concept statements increased the likelihood of FASB's bringing financial reporting requirements for nonprofits closer to those of business organizations.

In 1984, GASB was created to replicate FASB's function for governmental organizations. In the wake of the financial crisis of New York City and other goverments in the 1970s, both the accounting community and the public became painfully aware of the importance of improving governmental accounting. Those involved in governmental accounting were concerned that FASB was too busy to improve governmental accounting standards, a task GASB has made substantial progress in achieving. GASB accounting standards are contained in the publication, *Codification of Governmental Accounting and Financial Reporting Standards as of May 31, 1990* (GASB, 1990). It is generally referred to as the *GASB Codification,* and we will cite it as such.

In addition to general government operations, GASB standards apply to colleges, universities, and other organizations operated by a government.

---

[3]FASB, Statement of Financial Accounting Concepts No. 4, *Objectives of Financial Reporting by Nonbusiness Organizations* (December 1980).

[4]FASB, Statement of Financial Accounting Concepts No. 6, *Elements of Financial Statements* (1985).

Thus, private colleges and hospitals may follow accounting principles (promulgated by the FASB) that differ from those for government-run colleges and hospitals (promulgated by the GASB). FASB, GASB, AICPA, and industry bodies are attempting to work together to remedy this situation.

Impact of Accounting Standards

Perhaps, at this point, you are thinking that the discussion is as dry as dust and about as relevant. But understanding what accounting does and does not measure is very important. For example, consider the theft of paintings from the Gardner Museum in Boston in 1990. The stolen paintings included a Rembrandt and a Vermeer, a Dutch master whose work is particularly valuable because he produced very few paintings. What was the impact of the theft on the Gardner's Balance Sheet? Zero. No impact. The paintings were never included among the Gardner Museum's Balance Sheet assets.

How can assets that are owned by the organization and worth millions of dollars be omitted from the financial statements? According to GAAP, the omission of major assets is perfectly fine. Museums are not required to include the value of their vast collections and colleges and universities need account only selectively for their substantial investments in buildings in their financial statements.

FASB recently reviewed these two aspects of GAAP and found them wanting. It developed standards requiring all nonprofits under its jurisdiction to recognize the cost of long-lived tangible assets in their external financial statements.[5] Thus, colleges and universities must now recognize the use of their buildings, and museums must account for the value of their collections. After all, reasoned FASB, museum collections can be worth billions of dollars and museum executives selectively "de-accession" (a polite word for sell) them. The presence and sales of these valuable assets should be reflected in the financial statements. And colleges and universities use up their buildings just like other organizations. They too should account for this use.

Although this sounds reasonable enough, a firestorm of controversy erupted around both issues. Irate museum and higher education executives and board members complained of the cost of the valuation process; figures like $50 billion for the extra accounting were bandied about. Others argued that the accounting was intrinsically infeasible. "How could rare art or college buildings be valued?" they demanded. (Of course, the presence of active art auction and real estate markets diminishes the force of this point, and

---

[5]Statement of Financial Accounting Standards No. 93, *Recognition of Depreciation by Not-for-Profit Organizations* (Stamford, CT: FASB, August 1987), and Statement of Financial Accounting Standards No. 99, *Deferral of the Effective Date of Recognition of Depreciation by Not-for-Profit Organizations* (Stamford, CT: FASB, September 1988).

the fact that most nonprofit organizations inventory and value such items for insurance purposes further erodes it.) Last, some found the very notion preposterous. "If there ever was a bean-counting rule, this is it!" noted one expert.[6]

The FASB tried to respond to these comments. Its members even undertook field trips sponsored by nonprofit managers determined to show the FASB the error of its ways. Like dutiful school children, the FASB's board members trudged through the American Museum of Natural History in New York City. While they undoubtedly learned a great deal about the insects in the museum's fabulous collection, FASB, so far, has yielded not an inch.

Other Sources of Accounting Standards

Federal government accounting is the combined responsibility of the General Accounting Office (GAO, an arm of the U.S. Congress headed by the Comptroller General), the U.S. Federal Department of the Treasury (headed by the Secretary of the Treasury), and the Office of Management and Budget (headed by its director). Federal accounting standards are embodied in three U.S. Government publications: *Treasury Financial Manual*,[7] *GAO Policy and Procedures Manual for Guidance of Federal Agencies, Title 2—Accounting*,[8] and *U.S. Government Standard General Ledger*.[9]

The AICPA is the primary professional association of certified public accountants (CPAs). Because CPAs work with accounting and auditing on a daily basis, they provide valuable input into the standard setting process. Four of the *Audit Guides* published by AICPA also provide accounting standards for several types of nonprofit organizations:

Audits of Colleges and Universities, 2d ed., New York: AICPA, 1975.

Audits of Providers of Health Care Services, New York: AICPA, 1991.

Audits of Voluntary Health and Welfare Organizations, 2d ed., New York: AICPA, 1988.

Audits of Certain Nonprofit Organizations, Statement of Position 78-10. New York: AICPA, 1987.

If the issues it covers are not superseded by GASB pronouncements, the AICPA *Audits of State and Local Governmental Units* (1989) is also relevant.

[6]Alison Leigh Cowan, "Pricing the Priceless: Museums Resist, Accountants Insist," *The New York Times*, 1 May 1990, pp. C13, C16.
[7]Department of the Treasury, *Treasury Financial Manual* (1986).
[8]General Accounting Office, *GAO Policy and Procedures Manual for Guidance of Federal Agencies, Title 2—Accounting* (1984).
[9]Office of Management and Budget, *U.S. Government Standard General Ledger* (1986).

Each type of nonprofit has at least one representative organization that provides guidance to accounting standard setters. Although past accounting bodies' pronouncements frequently conflicted with industry standards, today the industry guides primarily elaborate on the standards provided by the accounting bodies and provide guidance on issues not covered by them. Industry groups have worked closely with accounting standard setters to arrive at the mutually acceptable positions reflected in the current standards. This situation is a welcome improvement from the past, when several conflicting sets of standards were advocated by different authoritative bodies. Postsecondary education is represented by the National Association of College and University Business Officers (NACUBO), local governments by the Government Finance Officers Association (GFOA), health care organizations by the Healthcare Financial Management Association (HFMA), and other nonprofits by a variety of units, most prominently the United Way. Publications that provide additional accounting standards, include the following:

Bean, David R.; Stephen J. Gauthier; and Paul E. Glick. *Governmental Accounting, Auditing and Financial Reporting*. Chicago, IL: Government Finance Officers Association, 1988.

National Assembly of National Voluntary Health and Social Welfare Organizations, Inc., National Health Council, Inc., and United Way of America. *Standards of Accounting and Financial Reporting for Voluntary Health and Welfare Organizations*. 3d ed., Alexandria, VA: United Way, 1988.

National Association of College and University Business Officers. *College and University Business Administration: Administrative Service*. Washington, DC: National Association of College and University Business Officers. Published in looseleaf form with periodic supplements.

National Center for Higher Education Management Systems. *Higher Education Finance Manual*. Washington, D.C.: U.S. Government Printing Office, 1980.

Office of Management and Budget. *Audits of Institutions of Higher Education and Other Nonprofit Institutions*. Circular A-133, April 1990.

United States Congress. *The Single Audit Act of 1984*, Public Law 98-502, 31 U.S.C. 7501-7507, 1984.

United Way of America. *Accounting and Financial Reporting, A Guide for United Ways and Not-for-Profit Human Service Organizations*. Alexandria, VA: United Way of America, 1989.

Regulators also can affect financial reporting standards, although they are less directly involved. Many state Offices of the Attorney General are responsible for regulating organizations that solicit charitable contributions within the state and promulgate accounting requirements that require filing of special forms. The U.S. federal government's Medicare and Medicaid health insurance programs, with regulatory and funding jurisdiction over health care provision for the elderly and the poor, require specific financial data. Regulatory agencies often are empowered to require the provision of different information, or information prepared on a different basis from GAAP requirements. Fortunately, the spirit of cooperation among regulators and accounting standard setters is also growing, although many differences in reporting requirements remain.

Funding agencies also wield considerable influence on nonprofit accounting. Many require separate accounting for the money they provide, in addition to the audited general purpose financial statements of the organization. The old variant on the Golden Rule, "(S)he who has the gold makes the rules," is relevant here; most organizations comply with these specialized accounting requirements, even if they impose substantial additional accounting effort. Some large funding agencies, such as the United Way, actively help set standards for the voluntary health and welfare organizations they typically finance. They also provide substantial accounting guidance and assistance to individual nonprofit organizations.

Audits

Audit is derived from the Latin "to hear," because the citizenry in ancient Rome publicly listened to the governors reading of the accounts of how city funds were spent. The audit made the Roman city governors accountable to the citizenry for their actions. Today, that practice has been replaced with a *financial audit* in which an auditor examines the accounting systems and information of an organization and concludes whether the financial statements fairly represent its financial activities and status. The audit must be performed by a licensed CPA, who renders a formal opinion on the fairness of the financial statements and the degree of their compliance with GAAP. CPAs are licensed after passing examinations and meeting educational and work experience requirements. The financial audit is the most common type of audit because banks, funders, and regulators require that most organizations' annual financial statements be audited.

Operational or *performance* audits also are conducted, most notably in governments. This type of audit assesses the quality of the performance of the organization, not the fairness of presentation of the financial statements. The General Accounting Office of the U.S. federal government probably is the best known of the organizations that perform such audits. Consulting firms and internal audit departments also conduct performance audits.

The hierarchy of accounting standards requires that auditors of nonprofit organizations use the relevant FASB or GASB pronouncements if they provide guidance. If they do not, the next source of authority is the relevant AICPA

Audit Guide. If no guidance is provided there, the final sources of authority are the accounting manuals published by representative groups within the nonprofit sector and their normal industry practices.

The *single audit* concept states that one audit should be sufficient to meet the needs of all those who might require that an organization be audited. Together, the Single Audit Act of 1984 and the Federal Office of Management Budget Circulars A-128 and A-133 require governments and nonprofit organizations that receive federal domestic assistance to have a single audit. Some claim that the cost of a single audit should be less than the total cost of separate financial and individual grant audits for organizations with multiple programs, funding sources, and regulatory bodies.

Sources of Accounting Research

To the surprise of many who view accounting, and sometimes accountants, as cast in concrete, considerable accounting research is conducted whose purpose is to increase accounting's relevance to changing social and economic circumstances. Because accounting is a complex social and technical phenomenon, many different types of research are conducted. Much of it focuses on the effects of accounting information on individual financial statement users and the stock markets. Other research assesses the effects of different managerial control systems on managers and organizational performance.

Academic journals such as *The Accounting Review* (American Accounting Association), *Accounting, Organizations and Society* (Pergammon Press), *Journal of Accounting Research* (Institute of Professional Accounting), and *Journal of Accounting and Public Policy* (North Holland), present contemporary accounting, theory, practice, and policy to a broad, but primarily academic, audience. Research that focuses on the management and accounting practices of nonprofit organizations appears in a wide range of accounting and industry journals, such as *The NonProfit Times* (Davis Information Group), *Nonprofit World Report* (Society for Nonprofit Organizations), *Administration in Social Work* (Haworth Press), and *Voluntary Action Leadership* (Volunteer—the National Center). The research of academic and practicing accountants who specialize in nonprofit organizations is published in the *Research in Government and Nonprofit Accounting* (JAI Press, Inc.) and *Financial Accountability and Management in Governments, Public Services and Charities* (Basil Blackwell, Ltd.).

Research of interest to the many different groups within the nonprofit sector is published in sector journals. Research relevant to to government accountants or financial managers is published in *The Government Accountants Journal* (Association of Government Accountants). Research of interest to state or local government general managers is in *Government Finance Review* (Government Finance Officers Association) and *Government Executive* (Times Mirror Co.). Research for educational managers is in *AGB Report* (Association of Governing Boards of Universities) and for financial managers is in *Business Officer* (National Association of College and University Business Officers). In health care, *Hospitals* (American Hospital Association) is a management-oriented research publication, while *Healthcare Financial Management* (Health-care Financial Management Association, Oak Brook, IL) publishes more technical research. Other publications will be noted in the chapters that address the specific types of profit organizations that they cover.

Unfortunately, little of the research conducted to date has provided definitive answers to the questions it addressed, and changes in the environment or technology can quickly render even valid findings and solutions obsolete. Nevertheless, research can provide useful insights, and wise practitioners should be aware of the theories currently in vogue. For this reason, we will try to provide relevant research findings where appropriate.

WHAT LIES AHEAD IN THIS BOOK?

This chapter has introduced you to the nature and purpose of accounting, both generally and specifically for nonprofit organizations; the basic financial accounting statements; and the conventions and standards underlying their preparation. The next two chapters are, of necessity, more technical and detailed because they address the individual components of each of the financial statements. Keep in mind that accounting is a language, used for communication about financial events among various interested parties, each with his or her own perspective. Like all languages, it is simultaneously important and complex.

Once you have mastered the language, we will use it for financial analysis purposes in Chapters 5 and 6, with a special focus on nonprofit organizations. The last chapter in Part One will demonstrate the mechanics of accounting that produce financial statements.

Suggested Reading

Accounting

The Accounting Review and *Accounting Horizons*. American Accounting Association, Sarasota, FL. Quarterly.

Accounting, Organizations, and Society. Pergammon Press, Elmsford, N.Y. Bi-monthly.

Journal of Accounting and Economics. Elsevier Science Publishing, B.V. Amsterdam, Netherlands. Quarterly.

Journal of Accounting and Public Policy. North Holland, New York, N.Y. Quarterly.

Journal of Accounting Research. Institute of Professional Accounting, Graduate School of Business, University of Chicago, Chicago, IL. Semiannual.

Nonprofit Organizations, General

The NonProfit Times. Davis Information Group, Hopewell, NJ. Monthly.

Nonprofit World Report. Society for Nonprofit Organizations, Madison, WI. Monthly.

Voluntary Health and Welfare Nonprofit Organizations

Administration in Social Work. Haworth Press. New York, NY. Quarterly.
Voluntary Action Leadership. Volunteer—the National Center, Arlington, VA. Quarterly.

Government Organizations

Financial Accountability and Management in Governments, Public Services and Charities. Basil
   Blackwell, Ltd., Oxford, England. Quarterly.
The Government Accountants Journal. Association of Government Accountants, Alexandria, VA.
   Quarterly.
Government Executive. Times Mirror Co., Washington, DC. Monthly.
Government Finance Review. Government Finance Officers Association. Newsletter. Chicago,
   IL. Biweekly.
Research in Government and Nonprofit Accounting. JAI Press, Inc., Greenwich, CT. Annually.

Colleges and Universities

AGB Reports. Association of Governing Boards of Universities, Washington, DC. Bimonthly.
Business Officer. National Association of College and University Business Officers, Washington,
   DC. Monthly.

Health Care Nonprofit Organizations

Hospitals. American Hospital Association. Chicago, IL. Semimonthly.
Healthcare Financial Management. Healthcare Financial Management Association. Oak Brook,
   IL. Westchester, IL, Monthly.

DISCUSSION QUESTIONS

1. Discuss the purposes of a Balance Sheet, Income Statement, and Statement of
   Cash Flow.

2. What kinds of questions do the financial statements discussed in this chapter
   help you to answer?

3. In what ways would the Balance Sheets in the tables be different if they were
   prepared under cash accounting? Why?

4. What are the basic accounting conventions? What are their implications for the
   usefulness of financial accounting information for the following purposes:
   a. Determining how much insurance will cover the organization's assets in
      case they are destroyed or lost
   b. Setting the price for a ten-year membership that entitles the user to access
      all of the nonprofit organization's services
   c. Determining if the nonprofit organization can obtain a loan to finance the
      purchase of a new building
   d. Evaluating how energetic a nonprofit hospital's physicians have been in refer-
      ring patients to the hospital
   e. Predicting when the building of a nonprofit college will need to be replaced

5. Should the "cost convention" be changed to recognize events at their market
   value? Why or why not?

6. What is the effect of electronic information technology on accounting?

7.   In what sense is accounting a social subject rather than a technical one?

8.   Why are skilled, experienced business exeutives often unable to understand the accounting statements of nonprofit organizations?

9.   Who are the groups responsible for setting accounting standards? Do you think they adequately represent your interests as a taxpayer and user of services provided by nonprofit organizations? Support your answer.

EXERCISES *

1.   Identify each of the following as an asset, a liability, a revenue, a deferred revenue, or a fund balance item. The transaction can also be none or more than one of the above.
   a.   The land on which the organization is located and which it owns
   b.   Salaries owed to employees
   c.   Grants awarded of $100,000 to be paid next year for specific purposes by the *XYZ* Foundation
   d.   Grants awarded to the organization for which a prepayment of $15,000 has been received from the *MNA* Foundation
   e.   Short-term government bonds owned by the organization
   f.   The organization's reputation
   g.   Prepaid rental expense for the next year
   h.   The costs of incorporation
   i.   A 25-year mortgage on the organization's building
   j.   The retained income of the organization
   k.   The supplies held in various cabinets and rooms
   l.   A loan made to the organization by a local bank

2.   Identify each of the following transactions as being a revenue, an expense, an expenditure, a cash inflow, a cash outflow, or as being none or more than one of the above.
   a.   Bills sent out for services rendered
   b.   The expectation that 10 percent of the bills will not be paid
   c.   Cash paid for bandages by a hospital
   d.   The use of some bandages from a hospital's inventory
   e.   Salaries paid in cash
   f.   Nurses' salaries of $140,000 in the month earned but not yet paid
   g. $1,000,000 borrowed, with interest of 8 percent and principal payable annually over a 20-year period
   h.   Interest of $80,000 paid in cash
   i.   A principal payment of $50,000 in cash.
   j.   The purchase of a $100,000 piece of equipment for cash
   k.   The securities owned declared dividends of $10,000. The dividends have not yet been received in cash

*Professor Regina E. Herzlinger prepared these and all the remaining exercises in this book. Copyright © Regina E. Herzlinger, 1993.

3. How much cash flowed in and out of this organization during the month, given the following information?

a.	Beginning accounts receivable	$50,000
b.	Ending accounts receivable	70,000
c.	Revenues for the month	60,000
d.	Loan granted and received in cash	30,000
e.	Sale of office equipment valued at $2,000 for $2,500	2,500
f.	Interest owed at end of month, but not paid	500
g.	Inventory supplies purchased and paid for	5,000
h.	Supplies used during the month	700
i.	Salaries and benefits paid during the month	30,000
j.	Salaries and benefits owed at the end of the month	35,000
k.	Outstanding bills to suppliers at the end of the month	5,000

Case

CASE STUDY

This case highlights the real-life importance of the differences between accrual and cash accounting. It describes the debate between the management of the New Hampshire/Vermont Blue Cross, a nonprofit health insurance company, and the government regulators who determine the premiums the organization can charge for its health insurance coverage.

With a cash basis of accounting, the Blue Cross organization's financial performance looks very different from the one depicted by an accrual accounting basis. Which one is right? The organization's future depends on the answer.

This case may appear complex to some readers because it is drawn from a complex, real-life situation and has not been artificially simplified. If this is the case, come back to it after you have finished Part One of this book. (Professor Herzlinger is grateful to her colleague, Ed Barrett, for drawing her attention to this incident as a case possibility.)

CASE 2.1 New Hampshire-Vermont Hospitalization Service

The last two paragraphs of the letter read:

Blue Cross is at present insolvent. Its liabilities exceed its assets. It's operating, in effect, by using Peter's money to pay Paul; i.e., current expenditures are being met from funds held to meet claims incurred on which payment will be due in the future.

Whatever may be said for cash-basis operations for a short period in an emergency, continuation of that condition due to inadequate rates has placed Blue Cross on the verge of total collapse which is highly likely in the next three or four months if adequate rate levels are not promptly instituted.

This case was prepared by Arva Clark and William C. Hsaio under the supervision of Professor Regina Herzlinger.

Copyright © 1991 by the President and Fellows of Harvard College. Harvard Business School Case No. 4-175-243. Revised January 1993.

The letter was addressed to Oliver R. Fifield, acting president of the New Hampshire-Vermont Hospitalization Service (Blue Cross) and signed by an actuary from the company's auditors, Peat, Marwick, Mitchell, and Company of New York. Three weeks later, New Hampshire-Vermont Blue Cross applied to the insurance commissioners of New Hampshire and Vermont for rate adjustments to go into effect on February 1 of the next year.

Without the proposed rate changes, Mr. Fifield warned, Blue Cross would lose more than $3 million for the year. But as public hearings on the rate filing opened in January, the insurance commissioners were skeptical. In response to a previous Blue Cross rate filing, the Vermont commissioner had written that although the Plan might become "technically insolvent from time to time," it had "sufficient cash and liquid assets to meet its current obligations."[1] Neither commissioner believed that the situation had changed in the intervening years.

BLUE CROSS

During the 1930s Depression, U.S. hospitals experienced a sharp drop in their major source of income, payment from clients for services rendered. Faced with unpaid bills and empty beds, hospitals in several communities joined together to establish local nonprofit corporations selling prepaid hospitalization insurance to groups of employees working for a single organization. So receptive were individual subscribers and member hospitals to the concept that Blue Cross was well on its way to becoming a national institution by the end of the Depression.

Today there are many Blue Cross plans throughout the United States. Each plan is an autonomous, nonprofit corporation serving members in a contiguous area within one or more states. A plan is usually established under special state legislation. This "enabling act" usually requires that hospital contracts and membership rates be approved by the state insurance department. The state insurance department usually also has the right to inspect the plan's operating records.

RATE FILINGS

In return for a yearly premium, Blue Cross guarantees its members certain benefits and total or partial payment for services received while hospitalized. Hospitals send each member's bills directly to the plan. How much Blue Cross reimburses the hospitals for subscriber benefits is determined by the Blue Cross-Hospital contract.

In forecasting its finances for any given year, a Blue Cross plan may find it difficult to predict its liabilities accurately. Revenue, which consists of premiums and investment income, is known and stable. Administrative expenses are relatively fixed; most plans pay less than ten cents of every premium dollar for administration. But the major portion of a plan's liabilities, claims for hospital services rendered to plan members, can vary considerably from year to year. For any given period, a plan must account for three types of claims: claims filed by members that have been processed and paid; claims filed by members, not yet processed and paid; and claims not yet filed for services already rendered.

The third type of liability is unique to the insurance industry, and may equal close to 100 percent of a company's assets. In addition, Blue Cross must project

[1]From the Rate Order issued by the Insurance Commissioner of Vermont, May 14, 1973.

increases in hospital costs for the premium year. If premiums received from subscribers are not adequate to cover these costs because they were incorrectly projected, cash flow problems may become acute. To counter the danger of insolvency, each Blue Cross plan maintains a contingency reserve, a surplus of liquid assets sufficient to cover its estimated operating expenses for a given period, perhaps one to three months. When its contingency reserve is lower than is considered safe, or is depleted, a plan makes a rate filing, a request to the insurance department under whose jurisdiction it operates for an adjustment in premium rates.

Insurance commissioners have always considered it important to ensure that a Blue Cross plan can meet its obligations to its members. However, huge health care cost increases caused some commissioners to broaden their interpretation of their regulatory authority. They began to question the process whereby Blue Cross routinely passed along increasing hospital costs to subscribers through higher premiums without first evaluating how hospitals are determining their costs and whether higher charges are justified. They hoped that their demands of better management from Blue Cross would translate into the same demand of the hospitals that depend on it for financial stability. Some commissioners also challenged the contingency reserve concept, asking whether Blue Cross allows itself too comfortable a margin for forecasting error at the expense of its subscribers.

THE PRESENT RATE FILING

Since 1944, one Blue Cross plan, the New Hampshire-Vermont Hospitalization Service (NHVHS), served all of New Hampshire and Vermont. The plan held contracts with all 47 regular (nongovernmental), short-term acute care hospitals in the two states. The Blue Cross-Hospital contracts gave the plan the right to audit each hospital's accounts annually and to pay for services to members on the basis of costs *or* charges, "whichever is lower."

In its present rate filing, Blue Cross sought to wipe out its deficit and to establish a contingency reserve of 1.5 months of operating expenses as of January 31, three years in the future. As usual, the plan based all its financial projections on the combined experience of members from both states.

The New Hampshire and Vermont insurance departments held public hearings to allow Blue Cross to present its case. Much of the testimony focused on the issue of cash accounting versus accrual accounting. The insurance departments analyzed the plan on a cash basis and found it solvent as of December (see **Exhibit 1**). Financial statements prepared on an accrual basis, the accounting method favored by NHVHS, showed that the plan was insolvent (see **Exhibits 2**, **3**, and **4**).

To learn exactly how NHVHS had computed its current deficit, the commissioners questioned a Blue Cross consultant about the propriety of the two asset and four liability accounts that do not appear in the statements prepared on a cash basis. The two asset accounts were (1) the plan's marketable equity securities carried at historical cost, significantly below market value; and (2) its bonds carried at amortized costs, somewhat above their market value. In their previous ruling, the commissioners had objected to both, as well as to the plan's assets being carried at historical cost. They argued that the plan's reported assets should reflect their real present value in order to give "a more complete picture of the true worth of the corporation."

At the hearing, the consultant defended both items as standard accounting procedure. "In addition," he said, "the ethical propriety of Blue Cross carrying these [stocks] at a higher market value—in a world where the Dow Jones is known to drop by approximately 20 percent in one month's time—is highly questionable."

The four liability accounts that the commissioners questioned were:

(1)   Unpaid claims (the amount owed on claims incurred, but as yet unreported).

(2)   Unpaid claims adjustment expense (the administrative cost of processing those unpaid claims once they are reported).

(3)   Accrued vacation allowances (the amount due employees for vacation time already earned, but not taken).

(4)   Unearned subscription income (cash payments received for coverage not in effect until the following fiscal year).

In their previous ruling, the commissioners had disallowed the second and third items as legitimate liabilities, saying they should rather be considered "liquidation basis" reserves:

> In both instances, claims and vacation expenses are paid as they arise. For example, claims personnel of the plans are working every day with both current claims and claims which arose out of illnesses months, or even years, removed. The cost of processing such old claims are included in current claims expense. Similarly, vacations during the normal course of a working year are included in current payroll figures. In most instances, there would not be an extra payment as such to the worker. He would simply receive his paycheck as normal. The only difference would be that he would not be physically present at the office for a number of days. In the context of an ongoing public service corporation, as we have here, the likelihood of the plans being liquidated, and therefore having to call upon these full reserves to meet their obligations rather than absorbing them in current expenses, is extremely remote.

They had also questioned the propriety of the first, and by far the largest, liability account, unpaid claims, questioning the plan's ability to predict unpaid claims with accuracy. In his decision, the Vermont commissioner had noted that:

> The figures shown for claims unpaid are estimates, and for years the [Blue Cross and Blue Shield] plans have used an actuarial technique known as "least squares per premium projection" in computing the estimate . . . [in past years] there has been an astonishing amount of variation or fluctuation between the amounts that were estimated and the actual results. . . .In computing its reserve for claims unpaid, Blue Cross took the mathematical estimate and added a "safety factor" of $100,000.

At the January hearing, the consultant defended all four as legitimate liability accounts, consistent with the accrual basis of accounting, since they provided an "accurate portrayal of the expenses related to providing service to the prior years' policyholders." He further noted that in the past year Blue Cross subscribers paid approximately $6 million less than the cost of services provided to them during that year. During that year, he said, Blue Cross used cash received for that year's premiums to pay claims related to the past year's experience and would have to do the same in the future unless rate increases were approved. The plan was in an especially precarious position because, in its attempt to remain solvent during the year, it had sold virtually all its regular investment portfolio and its computer software program and had recalled most of its cash advances to member hospitals (used by the hospital to meet their cash flow needs). He argued that using next year's premiums to pay current expenses was putting the whole concept of a prepaid hospitalization plan into jeopardy.

The insurance commissioners also questioned the concept of surplus itself. They wondered whether it was appropriate for a nonprofit organization such as Blue Cross to maintain a contingency reserve to protect it from fluctuations in its financial experience. They had expressed their doubts on several occasions. In one order, the Vermont commissioner wrote: "Blue Cross and Blue Shield, according to New Hampshire law, are not insurance companies. . . . In most respects they are exempted from the provisions of the code which regulates insurance companies. With respect to surplus levels, it should be noted that [the laws] do not require that Blue Cross maintain *any* surplus."

To bolster its case, NHVHS distributed a position paper prepared by the national Blue Cross Association, which identified several contingencies that might affect a plan's financial state adversely:

(1) Incorrect estimates of claims cost per contract, of administration and other expenses, and of unpaid claims liabilities;

(2) Unanticipated financial demands related to improvements in health care provided by community hospitals;

(3) Fluctuation of stock and bond values; and

(4) Natural disasters, epidemics, and other catastrophes.

Based on national experience, the Association recommended a contingency reserve of at least 17 percent of the sum of claims expense and administrative expense, both measured over the most recent 12-month period.

ISSUE

The insurance commissioners had to determine whether NHVHS was actually insolvent, and resolve the contingency reserve issue. How much of a surplus would give NHVHS just the right amount of "cushion"—not so small that members' interests were endangered, not so large that the plan lost its incentive to maintain rigorous management controls?

Notes

All material on the New Hampshire-Vermont Hospitalization Service's rate filings comes from the public record: Vermont Insurance Commissioner's Rate Order of May 14, 1973; Blue Cross's Rate Filing of December 23, 1973; and the transcript of the 1974 public hearings on the plan's December filing held in Concord, New Hampshire and Montpelier, Vermont, on January 28 and 29, respectively.

Background material on the establishment of Blue Cross in the United States comes from *Doctors, Patients, and Health Insurance*, by H.M. Somers and A.R. Somers, The Brookings Institution, (Washington, DC: May 1961).

Background material about the New Hampshire-Vermont Hospitalization Service comes from that organization's publication entitled: "The Blue Cross and Blue Shield System in New Hampshire and Vermont," undated (mimeo).

EXHIBIT 1 **New Hampshire-Vermont Hospitalization Service Projected Statement of Cash Receipts, Disbursements, and Balances for Current and Next Year[a] (thousands of dollars)**

	Current Year			Next Year				
	Actual, Ten Months Ended Oct. 31	Projected, Nov. and Dec.	Projected, Year Ending Dec. 31	1st Quarter Jan.-Mar.	2d Quarter Apr.-Jun.	3d Quarter Jul.-Sep.	4th Quarter Oct.-Dec.	Projected, Year Ending Dec. 31
Cash balance, beginning	$ 419	$2,613	$ 419	$ 2,270	$ 2,042	$ 712	$ 1,321	$ 2,270
Cash receipts from operations:								
Subscription income	$34,951	$7,767	$42,718	$11,939	$12,155	$12,168	$12,383	$48,645
Cash disbursements for operations:								
Hospital settlements	$ 1,139	$ 100	$ 1,239	$ 500	$ 100	$ -	$ -	$ 600
Claims paid	35,785	7,417	43,202	10,962	12,788	10,962	12,788	47,500
Net operating expense	2,554	692	3,246	686	645	656	996	2,983
Total cash disbursements	$39,478	$8,209	$47,687	$12,148	$13,533	$11,618	$13,784	$51,083
Net cash disbursements from operations	$ (4,527)	$ (442)	$ (4,969)	$ (209)	$ (1,378)	$ 550	$ (1,401)	$ (2,438)
Other receipts and (disbursements):								
Investment income from & sale of	4,750	44	4,794	70	70	70	70	279
Return of hospital advances	1,987	55	2,042	42	-	-	-	42
Capital equipment expenditures	(16)	-	(16)	(130)	(22)	(10)	-	(163)
Cash inflow (outflow)	$ 2,194	$ (343)	$ 1,851	$ (227)	$ (1,331)	$ 609	$ (1,331)	$ (2,280)
Cash balance, ending	$ 2,613	$2,270	$ 2,270	$ 2,042	$ 712	$ 1,321	$ (10)	$ (10)

[a]Numbers do not balance precisely because of rounding.

Source: Computations based on table provided by NHVHS.

EXHIBIT 2 New Hampshire-Vermont Hospitalization Service,
Projected Accrual Basis Statement of Income and Expenses for the
Current Year Ending December 31 (thousands of dollars)[a]

	December	Percentage	Year to Date	Percentage
Subscriber payments	$4,167		$42,423	
Other income	23		209	
Total operating income	4,191	100.0%	42,631	100.0%
Claims incurred	3,680	87.8	45,441	106.5
Total operating expenses	494	11.7	5,205	12.2
Less: reimbursed expense	164	3.9	2,141	5.0
Net operating expense	330	7.8	3,064	7.1
Total claims and operating expense	4,010	95.6	48,505	113.7
Net operating income	181	4.3	(5,874)	(13.7)
Investment income—real estate	3		32	
Investment income—other	34	0.8	284	0.6
Gain (loss) on sale of assets	-	-	(318)	(0.7)
Net income before extraordinary items	219	5.2	(5,875)	(13.7)
Extraordinary items	(24)	(0.5)	(223)	(0.5)
Net income	$ 195	4.6%	$ (6,098)	(14.3)%

[a]Numbers do not balance precisely because of rounding.

Source: NHVHS

EXHIBIT 3 New Hampshire-Vermont Hospitalization Service,
Projected Accrual Basis Balance Sheet as of December 31
of the Current Year (thousands of dollars)[a]

Assets		Liabilities	
Cash	$ 2,597	Claims, unpaid, reported	$ 1,313
Securities	1,587	Claims, unpaid, unreported	7,412
Real estate (net of depreciation		Total claims unpaid	8,725
of $294)	2,637	Unearned subscriber payments	997
Accounts receivable	3,630	NH-VT. physician service	377
Deposits with InterPlan Bank	113	Outstanding checks	1,271
Deposits—advances to hospitals	47	Other liabilities	1,661
Equipment, furniture, fixtures		Unpaid claims adjustment	
(net of depreciation of $32)	78	expense	307
Software program (net of		Contingency reserve	(2,645)
amortization of $9)	6		
Total assets	$10,694	Total liabilities	$10,694

[a]Numbers do not balance precisely because of rounding.

Source: NHVHS

EXHIBIT 4   **New Hampshire-Vermont Hospitalization Service, Projected Accrual Basis Balance Sheets for Selected Months in Next Year[a] (thousands of dollars)**

	Next Year				
Assets	*Jan.*	*Apr.*	*Jul.*	*Oct.*	*Dec.*
Cash	$ 2,103	$ 2,098	$ 899	$ (201)	$ (10)
Accounts receivable from subscribers	596	601	607	627	616
Other receivables	2,596	2,596	2,765	2,703	4,658
Investments (securities at cost, real estate at depreciated value)	414	412	410	409	407
Property, plant, and equipment at depreciated value	2,454	2,436	2,417	2,398	2,386
Total assets	$ 8,164	$ 8,144	$ 7,098	$ 5,936	$ 6,058
Liabilities					
Unpaid claims	$ 8,904	$ 9,575	$ 9,065	$ 8,941	$ 9,802
Unearned subscription income	992	992	992	992	992
Other liabilities	1,862	1,795	2,012	2,012	1,683
Total liabilities	11,758	12,362	12,069	11,944	12,477
Contingency reserve	(3,594)	(4,218)	(4,971)	(6,008)	(6,419)
Total liabilities and reserve	$ 8,164	$ 8,144	$ 7,098	$ 5,936	$ 6,058

[a]Numbers do not balance precisely because of rounding.

Source: Figures taken from table provided by NHVHS.

3   The Balance Sheet

A SET OF FINANCIAL STATEMENTS TYPICALLY contains a Balance Sheet, a Statement of Revenues and Expenses, and a Statement of Changes in Financial Position. Each statement describes different aspects of the economic status of the organization and its performance over some period of time. Statements are prepared at least once per *fiscal year* or operating cycle, a period of time that does not necessarily coincide with a calendar year. (For example, the operating cycle of a college typically begins in September when students arrive.) The statements are usually accompanied by notes that disclose the accounting methods used and other relevant information to help users interpret the financial statements. If the financial statements were audited by a certified public accountant, an audit opinion will also accompany them.

The next two chapters describe the financial statements of the real nonprofit public broadcasting station we have called RSUS. Although the description may initially appear to be simple, do not confuse our simple language with simplistic discussion. Each item is discussed in depth.

In what follows, the same account or activity may be called by several different names. The language of financial management is very flexible; it employs many synonyms. This fact is often frustrating for beginning speakers of the language, who would understandably prefer the book to contain only one name per account or event. But if we used only one name, we would defeat our purpose of helping managers function in the messy reality of the world. You would be ill served if we created an artificially neat world. In the following discussions, we will note the several names commonly used for the economic transactions we are describing. The most frequently used one will be our major title, others will be identified in parentheses. We will also identify terms with unique accounting definitions with the sobriquet ''accountingese.''

OVERVIEW OF THE BALANCE SHEET

The Balance Sheet reflects the current financial position of the organization at a given time. For that reason it is sometimes called a Statement of Financial Position. It accounts for the various types of items owned by the organization (Assets) and the sources of financing for those items (Liabilities and Fund Balances). Each Balance Sheet account is a summary of the amounts from several subsidiary accounts. For example, although most organizations have several bank accounts, their Balance Sheet has only one cash account; it is the sum of the cash amounts in the several bank accounts. The Balance Sheet presentation format can be layered, with Assets on top and Liabilities and Fund Balances on the bottom, or side-by-side, with Assets on the left and Liabilities and Fund Balances on the right.

Every significant monetary transaction in which an organization engages is ultimately recorded on the Balance Sheet. Assets are the things of value the organization owns—the items in which its resources are invested. Liability and Fund Balance accounts represent the sources financing the Assets and frequently are collectively referred to as *capital*. Liabilities are debts owed and Fund Balance is the amount of income retained by the organization.

The Balance Sheet for RSUS for the fiscal years 19X7 and 19X8 is shown in Table 3-1. It will be used as the basis for the ensuing discussion. Please do not be intimidated by its daunting appearance. At the end of this chapter, you should understand every account it contains.

ASSETS

Assets are classified as *current* and *noncurrent* assets, based on the amount of time required to *liquidate* them, or turn them into cash. (*Liquidity* is accountingese for a measure of the fortunate financial condition of having lots of freely available cash and cash-like assets.) Current assets are those expected to be converted to cash within the next operating cycle (usually a year). Noncurrent assets are expected to remain in their noncash form for longer than a year, and are categorized as *investments*, *fixed assets* or *other assets*. Assets are valued at the lower of historical cost or market, reflecting the application of the conservatism convention.

Current Assets

Current assets are typically listed in descending order of liquidity. It is important to distinguish current assets from other assets because they are readily available to pay debt obligations, unlike other assets. The Balance Sheet shows that RSUS's $472,234 of current assets in 19X8 decreased slightly from the $489,935 in current assets in 19X7.

TABLE 3-1   **RSUS Balance Sheet**

RSUS
Balance Sheet
For the Years Ending June 30, 19X7 and June 30, 19X8

Assets

	June 30, 19X8		June 30, 19X7	
Current assets				
Cash		$ 310,010		$ 185,499
Certificate of deposit		100,000		100,000
Other marketable securities (market				
value 19X8, $6,528; 19X7, $6,224)		6,465		6,009
Receivables		10,399		165,263
Interest	$ 6,212		$ 4,946	
Employees	2,239		927	
Agencies	1,948		6,612	
Grant awards	-		152,778	
Prepaid expenses		5,360		3,164
Inventory		40,000		30,000
Total current assets		$ 472,234		$ 489,935
Property, plant, and equipment				
Studio and offices	22,621		14,984	
Telecasting equipment	1,263,472		1,166,575	
Mobile equipment	6,875		5,352	
Office furniture and equipment	56,998		50,286	
Property rights acquired under long-				
term lease	-		97,761	
Allowance for depreciation	(548,905)		(426,114)	
Net Property, plant, and equipment		$ 801,061		$ 908,844
Time deposits designated for capital im-				
provements and production		133,653		128,723
Total assets		$1,406,948		$1,527,502

Liabilities and Fund Balance

	June 30, 19X8		June 30, 19X7	
Current liabilities				
Accounts payable		$ 12,906		$ 170,648
Salaries and wages payable		18,547		9,337
Payroll taxes payable		3,087		3,454
Current portion of installment contract				
payable		22,134		-
Current portion of capitalized lease				
obligation				32,587
Total current liabilities		$ 56,674		$ 216,026
Deferred grant award revenue		25,000		25,000
Deferred production revenue		10,000		
Installment contract payable, less portion				
classified as a current liability		8,255		
Capitalized lease obligation, less portion				
classified as a current liability				65,174
Fund balance		1,307,019		1,221,302
Total liabilities and fund balance		$1,406,948		$1,527,502

Cash   The most liquid asset is cash because it can be used directly at any time to purchase other assets or services or to pay liabilities. Cash can take a number of forms. Most cash is held in checking and savings accounts. The small amount in currency is usually in *petty cash* funds, small pools of cash used to buy inexpensive items on an as-needed basis. Temporary investments of excess cash in highly liquid, short-term investments, such as money market funds and Treasury bills, are called *cash equivalents*. They can be combined with cash on the Balance Sheet in an account called *cash and cash equivalents*. RSUS had cash balances of $310,010 in 19X8 and $185,499 in 19X7.

Marketable Securities   The resources invested on a short-term basis in various securities, such as stocks, bonds, and governmental financial instruments, are called *marketable securities*. The purpose of this investment is to earn a return. Although marketable securities can take many forms, they can all be quickly bought and sold in an existing organized market. If securities are held for other, longer-term purposes, or cannot be quickly sold, they are reported as *investments* in the Other Asset section of the Balance Sheet, as discussed below.

The more common forms of marketable securities are stocks, bonds, notes, and bills. Stocks of corporations are sold on the stock exchanges. Common stocks represent shares in the ownership of the corporation and carry voting rights. Although the owners of common stock frequently receive a dividend, they are not guaranteed that a dividend will be declared. The value of common stock changes with the growth and earnings of the company and the vagaries of the stock markets. For example, when General Motors was growing rapidly, its stock was worth more, relatively, than it is today. The owners of preferred stock do receive a guaranteed dividend but do not have ownership rights in the corporation. They cannot vote on the nominees for the corporation's board of directors, for example, but holders of common stock can do so. *Bonds*, *notes*, and *bills* are debt instruments (IOUs) issued by state, local, and federal governments and by corporations and, sometimes, private parties. The issuing organization promises to repay the buyer of the IOU the amount of money borrowed (called the *principal*) plus interest for the use of the money.

Some types of marketable securities, such as bank certificates of deposit, may be disclosed separately because they are less risky than other types of marketable securities, and are more like cash. RSUS separately listed a $100,000 certificate of deposit in 19X7 and 19X8. RSUS also held other marketable securities that cost $6,009 in 19X7 and $6,465 in 19X8 and had market values of $6,224 in 19X7 and $6,528 in 19X8. That is, the securities owned on June 30, 19X8, could have been sold to yield a market value of $6,528 on that date and had been purchased for $6,465.

Nonprofits value marketable securities for financial reporting purposes in three basic ways: (1) at their market value on the statement date, (2) at their historical cost, or (3) at the lower of their historical cost or their market on the statement date. In addition to these broad categories, there are myriad variations that depend on the type of nonprofit, the type of security, the purpose for holding the security, and other factors. Generally, an organization must use the same method for valuing all its marketable securities. Whatever basis of measurement is used, both cost and market value should be disclosed either in the statement itself or in a footnote.

Revenue earned from marketable securities consists of interest and dividends, and may be called *investment income, endowment income, dividends, interest earned* or some other descriptive title. It is reported as revenue, with a corresponding addition to a cash or receivable account, depending on whether or not it has been received in cash.

In addition to these traditional investment earnings, organizations also report gains or losses from owning appreciated or depreciated marketable securities. These are referred to as *realized* if the securities were sold, or if the decline in market value is expected to be permanent, and as *unrealized* if the securities were not sold and the gains and losses thus reflect only changes in market value. Realized gains and losses occur under all valuation methods. The *market basis* of valuing marketable securities also recognizes unrealized gains and losses whenever a change in market value occurs. The *lower of cost or market basis* recognizes unrealized gains or losses when the market value of securities decreases below cost, or increases after having been *written down* to a lower market value in a prior period. Businesses must use the lower of cost or market method unless special industry standards allow them to use market or other valuation methods. Various nonprofits have different options for valuing marketable securitis.

The following example may help to clarify the various methods. In November of 19X0, we paid $10 to buy a share of stock in Health Inc., a mythical company whose stock is sold on the New York Stock Exchange. At the end of November, the stock paid its owners a dividend of $0.50 per share. By December 31, 19X0, dramatic events caused its market value to drop to $9 a share, a decline that was not expected to be permanent. We still owned the stock on that date. Under all valuation methods, our statement of revenues and expenses would show dividend income of $0.50. With the lower of cost or market or the market bases of valuation, our Balance Sheet at December 31, 19X0, would show marketable securities valued at $9 and our statement of revenues and expenses would show an Unrealized Loss of $1. With the cost basis of valuation, our Balance Sheet at December 31, 19X0, would show marketable securities valued at $10 and our statement of revenues and expenses not record any loss until the security was sold.

Now suppose that unexpected good news caused the market value of the stock to increase to $13 a share on December 31, 19X1. Applying the lower of cost or market basis of valuation, the Balance Sheet at December 31, 19X1, would show marketable securities valued at $10, with an unrealized gain of $1 in the statement of revenues and expenses. With the market basis, the Balance Sheet at December 31, 19X0, would show marketable securities valued at $13 and our statement of revenues and expenses with an unrealized gain of $4 (current market value of $13 − last market value of $9). Using the cost basis, the Balance Sheet at December 31, 19X1 would show marketable securities valued at $10 and our statement of revenues and expenses would show neither a gain nor a loss related to marketable securities.

Finally, suppose we sold the stock during 19X2 for $11.25. Under all three methods, the marketable securities asset value at December 31, 19X2, is zero, and cash is increased by $11.25, the amount for which the stock was sold. However, the amount of the realized gain or loss on the sale of marketble securities will differ under the various methods. Applying either the cost or lower of cost or market basis, our statement of revenues and expenses would show a realized gain of $1.25 ($11.25 − $10.00). Using the market basis, our statement of revenues and expenses would show a realized loss of $1.75 ($13.00 − $11.25).

Table 3-2 provides a clear example of the impact of the flexibility of accounting. Note that the value of the stock in 19X1 ranged from $10 to $13 and that the gain in that year was from $1 to $4. All of these values are sanctioned by GAAP under certain conditions. Readers of the financial statements must

TABLE 3-2   **Effect of Alternative Marketable Securities Valuation Methods**

	Marketable Security Value	Unrealized Gain (Loss)	Realized Gain (Loss)
December 31, 19X0			
Market	$ 9.00	$(1.00)	-
Lower of cost or market	9.00	(1.00)	-
Cost	10.00	-	-
December 31, 19X1			
Market	$13.00	$4.00	-
Lower of cost or market	10.00	1.00	-
Cost	10.00	-	-
December 31, 19X2*			
Market	-	-	$(1.75)
Lower of cost or market	-	-	1.25
Cost	-	-	1.25

*Stock sold during 19X2 for $11.25.

understand that the financial values they contain, as in our example, are not cast in concrete, and can be readily changed by a change in accounting methods.

Mutual funds, real estate investment trusts, commodities, futures contracts, options, and even junk bonds are all popular investments. New financial instruments and markets are constantly being invented. Discussion of these other investment possibilities is beyond the scope of this text, and many nonprofit and other investors have found them beyond the scope of their ability to manage successfully. If a small nonprofit has a large investment in any of these, a red flag of concern should be raised. Any organization with a sizable investment portfolio today probably requires sophisticated investment advice and professional investment management.

Receivables The amounts owed to an organization are *receivables*. *Accounts receivable* are revenues not yet collected in cash—the amounts still owed by customers or clients for goods or services the organization has already delivered. Other types of receivables typically found in nonprofits include *membership dues receivable* (dues for memberships applied for and approved, but not yet paid for), *grants receivable* (grants awarded but not yet received), *pledges receivable* (pledges made but not yet received), *interest receivable* (interest earned but not yet received), and *employee advances or loans receivable* (amounts of money lent to employees and not yet repaid).

All receivables are valued at the amount that can realistically be collected. The amount that will not be collected is estimated, and placed in an account called *allowance for uncollectible receivables*, (or *allowance for bad debts* or *allowance for doubtful accounts*). It is deducted from the total receivables account. The accounts receivable are typically shown net of this allowance on the Balance Sheet, as follows:

Accounts receivable (net of allowance for bad
   debts of $XXX) $YY,YYY

The amount estimated to be uncollectible is calculated on the basis of the organization's prior experience with collections of similar types of receivables. The allowance can be calculated as a percentage of revenues or as a percentage of receivables. A good way of calculating it is to group the receivables by the amount of time they have been owed (*outstanding*); this process is called *aging the receivables*. The appropriate estimated uncollectible rate is then applied to each group. The older the receivable, the higher the probability of its not being collected. An example of this process is shown in Table 3-3. The accounts receivable of $600,000 would be valued at the net amount expected to be collected of $533,000, and the Balance Sheet would disclose the allowance for bad debts of $67,000.

Accounts receivable frequently represent a large proportion of the current assets of private nonprofit organizations. For example, more than one-third of the 19X7 current assets of RSUS are receivables. Because of their relative magnitude, a great deal of care should be taken to manage and account for

TABLE 3-3   **Aging of Receivables and Calculation of Allowance for Bad Debts**

Age	Accounts Receivable Amount	Estimated Percentage Uncollectible	Allowance for Bad Debts
Less than 1 month	$100,000	2%	$ 2,000
1 to 4 months	400,000	10	40,000
4 to 8 months	50,000	20	10,000
Over 8 months	50,000	30	15,000
Total	$600,000		$67,000

receivables correctly. A nonprofit organization that does not bill promptly or control its billing and collection process is providing free loans or free services to those who do not pay promptly. While it might be appropriate for an organization to provide such loans or free services to certain constituencies, it should be done as a deliberate matter of policy, not as an accidental result of a poorly managed billing and collections process. A long receivables cycle (accountingese for a long period of time before cash payment is received) may be the cost of doing business with certain clients or government agencies, but this too should be a matter of deliberate policy. Also, if billings and receivables are poorly managed, the accuracy of the amount of receivables in the financial statements is suspect.

In 19X7, RSUS had total receivables of $165,263, consisting of grants receivable of $152,778, interest receivable of $4,946, employee receivables of $927 and amounts due from various agencies which have not yet been paid in cash (agencies receivables) of $6,612. The absence of an allowance for uncollectible receivables, indicates that RSUS expects all the amounts listed as receivables to be collected in full. The drastic decrease of receivables to $10,399 by 19X8 was primarily caused by the absence of grants receivable. A change of such magnitude from one year to the next deserves investigation of its cause. There may well be a satisfactory explanation for the change, and management should be able to provide that explanation to an inquiring board. Frequently, such a large change, in either direction, may signal a need for investigation.

Prepaid Expenses   Intangible, valuable rights to future services, such as insurance policies and rent, that are owned and will be used in the upcoming year are *prepaid expenses*. Although these items are intangible, they are nevertheless assets because they are of future value to the entity and are owned by it. When items are prepaid more than one year in advance, the portions pertaining to later years may be listed under other assets, and are called *deferred charges*. RSUS's small prepaid expenses probably represent insurance policies.

Inventories The cost of material and supplies currently owned that will be used in the forthcoming operating cycle are accounted for in *inventories*. They may consist of goods to be sold or supplies to be used, and may have been purchased or manufactured by the organization. As inventories are used up in operations, the reduction of their value is accounted for as a *supplies* expense or a *cost of goods sold* expense. Unless they are engaged in manufacturing or retail sales, most nonprofits have relatively small inventories. RSUS's inventory probably consists of supplies such as videotapes and films.

Many organizations cannot accurately value the inventory they have on hand because they do not carefully account for additions to inventory or uses of inventory. If the amounts are relatively small, it may be reasonable to expense all purchases immediately, even though some supplies may remain on hand at the end of the period. However, it is important to monitor supplies and cost of goods sold expenses, and physically to examine the inventories periodically, to make sure that there is no pilferage or waste due to obsolescence or damage. The monitoring approach should be tailored to the nature of the inventory. Certain types of items are more likely to be pilfered (such as narcotic drugs in a pharmacy). Others are more susceptible to damage by improper storage (such as paper). Still others have limited shelf lives and are thus susceptible to obsolescence (such as food). Management and staff are usually well aware of which items are most susceptible to each type of risk, even if the proper control mechanisms are not yet in place.

The two procedures of controlling and accounting for inventory are called the periodic and the perpetual methods. They provide different levels of control over the items in inventory and require different amounts of effort and recordkeeping to implement. The *periodic inventory method*, as its name suggests, values inventory at specific points in time, rather than continuously. It is implemented by valuing the inventory at the beginning of the period, adding to it the value of the items purchased during the period, and subtracting from that sum the value of the inventory remaining at the end of the period. The ending inventory value is obtained by taking a physical count of the items on hand at the end of the period and valuing them at their purchase price. This method provides accurate inventory values at the end of the period, but does not provide good control over inventory during the period.

For example, in the beginning of its fiscal year 19X8, RSUS had $30,000 in its inventory. (This is the amount it had in inventory as of the last day of fiscal 19X7 and, therefore, the amount in inventory on the very first moment of fiscal year 19X8.) If it purchased inventory costing $31,775 in 19X8 and determined that the ending value of the inventory in 19X8 was

TABLE 3-4 **Calculation of Inventory Use or Supplies Expense**

Beginning inventory	$30,000
Plus purchases of supplies during fiscal 19X8	31,775
Inventory available for use during year	$61,775
Less inventory value as of the end of fiscal 19X8	40,000
Inventory used or supplies expense 19X8	$21,775

$40,000, then the supplies expense is calculated as shown in Table 3-4. Note that the supplies expense of $21,775 represents the cost of supplies inventory used up or *consumed* during the year. It is a different amount from the expenditure for supplies of $31,775, which represents the inventory *acquired* during the year.

The *perpetual inventory method*, in contrast, measures and controls inventory use throughout the period instead of measuring it only at the end of the period. It requires extensive recordkeeping on purchases and a requisition system that documents every withdrawal from inventory. The requisitions record how much was taken, why, when, and by whom. The inventory on hand also is physically counted and valued under this method as a check on the accuracy of the perpetual inventory records. Any discrepancies found are investigated and adjusted to the correct amount. The physical count may be taken at times other than the end of the accounting period. If the discrepancies are found to be minimal and the perpetual inventory values reliable, the perpetual inventory amounts at the end of the accounting period will be used for the Balance Sheet inventory values.

A perpetual inventory system helps protect the organization against theft and damage. But this system is expensive because it accounts for every item separately and continuously. It is worthwhile only for organizations with inventory items that are few in number, individually identifiable, or very expensive, or those that must be carefully controlled, such as radioactive materials in nuclear laboratories. Organizations may choose to use a perpetual inventory system only for some items, and use a periodic inventory or immediate expense approach to account for other, less important, items.

The periodic and perpetual methods account for the physical items in inventory. Either method should result in an identical count of the number of items in inventory at the end of the period.

The issue of how to value the items in inventory and those sold or used in operations is a more complex one. As an example, consider the following inventory valuation problem. A museum shop purchased 50 statues of King Tut at $20 each and sold all of them for $40 each. With this successful record, the museum bought 100 more statues, which now cost $30 each, and sold them for $55. Ten were left in inventory at the end of the period.

Calculating the number of items involved is straightforward: the beginning inventory was zero, 150 statues were purchased during the period, and 10 were left at its end. Therefore, 140 statues were sold during this period. It is also straightforward to determine the revenues: 50 at $40 plus 90 at $55 equals $6,950 of revenues.

But what is the value of the ending inventory and what is the cost of the items sold? Several alternative methods may be used to calculate the monetary amounts. Although each method is likely to generate different amounts, all of them are acceptable accounting methods.

The *first-in, first-out (FIFO)* inventory valuation method assumes that the first 140 statues to arrive were the first to be sold. Therefore, the ending inventory consists of the last 10 items purchased, which cost $30 each. The cost of the goods sold consists of 50 items at $20 each and 90 items at $30 each, for a total expense of $3,700 [($20 × 50) + ($30 × 90)].

The *last-in, first-out (LIFO)* inventory valuation method assumes that the museum will always want to have a certain amount of inventory available and that it will never sell the first items to arrive but rather will sell the last ones. A coal bin is often used to illustrate the LIFO inventory method. Under LIFO, the 10 items left in the ending inventory are those that arrived first, at a cost of $20 each. Of the 140 items sold, 100 cost $30 each and 40 cost $20 each, for a cost of goods sold of $3,800 [($30 × 100) + ($20 × 40)]. An advantage claimed for the LIFO method is that it expresses the cost of the items sold more nearly in terms of their replacement costs than the FIFO method. In practice, relatively few nonprofit organizations use LIFO, but it is an available option of which financial statement readers should be aware.

The *weighted average* method of valuing inventory holds that each unit should be valued at its average cost—in this case the total purchase price of $4,000 [($20 × 50) + ($30 × 100)] divided by the total units purchased of 150, or $26.67. The ending inventory of 10 statues would have a value of $268 (10 × $26.67) and the cost of goods sold would be $3,734 (140 × $26.67).[1]

The *specific identification* method identifies which specific items are left in inventory, and values them at the amount they actually cost. Its use is limited to situations where the items in inventory can be so identified, and is likely to be reserved for expensive items, each of which has a significantly different cost. If three of the remaining statues were from the first batch, and the other seven from the second, the ending inventory would be $270 [($20 × 3) + ($30 × 7)]. In practice, the museum store might value large pieces on a specific identification basis, and smaller, relatively homogeneous items using one of the other methods.

The values of the ending inventory, cost of goods sold and *gross margin* (difference between revenue and cost of goods sold) under the different methods are shown in Table 3-5.

---

[1]We have rounded the accounting values to the nearest dollar rather than accounting for pennies.

TABLE 3-5 **Effects of Different Inventory Valuation Methods**

Inventory Valuation Method	Ending Inventory	Cost of Goods Sold	Gross Margin[a]
FIFO	$300	$3,700	$3,250
LIFO	200	3,800	3,150
Weighted average	268	3,734	3,216
Specific identification	270	3,730	3,220

[a]Gross Margin = Revenues of $6,950 − Cost of Goods Sold

Note that a simple accounting decision can change expenses and the gross margin significantly (by up to $100 for this example). And any one of the four methods for valuing inventory and cost of goods sold may be used. The method used to value inventory is disclosed in a footnote to the financial statements. The knowledgeable reader should understand the impact of this choice on the financial statements.

Investments

Investments are made either to establish a long-run relationship between two organizations (usually effected with the purchase of a substantial percentage of the common stock of one organization by the other) or to secure a long-term gain from purchasing assets with the sole intention of holding them for longer than a year, such as direct real-estate investments or purchases of securities. For example, when Boston University invested nearly $60 million in a start-up biotechnology firm, it should have classified this transaction as a noncurrent asset (investment) because it could not recover its money for many years. These assets are sometimes called *long-term* or *noncurrent investments*. (If they are in the form of securities, they are distinguished from marketable securities by management's intentions about the length of time the securities will be held.)

Long-term investments and marketable securities can provide income for an organization in two ways: (1) from the dividends paid on common and preferred stocks, the interest paid on bonds, the rental income from real estate, and the profits from business operations and (2) from the increase in the value of the investment. Although there are exceptions, investments generally are accounted for as discussed above under marketable securities.

For example, consider a nonprofit organization that bought 100 shares of stock at $10 each, received dividends of $0.50 per share, sold 30 shares at $20 each during the year, and kept the remaining 70 shares, which had a market value of $16 per share at the end of the year. It had dividend income of $50 (100 shares × $0.50), a realized gain of $300 [($20 sale price − $10 cost) × 30 shares] on the 30 shares of stock sold, and an unrealized gain of $420 [($16 market − $10 cost) × 70 shares held] on the 70 remaining shares of stock. The unrealized gain is reflected in the financial statements only if the organization accounts for investments on a market basis. Had the market value instead dropped temporarily to $8 per share at year end, the investment would be reduced by the $140 unrealized loss [($10 cost − $8 market) × 70 shares held] under either the market or the lower of cost or market bases. A permanent drop in market share would also be reported under the cost basis, as well as under the market and LCM bases.

RSUS's time deposits designated for capital improvements and production of $133,653 in fiscal year 19X8 and $128,723 in 19X7, represent resources set aside solely for the purpose of capital improvements and program production. Their classification as long-term assets indicates that these investments are not expected to be liquidated in the upcoming fiscal year. The classification of securities as current marketable securities versus noncurrent invesments based on management intention means that investments in them are often much more liquid than other types of noncurrent assets.

Fixed Assets

Fixed assets represent the bulk of RSUS's noncurrent assets, a pattern found in many nonprofits. Also referred to as *plant, property, and equipment*, these assets consist of any land, buildings, equipment, furniture, and fixtures that the organization owns, that have value, and that are used in operations. (Similar types of assets held solely for resale purposes would be accounted for as investments.) They are considered a relatively fixed or permanent part of the organization, and are accounted for at their *original*, or *historical*, cost when purchased. In theory, any tangible item used in operations that has an expected useful life of more than one year should be accounted for as a fixed asset. In practice, small items such as staplers or floppy disks for computers are accounted for as supplies and expensed when purchased. As long as the amounts are not material, this practice is acceptable.

The original cost of the studio and offices of RSUS was $22,621 in fiscal year 19X8, and $14,984 in fiscal year 19X7. The difference of $7,637 between the 19X7 and 19X8 values represents the net cost of purchases of studio and/or office space less the cost of any such items that were disposed of in 19X8. It is easy to see that the telecasting equipment, in terms of cost, represents the largest portion of the value of RSUS's fixed assets.

An *allowance for depreciation* totaling $548,905 in 19X8 and $426,114 in 19X7 is subtracted from the original cost of all property, plant, and equipment accounts to arrive at the net amount included as an asset on the Balance Sheet. This net amount frequently is called *net book value. Depreciation expense* accounts for the use of fixed assets over time. The allowance for depreciation is the cumulative amount of depreciation expense recorded for these assets since they were acquired and represents a reduction in the value of the fixed assets. When a fixed asset is disposed of, its accumulated depreciation is removed from this account.

The relationship between the allowance for depreciation and the original cost of the fixed assets indicates how used up the assets are. For example, in 19X8 the original cost of RSUS's assets was $1,349,966, the allowance for depreciation was $548,905, and the ratio of the two was approximately 41 percent. (Original cost = net book value of $801,061 + allowance for depreciation of $548,905.) On average, the fixed assets were 41 percent used up. Of course, the depreciation expense estimates are generally conceded to be only crude approximations to the rate of using up an asset.

Calculating depreciation expenses requires estimating the useful *life* of the asset and its *salvage value* at the end of this period, and choosing a *method for allocating* the cost less the salvage value over the life. Estimates of the life of an asset and its ending salvage value can be based on asset guideline periods published by the Internal Revenue Service. However, nonprofits are not required to use these estimates—if they are not consistent with managerial judgments, then the management should prevail.

Many methods exist for allocating depreciation over the life of an asset. All of them allocate only the *net cost* of the asset (original cost less salvage value). The simplest and most common is the *straight-line method*, which calculates each year's depreciation expense by dividing the asset's net cost by its estimated years of life. This method assigns the same amount of depreciation expense to each year of an asset's life. *Accelerated depreciation* methods assign higher expenses in the early years of life than in later ones, with the reasoning that a fixed asset will be consumed at a faster (accelerated) rate in the early years than in the later ones. This assumption might appear counter-intuitive but most fixed assets endure harder wear and tear, and suffer a greater decline in value, during the early years of their life. Automobiles are a common example of this effect.

The two common ways of calculating accelerated depreciation are the double-declining balance method and the sum-of-the-years' digits method. The *double-declining balance*, as its name suggests, results in a depreciation rate double that of the straight-line rate. For example, if an asset is estimated to have a five-year life and no salvage value, under straight-line, its depreciation rate will be 20 percent or one-fifth of its original cost every year. Its double-declining rate will be double that, or 40 percent, of the declining value of the asset. The *sum-of-the-years' digits* method of computing depreciation expense calculates each year's depreciation as the ratio of the value of that year in the asset's life to the total of the sum-of-the-years' digits in its life. The denominator is quite literal. Thus, for an asset with a two year life, it is three, the sum of the digits one and two. For an asset with a five-year life and no salvage value, in its first year the depreciation expense will be equal to $33\frac{1}{3}$ percent $(\frac{5}{5+4+3+2+1} = \frac{5}{15})$ of its original cost.

Other depreciation methods, such as those based on the productive capacity of the asset rather than its life, may also be used for financial reporting purposes. They require estimation of the productive capacity and use of fixed assets. The choice of depreciation methods, as well as of life and salvage value, are matters of managerial judgment. Once the method is chosen, however, it should be used consistently over time. In practice, straight line is the method most commonly used by nonprofits. Allowable depreciation methods for other types of reporting may be limited or dictated by regulatory or funding agencies, especially those whose payments are based on reimbursement of service cost.

The choice of depreciation method, like the choice of inventory valuation method, will have a substantial impact on the value of the fixed assets and the depreciation allowance and expense at any given time. The impact of this decision is illustrated in Table 3-6 for a $100,000 fixed asset with no salvage value and a five-year life.

Note the dramatic difference in the net book values and the depreciation expenses under each of these methods. For example, assume an organization has revenues of $30,000 and accounts receivable of $30,000 and the $100,000 fixed asset, purchased in the beginning of the year, as its only assets. Its end-of-year Balance Sheet and Operating Statement would look very different under each method of depreciation, as shown in Table 3-7.

The difference in total assets is as much as $20,000, and the *only* reason for that difference is the method of calculating depreciation. Similar dramatic differences occur on the Statement of Revenues and Expenses shown in Table 3-8. This entity either lost $10,000, or earned a profit of $10,000, or lost only $3,333. The differences in profit depend solely on the method of depreciation used.

TABLE 3-6 **Effects of Different Depreciation Methods**

	Depreciation Expense			Net Book Value		
Year	Straight Line	Double-Declining Balance	Sum-of-the-Years' Digits	Straight Line	Double-Declining Balance	Sum-of-the-Years' Digits
1	$20,000	$40,000	$33,333	$80,000	$60,000	$66,667
2	20,000	24,000	26,667	60,000	36,000	40,000
3	20,000	14,400	20,000	40,000	21,600	20,000
4	20,000	8,640	13,333	20,000	12,960	6,667
5	20,000	5,184	6,667	0	7,776*	0

*In practice, organizations often change to straight-line accounting at the point where the straight-line depreciation expense becomes greater than the double-declining expense. This would be somewhere between Years 3 and 4 in this example. If strict double-declining were used, some residual value would always exist at the end of the asset's life.

TABLE 3-7 **Effect of Different Depreciation Methods on Balance Sheet Assets**

	Balance Sheet As of End of Year 1					
	Straight Line		*Double-Declining Balance*		*Sum-of-the-Year's Digits*	
Accounts receivable		$ 30,000		$30,000		$30,000
Equipment:						
Original cost	$100,000		$100,000		$100,000	
Less accumulated depreciation	(20,000)	80,000	(40,000)	60,000	(33,333)	66,667
Total assets		$110,000		$90,000		$96,667

TABLE 3-8 **Effect of Depreciation Methods on the Operating Statement**

	Statement of Revenues and Expenses for Year 1		
	Straight Line	*Double-Declining Balance*	*Sum-of-the-Years' Digits*
Revenues	$30,000	$ 30,000	$30,000
Depreciation expense	(20,000)	(40,000)	(33,333)
Income (loss)	$10,000	$(10,000)	$ (3,333)

Some nonprofits lack adequate systems for tracking and valuing their fixed assets. Depreciation expense can be accurately calculated only by keeping good accounting records for each fixed asset and by carefully considering the appropriate asset life and method of depreciation.

This problem is particularly unfortunate for nonprofits that are reimbursed on the basis of their costs, such as hospitals or grant-receiving organizations. In inflationary times, even the full amount of depreciation expense included in the reimbursement is less than the amount of money needed to replace the asset. Depreciation expense allocates the original cost of the existing fixed assets, not the greater amount of money that firms usually need for their replacement. Depreciation expense is a method for allocating the original cost of a fixed asset over time, not a method for determining the current value of replacing the asset. The historical cost and related allowance for depreciation are of little value for managerial decisions such as the amount of insurance coverage needed to replace fixed assets destroyed in a fire. An independent appraisal of replacement costs is a more appropriate source of such data than the fixed asset values in the financial statements.

Other Assets

Intangible assets, which would be classified as *other assets*, are long-lived assets that have no physical reality, such as patents, copyrights, goodwill, and trademarks. They are valued at their cost of acquisition and reduced in value over their estimated useful life by a process called *amortization*. Amortization of these assets is conceptually equivalent to depreciation of fixed assets. Only the name is different. Intangible assets must be amortized over not more than a 40-year period or the legal life for patents. But as with depreciation, there is considerable latitude in the life and method of amortization.

Only the direct costs of acquiring the patent or trademark may be recorded (in accountingese, *capitalized*) as assets. The costs of research and development associated with acquiring a patent or of the public relations efforts to generate goodwill must be expensed. This accounting rule was adopted primarily because of the difficulty in determining what future benefits can be derived from the amounts already expended. In practice, long-term intangible assets are uncommon in nonprofit financial statements. They occur primarily when one organization acquires another for more than the fair market value of the net assets. The difference between the acquisition price and the fair market value of the net assets is shown as *goodwill*.

Other types of noncurrent assets that appear on nonprofit Balance Sheets usually represent a relatively small fraction of the total assets. Colleges and universities may have *loans to students and faculty* that will not be paid back within the next year. If the assets have relatively small values, and consist of several different types of assets, they may be listed simply as other assets. If the amounts are relatively large, they should be listed separately with a title that describes their nature. In the example, RSUS does not happen to own any of these other types of assets.

LIABILITIES

Liabilities and Fund Balances represent the sources of the capital used to finance the assets contained on the other side (or top) of the Balance Sheet. *Liabilities* are amounts owed to external, or ''third,'' parties (those outside the entity). As with current assets, current liabilities are expected to be paid within a year. Longer-term (or noncurrent) liabilities are those that will not have to be repaid until some time after the end of the upcoming year. They include the noncurrent portions of notes, mortgages, bonds, and other borrowing instruments, deferred revenues, pension and related benefits, contingent liabilities, and warranty liabilities. *Fund balances* (or *net assets*) represent the amounts cumulatively provided or used by the organization through its operations. In fiscal year 19X8, RSUS's sources of capital were the following (refer to Table 3-1 on page 61): current liabilities of $56,674; long-term liabilities and deferred revenue of $43,255; and a fund balance of $1,307,019. The bulk of its financing was internally generated.

Current Liabilities

As with assets, liabilities are distinguished by the period of time in which they will be liquidated, or repaid. *Current liabilities* must be repaid within the next year, or operating cycle, of the organization. The total amount of current liabilities has diminished substantially for RSUS—from $216,026 in 19X7 to $56,674. As with current assets, such a substantial change should warrant further investigation. The most typical current liabilities are *accounts payable*, and *payroll and fringe benefits payable*. *Notes, mortgages,* and *leases payable*, and *deferred revenues* are also divided between current and long-term, based on whether they are due within the upcoming year or later.

Accounts Payable   A substantial fraction of the current liabilities are *accounts payable*. They represent money owed to suppliers of goods and services received by the organization, are usually due within 30 days of the invoice being sent, and, therefore, are expected to be liquidated well within the next operating cycle. Accounts payable are a source of funds because they represent the value of goods and services received and perhaps used by the organization prior to a cash payment having been made. (When an expense has been incurred, but the amount is not yet payable, the resulting liability may be called an *accrued* expense. This commonly occurs with interest and payroll expenses.)

Payroll and Fringe Benefits   *Personnel expenses* include *gross pay* (total *salaries and wages* for both regular and overtime pay earned by employees) and *fringe benefits* (payroll taxes and other payroll related benefits, such as health insurance, retirement benefits, and workers' compensation). They are often the largest expense of a nonprofit organization. Salaried employees (also called *exempt* employees) are those who are not paid overtime if they work more than 40 hours a week. Employees who are paid wages, under the provision of the U.S. Fair Labor Standards Act, must be paid for overtime if their work week exceeds 40 hours a week.

Payroll (or *salaries and wages*) *payable* represents money owed but not yet paid to employees for time they have worked. Payroll payable typically reflects the amount of net pay owed to employees. It is calculated by subtracting the *payroll deductions* (for income taxes and other items for which the employee pays) from the gross pay. The amounts of deductions are governed by law (for income and other taxes) or by contracts between the employer and employee (for deductions such as union dues or insurance premiums). Separate payable accounts are maintained for taxes and other amounts deducted from employees' earnings by the employer as an agent for the federal and state governments and other organizations. Employee deductions are made for the federal government for *FICA* taxes (the Federal Insurance Contribution Act, commonly known as *Social Security*) and for federal income taxes (*FIT*) withheld.

In addition to amounts deducted from employees' gross pay, the employer also incurs expenses for FICA taxes and usually expenses for at least part of the employee's insurance premiums and retirement benefits. Liabilities to a state government usually account for state income taxes withheld from employees and for unemployment insurance, usually an expense of the employer. Liabilities to private or public insurance companies and pension funds are for various pension, insurance, and other benefit plans. They typically consist of a combination of deductions from employee's gross pay and a portion that represents the employer's expense.

Although these many items may be combined into as a single line item, fringe benefits payable, on the Balance Sheet, individual accounts must be maintained internally to track the amounts paid and owed, not only by the type of item, but by individual employee as well. This can make payroll accounting very tedious and complex. The RSUS payroll taxes payable of $3,087 in 19X8 represent the amounts deducted from employees' earnings and amounts owed by RSUS for its portion of the taxes that it has not yet forwarded to the government as of the Balance Sheet date.

Notes Payable Short-term borrowings by the organization that must be repaid before the end of the next operating period are *notes payable*. Such borrowings are common among organizations with seasonal cash flows patterns such as a college that has large cash inflows when tuition payments are made at the beginning of each term, but relatively uniform monthly cash outflows. The resulting uneven pattern of net cash flows may require short-term financing to cover cash outflows between the points when the cash inflow from tuition payments are received.

The cost of borrowing is the *interest expense*, calculated as the amount of money currently borrowed (*principal*) times the *stated annual interest rate* times the *amount of time* for which the money has been borrowed, stated as a portion of a year. The formula for interest expense is:

$$\text{Interest Expense} = P \times I \times T$$

where P = the principal amount borrowed
   I = the interest rate for the year
   T = the time for which interest is owed, as a fraction of the year.

For example, the interest expense on a $20,000, 10 percent loan that was used for half a year is $1,000 $[(\$20,000)(0.10)(\frac{1}{2})]$. The interest rate and the time period can both be stated on another basis, such as days or months, but both must be stated in the same units of time.

In 19X8, RSUS had $22,134 in *short-term notes payable*, which it refers to as an *installment contract payable*. To incur this debt, in 19X8 RSUS borrowed $30,389, repayable in installments: $22,134 of these borrowed funds were classified as a current liability because they were to be repaid during the upcoming fiscal year 19X9, and the remaining $8,255 were classified as a long-term liability because they were to be repaid only after the end of the upcoming fiscal year. (The $8,255 are accounted for as installment contract payable below the current liabilities.)

Leases

Leases are agreements to rent or buy something (typically land, buildings, or equipment) in exchange for a specified series of payments over a certain amount of time. There are two types of leases. One, an operating lease, is a rental agreement. The other, a capital lease, is essentially a purchase financed by borrowing from the leasing company.

Capital leases must meet one of the following four conditions:

(1) Title is transferred to the lessee by the end of the lease term.

(2) The lease contains a "bargain purchase right" option at less than the fair value at the time of the option.

(3) The lease term is at least 75 percent of the leased property's estimated economic life.

(4) The present value of the minimum lease payments is 90 percent or more of the fair value of the leased property.

When a capital lease is first created, it is entered on the Balance Sheet as an asset (items of value that are owned by the entity) with a corresponding liability (*lease payable*) (See Table 3-9). The asset amount is amortized or depreciated in a manner similar to that of other fixed assets, and the liability is diminished in size as payments become due and are made. The liability is equal to the amount of money the organization would need at the present time in order to pay off the entire amount of the lease obligation (the so-called "net present value" of the liability).

When the first payment on the lease is made, the cash and the current lease payable accounts are each reduced by the amount of the payment. The current lease payable account is then adjusted to reflect the lease payments due the next year and the long-term lease payable is reduced by the same amount. For example, if a payment of $10,000 was made immediately and the lease payment for Year 2 is $8,000, the effect of these two transactions on the Balance Sheet will be as shown in Table 3-10. Note that the asset

TABLE 3-9 **Accounting for a Lease Acquisition**

Balance Sheet
XYZ, **Inc.**
As of the Date of Acquisition of the Capital Lease

Assets		*Liabilities and Fund Balance*	
		Various liabilities	$YYY
Cash	$YYY	Current lease	
Property acquired		payable	10,000
under lease	100,000	Long-term lease	
		payable	90,000
		Total liabilities and	
Total assets	$YYY + 100,000	fund balance	$YYY + 100,000

TABLE 3-10 **Accounting for a Lease Payment**

Balance Sheet
XYZ, **Inc.**
As of the Date the First Lease Payment is Made

Assets		*Liabilities and Fund Balance*	
		Various liabilities	$XXX
Cash	$XXX − 10,000	Current lease	
Property acquired		payable	10,000 − 10,000
under lease	100,000		+ 8,000
		Long-term lease	
		payable	90,000 − 8,000
		Total liabilities and	
Total assets	$XXX + 90,000	fund balance	$XXX + 90,000

balance is no longer necessarily equal in amount to the total lease liability balance. (In Table 3-10 we ignored the depreciation of the leased asset and focused only on the accounting for the payment of the lease in order to clarify the exposition. The leased asset should be depreciated in the same manner as any other asset.)

Leases that do not meet any of the four criteria are classified as *operating leases*. Because they are merely rentals, operating leases do not require recognition of an asset or liability. Rather, the lease expenses are recorded as they become payable, and footnote disclosure reveals the magnitude and length of the lease commitments if they are significant.

In fiscal year 19X7, the RSUS capital lease liability is shown in two accounts: *current portion of capitalized lease* of $32,587 to be repaid in the upcoming fiscal year and the remainder of the lease liability of $65,174 (*capitalized lease obligation*) to be repaid in years subsequent to fiscal year 19X8. The corresponding asset, *property rights acquired under long-term lease* of $97,761, is equal to the sum of the current and long-term lease liabilities ($32,587 + $65,174).

There is no entry under either the asset or liability lease accounts in fiscal year 19X8, indicating that the lease obligation was paid off in the course of the year. This is somewhat unusual and is an item an alert financial statement user should question. Either the lease contract was broken and satisfactorily resolved, or the lease was repaid in advance of coming due and the assets are now included in one of the other fixed asset categories.

(This discussion of leases deals with one of the most complicated accounting issues extant. We will turn to this topic again in Chapter 14.)

Deferred Revenues

Deferred revenues represent services that have not yet been provided, even though cash payment for these services has already been received or a receivable for the amount due has been recorded as an asset. RSUS has two deferred revenue accounts in fiscal year 19X8. The *deferred grant award revenue* of $25,000 represents money received from a donor who designated that it be spent for capital improvements. The *deferred production revenue* of $10,000 represents money received and designated to be spent for production purposes—that is, for producing new programs, perhaps on a specific topic. The corresponding assets are included among the $133,653 of long-term assets in the *time deposits designated for capital improvements and production*.

Deferred revenues are classified as current liabilities only if the services they represent will be rendered in the upcoming fiscal year. By classifying them as long-term liabilities, RSUS is indicating that these services will not be provided until the period after the upcoming fiscal year. This is consistent with the noncurrent classification of the related assets. When the services are actually rendered, the deferred revenue account will be decreased by their value and the revenue account will be increased by that same amount. Although deferred revenues should theoretically be reclassified as current liabilities at the beginning of the period in which they are to be spent, in practice all deferred revenues may be classified together in an account that immediately follows current liabilities on the Balance Sheet.

Long-term Debt

Long-term debt is a debt that does not have to be repaid within the up-coming year. The portion of the debt that must be paid within the upcoming year should be classified as a current liability, and the long-term amount owed correspondingly reduced. Money is borrowed on the basis of a legal document that specifies the interest rate, the rate of repayment, and the life (or *term*) of the loan. Loans *secured* (or *collateralized* or *backed*) by specific assets (which may be referred to as the *loan collateral*) give the lender first claim against the assets that secure the loan in the case of default (nonpay-ment) or bankruptcy. Any such agreement would be specified in the loan document.

Several common loan repayment plans or patterns exist. One specifies periodic (monthly, quarterly, or semiannual) payments of interest and repay-ment of principal in a lump sum at the end of the loan term. The principal payment is called a *balloon payment* because it swells like a balloon at the end of the term. Another repayment plan requires periodic repayment of principal, as well as of interest.

The three main types of long-term loan instruments are bonds, mortgages, and notes. As with other forms of financial securities, new types of borrow-ing contracts are continually developed to meet specific organizational needs and market demands. The advice of professional investment advisers and securities lawyers is recommended if an organization is considering an unusual form of borrowing because the legal issues can be complex.

Long-term *notes* typically have no collateral and represent borrowings from a private financial institution or from an individual or other organiza-tion. RSUS has a long-term note, called *installment contract payable*, of $8,255 in fiscal year 19X8. Although RSUS has no other long-term notes, many non-profit organizations also have mortgages and long-term bonds payable.

Mortgages are long-term borrowings that are secured by real estate. If mortgage payments are not made, the lenders have the right to confiscate the asset and sell it to recover their money. When the mortgage is issued, the entity recognizes an increase in cash and a liability called *mortgage payable* on its Balance Sheet. The portion of the principal to be paid during the next operating cycle is recognized as a current liability, *current mortgage payable*.

Mortgage payments usually consist of equal monthly amounts during the life of the mortgage. Each payment includes both principal and interest. In the initial years, most of each payment pays for interest expense, while in the later years, most of each payment repays loan principal.

For example, if a charitable organization has a five-year, $300,000 mort-gage on its building and agrees to make equal semiannual payments with an annual interest rate of 8 percent, the amount of each payment will be $36,990. In the first payment of the $36,990, $12,000 will be for interest expense and only $24,990 will be for principal. [Interest = ($300,000)(0.08)($\frac{1}{2}$) = $12,000.] In the second payment of $36,990, the interest expense declines to $11,000 and the principal repayment increases to $25,990 [Principal = $300,000 − $24,990 = $275,010; Interest = ($275,010)(0.08)($\frac{1}{2}$) = $11,000.40].

The mortgage contract typically lists all the payments due for the entire mortgage period and indicates how much of each payment is interest and how much is principal. If a payment is late, however, the amount of interest and principal for each of the subsequent payments will change. Although calculators and spreadsheets simplify the calculation of net present values and periodic payments, the concepts remain difficult to comprehend. These concepts, and the related calculations of present values and periodic payments, will be discussed in detail in Chapter 14 of Part Two.

The accounting effects of entering into the mortgage described above are illustrated in Table 3-11. Immediately after the first payment of $36,990, the Balance Sheet would appear as shown in Table 3-12.

The distinction between interest and principal payments is particularly important for cost-reimbursed nonprofit organizations that receive reimbursement for their interest expenses but not for principal payments. They will have larger cash inflows from reimbursement for interest in the early years of a mortgage and smaller ones in its later years, even though the total amount of the mortgage payment remains the same.

Bonds are financial securities that are usually publicly traded in a bond market and are purchased by several different investors. Some nonprofits use their marketable securities and investments as collateral for borrowing (*collateral trust bonds*), but many bonds have no collateral. Bonds may also require the use of *sinking funds*, which involve setting aside money each year to pay off the bonds, even though no payment may be due to external parties.

Bonds payable represents the amount of principal the organization will have to repay, called the *par value* or *face value* of the bond. It is frequently different from the bond *proceeds* (the amount of money the borrower actually

TABLE 3-11   Balance Sheet at Mortgage Issuance Date

Balance Sheet
XYZ, Inc.
As of Date of Issuance of Mortgage

Assets		Liabilities and Fund Balance	
Cash	$300,000	Mortgage payable	$300,000
Other assets	XXX	Fund balance	XXX
Total assets	$XXX + 300,000	Total liabilities and fund balance	$XXX + 300,000

TABLE 3-12 **Balance Sheet at Date of First Mortgage Payment**

Balance Sheet
XYZ, Inc.
As of Date of First Mortgage Payment

Assets		*Liabilities and Fund Balance*	
Cash	$300,000 − 36,990	Mortgage payable	$300,000 − 24,990
Other assets	XXX	Fund balance	XXX − 12,000
		Total liabilities and	
Total assets	$XXX + 263,010	fund balance	$XXX + 263,010

receives). For example, a hospital that issues a 10-year, $10,000,000 bond and records a $10,000,000 bond payable account may receive only $9.3 million in cash or, perhaps, receive $10.7 million in cash. Why? One reason is that the investment bankers, accountants, and lawyers who helped to obtain the loan take their substantial fees from the loan proceeds. Their payments are usually recorded as deferred charges in the Asset section of the Balance Sheet and amortized over the life of the bond.

Another, more important reason that the face value may differ from the bond proceeds has to do with interest rates. Bonds are usually sold either at a *discount* (an amount less than the face value) or at a *premium* (more than its face value) because their stated interest rate is higher or lower than the market interest rate for securities of the same risk level. The discount is deducted from the face value of the bond liability account, or the premium added to it, so that the liability that is initially recorded reflects the actual amount of the bond proceeds, rather than the face amount that will be paid in the future. Recording bonds that sell at a premium or a discount is discussed in more detail in Appendix A on page 88.

Pension Liabilities

Pension liabilities and *other post-retirement benefits* are incurred in organizations that have formal agreements to pay benefits to their employees after they retire. Accrual accounting requires that these expenses be recorded during the employees' period of employment, rather than being recorded only when paid to the employees after their retirement. They are expenses because they represent the use of resources consumed in conducting current operations.

The two major types of plans receive different accounting treatment. In a *defined contribution plan*, the employer promises to contribute a given amount to the plan, and the expense is equal to the contribution promised by the employer. The contribution is a liability until it is paid in cash to the plan. The plan may be administered as part of the organization itself, or it may be a separate legal entity. When the cash payment is made, the liability is discharged, and is no longer reflected on the Balance Sheet. It is relatively straightforward to calculate the amount of liability at any given time for this type of plan.

But computing the liability of a *defined benefit plan*, where the employer promises to deliver a certain level of benefits upon the employee's retirement, is much more complex. The assets at any given time should be equal to the amount of money needed right now if the organization is to honor its promises in the future. If this money has been set aside in cash, there will be no liability. The amount that has not been set aside will be recognized on the Balance Sheet as a *liability*. The value of the liability under this type of plan is much more difficult to estimate at any time because it will be affected by the rates of return earned on the plan's investments, by changes in the prices of the services that an employer had promised to provide to retirees, and by changes in the employees' longevity and health status.

Accountingese labels the process of actually paying cash to meet the liability as *funding the benefits*. (This usage should not be confused with "fund" accounting for nonprofit organizations. They are two different uses of the term *fund*; here the word is a verb that means *to provide cash*.)

In addition to the liability for expenses of benefits earned by employees in the current period, some organizations also have a liability for past expenses that have not yet been funded. Further liabilities may arise from the fact that pension benefits may be improved over time, and these improved levels have not been funded either. The liability for these *prior service costs* need not be shown in the financial statements, but their amount must be disclosed in the notes to the statements. This past service liability must be funded over a period of not less than 10 nor more than 40 years. (When the accounting standards were changed to require disclosure of pension liabilities, this grace period was provided to cushion the shock of incorporating such large liabilities on the organizations' financial performance.)

Benefit accounting is important because they are among the most pressing liabilities of many state and local governments. Most of these liabilities are for past service costs and their extent is revealed only in the footnotes to the financial statements, if at all. In an early study of unfunded pension obligations, John Nuveen and Company, Incorporated, found that the per-capita liability for these pensions exceeded the per-capita debt burden in a number of state and local governmental units. For example, the Commonwealth of Massachusetts had a per-capita pension liability of $667 and a per capita debt burden of $490; the city of Boston had even more dramatic differences—its per-capita pension burden was $1,725 while the per-capita debt burden was $740.[2]

As of 1990, pension liability data are still not easy to acquire, as we discovered when we attempted to update the Nuveen data. A bond analyst noted, "We should probably pay more attention to pension liability data, but do not because it is more difficult to get than data provided in the basic financial statements." Pension liability data were obtained through telephone conversations with state and city officials and data from a Massachusetts and a Boston bond prospectus. Debt data were obtained from the *U.S. Statistical Abstract*. Based on these sources, it appears that as of June 30, 1989, Massachusetts per capita pension liability had more than doubled, to approximately $1,434, and its per capita debt had grown to approximately $3,285 in 1987. Boston, on the other hand, had decreased its per-capita pension liability to approximately $606 and increased its per capita debt to approximately $1,363 in 1987.[3]

Warranty Liabilities

Warranty liabilities represent liabilities for warranties (guarantees) on goods or services sold by the entity. They are a source of funds in the sense that the buyer has paid for the guarantee, usually as part of the purchase price of the good or service, in advance of receiving the warranty services. The amount of these liabilities is estimated on the basis of experience with claims for similar items under similar warranty agreements in the past.

Contingent Liabilities

Contingent liabilities are recognized when it is likely, but not certain, that the value of an asset has been impaired or a liability has been incurred. Among such events are guarantees of the indebtedness of others, pending litigation, and other kinds of claims. Contingent liability disclosures are particularly relevant for such organizations as hospitals threatened by large malpractice settlements or local governmental units sued for dereliction of responsibilities, such as allowing pollution.

A contingent liability must be recognized when both of the following two elements exist:

(1) It is probable that the value of an asset has been impaired or a liability has been created.

(2) The amount of the loss can be reasonably estimated.

---

[2]Nuveen Research, *Public Employees Pension Funds: Impact on State and Local Credits* (Chicago, IL: John Nuveen and Co., Inc., July 1976).
[3]*U.S. Statistical Abstract*, (Washington, DC: Government Printing Office, 1991), Tables 466 and 481.

Losses that are less than likely but more than remote should be revealed in the footnotes to enable the readers of the statements to make their own assessments about the likelihood of various future cash drains on the organization.

A contingent liability is classified as a long-term liability on the Balance Sheet. If it were certain enough to be classified as current, it is unlikely it would still be contingent. When a contingent liability is recognized, a corresponding loss (expense) that will reduce the period's earnings is also recognized.

FUND BALANCE

The major source of capital for RSUS is the *fund balance*, also called *net assets*. It represents the cumulative amount of the difference between revenues and expenses for RSUS from the date the organization came into existence. In contrast to liabilities, which are generated by borrowing funds, the fund balance represents capital that was generated by the operations of RSUS. It is owned by RSUS and does not have to be repaid. In a for-profit organization, the comparable amount is *owners equity*, which represents the claims of owners against the assets of the company. Because a nonprofit entity has no owners, its organizational charter or incorporation documents usually specify how to distribute its fund balance if the organization is dissolved.

Some nonprofit organizations mistakenly think their fund balance should be zero. If they follow this policy, they lose the ability to finance acquisition of assets from any sources other than liabilities. The following illustration will help to clarify this concept.

Assume that a nonprofit organization has the Balance Sheet shown in Table 3-13. Suppose the organization incurs a loss of $100,000 in Period 2. Therefore, its fund balance at the end of that period will be zero. If the organization wishes to maintain its present size and to have the same total amount

TABLE 3-13 **Beginning Balance Sheet for Fund Balance Example**

ABC, Inc. Balance Sheet, as of End of Period 1			
Assets		*Liabilities and Fund Balance*	
Current assets	$ 200,000	Liabilities	$1,100,000
Fixed assets	1,000,000	Fund balance	100,000
Total	$1,200,000	Total	$1,200,000

TABLE 3-14 **Balance Sheet After Loss and Borrowing**

ABC, Inc.
Balance Sheet—Scenario 1, Period 2
After Incurring a $100,000 Loss and Borrowing $100,000

Assets		*Liabilities and Fund Balance*	
Current assets	$ 200,000	Liabilities	$1,200,000
Fixed assets	1,000,000	Fund balance	-0-
Total	$1,200,000	Total	$1,200,000

of capital invested in it, its liabilities must increase by $100,000, as illustrated in Table 3-14.

It is extremely unlikely, however, that this organization could persuade anybody to lend it the needed $100,000. It will, therefore, be forced to shrink by reducing its fixed or current assets, as illustrated in Table 3-15. Had the organization's fund balance been larger at the beginning of Period 2, a shrinkage in its size would not have been necessary.

The fund balance may be divided into several sections to reflect the actions and intentions of the board and management. Money that has been internally designated—that is, set aside by the board—for certain purposes, is indicated by a *reserved* portion of fund balance. It is not uncommon for fund balances to include *reserves for capital improvements*, *quasi-endowments*, and other special purposes. These reserves indicate the board's choice to reserve those portions of the fund balance for longer term special purposes, rather than current operations. These decisions can always be reversed at

TABLE 3-15 **Balance Sheet After Loss and Shrinking Fixed Assets**

ABC, Inc.
Balance Sheet— Scenario 2, as of End of Period 2
After Incurring a $100,000 Loss and Shrinking Fixed Assets by $100,000

Assets		*Liabilities and Fund Balance*	
Current assets	$ 200,000	Liabilities	$1,100,000
Fixed assets	900,000	Fund balance	-0-
Total	$1,100,000	Total	$1,100,000

the discretion of the board. (The use of separate funds and accounting is necessitated by external designation of resources for specific purposes. This topic is addressed in depth in Chapter 6.)

Proposed new accounting standards would eliminate the need to report separate funds, but would require the net assets (the proposed term for the fund balance) to be presented in three classes: unrestricted, temporarily restricted, and permanently restricted. Disclosure of the nature and amount of restrictions and their expected expiration date would also be required.[4] The unrestricted net assets could be subdivided to disclose board designated amounts.

SUMMARY

This chapter addressed the nature of the individual Asset and Liability and Fund Balance accounts of a Balance Sheet. Generally accepted accounting principles permit the use of many alternative valuation methods. The different methods for valuing key Balance Sheet accounts, such as inventories and fixed assets, were described and compared, along with their likely impact on the Balance Sheet and Statement of Revenues and Expenses.

You should now have a good understanding of the types of accounts commonly found in the Balance Sheet and of the conceptual basis of the accounts classified as assets, liabilities, and fund balances.

APPENDIX A Recording Bond Premiums and Discounts

Bond discounts occur when the face, or stated, interest rate is lower than the market interest rate. For example, suppose a $10 million 10-year hospital bond carries an annual stated interest rate of 8 percent, with semiannual interest payments. The bond will pay semiannual interest of $400,000 ($10,000,000 × 0.08 × 0.5). If investors can obtain a return of 9 percent on equally risky investments, investors will not be willing to pay the full face value for the bond. The bond will sell at a discount—the amount that will yield the 9 percent market rate of interest. The amount that will earn a return

[4]FASB, Invitation to Comment, *Financial Reporting by Not-for-Profit Organizations: Form and Content of Financial Statements* (August 29, 1989): 36.

of 9 percent is $9,349,600, implying a discount of $650,400 on the bond offering ($10,000,000 − $9,349,600). Table 3-16 shows the calculation of the amount that investors will be willing to pay for the bond. Present value calculations are addressed in Part Two.

Conversely, if the market rate of interest is 7 percent for equally risky bonds, investors will be willing to pay more than the $10,000,000 face value for the hospital bonds that carry an 8 percent interest rate. They will be sold at a premium of $710,700; the organization will receive cash of $10,710,700 for them, as calculated in Table 3-17.

The Balance Sheet will recognize both the face amount of the bond payable and the premium or discount on the bonds. A discount will be subtracted from the par value of the bond payable, and indicates that the bond's stated interest rate was not sufficiently high to sell it at par value. In the discount example above, when the bond is first sold, the Balance Sheet will be as shown in Table 3-18.

After six months, the organization will pay interest expense of $400,000, one-half year's interest on the $10,000,000. In addition, it will *amortize the discount* gradually, eliminating the difference between the $10 million loan it must repay and the $9.3 million it received, by recognizing the implicit additional interest expense. As with any amortization, there are many methods for doing it. The simplest, the straight-line method, amortizes an equal amount of $32,520 each time interest is paid ($650,400 discount ÷ 20 periods) and declares it as an additional interest expense. The total amount of interest expense will therefore consist of $400,000 of interest paid to the bondholders plus a $32,520 reduction in the amount of the bond discount, for a total expense of $432,520.

TABLE 3-16   Sample Calculation of a Bond Discount

Present value of $10 million principal to be repaid in 10 years at 9 percent	= $4,146,400
Present value of a stream of $400,000 interest every six months for 10 years at 9 percent	= 5,203,200
Present value of 8 percent bonds priced to yield 9 percent	= $9,349,600

TABLE 3-17   Sample Calculation of a Bond Premium

Present value of $10 million principal to be repaid in 10 years at 7 percent	= $5,025,700
Present value of a stream of $400,000 interest every six months for 10 years at 7 percent	= 5,685,000
Present value of 8 percent bonds priced to yield 7 percent	= $10,710,700

TABLE 3-18 **Recording a Bond Sold at a Discount**

Balance Sheet
XYZ, Inc.
As of Date of Bond Sale

Assets		*Liabilities and Fund Balance*	
Various assets	$XXX	Various liabilities	
Cash	9,349,600	and fund balance	$XXX
Bond discount	650,400	Bond Payable	10,000,000
		Total liabilities and	
Total assets	$XXX + 10,000,000	fund balance	$XXX + 10,000,000

Another way to think about this very complex event is the following: The bond was discounted because it did not yield a high enough interest amount with its promise to pay out $400,000, or 4 percent interest semiannually. It was discounted so that it pays an effective semiannual interest rate of 4.5 percent (as shown in Table 3-16, the effective annual interest rate is 9 percent; half of that is the semiannual rate of 4.5 percent). The interest expense of $400,000 understates the higher interest rate that was necessary to sell the bond. That is why the bond discount is amortized and added to the $400,000 interest expense.

A premium will be accounted for as an addition to the bond liability. After six months, the organization will make an interest payment of $400,000 and also recognize the fact that the interest expense of $400,000 was reduced by the bondholders' willingness to pay more than $10 million for their bonds. Using the straight-line method, the premium will be amortized by $\frac{1}{20}$, or $35,535 ($710,700 $\times$ $\frac{1}{20}$), for a total interest expense of $364,465 ($400,000 − $35,535) for each half-year period in the bond's life. (The "effective-yield" method, which amortizes the premium or discount to maintain a constant 9 percent or 7 percent yield over time, is more accurate but rarely used.) Another way to think about these transactions is that they reduce the bond's promised interest payment of $400,000, which was higher than its buyers expected, to the interest amount based on the rate the buyers expected.

The difference between accrual and cash accounting for the interest expense can have important implications for an organization that is reimbursed for its costs and that calculates its costs on an accrual basis. For example, if the hospital above sells its bonds at a discount, the interest expense will exceed the hospital's bond-related cash outflow by $32,250. If it is reimbursed on the basis of its interest expense, not on the basis of its cash interest payments, it will therefore have a surplus cash flow of $32,250—the annual amortization of its discount. Conversely, if the hospital sells its bonds at a premium, it will receive $35,535 less cash from its reimbursers than it pays out.

DISCUSSION QUESTIONS

1. What is the distinction between current and noncurrent assets? Why is the distinction important?

2. Name the common assets and discuss how are they valued for a nonprofit organization with which you are familiar.

3. Discuss the characteristics necessary to classify an item as a marketable security.

4. What is the purpose of the allowance for uncollectible accounts?

5. For each of the following, decide whether you should use a perpetual or a periodic inventory system, or no inventory system: paper clips, a hospital's inventory of prescription drugs, clothing to be sold in a resale shop, the books in a college book store.

6. Discuss the effects on the Balance Sheet of choosing each of the various inventory valuation methods (FIFO, LIFO, average and specific identification) and depreciation methods (straight-line, double-declining balance, sum-of-the-years-digits).

7. Distinguish between long-term investments and marketable securities, and discuss why they are classified separately on the Balance Sheet. Do you think this treatment is appropriate?

8. Why are current liabilities distinguished from other liabilities? What is the relationship between current assets and current liabilities?

9. Name the most common liabilities and how they are valued for a nonprofit organization with which you are familiar.

10. Why is the current portion of a long-term liability reclassified as a current liability each year?

11. What are deferred revenues? Why aren't they recognized immediately as revenues when they are received? What events reduce the amount of deferred revenues?

12. What is the significance of recording pension and other post-retirement benefit liabilities at the time they are earned, rather than when they are paid? Why do you think most organizations did not record these liabilities until they were required to do so by a change in accounting standards?

13. Does a long-term liability that is repaid with periodic payments of equal amounts contain increasing, decreasing, or equal amounts of interest expense in successive payments? Why?

14. What is a fund balance? What economic events created it? How does it change? What happens to it if the organization is dissolved?

15. For those who have read Appendix A, discuss the purpose and effects of recording and amortizing a bond premium or discount instead of using the face value and stated interest.

EXERCISES

1. The county welfare department purchased a minicomputer for $55,000. It was probably going to be obsolete in five years, at which time it could be sold for $5,000.

    a. What is the computer's annual depreciation expense and net book value on a straight-line basis?

    b. What is the computer's depreciation expense and net book value for years 1 through 5 using the double-declining balance method?

    c. What is the computer's depreciation expense and net book value for years 1 through 5 using the sum-of-the-years' digits method?

    d. What are the implications of the differences in expenses and net book values among the three methods for taxpayers? the welfare department's clients? the "county efficiency agency" that evaluates each county department's efficiency?

2. The Appalachian Handicraft Co-op Shop had revenues for the month of $47,500. It also had the following transactions in sequential order:

    -   Bought $30,000 worth of handicrafts at an average cost of $20 per item.
    -   Sold 1,200 items at $25 each.
    -   Bought another 600 items at an average cost of $30 per item.
    -   Sold 500 items at $35 each.

    It had no beginning inventory.

    a. What is the cost of goods sold, profit, and ending inventory under LIFO? under FIFO? under average cost?

    b. How would you interpret these differences in values if you were a volunteer working in the co-op? a customer of the co-op? a supplier of handicrafts to the co-op?

3. The Bakron University issued a $6,000,000, 20-year dormitory bond with a 5 percent interest rate, with interest to be paid annually. Calculate the yearly interest expense under each of the following conditions.

    a. The bonds sold for $6,600,000.

    b. The bonds sold for $5,400,000.

    c. The bonds sold at face value.

Case

CASE STUDY

This case study, WJAC, is synthesized from a variety of real-life experiences. It will give you the opportunity to practice the preparation of two Balance Sheets. Remember that in accounting, as in most other skills, practice makes perfect.

CASE 3.1 WJAC—The Birth of a Television Station

As an undergraduate student in English, a Master's student in Communications, and director of community programming in the local CBS affiliate, George Hart had one vision guiding him. Now he was close to fulfilling his long-held dream of founding WJAC, an educational television station.

The station would be located in Clifton, the commercial center of the northeast section of the state. The University of Clifton had agreed to sponsor station WJAC and to provide $10,000 in operating funds for its first year of operation and The Ford Foundation had given the station a $100,000 grant for acquiring fixed assets. The only substantial barrier remaining between him and the reality of running the station was the additional $12,000 he needed to operate it. Major General John Woodward (Ret.) agreed to provide those funds as a no-strings attached gift if Mr. Hart would agree to provide Woodward, who had come from the comptroller's office in the Pentagon, with a set of *pro-forma* statements for the first year of operation.

Mr. Hart didn't find the request too onerous. He felt that the station had to be managed in a professional, businesslike manner. So, to comply with Major General Woodward's request, he began to list those activities which were to take place during the station's period of organization, prior to beginning operations:

(1) The Ford Foundation grant of $100,000 for the purpose of purchasing fixed assets in the first two years of operation, would be received in cash.

This case was prepared by Professor Regina E. Herzlinger.

(2) A University of Clifton operating grant of $10,000 would be received, to be used as needed for operations.

(3) The Woodward gift of $12,000 would be received in cash.

(4) Costs of incorporation of $4,000 would be paid for in cash.

Mr. Hart then compiled the following list of activities that he expected to undertake during the course of the first year of operations:

(1) Expected pledges from the community of $5,000, $2,000 of which would be received in cash by the end of the year.

(2) Purchase of $4,000 of materials and supplies, all paid for in cash.

(3) Purchase of a camera and other fixed assets for $87,000. The camera would cost $48,000 and have an estimated 5-year life. Various other equipment would cost $12,000, furnishings would cost $7,000, and improvements to the free space at the University of Clifton would cost $20,000. The equipment was estimated to have a 10-year life, the furnishings a 7-year life, and the improvements a 40-year life. All fixed assets were to be paid for by the end of the year.

(4) Expected payroll expenses of $12,000 for Mr. Hart and his very small part-time staff to be paid for in cash.

(5) Other operating expenses of $4,000, to be paid as incurred.

(6) Inventory of materials and supplies at the end of the year of $1,000.

(7) The University of Clifton guaranteed that WJAC could continue to use the free space for the next ten years.

ASSIGNMENT

a. Prepare a Balance Sheet for WJAC as of the beginning of the first year of operation.

b. Prepare a WJAC Balance Sheet as of the end of the first year of operation.

c. Is the University of Clifton's promise to provide free space for the next ten years an asset, and why?

4 | Other Financial Statements and the Auditor's Opinion

Whereas the balance sheet describes the organization's current financial position, other financial statements describe how the organization attained it. The *Statement of Revenues and Expenses* and *Changes in Fund Balance* (generally called the *Activity Statement* or *Operating Statement*) describes the financial activities that caused changes in net worth for the year preceding the most recent Balance Sheet date. A *Cash Flow Statement* provides information about the sources and uses of cash in the year that elapsed between two Balance Sheets. *Notes to the financial statements* are also an integral part of the financial statements. They disclose the accounting practices followed, provide additional detail about some accounts, and reveal any material information relevant to the financial operations and status of the organization. They are like a notation on a thermometer that informs the reader whether it measures on a Fahrenheit or Celsius scale.

With the Balance Sheet, discussed in Chapter 3, these statements comprise the primary financial information available to users outside the organization. They are called the *general purpose* or *external financial statements*. If the financial statements are audited by an independent auditor they will be accompanied by an *audit opinion* on the fairness of the data presented in the statements. We discuss each of these topics in this chapter.

STATEMENT OF REVENUES AND EXPENSES AND CHANGES IN FUND BALANCE

Understanding, evaluating, and predicting the financial consequences of an organization's operations is very important. An Operating Statement contains information about the financial activities that moved the organization from its net asset position at the last Balance Sheet date to its current level. It enables the user to assess the following dimensions of financial performance:

Do revenues equal or exceed expenses? If they do not, the organization is jeopardizing its ability to survive. If they do, the amount by which revenues exceed expenses is important. A wafer-thin margin increases the organization's vulnerability to future financial downturns. On the other hand, an exceedingly large margin may mean that the organization is delivering too few services or charging excessively high prices.

Do programmatic revenues and expenses appropriately match? If not, is the organization's purpose to subsidize the programs—as, for example, education is subsidized in most colleges and universities—or is the subsidy an accidental one?

Are expenses that are likely to last for a long period of time, such as those of tenured faculty or a new building, matched with revenues and other resource inflows that will last for an equal or longer period of time, such as bond proceeds or the income from a large pool of invested capital?

Are the revenue sources diversified, or are all the organization's eggs in one basket?

Are expense levels commensurate with the mission, scope, and needs of the organization? For example, is enough money being spent to maintain the physical plant in adequate condition? Is an excessively large amount spent in administration rather than in the delivery of services?

Are revenues sufficient, deficient, or excessive for fulfilling the organization's mission?

We will return to this subject of financial analysis in Chapter 5. A single operating statement may be presented, or a Statement of Revenues and Expenses (showing the detail of the resource flows) can be presented with a separate Statement of Changes in Net Worth that incorporates the summary figure from the Statement of Revenues and Expenses.

Nonprofit and For-profit Operating Statements

The title that for-profit organizations bestow on their operating statement, the Income Statement, appropriately reflects their focus on generating income. Nonprofit organizations use many variations on the title, such as the Statement of Revenues and Expenses and Changes in Fund Balances, and Statement of Revenues and Expenditures and Changes in Fund Balances. The title Statement of Changes in Net Assets has most recently been proposed.

The difference between for-profit and nonprofit Operating Statement titles is more than symbolic. It reflects the nonprofit organizations' focus on the flows of financial resources, rather than on net income. The primary objective of nonprofit organizations is to provide services, not to earn a profit. Financial operations support and enhance their ability to provide services by balancing sources and uses of financial resources. Nonprofits must manage their financial operations prudently to ensure that they own financial resources adequate for continued service provision. For them, financial success should not be an end in itself. The various nonprofit operating statement titles more appropriately reflect these organizational objectives than the title Income Statement.

Classification and Analysis of Resource Flows

The *Statement of Revenues and Expenses and Changes in Fund Balance* contains the organization's resource inflows from revenues and other types of support and the resource outflows used in operations (expenses). The difference between resource inflows and outflows is the change in the fund balance (net assets) of the entity for the period.

Resource Inflows   Resource inflows are generated from sales of goods and services, government appropriations, grants, gifts, and investment income. Resource inflows are recognized most often when a bill is sent. This event may occur before, after, or at the same time cash is received. Most frequently, a revenue is matched with an increase in the cash or receivables assets, or by a decrease in the deferred revenue liability account.

Resource inflows can be categorized or classified by:

- Their *nature*, such as grants, contributions, contracts, service revenues, and investment income.

- Their *source*, such as governments, foundations, and private contributors.

- The *organizational units or programs* to which they relate. For example, colleges and universities frequently report the revenues earned by separate organizational units, such as dormitories and bookstores; hospitals report outpatient, inpatient, and ancillary operation revenues; and voluntary health and welfare organizations may report revenues by the programs that generated them, such as counseling, day care, and so on.

These classifications help the reader of the statement judge the stability and quality of the organization's revenue base. In the for-profit sector, this type of information is considered so desirable that organizations with audited financial statements frequently report the separate revenues of their significant lines of business. Nonprofit organizations generally are required to classify their resource inflows by source and nature of the revenue. The specific classification scheme recommended for each type of nonprofit entity is provided in the relevant source of GAAP for that type of organization, as discussed in Part Three.

Because revenues are influenced both by internal factors under the organization's control and external factors in the environment outside the organization's control, knowledge of their nature and source is important.

Revenues based on *service fees*, like a hospital's, or *sales of goods*, depend on the prices charged, volume of demand, quality, and success with which they are marketed to potential consumers and funders, as well as on the condition of the overall economy. If third-party payers are involved, the organization may not have much control over pricing. *Gifts (donations or contributions)* depend on the organization's fund-raising efforts, social values and mores, the economy, tax law, and a variety of other factors. *Investment income* depends on prudent investment management practices and on the general state of the economy and specific financial markets. *Grants* depend on the organization's proposals and the availability of funding for the programs it conducts. Some grants have a built-in limited life, require matching by contributions from the general public, or are contingent on producing certain outputs or expending specified amounts. *Government appropriations* are susceptible to change in the political agenda and the status of the budget. A newly-elected governor or depletion of a state's budget can spell the end of revenues from the state government.

　　Knowing which organizational unit or program generated the revenue is important both for predicting the stability of resource inflows and for determining the net cost or contribution of a unit or program. For example, if demand for a specific type of program is waxing or waning, the revenues related to that program will likely follow suit. Also, an organization might choose to continue a program whose resource inflows are equal to or greater than its outflows, but choose to discontinue it if the reverse is true. It is especially important to identify the resource inflows of programs or units intended to be self-supporting. The organizational unit classification usually is not used in financial reporting for nonprofit organizations, but should be maintained and made available in the managerial accounting reports.

　　RSUS's Statement of Revenues and Expenses for 19X7 and 19X8, shown in Table 4-1, identifies revenues both by source and by nature. RSUS displays the statements for both the current and the previous year to allow the reader to judge the changes between the two years' activities.

　　Comparison of the two years indicates both good and bad revenue news. While there is only a slight increase in the amount of total revenues from 19X7 to 19X8 of $6,253 ($1,245,730 − $1,239,477), there is substantial change in their composition. If the 0.5 percent ($6,253 ÷ $1,239,477) increase in the total revenues is less than the inflation rate between 19X7 and 19X8, RSUS earned less revenue this year than last in inflation-adjusted dollars. As a result, the bad news is that the purchasing power of RSUS's revenues diminished over the course of the year. The change in revenue composition, characterized by large increases in revenues from *program underwriting by corporations* and *production sales to other stations* and an offsetting decrease in *government grant awards* is good news. This change in the composition of revenues provides a more diversified base of support—governments supplied about two-thirds of the revenue in 19X7 ($819,487 ÷ $1,239,477 = 66 percent) and less than one-half in 19X8 ($594,139 ÷ $1,245,730 = 48 percent).

TABLE 4-1   **RSUS Activity Statement**

RSUS
Statement of Revenues and Expenses and Changes in Fund Balance
For Years Ended June 30, 19X8 and 19X7

	Year Ended June 30	
	19X8	19X7
Revenues:		
Government grant awards	$ 594,139	$ 819,487
Auction	198,011	179,864
Foundation and public contribution	248,852	213,009
Program underwriting by corporations	35,055	3,975
Production sales to other stations	129,678	1,680
Services and other to other entities	39,995	21,462
Total revenues	$1,245,730	$1,239,477
Expenses:		
In-school services	$ 78,027	$ 64,354
Programming and production	390,108	182,387
Engineering and technical	150,592	99,593
Promotion, development, and auction	177,297	142,254
Administrative and general	241,198	143,002
Depreciation	122,791	80,220
Total expenses	$1,160,013	$ 711,810
Difference between revenues and expenses	$ 85,717	$ 527,667
Fund balance at beginning of year	1,221,302	693,635
Fund balance at end of year	$1,307,019	$1,221,302

See notes to financial statements.

This diversification diminishes RSUS's dependence on any one source of funds. The large increase in sales to other organizations (production sales to other stations plus services and other to other entities) from $23,142 ($21,462 + $1,680) in 19X7 to $169,673 ($129,678 + $39,995) in 19X8 is particularly encouraging because those sources of revenue are more controllable by RSUS than its other revenue sources.

Resource Outflows   Recall that expenses represent the value of the resources consumed or used up and may occur before, after, or simultaneously with a cash outflow. They are different from expenditures which are the values of goods or services purchased and received and which may occur before, after, or simultaneously with a cash outflow. Expenditures may occur before or with the cash outflow, but not after. In this chapter, we will use expenses as the measure of resource outflows. Most nonprofit organizations are now required to use accrual accounting and to recognize expenses rather than expenditures.

Like revenues, expenses may be classified in several ways: function (or program), organizational unit, activity, and nature or object of the expense. Each type of classification is useful for different monitoring and decision-making tasks. The accounting system should be sufficiently detailed to allow preparation of financial statements on the basis of any of these classifications, or combinations of classifications, as required by legislation or management. Two of the most common and important classification schemes, functions and objects of expense, are discussed in this chapter. Another important classification, by fund, is deferred until Chapter 6 because it is unique to nonprofit accounting. Because classification of expenses by organizational unit is most relevant for the managerial purposes of evaluating the performance of individual organization units, it is discussed in Part Two.

The current trend is toward financial reporting on a *functional basis*—that is, on the basis of the functions performed by the organization. This basis is consistent with for-profit financial reporting and enables evaluation of the absolute and relative amounts of resources devoted to each program. Expenses are most naturally recorded on an *object of expense basis*—such as salaries, benefits, and utilities—because these expense categories relate to events that are clearly observable and easily tracked. For example, when salaries and wages are earned by employees, they are recorded as personnel expenses and when a utility bill is paid, it is recorded in the utilities, or occupancy, expense account. Many organizations develop their budgets on the basis of objects of expense. To illustrate them, codes for the objects of expense commonly used by broadcasting stations such as RSUS are shown in Table 4-2.

Functional statements that disclose how much was spent on a certain function, such as engineering in RSUS, rely on distribution of the objects of expense to the function. For example, personnel and utility expenses must be distributed to the engineering function. In some cases this is accomplished by direct charges. For example, engineering personnel charge their time to the engineering and the programming and production function. In cases where direct charges are not possible, such as occupancy expenses, the total amount of occupancy expense is allocated among the various functions on some basis, such as the percentage of the building floor space they use. (The allocation process is discussed in detail in Part Two.) Thus, each expense is eventually identified by several characteristics, including object, function, and organization unit.

As shown in Table 4-1, RSUS categorizes its expenses primarily by function, such as engineering, but also by an object of expense, *depreciation*. Inconsistent classification of expenses is not uncommon among nonprofit organizations. Many organizations that use functional expense categories also separately disclose interest and depreciation expense.

TABLE 4-2 **Object of Expense Classification for RSUS**

Salaries and Wages (01-19)

01-13	Salaries and wages—regular
14	Salaries and wages—overtime
15	Salaries and wages—vacations
16	Bonuses
17	Pension costs
18	Other employee benefits
19	Payroll taxes

Direct Program Costs (20-39)

20	Talent fees
21	Amortization of broadcasting rights to feature films
22	Amortization of broadcasting rights to other programs
23	Program rights
24	Network co-op fees
25	Film expense
26	Film shipping charges
27	Studio sets and props
28	Other program materials and supplies
29	Outside origination costs
31	News services
32	Music recordings and transcriptions
33	Music license fees
35	Depreciation
39	Other program expenses

Technical Expenses (40-49)

40	Transmitter tubes expense
41	Studio and mobile unit tubes expense
42	Line charges
43	Tape expense
44	Equipment parts and supplies
45	Depreciation
49	Other technical expenses

Promotion and Other Services (50-69)

50	Advertising—audience
52	Promotion and publicity—audience
56	Promotion and publicity—trade
58	Rating services (market research)
60	Commissions, national representatives
69	Other selling, promotion, and publicity expenses

Miscellaneous (70-99)

70	Travel and entertainment
71	Motor vehicle operating expense
72	Telephone and telegraph
73	Light, heat, and power
74	Rent
75	Depreciation and amortization
76	Maintenance and repairs
77	Stationery and office supplies
78	Postage
79	Membership dues and subscriptions
81	Insurance
90	Charitable contributions
91	Legal and auditing fees
92	Provision for uncollectible receivables
99	Other general and administrative expenses

RSUS' expenses increased considerably from 19X7 to 19X8, particularly for *programming and production, engineering and technical,* and *administrative and general expenses.* The rise in general and administrative expenses is not readily explainable and should be flagged as an item that warrants further investigation. The increase in programming and engineering expenses was probably caused by the increase in sales to other stations and entities. However common-sense this explanation seems, its accurancy should also be substantiated.

The *difference between revenues and expenses* or *surplus* declined sharply from 19X7 to 19X8, although it remains positive. The results are not surprising; revenues increased much less than expenses in the period. Because this difference represents the ability of the organization to finance itself internally, the decline may be a source of concern. The smaller the surplus, the smaller is the organization's internal financing ability and the greater is its need to finance its expansion or meet unforseen contingencies via external sources. On the other hand, the 19X8 surplus, equal to approximately 7 percent of revenues ($85,717 ÷ $1,245,730), generally is considered an adequate margin. It is likely that RSUS's 19X7 surplus of 43 percent of revenues ($527,667 ÷ $1,239,477) was too high, rather than 19X8's being too low.

The reconciliation of the fund balance in the last two lines of Table 4-1 shows that the 19X8 fund balance is merely the 19X7 fund balance of $1,221,302 with 19X8's difference between revenues and expenses of $85,717 added to it. This simple reconciliation is typical of for-profit and smaller nonprofit organizations. (The Statement of Changes in Fund Balance becomes much more complex with the use of fund accounting, which will be discussed in Chapter 6.) This simple statement makes it clear that an *excess of revenues over expenses* or *surplus* (analogous to a profit in a for-profit organization) increases the fund balance and adds to the organization's ability to internally finance its activities. Conversely, an *excess of expenses over revenues*, or *deficit*, (analogous to a loss) represents a consumption of previously accumulated resources, a decreased ability to finance continuing operations internally, and a threat to the organization's existence if expenses continue to exceed revenues indefinitely.

Comparisons Over Time

Much of our discussion of the RSUS operating statement involved comparison of the two years 19X8 and 19X7. This common type of comparison reveals patterns of change or stability in operations. Another comparison frequently used is between actual performance and budgeted or planned performance. It is discussed in Part Two as part of the topic of budgeting because it is primarily a management tool. Only governments disclose the budget in their general purpose external financial statements.

Unusual Items in Operating Statements

Because operating statements are frequently compared from one year to the next, the results of continuing operations are reported separately from discontinued ones so that readers can be relatively sure that they are looking at the results of the same entity, over time. Additionally, *extraordinary events* are distinguished from ordinary events so that the reader can readily separate the results of recurring activities from those that are unusual in nature, occur infrequently, and are significant in amount. Extraordinary events are rare. Under these criteria, the disposal of part of the entity—for example, the sale of a Girl Scout camp—would not qualify as an extraordinary event because disposition of part of the business is part of the normal business operations.

Items caused by events of prior periods that were not settled until this period, such as the resolution of a longstanding lawsuit, must be accounted for in the current year's financial statements. The only sanctioned *prior period adjustments* to the financial statements are for the correction of errors in earlier statements and some tax considerations (FASB Statement, Number 16). Thus, the financial consequences of long-standing litigation that was resolved in this fiscal period must be revealed in this year's statements.

STATEMENT OF CASH FLOWS

The third major financial statement is the *Statement of Cash Flows*, which details where cash was obtained and how it was used. It is also called the *Statement of Changes in Financial Position (Cash Basis)* because it highlights the changes in a Balance Sheet account, cash, between two periods. (Recall that the Balance Sheet is also called the Statement of Financial Position.) It is possible, although not usual, to prepare a Statement of Changes in Financial Position on the basis of financial accounts other than cash, such as cash and marketable securities, current assets less current liabilities, and all financial resources.

The Statement of Cash Flows is the most recent addition to the family of general purpose financial statements. Although required for only a few nonprofit organizations at this time, it is recommended for others and must currently be included in the financial statements of for-profit organizations. It is very useful for assessing the entity's financing strategy. As a manager or board member, you might find it worthwhile to have one prepared even if it is not required because it answers three fundamental questions:

(1) How much cash was derived from internal sources versus sources external to the entity? Are the internal sources derived from operations or from selling assets? The former is generally preferable to the latter source.

(2) What were the major uses of cash? Was it expended for repayment of debt or for investment in activities to maintain or expand the entity?

(3) Is there an appropriate match between the sources and uses of cash? Are short-term sources being applied to short-term uses and long-term sources being applied to long-term investments?

Because the statement is relatively new and accounting standards for it have evolved over the last two decades, a variety of ways may be used to prepare the Statement of Cash Flows. Two methods, direct and indirect, are most commonly used.

Both methods classify cash inflows and outflows as operating, investing, and financing activities. *Operating activities* are those related to accomplishing the organization's primary mission. Nonprofit *financing activities* are those involved in obtaining and repaying borrowed resources. (For-profit organizations' financing activities also involve issuing stock.) *Investing activities* are those of buying or selling fixed assets for use in operations and assets designed to earn income, such as marketable securities.

The direct and indirect methods differ only in the way that they derive cash provided by operations, not in the amount derived. The Statement of Cash Flows for RSUS shown in Table 4-3 uses the *indirect* or *reconciliation* method. It derives the cash provided by operations by adding to the difference between revenues and expenses all the noncash items included in the operating statement. They include only depreciation in this case. The *direct* method shows total cash receipts and cash disbursements, rather than working back from the difference figure. (Table 4-3 and the indirect method are explained in detail in the following pages.)

Cash flows from financing and investing activities and the total change in cash are the same under either the direct or indirect method. The cash increase of $124,511 during 19X8 can be calculated by subtracting the 19X7 cash balance of $185,499 from the 19X8 cash balance of $310,010. For the Statement of Cash Flows, cash includes cash equivalents, highly liquid short-term investments that can be converted to cash quickly, such as money market account deposits and U.S. Treasury bills.

The Statement of Cash Flows provides information on the changes in other Balance Sheet accounts that caused this change in cash. (The beginning and ending figures are from the RSUS Balance Sheet in Table 3-1; the operating data are from Table 4-1.)

Cash provided by operations consists of cash generated from and spent on the operations of the firm. With the indirect method, it is calculated as the difference between revenues and expenses (the *difference*), as derived on the operating statement, adjusted for all noncash items included in that figure.

The purpose of this computation is to adjust the accrual basis difference to a cash basis, the reverse of the process we used in Chapter 2. It may be easier to comprehend in words than in figures. Accrual accounting includes measures of revenues that have not been received in cash, such as accounts receivable, and expenses that have either not been paid for in cash, such as accounts payable, or that do not require use of cash, such as depreciation. Thus, the difference includes many non-cash items: revenues that have not yet been received in cash, expenses that have not yet been paid for in cash, and expenses that were paid for in cash in prior periods. The difference can be converted to a cash basis by converting all the noncash revenues and expenses that it contains to the cash basis.

Depreciation expense is the most common noncash component of operating expenses. It is added back to the difference because it did not require a cash outflow. On the other hand, increases in an operating asset such as

TABLE 4-3 **RSUS Statement of Cash Flows**

Statement of Cash Flows
RSUS
For the Year Ending June 30, 19X8

Cash flows from operating activities:		
Excess of revenues over expenses		$ 85,717
Noncash expense—depreciation	$122,791	
Decrease in receivables	154,864	
Increase in salaries and wages payable	9,210	
Increase in deferred revenue	10,000	
Increase in prepaid expenses	(2,196)	
Increase in inventory	(10,000)	
Decrease in accounts payable	(157,742)	
Decrease in payroll taxes payable	(367)	126,560
Cash provided by operations		212,277
Cash flows from investing activities:		
Increase in fixed assets and property rights	$ (15,008)	
Increase in other marketable securities	(456)	
Increase in time deposits	(4,930)	
Net cash outflows from investing activities		(20,394)
Cash flows from financing activities:		
Increase in current portion of installment contract payable	$ 22,134	
Increase in installment contract	8,255	
Decrease in current capitalized lease obligation	(32,587)	
Decrease in long-term capitalized lease obligation	(65,174)	
Net cash outflows from financing activities		(67,372)
Net increase in cash		$124,511
Cash balance, June 30, 19X7		185,499
Cash balance, June 30, 19X8		$310,010

inventory between two accounting periods decrease the amount of cash provided by operations. They represent cash paid for assets not yet declared as expenses. Conversely, increases in operations-related liabilities (such as accounts or payroll taxes payable) increase the amount of cash provided by operations because they represent expenses that did not require cash outlays. And decreases in operating assets, such as accounts receivable, in a sense free up the cash once invested in them to be used in operations.

To illustrate the adjustment process, let us return to RSUS's Operating Statement and Balance Sheet. RSUS had an excess of revenues over expenses (difference) of $85,717 in 19X8. The depreciation expense used to arrive at this figure did not involve any flow of cash. Therefore, to calculate the cash provided by operations we add back the noncash depreciation expense of $122,791 to the difference of $85,717. We also add back the items from the Balance Sheet that generated more cash than they did revenue, or used less cash than was reflected in expenses: the decrease in receivables of $154,864, the increase in salaries and wages payable of $9,210, and the increase in deferred revenues of $10,000. We deduct the items that generated less cash than they did revenue, or used more cash than was reflected in expenses: the increase in prepaid expenses of $2,196, the increase in inventory of $10,000, the decrease in accounts payable of $157,742, and the decrease in payroll taxes payable of $367. These adjustments of the difference to a cash basis total an additional $126,560 of cash inflows, for a total cash provided by operations of $212,277.

Cash flows from investing include the purchase and sale of the things of value the organization owns, typically fixed assets, marketable securities, or investments. Asset sales may occur because the asset is obsolete and no longer useful to the firm. They are akin to a garage sale. But excessive, persistent asset sales are very worrisome if they are the primary source of the cash the organization requires to stay afloat. They are a form of self-cannibalization and impair the organization's ability to survive. Cash outflows for purchase of assets that will be productively employed for the expansion or maintenance of present operations are usually desirable. There is, however, always a danger of overexpansion or of acquisition of assets that will be less productive than the ones presently used.

The net cash outflows from RSUS's investing activities totaled $20,394. The investment in fixed assets of $15,008 was composed of a $112,769 increase in fixed assets and a $97,761 decrease in property rights under lease. The two were *netted* (one subtracted from the other and only the difference shown) because the property rights were merely reclassified as fixed assets when the lease liability was paid. The remainder of the investments consisted of increases in other marketable securities of $456 and time deposits of $4,930.

Cash flows from financing are increasingly frequent in nonprofit organizations. If the entity can easily repay the cash, borrowing is not a cause for alarm. But borrowings sometimes are used inappropriately. As a general rule, short-term sources of cash (sources that are likely to disappear or need to be repaid quickly) should not be used to finance long-term investments. Conversely, long-term borrowings should not be used to finance operations. In a growing organization, the cash inflows generated with debt will usually outstrip the outflows for debt repayment. The reverse pattern will hold in shrinking organizations.

For RSUS, inflows from borrowing consisted of the increase in installment contract payable ($22,134 current and $8,255 long-term). Outflows from financing activities, to repay debt, were reflected in a decrease in capitalized lease obligation of $32,587 current and $65,174 long-term. The decrease in both current and long term lease obligation indicates that the lease was paid off before it was due, meaning the organization had excess cash available. Net cash outflows from financing activities were $67,372, primarily for the lease repayment.

The *net increase in cash* of $124,511 emanated entirely from operations, rather than financing or investing, and reflects a generally healthy financing strategy. RSUS generates sufficient cash flows internally to self-finance. It used the cash to reduce debt significantly, by $67,372, and to increase investments in plant and other assets modestly, by $20,394. One cloud on the horizon is that RSUS's 19X8 investment in fixed assets was much less than the depreciation expense. RSUS does not appear to be replacing assets sufficiently to maintain its physical facilities. Another concern is with the sheer magnitude of the cash flow from operations, and whether it is sustainable or appropriate for a nonprofit organization. The concern is heightened because RSUS does not appear to be reinvesting these large cash flows to create larger operating capacity. On the other hand, the substantial increases in its expenses indicate that it is using its resources to provide more services.

NOTES TO THE FINANCIAL STATEMENTS

The *notes to the financial statements* are an integral part of an organization's financial statements. They provide information necessary for fair presentation of the financial results that is not included in the bodies of the statements themselves. The notes explain the basis of accounting used in preparing the financial statements, disclose additional detail to support the numbers appearing in the body of the financial statements, and provide any additional relevant data. Their purpose is to help the reader understand and interpret the financial statements.

The first note contains a statement of significant accounting policies. It is important because of the variety of accounting policy alternatives available within GAAP. In nonprofit organizations, the accounting policies discussed typically include the methods of revenue recognition, the valuation of donated goods and services, the treatment of inventory, and depreciation. Any accounting policy that is significant to the organization should be disclosed. The remaining notes explain individual items on the various statements, as needed.

The notes to the RSUS financial statements (Table 4-4) begin with a statement of significant accounting policies. The most interesting policy relates to gifts-in-kind, and indicates that RSUS may be understating its revenues and expenses because it does not recognize donated services and free use of land and buildings. RSUS defers grant revenue recognition until the expentures for which the grant was provided are made. RSUS values fixed assets at cost or donated value, less accumulated depreciation, which is calculated using the straight-line method. The useful lives on which the depreciation calculations are based are also disclosed.

Note B explains the long term capital lease, which was in effect a purchase of equipment. Had the lease not been canceled, presumably by early repayment, the payment schedule, amounts, and interest rate would also have been disclosed. It was not necessary to disclose these items because the lease obligation was completely discharged by the end of 19X8. Note C discloses that no provision was made for federal or state income taxes, because RSUS is tax exempt. Because most television stations are operated on a for-profit basis, this disclosure is useful to readers who are unaware that RSUS is a nonprofit organization. Note D discloses that $25,000 of RSUS's cash is restricted for expenses related to relocating the station. Note E discloses a very high interest rate of 17.12 percent on a sales contract, and the type and amount of assets used as collateral for the borrowing. With RSUS's cash-rich position, repayment and renegotiation of the loan may be desirable. Note F discloses the amounts contributed to tax-sheltered annuities and charged to operations for retirement benefits.

The notes enhance our understanding of RSUS's financial status. They explain that the station's increase in fixed assets of $112,769 consists of the purchase of fixed assets of only $15,008 and a reclassification of $97,761 for the color camera, purchased under lease in 19X7, from the account called *property rights under lease* to *fixed assets*. They also reveal that the organization has made some provisions for retirement expenses. A large liability for unfunded expenses is thus unlikely. In addition, we find that the depreciation expense may be understated with a straight-line policy. Accelerated depreciation for equipment may be a more accurate reflection of the rapid rate of technological obsolescence of broadcasting cameras and transmission mechanisms. But revenues are also understated because the station does not recognize in-kind donations. Last, $25,000 of RSUS's cash cannot be freely used. It is restricted for future expenditures of moving.

THE AUDITOR'S OPINION

The financial statements and accounting records of many nonprofit organizations are examined by an independent certified public accountant (CPA) in a process of examination called a *financial audit*. Its purpose is not primarily to uncover fraud (although this may happen in the course of the examination), but to render an opinion on whether the financial statements present fairly all matters material to the financial condition of the organization in accordance with generally accepted accounting principles (GAAP).

TABLE 4-4   **RSUS Notes to the Financial Statement**

Notes to the Financial Statements
RSUS
Years ending June 30, 19X8, and June 30, 19X7

Note A: Summary of Significant Accounting Policies

Revenue Recognition

Revenues received or to be received from grants are recorded as deferred revenue when awarded. Revenue is recognized to the extent expenditures have been made for the purposes specified in the grant.

Gifts-in-kind

Substantial income is received in the form of gifts-in-kind, which include (a) the use of land, buildings, and equipment without charge; (b) donated equipment and materials to be used in the station's operations or to be sold during the annual auction; and (c) donated services.

To the extent measurable by appraisal, gifts of tangible property, which are material in amount, have been recorded in the financial statements at such appraised values. Gifts consisting of the use of land, buildings, and equipment without charge and donated services are not reflected in the financial statements.

Depreciation

Property, plant, and equipment are carried at cost or donated value less accumulated depreciation.

Depreciation of plant and equipment is provided at annual rates expected to amortize the cost of such assets over their estimated useful lives using the straight-line method as follows:

Studio and offices	10-15
Telecasting equipment	5-20
Mobile equipment	3
Office furniture and equipment	10

Note B: Property Rights Acquired Under Long-Term Lease

In 19X7, the Company entered into a long-term lease agreement for color camera equipment. Since the lease was in substance a purchase, it was capitalized.

In 19X8, the lease was canceled by the Company and the lessor. At the time of cancellation the capitalized lease obligation was removed from the records and the color camera equipment was reclassified from property rights acquired under long-term lease to telecasting equipment.

Note C: Federal Income Taxes

No provision for federal or state income taxes has been made in the financial statements, as the Company is exempt from the payment of such taxes.

Note D: Cash Contribution Restricted by Donor

In June 19X6 a $25,000 grant was received from a private foundation which was designated to be used for expenses incurred when the station moved to a new location. This amount has been classified as Deferred Grant Award Revenue in the financial statements.

TABLE 4-4   (Continued)

Note E: Installment Contract Payable

The amount due under the installment contract payable represents a 17.12 percent conditional sales contract payable to a corporation. The contract extends through December 1, 19X9. Collateral consists of telecasting equipment with a net carrying amount of $62,504.98.

Note F: Retirement Benefit Plan

Contributions are made to tax-sheltered annuities for certain employees. Amounts charged to operations under these annuity plans amounted to $26,322.79 and $7,371.67 in 19X8 and 19X7, respectively.

One way to understand a financial audit is to examine the letter that conveys the *auditor's report* or *opinion* and accompanies the *audited financial statements*. Table 4-5 shows a sample auditor's report. Several variants of the audit report may be used at present, although the auditor's report for nonprofit organizations should reflect the most current AICPA standards.

The auditor's report is addressed to the city council, board of directors, or other relevant governing body of the organization. It is dated and signed by a partner of the CPA firm that performed the audit. The opinion is issued for the financial statements taken as a whole. The auditor may not issue a piecemeal opinion that renders different judgments on different parts of the financial statements.

Each paragraph of the report is carefully worded. The first (*introductory*) paragraph discloses the organization units, financial statements, and time period audited and then states that the financial statements are the responsibility of management and that the auditor's responsibility is to express an opinion on those statements. The second (*scope*) paragraph states that the audit was performed in accordance with *generally accepted auditing standards* (*GAAS*) and briefly discusses the nature of those audit standards and the audit work done. It concludes with the representation that the audit provides a reasonable basis for the opinion that is expressed in the following paragraph. The introductory and scope paragraphs are the same for either a qualified or unqualified opinion.

The *opinion* paragraph or paragraphs express the auditor's opinion on the financial statements. The most desirable and common is an *unqualified*, or *clean* opinion which is usually contained in a single paragraph. An example of an unqualified opinion is shown in Table 4-5. An unqualified opinion may be accompanied by an additional explanatory paragraph if material uncertainties exist or if a change in accounting principles or application thereof

TABLE 4-5 **Sample Independent Auditor's Report**

We have audited the accompanying balance sheet of *X* Organization, as of June 30, 19XX, and the related statements of revenue and expenses and changes in fund balance, and cash flows for the year then ended. These financial statements are the responsibility of the organization's management. Our responsibility is to express an opinion on these financial statements based on our audit.

We conducted our audit in accordance with generally accepted auditing standards. Those standards require that we plan and perform the audit to obtain reasonable assurance about whether the financial statements are free of material misstatement. An audit includes examining, on a test basis, evidence supporting the amounts and disclosures in the financial statements. An audit also includes assessing the accounting principles used and significant estimates made by management, as well as evaluating the overall financial statement presentation. We believe that our audit provides a reasonable basis for our opinion.

In our opinion, the financial statements referred to above present fairly, in all material respects, the financial position of *X* Organization as of June 30, 19XX, and the results of its operations and its cash flows for the year then ended in conformity with generally accepted accounting principles.

Source: Adapted from AICPA Auditing Standards Board, Statement on Auditing Standards 58, "Reports on Audited Financial Statements."

had a material effect on the comparability of financial statements. It is issued in situations whose unusual items deserve disclosure, but are not sufficiently large to require the opinion to be qualified.

If the auditor is unable to issue an unqualified opinion, the report usually contains additional paragraphs disclosing the nature of the limitations and is a *qualified* opinion. It states that except for the omissions, the statements present the financial position fairly. The reason for the qualification must be disclosed, and the effect of the omission should be stated, if possible.

The opinion paragraph of an unqualified opinion includes the key phrases *present fairly* and *in conformity with generally accepted accounting principles.* The former means that the financial statements are free from material error, provide adequate disclosure, and are unbiased; in essence, that the statements are reasonably accurate and complete. The latter means that the organization has used accounting principles endorsed by authoritative organizations. Earlier auditor's reports also included the phrase *on a basis consistent with,* to indicate that the same accounting principles were used to prepare these statements in the current and prior periods. Consistency, which enables readers to compare statements to reveal changes in the organization's financial circumstances, is now mentioned only if statements are not consistent. The nature of the inconsistency and the reason must be disclosed. If these conditions are met, and no other important considerations exist, the CPA will issue an unqualified opinion.

A qualified opinion states that the financial statements present fairly and in accordance with GAAP, *except for* the effects of the matters to which the qualification relates. An opinion may be qualified for a number of reasons. It may be used to indicate a lack of sufficient evidence, a limitation in the scope of the examination, a departure from generally accepted accounting principles, an inadequate disclosure of information in the financial statements, a material change in the application of accounting principles from one year to the next, or a high probability of loss or failure. An except for opinion conveys the judgment that the exception does not have a significant material effect on the fairness of the presentation of the organization's financial position. Otherwise, the auditor must issue an adverse opinion or disclaim an opinion.

Prior to the current auditing standards, two other types of opinions were also used. A *subject to* qualified opinion indicated the existence of a matter that could have a significant material effect on the financial condition of the organization and whose outcome is uncertain. A major lawsuit involving significant monetary damage claims against the organization might lead to a subject to opinion. A *going concern* qualification indicated the auditor's opinion that the organization was in such vulnerable financial condition that it might not survive. The financial statements of some hospitals, colleges and municipalities that were teetering on the brink of bankruptcy received going concern qualifications. Current auditing standards eliminated both subject to and going concern opinions. The circumstances that would previously have led to either a subject to or going concern opinion must now be disclosed in an explanatory paragraph, and the opinion be either qualified or unqualified; the auditor is thus now required to decide whether the circumstances warrant qualification.

In extreme circumstances, the auditor may also render an *adverse* opinion or a *disclaimer* of opinion. Financial statements accompanied by either of these opinions are of little value, although an adverse or disclaimer of opinion itself often signals problems.

An *adverse* opinion indicates an auditor's judgment that the financial statements do not fairly present the financial position of the organization. Adverse opinions are rare because the management of most organizations is usually willing to make the changes necessary to obtain at least a qualified opinion.

A *disclaimer* of opinion indicates no opinion of any type on the financial statements. Disclaimers have sometimes been used in organizations that had primitive accounting and control systems that prohibited the auditor's verifying the financial statements. Auditors are specifically prohibited from using a disclaimer to whitewash a situation. If they have reason to believe that the statements are materially deficient, or that GAAP has not been followed, then an adverse opinion must be issued. Disclaimers are most commonly used in situations where the degree of uncertainty and materiality are too great to issue a qualified opinion.

An auditor's opinion is used by parties external to the organization, particularly those who have a financial interest in it, such as potential donors or grantors, or those who have served on its board. Qualified opinions are fairly common in the nonprofit sector, but adverse opinions or disclaimers of opinion are viewed with concern.

The auditors' report on RSUS's financial statements is shown in Table 4-6. It received a clean or unqualified opinion.

The auditor's opinion of the financial statements is couched in terms of "conformity with GAAP" and "accordance with generally accepted auditing standards" (GAAS). This judgment requires the promulgation of standards and principles. GAAP for governmental organizations, including government-run universities and hospitals, are set by the GASB; for all other organizations, they are provided by the FASB. Together with the AICPA, which has primary responsibility for GAAS as well as significant influence on GAAP,

TABLE 4-6   **RSUS Auditor's Report**

Opinion of the Auditors Phinney and Rogoff
Certified Public Accountants

August 8, 19X8

Board of Directors

We have audited the accompanying balance sheets of RSUS as of June 30, 19X8, and June 30, 19X7, and the related statements of revenues and expenses and changes in fund balances and cash flows for the years then ended. These financial statements are the responsibility of RSUS management. Our responsibility is to express an opinion on these financial statements based on our audit.

We conducted our audit in accordance with generally accepted auditing standards. Those standards require that we plan and perform the audit to obtain reasonable assurance about whether the financial statements are free of material misstatement. An audit includes examining, on a test basis, evidence supporting the amounts and disclosures in the financial statements. An audit also includes assessing the accounting principles used and significant estimates made by management, as well as evaluating the overall financial statement presentation. We believe that our audit provides a reasonable basis for our opinion.

In our opinion, the financial statements referred to above present fairly, in all material respects, the financial position of RSUS at June 30, 19X8, and June 30, 19X7, and the results of its operations and its cash flows for the years then ended, in conformity with generally accepted accounting principles.

Phinney and Rogoff

these organizations comprise the primary standard setters for accounting and auditing. (The specific roles of these and other institutions involved in the process of developing accounting principles and setting audit standards were discussed in more detail in Chapter 2, along with a listing of relevant *Audit Guides* for the various types of organizations.) It is not always easy to determine GAAP and GAAS in an environment of conflicting pronouncements and ambiguous jurisdiction, so be prepared to encounter some variety in actual financial statements and audit reports.

REPORTING TO REGULATORS

Nonprofit organizations are closely regulated by the Internal Revenue Service (IRS) and by many state governments. The financial reports to be filed with regulatory agencies usually differ in some respects from those filed with external parties under GAAP. Regulators may require additional or reformulated information. Because of the potentially disastrous consequences of noncompliance, nonprofit accounting systems must meet the needs of these regulatory requirements as well as GAAP. CPAs who perform financial audits also typically assist with the preparation of the required filings and are aware of the filing requirements for different types and sizes of agencies.

The Internal Revenue Service

The IRS exempts most nonprofit organizations from paying federal income taxes and requires them to file financial statements and other documents to ensure that they fulfill the requirements for the exemption. The major classes of exempt organizations, as specified by the Internal Revenue Code, are:

501(c)2: "Corporations organized for the exclusive purpose of holding title to property, collecting income therefrom, and turning over the entire amount thereof, less expenses, to an organization which itself is exempt under this section."

501(c)3: "Corporations, and any community chest, fund or foundation, organized and operated exclusively for religious, charitable, scientific, testing for public safety, literary, or educational purposes . . . or for the prevention of cruelty to children or animals, no part of the net earnings of which inures to the benefit of any private shareholder or individual, no substantial part of the activities of which is carrying on propaganda, or otherwise attempting to influence legislation . . . and which does not participate in, or intervene in (including the publishing or distributing of statements), any political campaign on behalf of (or in opposition to) any candidate for public office."

501(c)6:   "Business leagues, chambers of commerce, . . . not organized for profit . . ."

501(c)7:   "Clubs organized for pleasure, recreation, and other nonprofitable purposes . . . no part of the net earnings of which inures to the benefit of any private shareholder."

These are commonly known as foundations (501(c)2), charitable organizations (501(c)3), associations (501(c)6) and social clubs (501(c)7). Collectively, they may be referred to as *501(c) organizations*, from the section of the IRS Code that confers their tax exempt status.

Organizations classified as exempt from federal taxation are required to file annual "informational" returns (Form 990) with the IRS. These returns require data about revenues, expenses and disbursements, and assets and liabilities, as well as supplementary information about compensation for officers and employees. In addition, if the organization has unrelated business income—that is, income that is not substantially related to its basis for receiving tax exempt status—it must file a form declaring such income and pay tax on that amount. This is known as Unrelated Business Income Tax (UBIT). Unrelated business activities of nonprofits are subject to close scrutiny, primarily because of complaints from small business competitors that nonprofit organizations have an unfair advantage because they are tax exempt.

The tax law continues to add restrictions and disclosure requirements. The Tax Reform Act of 1969 restricted the base of support of nonprofit organizations to curb the creation of individually-financed private foundations with a primary purpose of avoiding tax payments. In 1986, the House Ways and Means Oversight Committee began a review of the tax treatment of the income producing activities of nonprofit organizations that is likely to result in tighter monitoring and taxation of UBIT. The 1989 Form 990 requires much more detailed reporting of income than in the past. Other recent IRS actions require organizations requesting contributions to disclose clearly how much of the contribution, if any, is tax deductible for the donor.

Although a nonprofit organization's accounting system must allow it to meet the IRS reporting requirements, it should be structured so that it can also provide adequate information for managerial needs and for financial reporting. Tax reporting, financial reporting and managerial accounting do not always follow the same principles.

Other Federal Agencies

Various other federal agencies also may impose reporting requirements on nonprofit organizations. For example, federal research agencies, such as the National Science Foundation, require grant and contract reports from universities, hospitals, and any other organizations that receive grants. The National Center for Education Statistics of the U.S. Department of Education conducts an annual survey on a variety of financial and other factors related to higher education institutions, as do other federal agencies. Whether mandatory, such as grant reporting, or voluntary, as with surveys, there are many reports that an organization must prepare and submit to various federal agencies.

State and Local Governments

State and local authorities also require various data from nonprofit organizations to confer exemptions from income, sales, and property taxes, and to permit the organization to solicit funds. Many state attorneys general regulate nonprofit organizations. They may require organizations to file a copy of their federal 990 tax forms or audited financial statements and other supplemental data. Some states require that a nonprofit spend less than a prespecified percentage of its total revenues on fund raising or administrative expenses, to safeguard the public against sham nonprofits that spend only a small fraction of their revenues on delivering services.

Effectiveness of Regulation

Despite regulatory efforts, drastic improvements are needed. The Comptroller General of the United States claims that the weaknesses in the system that allowed a single U.S. Department of Housing and Urban Development (HUD) employee to steal some $5 million are widespread and systemic (she was nicknamed "Robin HUD" because she claimed to distribute her theft proceeds to charity). Alleged offenders range from the former secretary of the agency and his top aide, through closing agents and low level employees in several field offices, to private sector HUD contractors. The charges include influence peddling, political favoritism, mismanagement, and outright theft. Losses are estimated in the billions of dollars. Ironically, in its 1987 annual Financial Integrity Act report, HUD itself disclosed that inadequate controls in the property disposition process provided the potential for closing agents to manipulate or otherwise take funds for their own use.[1] Had these weaknesses in internal control and accountability been corrected then, billions of dollars could perhaps have been saved and the costly erosion of public confidence could have been avoided.

Eliminating, or at least reducing, such abuses does not mean simply adding more controls to an already cumbersome regulatory system; it means redesigning the control system and educating and informing its operators: elected officials, managers, and, ultimately, the general public. A vital part of any accounting control system is a pool of interested, vigilant users of

[1]Phil Kuntz and Joan Biskupic, "New Investigations Launched as HUD Scandal Widens," *Congressional Quarterly Weekly Reports* (June 17, 1989): 1477-8; and Charles A. Bowsher, *Facing Facts*, Comptroller General's 1989 Annual Reports, United States (Washington, DC: General Accounting Office, 1989), p. 11.

the information. The lack of public accountability, the mountain of confusing data, and the absence of an interested, informed user population may be the weakest links in the existing chain of control.

SUMMARY

Financial statements that reflect the activity of the period are important for understanding and evaluating the performance of nonprofit organizations. All nonprofit organizations are currently required to present an operating statement that includes the revenues, expenses, and resulting change in fund balance during the period. A growing number are also required to present a Statement of Cash Flows that discloses information on the sources and uses of cash from various types of activities during the period. Each statement provides uniquely useful information. Their utility is enhanced by the audit process and the notes to the financial statements.

The wide variety of accounting methods and statement formats in use contributes to the difficulty of comparing the performance of different organizations. The many sources of authority on accounting standards for nonprofit organizations are currently developing better, clearer, more uniform financial reporting standards. Nevertheless, serious problems remain with the caliber of nonprofit accounting and auditing.

DISCUSSION QUESTIONS

1. What types of items should be included in an operating statement, and why would they be important to financial statement readers?

2. What is the relationship between the fund balance and the operating statement?

3. What is the purpose of the Statement of Changes in Fund Balance?

4. Discuss the value of the Statement of Cash Flows. Provide examples of the questions it can answer that cannot be answered from the operating statement.

5. Depreciation expense is sometimes referred to as a "source of cash." Is this statement correct? If not, how do you think it originated? If yes, why is it correct?

6. Why are notes to the financial statements needed? Can you think of any items that were not mentioned in the text that should be disclosed in notes to the financial statements?

7. What is the purpose of the auditor's opinion? What information does it convey about the financial statements? Does a clean opinion mean that the organization is in sound financial health?

8. How are the reports required by regulators different from general purpose financial statements?

EXERCISES

1. The Cleveland Volunteers have lost parts of their accounting records. Can you help them calculate the missing items? As of the end of the period, the records show the following:

Cash	$25,000
Net accounts receivable	5,000
Marketable securities	5,000
Net book value of fixed assets	18,000
Note payable	5,000
Salaries payable	3,000
Mortgage payable	12,000

    In addition the records show the following:

Bills sent for services rendered of	$20,000
Depreciation expense	1,600
Equipment purchase	1,000
Supplies purchase	800
Supplies expense	500
Administrative salary expense	2,000
Fund-raising salary expense	1,000
Interest expense	400
Program salary expense	15,000
Salaries paid	15,000

    a. What was the difference between revenues and expenses for the period? Does this represent an increase or decrease in the fund balance?
    b. What was the fund balance at the end of the period?
    c. What was the fund balance in the beginning of the period?

2. The Belton Independent School in Nebraska had the following transactions in the first year of its existence:

Salaries owed, teachers	$111,000
Salaries owed, administration	39,000
Salaries owed, fund raisers	14,000
Bills for tuition	150,000
Gifts received in cash	50,000
Bills received for utilities, supplies, and food	20,000
Bills received for textbooks purchased	5,000
Bills sent for student fees	15,000
Cash inflow (including the gift)	165,000
Cash outflow	160,000

    Because Belton School will not give credit for courses or admit students for the next year unless their bills are fully paid, it expects a bad debt expense of only 5 percent of the amount of bills sent.

    Construct a Balance Sheet and an Operating Statement for the first year based on the information provided.

3. The Belton Independent School hired an accountant who discovered the following errors in the financial records shown in Exercise 2 while performing the audit:

    a. The administrative salaries owed of $39,000 were for a 13-month period and included the first month of the second year.
    b. The bills for tuition did not include the $15,000 for summer school tuition for the summer school session that had been completed.
    c. Included in the $20,000 bill for utilities, supplies, and food was a $5,000 bill for supplies. As of the end of the first year, $1,000 of the supplies was still in inventory.

    Correct the financial statements for Year 1 in light of these facts.

4. The Museum of Normont in Alabama has the following Statement of Cash Flows and Balance Sheet as of the beginning of the year:

**Statement of Cash Flows
from Beginning to End of the Year**

Sources of Cash		Uses of Cash	
From operations (including an adjustment for depreciation expense of $5,000)	$15,000	To repay long-term borrowing	$ 5,000
From short-term borrowing	5,000	To purchase:	
		Fixed assets	10,000
		Inventory	3,000
From reduction of assets:			
Sale of fixed assets	8,000		
Accounts receivable	10,000		

**Balance Sheet
as of the Beginning of the Year**

Assets		Liabilities and Fund Balance	
Cash	$ 10,000	Notes payable	$ 10,000
Inventory	10,000	Long-term debt	30,000
Accounts receivable	20,000	Fund balance	100,000
Net value of fixed assets	100,000		
Total	$140,000	Total	$140,000

Construct the Balance Sheet as of the end of the year.

5. The Portland Nonprofit Services has revenues of $500,000, salary and wage expense of $300,000, supplies expense of $50,000, interest expense of $20,000, and depreciation expense of $60,000. What was its total cash flow from operations?

6. Using the data below, prepare a Statement of Cash Flows for The Children's Workshop in Michigan for 19X8.

Balance Sheet
The Children's Workshop
(dollars in thousands)

	19X7	19X8	Difference
Assets			
Cash	$ 46	$ 47	+$ 1
Marketable securities	16	18	+ 2
Accounts receivable	50	54	+ 4
Inventories	38	36	− 2
Fixed assets—original cost	490	525	+ 35
Less accumulated depreciation	100	120	+ 20
Total assets	$540	$560	
Liabilities and Fund Balance			
Accounts payable	$35	$30	− 5
Notes payable	40	42	+ 2
Long-term debt	162	168	+ 6
Fund balance	303	320	+ 17
Total liabilities and fund balance	$540	$560	

Statement of Revenues and Expenses
for the Years 19X7-19X8
The Children's Workshop
(dollars in thousands)

Revenues		$340
Expenses:		
Salaries and wages	$233	
Supplies	20	
Space expense	50	
Depreciation expense	20	323
Total income		$ 17

Additional information: debt was increased by $50 thousand; it was used to finance the purchase of fixed assets, in the amount of $50 thousand.

Cases

CASE STUDIES

The WJAC case, 4.1, is synthesized from a number of real-life situations. It is in the seemingly contradictory position of increasing its income while decreasing its cash. The case should enable you to better understand the differences between cash and accrual accounting and the impact of a financing strategy on both cash and income.

The Guaranteed Student Loan Fund, Case 4.2, contains the financial statements of the U.S. government insurance funds for student loans. It puts you in the role of the auditor and asks what kind of opinion these statements should receive. The case presents you with yet another opportunity to analyze financial statements and to understand the relationship to the auditing process. Although the case describes events dating back more than two decades, they are still relevant today. By 1992, the value of the defaults on student loans exceeded $3.6 billion.[1]

CASE 4.1 WJAC—Financing a Growing Organization

BACKGROUND

In December 19X6, Susan Fried, treasurer of WJAC, was preparing a loan request to the Clifton Trust Company. The loan was to meet the cash needs of the station in the year 19X7.

WJAC had become one of the larger public television stations. It had a substantial base of community support, produced a number of programs for national distribution, and provided both regularly scheduled and special coverage of local events. The programming efforts began modestly with a series, "How Things Work," conducted by an eccentric and engaging professor of engineering, whom George Hart,

This case was prepared by Professor Regina E. Herzlinger.

Copyright © 1977 by the President and Fellows of Harvard College. Harvard Business School case 9-177-158. Revised January 1993.

[1]Michael Rust, "Taking the Rap for Bum Loans," *Insight* (June 22, 1992): 14.

the station director, had casually met at a party. The show became a surprising success and provided the base for WJAC's later programming efforts.

The station had also done well financially. As can be seen from **Exhibits 1** and **2**, WJAC's profitable operations enabled it to acquire a substantial amount of assets. It had broken even every year since its incorporation and continued profitable growth was anticipated. The Ford Foundation and the National Endowment for the Arts had given the station many grants in the past for program development and these were expected to continue. Further, WJAC's newly appointed director of development, Linda Brown, had convinced a large manufacturer to underwrite new episodes of the "How Things Work" series. She was expected to continue to find new sources of financing from the business community in the future.

To provide the plant for this anticipated growth, WJAC substantially expanded its facilities in the past three years. The capital expansion was to be completed in 19X7, with the installation of the new equipment acquired in that year.

The Loan

WJAC had borrowed seasonally from the Clifton Trust Company for the past few years. The bank loan was granted under the following conditions:

(1) It was to be completely paid off for one month during the course of the year.

(2) The monthly cash and accounts receivable balances had to be equal to (or greater than) 120 percent of the loan.

(3) A compensating cash balance equal to $200,000 had to be maintained at all times. If the loan were to go above $2,000,000, the cash balance must increase by 10 percent of the amount by which the loan is greater than $2,000,000.

In the past, WJAC had no difficulty meeting these requirements. However, in 19X6, the station had been unable to liquidate for a period of a month. Although the Clifton Bank extended the necessary credit, the bank's loan officer expressed his concern over the situation and asked for a monthly cash budget to justify the amount and timing of the 19X7 seasonal financing. Ms. Fried began to collect the data needed to prepare such a budget.

WJAC derived its revenues from three main sources: contributions, memberships, and grants. Ms. Fried calculated the accounts receivable balance for each of these sources, by month, for the year 19X7. These estimates were based on a continuation of WJAC's normal procedures for collecting pledges and grant revenues and are contained in **Exhibit 3**. Total grants awarded in 19X7 were expected to amount to $8,606,000.

Expenses were scheduled to be level throughout the year 19X7, except for purchases of supplies which were normally made twice a year in December and June. In 19X7, $200,000 of supplies would be purchased in June and $700,000 in December, on terms of net 30 days. The supplies inventory at the end of December was expected to be $600,000. Depreciation expense would be $500,000 for the year. Other expenses were expected to run at an even rate of $710,000 a month throughout the year. Payroll and program purchase expenses accounted for $700,000 a month of other expenses. These expenses were paid on the Monday of the first week following the end of the month. The other $10,000 a month of expenses were paid for as incurred.

The new equipment, costing $400,000, was to be delivered in September and paid for in four equal monthly installments beginning in September. Additionally, small equipment purchases of $20,000 were to be delivered and paid for on delivery for every month of 19X7.

In 19X3, WJAC borrowed $4,000,000 from a life insurance company, repayable over a 16-year term, in equal payments in June and December of each year. Interest at 5 percent annually on the unpaid balance was also payable at these dates. Ms. Fried calculated that the total mortgage interest payments for 19X7 would be $172,000. The seasonal loan interest expense was at the annual interest rate of 8 percent of the unpaid balance of the loan, payable monthly.

Ms. Fried thought it prudent to maintain the cash balance of WJAC at $200,000 at all times. Also, the bank wanted to have at least this amount on deposit.

ASSIGNMENT

1. Calculate the cash inflows and outflows for every month in the year 19X7. What are WJAC's monthly loan requirements?

2. Calculate the projected Balance Sheets and Income Statement for WJAC for 19X7.

3. Prepare the actual Statements of Cash Flows for WJAC for 19X4 through 19X6, and the projected Statement of Cash Flows for 19X7.

4. What financing strategy would you recommend for WJAC?

EXHIBIT 1   WJAC, Inc., Balance Sheet as of December 31, 19X4-19X6 (in thousands of dollars)

	19X4	19X5	19X6
Assets			
Cash	$2,688	$ 229	$ 208
Accounts receivable	2,942	3,372	4,440
Inventory	700	700	500
Total current assets	$6,330	$4,301	$ 5,148
Plant and equipment	2,643	4,838	5,809
Total assets	$8,973	$9,139	$10,957
Liabilities and Fund Balance			
Bank loan	$ 0	$ 0	$ 1,620
Accounts payable	420	720	780
Accrued payroll and programming expenses	472	583	646
Mortgage, current	250	250	250
Total current liabilities	$1,142	$1,553	$ 3,296
Other payable	270		
Mortgage payable	3,750	3,500	3,250
Fund balance	3,811	4,086	4,411
Total liabilities and fund balance	$8,973	$9,139	$10,957

EXHIBIT 2   WJAC, Inc., Income Statements, 19X4-19X6 (in thousands of dollars)

	19X4	19X5	19X6
Grants and other revenues	$3,303	$4,060	$5,263
Memberships	1,202	1,361	1,874
Contributions	1,041	1,412	1,702
Total revenues	$5,546	$6,833	$8,839
Expenses[a]			
Programming	$4,071	$4,805	$6,307
Transmission	271	332	473
Public relations and community development	1,082	1,421	1,734
Total expenses	$5,424	$6,558	$8,514
Net income	$ 122	$ 275	$ 325

[a]Expenses include Depreciation of $355, $370, and $470 and General and Administrative Expenses of $1,549, $1,688, and $2,142 in the years 19X4-19X6, respectively.

EXHIBIT 3   WJAC, Inc., Estimated Monthly Revenues and End of Month Receivables for 19X7 (in thousands of dollars)

	Memberships		Contributions		Grants	
	Revenues	End of Month Receivables	Revenues	End of Month Receivables	Revenues	End of Month Receivables
January	$ 20	$ 981	$ 4	$ 751	$ 230	$2,695
February	44	1,000	25	771	260	2,722
March	68	1,027	46	794	362	2,795
April	68	1,054	46	817	362	2,868
May	92	1,084	67	848	429	2,953
June	288	1,130	250	888	793	3,100
July	540	1,168	508	921	1,061	3,206
August	440	1,206	408	1,054	861	3,312
September	316	1,240	287	1,083	695	3,407
October	192	1,270	167	1,110	529	3,492
November	192	1,300	167	1,137	529	3,577
December	144	1,342	108	1,170	461	3,683

CASE 4.2 The Guaranteed Student Loan Program

PURPOSE OF THE PROGRAM

The Guaranteed Student Loan Program (GSLP) was established under the Higher Education Act of 1965 to provide low-interest insured loans to students in post-secondary and vocational schools. The program, which was designed to benefit low- and middle-income students, was administered by the Department of Education (DE). It began operations in fiscal year 1968.

The GSLP was intended to serve three basic purposes: (1) to encourage states or private nonprofit institutions to establish adequate student loan-insurance programs by guaranteeing a portion of all loans they agreed to insure; (2) to provide a federal student loan-insurance program for students or lenders who do not have reasonable access to a state or private nonprofit program; and (3) to pay part of the interest charged to students on loans insured by the federal government, the state, or private nonprofit institutions.

OPERATION OF GSLP

To accomplish its goals, the program was divided into two discrete components: a federal loan *insurance* program, and a state or private nonprofit agency loan *reinsurance* program. Under the federal insurance program, the government promised to reimburse the lender for 100 percent of the unpaid principal balance of any defaulted loan. Upon payment of a lender's claim, the government acquired title to the borrower's note for the loan. If default resulted from a simple failure to pay, the government then attempted to collect the loan; if it resulted from the death or total and permanent disability of the borrower, the borrower or surviving family was released from any obligation for the unpaid balance.

Under the reinsurance program, the DE was authorized to reimburse state or private agencies for 80 percent of all losses on loans made prior to December 15, 1968. On loans made on or after that date, the DE was authorized to repay 100 percent of the amount owed when default resulted from death or disability of the student borrower, regardless of whether the guaranty agency had signed a reinsurance agreement.

Under the state program, however, the DE did not acquire title to the borrower's note on any claim it paid. Even after the DE reimbursed a guaranty agency for a defaulted claim, that agency retained full collection responsibility, and was required to return to the DE 80 percent of any amount it subsequently recovered from the borrower.

This case was prepared by B. S. Chakravarthy under the direction of Professor Regina E. Herzlinger.

FINANCING THE PROGRAM

The insurance and reinsurance of loans provided under the GSLP was funded by the revolving Student Loan Insurance Fund (SLIF). The fund was financed by direct appropriations from Congress, insurance premiums collected from participating lenders (only on loans made under the federal program), and proceeds from the collection of defaulted loans. The premium was computed at one-fourth of one percent a year on the unpaid principal of the loan, from the date of disbursement of the loan to the student borrower, to the anticipated date of their graduation plus 12 months. The entire premium was collected in advance.

Loans were repaid over a period between five and ten years, beginning not earlier than nine nor later then twelve months following the date on which a student ceases to be enrolled at least half-time at an eligible institution. However, as the act required the student to repay at a rate of not less than $360 a year, the actual repayment terms will depend on the student's total indebtedness. Borrowers did not need to make principal payments for up to three years while they were members of the Armed Forces, volunteers in certain agencies, or pursuing a full-time course of study at an eligible school.

The payment of interest expenses on behalf of eligible students, as well as the salary and office administration expenses under the program, were funded by separate provisions. Death and permanent disability claims on loans insured after December 15, 1968, were also funded by sources external to SLIF. **Exhibit 1** shows a flow diagram of receipts and disbursements under SLIF.

THE ROLE OF THE GAO

The General Accounting Office (GAO) was required by law to audit the SLIF. **Exhibits 2** through **4** present information from the GAO examinations of financial statements of the Student Loan Insurance Fund for fiscal years 1968, 1969, and 1970.

ASSIGNMENT

1. If you were a GAO auditor, what opinion would you give the SLIF financial statements?
2. Is there any information the government needs that the accounts fail to provide?
3. What changes if any would you recommend to be made in the SLIF accounting procedures?

EXHIBIT 1 **SLIF Receipts and Disbursements**

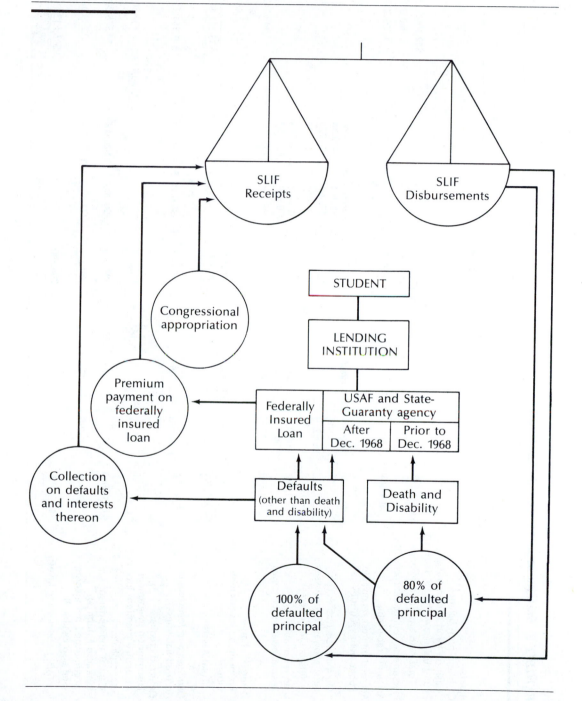

EXHIBIT 2 **Statement of Financial Condition**

	1968	1969 Insured	1969 Reinsured	1969	1970 Insured	1970 Reinsured	1970
Assets							
Cash and fund balance:							
Cash on hand and in transit				$ 6,877			$ 32,017
Fund balance with U.S. Treasury				4,095,540			12,077,536
Total cash and fund balance	$3,793,512			$4,102,417			$12,109,553
Investments—public debt securities[1]				412,000			900,000
Accounts receivable	405,164			485,807			1,199,255
Accrued interest receivable:							
Public debt securities	-			-			17,031
On loan receivables	15	$ 1,051	$ 214		$ 28,294	$ 47,684	
Less: allowance for losses	-	578	118		15,562	26,226	
Net accrued interest	15	473	96	569	12,732	21,458	34,190
Loan receivable	1,800	66,055	21,096		1,764,743	2,567,795	
Less: allowance for losses	-	36,330	11,603		970,609	1,412,287	
	1,800	29,725	9,493	39,218	794,134	1,155,508	1,949,642
Deferred charges:							
Premium on investments				9,595			-
Other[2]	-			157,384			2,481
Total Assets	$4,200,491			$5,206,990			$16,212,152
Liabilities and Investments							
Accrued liabilities[3]		$ 14,135	$228,709	$ 242,844	$ 536,620	$ 614,691	$ 1,151,311
Deferred credits:							
Discount on investments				$ 8,036			$ 4,526
Insurance premium income[4]				1,188,219			2,730,142
				1,196,255			2,734,668
Total capital:							
Capital appropriated[5] (See also Exhibit 4)	$3,750,000			3,487,675	3,750,000	10,826,000	14,576,000
Accumulated net income[6][7] (See also Exhibit 4)	450,491	113,242	166,974	280,216	(377,303)	(1,872,524)	(2,249,827)
Total Liabilities and Investments	$4,200,491			$5,206,990			$16,212,152

Notes to Exhibit 2/Case 4.2

Note 1   Moneys on the SLIF which are not needed for operations may be invested in bonds or other U.S. Government guaranteed obligations.

Note 2   1969—Other deferred charges are unpaid defaulted loans guaranteed by the U.S. Government.

Note 3   In 1969, accrued liabilities represent claims payable to lenders and state or private guaranty agencies and consisted of:

Insured loan claims due state	$ 14,135
Reinsured loan claims due state and private guaranty agencies	228,709
Total	$242,844

In 1970, accrued liabilities represented claims payable to lenders and state or private guaranty agencies and consisted of:

Insured loan claims due lender	$ 536,620
Reinsured loan claim due state and private guaranty agencies	614,691
Total	$1,151,311

Note 4   In 1969, a major change in the method of statement preparation involved the deferring of insurance premium income over the average length of loans. The best estimate of expected loss for the $206,286,220 of insured loans was $1,325,000.

Note 5   1969—Reduced by reinsured claims processed:

1968 Ending	$3,750,000
Less: Cost funded by appropriation (Exhibit 4)	262,325
	$3,487,675

Note 6   In 1968, the reserve for losses was based on the loan principal insured less write offs due to death and disability, $10,840. The residual amount of $61,272,966 × 0.725 percent (estimated loss rate) gave a reserve for losses of $444,229. The loss rate is the average between the actual expense of eight agencies (1.2 percent) with similar insurance problems over an 11-year period, which included loans in repayment status, and the established annual insurance rate (0.25 percent) based on loans in school status. Out of the accumulated net income of $450,491 in 1968, the reserve for losses was $444,229.

Note 7   The 1968 statement excluded unfunded contingent liabilities for loans insured of $61,283,806. The contingent liabilities were computed on the basis of 73,458 loans insured at an average principal of $834.27 per loan.

The 1969 contingent liability for loans underwritten was:

Insured loans	$205,256,220
Reinsured loans	496,115,602

The 1970 financial statements which the Office of Education submitted to the U.S. Treasury included a schedule showing the fund's estimated net contingent liability of $465 million for federally insured loans and $1.13 billion for reinsured loans that had been disbursed as of June 30, 1970. The Office of Education determined these amounts after considering the amount of claims paid on defaulted loans and an estimated amount for repayments made by student borrowers. Additional amounts of $173 million for federally insured loans and $132 million for reinsured loans were shown on the schedule as the potential contingent liabilities for loans that had been approved but had not been disbursed as of June 30, 1970.

EXHIBIT 3 **Statement of Income and Expense**

	1968	1969			1970		
	Total	*Insured*	*Reinsured*	*Total*	*Insured*	*Reinsured*	*Total*
Income:							
Insurance premiums[a]	$461,316	$210,077	$ -	$210,077	$ 553,121	$ -	$ 553,121
Interest on public debt securities	-	-	-	-	48,194	-	48,194
Amortization of discount on investment—public service securities	-	4,765	-	4,765	-	-	-
Interest on loans receivable	15	1,036	214	1,250	27,276	47,470	74,746
Total Income	$461,331	$215,873	$ 214	$216,092	$ 628,591	$ 47,470	$ 676,061
Expenses:							
Loss on loans (death and disabilities)[b]	$ 10,840	$101,035	$ 83,844	$184,879	$ 169,874	$ 397,851	$ 567,725
Estimated losses on accrued interest receivable	-	578	118	696	14,984	26,108	41,092
Estimated losses on loans receivable	-	36,330	11,603	47,933	934,278	1,400,684	2,334,962
Total Expenses	$ 10,840	$137,943	$ 95,565	$233,508	$1,119,136	$ 1,824,643	$ 2,943,779
Net income or (deficit)	$450,491	$ 77,935	$(95,351)	$ (17,416)	$ (490,545)	$(1,777,173)	$(2,267,718)

[a] Insurance premium for 1968 was computed on the basis of an average of $6.28/loan. The average premium was based on the billing, dated June 4, 1968, of $140,870 for 22,441 loans.

[b] Losses by death or disability of loans made after December 15, 1968, were paid by higher education activities and appropriations. These losses are excluded from the statements. Cumulative through June 30, 1970, claims of $305,000 were received, $200,000 for insured and $105,000 for reinsured.

EXHIBIT 4 **Statement of Changes in Accumulated Net Income**

	Insured	Reinsured	Total
Balance at beginning of period	$ 450,491	$ -	$ 450,491
Less adjustment to defer income of prior year	415,184	-	415,184
Adjusted balance at beginning of period	35,307	-	35,307
Add net income or (deficit) for current period (see Exhibit 3)	77,935	(95,351)	(17,416)
Total	113,242	(95,351)	17,891
Add costs funded by appropriations	-	262,325	262,325
Balance at end of period	$ 113,242	$166,974	$ 280,216

Note: Computations for capital appropriation and accumulated net income, shown in Exhibit 2 at end of fiscal year 1969, are shown below:

Capital appropriated beginning of 1969	$3,750,000	$ -	$3,750,000
Appropriations for reinsurance costs from insurance funds	(262,325)	-	(262,325)
Capital appropriated at end of 1969	$3,487,675	-	$3,487,675
Accumulated net income at end of 1969	113,242	166,974	280,216
Appropriated capital and accumulated net income, end of 1969 (first item in Exhibit 5)	$3,600,917	$166,974	$3,767,891

EXHIBIT 5 **Statement of Changes in Investment of the U.S. Government**

	Insured	Reinsured	Total
Balance at beginning of period	$3,600,917	$ 166,974	$ 3,767,891
Funds appropriated for reinsurance claims	-	10,826,000	10,826,000
Adjustment for fiscal year 1969 reinsured claims paid from insured loan funds	262,325	(262,325)	-
Net income or (deficit) for year ended June 30, 1970 (see Exhibit 3)	(40,545)	(1,777,173)	(2,267,718)
Balance at end of period	$3,372,697	$ 8,953,476	$12,326,173

Note: Computations for capital appropriation and accumulated net income, shown in Exhibit 2, at the end of fiscal year 1970, are shown below:

Capital Appropriation			
Capital appropriation beginning of 1970	$3,487,675	-	$ 3,487,675
Funds appropriated in 1970 for reinsurance claims	-	$10,826,000	10,826,000
Adjustment for fiscal year 1969 reinsurance claims paid from insured loan funds	262,325	-	262,325
Capital appropriation end of 1970	$3,750,000	$10,826,000	$14,576,000
Accumulated Net Income			
Accumulated net income end of 1969	$ 113,242	$ 166,974	$ 280,216
Adjustment for fiscal year 1969 reinsurance claims paid for insurance loans	-	(262,325)	(262,325)
Income in 1970 (Exhibit 3)	(490,545)	(1,777,173)	(2,267,718)
Accumulated net income end of 1970	$ (377,303)	$ (1,872,524)	$ (2,249,827)

5   Financial Analysis

FINANCIAL STATEMENTS SHOULD ENABLE READERS TO evaluate the organization's financial performance. *Financial analysis* is the process of using the information provided by the financial statements to calculate the financial ratios and other measures that enable such judgment. Financial analysis enables the user to answer four fundamental questions:

(1) *Are the organization's goals consistent with the financial resources it needs to finance them?* In the ebullient financial climate of the 1960s, many nonprofit organizations undertook programs that exceeded their financial capacity. Just like small children who take much more food than they can possibly eat, these organizations' eyes were bigger than their stomachs. The recessionary economy of the 1970s forced some of these overcommitted organizations to bankruptcy, while others were significantly cut back. That cycle may be repeated. The boom of the 1980s may lead to severe cutbacks in the 1990s. Many hospitals are already closing their doors, some cities, Philadelphia for example, are near bankruptcy, and Stanford University is but one of the many colleges and univerities that are in the throes of major cost reductions.

Yet other nonprofit organizations have overly modest goals, given the size and quality of their financial resources. They seem to forget that the purpose of a nonprofit is to provide services—not to conserve large amounts of capital.

This question assesses whether the organization's financial position can accomplish its goals and if the financing methods are appropriate for its goals. Because the purpose of a nonprofit is to provide services, not to conserve large amounts of capital, an overcapitalized organization may be as worrisome as an undercapitalized one. The complementary assessment of the impact of the organization's financing methods on its goals is also an important one.

(2) *Is the organization maintaining intergenerational equity?* Every dollar used now represents a dollar of services foregone by future generations. For example, when the national YWCA undertook elimination of racism as its goal, local chapters were understandably enthusiastic about its accomplishment. But realistically, the YWCA could not single-handedly eliminate racism; the problem dwarfed its resources. The YWCA Boston chapter nearly depleted its resources in the 1970s in its effort to accomplish this goal. It decided to trade a significant reduction in the maintenance of its financial and physical resources for the attainment of this noble goal. Its actions depleted past resources and diminished future ones for the benefit of the present generation.

Were the Boston YWCA's actions appropriate? That question can only be answered by its board. But the actions clearly raised the question of intergenerational equity. The young women of Boston in the 1990s pay the price for the decisions made by a prior generation. Absent new funds, they cannot receive the same level of the traditional YWCA services as their forebears. On the other hand, the 1970s generation did its utmost to achieve a new goal that would benefit the young women of the 1990s.

(3) *Is there an appropriate match between the sources of resources and the uses to which they are put?* In general, long-term uses should be matched with long-term sources of capital, and short-term uses should be financed by short-term sources. Thus, long-term investments in fixed assets and commitment to tenured faculty should be financed with long-term sources of funds, such as a mortgage or an endowment fund, and not with short-term sources, such as operating grants and contracts. As many colleges discovered to their chagrin, when the short-term grant disappeared, the long-term commitment to a tenured faculty member remained. This fundamental mismatch between sources and uses caused considerable strife as tenured faculty were asked to leave.

(4) *Are present resources sustainable?* The more dispersed the resources, the better is the organization's ability to maintain them. Organizations with several sources of revenues, expenses, assets, and liabilities are much less vulnerable to a change in any one of them. A firm beholden to one or a few suppliers is likely to be held hostage by them. For example, colleges with only a few star professors may be forced to pay them high salaries to maintain their presence. And health care organizations that provided services primarily to the elderly were sent financially reeling by the federal government's reductions in Medicare health insurance reimbursements for the elderly.

Of course, dispersion of financial resources has its costs as well. All additional sources of revenues require extra management effort that must be weighed against the advantages that diversity brings. Nonprofits should avoid the inappropriate diversification that has caused undesirable results for so many corporations in recent decades. Diversification must be limited to activities that are consistent with the organization's mission and strengths.

Financial analysis also is used to indicate red flags of danger and to evaluate creditworthiness. These uses and the four fundamental questions are discussed in this chapter. It should be noted that in itself financial analysis seldom provides final answers; rather, it indicates where further investigation is warranted. Further investigation may take the form of acquiring and analyzing operating or management accounting data; visiting the organization; interviewing employees, clients, or suppliers; doing library searches; and examining credit reports.

USE OF FINANCIAL ANALYSIS TO ANSWER THE FOUR KEY QUESTIONS

Financial analysis can help answer the four important and difficult questions presented above. The analytic process usually involves calculating a set of ratios for the organization and comparing the ratios to industry averages and to the organization's own past performance. It is similar to a physician's diagnostic process in which a set of important measurements, such as temperature and blood pressure, are compared to the measurements for a similar group of people and to the individual's own history. Then the physician uses the comparisons to reach a diagnosis and plan of treatment, if needed.

Of course, the ratios and financial data do not in themselves answer the four questions any more than bodily measures provide a medical diagnosis. Rather, they assist the decision maker to understand the current status of the organization, the likely causes of its status, and the appropriate tactics that will sustain or improve future performance. The ratios will be related to each of the four questions to help you understand their meanings. The RSUS financial statements that were discussed in Chapters 3 and 4, and shown here as Tables 5-1, 5-2, and 5-3, will be used to illustrate their application.

Measures of the Consistency Between Financial Resources and Activities

Organizations, like people, may have excessively high or modest ambitions in relation to their personal competencies. Many measures help us better match our ambitions with our abilities. For example, IQ and other achievement and aptitude tests may help us gauge whether a career as a nuclear physicist is in the offing and tests of psychological traits help us assess the kind of work and social environment best suited to our personality.

TABLE 5-1   **RSUS Balance Sheet**

RSUS
Balance Sheet
For the Years Ending June 30, 19X7 and June 30, 19X8

Assets

	June 30, 19X8		June 30, 19X7	
Current assets				
Cash		$ 310,010		$ 185,499
Certificate of deposit		100,000		100,000
Other marketable securities (market				
value 19X8, $6,528; 19X7, $6,224)		6,465		6,009
Receivables		10,399		165,263
Interest	$ 6,212		$ 4,946	
Employees	2,239		927	
Agencies	1,948		6,612	
Grant awards	-		152,778	
Prepaid expenses		5,360		3,164
Inventory		40,000		30,000
Total current assets		$ 472,234		$ 489,935
Property, plant, and equipment				
Studio and offices	22,621		14,984	
Telecasting equipment	1,263,472		1,166,575	
Mobile equipment	6,875		5,352	
Office furniture and equipment	56,998		50,286	
Property rights acquired under long-				
term lease	-		97,761	
Allowance for depreciation	(548,905)		(426,114)	
Net Property, plant, and equipment		$ 801,061		$ 908,844
Time deposits designated for capital im-				
provements and production		133,653		128,723
Total assets		$1,406,948		$1,527,502

Liabilities and Fund Balance

Current liabilities				
Accounts payable		$ 12,906		$ 170,648
Salaries and wages payable		18,547		9,337
Payroll taxes payable		3,087		3,454
Current portion of installment contract				
payable		22,134		-
Current portion of capitalized lease				
obligation				32,587
Total current liabilities		$ 56,674		$ 216,026
Deferred grant award revenue		25,000		25,000
Deferred production revenue		10,000		
Installment contract payable, less portion				
classified as a current liability		8,255		
Capitalized lease obligation, less portion				
classified as a current liability				65,174
Fund balance		1,307,019		1,221,302
Total liabilities and fund balance		$1,406,948		$1,527,502

TABLE 5-2 **RSUS Activity Statement**

RSUS
Statement of Revenues and Expenses and Changes in Fund Balance
For Years Ended June 30, 19X8 and 19X7

| | Year Ended June 30 | |
	19X8	19X7
Revenues:		
Government grant awards	$ 594,139	$ 819,487
Auction	198,011	179,864
Foundation and public contribution	248,842	213,009
Program underwriting by corporations	35,055	3,975
Production sales to other stations	129,678	1,680
Services and other to other entities	39,995	21,462
Total revenues	$1,245,730	$1,239,477
Expenses:		
In-school services	$ 78,027	$ 64,354
Programming and production	390,108	182,387
Engineering and techical	150,592	99,593
Promotion, development, and auction	177,297	142,254
Administrative and general	241,198	143,002
Depreciation	122,791	80,220
Total Expenses	$1,160,013	$ 711,810
Difference between revenues and expenses	$ 85,717	$ 527,667
Fund balance at beginning of year	1,221,302	693,635
Fund balance at end of year	$1,307,019	$1,221,302

Similar measures assess the range of the possibilities available to a non-profit organization. A wealthy organization, like a high IQ extrovert, can contemplate a wide range of activities, while one with less wealth may have fewer options. Organizational wealth can be measured with a number of ratios; liquidity and long-term solvency are the two most commonly used. *Liquidity*, also called *short-term solvency*, measures the organization's ability to meet its needs for cash in the short term. *Long-term solvency* measures the organization's reliance on debt in its capital structure and its ability to repay the debt and the related interest charges as they become due over the long-term. The use of debt as a source of capital carries a risk because it commits the organization to fixed payments in the future. Highly liquid and

TABLE 5-3 **RSUS Statement of Cash Flows**

Statement of Cash Flows
RSUS
For the Year Ending June 30, 19X8

Cash flows from operating activities:		
Excess of revenues over expenses		$ 85,717
Noncash expense—depreciation	$122,791	
Decrease in receivables	154,864	
Increase in salaries and wages payable	9,210	
Increase in deferred revenue	10,000	
Increase in prepaid expenses	(2,196)	
Increase in inventory	(10,000)	
Decrease in accounts payable	(157,742)	
Decrease in payroll taxes payable	(367)	126,560
Cash provided by operations		212,277
Cash flows from investing activities:		
Increase in fixed assets and property rights	$ (15,008)	
Increase in other marketable securities	(456)	
Increase in time deposits	(4,930)	
Net cash outflows from investing activities		(20,394)
Cash flows from financing activities:		
Increase in current portion of installment contract payable	$ 22,134	
Increase in installment contract	8,255	
Decrease in current capitalized lease obligation	(32,587)	
Decrease in long-term capitalized lease obligation	(65,174)	
Net cash outflows from financing activities		(67,372)
Net increase in cash		$124,511
Cash balance, June, 30, 19X7		185,499
Cash balance, June 30, 19X8		$310,010

solvent organizations face little financial risk; their cash surpluses and low debt levels protect them.

Is the wealthy organization living up to its potential? *Activity* or *asset turnover* ratios that measure the use of specific assets provide one answer to the question. Organizations with high asset turnover generate a large amount of operating activity from their assets. A low asset turnover organization may have many financial assets that are left relatively idle. An organization with more assets than those needed to finance two years of spending is flagged as suspect by one evaluator of charities.[1]

The consistency between goals and financial resources must also be evaluated from the perspective of appropriateness. Financial resources may be obtained or spent, at times, in a manner that is inconsistent with the organization's goals. For example, the appropriateness of the head football and basketball coaches at Ohio State University reportedly earning six times as much as the average full professor should be evaluated.[2] So should the appropriateness of museums displaying collections designed to promote the sponsor's products, such as the Daimler-Benz sponsored exhibition at the Guggenheim Museum in New York City that displayed paintings of the company's Mercedes-Benz cars.[3] It is possible that in these cases the need for financial resources may have compromised the organization's goals.

A wise board and management should continually examine both sides of this question: Are financial resources affecting the organization's mission in inappropriate ways and is the mission consistent with the organization's financial ability?

Measure of Intergenerational Equity

An organization that does not save sufficient income for maintenance of the purchasing power of its fund balance is using past savings to finance the present. Conversely, an organization whose fund balance increases by more than the rate of inflation is using the present to finance the future. Another way of understanding these admittedly difficult propositions is to think about them in personal terms. If you do not add enough money to your savings to maintain their purchasing power, you are depleting your past savings to maintain your present activities. Conversely, if your savings increase by more than the rate of inflation, you are consuming less than you currently have available, in order to benefit the future.

You may have precisely one of these goals in mind. Retired people commonly use the savings they accumulated in the past to pay for present expense and younger people save for their retirement. Financial analysis can help identify whether an intergenerational transfer is taking place, but it cannot answer the question of whether the intergenerational transfer is appropriate; that question is separate from the measurement of its magnitude.

[1]Alison Leigh Cowan, "The Gadfly Who Audits Philanthropy," *The New York Times,* 7 October 1990, p. F9.
[2]Brenton Welling, "How Sports Mania is Sacking America's Schools," *Business Week* (September 24, 1990): 18.
[3]Lee Rosenbaum, "Art's Cozy Relationship with Business," *The New York Times Forum*, 9 September 1990, p. F11.

Some intergenerational transfers can be simply measured with the ratio between the surplus or difference between revenues and expenses (the equivalent to a for-profit's income or loss) and the fund balance. If this ratio is less than the rate of inflation, the organization is using some of its past savings for present operations. If the ratio is larger than the rate of inflation, the organization is saving some of the results of the present to finance the future. Thus, a ratio different from the rate of inflation indicates the presence of intergenerational transfers.

Sounds simple enough, doesn't it? Unfortunately, this measure is useful only when applied to surplus and fund balance accounts that reflect current values. But the cost principle of accounting values financial activities at their historical cost, not their current values. We will discuss below how to adjust historical cost accounts to their current values so that intergenerational transfers can be better measured.

Intergenerational transfers are sometimes effected through commitments such as long-term debt, pensions, and other post-retirement benefits not fully disclosed in the financial statements. Indeed, the reluctance of current accounting standards to recognize the full cost of some of these activities may be viewed as a reason for engaging in them—"nobody will know." But responsible managers and boards must consider the intergenerational impact of any proposed action, whether it is reflected immediately on the external financial statements or not.

Measures of the Match Between Sources and Uses of Capital

Answering this question requires classifying all revenues, expenses, assets, and liabilities as either long-term or short-term and then examining the relationships between them. Long-term fixed expenses should be matched with long-term stable revenues. If the ratio of long-term stable revenues to long-term fixed expenses is less than one, the organization is in some financial jeopardy; in the long-term, its expenses will not be covered by its revenues. Similarly, long-term assets should be financed with long-term sources of capital, such as the fund balance and long-term debt, rather than with short-term borrowing or short-lived revenues.

Variability and *controllability* indicate whether resources are short or long term. Variability is measured by the amount and direction of change in financial results from year to year. A grant received for only one time, for example, is highly variable and may be uncontrollable. It is therefore a short-term resource. Endowment income is controlled by the organization but it may be highly variable, depending on the investment strategy pursued. If endowment income varies considerably from one period to the next because of the investment strategy chosen, it should be considered as a short-term revenue source. On the other hand, if endowment income over time has proven to be very stable, it should be classified as a long-term revenue source.

Measures of the Sustainability of Financial Performance

The warning not to put all your eggs in one basket finds its financial equivalent in measures of the *dispersion* of the sources and uses of capital. These measures are key to evaluating sustainability. Dispersion simply measures the fraction of the total category accounted for by one activity in that category: the higher the concentration, the lower the dispersion. For example, an organization whose endowment income accounts for 80 percent of all revenues has a high concentration of revenues. It is very vulnerable to the effects of a downturn in endowment income. But an organization with ten sources of revenue, each of which accounts for 10 percent of its total revenues, is on a more stable footing. Its dispersion ratio is low. If the stock market tumbles, for example, the latter organization, which depends on endowment income for 10 percent of its revenues is in a much more stable situation than the former, whose revenues are primarily composed of endowment income.

Using Ratio Analysis: Some Caveats

We will use the RSUS financial statements to illustrate how ratios can be applied to answer the four key questions. The particular ratios we specify in the discussion do not begin to exhaust the possible measures that can be used to answer the questions posed. The ratios we cite are those most frequently used, but your analysis need not be limited to them. Also note that ratios can be measured in many different ways. The formulas we provide are guidelines, not commandments. They are meant to illustrate how the process of financial analysis is conducted—not to put it in a straitjacket.

Success or failure should be measured relatively, rather than in absolute magnitude of the ratios. A low ratio is neither good nor bad. It must be compared to the ratios characteristic of that type of organization, just as the naturally low height of shrubs cannot be compared to the great height of maple trees. For example, when the average investor earns 10 percent on funds invested and your organization achieves a financial asset turnover ratio of 15 percent, the result is impressive, if it has been achieved with investments equal in risk to those earning 10 percent. And, if the average hospital's ratio for some activity is 0.8 and your hospital's is 1.0, then your hospital is getting more operating performance from its assets than the norm. Relative performance should also be measured across time. Thus, if your hospital's ratio declined from 1.1 last year, its performance on this dimension has deteriorated, even though it is still doing better than the average hospital.

MEASUREMENT OF THE CONSISTENCY BETWEEN RESOURCES AND ACTIVITIES

The key ratios for assessing the match between an organization's resources and activities are those of liquidity, solvency, and asset turnover. The first two measure an organization's wealth and the financial risk it has incurred by financing with debt that must be repaid. The latter measures how actively the organization is using its resources to carry out its goals.

Liquidity Ratios

Liquidity, the ability to pay for current obligations or liabilities, is traditionally an important aspect of financial analysis. Its importance was accentuated by the highly publicized inability of some cities and hospitals to meet their current obligations. Short-term solvency ratios are important to the holders of these current obligations—suppliers, bankers, and employees. The most common measures of liquidity are the current ratio, working capital, the quick ratio, and dynamic working capital. The following paragraphs define and describe these measures.

$$\text{Current Ratio} = \frac{\text{Current Assets}}{\text{Current Liabilities}}$$

Current assets are those that can be converted into cash in the normal next cycle of operations. They include cash, short term investments, accounts receivable, inventories, and any other assets that can be liquidated. Current liabilities are those that must be paid during the coming period.

The *current ratio* measures the availability of current assets to pay for those liabilities that must be met during the next operating cycle. At a minimum, this ratio should be equal to one, or the organization may well become insolvent. A very high current ratio, on the other hand, may imply excessive investment in current assets of resources that could otherwise be used to provide services. An organization whose cash flows are very stable over time can operate with a lower current ratio than one with highly variable ones. Some nonprofit organizations are characterized by low current ratios. For example, some hospital current ratios are dangerously close to one.

RSUS's current ratio was 8.3 in 19X8 ($472,234 ÷ $56,674) and 2.3 in 19X7 ($489,935 ÷ $216,026). The ratios are high and increasing substantially over time. RSUS appears to have an excessively high current ratio in both years.

$$\text{Working Capital} = \text{Current Assets} - \text{Current Liabilities}$$

The difference between current assets and current liabilities is called the *working capital* of the organization. It is the capital needed to carry out the day-to-day work and should always be positive. The RSUS 19X8 working capital of $415,560 ($472,234 − $56,674) compares favorably to the working capital in 19X7 of $182,874 ($489,935 − $216,026). Working capital increased by $232,686 ($415,560 − $182,874) during 19X8.

$$\text{Quick Ratio} = \frac{\text{Cash + Marketable Securities + Accounts Receivable}}{\text{Current Liabilities}}$$

The *quick ratio* measures the coverage of current liabilities provided by those assets that are the most cash-like in their ability to be liquidated at full value. It differs from the current ratio by excluding inventories and prepaid expenses from the numerator. These assets cannot be as readily converted to cash as receivables and securities. The distress value of a quick inventory sale and the prorated redemption value of prepaid expenses are likely to be far lower than their balance sheet values. This ratio is a harsher measure than the current ratio of the entity's short-term liquidity. It views the organization not as a going concern, but as one that must liquidate its assets in order to meet current liabilities.

RSUS had a 19X8 quick ratio of 7.5 ($426,874 ÷ $56,674) and a 19X7 quick ratio of 2.1 ($456,771 ÷ $216,026). Again, both quick ratios indicate RSUS's high, probably excessive, level of short-term solvency.

The current and quick ratios are *static*; they measure short-term solvency at only one point in time. Their values can change dramatically from one period to another, as illustrated by the RSUS quick ratios calculated above that changed from 2.1 to 7.5 in only one year. As a further example, suppose an organization has total current assets of $100,000 in cash and total current liabilities of accounts payable of $20,000, giving healthy current and quick ratios of 5. If the organization uses $80,000 of its cash as a down payment for a building, the current ratio will slide to a danger level of 1, consisting of $20,000 of current assets of the remaining cash and $20,000 of accounts payable.

$$\text{Dynamic Working Capital} = \frac{\text{Working Capital}}{\text{Cash Flow from Operations}}$$

Dynamic, or *flow*, ratios that measure the flow of resources over time, are particularly useful for organizations with variable patterns of resource flows. The dynamic ratios are also more difficult to manipulate than static ones. For example, a good current or quick ratio can be created in the short run by selling off fixed assets for cash. As a result of the sale, cash will increase, as will the current and quick ratios, by depleting the organiation of needed fixed assets. Such manipulation would be revealed in the dynamic or flow ratios because the cash flow from operations would be unaffected by the asset sale.

If a Statement of Cash Flows is not available, cash flow from operations (or simply cash flow) is calculated by adjusting the difference between revenues and expenses for non-cash operating items, such as depreciation expense and changes in accounts receivable, accrued payroll, and other operations-related Balance Sheet accounts. The RSUS 19X8 annual cash flow from operations was $212,277 (Table 5-3). Dividing RSUS 19X8 working capital by cash flow from operations ($415,560 ÷ $212,277) indicates that RSUS has about twice as much working capital as the cash it generates from operations. Once more, this ratio underscores RSUS's sound short-term solvency.

Long-Term Solvency Ratios

Long-term solvency ratios are useful in estimating an entity's ability to meet its future commitments to pay outside parties, especially the principal and interest payments of its long-term debts. They measure whether operating cash flows are adequate for meeting scheduled payments (coverage) and whether sufficient assets are available for creditors if the organization incurs future operating losses (leverage). These ratios are widely used by the bankers and bond rating agencies who help the organization to issue long-term debt. Favorable long-term solvency ratios indicate an organization with little risk of bankruptcy.

Leverage Ratios   The relative proportion of debt in the organization's capital structure is measured by *leverage ratios*. *Total capital* is equal to total assets. *Capital structure* measures the relative mix in the of total capital of debt and fund balance sources. The term *leverage* originated in the for-profit sector, where a small amount of investor capital is "leveraged" with borrowed capital that increases the amount that the investors will earn, just as a crowbar is used as a lever to lift large weights. The term *highly leveraged* means a high proportion of debt relative to the level of equity. Several ratios are used to measure leverage.

$$\text{Debt to Asset Ratio} = \frac{\text{Total Liabilities}}{\text{Total Assets}}$$

The *debt to asset ratio* (also sometimes called the *debt to total capital ratio*) measures the percentage of the organization's total assets financed by borrowing of all types, both short and long-term.

Another ratio that contains essentially the same information is the *debt to equity ratio*:

$$\text{Debt to Equity Ratio} = \frac{\text{Total Liabilities}}{\text{Fund Balance}}$$

This ratio compares the long-term resources provided externally through debt with those provided internally through the fund balance. It is simply another way of measuring the relative mix of internally and externally provided capital, or capital structure.

$$\text{Long-Term Debt to Capitalization} = \frac{\text{Long-Term Debt}}{\text{Capitalization}}$$

Some leverage ratios are based only on the *capitalization*, or long-term financing, of the organization which includes long-term debt and equity. Long-term debt includes all liabilities that are not current. Capitalization is easily calculated by subtracting current liabilities from total liabilities and fund balance. It can also be calculated by adding all noncurrent liabilities and the fund balance. Capitalization-based leverage ratios focus on the long-term sources of financing for the organization. Other variations include the current portion of any interest-bearing liabilities in both the numerator and denominator, or exclude noncontractual long-term liabilities. The higher these ratios, the greater the need is to set aside some fixed portion of cash flow to meet recurring principal and interest payments. High leverage ratios increase financial risk, the danger that in times of fluctuating cash inflows the organization will be unable to meet its payment obligations to external parties.

The proportion of debt in the total capital structure of private nonprofits has been growing rapidly in recent times. It is more than 50 percent in many hospitals and educational institutions. Some organizations typically have more debt than others, usually because they also have high proportions of the fixed assets which are most commonly financed with debt. These ratios must be adjusted if the value of the fund balance is understated because the long-term fixed assets are worth more than their Balance Sheet values.

The RSUS debt to capital ratio is very small. In 19X7, it was 0.06 [($25,000 + $65,174) ÷ $1,527,502] and in 19X8, it was 0.03 [($25,000 + $10,000 + $8,255) ÷ $1,406,948]. The debt to equity ratio was 0.071 in 19X8 [($56,674 + $25,000 + $10,000 + $8,255) ÷ $1,406,948] and 0.2 in 19X7 [($216,026 + $25,000 + $65,174) ÷ $1,527,502]. Using the same numerators and changing the denominator to fund balance instead of total assets yields liability to equity ratios of 0.076 in 19X8 ($99,929 ÷ $1,307,019) and 0.25 in 19X7 ($306,200 ÷ $1,221,302). The RSUS long-term debt to capitalization ratio was 0.032 in 19X8 [($25,000 + $10,000 + $8,255) ÷ ($1,406,948 − $56,674)] and 0.069 in 19X7 [($25,000 + $65,174) ÷ ($1,527,502 − $216,026)]. There was less change from 19X7 to 19X8 in this ratio than those using total liabilities because of the large decrease in current liabilities. In 19X8 and 19X7, the debt to equity ratio was a very conservative 0.07 ($90,174 ÷ $1,221,302) and 0.06 ($43,225 ÷ $963,636), respectively, for RSUS. Again, RSUS appears to be very conservative in its financing. It has many liquid assets and very little debt. If it wanted to expand, RSUS has sufficient financial capacity to handle more long-term debt.

Coverage Ratios   The ability of an entity to generate sufficient cash flow to meet its commitment for future payments is measured by *coverage ratios*.

$$\text{Times Interest Earned Ratio} = \frac{\text{Cash Flow from Operations} + \text{Interest Expense}}{\text{Interest Expense}}$$

This *times interest earned ratio* measures the relationship between the cash flow from operations and the amount of cash needed to pay the interest on its long-term debt. We cannot calculate this ratio (or any other ratio that requires interest expense) for RSUS in 19X7 from the information in the financial statements alone because the lease interest expense is not reported separately. However, the footnotes in Table 4-4 disclose that the installment contract carries a 17.12 percent interest rate; RSUS, therefore, will have an interest expense of $5,203 [(0.1712)($22,134 + $8,255)] in 19X9 if none of the installment contract is paid off before the end of the coming year. If we assume that a comparable 17 percent interest rate was paid on the lease obligation in 19X8, and that it was paid off on the last day of the year, the 19X8 interest expense was $16,619 [(0.17)($65,174 + $32,587)].

This provides us with an estimate of the 19X8 times interest earned ratio of 13.8 [($212,277 + $16,619) ÷ $16,619]. The net cash flow provided by operations before interest expense was nearly 14 times the amount needed to cover interest payments in 19X8—a very healthy ratio.

$$\text{Times Fixed Charges Ratio} = \frac{\text{Cash Flow} + \text{Interest} + \text{All Fixed Charges}}{\text{Interest} + \text{Lease Payments} + \text{Other Fixed Expenses}}$$

The *times fixed charges ratio* measures the ability of the entity's cash flow to meet all its fixed commitments, such as interest and lease payments. Principal payments are often included in the denominator as well. Including the principal payments required to be made in 19X8 (based on the amount of capitalized lease obligation listed as current in the 19X7 Balance Sheet), the RSUS times fixed charges ratio is a healthy 5.3 [($212,277 + $16,619 + $32,587) ÷ ($16,619 + $32,587)]. For every dollar of fixed payments, RSUS generates around $5.31 of cash from operations.

Asset Management Ratios

Asset management ratios usually relate investments in assets to the revenues or other outputs that they generate. A high asset turnover ratio is usually desirable because it indicates that the organization provides many services or products for every dollar invested in its assets. This goal is particularly appropriate to nonprofit organizations whose purpose is to provide as many goods and services as possible with their available resources. If the level of service provision is not appropriately reflected by revenues, then the organization should calculate ratios that measure service provision directly, such as the number of teaching hours or students taught per invested dollar. Asset managment is particularly crucial in periods of rapid growth, during which many organizations are traditionally distracted and characterized by poor asset management practices.

As with other ratios, the magnitude of the asset turnover ratio varies with the type of organization and the class of assets. Because hospitals require considerable assets to deliver their services, the hospital asset turnover ratios are lower than those of a social work agency that requires fewer assets. The low asset turnover ratio of hospitals and the high ratio of social work agencies is neither good nor bad.

Excessively low ratios often indicate the presence of assets that are not generating sufficient services. The money invested in these assets could be transferred to others that would yield more services or revenues. However, unusually high ratios should be investigated as well. Remember that a high ratio can be caused by high revenues or low asset values. If the asset values are lower than normal because the organization purchased them at bargain prices, that is cause for celebration. However, if a high ratio stems from assets on the verge of obsolescence, it may be a short-term phenomenon. Soon, the organization will replace them, at a much higher cost than the book value of the existing assets.

Revenue is usually a good surrogate for service output in colleges because they record revenues even for students who receive free services. However, recorded revenue seldom accurately reflects service output in other types of nonprofits because they do not record revenues for clients who receive free services. For these other types of nonprofits, an expenses/asset ratio may better reflect the level of services than revenue/assets ratio. This topic will be addressed in greater detail in the chapters on specific types of nonprofit organizations in Part Three of this book.

$$\text{Asset Turnover Ratio} = \frac{\text{Total Revenues}}{\text{Average Total Assets}}$$

The *asset turnover ratio* measures the relationship between the total investment in assets and the amount of revenues they generated. If this ratio differs significantly from industry averages or from past experience, it should be investigated. It is a particularly important ratio for such organizations as hospitals that have large capital investments. In 19X8, this ratio for RSUS was 0.85 [$1,245,730 ÷ [($1,406,948 + $1,527,502) ÷ 2)]], indicating $0.85 in revenues generated for every dollar of investment in assets.

If the data are available, asset management ratios should be applied to three separate revenue and asset classes:

- *Operating revenues and assets*, such as patient care revenues and the related assets in a hospital, are provided by and used for the fundamental purposes of the organization.

- *Investment revenues and assets* are the assets devoted to earning a financial return, and the income generated by them, primarily endowment assets and income.

- *Other revenues and assets* relate to auxiliary enterprises and other activities that are not a primary part of the organization mission, such as a hospital parking garage.

If these categories are intermingled, the resulting ratio will be much less meaningful. Consider the following extreme example: Hospital *A* with $10 million of fixed assets and $6 million in investments, earns $2 million in revenue on its investments and has no other sources of revenues. Its overall asset turnover ratio is 0.125 [$2 ÷ ($10 + $6)]. Hospital *B* achieves the identical ratio with $16 million in fixed assets and $2 million in patient revenues. Which hospital comes closer to fulfilling its goals? Unquestionably, Hospital *B*. By providing $2 million of patient services, it is more nearly fulfilling its purposes than Hospital *A* that provides no patient services at all. An asset turnover ratio that combines all classes of revenue and assets masks this difference in achievement. Unfortunately, RSUS does not provide sufficient information to enable us to segregate its revenues and assets into three classes.

Analyses of separate asset categories are traditional and important aspects of financial analysis in all organizations. The performance of any significant type of asset should be evaluated. The most commonly evaluated assets are fixed assets, accounts receivable, and inventory, because they tend to be the largest and most susceptible to poor management.

$$\text{Fixed Asset Turnover Ratio} = \frac{\text{Total Revenues}}{\text{Average Fixed Assets}}$$

The *fixed asset turnover ratio* calculates the revenue generated per dollar of investment in fixed assets. It is a useful ratio for organizations whose fixed assets have increased sharply from one year to the next and for capital-intensive nonprofits. For example, the dollars of revenue generated per bed is an important statistic in evaluating a hospital's fixed asset management. However, the usefulness of this ratio is limited by the use of book, rather than market, values for fixed assets in the financial statements. It must be used with special care when comparing two organizations whose fixed assets are of substantially different ages. In 19X8, the fixed asset turnover ratio for RSUS was 1.46 [$1,245,730 ÷ ($\frac{1}{2}$)($801,061 + $908,884)], indicating $1.46 in revenues generated for every dollar invested in fixed assets.

$$\text{Accounts Receivable Turnover Ratio} = \frac{\text{Sales Revenue}}{\text{Accounts Receivable}}$$

The analysis of accounts receivable turnover is particular!y crucial, as the following ditty notes:

Though my bottom line is black, I am flat upon my back,
My cash flows out and customers pay slow.
The growth of my receivables is almost unbelievable;
The result is certain—unremitting woe!
And I hear the banker utter an ominous low mutter.
"Watch cash flow."[4]

The *accounts receivable turnover ratio* measures how many times the receivables turn over—that is, are collected in cash and replaced with new revenues—during the course of the year. A higher turnover ratio is generally better. Reversing the numerator and denominator of this ratio provides exactly the same information, but the is ratio stated as *receivables to revenues ratio*, and indicates the percentage of revenues tied up in receivables.

$$\text{Days Receivables Ratio} = \frac{\text{Accounts Receivable} \times 365 \text{ Days}}{\text{Sales Revenue}}$$

The *days receivables ratio* measures the average number of days between the creation of an account receivable and its collection in cash. Again, it is a different way of looking at the same phenomenon. A ratio that lengthens substantially over time, or is worse than the industry standard, signals a need for further investigation of the receivables collection process. An unusually long collection period means that the organization is lending its money, often without interest, to the entities that owe it money, such as service recipients, third party payers, or granting agencies. While these resources are on loan, the organization may be paying finance charges and forgoing the provision of other services. A high number of days receivables ratio may also indicate that many of the receivables are not collectible. Determining the underlying cause requires data that are not provided by the financial statements, but are available to management and board members. An unusually short collection period may also be undesirable because it may indicate that good opportunities for sales or service provision are being missed because of harsh credit terms.

To minimize the effect of short-term fluctuations, the beginning and end of the period receivables are sometimes averaged. Averaging is particularly desirable in an organization that has experienced a substantial change in its receivables between one period and the next. For RSUS, the average receivables balance for 19X8 was $87,831 [($10,399 + $165,263) ÷ 2]. It therefore

[4]Herbert S. Bailey, Jr., "Quoth the Banker, 'Watch Cash Flow'," *Publishers Weekly* (January 13, 1975): 34.

experienced average days' receivables of 25.73 [($87,831)(365) ÷ $1,245,730] —a low amount. Using only the ending accounts receivable, we can compare the 19X8 and 19X7 ratios. In 19X8 it was 3.05 [($10,399)(365) ÷ $1,245,730] and in 19X7 it was 48.67 [($165,263)(365) ÷ $1,239,477]. While this ratio was at a reasonable level in 19X7, it has declined so sharply that one wonders if revenues are lost because of an overly stringent credit and collection policy. If so, such a policy is particularly inappropriate for RSUS. With its large liquid assets and small debt, it need not speed up collection of receivables for liquidity purposes. On the other hand, the decline may have been caused by a reduction in grants receivable, rather than an increasingly stringent collection policy.

If data are available, it may be useful to calculate ratios for different types of receivables and revenues. For example, for RSUS, it might be useful to calculate separate grant, interest, and agency receivables turnover ratios. Unfortunately, interest revenue is not disclosed separately and the relationship between agencies receivables and revenues is unclear. This leaves the grant receivables turnover ratio. Assuming all grants were government grants, it increased from 5.4 times in 19X7 ($819,487 ÷ $152,778) to infinity, because no grants were receivable at the end of 19X8.

$$\text{Inventory Turnover Ratio} = \frac{\text{Cost of Goods Sold}}{\text{Average Inventory}}$$

The *inventory turnover ratio* presents the number of times inventory is sold and replaced during the year.

$$\text{Days Inventory Ratio} = \frac{\text{Average Inventory} \times 365 \text{ Days}}{\text{Cost of Goods Sold}}$$

The *days inventory ratio* restates the same information in terms of the number of days of goods in inventory.

Because resources are required to keep inventory on hand, and because it may become obsolete, an efficient organization should minimize the amount of inventory it holds and maximize inventory turnover, without losing opportunities to generate revenue. These objectives drive the *just-in-time* approach to manufacturing. The ideal state in the just-in-time approach is to carry no inventory, with the needed materials arriving on the loading dock just in time to be put into production. When the product is completed, it is also shipped to the customer immediately, rather than being put into inventory.

Inventory management ratios are particularly useful for organizations whose inventory represents a substantial fraction of the assets, as in a museum's gift shop or thrift store. An abnormally high or low ratio, in relation to past performance or to the industry, signals that inventory management should be investigated. In a nonmanufacturing or nonretailing entity, the relevant denominator is the supplies expense, which is calculated to determine the average days of supplies inventory on hand. We do not know the supplies expense for RSUS, but because inventory accounts for only 8 percent of the current assets in 19X8, it is not likely to be a significant financial factor.

$$\text{Days Payables Ratio} = \frac{\text{Accounts Payable} \times 365 \text{ Days}}{\text{Purchases}}$$

The *days payable ratio* states the number of days of purchases for which payment has not yet been made. A *payables to purchases* ratio can also be calculated by omitting the number of days. A *payables turnover ratio* could also be calculated, in the same way as the other turnover ratios calculated above. The number of days payables tends to be an especially convenient measure because credit terms are usually stated in terms of days.

Managing purchases and payables is also a significant job for most types of nonprofit organizations. Their objective is to pay bills on time so that interest charges and bad credit relations are avoided, but not to pay them earlier than necessary. If bills are paid before they are due, the organization is forgoing the interest that it could have earned on the money. The lost interest indicated by an excessively short payables period is significant only for organizations with large amounts of purchases. However, a long or lengthening payables period is common for an organization that is having trouble paying its bills. It is an important danger signal for any size and type of organization.

This ratio can be calculated most readily for a retail organization, such as a gift shop, whose purchases equal the cost of goods sold plus the difference between beginning and ending inventories. The data needed to calculate this ratio are not available for RSUS, and cannot be reasonably estimated from the financial statement data. This is not uncommon.

Are RSUS Goals and Resources Consistent?

Our ratios indicate RSUS as very liquid and solvent and with low asset turnover ratios. What do these ratios mean? RSUS either has excessive assets for the level of services it is delivering or should be providing many more services for its asset level. The organization should either sell some assets and use the resulting cash to provide more services or increase its service levels. The latter may indeed be RSUS's strategy. It may be building its assets now so that it can provide greater levels of services in the future.

MEASUREMENT OF INTERGENERATIONAL EQUITY

Profitability in Nonprofit Organizations

Paradoxically, the nonprofit status is not equivalent to the absence of profits ("profit" is referred to more obliquely as *excess of revenues over expenses*, or *surplus*, in the nonprofit language). Quite to the contrary, non-profits must earn a profit, however it is labeled, for the following reasons:

(1) To replace assets because asset values are reported at cost rather than at their substantially higher replacement value

(2) To help finance expansion because an organization cannot rely entirely on borrowing capital for expansion

(3) To protect against uncertainties and variability in earnings

If a nonprofit organization does not earn sufficient profit, or surplus, or return, to preserve the purchasing power of its fund balance, then the current period has consumed some of the reserves generated by prior ones. For these reasons, the profitability of a nonprofit organization should be measured.

$$\text{Profit Margin Ratio} = \frac{\text{Surplus}}{\text{Revenues}}$$

The ratio of surplus to revenues, which is referred to as the *profit margin ratio* even in nonprofit organizations, measures the percentage of every revenue dollar that was not used to cover expenses. It could also be called the *surplus margin ratio*. The RSUS ratio of 7 percent for 19X8 ($85,717 ÷ $1,245,730) and 43 percent for 19X7 ($527,667 ÷ $1,239,477) indicates a significant decline in profits for RSUS in 19X8, from a very high profit rate in 19X7 to a more normal rate in 19X8.

$$\text{Operating Margin Ratio} = \frac{\text{Surplus Before Interest Expense}}{\text{Revenues}}$$

The *operating margin ratio* is a variation of the profit margin ratio and measures the operating surplus separately from the financing expense. It thus separates the effect of the financing decisions that determine interest expense from the operating decisions. RSUS's small interest expense in 19X8 has a negligible effect on this ratio.

Return on Fund Balance (ROFB)

While profitability ratios compare the surplus earned to revenues, ROFB measures compare the surplus earned to the amount of investment required to earn them. They indicate whether a nonprofit organizations has preserved the purchasing power of the capital invested in it.

$$\text{Return on Fund Balance} = \frac{\text{Surplus}}{\text{Fund Balance}}$$

The *return on fund balance* is the single best indicator of intergenerational transfers. It measures the return, or surplus, earned per dollar of fund balance. Many possible variants of this ratio exist: The numerator, or surplus, can be adjusted for the impact of interest expense, or can be separated into operating, investing, and financing components. The denominator, or investment, can be defined as total assets or total permanent capital rather than as fund balance.

For RSUS, the return on the beginning fund balance in 19X8 was 7 percent ($85,717 ÷ $1,221,302), and in 19X7 it was 76 percent ($527,667 ÷ $693,635). The 19X8 ratio is only slightly above the inflation rate of 6 percent for that year and indicates a very small transfer from the current to future generations. The 19X7 ratio is excessively high for a nonprofit organization. Although many different measures of inflation rates are available, the Consumer Price Index (CPI) is usually adequate, except for nonprofits whose inflation differs significantly from the CPI—hospitals or colleges, for example.

Another way of looking at the return on fund balance (ROFB) is shown in the following equation:

$$\text{ROFB} = \frac{\text{Surplus}}{\text{Revenues}} \times \frac{\text{Revenues}}{\text{Fund Balance}} = \text{Profitability} \times \text{Fund Balance Turnover}$$

This equation highlights the fact that an acceptable return can be obtained only with careful management of two different aspects of operations:

(1) Profitability or return must be sufficiently high to enable maintenance and expansion of the entity. Good profitability requires careful management of the relationship between revenues and expenses.

(2) The level of capital invested to produce a given level of revenue must be carefully managed to ensure an appropriate balance between the two.

In addition to measuring intergenerational transfers, ROFB is also a useful managerial tool. Decomposing the ROFB measure into the financial elements that cause it enables assigning responsibility to specific managers. Figure 5-1 shows the links between each of the factors and their managers. When presented in this fashion, each factor in the ROFB is clearly linked to a particular management group. For example, revenues are clearly linked to the program, marketing, and fund raising managers.

Is There Intergenerational Transfer in RSUS?

Based on the measures above, in 19X7 RSUS was unquestionably transferring assets from the present generation to future ones, as indicated by its ROFB of 76 percent. By 19X8, RSUS was earning a return on its fund balance slightly more than sufficient to maintain present capacity—it was neither excessively high nor low.

FIGURE 5-1 **Components of Return on Fund Balance**

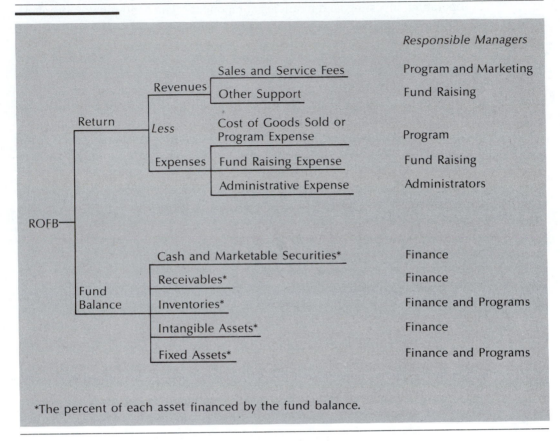

*The percent of each asset financed by the fund balance.

Incorporating Inflation in Intergenerational Equity Analysis

Unfortunately, the historical cost basis of accounting renders the above analysis almost meaningless for organizations with substantial fixed assets or debts that are more than five years old. In such organizations the values that accountants assign to fixed assets and debt are likely to be very different from their replacement values. An organization must be concerned with the costs of replacing itself, not with historical costs. For example, retired persons who want to sell their homes and move to a warmer climate consider the sales value of their present house and the cost of buying a replacement. The original cost of their present house is irrelevant (except for tax computations). Unfortunately, financial accounting ignores this concern because it values all at original cost.

How can we adjust assets and liabilities for the effect of inflation? The answer is complicated. Conceptually, inflation adjustment requires the following revaluations:

(1) Changing the values of fixed assets from their original to their replacement values. For example, if an asset that originally cost $100 now requires $300 for its replacement, its new value increased by $200 from its original Balance Sheet measure of $100, with a corresponding increase credited to the fund balance. As in this example, most fixed assets cost more to replace than their original cost. But some cost less. For example, the costs of computers with equivalent computing power have decreased consistently over the past three decades.

(2) Changing the allowance for accumulated depreciation. If the asset in (1) is 6 years old, has a 10-year life, and has been depreciated on a straight-line basis, then for the past 6 years the depreciation expense has been understated. It was computed at $10 a year ($100 ÷ 10 years) rather than $30 a year ($300 ÷ 10 years). The fund balance should thus be adjusted for the 6 years of understated expenses of $20 a year ($20 = $30 replacement cost depreciation − $10 historical cost depreciation). Thus, the fund balance should be decreased by $120 and the allowance for accumulated depreciation increased by $120 [($20 a year understatement)(6 years)].

(3) Changing the value of long-term fixed debt to its replacement cost. If the debt carries an interest rate lower than the market interest rate, the borrower has a gain on the debt. Why? Because lenders will eagerly encourage early repayment of a low interest rate loan so that they can lend out the money at the new, higher rates. For example, consider a one-year loan of $1,000 with a 5 percent interest rate. If the lender's cost of money is 10 percent, the present value of the loan is $954.46.[5] That is, the lender can invest $954.46 in a 10 percent savings account and collect $1,050 at the end of one year, a sum equivalent to the original loan of $1,000 and interest of $50.

The lender will offer the borrower the option of repaying the loan for a sum greater than $954.46 and less than $1,000, plus accumulated 5 percent interest. If the borrower agrees, the lender will relend this payment at a higher interest rate. For example, if the deal between them is struck at $975, the borrower can repay a liability shown on the Balance Sheet at $1,000 for only $975, a gain of $25. The lender who then relends the $975 at a higher interest rate of, for example, 12 percent, will earn $117 in a year [($975)(12%)]. The sum of $1,092 ($975 + $117) is greater than the $1,050 the lender would have received from the original 5 percent loan. (We will return to this subject of the time value of money in Part Two.)

---

[5] "Present value" is the technical term for the amount of money that when invested right now, in the present, will equal a specified future value.

The mechanics that account for these revaluations are the following:

(1) Increase fixed assets and the fund balance by $200 each.

(2) Increase accumulated depreciation and decrease the fund balance by $120.

(3) Reduce debt and increase the fund balance by $25.

The net effect of these three changes on the fund balance is to increase it by $105 ($25 for the gain on early replayment of debt + $200 for fixed asset revaluation − $120 for additional depreciation). The increased fund balance correctly reflects the larger investment needed to replace assets. It reduces the organization's ROFB, providing a more realistic appraisal of whether an intergenerational transfer has taken place. For example, if on a historical cost basis the surplus was $200 and the fund balance was $500 for an ROFB of 40 percent, the adjustments for inflation will produce a surplus of $180 ($200 − $20 incremental depreciation expenses), and a fund balance of $605 ($500 + $105) for an inflation-adjusted ROFB of 29.7 percent.

The United States and many European countries have been blessed with generally low rates of inflation. So, if you are feeling confused, it is for lack of experience in adjusting for the ravages of inflation. People who live in countries with high inflation rates find this way of thinking to be second nature. Let us try this topic of inflation accounting in a different way, by examining the Balance Sheet in Table 5-4. It shows a simple organization: fixed assets that cost $100, less depreciation of $60; investments at $1,460; debt at $1,000; and fund balance of $500, all valued at historical cost.

The organization experienced the inflationary events described above. The cost of replacing its fixed assets increased to $300 and of replacing the debt dipped to $975. The fixed assets are six years old and have been depreciated on a straight-line basis. Table 5-5 shows the inflation-adjusted statements of the organization. The total assets value has increased by $80 (net replacement value of $120 − net historical cost value of $40), as has the total source of capital—the net of the debt reduction of $25 and the fund balance increase of $105.

If you are still confused, rest assured that you are not alone. Let us forget about the accounting and look at the big picture. Inflation makes things more expensive. So the effect of inflation on an organization is to increase the amount of money needed to run it. An ROFB measured on a historical cost basis does not measure the increased costs brought about by inflation. Adjusting the financial statements to an inflation-adjusted basis shows us more precisely what the ravages of inflation have been. It will depress the ROFB, by increasing the values of the required investments and the expenses associated with them.

TABLE 5-4   **A Simple Organization, Historical Cost Balance Sheet**

A Simple Company
Historical Cost Balance Sheet
End of Year 6

Assets		*Liabilities and Fund Balance*	
Investments	$1,460	Debt	$1,000
Fixed assets (net of depreci-		Fund balance	500
ation $60)*	40	Total liabilities and	
Total assets	$1,500	fund balance	$1,500

*Original Cost ($100) − Accumulated Depreciation ($60)

TABLE 5-5   **A Simple Organization, Inflation-Adjusted Balance Sheet**

A Simple Company
Inflation Adjusted Balance Sheet
End of Year 6

Assets		*Liabilities and Fund Balance*	
Investments	$1,460	Debt	$ 975
Fixed assets (net of depreci-		Fund balance	605
ation $180)*	120	Total liabilities and	
Total assets	$1,580	fund balance	$1,580

*Replacement Cost ($300) − Accumulated Depreciation ($180)

MEASUREMENT OF THE MATCH BETWEEN SOURCES AND USES OF MONEY

RSUS's sources and uses of money match up very well. In 19X8, its total capital of $1.4 million was 57 percent invested in long-term fixed assets ($801,061 ÷ 1,406,948), and more than 90 percent of its capital derived from a fund balance of $1,307,019. It can well afford to invest in additional fixed assets or to consume some of its fund balance in providing additional services.

It would be desirable to evaluate whether long-term, fixed expenses—such as those of essential, highly valued, personnel or minimum maintenance of buildings and equipment—are matched with similar long-term revenues. Generally, long-term expenses consist of the following items: tenured employees, minimum replacement and maintenance expenses, and minimal administrative and service expense. They are the ongoing expenses that are critical to the long-term survival of the organization. They are ideally matched with stable long-term revenues that are controlled by the organization, such as program fees, tuition, and endowment earnings.

Long-term expenses should not be matched with short-term revenues, whose magnitude cannot be readily controlled and that are subject to yearly oscillations. For example, maintenance expenses financed by short-term government grants cannot be carried out in those years that grant monies disappear. Maintenance expenses would more appropriately be financed by revenues such as endowment earnings that provide greater assurance of resources sufficient to implement the required maintenance schedule. The best information on the level of control over expenses and their variability is available through the managerial accounting systems that we will discuss in Part Two. However, in the absence of managerial accounting data, the degree of control over expenses and their variability can be roughly estimated with financial statement data.

There are two different and complementary ways of approaching the problem. If several years of data are available and there is sufficient variability in the level of expenses during those years, an econometric analysis can be performed. Time periods (on the horizontal axis of the graph) are plotted against corresponding periodic expense levels (on the vertical axis), and a straight line is drawn through the points on the resulting graph. The level of expenses at which the line intersects the vertical axis is the *fixed* or *base expense level* the organization needs to continue operations. Any expenses above that level are considered discretionary, and management can eliminate them if necessary. [Expenses should be adjusted for the effects of inflation so that all years of data are stated in constant (equivalent purchasing power) dollars.]

An alternative procedure examines the individual components of expense, and differentiates those that can be controlled by management from those that cannot. The fixed charges (such as depreciation, interest, and long-term lease payments) form the base of expenses that cannot be controlled. (If cash flows are examined instead of expenses, depreciation would be replaced by principal payments.) It is very helpful to have statements that show the object of expense, as well as the program purpose, when trying to assess how effectively expenses can be controlled. Unfortunately, neither type of analysis can usefully be performed for RSUS with the available data.

MEASUREMENT OF RESOURCE SUSTAINABILITY

Analysis of resource sustainability attempts to measure whether current organization performance can be sustained by examining the dispersion of assets, liabilities, fund balance, revenues, and expenses. More dispersed resources are generally more sustainable, unless dispersion becomes excessive.

Asset and Capital Dispersion

Table 5-6 shows, in the 19X8 and 19X7 columns, the total assets and capital of RSUS for 19X8 and 19X7, and the relative proportion of each type of asset to total assets and of each type of capital item to total capital. This is a form of *common size financial statement*, so called because the relative percentages can be compared among organizations of different sizes. It also indicates the absolute dollar change from 19X7 to 19X8 in the Dollar Change column and the percentage increase or decrease from 19X7 to 19X8 in the Percent Change column.

Although each of these measures is useful for understanding some aspect of the organization's operations, the statement is particularly useful for evaluating changes in dispersion. Comparing an organization's current to its prior year common size statements highlights changes in the relative proportion of resources each type of revenues contributed and each type of expense consumed. Comparisons to industry averages or similar organizations' common size statements for the year indicate how the organization compares to others. The percentage change from the prior year highlights the amount of change in a specific line item, which may help to detect rapid and potentially troublesome growth in what is currently a relatively small line item. The absolute dollar change serves as a convenient check on whether the amount involved is large enough to bother with. The relative proportion, or *common size ratio*, for each line item is calculated as follows:

$$\text{Common Size Ratio} = \frac{\text{Line Item Amount}}{\text{Total Category}}$$

The table also shows the absolute dollar change from 19X7 to 19X8 in the Dollar Change column and the percentage increase or decrease from 19X7 to 19X8 in the Percent Change column.

For example, the cash common size ratio for 19X8 is 22.0 percent ($310,010 ÷ $1,406,948), and for 19X7 it is 12.1 percent ($185,499 ÷ $1,527,502). Cash increased from 12.1 percent to 22.0 percent of all assets over the period. The cash Dollar Change is an increase of $124,511 ($310,010 − $185,499), which is equivalent to a Percentage Change of plus 67.1 percent ($124,511 ÷ $185,499). All the entries in Tables 5-6 and 5-7 are calculated in this manner.

TABLE 5-6 **RSUS Balance Sheet Measures**

	A	B	C = A − B	D = C ÷ B
			Dollar	Percent
	19X8	19X7	Change	Change
Totals	$1,406,948	$1,527,502	$(120,554)	(7.9)%
Assets:				
Cash	22.0%	12.1%	$ 124,511	67.1%
Certificate of deposit	7.1	6.6	0.0	0.0
Other marketable securities	0.6	0.4	456	7.6
Accounts receivable	0.7	10.8	(154,864)	(93.7)
Prepaid Expenses	0.4	0.2	2,196	69.4
Inventory	2.8	2.0	10,000	33.3
Total current assets	33.6	32.1	(17,701)	(3.6)
Fixed assets	56.9	59.5	(107,783)	(11.9)
Time deposits	9.5	8.4	4,930	3.8
Total	100.0%	100.0%	$(120,554)	(7.9)%
Liabilities:				
Accounts payable	0.9%	11.2%	$(157,742)	(92.4)
Salaries and wages payable	1.3	0.6	9,210	98.6
Payroll taxes payable	0.2	0.2	(367)	(10.6)
Current debt payable	1.6	2.1	(10,453)	(32.1)
Total current liabilities	4.0	14.1	(159,352)	(73.8)
Deferred revenues	2.5	1.6	10,000	40.0
Installment contract	0.6	4.3	(56,919)	(78.3)
Fund balance	92.9	80.0	85,717	7.0
Total	100.0%	100.0%	$(120,554)	(7.9)%

Each of these measures is useful for understanding some aspect of the organization's operations. Comparing these Balance Sheet ratios from year to year highlights changes in the organization's status from year to year.

RSUS's assets are well dispersed. Because they are not overly concentrated in any one investment, they are not greatly exposed to changes in the values of any one type of asset, such as a substantial decrease in the value of the items held in inventory. The $233,653 ($100,000 + $133,653) of investments in certificates of deposit and time deposits and the $310,010 in cash are the assets most vulnerable to changes in interest rates. They account for a large 38.6 percent of all the 19X8 assets.

On the other hand, RSUS's capital sources are primarily concentrated in the fund balance. Although earnings retained in the fund balance are the very best source of funds and indicate a high degree of financial security and stability, this large concentration may indicate excessive conservatism in the levels of services it is providing relative to those it could afford to provide. (The fund balance represents resources contributed in the past that an organization has chosen to invest for use in the future, instead of using them to provide service.) In the future, RSUS could afford to make its capital mix more dispersed, with more money emanating from short- and long-term debt, in order to provide more services.

Revenue and Expense Dispersion

Table 5-7 contains the totals, common size calculations, dollar changes, and percent changes for revenues and expenses for 19X7 and 19X8.

Revenues   Revenue dispersion in RSUS increased from 19X7 to 19X8, which means that there is less reliance on any single revenue source. As shown in Table 5-7, government grants, which accounted for 66.1 percent of RSUS's revenues in 19X7, declined in relative importance to 47.7 percent in 19X8. This was due to a very large absolute dollar decrease of $225,348 ($819,487 − $594,139) and a percentage decrease of 27.5 percent ($225,348 ÷ $819,487) in grant awards from 19X7 to 19X8. Even after the decrease, RSUS still relies on grants for nearly half its revenues. It is important to also consider the nature of the revenue source, which requires knowledge of the environment in which the organization operates. Generally, government grants are not considered highly sustainable revenue sources because a political change, over which an individual organization has little control, can eliminate them. For example, the National Endowment for the Arts substantially altered its grant strategy after a 1990 furor about its grants to artists who produced what some considered to be obscene and perverse works of art.

Happily, RSUS increased the proportion of revenues originating from more sustainable sources, such as the public's support of the station and the sale of its productions and services to other stations. They are sustainable because RSUS's management can affect their size more readily than it can governmental grants, in which the influence of any one station is much smaller. The decrease in government grants was approximately offset by increases in every other type of revenue. This indicates that RSUS is developing a broader base of revenue sources, which improves revenue quality. The increases in diversity of the revenue sources and in the presence of controllable types of sources are both positive signs.

Expenses   Expense ratios measure the dispersion, or relative resource consumption, of various aspects of operations. They indicate the relative amount of the total expenses devoted to each program or support function.

TABLE 5-7 **RSUS Revenue and Expense Dispersion Measures**

| | A | B | C = A – B | D = C ÷ B |
| | | | Dollar | Percent |
	19X8	*19X7*	Change	Change
Revenues:				
Total revenues	$1,245,730	$1,239,477	$ 6,253	0.5%
Government grants	47.7%	66.1%	(225,348)	(27.5)%
Auction	15.9	14.5	18,147	10.1
Foundations and public contributions	20.0	17.2	35,843	16.8
Corporation underwriting	2.8	0.3	31,080	781.9
Production sales to other stations	10.4	0.5	127,998	7,618.9
Services to other entities	3.2	1.7	18,533	86.4
Expenses:				
Total expenses	$1,160,013	$711,810	$448,203	63.0%
Program:				
In-school services	6.7%	9.0%	13,673	21.2%
Programming and production	33.6	25.6	207,721	113.9
Engineering and technical	13.0	14.0	50,999	51.2
Promotion, development, and auction	15.3	20.0	35,043	24.6
Administrative and general	20.8	20.1	98,196	68.7
Depreciation	10.6	11.3	42,571	53.1

Expense amounts and ratios are shaped by the cost-accounting techniques used to calculate the different program, fund raising, and administrative expenses. The allocation of expenses to a particular category may vary across organizations and with time. (We will address this subject in Part Two of this book.) For now, we will use the expense amounts as given because no additional information is available from RSUS's financial statements with which to adjust them.

$$\text{Expense Ratio} = \frac{\text{Expense Category Amount}}{\text{Total Expenses}}$$

The relative amounts devoted to programming and production increased by a whopping 113.9 percent, or $207,721, in 19X8, growing from 25.6 percent to 33.6 percent of total expenses. On the one hand, this is a welcome sight because it demonstrates that RSUS is devoting more of its resources to providing services in the form of producing new programs. Presumably this increase was mirrored by the substantial increase in production sales to other stations noted in the revenue section above. Because of the very large increase in total expenses, the increase in programming and production expense did not cause an absolute dollar decrease in the resources devoted to other activities. For example, although in-school services decreased as a percentage of total expense, from 9.0 percent to 6.7 percent, they increased by $13,673, a 21.2 percent increase over the 19X7 spending level. Thus the decrease in the percentage from 19X7 to 19X8 does not reflect a cutback in in-school services; it merely means that in-school services did not increase quite as much as other types of activities. On the other hand, the large increase in production expenses decreases the dispersion of expenses and, hence, their sustainability.

In many organizations, administrative expense can balloon suddenly and perniciously. This increase is unwelcome when considering the organization's substainability. While the increase in general and administrative expenses at RSUS is not good news, it is hardly of disastrous proportions at this time. However, it is always advisable to question the cause of an increase in administrative expenses. Although they increased only slightly as a percentage of total expenses, from 20.1 percent to 20.8 percent, they represent an absolute dollar increase of $98,196. It may be useful for management or board members to request the subdivision of general and administrative expenses into their component parts, such as maintenance, legal, data processing, and accounting expenses and to analyze the growth of each. And, to the extent possible, it is useful to determine expenses per unit of output, such as maintenance and utilities expenses per square foot, data processing expenses per computer resource unit, and accounting expenses per bill or invoice.

An increase in promotion expenses (also called fund raising or development expenses) is another area that may be cause for concern. Promotional expenses are analogous to marketing expenses in a for-profit organization. On the one hand, because promotion represents resources devoted to raising more money, rather than to the service mission of the organization, a lower percentage of expenses devoted to fund raising is generally considered better. On the other hand, organizations that spend too little in this area may have poor fund raising results. An often-used rule of thumb is that fund raising should not exceed 25 percent of expenses, but most well-established organizations should have an even lower percentage.

The RSUS promotion expense increased by $35,043, or by 24.6 percent from 19X7 to 19X8. Although promotion expenses had the largest relative decrease for RSUS, from 20.0 percent of expenses in 19X7 to 15.3 percent in 19X8, the significant change in total expenses between 19X7 and 19X8 makes this a less relevant indicator than the relationship between fund raising expenses and revenues generated by fund raising. This example indicates the importance of examining absolute dollar amounts as well as percentages of totals.

The purpose of fund raising expenses is to generate financial support for the organization. The *fund raising return ratio* measures the return generated by fund raising expenses, which indicates the success of the fund raising efforts.

$$\text{Fund Raising Return Ratio} = \frac{\text{Revenues Generated From Fund Raising}}{\text{Fund Raising Expenses}}$$

This important return ratio should at least equal one, and in the long run should average at least a four-to-one return for every dollar spent on fund raising.

Depending on the nature of the promotional activities, there may be a lag between the time when the expenses are incurred and when the resulting revenues are received and recognized. Whether revenues are recognized at the point of a pledge or only when the cash is received, fund raising expenses are incurred months in advance of that time. If this time lag is substantial, it may be useful to compare the fund raising expenses of one year to the fund raising results of the following year.

The *object of expense ratio* measures each object of expense (such as salaries, utilities, or postage) as a proportion of total expenses and indicates whether an appropriate balance is being maintained among different components of expense.

$$\text{Object of Expense Ratio} = \frac{\text{Object of Expense Amount}}{\text{Total Expenses}}$$

This ratio cannot be calculated from the normal financial statements, except for those of voluntary health and welfare organizations, which are required to prepare a Statement of Functional Expenses that provides the necessary data. These ratios should be requested by managers or board members from those who have access to internal supplementary data. Large changes in certain types of items as a proportion of total expenses may critically affect sustainability.

OTHER RATIOS

In addition to these general purpose ratios, each nonprofit sector uses its own unique ratios. Hospitals analyze their activities on a patient-day or per-bed basis; educational organizations use a per-student or per-course bsais; voluntary health and welfare organizations use a per-case or per-encounter basis; and performing arts organizations may use per-performance measures. It is useful for any organization to calculate revenues and expenses, and sometimes assets (such as endowments) per whatever it perceives to be the relevant output measures. Efficiency ratios measure the amount of output produced per unit of input. Such ratios may be provided as supplementary data in annual reports, but generally cannot be calculated from the data available in the financial statements alone.

RED FLAGS IN FINANCIAL ANALYSIS

A substantial change in the size of some ratios, either in relationship to past performance or in relationship to organizations similar in purpose, often indicates that something is awry. Financial analysts refer to these signals as "red flags." Presented below are the red flags that usually indicate serious financial troubles.

(1) *Reductions in administrative or marginal programmatic expenses.* In the short run, discretionary supporting expenses such as maintenance or fund raising that support the organization's primary functions can be reduced without causing immediate negative repercussions. Expenses such as libraries, out-reach activities, and information centers do not produce readily measurable outputs and are therefore ripe candidates for cuts when expenses must be reduced. But in the long run, continued deferral or reduction of such expenses will inevitably cause serious negative consequences. The likely collapse of many U.S. bridges is the result of many years of deferred maintenance. For example, repairing New York City's long-neglected bridges will require $3.2 billion that the financially-distressed city does not have.[6] Similarly, college administrators in the midst of tight economic circumstances now consider correction of the serious under-maintenance of physical plant to be one of their most serious challenges for the 1990s. (Of course, reduction of an unnecessarily high expense is cause for rejoicing, rather than concern.)

(2) *Increases in short-term liabilities.* "Sitting on the payables" is an instinctive reaction; like an individual, an organization short of cash does not pay its bills. This condition is revealed by a slow turnover of accounts payable. Some may even send checks they know will bounce, hoping for just one more delivery of supplies. Inevitably, these stratagems only hamper the organization's ability to obtain the services and supplies it needs. Suppliers will refuse to provide goods except on cash-only or COD terms, both of which are more expensive than normal credit terms. Bounced checks also lead to bookkeeping headaches, bad bank relations, and expensive service charges.

[6]Calvin Sims, "New Problems Are Found on Bridges," *The New York Times*, 15 September 1990, p. 276.

And the bad will and damage to the organization's reputation can last far beyond the time when the organization returns to a better financial status.

(3) *Reductions in the level of fixed assets* may indicate that fixed assets are being sold to finance operations. If a troubled nonprofit sells its buildings and equipment and uses the proceeds for operational purposes, its self-cannibalization is likely to be destructive in the end.

(4) *"Soft" or short-term sources of revenues* may indicate that the organization is pulling out the stops in an effort to find financial inflows, or is over-committing itself to future outflows. When soft revenues are matched with soft or short-term resource outflows, the organization does not put itself at financial risk. However, if they are used for outflows that will continue long after the soft revenues are gone, without plans to generate revenues to continue their support, the organization may face serious problems.

(5) *Large gift horses* should be looked in the mouth because some carry continuing streams of hidden costs with them. For example, many large gifts of new buildings to educational institutions were later discovered to carry equally large , unfunded, hidden price tags of the annual operating expenses they require for service, support, and maintenance.

(6) *Continuing losses or declines in the margin between revenues and expenses* generally indicate an organization that is unable either to plan properly or to implement its plans effectively. If these conditions persist, it will have to shrink in size to continue operating. Losses or declines in the surplus are usually a signal of problems unless the surplus was previously very high, as in RSUS, or the reduction was caused by carefully planned increased program or service expenses.

(7) *Reduction in receivables and inventory turnover* may indicate a sloppy or distracted management. Excessively slow turnover of these assets means that resources that could be used to provide services are tied up in inventories and receivables. While seldom a signal of immediate severe distress, if inventories or receivables are material, slowdowns in turnover may signal management inefficiency that should be corrected.

LIMITATIONS OF ACCOUNTING INFORMATION

By now, you are probably dizzy from crunching numbers. Let us step back to get a view of the financial analysis forest, instead of focusing on individual trees. We will do this with a discussion of the financial accounting data limitations you must bear in mind when interpreting the results of your financial analysis.

It is important to remember the limits imposed by potentially unreliable accounting information, flexible GAAP, and historical cost for interpreting or predicting financial results.

Quality of Accounting Data

The near default of New York City in the 1970s also provided telling documentation of the poor quality of its accounting data.[7] The disclosure of New York's situation was soon followed by revelations from other state and local governments that they too were on the verge of bankruptcy, with huge unfunded pension liabilities. Prompted by claims that the fiscal failures could be partially traced to the lack of meaningful accounting information, the large CPA firms, such as Coopers and Lybrand and Arthur Andersen, joined in issuing proposals for reform of government accounting. Although some progress has been made, accounting data quality may still be poor in many cases.

In government accounting there is no shortage of evidence that things are not all they might be. In 1989, a government finance officials organization reported that of the 1,485 annual government reports submitted, it awarded 1,333 Certificates of Achievement for Excellence in Financial Reporting (its more positive new name for the prior Certificate of Conformance).[8] Although the numbers increased from the 889 submissions and 705 Certificates of Achievement awarded in 1984, they were but a fraction of the total population of more than 80,000 governmental units (municipalities, counties, school districts, councils, retirement systems, and other) that are eligible to apply.

The federal government's accounting problems seem only to be getting worse. Problems in accounting for federal expenditures make dull copy by now, but the billions of dollars involved compel reiteration. Even when the government is engaged in business-like activities, its accounting statements are inadequate. For example, for many years the Student Loan Insurance Fund may or may not have had a deficit in the investment of the U.S. government account of $1.5 billion. The deficit was variously estimated at $3 or $4 billion or at a somewhat smaller $1.5 billion. It was impossible to narrow this error range. In recognition of this dubious distinction, the General Accounting Office (GAO) gave the financial statements of this fund a relentlessly consecutive string of adverse opinions.

In private nonprofit organizations, an audit opinion generally reflects the quality of the accounting systems; qualified audit opinions are not uncommon.

Uniformity of Accounting

As discussed above, GAAP is sufficiently flexible to allow the same economic event to be accounted for quite differently in different organizations. Although flexibility permits managers to use those accounting procedures

---

[7] As cited in General Accounting Office, *New York City's Efforts to Improve Its Accounts System*, Appendix I, (Washington, DC: General Accounting Office, 1977).
[8] Government Finance Officers Association, "Certificate of Achievement for Excellence in Financial Reporting, 1989 Results," available on request from GFOA.

that best reflect their unique strategies and situations, flexibility also makes it difficult to compare the financial data of different institutions. For example, we demonstrated in Chapter 3 that the choice of depreciation method could make the difference between an excess of revenues over expenses and a deficit. Although many studies indicate that the capital markets are not fooled by accounting maneuvers, managers should be aware of this flexibility in analyzing the financial results, especially when comparing their data to those of other organizations.

The desire for uniformity has been a theme in nonprofit accounting that can be traced back to the early twentieth century for American colleges and universities. Yet, some of the accounting or reporting practices of nonprofit organizations are more uniform than those of the for-profit sector. Many colleges and universities and voluntary health and welfare organizations have adopted recommended accounting classifications for revenues and expenses and, in a number of states, hospitals use either uniform reporting systems or uniform charts of accounts. In the for-profit sector, only regulated industries, such as utilities, have comparable degrees of uniformity.

Nevertheless, some argue for even greater uniformity to minimize accounting flexibility and prescribe inventory and depreciation methods, asset lives, and many other accounting matters that are presently discretionary. Proponents argue that such uniformity is particularly necessary for making valid comparisons among nonprofit organizations because they do not compete in the marketplace for equity capital as do for-profit organizations.

Opponents of greater accounting uniformity point out that the resulting statements may not necessarily reflect financial results as they are viewed by managers. Differences in accounting frequently reflect the legitimate differences in strategies and economics that a uniform accounting system cannot accommodate. For example, an urban teaching hospital must acquire new technology frequently for teaching and research activities and is likely to use it much more than a small rural hospital. As a result, the urban hospital should have a shorter asset life and should use a more rapid depreciation method than the rural one.

This issue cannot be simply resolved. If the funding sources for nonprofits become increasingly concentrated, the pressure for uniformity will mount. The example of regulated industries that must use uniform accounting systems is not an altogether happy one. Many have been hampered from developing accounting systems that meet their own managerial needs because their energies have been diverted to meeting the required outside needs for information.

Current Value Accounting

Under GAAP, assets are valued at their purchase cost or at market value when donated. Neither replacement nor market value is contained in the financial statements. The resulting Statement of Revenues and Expenses is a heterogeneous amalgam of current dollars for revenues and past dollars of various vintages for expenses. The Balance Sheet consists of several layers of dollars, with some assets, such as accounts receivable, stated in current dollars and some, primarily fixed assets, stated in the dollars of the time of their purchase. Very old nonprofit institutions may have Balance Sheet values for assets acquired in the seventeenth and eighteenth centuries that are ludicrously small.

One way to deal with the heterogeneity of values is to inflate all dollars so they are stated in equivalent purchasing power terms. Accountants had suggested inflation adjustment for quite some time, but the very low U.S. inflation rates—on the order of 1 percent to 3 percent—made it hardly worth the bother. The double digit inflation rates the U.S. experienced in the 1970s increased the interest in inflation accounting. And inflation is not about to go away—it has been a rather persistent aspect of the world economy, dating back to the year 1500![9]

The December 1979 FASB statement, *Financial Reporting and Changing Prices*, required certain supplemental disclosures. A five-year comparison of certain financial data and a current year Income Statement were among the disclosures required. The supplemental Income Statement was to be prepared on a constant dollar or a current cost basis. (Alternatively, a reconciliation of historical cost income to income on a constant dollar or current cost basis may be presented.) The *constant dollar* is essentially price level or general purchasing power accounting. The *current cost* basis adjusts the historical cost income statement for the current cost of inventory, property, plant and equipment, cost of sales, and depreciation.

Although such statements are not currently required of either for-profit or nonprofit organizations, they can be of value in assessing intergenerational equity. The benefits of current cost accounting can be approximated with relatively simple estimates and adjustments, primarily involving fixed asset valuation, and possibly long term debt. The battle between historical and current value accounting is likely to rekindle whenever inflation rates are high. It is most important to nonprofit organizations, such as hospitals that are capital intensive and to those that are reimbursed for their costs. Many feel that "cost" defined on a historical cost basis is an inadequate basis for reimbursement.

SUMMARY

Financial statements can be useful for understanding the financial condition of an organization. They can help answer four specific quesions: Are the organization's finanical resources consistent with its goals? Is intergenerational equity being maintained? Are sources and uses of capital well matched?

[9]With thanks to Mr. Davis Hussy, Principal, Harbridge House, Europe, for bringing this point to Professor Herzlinger's attention.

How sustainable is the organization's financial performance? Liquidity and solvency, asset management, return on fund balance, variability analyses, and dispersion ratios are particularly helpful in answering these questions and can generally be constructed from the data in the financial statements. Their interpretation must be tempered with considerations of the underlying data quality, the effects of flexibility in accounting, and the limitations of historical cost accounting.

APPENDIX A Financial Analysis Research on Risk and Interest Rates

Financial analysis is used for a variety of purposes. Its uses include the evaluation of the financial risk of the organization, its creditworthiness, and the interest rates for its debt. We will discuss the research findings relevant to these topics.

Research on Financial Distress or Failure

In the 1970s, a number of private colleges and universities closed their doors or averted closure only by becoming public institutions; private voluntary organizations went bankrupt; and some governmental entities were unable to meet their fixed financial obligations. The 1980s saw hospitals added to this group. The 1990 drop in the Massachusetts bond rating to the lowest in the nation is merely a harbinger of distress yet to come for many other state and local governments. Some organizations will file for bankruptcy, or fail, each year, due to poor management or other factors.

Organizations that do not technically fail may experience *financial distress*, defined by one expert as "severe liquidity problems that cannot be resolved without a sizable rescaling of the entity's operations or structure."[10] Potential creditors and funding agencies, depending on their priorities and strategies, may want either to avoid providing resources to financially distressed organizations or to provide sufficient infusions of resources to save them.

Many studies have attempted to determine the information that best predicts financial distress or failure in the for-profit sector. One approach uses ratios to predict whether an organization will fail. Generally, the results indicate that the financial ratios of failed firms differ significantly from those that survive.[11] The four factors that showed the best predictive ability (greatest

[10]George Foster, *Financial Statement Analysis*, 2d ed. (Prentice-Hall, 1986), p. 632.
[11]Foster, *Financial Statement Analysis*.

difference between bankrupt and nonbankrupt firms) were profitability, leverage, cash flow or earnings coverage of fixed payments, and mean stock returns and volatility. Consistent with prior research, a 1983 study of 75 variables and 3,645 firms found that liquidity and activity/turnover ratios were generally not good predictors of failure.[12]

Another commonly used approach combines several ratios in a mathematical model to predict the probability that an organization will fail. Different sophisticated mathematical techniques have been used in these studies. In a seminal study, Altman calculated a *Z score*[13] for each organization. Only failed institutions had *Z* scores lower than 1.81. The following formula was used to calculate *Z* scores:

$$Z = 0.012X_1 + 0.014X_2 + 0.033X_3 + 0.006X_4 + 0.999X_5$$

where X_1 = working capital/total assets; X_2 = retained earnings/total assets; X_3 = earnings before interest and taxes/total assets; X_4 = market value of equity/book value of total liabilities; and X_5 = sales/total assets. Commercial services now use multivariate approaches to conduct research on financial distress analysis.[14]

The studies of failure prediction for nonprofit organizations are few. One of the earliest found private college failure correlated with relatively large student aid bills, large increases in wage bills, and a deficit in the current funds. A study of public and private colleges and universities found that the flow of resources for wages, student aid, plant maintenance, and library activities were good discriminators of failure.[15] Nondistressed institutions spent more on an absolute basis on these functions than did distressed ones. However, on a relative basis, the nondistressed institutions spent proportionately less on wages, maintenance, and libraries than distressed ones.[16]

One researcher of municipalities found four significant basic indicators of funds flow: long-term debt per capita, short-term debt per capita, expenditures per capita for nine municipal functions, and the ratio of the city's

[12]M. E. Zmijewski, "Methodological Issues Related to the Estimation of Financial Distress Prediction Models," *Studies on Current Econometric Issues in Accounting Research*, Supplement to *Journal of Accounting Research*, 1984, pp. 59-82. (As cited by Foster, *Financial Statement Analysis*, pp. 545-546.)

[13]E. I. Altman, "Financial Ratios, Discriminant Analysis and the Prediction of Corporate Bankruptcy," *The Journal of Finance* 23 (September 1968): 589-609.

[14]Foster, *Financial Statement Analysis*, p. 553-558.

[15]Earl Cheit, *The New Depression in Higher Education* (New York, NY: McGraw-Hill, 1971); and *The New Depression in Higher Education—Two years Later* (New York, NY: McGraw-Hill, 1973).

[16]Katherine Schipper, "Financial Distress in Private Colleges," *Studies on Measurement and Evaluation of the Economic Efficiency of Public and Private Nonprofit Institutions*, Supplement to *Journal of Accounting Research* (1977): 1-45.

revenues from internal sources to its full value taxable property base.[17] He found capital outlay expenditures per capita highly significant in explaining negative cash flows.[18] Another researcher found operating surpluses to be correlated with debt variables, capital expenditures, and wages.[19]

A study of private nonprofit hospitals found them to use the same financial strategy as for-profit ones.[20] If this study can be generalized, then the variables that are significant in the for-profit sector can be used in the nonprofit one.[21]

Credit Research

The central concern of those who use financial analysis to evaluate an organization's ability to discharge its debt obligations is whether the entity will be able to pay the interest and principal when due.

Bond rating agencies (bond raters), such as Standard and Poor's (S&P) and Moody's, use financial analysis with other information to assess bond riskiness and determine the *bond rating*. The rating indicates the *bond quality*, or how likely the borrower is to pay interest and principal when due. Although different firms have somewhat different rating schemes, the grade of AAA is the best grade of bond, and anything below BBB or Baa is considered a *junk bond*, that is, not of sufficient quality for prudent investors to buy. Bond raters willingly provide guidance on what factors they examine to assign a rating, but caution that the analysis is a judgmental, rather than a mechanical, process. Two useful guides are *S&P's Municipal Finance Criteria*[22] and *Moody's on Muncipals.*[23]

Although financial analysis is only a part of the bond rating process, it is considered very important. It uses the financial statement data to assess the organization's ability to meet the proposed debt obligations. The financial factors examined include the liquidity, leverage, coverage and profitability ratios discussed earlier. The five-year trends of these ratios for the organization are calculated and compared to those of similar organizations. Notes

[17]Terry N. Clark, "Fiscal Management of American Cities" (Working Paper No. 83, Comparative Study of Community Decision Making, University of Chicago, April 1977).

[18]Terry N. Clark, et al., "How Many More New Yorks?" *New York Affairs* 3 (Summer/Fall 1976): 18-27.

[19]Jean Greenblatt, "Determinants of Municipal Operating Deficits" (M.A. thesis, Cornell University, 1976).

[20]Richard A. Elnicki, *Hospital Working Capital, An Empirical Study*, Proceedings of the Conference of Measurement and Evaluation of the Efficiency of Nonprofit Institutions (Chicago, IL: University of Chicago, May 1977).

[21]Ibid., p. 11.

[22]Standard and Poor's, *S&P Municipal Finance Criteria*, 1989.

[23]Moody's Investors Service, *Moody's on Municipals: An Introduction to Using Debt*, 1989.

to the financial statements are carefully examined to assess the liquidity of the various assets, including restrictions on them; contingent liabilities; and other factors that could affect the organization's ability to pay. Assets held by outside trustees are generally excluded from the assets of the organization, even when they are reported on the Balance Sheet. If the organization receives significant third-party reimbursements, the relevant reimbursement agreements and practices will be considered. In short, the financial statements are reviewed with a fine tooth comb to find positive evidence of the organization's likely ability to meet its debt obligations when due and negative evidence of an inability or unwillingness to meet those obligations.

A number of studies have attempted to model the process the rating services use to arrive at their ratings. One early study found that total assets, working capital/sales, net worth/total debt, sales/net worth, and profit/sales were in combination the best predictors of a bond's rating.[24] Another found that earnings variability, reliability in meeting obligations, capital structure, and bond marketability led to a model that had fair success in predicting ratings.[25] Similar results were obtained in studying the determinants of bond ratings of state and local governments.[26]

How loan applications are evaluated and rated has also been investigated. One approach asked loan officers how important various factors are in the loan decisions.[27] Debt/equity and current ratios were listed as the most important. Another approach parallels the bond rating research above, attempting to develop a mathematical model that will replicate loan officer decisions. Again, the research does not provide definitive results and primarily involves for-profit rather than nonprofit organizations.

In summary, the research confirms that some financial ratios are useful in predicting financial distress, debt default, and interest rates, and that different ratios are useful under different circumstances. To date, no magic formula for predicting failure or default has emerged. Unhappily, there is no short cut for understanding the organization, its management, and its financial information in depth.

[24]J. O. Harrigan, "The Determination of Long-Term Credit Standing with Financial Ratios," *Empirical Research in Accounting: Selected Studies, 1966,* Supplement to Vol. 4, *Journal of Accounting Research* 1966, pp. 44-62.

[25]R. R. West, "An Alternative Approach to Predicting Corporate Bond Ratings," *Journal of Accounting Research* (Spring 1970): 118-127.

[26]See, for example, W. T. Carleton and E. M. Lerner, "Statistical Credit Scoring of Municipal Bonds," *Journal of Money, Credit, and Banking,* 1969, pp. 750-764; Jerome S. Osteryoung and Dallas R. Blevins, "A New Approach to Ratings of State GO's," *Journal of Portfolio Management* (Spring 1979), pp. 69-74; and Daniel Rubinfeld, "Credit Ratings and the Mart for GO Municipal Bonds," *National Tax Journal,* 1973, p. 1727.

[27]C. Gibson, "Financial Ratios as Perceived by Commercial Loan Officers," *Akron Business and Economic Review* (Summer 1983): 23-27.

DISCUSSION QUESTIONS

1. Consider a nonprofit organization with which you are familiar—perhaps your school or local government. Present an example of actual events in that organization that illustrate each of the four key questions of financial analysis.

2. Listed below are typical examples of financial events in nonprofit organizations. For each of them, indicate which of the four questions should be asked about this event. (You may find more than one of the four questions appropriate.)

   A loss
   A high profit
   Investment of most of the endowment in the stock of one company
   Receipt of a large grant
   An increase in the pensions of past and current employees
   A large number of unused buildings that are owned by the organization
   A bridge, highway, or building that is in poor physical condition

3. Define liquidity and solvency. How are they measured?

4. What are the ratios that measure profitability? Dispersion? Asset management?

5. How would you use the ROFB measure in a nonprofit organization? What managers would you hold responsible for attaining a certain level of ROFB?

6. Explain whether or not the following statements are correct and your reasoning.

   The ratio of the surplus to the fund balance should always be positive and greater than the rate of inflation.
   The current ratio should always be greater than one.
   An opera company that has one nationally recognized performer will never get into financial problems.
   Working capital should always be a negative number.
   High leverage is always financially dangerous.
   Low leverage is always financially prudent.
   Low asset turnover ratios inevitably indicate that assets are not being used appropriately.
   An organization with a high profit margin will invariably earn a high ROFB.
   Inflation does not affect the finances of nonprofit organizations.
   Inflation affects the value of the debt, fixed assets, and fund balances of nonprofits organizations.

7. What factors do you consider to be most important in measuring the financial performance of a nonprofit organization? How would you measure them?

8. What is the difference between historical and current costs? Which is the better measuring method and why?

9. Do you think the flexibility of accounting methods is desirable or undesirable? What, if any, changes should be made to accounting principles?

EXERCISES

1. The Balance Sheets for two consecutive years and the activity statement of the Rose Independent School of Indiana are presented below:

Balance Sheet
(as of the end of Year 1 and Year 2)

Assets	Year 1	Year 2	Liabilities and Fund Balance	Year 1	Year 2
Cash	$ 30,000	$ 20,000	Accounts payable	$ 15,000	$ 15,000
Accounts receivable	40,000	50,000	Salaries payable	35,000	40,000
Inventory	5,000	6,000	Note payable	20,000	15,000
Prepaid expenses	5,000	4,000	Long-term debt	100,000	80,000
Land	20,000	20,000			
Buildings and equipment,			Fund balance	30,000	60,000
net book value	100,000	110,000	Total liabilities and		
Total assets	$200,000	$210,000	fund balance	$200,000	$210,000

Statement of Revenues and Expenses
(For the Period Between Years 1 and 2)

Revenues		$400,000
Tuition	$200,000	
Room and board	100,000	
Fund raising	100,000	
Expenses[a]		370,000
Instructional expenses	220,000	
Administrative expenses	110,000	
Fund raising expenses	40,000	
Excess of revenue over expenses		$ 30,000

[a]Includes Depreciation Expense of $10,000

The School's long-term debt consists of a 5-year note issued in Year 1 to be repaid in equal annual payments of principal and with an annual interest rate of 8 percent. The note payable is noninterest bearing.

a. Use a Statement of Cash Flows to explain why the cash balance went down between Years 1 and 2.
b. What financing strategy is the school using?
c. Use financial ratios to comment on other aspects of the school's management. What appears to be strong? Weak?

Case

CASE STUDY

This case study, Community Television of Southern California: KCET, enables you to evaluate the station's financial status. The case is not simple. It contains the actual financial statements of the station. A useful approach to the case might be first to evaluate the impact of the notes in **Exhibit 5** on the values contained in the financial statements in **Exhibits 2** through **4**. You could then construct a set of financial ratios for KCET for two years and evaluate the answers they provide to the four questions. As a clue, one of the four questions could be answered in a way that will cause concern about KCET's financial situation. Also note that the station is still going strong, both financially and programatically.

CASE 5.1 Community Television of Southern California: KCET

The annual report of KCET for the 19X7 fiscal year began with a foreword written by Dr. James Loper, its president and chief executive officer:

> By their very nature, annual reports deal in terms of money: How money was obtained and how it was spent.
>
> Our annual report includes a formal and precise accounting of the money entrusted to us, and how it has been spent during our fiscal year which ended June 30, 1977.
>
> But ours is unlike most other companies. Our product is not for sale in supermarkets or in department stores. Our reason for existence is not expressed in profits.
>
> We are not in the business of making money. We are in the far more rewarding business of enriching our community.

This case was prepared by Professor Regina E. Herzlinger.

Copyright © 1978 by the President and Fellows of Harvard College. Harvard Business School case 9-179-046. Revised January 1993.

Our product is information. Involvement. Entertainment. Music. News. Sports. Dance. . . . It is education. The ABCs. How to cross a street safely. How to cook. How to cope. How to relax. How to laugh. How to love. How to survive. . . . It is drama. Great drama. Disturbing drama. Delightful drama. . . . It is probing. Recording. Questioning. Portraying. Demanding. Revealing. Exchanging ideas. . . .It is wondering. The wonder of the stars. Of the sea. Of the earth. Of seeing. Of hearing. Of being.

It is a business bounded only by our imagination, our energy, our resources, and the support of our community.

HISTORY OF KCET

The station was incorporated in 1962 to operate a noncommercial educational television facility in Southern California. Los Angeles was the last major American city to incorporate such a station; but its proximity to the centers of motion pictures and television production soon enabled it to overcome this disadvantage. KCET was not only well entrenched and respected in the local community, but also a major producer of programs which were broadcast by the nation's other 265 public television stations. It had won 31 national and local Emmys. The history of KCET was mirrored in the rapid growth of the public broadcasting system as a whole. From its humble beginnings, in the late 1940s, the public broadcasting industry had grown to a half a billion dollar a year sector. It consisted of hundreds of public radio and television stations; KCET was among the leaders of the stations and one of the five or so television stations that served as producers of national, as well as local productions.

KCET had revenues of $13.4 million a year and a fund balance of $3.7 million. It was housed in a Broadcast Center, newly constructed in 19X7—complete with 128 offices, an auditorium, and related space. The building was on a 4.5-acre movie lot purchased with the aid of a $2.5 million loan from the Ford Foundation. The site also houses KCET's production studios.

SOURCES OF FINANCIAL SUPPORT

KCET derives its support from a number of sources:

(1) *Subscriptions* provide a broad base of support from the 119,865 Southern California residents who contributed $15 or more to the station.

(2) *Contributions* provided by corporations and individuals are other diversified funding sources. The contributions are for capital and operating purposes.

(3) *Grants* by the federal government, corporations, foundations, and others for the production of programs are the largest single source of funds.

(4) *Facility and operating grants* for the purposes of operations and of expanding KCET's physical plant are the fourth major source of support. KCET has a capital campaign with a goal of $10.58 million, of which $6.08 million must be raised from the community and the remainder of which will be provided on a matching basis by the Ford Foundation. The Ford offer is open to December 19X8, and as of the end of 19X7, $3.9 million has been raised from the community. The Ford Foundation, over the years, had given over $8 million to KCET, and over $200 million to the industry, but by 19X8 ceased its contributions to public broadcasting.

USE OF FUNDS

The upgrading of technical facilities and studios at KCET is budgeted at $3,195,000. Much of this work had already been completed. Additional property and construction and furnishings of the new Broadcast Center cost $2,185,000. Actual construction cost was $38 per square foot. Additionally, $3,750,000 is earmarked for national program production, and $1,450,000 is for program development and working capital.

Dr. Loper feels that because of its location and staff, KCET's comparative advantage, now and for the future, is in serving as a production center. The advances of broadcasting technology and the use of satellites for broadcasting purposes also underscored the importance of diversifying from a primarily local and broadcasting oriented station to a nationally oriented production center.

ASSIGNMENT

1. **Exhibit 2** through **5** contain the financial statements of KCET. Evaluate the station's financial condition.
2. What financing strategy do these statements reveal?
3. Are the results of operations, the financing strategy, and the financial position consistent with the station's goals?

EXHIBIT 1   Audit Opinion

Report of Certified Public Accountant

The Board of Directors—Community Television of Southern California

We have examined the accompanying statement of assets and liabilities of the Community Television of Southern California at June 30, 19X7 and June 30, 19X6 and the related statements of revenues and expenses and changes in financial position for the years then ended. Our examinations were made in accordance with generally accepted auditing standards, and accordingly included such tests of the accounting records and such other auditing procedures as we considered necessary in the circumstances.

In our opinion, the financial statements mentioned above present fairly the financial position of Community Television of Southern California at June 30, 19X7 and June 30, 19X6 and the results of operations and changes in financial position for the years then ended, in conformity with generally accepted accounting principles applied on a consistent basis.

Arthur Young & Company

Los Angeles, California
August 23, 19X7

EXHIBIT 2 **KCET Balance Sheet As of June 30, 19X7 and 19X6**

	19X7	19X6
Assets		
Current Assets:		
Cash	$ 161,204	$ 401,684
Grants and accounts receivable (Notes 1 and 7)	7,537,524	3,665,585
Prepaid expenses	80,285	235,098
Film rights, at cost (Note 1)	409,559	300,577
Capital improvement fund (Notes 3 and 4)	-	38,927
Total current assets	$ 8,188,572	$ 4,641,871
Property, Plant and Equipment at Cost (Notes 1 and 4):		
Land	552,936	552,936
Buildings and improvements	4,612,626	2,689,624
Building (at transmitter site)	105,663	105,767
Antenna, transmitter and other broadcasting and studio equipment	3,701,616	3,392,994
Furniture, fixtures, and automobiles	344,483	140,698
Construction in progress	-	726,476
	$ 9,317,324	$ 7,608,495
Less accumulated depreciation	3,617,653	3,280,898
Net property, plant, and equipment	$ 5,699,671	$ 4,327,597
Other Assets:		
Long-term portion of grants receivable (Note 5)	2,270,338	1,647,194
Other	27,555	113,046
Total other assets	2,297,893	1,760,240
TOTAL ASSETS	$16,186,136	$10,729,708
Liabilities and Net Assets		
Current liabilities:		
Accounts payable and accrued expenses (Note 7)	$ 1,547,616	$ 1,462,239
Unexpended grant funds (Notes 1 and 5)	6,362,735	2,715,079
Long-term debt due within one year (Note 4)	1,140,171	473,099
Total current liabilities	$ 9,050,522	$ 4,650,417
Deferred revenue:		
Funds held in trust (Note 1)	12,263	12,341
Unexpended grant funds (Note 5)	2,617,389	1,647,194
Long-term debt due after one year (Note 4)	836,206	1,478,348
Other payables	-	15,738
TOTAL LIABILITIES	12,516,380	7,804,038
Commitments (Notes 4 and 6)		
Net assets represented by:		
Balance at beginning of year	2,925,670	1,953,420
Contributions to capital improvement fund (Note 3)	742,053	730,860
Excess of revenues over expenses for the year	2,033	241,390
NET ASSETS	3,669,756	2,925,670
TOTAL LIABILITIES AND NET ASSETS	$16,186,136	$10,729,708

See accompanying notes.

EXHIBIT 3 **KCET Statement of Revenues and Expenses**
Years Ended June 30, 19X7 and 19X6

	19X7	19X6
Revenues:		
From operations:		
Restricted program grants		
Federal agencies	$ 1,303,305	$ 873,198
Public television agencies	2,031,408	2,670,109
Corporations	2,814,196	973,015
Foundations	1,481,414	2,203,348
Total restricted program grants	7,630,323	6,719,670
Facilities:		
Public television agencies	576,815	448,716
Instructional broadcast	95,756	96,120
Other	69,595	47,897
Total facilities	742,166	592,733
General operating grants	1,200,000	1,234,014
Interest and other income (Note 7)	135,484	423,049
Total from operations	9,707,973	8,969,466
Subscriptions	2,520,479	2,196,539
Contributions (Note 1)	1,167,532	1,084,254
Total revenues	13,395,984	12,250,259
Expenses (including interest of $129,214 in 19X7 and $160,413 in 19X6):		
Programming (including production and engineering)	9,668,530	8,575,885
Transmission	595,404	498,981
Public information	396,711	381,616
Community development	579,630	552,956
Subscriber services	461,708	450,238
Volunteer services	61,721	56,846
Auction	244,111	189,043
General and administrative	1,386,136	1,303,304
Total expenses	13,393,951	12,008,869
Excess of revenue over expenses	$ 2,033	$ 241,390

See accompanying notes.

EXHIBIT 4   KCET Statement of Changes in Financial Position
          Years Ended June 30, 19X7 and 19X6

	19X7	19X6
Source of funds:		
Current year's operations:		
Excess of revenues over expenses	$ 2,033	$ 241,390
Expenses not involving the use of working capital in current period—depreciation	409,858	350,928
Working capital provided by operations	411,891	592,318
Contributions to capital improvement fund (Note 3)	742,053	730,860
Additions to long-term debt	1,174,614	-
Increase/decrease in deferred revenue—unexpended grant funds	970,195	(2,806)
Other—net	69,675	(1,854)
Total source of funds	$3,368,428	$1,318,518
Application of funds:		
Addition to plant and equipment	1,781,932	728,839
Reduction of long-term debt	1,816,756	165,587
Increase (decrease) in long-term portion of grant receivable	623,144	(2,806)
Total application of funds	4,221,832	891,620
Increase (decrease) in working capital	(853,404)	426,898
Working capital deficiency at beginning of year	(8,546)	(435,444)
Working capital deficiency at end of year	$ (861,950)	$ (8,546)
The increases/decreases in working capital are as follows:		
Current assets:		
Cash	$ (240,480)	$ (126,847)
Commercial paper	-	(250,000)
Grants and accounts receivable	3,871,939	(1,501,751)
Prepaid expenses	(154,813)	163,896
Film rights	108,982	231,751
Capital improvement fund	(38,927)	(111,560)
	3,546,701	(1,594,511)
Current liabilities:		
Accounts payable and accrued expenses	(85,377)	(344,010)
Unexpended grants fund	(3,647,656)	2,265,909
Long-term debt due within one year	(667,072)	99,510
	(4,400,105)	2,021,409
Increase (decrease) in working capital	$ (853,404)	$ 426,898

See accompanying notes.

EXHIBIT 5 Notes to Financial Statements, June 30, 19X7

1. Summary of Significant Accounting Policies

Contributions and grants Contributions are recorded as income as they are received. Grants which are restricted as to purpose are taken into income as funds are expended. Grants which are both restricted as to purpose and must be matched by contributions are taken into income as the grant funds are matched and expended.

Contributions of other than cash are recorded at the fair market value at the date of gift.

Pledges, which will be recorded as contributions to the capital improvement fund (Note 3) when the funds are received, amounted to $505,000 at June 30, 19X7.

Depreciation Depreciation is provided using the straight-line method over the following estimated useful lives: studios, buildings, and improvements—25-40 years; building (at transmitter site)—10 years; antenna, transmitter, and other broadcasting and studio equipment—5 to 10 years; furniture, fixtures, and automobiles—5 to 10 years.

Funds held in trusts The Company is the beneficiary of two trust funds. Contributions to the trusts are recorded as income as funds become available to the Company. Future distributions from the trusts must be deposited in the capital improvement fund (Note 3) and are security for the Ford Foundation note (Note 4).

Film rights Film rights are amortized over their expected usage of the rights and are net of accumulated amortization of $303,252 in 19X7 and $272,171 in 19X6.

2. Organization

The Company is a nonprofit corporation exempt from federal and state income taxes and it commenced broadcasting as Station KCET, Channel 28, on September 28, 1964. Under terms of grants from the Department of Health, Education and Welfare used to partially finance the Company's broadcasting equipment, the Company must comply with the Educational Television Facilities Act and certain other federal rules and regulations for a period of ten years from the date of the latest grant.

3. Capital Improvement Fund

During fiscal 19X3 the Company began a campaign to raise funds for its capital improvement program. This program included completion of the present studio and facilities, construction of a new office building and the retirement of all long-term debt. Contributions to the fund during the years ended June 30, 19X7 and 19X6 of $742,053 and $730,860, respectively, have been credited to net assets.

EXHIBIT 5 (Continued)

---

4. **Long-term Debt**

Long-term debt consists of the following at June 30:

	19X7	**19X6**
$7\frac{1}{2}$% note payable to the Ford Foundation	$ 900,603	$1,650,000
Note payable to Security Pacific National Bank	910,000	255,386
$7\frac{3}{4}$% note payable to bank, due $800 monthly (including interest) through July 19X0, secured by real property	19,449	27,209
$6\frac{1}{4}$% note payable to bank, due $442 monthly (including interest) through July 19X0, secured by real property	11,325	16,130
Note payable to Security Pacific National Bank	135,000	-
Other	-	2,722
	1,976,377	1,951,447
Less amounts due within one year	1,140,171	473,099
Long-term debt due after one year	$ 836,206	$1,478,348

The repayment terms of the Ford Foundation note, as amended, provide for minimum payments totaling $275,000 in fiscal 19X8 (including interest), with all remaining principal and interest due by December 31, 19X8. In addition to the minimum payments, all future contributions to the Capital Improvement Fund are to be applied proportionately to the principal balances of the Security Pacific National Bank note and The Ford Foundation note.

Under the Ford Foundation loan agreement, the Company has pledged all of its assets as security for the loan. The agreement prohibits the Company from selling substantial parts of its assets, acquiring other businesses, and further borrowings in excess of $250,000, except for the Security Pacific National Bank note.

During fiscal year 19X6, the Company entered into a $1,250,000 loan agreement with Security Pacific National Bank in connection with the construction of a new office building. The terms of the loan agreement provide for interest at one-half to three-fourths percent above prime rate. Principal payments are being made on a *pro rata* basis with the Ford Foundation note with minimum principal reductions of $710,000 in fiscal year 19X8 and $200,000 in fiscal year 19X9. The loan is secured on a *pro rata* basis with the Ford Foundation note by all the Company's assets, including the new office building.

During fiscal year 19X7, the Company entered into a $180,000 loan agreement with Security Pacific National Bank in connection with the installation of a telephone system in the new office building. The terms of the loan agreement provide for interest at one-half to three-fourths percent above prime rate. Principal payments are due $90,000 in fiscal 19X8 and $45,000 in fiscal 19X9. The note is secured on a pro rata basis with the Ford Foundation and Security Pacific construction loans by all the Company's assets.

EXHIBIT 5 (Continued)

5. Unexpended Grand Funds

During 19X4, the Company was awarded a $4,500,000 matching grant from the Ford Foundation. The Ford Foundation has released $3,599,397 of grant funds through June 30, 19X7, and the remaining $900,603 will be advanced only in amounts equal to the amount by which the principal of the note payable to the Ford Foundation is reduced below $900,603 (Note 4).

The Ford matching grant must be matched by obtaining an equal amount of contributions to the capital improvement fund (Note 3) by December 31, 19X8. However, up to $1,350,000 may be matched by certain other contributions and revenues. Through June 30, 19X7, the Company received matching contributions of $2,543,581 and met the conditions allowing the $1,350,000 of grant funds to be matched by certain other contributions and revenues. At June 30, 19X7, $606,419 of future matching contributions is required under the grant.

The Ford matching grant is to be utilized $3,750,000 for national programming and $750,000 for program development and working capital. Additional amounts of $546,000 on national programming remain to be utilized under the grant.

6. Lease Commitments

The Company leases its transmitter site and various equipment. The terms of these agreements require aggregate annual rental payments (net of transmitter site sublease revenues of $24,000 and $14,000 in 19X8 and 19X9, respectively) approximating $76,000 in 19X8, $73,000 in 19X9, $80,000 in 19Y0, $79,000 in 19Y1, and $30,000 a year through 19Y4, aggregating $398,000. Rent expense, which is reduced in both years by sublease revenues of $25,920, amounted to $86,572 in 19X7 and $55,899 in 19X6.

7. Refund of FICA Taxes

The Company is a nonprofit organization that is not required to participate in the Social Security program. The Company has elected to participate under the program for calendar year 19X6 and future years.

During fiscal year 19X6 the Company requested a refund of certain FICA taxes paid by the Company and its employees for calendar years 19X2 through 19X5. For those employees electing to participate in the claim, management requested a refund of taxes paid.

Refunds of $695,914 are included in grants and accounts receivable in 19X6. One-half of all sums to be refunded to the Company must be paid to the employees on whose behalf the request for a refund was made, and accordingly is included in accounts payable and accrued expenses at June 30, 19X6. Refunds aggregating $347,957 are included in interest and other income in fiscal year 19X6.

6 Unique Aspects of Accounting and Financial Analysis for Nonprofit Organizations

NONPROFIT ORGANIZATIONS' FINANCIAL STATEMENTS SHOULD ENABLE their readers to evaluate the following two issues:

(1) Were donated or restricted resources used in a manner consistent with the instructions of those who gave them?

(2) Is the organization financially stable in the sense that the inflow of financial resources is generally equal to or greater than the outflow?

Answering the first question requires *fund accounting* in nonprofit financial statements that tracks carefully how donated resources were used. The second question requires that all *resource inflows and outflows* be highlighted in a financial statement that focuses on financial stability. This statement's purpose differs from a for-profit organization's Income Statement. The latter focuses on the profitability of for-profit organizations, while the nonprofit statement focuses on the relationship between inflows and outflows. After all, the purpose of a nonprofit organization is to provide important goods and services, not to earn a profit. Its financial management must ensure that it is financially stable so that it can continue to fulfill its mission.

FUND ACCOUNTING

For-profit organizations acquire resources by selling goods or services, borrowing money, and selling their stock. These resources are usually not restricted; they may be used in any legal manner the management believes will generate a profit or otherwise benefit the organization and its owners. In contrast, the resources donated or granted to a nonprofit frequently are intended for the specific purposes to which the organization is devoted, such as cancer research or drug abuse treatment. Donors often further restrict the use of the resources to specific purposes (such as a pediatrics program), specific types of expenditures (such as a particular building or room), and even specific time periods (such as the current fiscal year). Thus, financial accounting systems must satisfy much more extensive *stewardship* requirements in nonprofit organizations than in for-profit organizations of comparable size.

To satisfy this stewardship purpose, nonprofit accounting entries are classified by *funds*. Each fund is like a cookie jar in which resources restricted for different purposes are stored. A fund is a separate accounting entity that records the sources and the uses of the resources it contains. Funds are separated from each other because their resources are restricted to certain specified purposes. The quantity of resources in each fund and its sources and uses are accounted for in the process called *fund accounting*.

The financial statements of many nonprofit organizations are currently presented by fund, as shown in Table 6-1. Although a financial statement that combines the separate funds may, at times, be used to depict the financial situation of the organization as a whole, most organizations also present a separate Balance Sheet for each fund and a separate Statement of Revenues, Expenses, and Changes in Fund Balance for each fund that earns revenues or incurs expenses.

The Statement of Changes in Fund Balance may be shown as a separate statement or may be combined with the Statement of Revenues and Expenses. In either case, it contains a summary of all the inflows and outflows that affected the fund balances during the accounting period. The fund balance or *net assets* account represents the cumulative net amount of resources, or the net worth, of a fund. It is the equivalent of the retained earnings portion of the owners equity section of a for-profit Balance Sheet. (Because nonprofit organizations have no owners, they lack the equivalent account on their Balance Sheet to the stock portion of the owners equity account in a for-profit organization.) In general, an organization should have only as many funds as are required by law and sound administration. An excessive number of funds results in inefficiency, undue complexity, and inflexibility.

History of Fund Accounting

Fund accounting has been traced as far back as the Roman Empire, which established a fund financed by road tolls. The fund's resources were to be devoted to the construction of walls that would protect the cities from invasions by barbarians. The use of fund accounting grew in England because Parliament wanted to check whether the monarchy was spending the resources it appropriated in the manner intended.[1]

[1]George Burton Adams, *Constitutional History of England* (New York, NY: Holt, Rinehart, and Winston, 1921), pp. 348-349.

TABLE 6-1 **Structure of Simple Fund Accounting Statements**

(These statements do not convey dollar magnitudes.)

Balance Sheet*
(Layered Format—Traditional)

Assets		*Liabilities and Fund Balance*	
		Fund A	
Assets	$ AA,AAA	Liabilities	$ AA,AAA
		Fund balance	$ AA,AAA
Total assets	$ AA,AAA	Total liabilities and fund balance	$ AA,AAA
		Fund B	
Assets	$ BB,BBB	Liabilities	$ BB,BBB
		Fund balance	$ BB,BBB
Total assets	$ BB,BBB	Total liabilities and fund balance	$ BB,BBB
		Funds A and B Combined	
Assets	$CC,CCC	Liabilities	$CC,CCC
		Fund balance	$CC,CCC
Total assets	$CC,CCC	Total liabilities and fund balance	$CC,CCC

Balance Sheet*
(Columnar Format—Proposed)

	Fund A	*Fund B*	*Funds A and B Combined*
Total assets	$ AA,AAA	$ BB,BBB	$CC,CCC
Total liabilities	AA,AAA	BB,BBB	CC,CCC
Net assets	AA,AAA	BB,BBB	CC,CCC
Total liabilities and net assets	$AAA,AAA	$BBB,BBB	$CC,CCC

Statement of Revenues and Expenses and Changes in Fund Balance
(or Statement of Changes in Net Assets)

	Fund A	*Fund B*	*Funds A and B Combined*
Revenues:	$ AA,AAA	$ BB,BBB	$CC,CCC
Expenses:	AA,AAA	BB,BBB	CC,CCC
Difference between revenues and expenses	A,AAA	B,BBB	C,CCC
Beginning fund balance	AA,AAA	BB,BBB	CC,CCC
Ending fund balance	$AAA,AAA	$BBB,BBB	$CC,CCC

*Only one of the alternative Balance Sheet formats would be presented.

The United States adopted the English system of fund accounting. Early discussion of "methods of keeping books of account" for schools, hospitals, or other charitable institutions stressed that "funds" designated for investment or other special purposes should not be co-mingled with those available for current operations. At that time, a fund was likely to require a separate cash box and a physically separate set of books.[2]

Today, only the accounting systems separate one fund from another. The addition of a fund code to the other accounting codes replaces the need to physically segregate resources.

Types of Funds

Funds are defined by the purposes for which they are intended. Funds containing resources for *current operating* purposes are distinguished from funds whose resources are part of the *permanent capital* of the organization and cannot be used in current operations. Permanent capital is further distinguished between resources to be permanently invested in income-generating assets and those to be invested in the fixed assets used by the organization. Other funds may contain resources held in trust or as an agent for an outsider.

Resources available for use in current operations are differentiated between those *restricted* by the donor to certain purposes and those that are *unrestricted* and may be used as the management of the organization chooses.

These types of funds are common to all types of nonprofit organizations, although additional types of funds are found in governmental units. Each type of fund is intended to serve a particular purpose. Different types of nonprofit organizations may use slightly different fund types because of the nature of their operations and their past accounting practices. The fund terminology should follow the definitions found in the appropriate standard setting documents (*Audit Guides* or *Statements of Position*). They will be discussed in detail in the chapters on specific organizations in Part Three. Nonprofit organizations differ among themselves in their nomenclature for funds. No matter what their title, all funds should enable readers to understand whether their resources are restricted or unrestricted and current or permanent.

Most nonprofit organizations have provisions for the use of general and restricted operating funds, agency funds, and other permanent funds, as illustrated for governmental units in Table 6-2. Governmental organizations were selected for this illustration because they use the most extensive set of fund types, some of them illustrated in Table 6-2.

---

[2]William Holmes, Linda H. Kistler, and Louis S. Corsini, *Three Centuries of Accounting in Massachusetts* (New York, NY: Arno Press, 1978).

TABLE 6-2 **Common Funds**

Current Funds

Unrestricted or General Funds—account for all resources not required to be accounted for by another fund

Restricted or Special Revenue Funds—account for the proceeds of specific revenue sources, usually those legally restricted to expenditures for specified operating purposes

Debt Service Funds**—account for the accumulation of resources and payments of principal and interest on long-term debt

Capital Projects Fund**—accounts for resources to acquire major capital facilities

Permanent Funds

Plant, Property, and Equipment Fund*—accounts for resources that are invested in plant, property, and equipment, and those reserved for acquiring or renovating plant, property, and equipment, and for payments of debt used to finance these activities

Endowment Funds—account for assets
    True endowment
    Term endowment

Trust and Agency Funds—account for resources the organization holds as an agent or trustee, has no fund balance, only assets and liabilities

Proprietary Funds

Enterprise Funds**—account for operations financed and operated similar to for-profit enterprises, whose operations are intended to be supported by user charges

Internal Service Funds**—account for goods provided by one department to other departments on a cost reimbursement basis

*In governmental accounting, this fund is separated into two groups: one for *General Fixed Assets* and the other for *Long-Term Debt.*

**Primarily used in governmental accounting; would be combined with another fund by private nonprofit organizations.

General, Current, or Unrestricted Operating Fund   The terms *General Fund, Unrestricted Current Operating Fund,* and *Unrestricted Current Fund* are used interchangeably to describe the fund that accounts for resources whose use is not restricted by law or by anyone outside the organization. Internal restrictions imposed by the board or management of an organization are not binding unless they constitute a legal restriction that cannot be reversed. Internally restricted resources remain part of the Current Unrestricted Fund and are usually disclosed as a designated or reserved portion of its fund balance.

The resources in this fund are used for and derived from the current, ongoing operations of the organization. The fund includes all resources that are not legally required to be separated or not significant enough to warrant creation of a special fund. Nonprofit organizations vary in the activities they include in this fund. For example, one town may account for libraries in a Special Revenue Fund because of legal requirements, while another may include the resources of its libraries in the General Fund.

Restricted Current Operating or Special Revenue Funds   The term *Restricted Current Operating Fund* (or an abbreviation thereof, frequently just *Restricted*) is found in most nonprofit organizations, while *Special Revenue Fund* is a term found almost exclusively in governmental organizations. In both cases, the fund accounts for resources restricted by law or contractual agreement to use for a specific, current operations purpose. These resources frequently are used in ways similar to those of the Current Unrestricted Fund resources. For example, in a college both funds typically pay for instruction or research. The distinguishing factor between them is that Special or Restricted Fund resources can be used only for the purposes to which they are restricted, while Current Unrestricted Fund resources may be applied to whatever organizational purposes the board and management specify.

Several such funds often are combined under one heading as Special or Restricted Funds in the financial statements. A supporting schedule showing the individual funds also may be presented in the general purpose financial statements and must typically be prepared for the person or organization that provided the resources.

Plant Fund   Also called the *Fixed Asset Fund* or the *Plant, Property, and Equipment Fund,* the *Plant Fund* may be used to account for three categories of resources:

(1) Resources invested in fixed assets.
(2) Resources not yet expended, but designated by an external party to acquire, renew, or replace fixed assets. (Resources set aside at the discretion of management are accounted for as a reserved portion of general fund balance until they actually are expended for fixed assets.)

(3) Resources legally required to be set aside for payment of principal (debt retirement) and interest (debt service) on debt used to finance acquisition of fixed assets.

Some institutions prepare Balance Sheets for each subgroup of the Plant Fund, some combine the three, and some combine the second and third subgroups and list the first separately.

The Plant Fund assets consist of the resources legally designated to finance fixed assets and the historical cost of the fixed assets themselves. The liabilities and fund balance of the Plant Fund account for the debt related to fixed assets and the fund balance in each, or all, of its subgroups. The resources in this fund originate from gifts, restricted fees and donations, and transfers from current funds.

In governmental organizations, the investment in fixed assets and its related long-term debt are contained in two separate entities referred to as *groups of accounts* instead of funds, called the *General Fixed Assets Account Group (GFAAG)* and the *General Long-Term Debt Account Group (GLTDAG)*. Resources acquired for the construction or acquisition of governmental fixed assets are accounted for in a *Capital Projects Fund*. After the assets are built or acquired, they are transferred from the Capital Projects Fund to the GFAAG.

Endowment and Similar Funds   The resources in *Endowment and Similar Funds* are permanently or temporarily restricted by their donors to investment that generates income. The assets of these funds cannot be consumed; they must remain intact. The amount that must remain intact is referred to as the endowment *principal*. It is invested in income-yielding assets, such as bonds, stocks, or real estate. The donor may specify the kinds of investments that may be made. Endowment Funds are also called *nonexpendable trust funds* in governmental organizations.

There are three categories of Endowment and Similar funds. The principal of *true endowment funds* has been designated by the donor to remain permanently intact for investment; the resulting income must also be used in the manner designated by the donor. The principal of *Term Endowment Funds* must remain invested for a fixed period, after which it can be used for other purposes designated by the donor. *Quasi-Endowment funds* or *funds functioning as endowment* are resources whose investment is designated by management and the board of directors, not by the original donor. All organizations, except colleges and universities, are now required to report these resources in the unrestricted current fund, usually as reserves for investment. In the past, managerially- or board-designated resources usually were combined with true Endowment Funds and may still be reported with Endowment Funds by colleges and universities. Nonprofit organizations with embarrassingly large operating surpluses are no longer able disguise this fact by transferring the extra resources to the Endowment Fund, except for colleges and universities. The distinction between externally restricted and internally reserved resources must be clearly disclosed.

The dividend, interest, rent, and royalty income (the *investment income* or *endowment income*) these assets generate must be used in the manner intended by the donor. Most endowment income is available for general operating purposes, although its use may be restricted by the donor, such as income from an endowment fund that may be used only for scholarships for children of Lithuanian farmers. At times, the income may not even be available for current operations. For example, some endowment income may be used only for buying new equipment. The income can also be restricted to the Endowment Fund for a specified period of time or until the endowment principal plus income reaches a certain size.

Agency, Annuity, and Life-Income Funds   *Agency Funds* are those in which the nonprofit organization acts as an agent for collecting, holding, and disbursing assets of others. These funds generally have liabilities to their donors rather than fund balances. *Annuity and Life-Income Funds* are resources received by an institution under an agreement in which the donors or the designated beneficiaries receive contracted payments from the institution during their lives, generally paid from the income generated by investing the assets or the principal. On the death of the donors or beneficiaries, or after a certain period of time, the resources become available for use by the organization in accordance with the donors' stated restrictions. At that time, the balance is transferred to the appropriate fund, i.e., Endowment, Plant, or Current Fund. Changes in the U.S. government income and estate tax laws affect this fund. For example, the tax law revisions in 1969 resulted in an increase of this kind of activity (referred to as deferred giving programs, pooled income funds, etc.).

Enterprise and Internal Service Funds   These proprietary funds are used in governments to account for resources generated and used for activities that are not central to the mission of the nonprofit organization. *Enterprise Funds* are intended to be self-supporting on the basis of their charges to users, and sometimes are expected to generate profits to support other parts of the organization. The most common example is a municipal-owned public utility. *Internal Service Funds* are similar, except that they sell their outputs internally, to other departments of the same organization; an example is a municipal garage that repairs vehicles owned by the municipality.

Because these funds are similar in purpose and operation to private businesses, accounting standards applicable to privately owned enterprises of the same type are recommended. For example, rather than a fund balance account, they have a retained earnings account as a business would have. Fixed assets and long-term debt and current assets and liabilities related to the business are accounted for within the Enterprise Fund. The governing body and laws of the entity determine which, if any, activities should be accounted for in an Enterprise Fund instead of a General or Restricted Current Operating Fund.

ACCOUNTING FOR RESOURCE FLOWS

Fund accounting enables outsiders to monitor the organization's fulfillment of its stewardship responsibilities. Reporting the flow of resources enables outsiders to evaluate the financial stability of the organization. Resource flows must be measured and reported for each individual fund.

Resource inflows occur for operating and nonoperating purposes. Most resource inflows result from operations and are reflected in the Statement of Revenues and Expenses. The most common *operating resource inflows* are fees for services rendered, contributions, membership fees, grants, and taxes. *Nonoperating resource inflows* include investment income, endowment gifts, capital campaign contributions, and the results of the gift shop or garage. Some are reflected in the Statement of Revenues and Expenses of the funds into which they flow, while others are treated as direct additions to the fund balance. The treatment of inflows varies among types of organizations and may depend on the individual organization's mission statement. Because proceeds of borrowing do not affect the fund balance, they are reflected only in the Balance Sheet and Statement of Cash Flows.

Resource outflows are recognized whenever an event that uses resources occurs, as when labor and materials are used in operations. All resource outflows must be accounted for in the financial statements, within the fund providing the resources.

Governmental organizations traditionally account for resource outflows as soon as a purchase order or a contract for the provision of future goods or services was signed, giving rise to an *encumbrance*. Resources are said to be *encumbered* when the organization makes the commitment to purchase goods or services. Most other nonprofit organizations, and most for-profit organizations, account for resource outflows at a later time, when a liability is incurred or a payment is made, whichever occurs earlier.

Encumbrance accounting presents a clear picture of the resources that remain available for use in the current period. It gained the force of law in many governments because it assigns responsibility for spending the taxpayers' money to the elected officials who commit to the expenditure, rather than to the ones who happen to be in office when the bills come due. Encumbrance accounting records all resource outflows to which the incumbent officials committed the organization. Comparable tracking functions are performed less formally by project management or purchase order systems within other organizations; these are not reported in the financial statements, but are used internally by management.

Resource Flows Among Funds

The existence of separate funds within the nonprofit organization requires the recognition of resource flows among them. Such flows may be *transfers* or *loans*. Every transfer and loan from one fund must be matched with equal transfers and borrowings from another fund or funds. Resource flows among funds must be accounted for as carefully as resource flows into or out of the organization.

Interfund transfers represent a permanent movement of the resources of one fund into another. Transfers may be *mandatory*, such as a bond covenant that requires the transfer of resources out of the Current Fund into a Debt Service Fund. *Non-mandatory* transfers occur when the management of the organization decides that resources held in one fund could be better used in another. The most frequent non-mandatory transfers move resources from the operating funds to the Plant Fund when fixed assets are purchased with operating fund resources.

Non-mandatory transfers are made at management's discretion and the transfer can be reversed. Mandatory transfers, in contrast, must be made and cannot be reversed. Increasingly, transactions once reflected as non-mandatory transfers must be accounted for as reserves of the general fund balance instead of interfund transfers, to reflect their discretionary and reversible nature. Interfund transfers are now primarily used for legally mandated transfers of resources among funds or for economic transactions that have taken place, such as the acquisition of fixed assets with current fund resources.

Interfund loans represent a temporary movement of resources from one fund to another. The lender fund receives an IOU from the borrowing fund, which it recognizes as an asset, a *receivable due from* the borrowing fund. The borrower fund recognizes its liability to repay the debt in a *payable due to* the lender fund. Such loans are not uncommon. For example, the Current Fund frequently provides a start-up loan to the Plant Fund when a construction project is begun. If the loans involved represent a substantial portion of the fund's resources or if they seem unlikely to be repaid, their existence may be a red flag of pending financial problems.

ILLUSTRATIVE FINANCIAL STATEMENTS[3]

All types of nonprofit organizations generally prepare a Balance Sheet and a Statement of Changes in Fund Balance for each fund, and some are required to prepare a Statement of Cash Flows or Changes in Financial Position for one or more funds. In addition, they prepare a Statement of Revenues, Expenses, and Changes in Fund Balance for any funds that had such activities during the year. These financial statements are discussed in the following paragraphs.

[3]I am very grateful to David Sherman, who, as my then-Research Assistant, prepared these statements and analyses—Regina Herzlinger.

Balance Sheet

In what follows, two versions of the Balance Sheet of Pepys College are compared to illustrate why fund accounting is important in nonprofit organizations. The for-profit financial statement format (Table 6-3), labeled the Combined Balance Sheet of Pepys College, is simple but misleading. It might lead to the erroneous conclusion that Pepys College is in a very strong financial position because it has

(1) Net worth of $9.85 million

(2) Nearly $3 of current assets for every $1 of current liabilities

(3) No intangible assets, and

(4) A small amount of debt that could easily be retired by liquidating some investments.

A more accurate and much less rosy picture is presented by the Balance Sheet prepared with fund accounting (Table 6-4). (Note that the numbers in the ensuing discussion, like those in the Balance Sheet, are rounded to the nearest thousand.)

(1) The Unrestricted Current Fund is seriously cash short, with current assets of $655 and current liabilities of $1,355. Its $700 fund balance deficit signals a problem. The $600 loan from the Plant Fund to the Unrestricted Current Fund may indicate that the Plant Fund

TABLE 6-3 **Pepys College—Combined Balance Sheet (For-Profit Format)**

PEPYS COLLEGE
Combined Balance Sheet at 19XX
(in thousands of dollars)

Assets		*Liabilities and Fund Balance*	
Cash	$ 515	Accounts payable	$ 55
Accounts receivable	160	Other liabilities	200
Other assets	30	Current liabilities	$ 255
Current assets	$ 705		
		Mortgage payable	500
Investments at market	5,600	Fund balance	9,850
Fixed assets	4,300	Total liabilities and	
Total assets	$10,605	fund balance	$10,605

TABLE 6-4 **Pepys College—Fund Accounting Balance Sheet**

PEPYS COLLEGE
Fund Accounting Balance Sheet at 19XX
(in thousands of dollars)

Unrestricted Current Fund

Cash	$ 465	Due to plant fund	$ 600
Accounts receivable	160	Due to restricted fund	500
Other assets	30	Accounts payable	55
Current assets	$ 655	Other liabilities	200
		Current liabilities	$1,355
		Fund balance	(700)
Total assets	$ 655	Total liabilities and fund balance	$ 655

Restricted Current Fund

Due from unrestricted fund	$ 500	Fund balance	$ 500
Total assets	$ 500	Total liabilities and fund balance	$ 500

Plant Funds

Due from unrestricted fund	$ 600	Mortgage payable	$ 500
		Unexpended fund balance	100
Fixed assets	4,300	Expended fund balance	4,300
Total assets	$4,900	Total liabilities and fund balance	$4,900

Endowment and Similar Funds

Cash	$ 50	Fund balance	
Investments at market	5,600	For restricted	$2,240
		For unrestricted	3,300
		Quasi-endowment	110
Total assets	$5,650	Total liabilities and fund balance	$5,650

mortgage was incurred to cover cash shortages in the Unrestricted Current Fund. It was not needed to finance land and buildings. The $500 loan from the Current Restricted Fund indicates that these assets were also borrowed to finance the deficit. One wonders if these loans can be repaid. The $500 of restricted gifts must be returned to the donor if they are not used for the designated purposes. If Pepys College were forced to return these restricted resources, it would be a candidate for bankruptcy. (Some argue that resource inflows of restricted resources should be classified as deferred revenue liabilities instead of fund balance, because they are not earned until they are used for the designated purpose. If their accounting were used, the Restricted Current Fund would have shown a $500 Liability, rather than a $500 Fund Balance.)

(2) The Endowment Fund cash of $50 is part of the Endowment Fund's income-earning investments, and is thus not available for meeting the unrestricted current fund's need for working capital. The Endowment Fund investments cannot be liquidated except for the $110 of quasi-endowment, which the institution added to endowment to provide investment income for operating purposes. This would be more appropriately accounted for as a reserved portion of the Unrestricted Current Fund balance, although many organizations continue to account for quasi-endowments in the Endowment Fund. If this amount were spent, however, it would eliminate some of the endowment income that is currently being provided to support operations.

(3) Although Plant Fund assets potentially could be sold, that would impair the organization's ability to operate. Also, plant resources may not be available for such purposes because of restrictions on them. The organization has received a $100 gift restricted for additions to plant, as indicated by the unexpended plant fund balance of that amount. Resources that management set aside from current operating funds for addition to or replacement of plant would be shown as a reserve of fund balance in the Unrestricted Current Fund. It is questionable whether the unexpended fund balance of $100 is sufficient to maintain the plant assets at the level needed to support operations.

The fund accounting indicates that the true financial status of Pepys College is substantially weaker than that disclosed by a single combined Balance Sheet. The combined fund balance of $9,850 masks the fact that $10,440 of the fund balance is restricted ($500 restricted current fund + $4,400 plant fund + $5,540 endowment fund). The unrestricted fund balance is in a deficit position of $590 ($110 quasi-endowment − $700 unrestricted current fund). Pepys College has used $590 of future resources to pay for its present operations. How long can it keep this up? Although the restrictions on assets and fund balances probably would be disclosed in elaborate footnotes to the combined financial statements, footnotes are generally not read as carefully as the financial statements themselves. Fund accounting incorporates these important revelations into the body of the statements.

Statement of Revenues, Expenses, and Other Changes in Fund Balance

The portion of the Statement of Revenues, Expenses, and Changes in Fund Balance that accounts for operating activities is analogous to the profit organization's Income Statement. The Statement of Changes in Fund Balance accounts for transfers among funds and for direct additions to and deductions from the fund balance. It reflects net resource flows from revenues and expenditures, as well as all mandatory and discretionary transfers of capital among funds. It can be presented either as a separate statement or combined with the Statement of Revenues and Expenses, with the choice of treatment governed by organizational preferences, consistency, and space constraints. It is analogous to a Statement of Changes in Retained Earnings.

The Pepys College Statement of Revenues, Expenses, and Changes in Fund Balance shown in Table 6-5 can raise several questions for its reader. Again, the numbers here are in thousands of dollars.

Current Fund—Unrestricted   This statement tells us that Pepys College had current unrestricted expenses of $19,353 in the past fiscal year, which exceeded the total support of $18,643 by $710. The organization's management elected to transfer $26 to the Plant Fund, which either reflects their judgments about the need to maintain the plant at a certain level or is required by the mortgage. The net effect of these activities was to reduce the Unrestricted Current Fund balance by $736, from a small surplus of $36 to a large deficit of $700.

The questions generally raised about the Current Unrestricted Funds are:

- Do operating revenues cover operating expenses and mandatory transfers?
- Are non-mandatory transfers justified?
- Are transfers for the replenishment of fixed assets covered by operating revenues?
- Are "soft" unstable revenues, such as government grants, matched with variable, "soft" expenses, such as temporary employees?

Current Fund—Restricted   The Current Restricted Fund received $700 of contributions, $83 of investment income and $53 of grants, but expended only $243 for student aid and $100 for education. Its fund balance increase, from a very small $7 to a substantial $500, raises several questions. Could some of the unrestricted expenditures have been covered by restricted funds? Or did Pepys delay spending for restricted purposes because it had transferred the money to cover unrestricted expenses? Must the restricted resources be returned to the donor if they are not spent for the specified purpose within a certain period of time? Does Pepys manage the Current Restricted Fund with any set policy?

General questions about this fund include:

- Do excessive constraints on development policies or other factors result in too few restricted gifts?

TABLE 6-5 **Pepys College Statement of Revenues and Expenses**

Pepys College—Fund Accounting
Statement of Revenues, Expenses, and Other Changes in Fund Balance
For the Year Ended June 30, 19XX
(in thousands of dollars)

	Current Unrestricted	Restricted	Plant	Endowment	Total
Revenues and other support:					
Tuition	$15,970				$15,970
Contributions	2,547	$700	$ 100		3,347
Investment income	126	83			209
Grants		53			53
Total support	$18,643	$836	$ 100		$19,579
Expenses:					
Education	$17,254	$100	$ 201		$17,555
Student aid	23	243			266
Auxiliary enterprise	2,065		45		2,110
Other	11				11
Total expenses	$19,353	$343	$ 246		$19,942
Excess of support over expenses	$ (710)	$493	$ (146)		$ (363)
Transfers in (out):					
Plant renewal	(26)		26		
Total transfers	$ (26)		$ 26		
Net increase/decrease for the year	$ (736)	$493	$ (120)		$ (363)
Beginning fund balance	36	7	4,520	$5,650	10,213
Ending fund balance	$ (700)	$500	$4,400	$5,650	$ 9,850

- Are restricted funds being used to finance current operating expenditures that would be financed by the Current Unrestricted Fund if restricted funds were not available?

- May restricted funds be used to finance current unrestricted expenditures?

- What policies determine the use of restricted current funds?

Plant Funds These funds increased by the $100 of contributions and the $26 transferred from the Current Unrestricted Fund. However, they decreased by $246, an amount $120 greater than the increases provided. One can question whether the amount transferred from Current Unrestricted Funds is an adequate addition to the Plant Funds. An important related issue is whether the prices charged for the services rendered by the Current Fund adequately cover the wear and tear on plant assets. These questions must be answered in light of the institution's ability to generate Plant Fund gifts when major additions are required in the future. If their replenishment cannot be funded by capital fund drives, the current fund transfer is, in effect, a provision for depreciation or replacement of plant, and pricing decisions must take that into account.

Endowment Funds   There were no new contributions to endowment, the endowment principal did not appreciate, and the investments generated only $209 of income, an unimpressive 3.8 percent rate of return ($209 ÷ $5,650). This combination of factors may indicate that the fund's assets are tied up in low yield, long-term interest bearing assets and lead one to question how well the endowment resources are invested, and whether the development office is devoting sufficient effort to generating new endowment gifts.

General questions that arise with respect to endowments are:

- Is the principal growing fast enough to assure that the endowment income will keep pace with inflation?
- Are contributions being solicited primarily to cover current financial requirements at the cost of receiving endowment gifts or *vice versa*?
- To what extent are increases in endowment internally designated?
- What is the nature of restrictions on income generated by endowment investments?

Total, All Funds   The amounts in the Total column reflect the total flow of financial resources to and from the organization. It is a useful summary of the effects of the activities of the various funds. The net interfund transfers are always eliminated because they represent flows among the different funds within the entity. Although the net decrease of $363 in the total fund balance is a red flag of problems, additional information about the individual funds is needed to evaluate the financial management of the institution. With disclosure of the individual funds and the organization totals, this statement permits the educated user to understand the mix of resources that flow into the institution, the magnitude of resources added to or depleted from the capital base of the institution during the year, and how restricted fund expenditures are used. Both the detail of the individual fund statements and the overall picture provided by the Total column are important.

CONTROVERSIAL ITEMS IN ACCOUNTING FOR NONPROFIT ORGANIZATIONS

Many aspects of nonprofit accounting are unresolved and controversial. The issues surrounding general financial statements form and content, the accounting treatment of funds, depreciation, endowment income, and donated goods and services will be addressed in the following paragraphs.

Financial Statement Form and Content

The different accounting practices among nonprofit organizations stem from differences in their purposes and activities, from the plethora of players involved in setting accounting standards in the past, and from their development for different types of organizations at different times. Recently, within any one type of nonprofit organization, various groups are likely to be working together to develop a common set of standards. Though this new-found harmony has led to more consistent accounting standards within a type of organization, such as private colleges, it has not affected the differences in accounting among different types of nonprofit organizations, such as colleges and governments. (The major players in the nonprofit accounting standards arena were introduced in Chapter 2.) For example, only voluntary health and welfare organizations must produce a Statement of Functional Expenses that shows the magnitude of each type of expense by program. Not all organizations are required to provide Statements of Cash Flow or Changes in Financial Position. Definitions of fund groups, levels of aggregation, and statement form also differ widely among organizations.

Because current financial reporting standards provide inconsistent recommendations for displaying financial information in general purpose external financial statements of nonprofit organizations, the FASB undertook the project that led to the issuance in August 1989 of its *Invitation to Comment, Financial Reporting by Not-for-Profit Organizations: Form and Content of Financial Statements*.[4] The statement is likely to lead to much more consistent financial reporting among nonprofit organizations than presently exists. However, until it is issued, current standards remain in force.

The FASB document recommends a Balance Sheet, Statement of Changes in Net Assets, Statement of Cash Flows, and notes to the financial statements. [para. 22] (The Statement of Changes in Net Assets is an operating statement, currently referred to as a Statement of Revenues, Expenses, and Changes

---

[4]Financial Accounting Standards Board, *Invitation to Comment, Financial Reporting by Not-for-Profit Organizations: Form and Content of Financial Statements* (Stamford, CT: August 29, 1989, NO.084-B).

in Fund Balance.) A Statement of Functional Expenses would not be required, but rather presented as supplementary information, if an organization chooses to provide it. Comparative statements are encouraged but not required.

The FASB's proposed Balance Sheet would present a single total column for assets, liabilities, and net assets with optional disaggregation by net asset class, managed fund group, or segment. If presented, the disaggregated statement would be in columnar format, and the basis for disaggregation disclosed. [para. 111] Net assets would be classified as unrestricted, temporarily restricted, and permanently restricted in the Balance Sheet, with disclosure of the nature and amount of restrictions on net assets. If an organization does not maintain the asset composition needed to meet donor restrictions, the amounts and circumstances should be disclosed. [para. 115]

At a minimum, the Statement of Changes in Net Assets would include the components of revenues, expenses, gains, and losses classified by class of net assets (unrestricted, temporarily restricted, and permanently restricted). The changes in net assets, reclassification of net assets, and the beginning and ending balances of net assets would be shown by class either in the Statement of Net Assets or in a separate reconciling statement. [para. 225]

Its Statement of Cash Flows would be classified by operating, capital, financing, and investing activities. Single column presentation is encouraged; if disaggregated, it should be on the same basis as the Statement of Changes in Net Assets, and a Total column should be shown. The direct method of presentation should be used. [para. 268-269]

The *Invitation to Comment* will be subject to the FASB exposure and deliberation process before it becomes a standard. Many of its recommendations are likely to be adopted, while others will be modified, dropped, or added. This deliberate standard setting process, in which all constituencies can voice their opinions and concerns, has contributed greatly to the development of acceptable standards. Other matters, related to recognition and measurement, are not addressed in this Invitation, but are being addressed by the FASB project on accounting issues for nonprofit organizations and by other FASB projects.

Fund Accounting

The value of fund accounting has long been questioned. Although some argue that fund accounting is confusing and obfuscating, many others, including the senior author of this book, find fund accounting essential for nonprofit accounting and even urge its adoption in business organizations.[5] The current trend is toward a summarized version of fund accounting for

---

[5]Regina E. Herzlinger and David H. Sherman, ''Advantages of Fund Accounting in Nonprofits,'' *Harvard Business Review* (May-June 1980): 94-105.

reporting on the stewardship aspects of management performance, with resources classified as unrestricted, temporarily restricted, and permanently restricted. Additional fund detail reporting is optional. The accounting standard setters carefully state that they are addressing only the financial reporting issues, not the underlying accounting system, which they explicitly recognize will require much more detail both for legal compliance and management purposes.

Depreciation Accounting

Depreciation has been one of the most hotly debated issues in nonprofit accounting, and was the focus of a FASB/GASB jurisdictional dispute. The FASB's SFAS 93 and 99 require nonprofit organizations to recognize the cost of consuming long-lived tangible assets, through depreciation, in their general purpose financial statements. These standards took effect for fiscal years beginning on or after January 1990. Governmental organizations, however, recognize depreciation expense only in their business-like activities (proprietary funds), such as Enterprise Funds.

The arguments against recognition of depreciation were succinctly stated by the National Committee on Municipal Accounting in 1936:

> There seems to be little occasion for recognizing in the general accounting records the depreciation of general municipal buildings and equipment. The reasons are:
>
> 1. It is not necessary to know the depreciated or replacement values of municipal properties, since property values cannot be used as a basis for credit.
>
> 2. Since the municipality as a whole is concerned with operating profit or loss only in the case of utilities and other self-supporting activities, it is not necessary to account for depreciation in the general accounts.
>
> 3. If depreciation is accounted for, the depreciation reserve has no importance unless a cash fund of an equal amount is set aside to replace worn-out properties. This is usually impractical, where not illegal.[6]

The opposite case is made by Emerson O. Henke:

> Given a stable price level or appropriate adjustments to compensate for its instability, the distinction between capital and revenue expenditures and the related recording of depreciation can help to disclose the following:
>
> 1. The fees to be charged where all or a portion of depreciation is to be recovered in such fees;

[6]National Committee on Municipal Accounting, *Municipal Accounting Statements*, Bulletin No. 6 (Chicago, IL: Municipal Finance Officers Association, 1936), p. 119.

2. The full costs of operations;

3. The full costs by functions on a basis that will facilitate inter-entity comparisons;

4. The amount of resources available to the entity at a particular instant of time and the changes in those resources over a period of time;

5. The extent of maintenance or erosion of invested capital.[7]

Other critics argue that depreciation based on historical cost cannot be a useful measure for nonprofit organizations. First, it accounts for a managerially irrelevant number—the past costs of acquiring existing assets—rather than the market value of assets or the costs of replacing assets as they wear out. If fees are set to cover "costs," these critics contend, current users should pay the cost of replacing the assets they consumed regardless of what such assets originally cost. Depreciation based on historical cost does not measure current "plant preservation" costs. It also does not address the cash flow issues of *funding* (accountingese for providing money) plant replacement expenditures and does not provide a basis for treating separately those classes of plant assets, such as buildings, that were originally donated and will probably be donated again when they wear out.

Overall, these critics contend that depreciation accounting is retrospective in orientation and needs to be replaced with a prospective cost concept for "plant preservation." A prospective cost approach would charge current operations for the cost of maintaining the plant in its current condition. It would distinguish between assets to be replaced out of general funds and those to be replaced by donations or special appropriations. Their thinking is consistent with the "current cost" or "inflation" accounting approaches we discussed in Chapter 5.

This approach recommends that the cost of plant assets whose replacement is financed by operating revenues be charged as an operating expense during the years the assets are consumed. The accounting procedure to accomplish this purpose involves calculating the average amount that should be set aside each year in order to provide sufficient money for the replacement of operating equipment. Once the required average annual expenditure is calculated, this amount would be charged against operations as the *provision for plant replacement, renewal, and special maintenance*. A corresponding amount of cash would be set aside within the Unexpended Plant Fund and invested to earn interest until replacement or renewal expenditures are required or a liability for that amount would be recognized.

SFAS 93 and 99 do not debate depreciation, except to note that it has long been required in business and some nonprofit financial statements. They state unequivocally that it will now be required under GAAP of all nonprofit

---

[7]Emerson O. Henke, "Accounting for Nonprofit Organizations: An Exploratory Study," *Indiana Business Information Bulletin No. 53* (Bureau of Business Research, Graduate School of Business, Indiana University, 1965), p. 49.

organizations that follow FASB standards. This change affects primarily colleges and universities and religious institutions. Works of art or historical treasures are excluded from depreciation.

Many interested parties still resist the requirement to depreciate. There is widespread recognition that information other than historical cost based depreciation is needed for many operating decisions, such as fee setting.

Jurisdiction of Standard Setters

The existence of both private and government-operated colleges and hospitals has led to a jurisdictional dispute between the GASB and the FASB. The Financial Accounting Foundation, which oversees both boards, has decided that the GASB has jurisdiction over all government operated institutions. As a result, hospitals and higher education institutions may employ different accounting standards, depending on whether they are private or government operated. With fiscal years beginning on or after January 1, 1990, nonprofit organizations that fell under the FASB's jurisdiction were required to depreciate fixed assets; those that fall under GASB jurisdiction were not.[8]

Measuring and Allocating Income from Endowment Funds

Endowment Funds create two accounting problems: how to allocate the total endowment income to different funds and how to measure endowment income. The latter remains a controversial issue, while the issue of accounting for the share of income earned by different endowment funds is more easily resolved.

Allocating Income from Endowment Funds   Although endowment resources designated for different purposes are accounted for in separate funds, they typically are invested in a single pool of financial instruments, such as stocks, bonds, and interest bearing accounts. The investment income from the endowment pool must be allocated among the different funds based on their relative share of the endowment capital amount. This investment policy thus creates a problem in accounting for the endowment income earned by each fund.

The *unit method*, widely adopted since the mid 1960s, distributes income, gains, and losses to funds based on their market value, rather than their *book value* (accountingese for the value of the investments when first donated). Basing distributions on book value allocates disproportionately more income to recent endowments than to older endowments whose investments have

---

[8]Financial Accounting Standards Board, Statement of Financial Accounting Standards No. 93, *Recognition of Depreciation by Not-for-Profit Organizations*, August 1987; and Financial Accounting Standards Board, Statement of Financial Accounting Standards No. 99, *Deferral of the Effective Date of Recognition of Depreciation by Not-for-Profit Organizations*, September 1988.

increased in market value since they were made. Because the book value method ignores the appreciated value of the older investments, its effect is to distribute income earned by the old fund to the new fund.[9] This inequity is illustrated in the example below:

Example

	Portfolio Value				Investment Income			
		Book		Market		Book		Market
Old Fund	$(\frac{2}{3})$	$20,000	$(\frac{4}{5})$	$40,000	$(\frac{2}{3})$	$5,000	$(\frac{4}{5})$	$6,000
New Fund	$(\frac{1}{3})$	10,000	$(\frac{1}{5})$	10,000	$(\frac{1}{3})$	2,500	$(\frac{1}{5})$	1,500
		$30,000		$50,000		$7,500		$7,500

Long ago, the initial $20,000 was received for the endowment fund. Years later, a new gift of $10,000, the income of which is restricted for different purposes from the original endowment, is received. It is added to the existing investments to create a pool of investments with a cost or book value of $30,000. The old endowment is worth $\frac{2}{3}$ of the book value ($20,000 ÷ $30,000). However, the original investments have appreciated to $40,000 by this time, so after the new money is added, the market value of the investments is $50,000. The old endowment is worth $\frac{4}{5}$ of the market value ($40,000 ÷ $50,000).

If the investments earned $7,500 of dividend and interest income in the following year, under the unit method the income would be distributed based on market values. The old fund would be allocated $6,000 [$(\frac{4}{5})$($7,500)] and the new one would be allocated $1,500 [$(\frac{1}{5})$($7,500)]. Under the book value method, the income distribution would be based on the relationship of income to book value. The old gift would be allocated $5,000 [$(\frac{2}{3})$($7,500)] and the new gift would be allocated $2,500 [$(\frac{1}{3})$($7,500)].

The unit method was adopted by many institutions with investments acquired long ago. Because the effort required to adopt the unit method retroactively would have been overwhelming, the institutions selected a recent date to convert to the unit method. Although this solution did not correct past inequities, it did assure that funds were fairly treated from that point onward.

Measuring the Income from Endowments   Until the 1960s, most endowment funds were invested in assets that provided a good cash yield in the form of dividends from stocks, interest from bonds, royalties from donated books and patents, and rents. In the 1960s, the stock market for certain equities grew rapidly in value. During this time, many nonprofit

---

[9]See William L. Cary and Craig B. Bright in *The Law and the Lore of Endowment Funds*, rev. ed. (New York, NY: Ford Foundation, 1974).

organizations were expanding in response to the changing needs of society, and these new ventures needed financing. Thus, private nonprofits saw these equities as a golden investment opportunity to meet their strong need for new sources of financing.

Securities whose value was appreciating most rapidly—called *growth stocks*—usually paid lower dividend rates than securities with lower appreciation rates. Standard accounting procedures recognized as endowment income only dividends, interest, rents and royalties, and gains and losses realized on sales of securities. Managers who invested in growth stocks to increase the long-term value of their endowments faced the prospect of a decreased present income under these accounting procedures.

The concept called *total return* was devised to enable them to account for income derived from the increase in value of growth stocks. (Its most eloquent proponents were W.L. Cary and C.B. Bright, who publicized it under the auspices of the Ford Foundation.)[10] The total return concept defined income from endowments as consisting of changes in the market value of the equities, as well as their cash dividend payments. The advocates of this concept argued that as long as the *corpus* of the endowment was maintained at its inflation-adjusted level, the legal requirements for the maintenance of principal were fulfilled. Any excess between the market value of the principal and its inflation-adjusted value could be considered to be part of the income generated by the endowment. For example, if an endowment was received a year ago at a value of $100, and inflation grew by 10 percent during the course of the year, the inflation-adjusted end-of-year value of the endowment should be $110. If the actual market end-of-year value is $115, the $5 difference between the market and the inflation-adjusted value can be considered as income.

Transition from a cash-yield concept of endowment management to a total return concept required a number of changes. First, the concept required legal sanction. It came from the Uniform Management of Institutional Funds Act, which has served as the pattern for such legislation in most states. Next came the problem of managing a portfolio to achieve a maximum total return. For most endowment funds, this required investing a greater fraction of their assets in equities. Their heavier participation in the equity market usually meant that the homegrown board of trustees variety of investment managers were replaced with outside professionals, which in turn required the board to better articulate its policies for investment management. Specifically, the board had to consider the following:

(1) The risks it was willing to take in order to earn higher rates of return. In general, in an expanding market, the higher the risk taken, the bigger the returns. But this relationship is reversed in a declining stock market.

---

[10]Cary and Bright, *Law and Lore of Endowment Funds.*

(2) Its assessment of the long-run inflation rate.

(3) Given the expected return from the endowment (from 1 above) and the expected inflation rate (from 2 above), the board had to stipulate the *spending rule*—the amount of endowment principal it was willing to spend for current operating purposes.

A frequent spending rule was that 5 percent of a three-or-five year moving average of the market value of the endowment portfolio would be considered its total return. If cash yields amounted, for example, to only 2 percent of this market value, the remaining 3 percent would be realized by the sale of Endowment Fund equity assets.

The accounting profession was reluctant to accept the total return concept. The *Audit Guides* limit recognition of endowment income to earnings from dividends, interest, royalties, and rents. The fraction of the total return realized through the sale of endowment assets—the 3 percent in our example above—is accounted for as a *transfer*, not as a *revenue*. The accounting distinction is that transfers are diminutions of capital in the donor funds, while revenues are additions to capital. This accounting position raised a furor among total return advocates.

The initial wave of enthusiasm over the concept of total return faltered with the stock market in the 1970s. A number of endowed institutions retracted from their whole-hearted support of the concept. The reasons for this retrenchment are vividly illustrated in Figure 6-1, which shows the history of endowment earnings in this period of time for college and university endowments. Note that endowment earnings were negative in the period mid-1972 to mid-1974, and at zero in years 1982, 1984, and 1988. The portfolios of the endowment funds are generally more risk-averse than the Dow-Jones or Standard and Poor's average of stock market performance. Therefore, endowment funds will not fare as well as the market as a whole in a growing market, (1973-1976 for example, and 1985-1987 in Figure 6-1) nor will they drop as much as the market as a whole in a declining market (see 1976-1979 and 1987-1988). The furor regarding the accounting treatment of total return revenues is likely to continue to heat up and cool down with the stock market.

By 1988, the total return concept was legalized in most states. Most organizations used a spending rule that was more conservative than spending all of the total return, but not necessarily limited to spending interest and dividends. Many endowed institutions have become more sophisticated investors, and have articulated investment and spending policies more thoroughly as a result of the experiences in the 1970s and 1980s.

Valuing Donated Goods and Services

Donated goods and services provide a substantial fraction of the resources of some nonprofit organizations. Donated services are most prevalent in voluntary health and welfare organizations and other nonprofits that rely

FIGURE 6-1 **Endowment Earnings Compared to Stock Market**

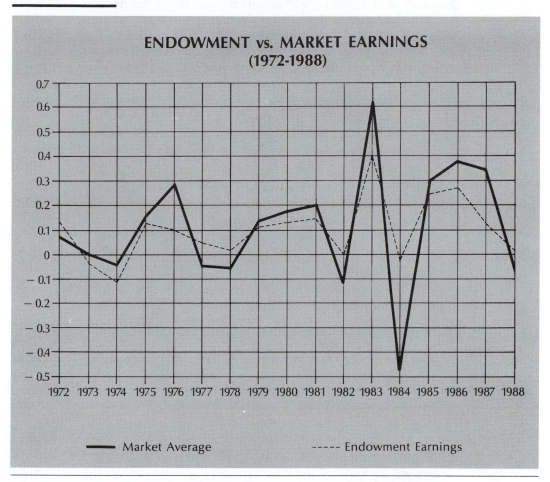

ENDOWMENT vs. MARKET EARNINGS
(1972-1988)

—— Market Average   ----- Endowment Earnings

Source: 1972-78, D. Kent Halstead, NACUBO; 1979-88, *NACUBO Endowment Study* (Boston, MA: Cambridge Associates, 1988).

heavily on volunteers, while donated goods are of importance to museums and cultural institutions that rely on donated art objects. Most observers agree that these resources should be accounted for as donated revenues and corresponding expenses, to reflect more accurately the level of resources obtained and used by the organization. The unresolved accounting question is when and how to value these resources.

Obtaining objective market values for donated resources, such as the value of Mr. Smith's time when he functions as a Boy Scout troop leader or the portrait of Uncle Ben donated to the Metropolitan Museum of Art, is frequently difficult. Some managers find volunteers difficult to manage and lacking the qualifications of salaried persons fulfilling the same jobs. To them, it is unclear that the volunteered resources have any value.

The Statement of Position for Certain Nonprofit Organizations cites the following standards for volunteers whose time should be valued.[11] These standards are representative of the current approach to valuing donated services, although standards differ somewhat for other types of organizations.

(1) The services performed are significant and essential to the organization and would be performed by salaried personnel if volunteers were not available for the organization to accomplish its purpose and the organization would continue this program or activity if volunteers were not available.

(2) The organization controls the employment and duties of the donors of the services. The organization is able to influence the activities of the volunteers in a way comparable to the control it would exercise over employees with similar responsibilities. That includes control over the time, location, duties, and performance of the volunteers.

(3) The organization has a clearly measurable basis for the amount to be recorded.

(4) The program services of the reporting organization are not principally intended for the benefits of the organization's members. Contributed services would not normally be recorded by membership organizations, such as professional and trade associations, labor unions, political parties, fraternal organizations, and social and country clubs.

The "fair" value of donated goods is also open to question. The most frequently used method of valuing goods is to employ an appraiser who will determine the value of the property. IRS challenges to taxpayers' claims of the value of donated goods are not infrequent. These challenges are argued by the IRS and the donor before the Tax Court. The Tax Court tends to rely heavily on the testimonies of expert witnesses and appraisers regarding valuation claims.[12]

[11]American Institute of Certified Public Accountants, Accounting Standards Executive Committee, *Proposed Statement of Position on Accounting Principles and Reporting Practices for Nonprofit Organizations Not Covered by Existing AICPA Audit Guides* (New York, NY: AICPA, December 1978). See also, *Audits of Voluntary Health and Welfare Organizations* (New York, NY: AICPA, 1974).

[12]Ted D. Englebrecht and Robert W. Jamison, Jr., "An Empirical Inquiry into the Role of the Tax Court in the Valuation of Property for Charitable Contreibution Purposes," *The Accounting Review* LIV, 3 (July 1979): 554-562.

SUMMARY

Accounting for nonprofit organizations is both similar to and different from accounting for for-profit organizations. The basic financial statements and the accounting conventions, such as accrual accounting, are similar. But the different legal and social environments of nonprofit organizations lead to the unique accounting requirements of fund and resource flow accounting. Financial analysis, too, differs in nonprofit accounting because nonprofit organizations obtain and must use financial resources in ways different from for-profit organizations.

DISCUSSION QUESTIONS

1. Define the following terms: fund accounting, stewardship, and flow of resources.

2. What are the purposes of accounting for nonprofit organizations and what are the primary unresolved controversies surrounding nonprofit accounting?

3. List and define the funds used in accounting for nonprofit organizations.

4. What does the account "due from plant fund" mean, when it is listed in the Current Fund?

5. What is an interfund transfer?

6. What is an encumbrance? When and why is it recognized in the accounting statements?

7. What are the controversial issues in accounting for depreciation in nonprofit organizations? How do you think they should be resolved?

8. What is an Endowment Fund?

9. What is the unit method for accounting for income in the Endowment Fund?

10. Define the total return policy. Under what circumstances would you recommend that it be used?

11. Classify the following events into the appropriate funds and accounts.
    a. You donated your time as a guide in the local museum.
    b. The college's building was depreciated in value.
    c. You gave a local hospital a donation and specified that it be used only for cancer patients.
    d. The nonprofit organization borrowed money from the Endowment Fund to finance its current operations.
    e. A nonprofit hospital received a $1 million grant to research diabetes.
    f. The hospital referred to in 11(e) spent $500,000 on diabetes research.

EXERCISES

1. Analyze the Omaha Rouse College Statement of Revenues, Expenses, and Changes in Fund Balances shown below.

Rouse College
Statement of Revenues, Expenses, and Changes in Fund Balances
For the Year Ended June 30, 19X8

	Current Funds			Endowment and Similar Funds
	Unrestricted	Restricted	Plant Fund	Funds
Revenue and other additions:				
Student income	$13,072,013			
Investment income	1,675,911	$3,083,477		
Gifts	2,128,592	895,255	$ 3,779,267	$ 1,000,000
Realized gains on investments				845,990
Grants	48,534	515,639		
Other income	931,400	70,416		
Total revenue and other additions	17,856,450	4,564,787	3,779,267	1,845,990
Expenses and other deductions:				
Educational and general	14,123,394	2,603,866	1,723,879	
Student aid	18,328	1,826,936		
Auxiliary enterprises	4,340,643	21,503	570,213	
Other deductions	70,488	112,482		
Total expenses and other deductions	18,552,853	4,564,787	2,294,092	
Interfund Transfers:				
Use of appreciation—total return	433,613	1,142,192		(1,575,805)
Transfers from/to plant	18,509	(109,722)	91,213	
Total transfers	452,122	1,032,470	91,213	(1,575,805)
Net increase/decrease for year	(244,281)	1,032,470	1,576,388	270,185
Beginning balance, July 1, 19X7	1,458,496	3,216,797	37,129,878	35,698,475
Ending balance, June 30, 19X8	$ 1,214,215	$4,249,267	$38,706,266	$35,968,660

2. Analyze the Statement of Revenues, Expenses, and Changes in Fund Balances of the New Orleans George College shown below:

George College
Statement of Revenues, Expenses, and Changes in Fund Balances
For the Year Just Ended
(in thousands of dollars)

	Current Unrestricted	Restricted	Plant	Endowment	Total
Revenues and other support:					
Tuition	$200				$ 200
Gifts	300		$ 100		400
Grants	10				10
Realized gains and losses				$ 70	70
Investment income	50	$30			80
Total revenues	560	30	100	70	760
Expenses:					
Education	150				150
Administrative	30				30
Utility and maintenance	30				30
Scholarships		10			10
Other	10				10
Total expenses	220	10			230
Excess of revenues over expenses	340	20	100	70	530
Transfers among funds:					
Non-mandatory:					
Purchases of plant	(40)		40		
Use of endowment gains	34	3		(37)	
Mandatory:					
Provision for debt retirement	(50)		50		
Total transfers	(56)	3	90	(37)	
Net change in fund balance	284	23	190	33	530
Beginning fund balance	(309)	28	6,213	2,617	8,549
Ending fund balance	$ (25)	$51	$6,403	$2,650	$9,079

CASE STUDY

This real-life case study is the first to introduce you to fund accounting statements. Evaluate them to assess the financial condition of the Girl Scout council it depicts. What answers do they provide for the four questions discussed in Chapter 5?

CASE 6.1 Guilford County Girl Scout Council

The Girl Scout Council of Guilford County was one of the best in the country, in membership, achievement, and financial situation. Two years ago, it served over 30,000 girls, or one out of every six girls of eligible age in the county, and over 8,000 adults. The council had many special projects for girls in disadvantaged areas as well as innovative programs in adult education for its volunteers; programs in arts, physical education, the outdoors, interpersonal behavior, science, and careers for its girls; and an early childhood program for girls younger than Brownies. These programs were recognized and emulated by other Girl Scout councils.

The financial position of the council was noteworthy as well. It ended the last fiscal year with total current unrestricted fund assets of $1,581,570, a substantial increase from the prior four year level of $266,000. In addition, over that period of time, it had accumulated an endowment fund with assets of $517,721. (See **Exhibits 1** through **4** for the financial statements.)

When asked how she had achieved these results, Executive Director, Georgie Black, a forthright and aggressive woman, replied:

> When I came here, I changed a number of things. First, I went out to recruit the best people for our Board. People, not women. Our Treasurer and the Chairperson of our Finance Committee are both experts in financial management. They are also male, as are other members of my Board.

This case was prepared by Professor Regina E. Herzlinger. It is based on a real organization whose identity has been disguised.

Copyright © 1979 by the President and Fellows of Harvard College. Harvard Business School case 9-180-091. Revised January 1993.

I then developed a new funding philosophy. I'm an independent. I don't like others having me under their control and I don't want to be on the bottom of the missionary barrel. In dealing with organizations like the United Way, I want to be their associate, to deal with them from strength, not from weakness.[1]

In order to do this, the Board and I decided to establish a $2 million trust fund. The income from that fund would make us less dependent on all other sources. We could walk to the beat of our own drummer.

Raising the trust fund money wasn't so hard. My Board and I know the community. We know who gives grants and we know for what purpose. I know how to approach them. Our single largest donor has been the Joffee Foundation, which gave us a $500,000 gift. I got to know the secretary of the foundation and I sent Councilman Norriss to see her with a bouquet of flowers so big that he couldn't get them through the door. Well, all the flowers in the world wouldn't have helped if our proposal wasn't right. But it was. We knew what the foundation wanted. And we drew its secretary into helping us draft it.

Two years ago, the Board reaffirmed the Trust agreement as follows:

> . . . Resolved that we re-affirm the intention of the trust fund and support all and any efforts of the Finance Committee to increase and enhance the assets thereof and be it further resolved that we shall deliver all possible monies into said trust fund to protect the future integrity and right of self determination of the Girl Scout Council of Guilford County.

Getting money is just one piece, however. The other is knowing how to spend it. We have had a balanced budget every year since I've been here. We budget by programs and then get revenues for them. If we can't get the revenues, we cut back on the programs.

ASSIGNMENT

1. Evaluate the financial condition of the Girl Scout Council of Guildford County as of last year.
2. Do you think the council should have an endowment fund? If so, how large should such a fund be?
3. Recommend any changes you think are needed.

---

[1]The United Way collects funds which it then allocates to qualifying charitable organizations.

EXHIBIT 1 **Balance Sheet, December 31, 19X8, 19X7, and 19X5**

Assets	19X8	19X7	19X5
UNRESTRICTED CURRENT FUND			
Cash	$ 60,590	$ 56,719	$ 24,467
Accounts receivable	1,027	728	
Notes receivable (Note 5)	-	-	148,990
Resale inventory and supplies	29,200	51,483	27,340
Prepaid expenses	7,192	6,928	10,535
Investments (at cost)			7,299
Maintenance reserve fund (Note 3)	1,483,561	1,137,402	456,604
Total assets	$1,581,570	$1,253,260	$ 677,235
RESTRICTED CURRENT FUND			
Cash	$ 15,332	$ 10,357	$ 8,816
	$ 15,332	$ 10,357	$ 8,816
ENDOWMENT FUND			
Cash	$ 9,399	$ 9,777	$ 10,371
Maintenance Reserve Fund (Note 3)	508,322	508,322	3,559
	$ 517,721	$ 518,099	$ 13,930
LAND, BUILDING AND EQUIPMENT FUND			
Cash	$ 6,103	$ 2,987	$ 4,197
Land, building, and equipment, at cost less accumulated depreciation (Notes 1 and 2)	1,491,035	1,553,247	1,620,904
	$1,497,138	$1,556,234	$1,625,101
CUSTODIAL FUND			
Cash	$ 4,201	$ 4,444	$ 1,613
	$ 4,201	$ 4,444	$ 1,613

Liabilities and Fund Balances	19X8	19X7	19X5
UNRESTRICTED CURRENT FUND			
Accounts payable and accrued liabilities	$ 23,315	$ 20,568	$ 13,552
Deferred pledge	4,000	-	-
Fund balances:			
Designated by the board of directors for future activities (Note 3)	1,519,638	1,137,402	456,604
Net unrealized loss on marketable equity securities (Note 3)	(40,077)	-	-
Undesignated, available for general activities	74,694	95,290	207,079
Total fund balances	1,554,255	1,232,692	663,683
Total liabilities and fund balances	$1,581,570	$1,253,260	$ 677,235
RESTRICTED CURRENT FUND			
Support for revenue designated by donor for future periods (Note 1)	$ 15,332	$ 10,357	$ 8,816
Fund balance	-	-	-
	$ 15,332	$ 10,357	$ 8,816
ENDOWMENT FUND			
Deferred pledge (Note 3)	$ 350,000	$ 450,000	$
Fund Balances:			
Restricted—The Joffee Foundation Grant (Note 3)	150,000	50,000	-
Designated by the board of directors for future activities	8,322	8,322	3,559
Undesignated	9,399	9,777	10,371
Total fund balances	167,721	68,099	13,930
	$ 517,721	$ 518,099	$ 13,930
LAND, BUILDING AND EQUIPMENT FUND			
Interest payable	$ 2,631	$ 2,987	$ 4,197
Notes payable (Note 2)	206,505	224,455	257,445
Fund balance	1,288,002	1,328,792	1,363,459
	$1,497,138	$1,556,234	$1,625,101
CUSTODIAL FUND			
Accounts payable	$ 4,201	$ 4,444	$ 1,613
	$ 4,201	$ 4,444	$ 1,613

See accompanying notes.

EXHIBIT 2 **Statement of Public Support, Revenue, Expenses, and Changes in Fund Balances Years Ended December 31, 19X8, 19X7, and 19X5**

	Unrestricted	Board Designated	Restricted	Endowment Fund	Land, Building and Equipment Fund	Total All Funds 19X8	19X7	19X5
Public support and revenue:								
Public support:								
Contributions:								
United Way	$240,593	$ -	$ -	$ -	-	$ 240,593	$ 245,853	$ 212,381
Foundations, trusts and other	20,565	84,655	7,203	100,000	20,672	233,095	103,373	105,166
Special fund-raising events (net of direct costs of $411,144 in 19X8, $353,790 in 19X7, and $300,930 in 19X5) (Note 1)	-	491,974	-	-	-	491,974	448,323	356,764
Sustaining membership participation	122,691	-	-	-	-	122,691	142,738	106,063
Total public support	383,849	576,629	7,203	100,000	20,672	1,088,353	940,287	780,374
Revenue:								
Program service fees	171,386	-	-	-	-	171,386	163,115	194,743
Investment income (Note 3)	-	97,581	-	-	-	97,581	83,259	21,276
Other income	6,433	-	-	215	516	7,164	31,204	17,884
Sale of property (Note 5)	-	-	-	-	-	-	-	94,849
Total revenue	177,819	97,581	-	215	516	276,131	277,578	328,752
Total public support and revenue	561,668	674,210	7,203	100,215	21,188	1,364,484	1,217,865	1,109,126
Expenses:								
Program services—camp, various summer programs, public education and community services	641,044		7,203	-	88,631	736,878	706,703	641,759
Supporting services—management and general, and fund raising	196,701	-	-	-	9,840	206,541	163,986	133,122
Total expenses	837,745	-	7,203	-	98,471	943,419	870,689	774,881
Excess (deficiency) of public support and revenue over expenses	(276,077)	674,210		100,215	(77,283)	421,065	347,176	334,245
Other changes in fund balances:								
Funds appropriated	255,481	(291,974)	-	-	36,493	-		-
Distribution of endowment funds	-	-	-	(593)	-	(593)	(743)	-
Net unrealized loss on marketable equity securities	-	-	-	-	-	-	-	-
Property returned to owner	-	(40,077)	-	-	-	(40,077)	-	(14,700)
Fund balances, at beginning of year	95,290	1,137,402		68,099	1,328,792	2,629,583	2,283,150	1,721,527
Fund balances, at end of year	$ 74,694	$1,479,561		$167,721	$1,288,002	$3,009,978	$2,629,583	$2,041,072

See accompanying notes.

EXHIBIT 3 **Statement of Functional Expenses**
          Years Ended December 31, 19X8, 19X7 and 19X5

	19X8			19X7	19X5
	Program Services	*Supporting Services*	*Total*	*Total*	*Total*
Salaries	$324,970	$108,421	$433,391	$410,397	$366,508
Payroll taxes	23,275	7,901	31,176	32,507	29,389
Employee benefits (Note 4)	28,970	10,330	39,300	32,740	28,002
Total salaries and related expenses	377,215	126,652	503,867	475,644	423,899
Professional services	-	16,574	16,574	12,826	7,390
Supplies	61,958	6,339	68,297	48,039	41,844
Telephone	9,297	2,009	11,306	10,454	8,726
Postage	537	3,681	4,218	2,406	4,694
Occupancy	50,688	34,418	85,106	72,665	53,287
Equipment rental	15,166	-	15,166	14,004	23,084
Local transportation	22,683	962	23,645	23,514	21,332
Conferences and conventions	8,430	-	8,430	3,336	9,216
Programmed special events	73,480	-	73,480	78,282	58,381
Printing	9,004	-	9,004	7,255	4,580
Interest expense	10,471	3,490	13,961	15,020	18,422
Other	19,889	6,066	25,955	25,173	25,876
Total expenses before depreciation	658,818	200,191	859,009	788,618	700,731
Depreciation of buildings and equipment (Note 1)	78,060	6,350	84,410	82,071	74,150
Total expenses	$736,878	$206,541	$943,419	$870,689	$774,881

See accompanying notes.

EXHIBIT 4 **Notes to Financial Statements, December 31, 19X8**

1. Summary of Significant Accounting Policies

The accounting policies that affect the more significant elements of the financial statements of the Girl Scout Council of Guilford County the Council) are summarized below.

Basis of Presentation The Council is a nonprofit corporation which has qualified for tax-exempt status. Accordingly, no provision for taxes based on income has been made in the accompanying financial statements.

Land, Buildings, and Equipment Land, buildings, and equipment are recorded at cost, when purchased, and at market value at date received when received as gifts. Depreciation of buildings and equipment is based on the straight-line method over estimated useful lives of 20 to 30 years for buildings and improvements and 5 to 10 years for furniture and equipment.

At December 31, 19X8, and 19X7, the costs of such assets were as follows:

	19X8	19X7
Land	$ 505,996	$ 505,996
Buildings	1,470,757	1,464,070
Furniture and equipment	178,700	163,189
	$2,155,453	$2,133,255
Less accumulated depreciation	664,418	580,008
	$1,491,035	$1,553,247

Items costing a nominal amount and repair and maintenance costs are charged to expense as incurred, whereas expenditures that materially extend asset lives are capitalized. Upon retirement or disposal, the related cost and accumulated depreciation of the asset is removed from the accounts and any gain or loss is included in income.

Special Fund-Raising Events The Council records product sales (cookies and calendars) net of retentions (approximately $190,000 in 19X8 and $166,000 in 19X7) paid to various troops for their sales assistance.

Support and Revenue Designated for Future Periods The Council receives certain revenue and support that have been designated by the donor as applicable to future periods. Such revenue is recognized in the period that the funds are expensed for the purpose intended by the donor.

Custodial Fund The Custodial Fund accounts for assets (troop treasuries) received by the Council that are held and disbursed as instructed by the person or troop from whom they were received.

Donated Services No amounts have been reflected in the statements for donated services inasmuch as no objective basis is available to measure the value of such services; however, a substantial number of volunteers have donated significant amounts of their time to the Council's administrative and fund-raising activities.

EXHIBIT 4 (Continued)

---

2. **Notes Payable**

Notes payable at December 31, 19X8 and 19X7 consist of the following:

	19X8	19X7
7 percent note payable to bank, secured by deed of trust on administration building having a net book value of $463,069, due in monthly installments of $708 including interest through 19Z8	$ 89,586	$ 91,723
6 percent note payable, secured by deed of trust on Camp Elbinger property having a net book value of $214,398, due in annual installments of $23,777 including interest through 19Y4	116,919	132,732
	$206,505	$224,455

3. **Maintenance Reserve Fund**

During 19X4, a separate qualified nonprofit trust known as the "Friends of the Girl Scouts' Trust" (the Trust) was established by the Council for the future benefit and preservation of girl scouting in the territory covered by the Council's charter. The Trust is administered and controlled at the discretion of a Board of Trustees in accordance with the terms of the trust agreement. In accordance with such agreement, the Trust is revocable at the discretion of the Council's Board, and is therefore accounted for as a Board-designated asset of the Council as titled "Maintenance Reserve Fund."

During 19X8, the Trust earned investment income of $97,581 and received designated donations of $84,655, which were recorded as revenue and public support, respectively, and reinvested by the Board of Trustees. The Council's board approved donations to the Trust of $200,000. Restricted donations of $100,000 were received and recorded as public support in the Endowment Fund.

At December 31, 19X8, a valuation allowance has been charged directly to the fund balance. This valuation allowance represents the excess of aggregate cost over aggregate quoted market value of marketable equity securities in the Trust's pooled investment portfolios and amounts to $40,077 at December 31, 19X8 (which represents the net of gross unrealized gains of $26,343 and gross unrealized losses of $66,420).

Net realized gains (losses) resulting from sales of marketable equity securities included in net earnings for the years ended December 31, 19X8 and 19X7, were ($1,094) and $7,786, respectively. The cost of securities sold was based primarily on the specific identification method.

EXHIBIT 4 (Continued)

Securities and other assets of the Trust are summarized as follows:

	19X8			**19X7**
	Current Fund Board Designated	Endowment Fund[a]	Total	Total
Time certificates of deposit	$ 526,187	$ -	$ 526,187	$ 308,270
Cash in savings accounts	1,245	-	1,245	28,539
Securities	991,321	-	991,321	652,000
Investment in limited partnership	100,000	-	100,000	50,000
Total investment	$1,618,753	$ -	$1,618,753	$1,038,809
Notes receivable	-	-	-	142,332
Long-term pledges	4,000	350,000	354,000	450,000
Other assets	19,130	-	19,130	14,583
	$1,641,883	$350,000	$1,991,883	$1,645,724
Allocation of pooled investment[b]	(158,322)	158,322	-	-
Total all "Maintenance Reserve Fund" assets	$1,483,561	$508,322	$1,991,883	$1,645,724

[a]In March and November 19X8, the Trust received the second and third installments of a $500,000 grant from The Joffee Foundation. The grant is payable in semiannual installments of $50,000. Pursuant to the terms of the grant, all principal is to be placed in an endowment fund, with interest therefrom used for operations, maintenance, and replacement of the Council's program facilities.

[b]Investments of the current and endowment funds have been pooled together. Investments in securities, except bonds that are expected to be held until maturity, are stated at the lower of aggregate cost or market value (market at December 31, 19X8). Their cost aggregated $1,031,398 at December 31, 19X8.

4. Pension Plan

The Council provides under the National Girl Scout Council pension plan a noncontributory defined benefit plan for all full-time employees. All prior service costs have been fully funded. The current cost to the Council paid to the National Council plan was approximately $28,000 in 19X8 and $24,000 in 19X7.

5. Notes Receivable

In 19X5, a camp was sold for $207,921 with a net profit of $94,849. The proceeds from the sale, a $150,000 note (secured by the property, bearing interest at 8 percent, and due in 120 monthly installments of $1,250 with the balance at maturity) and $57,921 in cash, were transferred to the current fund net of $77,241 of property and equipment acquired with unrestricted current funds. Subsequently, in 19X6, the note was transferred to the Friends of the Girl Scouts Trust.

7 The Mechanics of Accounting

ALL ORGANIZATIONS HAVE SYSTEMS TO RECORD the accounts that appear in the financial statements discussed in Chapters 3 and 4. If the accounting systems are not sound, the financial statements will be inaccurate. This chapter introduces the mechanics of accounting and the internal control systems that ensure reliable accounting information.

The accounting process that maintains these records can be complex and confusing, but it is the heart of financial management. Although it is not the purpose of this book to train accountants, understanding the mechanics of accounting described in this chapter is key to understanding financial statements. Virtually all those who persist eventually experience an "Ah ha!" moment, in which the various names and mechanics they have been studying crystalize into comprehension of the financial statements.

DOUBLE-ENTRY BOOKKEEPING

Just as there are two sides to every story, there are two sides to every economic transaction. For every use of funds, there is an equal source of funds. The accounting entries for recording the two sides of every transactions are called *debits* (uses of funds) and *credits* (sources of funds). They are defined as follows:

Debit = Increase in an asset *or*
              Decrease in a liability or fund balance account

Credit = Decrease in an asset *or*
              Increase in a liability or fund balance account

Double-entry bookkeeping is the standard for accounting systems. It is called *double-entry* because it records the two sides of every transaction in at least two accounts. It is the mechanism for ensuring that the two sides *balance*—that the total amounts recorded on both sides of the transaction are equal. For example, when a cash sale is made, double entry bookkeeping is used to enter the data in the cash and the revenue accounts that reflect the two sides of this transaction. *Bookkeeping* refers to the process of entering and maintaining data in the accounting system.

Every debit entry must have an equal and corresponding credit entry if the accounting transaction is to balance. The words debit and credit are conventions. They do not correspond to the ordinary usage of these words; there is nothing good about a credit or bad about a debit. Debit and credit are abbreviated, for reasons unknown to us, as *Dr.* and *Cr.* (Some claim that the abbreviations are based on the Latin roots of the words.)

One way of visualizing how debits and credits are used in accounting is to think of every account on the Balance Sheet as having a large T beneath it, with *Dr.* above the left side of the cross on the T, and *Cr.* above its right side. All *debits* will be entered on the *left*-hand side of the T and all *credits* on the *right*-hand side. Asset accounts will have debit balances (on the left-hand side of the T) and Liability and Fund Balance accounts will have credit balances (on the right-hand side), as shown in Figure 7-1.

Debits on the left, credits on the right. Sounds easy enough; but in reality, mastering the mechanics of bookkeeping requires a great deal of patience and persistence. Do you know the old joke about a bookkeeper who began the workday by first opening his left desk drawer and then, his right-hand drawer? When a curious co-worker asked him why, the bookkeeper opened the drawers to reveal a large DEBIT pasted in the left-hand one and a large CREDIT pasted in the right-hand one.

If the mechanics of accounting were easily mastered, this old joke would not be as frequently repeated and as well received as it is. The best way to feel comfortable with these mechanics is to practice doing them. Accounting is a language; as with all languages, it is best learned with repeated practice in its use. A simple and then a more complex example of bookkeeping mechanics are provided to assist in the process.

FIGURE 7-1   **Balance Sheet T-Accounts**

Assets		Liabilities		Fund Balance	
Debits	Credits	Debits	Credits	Debits	Credits
XXX			XXX		XXX

A Simple Example

The simple Balance Sheet in Table 7-1 represents the financial position of RSUS at the beginning of its first period of operations. It reflects a then-new organization that has received a single cash donation of $5,000 and, thus, contains only one asset, cash, and one fund balance account. Balance Sheet accounts are *permanent accounts*; the balances in them at the end of each year are carried forward as the beginning balances for the next year, as long as the organization exists. Income Statement accounts, in contrast, are *temporary* because they are closed down and transferred to the permanent fund balance account on the Balance Sheet.

During Year 1, the following transactions occurred:

(1) Provided services for which $8,000 was billed and received $1,000 of cash donations.

(2) Incurred, but did not pay for, expenses of $6,500 for salaries and $2,000 for supplies.

(3) Received $6,000 cash as payment for services billed.

(4) Paid cash of $7,500 for the amounts owed for expenses.

To record the effect of these four transactions on our Balance Sheet, it will be helpful to make a T-account for each Balance Sheet account. The next step is to analyze where (which side of what account) to *post* each transaction. (In accountingese, to *post* means to *enter* or *write down*.)

Each transaction will be discussed separately, as follows:

(1) The first transaction indicates a credit to revenues of $9,000 ($8,000 to service fees and $1,000 to donations). The debit portion of this transaction is recorded as an increase in the accounts receivable

TABLE 7-1 **RSUS Balance Sheet, Beginning of Year 1**

RSUS			
Balance Sheet			
As of the Beginning of Year 1			
Assets		*Liabilities and Fund Balance*	
Cash	$5,000	Fund balance	$5,000
		Total liabilities and	
Total assets	$5,000	fund balance	$5,000

asset of $8,000, and an increase in the cash asset of $1,000. It is a debit because these assets are increased. The corresponding credit ultimately increases the fund balance through the revenue accounts. The Balance Sheet thus has matching debit and credit entries.

The credit portion of this transaction is troublesome, isn't it? Remember that the fund balance represents the cumulative earnings of the entity and that revenue is an increase in those earnings and therefore ultimately an increase in the fund balance. Instead of crediting the fund balance account directly, the credit entries are made to the two revenue accounts, to facilitate constructing the Statement of Revenues and Expenses.

(2) The second transaction represents expenses of $8,500, which ultimately decrease the cumulative earnings of the entity, and, therefore, the fund balance—a debit entry. Again, instead of a debit directly to the fund balance account, a debit is posted to the salaries expense account of $6,500 and to the supplies expense account of $2,000. The corresponding credit entry of $8,500 is posted to the accounts payable liability account because payment for these expenses is still owed. A credit entry records an increase in a liability.

(3) The third transaction tells us that $6,000 of the accounts receivable have been received in cash. This decreases the accounts receivable asset account by $6,000 (a credit entry) and increases the cash asset account by $6,000 (a debit entry). The $6,000 is not recorded as revenue at this point, because we already recognized it as a revenue in transaction (1).

(4) The last transaction reflects the reduction of the outstanding bills with payment of $7,500 in cash. It is entered with a debit to the accounts payable account (decrease in a liability) and a corresponding credit to the cash account (decrease in an asset). We do not recognize the $7,500 as an expense, because the $8,500 of expenses to which this payment relates were already recognized in transaction (2).

Figure 7-2 illustrates and summarizes the impact of these transactions on the T-accounts of the organization's Balance Sheet. The account balances at the beginning of the period are indicated with (BB); transaction numbers are shown in parentheses; closing entries, which are discussed below, are designated (C); and account balances at the end of the period are indicated by (EB). This coding scheme makes it possible to know which transaction each debit and credit reflects. Without it, tracing the activities through the accounts is virtually impossible. A similar referencing system is used to trace transactions in real accounting systems.

FIGURE 7-2 **T-Accounts for RSUS, Year 1**

T-Accounts for RSUS
As of the End of Year 1

Permanent Accounts—Balance Sheet

	Assets				**Liabilities** **and Fund Balance**		
	Cash				*Accounts Payable*		
	Dr.	Cr.			Dr.	Cr.	
(BB)	$5,000					(BB)	$ 0
(1)	1,000					(2)	6,500
(3)	6,000	(4)	$7,500	(4)	$7,500	(2)	2,000
(EB)	$4,500					(EB)	$1,000

	Accounts Receivable				*Fund Balance*		
	Dr.	Cr.			Dr.	Cr.	
(BB)	$ 0					(BB)	$5,000
(1)	8,000	(3)	$6,000			(C)	500
(EB)	$2,000					(EB)	$5,500

Temporary Accounts
Statement of Revenues and Expenses

	Revenues				**Expenses**		
	Service Fees				*Salaries*		
	Dr.	Cr.			Dr.	Cr.	
(C)	$8,000	(1)	$8,000	(2)	$6,500	(C)	$6,500
			$ 0		$ 0		

	Donations				*Supplies*		
	Dr.	Cr.			Dr.	Cr.	
(C)	$1,000	(1)	$1,000	(2)	$2,000	(C)	$2,000
			$ 0		$ 0		

Revenue and expense accounts are used to track the details of the changes in fund balance during the accounting period. They are *temporary* accounts that are *closed* (accountingese for *reduced to a zero balance*) at the end of each year. Each year, all revenue and expense accounts begin the period with a balance of zero. The entries marked (C) close the temporary accounts for the year by entering the debit or credit amount needed to bring each account balance to zero. The difference between all the revenue and expense accounts is the net change in the fund balance for the period. When this difference is entered in the fund balance account, it balances the closing entry. The difference between total revenues and total expenses of the period is permanently reflected with this entry to the fund balance account. All the transactions that affect the fund balance are reflected and summarized in a Statement of Revenue and Expenses, as illustrated in Table 7-2.

Ending balances are arrived at by calculating the difference between the total debits and total credits in each account. Does the ending Balance Sheet balance? Well, if the beginning accounts balanced *and* all the transactions including the closing entry balance (if for every debit there is an equal and corresponding credit) *and* all the arithmetic is correct, then the ending accounts must also balance. This is a mathematical certainty, but a rare event, particularly for beginning students of the subject. When accounts in the end of the period Balance Sheet shown in Table 7-3 were closed, the total of the assets is the same as the total of the liabilities plus fund balance accounts. Our books are in balance.

TABLE 7-2 **RSUS Statement of Revenues and Expenses, Year 1**

RSUS
Statement of Revenues and Expenses
From the Beginning to the End of Year 1

Revenues:	
Services fees	$8,000
Donations	1,000
Total revenues	9,000
Expenses:	
Salaries	6,500
Supplies	2,000
Total expenses	8,500
Excess of revenue over expenses	500
Add: Beginning fund balance	5,000
Ending fund balance	$5,500

TABLE 7-3 **RSUS Balance Sheet, End of Year 1**

	RSUS **Balance Sheet** **As of the End of Year 1**		
Assets		*Liabilities and Fund Balances*	
Cash	$4,500	Accounts payable	$1,000
Accounts receivable	2,000	Fund balance	5,500
Total assets	$6,500	Total liabilities and fund balance	$6,500

Learning these mechanics takes a great deal of practice. It may be helpful to remember that in double-entry bookkeeping there are only four types of transactions:

(1) An increase in an asset (debit) that is matched by a corresponding increase in a liability or fund balance account (credit)

(2) A decrease in an asset (credit) that is matched by a corresponding decrease in a liability or fund balance account (debit)

(3) An increase in an asset (debit) that is matched by a decrease in another asset (credit)

(4) An increase in a liability or fund balance account (credit) that is matched by a decrease in another liability or fund balance account (debit)

It is sometimes useful to visualize the Balance Sheet as consisting of two sides of equal weight. If we add a weight to one side, balance will be maintained only if we add an equal weight to the other side or if we subtract the same weight from the side to which the weight was added. In accountingese, the addition and subtraction of weight is equivalent to saying that every debit must be matched with an equal amount of credit.

The Perspective of a New Practitioner

At this point, most newcomers to the field of accounting begin to feel a bit uneasy. If you are beginning to have this feeling, the following essay will show that you are in good company.

We begin with a "T," which, as a convenient mnemonic device, we may consider to stand for "tally." On the left side of the "T," assuming of course that we are standing in front of the "T," and not behind it, we place our debits. Debits, as everyone knows, are defined as those figures we place on the left side of the "T." Accounting procedures have a kind of pristine beauty in their logic to which the layman is often curiously insensitive.

On the right side of the "T," assuming, of course, that we are standing in front of the "T," and not behind it, we place our credits. A credit, by definition, is anything that we place on the right side of the "T," or, to look at it another way, it is anything that is the precise antithesis of a debit. If you make the vertical line on the "T" heavy and black, you will never confuse credits and debits.

Now we come to the question of what to write on top of the "T." Actually, one has great freedom in this matter; one can write almost anything he pleases on top of the "T," and most experienced business managers do. One also has great freedom in the number of "T's" he writes. One could have a "T" for paperclips, a "T" for telephone—which is particularly appropriate. . . . It may be stated as a general and universally recognized truth that an administrator's success in fiscal matters is in direct proportion to the number of "T's" he contrives to fill out in a month's time. . . .

One now comes to the moment to add up all the numbers on each side of the "T's." At this point, the administrator might be wise to consider renting a computer. In any case, both columns must be added up and they must both add up to the same sum. But they won't. They just never do. And at this point, to speak baldly, one must cheat . . . so that both sides will balance. The vast majority of people, looking at your books, will see only that both sides balance, and will, therefore, infer that you are neither losing money nor making a profit unseemly for a nonprofit institution. This is the true genius of double-entry bookkeeping: It doesn't matter whether you win or lose, so long as you have your accounting procedures down to a "T."[1]

A More Complex Example

Having bolstered our spirits, let us proceed to the more complex example of the mechanics of double-entry bookkeeping provided by the second year of operations of RSUS. The balances in the accounts of the ending Balance Sheet for Year 1 (Table 7-3) are, by definition, the amounts of the accounts in the beginning Balance Sheet for next year. The economic events described below occurred during the fiscal year, with the postings to the T-accounts as shown in Figure 7-3. A single T-account is used for expenses and revenues, with each entry identified by its related revenue or expense account name as well as its transaction number. This summary approach works well only with a small number of transactions.

(1) RSUS boomed. It had $50,000 in service fees revenue, $14,500 of which was received immediately in cash and $35,500 of which was billed. It also received an additional $30,000 of donations in cash.

[1]William S. Kilbourne, Jr., *A Succinct and Lucid Explanation of Debits and Credits* (Boston, MA: National Association of Independent Schools, 1979).

FIGURE 7-3 RSUS T-Accounts, Year 2

Permanent Accounts

Asset Accounts

Cash				Accounts Receivable				Inventory			
(BB) $ 4,500	(BB) $12,375			(BB) $ 2,000	(2a) $29,500			(BB) $ 0			
(1a) 14,500	(4b) 3,000			(1a) 35,500				(3) 12,375	(8) $ 9,000		
(1b) 30,000	(4c) 1,800			(EB) $ 8,000				(EB) $ 3,375			
(2a) 29,500	(5) 1,000										
(6) 2,000	(7a) 12,000			Allowance for Bad Debt							
	(10b) 43,000				(2b) $ 1,300						
(EB) $7,325					(EB) $ 1,300						

Furniture and Equipment		Accumulated Depreciation		Prepaid Rent	
(BB) $ 0			(BB) $ 0	(7a) $12,000	(7b) $ 6,000 (BB)
(4a) 15,000			(9) 1,500	(EB) $ 6,000	
(EB) $15,000			(EB) $ 1,500		

Liability and Fund Balance Accounts

Accrued Payroll			Accounts Payable			Fund Balance	
(10b) $43,000	(BB) $ 0	(5)	$ 1,000	(BB) $ 1,000			(BB) $ 5,500
	(10a) 46,000			(EB) $ 0	(C)	$65,600	(C) 80,000
	(EB) $ 3,000						$19,900

Mortgage Payable		Deferred Revenues	
(4b) $ 3,000	(4a) $15,000 (BB)	(6) $ 2,000 (BB)	
	(EB) $12,000	(EB) $ 2,000	

Temporary Accounts

Expenses				Revenues			
(2b) $ 1,300 Bad debt					(1a) $50,000 Service Fees		
(4c) 1,800 Interest				(C) $80,000	(1b) 30,000 Donations		
(7b) 6,000 Rent					$ 0		
(8) 9,000 Supplies							
(9) 1,500 Depreciation							
(10a) 46,000 Personnel	(C) $65,600						
$ 0							

*BB = beginning balance
EB = ending balance

The first transaction, (1a), is recorded as a credit of $50,000 to the revenue T-account and debits of $35,500 to the accounts receivable T-account and $14,500 to the cash T-account. The second, (1b), is recorded as a credit of $30,000 to the revenue T-account and a debit of $30,000 to the cash T-account.

(2) At the end of the year, $8,000 in bills had not yet been paid by RSUS's customers. Of the total, $4,000 in bills were less than 30 days old; $3,000 were between 30 and 60 days old; and the remaining $1,000 were more than 60 days old. So far, RSUS had collected 95 percent of all bills less than a month old, 80 percent of the bills that were between 30 and 60 days old, and only 50 percent of the bills that were more than 60 days old.

RSUS began the year with an accounts receivable account balance of $2,000 that could have been collected, to which was added the $35,500 billed to customers during the year. Thus, a total of $37,500 of accounts receivable could have been collected in cash. Since $8,000 remains uncollected at the end of the year, the difference of $29,500 is the amount that was collected in cash ($37,500 − $8,000). This is reflected with a credit, (2a), to the accounts receivable account and a debit to the cash account of $29,500 each.

We must also record the amount of bad debt expense expected for this year's operations. Based on past experience, only $6,700 [(0.95)($4,000) + (0.80)($3,000) + (0.50)($1,000)] of the $8,000 ending balance of accounts receivable is likely to be collected. RSUS thus estimates a bad debt expense of $1,300 and a corresponding reduction of the value of its accounts receivable. This is reflected, (2b), by a debit of $1,300 ($8,000 − $6,700) to the bad debt expense account and a credit to the allowance for bad debts account. The allowances for bad debts account will be used to reduce the volume of the accounts receivable to the amount that can realistically be collected. The allowance for bad debts account is called a *contra-account* and presented as a deduction from accounts receivable. It has a credit balance.

(3) During the year, $12,375 of inventory was purchased, all of it paid for in cash by the end of the year. This transaction is an exchange of one asset, cash, for another, inventory. We thus credit the cash account by $12,375 and debit the inventory account by the same amount.

(4) At the beginning of the year, RSUS bought $15,000 worth of furniture and equipment. It obtained a five-year, 12 percent mortgage to finance the purchase. The mortgage required equal annual payments of principal and an annual payment of the interest on the outstanding balance of the loan. RSUS made such payments by the end of the year, in cash.

The purchase increased a new asset, furniture and equipment, via an equal increase in a new liability, mortgage payable. In transaction (4a), we create two corresponding new T-accounts, label them, and debit furniture and equipment and credit mortgage payable by $15,000 each. One-fifth of the mortgage was paid in cash by year end (the principal payment). Thus, in (4b), the mortgage payable and cash accounts are each reduced by

$3,000 ($15,000 ÷ 5). The interest expense of $1,800 ($15,000 × 0.12) was also paid in cash. It is recorded in (4c) with a debit of $1,800 to the interest expense account, and a corresponding credit of $1,800 to the cash account.

(5) All the amounts owed for items purchased during the previous year were paid. This is recorded by a debit to accounts payable of $1,000 and an equal credit to cash.

(6) RSUS announced its intention to start a newsletter to inform its patrons about upcoming programs and events. After it aired this announcement, it received $2,000 of cash payments for subscriptions in advance of any newsletters being delivered.

The $2,000 is therefore a liability for RSUS until it sends out the newsletters for which payment was made. It is recognized as a $2,000 debit to cash and a corresponding equal credit to an account that reflects this liability, deferred revenues.

(7) At the beginning of the year, RSUS paid $12,000 in cash for the next 24 months of rent. The exchange of $12,000 in cash for another asset, prepaid rent, is reflected in transaction (7a) by a credit to cash of $12,000 and an equal debit to prepaid rent. By year-end, RSUS used up 12 months of the prepaid rent. This was recorded, in (7b), as a reduction of the asset, a credit entry to the prepaid rent account of $6,000 [($12,000 ÷ 24 months) × 12 months used] and a debit to the rent expense account of $6,000.

(8) A physical count of inventory items on hand at the end of the year indicated an inventory value, at cost, of $3,375. The inventory account started the year with a zero balance, to which goods costing $12,375 were added during the year, per transaction (3). Had no inventory been used, the value of the inventory at the end of the year would have been $12,375. Since the end-of-year inventory value was $3,375, we calculate that inventory costing $9,000 ($12,375 − $3,375) was used during the year. The accounting transaction to reflect this is a credit to inventory, to reflect its reduction by $9,000, and a corresponding debit to supplies expenses of $9,000 to reflect the value of the inventory used.

(9) Because the furniture and equipment purchased were expected to have a ten-year life, with no salvage value at the end of that time, the depreciation expense for the year was $1,500 ($15,000 ÷ 10). This transaction reduced the amount in the furniture and equipment account through a credit to the accumulated depreciation account. The corresponding debit is to the depreciation expense T-account. Accumulated depreciation is another Balance Sheet *contra* account. It is shown on the asset side of the Balance Sheet, but unlike other asset accounts, the *contra* has a credit balance. It is subtracted from the corresponding fixed asset account.

(10) There were personnel (salary and benefits) expenses of $46,000 during the course of the year, of which $3,000 was still owed to employees at the end of the year. The expense and liability are recorded in (10a) by a $46,000 debit to the personnel expense account and an equal credit to the

accrued payroll liability account. Because there were $46,000 of expenses during the year but only $3,000 was still owed at the end of the year, $43,000 of the accrued payroll must have been paid in cash ($46,000 − $3,000). We record the payment transaction in (10b) by a debit of $43,000 to the accrued payroll account and a corresponding credit to cash.

Preparing Financial Statements

After the transactions are posted to the T-accounts, we calculate the balance in each account, and then make the final entry to close the revenue and expense accounts to the fund balance, as illustrated in Figure 7-3. The Balance Sheet (Table 7-5) and the Statement of Revenues and Expenses (Table 7-4) can then be derived directly from the T-account ending balances. The mortgage payable of $12,000 has been split into its current ($3,000) and long-term ($9,000) components for the financial statement presentation. It is common to maintain a single account for the liability and to calculate the current portion as needed for financial statements.

Recall that the fund balance account represents the cumulative difference between all the revenues and expenses of the organization since its inception. At the beginning of the year, the fund balance was $5,500. During the year, RSUS generated $80,000 in revenues, which increased the fund balance, and consumed resources, reflected as expenses, of $65,600, which decreased the fund balance. The net addition to the fund balance for the year is the difference between revenues and expenses of $14,400.

THE ACCOUNTING SYSTEM

Although a very small organization may have accounts only for the items listed on the Balance Sheet and Statement of Revenues and Expenses, most organizations have many additional accounts. The accounts that appear on the financial statements are often referred to as *control* accounts. The other accounts are usually *subsidiary* to the control accounts and provide the additional detail needed for managing the organization. For example, whereas it is sufficient for external parties to know the total cash balance of the organization, management should be able to account separately for the amounts in petty cash and in each individual bank account if there are more than one.

Chart of Accounts

The fundamental building block of any accounting system is the *chart of accounts* that identifies by name and number the accounts the organization will use. The chart of accounts used by RSUS is shown in Table 7-6. In large organizations that employ several people for bookkeeping, the chart

TABLE 7-4   **RSUS Statement of Revenues and Expenses, Year 2**

Statement of Revenues and Expenses
RSUS
For Year 2

Operating revenues:		
Services fees	$50,000	
Donations	30,000	$80,000
Expenses:		
Bad debt	$ 1,300	
Rent	6,000	
Supplies	9,000	
Depreciation	1,500	
Personnel	46,000	
Interest expenses	1,800	65,600
Excess of revenues over expenses		$14,400
Add: beginning fund balance		5,500
Ending fund balance		$19,900

TABLE 7-5   **RSUS Balance Sheet, Year 2**

Balance Sheet
RSUS
As of the End of Year 2

Assets		*Liabilities and Fund Balance*	
Cash	$ 7,325	Accrued payroll	$ 3,000
Accounts receivable (net of		Current mortgage payable	3,000
$1,300 bad debt		Deferred revenues	2,000
allowance)	6,700	Long-term mortgage	
Inventory	3,375	payable	9,000
Prepaid rent	6,000	Total liabilities	$17,000
Furniture and equipment			
(less accumulated depre-			
ciation of $1,500)	13,500	Fund balance	19,900
		Total liabilities and	
Total assets	$36,900	fund balance	$36,900

TABLE 7-6 **RSUS Summary Chart of Accounts**

Summary Chart of Accounts
RSUS

1—Assets
   10 Cash
   11 Temporary investments
   12 Receivables
   13 Inventories
   14 Broadcasting rights
   15 Prepaid expenses
   16 Property, plant, and equipment
   17 Deferred charges
   18 Other assets
   19 Intangibles

2—Liabilities
   20 Notes and accounts payable
   21 Taxes and other amounts withheld
      from employees
   22 Accrued expenses
   25 Deferred credits
   26 Long-term debt
   29 Other liabilities

3—Fund Balance
   30 Fund balance

4—Operating Revenues
   40 Local sales
   41 National sales
   42 Network sales
   43 Talent and facilities sales
   49 Agency commissions

5—Operating Expenses
   50 Program and production
   51 Transmitter
   52 Studio
   53 News and public affairs

6—Selling Expenses
   60 Sales department
   61 Advertising and promotion

7—General and Administrative Expenses
   70 Station manager's office
   71 Accounting department
   73 Building and grounds
   79 General overhead

8—Other Revenues and Other Expenses
   80 Other revenues
   85 Other expenses
   87 Extraordinary items

of accounts will be supplemented by lengthy, clear definitions of each account. The purpose of these definitions is to ensure that different bookkeepers will classify similar transactions in the same way.

Developing and defining a chart of accounts deserves a great deal of attention. From their inception, the accounts should describe the economic events that the management of the organization wishes to describe. Unfortunately, charts of accounts are often allowed to grow haphazardly over time, with random accounts inserted to meet long-forgotten needs. For example, a $250 million hospital has a $25 taxi fund in its chart of accounts. First established in 1940, the purpose of the account has long been forgotten and its small amount is hardly worthy of a separate account title. The chart of accounts should be reviewed regularly to purge such accounts as the taxi fund and ensure that appropriate accounts are added as the organization's purpose and activities change.

Some nonprofit organizations lack a formal chart of accounts. As a result, they cannot ensure consistency of accounting over time and across different units of the same organization. Many small nonprofits that have had the same bookkeeper for years have not bothered to establish such a chart; but what will happen to the accounting system when the bookkeeper leaves? (Small nonprofits are not alone in this area. The multibillion dollar a year New York City did not have a complete Chart of Accounts until 1977!)

Keeping the Books

T-accounts *per se* are not used in operating accounting systems. Instead, two sets of documents are used to keep track of the accounting information. The accounts are kept in a book, or set of books, called the *general ledger*, with a separate page for each account. The ledger page for an account is functionally equivalent to our T-account, although it will typically contain many more entries. Periodically, usually monthly, transactions are entered in each account, and its current balance is calculated.

The entries in the ledger are copied from *journals*, which contain detailed transactions posted in chronological order. An accounting journal is analogous to any other journal that keeps track of particular activities; in this case, the activities are economic in nature. Several special journals are commonly used. Each records only one type of high-volume transaction, such as sales, payroll, cash receipts, and cash disbursements. The *general journal* summarizes the transactions from these journals, other regularly occurring entries, and any other journal entries that are occasionally necessary. Although these are common accounting terms, many other variations on accounting system structure and terminology are in use today.

A journal entry, by convention, places the debit on the left and the credit on the right, as in T-accounts. Each journal entry includes the date, the accounts affected, the amounts of the debits and credits, a description explaining the purpose and the source of data for the entry, and a journal entry number that identifies the entry when it is posted in the general ledger. The journal entries for the transactions (1a) and (2) of the second year of operations for RSUS are given as follows.

Date	Accounts	Dr.	Cr.
May 5	Accounts receivable	$35,500	
	Cash	14,500	
	Revenue		$50,000
Dec. 12	Cash	$29,500	
	Accounts receivable		$29,500

Periodically, the balance in each of the general ledger accounts is calculated, and a listing of the balances called a *trial balance*, is prepared. It is usually prepared monthly or quarterly throughout the year, whereas formal Balance Sheets and Revenue and Expense Statements are typically prepared less frequently, perhaps only annually. Both journals and ledgers are now commonly kept on computer, rather than manually.

As with the T-accounts, a cross-referencing system enables data to be traced from the initial transactions in the journal through the accounting system, and *vice versa*. Although the fact that "the books balance" ensures that total debits equal total credits, it does not ensure that the debits and credits were entered in the correct accounts. A good accounting system provides a visible *audit trail* that provides evidence of the accuracy and completeness of the accounting for economic activities in the system. It is based on a set of standardized procedures, with built in checks and balances called *internal controls* that prevent errors from occurring in the first place and facilitate the discovery and correction of errors when they do occur.

No matter how well an accounting system is designed, it will not be effective unless the people responsible for operating it follow the prescribed procedures. Even the best designed system can be used badly or incorrectly by careless or poorly trained personnel. One of the most important checks and balances in such a control system is an attentive management and board, who carefully analyze the periodic statements and investigate any unusual or questionable amounts.

SUMMARY

Accounting statements are compiled through the use of double-entry bookkeeping, which specifies that every accounting entry debit must have an equal and corresponding credit. A debit is an increase in an asset or a decrease in a liability or fund balance. A credit is a decrease in an asset or an increase in a liability or fund balance. Temporary revenue and expense accounts are used to accumulate the revenue and expenses accounts that affect fund balance. Transactions are first recorded chronologically in a journal, then summarized by account through entry in a ledger, from which the financial statements are prepared. The integrity and value of the resulting financial statements are directly dependent on the design and the execution of the accounting procedures.

DISCUSSION QUESTIONS

1. Define a debit and a credit.
2. Why must debits equal credits?

3. Do the following accounts have a debit balance or a credit balance? Also identify each as being an asset or liability or a contra-account.
   a. Accounts receivable
   b. Accumulated depreciation
   c. Accounts payable
   d. Fund balance
   e. Marketable securities
   f. Fixed assets
   g. Salaries payable
   h. Inventory
   i. Deferred revenues
   j. Cash
   k. Allowance for bad debts

4. What is a Chart of Accounts and why is it important for an organization to have one?

5. What is internal control? Whose responsibility is it?

EXERCISES

1. Describe the debit and credit entries for each of the following events, using both a T-account and a journal entry format:
   a. Revenues earned and bills sent out for them of $10,000
   b. Cash received for issuing a bond for $150,000 of principal with 10 percent interest
   c. Travel expenses incurred but not paid for of $3,000
   d. Depreciation expense for the use of an asset of $21,000
   e. Cash sales of $350,000
   f. Payroll expenses, $200,000 of which were paid for in cash and $31,000 of which have not yet been paid
   g. Receipt of cash of $18,000 for goods or services not yet provided
   h. Expected uncollectibles of 8 percent of the $55,000 owed to the organization

2. What is the closing entry for an organization that incurred $365,700 of expenses and earned $389,600 of revenues during the year? What would the entry be if expenses were $365,700 and revenues were $354,200? What is the ending fund balance in each case if the beginning fund balance was $56,000? If it was $8,000?

Cases

CASE STUDIES

These case studies were prepared by Professor Herzlinger to give those of you who want to practice the mechanics of accounting the opportunity to do so. The case studies do not depict real organizations, but they do describe the real economic events for which accounting entries are prepared most frequently.

CASE 7.1 Lourdville Health Center

The beginning-of-year balance sheet for the Lourdville Health Center in North Carolina is given below:

Balance Sheet
Lourdville Health Center
As of the Beginning of the Year

Assets		Liabilities and Fund Balance	
Cash	$ 20,000	Accounts payable	$ 30,000
Net accounts receivable	60,000	Current mortgage	20,000
Inventory	20,000	Mortgage	80,000
Fixed assets (net of $20,000 of accumulated depreciation)	100,000	Fund balance	70,000
Total	$200,000	Total	$200,000

Professor Regina E. Herzlinger prepared this case for class discussion rather than to illustrate either effective or ineffective handling of an administrative situation.

Copyright © 1993 by the President and Fellows of Harvard College. Harvard Business School case 193-119.

The following transactions occurred during the year:

(1)	Bills sent out for services provided	$90,000
(2)	Expected bad debts	4,500
(3)	Inventory purchased, on credit	10,000
(4)	Inventory value at end of period	25,000
(5)	Purchases on credit of furniture	$ 5,000
(6)	Depreciation expense	4,000
(7)	Unpaid bills owed by the Center, including fuel and utilities, as of the end of the year	40,000
(8)	Salary expense, paid in cash	60,000
(9)	Bills received for fuel and utilities	14,000
(10)	Bills sent out for services provided not yet paid to the Center at year-end	50,000

Note: The mortgage of $100,000 was obtained at the beginning of the year. It is to be repaid in five equal annual installments and has an 8 percent annual interest rate. The principal and interest payments owed were paid in cash at year end.

ASSIGNMENT

a. Post the year's transactions for the Lourdville Health Center, using the following T-accounts: Cash, Net Accounts Receivable, Inventory, Fixed Assets—Original Cost, Accumulated Depreciation, Accounts Payable, Current Mortgage, Mortgage, Fund Balance, Revenues, Bad Debt Expense, Salary Expense, Depreciation Expense, Fuel and Utilities Expense, Supplies Expense, and any other accounts you find relevant.

b. Compile an end-of-the-year Balance Sheet and Statement of Revenues and Expenses and Changes in Fund Balance.

CASE 7.2 The Museum Accounting Methods Controversy

St. Paul's Museum of Fine Arts was an old and conservative institution. Its Museum of Modern Art (MOMA) was a newcomer, making a name for itself because of its daring and innovative exhibits. Accounting policies reflected their philosophies. The Fine Arts Museum was very conservative and MOMA an accounting radical.

Professor Regina E. Herzlinger prepared this case for class discussion rather than to illustrate either effective or ineffective handling of an administrative situation.

Both museums had shops of virtually identical size and level of activity. In the past year, the following activities occurred:

(1) Revenues of $3,000,000.
(2) A beginning inventory of 20,000 items purchased at a cost of $40 each.
(3) Purchases for inventory of 40,000 items at a cost of $50 each.
(4) An ending inventory of 10,000 items.
(5) Fixed assets which had been purchased five years ago at a cost of $200,000. When acquired, it was anticipated that they would last for ten years with no salvage value.
(6) Administrative and selling expenses of $100,000.

ASSIGNMENT

Use T-accounts for revenues and expenses.

a. What was the income for the Fine Arts' museum shop for the year? Use LIFO and double-declining balance depreciation to calculate income.
b. What was the income for MOMA's museum shop? Use FIFO and straight-line depreciation to calculate income.
c. Which one was really more profitable and why?
d. Why is the use of FIFO and straight-line depreciation considered to be less conservative than LIFO and accelerated depreciation?

It may be useful to review the inventory and depreciation methods discussed in Chapter 3.

CASE 7.3 Vocational Education Club— The Missing Cash Dilemma

The head of the Vocational Education Department and the Home Economics teacher suddenly eloped on New Year's Day, taking with them all the cash in the Vocational Education Club treasury and the ledgers. All they left was a journal for the current year (the one in which the department was first started). Nobody knew how much cash they had taken. Do you?

Date	Account	Dr.	Cr.
January 1	(1) Accounts receivable	$100,000	
	Revenues		$100,000
Every month for	(2) Salary expense	5,000	
12 months	Salaries payable		5,000
February 1	(3) Inventory	6,000	
	Accounts payable		6,000
March 1	(4) Cash	100,000	
	Accounts receivable		100,000
March 1	(5) Fixed assets	20,000	
	Accounts payable		20,000
March 31 and every	(6) Salaries payable	5,000	
month thereafter	Cash		5,000
July 1	(7) Accounts payable	15,000	
	Cash		15,000

Note: The ending value of the inventory was $2,000; the fixed assets had a ten-year life with no ending value.

ASSIGNMENT

a. Post the journal entries to T-accounts.
b. Compile a balance sheet as of year-end, using straight-line depreciation.
c. What is the ending cash value?

CASE 7.4 Alexander Hospital Gift Shoppe

The beginning of the year Balance Sheet of Alabama's Alexander Hospital Gift Shoppe is shown on page 244. Prepare the postings to the T-accounts, a Balance Sheet, and a Statement of Revenues and Expenses to account for the following economic events that occurred during the fiscal year:

(1) The Shoppe had $30,000 in sales revenue, of which $28,500 were in cash and $1,500 were on a credit basis.

Professor Regina E. Herzlinger prepared this case for class discussion rather than to illustrate either effective or ineffective handling of an administrative situation.

Copyright © 1993 by the President and Fellows of Harvard College. Harvard Business School case 193-117.

(2) At the end of the year $800 in bills had not yet been paid by the Shoppe's customers. Of the total, $400 in bills were less than 30 days old, $200 were between 30 and 60 days old, and the remaining $200 were more than 60 days old. In the past the Shoppe had collected 95 percent of all bills less than a month old, 80 percent of the bills that were between 30 and 60 days old, and only 50 percent of the bills that were more than 60 days old.

(3) During the year, $10,000 of inventory was purchased, all of which had been paid for in cash by the end of the year.

(4) At the beginning of the year, the Shoppe bought $8,000 worth of furniture and equipment. It secured a 20-year, 9 percent loan to finance the purchase that called for equal annual payments of principal every year and for interest on the outstanding balance of the loan. The Shoppe made such payments by the end of the year.

(5) The note payable was completely paid off at year end. It had a 7 percent annual interest rate.

(6) The Gift Shoppe proposed to start a newsletter, "Mental and Physical Fitness," to keep people aware of the latest findings in medical, nutritional, and psychiatric research. In response to a letter soliciting subscriptions for the upcoming year, it received $5,000 of cash payments for subscriptions.

(7) At the beginning of the year, the Gift Shoppe paid the Alexander Hospital $2,400 in cash for the next 24 months of rent.

(8) The inventory on hand at the end of the year had cost $14,000.

(9) The depreciation expense for the year was $2,000.

(10) There were salary and benefits expenses of $12,000 during the course of the year, of which $1,000 was still owed to employees at the end of the year.

The Alexander Hospital Gift Shoppe
Balance Sheet
As of the Beginning of the Year

Assets			Liabilities and Fund Balance	
Cash		$ 5,000	Salaries payable	$ 1,500
Net accounts receivable		500	Note payable	2,000
Inventory		15,000	Total liabilities	3,500
Furniture and equipment				
Original cost	12,000			
Less: Accumulated				
depreciation	5,000	7,000	Fund balance	24,000
			Total liabilities and	
Total assets		$27,500	fund balance	$27,500

Part Two

Managerial Accounting and Control Systems in Nonprofit Organizations

8 Managerial Accounting and Control Defined

THE FIRST PART OF THIS BOOK discussed how to prepare and analyze financial data with the techniques of financial accounting and the process of financial analysis. Part Two discusses how nonprofit organizations can help to secure their futures with the techniques of managerial accounting and the process of managerial control. Thus, while these two parts of the book share the goal of enabling managers to achieve better financial results for their nonprofit organizations, they differ in the techniques and procedures they discuss for achieving it.

This chapter will explain the purpose of managerial accounting and control systems, the difficulties encountered in their implementation, and the contents of the remainder of Part Two.

WHAT ARE MANAGERIAL CONTROL SYSTEMS?

Managerial control systems help organizations to *plan* the results they hope to attain, to *measure* and *analyze* the differences between planned and actual results, and to *motivate* closing of the differences between the two. They are the organizational equivalent of a thermostat. Like this device, they are set to a pre-specified level, called a plan or budget. They continually monitor the differences between actual and specified results, and they activate mechanisms to align actual results with those planned.

Three activities enable good managerial control: (1) planning and budgeting to delineate intended results; (2) managerial accounting to measure actual results and analyze the reasons for the variances, if any, from the plan; and (3) motivating mechanisms to hold people responsible for attaining planned results and reward them for their accomplishment. These activities are normally described and implemented in a chronological cycle that begins with the planing process and proceeds to motivational devices. As indicated in Figure 8-1, the different parts of the cycle are inextricably linked

FIGURE 8-1 **Managerial Control Cycle**

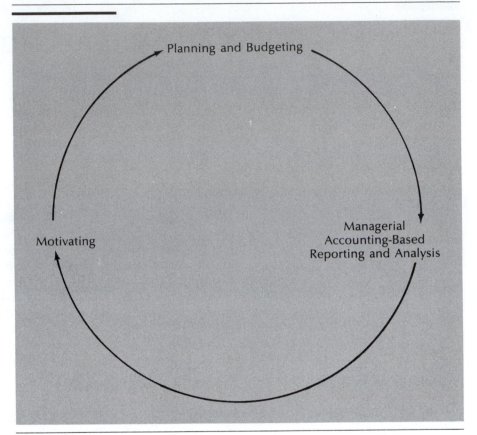

to each other: the planning process produces the standards against which actual results are measured; the measurement process, in turn, motivates managerial performance; and the results achieved by the motivational devices are used to help create a new plan for the next period.

Managerial control systems help to understand the past and shape the future. These systems are useful for evaluating whether past plans were appropriately executed. The impact of managerial control systems in shaping future plans can also be substantial. In some businesses, top managers use them interactively with their subordinates to probe and learn more about areas of crucial strategic importance and uncertainty.[1]

Some authors insert another activity in the cycle, one that they call "programming." In their eyes, programming succeeds the planning process and

[1]Robert Simons, "Strategic Orientation and Top Management Attention to Control Systems," *Strategic Management Journal* 12 (1991): 49-62.

converts plans into the action programs that will implement them. They define it as the activity during which major financial decisions are considered; for example, the step in which the U.S. Department of Defense decides which weapons systems and troop deployment patterns are most likely to achieve its plans. Here, this step is considered as an inseparable part of the planning process.

IMPACT OF MANAGERIAL CONTROL SYSTEMS

Managerial control systems can make substantial differences in the success of an organization. For example, Au Bon Pain, a Boston-based bakery-resturant chain, experienced explosive growth after implementing a new managerial control system. The prior system had placed considerable responsibility for planning, reporting, and analysis of results in the hands of corporate managers. The individual restaurant managers were paid a relatively low salary and a small share of the revenues of the restaurants. The new system completely reversed its predecessor. Planning was now performed primarily by the individual restaurant managers. Corporate planning was restricted to the design of the stores, menus, and operating systems. Restaurant managers could now hire staff, whose hours and pay they determined, decide on hours of operation, and even offer new, off-site businesses such as catering.

Reporting on performance was no longer solely a corporate function. Instead, a firm was hired to monitor the performance of the store from the perspective of the customer. The firm sent "mystery shoppers" to score individual restaurants on the following: Was the customer verbally acknowledged within three seconds of reaching the counter and served within one minute? Was the store's stock sufficient to fill all orders? Were the dining, serving, and restroom areas clean?

Failure to score well in the "mystery shopper" ratings prohibited restaurant managers from participating in Au Bon Pain's new motivational system. This new system reduced a manager's salary but increased his or her incentive compensation to half of the restaurant's negotiated profits. Some of the Au Bon Pain managers approached six figure incomes, while the company achieved record earnings and customer satisfaction. Most of these results could be traced to the new managerial control system. The new managerial control system changed the methods for planning, reporting, and motivating.

MANAGERIAL CONTROL SYSTEMS IN PRACTICE

Excellent managerial control systems are notable mostly for their absence. Their paucity is not surprising; they are difficult to implement, requiring substantial time and effort to speculate about the future. They require creative motivational devices and detailed, precise systems to measure and analyze results. They simultaneously demand vision and passion for detail. Most managers have one or the other quality, but few have both. In practice, many managerial control systems are mechanistic exercises, the products of mindless number-crunching. Next year's plan? Why it is the same as last year's, plus inflation. Why did we fail to achieve budgeted results? The economy is terrible. It is not our fault. How do we motivate employees? We inform them of our expectations at a yearly meeting.

Such mechanistic systems waste time and money. But the more important loss is the organization's inability to capture the benefits of a well-functioning managerial control system.

Excellence in managerial control systems is particularly difficult to attain in nonprofit organizations. For example, while the city of Philadelphia projected its 1991 deficit at $60 million, Moody's debt rating service estimated it as nearly three times as large.[2] And the Boston City Council finally voted to eliminate the long-established School Committee when, after many years of deficit spending, it once again overspent the school budget by $11 million.[3]

Indeed, some of the disquieting financial problems of major U.S. universities in 1992 can be traced to an absence of managerial control. Buoyed by a booming economy that increased their endowments and enabled ever-greater tuition increases, many universities greatly increased their expenses. They did not carefully plan or budget, they neglected reporting and analysis, and they did not focus on motivation to enhance performance. In 1992, the bubble burst: the U.S. economy was in recession and endowment earnings plummeted. Columbia University's 1993 deficit was projected at a staggering $83 million; Yale University closed some of its educational departments; and Stanford tried to pare $43 million from its budget.

Many of these problems are caused by the intrinsic characteristics of nonprofit organizations.[4] Most nonprofits lack a market signal of success or failure because they derive the bulk of their revenues from sources other than their customers. After all, many are charitable organizations whose very purpose is to enable the poor to use services they cannot otherwise afford. Many are also monopolies. As a result, nonprofits cannot benefit from the single most powerful element of a managerial control system, the paying customer who chooses the best of alternative suppliers.

When consumers felt that cars produced by American manufacturers were not nearly as good a value as automobiles manufactured elsewhere,

[2]"The City of Brotherly Love Keeps Taking It On the Chin," *Business Week* (September 10, 1990): 80.

[3]"Boston Votes to Abolish School Board," *The New York Times*, 6 December 1990, p. A22.

[4]See Regina E. Herzlinger, "Managing the Finances of Nonprofit Organizations," *California Management Review* 21, no. 3 (Spring 1979): 60-69; and "Why Data Systems in Nonprofit Organizations Fail," *Harvard Business Review* (January 1977): 81-86, for further discussion.

they made their feelings clear by buying Japanese and European vehicles. But the clients of many nonprofit organizations lack this pocketbook vote. They may use the services of wildly inefficient or ineffective nonprofit organizations only because they do not pay the costs of that inefficiency or lack a choice among service-providing sites. These nonprofit organizations cannot receive the same kind of clear message delivered to the American car companies who lost their market share.

Also complicating the managerial control process is the fact that most nonprofits produce services rather than goods. Services are difficult to measure because they evanesce, disappearing at the point of production. Goods do not. As in science, measuring the properties of a solid quantity is simpler than measuring those of a gas. This measurement problem is not unique to nonprofits. It also plagues service-producing businesses, such as restaurants, hotels, banks, airlines, and retail stores. They too experience substantial difficulties in measuring the many attributes of their services.

Consider, for example, the complexity of measuring the relatively simple services performed by the McDonald's fast food restaurants. The attributes to be measured must include speed of service, courtesy, low-cost, cleanliness, taste, nutrition, freshness, and responsiveness to customer requests. But this complexity is dwarfed by that of measuring the attributes of the professional services produced by nonprofits: education, health care, human services, defense, regulation, culture, and fellowship. Compare the complexity of measuring McDonald's services to the complexity of measuring the services in a first-grade class—the intellectual, social, and emotional developments of the child, the effectiveness of parent-teacher interaction, and the safety, comfort, and sanitation of the classroom. Further, in contrast to McDonald's services, many of the school's services lack well-accepted measuring rods. Even traditional achievement tests of learning are continually critiqued for their inaccuracy and biases.

Managerial control difficulties are increased by the absence of well-accepted production processes for professional services. For example, although the New England states consume many more per-capita health care resources than the western states, nobody knows if New England's doctors and hospitals produce better or worse health care than those of the West. This question cannot be answered because of the absence of well-accepted standards that relate the use of health care resources to health status. Such standards are absent for many other professional services as well. Thus, while a low student-to-teacher ratio is frequently cited as essential to effective education, the student-to-teacher class ratio at the Harvard Business School, renowned for the excellence of its teaching, is frequently as high as 80-to-1.

How many police are needed to provide a safe environment? How many social workers to protect the rights of children? How many violins to produce a beautiful sound? How large a curatorial staff to display a museum's collection? Because all these questions lack universally accepted answers, the managerial control process of planning results becomes subjective and ambiguous.

Last, the professionals who frequently serve as the managers and the primary employees in many nonprofit organizations complicate the motivational process. Professionals who are also managers embody two separate, frequently conflicting, allegiances: one to the mores of their profession and another to their organization. All professions view their need for resources as imperative, while the managers of all organizations, no matter how wealthy, must constrain and ration spending. Thus, while the professors in the English department argue for more faculty slots and higher salaries to maintain excellence, the ex-professor who is now the college's president must struggle to simultaneously empathize with and reject some former colleagues' requests.

Then too, some of the motivational devices appropriate for traditional organizations are ill-suited for professional ones. For example, a hierarchical, pyramidal organizational structure that motivates with promises of promotions up the career ladder is irrelevant to most professionals. They seek peer recognition, not managerial promotions. No wonder the deans of schools carefully refer to themselves as "First Among Equals." In doing so, they acknowledge their allegiance to the flat, collegial organizational structure of professional organizations and disavow the legitimacy of managerial hierarchies.

Many professionals are resistant to business-like efforts to plan and control their nonprofit organization. When the curator of a large museum proposed short-term rentals of a fraction of its vast, unused art objects to smaller museums, he expected plaudits. His plan would simultaneously shore up his museum's sagging finances and enable smaller museums to access world-class art. But instead, the plan caused a furor. The museum's professional staff considered it "callous" and "fraught with hazards," reported *The New York Times* in the front page of its Art section.[5] They wanted the *status-quo* maintained. It is difficult to implement managerial control systems in such resistant environments.

Despite these characteristics, many nonprofit organizations have excellent managerial control systems. And some have even overcome these substantial impediments and installed model systems. For example, the Archdiocese of Chicago reversed its flagging fortunes, marked by a 1989 deficit of $4 million, with a new managerial control system. It succeeded despite the absence of such systems in the past and the lack of business training in the background of most priests. The Archdiocese's new system consists of a planning and budgeting process that includes mechanisms for measuring actual performance, such as quarterly reports of performance. It also makes use of motivational devices, such as consultations for pastors who exceed their budgets. One pastor recalled that in the past, "We didn't have a plan."

---

[5]Michael Kimmeman, "What on Earth Is the Guggenheim Up To?" *The New York Times*, 14 October 1990, Section 2, pp. 1-2.

The new system, in contrast, has resulted in restructuring the archdiocesan offices, in more equitable tuition pricing in its 138 schools, and in the sale of unnecessary assets.[6]

Other nonprofits can also succeed in installing managerial control systems. To do so, they must explicitly confront the difficulties they face in installing such systems. Lack of "paying customer" feedback can be partially corrected with detailed customer surveys. The absence of standards of production calls for a careful planning process. And the resistance of professionals to managerial control requires the design of creative motivational systems. All of these will be discussed in the upcoming chapters.

WHAT IS MANAGERIAL ACCOUNTING?

Financial and managerial accounting are conventionally distinguished by their intended audience. Financial accounting statements are said to be primarily for the use of those *external* to the organization, while managerial accounting data are for *internal* users. But this distinction is not telling. After all, internal users such as employees are vitally interested in the results depicted in financial statements, while external users such as board members inevitably find some of the managerial accounting of value.

The more telling distinction between financial and managerial accounting is in the extent of their codification. Financial accounting is steeped in the well-developed standards of generally accepted accounting principles. Managerial accouting data, in contrast, are rarely audited and not irrevocably wedded to generally accepted accounting principles. The following old joke told about all accountants is more accurately aimed at the subset of managerial accountants:

Question: How can you spot accountants?

Answer: When you ask them the sum of two plus two, they respond: "What number are you looking for?"

The flexibility of managerial accounting results directly from its purpose. It must be *relevant* for answering a vast array of managerial questions. Among the key questions it answers are: How much does something cost? Should we invest in this activity? What are the appropriate prices for our services? Strictly codified accounting standards will inevitably produce data that are irrelevant for certain questions. For example, if accounting for the cost of a hospital service, say an X ray, were required to *include* depreciation expense, the resulting data would be useless for projecting the cost of providing

---

[6] "Chicago's Catholic Church: Putting Its House In Order," *Business Week* (June 10, 1991): 60-65.

only one more X ray; but, if the accounting were required to *exclude* depreciation, the resulting data would be useless for long-run investment planning.

Why should depreciation expenses be excluded as an element of the cost of producing only one more unit of the service? Because the expense remains the same in the short run and will not change with the production of only one more X ray. But depreciation expense should be included as an element of the costs of continued production of the service because the expense varies considerably in the long run, as different types of X ray equipment are added to or subtracted from the hospital.

Inevitably, as in this example, an accounting system that required *either* inclusion *or* exclusion of certain expenses creates data that are incorrect for answering certain managerial questions. (The concept this example illustrates will be fully discussed in Chapter 13.)

Although the flexibility of managerial accounting helps to create data that are relevant to the question being asked, the relevance comes at a price. The paucity of standards may result in the use of accounting data that are totally inappropriate for the issue being examined. Those preparing the data may not understand the question or may even willfully choose to present misleading data. There are many instances of both; for example, some nonprofits will "creatively" account for the costs of a service at its very highest levels when they ask the public for donations or grants to cover its costs. In 1992, when the U.S. Congress charged some research universities with manipulating their costs to obtain unduly large U.S. government reimbursement of their research costs, many top level university managers and board members were stunned. They were simply not aware of the possibility of such problems in managerial accounting.

The flexibility of managerial accounting data demands a deep understanding of how they are prepared and the resulting limitations in their use. Simply put, managerial accounting requires much more knowledge of the user than does financial accounting.

WHAT LIES AHEAD?

The following four chapters discuss the three activities in a managerial control system: planning and budgeting, measuring and analyzing variances between planned and actual results, and motivating to achieve planned performance. Each activity is discussed in a separate chapter. The discussion delineates the ideal characteristics of each activity, identifies major difficulties in its implementation, and presents examples of successful practice. The last chapters in Part Two discuss the analytic techniques for financial decision-making. Because of the managerial orientation of this book, they are discussed last rather than first. As in Part One, techniques are discussed only after their purposes are clarified.

Although these six chapters distill a large body of knowledge and present it in the context of nonprofit organizations, do not be misled by their brevity and relevance to assume that their contents are simple. Many intelligent people experience difficulty in understanding and applying the economic and psychological concepts that underlie the subject. As one successful manager observed: "When I was a student, I found managerial accounting a tough subject. But now that I am a manager, the real tough nut is in implementing managerial control. The difficulties of *implementing* effective control systems dwarf those of *understanding* the subject matter."

SUMMARY

This chapter introduced the managerial control systems used to plan and secure the nonprofit organization's future and the language of managerial accounting, which is used to measure the events that take place in managerial control systems. The process of managerial control is crucial to the success of an organization, but is difficult to execute well, particularly in nonprofit organizations. It consists of three activities: planning and budgeting, reporting and analysis, and designing motivational devices. Because managerial accounting is much less codified than financial accounting, it requires much deeper comprehension.

Suggested Reading

Herzlinger, Regina E. "Management Control Systems in Human Service Organizations." Paper delivered at the Conference on Human Service Organizations and Organization Theory, Center for Advanced Study in the Behavioral Sciences, 23 March 1979, at Stanford University, Palo Alto, California.

Herzlinger, Regina E. "Managing the Finances of Nonprofit Organizations." *California Management Review* (Spring 1979): 60-69.

Herzlinger, Regina E. "Why Data Systems Fail in Nonprofit Organizations." *Harvard Business Review* (January-February 1977): 81-86.

Herzlinger, Regina E., and Nancy M. Kane. *The Bank, The Insurance Company, and the Factory—Administrative Mechanisms for Income Redistribution.* Cambridge, MA: Ballinger Press, 1979.

Ramanathan, Kavasseri V. *Management Control in Nonprofit Organizations.* New York: John Wiley & Sons, 1982.

Ramanathan, Kavasseri V., and Larry P. Hegstad. *Readings in Management Control in Nonprofit Organizations.* New York: John Wiley & Sons, 1982.

Wildavsky, Aaron. *The Politics of the Budgetary Process.* Boston: Little, Brown, 1974.

Ziebell, Mary T., and Don T. DeCoster. *Management Control Systems in Nonprofit Organizations.* San Diego: Harcourt Brace Jovanovich, Publishers, 1991.

DISCUSSION QUESTIONS

1. What are managerial control systems?

2. What are the three activities of managerial control?

3. What are the difficulties in implementing managerial control systems in non-profit organizations? How should managers deal with them?

4. What is managerial accounting?

5. How does managerial accounting differ from financial accounting?

6. Describe the managerial control system of a nonprofit organization with which you are familiar. Evaluate the system, recommend any needed changes, and specify how you would implement them. What results do you expect the new system to achieve that the old system did not?

Cases

CASE STUDIES

The Massport case, 8.1, presents a classic contrast between two different styles of managerial control—one centralized and the other decentralized—and their use by two different directors of Massport. One director, an accountant, went on to become Governor of Massachusetts; the other was widely hailed as an excellent civil servant. The case provides an example of how smart managers control organizations.

Case 8.2 describes the management control system used by Humana, a for-profit hospital chain. The system is highly centralized with detailed reporting and clear incentive systems. Does this system help or hinder Humana? Can it and should it be employed in a nonprofit setting? We will return to this case after Chapter 14.

CASE 8.1 Massport

The panaoramic view from the office of David W. Davis, the executive director at the Massachusetts Port Authority (Massport), includes the Port of Boston and Logan International Airport—its largest facilities. Tugboats bustled back and forth across the harbor and jumbo jets took off and landed on the other side of the harbor as Davis spoke in his calm and reflective manner about the position he occupied and the changes he had brought about in the control of the agency:

> My ideas about management led me to believe that performance is better in a decentralized organization where there is clear responsibility and accountability at the operational levels. Also a decentralized management system would permit me to spend more of my time building linkages between Massport and the outside world. I viewed Massport as an economic development agency which should be concerned with issues of international trade and the environment and national economic and commerce concerns.

Research Assistant Frances Jones prepared this case under the supervision of Professor Regina E. Herzlinger.

Copyright © 1991 by the President and Fellows of Harvard College. Harvard Business School case 179-169. Revised January 1993.

The board was concerned that it wasn't getting information, but there just wasn't much to give. The accounting system responded to the requirements of the trust agreement which is the basis of our financing and not to the management of the agency. There were no profit and loss statements for the different facilities, so we could not evaluate performance of the separate units that comprise Massport.

We changed the budgeting system from one that was top-down to a bottom-up process. Much time was spent in educating people about the process and substance of these changes. Some folks could make the shift and some couldn't—not so much because of their abilities, but because of their attitudes. Some managers eventually left. The new managers are deeply committed to these management systems.

MASSPORT

The Massachusetts legislature (Acts of 1956) established the Massachusetts Port Authority to operate, maintain, and build additional facilities for the "development and improvement of commerce" in metropolitan Boston. The Authority operated the following facilities:

(1) *Logan International Airport*, one of the country's largest;
(2) *Tobin Memorial Bridge*, a toll bridge providing an expressway connector to Maine and eastern New Hampshire;
(3) *The Port of Boston*, consisting of freight handling and storage facilities; and
(4) *Hanscom Field*, a general aviation facility located west of Boston.

The Authority's board consists of seven members appointed by the governor, serving seven-year terms.

Massport was organized along functional and programmatic lines. There were separate aviation, maritime, and bridge units, and a number of administrative departments. All of the operating and staff managers, but for the controller, had joined Massport after 1975.

The enabling legislation established Massport as "a body politic and a public instrumentality of the Commonwealth" with the power to issue revenue bonds; however, it has no taxing authority and its bonds are not backed by the general taxing ability of the Commonwealth.

The Authority usually generated a surplus in its operating funds. It had over 700 employees, of whom 420 were covered by collective bargaining agreements.

MASSPORT UNDER EDWARD KING

Under Edward J. King, Massport's executive director prior to Davis, operating revenues grew from $12.9 million to $47 million. Logan International Airport was the focus of King's development efforts at Massport. It was transformed from a mid-sized turboprop airport to a modern international facility.

A close top-level associate of Edward J. King's who worked with him before, during, and after his years at Massport described King and his style of management at Massport:

Ed King draws people. He's a leader: shrewd, fair, and strong. After graduating from Boston College, he played professional football for three years. He then studied accounting and was a practicing accountant for six years. He became comptroller at the Port Authority in 1959, the first employee they hired. He was made secretary-treasurer in 1960. Soon after, the executive director became ill and Ed took over the job.

Back then, the Authority had a lot of problems, particularly with money. We had almost no capital, and the seaport and the airport were in deficit. The bridge made perhaps $2.5 million. Also, it wasn't even clear who the people on the payroll were.

Management control was executed by sitting down every month and going through every item in the budget. We knew everything—down to the price of road salt. Ed was involved in all the concession negotiations, all the labor negotiations. He knew every employee. He's a very hard negotiator—businesslike, tough, but not in a vulgar way. Those same poeple support him now—they wouldn't have respected a soft touch.

In the early days we checked every invoice. The budget was a tool to show what we expected. The *real* control was to know every employee and to check every expense. King didn't let out any concessions at Massport, and after various unsuccessful attempts to lease out the airport's garage management, took that over as well. Ed wanted to do what was best for Massport, not for himself.

During King's tenure, the composition of the board changed. It became increasingly interested in operating Massport as a social entity. King felt it should be operated like a business. Also, the board felt that it wasn't getting the information it needed. These differences led to his termination in December of 1974. He was elected governor of Massachusetts in 1979.

MASSPORT UNDER DAVID DAVIS

Born in Nebraska, educated in California, Davis was a budget specialist with a broad background in government and nonprofit institutions. Davis had moved from job to job along with his mentor, until his job at Massport.

When Davis came to Massport, his situation was admittedly a "lonely one." Virtually all of the staff had been hired by Ed King. One of the first persons Davis hired was Arthur Segel, a 24-year-old native of Massachusetts, who had just completed an MBA at Stanford. Davis told the story of how he hired Arthur:

He called me up and said he thought I needed him. He was quite insistent. I told him to come in to see me, but it was a short interview because I had a luncheon engagement. I told him to get me a resume and I'd get back to him. Forty-five minutes later, at the restaurant, I looked up and there was Arthur, resume in hand.

For the first year, Segel served as Davis' assistant, spending much of his time talking to people at all levels of the organization. Davis stated:

I wanted an active administrative assistant, but one who wouldn't be mistaken for me. As it turned out, Arthur was doing more financial analysis than the accounting department was. Arthur's style was "precipitous," but coupled with enormous energy and charm. The organization liked Arthur.

Davis described his method of organizing projects, his use of the new management system, his system of incentives and disincentives in management:

There are other incentives besides monetary ones. It's important to foster a feeling of belonging. I can accomplish this by being interested in the activities and the performance of managers. It's really a matter of "organizational style," something that's very intangible and difficult to define. Because of the collegial atmosphere and my desire for multiple inputs and decentralization, I am not a snap decision maker. Frequently, I'm the referee. If you want someone who has it all laid out, that's *not* me. We have a team approach to accomplishing major tasks. The team leaders report to me. My instructions to them are generally pretty vague—they know that I expect coordination with appropriate departments.

I keep an eye on the long term by using a task list—with the task, participating departments, and steps. I have a staff meeting with all department heads twice a month, and I try to follow up on the list every other meeting. I view the new management system as a way of integrating the organization. Also, it supplies the information needed to hold managers responsible for their performance. Finally, it forms a kind of contract between me and the pieces of the organization. The budget clarifies the priorities and the plans and provides for sufficient moves so that there is no ambiguity about the goals of the Authority.

Installation of the New Control System

During Davis' first summer as director, the accounting firm of Coopers & Lybrand was hired to install a "what if" model to produce long-term forecasts of financials. That process took most of the first year.

In the early fall, Davis changed Arthur Segel's position to that of director of budgets and federal relations, where he took charge of planning and implementing the new budgeting and other control systems that Davis felt were needed. Also, a finance committee of the board of directors was formed. Michael Christian, member of the board and chairman of the finance committee, related that:

I'd wanted to start a finance committee for a while. I was concerned about the integrity of our finance, of our cash management. Arthur Segel became secretary to the finance committee and he has guided our actions. The committee has been the place to discuss his ideas and we've given him support and advice.

Segel documented his activities through a series of status reports to the finance committee. He reported:

We initially went out into the field to review the chart of accounts with the unit managers, to revamp the accounts to their liking, to reissue account descriptions, and to insist that all coding be done in the field for the first time. Since January we have provided internal-auditing support to help in their coding. In return, we promised a monthly line-item expense and payables computerized report by manager. To make these reports more meaningful we have worked with every unit manager and department head to develop a month-by-month budget per account. In this way managers at all levels will finally receive expense information from an accounting system that they constructed themselves. More importantly, we have begun involving all levels of the organization in a more meaningful budget process. These are literally the first financial reports that managers throughout the organization have ever received.

We are beginning a job-costing system to be introduced next fiscal year which will help us identify the true cost of each of our structures. As important as understanding our true costs per building, we will also then be able to pass on those costs most accurately to our tenants.

We introduced a capital budget by developing a five-year capital plan with each of the operating heads and the engineering department. The short-term mandate was to reach an agreement on the list of projects for the next construction season and to match those "wish lists" with what we expect our cash situation to be.

According to Segel, the most important products of the budget process were the organization charts and statements of goals and objectives that the units produced. For example, the objectives of the building maintenance department were as follows:

- Reduce lost time by accident from 9 to 5 by the end of next year.
- Reduce overtime from current level of 11 percent to 7 percent overall by the end of the fiscal year.
- Reduce energy usage by close surveillance of using departments and use of shutdown cards to calculate the savings with a goal of 10 percent below budgeted quantities based on usage.
- When cleaning contract is to be rebid, include an item-to-program nonroutine project cleaning by work order based upon need at period intervals.
- By winter, develop a mechanical means of removing snow around lights to reduce electrical costs during snowstorms and provide for quicker results.

A contract was let to install a database-oriented, modular accounting system. The introduction of the system resulted in changes in the operating budget over and above the developmental changes which the budgeting and finance department had identified earlier. Personnel procedures and problems were identified as particularly thorny.

THE BUDGETING PROCESS

A report on the budgeting process concluded:

> Lacking background information critical to the evaluation of the budget submitted for its approval, board members required the budget department to prepare a financial framework within which the feasibility of budget requests could be measured, and called unit managers and department heads before them to present the rationale behind their requests. The managers were not consulted about cuts and changes in this budget during the budget review process. Throughout the budgeting process, information about the status of submissions was scant and provided on a highly informal basis.

Indeed, many departments and unit managers complained that their budgets were cut without their being informed of the cuts.

The chairman of the board of directors, Robert Weinberg, felt that people were not expecting the kind of disruption that occurred.

> You have to think through all the human relationships involved in the established patterns, not just procedures. The rules of the game were being changed. Before, amending a budget was an extermely laborious procedure, so the practice had been to pass a high budget and underspend. There was no history of budgetary politics at Massport.

THE CURRENT SITUATION

Several unit managers were interviewed about the new budgeting and accounting systems. Their responses varied, but most were willing to give it a try. Managers had just received expense reports for August, and they were working on ironing out bugs. According to the budget director, summer expenditures are characteristically low, and she felt that it would take until the middle of the fiscal year for managers to have a clear sense of where they were.

One of the managers interviewed said:

> I think it's good from an operational point of view, as a manager at a facility. When it works, you know where you are. Before, coding was done uptown; you got no cost figure at all.

> Actually, I can tell pretty well what it costs me here because I've been here 31 years. But now the people at High Street (the administrative offices) and I have the same information. One thing bothers me. I know some vendors weren't paid in August that should have been. I hope it catches up with itself. With the complex union situation here, small problems, like no clean clothes or something, can become very big. I'd rather have more control of my payables. But I get a good response if I need something quickly and I call the purchasing agent.

> Managers *have* gotten more responsibility. I don't know about the other people, but *I* intend to come in close to budget. It's my job to see that Massport's money is spent the right way.

Another manager, the chief of an emergency service unit, and his assistant were less sanguine about the system:

> We went into this as a positive thing—we wanted to know where we were. But now we're being held accountable without knowing where we are. We're supposed to get printouts monthly, but so far we've only gotten July—we haven't seen anything since. One problem is that the purchasing department doesn't have enough staff. But here, we need to replace used equipment immediately for safety reasons. And now vendors aren't being paid. One branded us "just another government agency."

> If the system worked correctly, if there was expedience in it, it would be okay. I like the format of the budget; the categories are useful. But the narrative portions are, for the most part, a waste of time—of course we're going to respond to 100 percent of all emergencies. It doesn't fit here; nothing in this unit is *routine*. We can't predict our costs accurately.

A third unit manager interviewed was the head of the field maintenance unit at the airport, which is responsible for motor vehicle service as well as snow removal, mowing, and similar activities.

> It's been hard for us, hard to get out of old habits. We have three supervisors here—one has been here 30 years, the other two about 20 years each. I've been here 20 years.

> Budgets were a new thing for me. It was a very complicated process. We had to figure out costs for all of our own vehicles, and then all the other units whose vehicles we service wanted to know costs for *their* budgets. There were quarrels over whose budget an item should be in.

ASSIGNMENT

1. Evaluate the new system and contrast it to the old one.
2. Recommend changes in the structure of the new system if you think they are needed.
3. Recommend changes in the way it was implemented if you think them warranted.

CASES 8.2 AND 14.3 The Hospital Replacement Decision

Kelly Bolton, Humana's regional vice president of the Hospital Division for the Sunbelt, was reviewing a memo from corporate about his feasibility study for a replacement hospital (see **Exhibit 1**). The memo questioned several of the key assumptions made in preparing the financial projections. Under corporate's alternative assumptions, the internal rate of return for the replacement facility would fall from regional's 15 percent to 10 percent.

He wondered how to proceed. The initial proposal was submitted three years before. The next step in the capital budgeting process would require the hospital division's president to present the project to the Management Committee of Humana. Should he defend the original assumptions or adopt corporate's alternative assumptions? Or, should he simply withdraw the project proposal?

He realized that his decision could affect his region's budget performance, the incentive compensation of his hospital administrators, his relations with corporate, and morale within the region and the community where the replacement facility would be built. To help clarify the factors involved, Bolton decided to review the background of the replacement hospital proposal and the history, management style, organizational structure, and management control systems and policies of Humana. (His review of management systems was limited to the Hospital Division.)

MANAGEMENT STYLE

Humana had the same top management in 1988 as it did when it was founded in 1961: David Jones as chairman and Wendell Cherry as president. Their management philosophy permeated the organization. Commented Wendell Cherry:

> Our value added is from management. We don't tell the doctors how to practice medicine, but we do know how to manage an organization. We centralize our management systems to insure that our know-how is shared with all of our institutions.

Centralized management included strong financial systems, measurement of performance against specific goals, standardization of policies and procedures, a highly leveraged compensation structure, and clear delineation of responsibility. Hospital administrator John Morse, an ex-naval officer and Wharton MBA, summarized the management environment at the company:

> The philosophy at Humana is very clear to all. The company is highly systems oriented and emphasizes standardization of policies and procedures. At Humana, unlike some of the other hospital management companies, there is a clear delineation of the responsibility of corporate versus the responsibility of the hospital; there are few gray

Richard B. Siegrist prepared this case under the supervision of Professor Regina E. Herzlinger.

areas. The hospital administrator and staff influence the hospital's direction but many decisions are made by corporate. But the administrative staff has a great deal of operational power. And, we're prepared to move up the ladder because we understand Humana's policies so clearly.

ORGANIZATIONAL STRUCTURE

Humana had a classical organizational structure. The president and chief operating officer, Wendell Cherry, as well as the heads of the corporate departments of Internal Audit, Legal, Finance and Administration, and Communications and Planning reported directly to David Jones, the chief executive officer, as did the hospital and group health division heads. Mr. Jones also served as chairman of the board of directors and chairman of the Management Committee which developed corporate strategy and management policies, determined earnings goals, and reviewed major capital expenditure proposals.

The Hospital Division, the mainstay of Humana's operations, was divided into six geographic regions: Central, Delta, Mid South, Florida, Western, and Pacific. They were headed by regional vice presidents who reported to the president of the Hospital Division. Each region contained 15 to 20 individual hospitals. The regional vice presidents were responsible for growing the business of their regions.

The hospital administrators in a region reported to the regional vice president. Each hospital administrator was responsible for the operation and performance of his or her hospital and for supervising the various departments within the hospital itself. The management structure of a hospital varied depending on the number of beds, size, and revenue of the hospital.

CAPITAL BUDGETING PROCESS

Humana's annual capital spending plan forecasted capital expenditures for the next three years. It classified capital expenditures into four areas: existing hospital operations; development (including the acquisition of hospitals and construction of new hospitals in new markets); Health Services Division (which encompassed expenditures for alternative health care delivery system projects); and other (such as new corporate offices and equipment, aircraft, computers, etc.). Existing operations outlays were divided into specific type: hospital replacements, expansion of existing hospital facilities, renovation or expansion of ancillary or outpatient services, equipment purchases, and nonrevenue-producing construction (such as a new roof or air conditioning system).

The Corporate Budget Department performed a preliminary review of the budgets, but the specific projects included in the budgets were formally reviewed and approved at a later time. To estimate total spending, the department attached probabilities of approval to the projects in the hospital capital budgets. While no specified limit was placed on the total capital spending, the Planning Department's five-year business plan, updated every six months, served as a backdrop to these decisions. Capital expenditures were assumed to be financed 25 percent from operations and 75 percent from new long-term debt.

Specific capital projects required formal approval before they could proceed. Hospital administrators could approve all projects within their limits ($6,000 typically). The regional vice president could approve projects less than $20,000. Projects greater than $20,000 were sent to the Capital Expenditure Request (CER) Committee for review. Its recommendations were to the vice president of administration who, in turn, made recommendations to the president of the Hospital Division. The president of the Hospital Division could approve projects under $1 million. All other projects were presented to the Management Committee for approval, by the president of the Hospital Division and the regional vice president involved.

The hospital administrator prepared financial feasibility studies for all capital expenditure requests, containing ten-year *pro forma* income statements. The related balance sheet was prepared by the Hospital Division's budget department. An after-tax internal rate of return for the project over the ten-year period was computed with 15 percent being the usual minimum requirement. The Corporate Budget Department reviewed all feasibility studies and communicated reservations to the responsible regional official, typically the regional vice president. Outstanding issues were resolved prior to the presentation of any project to the Management Committee for approval.

In evaluating specific projects, the Management Committee did not apply a uniform required rate of return. Rather, it estimated the company's cost of capital and performed a discounted cash flow analysis based on the risks. Project approval decisions were not based solely on the numbers. Intangible considerations could have a significant influence on the approval or rejection of a capital project.

ANNUAL BUDGETING PROCESS

The budgeting process at Humana was a combination of a top-down and bottom-up approach. The Management Committee set an overall budget, by reviewing macroeconomic conditions and environmental factors to arrive at assumptions about the next year and budgeting an earnings per share figure on the basis of Humana's past performance, Wall Street expectations, and intuition about what was attainable. It received a consolidated income statement and balance sheet (factoring in predicted capital expenditures) for the budget year, as prepared by the Planning Department. This budget was then broken down into four areas: hospital operations, development, health services division, and other. The hospital operations budget was further divided into regional budgets. Pre-tax margin was the key figure in that budget.

Simultaneously, the hospital administrators built up budgets for their hospitals from the department level. The bottom-up budgets were summed by region and compared with the regional budget developed by the Management Committee. If a profit shortfall existed in a region, it was made up by reducing the individual budgets of the hospitals within that region. Each region stood on its own. Altered rarely were the top-down regional budgets or the overall EPS target.

Approved capital expenditures were factored into the hospital and regional budget. The hospital was charged imputed interest of 14 percent on the total capital expenditure, including any additional working capital required, and received imputed interest of 8 percent on any free cash it provided to corporate. Capital expenditures did not change regional pre-tax margin targets. The hospital with the capital expenditure may have received a budget exception for its targeted pre-tax margin, but the other hospitals in its region were expected to make up that shortfall in profit.

PERFORMANCE MEASUREMENT

Performance measurement at Humana used three primary systems: the general ledger, productivity management, and patient business systems.

- The general ledger system was centralized at corporate headquarters. Each hospital submitted monthly data via computer terminal to headquarters. Corporate processed the information and sent back a variety of reports. The key general ledger report was the hospital budget analysis (see **Exhibit 2**), which compared the current month and year-to-date income statements with their budget. No adjustment was made for differences between budget and actual in number of patient days or case mix. The report highlighted pre-tax margin, accounts receivable days outstanding, occupancy, and paid hours per patient day. If the hospital administrator could attain the targeted pre-tax margin figure, line item variances from budget were of lesser importance.
- As a complement to the financial orientation of the general ledger system, Humana used its productivity management system which measured labor productivity for salaried labor, but not physicians, based on standards for labor hours per unit of activity (e.g., per-calendar day, test, dose, visit, etc.). (See **Exhibit 3**.) The standards were determined using time and motion studies and were considered to be ideals. Because they might not be attainable in the short run, Humana also set budgeted targets for each department. Biweekly comparisons were made between actual, budget, and standard hours per unit of activity for each department within a hospital. Specific departments were compared on a regional and companywide level (see **Exhibit 4**). Performance ratios of actual-to-standard and actual-to-budget were used for the comparison (a ratio of greater than 1 or 100 percent indicated favorable performance).
- The third performance measurement system, patient business system, tracked patient origin, charges generated, patient days, admissions, and bad debt by physicians. The information was used to evaluate the revenue-generating and marketing performance of individual physicians and hospitals.

INCENTIVE COMPENSATION SYSTEM

Incentives accounted for a large portion of the total compensation of Humana managers. Each manager was paid a base salary and a bonus based on performance in relation to specified goals. Under the highly leveraged compensation structure, a manager who performed well could make more money at Humana than at the other hospital management companies. The performance measure used and the magnitude of the bonus in relation to base salary varied by level and by type of management (e.g., operations or corporate).

Hospital administrators received a basic bonus of up to 50 percent of their salary if they met predetermined performance goals for their hospital. The key performance measures were pre-tax profit, days of accounts receivable outstanding, bad debts, and growth in census. They were then eligible for an additional stock bonus at market value for up to 50 percent of their salary. Under this system, a six-figure salary was possible for a young Humana hospital administrator. Regional vice presidents received similar incentive compensation, but their performance goals were based on the performance of their region. Corporate managers received bonuses based solely on EPS. Four levels existed in the structure for corporate bonuses, ranging from 25 percent to 60 percent of salary.

RECRUITING, TRAINING, AND PROMOTION

New managers were brought into the company at the entry level. Each year 60 to 70 recent college graduates were recruited to participate in Humana's one-year administrator training program or two-year financial manager training program, which combined formal classroom study with on-the-job training. They then became hospital assistant administrators or assistant financial managers. Approximately half of the operating executives at Humana had gone through these entry-level training programs. Because hospital operations and corporate staff remained relatively separate and few people moved back and forth between the two, some tension existed between the two groups.

The size of the hospital determined the salary range, type of company automobile, prestige, etc. Accordingly, the typical advancement pattern was to move from smaller to larger hospitals. No purely lateral or downward moves were permitted. The company's regional vice presidents had moved up through the hospital ranks. Almost every position was posted and filled internally; outsiders were rarely hired, except at entry level.

There was a fairly high turnover in the training program and some turnover at the hospital administrator level, but almost none at the regional vice president or corporate levels.

ASSIGNMENT

1. Should Humana invest in this hospital? Be prepared to discuss both the financial and managerial implications of your decision.
2. What are the key success factors which will enable Humana to maintain its rapid rate of growth?
3. Outline the control and human resource management systems used by Humana. Do they help or hinder Humana in achieving the key factors you identified in Question 2?

EXHIBIT 1 **The Hospital Replacement Decision**

Memo To: Kelly Bolton
    From: Jane Lloyd, Corporate
 Subject: Feasibility Study: Replacement Hospital

Attached is the completed financial feasibility for a replacement facility. Please review the assumptions closely to be sure they accurately reflect your assessment of the existing market. Based on these assumptions, this project generates the minimum return required for capital projects (15 percent).

Pursuant to our telephone conversation, however, listed below are reservations raised about these assumptions:

Marketing Considerations

- Certificate of need application for the new facility indicates that the SMSA has had minimal population growth, and a higher than average percentage of the population is over age 65.
- Two nearby hospitals have spent considerable capital funds over the years to increase their market share. Both would represent formidable opponents in any market share battles.
- There currently is an out-migration of patients to nearby communities. Though I have not confirmed this, it could be that the patients going to the city require the sophisticated services of the teaching hospitals, and we are capturing some of the remaining patients at our other hospitals in this area. Therefore, the actual significance of this out-migration may not be what it seems.
- The ability of the new hospital to increase patient days from the current 26,000 annual volume is conditional upon the ability of five recruited physicians to establish successful practices. Again, given the stable nature of this market, this will be difficult.

Patient Days

- The attached pro-formas assume patient days in the first year of approximately 32,000 due to: (1) impact of recruited physicians; and (2) new location of hospital, and assume subsequent years will grow at a compound annual growth rate of 2.4 percent. This compares to a less than 1 percent growth rate during the '70s.
- Based upon information presented in the above sections and the existing volume of 26,000 patient days, the likelihood of this occurring could be seriously questioned.

Cost-Based Patient Days

- The pro-forma assumes that the cost-based patient days will be 57 percent during the first year of operation versus approximately 63.4 percent for the current year. This is based upon the assumption that when the hospital operated at a 32,000 annual patient day volume (1978), 57 percent of the patient days were cost-based.
- Therefore, the new hospital will not only result in a substantial increase in patient days (32,000 − 26,000 = 6,000), but 70 percent of the increase in patient days will be charge paying.
- Again, given the market, the likelihood of this occurring could be seriously questioned.

EXHIBIT 1 (Continued)

Based on this information, a hypothetical pro-forma was developed changing only the following assumptions:

- Patient days
  —First year operation: 26,000 (actual)
  —Subsequent years: Grow by 0.5 percent per year (latest SMSA GROWTH)
- Cost-based patient days
  —Actual (63.4 percent) held constant for subsequent years.

The pro-forma return for this project is reduced from 15 percent to 10 percent, well below the required return. Pre-tax margins are depressed to the extent that this year's actual margin (8 percent) is not obtained until the seventh year of operation.

Prior to submitting the enclosed feasibility for approval, I believe we should take one last look at the assumptions to be sure they are reasonable.

Hospital Financial Profile[a]
($000)

	FY 'X0 Actual	% of Revenue	FY 'X1 Actual	% of Revenue	FY 'X2 Actual	% of Revenue
Project: Replacement Facility						
Summary Income Statement						
Inpatient Revenue	$8,841	95%	$10,307	95%	$10,094	95%
Outpatient Revenue	449	5	540	5	530	5
Gross Patient Revenue	9,290	100	10,847	100	10,624	100
Revenue Adjustment[b]	(1,265)	(14)	(1,725)	(16)	(1,810)	(17)
Net Revenue	8,025	86	9,122	84	8,814	83
Operating Expenses	5,853	63	6,659	61	6,549	62
Fixed Expenses	1,102	12	1,159	11	1,274	12
Total Expenses	6,955	75	7,818	72	7,823	74
Pre-Tax Profit	$1,070	11%	$ 1,304	12%	$ 991	9%
Financial/Operating Statistics						
Patient Days	32,093		31,834		26,801	
Occupancy	64%		63%		53%	
Beds	138		138		138	
Gross Revenue/P.D.	$289.46		$340.74		$396.42	
Pre-Tax Profit/P.D.	$33.35		$40.96		$36.98	

[a]All financial data include operations of the medical office building.
[b]Includes contractual allowance, other deductions from revenue, bad debts, and other income.

EXHIBIT 1 (Continued) **Projected Income Statement—Kelly Bolton's Estimates (000)**

	1	2	3	4	5	6	7	8	9	10	CGR (%)[a]
Gross Revenue	$17,661	$20,401	$23,549	$27,162	$31,305	$35,130	$39,425	$44,242	$49,649	$55,716	13.6
Bad Debts	618	714	824	951	1,096	1,230	1,380	1,548	1,738	1,950	13.6
Contractual Allocation	1,361	1,775	2,599	3,525	4,572	5,622	6,780	7,949	9,288	10,797	25.9
Net Revenue	$15,681	$17,912	$20,126	$22,686	$25,638	$28,279	$31,265	$34,744	$38,623	$42,969	11.9
Expenses:											
Operating Expenses	$10,522	$12,047	$13,783	$15,755	$17,997	$20,017	$22,264	$24,763	$27,542	$30,633	12.6
Management Fee	870	1,005	1,160	1,338	1,542	1,731	1,942	2,179	2,466	2,745	13.6
Depreciation	1,197	1,197	1,197	1,197	1,197	1,197	1,047	1,047	1,047	1,047	-1.5
Amortization	0	0	0	0	0	0	0	0	0	0	0.0
Interest	1,849	1,812	1,769	1,719	1,661	1,496	1,321	1,176	1,078	980	-6.8
Total Expenses	$14,437	$16,060	$17,909	$20,009	$22,397	$24,441	$26,573	$29,165	$32,113	$35,404	10.5
Pre-Tax Income	$ 1,244	$ 1,852	$ 2,217	$ 2,677	$ 3,241	$ 3,838	$ 4,692	$ 5,580	$ 6,510	$ 7,564	22.2
Income Tax	$ 310	$ 892	$ 1,069	$ 1,291	$ 1,562	$ 1,850	$ 2,261	$ 2,689	$ 3,138	$ 3,646	31.5
Net Income	$ 933	$ 959	$ 1,149	$ 1,387	$ 1,679	$ 1,988	$ 2,430	$ 2,890	$ 3,372	$ 3,918	17.3
Operational Statistics											
Revenue/Day	$ 542	$ 602	$ 668	$ 741	$ 823	$ 914	$1,014	$1,126	$1,249	$1,387	11.0
Operational Expense/Day	$ 324	$ 356	$ 391	$ 431	$ 474	$ 521	$ 573	$ 630	$ 694	$ 763	10.0
Management Fee/Day	$ 27	$ 30	$ 33	$ 37	$ 41	$ 46	$ 51	$ 56	$ 62	$ 69	11.0
Pre-Tax Management	7.0	9.1	9.4	9.9	10.4	10.9	11.9	12.6	13.1	13.6	7.6
Net Cash Flow	$1,220	$2,243	$2,254	$2,336	$2,460	$1,544	$1,741	$2,690	$3,121	$3,606	12.8
Bed Size	128	128	128	128	128	128	128	128	128	128	0.0
Patient Days	32,093	33,401	34,733	36,090	37,474	37,886	38,303	38,724	39,150	39,580	2.4
Occupancy	68.7	71.5	74.3	77.2	80.2	81.1	82.0	82.9	83.8	84.7	2.4
Projected Fund Flow (000)											
Net Income	$ 933	$ 959	$1,149	$1,387	$1,679	$1,988	$2,430	$2,890	$3,372	$3,918	
Depreciation	1,197	1,197	1,197	1,197	1,197	1,197	1,047	1,047	1,047	1,047	
Deferred Taxes	515	584	483	415	354	-171	-146	-165	-165	-165	
Amortization	0	0	0	0	0	0	0	0	0	0	
Tax Effected Interest	958	938	916	891	861	775	684	609	558	508	
AWC	-1,425	-230	-265	-303	-352	-333	-376	-429	-480	-541	
Reinvest Assumpt.	0	0	0	0	0	0	0	0	0	0	
Net Funds Flow	$ 2,178	$3,448	$3,480	$3,586	$3,738	$3,456	$3,639	$3,952	$4,333	$4,766	

[a]CGR = compounded growth rate.
Initial Investment $19,252,000. IRR (including residual value of two times the last year's income) = 15%.

EXHIBIT 1 (Continued) Replacement (Alternate Case) Income Statement—Jane Lloyd's Corporate Estimates (000)

	1	2	3	4	5	6	7	8	9	10	CGR (%)[a]
Gross Revenue	$14,578	$16,264	$18,143	$20,239	$22,577	$25,186	$28,097	$31,344	$34,966	$39,006	11.6
Bad Debts	510	569	635	708	790	882	983	1,097	1,224	1,365	11.6
Contractual Allocation	850	1,090	1,719	2,398	3,137	4,007	4,948	5,849	6,877	8,028	28.2
Net Revenue	$13,218	$14,605	$15,789	$17,133	$18,650	$20,297	$22,166	$24,398	$26,865	$29,613	10.5
Expenses:											
Operating Expenses	$ 8,686	$ 9,603	$10,618	$11,740	$12,980	$14,352	$15,867	$17,543	$19,398	$21,446	10.6
Management Fee	718	801	894	997	1,112	1,241	1,384	1,544	1,723	1,922	11.6
Depreciation	1,197	1,197	1,197	1,197	1,197	1,197	1,047	1,047	1,047	1,047	-1.5
Amortization	0	0	0	0	0	0	0	0	0	0	0.0
Interest	1,849	1,812	1,769	1,719	1,661	1,496	1,321	1,176	1,078	980	-6.8
Total Expenses	$12,450	$13,413	$14,478	$15,653	$16,950	$18,286	$19,619	$21,310	$23,246	$25,395	8.2
Pre-Tax Income	$ 768	$ 1,192	$ 1,311	$ 1,480	$ 1,700	$ 2,011	$ 2,547	$ 3,088	$ 3,619	$ 4,218	20.8
Income Tax	$ 82	$ 575	$ 632	$ 713	$ 819	$ 969	$ 1,228	$ 1,489	$ 1,745	$ 2,055	42.9
Net Income	$ 686	$ 617	$ 679	$ 767	$ 881	$ 1,042	$ 1,319	$ 1,599	$ 1,874	$ 2,163	13.7
Operational Statistics											
Revenue/Day	$ 542	$ 602	$ 668	$ 741	$ 823	$ 914	$1,014	$1,126	$1,249	$1,387	11.1
Operational Expense/Day	$ 324	$ 356	$ 391	$ 431	$ 474	$ 521	$ 573	$ 630	$ 694	$ 763	9.0
Management Fee/Day	$ 27	$ 30	$ 33	$ 37	$ 41	$ 46	$ 51	$ 56	$ 62	$ 69	11.1
Pre-Tax Management	5.3	7.3	7.2	7.3	7.5	8.0	9.1	9.9	10.4	10.8	8.3
Net Cash Flow	$1,204	$1,985	$1,882	$1,834	$1,803	$ 696	$ 741	$1,527	$1,770	$2,038	6.0
Bed Size	128	128	128	128	128	128	128	128	128	128	0.0
Patient Days	26,493	26,626	26,759	26,893	27,027	27,162	27,298	27,435	27,572	27,710	0.5
Occupancy	56.7	57.0	57.3	57.6	57.8	58.1	58.4	58.7	59.0	59.3	0.5
I.R.R.	7.97	0.00	0.00	0.00	0.00	0.00	0.00	0.00	0.00	0.00	-100.0
I.R.R. (Resid)	10.01	0.00	0.00	0.00	0.00	0.00	0.00	0.00	0.00	0.00	-100.0
Cash Flow Comp.											
Net Income	$ 686	$ 617	$ 679	$ 767	$ 881	$ 1,042	$1,319	$1,599	$1,874	$2,163	$11,627
Depreciation	1,197	1,197	1,197	1,197	1,197	1,197	1,047	1,047	1,047	1,047	11,370
Deferred Taxes	515	584	483	415	354	-171	-146	-165	-165	-165	1,539
Amortization	0	0	0	0	0	0	0	0	0	0	0
AWC	-927	-104	-118	-128	508	-157	-826	-301	-333	-375	-2,761
Principal Payments	-267	-309	-359	-417	-1,137	-1,215	-653	-653	-653	-653	-6,316
Reinvest Assumpt.	0	0	0	0	0	0	0	0	0	0	0
Net Cash Flow	$1,204	$1,985	$1,882	$1,834	$ 1,803	$ 696	$ 741	$1,527	$1,770	$2,017	$15,459

[a]CGR = compounded growth rate.

EXHIBIT 1 (Continued) **Notes to Projected Income Statement**

1.   Revenue

Total patient days have declined at the present hospital from 38,782 eight years ago.

The primary factors contributing to this decline in patient days are:

- Deteriorating condition of the existing facility
- Existing facility location in downtown
- Nearby hospital completing a $20.0 million renovation and expansion project last year
- Another nearby hospital expanding bed capacity three times during the last eight years
- Local unemployment rate of 19 percent
- Failure to attract new physicians to the hospital (no physicians have been recruited in six years)

These factors have contributed to the hospital's loss of market share from 19.5 percent of total SMSA patient days eight years ago to 15.4 percent now.

To resolve this problem, a new 128 bed facility is proposed which will address these problems in the following manner:

- New location to enhance geographic accessibility to the hospital
- New physical plant to aid in attracting needed physicians to the area (in anticipation of the new hospital, five physicians have been recruited)

Therefore, it has been assumed that the new facility will have approximately 5,300 more patient days in the first year of operation than experienced this year. This patient day volume (32,093) is approximately equal to the hospital's patient day volume four years ago. Patient days are projected to grow at a rate which will produce a patient day volume in 1994 which is approximately equal to the actual patient days for this facility eight years ago.

Year	Incremental Patient Days	Increase Days	%	128 Bed Occupancy
1	32,093	-	-	68.7%
2	33,401	1,308	4.1	71.5
3	34,733	1,332	4.0	74.3
4	36,090	1,357	3.9	77.2
5	37,474	1,384	3.8	80.2
6	37,886	412	1.1	81.1
7	38,303	417	1.1	82.0
8	38,724	421	1.1	82.9
9	39,150	426	1.1	83.8
10	39,580	430	1.1	84.7

Revenue per patient day, including effects of intensity increases, is projected to grow by 11 percent per year. No additional rate increases are projected to cover the cost of the new facility.

EXHIBIT 1 *(Continued)* Notes to Projected Income Statement

2.   Contractual Allowance

> For the past four years, patient days have declined by 5,300 of which 70 percent (3,700 patient days) were charge-paying patient days. Therefore, it has been assumed that 70 percent of the increase in patient days will be charge-paying resulting in total charge-paying patient days being approximately 43 percent of the total during the first year of operation.
>
> Subsequent years are projected assuming 43 percent of total patient days are charge-based.

3.   Other Deductions From Revenue

> Estimated to be 0.7 percent of revenue, which is consistent with the hospital's current experience.

4.   Bad Debt

> Estimated to be 3.5 percent of revenue. This is higher than the actual experience (2.1 percent) because of planned increases in ER and outpatient business.

5.   Other Revenue

> Estimated to be 2.2 percent of revenue, which is consistent with the hospital's current experience.

6.   Payroll and Other Operating Expenses

> These are projected using current expense/patient day increased at a 10 percent annual inflation rate.

7.   Management Fees

> Management fee is projected at 5.0 percent of revenue.

8.   Depreciation

Building	20 Years	$13,999,000
Fixed, major and minor moveable equipment	10 Years	3,752,860
(Groups I, II, & III)		

> Additionally, equipment originally costing $1.5 million (with accumulated depreciation of $600,000) will be transferred from the old facility to the new facility. The net book value ($900,000) was depreciated over six years, the average remaining useful life of the transferred equipment.

9.   Interest

> Fixed, major and minor moveable equipment are 70 percent financed at 15 percent, payable in 84 equal monthly installments. The building is 70 percent

EXHIBIT 1 (Continued) **Notes to Projected Income Statement**

financed at 15 percent. Interest payments only are made for the first five years with the principal balance retired in 15 equal annual installments thereafter.

Additionally, the existing facility will have unretired Hospital Revenue Bonds when the new facility opens. It is assumed that the new facility will retire these bonds during the first year of operation. This additional expenditure has been added to the project cost of the new facility for the internal rate of return calculation.

10. Other Fixed Expenses

Estimated to be 0.8 percent of revenue, which is consistent with the hospital's current experience.

11. Income Taxes

Income taxes are calculated using an effective annual rate of 48.2 percent, less the applicable investment tax credit.

12. Return on Equity

Computed at 15 percent of past year's Stockholders' Equity less Inter-Company Receivables.

EXHIBIT 2 **The Hospital Replacement Decision—General Ledger System**

1. Hospital Division
P.D. = Patient Day
Ingersoll Memorial Hospital*

Hospital Budget Analysis

	May Budget			May Actual			Variance	
	Amount	%	$/P.D.	Amount	%	$/P.D.	Inc./Dec.—$	%
Routine Services	$ 977,787	35%	$181.27	$ 981,262	33%	$181.38	$ 3,475	-
Inpatient Ancillary Revenue	1,581,985	56	293.29	1,698,539	57	313.96	116,554	7%
Total Inpatient Revenue	2,559,772[a]	91	474.56	2,679,801[a]	91	495.34	120,029[a]	5
Outpatient Ancillary Revenue	261,818	9	48.54	275,727	9	50.97	13,909	5
Total Gross Patient Revenue	2,821,590[a]	100	523.10	2,955,528[a]	100	546.31	133,938[a]	5
Contractual Adjustments	252,273-	9-	46.77-	349,853-	12-	64.67-	97,580	39
Other Deductions from Revenue	24,677-	1-	4.57-	47,183-	2-	8.72-	22,506	91
Provision for Bad Debt	42,561-	2-	7.89-	36,413-	1-	6.73-	6,148-	14-
Other Income	36,815	1	6.83	36,729	1	6.79	86-	
Net Revenue	2,538,894[b]	90	470.69	2,578,807[b]	87	472.98	39,913[b]	1
Payroll	908,582	32 (51%)	168.44	901,719	31 (52%)	166.68	6,863-	1-
Employee Benefits	168,494	6 (9)	31.24	152,800	5 (9)	28.24	15,694-	9-
Supplies	388,356	14 (22)	72.00	384,301	13 (22)	71.04	4,055-	1-
Professional Fees	62,712	2 (3)	11.63	65,252	2 (4)	12.06	2,540	4
Other Operating Expenses	269,981	10 (15)	50.05	241,709	8 (14)	44.68	28,272-	10-
Total Operating Expenses	1,798,125[a]	64 (100%)	333.36	1,745,783[a]	59 (100%)	322.70	52,342-[b]	3
Management Fees	114,532	4	21.23	114,532	4	21.17		
Depreciation & Amortization	166,152	6	30.80	161,151	5	29.79	5,001-	3-
Interest	137,085	5	25.41	135,105	5	24.97	1,980-	1-
Inter-Company Interest	21,000-	1-	3.89-	43,456-	1-	8.03	22,456-	107
Other Fixed Expenses	32,347	1	6.00	33,851	1	6.26	1,504	5
Total Fixed Expenses	429,116[a]	15	79.55	401,184[a]	14	74.16	27,932[a]	7-
Total Expenses	2,227,241[b]	79	412.91	2,146,967[b]	73	396.85	80,274-[b]	4-
Net Pre-Tax Profit/Loss (CR)	311,653	11	57.78	411,840	14	76.13	100,187	32
Over/Under (CR) Budget				100,187				
Licensed Beds	400 Beds			400 Beds			Beds	
Patient Days/Occupancy %	5,394 P.D./44%			5,410 P.D./44%		AR Days Outstanding	16 P.D./%	
Total Paid Hours/Inpatient Day	19.61			19.82		Actual 40	0.21	

*Name has been changed.
[a]Major importance
[b]Important

EXHIBIT 3 **The Hospital Replacement Decision—Bi-Weekly Productivity Management Report**

Tully Memorial Hospital*
Licensed Beds 155   % Occupancy 53

IV—Mid-South
Inpatient Day 1,141 Avg. Daily Census 82

Department	Volume	Unit Measure[a]	Regular Hours	O.T. Hours	Total Prod. Hrs.	Total Paid Hrs.	Index (Hours/Unit)				Ratio	
							Std.	Budget	Actual	YTD	Std.	Budget
600 NURS AD	14	CAL D	160.0	0.0	160.0	160.0	11.43	15.90	11.42	14.08	100%	139%
601 NURS AD	14	CAL D	428.6	0.8	429.4	440.4	22.80	21.20	30.67	28.42	74	69
610 MED/SUR	1,098	PAT D	5,086.8	19.9	5,106.7	5,994.1	4.900	4.934	4.561	4.784	105	106
650 I.C.U.	43	PAT D	631.8	7.6	639.4	727.0	15.00	15.71	14.87	16.52	101	106
688 INSU ED	14	CAL D	72.0	0.0	72.0	80.0	5.143	5.300	5.143	4.691	100	103
689 PSRO AC	14	CAL D	32.0	0.0	32.0	32.0	2.286	8.500	2.286	2.666	100	372
NURSING SVC. SUBTOTAL			6,411.2	28.3	6,439.5	7,433.5						
701 SURGERY	90	VISIT	700.3	24.8	725.1	810.1	9.390	8.514	8.057	9.185	117	106
704 RECY RM	0	VISIT	154.7	1.5	156.2	226.2	0.000	1.887	0.000	2.427	0	0
712 PHARM	16,981	DOSES	409.8	0.0	409.8	451.1	0.028	0.034	0.024	0.026	116	141
718 M&S SUP	6,106	LINEI	400.0	0.0	400.0	407.5	0.069	0.089	0.066	0.064	105	136
722 ANESTHE	14	CAL D	0.0	0.0	0.0	0.0	0.000	0.000	0.000	0.000	0	0
728 X-RAY	613	PROCS	585.4	52.4	637.8	671.8	1.017	1.017	1.040	1.046	98	98
729 ULTRASO	11	PROCS	80.0	0.0	80.0	80.0	3.590	0.000	7.273	4.492	49	0
736 LABORAT	33,818	C A P	618.0	3.4	621.4	675.4	0.019	0.019	0.018	0.018	103	103
744 E.K.G.	159	TESTS	75.0	0.0	75.0	75.0	0.500	0.500	0.472	0.455	106	106
748 E.E.G.	9	TESTS	13.5	0.0	13.5	13.5	1.500	0.000	1.500	1.522	100	0
754 RESP TH	1,365	TREAT	458.5	0.0	458.5	474.5	0.377	0.300	0.336	0.327	112	89
762 PHYS TH	1,119	MODAL	517.7	0.0	517.7	577.7	0.353	0.438	0.463	0.364	76	95
763 NUC MED	14	CAL D	80.0	0.0	80.0	80.0	5.714	5.300	5.714	5.743	100	93
768 SOC SV	14	CAL D	80.0	0.0	80.0	80.0	5.714	5.300	5.714	5.328	100	93
780 EMERGEN	204	VISIT	287.4	0.0	287.4	399.9	1.599	1.599	1.409	1.758	113	113
800 DIETARY	5,411	MEALS	1,396.9	0.0	1,396.9	1,452.9	0.264	0.264	0.258	0.264	102	102
810 HOUSEKP	1,141	T.P.D.	1,107.5	0.0	1,107.5	1,130.0	1.204	1.104	0.971	1.097	124	114
820 LINEN	14	CAL D	75.0	0.0	75.0	75.0	5.357	5.300	5.357	5.221	100	99
830 PLANT	14	CAL D	378.5	0.0	378.5	446.5	27.04	26.50	27.03	30.57	100	98
832 SYSTEMS	14	CAL D	78.0	0.0	78.0	78.0	5.571	5.300	5.571	5.030	100	95
835 SECURITY	14	CAL D	133.0	0.0	133.0	140.5	9.500	9.500	9.500	9.551	100	100
840 MED REC	1,141	GTPD	476.3	0.0	476.3	529.8	0.493	0.446	0.417	0.420	118	107

EXHIBIT 3 (Continued)

Department	Volume	Unit Measure[a]	Regular Hours	O.T. Hours	Total Prod. Hrs.	Total Paid Hrs.	Index (Hours/Unit)				Ratio	
							Std.	Budget	Actual	YTD	Std.	Budget
855 UTIL RE	14	CAL D	48.0	0.0	48.0	48.0	3.429	0.000	3.429	2.741	100	0
900 ADMIN	14	CAL D	395.0	0.0	395.0	395.0	22.20	21.20	28.21	20.31	79	75
902 ACCTG	14	CAL D	308.4	0.0	308.4	308.4	22.02	23.30	22.03	20.85	100	106
903 FIN MGT	14	CAL D	160.0	0.0	160.0	160.0	11.43	15.90	11.42	10.85	100	139
904 CREDIT	14	CAL D	380.4	0.0	380.4	387.9	27.17	31.90	27.17	26.62	100	117
905 PATBILL	14	CAL D	130.4	0.0	130.4	167.9	9.31	10.60	9.314	9.691	100	114
906 ADMIT	14	CAL D	187.7	0.0	187.7	232.7	13.41	20.20	13.40	16.94	100	151
907 RESERV	14	CAL D	70.0	0.0	70.0	70.0	5.000	7.440	5.000	5.242	100	149
908 D.P.	14	CAL D	194.9	0.0	194.9	194.9	13.92	15.40	13.92	14.74	100	111
910 P.B.X.	14	CAL D	233.4	0.0	233.4	270.9	16.67	22.30	16.67	18.58	100	134
912 MAT MGT	14	CAL D	222.5	0.0	222.5	231.1	15.89	15.90	15.89	17.68	100	100
914 SPEE BUS	14	CAL D	197.0	0.0	197.0	197.0	14.07	13.30	14.07	13.31	100	95
916 PERS	14	CAL D	232.4	1.5	233.9	233.9	14.30	13.30	16.70	13.98	86	80

*Name has been changed.
[a]CAL D = Calendar Days
PAT D = Patient Days
PROCS = Procedures.

EXHIBIT 4 The Hospital Replacement Decision—Humana Inc.: Gross Revenue and Operating Expense Analysis

Period Covered: Fiscal Year

Department: Radiology

Patient Days	Hospital[a]	Volume	Volume per Patient Day	Rank	Average Rates	Rank	Payroll as a % of Revenue	Rank	Supplies as a % of Revenue	Rank	Prof. Fee as a % of Revenue	Rank	Other as a % of Revenue	Rank	Profit Margin (%)	Rank	Profit per Patient Day	Rank
23110	1	10283	0.44	77	$41.09	72	16.59	57	11.21	28	0.00	0	2.61	1	69.59	1	$12.71	7
43745	2	33221	0.76	31	43.47	68	16.02	50	11.07	27	0.00	0	3.71	4	69.20	2	22.84	2
63959	3	42229	0.66	39	52.88	41	13.01	11	13.29	53	0.00	0	4.65	7	69.06	3	24.11	2
17474	4	16760	0.96	10	86.54	2	10.00	2	7.32	6	0.00	0	14.00	60	68.69	4	57.02	5
20794	5	18599	0.89	16	29.21	84	14.07	23	13.79	57	0.00	0	3.47	3	68.67	5	17.94	1
91121	6	56659	0.62	48	64.10	18	13.26	17	12.16	38	0.55	10	6.68	12	67.91	6	27.07	
37798	7	41229	1.09	2	74.65	7	12.77	9	9.17	13	0.00	0	9.64	38	67.87	7	55.26	1
17264	8	17612	1.02	8	66.25	15	16.01	49	5.92	1	0.00	10	10.85	45	67.22	8	45.43	3
85390	9	51577	0.60	54	67.95	12	13.13	13	13.15	50	0.00	0	6.86	16	66.85	9	27.44	5
33652	10	16601	0.49	69	67.38	14	14.77	30	12.06	36	0.61	11	6.84	15	65.73	10	21.85	8
24908	11	11368	0.46	76	58.14	25	13.32	19	10.03	18	1.11	14	10.38	42	65.15	11	17.29	1
27609	12	9744	0.35	84	39.50	77	13.87	22	9.95	17	0.00	0	11.04	46	65.14	12	9.08	4
66304	13	56397	0.85	22	47.44	58	14.97	31	13.77	56	0.00	0	6.37	10	64.89	13	26.18	2
97787	14	46017	0.47	73	61.52	19	14.99	33	12.35	39	0.00	0	8.12	27	64.54	14	18.68	2
38266	15	35015	0.92	15	64.20	17	16.54	55	11.58	31	0.00	0	8.92	35	62.97	15	36.99	7
53568	16	25560	0.48	71	74.73	6	13.29	18	12.79	47	0.00	0	11.08	47	62.84	16	22.41	3
21559	17	17161	0.80	25	49.44	51	14.70	29	14.01	60	0.00	0	8.44	31	62.84	17	24.73	2
46716	18	40496	0.87	20	45.62	64	15.15	37	10.32	19	0.26	5	11.46	49	62.82	18	24.84	6
16848	19	9043	0.54	65	39.77	76	16.62	58	16.34	75	0.00	0	4.37	6	62.67	19	13.38	4
42434	20	35286	0.83	23	39.86	75	15.28	38	15.74	71	0.00	0	6.76	13	62.22	20	20.62	1
31834	21	17866	0.56	61	64.52	16	14.32	25	12.03	35	0.72	12	10.71	44	62.22	21	22.53	5
28360	22	13205	0.47	74	51.31	46	14.98	32	12.72	46	0.00	0	10.17	40	62.13	22	14.84	5
163703	23	111970	0.68	38	99.48	1	10.36	3	7.93	9	15.13	21	4.67	8	61.91	23	42.13	6
64452	24	37523	0.58	58	52.65	42	16.43	53	14.75	66	0.00	0	7.33	20	61.49	24	18.85	5
40971	25	41926	1.02	7	51.13	47	13.11	12	13.98	59	0.00	0	11.68	51	61.22	25	32.03	4
31294	26	32671	1.04	4	40.86	73	17.48	63	13.50	54	0.00	0	8.11	26	60.91	26	25.98	6
40058	27	19084	0.48	72	53.96	35	11.21	7	9.11	12	3.57	18	15.21	64	60.90	27	15.66	1
30028	28	19159	0.64	44	73.73	8	15.47	42	10.97	26	0.00	0	13.00	57	60.56	28	28.49	5
20429	29	12363	0.61	53	47.76	56	14.52	27	13.03	49	0.03	4	12.06	53	60.36	29	17.45	1
27803	30	17193	0.62	50	38.00	80	17.17	59	15.81	73	0.00	0	7.36	22	59.72	30	14.03	5
18787	31	19318	1.03	5	79.80	4	10.75	6	13.27	52	0.00	0	16.53	71	59.45	31	48.79	6
63784	32	39607	0.62	49	45.22	66	15.86	46	15.77	72	0.00	0	9.40	36	58.98	32	16.56	5
55045	33	32638	0.59	55	53.90	36	14.31	24	14.18	62	0.00	0	13.02	58	58.49	33	18.69	4
31887	34	20596	0.65	43	37.80	81	19.06	72	15.35	69	0.00	0	7.34	21	58.25	34	14.22	6
59018	35	60457	1.02	6	40.52	74	14.67	28	14.81	67	0.00	0	12.40	54	58.11	35	24.12	2

Percentiles:

High (Outstanding)		111970	10.30		99.48		9.99		5.92		0.00		2.61		69.59		57.02	
90th		51577	0.98		70.68		12.77		7.93		0.03		5.34		66.85		32.03	
80th		41229	0.88		64.20		13.26		9.95		0.32		6.91		62.84		25.98	
70th		35638	0.80		57.71		14.47		10.97		0.55		8.11		60.91		23.01	
60th		32638	0.72		54.93		15.05		11.97		1.11		8.88		58.25		21.85	
(Median) 50th		20825	0.65		52.01		15.51		12.51		2.58		10.60		57.01		18.69	
Low (Poor)		1450	0.32		4.66		32.76		24.71		30.80		27.32		19.18		4.44	

[a]Hospital's identity is disguised by a number.

9   Planning and Budgeting

The first part of a managerial control system is the planning and budgeting process. This chapter discusses the process, formats, and techniques of planning and budgeting. It focuses on *expenses*. Chapter 10 discusses the planning for the separate components of the *revenues* and *profits* of nonprofit organizations.

PLANS AND BUDGETS

Planning is comprehensive. It must involve consideration of all the factors which can influence the organization's situation and decisions about how to manage these factors. It begins with the organization's mission and ends with the plans or activities that will enable its attainment. The financial portion of these plans must specify the revenues, expenses, profits, assets, and liabilities that will enable the organization to achieve its mission. Financial planning is very complex. As an example of its complexity consider the difficulty of incorporating the potential impact of the economy in the plans. Although managers do not control the economy, they must, nevertheless, incorporate its likely effects on employee salaries, the cost of materials and supplies, interest expenses, the prices they can charge, and the returns expected from the financial investments.

Despite its complexity, financial planning is a key managerial activity. The heart of good management is the attainment of carefully considered plans. Unanticipated results, whether positive or negative, are the *bete noire* of a professional manager. One corporate CEO hired a consultant to help him bury a few million dollars of unexpected profits on the corporation's Balance Sheet. Although the unexpected news was positive—it was after all a profit rather than a loss—the CEO thought that any *unexpected* event, whether good or bad, reflected poorly on his managerial skills. Instead, he wanted to predict the arrival of these profits in the subsequent year and then unearth them from their Balance Sheet hiding place. To that CEO, and many others, good managers predict income and create it; they are not merely the beneficiaries of good fortune.

Good plans provide many benefits. They embody a clear road map for the organization's employees, board members, managers, and clients. They say, "Here is what we are and what we hope to become." One superlative CEO noted: "I will succeed as a leader of this organization only when every one of my employees understands my plan. When they do, I will feel comfortable about their ability to react appropriately to any of the thousands of situations in which they represent me. The plan will give them a clear measure of what I hope to achieve and enable them to gauge whether their actions are consistent with achieving those ends."

But despite its importance, in many organizations planning is either neglected or performed in a cursory, mechanistic fashion: Next year's plan equals last year's actual results plus inflation. Or managers are pushed to deliver meaningless corporate goals: "Can you do 14 percent more next year?" prods the CEO. "Uh huh," responds the manager. Because neither has any idea how this 14 percent increase will be generated, it rarely happens.

A well implemented planning process can also serve as a training ground for managers and helps professionals to understand managerial constraints. One professional who subsequently became a manager stated: "I did not really understand management until I was given the responsibility for developing my department's plan. Creating the plan caused me to think about marketing and its effect on revenues, production and its effect on expenses, and finance and its effect on the money we have available. I saw the forest instead of the trees. When I started the planning process, I was a professional. When I finished, I was a manager."

STYLES OF FINANCIAL PLANNING AND BUDGETING

Some organizations create their plans in a *centralized* fashion. Their top management and board decide on the goals which will achieve the organization's mission and on their financial requirements. Middle and lower level managers receive these plans but are not involved in their creation. Other organizations create their plans in a *decentralized* manner. Their top management and board elucidate the mission and then ask other management levels to develop the required plans and budgets. For example, William Massey, a top Stanford University financial manager, describes his version of decentralized planning and budgeting: "General funds are allocated to operating units as lump sums and the unit head is given authority to spend these funds as he or she sees fit, subject to policy constraints such as salary increase guidelines or limits of tenure-line faculty . . . The (size of the allocation) can be based on the unit's needs, its opportunities, the institution's priorities and particular incentive considerations. . . ."[1]

The process of planning is central to its success. It is at least the equal in importance to the format of the plans or the planning techniques discussed later in this chapter.

Good plans result from a careful planning process. Whether centralized or decentralized, they should simultaneously reflect top management's goals and middle management's assessments of the results it can attain. In planning terminology, the plans must reconcile "top-down" views—for example, of the accomplishments needed to attract donors or clients—with "bottom-up" perceptions, such as the minimum budget needed for research. Professional planners can be helpful. They can present analyses of the sector and the economy, compile inflation projections and regulatory trends, suggest alternative scenarios, and manage the flow of paper in the process. But planners can become impediments if they are allowed to usurp managerial prerogatives and create the plan, rather than facilitate its creation.

CALENDAR FOR THE FINANCIAL PLANNING PROCESS

The planning process requires considerable amounts of time and effort. Some organizations appropriately begin next year's planning process six months before the end of the current year. They involve virtually all layers of management in the process, requiring them to acknowledge their responsibility for attaining the final plan by "signing-off" on it. The process is iterative. Many versions of the plan are continually honed before the final document emerges.

An Example of the Financial Planning Process

A 900-student, private nonprofit elementary and secondary school provides a good example of the process of financial planning. The school's plan clearly articulates its goals and then specifies the financial resources needed to achieve them. The school's primary goals are to foster the intellectual development and the diversity of its student body. The first goal requires salary and benefit packages sufficient to attract and retain very good teachers, while the second requires adequate financial aid resources to enroll students who could not otherwise afford to attend the school.

How much money does accomplishment of these goals require? The school computes that raising its median teachers' compensation to the level paid by the top 10 percent of the private schools with which it competes

---

[1]William Massey, "Improving Academic Productivity: The Next Frontier?" *Capital Ideas* (September-October 1991): 8.

for teachers will require an additional $1.2 million a year in expenses. The financial aid resources needed for a diverse student body require yet another $1 million annually.

How can the additional $2.2 million in revenues be obtained? To answer this question, the school examined alternative revenue sources. It rejected tuition as a major source because its tuition levels were already equal to those of competitive schools. But it felt that it could create an endowment pool that had sufficient capital to earn $2.2 million annually. Although the school's ability to raise an endowment pool of such size remains to be seen, its present endowment level per student is less than half that of its sister schools. Because the school's alumni are as successful and numerous as those of the other private schools, the school felt, with some justification, that it could increase its endowment to the level needed.[2]

Steps in the Financial Planning Process

The planning process followed by the school is instructive. It first drew up a "wish list" of the projects that would enable it to achieve its goals. It then delineated the expenses associated with these projects and assigned priorities to the projects. For example, a project for better integration of the management information systems among the school's three geographically separate campuses received a lower priority than some other projects because it was less immediately associated with achievement of the school's goals of excellence and diversity and required significant expenditures. With this wish list in hand, the school evaluated the feasibility of financing the projects by specifying the amount of money that could be obtained from each of the separate revenue sources, such as operating revenues, gifts, and endowments. It then ascertained how many projects the resulting total revenues could finance. Low-priority projects were deleted from the plan or postponed.

A good financial planning process should follow the same iterative pattern of creating a wish list, assigning priorities, and identifying the projects that can realistically be funded. Some nonprofits skip the last step, hoping that needed resources will magically materialize. This is the "God will provide" theory of financial planning. But in planning, as elsewhere, God helps those who help themselves. Unrealistic plans are self-defeating: they create inevitable failures.

PLAN STATEMENTS

Plan statements should express both the organization's *mission*, or purpose, and the *objectives* it must attain in order to accomplish this mission. The mission statement should clarify the organization's reason for being and

[2]Buckingham, Browne & Nichols, *A Look Ahead* (Cambridge, MA: 1990).

constituency. For a local art gallery, the mission might be to enable the townspeople to see the work of local artists; for a town library, the mission might be to provide town residents easy access to master works of scholarship and literature; for a liberal arts college, the mission might be to produce graduates with a sound humanistic education.

The objectives statements, in contrast, should be much more concrete. Objectives should state both the aims of the organization and the resources required to achieve them. For example, a state government's Division of Social Services has "family preservation" as its mission, and as its objectives times the resolution of 75 percent of its cases within the existing family and safely returning home 75 percent of the children once placed outside the home.[3] Objectives should specify effectiveness and efficiency. Nonfinancial measures of the results of the organization are usually termed *effectiveness* measures. The relationship between the effectiveness measures and the resources they required is a measure of the organization's *efficiency*. Put somewhat differently, effectiveness objectives state where the organization is going, whereas efficiency objectives state how much it will take to get there. For example, the effectiveness objective for a Registry of Motor Vehicles is a 25 minute average wait for license and registration renewal; the efficiency objective specifies the number of employees needed to attain that objective.

Statements of mission must reflect the social obligations of a nonprofit organization. If they do not, the organization is in danger of losing touch with its fundamental purpose. Thus, a college that proudly trumpets that it has achieved its *mission* of raising $50 million in endowment is really expressing its attainment of an objective that will help the college to attain its ultimate mission of education. The roles of the two should not be confused.

The 1991 closing of Tarkio College in Missouri presented a vivid example of the problem created by confusing objectives with social missions. When a new Tarkio College manager accomplished his goal of eliminating the college's $1.4 million deficit, he was widely congratulated. But subsequent investigation showed that the deficit was eliminated with U.S. government education loans and grants given to students, many of whom were not prepared for a college education. (They provided new revenues to cover the college's existing expenses.) The college had forgotten its social mission of education in order to achieve its objective of financial survival. By losing touch with its mission, the college's ultimate closure was tainted with charges of scandal and abuse. What should have been the dignified closure of a nearly century-old institution that had outlived its social mission instead became a media circus.[4]

[3]Robert Keogh, "Experts Question Program Budgeting," *Boston Business Journal* (February 3, 1992): 1.
[4]Anthony DePalma, "A College Acts in Desperation and Dies Playing the Lender," *The New York Times*, 17 April 1991, p. 1.

Phrasing the Statements of Mission and Objectives

Statements of mission and objectives are important to people both inside and outside the organization. A recent survey found mission statements ranked number one in importance and objectives as number six for the officials of charity organizations and its external auditors and contributors.[5]

To accomplish their purposes, plans must be expressed in language that is both evocative and detailed. If the organization intends to accomplish an important mission for a specific group, the plan should say so: "We will graduate the best history students among the four-year liberal arts colleges in New England." "We will help 100 homeless schizophrenics to find housing." "We will reduce the burglary rate of the town of Belmont." These spare statements are nevertheless evocative, clearly explaining the organization's purpose.

Plans stated in excessively grandiose fashion frequently achieve opposite results from those intended. They are perceived as meaningless or pompous. For example, a hospital whose stated mission is "to achieve optimum health" clearly cannot attain it. Achieving optimal health status is beyond the resources of any hospital. The statement is worse than useless, because it undermines the confidence of the reader in the hospital's competence or sincerity. On the other hand, the statement that "we will provide modern imaging technology," or "caring patient services," or "prenatal services to the 200 neighborhood women who are poor" reflects an important mission that the hospital has a good possibility of achieving.

Quantitative objectives statements are useful because they focus purpose. But, excessive quantification of the objectives can undermine the evocative quality of the mission. For example, the statement "We will help the 732 people whose income is at the bottom ten percent of the distribution to find jobs in 1993" dilutes the power of the more general statement of "serving the poor." A good plan generally contains two sets of statements: one set is brief and evocative and the other detailed and precise. The former inspires, while the latter focuses action.

THE RELATIONSHIP BETWEEN PLANNING AND BUDGETING

The budget is a short-run version of a long-run plan. Many different kinds of budgets exist, although budgeting is often discussed as if there were only one. The "budget" takes many forms—it can manifest itself as a budget for operations, or for multi-year capital requirements, or as a head count of

[5]Noel Hyndman, "Contributors to Charity: A Comparison of Their Information Needs and the Perceptions of Such Needs by the Providers of Information," *Financial Accountability and Management* (Summer 1991): 75.

personnel—and it can be expressed in cash or accrual accounting terms. These budgets serve different purposes, as detailed below:

- *Cash* budgets forecast the sources and uses of cash. They are used to predict when money should be invested or obtained from sources outside the organization.

- *Accrual* budgets are used to compare actual operating results with those budgeted.

- *Operating* budgets specify the revenues and/or expenses associated with operating the organization.

- *Capital* budgets anticipate the proposed investments in buildings and equipment.

All of these budgets should be grounded in a consistent set of projections about the future, but they should be separated from each other because they serve different purposes. For example, *operating budgets* that predict the operating revenues and expenses by week, month, quarter, or year must be kept separate from *capital budgets* that articulate the organization's plans for acquiring large assets. Because capital acquisitions are large and made on an erratic basis while operating expenses have much smoother patterns from one period to the next, blending the two budgets into one reduces the ability to make valid comparisons of the budget from one period to the next.

PLANNING AND BUDGETING FORMATS

Financial plans can be presented in the three different formats described below. Each format serves a different purpose.

(1) *Line-item or object of expense formats* delineate the amount the organization expects to spend for certain types of expenses or to receive from certain sources of revenue. For example, a government line-item budget lists the appropriations made by the legislative branch for such items as salaries, consultants, and pensions. This budgetary format enables the legislature to control whether actual expenditures by the executive branch have conformed to its appropriations. The format is less useful for planning and evaluation of outputs because it does not clarify what the expenditures accomplished. Line-item budgets devote equal attention to every item even if they are not of equal importance. For example, a $170 million Boston school system budget devoted equal space to the line item for teachers' salaries of $140 million and to the line item for uniforms of only $30,000.

(2) *Responsibility center formats* are used to hold different parts of the organization responsible for the revenues and expenses they control. They present the financial information in a way that is consistent

with the organization structure. In an elementary school, for example, a responsibility center budget measures the principal's office and each of grades kindergarten through six. Most large organizations have responsibility center budgets.

(3) *Program formats* delineate the revenues and expenses associated with achieving each of the organization's programs or purposes. They organize information in a way that clearly highlights the resources associated with each of the organization's main activities. They enable evaluation of the appropriateness of the organization's expenditures. In one case, some managers were stunned when a new program format for a nonprofit's budget revealed the high level of spending on administration.

Program costs are rarely available. Indeed, the damning revelation that New York City spent less than one-third of its public high school funds in the classrooms could be reached only with a doctoral dissertation on the subject.[6] A program budget would have routinely revealed this information. Some cynically assert that this very quality accounts for the scarcity of programmatic information.[7] Managers do not want this kind of information to be easily accessed. It is too revealing!

Program formats are rarely useful for control purposes because the organization structure and the program structure rarely coincide. An elementary school, for example, might have programs for reading, mathematics, athletics, special education, and administration, while its organization structure consists of the separate grades and the principal's office.

The program structure consists of the key *programs* and *subprograms* of the organization, the *program elements*, or the fundamental building blocks of the program, and the *objects of expense* used to carry out the program elements. A sample program structure for a museum is presented in Table 9-1. It consists of the key programs of the institution (curatorial, educational, operation and maintenance, and administrative), the subprograms (college courses, high school and elementary school activities, and adult education), and the program elements or basic activities used to carry out the programs. In the educational area, the program elements consist of the individual courses taught in each of the subprograms. The objects of expense are the fundamental resources for which funds are expended, such as salaries for personnel resources and utilities for heat, light, and power resources.

Programs should be defined so that they have measurable outputs. A frequent shortcoming in the design of a program budget is the selection of programs whose outputs are not measurable. A social service agency's program of "promoting welfare" is so fuzzy that almost any set of expenses

---

[6]Dana Wechsler, "Parkinson's Law 101," *Forbes* (June 25, 1990): 52-56.
[7]Keogh, "Experts Question Program Budgeting."

TABLE 9-1 **Program Structure for a Museum**

	Programs	Subprograms	Program Elements	Objects of Expenses
1.	Curatorial	Regular exhibits Special exhibits	Curatorial departments	Salaries, benefits, and other direct expenses
2.	Educational	College High school and elementary school Adult education	Courses taught	Salaries, benefits, and other direct expenses
3.	Operation and maintenance	Operations Maintenance	Security Operations Maintenance	Salaries, benefits, utilities, and other direct expenses
4.	Administrative	Fiscal General	President Treasurer Controller	Salaries, benefits, utilities, and other direct expenses

could be attributed to it, and its outcomes are not clearly measurable. This program does not achieve its intended purpose of enabling the reader to judge the appropriateness of the monies spent for the results achieved.

PLANNING AND BUDGETING TECHNIQUES

The two most frequently used planning techniques are *incremental planning* and *zero-base planning*. They will be discussed in detail below, as will the less-frequently used *formula budgeting* technique.

Most planning is incremental. It accepts the organization's present goals and strategies and plans for their extension in the future. However, incremental planning is not appropriate for activities that are not faring well, and it is not feasible for new organizations. In these situations, the plan must consider the organization without any constraints and create the new activities that will either supplant or newly implement the organization's goals. Zero-base planning is a process for creating such a plan. For example, a large company that was losing market share and whose expenses were considerably above its competitors underwent a zero-base planning process. The process reduced and reorganized the company's expenses, and, as a result, its competitive position was enhanced.[8]

[8]Management Analysis Center, *MAC Classics* (Cambridge, MA: Spring 1990).

It is important to distinguish the circumstances that require the two types of planning because zero-base planning requires more effort than the incremental variety. It should be used sparingly, only when fresh, creative efforts for achieving the organization's goals are required. When first popularized in the late 1970s by President Carter and Texas Instruments, zero-base planning was widely and indiscriminately implemented. No wonder later surveys found managers disappointed in its impact; it was frequently used in activities that did not warrant the massive effort it required.[9] This is not to suggest that incremental planning is effortless. It too necessitates careful consideration, but it requires considerably less effort than the zero-based variety.

Incremental Planning

How is incremental planning implemented? It begins with the revenues and costs of existing programs and projects their future costs and revenues by delineating the separate impact of each of the six factors that can change them: inflation, volume, price, efficiency, technology, and quality. For example, these six factors will affect a Canadian government program that provides translation services in English and French as follows: *Inflation* will change wages and other expenses. Changes in the *volume* of translation services will affect both costs and revenues. Higher or lower *prices* will have a commensurate effect on translation revenues. New *technology*, such as new word processors and computer-based translating systems, will affect costs and, possibly, efficiency. Changes in *efficiency* and *quality* will also affect costs and possibly revenues.

The combined impact of these six factors will delineate the future budgets and plans for the organization. Each of the six factors will be discussed separately below. The relationship between volume and costs will receive a particularly extensive discussion because volume frequently plays the major role in explaining changes in the budget.

Inflation   All the separate objects of expense should be listed so that the inflation or deflation expected for each of them in the forthcoming year can be specified. For example, union negotiations will determine future wage rates for union members, and nonunion employees receive raises known well in advance of the year. The inflation indices for various items can be reasonably estimated well in advance of the forthcoming period. Because different objects of expense inflate at different rates, separate inflation indices should be used for different items. Utilities and fuel expenses have at times inflated at rates far above those of other items. On the other hand, it is neither necessary nor appropriate to determine a different inflation rate for each object of expense.

[9]Robert N. Anthony, "Zero-Base Budgeting Is a Fraud," *The Wall Street Journal*, 27 April 1977, p. 26.

Volume The relationship between various revenue and expense items and the expected volume of activity should be defined.

Unfortunately, this relationship is unknown in most service-producing organizations. For example, consider a police force. How many police officers should be out walking a beat? Is one police officer needed per 1,000 people? More? Less? No one can supply a definitive answer to these questions. When New Haven's new police chief found less than half of his force out on the streets, he eliminated a large number of administrative jobs and newly placed many police on foot patrol. Did he receive kudos for his move? Not from his force, most of whom think the organization's purposes are better served if they have a desk job or ride in a car rather than doing foot patrol work.[10] As indicated in this example, most service organizations simply do not know what the relationship between cost and volume should be.

To compensate for this lack of knowledge, the relationship between cost and volume is usually derived by evaluating historical data of the relationship between the two. What follows will describe some of the mathematics required in this process. But do not lose the forest for the trees. Remember, the sole point of the mathematics is to derive a relationship between volume and cost. If the relationship between them is clear and generally accepted, there is no need to engage in such mathematical manipulations.

The cost-volume relationship is estimated by plotting historical data and fitting them into a pattern that can be expressed with a mathematical relationship. The relationship between volume and cost is usually assumed to be *linear*. In English this means that it can be drawn as a straight line in which every increase of volume causes the same increase in costs or revenues. For example, if every additional student requires an additional $200 of annual book expenses, the relationship between the number of students and book expenses is linear. In algebra, such a relationship is characterized by a constant slope. Econometric studies of cost functions buttress the validity of the linearity assumption.[11]

Figure 9-1 shows three kinds of common cost-volume relationships, using the translation service as an example. The costs in Figure 9-1A have a pattern of a horizontal straight line (slope of zero) and are classified as *fixed expenses.* They remain at the same level, no matter what the volume of words translated. For example, the salary of the chief administrator of the translation service or rent expense are fixed costs. The costs in Figure 9-1B vary by steps with increases in volume and are classified as *semivariable expenses.* The salaries of the translators follow this pattern. An increase in the number of words translated means an additional translator must be added. This would cause a jump in the cost of salaries. These costs are sometimes referred to as *step functions* because they look like a set of steps. The costs in Figure 9-1C vary directly with changes in volume and are classified

[10]Bob Cohn, "A People's Cop Ruffles His Macho Men," *Newsweek* (August 27, 1990): 38.
[11]J. Johnston, *Statistical Cost Analysis* (New York, NY: McGraw-Hill, 1960).

FIGURE 9-1   **Illustrative Cost-Volume Relationships (Constant Dollars)**

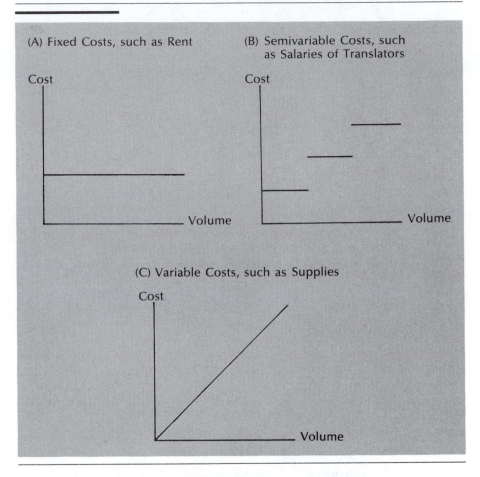

as *variable expenses*. There are few examples of truly variable expenses in the translation service, but the cost of paper could vary directly with the volume of words translated.

The expense data used for this analysis must be measured in constant dollars. If they are not, a relationship between cost and inflation may be misinterpreted as a relationship between cost and volume. For example, costs and volume that both grow by 10 percent in a year may be interpreted as a cost equation with a slope of one; that is, every unit increase in volume brings about an equal increase in costs. But if inflation grew at 10 percent during the year, real costs did not increase at all while volume advanced by 10 percent.

If visual examination is not sufficient for fitting the data to a straight line, more formal mathematical techniques can be used to derive the relationship between cost and volume. *High-low analysis* calculates the slope of the line based on the highest and lowest data points, or the mathematical relationship between the highest and lowest volumes and highest and lowest costs. The resulting slope can then be used to project next year's costs given next year's projected volume.

As an example of high-low analysis, consider the translation service data shown in Table 9-2. The highest supplies expense of $1,798 is associated with a volume of 17,074 thousand words: the lowest supplies expense of $901 is associated with a volume of 8,905 thousand words translated. The difference between the high and low expenses and its relationship to a change in volume can be expressed as follows:

$$\frac{\text{Change in Expenses}}{\text{Change in Volume (in thousands of words)}} = \frac{\$1,798 - \$901}{17,074 - 8,905}$$

$$= \frac{\$897}{8,169}$$

$$= \$0.11 \text{ per thousand words}$$

This calculation implies that every extra thousand words requires an additional supplies expense of 11 cents. If the volume of words to be translated in the next year is expected to be 20 million, the expected supplies expense will be $2,200 [($0.11 per thousand words)(20 million words)].

If the data are excessively variable for the use of high-low analysis, the technique of *least-squares regression* (or linear regression) analysis is useful for expressing the relationship between cost and volume. This technique minimizes the discrepancy between the actual data and the line it selects to represent the relationship. (A detailed disucssion of the technique is included in Appendix A at the end of this chapter for those who are comfortable with mathematical techniques or who want to learn more about it.)

TABLE 9-2 **Deriving Cost-Volume Relationships with High-Low Analysis**

Year	Supplies Expense (in constant dollars)	Volume of Words Translated (in thousands)
19X9	$1,798	17,074
19X8	1,701	16,102
19X7	1,102	11,108
19X6	1,501	14,981
19X5	1,402	14,032
19X4	1,199	12,063
19X3	1,301	12,853
19X2	998	10,107
19X1	901	8,905

Quality   The extra costs required to achieve higher quality, or the cost savings that could be achieved by lowering quality, are adjusted with explicit judgments. For example, the expense of hiring a high-cost translator with special qualifications to improve the quality of the service would be added here.

Efficiency   Changes in efficiency will increase or decrease the budget. If large changes in volume are expected, efficiency is likely to decrease in the short run because of the disruptions they inevitably cause. But if volume is expected to remain stable, efficiency will probably increase because people become more efficient over time as they repeatedly perform the same task. If the organization has adopted a new technology or created a new system for performing the work, these changes will also affect efficiency. For example, if the translation service purchases a computer system that recognizes voices and performs translations automatically, the efficiency of translation will be affected.

Prices   Changes in prices will change revenues. The considerations in setting prices in nonprofit organizations will be discussed in Chapter 10.

Effect of Six Factors   To illustrate how the six factors are incorporated in the incremental budget process, consider the translation service budget presented in Column A of Table 9-3. Its future budget will be estimated with the techniques of incremental budgeting. In addition to inflation, the service expects an increased volume of two million pages, increased sales prices of 10 percent, the purchase of a new machine that increases depreciation expenses by $400,000, no change in quality, and a decrease of 5 percent in translators' efficiency. Columns B through G delineate the impact of each of the six factors on the future. Column H reflects the plan for the future after consideration of the effect of each of the factors. For example, the translators' expenses begin at $6 million; $600,000 are added for the expected impact of inflation; $1.32 million are added for their increased volume of 2 million pages [$1.32 = ($6 + $0.6)(2 million pages ÷ 10 million pages)]; and $0.396 million for the 5 percent decrease in efficiency [$0.396 = ($6 + $0.6 + $1.32)(0.05)]. For the translators, budgeted expenses will grow by $2.316 million. Revenues have grown by $3.2 million through projected volume and price increases, and expenses reflect an additional $3.432 million of required spending because of the impact of inflation, volume, technology, and efficiency.

Although Table 9-3 may look like just another table to you, it contains an example of the heart and soul of an effective plan. Its format forces managers to specify why they expect the future to differ from the past. It is also a valuable format for control and evaluation because it isolates the effects of each of the six variables. For example, if the actual increase in pages translated is one million rather than the two million expected, the supplies budget should be adjusted to an addition of only $180,000, rather than the $360,000 increment originally budgeted.

TABLE 9-3 **Incremental Planning for the Translation Service (all financial data in millions of Canadian dollars)**

(A) Revenues, Expenses, and Volume, Last Year	(B) Impact of Inflation		(C) Impact of Volume		(D) Impact of Technology	(E) Impact of Quality	(F) Impact of Efficiency	(G) Impact of Prices	(H) New Budget
	Expected Rate of Inflation	*Dollar Effect*	*Expected Change in Volume*	*Dollar Effect*					
Volume: 10 million pages									
Revenues: $10	no change	-0-	+2 million pages	+$2	no change	no change	no change	+$1.2	$13.2
Expenses:									
Translators: $6	10%	+$0.6	+2 million pages	+$1.32	no change	no change	+$0.396	no change	$8.316
Administration: $1	10%	+$0.1	+2 million pages	no change	no change	no change	no change	no change	$1.1
Supplies: $1.5	20%	+$0.3	+2 million pages	+$0.36	no change	no change	no change	no change	$2.16
Depreciation: $0.5	no change	-0-	+2 million pages	no change	+$0.4	no change	no change	no change	$0.9

Zero-Base Planning

The technique of zero-base planning is particularly useful for new programs or ones that need large-scale overhauling. The underlying concept has been traced as far back as 1934 when an author noted:

> It must be a temptation to one drawing up an estimate to save himself trouble by taking last year's estimate for granted, adding something to any item for which an increased expenditure is foreseen. Nothing can be easier, or more wasteful and extravagant. It is in that way obsolete expenditure is enabled to make its appearance year after year, long after reason for it has ceased to be.[12]

Zero-base planning reconceptualizes the program by breaking it down into the most fundamental activities needed to accomplish its aims. These activities are called *decision packages*. Each decision package is budgeted at the level needed to attain minimum, maintenance, and improvement performance. These budgets are then ranked to indicate their relative importance. (Because it results in a budget, the process is commonly referred to as *zero-base budgeting*.)

Easy to say, but not so easy to do. As an example, consider the process for a hospital division that prepares the estimates for all proposed construction projects and monitors the progress of the work. The division is divided into two decision packages: estimation and monitoring. The division manager prepares three financial estimates for each of these decision packages: the *minimum budget* is the bare bones amount needed for this decision package to function, the *maintenance budget* is the amount needed to carry on the same work in the forthcoming year as in this year, and the *improvement budget* describes the extra work that could be performed with successive small increments to the budget. These budgetary estimates are accompanied by detailed descriptions of the results to be accomplished by each budget and the consequences of its not being done. The budgetary levels are then ranked in order of preference, as illustrated in Table 9-4.

The zero-base planning process can result in substantially different program and budget compositions from those of the past. For example, referring to Table 9-4, if last year's budget was $160,000 for minimum and maintenance funding of the estimation and monitoring functions ($50,000 + $60,000 + $15,000 + $35,000), and if $170,000 were budgeted for the forthcoming year, only the decision packages ranked 1 through 4 would be implemented. Although approximately the same total amount of money is budgeted in both years, the zero-base planning process has created substantially different patterns of use. In the forthcoming year, monitoring will employ $120,000 of the budget (the decision packages ranked 1, 2, and 3), as opposed

[12]Arthur Eugene Buck, *The Budget in Government Today* (New York, NY: McMillan Co., 1934), p. 12, as cited by L. Allan Austin, *Zero-Base Budgeting: Organizational Impact and Effects* (New York, NY: AMACOM, 1978).

TABLE 9-4 **Decision Package Expense Estimates and Rankings**

Package	Minimum	Maintenance	Improvement Level 1	Improvement Level 2
Estimation	$50,000	$ + 15,000	$ + 10,000	$ + 40,000
Monitoring	60,000	+ 35,000	+ 25,000	+ 30,000

Rank	Decision Package Level	Amount	Cumulative Total
1	Monitoring—Minimum	$ 60,000	$ 60,000
2	Monitoring—Maintenance	+ 35,000	95,000
3	Monitoring—Improvement 1	+ 25,000	120,000
4	Estimation—Minimum	+ 50,000	170,000
5	Estimation—Maintenance	+ 15,000	185,000
6	Monitoring—Improvement 2	+ 30,000	215,000
7	Estimation—Improvement 1	+ 10,000	225,000
8	Estimation—Improvement 2	+ 40,000	265,000

to only $95,000 in the prior year ($60,000 of minimum and $35,000 of maintenance expenses), and the estimation budget will be commensurately reduced from $65,000 in the prior year to $50,000 for this year. If the total budget is raised to $215,000, decision packages 5 and 6 will also be implemented. If the budget were cut to $120,000, only decision packages 1, 2, and 3 would be carried out.

As in this example, the zero-base process usually does not really require an analysis from a funding base of zero, but rather a fresh appraisal of a situation. The activities required for a successful zero-based process are the following:

(1) Clearly define the decision packages. If they are not clearly defined, the plan will be inundated by thousands of meaningless packages.

(2) Articulate the minimum, maximum, and maintenance packages, and state whether they include the effect of inflation. If they do, then the inflation guidelines must be specified.

(3) Disseminate the criteria to be used for ranking purposes to enable better understanding and, therefore, greater support of the process by lower-level managers.

(4) Clarify the degree of involvement of various managers in the process and the reasons for the involvement.

Zero-base planning is usually implemented by a task force of program managers and informed outsiders. To be effective, it must be performed in an open and candid environment. Many past efforts failed because managers felt they were merely going through the motions without top management's support. Such results are doubly pernicious because the managers involved may start playing budgetary games rather than presenting their expert, candid evaluation of the resource use best suited for the organization.[13] For example, they may rank key decision packages at the bottom of their list, knowing that these packages would always be funded, or they may rank administration very high in order to protect their jobs. Sometimes they may mechanistically compute minimum estimates as a certain percentage reduction from present budgets rather than as the result of careful consideration of the appropriate size of the minimum budget.

Formula Budgeting or Planning

Some financial planning is performed with the use of a formula based on average costs, such as "the average student's education costs $25,000 a year," or "the average patient's hospital care required $7,000 per stay." The plan or budget is then computed by multiplying the average cost by the expected volume of students or hospital stays.

Formula budgeting will almost always lead to an *incorrect* budget or plan. It can be used only if the future is expected to be an exact replica of the past. If the future is expected to differ from the past, only incremental or zero-base techniques are appropriate.

As an example of inappropriate formula budgeting, consider a city that uses "EDUs" as the basis for its budget, in which the "EDU" is a function of both the number of people who live in the city and those who work but do not live there. The city computes its budget by multiplying the cost per "EDU" of each of its programs, such as the costs of the police or school per "EDU," by the number of "EDUs" it expects. This budgetary computation has little economic value. Consider the town's aquatics program as an example. Because it is used primarily by town residents, its costs are unaffected by the number of nonresidents. But this town's formula budgeting technique causes the budgeted costs of the aquatics program to increase when the number of nonresidents who work in the town increases![14]

ACCOUNTING IN PLANS AND BUDGETS

Plans and budgets should account for all relevant revenues, expenses, assets, and liabilities. But they may not. Sometimes relevant items are overestimated, sometimes they are underestimated, sometimes they are totally absent, and sometimes they are misclassified, as detailed below.

---

[13]Regina E. Herzlinger, "Zero-Base Budgeting in the Federal Government," *Sloan Management Review* (Winter 1979): 3-14.
[14]Charles D. Francis and Alan J. Borwick, "The Equivalency Factor: Municipal Budgeting by the Household," *Government Financing Review* (August 1990): 7-13.

Items that are frequently underestimated or absent include pension and other long-term employee benefit expenses and liabilities and the expenses of loan guarantees. Sometimes important information is absent because the organization does not spend the funds needed to obtain it. For example, budgeted expenses for bridge repair were increased only after the city budgeted enough money for bridge inspection.[15]

Items that are frequently overestimated include tax revenues, revenues from operations, gifts and donations, and other revenues and associated asset items. For example, in 1989 the U.S. government's Export-Import Bank still listed as assets the loans it made to Cuba before the anti-U.S. Castro regime took office. Only after the auditors issued an adverse opinion did the bank create a $4.2 billion reserve for losses on these noncollectible loans.[16] Many financially troubled institutions are prone to such overestimates, hoping that salvation is just around the corner.

Items that are frequently misclassified include capital expenditures that are classified as if they were operating expenses. Also, some expenses from past periods may be recognized only when cash is spent. For example, the $115 billion spent by the U.S. government by 1992 to "bail out" failed savings and loans and banks is an expense of prior periods. It should have been recognized as an expense in the past when the banks failed. Instead, it is recognized in the present when the cash payments are incurred.[17]

THE ROLE OF THE BOARD
AND TOP MANAGEMENT

The board and top management should seek satisfactory answers to the following questions about the process:

Does a plan exist?

Is there a satisfactory mission statement? Objectives statement?

Do budgets exist? If so:
    How many types and for what purpose?
    Are they consistent with the plan?
    Do they include all relevant financial items?
    Are they presented in an appropriate format?

Is there a well-deliberated planning and budgeting process? If so:
    Is it centralized or decentralized?
    Does it have a clear calendar?

[15]Calvin Sims, "New Problems Are Found on Bridges," *The New York Times*, 15 September 1990, p. 27.
[16]Dana Wechsler, "Phony Bookkeeping," *Forbes* (May 14, 1990): 112.
[17]Roula Khalaf, "Lies, Damned Lies, and the Budgeted Deficit," *Forbes* (December 9, 1991): 71-74.

SUMMARY

This chapter discussed the process, formats, and techniques for planning and budgeting. Planning and budgeting are key to effective managerial control. A good planning process clearly articulates the organization's social mission and the effectiveness and efficiency objectives that will enable attainment of the mission. Budgets are short-run versions of the long-term plans. Plans and budgets can extend to many different activities and can be expressed in many different formats. Each format—whether organized by program, responsibility center, appropriation, or object of expense—serves a different purpose. The three primary techniques for planning and budgeting are incremental, zero-base, and formula. Incremental budgeting should be used most frequently, zero-base budgeting should be used primarily for troubled or new organizations, and formula budgeting should be used only if the future is expected to be an exact replication of the past.

Managers and board members must insure adherence to the planning process. It is a time-consuming and challenging process and frequently is neglected or performed mechanistically. But the rewards of a well-implemented process are many.

Suggested Reading

Hofstede, Geert H. *The Game of Budget Control.* The Netherlands: Goreum & Comp., N.V., 1967.
United Way of America. *Budgeting: A Guide for United Way and Not-for-Profit Human Service Organizations.* Alexandria, VA: United Way of America, 1975.

APPENDIX A   The Least-Squares Technique of Estimating Cost-Volume Relationships

The least-squares method fits a straight line with the following formula:

$$\text{Total Cost} = a + b(\text{Volume})$$

where a = fixed costs when volume is zero
         b = change in costs with a change in volume (slope)

The parameters *a* and *b* are derived by solving the equations below using the techniques for solving simultaneous equations:

(Sum of the Volumes × *a*) + (*b* × Sum of the Volumes Squared) (1)
= Sum of the Product of Volume and Cost

(Number of Observations × *a*) + (*b* × Sum of the Volumes) (2)
= Sum of the Costs

An example of the use of the least-squares technique is presented using the cost and volume data of Table 9-5. Substituting these values into Equations (1) and (2) leads to the following results:

$$(303 \times a) + (b \times 20{,}929) = \$25{,}575.46$$
$$(6 \times a) + (b \times 303) = \$431.79$$

Solving these two equations yields values for *a* and *b* that are used to define the following line:

$$\text{Total cost} = \$38.13 + \$0.67(\text{Volume}) \qquad (3)$$

This equation says that the fixed component of costs is $38.13 and the variable component is an extra $0.67 for every increased unit of volume. If 10 units are to be produced next year,

$$\text{Total Cost} = \$38.13 + (\$0.67 \times 10) = \$44.83$$

Before using these equations to project the effects of volume on costs, it is important to examine how much of the variation in the data they explain. This explanation is partially provided by a statistic with the ominous title of the *coefficient of determination* or R^2. It measures the relationship between the variation in the data explained by this estimated equation and the total variation in the data. In this case, Equation (3) has an R^2 of 0.95; that is, it explains 95 percent of the observed variations in the data.[18]

A low R^2 statistic may indicate either that the relationship between costs and volume is nonlinear or that costs are primarily related to factors other than volume. If costs are related to more than one variable, the technique of *multiple regression* should be used. For a detailed discussion of this topic, see J. Johhnson, *Econometric Methods*, New York: McGraw-Hill, 1984; Roger

---

[18]The R^2 is calculated using the following formula:

$$R^2 = \frac{\left[\text{Sum of Volume} \times \text{Cost} - \dfrac{\text{Sum of Volume} \times \text{Sum of Cost}}{\text{Number of Observations}}\right]^2}{\left[\text{Sum of Volume}^2 - \dfrac{(\text{Sum of Volume})^2}{\text{Number of Observations}}\right]\left[\text{Sum of Cost}^2 - \dfrac{(\text{Sum of Cost})^2}{\text{Number of Observations}}\right]}$$

TABLE 9-5 **Data for Least-Squares Calculation**

Year	Volume	Cost (in constant dollars)	Volume Squared	Cost × Volume
1	20	$ 52.80	400	$ 1,056.00
2	100	99.02	10,000	9,902.00
3	40	63.10	1,600	2,524.00
4	15	47.50	225	712.50
5	80	101.60	6,400	8,128.00
6	48	67.77	2,304	3,252.96
Totals	303	$431.79	20,929	$25,575.46

C. Pfaffenberger and James H. Patterson, *Statistical Methods for Business and Economics*, Homewood, IL: Irwin, 1987, pp. 658 and 670; and Robert S. Pindyck and Daniel L. Rubenfeld, *Econometric Models and Economic Forecasts*, New York: McGraw-Hill, 1981.

DISCUSSION QUESTIONS

1. Why is planning important to an organization? What can it accomplish?

2. Describe the characteristics of a good planning process.

3. What are missions? How are they distinguished from objectives? Give an example of each for a nonprofit organization with which you are familiar.

4. What is the difference between effectiveness and efficiency?

5. How are budgets related to plans?

6. List as many types of budgets as you can.

7. What is the difference in nature and purpose of the following budgetary formats: line item, responsibility center, and program?

8. What is incremental budgeting? How is it distinguished from zero-base budgeting?

9. Describe how each of the following factors are incorporated in an incremental budget: inflation, prices, volume, efficiency, technology, and quality.

10. What is fomula budgeting?

11. Specify the circumstances under which each of these three budgeting techniques is best used: incremental, zero-base, and formula.

12. What accounting considerations are relevant for planning and budgeting?

13. What role should the organization's board and top management play in the planning and budgeting process?

14. Describe and evaluate the planning and budgeting process in a nonprofit organization with which you are familiar. What changes do you recommend and why?

Cases

CASE STUDIES

Case 9.1 enables you to review the mechanics of the budgeting process. Despite its brevity, it is quite detailed and realistic. It is a good introduction to the budgeting process. Case 9.2 describes the politics of the budgetary process in the context of a large school system in Boston. Case 9.3 contrasts a budget prepared on a program basis with a line-item one. Compare the two exhibits and ask yourself what information each provides and how it helps you to evaluate the efficiency of the system. Case 9.4 traces the steps by which a line-item budget is transformed into a program budget. It provides a good sense of the possibilities and limitations of program budgeting.

CASE 9.1 Davis Graduate School

The Davis Graduate School was an old, well-established institution. Ella Joffe, its newly hired budget officer, was trying to calculate its revenues and expenses for the following year using the projections listed below:

(1) The Davis School had a large two-year Master's program, with 800 students enrolled each year, for a total student body of 1,600. The Doctoral program had an enrolled student body of 200. The Continuing Education program, which conducted a number of residential nondegree programs, had the equivalent of 1,000 full-time students. The school had little difficulty in attracting applicants and Ms. Joffe expected these enrollment figures would continue for the upcoming year.

(2) The tuition for the next year would be $10,000 per Master's student, $5,000 per Doctoral student, and $2,000 per full-time equivalent continuing education student.

This case was prepared by Professor Regina E. Herzlinger.

Copyright © 1991 by the President and Fellows of Harvard College. Harvard Business School case 180-038. Revised January 1993.

(3)   The Master's program had seven courses that were required to be taken by all students in the first year. There were ten sections in each course, with 80 students per section. Each section of a course had one faculty member assigned to it. The second year offered 80 one-semester courses, each of which had a faculty member assigned to it.

(4)   Faculty members received credit for one-fifth of their time for every course they taught in the second year of the Master's program. They received two-fifths credit for every course section taught in the first year of the program.

(5)   The Master's program faculty did a substantial amount of course development work. Historically, each unit of time spent in teaching was matched with 0.7 units of time spent in course development.

(6)   There were 11 full-time equivalent (FTE) faculty assigned to the Doctoral program and 38 FTE faculty assigned to the continuing education program for the next year.

(7)   The Davis School also had an active research program. For the next year, the FTE of 20 full, 5 associate, and 10 assistant professors were to be doing research. Each faculty on research employed a half-time assistant.

(8)   There were 89.4 full professors with an average salary of $40,000, 14.9 associate professors with an average salary of $30,000, and 44.7 assistant professors with an average salary of $20,000. The research assistants had a salary of $12,000 a year.

(9)   The average secretarial salary was $16,000 a year. For teaching faculty, one-half secretary was assigned to each full professor, one-third to each associate professor, and one-fourth to each assistant professor. Each faculty member on research received the equivalent of a half-time secretary.

(10)   Each faculty member was permitted to attend one professional conference a year. The expected total travel cost was $500 for the average trip and living expenses. Historically, only 70 percent of the faculty attended such conferences.

(11)   The administration of the school was conducted by a dean, four associate deans, and three assistant deans for personnel, administration, financial management, and buildings and grounds. The total salary of these deans was to be $400,000. Each dean had a full-time secretary.

(12)   Each of the associate deans had administrators working for them, at an average salary of $25,000 each. Three associate deans employed two such people per dean. The other associate dean for continuing education employed five such people and two secretaries who worked for these administrators.

(13)   The average benefits expense was 30 percent of salary for the faculty and deans and 25 percent for the other employees.

(14)   The other administrative salary expenses were $3,500,000.

(15)   The nonsalary expenses consisted of student aid of $1,000,000, utilities of $1,200,000, nonconference travel of $900,000, supplies and other of $500,000, and library, duplicating, and other expenses of $1,500,000 a year.

(16)   The auxiliary services of dormitories, dining halls, and health care were separately budgeted and operated on a break-even basis.

(17)   In addition to its tuition revenue, the Davis School expected to receive grants and contracts of $200,000 and endowment income of $2,000,000. The endowment income was unrestricted except for $600,000 for student aid.

ASSIGNMENT

1. Calculate the school's revenues and expenses for the upcoming year.
2. What recommendations would you make on the basis of these budgeted figures?

CASE 9.2 The Budget Crisis of the Boston School Committee

Kathleen Sullivan, an elected member of the Boston School Committee, and founder and chairperson of the new subcommittee on the budget, did not know what step to take next. As shown in **Exhibit 1**, the Boston School Department's business manager had estimated next year's expenditures at $170 million, while City Hall had estimated them at $148 million. In an attempt to close that gap, Ms. Sullivan had conducted 17 budget hearings, only to come to the unsettling conclusion that the School Committee was not in control of the School Department Budget.

She found three major problems in managing the budget:

First of all, even when the Budget Subcommittee developed specific forms and instructions, School Department personnel did not know how much their programs, departments, or schools cost. Furthermore, we did not know what questions to raise once some of the data were broken down. Finally, court involvement further complicated matters. We voted to close 17 schools because of the loss of between 17,000 and 20,000 students over the past three years. On May 3, [U.S. District] Judge Garrity announced he would only allow us to close 3 schools. By the first Monday in April, we had not achieved our goal of any budget reductions. (Boston was in the midst of a court-ordered desegregation of its schools then.)

In the past 10 years, the School Department's budget had more than doubled, growing from 22 percent to 35 percent of the city's total budget. At the same time, the number of students in the system had steadily declined, and by most accounts, so had the quality of education. Immediate city and court pressure was being put on the School Committee to cut its current budget request. But even more important to Ms. Sullivan was that the committee develop a long-term plan to regain budgetary control of the system, and to raise the quality of educational services being provided.

THE BOSTON SCHOOL COMMITTEE

Since 1905 the Boston School Committee had been composed of five persons elected at large every two years. The role of the committee was to delineate, implement, and evaluate the policies and programs of the Boston School Department. While

Frances Jones and Arva Clark prepared this case under the supervision of Professor Regina E. Herzlinger.

most public school systems in the nation were funded largely through direct local tax appropriations, the Boston system received its local revenue through the City of Boston.

Within the monetary constraints set by the city, the committee and the school superintendent it elected traditionally had control over the school system. Reporting to the superintendent were the following assistant superintendents: instruction, pupil services, vocational and occupational education, special programs, operations, personnel support services, and business. Reporting to the deputy superintendent of operations were nine assistant superintendents, each responsible for the schools in one geographical area. In each area there were one or more high schools, typically two or three middle schools, and about a dozen elementary schools.

The committee voted on all academic and nonacademic appointments. Academic appointments were nominated by the superintendent; nonacademic appointments, which were all civil service jobs, were nominated and elected by the committee alone. All salaries and terms of employment were set by union contracts, which were negotiated by the School Committee. Hiring and firing of academic personnel had to be done before the school year started in order to avoid disruption of students' education. As of April, the Boston School Department had 7,126 employees: 5,171 teachers, 55 administrators, 1,050 aides, 33 school secretaries and clerical, 544 custodians, 144 cafeteria workers, and 129 physicians and nurses.

Positions on the School Committee, although unpaid, had long been prized as a political stepping-stone because of the public exposure and patronage they afforded. Committee members frequently clashed with each other and the superintendent during their heavily publicized committee meetings.

THE SCHOOL BUDGET CRISIS

By city law, the School Committee was required to submit to the mayor estimates of the next fiscal year's (July 1-June 30) expenditures by the first week in February. The city had to respond by March with an appropriation equal to, or greater than, that of the current year. Last year, the city had allocated the School Department $142 million.

The School Committee and most of the School Department staff were not well acquainted with budgetary procedures. As a result, the primary responsibility for preparing the estimated budget fell to the business manager, Leo Burke.

In September, as in past years, Burke sent out requests for budgetary information for the next fiscal year to the heads of Boston's 161 schools and to the system's administrative departments. The information requested included number and reason for personnel reductions and expansions; current year's allowances and next year's estimates of expenses for supplies, services, auto mileage, and other expenses.

To estimate next year's personnel expenses, the principals had to estimate next year's enrollment. The following August, one month before school was to begin, the Office of Implementation would provide the superintendent with an enrollment estimate based on applications received. But for this early projection the principals relied on a formula prescribed by the Office of Attendance, which instructed them to count (1) all students who had newly applied for admission to a Boston public school; and (2) all students who had attended a Boston public school at least one day in the previous year, whether or not they had returned an application indicating their school assignment preference for the coming year. The actual enrollment had fallen about 10,000 pupils short of the enrollment projected by this formula this year.

Principals then applied the projected enrollment to guideline staffing ratios issued by the superintendent's office, to give them their projected personnel needs. Many of the ratios were set by collective bargaining agreements between the School Committee and various unions (i.e., no fewer than one classroom teacher per 26 elementary-level students; no more than 25 periods taught by each secondary-level teacher). Others were mandated by the state, and some, including those for administrative staff, custodians, and educational aides, were set at the discretion of the superintendent.

Burke spent November and December assembling a projected budget for the entire system. He estimated salaries by applying the current pay scale, adjusted for yearly increases, to the personnel estimates he had received. Instruction materials were estimated on a per-capita basis, using a base figure adjusted annually for inflation. The demand for temporary teachers, secretaries, aides, lunch monitors, and lab assistants was estimated based on previous years' experience.

Each school's total was then added, together with the totals of each administrative department, to provide a budget for the entire system. The appropriations for each individual school were not listed on the final budget, nor were they published or distributed to the principals. Instead, as additional funds were needed during the year, each principal checked with Burke to see if money was left in the school's budget. Principals were urged to keep their own running tallies, but many did not, according to Burke. At the end of the year, Burke prepared a list of expenditures broken down by school, and a financial statement to be submitted to the city, using the format shown in **Exhibit 2**.

On January 28, Burke submitted a preliminary budget to the board of superintendents and the School Committee (see **Exhibit 1**). It exceeded the prior year's budget by $28 million. On February 4, the School Committee forwarded the budget to the mayor, as required by law. But Sullivan, doubtful that the city would provide an additional $28 million, had written Superintendent Fahey on February 2 requesting that Fahey prepare an alternative budget reflecting a 20 percent reduction in funding. (Fahey was appointed superintendent after the abrupt departure of her predecessor. Boston school superintendents usually did not have long tenure in that role.)

Sullivan and her newly formed Budget Committee then held 17 budget hearings during February and March with School Department area and community superintendents, during which $12 million was cut from the original February estimate. At the final budget hearing at the end of March, Superintendent Fahey at last presented her revised budget. Instead of reducing the department's request, she asked for a $13 million increase, thereby offsetting the Budget Committee's reduction and raising the total budget request to $171,884,950.

On March 26, the city auditor informed the School Committee that its appropriation would be $148,668,734. On April 7, the School Committee submitted its final budget estimate of $171,816,260 to the mayor.

In past years the city had always funded any School Department deficit remaining at the end of a fiscal year (last year, that debt had reached $12.5 million). But the mayor, who was already contemplating a politically unpleasant but financially necessary increase in the city's property tax rate—then at $196 per $1,000 assessed value—vowed to make the School Department stay within its appropriations.

In addition, the School Department faced an imminent deficit for the current fiscal year. Although staffing had been planned under the expectation that 85,000 students would attend Boston schools, the actual enrollment was around 76,000. The School Committee's belated attempt to cut the teaching staff was thwarted in March by Judge Garrity, who would allow only 149 of a proposed 370 teachers and aides to be released. On April 28, Mayor Kevin White announced that schools must close early due to the budget overruns. On May 10, Judge Garrity ordered the mayor to keep the schools open, and provide funds to do so. The mayor complied. Both the mayor and Judge Garrity were frequently accused of "bankrupting the city."

WHAT WENT WRONG?

A number of problems were apparent to those involved, chief among them that Sullivan's new School Committee had inherited a legacy of fiscal indifference. Voters in the past had elected committee members according to their political camp with little regard for management skill; at the same time, the committee lacked both the staff and information needed to control the budget, even if they so desired. As a result, past committees had neither the incentive nor the power to counter the demands of the 11 strong unions representing both academic and nonacademic groups. A Boston Municipal Research Bureau study showed that teachers' salaries in Boston exceeded those in even affluent suburbs by at least 7 percent. Custodian salaries and benefits, according to another survey, were found to be from 12 percent to 36 percent greater than the average custodian pay of representative cities and towns across the state. In addition, teacher productivity was considerably below the 625 "pupil contact hours" provided for in union contracts. In 11 high schools surveyed, the average was 467 hours.

Finally, school desegregation had greatly increased the system's budget. A whole new department—the Office of Implementation—was set up by court order at the outset of desegregation to oversee its progress. Twenty additional teachers were funded, 1,015 transitional aides were hired (although there had been appropriations for only 600 passed by the School Committee), and the superintendent's administrative staff grew from 42 to 78. All of these expenses, added to the cost of transportation, safety officials, and teacher and administrative overtime, led to a deficit of $20,000,000 by the end of the current year, which the city was ordered to cover.

The pressure on Sullivan and the rest of the School Committee to control its budget mounted as the city faced its own fiscal crisis. In ten years, the city budget had almost doubled. At the same time, the total value of the city's taxable land, buildings, and property had barely remained stationary, as middle-class families and businesses left the city. The only immediate solution the mayor could find was to raise the tax rate—already among the highest in the country—a solution that many acknowledged would only worsen the city's economic future.

Ms. Sullivan knew that finding a way to control the system's budget, at the same time as improving the quality of the education it delivered, was the most important task facing her committee. She wondered how to do it and how her father, the owner of the Patriots football team and a popular Boston figure, could help.

EXHIBIT 1 **The Budget Crisis of the Boston School Committee**

Office of the Business Manager

To the School Committee of the City of Boston:

I submit herewith estimates of proposed expenditures for general school purposes for the fiscal year in accordance with Section 109 of the Rules of the School Committee.

The preliminary estimates for the year exceed the budget for last year by $28,266,216. The following are the increases by function:

Function	Estimated Budget	Budget, Last Year	Increase (Decrease)
Administration	$ 6,686,110	$ 4,723,130	$ 1,962,980
Instruction	124,079,730	105,562,760	18,516,970
Attendance and health services	2,681,240	2,597,370	83,870
Pupil transportation services	11,039,440	5,939,200	5,100,240
Operation of plant	15,439,500	14,602,010	837,490
Maintenance of plant	808,790	610,870	197,920
Fixed charges	6,539,000	3,963,000	2,576,000
Food services (deficit)	2,227,230	3,669,244	(1,442,014)
Community services	1,083,910	651,150	432,760
Totals	$170,584,950	$142,317,734	$28,266,216

Respectfully submitted,
Leo Burke
Business Manager

EXHIBIT 2   **The Budget Crisis of the Boston School Committee—Statement of Appropriations, Other Credits, Expenditures for All School Purposes Business Manager's Report (000 omitted)[a]**

School Committee General School Purpose	Appropriations and Other Credits			Expenditures			Unexpended Balance or (Deficit)
	Salaries	Other Expenses	Totals	Salaries	Other Expenses	Totals	
1. Administration							
A. General administration	$ 226	$ 317	$ 542	$ 241	$ 382	$ 623	$ (80)
B. Business administration	505	33	537	511	58	569	(31)
C. Educational administration	1,545	417	1,962	2,661	540	3,202	(1,240)
Totals	$ 2,276	$ 767	$ 3,041	$ 3,413	$ 980	$ 4,394	$ (1,351)
2. Instruction							
A. Educational director and supervision	$ 4,016	$ 239	$ 4,255	$ 4,487	$ 251	$ 4,738	$ (483)
B. Elementary schools	42,374	1,935	44,309	42,140	974	43,115	1,195
C. Latin and day high schools	22,079	1,045	23,123	27,530	843	28,373	(5,250)
D. Junior high and middle schools	14,810	528	15,338	17,712	380	18,091	(2,754)
E. Special education	3,309	1,085	4,394	3,351	1,106	4,457	(62)
F. Physical education	524	284	808	497	199	696	112
G. Evening and summer schools	437	32	479	487	29	516	(47)
H. Other education—instruction	863	1,030	1,893	2,071	1,176	3,247	(1,354)
I. Stores and other expenditures	0	150	150	0	836	836	(686)
Totals	$ 88,412	$ 6,328	$ 94,739	$ 98,276	$ 5,794	$104,069	$ (9,329)
3. Attendance and health services							
A. Supervisors of attendance	$ 796	$ 29	$ 825	$ 772	$ 21	$ 793	$ 32
B. School physicians and nurses	1,764	98	1,862	1,701	59	1,760	102
Totals	$ 2,560	$ 127	$ 2,687	$ 2,473	$ 80	$ 2,553	$ 134
4. Pupil transportation services	$ 0	$ 502	$ 502	$ 0	$ 4,816	$ 4,816	$ (4,314)
5. Operation of plant							
A. Office of schoolhouse custodian	$ 200	$ 6	$ 205	$ 211	$ 10	$ 221	$ (16)
B. Custodians	7,069	0	7,069	6,302	0	6,302	767
C. Heat for buildings	0	2,847	2,847	0	1,939	1,939	908
D. Utilities, except heat for buildings	19	2,463	2,481	20	3,350	3,370	(889)
E. Supplies, except utilities	0	360	360	0	244	244	116
F. Supply room	269	29	298	252	31	284	15
Totals	$ 7,557	$ 5,704	$ 13,261	$ 6,785	$ 5,574	$ 12,360	$ 902

[a]Omitted for case purposes. The actual report showed numbers to the penny.

EXHIBIT 2 (Continued)

School Committee General School Purpose	Appropriations and Other Credits			Expenditures			Unexpended Balance or (Deficit)
	Salaries	Other Expenses	Totals	Salaries	Other Expenses	Totals	
6. Maintenance of plant	$ 0	$ 443	$ 443	$ 0	$ 414	$ 414	$ 29
7. Fixed charges	$ 3,076	$ 123	$ 3,199	$ 2,947	$ 145	$ 3,092	$ 107
8. Food services (deficit appropriation)	$ 3,203	$ 0	$ 3,203	$ 2,036	$ 0	$ 2,036	$ 1,167
9. Community service							
Budget appropriation	$ 318	$ 6	$ 324	$ 306	$ 209	$ 515	$ (191)
Unliquidated reserves (1971, 1972, 1973-74)	107,401	13,999	121,400	0	134,248	134,248	(12,848)
Pensions to teachers	0	3,360	3,360	0	2,679	2,679	681
	(203)	0	(203)	112	0	112	(315)
Total appropriation	$107,198	$17,359	$124,557	$116,349	$20,690	$137,039	$(12,482)
Income accounts							
A. School Lunch Account—Chap. 417 of 1950	$ 7,160	$ 0	$ 7,160	$ 233	$ 5,149	$ 5,382	$ 1,778
B. Physical Education—G.I. Chap. 71, Sec. 47	0	22	22	0	0	0	22
C. Grants—Federal and Others	13,307	0	13,307	11,520	2,905	14,426	(1,118)
D. Special Education CH776—Advance	3,436	0	3,436	2,199	0	2,199	1,237
E. Court judgment	4,821	0	4,821	0	0	0	4,821
Total general school purposes	$135,922	$17,381	$153,303	$130,301	$27,744	$159,045	$ 5,742
Planning and Engineering							
Administration	$ 1,150	$ 272	$ 1,422	$ 1,216	$ 177	$ 1,393	$ 29
Maintenance of grounds	0	141	141	0	134	134	7
Maintenance of buildings	0	3,420	3,420	0	3,191	3,191	229
Maintenance of equipment	0	150	150	0	106	106	44
Acquisition of equipment	0	0	0	0	0	0	0
Replacement of equipment	0	100	100	0	74	74	26
Vocational education	0	9	9	0	0	0	9
Unliquidated reserves (1971)	0	10	10	0	2	2	8
Total appropriation	$ 1,150	$ 4,102	$ 5,252	$ 1,216	$ 3,684	$ 4,900	$ 352
Summary							
School Committee general school purposes	$135,922	$17,381	$153,303	$130,301	$28,744	$159,045	$ (5,742)
Planning and engineering	1,150	4,102	5,252	1,216	3,684	4,900	352
Total all school purposes	$137,072	$21,483	$158,555	$131,517	$32,428	$163,945	$ (5,390)

Note: Although the School Committee under existing statutes makes appropriations for all school purposes, the actual expenditures for the department of planning and engineering are made by that department.

CASE 9.3 Somerstown Public Schools

Dr. John Nelson, superintendent of the Somerstown, New Jersey, public schools, reflected on the recently implemented program budgeting system:

> Although we have been developing our program budgeting system for almost a year and a half, we have a long way to go before we will be satisfied. Program budgeting has yet to reach the point of being in the mainstream of our operations. For example, our budget was approved by the school board by line item, although we prepared it in both program and line-item format; our accounting will continue to be line item; and both budgeting and accounting continue to be central office activities, with limited teaching staff involvement. Most important, program budgeting has yet to result in any major changes in our total educational program.

BACKGROUND

Somerstown, New Jersey, located within easy commuting distance of downtown Philadelphia, like many suburban communities, was a town in the midst of rapid change. Until the mid-1950s it was a small farming community, raising tomatoes for the nearby Camden, New Jersey, Campbell Soup Company plant, and raising apples. Then the combination of the sprawling metropolitan area and the sale of several large farms for both industrial and residential developments began to take effect. Population increased from less than 5,000 to nearly 15,000 during the 1980s. The new families were young, well educated, with children. Soon, Somerstown had a higher percentage of its population in its local school system than any of its neighboring towns.

The combination of the large number of school-age children, resulting in school budgets representing approximately 75 percent of the town's budget, and the diverse educational philosophies espoused by the older, conservative farmers on the one hand, and the younger and more liberal professionals on the other, tended to keep the schools continually in the center of controversy.

Somerstown had two, or more accurately, one and a third, school systems. First, there was the Somerstown Public School System, consisting of Grades 1 through 8. Second, there was the Wampanoag Regional High School, Grades 9 through 12, for the three communities of Carleton, Somerstown, and Winsor. Each was independent in that it had its own staff, administration, and school board. There were, however, frequent attempts by both staffs, administrations, and school boards to coordinate educational programs.

Professor Robert A. Howell prepared and Professor Regina E. Herzlinger revised this case.

Copyright © 1991 by the President and Fellows of Harvard College. Harvard Business School case 171-369. Revised January 1993.

THE PROGRAM BUDGETING SYSTEM

Dr. Nelson continued:

We began our program budgeting efforts two years ago. One of the school board members is a business school professor, and at his urging and with his help, he and I developed a very detailed program structure and recast our budget into program format. Then my staff and I prepared the next year's budget in both program and line-item format. That version provided costs by level, building (we have seven), and program for both elementary and junior high. At the elementary level our program was a grade; at the junior high, it was a subject.

Our current budget has omitted the individual building as a primary dimension. More important, we have shifted to a subject orientation at the elementary level. And we have put much more emphasis on our planning at the individual program level.

Let me show you the line-item budget, then the program budget we now have. You can draw your own conclusions regarding the relative usefulness of each.

With that, Dr. Nelson described both the line-item and program budget schedules shown in the exhibits. The following paragraphs summarize his remarks:

Exhibit 1 is the current Somerstown Public Schools Budget in line-item format. In addition to the summary page, the details for two line items, 2,300 teachers and 2,400 texts, are shown. As one can see, teachers' salaries, representing more than 50 percent of the total budget, are presented as a single "line." Teachers and texts applied to the same educational program are included in different line items.

Exhibit 2 is the current Somerstown Public Schools Budget in program format, including detail by organizational unit and expenditure types.

Exhibit 3 provides further explanation and cost information for the reading program, elementary level. The program approach consolidates all expenditures that can be clearly identified, such as teachers and texts, with a given program.

ASSIGNMENT

1. Is the programmatic method of collecting expenses any better than the line-item method? Would a different program structure be more useful?
2. The program budget indicates that the reading program in Grades 1 to 5 will cost $249,609. How was this number obtained? What is the cost per child for reading in Grades 1 to 5? Is this too much, just right, not enough? What additional data might you need to answer this question?

EXHIBIT 1   Somerstown Public Schools—Line-Item Budget

Code	Description	Current Budget	Last Year's Budget
1100	School committee	$ 2,190	$ 2,063
1200	Superintendent's office	83,322	78,540
	Total administration	85,512	80,603
2100	Supervision	9,420	15,930
2200	Principals	177,350	155,197
2300	Teachers	1,756,058	1,579,922
2400	Texts	38,126	37,025
2500	Library	20,693	19,745
2600	Audiovisual	23,331	19,664
2700	Guidance	83,526	62,350
2800	Pupil personnel	17,130	15,235
	Total instruction	2,125,634	1,905,068
3100	Attendance	200	200
3200	Health services	41,482	35,023
3300	Transportation	165,703	166,753
3400	Food services	11,116	10,079
3500	Student activities	2,512	2,246
	Total other services	221,013	214,301
4100	Operation	194,618	171,685
4200	Maintenance	57,959	61,518
	Total operation and maintenance	252,577	233,203
7200	Improvement	0	0
7300	Acquisition	14,469	10,355
7400	Replacement	2,552	3,870
	Total improvement, acquisition, replacement	17,021	14,225
9100	Tuition	8,243	2,600
	Total budget	$2,710,000	$2,450,000

Teachers—Detail:
Current: (92 + 46.5)
New: (1.5)
Sabbatical: (2.0)

Code	Description	Current Budget	Last Year's Budget
2300-11-1.1	Classroom	$1,395,027	$1,255,541
1.2	Specialists	147,579	133,175
1.4	Substitutes	20,000	18,000
1.5	Tutors, physical handicap	1,500	1,500
1.6a	Curriculum workshops	15,000	10,000
1.6b	Professional advancement	5,000	4,000
2.a	Aides, academic	10,942	7,680
2.b	Aides, noon	18,400	18,400
4	Contracted services	1,950	9,137
5.1	Supplies, routine	12,800	14,000
5.2	Elementary	46,504	40,403
5.3	Junior high	21,256	18,440
6.1a	Travel in-state	2,245	2,215
6.2a	Travel out-of-state	1,715	1,460
2300-11	Total basic education teachers	1,699,918	1,533,951
2300-12	Total special education teachers	56,140	45,971
2300	Total teachers	$1,756,058	$1,579,922

Texts—Detail:

Code	Description	Current Budget	Last Year's Budget
2400-11-5.2	Elementary text	$ 26,347	$ 24,925
5.3	Junior high text	11,429	11,850
2400-11	Total	37,776	36,775
2400-12-5.1	Special class text	350	250
2400	Total text	$ 38,126	$ 37,025

EXHIBIT 2 **Somerstown Public Schools—Current Budget by Program: Summary of Expenditures**

Code	Program Title	Total Budget	Percent Total	$ per Student	Allocated by Organization				Allocated by Expenditure Type		
					Elem. (1-5)	Hoyes (6)	Jr. High (7-8)	District-wide	Certified Salaries	Noncert. Salaries	Other Expenses
Instructional Programs											
	Basic Education:										
60	English, language arts, 1-8	$ 306,713	11.32	$ 96	$ 182,310	$ 32,328	$ 92,075	$ -	$ 285,456	$ -	$ 21,257
61	Reading 1-8	292,619	10.80	122	249,609	37,725	5,285	-	260,435	3,300	29,884
62	Science 1-8	168,967	6.23	53	54,398	33,584	80,985	-	142,172	5,555	21,240
63	Health 1-8	39,501	1.46	13	31,303	4,995	3,203	-	35,006	-	4,495
64	Mathematics 1-8	228,675	8.44	72	130,708	21,684	76,283	-	215,889	-	12,786
65	Social studies 1-8	169,803	6.27	53	69,412	25,310	75,081	-	145,448	-	24,355
59	Physical education 1-8	122,011	4.50	59	77,395	13,808	30,808	-	111,376	2,090	8,545
66	Typing 7-8	23,790	0.88	33	-	-	23,790	-	19,824	-	3,966
67	Foreign language 7-8	21,645	0.80	43	-	-	21,645	-	20,229	-	1,416
68	Home economics 7-8	26,914	0.99	68	-	-	26,914	-	25,458	-	1,456
69	Industrial arts	37,277	1.38	86	-	-	37,277	-	32,031	-	5,246
57	Art 1-8	119,220	4.40	37	79,410	15,790	24,020	-	109,342	-	9,878
58	Music 1-8	126,143	4.65	44	84,980	15,046	26,117	-	114,106	-	12,037
00	Nonprogram	65,387	2.41	21	-	-	-	65,387	47,000	-	18,387
	Total Basic Education	1,748,665	64.53	-	959,525	200,270	523,483	65,387	1,563,772	10,945	173,948
76	Special education	56,490	2.08	1,027	-	-	-	56,490	52,485	2,430	1,575
77	Tuition pupils	8,043	0.30	731	-	-	-	8,043	-	-	8,043
74	Adult education	200	0.01	29	-	-	-	200	-	-	200
	Total Instructional Programs	1,813,398	66.92	-	959,525	200,270	523,483	130,120	1,616,257	13,375	183,766
Instructional Support Programs											
71	Learning resources—Libraries	20,693	0.76	7	4,140	885	15,668	-	11,739	-	8,954
72	Guidance 1-8	83,526	3.08	26	31,998	16,064	35,464	-	72,715	4,681	6,130
73	Health services	41,482	1.53	13	-	-	-	41,482	25,490	3,609	12,383
81	Facilities	273,918	10.11	-	124,793	29,122	55,294	64,709	-	130,318	143,600
85	School management	175,350	6.47	55	108,342	22,903	44,105	-	136,285	34,336	4,729
86	Central office management	101,452	3.74	32	-	-	-	101,452	57,600	33,442	10,410
80	Transportation	165,703	6.11	36	-	-	-	165,703	2,850	-	162,853
84	Food service	11,116	0.41	3	-	-	-	11,116	10,541	-	575
00	Nonprogram	19,150	0.71	6	-	200	550	18,400	750	18,400	-
	Total Instructional Support Programs	892,390	32.93	-	269,273	69,174	151,081	402,862	317,970	224,786	349,634
Community Service Programs		4,212	0.16	1	-	-	-	4,212	-	-	4,212
	Grand Total	$2,710,000	100.00	-	$1,228,798	$269,444	$674,564	$537,194	$1,934,227	$238,161	$537,612

EXHIBIT 3 **Somerstown Public Schools—Current Education Program**

Summary Description of Existing Elementary-Grade Program

1. *Brief summary of program:* Multibasal program augmented by teacher-chosen materials designed to help children grow in five stages of reading: (1) readiness, (2) beginning reading, (3) stimulating rapid growth, (4) establishing power, and (5) refining tastes. One reading director, two reading consultants, and one reading aide assist teachers in choosing appropriate materials and executing effective reading programs.

2. *Student text materials:* (listed)

3. *Teacher's resources guides:* (listed)

4. *Certified staff:* 21.7

5. *Noncertified staff:* 1

6. *Instructional time provided,* based on 180 days per year:

	Hours Per Day	Total Hours Per Year
Grades 1-3	2.0	360
Grades 4-5	1.5	270

7. *Number of teaching stations required:* 47

8. *Methods of evaluation—students:* Use of tests, designed (1) by teachers, (2) by consultants, (3) systemwide, and (4) by textbook publishing companies, with results evaluated by reading consultants, principals, and teacher/observers.

9. *Methods of evaluation—staff:* Use of various levels of committee assessment, including reading department, principals, reading consultants, grade-level committees, primary and intermediate subgroups.

10. *Methods of evaluation—program:* Use of committees of teachers and reading consultants together.

Multiyear Financial and Statistical Plan

	Budget Year	Next Year	Year after Next
I. Multiyear Financial Plan			
1. Salaries—certified	$219,609	$236,245	$255,904
2. Salaries—noncertified	3,300	3,600	3,950
3. Extra-duty compensation	-	-	-
4. Equipment	1,200	3,000	4,000
5. Supplies	2,500	4,000	5,000
6. Workbooks	9,000	13,000	14,000
7. Textbooks	13,000	13,000	14,000
8. Other expense	1,000	1,500	1,500
9. Total	249,609	274,345	298,354
10. Offsetting revenues			

EXHIBIT 3 (Continued)

	Budget Year	Next Year	Year after Next
II. Multiyear Statistical Plan			
11. Total number of classes or sections	73	71	69
12. Number of certified staff (FTE)	21.7	22.5	21.8
13. Number of noncertified staff (FTE)	1	1	1
14. Number of teaching stations	47	47	47
15. Hours of instructional time per year	1-3: 360 4-5: 270	K-3: 360 4: 270	K-3: 360 5: 270
16. Total teacher hours of instruction	1-3: 15,120 4-5: _8,370_ 23,490	K-3: 20,520 4: _3,780_ 24,300	K-3: 19,800 4: _3,780_ 23,580
17. Student enrollment			
Kindergarten	-	260	260
Grade 1	369	328	267
Grade 2	374	376	335
Grade 3	373	377	379
Grade 4	370	376	380
Grade 5	423	-	-

CASE 9.4 Dearden College

Dearden College is a small, private, liberal arts college located in Fleming, Ohio. It grants a Bachelor of Arts degree. Originally founded as a men's college, after several heated trustee meetings it opened its doors to women four years ago.

The admissions office felt that the decision to go coed had significantly offset the negative reaction to the small, rural Ohio town in which the college was located. In the last four years, its applications from both men and women had increased and projected enrollment for next year was 3,000 students (all residents). Despite the strong enrollment figures and a large endowment, a deficit of $530,000 was projected (see **Exhibit 1**).

In its recent meeting, the trustee finance committee had not approved the proposed budget. Instead, it asked President Haas to review the budget with his business officer, academic department heads, and other department heads in order to reduce costs. The finance committee was unwilling to consider an increase in tuition and fees until it was convinced that adequate measures had been taken to control

Professor Claudine Malone prepared and Professor Regina E. Herzlinger revised this case. Copyright © 1975 by the President and Fellows of Harvard College. Harvard Business School case 178-025. Revised January 1993.

expenses. In addition, it felt that the budget, as submitted, gave no indication of where the college's resources were being consumed. They felt any cost reductions should be considered in light of explicit educational objectives. They asked President Haas and his business officers to prepare a budget format that would help them.

ASSIGNMENT

1. Restructure the preliminary budget in program format using the worksheet and data provided in Appendix A. All administrative expenses and plant expenses should be allocated to one of the programs.
2. What actions should President Haas take?

EXHIBIT 1   Dearden College Operating Budget ($ in 000s)

	Preliminary Budget Next Year	Actual Last Year
Revenues		
Student tuition and fees	$ 7,800	$ 7,280
Dining	2,700	2,520
Housing	3,300	3,080
Auxiliary enterprises	1,400	1,270
Gifts for current use	700	630
Endowment income	950	718
Reimbursement of direct and indirect expenses related to research grants	80	72
Total revenue	16,930	15,570
Expenses		
Salaries:		
Faculty (teaching and research)	6,856	5,962
Administration	1,210	1,052
Staff	2,800	2,435
	10,866	9,449
Student support:		
Library and audiovisual	433	363
Equipment and supplies	105	91
Food	2,086	1,812
Student activities and athletics	340	296
Scholarships	350	320
	3,314	2,882
Plant:		
Maintenance (salaries, supplies, and minor parts)	354	307
Utilities	400	320
Equipment	300	378
Interest	46	38
	1,100	1,043
General and administrative:		
Employee benefits	866	754
Insurance	62	54
Professional fees	40	35
Communications and data processing	430	398
Travel	84	73
Services purchased	45	39
Security	68	32
Health services	273	237
Miscellaneous	12	14
	1,880	1,636
Research costs (excluding faculty salaries)	300	261
Total expenses	17,460	15,271
Surplus (deficit)	$ (530)	$ 299

Dearden College Worksheet ($000)

Line Items		Administration	Instruction	Research	Plant	Housing	Dining Center	Health Services	Student Activities and Athletics	Development	Total	Adjustments	Adjusted Total
Salaries													
Faculty	(1)										$ 6,856		
Administration	(2)										1,210		
Staff	(3)										2,800		
Student Support													
Library and Audiovisual	(4)										433		
Equipment and Supplies	(5)										105		
Food	(6)										2,086		
Student Activities and Athletics	(7)										340		
Scholarships	(8)										350		
Plant													
Maintenance	(9)										354		
Utilities	(10)										400		
Equipment	(11)										300		
Interest	(12)										46		
General & Administrative													
Employee Benefits	(13)										866		
Insurance	(14)										62		
Professional Fees	(15)										40		
Communications and Data Processing	(16)										430		
Travel	(17)										84		
Services Purchased	(18)										45		
Security	(19)										68		
Health Services	(20)										273		
Miscellaneous	(21)										12		
Research	(22)										300		
Subtotal	(23)										$17,460		
Allocation In (Out)	(24)												
	(25)												
	(26)												
Total	(27)												

Programs

APPENDIX A

In trying to understand how the college's resources were being consumed, President Haas studied the data presented below. To this he added some notes to expedite the business office's first cut at a new budget format using the form they had recently worked out.

(1) Revenue from auxiliary enterprises represents the surplus of income over expenses for the bookstore, faculty club, and college printing office. It does not include any revenue from the college infirmary (health services). A health service fee of $75 is included in the total tuition charge of $2,600 per student.

(2) The health services expense includes expenses for medicine and drugs dispensed in the infirmary but not special prescriptions, which students pay for themselves. The health services expense also includes salaries for nurses and doctors but does not include any costs for plant, housekeeping, food, or utilities.

(3) For the next year, five FTE faculty were assigned to research. Average faculty salaries were budgeted for $52,000 per year. Salaries for faculty secretaries are included in the budget line for staff salaries. For budgeting purposes, each member of the faculty (whether a department head, teaching faculty, or assigned to research) is considered to have 0.3 secretaries at an average salary of $16,800 for an FTE. The budget line for salaries does not include fringes. Next year's teaching faculty (including department heads) number 145 FTEs.

(4) For budgeting purposes, administrators are assumed to have 0.1 FTE secretaries. The one exception is the development office. The director of development (salary $24,500) has a full-time secretary, and the office staff comprises an additional 2.5 FTE secretary/clerks as well as three administrators (average administrative salaries are $18,500).

(5) Salaries for librarians, library clerical, and the audiovisual staff are included in the budget line for library and audiovisual. However, the chief librarian's salary of $18,600 is included in the budget line for administrative salaries.

(6) The budget line for student activities and athletics includes all the expenses for the varsity sports program, as well as intramural athletic activities, the student association, required physical education classes, athletic equipment, travel for athletic activities, and other student organization expenses. Revenues from athletic fees and game receipts have been credited to these expenses. Salaries totaling $66,000 for the athletic director, assistant athletic director, and the director of student services have been included in the budget line for administrative salaries.

(7) Little information is readily available on the breakdown of plant expenses. The business office records indicate that the utilities for the dormitories have been budgeted for $100,000. The utility budgets are: the athletic buildings, $60,000; dining center, $40,000; infirmary, $18,000. It was not possible to separate administrative and classroom building utilities, since administrators and student activities personnel share space in the complex of classroom buildings. Nor was it possible to isolate housekeeping salaries and expenses

from other maintenance salaries and expenses. The salary for the director of the physical plant ($23,200) is in the budget line for administrative salaries. It was possible to allocate building space among the different users, as indicated below:

Program	% of Building Square Feet Used
Administration	5
Instruction	40
Research	10
Plant	1
Housing	40
Dining Center	1
Health Services	1
Student Activities	1
Development	1

(8) Professional fees cannot be identified by program. Nor have travel expenses ever been broken down by department. Travel requests have to be approved in advance by the business office except for the $2,000 in travel expenses included in the development office budget and the $4,500 in travel expenses designated for the recruiting office.

(9) The $430,000 budgeted for communications and data processing includes $128,000 for the college switchboard, telephones, and operators' salaries. The remainder covers computer rentals and data processing personnel salaries except for the $24,000 salary for the director of computer services included in the budget line for administrative salaries.

(10) Professional services purchased include legal fees, consulting fees, and auditing fees. Historically, legal fees have been very low because of the longstanding relationship between the college and the firm. Likewise, the fee for the annual audit was well below market.

(11) Maintenance of the athletic fields costs about $15,000 a year.

Notes: For this first budget review, no attempt will be made to examine the individual faculty department salaries and expenses. Where data are not immediately available on a direct-expense basis, make reasonable assumptions, using average salaries and average expenses.

10 Planning and Budgeting for Revenues

FINANCIAL PLANNING PRESENTS PROJECTIONS FOR THE organization's revenues, costs, and profits. The process of planning for costs was discussed in Chapter 9 as part of the planning and budgeting techniques section. This chapter discusses planning for revenues and profits.

REVENUE PLANNING

This process requires that all revenue sources be carefully analyzed and budgeted. They include revenues from operations, income from endowments and other capital invested for financial returns, gifts for operations, grants for various programs, and fees from ancillary activities. All of these sources can yield sizeable amounts. For example, fees from ancillary activities can provide such substantial income that a recent museum directors' conference devoted the bulk of its time to discussing restaurant and gift shop management and how to market reproductions of the museums' collections.

Two of the most important sources of revenue in nonprofit organizations are those earned from endowment and other invested capital and from selling the organization's services. These two revenue sources are dependent on two critical financial decisions—the investment decisions for endowment and the pricing decision for operating revenues. Each is separately discussed below. (Gifts and donations represent yet another important funding source, but because they are most critically dependent on marketing skills, rather than financial ones, they are not discussed here).

Effect of the Economy

Planning for endowment and operating revenues is complicated by the fact that they are heavily affected by the economy, a variable which no organization controls. The effects of the economy on revenues are many. Rates of inflation and economic growth affect the returns to be earned from invested capital. Employment and income patterns affect the need for various services and the amount people can pay for them. The effect of the economy on revenues is profound and rapid. For example, the interest rates paid by one-year U.S. Treasury bills fluctuated from 8 percent to 15 percent in one six month period from June to December of 1980.[1]

Thus, planning for revenues must incorporate projections about the future of the economy. Because no one projection is completely reliable, the planning process should also evaluate the effect of different economic projections—such as a depressed, steady, or booming stock market—on revenues. These projections do not necessarily require fancy computer models or massive expenses, just common sense. For example, a small nonprofit cultural organization should evaluate the effect of a booming, flat, or recessionary economy on its ticket sales. If it has endowment and other invested funds, it should evaluate the effect of the economy on these as well.

Role of Simulations in Revenue Planning

Some nonprofit organizations have such large and complex revenues and expenses that they must use simulation models to help them clarify the consequences of alternative scenarios. For example, service organizations whose revenues and expenses are interdependent because their revenues are reimbursed on a cost basis, such as research laboratories with government contracts whose payments are based on research ''costs,'' must ensure that all allowable avenues for maximizing reimbursement are explored. Simulations are computer-based models that ''simulate'' the results of different actions. In this case, they identify the cost-accounting methods that produce the highest costs and, therefore, the highest revenues. Although some view this process of maximizing costs, and thus revenues, as ''immoral,'' it is no more immoral than knowing the tax code well enough to avail oneself of every legitimate tax deduction.

The use of simulations is growing, especially in health care organizations. They are potentially valuable in virtually all types of organizations. Simulations incorporate projected costs, resource contributions, prices, and demand for services, including other assumptions that are anticipated to affect demand. Several scenarios are examined to determine their effects on the financial performance of the organization. The effect on financial performance of various managerial actions, such as raising prices or dropping unprofitable services, is then estimated.

Sometimes, a formal mathematical model of revenues may prove useful for identifying changes in future revenue sources that will have a large impact on the organization. For example, a 1988 model of college and university

[1]Paul V. Shantic and Robert R. Bryers, ''Hidden Risk: Problems in Local Agency Portfolio,'' *Governmental Finance Review* (August 1990): 14.

revenues identified stock market prices and trends in government spending as the factors with the highest impact on the finances of higher education. Their impact on finance was much larger than the effect of wage changes, price levels, or the Gross National Product.[2] Their importance might not have been identified without a formal mathematical model.

Lifetime

As discussed in Part One, the projected *lifetime* of the revenues should be matched with the lifetime of the expenses. Failure to do so may lead to disastrous results. For example, many institutions of higher education are now paying the price for failing to match the lifetimes of revenues and expenses as they struggle to find revenues to pay for the expenses of faculty whose life-long tenure was financed by long-gone short-term grants and contracts. Because endowments are the most permanent form of long-term capital, it is worthwhile to devote substantial effort to finding such capital.

The following sections discuss planning for each of the two major sources of revenues: endowment and operations. Endowment as used here includes all resources invested to produce revenues, whether or not they are placed in the endowment fund.

PLANNING FOR ENDOWMENT REVENUES

Endowment revenues are earned from investing endowment capital to earn income or capital gains. They are important in two ways. In many large nonprofit organizations they contribute a substantial portion of revenues. In addition, endowment revenues frequently play the unique role of providing funds for activities that cannot be financed in any other way. Despite the importance of revenues from endowments, some nonprofits do not budget or plan the earnings on endowment funds. Instead they view them as akin to the outcome of a throw of the dice—governed by fate, not management. This view has some validity. Earnings from endowment are somewhat unpredictable because they are affected by unexpected events such as oil crises or earthquakes. But they have predictable elements as well. For example, long-run average earnings from investments in the shares of stock purchased in stock markets (equity investments) have traditionally exceeded those from bonds or other debt instruments.[3] An endowment portfolio consisting solely of equity investments can reasonably be predicted to earn more in the long

---

[2]William Nordhaus, "Evaluating the Risks for Specific Institutions," in *Financial Planning Under Economic Uncertainty*, Richard E. Anderson and Joel W. Meyerson, eds. (San Francisco: Jossey-Bass, Spring 1990), p. 29.

[3]R. G. Ibbotson, R. A. Sinquefield, and J. P. Williamson, "Stocks, Bonds, Bills, and Inflation— Past (1926-1976) and the Future," *Journal of Finance* no. 1 (March 1980): 205-209.

run than a portfolio invested solely in bonds. Other elements of endowment earnings—such as the types of equity investments and the magnitude of the funds to be invested in debt, savings accounts, real estate, or other financial investments—should be planned as well.

Planning for endowment revenues involves two key decisions. One concerns the size of the endowment pool and the other its rate of return. A discussion of each follows.

The Size of the Endowment

How much endowment capital is enough? This decision can be made by planning future expenses (with the incremental or zero-base techniques discussed in Chapter 9), planning for revenues from sources other than endowments (such as gifts and grants), and then computing the revenue shortfall, if any, between the two. For example, if planned expenses require $9 million and revenues from the sale of services and from donors will provide only $8 million, the revenue shortfall of $1 million must be derived from endowment earnings.

How much endowment capital is needed to generate $1 million of earnings? The answer is found by dividing the required $1 million by the long-run rate of return expected on the endowment capital. For example, if the long-run rate of return is 5 percent of endowment capital, then $20 million of endowment capital ($1 million ÷ 0.05) are needed to generate $1 million. If the organization cannot acquire $20 million of endowment capital, it must reduce its planned level of expenses. If, for example, it can raise a maximum of $15 million in endowment capital, its expected endowment earnings will decline to $750,000 ($15 million × 0.05), and the organization must reduce its planned expenses by $250,000 ($1 million − $750,000).

The Rate of Return on Endowment

How is the expected rate of return from endowment derived? It results from three managerial decisions about how to invest capital, frequently referred to as the asset allocation, risk, and liquidity decisions.

The *asset allocation decision* apportions the fractions of the endowment portfolio to be invested in different financial instruments—so much is invested in common stocks (or equities), so much in debt instruments, so much in venture capital, and so much in real estate and other investments.

The *risk and liquidity decisions* delineate the amount of risk and liquidity for each investment. All financial instruments bear different risks and returns. For example, equities generally are considered to carry higher risks and also higher returns than debt instruments. Different financial instruments also bear differing liquidity characteristics. For example, debt instruments specify their interest payments and repayment amounts, while real estate investments yield a more unpredictable stream of rental payments and a more uncertain sales value. Thus, investments in debt can generally be more easily sold than those in real estate and are generally considered more liquid. The requirements for cash govern liquidity decisions. For example, if the organization needs to make a large repayment on a loan in five years, it must invest its capital in financial instruments that will insure that this sum is readily available, in cash, at that time.

As a practical matter, the asset allocation decision usually divides endowment capital investments between debt (also called fixed-income investments) and all other financial instruments. Because debt is generally considered to have lower risk and greater liquidity than most other alternative investments, it usually comprises between 40 percent and 60 percent of the endowment capital. The remaining endowment funds are then allocated to investments in stocks traded on the stock market, venture capital funds, mutual funds, real estate, and foreign investments. Although these instruments usually are more risky and less liquid than debt, they also hold the promise of larger returns.

Equity investments are frequently further subdivided into the more specific categories discussed below.

High or low capitalization stocks are differentiated by the total amount of money invested in them. A so-called "high cap" company has substantial levels of equity investment and a "low cap" one has relatively small dollar amounts of equity capital. A high cap company may have as much as $50 billion invested in it and many millions of stockholders and shares of its stock can be bought and sold without causing a sharp change in their market value. A high cap stock is thus more liquid than a low cap one with only a small number of investors. But more growth is generally anticipated from a low cap stock.

Growth stocks are the securities of companies from whom considerable future growth is expected. Examples of such companies are the biotechnology firms of the 1980s and the personal computer or software ventures of the 1970s. Because these companies are growing rapidly, they are unlikely to pay out their earnings as dividends, preferring instead to reinvest them in financing their growth. In contrast, *income stocks* are the securities of more stable companies, such as utilities. These companies pay out a substantial fraction of their earnings as dividends to stockholders. Growth and low cap stocks generally hold the promise of producing greater returns than income and high cap ones, but they are also more risky and less liquid.[4]

An Example of Planning for Endowment Revenues

Let's consider a nonprofit organization that currently has $100,000 of endowment capital. It projects the need for $8,000 a year in cash income from endowment. Five years from now it will need $60,000 for the down

---

[4]For further discussion, see *Handbook of Modern Finance* (New York: Warren, Gorham, and Lamot, 1986).

payment on a new building. The endowment fund is the only likely source of that sum. To date, the organization has deposited its money in a bank certificate of deposit that yields 7 percent a year, or $7,000. But the organization needs to earn more income.

The organization has narrowed its investment options to three. It can invest its money in the stock of a utility that is now selling at $10 a share and that pays dividends of at least $1 a share. Or, it can buy an AA-rated corporate bond that yields 9 percent a year that will be repaid in five years. Or, it can invest in an equity growth fund that has yielded an annual 15 percent return in the past. The utility has paid dividends continuously for the past 50 years. The growth fund is 5 years old.

If the organization chooses to invest all its capital in the equity growth fund, it is not completely certain of having $60,000 in five years with which to build its new building because the equity value may fall below that amount. On the other hand, if it invests all of its $100,000 in the 9 percent bond, it will give up the possibility of earning 10 percent from the utility stock or 15 percent from the growth fund. When the organization's managers considered investment in equity, they viewed the growth fund, with only five years of history, as being a riskier investment than the utility stock. But, because both equity investments had large capitalizations, they considered them equally liquid.

The managers documented their thoughts as shown in Table 10-1. They ranked risk and liquidity characteristics from 1 (best) to 5 (worst). They also considered the impact of alternative investment plans on income, risk, and liquidity. Ultimately, they chose investment plan (4) of Table 10-1, which gave them what they felt to be the best combination of these characteristics. For example, it improved expected returns from $9,000 with plan (1) to $9,900 with only a small decrease in risk and liquidity ratings.

Note that while there is no right or wrong investment plan, it is important that endowment income be planned with explicit consideration of risk, liquidity, and income.

Managing the Planning Process for Endowment Revenues

Planning for endowment revenues thus requires a series of decisions about the asset allocation of the endowment capital, the liquidity required, and the level of risk that can be tolerated. In combination, these decisions produce the rate of return that can be expected from the endowment. This rate, in turn, should be used to evaluate the adequacy of the amount of the endowment capital. If the amount is judged inadequate, the organization must either reduce its expenses or formulate realistic plans for generating additional endowment capital.

Every element of planning for endowment income should be documented. Liquidity requirements should be clearly depicted in a cash flow

TABLE 10-1 **An Example of Planning for Endowment Revenue (1 = Best, 5 = Worst)**

Investment Plan	Endowment Capital	Bond	Utility Stock	Growth Fund	Cash Income	Risk Level	Liquidity Level	Growth Potential
(1) All bonds	$100,000	$100,000	$ 0	$ 0	$ 9,000	1	1	5
(2) All utility stocks	100,000	0	100,000	0	10,000	3	3	3
(3) All growth equity funds	100,000	0	0	100,000	15,000	5	3	1
(4) 60 percent bonds, 30 percent utility stocks, 10 percent growth fund	100,000	60,000	30,000	10,000	9,900	2	1.2	4

plan that specifies the timing and magnitude of the cash required from the endowment. Risk levels should be specified with quantitative equity risk measures (called *betas*) and with qualitative discussions of the business and financial risk characteristics of other potential investments.[5] Asset allocation decisions should articulate the maximum and minimum percentages of endowment capital to be invested in different types of financial instruments. The expected rates of return should be clearly specified for each type of investment and for the portfolio as a whole.

The process of documenting these decisions will force planners to be articulate and specific about their decisions. It is also key to accountability. Frequently, the actual management of the funds is performed by firms that specialize in that type of investment. Such outside assistance usually requires payment of a sizeable fee. Planning documents that specify the risk, liquidity, and rate of return expected are useful in selecting and evaluating these endowment managers.

PLANNING FOR OPERATING REVENUES

Revenues derived from charging users for services are central to the financing of most nonprofit organizations. Some organizations derive almost all of their revenues from selling their services. Hospitals, for example, are almost totally funded by revenues from patient services. Other organizations, such as colleges and universities, are not so dependent as hospitals on revenues from operations. Nevertheless, even these organizations derive a significant proportion of their total funding from selling services to their users. Increasingly, even the government organizations that traditionally derived their revenues solely from taxes charge user ₁.es for providing services such as refuse collection. Only in purely charitable organizations, such as those providing services to the poor, are revenues from operations of relatively minor consequence.

Despite the importance of these revenues, many nonprofit organizations devote surprisingly little attention to delineating the prices they charge for services. Their prices often are either historical—"what we always charged"— or competitive—"what everybody charges." All too few nonprofit organizations analyze the economic and societal considerations on which their pricing should be based.

Setting the price for services provided is much more difficult in a nonprofit organization than in a business. The commercial enterprise has a clear objective in setting its prices: it will select those that maximize its profits. Nonprofits lack this clear objective. Their purpose is not to earn a maximum

---

[5]For further discussion see Eugene F. Brigham, *Financial Management: Theory and Practice* (Troy, MO: Dryden Press, 1985).

profit but rather to provide the maximum amount of services while remaining financially solvent. Their prices must reflect this dual purpose. They must provide both the needed financial resources and management of access to the organization's services.

Economic and social criteria should guide nonprofits in setting their prices. The following sections will discuss both, with the objective of providing a guide for nonprofits facing pricing decisions. But the discussion is merely a map: the decision about how to balance these criteria must reflect the unique circumstances of each individual case.

Economic Criteria for Setting Prices

What is the ideal price for a nonprofit organization's services? If the price were set at zero and the service provided for free, most users would not place appropriate value on the resources they receive. It is an all-too-human tendency to denigrate those things we receive for free. As a result, clients might use an excessive amount of the services because they appear to them to be free, or might not extract as many benefits from the services as they would if they paid for them. These reasons compel some mental health therapists to insist that even poor patients pay some fraction of the cost of their treatment. They believe that the act of payment will enhance the value the patients derive from the therapy.

An equally inappropriate price guideline for a nonprofit is one that maximizes profits. After all, it is not the purpose of a nonprofit to maximize profits. A profit-maximizing price is appropriate only when the organization is providing a service incidental to its main function for the convenience of the users, such as a college bookstore or a museum gift shop. In these cases, the profit-maximizing price is usually equivalent to the prevailing market price. But even in this profit-maximizing case, nonprofits must take care not to exploit the subsidies received as a result of their nonprofit status, such as the exemption from paying income taxes, and to compete unfairly with businesses that also provide these services. For example, nonprofit hospital pharmacies that undercut the prices of taxpaying pharmacies have been charged with unfair competition by commercial pharmacies. The taxpaying competitors argue that the nonprofits are unfairly exploiting the lower costs that result solely from their tax-exempt status.[6]

In most cases, the price charged for services should be greater than zero but less than the profit-maximizing price. An appealing price is one set at *marginal cost*—the value of the resources used to produce one additional service. For instance, the marginal cost of one additional hospital day is equivalent to daily expenses generated exclusively by the patient. These expenses

---

[6]Mary Wagner, "Pharmacy Directors Fear That Anti-Resale Law May Be Point of No Return for Drugs," *Modern Healthcare* (September 30, 1988): 38.

would include the cost of such items as laundry, drugs, food, housekeeping, nurses, and doctors. With prices set at marginal cost, users pay no more and no less than the costs of the resources expended for their benefit. If patients judge this marginal cost price to be higher than the value they received from the service, the service should not be provided to them. Alternatively, if users can find another, cheaper source for the service, they provide a signal to the nonprofit organization that its costs are too high.

What about users who cannot afford the marginal cost price? They should be provided with a subsidy—a scholarship or a discount—so that they can afford to buy the service, but the price should not be reduced below marginal cost. Why? Because prices set below marginal cost will cause the service to appear as unduly cheap and, thus, motivate either its excess consumption or its devaluation. (Additional coverage of this point is included in the social criteria section that follows.)

Unfortunately, when reality rears its head, two practical problems appear to mitigate the appeal of marginal cost pricing. One problem lies in the difficulty of identifying marginal cost. As an example, let's return to the hospital patient above. Should the cost of replacing the bed the patient used be included in marginal costs? Some would say "of course" because the bed would last longer if the patient had not used it. Therefore, the costs of replacing it should be included among the marginal costs. Others would argue that the bed will need replacing whether or not this patient used it; after all, everything wears out eventually regardless of how much it is used. To them, the cost of replacing the bed would not be an element of marginal cost. What about the orderlies who wheeled the patient to the room? Some would argue that the orderlies should not be included in the marginal cost calculation because they are employed by the hospital whether or not this patient uses their services. Others argue to the contrary.

The appealing theory of marginal cost pricing thus is undercut by the difficulty of measuring marginal costs. Yet another difficulty is that some measures of marginal cost pricing may not provide revenues for covering *fixed costs*—those costs that remain the same no matter how much or how little the service is used, such as the cost of a hospital building that will exist whether or not the patient visits it. Prices set at the marginal cost of providing one more unit of services may not generate sufficient revenues for covering fixed costs.

To deal with the financial problems this pricing strategy causes, the organization must either find other sources of revenues for covering fixed costs, such as gifts or grants for building, or redefine marginal costs as *long-term marginal costs*. The "long-term" implies that *all* the costs that vary with one additional service will be included in the marginal cost computation. Returning to the hospital example, the long-term marginal cost will include the cost of a new building because, in the future, the hospital plant will need to be replaced.

Average costs sometimes may represent a good approximation to long-term marginal costs. They equal the total costs of providing the service divided by the total quantity of services provided. For example, if a hospital spends $15 million for patient services and provides 3,000 hospital stays, its average cost per stay is $5,000 ($15 million ÷ 3,000 stays). When prices are set at average cost, the organization receives revenues equal to costs and, thus, experiences neither a profit nor a loss. Instead it receives the revenues that will enable it to recoup all the monies it spent for providing services. But because average costs are based on historical data, they do not account for the costs of *replacing* the resources consumed. Thus, they are not totally equivalent to the long-term marginal costs, especially for capital-intensive nonprofit organizations such as hospitals or colleges that are likely to incur substantially higher costs for replacing their existing capacity.

Average costs are translated into prices for specific services with one of the following techniques. A laboratory that performs diagnostic tests will be used for illustrative purposes.

(1) *Specific Costing.* The average cost of each specific service is traced. For example, if the laboratory performs two diagnostic tests, the cost of each is identified with requisition and time sheets that measure the quantity of materials and hours of time devoted to each test.

(2) *Relative Value Costing.* The average cost of the laboratory test is computed by dividing the total costs of the laboratory by a number that reflects the relative resource use of each test. For example, if Test *A* requires twice the resources of Test *B*, then the number of Test *A*'s performed will be multipled by two and added to the number of Test *B*'s performed. Thus, if 100 Test *A*'s and 500 Test *B*'s were performed and if the laboratory cost totals $1,400, the average cost of a test is $2 [$1,400 ÷ (2)(100) + 500]. Test *A* will cost $4 under this system and Test *B*, $2. (If you feel uncomfortable with this computation, check it by multiplying the number of Test *A*'s by $4 and the number of Test *B*'s by $2. The sum of the two should equal $1,400. Why?) Relative value costing is only as accurate as the estimates of the relative resource use of each of the services produced.

Yet another approximation to marginal costs is provided by *two-step pricing* in which the users pay those expenses that can be directly linked to their receipt of the service, and the community or members of the nonprofit pay the rest of the costs. In this way, the users are charged with the costs caused by their consumption—no more and no less—and the general community subsidizes the fixed costs of the services they consumed.

The economic considerations that should guide pricing in nonprofit organizations are shown in Table 10-2. But these criteria present only one side of the story. Nonprofit organizations exist to provide services that are

TABLE 10-2 **Economic Criteria for Setting Prices in Nonprofit Organizations**

Type of Service	Theoretical Pricing Criterion	Practical Price
Service provided is peripheral to main purpose of the organization	Profit-maximizing	Market price
Service provided is central to the purpose of the organization	Long-run marginal cost	Average cost or two-step price

important to society. These social purposes present many good reasons for deviating from these economic pricing criteria, as discussed below.

Social Criteria for Setting Prices

Nonprofit organizations exist to provide services that the business sector will not or cannot provide. Their pricing strategy must be guided by the purpose of the nonprofit organization and the class of service it provides. The discussion in the following paragraphs is summarized in Table 10-3.

Pricing Services for the Poor   One of the purposes of some nonprofits is to provide services for the poor. A business will not provide services to those who cannot afford to pay for them. After all, stockholders invest in the business to earn money, not to provide charity. If they choose, the stockholders can use the proceeds they earn from the business for many purposes, including charitable donations. In contrast, nonprofit organizations have no stockholders who expect financial returns. They can provide charitable services—indeed, that may be their main purpose. If so, their pricing strategy must reflect this charitable mandate.

If a nonprofit wishes to enable poor people to use its services, it should provide subsidies to them rather than reducing the price of the service. Reducing the price will provide a subsidy to *all* users, both rich and poor; it is much more effective to target the subsidy directly at those who need it. Price reduction also leads all users to devalue the service or to use it excessively.

As an example, consider the question of setting the tuition price at a nonprofit college. Suppose that on the basis of the economic criteria discussed above, our mythical college should set tuition charges at its average cost of $20,000 a year. The college's admissions officer expects 1,000 students next year, 80 percent of whom will require financial aid. But the college overseers are concerned that a $20,000 level of tuition will discourage poorer students from applying. Some of them suggest reducing tuition to $15,000.

What tuition should the college propose? Lowering tuition to $15,000 is equivalent to giving a $5,000 scholarship ($20,000 − $15,000) to every student enrolled. But 20 percent of the student body does not need this scholarship. These 200 students (20 percent of 1,000 admits) will generate $1 million in revenues for the college with tuition set at $20,000 rather than $15,000 [($20,000 − $15,000)(200 students)]. To put it another way, reducing tuition by $5,000 will deprive the college of $1 million in revenues that can be generated from students who can readily afford to pay them. A better pricing strategy would simultaneously set tuition at $20,000 and advise prospective applicants that scholarships will be readily available to those who cannot afford that level of tuition.

Pricing Public Goods   Services whose use cannot be restricted are frequently provided only by government organizations or private nonprofits under a government charter. Users cannot be charged for this service because it will be available whether or not the user pays for it and should not be charged because it benefits the community at large. A lighthouse is the classic example of such services; its light is available to all who need it whether or not they have paid for the service. All of us benefit when a lighthouse prevents accidents at sea. Other examples are the defense or police forces whose activities provide safety for all citizens, and not only for those who pay for them. Businesses normally do not provide such services because people can use them whether or not they pay for them.

Such services are called *public goods*. Their very nature prohibits charging a price for them. Instead they must be supported with a general tax or a levy on the entire community of potential users. The lighthouse, for example, can be priced with a levy assessed on all community residents who own a boat, perhaps by using a levy that is related to the cost of the boat, with the boat's cost as a surrogate for the owner's income. This levy can be financed in accordance with the potential users' income.

Pricing Services with Both Public and Private Benefits   Frequently, nonprofit organizations provide another class of services that benefits the public at large. These services are different from public goods because they can be targeted uniquely at one user. A vaccine that protects against an infectious disease is an example. Persons inoculated with this vaccine protect not only themselves but also society as a whole. They protect themselves because they will not catch the disease once they are inoculated; they protect society because when they are inoculated they will not spread the disease. Unlike a pure public good, such as a lighthouse, the vaccine can be withheld from those who will not pay for it.

When a nonprofit organization provides such services, its pricing strategy should reflect both perspectives. The price should be sufficiently low to encourage individuals to use the service and generate *public* benefits, but

TABLE 10-3 **Social Criteria for Setting Prices in Nonprofit Organizations**

Situation	Pricing Responses
Some users cannot afford the service.	Price at average cost and provide the user with a subsidy; do not reduce price.
Service is a public good.	Use a tax or levy on the entire community of users.
Service has substantial public benefits, low private benefits.	Price at marginal cost, with large subsidies to attract low-income users; use tax or levy to finance remaining costs.
Service has low public benefits, high private benefits.	Average cost or market pricing, with small subsidies.
Service has low public and private benefits.	Evaluate need for provision of service by a nonprofit organization.

not so low as to ignore the *private* benefits that use of the service creates for the individual. In the case of the vaccine, the nonprofit must set a price that simultaneously insures that all are inoculated and that those who can afford to pay for the vaccine do so.

More generally, for this type of service, the price should reflect the mix of public and private benefits provided by the service. The prices for services that produce large public benefits and small private ones should be subsidized to encourage people to use them. For example, consider the issue of setting tuition levels at different types of colleges. If good elementary and secondary school teachers are in short supply and of great value to our society—high *public* benefits—but receive relatively modest salaries—low *private* benefits—the tuition charges for those training to be teachers should be relatively low. On the other hand, if corporate lawyers and MBAs can earn significant income—high *private* benefits—and are not in short supply— low *public* benefits—there is less need to reduce the tuitions charged by law and business schools.

Services that produce large public and private benefits should not deviate from the economic criteria for pricing unless there is reason to believe that a high price will deter people from using the service even if a subsidy is available. For example, a vaccine against polio should be priced at its average cost because it provides substantial benefits both to its users and to society as a whole. But, if evidence shows that people will not protect themselves against the disease solely because of the price of the vaccine, the price should be subsidized. On the other hand, for services with low public and private benefits, the appropriate question is not what price should be charged but whether the service should be provided at all.

Subsidies

This discussion has repeatedly referred to subsidies for the user. Where do the funds for subsidies originate? Two sources prevail.

Lump Sum sources provided from general membership in the nonprofit, endowment earnings, taxes and/or special levies, or special gifts and donations.

Cross-Subsidization of the user who needs to be subsidized by one who does not. Hospitals have used cross-subsidized pricing for many years. They use revenues from private health insurance to subsidize Medicaid revenues and the poor who have no insurance. As shown in Table 10-4, the hospital sets its prices to different payers on the basis of their ability to pay. This Robin Hood pricing charges the rich to pay for the poor. The practice is usually referred to as cross-subsidization of prices.

An Example of Price Setting in a Nonprofit Organization

This section will illustrate how the pricing criteria are applied by using as an example a small, nonprofit nursery school that can set its price to maximize profits or at average costs or at marginal costs. The purpose of this discussion is to make the concepts discussed above more concrete. If you feel comfortable with the concepts, skip this section. If not, it is worthwhile to devote substantial time to the details of the example presented.

Prices to Maximize Profits In a profit business, prices will be set to maximize profits, that is, the difference between revenues and costs. First, we need to determine how these quantities are measured.

Revenues equal the price per unit of service multiplied by the quantity of services sold. In most cases, the lower the price, the greater the quantity that will be sold. For example, a nursery school in a small town might project

TABLE 10-4 **Example of Cross-Subsidized Prices for a Coronary Bypass Operation**

Patient	Cost of Operation	Insurer*	Price	Net Gain or Loss
A	$34,433	Medicaid	$10,710	$(23,723)
B	$39,082	Medicare	$27,160	$(11,922)
C	$41,738	Private insurance	$80,763	$39,025

*Medicaid and Medicare are governmentally provided health insurance policies for the poor and the elderly, respectively. Private insurance is paid for by employers who purchase it from private insurance companies.

Source: Glenn Kramor, "Coaxing the Stanford Elephant to Dance," *The New York Times,* 11 November 1990, p. 6.

that when it sets tuition at $1,000, no students will attend it; at a price of $550, 5 students will attend; and at a tuition of $100, 10 students will attend. This relationship is called the *demand function*. The equation that fits this pattern has a negative slope (i.e., the lower the price, the greater the quantity sold). For the nursery school, it is mathematically expressed as:

Demand Function = Price = $1,000 − ($90 × Quantity of Students)

Revenues equal the demand function (or price) multipled by the quantity of services. Thus, for the nursery school,

Total Revenues = Price × Quantity of Students

Costs are measured by a *supply function* that depicts the relationship between expenses and the quantity supplied. Some costs are fixed; they will remain the same no matter how much is supplied. In the nursery school the fixed costs are $2,000 and include the nursery school teacher and the space expenses, such as rent. Other costs are variable; their magnitude changes with quantity. For variable costs, the greater the quantity the greater the cost. The nursery school's variable costs of $100 cover the expenses of the supplies and materials per student.

The supply function equals the sum of fixed costs and the product of variable costs times quantity:

Supply Function = Fixed Costs + (Variable Costs × Quantity)

Thus, an equation for a supply function for the nursery school is:

Supply Function = Total Costs = $2,000 + ($100 × Quantity of Students)

An organization that wishes to maximize profits will choose the price and the quantity that lead to the greatest profit or difference between revenues and costs. To calculate total revenues it will multiply price, or the demand function, by the quantity to be sold. It will then subtract total costs, or the supply function, from total revenues. The difference between them is total profits.

An example of this procedure is presented in Table 10-5. It indicates that the nursery school maximizes its profits at a price of $550 and 5 students. At that point its profits equal $250, while at 4 and 6 students its profits are only $160.

Some find the following explanation of profit-maximizing pricing to be clearer. Perhaps you will be among them. Economists define the point of maximum profits as the quantity at which an extra dollar in total revenues is exactly equal to an extra dollar in cost; or in the nomenclature of economics, the point at which marginal (i.e., extra) revenues equal marginal

TABLE 10-5 **Pricing to Maximize Profits**

(A) Quantity of Students	(B) Price[1]	(C) Total Revenues[2]	(D) Total Costs[3]	(E) Profit or Loss = Total Revenues − Total Costs[4]
4	$640	$2,560	$2,400	$160
5	550	2,750	2,500	250
6	460	2,760	2,600	160

[1]Price = Demand Function = $1,000 − ($90 × Quantity of Students) = $1,000 − [$90 × (A)].
[2]Total Revenues = Quantity of Students × Price = (A) × (B).
[3]Total Costs = $2,000 + ($100 × Quantity of Students) = $2,000 + [$100 × (A)].
[4]Profit or Loss = (C) − (D).

costs. At a quantity below this point, extra expenditures will yield additional revenues greater than the change in total costs. Therefore, more units will be sold. At a quantity above this point, additional costs will be larger than the extra revenues they generate.

To return to our example, when the number of students increased from four to five, total revenues increased by $190 ($2,750 − $2,560), while total costs increased by only $100 ($2,500 − $2,400). The marginal revenue of the fifth student of $190 was greater than the marginal cost of $100. But when the number of students increased from five to six, the marginal costs of $100 ($2,600 − $2,500) was greater than the marginal revenue of $10 ($2,760 − $2,750). Therefore, the point where marginal revenues approximately equal marginal costs is five students.

Marginal Cost Pricing   From the point of view of society, prices for the services of nonprofit organizations should be set equal to the marginal or extra cost of producing one more unit. The marginal cost measures the value of the resources expended to produce one more unit, while price measures the value the consumer is willing to pay for that extra unit. If the marginal cost is lower than the price, the cost of the resources consumed is less than the value that people place on them. More output should be produced and sold in this case. Conversely, if the marginal cost exceeds the price, societal resources are being used inefficiently because the cost of the resources exceeds the value that people place on them.

Unfortunately, this pricing rule will, in most circumstances, cause the organization to lose money. In the nursery school example, the marginal or extra cost per student is $100 for the supplies. When price is set equal to $100, ten students will sign up for the school. The nursery school's profit picture will be as shown in Table 10-6.

TABLE 10-6 **Marginal Cost Pricing**

Price	Quantity[a]	Total Revenues	Total Costs[b]	Profit (Loss)
$100	10	$1,000	$3,000	$(2,000)

[a]Quantity = $\dfrac{\$1{,}000 - \text{Price}}{\$90}$

[b]Total Costs = $2,000 + ($100 × Quantity)

Average Cost Pricing The loss of $2,000 in Table 10-6 is exactly equal to the fixed costs of $2,000. Some consider these fixed costs irrelevant for pricing because they remain the same whatever the volume sold. In their view, the price should reflect only those costs that change with the quantity of sales. Nevertheless, fixed costs are real in the sense that they must be paid or replaced. If they are paid by setting a price equal to average cost, the volume sold will decline from 10 (at a price of $100) to 7 (the quantity at which the average cost most closely approximates the demand price), as shown in Table 10-7. Some would find this result socially undesirable, with irrelevant fixed costs causing an unnecessary decline in the number of students signing up for the school. After all, the fixed costs will remain the same whether 7 or 10 students enroll.

TABLE 10-7 **Calculation of Average Cost Prices**

Quantity	Total Costs	Average Unit Cost	Demand Price	Unit Profit (Loss) = Difference Between Average Cost and Demand Price
3	$2,300	$2,300 ÷ 3 = $767	$730	($37)
4	$2,400	$2,400 ÷ 4 = $600	$640	$40
5	$2,500	$2,500 ÷ 5 = $500	$550	$50
6	$2,600	$2,600 ÷ 6 = $433	$460	$33
7	$2,700	$2,700 ÷ 7 = $386	$370	($16)
8	$2,800	$2,800 ÷ 8 = $350	$280	($70)
9	$2,900	$2,900 ÷ 9 = $322	$190	($132)
10	$3,000	$3,000 ÷ 10 = $300	$100	($290)

Two-Part Pricing   A pricing strategy that attains the optimal level of use achieved by marginal cost pricing without burdening the organization with a loss equal to its fixed costs is one that charges a two-part price. One part is based on the marginal cost and the second part is based on the fixed costs. The marginal cost price is charged on the basis of usage and the fixed cost price, called a *lump-sum* or *basic price*, is charged because it entitles the payer with the right to use the service.

If the nursery school is part of a larger school system to which 200 families send their children, the lump-sum charge would be $10 per family ($2,000 of fixed costs ÷ 200 families) and the tuition per child would equal the marginal cost of $100. The $10 charge covers the fixed costs of running the nursery school and enables any of the 200 families to send a child to the nursery school. With tuition set at $100 per child, the optimal number of 10 children will attend the school. They are the children whose families judge the $100 price at least equal to the value of the service. Thus, the use of two-step pricing enables the school to cover its costs without restricting the number of children who can attend.

Governmental organizations can apply the two-step pricing policy through a combination of general taxes to cover fixed costs and user charges based on marginal costs. For example, the fixed costs of an adult education program, such as administration costs, can be paid through general taxes, while the marginal costs of each course, such as the cost of the instructor, can be paid with user charges. Private nonprofit organizations can apply this policy by thinking of their membership dues and contributions as sources of revenues for covering their fixed costs and of their charges for particular services as based on marginal costs. An art museum or orchestra, for example, can cover its fixed costs with donors' contributions and then charge another separate price that equals the marginal costs associated with particular exhibitions or performances.

Social Criteria   In practice, it is extremely difficult to apply these economic criteria because of the difficulty in identifying demand and supply functions. Most organizations cannot quantify the relationship between price and the quantity sold, cleanly separate fixed from variable costs, or even identify the activities that should be included among the relevant costs of the service. Not surprisingly, many pricing decisions are made in the absence of such data. Even when data are available, their reliability should be carefully considered, and other relevant factors, such as the wealth of the users and the relationship of public and private benefits, should always be considered. In the nursery school example, the economic status of the parents and their use of the time in which their children are in the nursery school are relevant social criteria for pricing. Low-income and working parents would create more powerful arguments for subsidies of prices than high-income and nonworking parents.

PLANNING FOR PROFITS
IN NONPROFIT ORGANIZATIONS

Should nonprofits earn a profit? Of course. Profits are needed for contingencies and to finance the replacement or expansion of the organization's assets. Some of these profits are not really profits but merely costs that are not recognized with conventional accounting. For example, profits to replace fixed assets are needed only because replacements costs are not recognized sufficiently with conventionally-recorded depreciation expense. They are not really profits.

How much profit is enough? The level of profits should be sufficient to enable an organization to sustain itself and to provide for contingencies and expansion. How is this level computed? Many organizations think that cumulative profits should include a kitty of liquid assets for financial contingencies equal to the sum of six months to a year of working capital and the amount of capital needed for replacement or expansion of assets. As an example of the latter, consider a shelter for the homeless that presently owns four six-year-old vans used for transporting its clients. It hopes to enlarge its fleet to ten vans, including replacement of the existing four, at a cost per van of $20,000. This organization will require $200,000 (10 vans × $20,000) for its maintenance and expansion. If it can borrow 50 percent of the $200,000, it will need $100,000 in cumulative profits to buy the ten vans, but if it can borrow only 10 percent of that sum, it will require $180,000 in cumulative profits.

Nonprofit organizations whose profits are inadequate for replacement of their plant and equipment must either find other sources of capital or contract in size. Conversely, nonprofits whose profits are substantially in excess of their needs should either increase their service levels or create new charitable activities. A deficit profit level is imprudent because it threatens the organization's ability to deliver future services, but an excessive profit level is unseemly, because it conflicts with the fundamental purpose of the organization.

SUMMARY

This chapter discussed planning for profits and for the two primary sources of revenues in nonprofit organizations: income from endowments and other invested capital and from operating revenues. Income from investments derives from the decision about how to invest the assets, the asset-allocation decision, and decisions about the risk and liquidity characteristics of the investments selected. These three decisions help to create the rate of return that will be earned from the investment.

The revenues from operations result from decisions about the prices to charge for the services or products of nonprofit organizations. Price setting should be governed by economic and social criteria and depends on the mix of public and private benefits the service creates. Economic pricing criteria include consideration of the long-run marginal and average costs of the service. In general, prices should not be reduced for low-income users; instead, low-income users should receive a subsidy that enables them to pay the price charged.

Profit planning in nonprofits insures that they can replace and renew fixed assets, respond to unforeseen problems, and finance expansion and growth.

Suggested Reading

Anderson, Richard A., and Joel W. Meyerson, eds. *Financial Planning Under Economic Uncertainty*. San Francisco: Jossey-Bass, Spring 1990.

Brigham, Eugene E. *Financial Management: Theory and Practice*. Troy, MO: Dryden Press, 1985.

Kotler, Philip. *Marketing for Nonprofit Organizations*. Englewood Cliffs, NJ: Prentice-Hall, 1982.

Lovelock, Christopher H., and Charles B. Weinberg. *Public and Nonprofit Marketing*. Palo Alto, CA: Scientific Press, 1978.

Mushkin, Selma. *Public Prices for Public Products*. Washington, DC: Urban Institute, 1972.

Shapiro, Benson P. "Marketing for Nonprofit Organizations." *Harvard Business Review* (September-October 1972): 123-132.

DISCUSSION QUESTIONS

1. What are the sources of revenues for nonprofits?

2. Define the following terms: asset allocation and risk and liquidity decisions.

3. What considerations govern planning for the income to be generated from endowment capital? Consider the results in Table 10-1. Can you create an alternative investment plan that improves on the fourth plan? Why?

4. An organization requires $20,000 in income from its endowment funds. If it can earn a 10 percent rate of return on endowment capital, how much endowment capital must it have to earn this income? Conversely, if it has $180,000 of endowment funds, what rate of return does it need to earn the required income?

5. What are the economic and social criteria for setting prices in a nonprofit organization?

6. When should users of the services of nonprofit organizations be subsidized?

7. Define the following pricing terms: profit-maximizing, marginal-cost, two-part, average cost, long-term marginal cost, and cross-subsidized pricing.

8. Think about the price charged by a nonprofit organization whose services you used. What economic and social criteria do you think guided setting this price? Were they appropriate? If not, how should the price have been delineated? Be as specific as possible in your answer.

9. What prices should be charged for the services of the following nonprofit organizations and why?
    a. Membership in a religious organization located in a lower-income area; a religious organization located in an upper-income suburb; price for attendance at a religious service at either one
    b. Tuition for degree students at a private university; at a public university
    c. Fees for hospital services in a nonprofit hospital; in a county hospital; in a for-profit hospital
    d. Fines for overdue books in a public library
    e. Attendance fee for an exhibition in a local museum
10. What considerations govern planning for the profits of a nonprofit organization?

Cases

CASE STUDIES

Case 10.1, a fictionalized case, enables you to review both the theory of total return and different formulas for applying it. Case 10.2 raises many of the issues relevant to a pricing decision: social impact, cost, and distributional effects. It is a good way to focus on these issues in the context of a small, voluntary organization. Case 10.3 is an excellent, but difficult, case for discussing every aspect of pricing that was mentioned in the text. It raises issues of costs, distributional impact, and elasticity of demand. Although the case describes a pricing decision made in the 1960s, the issues it raises are as fresh as today's newspaper.

CASE 10.1 Frank Renaut College

In late June, the finance committee of the board of trustees of the Frank Renaut College was completing the budget for the next fiscal year beginning July. The finance committee knew it had to resolve two questions that the board of trustees had debated for several years: how the college's current income on endowment should be defined, and then, how to calculate the amount of endowment earnings that should be used to support current operations.

Frank Renaut, a self-made entrepreneur, with the aid and encouragement of his friends founded the Frank Renaut College of Arts and Sciences. Until his death, Renaut generously supported the college and, during this period, Renaut College became a respected liberal arts educational institution with a distinguished faculty and a highly regarded student body. In his will, Renaut gave the college an endowment of $10 million provided that his contributions would be matched by gifts from his friends. At the beginning of fiscal year 1982, Renaut College had an endowment of $20,123,000, which has since grown as shown in **Exhibit 1**.

During the 1980s, Renaut College faced the same financial problems that troubled many colleges and universities, with its costs rising much more rapidly than revenues.

Peter M. Ferro prepared this case under the supervision of Professor Regina E. Herzlinger. Copyright © 1975 by the President and Fellows of Harvard College. Harvard Business School case 176-024. Revised January 1993.

In June of 1989, it became apparent that the current income (defined as cash dividends and interest payments) from the endowment would not provide enough revenue to balance the budget for the next fiscal year. Renaut College faced the choice of cutting back on its educational services or finding additional revenue. The board of trustees requested that the finance committee and its chairman, Ralph Nikky, develop a method of recognizing capital gains as income and investigate its effects on the financing of Renaut College and the future value of the endowment.

THE MEETING

In addition to Ralph Nikky, the chairman, the finance committee consisted of Andrew Cheng, the treasurer of Renaut College, Johanna Milberg, a New England banker, and Charles "Chuck" Moody, a Boston lawyer and former ambassador to Great Britain. In late June the committee met to decide what recommendations it would make to the board on the following day.

Nikky: Many college administrators who share our need for additional revenue have already tapped the appreciation of their endowment portfolio as a source of current income. If we are to adopt the same solution, we face a difficult problem. We must decide how to measure the amount of capital appreciation of the endowment that should properly be considered current income. This portion of capital gains, along with cash dividends and interest payments, should then be available to support the college's programs each year.

Moody: Frankly, I believe that using any part of the endowment—principal or appreciation—to cover operating deficits weakens the college's ability to survive and to educate in the future.

Nikky: I feel that just the opposite is true. If the policies of an educational institution prevent it from utilizing all available revenues to support the highest level of educational service it can provide, then that institution is failing in its educational responsibilities to the current generation of students.

Moody: I am concerned that we will adopt today a policy that in the long run will undermine the value of our endowment and the viability of this college. In the past, the cash we received from the endowment always seemed to be an adequate and reliable measure of endowment earnings. I am reluctant to abandon this clear and simple measure merely because we are facing a deficit next year. Perhaps a better course of action would be to cut expenses or reduce enrollment.

Nikky: Yes, it's true that an endowment portfolio invested in common stock is exposed to greater risk of price fluctuation—up and down—than a portfolio invested in bonds. In measuring true endowment earnings from a common stock portfolio, we must take care to focus on long-term trends and to smooth the effects of short-term price fluctuations. Therefore, my thinking is that an appropriate portion of the common stock should be added to the principal of the endowment in order to preserve the purchasing power. The remaining portion of the appreciation should be recognized as current income and should be available to support the college's educational programs.

Moody: Yes, but how are we to determine what portion is "appropriate"?

Nikky: Clearly, we should adjust the book value of the endowment to equal in current dollars the purchasing power of the original 1982 endowment. Since the economy has experienced 3 percent annual inflation over the decade, this means that we should increase its book value by 3 percent a year.

Remember, too, that we must consider the additional gifts to the endowment that we received afterwards. We can assume that these gifts were placed in the endowment at the end of each fiscal year. The formula, then, for calculating the adjusted book value at the end of each year is to take the adjusted book value at the beginning of the year plus 3 percent of the adjusted book value—this is to offset the inflation—plus the amount of gifts added to the endowment that year. The only thing that troubles me is that sometimes I think we should not use the inflation rate of the economy as a whole; maybe a rate of inflation based on the experience of educational institutions might be more appropriate.

But whatever inflation rate we settle on, the difference between the market value of the endowment at year-end and the adjusted book value at year-end would be the total financial gain of the endowment in real terms. The total financial gain at the end of the current year less the total financial gain at the end of the previous year equals the financial gain made from the endowment during the current year.

The financial gain made during the current year plus any cash dividends and interest payments received equals the total return received from the endowment.

We can then calculate the moving average of our total return from the three previous years, and use this three-year moving average as the budgeted income from our endowment for the current year. At the end of the current year, the difference between actual total return of the year and the three-year moving average would be placed in a reserve account. This reserve account would serve as our margin of safety in years when the three-year moving average—which we use to predict current endowment income—happens to be greater than the actual total return.

Milberg: I see what you are doing, Ralph. For example, if the three-year moving average of total return at the end of Year X was $2,000, we would plan in our budget for Year $X + 1$ an endowment income of $2,000. If the actual total return at the end of Year $X + 1$ were $2,200, then $200 would be added to the reserve. On the other hand, if the actual total return by the year's end turned out to be only $1,800, we would draw $200 from the reserve and add it to current income. In either case, the amount of endowment income recognized in Year $X + 1$ would be $2,000.

Nikky: That's exactly right, Johanna. And the use of the moving averges will tend to dampen the effect of those price fluctuations that troubled Mr. Moody so much, and the reserve account will stabilize the amount of income from the endowment we recognize each year. Sometimes, though, I wonder if a three-year moving average is adequate; maybe we should use five years.

Milberg: What will be the beginning balance in the reserve account, Ralph?

Nikky: I was thinking that it might be appropriate to set aside the total financial gain from 1982 to the end of 1989; this would provide a substantial beginning balance for our reserve account.

Moody: I don't know about Andy Cheng here, but I, for one, am unimpressed by your numerical gymnastics.

Nikky: There is no reason for this college—or any other—to accumulate capital in its endowment endlessly. Yes, we trustees do have moral duties to the donors. On one hand, it is the duty to preserve the principal of their gifts. My method accomplishes this by protecting the purchasing power of the donor's gifts to the college. But we also must ensure that each generation of students benefits to the fullest extent from their gifts. By not recognizing a portion of the appreciation of current income, the trustees are denying the current generation of students the benefit of the endowment to which they are entitled.

Cheng: If I accept your view—and I say "if" for I am still not completely convinced—how can we be certain of the correctness of your formula and of the estimates we use? Even more important, it will not be easy to present such a complex method with sufficient clarity that it wins acceptance by the full board.

Milberg: Ralph, I have a suggestion that may help in this matter. I believe there is a simpler method to work with. First, we calculate the gross rate of return on our portfolio over the last five years or so by taking the sum of the interest and dividend payments plus capital gains received each year and dividing it by the average market value of the endowment for that year. From this gross rate, we subtract the expected inflation rate so that the purchasing power of the endowment is protected. The difference between the gross rate of return and the inflation rate is what I call the spending rate, and represents the percentage of the market value that should be treated as income. In order to determine the amount of endowment income that should be recognized in any given year, we simply multiply the spending rate times the market value of the endowment—or perhaps it would be better to use a moving average of the market value at the end of the three previous years. The use of the spending rate times a three-year moving average of market value to predict endowment income in the fourth year would work well, and it would serve to reduce the influence of short-term price fluctuations.

I've completed some calculations using this method, showing that our gross rate of return averaged over the past few years has been about 11 percent. If we assume an inflation rate as high as 3 percent, we can maintain a spending rate of 8 percent. But since we are trying something new, it might pay to be conservative and use a spending rate of only 5 percent for the next fiscal year.

Cheng: I agree with that, Johanna. Why don't we use your method but with a 5 percent spending rate and present that proposal to the board tomorrow? What's your opinion, Ralph?

Nikky: Johanna's proposal is very interesting. However, I am not sure that its simplicity does not sacrifice some necessary safety that my method provides. Let's break for lunch now and meet again at 2:00 p.m. That will give each of us some time to consider the various methods available to us. Remember, we must report to the full board tomorrow.

ASSIGNMENT

1. Evaluate each of the various alternatives proposed in the finance committee's meeting.
2. Recommend which proposal the committee should present to the board of trustees.

EXHIBIT 1 **Frank Renaut College—Financial Information ($000)**

	1981	1982	1983	1984	1985	1986	1987	1988	1989 (pro-forma)
Revenues (excluding endowment income)[a]	$ -	$ 3,089	$ 3,359	$ 3,727	$ 4,104	$ 4,483	$ 4,849	$ 5,296	$ 5,925
Expenses	-	3,323	3,729	4,113	4,525	4,968	5,407	5,995	6,930
Gap	NA	(234)	(370)	(386)	(421)	(485)	(558)	(699)	(1,005)
Endowment income[b]	NA	454	502	579	608	659	702	770	820
Endowment funds:									
Renaut Fund	10,000	10,000	10,000	10,000	10,000	10,000	10,000	10,000	10,000
Capitalized gifts	10,123	10,591	11,357	13,201	14,171	15,137	16,300	17,464	18,864
Total book value	20,123	20,591	21,357	23,201	24,171	25,137	26,300	27,464	28,864
Total market value (at year-end)		24,389	27,776	30,955	34,530	38,549	44,046	50,761	

[a]Includes tuition and fees (55-60 percent), grants, auxiliary enterprises, and other.
[b]Dividend and interest payments.

CASE 10.2 Child Care Task Force

The Child Care Task Force (CCTF) was established in Chicago. It was organized by a group of women who had set up a day-care center and wanted to help others to do so. But they found that day-care centers faced formidable obstacles in financing, licensing, and management. Instead, they turned their attention to home day care, where caregivers take children into their homes on a weekly or monthly basis during parents' working hours. They began a number of projects to help home caregivers, including courses in home day care, an association with monthly meetings, publications, puppet shows, seminars, and outings for children.

The CCTF board also decided there was sufficient need for on-going information about sources of child care in Chicago's south side to warrant a referral service. A private foundation gave them a $10,000 starting grant for it, but additional funding sources were needed. Small grants and contributions from parents, caregivers, and board members, as well as a benefit, sale of publications, and subscriptions to the newsletter, saw them through their first year. But after two years, revenues—now obtained mostly from a $5 voluntary membership fee—had dropped to $20,000, two-thirds of their prior level.

In efforts to cut expenses, the two full-time staff members (a service coordinator and an administrative coordinator) had reduced their hours to half time, and the board members and other volunteers donated more time than usual to CCTF services. The referral line was cut back, operating for only 20 hours each week. Postering and advertising—two activities that generated business for the referral line—were also cut back.

The task force examined its budget, and decided that it could not cut expenses any more. Additional sources of funding would have to be found. Charging day-care providers or users for the CCTF's services was one possibility, but the board was uncertain how to do so. Other possibilities included grants by businesses, if the board could find a way to interest them in the Task Force's work.

RANGE OF SERVICES

To help them make a decision about pricing, the board categorized the services they provided, as indicated below:

(1) *Parents.* CCTF referred parents, usually by telephone, to the type of caregivers they sought. The information on caregivers was arranged by location, type and age of children cared for (handicapped, retarded, or disturbed children were specially noted), number of children in the facility, and some fee information. Babysitter information, with some less detail, was also provided. Parents also received a packet of information suggesting guidelines

Anne B. Moses prepared this case under the supervision of Professor Regina E. Herzlinger. Copyright © 1977 by the President and Fellows of Harvard College. Harvard Business School case 178-078. Revised January 1993.

for choosing a home caregiver or babysitter, enclosing a publication list and a request for donations, and a brief questionnaire which was to be returned to the Task Force.

Parents tended to use the referral service once every three to six months. When they re-used the service, it was because they lost a caregiver or needed a new or additional type of care. Some made several calls when first using the service until they found a caregiver who suited them.

(2) *Home caregivers.* Caregivers initially contacted the CCTF by phone. Before adding caregivers to their reference lists, the staff visited them at their homes. Visits usually lasted about an hour, during which time the caregiver was interviewed and given educational materials and advice on operating a day-care home.

Once they had been added to the referral lists, some caregivers were brought in to the rest of CCTF's system on the initiative of the service co-ordinator. Many caregivers maintained frequent contact with the referral service when they needed more children to care for, or when changing their hours, fees, or types of care. Some were also members of the Home Care-givers Association the CCTF had established in its early days.

(3) *Babysitters.* Babysitters also initially contacted the CCTF by phone. They were interviewed in the CCTF offices and given educational materials written for them by CCTF members. The babysitters usually earned more per hour than the home caregivers, although the home caregivers worked more hours each week.

(4) *Publications.* The CCTF sent six publications to interested parents, caregivers, day-care centers, and agencies.

(5) *General membership.* Membership services consisted primarily of a subscrip-tion to the CCTF newsletter, *Building Blocks*. Members included some, but not all, of the parents and caregivers who used the CCTF services, and other community-minded people and local agencies. A yearly subscription to the newsletter (which was also the membership fee) cost $5.00.

(6) *Telephone.* Although the bulk of phone calls handled by the referral line were with parents, most home caregivers and babysitters used the line to make their initial contacts with the service.

DEMAND FOR SERVICES

The market potential for the CCTF referral service appeared to be quite large. At that time, Chicago had 125,000 children six years or under with working par-ents, and about 200 licensed home caregivers. No other referral service in the city had the detailed information parents needed to find the type of care their child required.

In the CCTF referral service's two years of operation, it had served about 2,500 parents and 500 caregivers and babysitters. Most of its clients were concentrated in three adjacent neighborhoods in Chicago: Hyde Park, South Shore, and Woodlawn. However, calls came in to the referral line from as far away as 50 miles.

At one time, the CCTF had written a proposal for expansion into several new neighborhoods. Although the proposal was never funded, preliminary contacts with community representatives in three neighborhoods indicated substantial interest and the potential for volunteer support.

Response from parents who used the service was almost unanimously favorable; the guidelines, reassurances, helpful advice, and information available from the service coordinator were all greatly appreciated. Home caregivers also responded favorably to the home visits and the literature and ongoing contact with other caregivers the Task Force provided. In addition, the Task Force discovered that advertising the referral line and their other services often brought new caregivers into existence to fill the unmet demand for child care.

PRICING

The board felt there were three factors to consider in their pricing decision. The first was the users' abilities to pay. The babysitters generally earned more per hour than the home care people. The parents represented a widely diverse group ranging from faculty members of the nearby University of Chicago to lower-income, single-family households.

The second factor was the feasibility of receiving payment from each of the groups. While there was substantial personal interaction with the service providers, interaction with the parents was usually limited to telephone conversations. As a result, the parent group—which had the greatest ability to pay—was the one judged most difficult to collect from.

Finally, the Task Force felt that cost differences among their services ought to be reflected in the prices they set. To get a better notion of the costs of the services, the service coordinator and administrative coordinator estimated how much of their time they devoted to different activities, as indicated below:

	Time Spent by	
Service	*Service Coordinator (%)*	*Administrative Coordinator (%)*
Service 1—Parents	5.0	-
Service 2—Home caregivers	17.5	-
Service 3—Babysitters	10.0	-
Service 4—Publications	5.0	14.0
Service 5—General membership	2.5	14.0
Service 6—Telephone (includes calls to and from Services 1, 2, and 3)	38.0	-
General	22.0	72.0

In the average month, the Task Force calculated that, under Service 6, 250 calls were received; that 30 babysitters and 30 home caregivers were visited; and that 120 parents were sent publications. About 500 supporting members received a monthly newsletter.

The direct montly cost of the services included the following items:

Telephone	$47/month
Home caregivers' packets	$1.98 each
Packets for parents	$0.31 each
Postage and materials for members	$70/month[a]
Salary and benefits of service coordinator	$10,190/year
Salary and benefits of service administrator	$13,300/year

[a]Sent out to only 500 members.

In addition, there were other expenses for rent, accounting, secretarial assistance, fund-raising, and minor equipment purchases of $380.20 per month.

ASSIGNMENT

1. What are the costs of the six services?
2. What prices should be charged for them?
3. What other alternatives should the Task Force explore?

CASE 10.3 Post Office Department

Staff members in the Bureau of Finance and Administration of the Post Office Department were preparing to review the economics of the department's money order service. Money orders were one of the "special services" in addition to primary mail responsibility, that the Post Office was required by Congress to provide. The others were special delivery, registry, insurance, certified mail, cash on delivery, and postal savings.

Postal rates were officially exempt from the President's policy regarding user charges, which was expressed as follows:

> Where a service (or privilege) provides special benefits to an identifiable recipient above and beyond those which accrue to the public at large, a charge should be imposed to relieve the full cost to the federal government of rendering that service.

But no official statement had ever been made about the department's special services, and opinion was divided on pricing policy. The Postal Policy Act of 1958 had

This case was prepared by staff members of the Management Analysis Center Inc. of Cambridge, Massachusetts, under contract with the U.S. government. The dialogue in the case is fictitious. Harvard Business School case 193-115. Revised January 1993.

categorized all losses incurred for special services as public service losses, which meant they would automatically be sanctioned by Congress. Some postal officials took this to indicate that special services were also to be exempt from the full-costing policy. But the same act also authorized the Postmaster General to establish rates for special services, a responsibility previously reserved for Congress. This, plus the fact that special services had a clearly identifiable recipient, seemed to indicate that the services were not exempt.

The review, begun at the request of the Postmaster General, was intended to establish the costs to the department of providing each of its special services and to settle on an appropriate pricing policy.

BACKGROUND

Money orders were sold in all of the department's outlets. In addition, applications for money orders were provided to rural customers directly by the carriers. The cash that each post office received from money order sales was forwarded directly to the Treasury Department. The money order itself could be redeemed at any post office, at any bank, or at most retail merchants. The form was processed, like a check, through the Federal Reserve System and eventually honored by the Treasury Department.

Any post office that issued over 350 orders per day was felt to require a special window. Officials estimated that the 321 Class A, B, and C offices had special money order windows, while the remaining 33,719 offices issued money orders at general-purpose windows.

The revenue from the postal money order service had never equaled the full cost of providing the service. **Exhibit 1** shows the expenses allocated to the service under the Post Office Department's Cost Ascertainment System. A similar analysis for the intervening years showed that the money order service had always operated at a deficit.

The Cost Ascertainment System was based on time studies taken during one week per quarter at a selected sample of approximately 500 post office branches. This survey was used as the basis of distributing the direct expense for collection and delivery, mail handling, and window service to the various services provided by the Post Office Department. If the survey recorded idle time, the expense for this idle time was spread in proportion to the productive labor cost for each post office service.

In small post offices, the administrative costs of operations were also distributed on the basis of a time-study survey. Also, postal supply expenses that could be identified directly with a particular service were charged to that service. All other expense classifications contained in the cost ascertainment report were allocated to the services proportional to their share of direct costs.

Since the mid-1950s, the expenses allocated to the money order service had steadily declined in most categories, while the Post Office Department's total expenses had risen. The primary cause of this decline was a decrease in the number of money order transactions, as shown in **Exhibit 2**. In response to the changes in costs and quantities to money order transactions, three rate changes have been made since the end of World War II (see **Exhibit 3**).

COMPETITION

Postal money orders had two traditional sources of competition: the commercial money order firms, the largest of which was American Express, and the banks.

Although American Express' money order transactions totaled less than $100 million, it had money orders available in over 25,000 locations, including many super-markets and drug and department stores that offered extended evening hours for their purchase. Its sales program, aimed at potential outlets across the country, was aggressive and included mailings, promotion portfolios, films shown at trade associations, and incentive contests.

Commercial money order rates were generally equal to or higher than postal money order rates. Banks, on the other hand, usually undersold the Post Office on large money orders. Of 18 important banking firms across the country, 3 offered money orders at a single fee, while 5 had graduated fees. In every instance, their fees for money orders over $10 were less than the Post Office's. And, in all but two instances, their fees for money orders from $5-$10 were equal to or less than the Post Office fees.

In addition, banks offered indirect competition through their regular and special checking accounts, which were growing rapidly in public acceptance.

Both commercial and bank institutions offering money order service benefited from the "float" it created--the delay between the purchase and the redemption of a money order. The amount of this float was estimated at between six and eight days of sales.

The high-value money order customer represented a larger share of the Post Office Department's money order revenue than of the money order transactions. The Post Office Department's distribution of transactions and revenue was as follows:

Value of Money Order	Share of Total Revenues (1959)	Share of Total Transactions (1959)
$ 0.01-$ 5.00	19%	29%
5.01- 10.00	21	24
10.01- 50.00	50	39
50.01- 100.00	10	8

Despite the decline in postal money order volume after the mid-1950s, both commercial and banking money order suppliers believed that the total market for money orders had expanded. This expansion was attributed to the increase in population and greater dependence by the public upon charge accounts and other credit facilities.

THE MEETING

As a result of the Postmaster General's request, three staff members of the Bureau of Finance and Administration held an informal meeting to discuss the approach they should use in their analysis. Excerpts from this discussion are quoted below.

Carl Jacobson: There is no good reason the Post Office should continue to provide money order service for the public. It lost $12 million in 1964. The money order market is filled with competitors—American Express, Travelers Express, and every bank in the country. I just don't understand why the Post Office should continue to conduct a special service at a loss when the same service is provided by commercial competition.

Howard Whitmore: The Post Office provides a very real service in rural areas where commercial firms can't afford to provide it. We carry money right to the door of rural customers.

Also money orders are important for our COD service. After the cash for a collect parcel is collected by our carriers, it is returned to the mailer in a money order. These COD remittances represent 10 percent of our money order volume.

Paul Berman: What about this so-called loss on money orders? Certainly a loss under cost ascertainment's full-cost allocation of expenses does not mean that the Post Office is suffering an out-of-pocket loss. I went through the cost ascertainment expense categories in detail (**Exhibit 1**) and separated the expense into a fixed and an incremental component. After reviewing these expenses, I'm sure that money orders make a substantial contribution to the department's overhead.

Howard Whitmore: I think your approach makes it reasonable to ask "What costs would we still incur if the Post Office went out of the money order business?" In fact, practically all of the costs are fixed because a great many people who handle money orders for 25 percent or 50 percent of their time would not be eliminated if money orders were discontinued.

Carl Jacobson: I just cannot agree with this line of reasoning. If you take this viewpoint, it is impossible to make decisions regarding any of the department's services. For instance, assume that a worker at a general-purpose window spends 40 percent of his or her time on money orders, 30 percent on CODs, 15 percent on printed stamped envelopes, and 15 percent on postal savings. All of these activities are revenue-deficient activities. If we look at these activities individually, it appears that there is no direct labor cost for conducting the activity. The worker will be there in any event. However, if we look at all of the activities together, the entire cost of the worker becomes variable.

The point is that elimination or substantial curtailment of several revenue-deficient services promises far more in cost-saving possibilities than the sum of the estimated cost savings if each, in isolation from the rest, were considerd for termination. This doesn't mean that there was actually a loss on money orders in 1964. Items of expense such as overhead, operation, care of buildings, and so forth, are certainly fixed as Paul indicated. But I feel strongly that the expense for mail handling and window service must be viewed as primarily direct expense.

Paul Berman: No matter how you view these expenses, I think you must agree that our pricing policy should be designed to maximize revenue. This is a different consideration than the question of whether we should be in or out of the business.

The money order fee increases in 1957 and 1961 decreased money order revenue dramatically. This not only is costing the Post Office money but is slowly pricing us out of the money order business. I doubt if Congress would appreciate our taking over the function of determining what services the department will provide by gradually going out of the money order business. Also, haven't they indicated that they feel money order service is in the public interest by covering it under public service losses?

Howard Whitmore: There have been a number of questions raised here. Let's see if we can't make a better start on the problem by first doing some preliminary analysis. There are several interrelated questions to which we ought to be able to get some approximate quantitative answers, and based on that we can then see how to proceed for a more detailed and precise analysis.

The questions that I think we ought to address ourselves to are:

(1) What impact did the rate increases in 1957 and 1961 have on money order volume?
(2) What was the net effect of these two rate increases in terms of the overall financial performance of the department?
(3) What might we expect to happen if we changed rates again? We could have a 5 cent across-the-board increase, or we might even cut rates if the higher volume would justify it.
(4) Finally, would a single-fee rate structure, similar to that used by banks, improve the financial performance of money orders?

ASSIGNMENT

1. Evaluate Mr. Berman's and Mr. Jacobson's analyses.
2. Recommend a pricing policy for the Post Office's money order service.

EXHIBIT 1   **Post Office Department—Apportionment of Post Office Expenses ($000)**

	Fiscal Year 1955[a]		Fiscal Year 1964	
	Total Expense	Money Order Allocations	Total Expense	Money Order Allocations
Postmasters:				
First-class A, B, C offices	$ 82,437	$ 3,203	$ 4,299	$ 32
All other class offices	166,396	22,819	201,972	13,719
Total postmasters	$248,833	$26,022	$ 206,271	$13,751
Supervisors:				
First-class A, B, C offices			$ 168,983	$ 1,576
All other class offices			103,236	3,445
Total supervisors			$ 272,219	$ 5,021
Mail handling and window service:				
First-class A, B, C offices	$593,609	$17,142	$1,095,916	$12,469
All other class offices	239,668	34,827	520,387	27,365
Total clerical	$833,277	$51,969	$1,616,303	$39,834
Collection and delivery—rural carriers:				
All class offices	$194,945	$ 2,475	$ 251,526	$ 1,601
Building operation and maintenance	$118,198	$ 3,284	$ 246,910	$ 3,432
Postal supply services:				
Stamps and accountable paper	$ 14,560	$ 767	$ 17,758	$ 891
Facilities field personnel	3,164		6,900	57
Money order processing by Federal Reserve Board			450	261
Total postal supply	$ 17,724	$ 767	$ 25,108	$ 1,209
General overhead expense:				
Administration and regional operations costs	$ 21,013		$ 78,060	
Processing money orders—U.S. Treasury	516		600	
Operations costs	11,765			
Transportation costs	1,505		4	
Facilities costs	3,399		886	
Research development costs			10,512	
Total general overhead	$ 38,198	$ 4,480	$ 90,062	$ 2,610
Nonfund expense:				
Depreciation			$ 51,825	$ 465
Freight and expendable equipment			5,858	168
Supply items			737	
Maintenance building services			20,876	271
Unemployment compensation			8,100	129
Total nonfund			$ 87,396	$ 1,033
Redistribution of expense:				
Post office penalty				498
Post office registry				3,393
Total redistribution				$ 3,891

[a]Fiscal year 1955 includes both postmaster and supervisors under postmaster account.

EXHIBIT 2   **Post Office Department—Historical Statistical Information for Money Order Service**

Fiscal Year	Domestic Transactions (thousands)	Average Domestic Fee (cents)	Domestic Value of Sales ($ million)	Average Domestic Value (dollars)
1950	302,848	17.7¢	$4,641	$15.3
1951	321,797	18.4	5,236	15.3
1952	375,215	18.1	5,946	15.8
1953	368,762	18.3	6,032	15.4
1954	359,685	18.6	6,049	16.8
1955	349,273	18.6	5,865	16.8
1956	346,505	NA	5,926	17.1
1957	334,882	18.9	5,880	17.6
1958	311,025	22.6	5,442	17.5
1959	286,647	23.2	5,158	18.0
1960	273,633	23.4	5,031	18.4
1961	264,267	23.5	4,958	18.8
1962	251,842	25.3	4,787	19.0
1963	242,871	25.4	4,709	19.4
1964	235,414	25.6	4,719	20.0

NA = not available.

EXHIBIT 3   **Post Office Department—Domestic Postal Rate History for Money Order Service**

Value of Money Order	November 1, 1944	January 1, 1949	July 1, 1957	July 1, 1961
$ 0.01-$ 2.50	6¢	10¢	15¢	20¢
2.51- 5.00	8	10	15	20
5.01- 10.00	11	15	20	20
10.01- 15.00	13	25	30	30
15.01- 20.00	13	25	30	30
20.01- 30.00	15	25	30	30
30.01- 40.00	15	25	30	30
40.01- 50.00	18	25	30	30
50.01- 60.00	18	35	30	35
60.01- 70.00	20	35	30	35
70.01- 75.00	20	35	30	35
75.01- 80.00	20	35	30	35
80.01- 100.00	22	35	30	35

11 Measuring and Analyzing Actual Results— Managerial Accounting

THE PRIOR TWO CHAPTERS DISCUSSED THE first activity of the managerial control process, that of planning and budgeting. The second part of the managerial control process measures actual results and costs against those planned, identifies the variances between actual and planned results, and analyzes the causes of these variances. This chapter discusses each of these activities.

MEASURING RESULTS

Elliott L. Richardson, a distinguished and experienced public servant, highlighted the importance of measuring results:

> In the absence of rigorous evaluation, we cannot find out how well—or how poorly—a particular effort is succeeding. . . . Only thus . . . can we judge the value of pursuing the objective at all versus . . . devoting the same resources to some wholly different purpose.[1]

Organizational results, or outcomes, can be be measured with many different measuring rods. One is calibrated in financial terms. Revenues, the financial value of the services delivered in the period, are of critical importance, of course. But revenues provide only a limited measure of the output of nonprofit organizations. Many nonprofits earn no revenues because their services are not sold, and some of those that generate revenues price their services at a level that does not reflect their worth. More fundamentally, revenues cannot be the measuring rod for results because the purposes of

[1]Elliott L. Richardson, ''The Value of Evaluation,'' *The GAO Journal* (Spring 1991): 39.

nonprofit organizations are not financial. They exist to improve the educational, cultural, medical, and social state of humanity. Outcome measures should evaluate whether these missions have been attained.

Outcomes can be measured with three other dimensions. First, the outcome measure can delineate the *private* benefits to the organization versus the *public* benefits to society. Second, the outcome measure can be one of the *effectiveness* or one of the *efficiency* of the organization. Third, measures can focus on *quality* or *quantity*. Ideal measures of results incorporate all three dimensions.

Categories of Outcomes

The different measuring rods are combined in the four categories of outcome measures for nonprofit organizations that are presented below. They are presented in order of their increasing validity in measuring attainment of the organization's missions and objectives. While Category 1 of outcome measure is much easier to delineate than that of Category 4, it is also a less valid measure of the output of the organization.

Category 1 Measures—Inputs Nonprofit organizations frequently measure outcomes by measuring inputs, or the costs of the resources consumed. For example, the statement that ''the police department's expenditures were $570,000 in 19X9, a 20 percent growth over the 19X8 budget'' implicitly implies that the services rendered by the police department grew by 20 percent. But this implication is not necessarily a valid one. Costs and outcomes do not necessarily grow in an parallel fashion. Input measures do not measure social benefits, efficiency or effectiveness, or quality. They are usually measured in financial terms.

Category 2 Measures—Process Some nonprofit organizations measure outcomes by specifying the steps in the process of delivering their services and then measuring their attainment of those steps. This measure implicitly assumes that following a certain process will inevitably lead to the accomplishment of a certain level of outcome. Again, this assumption is not always correct. For example, at one time, the process of removing tonsils was believed to improve the patient's health. The number of tonsillectomies was used as a measure of health status: the greater the number of tonsils removed, supposedly the better the state of U.S. health. Today, tonsillectomies are no longer viewed as inevitably desirable and the process of removing tonsils is no longer equated with the desired outcome of good health. As in many other cases, the assumption that following a certain process inevitably leads to a specified output proved to be incorrect.

Process measures of outcomes are usually greeted with some doubt. One expert, for example, characterized measuring a state government's ability to attain its mission of highway safety with process measures such as drunk driving arrests and traffic tickets as "weird."[2]

Many nonprofit organizations find it difficult to specify the process that will produce the best results. We simply do not know the "best" process for education, social services, preventive health, etc. Our lack of knowledge about appropriate processes limits the usefulness of Category 2 measures. Such process measures delineate the *efficiency* of services delivered and their *quantity*. They do not measure benefits, effectiveness, or quality. They are not usually measured in financial terms.

Category 3 Measures—Program Output   This category measures the actual outcomes of the programs: the number of children enrolled, patients served, fires fought, and so on. In a way, it measures social benefits and effectiveness. The information for this category of measures is frequently difficult to gather, but it is a superior measure to Categories 1 and 2 because it focuses on those things achieved by the organization. Nevertheless, if it is the only outcome measure, it may motivate the organization to increase quantity at the expense of quality or efficiency because it only enumerates the number of services delivered and not their quality or efficiency. It is usually measured in nonfinancial terms.

Category 4 Measures—Program Effects   This category measures the impact of the services, not merely their magnitude. For example, it measures the increased literacy of children in a school, the increased life expectancy of those following a certain health program, and the decreased crime that results from a patrol program in a neighborhood, and it ideally relates these effects to their costs. Category 4 measures delineate public and private benefits, effectiveness and efficiency, quality and quantity, and financial and nonfinancial results. (Table 11-1 contrasts output, process, and effects measures.)

Data for this category of measures are exceedingly difficult to obtain and interpret correctly. For one, the causes of the observed impacts are unclear. Children in a special education program may become more literate because they are unusually intelligent or because their family environment is stimulating. The observed increases in their literacy may well result from circumstances other than the program. Then too, this type of measure requires data that are rarely available in either nonprofit or for-profit organizations. Counterbalancing the difficulty of obtaining and interpreting Category 4 measures is the fact that when they are measured and interpreted correctly they are the most valuable of the four categories for measuring outcome.

[2]Robert Keogh, "Experts Question Program Budgeting," *Boston Business Journal* (February 3, 1992): 3.

TABLE 11-1 **Sample Outcome Measures for Four Service Activities**

Category of Measure	Service Activities			
	Tax Enforcement	*Welfare Administration*	*Sewage Treatment*	*Fire Prevention*
1: Inputs	1. Number of tax agents employed	1. Number of social workers employed	1. Amount of money spent on sewage treatment	1. Number of fire-fighters employed
2: Process	1. Number of delinquent notices mailed 2. Number of field visits made	1. Eligibility error rate 2. Percent of assistance cases receiving checks late	1. Number of laboratory tests conducted	1. Number of inspections conducted 2. Number of public education brochures mailed
3: Outputs	1. Percent of accounts delinquent 30 days after due date 2. Percent of total tax levy delinquent 30 days after due date	1. Number of assistance cases open or active	1. Number of gallons of sewage treated	1. Number of fire alarm responses
4: Effects	1. Reduction in tax fraud and payment delays	1. Improvement in health and welfare of the poor	1. Percent of samples of effluent meeting EPA standards 2. Number of complaints received/ number of households served	1. Number of fires per capita 2. Total property loss from fires/total value of all property 3. Number of deaths and injuries per capita from fires

Source: Partially derived from Price Waterhouse and Company (PW), *Productivity Improvement Manual for Local Government Officials* (New York, NY: PW, 1977), p. 24.

Elliott Richardson provides a telling example of why it may be so difficult to obtain Category 4 measures:

I remember the time when, as Attorney General, I was invited to New York City to dedicate the new police headquarters. I was met at the airport by a deputy commissioner who was responsible for the city's battle against organized crime. I asked him how he was doing.

"Great," he said.

"Really?" I said. "What have you done?"

He recounted the number of people he had sent to jail. I said, "That's fine. But has that had any effect on organized crime?"

He continued in the same vein, telling me about the various indictments he had obtained and the dent they had made in the Colombo gang—or whatever—and how the NYPD now had the Mafia on the run. I said, "That's also fine. But have your efforts reduced any of the activities in which organized crime is engaged? Is there any less illegal gambling?"

He looked at me quizzically and asked, "What does that have to do with it?"[3]

Measuring Quality

Formal measures of the quality of the services are at least as important as financial measurements. One health care organization regularly monitors the following events to assure itself of the highest quality of care:

(1) Undesirable occurrences (e.g., all patients hospitalized after minor surgery)

(2) Patient advocacy notes (clinical care complaints referred by the patient advocate or by others)

(3) Quality assurance and risk management committee minutes

(4) Minutes of safety, disaster, and maintenance committees

(5) Incident reports (reports involving clinical issues referred by executive director)

(6) Other screens already in place for reviews mandated by the Board of Registration in Medicine

(7) Potential or actual claims (referred by loss control coordinator)

New England Critical Care, a company providing intravenous infusions in patients' homes, developed a detailed outcome measurement system that focused on quality, the company's distinctive attribute. Among the items included were patient ratings of the quality attributes that are important to them, such as the nurses' punctuality and their ability to painlessly and accurately insert a needle in a vein; ratings of the cleanliness of the vans used by the company to deliver infusion solutions; and evaluations of the van driver's neatness, friendliness, and punctuality.

As in these examples, the recipient's satisfaction with the services is an important measure of performance. Yet, many managers of nonprofit organizations shy away from such measures. They either ignore them or argue that

[3]Richardson, "Value of Evaluation," pp. 39-40.

clients are not capable of evaluating the services. For example, professors may say that their students are not competent to evaluate their teaching, and hospitals may feel that patients are similarly incapable of evaluating their services.

These claims have some validity; after all, the student usually does not know as much about the subject as the teacher. Nevertheless, people are surprisingly well-informed. For example, patients are much better predictors of their deaths than their physicians, even after the physicians have performed rigorous examinations of the patients.[4] And, when some professors first received feedback from systematic student evaluations, they were stunned to see that their lectures were considered dull or irrelevant. They had never before received any feedback from their students. No wonder they were shocked at the results. Many of these professors changed the style and content of their courses after receiving this feedback.

Similar results can be obtained in other organizations whose professionals are usually sheltered from client scrutiny. Lawyers can be asked to evaluate the performance of judges, and patients to evaluate the performance of nurses, aides, physicians, and other hospital personnel. The New York City Board of Education even plans to add a high school student as a non-voting member to provide this kind of feedback.[5] The U.S. General Accounting Office is currently researching what it calls Service Efforts and Accomplishments to provide such data for government services.

Peer Review

Many professionals prefer evaluation by their peers to evaluation by their clients because other professionals are well informed. But, *peer review* can result in less meaningful evaluations. For one, professionals may fear that a critical evaluation of a peer will be repaid in kind. Also, peer review substitutes professional criteria of performance for the criteria that are important to the client. For example, while the caliber and quantity of research is important to professors, the quality of teaching is much more important to students. The peer review process cannot duplicate the clients' perceptions and should not be a substitute for evaluations of the clients' feelings.

Examples of Measuring Results

Among the examples of some of the measures of results used in different nonprofit organizations are the following:

Hospitals: The Health Care Financing Administration of the U.S. government annually reports the hospital mortality rates of Medicare patients and

[4]Daniel Coleman, "Mortality Study Lends Weight to Patient's Opinion," *The New York Times*, 21 March 1991, p. B13.
[5]Joseph Berger, "School Board Offers to Add Student Voice," *The New York Times*, 3 January 1991, p. B1.

identifies the hospitals whose rates are higher than expected. For example, 15 hospitals have exceeded expectations for mortality in each of the four years of the report. These are measures of social effectiveness, quality, and quantity.[6]

Health Maintenance Organizations (HMOs): Some measurement systems enable HMOs to reward physicians who adhere to guidelines about how to practice medicine, such as guidelines on the number of immunizations or breast-cancer screenings performed.[7] These are process measures.

Local Governments: Among the measures of effectiveness and social benefits that local governments can readily use are jobs by sector, retail sales levels, value of taxable property, per capita income, percent of population below poverty level, population size and mobility, crime rate, and fire insurance ratings.[8]

An interesting score-card on the attainments of New York City's government is presented in Table 11-2. It contains some Category 4 measures (Streets Rated Acceptably Clean), many Category 2 process measures (Felony Arrests, for example), and even some efficiency data. John Palmer Smith, its author, has produced much more detailed analyses of many of the city's services. Table 11-3 contains an example of one such analysis for the police. It not only provides measures of outcome over time but also compares them to suggested goals.

[6]Stephen K. Cooper, "Hospitals Show High Mortality," *HealthWeek* (May 6, 1991): 3.
[7]Sharon McEachern, "Performance Scores Reward 'Star' Docs," *HealthWeek* (May 6, 1991): 24 and 36.
[8]Terry Michols Clark, ed., *Monitoring Local Governments* (Dubuque, IA: Kendall/Hunt Publishing Co., 1987), pp. 75-80.

TABLE 11-2 **Selected Indicators of New York City's Quality of Life, 1978-86, Selected Years**

	1978	1986	Percentage Change
Reported Crimes	1,213,940	1,687,200	39.0%
Felonies	499,080	554,811	11.2%
Felony Arrests	109,228	121,396	11.1%
Structural Fires	46,460	31,050	−33.2%
Streets Rated Acceptably Clean	63.1%	74.0%	17.3%
School System Dropouts	41.7% ('83)	35.3% ('85)	NA
Public Assistance Recipients	907,000	913,000	0.7%
Daily Adult Shelter Population	1,087 ('79)	8,069	133.4%

Source: Adapted from John Palmer Smith, "Quality of Life in the Big Apple: An Empirical Glimpse," *New York*, 3 NQ 3 (Spring 1986), p. NY2.

TABLE 11-3   **Indicators of Outputs, Quality, and Efficiency: Police Services**

	1978	1985	Goals 1989
Outputs			
Arrests	220,780	226,192	289,323
Felonies	109,228	111,383	144,662
Misdemeanors	85,312	110,525	No Goals
Violations	26,240	4,284	No Goals
Patrol Car Response to:			
"911" Calls	2,540,000	3,304,000	2,808
"Crime-in-Progress" Calls	NA	366,000	No Goals
Service Quality			
Arrest Rate, Felonies	21.9%	20.3%	26.4%
Rate of Solving Felonies	15.5%	17.0%	No Goals
Average Time to Dispatch Patrol Car to			
"Crime-in-Progress" (minutes)	2	1	1
Service Efficiency			
Arrests per Uniformed Employee Year	NA	7.4	9.0
Felony Arrests per Uniformed Employee Year	NA	3.8	4.5
Patrol Car Responses per Employee Year	86.5	107.2	91.9

Source: Adapted from Citizens Budget Commission, *The State of Municipal Services, 1978-1985*, (New York City: Citizen's Budget Commission, 1985): 5.

Colleges and Universities: One university assessed the effectiveness of its undergraduate college by interviewing hundreds of current students and alumni. The resulting measures of effectiveness were published in a widely circulated report.[9] The results of post-secondary institutions can be evaluated with comparative data gathered from over 500 colleges and universities. The data include input measures such as surplus or deficit relative to expenses, process measures such as the ratio between students and support staff members, and outcome measures of private benefits such as the percentage of alumni who contribute to the school and the total return on endowment.[10]

MEASURING INPUTS—COST ACCOUNTING

Costs, the resources consumed to achieve the outcomes, must be carefully measured and related to outputs. This process is usually termed *cost accounting*. It may seem that delineation of costs is a rather simple process;

[9]Richard J. Light, *The Harvard Assessment Seminars* (Cambridge, MA: Harvard Graduate School of Education, 1990).
[10]Barbara E. Taylor, Joel W. Meyerson, Louis R. Morrell, and Dabney G. Park, Jr., *Strategic Analysis* (Washington, DC: Association of Governing Boards of Colleges and Universities, 1991).

but as with many other aspects of accounting, it is not. The first decision in accounting for costs is the number of outcomes whose costs are to be measured. These are termed cost centers. The greater their number, the greater the expense and the accuracy of the cost accounting system. Costs are characterized by three dimensions. The next step in the measurement of costs requires decisions about each of these three separate attributes of costs, as discussed below.

Product Versus Process Costs

One attribute of costs that requires a decision is whether the *process* of delivering services or the ultimate *product* of the service delivery process should be measured. For example, in a hospital, this issue considers whether it is the *process* of delivering patient care or the output, or *product*, produced that should be costed. The cost-accounting systems used for these purposes are called process and product costing systems, respectively.

Process costing systems derive an average cost per unit by collecting all the expenses that are relevant to the process and dividing them by the total units produced. In a hospital, for example, process costing involves collecting all the expenses of the process of producing inpatient or outpatient care and dividing that total cost by the total number of days of care or the total number of outpatient visits. It results in the calculation of the average cost per patient day or per patient visit.

As shown in Table 11-4, the calculations for process costing in service-providing organizations are relatively straightforward. Unfortunately, the simplicity of process costing is not mirrored by its validity. Process costing ascribes the same cost to every outcome of the process. Thus, the hospital patient who receives a routine surgical procedure will have the same $400 cost per day as the patient in the intensive care unit who requires considerably more personnel, space, equipment, and supplies. If the hospital were producing only one product, this problem would not occur. However, most service-producing organizations provide a number of different products. As a result, the data produced by a process costing system are generally inaccurate. The greater the heterogeneity in the products provided by the organization, the greater the likelihood of inaccuracies in a process costing system.

TABLE 11-4 **Example of Process Costing in a Hospital**

(A) Process	(B) Expenses	(C) Output	(B) ÷ (C) Average Cost
Inpatient Care	$2,000,000	5,000 patient days	$400 per patient day
Outpatient Care	$100,000	2,500 visits	$40 per visit

The alternative *product costing system* traces the costs of particular products or outputs. In a hospital, this system would calculate the costs of certain diagnoses, episodes, types of visits, or patient-days. While product costing results in more accurate cost data, it is also more difficult to implement. Specifying the product being produced is one difficulty. In an outpatient clinic, for example, should the job of monitoring a patient with arthritis be classified by the primary diagnosis, by the chronic nature of the visit, or by the characteristics of the patient? And should the cost measure the entire episode of providing care to such a patient? Similar questions would arise in an educational setting: What are the appropriate measures of the products of the school?

Product costing also requires substantially more data collection than process costing. The expenses for each product, however defined, must be traced in this kind of system. This task involves time sheets and other detailed records of the expenses connected with particular products, as well as a precise accounting for the number of products produced.

The complexity of product costing is such that most nonprofit organizations use process costing systems despite their inaccuracies. Colleges and universities calculate the cost per student despite the fact that graduate students cost more to educate than undergraduates, that business students require fewer resources than physics students, and that a chemistry lab will have a higher expense than an algebra class. Highway departments calculate the cost per mile built, cleaned, or snowplowed despite the fact that the cost of performing these services on a superhighway is very different from doing them on a mile of dirt-packed road or on a steep hill. (The use of the relative value method discussed in Chapter 10 may increase the accuracy of process costs.)

Full Versus Direct Costs

The second attribute of costs that requires a decision concerns the expenses that should be measured. Should the costs of a particular process or product include only those expenses clearly and *directly* involved in the performance of the job? Or should they include *indirect* costs, such as the salary of the organization's chief executive officer, that cannot be clearly traced to any one output or process but that are necessary for the organization as a whole? These two different systems are referred to as direct and full cost systems, respectively.

Direct cost systems are relatively easy to understand. In a hospital, for example, these systems simply trace the expenses directly involved with the provision of inpatient and outpatient care—such as the expenses of the medical personnel directly involved, space, direct supplies and equipment used, and so on.

But direct cost systems may understate the costs of providing services. A *full cost system* includes some fair share of the overall indirect expenses in the measure of costs. These indirect expenses are generally referred to as *overhead* expenses and the process of distributing them is called *allocation*. (The allocation process can become so complex that many come to regard overhead as underfoot.)

The simplest method for overhead allocation involves distributing overhead expenses to particular processes or products via a measure that is related to the expense. For example, the overhead expense of the accounting unit could be distributed to a product or process on the basis of the relative number of bills issued; the expenses of fuel, on the basis of relative square or cubic feet of space heated or cooled; and the expenses of the cafeteria, on the basis of the number of meals consumed by the personnel in that department.

Table 11-5 illustrates this simple allocation methodology in the context of a small community health center that provides only two services: clinic visits and home health visits. The direct expenses of these services are $160,000 and $120,000, respectively. The indirect, or overhead, expenses of the health center are allocated to these services as indicated in the table. For example, the $90,000 indirect expense of accounting, medical records, and admissions is allocated to each of the services on the basis of the relative number of visits. The clinic visit function, which accounts for 57 percent of the direct expenses [$160,000 ÷ ($160,000 + $120,000)], receives only 50 percent of the $90,000 as its share of the accounting and medical records expenses because it accounts for only half of the total visits. After the allocation process was completed, the full costs of clinic visits grew from $160,000 to $310,000. The $140,100 increase is caused by the allocation of the overhead expenses to the clinic visits function.

TABLE 11-5 **Allocating Overhead Costs: Simple Method**

	Health Center Expenses	Clinic Visits	Home Health Visits	Basis of Allocation
Clinic visits, direct expenses	$160,000	$160,000		
Home health visits, direct expenses	120,000		$120,000	
Maintenance and utilities	60,000	50,000	10,000	Square feet
Accounting, medical records, and admissions	90,000	45,000	45,000	Number of visits
General administration	45,000	26,100	18,900	Direct expenses
Laboratory	55,000	29,000	26,000	Number of tests
Totals	$530,000	$310,100	$219,900	

This allocation method ignores the fact that the indirect cost functions provide services to each other. Utilities are used not only for inpatient and outpatient care, but also to heat, cool, and light the offices of all the indirect functions, such as the accounting department. The *step-down method* of allocating overhead expenses deals with this issue by allocating overhead expenses among the overhead departments, as well as among the service-providing units. (It is called a "step-down" because the resulting data look like a series of stairs.)

This method involves allocation of the indirect cost activities to each other as well as to the basic services whose full costs we are attempting to delineate. For the hospital illustrated in Table 11-6, the overhead functions of utilities, maintenance, and administration are to be allocated to the primary functions of research, operating room, inpatient floor, laboratory, and clinic.

The process begins with one indirect cost activity being allocated to all the other activities. In this case, it begins with the $160,000 of utilities expenses being allocated to all the other functions. The maintenance function costs that began at $120,000, increase to costs of $136,000 with the allocation of $16,000 of utilities expense. The new maintenance expenses of $136,000 then are allocated to the remaining primary functions and the overhead function of administration. Administration costs began at $70,000 and are increased by $24,000 of allocated utility expenses and $27,200 of allocated maintenance expenses. This allocation process continues sequentially through all the activities.

A number of iterations of this process may be used, culminating in the final allocation of the indirect costs to the primary functions of the organization. Table 11-6 contains only one iteration. The outcomes of the step-down method are influenced by the order of the allocation steps and the measures used to allocate overhead.

After the full costs of a department are identified, the full costs of an activity or a product within it are usually accounted for by measuring the amount of direct expenses it consumes and then allocating overhead costs to it via an *overhead rate*. This rate relates the total amount of overhead in the department to its direct costs. For example, the overhead rate for the hospital clinic in Table 11-6, is 0.9704 ($48,520 ÷ $50,000). Every dollar of direct expenses also incurs approximately $0.97 of overhead. Thus, if a particular clinic visit has direct expenses of $20, its overhead costs will be $19.41 ($20 × 0.9704).

Standard Versus Actual Costs

The third attribute of costs that requires a decision is whether to measure the process or product with its *actual* cost or with a *standard* of what the cost should be. For manufacturing firms this is a moot question; most of their cost-accounting systems are based on standard costs. Standard cost

TABLE 11-6 Allocating Overhead Expenses: Step-Down Method

	Utilities	Maintenance	Administration	Research	Operating Room	Inpatient Floor	Laboratory	Clinic	Total
Direct Expenses	$ 160,000	$ 120,000	$ 70,000	$100,000	$240,000	$150,000	$ 60,000	$ 50,000	$950,000
Allocate Utilities	− 160,000	+ 16,000	+ 24,000	+ 40,000	+ 16,000	+ 32,000	+ 16,000	+ 16,000	
New Totals	$ 0	$ 136,000	$ 94,000	$140,000	$256,000	$182,000	$ 76,000	$ 66,000	$950,000
Allocate Maintenance		− 136,000	+ 27,200	0	+ 20,400	+ 47,600	+ 20,400	+ 20,400	
New Totals		$ 0	$ 121,200	$140,000	$276,400	$229,600	$ 96,400	$ 86,400	$950,000
Allocate Administration			− 121,200	+ 24,240	+ 48,480	+ 24,240	+ 12,120	+ 12,120	
New Totals			$ 0	$164,240	$324,880	$253,840	$108,520	$ 98,520	$950,000

systems are in widespread use because they facilitate control and evaluation. They predict what costs should be and analyze the difference, or variance, between standard and actual costs. Standard cost systems thus help the managers of large organizations to better understand and control performance.

The mechanics of a standard cost system require an estimate of the standard amount of resources, such as labor, material, supplies, and overhead, that will be used in the production process. These standards are usually produced by industrial engineers who are carefully trained in the statistical and experimental techniques necessary to produce them. Time and motion studies are the key to the construction of standard personnel costs. Nonprofit organizations frequently lack both standards and the industrial engineering units to develop them. Instead, the budget can be used as a standard, particularly if it has been developed with the careful application of the techniques of incremental or zero-base budgeting discussed in Chapter 9. Alternatively, data on comparable organizations can be used as a standard.

Activity-Based Costing

Activity-based costing allocates expenses to the level of activity that consumes resources, rather than trying to allocate all expenses to individual units of final output.[11] It has recently been applied to manufacturing firms but has not yet been widely applied to nonprofit and service organizations. Activity costing has the potential to be very useful to nonprofit managers.

Different types of programs, services, clients, and resource providers can place different demands on an organization's resources and can result in different contributions to the benefits produced. Activity costing analysis clarifies the activities associated with each program or function, and it specifies their linkage to the generation of revenues or other benefits. By highlighting the relationships between activities and costs, it shows managers where they can take actions to increase benefits or reduce resource consumption.

As an example of the differences between activity-based costing and more traditional cost-accounting techniques, consider two services: one a high-volume area such as a multi-section freshman class in accounting, and the second a low-volume one, such as a seminar on Chaucer. With traditional accounting techniques, the costs of a section of each course may well be the same. As illustrated in Table 11-7, both course sections are likely to have the same costs assigned to them. After all, both course sections employ one teacher and use one classroom. Overhead rates will be allocated to each section on the basis of the school-wide rate of $1 of overhead for every dollar of teacher expenses.

[11]See, for example, one discussion of activity costing in Robin H. Cooper and Robert S. Kaplan, "Profit Priorities from Activity-Based Costing," *Harvard Business Review* (May-June 1991): 130-135.

TABLE 11-7   **Traditional Versus Activity-Based Costing**

	Traditional Cost-Accounting			Activity-Based Costing		
Section	Teacher	Overhead	Total Cost	Teacher	Overhead	Total Cost
Accounting	$10,000	$10,000	$20,000	$10,000	$ 1,000	$11,000
Chaucer	$10,000	$10,000	$20,000	$10,000	$10,000	$20,000

Overhead Allocation
Basis: $1 of overhead for every $1 of teacher expense

Overhead Allocation
For accounting: 10¢ overhead for every $1 of teacher expenses
For Chaucer: $1 overhead for every $1 of teacher expenses

But, these cost-accounting results seem counter to our intuition. The freshman accounting course runs multiple sections and should benefit from economies of scale that the single section course cannot enjoy. Its indirect costs per section should be much lower than those of the Chaucer course. Activity-based costing will trace the overhead expense tied to each activity within each course. For example, suppose the indirect, or overhead, costs consist entirely of the expenses associated with ordering a textbook for the students. Both courses will incur approximately the same total overhead costs because they are both doing essentially the same work. But the accounting course can spread its overhead costs over many sections, say ten, while the Chaucer course must absorb its costs in only one. Activity-based costing highlights this difference, as shown in Table 11-7.

The activity costing system refines the overhead allocation process. If producing an additional unit of service causes additional costs to be incurred, then these costs are charged directly to the units produced. However, costs incurred because of the organization's decision to offer a specific type of service or program are charged to the program level, not the individual unit level. The unit costs are direct; all others are overhead costs. Activity costing usually produces a hierarchy of expense levels, typically three or four. For example, the cost of program services might include separate expense levels for *service units* (such as an individual meal to a single homeless person), *batch* activities (serving lunch), *services or programs* (providing meals in general), and *facility sustaining activities* (owning and maintaining a building in which to conduct the organization's activities, including but not limited to serving meals).

As a further example, consider fund raising. Some of its expenses are directly related to producing an individual unit of output of the activity, such as the postage and materials costs of mailing a fund-raising letter. Other expenses are related to the batch, such as design and setup costs of the letter. Yet other costs relate to the fund-raising program, such as the salary of the development director. The final level of expenses includes the general costs of operating the organization, such as the executive director's salary, utilities, and maintenance. Traditional cost systems allocate all indirect costs to individual units on some simple basis such as labor or machine hours. The larger the proportion of costs driven by activities other than the number of units, the larger the difference between the costs calculated by the two systems and the greater the importance of using activity-based costing.

In many nonprofit organizations, a large proportion of costs are not related to the number of units produced. These cost characteristics have generally led to frustration with traditional cost systems that are extremely susceptible to the assumptions on which cost allocations are based and, therefore, to manipulation or error. Activity costing promises to provide nonprofit managers with better measures of their organizations' costs.

Nonprofit Cost-Accounting Practices

The cost-accounting systems of nonprofit organizations that receive considerable funds from outside donors or government contracts can be heavily influenced by the accounting requirements of these funding sources. For example, when the U.S. government began to pay hospitals a flat price for a Medicare patient's diagnostically-related group (commonly referred to as a DRG), some hospitals began the painful transformation of their cost-accounting system from an actual, process-measuring one to one that measured standard costs per product, or DRG. (The DRG is the flat price for hospital-based treatment of a group of diagnoses that U.S. health insurance for the elderly pays.)

Perhaps the greatest influence on the cost-accounting systems of U.S. nonprofit organizations is provided by the government overhead accounting requirements for organizations that receive research and other grants or contracts. The requirements stipulate the items of expense that may legitimately be included as an overhead cost and how these costs should be allocated to the grant or contract. Because the precise requirements change continually, we will not discuss them here but will, instead, focus on management's role in responding to external accounting dictates.

The government's standards provide guidelines, not requirements. As a result, overhead rates vary considerably. Among research universities, for example, Stanford's rate of 74 percent of the amount gained in government grants was the highest.[12] Nevertheless, failure to adhere scrupulously to the government's standards can be both humiliating and costly. For example, in

---

[12]Andrew Pollack, "Under Audit, Stanford Will Repay U.S.," *The New York Times*, 24 January 1991, p. A16.

March of 1991, early reports surfaced alleging that Stanford University over-charged the U.S. government for its overhead costs. Among the items Stanford was alleged to have inappropriately included were expenses for the university president's wedding reception and household furnishings.[13] By April, the U.S. government announced cutbacks in its payments to the university that could reduce its revenues by $20 million a year.[14]

Although, as of now, it remains unclear whether Stanford University committed any material violations of its agreements for overhead accounting with the government, it is amply clear that Stanford lost a public relations battle. As its president noted of the expenses: "They are in my judgment allowable. They just don't appear reasonable to most people."[15] In an effort to minimize the problem, other universities voluntarily offered to refund some overhead payments. For example, the Massachusetts Institute of Technology promised to repay $731,000—a sum that included funds reportedly used for government lobbyists.[16] Harvard University's Medical School followed a similar route.

It is easy to find fault in retrospect. Nevertheless, one wonders about the managerial oversight of overhead accounting that permitted universities to include expenses that the public would likely decide were only tangentially related to the government's interests.

The problems with overhead accounting requirements do not end here. Some nonprofit organizations, in an attempt to achieve the highest amount of reimbursement possible, will assign expenses as direct costs that, from a motivational perspective, more appropriately should be designated as over-head, or the reverse. As an example of the former, one university charged the services of an environmental control group that monitors environmental hazards directly to research contracts. Although this method of accounting insured that these direct costs would be repaid by the funders of the contract, it also motivated the contract manager to minimize use of these critically important environmental control services.

Conversely, another university increased the expenses of a support department because its research contracts permitted the department to be included as a component of overhead expenses. The higher the costs were in this department, the greater the overhead reimbursement the university would receive. But the department's managers viewed this process as "padding." It caused them to lose some of their interest in controlling costs. They felt that their attempts were in vain because the university's accountant would inevitably increase their costs.

[13]"The Cracks in Stanford's Ivory Tower," *Business Week* (March 11, 1991): 64-65.
[14]Andrew Pollack, "U.S. Sharply Cuts Funds to Stanford as Result of Inquiry on Overcharging," *The New York Times*, 26 April 1991, p. A16.
[15]"The Cracks in Stanford's Ivory Tower," p. 65.
[16]Philip J. Hilts, "M.I.T. Will Pay Back $731,000 to U.S., Including Lobby Funds," *The New York Times*, 24 April 1991, p. A16.

Managers should insure that external accounting requirements are not permitted to interfere with the managerial control process and cause costs to be misstated or misunderstood.

ANALYZING THE DIFFERENCES BETWEEN PLANNED AND ACTUAL RESULTS

Thus far we have discussed how to measure actual results and costs. This section discusses how to analyze the variance between the actual results and costs and those planned.

Sources for Standards of Performance

The plan or budget is key to this process. For a budget to be useful for analyzing results, it should have the following characteristics:

(1) *The budget should be time phased* in a manner that accurately reflects the events expected at different times. A monthly budget that is merely a yearly budget divided by twelve is not a very useful control device if expenses do not occur uniformly. Hospitals, schools, and government organizations all experience substantial monthly or seasonal variations in their inflows and outflows.

(2) *The budget should be matched with the accounting system.* A cash budget is not a very useful control device if the actual inflows and outflows are accounted for on an accrual basis.

If a budget does not have these characteristics, it may not be an adequate standard to use for variance analysis. In such circumstances, other standards must be sought. Frequently, data about comparable organizations are available. For example, the book *Strategic Analysis* contains comparative data for many dimensions of performance of post-secondary educational institutions. The data are sorted into five different types of institutions. With these data, an educational institution can compare its performance to the performance of similar institutions.[17]

But for many organizations, such data may be unavailable or the comparisons may prove difficult to assess. A technique called *data envelope analysis* (DEA) enables managers to rank themselves versus comparable organizations. The technique identifies the most and least efficient organizations in the group, via a mathematical analysis of the mix and volume of services and the resources used. For example, a DEA analysis performed for a group of government purchasing offices yielded the results shown, in condensed form, in Table 11-8.[18] The analysis revealed that Offices 6 and 7 were particularly

[17]Taylor et al., *Strategic Analysis.*
[18]H. David Sherman, *Service Organization Productivity Management* (Hamilton, Ontario: The Society of Management Accountants of Canada, November 1988), p. 89.

TABLE 11-8 **Sample Results of a Data Envelope Analysis of the Performance of a Large Procurement Office**

Office Number	Maximum Efficiency	Maximum Inefficiency
1	100.0	-
2	80.3	$ 98,086
3	100.0	-
4	94.1	60,062
5	95.1	15,246
6	70.0	261,391
7	84.3	375,230
8	100.0	-
9	100.0	-
10	93.4	23,338

Source: H. David Sherman, *Service Organization Productivity Management* (Hamilton, Ontario: The Society of Management Accountants of Canada, November 1988), p. 89.

inefficient. Another technique for developing standards is *best practice analysis*, in which experts identify the best process for accomplishing the desired results. This process can then be used as a standard.

Variance Analysis

The process of *variance analysis* isolates the causes of the differences between planned goals and actual results. Variance analysis is critical for evaluation of managerial performance because it separates those events that can be controlled by managers from those that cannot and also distinguishes the effect of the activities controlled by different managers. It can explain the differences between planned and actual performance of any financial measure. The following sections discuss variance analysis of revenues, expenses, and profits.

Variance Analysis of Expenses

The technique of variance analysis is found most frequently in manufacturing firms. It is used to separate variances from the plan that are caused by changes in the volume of sales activity from those that are caused by changes in the efficiency of production. (These two variances are referred to as *volume* and *efficiency* variances from plan.) These variances are distinguished because they are controlled by two different managers. Volume changes are controlled by the marketing staff whose job is to cause more or less volume to be sold, while efficiency changes are usually the responsibility of those managing production. The variances enable measurement of the separate effectiveness of these managers.

Variance analysis can also be useful in service organizations. If you are doing a variance analysis, you may find it much easier to visualize the analysis graphically, rather than mechanistically to insert numbers into formulas. The graph enables some people to visualize more clearly why planned and actual results differ. Figure 11-1 illustrates the graphical analysis for a hospital whose actual costs exceeded planned costs by $70 million. For some people, variance analysis is best understood by looking at the problem graphically. If you study Figure 11-1, you can see that the cross-hatched area represents the total variance, the difference between planned and actual events. Note that the cross-hatched area is composed of two sub-areas, each representing a different kind of variance.

The analytic process of variance analysis is comparable to taking partial derivatives in calculus. For those who have forgotten calculus or who may have skipped it altogether, it is the process of analyzing how one variable affects a system when everything is held constant except those things affected by a change in that variable.

The formulas for the variances for the hospital in Figure 11-1 are as follows:

$$\text{Total Variance} = \text{Actual Total Costs} - \text{Planned Costs}$$
$$= \$150,000,000 - \$80,000,000$$
$$= \$70,000,000$$

FIGURE 11-1 **Variance Analysis of Expense**

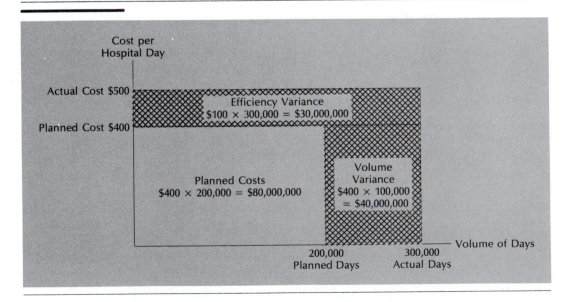

$$\begin{aligned}
\text{Efficiency Variance} &= (\text{Actual Cost per Day} - \text{Planned Cost per} \\
&\quad\ \text{Day}) \times \text{Actual Days} \\
&= (\$500 - \$400) \times 300{,}000 \\
&= \$30{,}000{,}000
\end{aligned}$$

$$\begin{aligned}
\text{Volume Variance} &= (\text{Actual Days} - \text{Planned Days}) \times \text{Planned} \\
&\quad\ \text{Cost per Day} \\
&= (300{,}000 - 200{,}000) \times \$400 \\
&= \$40{,}000{,}000
\end{aligned}$$

$$\begin{aligned}
\text{Total Variance} &= \text{Efficiency Variance} + \text{Volume Variance} \\
&= \$30{,}000{,}000 + \$40{,}000{,}000 \\
&= \$70{,}000{,}000
\end{aligned}$$

What Information Does This Analysis Convey?   The expense variance analysis illustrated in Figure 11-1 explains why actual hospital costs were $70 million higher than planned. Although the hospital's managers claimed that the increase occurred because the actual volume of hospital days was much higher than planned, the analysis does not confirm their explanation. Yes, the increased volume of 100,000 days caused total cost increases of $40 million, the volume variance, but costs increased by $70 million, not $40 million. The remaining variance was caused by the $30 million efficiency variance that occurred when the hospital's costs rose from a planned level of $400 to an actual level of $500 per day. Had the hospital maintained its actual costs at the planned level, its total costs would have been at least $30 million lower. The $70 million of cost variances were the product of increased volume ($40 million impact) and decreased efficiency ($30 million impact). Variance analysis isolated the cost impact of increased volume from that of decreased efficiency. It thus enabled better evaluation of the managers' performances.

Variance Analysis of Revenues

Variance analysis of revenues distinguishes the impact of volume and price on revenues. For example, if the planned price per day for the hospital above was $600, and the actual price was $700, then planned revenues were $120,000,000 ($600 per day × 200,000 days), while actual revenues were $210,000,000 ($700 per day × 300,000 days). In this case, the price variance is $30 million [($700 − $600) × 300,000], and the volume variance $60 million [$600 × (300,000 days − 200,000 days)]. (See Figure 11-2.) The revenue variance of $90 million ($210 million − $120 million) consists of the favorable volume variance of $60,000 and price variance of $30 million.

Note that whether the variance is positive or negative does not determine whether it is good news or bad. A positive expense variance is bad news; actual costs exceeded those planned. A positive revenue variance, on the other hand, is good news; actual revenues were higher than planned.

FIGURE 11-2   **Variance Analysis of Revenues**

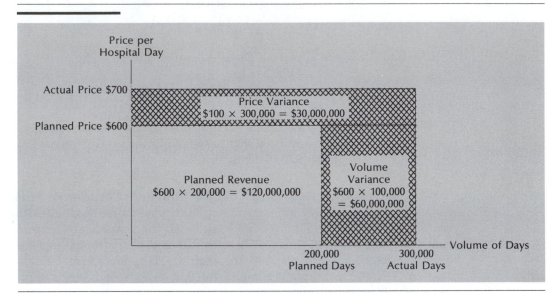

Variance Analysis of Profits

    Revenue and cost variances can be combined for a profit variance analysis that explains why actual profits differed from planned ones. The explanation helps to assign praise or blame to those managers responsible. In the hospital example, profits were planned at $40 million ($120 million in revenues − $80 million in costs), while actual profits were $60 million ($210 million − $150 million). Profits were $20 million higher than planned. (A negative profit variance contains good news; actual profits were higher than planned.) Although decreased efficiency reduced profits by $30 million, its negative impact was offset by a volume variance whose net effect on profits was a positive $20 million and a price variance that raised profits by another $30 million. The combined effect of these variances was $20 million, as shown in Table 11-9.

TABLE 11-9   **Profit Variance Analysis (in millions of dollars)**

	Actual	−	Planned	=	Total Variance	=	Volume Variance	+	Price Variance	+	Efficiency Variance
Revenues	$210	−	$120	=	$90	=	$60	+	$30	+	NA
− Costs	150	−	80	=	70	=	40	+	NA	+	$30
Profits	$ 60	−	$ 40	=	$20	=	$20	+	$30	+	$(30)

This analysis can answer many questions. For example, did the hospital's marketing directors do a good job this year? On balance, the answer appears to be "yes." When they raised the hospital's prices, they also managed to increase volume. The only negative effect of the greatly increased volume was possibly to decrease efficiency. But this negative effect was more than offset by the positive contributions to profits from increased prices and volume.

An Additional Example of Variance Analysis

Variance analysis is a difficult subject, but it is included here because of its importance. This is a subject best learned with tincture of time. To help you become more comfortable with the process, one additional example of variance analysis follows.

The actual revenues for a nonprofit opera are shown in Table 11-10. The planned ticket prices, sales, and revenues are presented in Table 11-11.

The difference between the actual and planned revenues (total variance) is $750,000 ($5,020,000 − $4,270,000). It resulted from the differences between the actual and budgeted price and volume of some productions. The formulas for these variances are as follows:

$$\text{Price Variance} = (\text{Actual Price} - \text{Planned Price}) \times \text{Actual Volume}$$

$$\text{Volume Variance} = (\text{Actual Volume} - \text{Planned Volume}) \times \text{Planned Price}$$

Table 11-12 exhibits the variances calculated by inserting the data from Table 11-10 and Table 11-11 in these formulas. The combination of the price and volume variances provides interesting information. In all cases, volume was higher than anticipated, even in the face of prices that were higher than

TABLE 11-10 **Actual Ticket Price, Volume, and Revenues**

	Actual Average Price	Actual Ticket Volume	Actual Revenues
Aida	$15	50,000	$ 750,000
La Traviata	16	60,000	960,000
Fledermaus	13	40,000	520,000
The Barber of Seville	16	100,000	1,600,000
Carmen	17	70,000	1,190,000
Total		320,000	$5,020,000

TABLE 11-11 **Planned Ticket Price, Volume, and Revenues**

	Planned Average Price	Planned Ticket Volume	Planned Revenues
Aida	$15	40,000	$ 600,000
La Traviata	15	50,000	750,000
Fledermaus	12	30,000	360,000
The Barber of Seville	16	100,000	1,600,000
Carmen	16	60,000	960,000
Total		280,000	$4,270,000

originally planned. Apparently, there is much greater support for these operas than originally anticipated. Next year's budgets should reflect these circumstances.

Analyzing Endowment Manager's Performance

Many nonprofits depend heavily on the earnings that managers generate from the endowment funds. When endowment earnings soar, managers eagerly claim credit but, when they fall, they blame the economy.

Where does the truth lie? Evaluating the causes of the results achieved by endowment fund managers involves yet another application of variance analysis. In this version, the manager is evaluated against a commonly-accepted benchmark of investment management performance. For example, managers of large cap equity funds can be evaluated against the performance of the S&P 500 Index—a measure of the returns generated by the stocks of 500 large cap companies. The manager who achieves a 15 percent return while the S&P 500 Index increases by 22 percent is not performing very well. But one whose return is a negative 10 percent while the S&P 500 index dips by 28 percent is doing a very good job indeed. Such analyses can be expanded to incorporate the riskiness of the investments. Managers of high-risk portfolios are expected to earn better returns than the S&P 500 because their investments are riskier than the average stock included in the Index. See Table 11-13 for a typical presentation.

Table 11-13 indicates that Equity Fund A has equaled the performance of the stock market as a whole, as measured by the S&P 500 Index, but Equity Funds B and C have not. One wonders why any of the fund managers continue to be paid when comparable returns can be achieved more cheaply by investing in the stocks constituting the S&P 500 Index. It is premature to judge the bond manager's performance, with only a few quarters of data,

TABLE 11-12 Volume and Price Variance Calculations

Production	Actual Price – Planned Price	×	Actual Volume	=	Price Variance	Actual Volume – Planned Volume	×	Planned Price	=	Volume Variance	Total Variance[a]
Aida	$15 – $15	×	50,000	=	$ 0	50,000 – 40,000	×	$15	=	$150,000	$150,000
La Traviata	$16 – $15	×	60,000	=	60,000	60,000 – 50,000	×	$15	=	150,000	210,000
Fledermaus	$13 – $12	×	40,000	=	40,000	40,000 – 30,000	×	$12	=	120,000	160,000
The Barber of Seville	$16 – $16	×	100,000	=	0	100,000 – 100,000	×	$16	=	0	0
Carmen	$17 – $16	×	70,000	=	70,000	70,000 – 60,000	×	$16	=	160,000	230,000
Total					$170,000					$580,000	$750,000

[a]Total Variance = Price Variance + Volume Variance

TABLE 11-13 **A Sample Endowment Manager's Performance Summary, June 30, 1990**

Manager	2d Quarter 1990	Year to Date 1990	Annualized Performance				
			2 Years	3 Years	4 Years	5 Years	6 Years
Equity Funds							
(1) Equity A	7.1%	3.1%	16.8%	10.2%	12.6%	17.12%	NA
(2) Equity B	2.6	0.6	12.0	8.5	9.4	13.7	NA
(3) Equity C	3.2	(0.4)	9.1	4.0	11.8	15.4	17.9%
Bond Funds							
(4) Bond A	2.4	3.7					
(5) Bond B	3.9	3.3					
(6) Bond C	3.8	1.0					
Benchmarks							
S&P 500 Index	6.3%	3.1%	18.4%	9.2%	13.0%	17.2%	19.4%
Bond Index	3.6	2.8					
90-day U.S. T-Bills	2.0	3.9					
Equity Median	5.8	2.9					
Equity Index	6.0	13.8					
Fixed-Income Median	3.5	2.4					

but the performance of Bond Fund A is sufficiently below that of the market measures to cause some concern in the second quarter of 1990.

Analysis of endowment fund performance should not be performed too frequently. The very best fund managers cannot continuously outperform the market every single month or quarter of a year, even though their *average* performance over a longer period is substantially better than the performance of the market as a whole. Instead, the performance of endowment fund managers should be evaluated at least annually and, if found wanting, the managers should not be given more than one or two more chances to improve. The many nonprofit managers who are commendably loyal to underperforming fund managers may fail to appreciate the substantial financial penalties that poor endowment management exacts.

MANAGING THE PROCESS OF MEASURING AND ANALYZING ACTUAL RESULTS

The process of measuring and analyzing actual results is sometimes called a *performance audit*. Its purpose is to insure that plans were attained at planned levels of effectiveness, efficiency, and quality. The U.S. General Accounting Office (GAO) pioneered audits of the effectiveness of government programs. Its evaluation staff has a broad diversity of competencies, ranging from backgrounds in sociology to accounting. The GAO disseminates its findings in reports that also contain the responses of the program's managers to the GAO findings.

The GAO defines performance audits to include *economy* and *efficiency* and *program audits*. Economy and efficiency audits determine whether the program is operating efficiently and is in compliance with its governing rules and regulations. Program audits, in contrast, determine whether the results desired by the legislature were achieved. The GAO has codified the standards for conducting government audits in its publication *Government Auditing Standards*.[19]

Although performance auditing is not frequently implemented in private nonprofit organizations, *audits of internal controls* are more prevalent. This type of audit evaluates the systems used by management to control the organization, such as the organization chart, the planning and budgeting process, the measurement and analysis of performance, and the motivational systems. It also evaluates the integrity of the accounting system by mapping the flow of financial and other transactions, delineating the checks and balances that exist, and sampling the data produced at various points in this flowchart.

Internal control audits frequently flag problems in managerial control. The internal control auditor is often an accountant who specializes in the services of that nonprofit organization. To maintain his or her independence, the internal auditor reports to the CEO—not to the accounting unit—and to the chairperson of the Audit Committee of the board, if such a committee exists. With this reporting structure, the auditor is, in theory, freer to critique the financial unit's performance.

The internal audit charter of Salick Health Care, Inc., a California health care organization, is presented in Table 11-14.

SUMMARY

The second activity in the managerial control process is that of comparing actual results to those planned. Actual result measures should focus on the private and public benefits; effectiveness and efficiency; and quantity and quality of results achieved. Client satisfaction surveys, peer review, and descriptions of the performance of similar organizations are all useful sources of such measures. Costs are measured on the basis of the product or process; they can include direct or full costs; and they can contain standard or only actual data. Full cost data include direct costs and an allocation of indirect costs, or overhead. Activity-based costing provides a more precise method for allocating indirect costs. Government cost-accounting regulations for programs

[19]Comptroller General of the United States, *Government Auditing Standards* (Washington, DC: U.S. Government Printing Office, 1988).

that are reimbursed for their "costs" should not play a major role in shaping managerial cost-accounting systems.

The standards of performance against which actual results are measured are derived from the budget or through other techniques. Variance analysis delineates the reasons that actual results differ from standard. The most common reasons are that the actual volume, efficiency, and price differed from the plan. It helps focus attention on different managers' responsibilities for the variances.

This part of the managerial control process is sometimes incorporated under the label of the performance audits that evaluate the U.S. government's programs. In private nonprofit organizations, the internal control audit is a useful part of this activity.

TABLE 11-14   Salick Health Care, Inc. (SHCI)—Internal Audits of SHCI Health Care System*

I. GENERAL AUDITING GOALS

SHCI's philosophy focuses on the internal audit as a management tool to assist in the overall direction of the organization. The broad objectives of any audit are to inform management of the status of systems reviewed and to identify ways to improve the system or controls employed. In carrying out these objectives, the internal audit may also assist in educating managers in the development and use of effective internal controls.

The audits are based on objective criteria to evaluate controls employed in SHCI's operations. Controls are related either to administrative (management-oriented) functions or accounting practices.

The sources of criteria regarding administrative controls are company policies, SHCI's contracts, industry standards, federal and state regulations (e.g., California Administrative Code and the Code of Federal Regulations), etc. The source of criteria for accounting controls are the American Institute of Certified Public Accountants and SHCI's established policies and procedures based on AICPA standards.

The method of selecting systems or entities for evaluation is generally based on their significance to the operation and their related financial exposure to SHCI. Internal audits should benefit the company in general and managers in particular. Auditing is not, however, a substitute for management and SHCI does not utilize audits in place of managements' responsibility for the operation and control of systems or operations.

An audit will:

- identify areas for corrective action to improve the overall performance of the unit,
- provide a learning experience for the personnel at the unit audited, the auditor, and other levels of SHCI's management, and
- provide the unit manager with additional support in carrying out his/her tasks.

Effective communication is a vital element needed to maximize the effectiveness of an audit. SHCI encourages its managers to take every opportunity during an audit to obtain an understanding of the purpose, scope, and results of the review.

*Reprinted with permission of Salick Health Care, Inc., Los Angeles, California.

TABLE 11-14 (Continued)

II. PURPOSE

SHCI's Internal Audit Department furnishes management at all levels with independent and objective reviews and analyses. These provide management with information regarding those segments of operation reviewed and suggestions on potential improvements which can be made.

III. ORGANIZATION

The Internal Audit Department is independent of the personnel and functions to be audited. The Director of Internal Audit reports operationally to the Chief Executive Officer of SHCI and periodically to the Audit Committee of the Board of Directors, which has oversight responsibility. This structure permits a greater degree of independence and objectivity, both in fact and in appearance.

IV. SCOPE AND OBJECTIVES

A. Controls—In general, all audits are designed to measure the effectiveness of administrative controls and/or accounting controls.
   1. Administrative controls are those designed to help ensure that company objectives are achieved while using resources efficiently and effectively.
   2. Accounting controls are those generally designed to help ensure that financial data reported are accurate and that company assets are adequately safeguarded by providing accountability over transactions.

B. Types of Audits—The audit emphasis will vary with each unit for two reasons. First, SHCI's contractual commitments may differ for each unit. Second, SHCI's financial exposure is likely to vary from unit to unit. Greater audit emphasis will be given to those areas having the greatest potential financial risk. Every audit and/or audit segment will address, however, one or more of the following questions:
   1. Is the unit achieving the operational and financial objectives that were established by management?
   2. Is the unit using resources efficiently and economically in achieving managements' objectives?
   3. Is the unit complying with company guidelines, contractual requirements, federal and state regulations and legislation, professional and/or industry standards, etc.?
   4. Is the unit employing adequate controls necessary for safeguarding company assets?
   5. Is the unit employing adequate controls to ensure that financial data generated are accurate, reliable, and meaningful?

V. PERFORMANCE OF THE AUDIT

A. Advance Notification—Generally, approximately one month's notification of an impending audit will be given. The purpose of the notification will be to discuss the nature and scope of the review to be conducted. Additionally, the auditor will determine that key personnel will be available and will coordinate efforts with other

TABLE 11-14 (Continued)

ongoing reviews. The first contact will be with the most senior manager having functional authority over the system or entity to be audited. Often, both a senior operational and a financial manager will be notified when an audit cuts across organizational boundaries. Notification to other levels of management will be made by senior management and/or the auditor, but at the discretion of senior management.

B. Conduct of the Audit—The audit will be conducted in a manner which minimizes disruption of the operation and keeps managers informed as to the status of completed segments. Interim information developed during the audit will not be disseminated until validated and discussed with supervisory and management personnel on site.

C. Audit Findings—At the conclusion of the audit or each audit segment, the auditor will present the unit manager with a recommendation worksheet. The worksheet will include:
    1. An assessment of the current status of the standards, procedures, and controls employed;
    2. A statement identifying accepted standards, procedures, and controls established by company management, state and federal regulatory agencies, industry standards, etc.;
    3. Reasons for deviation from accepted standards;
    4. The effect or impact due to deviation from accepted standards;
    5. Recommendations to improve controls and reduce financial exposure;
    6. The unit manager's initial indicating that he/she reviewed the worksheet.

The manager at his/her option, may include comments regarding agreement/disagreement with conclusions reached and/or action planned or taken. Every effort should be made to resolve the differences regarding the factual presentation.

D. Working Paper Verification—Some audit working papers are more sensitive or significant than others for providing a permanent record. These include cash count sheets, narcotic inventory sheets, and other similar schedules. These must be prepared in ink and signed and dated by both the unit manager and auditor. Corrections and revisions must be initialed by both parties.

    Copies of these schedules will be made available to the unit manager for his/her records upon request.

VI. AUDIT REPORTS AND RESPONSES

A. Oral Report.
    1. After the audit, the auditor will notify the unit manager of any additional findings which may have developed, based on further analysis of data obtained.
    2. Prior to issuing the written report, the auditor will brief regional and senior management on the audit results. They may provide additional information which might shed additional light on the audit conclusions. This contact will be documented in the audit working papers. Where appropriate, the auditor will include these views in the final report.

TABLE 11-14 (Continued)

B. Written Report.
    1. The auditor will prepare a report consisting of two sections: an executive summary and a full report. The executive summary is a synopsis of the audit conclusions and recommendations. The full report will consist of the following sections:
        a. Scope and Objectives
        b. Background Information
        c. Overall Opinion
        d. Section-by-Section Analysis
    2. The report will be distributed on a need-to-know basis. The report segments will be distributed to the following supervisors and managers:
        a. Supervisor(s)/Manager(s) in charge of the function(s) audited (billing supervisor, payroll manager, etc.)
        b. Treatment center/clinic management (medical directors and nurse managers)
        c. Regional Director
        d. Vice President and Corporate Controller
        e. Senior Vice President-Director, Professional Services
        f. Senior Vice President-Director of Operations
        g. Executive Vice President and Chief Financial Officer
        h. Chairman of the Board and Chief Executive Officer
        i. Chairperson, Audit Committee of the Board of Directors

Suggested Reading

Measuring Results and Costs

Brown, Richard E., and Hans-Dieter Sproghe. "Governmental Managerial Accounting: What and Where Is It?" *Public Auditing and Finance* (Autumn 1987): 35-46.

Epstein, Paul D. *Using Performance Measurement in Local Government*. New York: Van Nostrand Reinhold, 1984.

Horngren, Charles T., and George Foster. *Cost Accounting: A Managerial Emphasis*. Englewood Cliffs, NJ: Prentice-Hall, 1987.

Suver, James D., and Bruce R. Neumann. *Management Accounting for Health Care Organizations*. Oak Brook, IL: Hospital Financial Management Association, 1981.

Analyzing Variances

Finkler, Steven A. "Flexible Budget Variance Analysis Extended to Patient Activity and DRGs." *Health Care Management Review* (Fall 1985): 21-34.

Holder, William W., and Jan Williams. "Better Cost Control with Flexible Budgets and Variance Analysis." *Hospital Financial Management* (January 1976): 12-20.

Sherman, H. David. *Service Organization Productivity Management*. Hamilton, Ontario: The Society of Management Accountants of Canada, 1988.

Welleve, Anthony. "Variance Analysis: A Tool for Cost Control." *The Journal of Nursing Administration* (July-August 1982): 23-26.

Performance Auditing and Internal Control

American Institute of Certified Public Accountants. *Internal Control.* New York, 1979.

Association of Government Accountants. *Executive Reporting on Internal Controls in Government.* Washington DC: U.S. General Accounting Office, 1980.

Brown, Richard E., Thomas P. Gallagher, and Meredith C. Williams. *Auditing Performance in Government.* New York: John Wiley & Sons, 1982.

Herbert, Leo, Larry Killough, and Allen Walter Steiss. *Accounting and Control for Government and Other Nonbusiness Organizations.* New York: McGraw-Hill, 1987.

U.S. General Accounting Office. *Standards for Audit of Governmental Organizations.* Washington, DC: U.S. Government Printing Office, 1988.

DISCUSSION QUESTIONS

1. What are the dimensions for measuring the results of nonprofit organizations?

2. What are the categories of outcome measures?

3. How can quality be measured?

4. Define *peer review* and its role in the managerial control process.

5. What are the three different ways in which costs can be measured?

6. What is the most prevalent cost-accounting method in nonprofit organizations?

7. Define indirect costs, direct costs, allocations, the step-down method, and activity-based costing.

8. How does activity costing differ from other methods of full costing?

9. What is variance analysis?

10. What are the most frequently computed variances?

11. How are standards of performance delineated?

12. How should the performance of an endowment manager be evaluated?

13. Define performance audits, economy and efficiency audits, program audits, and audits of internal control.

14. Think about the process of measuring and analyzing results in a nonprofit organization with which you are familiar. How are results and costs measured? How are the differences between planned and actual performance analyzed? How is the process managed? What changes would you recommend in the process? What would be the impact of your recommended changes?

EXERCISE

The Oklahoma Museum's maintenance department cleans the two galleries in which the museum's collections are viewed by the public, as well as the museum's other space. The maintenance department's cleaning people are paid the rates shown in Table 1 on page 391. Its other costs are shown in Table 2. One of the museum's two galleries contains oil paintings whose condition requires an unusual maintenance program. The cleaners assigned to that gallery use twice as much time and supplies as the cleaners assigned to the other gallery. The galleries and the administrative and admissions areas each occupy one-third of the total square area of the museum. Cleaning the galleries is estimated to require half of the total supplies and labor hours. The two galleries each occupy the same amount of space.

Table 1

Maintenance Department: Labor Expenses

Salary and benefits cost per hour	$ 10
Number of hours worked per year	20,000

Table 2

Maintenance Department: Other Expenses

Supplies	$ 70,000
Administration of maintenance department	150,000
Rent	30,000

1.   What is the cost of cleaning the oil painting gallery?

2.   The cost of hiring an outside company to clean the oil painting gallery is $115,000 a year. The outside company's services are at a quality level equal to the museum's present maintenance staff. Should the museum hire the outside firm? If it does, all the expenses, except for labor and supplies, will remain the same.

Cases

CASE 11.1 Hyatt Hill Health Center

"These numbers don't mean a thing," said Hank Clemens. "They don't reflect what my department does and needlessly make us look terrible."

Mr. Clemens was talking to his fellow department heads, the administrative staff, and the executive director of the Hyatt Hill Health Center (HHHC) at their weekly executive committee meeting. The subject of Hank's ire was the control system which was recently installed in the health center.

This case was made possible by an organization which chose to remain anonymous. Professor Regina E. Herzlinger prepared this case.

Copyright © 1989 by the President and Fellows of Harvard College. Harvard Business School case 190-009. Revised January 1993.

BACKGROUND

The Hyatt Hill Health Center was established in New York City. It was sponsored by the Fowler Hospital, widely considered to be the leading hospital in the United States for the quality of its medical care, research, and teaching. The health center was established, on an experimental basis, to provide community-centered health care to the residents of the town of Bedford, in which it was located. Bedford was a lower-income area which suffered from a heavy incidence of medical, dental, and psychiatric problems. For example, over 40 percent of Bedford's adults needed dental plates, and a large proportion of its adult population were alcoholics and drug abusers.

Because there were few physicians residing in Bedford, its residents used the emergency room of the Fowler Hospital as a substitute for a family physician. As a result, they received sporadic therapeutic medical care and very few of them received any preventive care in the form of yearly check-ups, x-rays, and so on.

The purpose of the health center was to provide adequate preventive as well as therapeutic care and to do so by becoming an accepted force in the Bedford community. This wasn't an easy mission; Bedford was geographically isolated from the rest of New York City, and its residents, who were largely composed of one closely-knit ethnic group, were traditionally suspicious of any "outsiders." Despite the heavy incidence of emotional problems in the area, the residents of Bedford were particularly resistant to receiving the services of social workers and psychiatrists. The personnel in these departments spent a great deal of time in the community trying to break down this resistance.

Organization and Personnel

The Hyatt Hill Health Center is composed of the following departments: pediatrics, internal medicine, nursing, mental health, social service, nutrition, dental, and specialists. Most of its practitioners hold joint appointments at the Fowler Hospital, are considered to be of high professional caliber, and are incurring substantial opportunity costs by working at the health center. They are highly effective practitioners who have dedicated themselves to demonstrating that a community health center can indeed provide effective therapeutic and preventive medical care and, thus, have a significant impact on its target area.

In addition to its goal of delivering community health care, the HHHC also served as a training ground for members of the Fowler Hospital or NYC Department of Health staff who were interested in community medicine. Training activities were conducted in all of HHHC's departments but were particularly concentrated in the mental health, social service, and nutrition departments.

Funding

The health center, which has a yearly operating budget of nearly $1,000,000, is funded from a variety of sources, including the Fowler Hospital. It is hoped that the HHHC will eventually become financially self-sufficient and not require hospital funds for its operation. At the present time, the largest portion of its funds come from the federal government. In return, the health center must provide quarterly reports about the characteristics of its patients, the kinds of services they received, and the impact of the center on the community. To gather these data, all practitioners completed a form immediately after every encounter with a patient. The data on the encounter form are then entered into Fowler Hospital's system.

THE CONTROL SYSTEM—BACKGROUND

Late in 1989, a researcher of the costs of ambulatory medical care facilities visited the health center. At the time, Dr. Steven Kyler, the health center's executive director, was becoming increasingly concerned over the potential for the achievement of the HHHC's financial self-sufficiency goal. Although the center had a good financial accounting system for billing and external reporting, it had no managerial accounting data. Dr. Kyler thus didn't know the total costs of his departments, of different kinds of cases, and of his practitioners. Since the only financial data available to him were the costs of the different line items on his budget, Dr. Kyler couldn't really assess the feasibility of his center's accomplishing its financial self-sufficiency goals. He, thus, agreed to the installation of a management control system which would provide him with the data he wanted.

THE CONTROL SYSTEM—MECHANICS

The management control system was based on the existing data system and provided the following data for each of the HHHC's departments:

(1) Average monthly cost, per encounter and per hour spent in seeing patients, for each practitioner
(2) Average monthly cost of the different kinds of encounters entered on the encounter form
(3) A comparison of actual costs to a standard cost, based on the average costs, in the past, of that department

A sample of the data for the social service department is contained in **Exhibit 1**. The flow chart used to compute the costs is in **Exhibit 2** and the total cost data are in **Exhibit 3**.

These data were distributed to Dr. Kyler and his department chiefs about two weeks after the end of each month. They enabled the HHHC's management to compare the efficiency of different practitioners in performing the same kind of work. They also enabled comparison of the relative efficiency and utilization of capacity of different departments.

The key data input for the control system was the time entered by the practitioner on the encounter form for each service performed. To check on the validity of these data, a time sheet was completed by all the practitioners, on a daily basis, for a full month, once every three months. The direct patient care category on the time sheet was, by definition, identical to the time entered on the encounter form. Continuous comparisons were made on the total times derived from the two forms to ensure that the time entered was valid. The time sheet data for the social service department are in **Exhibit 4**.

As indicated by the time sheet categories, the HHHC's departments performed a number of activities other than that of providing direct patient care. Yet only the direct patient care activities generated revenue. If the HHHC were ever to be self-sufficient, the revenues created by the practitioners' medical care activities would have to absorb the costs of all their other activities. Thus, the financial data produced by the control system included the costs of all the time spent by the practitioners in HHHC—regardless of whether they spent it in seeing patients or in the other activities listed on the time sheets.

On the basis of these data, the social service department didn't seem to be very efficient. Its costs per encounter were higher than those of any other department, and its practitioners used less of their time for seeing patients than did those of the other departments. (See **Exhibit 5**.)

Dr. Kyler was quite disturbed by these data and discussed them with the head of the social service department at the executive committee meetings. "Why are your costs per encounter so high?" he asked. "Your department's average costs are twice as high as those of the medical department, and yet the social workers' salaries are half of those of the physicians. You fellows had better shape up. You're costing all of us a lot of money."

ASSIGNMENT

1. What is the purpose of the Hyatt Hill Health Center?
2. How do you interpret the patterns in **Exhibit 5**?
3. Is the control system consistent with the purposes of the health center? If not, how should it be modified?

EXHIBIT 1 **Hyatt Hill Health Center—Cost Data Social Service Department**

	Entire Department	Practitioners 1	2	3	4
Total Hours Available	400	100	100	100	100
Total Hours Spent in Patient Care	100	20	20	50	10
Hours Spent/Hours Available	25%	20%	20%	50%	10%
Cost per Hour Spent in Patient Care	$50.00	$62.50	$62.50	$25.00	$125.00
Cost per Encounter	$50.00	$125.00	$62.50	$20.83	$125.00
Initial Interview, Alone		$125.00	$62.50	$20.83	$125.00
Initial Interview, Family		$125.00		$20.83	$62.50
Additional Interviews, Alone			$62.50	$20.83	$187.50
Additional Interviews, Family				$31.25	

EXHIBIT 2 **Hyatt Hill Health Center**

Symbol	Meaning
$\$x$	Fixed cost of the department
$\$Y_j$	Salary per minute of Physician j
Z_j	Time, in minutes, that Physician j was available
N_{ij}	Number of encounters of Type i by Physician j
T_{ij}	Time spent on encounters of Type i by Physician j
NW_j	Number of walk-in patients treated by Physician j
Nr_j	Number of patients who made appointments treated by Physician j
Tr_j	Time spend on appointment encounters by Physician j

(1) The total time spent in patient care by Physician j:

$$T_j = \sum_i T_{ij}$$

(2) The direct labor cost of Physician j:

$$\$DLC_j = T_j \times \$Y_j$$

(3) The total time spent in nonpatient care activities by Physician j:

$$Q_j = Z_j - T_j$$

(4) The direct overhead cost of Physician j:

$$\$DOH_j = Q_j \times \$Y_j$$

(5) The total time spent in nonpatient care activities by physicians in the department:

$$Q = \sum_j Q_j$$

(6) The fixed overhead cost of Physician j:

$$\$FOH_j = \frac{Q_j}{Q} \times \$x$$

(7) The total cost of Physician j:

$$\$TC_j = \$DLC_j + \$DOH_j + \$FOH_j$$

(8) The proportion of the total cost of Physician j attributable to encounter of Type i:

$$\$TC_{ij} = \frac{T_{ij}}{T_j} \times \$TC_j$$

(9) The average cost of encounters of Type i for Physician j:

$$\$Ac_{ij} = \frac{\$TC_{ij}}{N_{ij}}$$

EXHIBIT 2 (Continued)

---

(10) The average cost per encounter for Physician j:

$$\$AC_j = \frac{\$TC_j}{\Sigma N_{ij}}$$

(11) The total costs of walk-ins and regular appointments for Physician j:

$$\$TCw_j = \frac{Tw_j}{t_j} \times \$TC_j$$

(12) The average cost of walk-ins and regular appointments for Physician j:

$$\$ACw_j = \frac{\$TCw_j}{Nw_j}$$

$$\$ACr_j = \frac{\$TCr_j}{Nr_j}$$

(13) The average cost for the department of walk-ins and regular appointments:

$$\$ACw = \frac{\displaystyle\sum_j TCw_j}{\displaystyle\sum_j Nw_j}$$

$$\$ACr_j = \frac{\displaystyle\sum_j TCr_j}{\displaystyle\sum_j Nr_j}$$

(14) The average cost for the department of an encounter:

$$AC = \frac{\displaystyle\sum_j TCw_j + \sum_j TCr_j}{\displaystyle\sum_j Nw_j + \sum_j Nr_j}$$

(15) The total cost for the department of encounters of Type i:

$$\$TC_i = \sum_j TC_{ij}$$

(16) The average cost for the department of encounters of Type i:

$$\$AC_i = \sum_j \frac{\$TC_i}{N_{ij}}$$

EXHIBIT 3 Hyatt Hill Health Center

	Salaries			Furniture and Equipment	Supplies	Rent	Heat and Power	Departmental Fixed Costs							
	Direct Patient Care	Direct Overhead	Fringe					Evaluation	Medical Records and Accounting	Administration	Service Reps	HHC Outpatient	General	Total	% of Total
Pediatrics	$ 2,400	$ 2,956	$ 610	$ 16	$ 441	$ 162	$ 20	$1,117	$ 817	$ 490	$ 220	$ 40	$ 330	$ 8,609	11.9%
Internal Medicine	3,336	1,331	653	23	467	189	33	894	1,170	533	239	43	359	9,270	12.9
Nutrition	537	260	68	4	-	42	7	381	264	189	81	15	127	1,975	2.7
Nursing	4,148	4,371	657	62	320	398	60	394	455	2,313	931	187	1,557	15,853	22.0
Dental	1,140	2,407	493	84	150	162	20	333	0	877	-	71	590	6,327	6.6
Mental Health	737	4,814	554	41	-	382	47	331	187	1,246	-	101	838	9,278	12.8
Social Services	502	4,906	421	30	-	301	40	458	258	1,720	243	139	1,158	10,176	14.1
Specialists	854	447	-	14	-	-	-	269	413	112	51	9	75	2,244	3.1
Eye Clinic	478	172	29	96	-	126	13	165	253	267	-	22	179	1,800	2.5
Laboratory	1,147	645	143	46	275	41	7	-	666	567	243	46	382	4,208	5.8
Radiology	139	392	49	189	272	68	7	-	387	189	80	15	127	1,914	2.7
Therapists	-	-	-	7	-	47	7	39	25	95	40	8	64	332	0.5
Total	$15,418	$21,701	$3,677	$612	$1,925	$1,918	$261	$4,381	$4,895	$8,598	$2,128	$696	$5,786	$71,986	

EXHIBIT 4 **Hyatt Hill Health Center—Social Service Department Time Allocation**

	Activity				
	Direct Patient Care	*Indirect Patient Care*	*Community Development*	*Training*	*Lunch, Breaks, Administrative Activities*
Time Spent (hours)	100	100	80	80	40
Percent of Total Time Available	25%	25%	20%	20%	10%
Monthly Costs of Activity	$1,250	$1,250	$1,000	$1,000	$500

EXHIBIT 5 **Hyatt Hill Health Center—Source of Difference Between Standard and Actual Cost per Visit, First Quarter**

Department	Standard Cost per Visit	Actual Cost per Visit	Difference (Variance) between Standard and Actual Cost	Differential Effect of Change in Efficiency[a]	Differential Effect of Change in Utilization of Capacity[b]
Social Service	$61.10	$27.31	+$33.79	+$5.37	+$28.42
Mental Health	53.65	27.77	+25.88	+0.23	+25.65
Dental Health	42.88	25.72	+17.16	+0.41	+16.75
Nutrition	34.97	20.45	+14.52	+6.04	+8.48
Pediatrics	25.64	22.16	+3.48	−0.57	+4.05
Internal Medicine	24.72	24.00	+0.72	−0.14	+0.86
Nursing	28.34	36.20	−7.56	−11.15	+3.29

[a]Efficiency effects result from changes in the time spent with each patient.
[b]Utilization of capacity effects result from changes in the percentage of their available time that practitioners devote to seeing patients.

CASE 11.2 Nasus School of Art

The Nasus School of Art was a community-based, start-up endeavor, offering courses in painting and sculpture to neighborhood children. Because its financial resources were limited, its instructors agreed to be paid for each child who attended a session, rather than a flat salary. But the materials cost could not be varied with the number of children.

The Nasus School was administered by volunteers and received rent-free space in a neighborhood church. One volunteer, Joe Doe, was in charge of the instructors; another, Josie Doesie, purchased the materials; and a third, David Ogilvy, was in charge of publicizing the school and recruiting students. The painting instructor was Ms. O'Keefe and the sculpture instructor was known as Michael-B. The school expected its total costs to be $365, but actual costs were $490. (See **Exhibit 1**.)

ASSIGNMENT

1. Why were actual costs different from those expected?
2. How much did Mr. Doe, Ms. Doesie, Mr. Ogilvy, Ms. O'Keefe, and Michael-B each contribute to the differences between expected and actual costs?

EXHIBIT 1 Nasus School of Art

	Painting		Sculpture	
	Standard	*Actual*	*Standard*	*Actual*
Pay per student/class	$5	$6	$9	$9
Materials/class	$30	$10	$150	$90
Number of students	10	20	15	30
Cost per student/class	$8	$6.50	$19	$12
Total cost	$80	$130	$285	$360

This case was prepared by Professor Regina E. Herzlinger.

CASE 11.3 North Shore Birth Center

INTRODUCTION

Dorothy Kuell, who prompted Beverly Hospital to set up a birth center, described the vision of the center's founders:

> At a birth center, birth would be a true family experience. There would be no limit on visiting hours or on the number of family and friends attending the birth. A mother would not be confined to one room: she could walk outside, sit in the living room, rest in the bedroom or take a bath.[1]

This vision became reality when the North Shore Birth Center opened in November 1980.

INDUSTRY OVERVIEW

History

The North Shore Birth Center was one of a growing number of alternatives to the hospital birth experience. Birth centers were the culmination of a long evolution in the preferred birthing location and the professional management of the delivery process.[2]

During the eighteenth and nineteenth centuries, childbirth in the United States underwent a gradual shift away from the earlier "social childbirth," in which the woman in labor was surrounded by female friends and relatives, and was attended by an experienced (often salaried) midwife. Male physicians gradually became more relied upon, especially in the event of delivery complications. In the 1950s, childbirth became more specialized, with obstetricians replacing general practitioners. The number of lay or "granny" midwives practicing in the U.S. declined from an estimated 20,700 in 1948 to approximately 1,800 in 1976, located mostly in low-income or remote areas where no professional services were available.

As management of the child delivery process became more technical, so did the birth setting. At the beginning of the twentieth century, over 95 percent of deliveries in the U.S. took place at home, but by 1955 almost 95 percent took place at the hospital. This shift was prompted by advances in medical science, particularly the development of anesthesia (which allowed hospitals to offer a "painless" delivery)

[1] Deborah Cramer, "Birth Without Doctors," *The Boston Globe*, 12 April 1981.
[2] L. Cannoodt, S. Sieverts, and M. Schachter, "Alternatives to the Conventional In-Hospital Delivery: The Childbearing Center Experience," *Acta Hospitalia* 22, no. 4 (Winter 1982).

Professor Regina E. Herzlinger prepared this case along with Joyce Lallman under the supervision of Professor Nancy Kane.

and safer surgical intervention techniques for obstetrical emergencies. Hospitals became the only setting with the technical and professional capacity necessary to respond to all medical complications.

During the last decade, the hospital delivery model was challenged. One article cites the following factors:

> The women's movement has affected maternity services, reacting against the perceived male domination of the medical profession. . . . In addition, from within as well as from outside the medical profession, there have been growing expressions of concern about the rising rates of cesarean deliveries, the increased levels of medication and the psychological consequences of the often impersonalized hospital atmosphere. Nurse-midwives have asserted their competence to perform uncomplicated maternity care and have begun to question much of present-day obstetrics as being needlessly (and perhaps dangerously) overmedicated.[3]

Birth Centers

Birth centers, in contrast to the hospital, were designed to offer a more homelike setting. Women and their companions often take classes in nutrition, relaxation, and breathing, and can spend up to ten times as many hours with nurse-midwives than they would spend with an obstetrician before a typical hospital birth.

Birth centers' costs were one-third the cost of a typical $2,500 to $3,500 hospital birth including physician fee. Many insurers included reimbursement of approved birth centers as a regular part of their medical coverge. "We're in favor of anything that saves money without endangering anybody," said a spokesperson for the industry. In 1984, 18 states had regulated birth centers, 20 (including the District of Columbia) were exploring or drafting regulations, and 13 had not started the rule-making process.

Birth centers cater only to low-risk natural childbirths, but they may in the future capture a substantial share of the $7 billion to $8 billion a year baby-delivery business. In 1983, Dr. John S. Short, executive vice president of Health Resources Corp. of America, Inc. (a multihospital system based in Houston), started a chain of birthing centers to be developed in joint ventures with obstetricians. He predicted that from 30 percent to 40 percent of births would be done in one-day stays within five years. Birth centers would compete on the basis of their lower costs. In his experience, a 7,500-square-foot center cost $1.2 million to build, with facilities for elective and emergency surgery. A 5,000- to 6,000-square-foot center without operating rooms would cost $500,000 to build. His first center experienced a 25 percent drop-out rate in the prenatal period.[4]

Safety Issues

The American College of Obstetricians and Gynecologists stated that the hospital setting provided the safest environment for mothers and infants during labor, delivery, and the postpartum period. From 10 percent to 20 percent of women using birth centers for delivery have to be transferred to hospitals. Dr. Bruce Shepard,

[3]Ibid.
[4]"Alternative Services," *Modern Healthcare* (December 1983).

author of "The Complete Guide to Women's Health," expressed reservations about birth centers despite his advocacy of more "humanistic" obstetrics:

> It's difficult to prove with statistics that the birth center is less safe than the hospital, but my strong inclination is that it would be less safe. I would rather see birth-center practices in fully equipped hospitals because when you have an emergency in obstetrics, you have just minutes for intervention. Between 10 percent and 30 percent of high-risk situations emanate from low-risk mothers. You can't select those that need to deliver in a hospital in advance.[5]

Other physicians, however, support birth centers. A representative of Dr. Short's birth center chain said, "We are already finding doctors more interested in the idea, either in joint ventures with entrepreneurs or in establishing their own centers. They want to protect their market, and they are responding to insurers' outcry about rising medical costs."

A matched sample of a large number of women at a birth center comparable to the one at Beverly Hospital and the maternity service at a large teaching hospital revealed more favorable outcomes for the women at the birth center. However, the percentage of babies with unfavorable risk profiles was higher at the birth center.[6]

Consumer Preferences

Consumer surveys indicated that although family involvement in the childbirth process has increased, most consumers preferred hospitals over birth centers; in one, 79 percent of the female respondents planning to have children preferred hospitalization to a free-standing birthing center.[7] Eighty-five percent preferred a doctor at childbirth, whether it be in a hospital or at a freestanding birthing center, instead of having a nonphysician practitioner or midwife; some 4 percent preferred birth in a hospital assisted by a nonphysician medical practitioner or midwife instead of a doctor; and 11 percent preferred childbirth in a separate birthing center not attached to a hospital but where a physician assisted with the birth.

The Childbearing Center in New York City, in operation since 1975, found that:

> The population delivering at [the Childbearing Center] is clearly atypical of the total childbearing population in New York City. The women are likely to be between 25 and 34 years of age, white, and better educated than the general population of women bearing children. Few of them depend on Medicaid (government health insurance for the poor). The occupation of almost half of the women is either professional or managerial.[8]

[5]J. R. Brandstrader, "As More Women Have Babies in Birth Centers, Doctors, Hospitals Rethink Obstetric Procedures," *The Wall Street Journal*, 29 November 1983.
[6]Gigliola Baruffi, Woodrow S. Dellinger, Jr., Donna M. Stobino, Alice Rudolph, Rebecca Y. Timmons, and Alan Ross, "A Study of Pregnancy Outcomes in a Maternity Center and a Tertiary Care Hospital," *American Journal of Public Health* 74, no. 9 (September 1984): 973-978.
[7]Bill Jackson and Joyce Jensen, "Home Care Tops Connsumer's List," *Modern Healthcare* 14, no. 6 (May 1, 1984): 88-90.
[8]Canoodt et al., "Alternatives to the Conventional In-Hospital Delivery."

Birth Rates

There were 3,680,537 births in the United States during 1982; the birth rate was 15.9 live births per 1,000 population; and the fertility rate was 67.3 live births per 1,000 women aged 15-44 years.

The birth rates per 1,000 population increased by 2 percent or less in four geographic divisions: New England, Middle Atlantic, South Atlantic, and West South Central. Rates declined by 1 percent in the rest of the U.S.[9] Massachusetts resident births continued to increase in 1981 to 73,931, a 1.8 percent rise over 1980. Of these births, 99.2 percent occurred in hospitals. Fifty-eight hospitals operated maternity units in 1981 with the number of births ranging from 61 at Nantucket Cottage Hospital to 7,099 at Brigham and Women's. Almost 26 percent of births occurred in only four hospitals. The total number of births which occurred en route, at home, or in a birthing center was 577; 45 of the 58 hospitals with maternity units had more births than the total of nonhospital births.[10]

NORTH SHORE BIRTH CENTER

Development

Prior to the establishment of the birth center, Beverly Hospital's 16-bed maternity unit was running at 50-60 percent occupancy. Births had dropped from 1,300 in the late 1960s to 518 in 1976, caused by a decline in the overall birth rate and by increased competition from other hospitals. The nearby Hunt Hospital in Danvers had 250 to 300 births per year in the early 1960s, but by 1976 it had 500 births per year. Home births in the Beverly area had been increasing, and were estimated at 100 to 120 per year in the late 1970s. The obstetricians at Beverly Hosital during this period developed innovative practices, even allowing fathers to attend deliveries except in those cases when anesthesia was administered. They also developed one of the first birthing rooms on the North Shore.

When Dorothy Kuell came to Beverly Hospital in 1977 as the new maternity coordinator, she joined local consumers and midwives in the effort to establish a birth center. The North Shore Health Planning Council recognized the need by including it in its health systems plan. The center opened in November 1980 with two certified nurse-midwives as staff. They were already well known by consumers who supported natural childbirth, and brought many potential clients with them.

Services

A client was first screened to determine risk status. Risky clients were referred to the maternity services within Beverly Hospital, where they were followed by an obstetrician and, if they chose, a nurse-midwife. "Normal low risks" returned to the birth center for education on such topics as nutrition and exercise. The client's partner was encouraged to accompany her on these visits, so the couple could do its own

[9]National Center for Health Statistics, *Monthly Vital Statistics Report* 33, no. 6 (September 1984).
[10]Registry of Vital Statistics, *1981 Annual Report of Vital Statistics of Massachusetts*, Massachusetts Department of Public Health, Document #1.

prenatal check-ups, urine tests, and record keeping. The nurse-midwives met weekly with the medical director to review client care and to refer high-risk clients. A client with no complications could deliver her baby without ever seeing a doctor or stepping into a hospital.

When a client was admitted to the birth center for delivery, the nurse-midwife performed a complete evaluation, including an admission exam and reassignment of risk status, if appropriate. The nurse-midwife stayed with the client during labor to provide continuous physical and emotional support, including breathing relaxation exercises, to determine client wishes regarding physical position during delivery (sitting, lying, or squatting), and to administer local anesthetics if deemed appropriate. Immediately after birth, a healthy baby was placed in the mother's arms to encourage bonding.

If any emergencies arose during or after the birth, the mother and/or baby were transferred immediately to the hospital. Those without complications were generally discharged before 12 hours postpartum; most went home after 5 hours.

Although Beverly Hospital administrators predicted about 75 births at the center the first year, between November 1980 and mid-January 1981, 61 clients were accepted into the program (see **Exhibit 1**). Of the total 70 intrapartum transfers and the 760 birth center births, there were 23 unexpected complications (see **Exhibit 2**). A survey of clients showed that 65 percent were from Beverly Hospital's normal service area and 35 percent were from towns outside this area (including towns as far away as Cambridge). When asked where they would have delivered if not at the birth center, 31 percent cited Beverly Hospital, 27 percent cited other hospitals, and 16 percent claimed they would have delivered at home (see **Exhibit 3**).

Operations

The center was located 400 feet from the driveway of the hospital's emergency room in a building constructed in 1950 as a residence for the hospital's chief administrative officer. It was equipped for use as a birth center at a cost of approximately $20,000 including $3,000 for an incubator, $5,400 for a handicapped ramp, walkway, and fire alarm system, and $3,200 for other building improvements. It consisted of a living room, kitchen, two bedrooms, two bathrooms, an office, and two exam rooms. The center would accommodate four women in labor or delivery at one time; there were two beds and two fold-out couches. The atmosphere was cozy; emergency equipment (such as oxygen) was hidden behind bedroom closet doors.

When the center first opened, it was staffed by two midwives. Because each birth was attended by both, they were on call continuously. In addition, they conducted home visits the day after each baby was born. Their starting salaries were about $18,000 per year.

By 1984, three midwives were employed (including the director). Two were at the center on any one day, except that all three were present on Thursdays for consultation with the medical director. Responsibility for being "in charge" of clinical services and births was rotated among the three midwives.

Administration

The director of the birth center had dual reporting responsibilities. For clinical purposes, the center was under the supervision of the chief of obstetrics. During their weekly meetings, they discussed prenatal patients' risk status. For administrative purposes, the center was considered another department of Beverly Hospital, and the director met weekly with the hospital's executive vice president. The birth center did not have its own business manager, but instead relied on the assistance of the hospital's business staff.

According to Beverly Hospital's budget director:

> The midwives at first had difficulty accommodating to institutional policies. When they were asked to choose which one would be the director, they resisted, saying, "No, we're all equals." They also resisted the idea of merit evaluation. They made their own statements to the press without consulting the hospital's public relations staff, and they made expenditures without proper budgetary authority. I've spent a lot of time teaching them about administration. When it comes to marketing, though, the midwives themselves are the best marketing tool—their clients respect them so much.

Ms. Ventre explained:

> I believe in consensus management and a system of peer review with input from the medical director. I feel it is important for the hospital to acknowledge that the birth center is an *alternative* service concept.

Charge Structure and Financing

In 1984, services cost an all-inclusive $1,045 at the birth center. Beverly Hospital's fees alone were $2,200, exclusive of physician fees (usually around $1,000). Birth center clients were encouraged to visit the hospital's business office when they first enrolled to determine whether they would be covered by insurance. In a survey of birth center clients, 32 percent were covered by Blue Cross, 35 percent were covered by commercial insurers, 5 percent were covered by Medicaid, and 27 percent were self-paying clients.

Charges for Beverly Hospital's in-house and birth center services can be found in **Exhibit 4**. If a birth center client was transferred to the hospital for delivery, the client paid the birth center rate for prenatal care, plus the regular hospital charge for the delivery, plus a transfer charge of $165 to cover the midwives' time. The bad debt rate at the center was slightly lower than the hospital's overall bad debt rate because many of the clients felt that they were "part of" the center. **Exhibit 5** contains the center's financial results.

BEVERLY HOSPITAL/BIRTH CENTER RELATIONSHIP

The birth center and Beverly Hospital had internal conflicts. Not unexpectedly, there were some difficulties in developing the initial protocols, which outlined the medical procedures to be followed at the birth center. Also, the midwives and physicians disagreed over certain issues, such as the point at which a woman experiencing a difficult labor should be transferred to the hospital's delivery room, or how the baby should be handled immediately after delivery. On the other hand, the hospital medical staff shared the midwives' concern for the mother-child relationship. For instance, after an extremely difficult and long labor the nurse picked up the newly delivered child to wash it. She was stopped by the anesthesiologist, who said, "Bring that baby back here! He hasn't bonded with his mother yet!"

Ms. Ventre mentioned her concerns:

Our situation sometimes leads to problems in how we are perceived by hospital personnel. Women come to the birth center with their own ideas. They've read the books and done their own research. If they get referred to the hospital, they may not be "good" patients from the physicians' perspective. They tend to challenge their physicians.

The positive effects of the birth center on Beverly Hospital may well outweigh the start-up difficulties. Dorothy Kuell explained:

Many of the midwives' ideas have spread to the hospital. We also have an assertive nursing staff at the hospital. The hospital set up a "women's health service," staffed by a certified nurse-midwife, who runs an in-house prenatal service and maternity service on similar protocols as the birth center.

Dr. Ramini, chief of obstetrics, noted:

Nurse-midwives have more training in natural childbirth than most obstetricians. Consequently, physicians look at birth as potentially hazardous, while nurse-midwives look at birth as a normal, healthy event with only an occasional problem.[11]

ASSIGNMENT

1. Was it a good financial idea for the Beverly Hospital to sponsor the birth center?
2. What managerial skills are critical to its success?
3. Does the birth center meet a social need or does it merely duplicate already existing facilities?

[11]"A Renaissance for Midwifery," *The Boston Globe*, 12 April 1981.

EXHIBIT 1 **North Shore Birth Center—Births by Hospital of Occurrence, 1970, 1975, 1980, and 1981**

Name and Location of Hospital	1970	1975	1980	1981	1980 / 1975	1981 / 1980
Addison Gilbert, Gloucester	443	342	372	333	+8%	(10.4%)
Anna Jacques, Newburyport	448	572	771	666	+35%	(14%)
Beverly Hospital, Beverly	951	560	711	852	+27%	+20%
Hunt Memorial, Danvers	397	487	480	500	0%	+4%
Lynn Hospital, Lynn	1,400	1,362	1,344	1,289	0%	(4%)
Salem Hospital, Salem	1,358	962	1,143	1,146	+19%	0%
Union Hospital, Lynn	854	0	0	0		

To:	Distance from Beverly Hospital	
	Distance (Miles)	*Drive Time (Minutes)*
Hunt Memorial, Danvers	4.2	12
Salem Hospital, Salem	4.5	19
Atlanti-Care Medical Centers:		
Union Hospital, Lynn	12.5	19
Lynn Hospital, Lynn	7.9	33
Addison Gilbert Hospital, Gloucester	13.4	18

Source: Beverly Hospital

EXHIBIT 2 **North Shore Birth Center—Birth Center Statistics**

	1983-84	1982-83	1981-82
Total Births	228	213	225
Transfers	19	16	23
Unexpected Complications	5	9	5
Risked Out	28	24	24
Infant Transfers	2	3	2

EXHIBIT 3   North Shore Birth Center—Survey of First 62 Clients

Residence of Birth Center Clients			Where Birth Center Clients Would Have Delivered Otherwise	
A. *Beverly Hospital's Normal OB Service Area*	40	65%	1. Beverly Hospital (Beverly)	19
1. Beverly	9		2. Beverly or Addison Gilbert	1
2. Manchester	3		3. Addison Gibert (Gloucester)	2
3. Gloucester	6		4. Hunt (Danvers)	2
4. Ipswich	6		5. Salem (Salem)	2
5. Danvers	5		6. Other Hospitals	10
6. Salem	4		a. New England Memorial	
7. Hamilton	2		(Stoneham)	2
8. Wenham	1		b. Mt. Auburn (Cambridge)	1
9. Magnolia	1		c. Mt. Auburn or Beth Israel	2
10. Essex	1		d. Beth Israel (Boston)	2
11. Boxford	1		e. Anna Jacques (Newburyport)	1
12. Topsfield	1		f. Taunton (Taunton)	1
			g. Leonard Morse (Natick)	1
B. *Other Towns*	22	35%	h. Winchester (Winchester)	1
13. Lynn	2		7. At home	10
14. Newbury	1		8. Unknown	17
15. West Newbury	2			
16. Middleton	1			
17. Marblehead	1			
18. Watertown	1			
19. Billerica	1			
20. Arlington	1			
21. Woburn	1			
22. Brighton	1			
23. Hardwick	1			
24. Andover	1			
25. Cambridge	1			
25. Somerville	1			
27. Taunton	1			
28. Littleton	1			
29. Medford	1			
30. Stoughton	1			
31. Haverhill	1			

EXHIBIT 4 **North Shore Birth Center—Beverly Hospital Corporation Special Services—Charges**

Service	Variable of Measure	Rate Effective 10/01/83
Delivery Room		
1. Delivery Room—C-Section	C-birth	$ 556.00
2. Del Rm—C-Section Recovery Rm	C-birth	134.00
3. Fetal Monitor	Delivery	70.00
4. Vaginal Delivery	Delivery	413.00
5. Birthing Room	Delivery	413.00
6. D-C After Delivery	Procedure	59.00
7. Birthing Room—Extended Stay	Per hour	25.00
8. Labor Room Nonstress Test	Test	30.00
9. Labor Room Stress Test	Test	40.00
10. Repair After Delivery	Procedure	178.00
11. Del Rm—Disposable Linensuit	Linensuit	6.00
12. Del Rm—Disposable Lap Sponge	Sponge	20.00
13. Delivery—Recovery Room	Delivery	119.00
14. Medical Labor Observation	Delivery	30.00
Alternative Birth Center		
15. ABC Prenatal and Delivery	Delivery	1,045.00
16. ABC Prenatal Only	Prenatal care	330.00
17. ABC Delivery Only	Delivery	715.00
18. ABC Visits	Visit	33.00
19. ABC Circumcision	Procedure	44.00
20. ABC—IUD	Procedure	83.00
21. ABC Transfers	Procedure	165.00

EXHIBIT 5 North Shore Birth Center

Obstetrical Service, Beverly Hospital Statistics, 1976-1984

	1976	1977	1978	1979	1980	1981	1982	1983	1984
Obstetrics—Unit Deliveries	518	568	639	670	711	744	865	876	913
Alternative Birth Center Deliveries	-	-	-	-	-	108	225	213	228
Total Deliveries	518	568	639	670	711	852	1,090	1,089	1,141
Number of Beds: In-House	16	16	16	14	14[a]	14	14	14	14
Birth Center	-	-	-	-	-	4	4	4	4
Occupancy (%) In-House	40%	43%	48%	52%	58.5%	73.3%	83.0%	79.6%	79.5%
Birth Center Gross Revenue						$ 82,600	$189,800	$210,400	$251,900
Birth Center Direct Expense						71,708	101,100	117,800	135,600
Birth Center Indirect Expense						61,733	75,251	83,241	94,920
Birth Center Total Expense						$133,441	$176,351	$201,041	$230,520

Direct Expense Breakdown—Obstetrics Service

	Salaries and Wages	M.D. Compensation	Supplies and Expenses	Major Movable	Reclassification	Recovery	Total
Obstetrics	$305,300	0	$20,400	$1,619	0	0	$327,319
Newborn	213,800	0	14,100	4,091	0	0	231,991

[a]Licensed beds reduced to 14—February 1979.

Note: Contractual Allowances and Bad Debts are not available on a department basis.

EXHIBIT 5 (Continued)

| | Gross Patient Service Revenue, by Service, FY Ending 9/30/84 | | |
	Routine	Ancillary	Total
Medical—Surgical	$ 9,304,837	$10,616,861	$19,921,698
Pediatric	468,892	559,616	1,028,508
Obstetrics	740,807	859,332	1,600,139
Psychiatric	1,194,313	149,504	1,343,817
Intensive Care	1,772,976	3,021,428	4,794,404
Newborn	493,950	65,240	559,190
Subtotal Inpatient	$13,975,775	$15,271,981	$29,247,756
Emergency	$ 1,947,755	$ 1,039,674	$ 2,987,429
Clinic	539,742	2,930,415	3,470,157
Satellite Clinic	0	2,786,660	2,786,660
Surgery	219,976	1,148,021	1,367,997
Dialysis	0	1,845,407	1,845,407
Subtotal Ambulatory	$ 2,707,473	$ 9,750,177	$12,457,650
Total Patient Care	$16,683,248	$25,022,158	$41,705,406

| | Ancillary Expenses, by Service ($ in thousands) | | |
	Total Ancillary	Direct	Allocated
Inpatient			
Medical—Surgical	$ 6,593	$ 4,256	$2,337
Pediatric	367	239	128
Obstetrics	869	565	304
Psychiatric	90	59	31
ICU	1,740	1,131	609
Newborn	187	122	65
Subtotal Inpatient	$ 9,846	$ 6,372	$3,474
Outpatient			
Emergency	$ 874	$ 568	$ 306
Clinic	2,277	1,480	797
Satellite Clinic	2,315	1,505	810
Surgery	658	428	230
Ambulatory Dialysis	1,642	1,067	575
Subtotal Outpatient	$ 7,766	$ 5,048	$2,718
Total	$17,612	$11,420	$6,192

EXHIBIT 5 (Continued)

Payor Mix by Service

	Total	Blue Cross	Medicare	Accident	Industrial Insurance	Commercial Insurance	Self-Pay
Medical–Surgical	52,873	4,054	32,315	4,104	356	10,872	1,172
Pediatric	2,758	1,068	102	291	13	1,112	172
Obstetrics	4,074	1,949	5	243	0	1,546	331
Psychiatric	4,659	1,336	538	1,246	0	1,036	503
Intensive Care	4,664	845	2,962	95	1	569	192
Newborn	3,414	1,640	0	214	0	1,283	277
Total Inpatient	72,442	10,892	35,992	6,193	370	16,418	2,647
			Visits				
Outpatient	49,040	18,534	8,015	2,893	2,224	13,003	3,771
			Dollars (000s)				
Gross Patient Service Revenue	$41,705	$9,353	$19,230	$2,494	$464	$8,205	$1,959
Deductions							
Contractual	$ 4,644	$ 941	$ 2,601	$1,080	$ 22	$ 0	$ 0
Free Care	584	0	0	0	0	0	584
Bad Debt	1,028	0	0	0	0	514	514
Total Deductions	$ 6,256	$ 941	$ 2,601	$1,080	$ 22	$ 514	$1,098
Net Revenue	$35,450	$8,412	$16,629	$1,415	$442	$7,692	$ 861
			Days				
Average Days Receivable	53	41	37	96	120	64	251

CASE 11.4 Nasus Clinic

The Nasus Clinic was a nonprofit organization that provided a complete range of ambulatory health care services to residents of Nasus, Louisiana. Its rates per visit were based on the expected costs for different kinds of visits. These costs were calculated on the basis of a thorough examination of the time physicians spend in providing different kinds of care and of the overhead expenses of the clinic.

In the past few months, the Internal Medicine Department in the clinic experienced a disturbing series of losses. The Nasus Clinic had an endowment principal of about $2 million, which yielded an income of about $140,000 a year for the past few years, but its trustees didn't wish to use this income to cover operating losses. They preferred to use these funds for acquisition of new equipment and wanted the medical department to generate sufficient revenues to cover its expenses.

The standard costs of the department for the physicians' time are displayed in **Table 1**. The physicians were paid at a rate of $36 an hour and were hired by the hour. The clinic had always used this method of payment in order to maximize its flexibility.

TABLE 1 **Standard Labor Costs, Visits, and Prices: Internal Medicine Department**

Type of Visit	Standard Time per Visit (minutes)	Standard Wage per Hour	Number of Visits in Standard Month	Price per Visit
Acute	20	$36	3,000	$26
Chronic	15	36	2,750	21
Treatment or lab	5	36	250	40
Checkup or physical	60	36	260	68

The standard overhead expenses are contained in **Table 2**. They were allocated to each visit category on the basis of the relative amount of time spent in each category. However, medical records and accounting each had a uniform charge per visit. Last month, the actual overhead expenses were $57,000. The actual labor costs for the last month are contained in **Table 3**. Actual prices did not differ from those expected.

Professor Regina E. Herzlinger prepared this case.

TABLE 2 **Standard Overhead Expenses per Month**

Free service and bad debt	$2,000
Rent	6,000
Medical supplies	4,000
Other supplies	2,000
Heat, light, and power	1,000
Depreciation	1,000
Administration	3,000
Medical records	$3/record
Accounting	$2/bill
Maintenance	1,500
Laundry	500
Nurse (1/2 time)	3,000
Reception	2,000
Total	$26,000 + $5/patient visit

TABLE 3 **Actual Labor Expenses, Internal Medicine Department**

	Actual Time per Visit (minutes)	Actual Wage per Visit	Actual Number of Visits
Acute	25	$40	3,000
Chronic	15	40	2,800
Treatment or lab	10	40	300
Checkup or physical	60	40	300

ASSIGNMENT

1. What are the standard and actual profits for the Nasus Clinic?
2. Why did the deviations from expected profits occur last month?
3. What should the Nasus Clinic do?

12 Motivating and Rewarding Performance

The third activity in the managerial control process motivates the attainment of planned performance. It relies on three activities: *holding managers responsible* for certain results, *measuring* their attainment of these goals, and *rewarding* or penalizing them in accordance with their ability to achieve the desired performance.

RESPONSIBILITY CENTERS

Sometimes managers are unaware of their responsibilities because the responsibilities have not been articulated. The diffidence in articulating managerial responsibilities is particularly marked in nonprofit organizations whose managers are also professionals. The reluctance to dictate professional responsibility—after all, it is ultimately up to the museum curators to organize their art exhibitions and they are the best judges of how to do so—is, perhaps unwittingly, extended to a reluctance to assign managerial responsibility. For example, one public television station had large and widely publicized cost overruns in producing programs because the production manager felt himself much more responsible for quality than for costs. His boss, the station's vice president for production, also felt that he was responsible primarily for programming quality. Neither felt any particular reason to worry about cost containment nor were they formally charged with responsibility for costs.

When sub-units within an organization are formally held responsible for clear measures of performance, many benefits can result. The problem at the public television station was solved by creating a new type of unit, whose manager, the new production coordinator, was jointly responsible to the vice presidents for finance and production. The coordinator integrated the demands of finance for cost control and the demands of production for high quality because he was clearly held responsible for both. With this new *responsibility center*, the station could more easily maintain its devotion to producing high-quality programs without continually fearing budget over-runs. The process of holding managers responsible for results is frequently called assigning *accountability*.

Types of Responsibility Centers

The nonprofit organizations that employ the concept of responsibility centers hold their managers accountable primarily for meeting budgeted expenses. This type of responsibility center is a *cost center*. A responsibility center whose management is held responsible for revenues as well as expenses is a *profit center*. One in which the manager is held responsible for the level of money invested, as well as the profits, is an *investment center*.

Financial responsibility should be commensurate with the manager's authority. The director of a hospital pharmacy should be held accountable for its revenues, costs, and inventory levels, but not for the total hospital's revenues, costs, or profits. After all, the pharmacy director cannot control total hospital performance. Marketing directors can be held responsible for their level of sales, selling expenses, and the prices they are able to obtain on sales, but they cannot be held responsible for the costs of the product they sell.

Some nonprofit organizations have fruitfully adopted the profit center concept. A large teaching hospital, for example, converted its outpatient department clinics from cost centers to group practices responsible for profits. Their providers and managers received bonuses based on their profits. After this change in responsibility, the group practices did not raise their fees for four years and yet maintained and even enhanced the hospital's medical reputation. All this was accomplished while the providers substantially increased their incomes. The new responsibility for profits motivated them to become more productive and increased their awareness of supporting expenses, which they dramatically reduced.

Some universities designate individual schools as profit centers, each separately responsible for matching its expenses with its revenues. Some do not permit cross-subsidization among the schools. For example, if the College of Arts and Sciences finds itself in a deficit position, it cannot rely on the wealthier professional schools of law, medicine, or business to bail it out. Although this profit center system reduces innovations in the less wealthy school because it does not subsidize any activities, it does enable these universities to maintain an unusually strong financial position.

Some universities extend the responsibility center concept to the services provided by the central administration, such as security. The individual schools must pay for their share of these services. If the central security budget is $1 million and the law school uses 20 percent of its resources, it will be charged $200,000. If the law school finds the security services ineffective or inefficient, it will protest to the central administration, and may even purchase security services externally.

In these settings, the responsibility center concept enables managers to broaden their vision. For example, the deans who otherwise might waste time and effort in asking for nonexistent university funding instead perform intelligent budgeting, fully cognizant of their funding constraints. Further, responsibility center deans who commit themselves to secure the revenues they need because they manage a profit center will, as a result, think longer and harder before expending these revenues. Last, the concept transforms professionals into managers.

But, it has its risks. For one, managers may be tempted to spend too little or to raise revenues at dizzyingly high rates in order to perform well under their cost, revenue, or profit center designation. These dangers are greatest if the managers plan to hold their current positions for only a short period of time and will not be forced to live with the long-term negative consequences of their actions. While these dangers are always present, responsibility centers may motivate greater negative behavior.

Responsibility center performance must be measured with comprehensive accounting principles. If it is not, the responsibility center may engage in undesirable performance. For example, inappropriate accounting measures allegedly caused the U.S. National Forest System to cut down trees that an ordinary business would have left standing. For one, when the Forest Services profit center sells its lumber, it must return only 50 cents per thousand board feet to the U.S. Treasury. It is permitted to keep the sizable difference between the price it receives for its lumber and the 50 cents it remits. Then too, the Forest Service is not charged for the cost of constructing roads into remote forest areas to reach the lumber.

The Forest Service's response to these measures of its performance is to cut down a great deal of lumber and to construct costly, intricate roads to reach it. The Service already has 342,000 miles of logging roads and plans to build yet another 262,000 by 2040. Critics contend that these roads are constructed to reach increasingly poor-quality timber and that they inflict considerable environmental damage. They recommend new measures of its performance that account for the full cost of logging, including the cost of raising the timber, building roads to reach it, and replacing it.[1]

Transfer Pricing

Responsibility center labels are most frequently attached to departments that perform the primary mission of the organization, such as a clinic in a hospital, or a school in a university. Some nonprofit organizations, such as the universities described above, extend the concept of responsibility centers by charging each support sub-unit within the organization with the responsibility for behaving as if it, too, were a separate, independent business.

---

[1]John Baden, "Spare that tree!" *Forbes* (December 9, 1991): 229-233.

Implementation of this concept requires a series of rules for valuing the internal sale and purchase of services, such as the sale of accounting services to the curatorial staff in a museum. This value, called a *transfer price*, is then compared to the expenses of the internal unit to judge its efficiency.

Charging for services which the buyer had previously thought to be free will lead to more prudent consumption of resources. Transfer prices can cause many other beneficial effects in increasing the quality or decreasing the costs of the internal providers. A large hospital, for example, used a transfer price of $20 per square foot to charge its group practices for the space they were using. The transfer price was based on the market price for new, well-maintained space at a nearby physicians' office building. The actual expenses of the hospital departments providing the space, such as maintenance and utilities, were $30 a square foot—50 percent over market. The transfer pricing mechanism not only identified the inefficiency of these departments—a fact previously disguised in the hospital's jumble of cost data—but also provided an incentive for the internal departments to become more efficient.

Transfer-pricing can be used for many support units, such as legal, purchasing, accounting, laundry, and kitchen. For example, some municipalities designate the motor pool as a profit center. Its transfer price is based on the prices charged by local garages. The motor pool's costs for providing such services as lubricating or servicing a car then are compared to the transfer price. The computing unit in some large nonprofits also may be designated as a profit center. Its services are transfer-priced at the charges of outside vendors, and the costs of its services are then compared to these prices.

Because the purpose of transfer pricing is to impose market discipline on transactions between two parts of the same firm, the transfer price should usually equal the market price. For example, a nonprofit health insurance company that provides both hospital and insurance services and that "sells" its hospital services to the insurance division can use market-based transfer pricing to compare the costs of the services provided by its own internal hospitals to the prices charged by hospitals that the company does not own. If its hospitals' costs are lower than the market-based transfer price, the hospital division's efficiency will be indicated by the high profits it will earn, as shown in Table 12-1. But if the hospital division's costs are higher than the market price, its inefficiency will be clearly documented with losses.

The use of transfer prices is desirable even in cases where market prices are not available. In the absence of market data, transfer prices can be based on standard direct costs or two-part pricing or can be negotiated between the buyer and seller. The pricing guidelines discussed in Chapter 10 are valid for transfer prices.

TABLE 12-1   **Use of Transfer Pricing to Evaluate Efficiency of Internal Production**

Given:	Market price for a hospital day is $500 so internal hospital gets paid for its services to the company's health insurance divisions at $500/day.			

Results:

Efficient Hospital Division		Inefficient Hospital Division	
Revenues:	$500/day	Revenues:	$500/day
− Costs:	$400/day	− Costs:	$700/day
Profits:	$100/day	Loss:	$(200/day)

Problems in Implementation of Transfer Prices

As described in Chapter 11, a full cost system measures direct costs and an allocated portion of the organization's indirect costs. A full-cost system may cause difficulties in implementing a transfer pricing system. For example, a full-cost system may motivate the town's motor pool to refuse to sell its services to the town's police department.

How does accounting create this perverse magic of causing one internal unit to refuse to provide services to another? Suppose the full costs of a tune-up are $100, and the motor pool refuses to provide one for a price less than that amount. If competing garages charge only $75 for a tune-up, the police department will prefer to send its cars to them rather than to the internal unit. What are the consequences of this set of events? The town will spend its taxpayers' hard-earned money paying for *both* the internal motor pool and the external garage.

But does not the city's motor pool lose $25 if it performs a $100 job for only $75? No. The $100 full cost is misleading. It consists almost entirely of expenses that will not increase with an additional tune-up. After all, the number of motor pool technicians, managers, and schedulers will neither increase nor decrease in number because of this additional tune-up. The only expenses likely to increase are those of the materials used in the tune-up. Their cost is much less than either $100 or $75. So if the motor pool accepted the internal job, it would receive revenues of $75 and spend only a few dollars for materials. It is clearly in the best interests of the town, the police, and the motor pool for the job to be performed internally—but the full-cost accounting system motivates precisely the opposite result.

The remedy for this problem is to use a direct cost system to evaluate whether a particular project will be performed internally and to use the full cost system to evaluate whether, over a long period of time, the internal unit's full costs lined up with the prices charged by its competitors.

FEEDBACK

Measurement of results is key not only to evaluation, as discussed in Chapter 11, but also to motivation. For example, three years of measurement and feedback may well have influenced the decline in the rates of patient morbidity associated with virtually all of the physicians illustrated in Table 12-2. (These data were provided by MediQual Systems, a Massachusetts company whose quality assessment system predicts the morbidity and mortality rates of different types of hospital procedures. These predictions are then compared to the actual results achieved by the hospital's physicians, as shown in Table 12-2.)

Good feedback systems must be timely and frequent and must measure those things for which managers are responsible. Managers must demonstrate their interest in the feedback reports by discussing them with their subordinates.

REWARDS

Rewarding managers for unusual performance can yield great benefits. For example, the "top 10" entries in Los Angeles County's Productivity and Quality Awards Program resulted in more than $68 million in estimated savings or increased revenues. The program rewards managers who submit ideas for increased productivity. The managers receive cash awards, up to $5,000,

TABLE 12-2   **Effect of Feedback on Incidence of Illness After Treatment for Heart Attacks and Shock, in a Hospital by Physicians, 1985-1987**

Physician	1985	1986	1987
a	7%	4%	5%
b	22	10	7
c	21	17	12
d	12	10	8
e	15	12	2
f	9	10	9
g	18	2	1
h	12	10	5
i	11	1	1

Source: MediQual Systems, Inc., Westborough, Massachusetts.

and attend a well-publicized awards luncheon. In two years, more than 600 ideas were submitted and virtually all departments participated.[2]

Managers frequently are rewarded with financial and other incentives in accordance with their ability to achieve specified goals. They may receive a share of the profits they earned, granted in cash or as a bonus. Portland, Oregon, permits city employees in its print shop to share in the profits that result from increased productivity.[3] Or there may be some other form of recognition, such as membership in a club composed only of those with exceptional organizational achievements or the receipt of an award as the employee of the month or the year. For example, the Riverside Methodist Hospital in Columbus, Ohio, recognizes its outstanding employees at a yearly celebration modeled after the scope and grandeur of Hollywood's Academy Awards presentation. Honored employees are brought to the festivities in a horse-drawn carriage and enter the large ballroom in which the ceremony is conducted on a red carpet. This festive event is recorded on videotape. The tape is presented as a memento to the employee and is broadcast on the hospital's internal television network.

Financial incentives often are structured to motivate employees to maintain a long-term connection with the firm. In these cases, incentive compensation is paid on a *time-vested* basis—the vesting specifies that employees will receive their incentive payment only after spending a certain period of time with the organization. (The incentive compensation funds are invested by the organization until they vest.) Compensation may also be *performance-vested*, so that it is paid out only if the organization as a whole reaches prespecified financial and other goals. In this way, employees are motivated to consider the effect of their performance on the organization as a whole, rather than to focus solely on the performance of their own responsibility centers.

Incentive compensation should be paid only if clearly articulated goals are achieved. Frequently, bonuses intended as rewards for exceptional performances come to be viewed as part of the manager's normal yearly compensation. This perception of bonuses defeats their purpose.

Problems in Implementation of Rewards Systems

Many systems for motivation and reward fail to achieve their intended results because they are poorly implemented. For example, one study found that 95 percent of the federal government employees who were supposed to receive performance ratings of "outstanding," "satisfactory," or "unsatisfactory," were rated "satisfactory." Their managers found it difficult to use the "unsatisfactory" rating because of the time and paperwork it involved

[2]Laura Jessee, "Productivity: Part of the Governmental Culture in Los Angeles County," *Government Finance Review* (December 1990): 17.
[3]"When City Hall Learns to Think Like a Business," *Business Week* (Quality 1991): 136.

and the "outstanding" category was also little utilized.[4] Similarly, while within-grade step increases were supposed to be based on merit, in practice, 99 percent of eligible employees received these raises, indicating that they were based simply on continued service. Dismissal, the ultimate step in dealing with nonproductive employees, was seldom utilized and, when attempted, it was sometimes overturned, on doubtful grounds, on appeal. The study cited the following case:

> An agency fired an employee for beating his supervisor with a baseball bat. The Federal Employees Appeals Authority overturned the removal, contending the agency had not given the employee adequate notice of the firing. The agency had to reinstate the employee in the same position, under the same supervisor, and reimburse the employee eight months' back pay.

Another study considered the impact of a U.S. government incentive award totaling more than $63 million, that granted nearly 210,000 quality pay increases and special achievement awards. The study concluded that the program "may have a more negative impact on employee productivity than would having no awards program at all."[5] The results of a questionnaire sent to employees of nine agencies indicated:

- Sixty percent felt their organization's program did little, or nothing at all, to change their job motivation.
- Forty percent said the current awards program made little or no contribution to their specific work group's productivity.
- One-third believed that improving their performance would probably not affect their opportunity to receive an award.
- Sixty percent were not sure cash awards are usually presented to those who are the most deserving.

State and local government employees and managers share the perception that rewards and performance are not necessarily in line. As shown in Table 12-3, few public sector personnel felt that their performance and promotional patterns were correlated. Private sector employees, in contrast, felt more positive about this relationship.

Motivational techniques must be intelligently designed and well implemented. If their design is flawed or their implementation perceived as insincere or careless, they will not be a useful component of managerial control.

---

[4]U.S. General Accounting Office, *A Management Concern: How to Deal with the Nonproductive Federal Employee* (Washington, DC: August 10, 1978).
[5]General Accounting Office, *Does the Federal Incentive Awards Program Improve Productivity?* (FGMSD-79-9, March 15, 1979).

TABLE 12-3 **Attitudes Toward Personal Development**

| | Responses (percent who agree) | | | |
| | Managers | | Employees | |
Questions	Public Sector	Private Sector	Public Sector	Private Sector
The better my performance the better will be my opportunity for promotion to a better job.	43.3	58.3	30.2	48.7
I receive enough feedback on how well I do my work.	45.3	41.5	30.0	48.5
I am satisfied with my advancement since starting work here.	55.7	48.6	29.3	38.0
I am satisfied with my opportunity to move to a better job.	24.4	35.6	19.0	22.9
I am satisfied with management's efforts to promote from within.	57.4	59.5	36.0	43.8

Source: National Center for Productivity and Quality of Working Life, *Employee Attitudes and Productivity Differences Between the Public and Private Sector* (Washington, DC: 1978), pp. 15, 17.

MANAGING THE MANAGERIAL CONTROL PROCESS

In the managerial control process, top management must ensure that plans are intelligently formulated, that managers are evaluated against the plans, and that the motivational process is effective. Management fuels this process with its interest and attention.

Committee Structure

Managerial and board-level committees are invaluable for the managerial control process. At a minimum four committees are helpful: a *financial planning* committee to prepare the long-run plans, a *budget* committee to prepare the budget, a *management review* committee to evaluate actual results and award performance rewards, and an *investment* committee to guide the process of investing endowment capital. To enable the committees to provide checks and balance on each other, most of their members should be assigned to only one committee. For example, the members of the management review committee must feel free to appraise the realism of the plans developed by the financial planning and budget committees. Some membership overlap is desirable, however, because it helps each committee to understand the work of the others. Board committees should meet regularly, two to four times a year. A more frequent meeting schedule may cause committee members to forget that their role is to oversee operations rather than to implement them. Board committees should receive staff support from the organization's management.

Most of the board members appointed to these committees should possess some relevant experience, either as senior operating managers or as financial managers, investors, or consultants. The management review committee should have the most senior members, ones with extensive general management experiences. The other committees will benefit from the presence of specialists in accounting, legal, finance, and consulting activities. If their membership is carefully chosen, the committees will provide a depth of experiences and a breadth of vision that managers cannot otherwise obtain.

Board members should be selected for their potential contribution to the organization, rather than the organization's potential contribution to them. Some people seek a seat on a nonprofit board to enhance their careers or to publicize themselves. Unless they have other sterling qualities, these self-seeking board members will do little for the organization. For example, an amateur athlete whose children had birth defects participated in an annual athletic competition as the board representative of a nonprofit organization that researched such defects. She actively enlisted media coverage of the event, osetensibly to publicize the organization, but the resulting publicity focused on her rather than on the organization.

To avoid such difficulties, the chairperson of the board must carefully explain to potential members why they were selected and what their responsibilities will be. In addition, the organization's charter should contain clear policy statements governing the use of the organization's name by board members. The selection of members with extensive managerial and other board experiences is also likely to minimize such problems.

Managerial Style

The organization's top management and board should also clearly delineate a philosophy about the "tightness" of its involvement with the managerial control process. Some are heavily involved, conducting extensive reviews of every little detail, while others prefer a more global and general involvement. Either style can be right if it is the product of extensive deliberations. But, it can be pernicious without such deliberations.

The tightness of managerial control should result from the top management's style. Some managers revel in details and are inspired by them. For example, the CEO of one large company was widely admired for his ability to estimate a factory's income after walking through it. His mind could integrate many details into a coherent picture of the whole enterprise. People with his cognitive style flourish when they are extensively involved in the managerial control process. But those with different ways of processing information will lose control when they are excessively involved. The detailed reviews they are asked to undertake will diminish their ability to envision the working of the organization as a whole. For them, a global review process that focuses in depth on a few key items is more desirable.

These cognitive styles are neither good nor bad—they are merely different. But their differences must be recognized and the managerial control process tailored to them. Failures in control occur when a top management that functions best with broad oversight is asked to conduct detailed reviews or when a detail-oriented management is matched with a broad overview control process. In the former instance, managers will lose their perspective and appear bored with the process while, in the latter, detail-oriented managers will charge their subordinates with inappropriately precise responsibilities.

Centralization Versus Decentralization

The nature of the organization's services is critical for determining the degree of involvement of top management. Organizations whose services must be tailored to the characteristics of different clients in different areas cannot and should not be led by managers who maintain tight involvement in the managerial control process. Instead, these managers must cede considerable responsibility and authority to those who directly supervise the delivery of services. A top management that insists on maintaining tight reins will hamper the ability of this type of organization to respond to local conditions. This kind of organization demands *decentralized* management.

On the other hand, an organization that delivers the same types of services to all clients will benefit from the extensive involvement of top management. These benefits will accrue from centrally standardized procedures and policies that reduce costs and make quality more uniform. This organization should have *centralized* management.

Centralized and decentralized organizations both require managerial control, but paradoxically, the control process is more extensive in a decentralized organization. Ensuring that actual results are consistent with those planned is much more difficult in an organization whose managers have considerable autonomy to respond to local conditions. The control process is relatively simpler in centralized organizations in which managers must adhere to tightly standardized plans.

Ironically, many organizations exercise loose control procedures in decentralized organizations and tight controls in centralized ones. Their equating decentralization with lack of managerial control usually leads to a troubled organization in which unexpected problems continually pop up in field operations. Conversely, centralized organizations with excessively tight controls may completely paralyze their managers, rendering them incapable of any independent action or creative thoughts.

SUMMARY

This chapter discussed the procedures of motivation, accountability, and rewards embedded in excellent managerial control systems. Managers are motivated when their responsibilities are clearly articulated and they receive extensive feedback about their performance. Managers held responsible for attaining budgeted costs have cost center responsibility. A profit center charges managers with responsibilities for both revenues and costs, as though they were in charge of an independent business. Transfer pricing simulates the environment of such a business for internal service units. Feedback informs managers whether they are performing as expected. Rewards, both psychic and financial, can yield significant benefits. Failures in motivation are most frequently the product of failures in implementing motivational systems. Decentralization or centralization are appropriate for different environments and organizations, and impose different requirements on management.

DISCUSSION QUESTIONS

1. What are the three activities that can motivate the achievement of planned results?
2. What is a responsbility center? Name the three most common types of responsibility centers.
3. Which of the three most common responsibility center designations should be assigned to the following units in a large university?
   a. The divinity school
   b. The medical school
   c. The data processing unit
   d. The dormitories
   e. The food services
   f. The grounds maintenance department
   g. The administration
   h. The environmental hazards monitors
4. Define transfer pricing. How should the transfer price be determined? If you have designated any of the units in 3(a) through 3(h) as profit or investment centers, specify how their transfer price should be determined when they provide service to some other part of the university.
5. List the desirable characteristics of a reward system for employees in nonprofits.
6. What is time- and performance-vested compensation?
7. What committees are essential for the managerial control process?
8. What is centralization? When should managers use a centralized style?
9. What is decentralization? When should it be used?
10. Describe the system for motivating performance in a nonprofit organization with which you are familiar. What are the activities for which managers are held responsible? What kind of feedback do they receive? How are they rewarded? Specify changes in this process that are needed, if any, and their impact.

Cases

CASE STUDIES

Case 12.1 describes the measurement system a newly appointed police chief installs in order to evaluate his officers and assign them where they are most needed. But the new system is installed in a college with a long tradition of decentralized management. Will it work in this environment? Is it measuring the right things?

Case 12.2 describes the initial impact of transfer pricing for translation services once provided free of charge by a Canadian province's government agency. When volume declined, the agency's supervisor ordered a reduction in its staff. But agency personnel claimed that the chargeback system was flawed and was causing the government to back away from its original bilingual policy.

CASE 12.1 Grayson University Police Department

Dave Nessum, recently appointed chief of police and director of security at Grayson University, sat at his desk in the basement of Howard Hall contemplating the problems of his new job.

Nessum had been appointed to his position on the first of January after a year-long selection process to replace the retiring chief. The special selection committee had been named by Grayson's president to include prominent faculty members as well as student leaders. Hundreds of applications were received from city police chiefs, FBI special agents, and other law enforcement officers. Nessum, a director of public safety in a small middle-income Minneapolis suburb, although an unlikely candidate, was urged to apply by an acquaintance at Grayson. His knowledgeable yet easy-going manner in interviews made him one of the finalists, but his eventual selection was a surprise to many, both at Grayson and within the law enforcement community.

Jeffrey Kahn prepared this case under the supervision of Professor Regina E. Herzlinger.
Copyright © 1979 by the President and Fellows of Harvard College. Harvard Business School case 180-044. Revised January 1993.

Now, in mid-May, Nessum mused: "It's much different from what I expected. I guess I didn't know quite what to expect. It's a question of getting our priorities straight. There's so much to do that you can almost start anywhere."

Nessum had been hired to "deal with the crime problem" at Grayson. Lacking detailed information about the scope of the problem, he decided to start by setting up an information system to describe patterns of crime at Grayson and to provide the tools for management control and evaluation of the department's work in combating it. He enlisted the help of a Grayson Business School student, Roger Cohen, who had called him in early January. Cohen had previously worked in the New York City Police Department and was eager to do an independent study/project with the Grayson police force as part of his work at the Business School.

Hoping to design and completely install the new system within three and a half months, Nessum and Cohen set to work in early February. By mid-May, after confronting problems with the members of the force, the university, and the system itself, it was clear to both of them that the system would not be in operation until July at the earliest. Said Cohen:

> The system is a good one. It's just that it takes time to effect change around this place. I don't mean simply the Police Department; it's all of Grayson that's involved. It seemed that every time we leaped over one hurdle there would be somebody shoving another in our path.

THE UNIVERSITY ADMINISTRATION

Nessum's immediate supervisor was the vice president of administration, who also controlled such diverse areas as buildings and grounds, personnel, real estate, and other centralized administrative tasks. However, the police chief was also responsible to the entire Grayson community of over 30,000 people.

Grayson University was firmly and proudly established on the principle of "every building on its own foundation," which meant that the 12 separate faculties (arts and sciences, business, law, etc.) were each self-supporting and in some ways self-sufficient. Universitywide overhead was kept to a minimum and most was directly allocated to the appropriate school; for many years the only major universitywide unallocated joint expenditures were the salaries of the president and his top assistants. In theory, the university was a form of decentralized free market where everyone was free to buy services outside the university if they were more cost effective than those internally available, and each school and department survived on the continuing demand for its form of service.

To the Grayson Police Department, this principle meant that officers were allocated on the basis of need as determined by the dean of a school. For example, the Business School would agree to hire a certain number of officers of a given rank on each shift, after which the various occupants of the Business School campus would be billed for the officers according to a formula based on the square footage of the building-base areas. The same method applied to the other school areas. The basic police budget was entirely allocated from the individual budgets of the various Grayson schools and amounted to $1.2 million. Of this sum, over 90 percent was in wages, salaries, and pension payments.

THE GRAYSON POLICE FORCE

Until World War II, the Grayson police force never contained more than five or six officers. During the war the organization expanded due to security requirements of many special government projects, and afterwards the expansion continued to counter the growing crime rate.

The entire Grayson campus over which this force had jurisdiction was contained within two square miles in downtown Stockton, except for the Business and Law Schools, both separate campuses located two and four miles away, respectively, in an adjacent city. Stockton itself was near the top of the FBI's list of per-capita crimes of violence and theft, and number one in per-capita auto thefts. Grayson Park, the campus epicenter, was one of the highest crime areas in Stockton. The remainder of the campus with its many wealthy students also had a notably high rate of crime. Most were simple property crimes, but some also involved personal violence.

In January when Nessum took over, the department consisted of 52 patrol officers and 22 "staff," all uniformed personnel above patrol officer level, which included 17 sergeants, 4 lieutenants, and 1 captain.

In general, the patrol officers were high school graduates with some college courses. Four had college degrees, while 20 did not possess high school diplomas. They ranged in age from 22 to 64 with a median age of 39 and an average of 11 years on the force. Many of the older officers had held previous positions in Grayson's buildings and grounds department. The staff was similar in background to the patrol officers although older, with the four lieutenants being between 35 and 48, and the oldest having 27 years in the department. All had taken some college courses. The force was well integrated racially although, as with many police forces, there was a heavy Irish-American contingent (four of the top five officers were of Irish lineage). The only female patrol officer was black and had been hired in the fall before Nessum arrived.

Within Grayson property, the officers had full police powers. All new personnel attended a four-week training session at the State Police Academy where they were instructed in criminal law, arrest procedures, and other areas of law enforcement, including, of course, weapons handling. All Grayson officers wore uniforms and carried pistols, and were sworn officers of the law under state statute.

While hierarchical in rank structure (**Exhibit 1**), the actual day-to-day organization appeared almost flat. Sergeants had the privilege of sometimes riding in cars or sitting at the reception desk to answer the telephone. There were no specialized departments or divisions, such as investigation or communication. Record keeping consisted of a single log typed by the desk sergeant, detailing whichever events were of interest during his working shift.

Both patrol officers and sergeants worked on assigned routes, and generally an officer patrolled the same route during the same hours until promoted or moved to fill a newly emptied spot. Many of the schools in the university got to know their assigned officers quite well. All officers and staff were assigned to one of three shifts (midnight to eight, eight to four, or four to midnight) and a lieutenant was in charge of each shift, his primary duty being to ensure that every route was covered. Each shift had approximately the same number of personnel who were assigned by seniority, with the day shift being the most popular and the midnight-to-eight the least. The Law School area, the most distant from the main campus, had two patrol officers and one lieutenant assigned especially for its coverage.

Within each assigned route, the shift routine consisted of walking a normal beat, watching and hopefully deterring, while waiting for any dispatches from headquarters. All officers were equipped with walkie-talkies. The dispatcher-sergeant handled all incoming phone calls, both routine and emergency. He also maintained a typed log-book account of his shift, although, depending on the amount of traffic and the esti-mated importance, not all phone calls or services were entered.

The nature of the work performed included a large proportion of duties peculiar to a university, such as opening the doors of students who had locked themselves out and standing by to transport students to and from the central health center. In addi-tion, there were the time-and-a-half details at hockey games, movie shows, speeches, and so forth.

While many officers held second jobs, this fact was not regarded as a problem for the organization, and most officers felt that one of the benefits of the job was its freedom and the lack of imposed constraints upon their lives.

DESIGNING THE SYSTEM

Nessum and Cohen felt that an information system should provide two types of information on the Grayson police force: *descriptive indicators* to display the type and pattern of crime and other demands for police service in the Grayson areas, and *per-formance measures* to show the degree to which the police were meeting the needs described.

They felt that the demand for police services should be measured by the number of calls into the Police Department requiring an officer to respond plus those incidents encountered by an officer in the field requiring action. Three facts were felt to be essential for each incident recorded: the geographic location, the time of occurrence, and the type of incident. By aggregating and cross-tabulating these facts, the watch commanders and other supervisors would be given a useful tool to tell them what kinds of incidents they could expect to encounter, where, and when.

The campus was initially redivided into 85 police zones formed by natural, social, and physical boundaries, disregarding in many cases the previous routes. The zones were then amalgamated into 15 police areas. Time of occurrence was measured as clock time, day of the week, and date. However, categorizing incidents took some rethinking. Most police forces used the FBI Uniform Classification Codes that divided incidents into violent person-directed crime, property-related felonies, and other mis-cellaneous noncriminal incidents. However, this system was inadequate for many of the duties performed at Grayson since major crimes were not the bulk of the work-load. Thus, a new system of 159 types of incidents was devised and cross-related to the FBI indices.

Nessum and Cohen decided that the only practical way to collect the second type of information—performance measurement—was to calculate response time, the amount of time it took from the initial call for a police service to the arrival of an officer at the scene. Various studies had shown that the improvement of police re-sponse time was one of the few changes that seemed to have an effect on the prob-ability of apprehending the perpetrator of a crime, as well as on community confi-dence in the police force. Types of incidents were classified into four priorities and, for each watch, response times could be ascertained for each priority.

After several false starts, in mid-February Nessum and Cohen designed an incident card to be filled out by the dispatcher for each occurrence, with blanks for all the required information plus space for any additional information. The right-hand side included space for all the information necessary to dispatch an officer to the scene; the left-hand side, to be filled out when the dispatcher had more time, provided most of the data for the management information system. Each incident was given a unique number, and a time clock was installed to stamp times for call receipt, dispatch, arrival on scene, and clearance.

Both men intended the system at first to be a simple means of gathering and displaying the information contained in regular reports. Later, however, they hoped to devise a system of interactive outputs that could answer specific queries about police problems. They chose the Business School's minicomputer system, because it could provide those interactive outputs at an affordable price. A programmer was hired to develop the necessary software. Working part time and after hours, an initial input program to record the gathered data was designed and ready within two weeks. By March 1 a terminal had been installed at the police station and linked via telephone to the computer. Shortly thereafter, a student was hired to start entering the data that had begun to be gathered in February after the printing of the initial incident cards. The input program was simple to use. Should the wrong type of data be entered (e.g., the day of the week instead of the place of the incident), the program would explain the error and request the correct information.

The third step was the development of useful output formats. It was decided that the initial output reports should be issued weekly. They would not be used by patrol officers or sergeants, but would provide information to lieutenants for resource allocation and to Chief Nessum for personnel evaluation as well as control.

A group of six basic reports was to be the weekly output, with the same report formats being used once a month to provide information on a year-to-date basis.

(1) *Area Time Report*. This report cross-tabulated, within a given watch, the time of an incident with the police area within which it occurred. By using this report, the staff could ascertain, for example, that from 4:00-6:00 P.M. on April 22 the largest number (21 percent) of reported crimes occurred in Area 6 (**Exhibit 2**).

(2) *Classification Time Report*. This report is also a cross-tabulation, but of types of incidents (classifications) with the time of occurrence. The report for April 22 shows, for example, that from 4:00-6:00 P.M. during that week 34 percent of all calls for service were of a public service nature, while 16 percent were alarms (**Exhibit 3**).

(3) *Classification Area Report*. Yet another cross-tabulation, this report compares incident classification with area (**Exhibit 4**).

(4) *Response Time Report*. Each report was broken down by the priority of a call as well as by watch. **Exhibit 5** shows, for instance, what percentage of Priority 1 crimes occurring in Area 4 during that week were responded to in 0-2 minutes, in 2-4 minutes, in 4-6 minutes, or in over 6 minutes.

(5) *Average Response Time Report*. This report summarized and aggregated all response times into averages for each priority and each watch. It also

displayed the standard deviation from the average. As shown below, the average response time for Priority 1 calls was 2.9 minutes with a standard deviation of 1.4 minutes.

Average Response in Minutes for Week Ending 4/22

	Priority 1	Priority 2	Priority 3	Priority 4
Watch 1	3.0	2.9	6.4	3.0
Watch 2	4.0	5.2	8.8	4.0
Watch 3	2.4	6.3	4.6	9.8
Overall	2.9	5.3	7.4	9.2
Standard deviation	1.4	16.9	13.5	12.1

(6) *Zone Report.* This report was a complete breakdown of all the 85 zones and all the 18 major incident classifications; it was cross-tabulated giving simultaneously a figure for this week and year to date. Previously, two weekly and one monthly reports on crime incidence and theft valuation had been prepared by the force captain. These had required about a day per week to develop and were presently distributed to almost 150 deans and other administrators. With all this information now to be computerized, it was felt that this zone report, along with a forthcoming theft valuation report, would supplant the older method.

A timetable was worked out so that the first two types of reports would be ready by April 1, while the weekly and monthly distribution reports would be developed somewhat later—it was hoped by mid-April.

As soon as a computerization was complete, a sergeant would generate a set of reports weekly and study them for trends and problems. They would be put on file, available to all watch commanders and supervisors, who once a week would meet to discuss the previous week's performance and determine what improvements could be made.

With this information, it was hoped that preventive patrol might be varied to suppress crime in high-crime areas and during peak hours of occurrence, subject to seasonal factors, weather conditions, and so forth. For example, if (as was the case) the reports revealed a very high number of bicycle thefts occurring from 12:00-3:00 P.M. at the bicycle racks in the southeast corner of Grayson Park, a special detail of plainclothes officers could be assigned to monitor that area during that time period, and apprehend the thieves.

PROBLEMS

Internal Resistance

The dispatchers, both sergeants and civilians, began filling out the new cards in February. Despite the many inevitable bugs in a new system, the dispatchers were among those most satisfied with the change taking place and seemed proud of their role in it.

Less happy were the patrol officers, who were also the least informed about the transformation. To the officer on the beat, computerization meant that he or she would now have to record the number of incident calls assigned to him or her and inform the dispatcher whenever he or she arrived at or left the scene of an accident. While no open resistance was being encountered, at least one official of the Grayson Police Officers Union had registered some anxiety over the speed with which changes were taking place, and the first annual contract bargaining session was scheduled for the sixth of May.

Not unexpectedly, the most resistance came from the lieutenants, who for many years had been running the day-to-day operations of the department. With no differentiation between staff and line in the existing organization, the lieutenants saw the administrative staff's move to set procedure as an incursion into their line functions. All of the lieutenants had been repeatedly asked by Nessum and Cohen for suggestions and questions concerning the new system, but few had responded.

Nessum and Cohen also encountered problems with the system itself. Originally, the major computer programs were to be ready by April 1. However, it was mid-April before they were completed and mid-May before the final distribution reports were done. In order to start with a full calendar year's worth of data, they wanted to enter a backlog of data along with the approximately 75 incidents added daily. The maximum number of incidents that could be entered by the program was about 35 per hour.

To solve the problem, they hired more operators to input the information and developed a new fast input program that asked fewer questions and allowed data to be entered as a string of numbers. This program was quickly put into effect, and by mid-April the data were almost entirely current. However, at that point it was discovered that fast input allowed incorrect data to be entered—data that would not have passed the old program. An additional arduous three weeks were spent cleaning out the electronic files by matching them with the printed ones, whereupon fast input was discarded in favor of the original program.

Chief Nessum called a meeting at the beginning of May to explain to the lieutenants the new system and their part in its use. Prior to this meeting, he and Cohen designed a simplified single-page weekly digest to be given to the lieutenants. This would provide some easily comprehensible and comparable measures of crime and incidence and response time by shift (**Exhibit 6**).

The weekly output form was explained and displayed at this meeting. For the first time it was apparent to the lieutenants that they would be evaluated by this system. An additional shock was the revelation that staff services had grown. Six people from outside the department had been hired to enter data—three civilians and three employees of the University Parking Office, recently annexed into the department—and the officers feared that students and clerks were replacing police personnel.

External Resistance

Nessum felt that in order for his new system to work, allocation of police resources could no longer be determined by individual schools: "People's perception of how much police protection they need usually bears little resemblance to their actual need. I would like to run a police department, not a contract guard service." He knew that he would have to get the university to recognize the police as a campus-wide resource that could not be funded in segments.

The proposal that Nessum was fighting for was called "University Assessment," the same system of overhead allocation that paid top administrators. While committed to the decentralized "every building on its own foundation" principle, Grayson had long ago realized that some services had to be centralized and centrally assessed. Therefore, the "University Assessment" was devised whereby most, although not all, units within the university paid into the central administration an amount based on a predetermined formula. There was, of course, continual opposition to any increases in the number of items funded under this assessment system, with individual financial autonomy being jealously guarded by the administrative deans of the component schools.

Some of the major opposition to the new financing scheme came from the Business School, which could both afford to pay for extra police protection and, because of its large exposed parking lot harboring the cars of the many top corporate executives attending the school, presently asked for and received a contingent of officers out of proportion to its incidence of crime. If priorities were set so that more officers were required elsewhere to thwart crimes of personal violence, Business School administrators felt that property crime at the otherwise relatively peaceful campus would soar.

With the school year drawing to a close, Nessum and Cohen both felt that much had been accomplished toward improving the department. Yet the overall schema, the system that encompassed the computerized information and redesigned organization, had yet to be fulfilled.

ASSIGNMENT

1. Evaluate the content of the new system. What changes would you recommend?
2. Evaluate the process of implementing the system. Why was this process chosen? What changes do you recommend?

EXHIBIT 1 Grayson University Police Department—Organization Chart, December

```
                              Chief
                                |
                              Captain ———— Secretary
          _____|_____
         |            |                    |                    |
    Lieutenant    Lieutenant           Lieutenant           Lieutenant
  12:00 P.M. to   8:00 A.M. to                              4:00 P.M. to
   8:00 A.M.      4:00 P.M.                                  12:00 P.M.

 Lieutenant (12:00 P.M. to 8:00 A.M.)
   |
   |——— GBS Sergeant ——— 3 Patrol Officers
   |——— Patrol Sergeant
   |         |——— Stockton 6 Patrol Officers
   |         |——— GBS 2 Patrol Officers
   |         |——— GLS 2 Patrol Officers
   |——— Student Security Patrol

 Lieutenant (8:00 A.M. to 4:00 P.M.)
   |——— GBS Sergeant ——— 2 Patrol Officers
   |——— Desk Sergeant
   |——— Patrol Sergeant ——— Stockton 1 Patrol Officer

 Lieutenant ——— GLS 2 Patrol Officers

 Lieutenant (4:00 P.M. to 12:00 P.M.)
   |——— Patrol Sergeant
   |         |——— GLS 7 Patrol Officers
   |         |——— GBS 3 Patrol Officers
   |——— GLS Sergeant ——— 2 Patrol Officers
   |——— GBS Sergeant ——— 3 Patrol Officers
```

Assigned sergeants   10
Swing sergeants   5
   Total sergeants   15

Assigned patrol officers   38
Swing patrol officers   16
   Total patrol officers   54

EXHIBIT 2 **Grayson University Police Department—Area-Time Report for Week Ending 4/22; Number of Incidents for Areas 1-6, Watch 3**

Week: 42
Julian Dates: 5103-5112

Area	16-18		18-20		20-22		22-0		Total	
1	2		1		2		1		6	
		4%		2%		4%		3%		3%
2	0		1		4		2		7	
		0%		2%		8%		5%		4%
3	5		0		7		1		13	
		10%		0%		15%		3%		7%
4	11		4		4		6		25	
		21%		9%		8%		15%		14%
5	0		0		0		0		0	
		0%		0%		0%		0%		0%
6	11		13		11		7		42	
		21%		30%		23%		18%		23%

EXHIBIT 3 **Grayson University Police Department—Classification Time Report for Week Ending 4/22, Watch 3**

Week: 42
Julian Dates: 5103-5112

Incident Classification	16-18		18-20		20-22		22-0		Total	
Violent crimes	1		2		1		0		4	
		2%		5%		2%		0%		2%
Property crimes	3		2		7		0		12	
		5%		5%		14%		0%		6%
Sex crimes	0		0		0		1		1	
		0%		0%		0%		3%		1%
Theft	2		1		1		5		9	
		4%		2%		2%		13%		5%
Missing property	2		3		1		4		10	
		4%		7%		2%		10%		5%
Narcotic violations	0		0		0		0		0	
		0%		0%		0%		0%		0%
Motor vehicle accidents	0		1		0		0		1	
		0%		2%		0%		0%		1%
Other (non-mv) accidents	1		0		0		0		1	
		2%		0%		0%		0%		1%
Disturbances	5		1		5		2		13	
		9%		2%		10%		5%		7%
Suspicious incidents	6		2		8		10		26	
		11%		5%		16%		25%		14%
Medical assistance	2		1		1		3		7	
		4%		2%		2%		8%		4%
Fire	0		0		1		0		1	
		0%		0%		2%		0%		1%
Traffic incidents	0		0		0		1		1	
		0%		0%		0%		3%		1%
Buildings and grounds	2		0		1		3		6	
		4%		0%		2%		8%		3%
Complaints	1		2		1		0		4	
		2%		5%		2%		0%		2%
Public service	19		18		18		9		64	
		35%		41%		35%		23%		34%
Services to agencies	0		0		0		0		0	
		0%		0%		0%		0%		0%
Alarms	11		11		6		2		30	
		20%		25%		12%		5%		16%
Total	55		44		51		40		190	
		29%		23%		27%		21%		100%

EXHIBIT 4 **Grayson University Police Department—Classification Area Report for Week Ending 4/22 for Areas 1-6, Watch 3**

Week: 42
Julian Dates: 5103-5112

Incident Classification	Area 1	Area 2	Area 3	Area 4	Area 5	Area 6
Violent crimes	0	0	0	0	0	0
	0%	0%	0%	0%	0%	0%
Property crimes	2	2	0	0	0	2
	33%	29%	0%	0%	0%	4%
Sex crimes	0	0	0	0	0	0
	0%	0%	0%	0%	0%	0%
Theft	0	0	0	1	0	1
	0%	0%	0%	4%	0%	2%
Missing property	1	0	2	2	0	2
	17%	0%	14%	8%	0%	4%
Narcotic violations	0	0	0	0	0	0
	0%	0%	0%	0%	0%	0%
Motor vehicle accidents	1	0	0	0	0	0
	17%	0%	0%	0%	0%	0%
Other (non-mv) accidents	0	0	0	0	0	0
	0%	0%	0%	0%	0%	0%
Disturbances	0	0	1	3	0	2
	0%	0%	7%	12%	0%	4%

EXHIBIT 5 **Grayson University Police Department—Response Time Report for Week Ending 4/22 for Areas 1-6, Watch 3**

Week: 42
Julian Dates: 5103-5112

Priority	Response (minutes)	Area 1	Area 2	Area 3	Area 4	Area 5	Area 6
1	0-2	0	0	0	0	0	1
		0%	0%	0%	0%	0%	50%
	2-4	0	0	0	1	0	1
		0%	0%	0%	50%	0%	50%
	4-6	0	0	0	1	0	0
		0%	0%	0%	50%	0%	0%
	6+	0	0	0	0	0	0
		0%	0%	0%	0%	0%	0%
Total		0	0	0	2	0	2

EXHIBIT 6 **Grayson University Police Department—Average Response Time Reported for Week Ending 4/22**

Week: 42
Julian Dates: 5103-5112

Response Time	W1	W2	W3	Average	Standard Deviation	Department Standard
Priority 1	3.0	4.0	2.4	2.9	1.4	2
Priority 2	2.9	5.2	6.3	5.3	16.9	4
Priority 3	6.4	8.8	4.6	7.4	13.5	7
Priority 4	3.0	4.0	9.8	9.2	12.1	10

Number of Incidents by Category	W1	W2	W3	Total
Violent crime	4	2	5	11
Index crime	12	43	26	81
All incidents	105	198	190	493

CASE 12.2 Province of Ontario Translation Services

In September, officials in the Ministry of Government Services (MGS), an executive department in the provincial government of Ontario, Canada, were considering how to respond to five months of declining workloads in the ministry's Translation Services. A new policy required for the first time that the Translation Services and a number of the ministry's other services charge their government clients. As soon as the policy was instituted, however, many government agencies started to have fewer manuals, forms, and other documents translated; to use bilingual (both English- and French-speaking) staff to translate official letters; or to send more work to private translation services.

By the end of May, Eugene Strauss, the MGS assistant deputy minister for Supply and Services, began to consider reducing the Translation Services staff. His target date for a final decision was September 30.

Ava Rosenfeld Clark prepared this case under the supervision of Professor Regina E. Herzlinger.

ONTARIO'S BILINGUAL POLICY

Ontario was the most heavily populated Canadian province. Almost three quarters of its people were of English ancestry. Another 500,000 residents had French-speaking ancestors, many of whom had emigrated to Ontario from the Province of Quebec. The remaining population was composed of a multitude of cultural groups.

Although most Ontarians spoke English, the province, like the rest of Canada, had been officially bilingual (English and French) since 1968. The Prime Minister of Ontario, William Davis, directed all departments and agencies of the Ontario government to provide a full range of bilingual services, especially in those areas of the province where there were large concentrations of people for whom French was the primary or sole language. He had expanded the Translation Services Bureau (TSB) to meet the demands placed on it by the government's bilingual program.

REORGANIZATION AND THE INTRODUCTION OF CHARGEBACK

MGS was formed to provide common support services such as vehicle service, mail service, printing and supplies, and translation to the other ministries. It was to "charge for services provided by the Ministry . . . to customer ministries on a full-cost basis," known as "chargeback." The customer ministries, in turn, were free to purchase those services wherever they could receive the best price, quality, and speed of delivery, either from the government or from the private sector. It was hoped that the new system would spur both government purchasers and providers to greater efficiency. The TSB was transferred to the new MGS. Following are the guidelines for those agencies adopting chargeback:

- All goods and services will be provided by the service agency on a pricing basis which reflects either total cost or the prevailing market price.
- Where true competitive market prices are readily obtainable from the private sector, the pricing structure will reflect the lower of market prices or total costs.
- Where market prices are not obtainable, the total cost to the service agency will be used as the pricing base.
- Selection of the actual pricing base will initially be the responsibility of the manager of the supplying service. But in subsequent fiscal years, prices will require approval by the Management Board.

The expenses included by each service agency in arriving at the total cost of its services were: salaries and wages; employee benefits; transportation and communications; service costs (e.g., mailing, equipment repairs); supplies; equipment and capital assets;[1] depreciation—to be calculated for all capital assets on a straight-line basis, amortized over the estimated life; and accruals—to be included in the total costs for a given accounting period when determined by the service agency to be a significant part of operating costs.

---

[1]Individual items used by the service agency in the provision of service that cost over $1,000 and had over one year's life expectancy were to be capitalized and depreciated over the estimated expected life of the item. Where the item's original cost could not be established, an estimated or appraised value was to be used.

Standard costs were to be developed from budgeted expenses and forecasted work volumes. The timing of billing was to be no later than the end of the month following that in which the service was rendered, with charges between ministries made through the existing system of journal vouchers.

CHARGEBACK FOR TSB SERVICES

TSB offered three primary services. It was originally established in 1959 to provide free translation and interpreting, usually of residency and work papers, to new immigrants into Ontario. In 1968, it also became responsible for the bulk of the English-to-French and all-languages-to-English translations required by the government's new bilingual policy. The bureau manager decided that, under chargeback, translation services to new immigrants, which then accounted for about one-third of the Bureau's work, would remain free of charge. Rates for the services were set as follows:

	Cost per Word		
Service	*General*	*Technical*	*Rush*
English to French	$0.09	$0.12	$0.15
Any language to English	0.07	0.10	0.12
Immigrants	Free on request		

The rates were set by MGS analysts and the bureau manager to be competitive with current commercial rates. They had originally planned to analyze the bureau's direct and indirect expenses in order to set service fees. (See **Exhibits 1** and **2** for data on the bureau's expenses.) But they decided that it would be too difficult to determine overhead expenses, and that whatever such an analysis might show, they would still have to set fees to compete with the private sector.

Private translation services in Ontario that specialized in English-to-French translations had no single price list, but usually charged clients by the number of English words to be translated and the overall length and complexity of the job. TSB, on the other hand, decided to charge clients according to the number of words in the target, rather than the original language. In the case of English-to-French translations, the French version is always longer.

For a short document, a private company's fee was usually 13 cents or 14 cents per word for relatively simple work, and 20 cents to 22 cents per word for technical work requiring more than the usual amount of research. Clients whose rush jobs required overtime were often charged an additional 25 percent. Occasionally, some clients were charged as little as 8 cents per word to keep translators busy during slack periods. Customers included advertising agencies, retail chains, and large manufacturing companies. Work received from government agencies was priced on the same basis as work for all other clients.

In determining their rates, most private translation firms included all employee salaries and benefits, utilities and rent, advertising, the cost of buying and servicing typewriters and the cost of other materials, transportation costs (most material was delivered to clients by taxicab), and profit margins.

Annual salaries for the 15 translators employed by a typical company then included $8,000 for a college student who worked during vacations, $14,000 for an experienced but relatively slow translator, $16,000 for a good, fast translator, and $24,000 for the head of a department—the person who checked the work of other translators.

TSB had a staff of 18, five of whom had been working for the agency for ten months or less and were still formally on probation (a period that lasted for one full year). All employees except the manager were required to belong to the Civil Service Association of Ontario. Under chargeback, TSB would still be authorized to send work to private translation services or free-lance translators, as it had done in previous years when the need arose.

EFFECT OF CHARGEBACK ON TSB SERVICES

Immediately after chargeback went into effect, many users cut down on the total number of items translated (see **Exhibit 3**). The Ministry of Treasury, Economics, and Intergovernmental Affairs, for example, ceased to publish its monthly "Quebec Log," a selection of Quebec newspaper commentaries on Toronto politics (translated from French into English by TSB). For small items, such as official letters, some agencies asked bilingual secretaries and other staff to serve as translators, instead of using TSB. A few agencies turned to private translation agencies for their English-to-French translations. Some government officials began to express concern about differences in quality in the translated documents that the ministries were providing for the public and inconsistency in the translation of government terminology. MGS suggested that the effect of the chargeback system on client ministries' use of TSB might be inconsistent with the government's statements on its bilingual policy.

In response to a July report that the use of TSB was still declining, Mr. Strauss directed that the agency's staff be reduced by September 30 if usage continued to decline.

ASSIGNMENT

1. Determine the impact of the chargeback policy on TSB's volume.
2. Evaluate the principles contained in the Management Board's recommendations.
3. Recommend specific staffing changes in TSB, if appropriate.
4. Evaluate the overall transfer pricing mechanism.

EXHIBIT 1 **Province of Ontario Translation Services—Translation Services Bureau Estimated Budget ($000)**

Classification	Last Year's Estimates Annualized	This Year's Estimated Changes				This Year's Estimates Total
		Cost Increases	Workload Changes	Service Level Changes	New Services	
Salaries and wages:						
Regular and probationary	$220.2	$10.5				$230.7
Unclassified—regular			$11.0			11.0
Unclassified—summer students	3.2					3.2
Total salaries and wages	223.4	10.5	11.0			244.9
Employee benefits	22.5	1.0	1.0			24.5
Transportation and communication	2.0	0.1				2.1
Services	50.6	2.0	2.0			54.6
Supplies and equipment	6.4	0.3	1.0			7.7
Activity subtotal	304.9	13.9	15.0			333.8
Less: Recoveries from chargeback						220.2
Activity total, net						113.6
Complement	18.0					18.0

Source: Translation Services Bureau, Government of Ontario

EXHIBIT 2 **Province of Ontario Translation Services—Translation Services Bureau Salary Data**

Position[a]	Salary
1. Manager	$21,897
2. Translator 3 (bilingual, E-F)	18,273
3. Translator 3 (bilingual, F-E, supervisor)	17,353
4. Translator 3 (multilingual, supervisor)	19,650
5. Translator 3 (bilingual E-F)	19,690
6. Translator 2 (bilingual, E-F)	14,442
7. Translator 2 (multilingual)	17,518
8. Translator 2 (bilingual, F-E)	16,271
9. Translator 2 (multilingual)	17,156
10. Translator 2 (bilingual, E-F)	15,019
11. Translator 2 (bilingual, E-F)	15,856
12. Translator 2 (bilingual, E-F)	14,396
13. Clerk General 4 (office manager)	9,640
14. Clerk General 4 (multilingual receptionist)	9,640
15. Clerical Stenographer/Typist (bilingual)	7,760
16. Clerical Stenographer/Typist (bilingual)	9,040
17. Clerical Stenographer/Typist (bilingual)	6,946
18. Clerk Typist 3	7,093

[a]Bilingual translators translated documents from English to French (E-F) or French to English (F-E). Multilingual translators translated documents from English into languages other than French or vice versa.

Source: Translation Services Bureau, Government of Ontario

EXHIBIT 3 **Province of Ontario Translation Services—Translation Services Bureau Statistics (volume by number of words)**

		Last Year				This Year			
		Bilingual		Multilingual		Bilingual		Multilingual	
		English to French	French to English	Government	Public	English to French	French to English	Government	Public
April	Internal[a]	69,489	38,707	52,606	51,174	73,581[c]	52,455	11,907	48,665
	Outside[b]	21,122	30,910	40,728	28,677	-	-	118,089	28,814
		90,611	69,617	93,334	79,851	73,581	52,455	129,996	77,479
May	Internal	50,185	51,224	46,528	71,652	49,315	49,003	20,450	57,326
	Outside	8,625	10,936	63,912	35,359	-	-	15,957	29,110
		58,810	62,160	110,440	107,011	49,315	49,003	36,407	86,436
June	Internal	47,141	40,078	57,437	47,025	49,920	20,970	17,037	42,973
	Outside	7,894	11,215	25,287	30,839	-	-	46,054	27,281
		55,035	51,293	82,724	77,864	49,920	20,970	63,091	70,254
July	Internal	36,370	39,853	37,175	50,451	62,851	44,928	19,311	57,666
	Outside	-	27,900	58,678	48,630	-	2,870	11,422	36,172
		36,370	67,753	95,853	99,081	62,851	47,798	30,733	93,838
August	Internal	119,338	44,553	59,077	83,861	72,780	17,757	13,884	49,913
	Outside	31,413	31,224	65,860	30,427	-	-	23,092	34,580
		150,751	75,777	124,937	114,288	72,780	17,757	36,976	84,493
September	Internal	40,558	63,691	29,174	69,947				
	Outside	14,921	9,935	38,292	32,700				
		55,479	73,626	67,466	102,647				
October	Internal	43,944	56,044	38,065	68,450				
	Outside	10,065	20,316	76,135	32,718				
		54,009	76,360	114,200	101,168				
November	Internal	48,726	65,405	87,301	59,349				
	Outside	53,334	11,587	95,189	38,075				
		102,060	76,992	182,490	97,424				
December	Internal	38,782	26,030	76,568	22,871				
	Outside	5,000	6,460	73,105	27,316				
		43,782	32,490	149,673	50,187				
January	Internal	54,005	67,219	93,974	33,830				
	Outside	43,850	16,908	46,064	43,844				
		97,855	84,127	140,038	77,674				
February	Internal	86,627	83,588	42,787	43,857				
	Outside	12,676	40,740	41,222	44,438				
		99,303	124,328	84,009	88,295				
March	Internal	57,935	96,388	28,803	54,549				
	Outside	5,000	52,810	64,679	35,963				
		62,935	149,198	93,482	90,512				

Note: All bilingual translations were done for government ministries. Multilingual translations included both government work and services for new Ontario residents.
[a]Internal = material translated by Translation Services Bureau.
[b]Outside = material translated by free-lance translators and private translation services.
[c]April totals included backlog from previous months for which client ministries were not charged.

Source: Translation Services Bureau, Government of Ontario

13 The Framework for Financial Decision-Making in Nonprofit Organizations

BECAUSE FINANCIAL RESOURCES ARE CONSTRAINED, ALL of us must make financial choices. We cannot buy everything. Instead, we must decide what and how much to buy, when to buy it, and how to finance our purchases. The process of making these choices is the topic of this chapter and Chapter 14.

When businesses consider such decisions, their profit objective helps them to evaluate their choices. They buy those things, in those quantities, and at those times that contribute to the greatest profits, and they finance their purchases with capital obtained at the lowest possible cost. But nonprofit organizations cannot rely on profit as the primary criterion of their financial decision-making because their purpose is not to make a profit but to serve society in other important ways. When nonprofits decide what and how much to buy, when to buy, and how to finance, they must consider the impact of these decisions on the society they serve, as well as on the organization's financial welfare.

Nonprofit organizations make many decisions, but the focus here is limited to the financial ones. Chapter 14 discusses the most frequent financial decisions—what and how much to buy, when to buy, and how to finance the purchase—in the context of nonprofit organizations. This chapter discusses how to manage the decision-making process and the framework for making financial decisions.

You may find some of the sections in these chapters repetitious. The same topic is discussed from a number of different perspectives because many people learn this subject best when they are provided with alternative ways of examining the same issue. If you find some of the economic discussions in these chapters a mere repetition of what you already understand, please go on to the next section. However, if you do not feel quite comfortable with the subject, you may find the slightly different expositions helpful.

MANAGING THE FINANCIAL DECISION-MAKING PROCESS

Good decisions can result only from intelligent consideration of a wide range of good alternatives. Many organizations, however, unnecessarily limit the number of alternatives they consider. Their stated reasons for narrowing the field are many, but one real reason prevails: a powerful person within the organization has already made the decision. In these organizations, the decision-making process becomes a method of rationalizing and defending decisions rather than one for shaping and investigating alternative ways of achieving the organization's goals. Even worse, it saps organizational creativity. Employees become political and expend energy in lining up behind the "right" decision rather than in fashioning original endeavors.

Some organizations try to avoid this problem through the creation of departments or units charged with the responsibility for creating and evaluating new ideas. But these units, too, can easily become political, lending their stamp of approval only to those ideas they think the boss wants.

How should the process be managed to ensure that fresh, creative approaches are presented and fairly analyzed? One critical dimension is the behavior of the organization's top management and board. Rigidly hierarchical and impersonal management limits the flow of good ideas, while managers who convey their willingness to listen are the fortunate beneficiaries of the best thoughts of their talented associates. Ironically, managers of organizations that are faring badly tend to become particularly inaccessible, defensively building barriers against the fresh ideas they so clearly need. For example, as the disasters of the Vietnam War escalated, President Lyndon B. Johnson reportedly reversed his previous gregarious habits and isolated himself in the White House.[1] A more positive model was presented by President Franklin Delano Roosevelt who reportedly opened his doors to many unusual types of advisors during the dark days of the Depression and World War II. Roosevelt is said to have listened intently, enthusiastically thanked the advisors, and then slowly and carefully considered the advice.[2]

For most decisions many alternatives exist, no one of which is clearly superior to the rest. However, when the decision-making process has become political, it will usually include a small number of alternatives, frequently only the *status quo* and the favored decision, and may be characterized by the massive superiority claimed for the favored option.

Both experienced and inexperienced managers and board members can help prevent the decision-making process from becoming political. Experienced ones can generate alternatives that contain the lessons of their

---

[1]George Reedy, *The Presidency in Flux* (New York, NY: Columbia University Press, 1973).
[2]Arthur M. Schlesinger, *The Age of Roosevelt* (Boston: Houghton Mifflin, 1957).

experiences, while the inexperienced can question the established dogma. Both points of view are useful. Some organizations encourage creativity with formal recognition of valuable new ideas that grant their originators financial rewards and visibility, such as designation as the "Entrepreneur of the Year."

The many managers who are legitimately concerned about the time demands of an open and creative process for financial decision-making should also consider the costs of constraining the process. In some cases, a closed political process sounds the organization's death knell.

FINANCIAL DECISION-MAKING IN NONPROFIT ORGANIZATIONS: BENEFIT-COST ANALYSIS

The process of allocating the funds of a nonprofit organization among competing activities is frequently called *benefit-cost analysis*. This nomenclature emphasizes the benefit-conferring nature of activities undertaken in nonprofits, and distinguishes their financial decision-making from that of for-profit businesses whose primary purpose is to earn a profit.

Benefit-cost analysis quantifies the benefits the proposed activity will generate, usually in monetary terms, and compares them to its costs. Measures of the relationship between benefits and costs help to assess whether the activity should be undertaken and, if so, they can also be used to determine the activity's priority ranking in commanding the organization's capital. Benefit-cost analysis first appeared in the U.S. in 1930, when Congress declared that the benefits of the federal flood control projects must exceed their costs. In their excellent *Cost-Benefit Analysis*, Peter G. Sassone and William A. Schaffer trace its subsequent dissemination through the federal government and among economists specializing in public expenditure analysis.[3] The technique was popularized in the 1960s by Secretary of Defense Robert McNamara, who used it to help set priorities in the weapons-acquisitions process. Since then, the benefit-cost technique has been applied to a wide variety of activities both in government and in private nonprofit organizations.[4]

Benefit-cost analysis entails the following five steps:

(1) The benefits and costs of the proposed activity are identified.

(2) Its benefits and costs are measured, frequently in financial terms.

---

[3]Peter G. Sassone and William A. Schaffer, *Cost-Benefit Analysis* (New York, NY: Academic Press, 1978).
[4]See, for example, Charles J. Hitch and Roland M. McKean, *The Economics of Defense in the Nuclear Age* (New York, NY: Atheneum, 1966).

(3) The financial benefit-cost relationships are ranked.

(4) The distribution of the benefits among different sectors of society is specified.

(5) A sensitivity analysis tests the sensitivity of the results to the assumptions made.

Each of these five steps will be discussed in detail.

Identifying Benefits and Costs

The positive results created by the activity are termed its *benefits*. Some of these benefits reflect the *direct* purposes of the program, while others occur *indirectly*. For example, the construction of a hydroelectric power station will yield the direct benefit of generating electric power, the project's intended purpose, and the indirect benefit of flood control. A vocational training program will yield the direct benefit of increased earning power for its participants and, perhaps, the indirect benefits of a more learned society and the reduced need for crime prevention. Many activities inevitably create negative side effects and these too should be articulated. A hydroelectric project may endanger some animal species or divert water needed elsewhere. These are *negative benefits*, or *costs*, to society.

Table 13-1 presents the way E. J. Mishan delineates the benefits of building a subway and the benefits of a program to eliminate disease. The users of the subway receive the direct benefits of the greater speed and comfort and possibly the lower costs of the subway as compared to alternate means of transportation. The users of other means of transportation benefit from reductions in congestion that occur when travelers are diverted to the subway.

The rise in land values in areas around the new subway line is not an additional benefit because it merely reflects the value of the reduced travel time for subway users. To put it another way, people are willing to pay more for land that is now easier and quicker to reach. The benefits of the increased speed and convenience are mirrored in the rise in the value of the land, but they have already been included among the direct benefits of the subway.

Measuring Benefits and Costs

Economists would have costs valued at the *opportunity cost* of the next best use of resources. For example, if the money invested in a new building could have earned 8 percent interest, the cost of the money invested in real estate is the 8 percent return the money could have earned elsewhere. In practice, the opportunity cost measures are difficult to delineate and costs are usually valued at actual expenditures.

TABLE 13-1   **Examples of the Benefits Associated with Various Activities**

Activity	Possible Benefits
A. Subway with a fare price set equal to its average operating costs	1. *For Users of Alternative Modes of Travel*—cost and time savings in comparison to their present mode of travel
	2. *For Nonusers*—decreased congestion, resulting in time savings
	3. *For Those with No Alternative Modes of Travel*—ability to travel
B. A program to eliminate disease	1. Avoided expenditures on medical care
	2. Avoided losses in production
	3. Avoided pain and discomfort

Source: Adapted with permission from E. J. Mishan, *Cost-Benefit Analysis* (London: George Allen Unwin, 1982), pp. 3-8.

Financial valuation of benefits is even more difficult. If the program creates results that can be sold, the benefits are partially measured by whatever people are willing to pay for them. The direct benefit of a hydroelectric project is partially measured by the market value of the electricity it sells. The direct benefit of a subway is partially measured by the value of its receipts.[5]

However, the subway has other benefits that should be measured. For most of its users, the subway generates benefits of reduced travel time and cost. The value of these benefits may be greater than the subway fare. Thus, the difference between the fare and the cost and time savings is a benefit that should be measured. The benefits of reduced congestion on other modes of transportation that result in reduced travel time and costs should also be measured.[6] Finally, the negative benefits of subway construction, if any, should be measured.

Guidelines can be used to measure benefits. In the case of the subway, the benefits to be measured accrue to the subway users and to those

[5]Prices reflect the *lowest* measures of the benefits to users. The market price is the one the very last buyer was willing to pay. It measures the value to the last buyer. But buyers before the last one are willing to pay a higher price. (Remember that the demand curve is downward sloping.) The benefits to them are higher than the price.

[6]E. J. Mishan, *Cost-Benefit Analysis* (London: George Allen Unwin, 1982), pp. 3-5.

using other modes of transportation. The value of the time savings created by the subway for each group can be estimated by the value of the wages travelers to work would earn during the time they save and the value to leisure travelers of their leisure time. Some negative benefits can be directly measured. If retail businesses directly surrounding the subway construction site are forced to close, the negative cost of the subway is the loss of their contribution to the economy. As in this example, different users frequently receive different benefits and the value to each should be measured. Some guidelines for valuing the benefits of other activities are shown in Table 13-2.

The valuation of benefits must always be related to the results that would have occurred without the activity. The benefits of the program are the values of the *additional* results that it caused. Thus, if the new subway does not decrease time or cost or does not increase comfort and access when compared to existing modes of transportation, it generates no benefits. And, if a vocational training program does not increase its participants' wage-earning ability, it too has not created benefits.

TABLE 13-2 **Guidelines for Valuing Benefits**

Item to Be Valued	Theoretical Measure of Value
Time saved	Marginal social product of labor, as measured by payments received per hour
Conversion of park land to an industrial park	Minimum compensation to be paid to existing park users that would cause them to agree to a conversion
Loss of life or physical impairment	A. Discounted present value of earnings lost because of premature death or physical impairment *or* B. The implicit value attached to human life when the society decides not to pursue life-saving activities
Pollution damage on property	Up to 100 percent of the prior market value of the property

Source: Adapted with permission from E. J. Mishan, *Cost-Benefit Analysis* (London: George Allen Unwin, 1982), pp. 295-362.

Whether the activity is a benefit or a cost depends on who is doing the analysis. For example, the West Side Highway to be built in New York City was to be funded primarily by the U.S. government. From the perspective of New York City, the new highway would have helped it to avoid some expenditures the city otherwise would have paid out of its own pocket and would have helped it to generate new real estate tax revenues from businesses attracted by the highway from other areas. But from the perspective of the U.S. government, neither of these is a benefit to the country as a whole. The benefit to the U.S. is in the real economic growth the project will create. Otherwise, the project has no benefits.

In practice, these measurement perspectives are not always applied. For example, when the federal government was deciding whether or not to fund the West Side Highway project, it accepted the avoidance of expenditures and the creation of new real estate taxes as a benefit of the project. But from the perspective of the U.S. as a whole, the fact that New York City can avoid spending money and charge more in real estate taxes is not a benefit; the real benefit is the additional economic growth that this project can help to create.

Sometimes, the results of an activity cannot be measured in financial terms. For example, the analysis of the alternative ways of building the West Side Highway included consideration of the effect on air, noise, and water pollution, on local street traffic, and on the other factors shown in Table 13-3. The analysts in this case preferred to express these effects in their natural physical dimensions rather than to convert them to monetary terms.

When results are stated in non-monetary terms, the analysis is referred to as a *cost-effectiveness analysis*. For example, a highway construction project's cost-effectiveness analysis evaluates the cost per mile of highway built instead of valuing the benefit of a mile of highway. Similarly, a cost-effectiveness analysis of various remedial education programs will focus on the cost per unit of student improvement rather than on the financial benefits that result from improved educational achievement.

Because "effectiveness" in a cost-effectiveness analysis is stated in non-monetary terms, its separate components cannot be added, unlike benefit-cost analysis in which financial measures of different results can be summed to one number. In Table 13-3, for example, air, noise, and water pollution cannot simply be added to each other. The reader is then left to judge the relative importance of each separate effect. Benefit-cost analysis, in contrast, adds all the effects into one financial result.

Ranking Benefit-Cost Relationships

The decision rules for ranking projects depend on the nature of the decision. If the activity must be implemented, and all methods yield equal quality, an appropriate decision rule chooses the implementation method that minimizes costs. For example, if the only school in town has burned down,

TABLE 13-3 **Other Effects of West Side Highway Project Alternatives**

Alternatives	New Housing	New Parkland	Morning Peak Hour Traffic (1995)	Local Street Traffic	Relocation	Air Pollution	Noise Pollution[a]	Water Pollution	Drivers Diverted to Transit Daily
Maintenance[b]	None	None	Volume exceeds capacity for most of highway	No change	None	No change in CO, hydrocarbons, or NO	During construction—1, after construction—3	No change	None
Reconstruction[b]	None	None	Volume exceeds capacity for 1/3 of highway	Insignificant change in cars; 9% fewer trucks	4 buildings (13 businesses)	Slight increase in CO levels; no change in others	During construction—2, after construction—5	No change	None
Arterial[b] (with railway)	None	2.81 inland acres; improved access to Battery Park	Volume exceeds capacity for 1/3 of highway; near capacity for rest	Insignificant change in cars; 6% fewer trucks	None	Largest in CO levels, exceeding federal standards	During construction—3, after construction—4	No change	9,000
Inboard[b] (with busway)	None	21 acres of waterfront park	Volume exceeds capacity for 1/3 of highway	Slightly fewer cars; 9% fewer trucks	48 buildings (89 residents and 91 businesses) 18 pier tenants	Slight decrease in CO (by diverting truck traffic)	During construction—5, after construction—2	Slight improvement from smoothing shoreline	10,500
Outboard[b] (with busway)	128 acres for future development	75 acres of waterfront park	Volume exceeds capacity for 1/2 of highway	Slightly fewer cars; 12% fewer trucks	40 buildings (80 residents and 101 businesses) 23 pier tenants	Slight decrease in CO (by diverting truck traffic)	During construction—4, after construction—1	Slight improvement from smoothing shoreline	10,500
Modified[c] Outboard	101 acres for future development	93 acres of waterfront park	Same as Outboard	Same as Outboard	47 buildings (109 residents and 92 businesses) 15 pier tenants	Same as Outboard	Same as Outboard	Same as Outboard	10,500

[a]The number 1 represents the lowest pollution levels, 5 the highest. *Source:* West Side Highway Project analysis.
[b]Based on construction to 72nd Street.
[c]Based on construction to 42nd Street, including transit system construction (without transit right-of-way costs).

Source: Regina E. Herzlinger, "Costs, Benefits, and the West Side Highway," *The Public Interest* 55 (Spring 1979): 90-91.

and the town's citizens insist that it be replaced, and all the replacement proposals provide the same amount of space and amenities, the decision-making methodology should rank projects in the inverse order of their costs. In this case, projects with the lowest costs should receive priority ranking. Decisions that should use this minimum cost criteria include activities that respond to regulatory requirements, to legislation, and to other purposes that users or citizens require, such as renovating out-of-date laboratory facilities in a college, installing an air-conditioning system that preserves art in a museum, and constructing new highway or airport space to relieve serious traffic congestion.

But many activities fall outside these categories. Whether they are implemented or not depends on the decisions of the managers. These activities are voluntary, not mandatory. For these types of activities, the relationship between benefits and costs must be evaluated. If the benefits are lower than the costs, the activity will usually not be implemented unless there are compelling nonfinancial reasons for doing so. (Some of these will be discussed in the next section.)

If the benefits are greater than the costs, the ranking of each activity depends on the nature of the activity and the amount of money available. If the activity cannot be proportionately increased or decreased in cost and if the organization's funding is limited, the appropriate criterion ranks projects by the magnitude of the difference between their benefits and costs. As in the example in Table 13-4, if the organization has only $100,000 to spend, it should pick Activity Y that yields benefits less costs of $200,000. If the activities can be contracted or expanded, Activity X should receive funding priority over Activity Y because it yields $4 of benefits for every $1 of costs while Y has a benefit-cost ratio of only 3 to 1.

TABLE 13-4   **Benefit-Cost Relationship of Two Different Activities**

Activity	(A) Benefits	(B) Cost	(C) = (A) − (B) Benefits Less Cost	(D) = (A) ÷ (B) Benefits Cost
X	$133,333	$33,333	$100,000	4
Y	$300,000	$100,000	$200,000	3

Although these decision rules are often applied to monetary resources, they should be applied to all types of scarce resources. For example, if the scarcest resources in a school are the teachers, activities should be ranked on the basis of benefits created in relationship to the teachers' time expended.

Thus, suppose Activities X and Y above create the relationship between benefits and teachers' hours shown in Table 13-5. In this example, Activity Y should be funded first if the organization's funding for teachers is limited and if the activities cannot be proportionately expanded or contracted. Activity X should be funded first if these conditions do not pertain.

TABLE 13-5 Relationships of Benefits to Teachers' Salaries and Hours

Activity	(A) Benefits	(B) Cost of Teachers' Salaries	(C) = (A) − (B) Benefits Less Cost of Teachers' Salaries	(D) Teachers' Hours	(E) = (A) ÷ (D) Benefits Teachers' Hours
X	$133,333	$16,667	$116,666	1,667	80
Y	$300,000	$60,000	$240,000	5,000	60

Linear programming can be used to rank activities with a number of scarce or limited resources. It is not commonly used in nonprofit organizations because it requires data that are usually not available. The data envelope analysis described in Chapter 11 is a more practical way of ranking activities characterized by many scarce resources.

The ranking methodologies described above assumed that the activities were independent of each other. If they are not, the benefits, if any, of each activity with and without the others should be measured in relationship to their cost or other scarce resource. For example, as shown in Table 13-6, the combination of Activities Y and Z yields significantly higher benefit-to-cost relationships than either activity by itself because of the synergy between them.

TABLE 13-6 Benefit-Cost Analysis of Complementary Activities

Activity	(A) Benefits	(B) Cost	(C) = (A) − (B) Benefits Less Cost	(D) = (A) ÷ (B) Benefits Cost
Y alone	$300,000	$100,000	$200,000	3
Z alone	$400,000	$150,000	$250,000	$2\frac{2}{3}$
Y and Z together	$1,000,000	$250,000	$750,000	4

Analyzing Distributional Effects

The results of an activity may yield positive benefit-to-cost relationships and yet not be desirable because they accrue to a group the organization does not wish to serve. For example, if a government activity with a high benefit-to-cost relationship benefits only the rich and uses monies collected from poor and middle-class taxpayers to achieve these results, many would refuse to invest in the activity.

Conversely, an activity may result in a low benefit-to-cost relationship and yet be deemed desirable because of the people who benefit from it. For example, consider a hypothetical activity that extends the lives of people who suffer from an inherited form of anemia. The benefits of this activity are valued partially by the increased income that the victims can earn in the newly-extended years of their lives. But, because many of those who suffer from the disease earn low incomes, the benefit-to-cost relationship is low. Should funding for extending human life be denied merely because the beneficiaries are poor? Many people would deplore such a result.

Distributional effects specify who benefits and who pays for an activity. Incorporating distributional effects directly into a benefit-cost analysis is difficult. It can be achieved by assigning weights to certain sectors of society, with higher weights given to those sectors that are deemed deserving of benefits. In the example above, the benefits of a program whose results accrue to the poor would receive a much higher weight than one whose benefits accrue to the rich. Activities that confer results on other sectors of society generally perceived to be deserving, such as the elderly or those living in rural or ghetto areas, can receive higher weights than others. Alternatively, the benefit-cost analysis can be conducted without incorporating distributional effects, and these effects can be separately considered.

Regardless of how distributional effects are included, the nonprofit organizations that neglect consideration of these effects run the grave risk of conducting activities that do not produce benefits for the organization's primary constituency. When a school offers a course in a frivolous subject, when a museum displays objects in programs that will attract primarily the educated elite, when a nonprofit hospital offers activities for the vain and worried-well, when a government subsidizes programs that will benefit only the rich, or when a social service agency caters primarily to those with only minor problems, it may be ignoring the distributional impact of its mission.

Measures of distributional impact are important because they reflect the fundamental purpose of the organization. If questions of distributional impact are left unasked, the nonprofit organization may become self-serving, fulfilling the needs of its well-heeled donors and board members rather than the broader commuity it is enfranchised to serve. A few well-to-do, private nonprofit hospitals, for example, strayed far from their charitable mandate to provide services to patients regardless of their ability to pay, when they rushed poor, uninsured patients into ambulances and ''dumped'' them into hospitals run by city and local governments. This practice became so prevalent that the U.S. Congress enacted "anti-dumping" legislation to prohibit it. Such regulation would have been unnecessary had the distributional impact of the hospital programs been regularly scrutinized.

Conducting a Sensitivity Analysis

Most financial decisions rely on assumptions about the future. The introduction of a new service program contains a host of assumptions about the number of clients for the new program, its revenues, and its expenses. All of these assumptions are uncertain, and they have a good chance of being wrong. This observation is not cynical but rather a factual assessment of our limited ability to predict the future correctly. For example, each of three experts who were asked to predict the course of the economy in the next two years presented a completely different view. At best, only one of the three can be correct, and all three can be wrong.[7]

When confronted with uncertainty about the future, most of us respond by asking for more information. In the real world, such requests must frequently remain unfulfilled because it is either not possible or very expensive to gather the requested information. But, if we permit uncertainty to paralyze us, civilization would not progress. For example, had Spanish royalty insisted on perfect information about the shape of the world before commissioning an investigatory journey, the European discovery of "the New World" might have been considerably delayed.

While we cannot eliminate uncertainty, we can reduce it. After all, most of us have intuitive feelings that some assumptions can be made with more confidence than others. *Sensitivity analysis* can help us to articulate why we are comfortable with accepting some assumptions and not with others by analyzing the effects of assumptions different from the ones we accepted.

To illustrate, let's consider the decision of whether to operate a nonprofit day-care program. The program is to be conducted in a small town of 25,000 residents, and there are 1,000 children between the ages of 3 and 5 who are potential candidates for the program. No other day-care facility exists in or near the town. The program will require rent and similar expenses of $6,000 a year and teachers' and aides' expenses of $20,000 a year. The charge of $1,500 per child per term is the standard rate in the region. Each child will require $200 of costs a year for supplies.

Is the decision to start this program a financially wise one? Sensitivity analysis will examine the realism of the assumptions about the revenues, costs, and number of children in the proposed program.

---

[7]Joel Kurtzman, "Now That the Recession is Official . . .," *The New York Times*, 13 January 1991, p. 4.

Break-Even Analysis   The break-even component of the analysis will determine the number of children necessary to generate revenues equal to the program's costs. We can then assess whether that break-even number of children is likely to enroll by comparing it to the number of children who are potential students in the program.

Break-even analysis is performed by equating the mathematical expression for total costs to the one for total revenues and finding the number of children who cause costs to equal revenues. We examined this topic in Chapter 10, but let us review it here.

Total costs can be expressed mathematially as $6,000 in rent and similar expenses plus $20,000 in teacher expenses plus $200 per child:

$$\text{Total Costs} = \$26,000 + (\$200 \times X)$$

where X = the number of children enrolled.

Total revenues can be expressed mathematically as $1,500 of tuition revenue per child multiplied by the number of children:

$$\text{Total Revenues} = \$1,500 \times X$$

where X = the number of children enrolled.

The break-even point occurs when total revenues equal total costs. If we equate the equation for total costs to the equation for total revenues, we can calculate the number of children needed to break even:

$$\text{Total Revenues} = \text{Total Costs}$$
$$\$1,500X = \$26,000 + \$200X$$
$$\$1,300X = \$26,000$$
$$X = \frac{\$26,000}{\$1,300}$$
$$X = 20 \text{ children}$$

The break-even point occurs at 20 children. If the program enrolls fewer than 20 children, it will operate at a loss. With 1,000 children as potential enrollees and no immediate competitors, it seems likely that the day-care center can easily enroll 20 children.

However, there are other circumstances that will cause the program to operate at a loss. Expenses can be higher than expected or revenues can be lower than expected. If the rent expense is higher than the projected $6,000 or if teacher or aide expenses are higher than the expected $20,000, the program will lose money. But, these events are unlikely to happen if the program signs year-long contracts with the landlord, teachers, and aides. If the supplies costs per child exceed the projected $200, the program will also operate at a loss. This, too, is unlikely to occur if these funds are tightly controlled. Finally, if revenues fall below the projected $1,500 per child the program will also lose money. However, if tuition is paid at the start of the school year, the likelihood of a tuition shortfall is also low.

The Process of Sensitivity Analysis   We have just performed a sensitivity analysis. We evaluated the impact of three critical assumptions on the decision to start a day-care center. We examined the realism of the assumptions about the volume of the program, its revenues, and its expenses.

The technique of break-even anlysis is invaluable for sensitivity analysis. It calculates the volume of activity at which revenues and expenses are equal to each other. The sensitivity analysis can then examine the likelihood of a loss if volume and revenues are lower than expected or if expenses are higher than expected.

Uncertainty about the future is the reason for performing a sensitivity analysis. The concept of uncertainty is sometimes expressed in probabilistic terms. But many people are confused rather than enlightened by this formal mathematical method of presentation.[8]

Break-Even Analysis Generalized   The technique of break-even analysis can be more generally expressed as the process for computing the level of volume, called X, at which total costs equal total revenues. The discussion below delineates how this form of analysis can be applied to any financial decision.

Total costs are generally expressed as a function of fixed costs (costs that remain the same regardless of volume) and variable costs (costs that vary directly with increases in volume). Total fixed costs do not change with volume. For example, the rent expense for the school building is independent of the number of children attending the school; it will not change if the number of students changes. Many personnel costs, such as salaries for tenured civil servants and faculty members, are also fixed; they will not vary with the amount of work to be done. Fixed costs may change for other reasons, such as management decisions or price changes, but they will not be changed directly by a change in activity level. The relationship between costs and volume for fixed costs is illustrated in Figure 13-1.

Variable costs change proportionately with volume. If each student in the day-care program uses supplies that cost $200, the variable supplies cost is $200 per student. The total supplies cost is calculated by multiplying the

---

[8]For those seeking a mathematical elucidation of sensitivity analysis, the following additional readings are recommended: Kenneth J. Arrow and Robert C. Lind, "Uncertainty and the Evaluation of Public Investment Decisions," *American Economic Review* (June 1970): 364-378; John S. Hammond, "Better Decisions with Preference Theory," *Harvard Business Review* (November-December 1967); Lorraine Datson, Lorenz Kruger, and Michael Herdelberger, eds., *The Probabilistic Revolution* (Cambridge, MA: MIT Press, 1987).

FIGURE 13-1 **Fixed Cost-Volume Relationship for Day-Care Program**

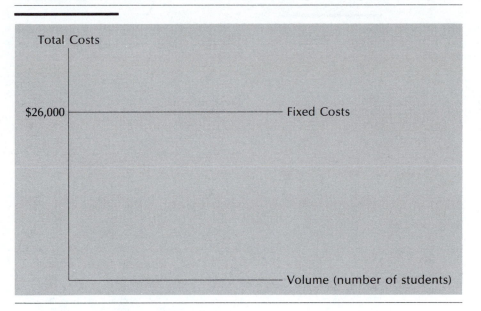

number of students by the per-student cost of supplies. With no students, the total supplies cost will be $0, and with 30 students, its costs will be $6,000 (30 × $200). The variable cost line has a constant slope—every change in volume will bring about the same change in total variable costs. For example, if the volume of students changes by 10, whether the change is from 10 to 20 students or from 30 to 40 students, the change in total supplies costs will be the same, $2,000. Items that can be purchased in units of one, such as supplies, are often variable costs.

The relationship between variable costs and volume is illustrated in Figure 13-2 for the proposed day-care program.

The total cost equation, the sum of fixed and variable costs, is generally described as follows:

$$\text{Total Costs} = \text{Fixed Costs} + (\text{Variable Costs})(X)$$

where X = volume.

Total revenues equal the price per unit of volume times the volume. They are generally described as follows:

$$\text{Total Revenues} = (\text{Price})(X)$$

where X = volume.

FIGURE 13-2   **Variable Cost-Volume Relationships for Day-Care Program**

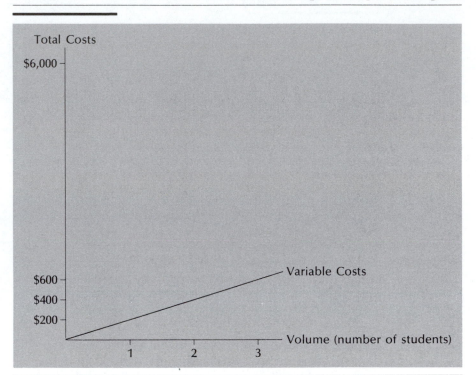

The break-even volume occurs where total revenues equal total costs. It is equal to fixed costs divided by the difference of price less variable costs:

$$\text{Total Costs} = \text{Total Revenues}$$
$$\text{Fixed Costs} + (\text{Variable Costs})(X) = (\text{Price})(X)$$
$$\text{Fixed Costs} = (\text{Price})(X) - (\text{Variable Costs})(X)$$
$$\text{Fixed Costs} = (X)(\text{Price} - \text{Variable Costs})$$
$$X = \frac{\text{Fixed Costs}}{\text{Price} - \text{Variable Costs}}$$

where X = break-even volume.

You may find it easier to conceptualize the break-even volume when it is graphically depicted, as in Figure 13-3. The break-even point is where total revenues equal total costs. In the case of the day-care center, it occurs at 20 children. If you examine Figure 13-3, you will see that it is the point where the graph for total costs intersects the graph for total revenues.

FIGURE 13-3   **Graphical Example of Break-Even Analysis**
               for Day-Care Program

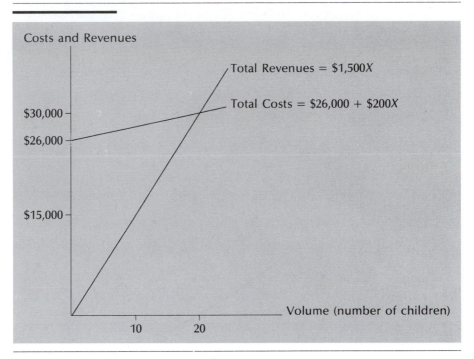

As a practical matter, computing the total costs equation is more difficult than illustrated because most programs involve hundreds of cost elements, not merely three. Then too, some costs are neither fixed nor variable.
For example, some regulations may require a day-care center to have a specific quantity of teachers' time for every additional five children enrolled.
Suppose this quantity of teachers' time costs $5,000. In this case the ex-
penses for teachers are neither fixed—they vary with every five children—
nor strictly variable. They remain the same from one to five children, climb
by $5,000 with the sixth child, and then, once again, remain constant through
the tenth child, and so on.

Such expenses are termed *semivariable*—a not too surprising name. Semivariable expenses complicate the break-even analysis because they change
the nature of the cost function. To return to our day-care center, the new
total cost function equals fixed costs of $6,000 for rent plus variable costs
of $200 per child plus costs of $5,000 for 1 to 5 children, or $10,000 for 6 to
10 children, or $15,000 for 11 to 15 children, or $20,000 for 16 to 20 children,
or $25,000 for 21 to 25 children, or $30,000 for 25 to 30 children. The graph
of the semivariable portion of the total costs is shown in Figure 13-4.

FIGURE 13-4 **Semivariable Cost-Volume Relationship for Day-Care Program**

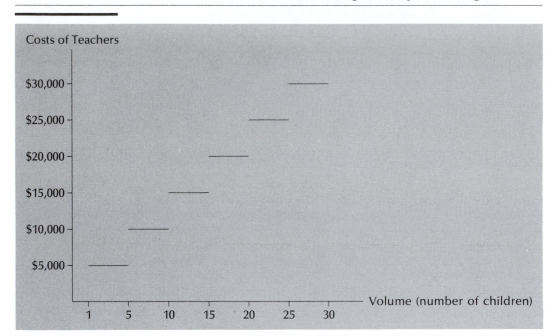

This version of the day-care program will break even at many points. The smallest point will occur with 20 children. For 21-25 children, the break-even point is approximately 24. As an example, we can start searching for the break-even volume at a level between 26 and 30 children. At that point, the total costs of the program are equal to the sum of $6,000 in rent and $30,000 for teachers and $200 per child, as shown in Figure 13-5. These costs equate to total revenues at a level of about 28 children:

$$\text{Total Revenues} = \text{Total Costs}$$
$$\$1,500X = \$36,000 + \$200X$$
$$\$1,300X = \$36,000$$
$$X = 27.7 \text{ children or } 28 \text{ children}$$

Sometimes a break-even point for a program with semivariable costs is computed by converting the semivariable costs into variable costs. In this case, the $5,000 of costs for every 5 children would be changed to $1,000 of variable costs per child. Although this conversion simplifies the computational process, it provides the wrong answer. Teachers are not paid at a flat rate per child but at a flat rate for teaching a certain amount of time. The statement of $1,000 of teacher's cost per child misrepresents their terms of

FIGURE 13-5 **Total Cost Calculation Example with Semivariable Cost Elements**

Expense Item	Nature of Cost-Volume Relationship	Cost Versus Number of Students					
		1-5	*6-10*	*11-15*	*16-20*	*21-25*	*26-30*
Teachers' salary and benefits	Semivariable	$5,000	$10,000	$15,000	$20,000	$25,000	$30,000
Supplies	Variable	$200 per student per year					
Rent	Fixed	$2,000 per year					
Heat, light, and power	Fixed	$1,500 per year					
Administrative salary	Fixed	$2,000 per year					
Administrative benefits	Fixed	$500 per year					

payment and therefore provides the wrong break-even quantity. Economic reality should never be sacrificed for mathematical tractability.

RELEVANT FACTORS AND CONTRIBUTION ANALYSIS

The only factors relevant to a particular decision are those that will change as a result of the decision. Factors that remain the same, that are unaffected by the decision, are irrelevant and should be ignored in the benefit-cost analysis. For example, a looming major oil crisis is an important world event but is irrelevant for most decisions. The decisions will remain the same, regardless of whether the oil crisis exists or not. Your decision of whether to eat a salad or a sandwich for lunch is likely to be totally unaffected by this major event.

Sounds simple enough, doesn't it? But, in practice, this principle is frequently violated. Consider the decision of what price to charge for the sale of out-of-date books in a college bookstore. Two years ago the store paid $20 per book and charged an initial price of $40 each for them. Five hundred books remain unsold. What price should be charged for them? The bookstore allocates $2 of overhead to each book sold to cover the costs of the $1 million it spends on rent, utilities, and salaried personnel. The number of books involved in this decision is less than 1 percent of the store's inventory. The manager estimates that at a price of $5 each she can sell the whole lot of 500 books; at $15 each she can sell 250 books; at $25 each she can sell 100 books; at $40, none. Should she charge a price of $5, $15, or $25? (Please think about this problem before going on to the next paragraph.)

And the correct answer is . . . $15. At a $15 price the store earns revenues of $3,750 (250 books × $15 each), while at the two other prices its revenues are only $2,500 [(500 books × $5 each) or (100 books × $25 each)]. But what about the costs of the books? At a price of $15 the store appears to lose $7 per book ($15 price − $2 overhead − $20 original cost of the book). However, the overhead costs of $2 per book will remain the same whether or not the books are sold. Whether it sells 500 books or no books, the store will have the same expenses for rent, utilities, and salaried personnel. These overhead costs are not relevant to the pricing decision because they are not affected by it. The $20 cost of the book is also irrelevant to the decision. The books were paid for long ago. The original cost of the books, referred to as a *sunk cost*, will not be affected by the price charged right now. The costs of overhead and even of the books themselves are not relevant to the issue of what price to charge right now.

Not so simple, is it? The key point to remember is that the analysis must consider only those factors that will be affected by the decision. A simple concept, but one that is hard to implement. Errors are frequent, as the following two studies illustrate:

(1) The Massachusetts Workfare program trains welfare parents to enter the work force and pays for the considerable child-care costs incurred during the training period. An evaluation of the program claimed that its benefits, as measured by the decline in the number of participants who require welfare assistance, exceeded its costs. But many of the participants would have left the welfare rolls without the program. The *relevant* factor is how many *more* welfare parents, if any, become welfare-independent as a result of the program.[9]

(2) An analysis of whether to replace an existing hospital also missed the point. It compared the revenues to be generated by replacing the hospital with the costs of constructing it. But the *relevant* revenues to the decision are the *incremental* revenues that will be generated by the new hospital. For example, if the old hospital generated $50 million in revenues and if its replacement will generate $60 million, the relevant factor for analyzing the new hospital proposal is the *incremental* $10 million in revenues ($60 million − $50 million). Even if the new facility is not constructed, $50 million of revenues will be generated. The $50 million revenues are thus not relevant to the analysis of whether to construct a replacement hospital because they are not affected by the decision.

[9]June O'Neill, *Work and Welfare in Massachusetts* (Boston, MA: Pioneer Institute, 1990).

Mechanics of Contribution Analysis

While the concept of considering only relevant factors is readily understood, it is difficult to translate into practice. The following three steps provide a mechanical way of performing the analysis correctly.

(1) List all the alternatives, including the *status quo*.

(2) List all the incremental cash flows associated with each alternative. (Note that cash flows, not accrual accounting revenues and expenses, must be used.)

(3) Choose the alternative with the highest positive or lowest negative cash flow.

As an example, let's return to the bookstore pricing case considered earlier.

(1) The four alternatives are do nothing, price at $5, price at $15, or price at $25.

(2) The cash flows associated with each option are shown in Table 13-7. Note that the cash flow for overhead is $1 million; it remains the same with each alternative.

(3) The price of $15 is best because it has the lowest negative cash flow. Put another way, pricing the book at $15 will reduce the negative cash flow by $3,750 when compared to the do-nothing alternative or $1,250 ($3,750 − $2,500) when compared to the $5 or $25 price.

TABLE 13-7 **An Example of Contribution Analysis**

		Alternatives		
	Status Quo	*1*	*2*	*3*
Price	$40	$5	$15	$25
Quantity Sold	× 0	× 500	× 250	× 100
Cash In	0	$2,500	$3,750	$2,500
Cash Out				
Books	0	0	0	0
Net Cash Flow (contribution)	0	$2,500	$3,750	$2,500

The cash flow associated with each of the alternatives is commonly labeled as its *contribution* to the overhead, fixed costs, and profits of the organization as a whole. Many students have found this concept more confusing than edifying. For example, in the bookstore case, the price of $15 makes the greatest contribution to overhead and other fixed costs. It contributed $3,750, or $1,250 more than the alternative prices of $5 and $25.

The Effect of Cost Accounting on Relevant Factor Analysis

Full cost accounting systems may undermine the consideration of only relevant factors because they present expenses that will not be affected by the decision as if they were relevant. Let's return to the issue of pricing the book. The bookstore uses a full cost system that allocates $1 million of overhead to each of the 500,000 books it sells at a rate of $2 of overhead per book ($1,000,000 ÷ 500,000). Books purchased for $20 each will thus carry a cost of $22: $20 in purchase price plus $2 of overhead. As shown in Table 13-8, if the book is sold for a price of $25, the full cost accounting system will record a profit of $3 per book ($25 price − $22 full cost). It will record a loss of $7 per book at the sale price of $15 ($15 price − $22 full cost). Nevertheless, the best option for the store is the price of $15, as shown in Table 13-7!

TABLE 13-8   An Example of Profit and Loss Analysis With a Full Cost System

	Revenues Less Full Costs	
Price	$25	$15
− Full Cost	− 22	− 22
Profit (Loss)	$ 3	$ (7)

Managers must understand that a full cost accounting system produces data that include irrelevant factors for much of their decision-making.

Common Errors in Decision-Making

The framework of using only relevant factors is frequently ignored in personal or professional decision-making. Some common examples are illustrated below:

(1) *"Bad" Stocks.* Ms. *X* purchased a stock for $10 as an endowment fund investment for her nonprofit organization. Its market value sank to $4. She would now like to buy another stock, whose value she thinks will increase substantially, but she does not want to sell her prior "bad" stock until its price returns to $10.

    Comment: The relevant factor in this case is whether the $4 currently invested will appreciate more if they remain invested in the "bad" stock, or if they are invested in the new stock that Ms. *X* wants to buy. The $10 she once paid is irrelevant for this decision.

(2) *New Products.* The *ABC* Hospital is considering whether to start a birthing center. Although considerable demand exists for birthing center services in the hospital's market, it is concerned that the birthing center will "steal" some mothers who would otherwise use the inpatient services of the hospital.

    Comment: The relevant factor in this case is whether a competitor to the *ABC* Hospital will open a birthing center. A competitor's birthing center will also "steal" the *ABC* Hospital's patients. The hospital must analyze whether it would rather lose patients to a competitor or to its own new birthing center.

(3) *Replacement of Equipment.* The *XYZ* College's copier is only two years old. When the machine was purchased, the college expected to use it for seven years. A highly automated new copier that was just introduced and that costs $35,000 would reduce the college's cost of operating a copier by $50,000 a year. The college is concerned about buying the new machine. After all, its current copier is only two years old and was expected to last for another five years.

    Comment: The relevant factors in this case are the $50,000 of annual savings and the cost of the new machine. With the new machine, the college will "save" $15,000 after one year ($50,000 in operating savings − $35,000 cost of new machine). After two years, it will "save" $65,000 with its purchase (first year savings of $15,000 + second years savings of $50,000). The old machine's cost and age are not relevant to this decision.

These examples illustrate the two most frequent errors in applying relevant factor analysis. One is to consider monies that were expended long ago, such as those spent on the old copier or the "bad" stock, as relevant. But these funds are long gone; they have no effect on the present decision. The old adage, "don't cry over spilt milk," is a common sense application of relevant factor analysis. The other common error is to exclude competitors as relevant factors in the analysis, as in the new product example. Many internal financial decisions are likely to cause a competitive response or are also being contemplated by competitors. Their reactions are relevant factors in the analysis.

APPLYING RELEVANT FACTORS

The following discussion focuses on two common types of nonprofit financial decisions and illustrates how the relevant factor framework is applied to them.

Make or Buy Decisions

Nonprofit organizations increasingly face so-called "make or buy" decisions. Economies of scale or staffing constraints imposed by civil service and union requirements enhance the appeal of "buying" efficient services from an outside supplier rather than "making" them internally.

Delineation of the financial consequences of such decisions may be difficult because the cost accounting system in many nonprofit organizations measures only the full costs of producing the services. Full costs may not accurately represent the savings that can be incurred with services provided externally rather than internally. All full cost data contain both fixed and variable costs. But fixed costs are irrelevant to the make or buy decision. They are independent of the activity because whether the decision is to make or to buy, these costs will be present. Only those costs that will change when the services are performed by external suppliers are relevant to the make or buy decision. The full cost data thus intermingle relevant and irrelevant costs.

For example, suppose a welfare agency is deciding whether or not to buy home care services, rather than to produce them internally. The agency is presented with the data in Table 13-9 as costs for providing the services internally. The general and administrative (G&A) expenses of $16,000 are allocated from the G&A costs of the welfare department's central office. They represent less than 1 percent of the total central office expense. The depreciation expense of $4,000 represents one-tenth of the cost of equipment purchased for $40,000. The equipment's current net book value is $8,000 and its estimated market value is $0. The personnel whose costs are $200,000 will be terminated if the welfare department's home care service unit is closed. The lease for the space; the maintenance and utilities expenses; and the cost of supplies, food, and miscellaneous items will be avoided if the unit is closed.

If an outside vendor offers to provide services at a cost of $285,000 for the present number of patients and at an equal level of quality, should the offer be accepted?

TABLE 13-9   **Costs for a Make or Buy Decision**

Salaries of personnel	$200,000
Rental of space	30,000
Maintenance and utilities	20,000
Depreciation of equipment	4,000
General and administrative	16,000
Supplies, food, and other miscellaneous expenses	20,000
Total expenses	$290,000

After a cursory inspection, the welfare agency appears to save $5,000 by purchasing outside ($290,000 − $285,000). But will it? Let's examine more closely the relevant expenses—those that will change as a result of the decision to buy outside rather than to make internally. The personnel salaries, rent, maintenance, utilities, and miscellaneous expenses will all be avoided if the decision to purchase services is made. Thus, a total of $270,000 in costs will be saved. But the general and administrative expenses of the central welfare office will continue; they will merely be allocated elsewhere if the home care unit is closed. The $16,000 of general and administrative expenses are not relevant to the decision to purchase services. The equipment's depreciation expense and net book value are also completely irrelevant to the decision. Because the equiment has no market value, the cash flow it might generate if the unit were closed is also not a relevant factor.

Therefore, $20,000 of costs—depreciation and general and administrative expenses ($16,000 + $4,000)—remain unaffected by the decision to buy outside. The costs that will be affected by the decision are the remaining $270,000 of expenses ($290,000 − $20,000) that can be avoided if the decision is made to purchase outside. Thus, purchasing the services will require spending $285,000, while producing them internally will cost only $270,000. The buy decision costs $15,000 more a year than providing the service internally.

In addition to the relevant factor analysis, two other factors must also be considered before concluding the make or buy decision: the sensitivity of the decision to the assumptions and its social impact. An inspection of the assumptions may reveal that the purchased services will have the capacity to provide home care to many more people, doubling the number of clients from 10 to 20. If so, the question is whether to spend $270,000 in providing services to 10 people or $285,000 to service twice that number. The purchase option appears to be more attractive when this assumption is reconsidered.

Among the social factors to be considered is whether the welfare department uses the unit to train people who have been on welfare. If it does, the benefits of the training should be considered in the make or buy decision.

For example, the trainees may be capable of operating home care centers themselves after their training experience. Such social benefits must be considered in the make or buy decision even if they cannot be quantified.

Expand or Contract Decisions

Organizations continually face "expand or contract" decisions. These are decisions about whether to continue or discontinue, or grow or shrink, some part of their services or programs. Among the many factors relevant to such decisions is their financial impact. But discerning what this impact will be may be difficult if only full cost data that include both relevant and irrelevant expenses are available. This decision requires separating those costs and revenues that change with the decision from those that remain unaffected by it.

Suppose Stone College is considering whether to close its fine arts program. Its deficit of $10,000 results from a shortfall between the tuition revenues from the students in the program of $120,000 and the expenses of $130,000, as displayed in Table 13-10.

TABLE 13-10 Costs for an Expand or Contract Decision

Salaries of faculty	$ 80,000
Depreciation of building	11,000
Utilities and maintenance	10,000
General and administrative	24,000
Supplies and miscellaneous	5,000
Total expenses	$130,000

The fine arts faculty members are not tenured. The program is housed in a building whose net book value is $50,000. While the building probably cannot be sold, it can be used to house the personnel presently occupying offices rented at a yearly expense of $30,000. The general and administrative expenses are allocated from Stone's central administration.

On a superficial level, the deficit of $10,000 could argue for the program's being closed. But on closer examination, the fact that the general and administrative expenses will remain the same and that the present rental expense of $30,000 a year could be avoided if the program were closed are also relevant factors. How do we put all this together? The cash flows that will accompany each decision are shown in Table 13-11. Please look the table over carefully. Make sure that you understand why it includes some items and excludes others. For example, why is the depreciation expense of $11,000 excluded? (Some people prefer to leave expenses, like general and administrative, that will not be affected by the decision in the cash flows. Because

TABLE 13-11 **Cash Flows for Expand or Contract Decision**

	Status Quo	Program Closed
Cash In	$120,000	$ 0
Cash Out		
Salaries	80,000	0
Utilities and maintenance	10,000	10,000
Supplies and miscellaneous	5,000	0
Rental of space	30,000	0
Total Cash Out	$125,000	$(10,000)
Net Cash Flow	$(5,000)	$(10,000)

the expense appears in the cash flows for *all* the alternatives, it will not affect the decision.)

A relevant factors analysis indicates that closing the program will result in
a net cash loss of $10,000. From a financial perspective, the program should
not be closed because the *status quo* generates a loss that is $5,000 lower
than the alternative ($5,000 − $10,000). But the sensitivity and distributional
analyses should also play a very important role in the final decision. Among
the factors to consider are the importance of the fine arts program to the
college's reputation and the likely effectiveness of alternative ways of eliminating the deficit, such as raising tuition for the fine arts students or attracting endowment gifts for its program.

SUMMARY

This chapter presented a framework for financial decision-making in nonprofit organizations. The primary criterion for ranking the priority of different activities is the relationship between their benefits and their costs.
A benefit-cost analysis should measure direct and indirect benefits and identify negative benefits, relate these benefits to the activity's costs, and rank
all activities on the basis of benefits less costs or benefits divided by costs.
The analysis should also specify the distributional impact of the activity on
different groups of people. It should include only those factors that are relevant to the analysis in the sense that they will be affected by the activity.
A sensitivity analysis that tests the sensitivity of the results to the assumptions made is also a crucial part of the effort.

Managers must ensure that these steps are incorporated into their organization's financial decision-making process. They should implement the process in a way that encourages employees to present creative ideas rather
than in a political manner that stifles new ideas.

Suggested Reading

Arrow, Kenneth J. *Studies in Resource Allocation Processes*. Cambridge, MA: Cambridge University Press, 1977.

Buchanan, James. *Cost and Choice*. Chicago, IL: University of Chicago Press, 1975.

Dasgupta, Ajit K., and D. W. Pearce. *Cost-Benefit Analysis*. New York, NY: Harper and Row Publishers, 1972.

Feldstein, Martin S. "Net Social Benefit Calculation and the Public Investment Decision." Oxford, England: *Oxford Economic Papers*, 1964, pp. 114-131.

Formaini, Robert. *The Myth of Scientific Public Policy*. New Brunswick, NJ: Transaction Publishers, 1990.

Lindbloom, Charles E. *The Policymaking Process*. Englewood Cliffs, NJ: Prentice-Hall, 1986.

McKean, Roland N. *Efficiency in Government through Systems Analysis*. New York, NY: Wiley, 1958.

Mishan, E. J. *Cost-Benefit Analysis*. London, England: George Allen and Unwin, 1982.

Musgrave, Richard, and Peggy Musgrave. *Public Finance in Theory and Practice*. New York, NY: McGraw-Hill, 1989.

Sassone, Peter A., and William A. Schaffer. *Cost-Benefit Analysis*. New York, NY: Academic Press, 1978.

DISCUSSION QUESTIONS

1. How does financial decision-making in nonprofit organizations differ from that in for-profit firms?

2. What is benefit-cost analysis?

3. What are direct and indirect benefits?

4. How should costs be measured?

5. What is cost-effectiveness analysis? How does it differ from benefit-cost analysis? Which analytic method is better?

6. What are the two major criteria for ranking benefit-to-cost relationships? Under what circumstances should each be applied?

7. What does the term *distributional impact* mean?

8. Think about an activity that was contemplated in a nonprofit organization with which you are familiar and present a benefit-cost or cost-effectiveness analysis of that activity.

9. What is sensitivity analysis? If you answered Question 8, present a sensitivity analysis for the activity you analyzed.

10. What is relevant factor analysis?

11. A hospital is deciding whether to close its radiology department and hire an outside firm to conduct the radiology work. Which of the following three expenses are relevant to the financial aspects of the decision? How much is the relevant expense?

    a. The X-ray machine, which has a present market value of $50,000 and an annual depreciation expense of $25,000

    b. The lead-lined room constructed at a cost of $800,000. It will be used as an ordinary hospital room if the radiology unit is closed.

    c. The X-ray technicians, who have one year left on their contract with the hospital. Their payroll is $200,000.

Cases

CASE STUDIES

Case 13.1 addresses all the key issues in relevant factor and sensitivity analyses. Despite its brevity, it will provide you with the opportunity to apply the contents of Chapter 13 to a set of commonly encountered financial decisions.

How much does the Engineering Center in Widener College cost? Case 13.2 enables you to conduct a real-life cost-accounting study because it depicts the data available in a typical nonprofit organization. (The data in the case are somewhat disguised.)

Case 13.3 delineates the benefits and costs of six alternative ways for reconstructing New York City's West Side Highway. Using an economic perspective, which of the six do you think is the best one? This case also illustrates how a political environment influences the economic decision-making process.

CASE 13.1 Janus Designs, Ltd.

Late in December, Mary Lindburgh, controller of Janus Designs, Ltd., met with Kurt Solamon, the marketing manager for the company's stoneware line to discuss the pricing of a relatively new addition to the product line. In keeping with company policy, the announced price would be adhered to for the year unless radical changes occurred in the market.

Janus Designs, Ltd., manufactured and sold housewares to retailers, primarily department and specialty stores. Last year, total sales were approximately $16.9 million. The stoneware line represented approximately half of the company's sales. The stoneware was high-quality, hand-painted, and artistically designed merchandise. Last

Kathleen A. McCarragher prepared this case under the supervision of Professors Regina E. Herzlinger and Norman Josephy. It is a version of "Atherton Company," Harvard Business School case 156-002.

year a new piece, a decorated serving dish, was added to the line. The dish was priced at $8.00 to distributors and was well received, with about 95,000 units sold. It was estimated that next year's sales would be 100,000 units.

Solamon was very eager to increase his product line's sales and profits. He felt that the new serving dish was overpriced and that dropping the price would create more demand for it. He was confident that his customers would respond to a lower price. Consumers had become somewhat price sensitive in this market in recent months as overall consumer spending had become more cautious. He also felt that this pricing decision would not affect competitors' pricing, as price was only one of many competitive factors in this diverse supplier group. His estimates of next year sales at alternative prices are given in **Exhibit 1**.

To help Solamon in making his decision, Mary Lindburgh compiled estimates of costs at the various levels of production. These estimates are in **Exhibit 2**. The estimates were based on last year's experience, adjusted for expected cost increases and efficiency increases.

The manufacturing process is labor intensive. The depreciation expense listed in **Exhibit 2** is attributable to the building which houses Janus' production facilities and administrative offices, and to the kiln used to fire all of their products. Both the kiln and the building had been constructed a year ago. The replacement cost of the building and the kiln were approximately equal to original cost. The depreciation was allocated to products on the basis of square footage used in the manufacture of that product. The company had adequate capacity; it had no alternative use for the space or kiln time utilized in the manufacture of the stoneware line. No additional space would be required if production of the dish were increased.

If Janus Designs increases the production of the dish above 125,000 units, it would be necessary to add one supervisor at an estimated annual cost of $23,200. This additional supervisor would not be required at either the 100,000 unit or 125,000 unit levels of production.

The Selling, General, and Administrative (SG&A) expenses listed in **Exhibit 2** are expenses incurred by Janus Designs as a whole and not only in this product line. The company followed the practice of allocating the SG&A expenses to the various departments at the rate of 130 percent of direct labor. That amount was calculated by allocating the total expected SG&A expenses to each department on the basis of its total direct labor expense at the expected level of production. In this case, the expected production level used was 100,000 units. However, the actual expenses incurred were not likely to be affected in any way by the volume of dishes produced and sold. The SG&A expenses included salaries of the president and corporate staff, marketing expenses, etc. The sales force sold the entire product line and was paid on a straight salary basis.

ASSIGNMENT

1. What price would you recommend to Kurt Solamon?
2. Calculate the department's income statement at each projected price-volume combination.
3. a.   At each price, how many dishes would have to be sold to cover the departmental overhead expenses? The departmental overhead *and* SG&A expenses?

b. How many dishes would have to be sold at $7.50 to earn the projected contribution from selling 150,000 units at $7.00 each; i.e., at what volume would Solamon be indifferent between the two alternative prices? How many dishes would have to be sold at $8.00 to earn the projected contribution from selling 150,000 units at $7.00 each?

c. What effects should the calculations above have on the decision about the price?

4. Assume for the purpose of answering only this question that this year will be the last year for manufacturing this dish. Material sufficient for production of 100,000 units is presently in inventory. It can be sold at a price of $0.75/unit or else used for production of the dish. It has no other uses. The purchase price for material is $0.78/unit. What quantity should be produced on the basis of this additional information?

5. Assume for the purpose of answering only this question that the labor used to make these dishes is in short supply. If the labor weren't used in making stoneware, it could be used for making some other dishes. The relevant data for alternative uses are presented below. Where should the labor be used—in making the stoneware or in other uses?

Alternative Uses for Labor

Alternative Use	Contribution/ Unit	Labor Hours/ Unit	Cost per Labor Hour
#1	$10/unit	1	$5/hour
#2	$20/unit	3	$5/hour
#3	$15/unit	2	$10/hour

EXHIBIT 1 Janus Designs, Ltd.

Projected Sales of Dishes	Price
100,000 units	$8.00 each
125,000 units	7.50 each
150,000 units	7.00 each

Current price = $8.00
Current sales = 95,000 units

EXHIBIT 2 Janus Designs, Ltd.—Estimated Cost per Unit

	100,000	125,000	150,000
Units of Production			
Expenses:			
Direct labor	$1.66	$1.66	$1.66
Materials	0.78	0.78	0.78
Other direct variables (miscellaneous supplies, spoilage, etc.)	0.23	0.23	0.23
Department overhead			
Depreciation	0.30	0.24	0.20
Supervisors' salaries	0.634	0.5072	0.5773
Selling, general, and administrative (SG&A)[a]	2.158	2.158	2.158
Total	$5.762	$5.5752	$5.6053
Price	$8.00	$7.50	$7.00

[a]SG&A is allocated at 130 percent of direct labor expenses.

CASE 13.2 Widener College

Joel Rodney, provost of Widener College, wanted to evaluate the economic condition of the Engineering Center. After decreasing substantially in recent years, the center's enrollment had increased by 50 percent last year to 193 undergraduates and 54 graduate students, and it looked as if it would continue to increase. Dr. Rodney felt that some increase in faculty might be required to meet this increased student load, but he wanted to be very cautious about increasing staff size from the present 11.9 full-time equivalent faculty. Widener College was not an institution with high faculty turnover; most of its staff had been there all their working lives. Further, the college's financial condition did not allow for many mistakes (see **Exhibit 1**). Dr. Rodney felt that he should look at the Engineering Center's revenues, costs, and enrollment for last year.

ENROLLMENTS

Dr. Rodney collected statistical data on enrollments for calculating tuition revenue and allocating costs.

Professor Regina E. Herzlinger prepared this case.

| | **Engineering Center** | | | **Total College** | |
	Majors	*Credit Hours*	*Course Enrollments*	*Credit Hours*	*Course Enrollments*
Freshmen	90	352	88		
Sophomores	51	742	218		
Juniors	25	800	225		
Seniors	27	756	210		
Total undergraduate	193	2,650	741	40,472	10,118
Graduate[a]	54	498	166	5,220	1,740
Evening and other[b]	-	-	-	15,410	5,212
Total all levels	247	3,148	907	60,002	16,070

[a]Forty-eight of the 54 engineering graduate students are part-time.
[b]Tuition per credit hour for evening and other programs varies by program.

REVENUES

Twenty-four engineering courses were taught each term, with an average tuition charge per credit hour of $85 per student. In addition to tuition, the Engineering Center had received $152,388 in research grants, of which it spent $83,907 on direct salaries and other direct expenses. Overhead expense was calculated by multiplying the direct expenses by the allowable overhead rate of 63.4 percent. The total amount expended on each grant was the sum of overhead plus direct expenses. Dr. Rodney thought the center should also be credited with some portion of the school's general unrestricted revenues (**Exhibit 1**).

EXPENDITURES

The internal accounting system collected expenditure data in nine categories: instructional, library, student services, maintenance, general institutional and administrative, student aid, auxiliary enterprises, research, and transfers. The expenses of the Engineering Center were directly accounted for in only the instructional category. All the other expenditure data were collected for Widener College as a whole. Some of them would have to be allocated back to the Engineering Center in order to calculate its full cost. **Exhibit 1** contains expediture data.

Dr. Rodney was concerned because the expenditure data did not include an explicit charge for space expenses. He noted that the cost of land, plant, and equipment was $22,660,609 and that no depreciation had been taken on them. Their total current market value was estimated to be $31,600,000. He estimated that on the average the fixed assets had about 30 years of useful life. Since the land on which Widener was situated had been donated to it in the early nineteenth century, he thought that its cost was probably a negligible part of the $22,660,609. Because most of the buildings had been built about the same time and for similar purposes, their original cost was roughly the same. In the past, Widener College had financed about 70 percent of the cost of its buildings through gifts, 20 percent through loans, and the remainder through operations.

Dr. Rodney also collected the following space utilization data:

Purpose of Space	Number of Square Feet
Instructional:	
Engineering	34,800
Other	155,600
Total Instructional	190,400
Library	71,453
Student service	168,239
Maintenance	3,000
Administrative	61,800
Auxiliary	157,300
Total	652,192

ASSIGNMENT

1. Calculate last year's revenues and costs of the Engineering Center.
2. Make recommendations to Dr. Rodney based on this analysis.

EXHIBIT 1   **Widener College**

Combined Statement of Revenues and Expenditures

	Unrestricted	*Restricted*	*Total*
Revenues			
Tuition and fees	$5,795,556		$5,795,556
Government grants and contracts	-	$417,635	417,635
State appropriations	170,300	-	170,300
Private gifts, grants, and contracts	319,038	191,931	510,969
Endowment income	25,548	3,384	28,932
Investment income	17,611	-	17,611
Miscellaneous	56,533	6,928	63,461
Total educational and general revenues	6,384,586	619,878	7,004,464
Auxiliary enterprises	1,692,566	-	1,692,566
Total revenues	8,077,152	619,878	8,697,030
Expenditures			
Instructional—engineering	499,632	-	499,632
Instructional—other	2,289,060	333,573	2,622,633
Research	-	87,565	87,565
Public service	-	51,807	51,807
Academic support	396,364	10,298	406,662
Student services	624,209	825	625,034
Maintenance and operations	884,371	6,824	891,195
Institutional support	1,033,749	-	1,033,749
Student aid—engineering	30,500	-	30,500
Student aid—other	427,904	128,986	556,890
Total educational and general expenditures	6,185,789	619,878	6,805,667
Mandatory transfers to:			
Plant fund			
Interest	170,181	-	170,181
Debt reduction	136,969	-	136,969
Reserves	41,000	-	41,000
Loan fund matching grant	22,207	-	22,207
Total mandatory transfers	370,357	-	370,357
Nonmandatory transfers to plant	43,154	-	43,154
Auxiliary enterprises (including mandatory transfers to reserves and debt service of $240,404 and $270,631)	1,672,132	-	1,672,132
Total expenditures and transfers	8,271,432	619,878	8,891,310
Excess (deficiency) of revenues over expenditures and transfers	(194,280)	-	(194,280)
Excess of transfers to revenues over restricted receipts	-	(18,451)	(18,451)
Net increase (decrease) in fund balances	$ (194,280)	$ (18,451)	$ (212,731)

CASE 13.3 West Side Highway

For many years, New York City debated the future of its dilapidated, elevated West Side Highway (WSH). The planners hired with federal government funds suggested that it be replaced with a below-grade highway built on hundreds of acres of infill land extending into the Hudson River. Construction cost of the 4.2-mile highway, known as Westway, and of the infill land surrounding it, was estimated at $1.2 billion. Under the terms of the Federal-Aid Highway Trust Fund, the government would pay up to 90 percent of the cost, once the project was approved.

As final approval looked imminent, opinion remained sharply divided in New York. Supporters of Westway heralded it as the best hope of the beleaguered city, "the twentieth century equivalent of Central Park." It would, they argued, revitalize Manhattan's West Side by diverting some traffic from its congested streets, opening up the waterfront, and creating additional parking and housing. The billion federal dollars that would finance Westway was money the city could not afford to turn down. And Westway would ease traffic flow into the heart of the business area in Manhattan.

But its opponents claimed that rather than revitalizing the West Side, Westway would destroy it. A bigger highway, they argued, could only lead to more traffic and worse pollution. Furthermore, the extra housing wasn't needed, the parks couldn't be maintained, and the city would see only a portion of that billion dollars because most of the money would be spent outside the city.

ALTERNATIVES CONSIDERED

The final plan for Westway was selected after careful consideration of six alternatives:

- *Maintenance.* The existing WSH would be repaired and maintained as an operating facility.
- *Reconstruction.* The existing WSH would undergo partial reconstruction to correct major structural difficulties, to make the road safer, and to enable trucks to use it.
- *Arterial.* The existing WSH would be torn down and replaced with an at-grade (level with surrounding area) arterial roadway of lower traffic capacity and an underground mass transit facility.
- *Inboard.* The existing WSH would be torn down and replaced with a six-lane interstate highway with a public transit system in the median strip. Some parts of the highway and transit system would be depressed, and approximately 21 acres of new land would be created.
- *Outboard.* The existing WSH would be torn down and replaced by a six-lane, limited-access interstate highway constructed in landfill beyond the existing shoreline and covered in sections, with an adjacent mass transit system and

Professor Regina E. Herzlinger prepared this case with Arva Clark and Barbara Fried.

a reconstructed West Street/Twelfth Avenue. Most of the existing waterfront facilities would be replaced with 243 acres of new landfill. Approximately 40 acres would be used for transportation facilities, 75 for recreation and open space along the river's edge, and 128 for housing and other development.

- *Modified Outboard.* A scaled-down version of the outboard, this was the proposal selected.

COST AND BENEFITS OF THE ALTERNATIVES

The planners did not provide a cost/benefit analysis of the alternatives, but rather described the impacts of each alternative on the environment, the economy, and the performance of the highway and traffic system. For some impacts, specific dollar estimates of the costs and benefits were provided, notably highway user cost savings and construction costs. **Exhibits 1** and **2** provide a compilation of the staff's findings for the six alternatives.

The total benefits in **Exhibit 1** were computed according to federal government procedures, which required that both be expressed in current dollars, and then discounted at the rate of 10 percent per annum. The "user cost savings" represent the time savings, where one person-hour = $3.64, and operating and accident cost savings resulting from the faster and smoother flow of traffic. They were accrued for 40 years, the highway's likely life span.

The anticipated regional income was derived from the multiplier effect on direct construction wages by which one dollar of wages paid into a region generates additional expenditures, wages, and profits in other sectors of the economy. Contemporary studies indicated that multipliers range from 2.0 for small metropolitan areas to 3.2 for larger areas. The multiplier used for New York City was 3.0, which the planners considered to be a conservative estimate. These benefits were accrued over the construction timetable in **Exhibit 2**.

The city's income from the 200 acres of land created by the modified outboard alternative was derived by assuming 200 dwelling units and associated commercial activities and parking per acre. Utilizing current values for construction, financing, maintenance, and rents, a market value of just over $1 million per acre was calculated. Each acre of land plus the more than $7.5 million worth of buildings assumed to be on it generated taxes of about $375,000 per acre annually under the constrained development conditions laid down by the city in agreement with local residents. It was assumed that each new acre of land created (except those used for highway purposes) would have this value, including the park, industrial, and community service landfill parcels. Since the decision to forego the monetary benefits of using the land for residential purposes is assumed to be a rational one, the nonmonetary benefits received by society from the other uses are equal to, or greater than, the benefits of residential development.

EVALUATION OF THE ALTERNATIVES

It was not the purpose of the planners to select a particular alternative but rather to outline the features of a number of alternatives so that public agencies and concerned individuals could comment on them. Nevertheless, their evaluation suggested that the "inboard" and "outboard" alternatives were probably superior to all others. They would add the least air, water, and noise pollution, largely because they would remove the most traffic from local streets and place the highway some distance from existing communities. Unlike the other alternatives, they would also create new land between the existing shorelines and the new highway, and this land could be used for new parks and housing. The economy of the area would be stimulated most by these two alternatives, since they would most improve the accessibility of Manhattan and would create the most jobs during construction. Finally, the inboard and outboard alternatives were estimated to provide greater reductions in highway user time, operating, and accident costs than the other alternatives. The inboard and outboard alternatives cost more to construct, but the benefits seemed to be larger too.

Opposition to these alternatives came from environmentalists, who were suspicious of the claim that larger highways would lead to cleaner air; mass transit advocates, who felt that the billion dollars might be better invested in improving the city's public transit system; and community residents, who feared a sudden large-scale redevelopment would fundamentally change the character of their neighborhoods.

Mass transit advocates proposed that the city build a new subway system in the corridor. To do this, the city applied for an "Interstate Transfer," with the approval of the governor. If the secretary of the U.S. Department of Transportation approved, the federal share of the estimated cost to complete the highway can be used to construct other roads or transit projects. Participation in transit projects was at the ratio of 80 percent federal and 20 percent other. This 20 percent can be a state contribution or shared by the state and city or other governmental entity.

ASSIGNMENT

1. Why was Westway selected from the alternatives?
2. How did the benefit and cost data affect the choice?
3. How should the benefit and cost data have affected the choice? Specify the relevant and irrelevant data contained in **Exhibit 1** and identify the data that should have been included in the analysis.

EXHIBIT 1 **West Side Highway—Cost and Benefits for Alternatives (milions of dollars)**

Alternatives	Source of Funding	Total Construction and Right-of-Way Costs[c] Undiscounted	Annual User Savings in 1995[d]	Property Tax Gains in 1995[d]	Increase in Regional Income during Construction[c]	One-Time Expenditures Avoided by City	Total Benefits Undiscounted
Maintenance[a]	70% Federal 30% City or State	$ 76	$ 0	$ 0	$25 × 3 = $75	$ -	$ 75.0
Reconstruction[a]	70% Federal 30% City or State	227	26.2	0	$65 × 3 = $195	-	1,249.4
Arterial (with railway)[a]	70% Federal 30% City or State	307	14.2	0	$90 × 3 = $270	-	836.3
Inboard (with busway)[a]	90% Federal (Interstate) 10% State	1,111	89.5	0	$315 × 3 = $945	-	4,529.8
Outboard (with busway)[b]	90% Federal (Interstate) 10% State	1,415	86.5	76	$400 × 3 = $1,200	61.5	4,658.4
Modified Outboard[b]	90% Federal (Interstate) 10% State	1,356	69.2	76	$285 × 3 = $855	61.5	6,068.0

[a]Based on construction to 72nd Street.
[b]Based on construction to 42nd Street, including transit system construction (without transit right-of-way costs).
[c]Timetable for construction expenditures given in **Exhibit 2**.
[d]Annual benefits presumed to accrue for 40 years, the expected lifetime of the highway.

EXHIBIT 1 (Continued)

Alternatives	New Housing	New Parkland	Morning Peak Hour Traffic (1995)	Local Street Traffic	Relocation	Pollution 1 = Least, 5 = Greatest			Drivers Diverted to Transit Daily
						Air	Noise	Water	
Maintenance	None	None	Volume exceeds capacity for most of highway. Average speed highway = 14.5 mph. Average speed streets = 5.7 mph	No change	None	No change in CO, hydrocarbons, or NO	During construction—1. After construction—3	No change	None
Reconstruction	None	None	Volume exceeds capacity for ⅓ of highway. Average speed highway = 18.4 mph. Average speed streets = 6.0 mph	Insignificant change in cars; 9% fewer trucks	4 buildings (13 businesses)	Slight increase in CO levels; no change in others	During construction—2. After construction—5	No change	None
Arterial (with railway)	None	2.81 inland acres; improved access to Battery Park	Volume exceeds capacity for ⅓ of highway; near capacity for rest. Average speed highway = 12.1 mph. Average speed streets = 5.7 mph	Insignificant change in cars; 6% fewer trucks	None	Largest increase in CO levels, exceeding federal standards	During construction—3. After construction—4	No change	9,000
Inboard (with busway)	None	21 acres of waterfront park	Volume exceeds capacity for ⅓ of highway. Average speed highway = 22.6 mph. Average speed streets = 6.8 mph	Slightly fewer cars; 9% fewer trucks	48 buildings (89 residents and 91 businesses) 18 pier tenants	Slight decrease in CO (by diverting truck traffic)	During construction—5. After construction—2	Slight improvement from smoothing shoreline	10,500
Outboard (with busway)	128 acres for future development	75 acres of waterfront park	Volume exceeds capacity for ⅓ of highway. Average speed highway = 23.6 mph. Average speed streets = 6.8 mph	Slightly fewer cars; 12% fewer trucks	46 buildings (89 residents and 101 businesses) 23 pier tenants	Slight decrease in CO (by diverting truck traffic)	During construction—4. After construction—1	Slight improvement from smoothing shoreline	10,500
Modified Outboard	101 acres for future development	93 acres of waterfront park	Same as Outboard	Same as Outboard	47 buildings (109 residents and 92 businesses) 15 pier tenants	Same as Outboard	Same as Outboard	Same as Outboard	Same as Outboard

EXHIBIT 2   **West Side Highway—Approximate Annual Construction Costs (in millions of dollars)**

Construction Year	Reconstruction	Arterial with Rail	Inboard with Busway	Outboard with Busway	Westway[a]
1	$ 18	$ 20	$ 92	$ 125	$ 120
2	14	25	123	159	152
3	16	43	101	106	102
4	19	40	119	144	138
5	20	39	153	152	146
6	23	34	157	209	200
7	27	25	149	191	183
8	19	28	141	165	158
9	24	24	53	112	107
10	19	29	23	52	50
11	19				
12	9				
Total	$227	$307	$1,111	$1,415	$1,356

[a]$\frac{\$1,356}{\$1,415}$ of the Outboard costs.

Source: Final Environmental Impact Statement, West Side Highway Project, Table 80.

14 Techniques for Financial Decision-Making

THIS CHAPTER WILL DISCUSS THE ASPECTS of the financial decisions made by all organizations: what and how much to buy, when to buy it, and how to finance the purchase.

Chapter 13 delineated the framework for evaluating whether a particular activity should be funded. This chapter extends the framework. Its considerations are key to conducting a benefit-cost analysis in a nonprofit organization. They affect the decisions of how much money should be allocated to different activities, when the activities should begin, and how to finance them.

WHAT AND HOW MUCH TO BUY?

All of us face financial decisions about how to allocate our money for various purchases. If we earn $30,000 a year, we must somehow allocate that money among consumption items, such as food, clothing, transportation, and entertainment; possible investments in education, houses, or cars; and savings. Similarly, a nonprofit organization must somehow decide how to allocate its funds among many activities.

Basic Decision Rule

The following decision rule helps to clarify how such decisions about the items and quantities to be purchased should be made. Although the rule frequently cannot be applied because it requires data that are difficult to obtain, it is included because it clarifies the decision-making process.

The decision rule states that we should buy the things that we can afford, that are within our budget, up to the point where the benefits we derive from spending a dollar more on each item purchased is equal. For example, suppose a social service agency has a $20,000 budget to spend on providing housing and food for its homeless clients. The decision rule states that it should buy as much as it can of both up to the point where one more dollar spent on food provides its clients with as many benefits as one more dollar spent on housing. If the clients derive more benefits from money spent on buying one more dollar of food rather than housing, it should continue to buy food up to the point that the incremental benefits from buying more food or more housing are equal or its budget is exhausted.

Hopelessly academic, you say? After all, we cannot measure the benefits that clients derive from spending one more dollar on either food or housing. Not necessarily. Consider a regulatory agency that must allocate its auditors' work between two different kinds of companies. The decision rule states that the agency should allocate its auditors' time so that each additional audit hour is used where it produces the greatest extra benefits. Fortunately, the agency derived the relationship between the extra benefits to be gained with audits of each kind of company and the amount of auditing work. If the relationship states that an extra audit hour in Company 1 produces greater additional benefits than one spent in Company 2—say $10,000 in regulatory fees in Company 1 versus $5,000 in Company 2—then the decision rule would recommend that auditors be reassigned from Company 2 to Company 1 up to the point where no further need for work exists in Company 1. The Internal Revenue Service (IRS) has used just this decision rule to help it allocate auditors among different kinds of taxpayers.

The decision rule can be applied to benefit-cost analysis as well. It states that money should be invested in a particular activity up to the point where benefits from the expenditure of one more dollar in that activity are equal to the benefit-cost ratio in the next best alternative activity. For example, suppose the IRS is interested in maximizing the benefits to U.S. citizens from its auditing activities by insuring that tax payments are fairly distributed across all sectors of U.S. society and that no one group is sheltered from its audits. It would compute as the benefit of its auditing activities the gain in the perceived fairness of its auditing and allocate auditors so that the gain in "fairness" per auditing hour was equal across different audit subjects.

The decision rule is also useful in evaluating how much and what to invest right now in activities that will yield benefits for many years in the future. For this decision, the rule is to invest up to the point where the incremental returns from all investments are equal for the last extra dollar of investment.

In applying this rule, it is important to distinguish between *incremental* and *average* returns. For example, consider the level of investment and the average and incremental return yields shown in Table 14-1. If we can invest only in Activities A and B, how much of our money should we invest in A and how much in B? Applying the decision rule leads us to invest up to $10,000 in A. Its average return is 4, while B's is only $2\frac{1}{2}$. For investments of $20,000, the average benefit-cost ratio of A is greater than B. If we consider only average returns, it appears we should continue investing only in A,

TABLE 14-1 **The Effect of Average and Incremental Returns on the Decision of What and How Much to Buy**

Amount of Total Investment	Average Return on		Incremental Return on	
	Investment A	*Investment B*	*Investment A*	*Investment B*
$10,000	4	$2\frac{1}{2}$	4	$2\frac{1}{2}$
$20,000	$3\frac{1}{4}$	$2\frac{1}{2}$	$2\frac{1}{2}$	$2\frac{1}{2}$
$30,000	$2\frac{1}{2}$	$2\frac{1}{2}$	1	$2\frac{1}{2}$

up to $20,000. But, at the level of investment between $10,001 and $20,000, we should be indifferent between A and B because both yield the same incremental return of $2\frac{1}{2}$ per dollar invested. Further, although the average returns of investments up to $30,000 are equal for A and B, our best strategy is to invest in A up to $10,000, invest in either A or B between $10,001 and $20,000, and invest only in B between $20,001 and $30,000. Following this strategy will lead to an average return on $30,000 of investment of 3, rather than $2\frac{1}{2}$ [($10,000 × 4 + $10,000 × $2\frac{1}{2}$ + $10,000 × $2\frac{1}{2}$) ÷ $30,000]. By examining the *incremental* returns earned with increasing levels of investments, we obtained a better return than the *average* one.

Time Value of Money

Long-run decisions are complicated by the fact that a benefit received right now has a different value from the same benefit received some time in the future. For example, $100 to be received two years from now has a lower value to us than $100 received right now. The different value of the same amount of money over time is referred to as the *time value of money*. All relevant financial factors must be adjusted for it. If they are not, the analysis will not reflect economic reality and the project may carry an unwarranted appearance of success or failure.

Before we plunge into the mechanics of this adjustment, let's step back and think about what it means. Suppose you or your child will enter college next year and you will need $25,000 to pay for each of the four years of college. Do you need $100,000 right now to pay $25,000 for each of the next four years? If you said "yes," re-read the prior paragraph. The correct answer is "no." The value right now of $25,000 to be spent in each of the next four years is less than $100,000. If you put an amount less than $100,000 in a savings bank or an investment instrument with a guaranteed interest rate, it will grow to become $100,000 sometime in the future when you need to spend it.

The amount of money that you need to invest now in order to have a certain amount of money in the future is called the *present value* of the future amount. You can think it it as the money you need now, in the present, so that you can afford future payments. For our college example, we need to calculate how much money we must set aside right now so that we have $25,000 every year for the next four years. To compute this amount, we must know how much interest we could earn on the money we set aside. Suppose we found a bank that will pay 8 percent interest annually on our deposit. We want to calculate the amount of money, X, that when deposited at 8 percent interest will yield $25,000 after one year. (Ignore income and other taxes for simplicity.) In this case X will equal $23,148 ($25,000 ÷ 1.08). The present value of $25,000 for the next four years is stated algebraically as:

$$\text{Present Value of \$25,000 a Year for Next Four Years} = \frac{\$25,000}{1.08} + \frac{\$25,000}{(1.08)^2} + \frac{\$25,000}{(1.08)^3} + \frac{\$25,000}{(1.08)^4}$$

This sum is cumbersome to compute unless you have a calculator or an electronic spreadsheet do it for you. To calculate present value manually, use the data in Table 14-4 at the end of this chapter; it contains the present value of $1 at various interest rates and periods of time. It shows the following present values for $1 for Years 1 through 4 at an 8 percent interest rate:

Year	Present Value Factor at 8 Percent
1	$0.926 = \dfrac{1}{1.08}$
2	$0.857 = \dfrac{1}{(1.08)^2}$
3	$0.794 = \dfrac{1}{(1.08)^3}$
4	$0.735 = \dfrac{1}{(1.08)^4}$

To calculate the present value of $25,000 in Year 1, we would multiply it by 0.926; in Year 2 by 0.857; in Year 3 by 0.794; and in Year 4 by 0.735. If we do so, and add the results, the present value is $82,800. In English, this means that if we invest $82,800 right now in an 8 percent bank account, we will have enough money on hand to pay out $25,000 a year for each of the next four years.

Although the present value factors contained in Table 14-4 are better than computing the quantity $(1 + i)^n$, the computation remains rather tedious. Fortunately, we can shorten the computational process even farther. Notice that we multiplied $25,000 by each year's present value factor and then added the results. Alternatively, we can add the present value factors and multiply their sum by $25,000. Both arithmetic operations will yield identical results, but one is simpler than the other.

Annuity tables, such as Table 14-5 at the end of this chapter, perform exactly this calculation for us. They add the present value factors for each of the years they contain. Thus, a two-year 8 percent annuity has a present value of 1.783—the sum of the first year's present value factor of 0.926 and the second year's present value factor of 0.857. (An annuity is an annually repeated event.) A four-year 8 percent annuity is equal to 3.312 (0.926 + 0.857 + 0.794 + 0.735). The present value of a four-year $25,000 annuity is $82,800 ($25,000 × 3.312).

Applying the Concept of Time Value of Money in Financial Decision-Making

The time value of money adjustments can help us to analyze what and how much to buy. A typical investment proposal involves the outlay of a large amount of money at the present time that will generate a stream of income some time in the future. For example, such a proposal might involve substituting a toll booth guard with a machine that accepts tolls, sounds alarms if needed, provides change, and keeps a count of the total revenues. If the machine costs $54,000, requires annual maintenance, operating, and insurance expenses of $2,000, and replaces a guard whose salary and fringe expenses are $20,000 a year, is it a good investment?

A simplistic answer to this question is provided by the calculation of the number of years required to "pay back" the initial investment. Every year the machine is in place it saves $20,000 (the expense of the guard) and costs $2,000 (the insurance expense), thereby generating net cash savings of $18,000 a year. The number of years required to *pay back* the initial investment of $54,000 can be calculated as:

$$\text{Payback Years} = \frac{\text{Initial Investment}}{\text{Annual Net Cash Savings}} = \frac{\$54,000}{\$18,000} = 3 \text{ years}$$

If the machine is expected to last less than three years, the payback criterion indicates that the investment is not worthwhile. If the machine's expected lifetime is more than three years, however, then an investment is worthwhile because the machine will have paid for itself by the third year. After that point, the net cash flows will be pure gravy.

The payback analysis assumes that a cash flow of $18,000 in Year 2 is equivalent in value to a cash flow of $18,000 in any year. But is it? If somebody offered to give you $18,000 two years from now in exchange for your giving up $18,000 right now, you should reject the proposal. Having $18,000 right now is worth more than $18,000 some time in the future. This is the (admittedly slippery) concept of the time value of money.

To answer the question of whether the machine is a good investment, we must compute the present value of its cash savings of $18,000 a year and compare them to the cost of the machine. If the machine lasts for four years, the present value of the savings of $18,000 that it generates, when valued at 8 percent, is $59,616 ($18,000 a year × 3.312). This amount is larger than the amount needed to purchase the machine. To put it another way, we spend $54,000 to save an amount equivalent to $59,616 at the time we buy the machine. It appears to be a wise investment.

Is 8 percent the right interest rate to use to compute the present value? Because the answer to the question of picking the "right" interest rate is complex, some people avoid it by computing the internal rate of return of the project. The internal rate of return is the interest rate that equates the present value of the cash inflows and outflows associated with the project.

We use the following steps to calculate the internal rate of return for the tollbooth machine:

(1) Divide the investment by the annual cash inflow:

$$\$54,000 \div \$18,000 = 3$$

(2) Look across the four-year row in Table 14-5 to find the number closest to 3. It occurs at an interest rate between 12 percent and 13 percent. This tells us that this project has an internal earning rate between 12 percent and 13 percent. If we earn less than this rate on alternative projects, this project is clearly desirable as an investment.

Unfortunately, although the internal rate of return is probably the simplest criterion for deciding what and how much to buy, it is frequently an erroneous one. To return to our example, suppose that we can invest $54,000 either in this machine or in a certificate of deposit that will pay 10 percent every year for four years. Suppose also that the best interest rate that we can obtain for investing the $18,000 a year of savings the machine generates is 5 percent. Which is the better option for investment of the $54,000—the four-year 10 percent certificate or the machine?

It might appear that the machine investment is the preferred investment because it yields an internal rate of return higher than 10 percent. But this analysis ignores the interest rate at which the savings from the machine can be invested. When this rate is included in the analysis, the certificate is the better investment. As shown in Table 14-2, the investment in a certificate is worth $79,061 at the end of four years, while the machine investment is worth only $77,582. The certificate option re-invests yearly interest at 10 percent, while the machine option does so only at a 5 percent rate.

The internal rate of return cannot serve as the sole criterion for decision-making. It must be complemented with considerations of the rates of return that can be earned by spinoffs from the investment. All of this complicated explication merely points out that we cannot use the criterion of internal rate of return to avoid consideration of interest rates.

TABLE 14-2   **Illustration of the Use of the Internal Rate of Return as a Criterion for an Investment**

	Option A: Buy a certificate of deposit that yields 10 percent a year for four years.		*Option B:* Buy a machine that generates savings of $18,000 a year for four years. Each year's savings can be invested at a 5 percent rate.
End of Year	**End of Year Value = Last Year's Value Plus Interest at 10 Percent**	**End of Year**	**End of Year Value = Last Year's Value Plus Interest at 5 Percent on Last Year's Value Plus $18,000**
1	$59,400 = ($54,000 + $5,400)	1	$18,000 = ($18,000)
2	$65,340 = ($59,400 + $5,940)	2	$36,900 = ($18,000 + $900 + $18,000)
3	$71,874 = ($65,340 + $6,534)	3	$56,745 = ($36,900 + $1,845 + $18,000)
4	$79,061 = ($71,874 + $7,187)	4	$77,582 = ($56,745 + $2,837 + $18,000)

Discount Rates

The interest rates that account for the time value of money are called *discount rates.* Although a few U.S. government agencies used a discount rate to account for the time value of money as early as the 1930s, the use of discount rates was fairly rare in government financial decision-making. At that time the substantial variation in the discount rates used by federal agencies was discovered. As a result, an agency, such as the Corps of Engineers, that used a low rate could very well decide to accept a project that the Defense Department, with a high rate, would reject. Because all the agencies were using the same source of funds, the federal treasury, the cause of the variation in discount rates was unclear. Some concluded that the primary reason for the use of different interest rates by different agencies was the absence of a theory on how to compute an appropriate discount rate.

Two schools of thought emerged about the correct discount rate for the federal government. One school maintained that the government's rate should reflect what its funds could earn in the private sector. After all, if the government could not equal or better the private sector's rate of return, it should leave the funds in that sector and not tax them away.[1] The second school of thought held that the market rate of return did not properly value the future against the present. For example, businesses might pollute the environment because they do not think about the future costs of cleaning

[1]William S. Baumol, "On the Social Rate of Discount," *American Economic Review* (September 1968): 788-802; Martin J. Bailey and Michael C. Jensen, "Risk and the Discount Rate for Public Investment," in M. C. Jensen, ed., *Studies in the Theory of Capital Markets* (New York, NY: Praeger, 1972).

up the environment, but only about minimizing their present expenses.[2] If the private sector's discount rate were used to decide what and how much the government should buy, proposals to create programs for the benefit of future generations would not be funded.

The first school advocated much higher interest rates than the second. Its reasoning generally prevailed and led to the requirement that all federal agencies use a discount rate that reflects the *opportunity cost* of diverting funds from the private sector. The second school of thought, advocates of the *social rate of time preference*, favored a significantly lower rate. A lower discount rate would have justified a greater rate of investment by the government for the future.

The same reasoning can be applied to private nonprofit organizations. They, too, could employ an opportunity cost discount rate, that is, the amount their funds could have earned if they had not been invested in the private nonprofit organization. For example, if the nonprofit's donors can earn 10 percent on their funds, the relevant discount rate when the nonprofit is deciding what and how much to buy is that 10 percent.

As a practical matter, private nonprofits cannot, of course, ascertain their donors' rate of return on invested capital. Instead, they can use indices of the rates of return earned by large institutions that invest on behalf of people similar to their donors, such as the pension funds of large companies. By using this rate for evaluating investments in projects, the nonprofit ensures that it analyzes proposals with the same financial measuring stick as that used by its donors. If the resulting discounted present value is negative, the project is not necessarily a poor one. However, management and the board must articulate the distributional impacts that justify investment in a project that earns lower returns than those earned in the private sector.

Manipulating Discount Rates

Some nonprofit organizations manipulate discount rates to enhance the attractiveness of unappealing proposals. When they do so, they rely on the user's inability to understand the manipulation.

In 1991, New York City's mayor found the money to fund salary increases for municipal workers despite the city's poor economic situation. Magic? Not at all. The mayor merely increased the rate of return the pension fund was assumed to earn. With this assumption, he could reduce the amount of money needed to fund the pensions. He then used the funds once expended for pensions to pay the municipal employees' raises. For example, if the pension fund needed $109 million to pay retirees a year from now, the assumption of a 9 percent discount rate would require $100 million in funding right now, while a 20 percent discount rate assumption would

[2]Stephen A. Marglin, ''The Opportunity Cost of Public Investment,'' *Quarterly Journal of Economics* (May 1963): 274-289.

require only $91 million in funding [$109 = $91 + (0.20)($91)]. By assuming a higher rate, $9 million of pension funds ($100 − $91) are freed up for other purposes.

By manipulating the discount rate, the mayor managed to give current employees a raise without increasing taxes. Can the city earn this higher rate of return? Don't hold your breath! The mayor's new discount rate is among the highest expected rates of return in the country and coincided with a new economic recession.[3] It is not likely to materialize.

Decentralized Decision-Making

Sometimes an organizational change can help answer the what and how much to buy question. A case in point is the Corporation for Public Broadcasting (CPB) which, in its early days, was under attack for funding an excessive number of politically liberal public television programs. But, if it had changed to a more politically conservative mix of programs, a new, vociferous group of critics would likely have emerged.

Rather than trying to improve its method of allocating funds to programs, the CPB changed its decision-making process. The CPB ceased direct funding of programs. Instead, it funded local, community-based public television stations that, in turn, made individual decisions to buy programs. The mechanism for accomplishing this decision-making process was a marketplace in which individual stations bid for programs offered by producers. The CPB's delegation of decision-making not only effectively silenced its critics but also led to efficiencies in program productions because the local stations, whose funds are more limited than CPB's, would not buy programs whose costs they considered extravagant. More recently, school systems in large urban areas have decentralized power to local schools to achieve the same results as the CPB.

When government organizations purchase goods and services from private companies that they once produced themselves, they too are changing the what and how much to buy decision-making process. This form of decision-making is called *privatization*. Marlborough, a Massachusetts town, presents a good example of the effects of privatization. After reducing its costs with the privatization of its billing, custodial, and landscaping services, it decided to hire private meter maids to ticket motorists who were parking illegally. Marlborough's downtown merchants had been complaining about motorists who blocked shoppers from parking in time-restricted meters because the motorists' cars were parked illegally for a whole day and about inconsistent enforcement of the law. In six months, the private meter maids reversed the situation. They not only collected $62,000 in parking fees— 10 percent more than in the past—but also caused wary parkers to increase

[3]Josh Barnabel, "City Hall Seeks Higher Estimate of Fund Return," *The New York Times*, 3 January 1991, p. 1.

their meter-feeding. Total meter revenues increased by over 30 percent, and the business community was well satisfied.[4]

But privatization is not always a panacea. For example, after decades of bemoaning the high costs of the guaranteed student loan program in which private banks lend educational funds to students, the Congressional General Accounting Office recommended that loans be made directly to students.[5]

WHEN TO BUY?

The second major financial decision concerns the timing of the investment. Should the purchase be made now or later? The answer to this question is simple in theory but difficult in practice. The timing of an action depends on our expectations of what will happen in the future. For example, large users of oil should buy large quantities of oil right now if they expect the price of oil to inflate wildly in the future. But if they expect the price to go down, they should buy as little oil as possible right now.

Three predictions about the future are key to the timing issue:

(1) Future price trends of the items to be purchased. If the price of the item whose purchase is being evaluated is likely to increase more than the discount rate, the item should be purchased as soon as the price increase is projected to outstrip the discount rate.

(2) Future technological innovations in the items to be purhased. If the item is likely to become technologically obsolete in the near future, its purchase should be deferred. For example, a hospital that is contemplating the purchase of an imaging device should postpone the purchase if it is aware that a new, vastly superior one is likely to be offered in the near future.

(3) General feelings of uncertainty and risk about the future. Some events appear to us to be much more likely to occur than others. We are generally confident about the sun's rising but may feel much less confident about the amount of sunshine that will be available. Thus, we feel less risk and uncertainty about an activity that is tied to the sun's rising, such as setting a time pattern, than to one that is dependent on the amount of sunshine, such as using solar panels as sources of energy.

In practice, most of us are not very skilled in predicting rates of inflation, technological innovations, or risk and uncertainty in the future. Even professional economists have poor records for predicting the economy. Nevertheless, virtually all professionals in financial decision-making agree

[4]Robert Duffy, "In Marlborough, More Revenue and Parking," *Boston Business Journal* (February 4, 1991): 8.
[5]Franklin Frazier, *Direct Student Loans Could Save Money and Simplify Program Administration*, (Washington, DC: U.S. General Accounting Office, October 29, 1991).

that the effect of inflation must be reflected by including the inflated values of benefits, costs, and discount rates in the analysis. These values should incorporate the inflated rates of the items being investigated rather than general inflation rates. Thus, if computers are expected to inflate at a lower rate than general inflation, an analysis that evaluates when to invest in new computers must incorporate rates of inflation relevant to them. Although greater diversity of opinion exists about how to adjust for risk, uncertainty, and likely innovations in technology, the adjustment principle that governs the analysis should remain the same: benefits, costs, and discount rates should be adjusted for the effects of these variables.

The resulting analysis can be simplified by first computing the minimum period of time required for the investment to break even if it is made right now. Then we determine whether a major change in inflation or technology can be reasonably expected before that minimum period has expired or whether our feelings of risk or uncertainty about the activity compel us to decide that a major change will occur before this period elapses.

Let's consider a hospital's contemplated purchase of an imaging device to illustrate this approach. Suppose the device costs $1 million and generates a present value of $500,000 of cash inflows every year. If the hospital buys it right now, and has an 8 percent discount rate, it will break even on its investment in roughly two years ($891,500 = present value of $500,000 a year of savings for two years, at 8 percent). The hospital now needs to evaluate whether a major technological innovation is likely within the next two years. If it occurs after the two year period, the hospital will have already recouped most of its $1 million investment in the device and can afford to purchase the next generation of technology. If it occurs before two years, the hospital may not recoup a large portion of its investment.

In reaching this decision, the hospital must also evaluate the number of people who could have benefited from earlier adoption of the technology and weigh the benefits to them versus the cost of early adoption. If the technology extends peoples' lives and confers benefits of $1.2 million a year, the benefit-to-cost ratio of the investment is 1.2 with only one year of use. The hospital must now evaluate the benefit-to-cost relationship of investment in this technology versus other uses of its funds.

HOW TO FINANCE IT?

The third financial decision faced by nonprofit organizations is how to finance their purchases or expenditures. The answer is simple—use the lowest-cost money available.

Nonprofit organizations have three sources of funds: operations, borrowing, or gifts from donors. Each of these sources and their costs will be discussed.

Funds from Operations

Private nonprofits can finance themselves with the profits they earn from their operations. Does profit have a cost or is it a cost-free source of financing? Profit is cost-free only if the organization lacks uses for the money other than the contemplated investment. But most organizations enjoy abundant options. They can provide additional services or invest in stocks, bonds, government securities, and so on. The cost of using profits to finance purchases is, therefore, the loss of the opportunity to invest the money elsewhere. The hospital that decides to use its profits to finance the purchase of an imaging device has lost the opportunity to invest the profits elsewhere.

Thus, the cost of using profits to finance purchases is the value of what they would have earned in the best alternative investments. The most practical measure of these foregone earnings is the long-run rate of return expected in the endowment funds. (See Chapter 10 for a discussion of how this rate of return is devised.)

Funds from Borrowing

Private nonprofit organizations and government organizations can borrow money from banks, and U.S. government organizations can borrow from the public. For private nonprofits the cost of their debt capital is simply the interest rate on the debt. (See the discussion of discounts and premiums on debt and their effect on interest rates in Chapter 4.) But, municipal debt, a form of government debt issued by state and local governments, carries a cost in addition to its interest expense. The recipients of interest on municipal debt are frequently exempted from paying income taxes on the interest they earn. Municipal debt can therefore yield lower interest rates and yet remain financially attractive to its buyers. For example, if a taxpayer pays 40 percent of income in taxes, the after-tax yield of an investment that pays 10 percent interest is only 6 percent. The taxpayer might therefore be willing to invest in a municipal debt instrument that yields only 7 percent interest. Although it pays less than the 10 percent the taxpayer can earn elsewhere, its after-tax yield of 7 percent is higher than the 6 percent after-tax return of the other investment.

The low interest rates of municipal debt are artificial—created by their tax exemption. If the interest were not exempted from taxes, the cost of the municipal debt would equal that of other debt instruments of equivalent risk. From the perspective of society, the market rate of interest is the correct measure of the cost to society of municipal debts; but from the perspective of the municipality, it is the actual rate associated with its borrowings.

Funds from Donors

Gifts and donations are the third source of funds for private nonprofits. They carry two costs. The first cost is that of raising the money. Fund-raising is very expensive in many organizations. In a 1991 survey of many nonprofits, it ranged from a low of 0 percent for a Shriners Hospital, to a high of 62 percent, with an average expense of 18 percent of direct public support.[6] The second cost associated with donated funds is the opportunity cost of using this money elsewhere. It carries the same cost as funds from operations.

Making the How to Finance Decision

The financing decision should be separated from the what to buy decision. For example, if a nonprofit can borrow money at 12 percent and invest it to yield 15 percent, the how to finance decision is clear. It should use borrowed funds at 12 percent to finance its purchases and invest its profits to yield 15 percent. If this organization used its invested capital to finance its activities, the cost of the capital is 15 percent—the returns lost by removing the funds from the investment pool.

Should the what to buy decision incorporate 12 percent, the cost of the borrowed capital, as the relevant interest rate? For government organizations the answer is no. Governments should use the opportunity cost of money invested by private citizens as their discount rate. After all, if governments did not tax this money away from their citizens, it would be invested to earn this rate of return.

Private nonprofit organizations, on the other hand, should use a weighted average cost of capital as their discount rate. A weighted average cost reflects the long-term proportions and costs of the money raised from its three different sources of capital. For example, if the private nonprofit expects the long-term sources and costs of capital shown in Table 14-3, its discount rate for evaluating what to buy decisions should be 14 percent.

The long-run rate should be used, instead of the 12 percent cost of borrowing money for this project, because few organizations raise money specifically for a particular project. Rather, they raise a pool of capital that will

[6]James Cook, "Charity Checklist," *Forbes* (October 28, 1991): 180-184.

TABLE 14-3 **An Example of Computing a Long-Run Cost of Capital for a Private Nonprofit**

Source of Capital	Amount	(A) Fraction of Total Capital	(B) Cost	(C) = (A) × (B) Weighted Average Cost of Capital
Profits	$1,000,000	$\frac{2}{3}$	15%	$\frac{2}{3}$ × 15% = 10%
Debt	500,000	$\frac{1}{3}$	12%	$\frac{1}{3}$ × 12% = 4%
Total	$1,500,000			14%

be used to finance a pool of projects. The long-run rate reflects the cost of this pool of capital.

SUMMARY

Nonprofit organizations face three financial decisions: What and how much to buy, when to buy, and how to finance the purchase. This chapter discussed the framework and rules for making these decisions. Nonprofit organizations should invest in each of many activities up to the point where the benefits obtained from the additional investment in each of the activities are equal. Their decisions about when to buy should reflect expectations about inflation, technology, and general risk and uncertainty. The financing decision should be governed by the cost of the money to be invested—the cost of capital.

When evaluating investments, a tax-raising government should consider as its cost of capital the opportunity cost of the returns that could have been generated in the private sector by the funds taxed away. Private nonprofits should use the same reasoning to determine the discount rate to be assigned to their profits and funds raised from donors. These rates should be blended with the costs of borrowing to determine the cost of the capital used to finance investments.

APPENDIX A   Deriving Present Values

To compute the present value of an amount of money needed a year from now, think about what will happen in a year to an amount of money that is placed in a bank account right now. If it will earn 8 percent interest, at the end of Year 1 its value will be 108 percent of its initial value:

$$\text{Value of } X \text{ at the End of the First Year} = X + (0.08)(X) = (1.08)(X)$$

where X = the amount of money invested right now in an 8 percent bank account. If we need \$25,000 at the end of Year 1, X will equal \$23,148 (\$25,000 ÷ 1.08).

How much money, Y, do we need right now to afford a payment of \$25,000 two years from now? (To check your understanding so far, consider the following question: Is Y smaller or larger than X? The answer is that Y is smaller because it can accumulate interest for two years, rather than only one year before we need to spend it.) How do we compute Y? Well, we know that at the end of the first year Y will grow to be $(1.08)(Y)$. During the second year the $(1.08)(Y)$ will grow by another 8 percent to become $(1.08)^2(Y)$:

$$\text{Value of } Y \text{ Invested Right} = \text{Value at End of First Year} + \text{Now After Two Years} \quad \text{Growth in Value During the Second Year}$$

$$= (1.08)(Y) + (0.08)(1.08Y)$$
$$= (1.08)^2(Y)$$

If we need \$25,000 at the end of two years, Y will equal \$21,425 [\$25,000 ÷ $(1.08)^2$]. Put another way, if we place \$21,425 in an 8 percent savings account, it will grow to \$25,000 after two years. The *present value* of \$25,000 two years from now at an 8 percent interest rate is \$21,425.

In general, the present value of any amount of money that we need at some period of time from now is equal to the amount we need divided by the quantity $(1 + i)^n$, where i equals the interest rate we can earn and n equals the period of time. It is algebraically expressed as:

$$\text{Present Value} = \frac{\text{Amount of Money Needed in the Future}}{(1 + i)^n}$$

where i = the interest rate to be earned and n = the number of years.

DISCUSSION QUESTIONS

1. What is the decision rule that helps to allocate the amount nonprofit organizations should invest in different activities?

2. What is the time value of money? How is it incorporated into nonprofits' investment criteria?

3. Define payback, internal rate of return, and present value. What are the strengths and weaknesses of each of them as investment criteria?

4. Does increasing the discount rate make a proposed activity more or less financially attractive?

5. What are the three major factors to be considered in deciding on the timing of an investment in a certain activity? How should each of them be considered?

6. What is the opportunity cost of capital?

7. For nonprofit organizations, what is the cost of funds from profits? Of funds from donors? Of funds from borrowing?

8. How should the cost of capital of the U.S. government be computed? Of state and local governments? Of private nonprofit organizations?

TABLE 14-4 **Present Value of 1 at Compound Interest**

n	1%	2%	3%	4%	5%	6%
1	0.99009901	0.98039216	0.97087379	0.96153846	0.95238095	0.94339623
2	0.98029605	0.96116878	0.94259591	0.92455621	0.90702948	0.88999644
3	0.97059015	0.94232233	0.91514166	0.88899636	0.86383760	0.83961928
4	0.96098034	0.92384543	0.88848705	0.85480419	0.82270247	0.79209366
5	0.95146569	0.90573081	0.86260878	0.82192711	0.78352617	0.74725817
6	0.94204524	0.88797138	0.83748426	0.79031453	0.74621540	0.70496054
7	0.93271805	0.87056018	0.81309151	0.72991781	0.71068133	0.66505711
8	0.92348322	0.85349037	0.78940923	0.73069021	0.67683939	0.62741237
9	0.91433982	0.83675527	0.76641673	0.70258674	0.64460892	0.59189846
10	0.90528695	0.82034830	0.74409391	0.67556417	0.61391325	0.55839478
11	0.89632372	0.80426304	0.72242128	0.64958093	0.58467929	0.52678753
12	0.88744923	0.78849318	0.70137988	0.62459705	0.55683742	0.49696936
13	0.87866260	0.77303253	0.68095134	0.60057409	0.53032135	0.46883902
14	0.86996297	0.75787502	0.66111781	0.57747508	0.50506795	0.44230096
15	0.86134947	0.74301473	0.64186195	0.55526450	0.48101710	0.41726506
16	0.85282126	0.72844581	0.62316676	0.53390818	0.45811152	0.39364628
17	0.84437749	0.71416256	0.60501645	0.51337325	0.43629669	0.37136442
18	0.83601731	0.70015937	0.58739461	0.49362812	0.41552065	0.35034379
19	0.82773992	0.68643076	0.57028603	0.47464242	0.39573396	0.33051301
20	0.81954447	0.67297133	0.55367575	0.45638695	0.37688948	0.31180473
21	0.81143017	0.65977582	0.53754928	0.43883360	0.35894236	0.29415540
22	0.80339621	0.64683904	0.52189250	0.42195539	0.34184987	0.27750510
23	0.79544179	0.63415592	0.50669175	0.40572633	0.32557131	0.2617926
24	0.78756613	0.62172149	0.49193374	0.39012147	0.31006791	0.24697855
25	0.77976844	0.60953087	0.47760557	0.37511680	0.29530277	0.23299863
26	0.77204796	0.59757928	0.46369473	0.36068923	0.28124073	0.21981003
27	0.76440392	0.58586204	0.45018906	0.34681657	0.26784832	0.20736795
28	0.75683557	0.57437455	0.43707675	0.33347747	0.25509364	0.19563014
29	0.74934215	0.56311231	0.42434636	0.32065151	0.24294632	0.18455674
30	0.74192292	0.55207089	0.41198676	0.30831867	0.23137745	0.17411013
31	0.73457715	0.54124597	0.39998715	0.29646026	0.22035947	0.16425484
32	0.72730411	0.62099292	0.38833703	0.28505794	0.20986618	0.15495740
33	0.72010307	0.52022873	0.37702625	0.27409417	0.19987254	0.14618622
34	0.71297334	0.51002817	0.36604490	0.26355209	0.19035480	0.13791153
35	0.70591420	0.50002761	0.35538340	0.25341547	0.18129029	0.13010522
36	0.69892495	0.49022315	0.34503243	0.24366872	0.17265741	0.12274077
37	0.69200490	0.48061093	0.33498294	0.23429685	0.16443563	0.11579318
38	0.68515337	0.47118719	0.32522615	0.22528543	0.15660536	0.10305552
39	0.67836967	0.46194822	0.31575355	0.21662061	0.14914797	0.10305552
40	0.67165314	0.45289042	0.30655684	0.20828904	0.14204568	0.09722219
41	0.66500311	0.44401021	0.29762800	0.20027793	0.13528160	0.09171905
42	0.65841892	0.43530413	0.28895922	0.19257493	0.12883962	0.08652740
43	0.65189992	0.42676875	0.28054294	0.18516820	0.12270440	0.08162962
44	0.64544546	0.41840074	0.27237178	0.17804635	0.11686133	0.07700908
45	0.63905492	0.41019680	0.26443862	0.18119841	0.11129651	0.07265007
46	0.63272764	0.40215373	0.25673653	0.16461386	0.10599668	0.06853781
47	0.62646301	0.39426836	0.24925876	0.15828256	0.10094921	0.06465831
48	0.62026041	0.38653761	0.24199880	0.15219476	0.09614211	0.06099840
49	0.61411921	0.48212975	0.23495029	0.14634112	0.09156390	0.05754566
50	0.60803882	0.37152788	0.22810708	0.14081262	0.08720373	0.05428836

TABLE 14-4 (Continued)

n	7%	8%	9%	10%	11%	12%
1	0.93457944	0.92592593	0.91743119	0.90909091	0.90090090	0.89285714
2	0.87343873	0.85733882	0.84167999	0.82644628	0.81162243	0.79719388
3	0.81629788	0.79383224	0.77218348	0.75131480	0.73119138	0.71178025
4	0.76289521	0.73502985	0.70842521	0.68301346	0.65873097	0.63551808
5	0.71298618	0.68058320	0.64993139	0.62092132	0.59345133	0.56742686
6	0.66634222	0.63016963	0.59626733	0.56447393	0.53464084	0.50663112
7	0.62274974	0.58349040	0.54703424	0.51315812	0.48165841	0.45234922
8	0.58200910	0.54026888	0.50186628	0.46650738	0.43392650	0.40388323
9	0.54393374	0.50024897	0.46042778	0.42409762	0.39092477	0.36061002
10	0.50834929	0.46319349	0.42241081	0.38554329	0.35218448	0.32197324
11	0.47509280	0.42888286	0.38753285	0.35049390	0.31728331	0.28747610
12	0.44401196	0.39711376	0.35553473	0.31863082	0.28584082	0.25667509
13	0.41496445	0.36769792	0.32617865	0.28966438	0.25751426	0.22917419
14	0.38781724	0.34046104	0.29924647	0.26333125	0.23199482	0.20461981
15	0.36244602	0.31524170	0.27453804	0.23939205	0.20900435	0.18269626
16	0.33873460	0.29189047	0.25186976	0.21762914	0.18829220	0.16312166
17	0.31657439	0.27026895	0.23107318	0.19784467	0.16963262	0.14564434
18	0.29586392	0.25024903	0.21199374	0.17985879	0.15282218	0.13003959
19	0.27650833	0.23171206	0.19448967	0.16350799	0.13767764	0.11610678
20	0.25841900	0.21454821	0.17843089	0.14864363	0.12403391	0.10366677
21	0.24151309	0.19865575	0.16369806	0.13513057	0.11174226	0.09255961
22	0.22571317	0.18394051	0.15018171	0.12284597	0.10066870	0.08264251
23	0.21094688	0.17031528	0.13778139	0.11167816	0.09069252	0.07378796
24	0.19714662	0.15769934	0.12640494	0.10152560	0.08170498	0.06588210
25	0.18424918	0.14601790	0.11596754	0.09229600	0.07360809	0.05882331
26	0.17219549	0.13520176	0.10639251	0.08390545	0.06631359	0.05252081
27	0.16093037	0.12518682	0.09760781	0.07627768	0.05974197	0.04689358
28	0.15040221	0.11591372	0.08954845	0.06934335	0.05382160	0.04186927
29	0.14056282	0.10732752	0.08215454	0.06303941	0.04848793	0.03738327
30	0.13136712	0.09937733	0.07537114	0.05730855	0.04368282	0.03337792
31	0.12277301	0.09201605	0.06914783	0.05209868	0.03935389	0.02980172
32	0.11474113	0.08520005	0.06343838	0.04736244	0.03545395	0.02660868
33	0.10723470	0.07888893	0.05820035	0.04305676	0.03194050	0.02375775
34	0.10021934	0.07304531	0.05339481	0.03914251	0.02877522	0.02121227
35	0.09366294	0.06763454	0.04898607	0.03558410	0.02592363	0.01893953
36	0.08753546	0.06262458	0.04494135	0.03234918	0.02335462	0.01691029
37	0.08180884	0.05798572	0.04123059	0.02940835	0.02104020	0.01509848
38	0.17645686	0.05369048	0.03782623	0.02673486	0.01895513	0.01348078
39	0.07145501	0.04971341	0.03470296	0.02430442	0.01707670	0.10203641
40	0.06678038	0.04603093	0.03183758	0.02209493	0.01538441	0.01074680
41	0.06241157	0.04262123	0.02920879	0.02008630	0.01385983	0.00959536
42	0.05832857	0.03946411	0.02679706	0.01826027	0.01248633	0.00856728
43	0.05451268	0.03654084	0.02458446	0.01660025	0.01124895	0.00764936
44	0.05094643	0.03383411	0.02255455	0.01509113	0.01013419	0.00682978
45	0.04761349	0.03132788	0.02069224	0.01371921	0.00912990	0.00609802
46	0.04449859	0.02900730	0.01898371	0.01247201	0.00822513	0.00544466
47	0.04158747	0.02685861	0.01741625	0.01133819	0.00741003	0.00486131
48	0.03886679	0.02486908	0.01597821	0.01030745	0.00667570	0.00434045
49	0.03632410	0.02302693	0.01465891	0.00937041	0.00601415	0.00387540
50	0.03394776	0.02132123	0.01344854	0.00851855	0.00541815	0.00346018

TABLE 14-5 **Present Value of Annuity of 1 at Compound Interest**

n	1%	2%	3%	4%	5%	6%
1	0.99009901	0.98039216	0.97087379	0.96153846	0.95238095	0.94339623
2	1.97039506	1.94156094	1.91346970	1.88609467	1.85941043	1.83339267
3	2.94098521	2.88388327	2.82861135	2.77509103	2.72324803	2.67301195
4	3.90196555	3.80772870	3.71709840	3.62989522	3.54595050	3.46510561
5	4.85343124	4.71345951	4.57970719	4.45182233	4.32947667	4.21236379
6	5.79547647	5.60143089	5.41719144	5.24213686	5.07569207	4.91732433
7	6.72819453	6.47199107	6.23028296	6.00205467	5.78637340	5.58238144
8	7.65167775	7.32548144	7.01969219	6.73274487	6.46321276	6.20979381
9	8.56601758	8.16223671	7.78610892	7.43533161	7.10782168	6.80169227
10	9.47130453	8.98258501	8.53020284	8.11089578	7.72173493	7.36008705
11	10.36762825	9.78684805	9.25262411	8.76047671	8.30641422	7.88687458
12	11.25507747	10.57534122	9.95400399	9.38507376	8.86325164	8.38384394
13	12.13374007	11.34837375	10.63495533	9.98564785	9.39357299	8.85268296
14	13.00370304	12.10624877	11.29607314	10.56312293	9.89864094	9.29498393
15	13.86505252	12.84926350	11.93793509	11.11838743	10.37965804	9.71224899
16	14.71787378	13.57770931	12.56110203	11.65229561	10.83776956	10.10589527
17	15.56225127	14.29187188	13.16611847	12.16566885	11.27406625	10.47725969
18	16.39826858	14.99203125	13.75351308	12.65929697	11.68958690	10.82760348
19	17.22600850	15.67846201	14.32379911	13.13393940	12.08532086	11.15811649
20	18.04555297	16.35143334	14.87747486	13.59032634	12.46221034	11.46992122
21	18.85698313	17.01120906	15.41502414	14.02915995	12.82115271	11.76407662
22	19.66037934	17.65804820	15.93691664	14.45111533	13.16300258	12.04158172
23	20.45582133	18.29220412	16.44360839	14.85684167	13.48857388	12.30337898
24	21.24338726	18.91392560	16.93554212	15.24696314	13.79864179	12.55035753
25	22.02315570	19.52345647	17.41314769	15.62207994	14.09394457	12.78335616
26	22.79520366	20.12103576	17.87684242	15.98276918	14.37518530	13.00316619
27	23.55960759	20.70689780	18.32703147	16.32958575	14.64303362	13.21053414
28	24.31644316	21.28127236	18.76410823	16.66306322	14.89812726	13.40616428
29	25.06578530	21.84438466	19.18845459	16.98371463	15.14107358	13.59072102
30	25.80770822	22.39645555	19.60044135	17.29203330	15.37245103	13.76483115
31	26.54228537	22.93770152	20.00042849	17.58849356	15.59281050	13.92908599
32	27.26958947	23.46833482	20.38876553	17.87355150	15.80267667	14.08404339
33	27.98969255	23.98856355	20.76579178	18.14764567	16.00254921	14.23022961
34	28.70266589	24.49859172	21.13183668	18.41119776	16.19290401	14.36814114
35	29.40858009	24.99861933	21.48722007	18.66461323	16.37419429	14.49824636
36	30.10750504	25.48884248	21.83225250	18.90828195	16.54685171	14.62098713
37	30.79950944	25.96945341	22.16723544	19.14257880	16.71128734	14.73678031
38	31.48466330	26.44064060	22.49246159	19.36786423	16.86789271	14.84601916
39	32.16303298	26.90258883	22.80821513	19.58448484	17.01704067	14.94907468
40	32.83468611	27.35547924	23.11477197	19.79277388	17.15908635	15.04629687
41	33.49968922	27.79948945	23.41239997	19.99605181	17.29436796	15.13801592
42	34.15810814	28.23479358	23.70135920	20.18562674	17.42320758	15.22454332
43	34.81000806	28.66156233	23.98190213	20.37079494	17.54591198	15.30617294
44	35.45545352	29.07996307	24.25427392	20.54884129	17.66277331	15.38318202
45	36.09450844	29.49015987	24.51871254	20.72003970	17.77406982	15.45583209
46	36.72723608	29.89231360	24.77544907	20.88465356	17.88006650	15.52436990
47	37.35369909	30.28658196	25.02470783	21.04293612	17.98101571	15.58902821
48	37.97395949	30.67311957	25.26670664	21.19513088	18.07715782	15.65002661
49	38.58807871	31.05207801	25.50165693	21.34147200	18.16872173	15.70757227
50	39.19611753	31.42360589	25.72976401	21.48218462	18.25592546	15.76186064

TABLE 14-5 (Continued)

n	7%	8%	9%	10%	11%	12%
1	0.93457944	0.92592593	0.91743119	0.90909091	0.90090090	0.89285714
2	1.80801817	1.78326475	1.75911119	1.73553719	1.71252333	1.69005102
3	2.62431604	2.57709699	2.53129467	2.48685199	2.44371472	2.40183127
4	3.38721126	3.31212684	3.23971988	3.16986545	3.10244569	3.03734935
5	4.01109744	3.99271004	3.88965126	3.79078677	3.69589702	3.60477620
6	4.76653966	4.62287966	4.48591859	4.35526070	4.23053785	4.11140732
7	5.38928940	5.20637006	5.03295284	4.86841882	4.71219626	4.56375654
8	5.97129851	5.74663894	5.53481911	5.33492620	5.14612276	4.96763977
9	6.51523225	6.24688791	5.99524689	5.75902382	5.53704753	5.32824979
10	7.02358154	6.71008140	6.41765770	6.14456711	5.88923201	5.65022303
11	7.49867434	7.13896426	6.80519055	6.49506101	6.20651533	5.93769913
12	7.94268630	7.53607802	7.16072528	6.81369182	6.49235615	6.19437423
13	8.35765074	7.90377594	7.48690392	7.10335620	6.74987040	6.42354842
14	8.74546799	8.24423698	7.78615039	7.36668746	6.98186523	6.62816823
15	9.10791401	8.55947869	8.06068843	7.60607951	7.19086958	6.81086449
16	9.44664860	8.85136916	8.31255819	7.82370864	7.37916178	6.97398615
17	9.76322299	9.12163811	8.54363137	8.02155331	7.54879440	7.11963049
18	10.05908691	9.37188714	8.75562511	8.20141210	7.70161657	7.24967008
19	10.33559524	9.60359920	8.95011478	8.36492009	7.83929421	7.36577686
20	10.59401425	9.81814741	9.12854567	8.51356372	7.96332812	7.46944362
21	10.83552733	10.01680316	9.29224373	8.64869429	8.07507038	7.56200324
22	11.06124050	10.20074366	9.44242544	8.77154026	8.17573908	7.64464575
23	11.27218738	10.37105895	9.58020683	8.88321842	8.26643160	7.71843370
24	11.46933400	10.52875828	9.70661177	8.98474402	8.34813658	7.78431581
25	11.65358318	10.67477619	9.82257960	9.07704002	8.42174466	7.84313911
26	11.82577867	10.80997795	9.92897211	9.16094547	8.48805826	7.89565992
27	11.98670904	10.93516477	10.02657992	9.23722316	8.54780023	7.94255350
28	12.13711125	11.05107849	10.11612837	9.30656651	8.60162183	7.98442277
29	12.27767407	11.15840601	10.19828291	9.36960591	8.65010976	8.02180604
30	12.40904188	11.25778334	10.27365404	9.42691447	8.69379257	8.05518397
31	12.53181419	11.34979939	10.34280187	9.47901315	8.73314646	8.08498569
32	12.64655532	11.43499944	10.40624025	9.52637559	8.76860042	8.11159436
33	12.75379002	11.51388837	10.46444060	9.56943236	8.80054092	8.13535211
34	12.85400936	11.58693367	10.51783541	9.60857487	8.82931614	8.15656438
35	12.94767230	11.65456822	10.56682148	9.64415897	8.85523977	8.17550391
36	13.03520776	11.71719279	10.61176282	9.67650816	8.87859438	8.19241421
37	13.11701660	11.77517851	10.65299342	9.70591651	8.89963458	8.20751269
38	13.19347345	11.82886899	10.69081965	9.73265137	8.91858971	8.22099347
39	13.26492846	11.87858240	10.72552261	9.75695579	8.93566641	8.23302988
40	13.33170884	11.92461333	10.75736020	9.77905072	8.95105082	8.24377668
41	13.39412041	11.96723457	10.78656899	9.79913702	8.96491065	8.25337204
42	13.45244898	12.00669867	10.81336604	9.81739729	8.97739698	8.26193932
43	13.50696167	12.04323951	10.83795050	9.83399753	8.98864593	8.26958868
44	13.55790810	12.07707362	10.86050504	9.84908867	8.99878011	8.27641846
45	13.60552159	12.10840150	10.88119729	9.86280788	9.00791001	8.28251648
46	13.65002018	12.13740880	10.90018100	9.87527989	9.01613515	8.28796155
47	13.69160764	12.16426741	10.91759725	9.88661808	9.02354518	8.29282245
48	13.73047443	12.18913649	10.93357546	9.89692553	9.03022088	8.29716290
49	13.76679853	12.21216341	10.94823436	9.90629594	9.03623503	8.30103831
50	13.80074629	12.23348464	10.96168290	9.91481449	9.04165318	8.30449849

Cases

CASE STUDIES

Case 14.1 combines all of the issues involved in a capital budgeting analysis in a realistic setting. It is an excellent vehicle for enhancing your command of the subject. Case 14.2 depicts the Federal Aviation Administration's decision about when to replace its VORTAC navigational system. The decision is exceedingly complex, replete with technological uncertainties, subtle options, and sophisticated discounting. But that's not all. Each option provides different levels of reliability. And alternative systems are backed by different political factions. This case is a paradigm for most public policy decisions. Case 14.3 expands a case presented in Chapter 8.

CASE 14.1 Leicester Polytechnic Institute

Leicester Polytechnic Institute is a small, private four-year college, located in Atlanta, Georgia. The school was founded by Robert Leicester, a successful industrialist and a "Georgia Booster," who thought that the Atlanta area should have a school to ensure a steady supply of top-notch engineers and other technical personnel. Over the years, Leicester Poly had fulfilled, and indeed exceeded, his expectations. It had an excellent reputation and many of its graduates held responsible positions in the major firms located in the Atlanta area. Their loyalty to the school was legendary and evinced itself not only in their gifts to the school but also in their rate of hiring and promoting the school's graduates. Leicester Poly's graduates had an average of three job offers and a number of the large, industrial concerns in the area were urging the institute to expand its capacity.

The administrators of the school thought that over the next 12 years at least 1,500 high-quality additional students could enter if there were sufficient space for them. A number of responsible people were consulted about the academic and financial viability of expanding the school's capacity. All agreed that it was desirable to do so. The issue was not whether to expand but how to do it.

Professor Regina E. Herzlinger prepared this case. It is based on "Atherton School Building," a case prepared by Gerard Johnson, under the supervision of Professor Robert N. Anthony.

Copyright © 1977 by the President and Fellows of Harvard College. Harvard Business School case 178-079. Revised January 1993.

ALTERNATIVE PROPOSALS

The current enrollment in the college was distributed among 70 classrooms in four physically separate locations. To meet the needs of the additional 1,500 students expected to be added to Leicester's enrollment over the next 12 years, projections called for 12 more classrooms after 2 years and an additional 12 classrooms 10 years thereafter.

The following choices were facing the school:

- Build one building with 12 classrooms now, and another 12-classroom building 10 years from now, or
- Build one 24-room building now.

The economics of construction were such that the total cost of the two smaller separate buildings was one and a half times the total cost of the one large building. Costs were expected to grow at 8 percent a year. As shown in **Exhibit 1**, the total cost of the first option was $9,489,000 (including the impact of inflation) and the total cost of the second was $4,023,500.

During the interim 10-year period, when the extra classrooms in the 24-room building would not be fully utilized, the various administrative agencies currently placed in the overcrowded administration building could usefully occupy the space. Plans called for the construction of a separate facility for this group at the end of the first 10 years anyway. In fact, the school would save approximately $26,000 annually in rent, which would have to be paid for the space needed by the administrative unit.

An additional issue was that of evaluating two competing proposals, both submitted by the same architectural consulting firm. Proposal A called for a conventional construction format. Proposal B called for a "systems building" format, a substantial departure from traditional school construction techniques, stressing modular flexibility.

The initial cost of the 24-room systems building exceeded the initial cost of a traditional building. (**Exhibit 2** summarizes the projected costs of the competing proposals.) According to the architects' report, either building would meet the requirements of Leicester Poly for the period of 20 years from the completion of the construction. In the tenth year, both proposals required the unavoidable cost of remodeling space, which would be much less expensive with the systems building whose inside walls were partitions. In the traditional building, the remodeling required altering the superstructure of the building. Both construction proposals would achieve the same effect in terms of educational quality and aesthetic appeal, but the systems building had lower maintenance expenses.

FINANCING ALTERNATIVES

An additional issue was that of recommending a financing alternative. Three options were considered—10- and 20-year bonds and use of the college endowment. The school had a $2 million unexpended fund balance in the plant fund, donated by former graduates and built up from past transfers of funds resulting from current operations. The endowment was currently earning an 8 percent return and it could be used to help finance the construction. The bonds would probably carry a 5 percent interest rate.

ASSIGNMENT

1. Should all 24 classrooms be built at the same time, or should 12 be built now and 12 be built in the future?
2. Which construction format, conventional or systems, should be used?
3. Which financing alternative should be chosen?

EXHIBIT 1 Leicester Polytechnic Institute—Preliminary Analysis

	Conventional	Systems
I. Build one building now and another ten years thereafter.[a]		
A. First building, 12 classrooms		
Construction cost[a] (at 75 percent of Option II)	$2,730,000	$ 3,844,317
Design and supervision	273,000	384,432
	$3,003,000	$ 4,228,749
B. Second building, 12 classrooms		
Construction cost[b]	$5,896,500	$ 8,303,725
Design and supervision	589,650	830,373
	$6,486,150	$ 9,134,098
Total cost	$9,489,150	$13,362,847
II. Build one building, 24 classrooms.		
Construction cost	$3,639,450	$ 5,125,909
Design and supervision	384,050	512,591
Total cost	$4,023,500	$ 5,638,500

[a]Does not include the cost of land which is already owned by the school.
[b]First building construction cost inflated by 8 percent per annum, compounded.

EXHIBIT 2 Leicester Polytechnic Institute—Construction Proposals

	Conventional	Systems
Initial cost	$4,023,500	$5,638,500
Annual maintenance—Years 1 through 9[a]	225,000/yr.	135,000/yr.
Remodeling and maintenance in Year 10	3,975,000	1,635,000
Annual maintenance—Years 11 through 20[a]	225,000/yr.	135,000/yr.

[a]Maintenance services are purchased from a cleaning service and are directly proportional to the size of the building.

CASE 14.2 Replacing the VORTAC Navigation System

BACKGROUND

The Federal Aviation Administration (FAA) is responsible for the safety of civil aircraft. It tests and approves aircraft designs, inspects aircraft and related equipment, and operates various forms of air traffic control. The latter entails coordinating aircraft movements while on the ground, during takeoffs and landings, and while flying between airports. By assuring that pilots follow correct flight paths and that there is adequate spacing between airplanes, the FAA can prevent most accidents. Air traffic is expected by the FAA to increase substantially by the year 2000—by a factor of at least three.

Navigational aids are an integral part of air traffic control between airports. The en route navigation system supplies pilots with the information necessary to determine their positions and to ensure that these correspond to the air traffic controllers' instructions. The current system had two basic components: VOR (Very-High Frequency Omni-Range) and TACAN (Tactical Air Navigation). VOR has a limited range of roughly 67 nautical miles. Constant signals are emitted from its antenna in all directions and provide instantaneous compass direction, or bearings, to airborne receivers. The signals are line-of-sight—they extend outward from the antenna in a conical pattern and are blocked by intervening obstacles, such as mountains. TACAN was initially deployed for the use of military aircraft and now serves both military and civilian traffic. It is maintained by the FAA but must be kept operational as long as the Department of Defense (DOD) deems necessary. TACAN serves as distance measuring equipment and provides the azimuth horizontal angular distance between the TACAN beacon and the instruments aboard an airborne craft.

A co-located VOR and TACAN are called a VORTAC unit. VORTAC can also refer to the system as a whole. The current en route system employs 708 VORTACs and 164 VORs. (This excludes special equipment necessitated by larger terminals, unusual terrain, and heavy traffic patterns.) Most are located redundantly so that at least two units can cover the same general area and, thus, serve as an added safety factor in the case of equipment failure.

The first VORTAC installations were commissioned in the mid-1940s and units were added through the mid-1960s. Further additions may be made as air traffic increases or moves to new areas. The newer units use solid-state technology. The older units use vacuum-tube design and, thus, suffer from relatively shorter part-life, longer warm-up time, and greater power consumption than the newer units. Some tubes can only be obtained by placing costly custom orders. Others are now supplied only by single manufacturers who can charge the higher prices afforded by this monopoly situation. The lack of standardization among units, the difficulties with parts procurement, and the existence of some very old components increase the operating and maintenance (O&M) costs. Almost all of the current ground systems use vacuum-tube hardware at least 15 years old and some of it is 30 or more years old.

THE ISSUE

In the 1980s, the FAA knew that it must develop a replacement program and has two major options. First, it can patch up the existing system with solid-state instruments and await new technologies such as LORAN-C or NAVSTAR-GPS. LORAN-C consists of widely spaced towers that emit pulsing signals which all types of vehicles can use to calculate their longitude and latitude. It is sponsored by the U.S. Coast Guard, which, like the FAA, is part of the Department of Transportation (DOT), and is already used by some seagoing, airborne, and land vehicles. NAVSTAR would use global positioning satellites to transmit signals to land, water, and air vehicles all over the world. It is sponsored by the Department of Defense and must still undergo some research and development. The earliest it could be operationalized is 1990.

The FAA's second alternative is to replace the present system with a second-generation VORTAC using standardized solid-state technology and a Remote Maintenance Monitoring System (RMMS) to further reduce O&M costs. This system could also, eventually, be replaced by LORAN-C or NAVSTAR.

THE EXISTING SYSTEM

The following inventory describes the types, numbers, and reliability of existing facilities:

Type	Number	Reliability
VOR		
Single	158	98.83%
Dual	714	99.36
TACR[a]		
Single	358	98.83
Dual	350	99.36

[a]TACR is the TACAN part of a VORTAC.

Each VOR and TACR is made up of a number of components. A single facility has only one type of each component at a facility; a dual one has a second unit for one or more of the components at a facility. The dualization provides a backup. If the first component fails, only a few seconds are required to switch from one unit to another and restore service. With a single system, a failure of the transmitter component shuts down that facility.[1] Traffic is then rerouted until a maintenance crew can effect repairs. The present mean-time-to-recovery is four hours (one-way travel time

---

[1]A detailed description of the mechanics and probabilities for breakdown involved in single vs. dual systems is presented in MITRE Report #7140, Economic and Performance Evaluation of Second-Generation VORTAC, the MITRE Corporation, Bedford, Massachusetts, 1977.

of two hours plus mean-time-to-repair of two hours). Reliability figures are based upon availability of service and usually expressed as a ratio:

$$\text{Reliability} = \frac{\text{Available Time}}{\text{Available Time + Downtime}}$$

where Available Time + Downtime = All the Hours in a Year.

Downtime is the result of scheduled shutdowns for maintenance and inspection and unscheduled line and power failures and equipment failures. The current scheduled downtime averages 62 hours per facility per year. The National Transportation Safety Bureau, which is responsible for investigating and determining the cause of airplane accidents, finds that the reliability factors of the VORTAC system are so high that few, if any, accidents can be attributed to VORTAC failure.

Costs of the Existing System

Manpower is the greatest single expense for the operation and maintenance of the system. Personnel expenses are allocated into five broad categories:

- *Electronics.* Time spent on the inspection and repair of components.
- *Plants and Structure (P&S).* Work done on access roads, power lines, and buildings.
- *Other.* Travel time, watch standing, training, and improvements.
- *Administrative Costs.* Calculated by multiplying the first three categories by 0.3.
- *Benefits.* Calculated by determining the various benefits afforded the different positions and grade levels associated with the numerous tasks.

The following table breaks down the labor costs associated with each type of facility:

Workload—Man-Hours per Month				
Facility	*Electronics*	*P&S*	*Other*	*Benefits*
VOR				
Single	21	4	23	9
Dual	28	15	31	13
TACR				
Single	63	4	45	21
Dual	68	4	42	21

Average salary = $22,800/year.

Each facility also incurs certain fixed costs. Spare parts must be kept on hand. FAA personnel perform a specified number of flight checks for each facility. This cost, jointly borne by a VOR and TACR, averages $1,818 for each of the 560 facilities. Leased phone lines connect the various sites with central monitoring stations. This cost, $2,450 a year per facility, can also serve both a VOR and TACR. Other expenses impose a per annum expenditure of $2,801 for single VORs, $3,380 for dual VORs, $2,150 for single TACRs, and $3,175 for dual TACRs. They include some utility charges, travel expenses, and miscellaneous items.

THE PATCH-UP PLAN

If the FAA decides to patch up the present system and await new technologies, the following equipment must be replaced to maintain operations to the year 2000:

VOR Transmitters (vintages 1943-46, 51-56)	23 single, 505 dual
VOR Monitors (vintage 1951-56)	130 dual
TACAN Beacons	54 single, 206 dual
TACAN Transmitter-Monitor-Control (TMC)	560 dual

Under this schedule, the O&M and other costs will remain the same as those of the current system. Each VOR consists of at least an antenna, a transmitter, a monitor, and a control. None of the antennas need to be replaced. A TACAN consists of a beacon and one unit which combines the functions of a transmitter-monitor-control (TMC). The dual equipment is used to provide the added safety of a backup unit. The Airways Planning Standards determine which units should be dualized by considering terrain, weather, traffic patterns, and breakdown probabilities. According to these standards, excess dualization now exists.

Contracts for electronic components would be let for complete lots with delivery schedules timed to match replacement plans which call for an even spread of the investment over five years. The estimated electronic equipment costs are:

Item	Dollars in Thousands
Single VOR Transmitter	$10.7
Dual VOR Transmitter	21.4
Single VOR Monitor	10.3
Dual VOR Monitor	18.3
Single TACAN Beacon	45.0
Dual TACAN Beacon	90.0
Dual TACAN TMC	70.0

Each component must have spare parts estimated to cost 35 percent of the purchase price. The installation and flight check costs depend on whether the new VOR and new TACR are co-located and whether the new equipment for a site is all being installed at the same time. The minimum per site cost is considered to be $13,752 while the maximum is $17,506. Retraining technicians will involve a three-week course at a tuition cost of $250/week given to two people for each facility. A total of 560 facilities will be affected.

But, it may be necessary to make further investments. Some predict that the entire system must be patched it if is to last past 1995.

SECOND-GENERATION ALTERNATIVE

The FAA prefers a second-generation option because the resulting O&M savings should more than pay for the investment. A variety of single and dual equipment configurations have been considered. All single configurations would produce a reliability factor of 99.30. The Airways Planning Standards (APS) permit 50 percent single units and 50 percent dual/single configurations. This results in a reliability factor of 99.40. The following table lists the respective configuration unit costs and the number of units required for APS:

Configuration Costs		
	Number	*Unit Costs*
VOR		
Single	95	$ 63,187
Dual/Single[a]	100	76,451
TACR		
Single	354	113,015
Dual/Single[a]	354	136,739

[a]Two transmitters and one monitor

The listed prices all include the cost of installation and of a Remote Maintenance Monitoring System (RMMS) capability which permits a monthly, rather than the current weekly, certification inspection. The RMMS places sensors in the equipment so that its status can be reviewed at a central location. It costs 5 percent of the total. Inventory costs call for an initial investment equal to 35 percent of the purchase price and a 2 percent annual investment thereafter.

The reduced workload accomplished through RMMS necessitates the training of one person per facility for a period of six weeks. Tuition costs $250/week and approximately 200 technicians would be trained each year. Regular relief personnel could not replace those being retrained. Expected workloads per facility are listed below:

Workload—Man-Years per Unit	
VOR	
Single	0.18
Dual	0.28
VORTAC	
Single	0.39
Dual	0.54

Telephone line and flight check costs would be the same for both first- and second-generation VORTAC. There would be some differences in other costs such as utilities and ground transportation.

Other Costs (per year per facility)		
	VOR	*VORTAC*
Single	$2,642	$4,727
Dual/Single	2,794	5,779

The timing of the replacements depends on which existing units are most in need of retirement, which occupy crucial positions, and which can be shut down and not disrupt the system. Cost savings also encourage the use of scheduled shut-down periods of equipment replacement. A tentative schedule for second-generation implementation places 20 percent of the replacements in each of five consecutive years.[2]

The International Civil Aviation Organization (ICAO) has agreed to use VORTAC as a standard until 1985. Since member countries are expected to spend one-half to one billion dollars in VORTAC equipment before that date, the ICAO will probably extend the VORTAC standard until 1995 to amortize this investment. The FAA also has a substantial investment in facilities and personnel dedicated to the operation of navigational aids. The majority of this personnel have competitive civil service status which generally permits removal only due to absence without leave, disobedience, insubordination, misrepresentation, untrustworthiness, inefficiency, or incompetence. And, the characteristics of the equipment and administration have interacted to form standardized pilot procedures, such as the Instrument Flight Rules. Their constant use over many years results in effective, unambiguous communications. If the rules must be changed to accommodate a radically different system, misunderstandings could develop.

Additionally, the owners of civilian aircraft have invested one billion dollars in navigation equipment. They may require some time to amortize this cost. If new equipment proves too expensive, not only may owners of aircraft which do not legally require these aids forgo investment but, also, the growth of civil aviation as a whole may be impaired.

If VORTAC remained in operation until 2010, further replacements must take place. This would include 700 TACAN/DME antennas at $20,000 plus $20,000 each for installation and 500 engine generators at $25,000 each which includes installation.

LORAN-C VS. NAVSTAR

LORAN-C

There are some definite advantages to eventually replacing the present short-range, line-of-sight system with a long-range, area navigation system (RNAV). The operating characteristics of VORTAC create limited and circuitous flight paths which lead to congestion, delay, and unneeded fuel consumption. RNAV can theoretically avoid these problems. It may eventually permit:

(1) Congested area by-pass routes;
(2) Multiple routes to allow the segregation of aircraft by operating characteristics;
(3) Pilot navigation of commonly flown radar vector paths which would reduce the workload of air traffic controllers;
(4) Improved alignment of routes; and
(5) Some increased instrument approach capability without further investments in airport air traffic control equipment.

There is a possibility that VORTAC itself could be modified to provide a partial RNAV capability. Satellites could potentially offer RNAV on a worldwide basis.

LORAN-C is an RNAV system already in operation for maritime traffic. It is also used by helicopters flying in the coastal zones (usually to offshore oil platforms).

___
[2]Actual implementation may not proceed at a uniform rate per year.

DOT has also sponsored some experiments with LORAN-C as a land navigation aid. However, it may prove a transitional system which should be limited or phased out with the development of NAVSTAR.

LORAN-C works by sending out differently timed, pulsing signals from a chain of stations—usually four, although only three are needed for effective operation. An airborne computer uses these signals to plot exact longitude and latitude. LORAN-C's low frequency radio beams follow the contours of the land. This allows a plane to fly in a straight line rather than zigzag to the VORTACs which must be placed to avoid interference with terrain or electrically radiating sources. The LORAN-C facilities have a range of 600 to 1,000 nautical miles and have demonstrated much greater accurancy than VORTAC. An article noted that its nominal accuracy is about one-quarter of a mile 95 percent of the time.[3] But, it has a much greater susceptibility to atmospheric noise (as with thunderstorms) and a longer time to recover a signal after interference. Proper VORTAC backup units offer a few seconds recovery time from initial equipment failure while LORAN failure can necessitate up to a two-minute period to resynchronize the pulsing signals.[4] Many of these problems are now under study and could be mitigated in the future.

There are now 15 LORAN-C stations in service for maritime traffic and an additional 5 may be approved to handle the land navigation needs of the 48 states. It may take a combined total of 28 stations to offer air navigation coverage with redundancy at all altitudes. Each station costs $6 million and has an annual O&M expense of $200,000. If LORAN-C also furnishes extensive instrument approach capability, it might require as many as 625 dual-monitoring stations. These would cost $30,000 each for equipment and installation and have annual O&M costs equal to 5 percent of the investment. This would replace some approach and landing, as well as en route, air traffic control systems. No studies have been undertaken to ascertain an appropriate division of responsibility between the Coast Guard and the FAA with such a system.

NAVSTAR-GPS

This concept uses satellites, globally located, for navigational purposes. This system could provide the same benefits as LORAN-C, and additional benefits of global coverage and better immunity to noise than LORAN-C. Its suitability for air navigation could not be determined until the 1980s, and it could not be used for civilian air navigation as soon as LORAN-C.

AVIONICS

The owners of private user equipment (avionics) will also be affected by changes in navigation systems. Avionics generally have a 20-year life span and annual O&M costs of 5 percent of purchase price. There is somewhere between one-half to one billion dollars invested in such equipment at this time. The FAA assumes that LORAN-C would not become operational for all aviation users until 1985. It is felt

[3]Frank McGuire, "LORAN-C—The Nanosecond Navigator," *Rotor and Wing* (April 1977): 25.
[4]Some of the on-board computers can continue functioning without interruption.

that there should be at least a ten year overlap period when VORTAC continues to operate so that avionics may be amortized. The following table presents the anticipated user population of 1980 by projecting a 2 percent growth rate for the five years from 1975. This growth rate was projected from the experience of the early 1970s. Class I and Class II planes are generally owned by private individuals. Class III and air carriers are for commercial and corporate purposes primarily.

A consulting firm has estimated likely equipment costs for 1980 of $2,050 per LORAN Receiver/Navigator; however, the Coast Guard indicates that some assumptions and component configurations employed by the consultant may have overstated LORAN-C costs. A single VOR costs $900, while a single TACAN/DME runs $1,800. Air carriers must purchase other equipment which raises the cost of either system to over $20,000. But, by 1985 advances in electronic fabrication may lower the carriers' costs by 50 percent.

Estimated 1980 User Population

Type of User	Number	VORTAC Requirements	LORAN-C Requirements
General Aviation			
Class I (1-3 places)	98,400	Single VOR	1 LORAN-C
Class II (4+ places)	57,800	Dual VOR	1.5 LORAN-C[a]
Class III (less than			
12,500 lbs)	39,600	Dual VOR + Single TACAN/DME	2 LORAN-C
Air Carrier (more than			
12,500 lbs)	3,210	All Dual + Extras	2 LORAN-C + Extras

[a]1.5 LORAN-C indicates that half the users would buy single and half would buy dual.

Present VOR sets can share some components with communications equipment, which can reduce the $500 normal communications equipment investment by 20 percent. On the other hand, LORAN-C may eliminate the need for Class III and above aircraft, which have special landing equipment, to purchase a microwave landing system. This could lead to savings of $1,700. VOR salvage and resale values are unknown.

ASSIGNMENT

Which options should the FAA choose and why, if the replacement begins in 1980?

CASE 14.3   Hospital Replacement Decision

Please return to Case 8.2 (page 263) and focus on the economics of the decision. Should the hospital be replaced?

Part Three

Financial Reporting and Analysis for Individual Sectors

15   Colleges and Universities

Institutions of higher education are being challenged to prepare students to deal with the complex problems facing the country, including the demands of increasingly competitive world markets and long-term economic and technological growth. Growing emphasis on the need to evaluate what colleges teach and what college students study and learn is, at least in part, a response to these issues.

Colleges and universities also face pressure to curb increasing costs. Rising tuition levels have caused considerable concern about students' ability to afford college education. As a result, the public has turned its attention to how higher education institutions spend their money and how much they charge students in tuition and fees.[1]

COLLEGES AND UNIVERSITIES ARE ENTRUSTED WITH the education and career preparation of our youth and, increasingly, of our adults. Our success as a society and economy hinges on their efficacy. But their costs are daunting. Trustees and managers find it increasingly difficult to obtain the resources they need to accomplish their educational objectives. This chapter discusses the current financial reporting standards of the higher education sector. It also illustrates financial analysis techniques for achieving better understanding and management of higher education institutions.

SECTOR OVERVIEW

Referred to as *colleges and universities*, *higher education*, or *postsecondary education*, this sector includes organizations that provide education beyond the high school level. Historically, it was composed primarily of nonprofit, four-year colleges and universities. But recent changes in demographics, pressures for career training, and the economics of learning have transformed it to include professional graduate schools, two-year colleges, and technical

---

[1]National Center for Education Statistics, *The Condition of Education 1989* 2, Postsecondary Education, ed. Curtis O. Baker (Washington, DC: U.S. Department of Education, National Center for Education Statistics, 1989), p. 1.

schools. A growing number of nondegree continuing education programs are offered by both nonprofit and for-profit organizations, and the number of degree granting for-profit institutions also has grown.

Sector Structure

Colleges and universities offer such a wide range of educational services that diversity is recognized as the hallmark of American higher education. Virtually all colleges and universities are nonprofit organizations, controlled either by state or local governments (*public*) or by independent nonprofit organizations (*private* or *independent*). They are either *two-year* or *four-year* institutions. Noncollegiate institutions provide a growing number of vocational training and adult and continuing education courses. Of the 3,587 *colleges and universities* and 8,469 *noncollegiate* postsecondary education institutions in the 1987-88 academic year, 6,229 were operated for profit as businesses (*proprietary schools*).[2] (The industry statistics and financial reporting standards discussed below do not apply to noncollegiate institutions, although the analytic techniques are relevant to all types of educational institutions.)

The data in Table 15-1 show that although the number of private nonprofit four-year colleges and universities dwarfs the number of public ones (1,536 versus 599 in 1987-88), enrollments show the reverse pattern. Of the nearly 13 million students, 43 percent are enrolled in public four-year schools, 36 percent in public two-year schools, and only 22 percent in private institutions. On average, private schools are much smaller than public schools, and are almost exclusively four-year institutions. Private four-year annual tuition and fees are nearly five times those of public four-year schools, and the proportionate gap is even greater between public and private two-year institutions.

Traditional higher education boomed throughout most of the twentieth century but leveled off in the 1980s. The number of institutions increased by about 26 percent during each of the decades of the 1960s and 1970s, but by only 6 percent from 1980 to 1986. Enrollment increased by 140 percent in the 1960s, 40 percent in the 1970s, and only 3 percent between 1980 and 1986.[3] Demographics indicate that the slow growth pattern of the 1980s is likely to continue, or worsen, in the 1990s, with 1995 enrollment projected to be below current levels.[4] While the expressed need for lifelong learning

[2]National Center for Education Statistics, *Digest of Education Statistics 1989 25th Edition* (Washington, DC: U.S. Department of Education, National Center for Education Statistics, 1989), p. 324, Table 301.

[3]*1989-90 Fact Book on Higher Education*, compiled by Charles J. Anderson, Deborah J. Carter, and Andrew J. Malizio with Biochi San (American Council on Education and Macmillan Publishing Company, 1989), p. 70 (Table 45), pp. 133-134 (Table 88).

[4]U.S. Department of Commerce, *Statistical Abstract, 1990* (Washington, DC: Government Printing Office, 1991), p. 128, Table 20.

TABLE 15-1 **Nonprofit and Public Institutions, Enrollment and Tuition, 1987**

| | Institutions | | Students | | | Tuition and Fees |
	Number	Percent	Total	Percent	Average	Average
Public four-year	599	17	5,434,010	43	9,072	$1,414
Public two-year	992	28	4,541,054	36	4,578	$660
Private four-year	1,536	43	2,558,075	20	1,665	$6,658
Private two-year	460	13	235,168	2	511	$3,684
Total all types	3,587		12,768,307			
Total public	1,591	45	9,975,064	79		
Total private	1,996	56	2,793,243	22		
Total four-year	2,135	60	7,992,085	63		
Total two-year	1,452	41	4,776,222	38		

Source: Adapted from *The Alamanac of Higher Education 1989-90*, The Editors of the Chronicle of Higher Education (The University of Chicago Press, 1989), p. 4.

is greater than ever, it is increasingly met by organizations other than traditional colleges and universities.

Financial Status

Table 15-2 contains historical data on current fund revenues and expenditures for all nonprofit higher education institutions, and a comparison of public and private institutions for 1985-86.

Revenues College and university current fund revenues exceeded $100 billion in fiscal year 1985-86, with only about a quarter of them from tuition and fees. The relative sources of revenue were fairly stable over the preceding ten years, with a 6 percent decrease in the share from government sources offset by increases from tuition and fees and other sources.

The importance of various revenue sources differs substantially between public and private institutions. Public institutions are financed primarily by state or local government appropriations (48.6 percent), with tuition and fees (14.5 percent), and federal government support, including grants (10.5 percent), contributing the next largest amounts. Private institutions are financed primarily by tuition and fees (38.6 percent), and secondarily by federal government support (16.5 percent). The surprisingly large fraction of government

TABLE 15-2 **Current Fund Revenue and Expenditure Data**

Distribution of Current Fund Revenue and Expenditures, Public and Nonprofit Higher Education Institutions Selected Academic Years 1975-76 to 1985-86 (in thousands)

	All Institutions			Public 1985-86	Private 1985-86
	1975-76	1979-80	1985-86		
Revenue by Source					
Educational and general:					
Student tuition and fees	$ 8,171,942	$11,930,340	$ 23,116,605	$ 9,439,177	$13,677,429
Federal government	6,477,179	8,902,844	12,704,750	6,852,370	5,852,380
State governments	12,260,886	18,378,299	29,911,500	29,220,586	690,914
Local governments	1,616,975	1,587,552	2,544,506	2,325,844	218,662
Endowment earnings	687,470	1,176,627	2,275,898	398,603	1,877,295
Gifts	1,917,036	2,808,075	5,410,905	2,109,782	3,301,124
Sales, services, and other activities	645,420	1,239,439	2,373,494	1,596,946	776,548
Auxiliary enterprises	4,547,622	6,481,458	10,674,136	6,684,794	3,989,342
Hospitals	2,494,340	4,373,384	8,226,635	4,708,930	3,517,705
Other sources	884,298	1,641,965	3,199,186	1,667,600	1,531,586
Total current fund revenue	$39,703,166	$58,519,982	$100,437,616	$65,004,632	$35,432,985
Expenditures by Function					
Education and General:					
Instruction	$13,094,943	$18,496,717	$31,032,099	$21,880,782	$ 9,151,318
Research	3,287,364	5,099,151	8,437,367	5,705,144	2,732,222
Public service	1,238,603	1,816,521	3,119,533	2,515,734	603,799
Academic support	2,472,393	3,876,388	6,667,392	4,693,543	1,973,849
Student services	1,624,643	2,566,732	4,562,938	2,921,758	1,641,180
Institutional support	3,615,423	5,054,411	9,350,786	5,667,144	3,683,642
Operation and maintenance of plant	3,082,959	4,700,070	7,605,226	5,177,254	2,427,972
Scholarships and fellowships	1,635,858	2,200,468	4,160,174	1,575,909	2,584,266
Mandatory transfers	546,498	732,385	1,192,449	735,695	456,754
Auxiliary enterprises	4,476,841	6,485,608	10,528,303	6,830,235	3,698,067
Hospitals	2,695,635	4,757,409	8,692,113	5,358,699	3,333,414
Independent operations	1,132,016	1,127,728	2,187,361	131,956	2,055,405
Total current fund expenditures	$38,903,177	$56,913,588	$97,535,742	$63,193,853	$34,341,889

Source: Adapted from *Digest of Education Statistics 1989 25th Edition*, National Center for Education Statistics (NCES), (U.S. Department of Education, 1989), Chapter 3, Tables 270, 271, 272, 278, 279, 280, pp. 293-303.

support of private institutions has been present since the earliest periods of American higher education:

> The crucial support by the state has often been clouded by the highly romantic regard held by Americans for unaided effort and by the confusion introduced by the use of such terms as "public" and "private" to describe institutions in a world that was itself in the process of defining the meaning of such terms.
>
> . . . On over 100 occasions before 1789, the General Court of Massachusetts appropriated funds for Harvard College. Indeed, Harvard, Yale, and Columbia could not have survived the colonial period without support of the state.[5]

Colleges and universities also earn revenues from affiliated hospitals and other auxiliary operations that provide students with services, such as food, housing, and books. Recent years have seen the introduction of a wide range of business activities whose purpose primarily is to earn profits that subsidize the costs of instruction or research. These activities include airports, day-care centers, travel agencies, and word processing units. The IRS closely monitors the tax-exempt status of such auxiliary units, as do small businesses that compete with them. For example, the sale of computers by educational institutions has become a source of serious contention between schools and small businesses. A coalition of small business groups is pressuring both federal and state lawmakers to tighten the restrictions on and monitoring of the commercial activities of nonprofit organizations.[6]

Charitable support of education provided $8.9 billion in 1988-89, an 8 percent increase over the preceding year.[7] Voluntary financial support more than doubled between 1980 and 1989, outpacing the general inflation rate.[8] The 1980s saw public higher education institutions increase their efforts to solicit voluntary support, resulting in increasing competition for charitable donations to education.

Expenditures In fiscal 1985-86 colleges and universities expended 32 percent of their current fund resources for instruction, 9 percent for research, 8 percent for plant operation and maintenance, 10 percent for institutional support, 20 percent for hospitals and auxiliary enterprises, and 4 percent for scholarships. While the relative proportions of expenditures by category have been stable, expenditure levels have increased at faster rates than inflation. Constant dollar revenue and expenditures increased 22 percent

---

[5]Frederick Rudolph, *The American College and University: A History* (New York, NY: Vintage, 1962), p. 185.
[6]"Tax Watch," *The Chronicle of Philanthropy* (May 29, 1990): 29.
[7]"Education Giving Rebounds in 1989," *The Chronicle of Philanthropy* II, no. 16 (May 29, 1990): 1.
[8]U.S. Department of Commerce, *Statistical Abstract, 1990*, p. 160, Table 270.

between 1980 and 1986, while full-time equivalent enrollment increased only 5 percent.[9] The Higher Education Price Index (HEPI) has outpaced annual increases in the Consumer Price Index (CPI) throughout most of the 1980s. These rapid increases in expenses and tuition have caused widespread concern about productivity in higher education and inspired efforts to improve it.[10]

Assets and Liabilities   Colleges and universities have significant assets, primarily in plant and endowment investments, and liabilities. Both assets and liabilities continue to grow.[11]

Since 1950 the book value of endowments has nearly doubled every ten years. The book value of endowments in 1981-82 was $23 billion, very close to their market value of $24 billion. Traditionally, the book and market values of endowments tended to be fairly close because many colleges and universities chose a conservative strategy of investing in fixed income instruments. But the changed investment strategies toward higher risk and return securities that accompanied the adoption of total return caused book and market values to diverge. For example, while the book value of endowments grew to $38 billion in 1985-86, their market value nearly doubled to $50 billion.

The 1960s were a period of substantial expansion of the fixed assets of most colleges and universities. In 1960 the gross additions to the plant fund amounted to $1.2 billion; by 1970, they were $4.2 billion. During the 1970s, the rate of growth of plant fund assets decreased, with fairly consistent expenditures of $4 billion to $5 billion per year. During the 1980s, plant fund expansion again increased, with annual expenditures more than doubling from $4.6 billion in 1978-79 to $10.1 billion in 1985-86. Total property value of physical plant at the end of 1985-86 was $122 billion, about double its 1975-76 level.

The 1985-86 plant fund liabilities of $25.7 billion were also about double their 1975-76 level. Of the 1985-86 plant additions, approximately one-third was financed by net borrowing. Colleges and universities can borrow from the federal and state governments, banks, and other financial institutions, using the common forms of nonprofit borrowing described in Chapter 3. Use of borrowing to finance college and university plant increased significantly in the 1950s and 1960s. Prior to that, plant was financed predominantly by capital donations and internally generated funds. In 1955-56 plant fund liabilities were only 10 percent of total property value. By 1969-70 liabilities were 22 percent, and in 1985-86 they were still at 21 percent of total property book value.[12]

[9]*1989-90 Fact Book on Higher Education*, p. 145.
[10]*Symposium on Improving Financial Condition Through Productivity*, National Center for Postsecondary Governance and Finance and the Forum for College Financing (October 26-27, 1989).
[11]*Digest of Education Statistics 1989 25th Edition*, p. 313 (Table 290), and p. 315 (Table 292).
[12]U.S. Bureau of the Census, *Statistical Abstract of the United States* (Washington, DC: U.S. Government Printing Office, 1977), p. 158.

Opportunities and Challenges

In 1971 Earl Cheit's *New Depression in Higher Education* set a gloomy tone for the future of private institutions in higher education.[13] But only a few four-year institutions folded during the early 1970s, most of them small.[14] One set of authors commented, "The main stream of private higher education is far from defunct. Reports of [its] demise are, like Mark Twain's death, greatly exaggerated."[15] The 1980s saw continued, although slower, growth and relative prosperity for American colleges and universities, but they are expected to face difficult times in the 1990s.

While higher education costs soar at rates in excess of general inflation, many traditional revenue sources are drying up. Enrollment increases are flattening; government financial support for research and student aid is capped by the U.S. electorate's resistance to increased tax payments; and middle-class families, with average annual incomes of $36,000, blanch at the $20,000 plus price tag for private college tuition and fees. Students are shopping for higher education in a much more intensive, cost conscious, and sophisticated manner. Surveys and ratings of school and program quality have proliferated, and are widely reported. The magazine *U.S. News & World Report* publishes an annual college guide that includes the results of an annual survey, a variety of articles related to higher education, and a directory of colleges and universities.[16] Advice on scholarship availability and college selection is sold commercially.

In the face of these financial pressures, individual colleges and universities are pursuing many strategies to reduce costs and increase revenues. No ready cures exist. Many of their expenses are fixed, as with tenured faculty and the large expenses of maintaining their physical plant. And few sources of increased revenues are apparent.

To reduce expenses, even the most august, seemingly financially secure institutions are employing drastic cost-cutting tactics, such as eliminating entire academic departments. This is an exceedingly difficult process because it involves fundamental decisions about the future of the institution. For example, to reduce its $50 million budgeted deficit, New York City's Columbia University not only deferred renovation of its library and elimianted subjects such as geography and linguistics and its school of library sciences, but also debated its mission as a research versus a teaching institution and the

---

[13]Earl F. Cheit, *The New Depression in Higher Education: A Study of Financial Conditions of 41 Colleges and Universities* (New York, NY: McGraw-Hill, 1971).

[14]National Association of Independent Colleges and Universities, *Openings, Closings, Mergers and Accreditation Status of Independent Colleges and Universities* (Washington, DC: November 1977).

[15]Howard R. Bowen and W. John Minter, *Private Higher Education: First Annual Report* (Washington, DC: Association of American Colleges, 1975), p. 101.

[16]U.S. News & World Report, *America's Best Colleges 1991* (Washington, DC: U.S. News & World Report, 1990).

role of its professional schools.[17] Some institutions are hoping to reduce their costs by merging and other cost-sharing efforts. For example, one group used a common formula to determine financial aid awards to its admits. It hoped this formula would eliminate financial competition, or bidding wars, among the members of the group for prized students because the common formula insured that a potential student received the same financial aid package from each college in the group.

Simultaneously, many institutions are developing new tactics for increasing revenues. Some offer nondegree programs for adults. Others use aggressive marketing campaigns. For example, one private college newspaper ad implied that its educational services were superior to those provided by public education.[18] Many adopt increasingly aggressive investment strategies to increase their income from investments. Research universities sometimes seek to use their research to bolster their financial position. Those that receive research grants that are reimbursed on the basis of the research costs sometimes ask their cost accountants to insure that as many costs as possible are allocated to the research function. Some create new departments whose purpose is to commercialize the fruits of the university's research by transferring it to the private sector. The departments frequently license rights to the research to businesses in exchange for royalties and fee payments and sometimes receive equity in new companies created to develop the research into commercial products.

The efficacy of these strategies to reduce costs and increase revenues is unclear; but they have unquestionably succeeded in creating storms of controversy about the proper role of colleges and universities. Institutions that cut costs inevitably engendered hostility among faculty, staff, and students. Noted one Yale student of its efforts to reduce its $15 million deficit by eliminating faculty in certain areas, "the university . . . has become a more economically driven place. . . . It's a lot less happy here, less humanistic, and I trace a great deal of that back to the administration."[19] And one academic noted of Columbia University's efforts, "Many departments now are . . . on the brink of becoming world class, only to have their advantages erode under these cost factors."[20]

Some cost-reducing strategies met with regulatory disapproval. The U.S. government filed an antitrust suit against the Massachusetts Institute of Technology (MIT) for its practice of using a common financial aid formula with 22 other institutions. While the others agreed to abandon the practice, MIT's administration decided to fight the Attorney General's charges that

[17]Anthony DePalma, "Short of Money, Columbia U. Weighs How Best to Change," *The New York Times*, 25 May 1992, p. 25.
[18]Anthony Flint, "Lasell College, Urban School May Pair Up," *The Boston Globe*, 19 July 1990, p. 49.
[19]Deborah Sontag, "Yale University President Quitting to Lead National Private School System," *The New York Times*, 26 May 1992, p. B-8.
[20]DePalma, "Short of Money."

students are entitled to the same benefits of price competition they would receive "in shopping for any other service." MIT argued that student aid was only one of many subsidies that it offered students because tuition payments cover only half of the costs of their education.[21]

The revenue-enhancing strategies also have not met with universal success. The proliferation of nondegree programs to nontraditional students increasingly calls to question the institution's primary social purpose. And the marketing campaigns that laud the virtue of one institution versus others have brought on the wrath of the competitors. For example, the ad touting the virtues of private education engendered a sharp rebuttal from public sector institutions and unseemly bickering between the two groups.[22] Some of the institutions that adopted aggressive investment strategies found the attendant higher risks devastating. For example, the University of Rochester's strategy of investing 75 percent of its endowment in small companies caused its endowment to grow by only 15 percent over a decade in which the endowment of comparable institutions tripled in value. The unfortunate choice of an aggressive investment policy resulted in earnings $60 million lower than could have been otherwise earned.[23] Similarly, the decision of the Massachusetts-based Boston University to invest a sizeable portion of its endowment capital in a biotechnology company that it formed with several faculty members caused considerable concern. For many years, the Massachusetts Attorney General, formally charged with reviewing the state's nonprofit organizations, worried aloud to the media about the lack of diversification of Boston University's endowment, especially when its major investment was in such a risky venture.[24] (Happily enough, the company seems to be faring well.)

But the biggest controversies surrounded those universities that attempted to maximize their research revenues. U.S. government officials charged as inappropriate some indirect costs allocated to the research function, such as Stanford University's inclusion of the costs of maintaining a yacht. In the wake of the resulting scandal, Stanford University's president resigned, the university withdrew $1.3 million in charges to the government that it admitted were inappropriate or errors, and it developed an accounting plan aimed at strengthening accountability for public funds.[25] Many wonder whether commercializing research will divert institutions from basic research because it is less likely to produce short-term financial success. And who owns research results? When MIT opened a technology licensing branch

[21]Peter Passell, "Fixing Prices for Virtue's Sake?" *The New York Times*, 13 May 1992, p. D2.
[22]"Public Educators Criticize Emmanuel Ad," *The Boston Globe*, 15 June 1990, p. 17.
[23]"Tempest In A B-School," *Business Week* (June 1, 1992): 38.
[24]Diana B. Henriques, "Good Science, Bad Grades in Boston," *The New York Times*, 3 May 1992, p. 15.
[25]Marilyn Chase, "Stanford President To Resign His Post In Wake of Scandal," *The Wall Street Journal*, 30 July 1991, p. B-9.

office in Japan, some U.S. congressional representatives wondered if it was selling to Japan the fruits of many decades of U.S. government research funding in MIT.

In the wake of these controversies, the American public sees a college education as simultaneously more important but produced in a questionable manner. It questions why tuition and fees grow faster than inflation but acknowledges that the earnings of college graduates continue to exceed by a wide margin the earnings of those without a college degree.

This environment presents many challenges for managers and trustees of nonprofit higher education institutions. In response to a 1989 spring survey of their concerns, 39 percent of the higher education administrators cited adequate finances, 44 percent cited maintaining enrollment, and 42 percent cited facilities and technology as challenges they expected to face in the next five years.[26] The changing U.S. economy, volatile capital markets, an expected faculty shortage, changing demographics of the college market, a government policy shift from higher to primary and secondary education, the potential for loss of tax benefits, and the globalization of the economy are seen as additional issues of concern for higher education.[27] The lack of consideration of the four financial questions in implementing the financial strategy of some institutions may have caused financial reversals and engendered unfortunate public skepticism. Wise financial management is key to dealing with all of these issues.

Data Sources

Statistical information about the number, size, and performance of institutions of higher education is widely available from a variety of sources. Both government agencies and independent education-related associations are involved in information gathering and dissemination.

A primary source of education statistics is the National Center for Education Statistics (NCES) which is part of the U.S. Department of Education. It surveys annually the population of higher education institutions on issues of enrollment, program offerings, minority representation, faculty, and finances. Its Higher Education General Information Survey (HEGIS) and the recently implemented, more comprehensive Integrated Postsecondary Education Data System (IPEDS) data bases provide much of the primary industry data used for educational evaluation and analysis. Two very useful annual NCES publications are the detailed *Digest of Education Statistics* and the postsecondary education volume of the more condensed and interpretive *The Condition of Education*.

[26]The Editors of The Chronicle of Higher Education, *The Almanac of Higher Education 1989-90* (Chicago, IL: The University of Chicago Press, 1989), p. 56.
[27]*Higher Education in a Changing Economy*, prepared for the American Council on Education and the Association of Governing Boards of Universities and Colleges by the Consortium on Financing Higher Education and by Coopers & Lybrand (1989).

The American Council on Education (ACE) publishes an annual *Fact Book on Higher Education*, (*Fact Book*), that provides detailed numerical current and historical data on revenues and expenditures of public and private institutions. The detail is accompanied by a ''highlights'' section that summarizes important points and trends.

The Chronicle of Higher Education is a weekly publication that might be considered *The Wall Street Journal* of higher education. The editors of *The Chronicle* and the University of Chicago Press annually publish *The Almanac of Higher Education*, (*Almanac*), which presents the position of higher education nationally and by state.

The National Association of Independent Colleges and Universities publishes *Independent Higher Education*, which contains extensive financial and statistical information. Institutions are classified in six categories to facilitate relevant comparisons.

The National Association of College and University Business Officers (NACUBO) is a source of data on the financial practices, performance, and status of colleges and universities. They produce an annual study of the size, growth, and performance of endowment funds, which can be useful for assessing endowment fund performance.

The Association of Governing Boards (AGB) of Universities and Colleges has worked with NACUBO to provide guidance and support to members of governing boards. They publish bimonthly *AGB Reports* that interpret the trends and issues in higher education for lay board members. They have produced several excellent publications that provide guidance and direction to boards in their use of financial and institutional information.

Many of these publications draw heavily on NCES data, as well as primary and other secondary sources. Each publication may present data in its own manner and format. It is not always easy, or even possible, to reconcile data from any two sources. Thus, great care is needed in combining or comparing data from multiple sources.

Data on individual nonprofit higher education institutions can be acquired from several sources. Most nonprofit organizations must file an IRS Form 990 with the federal government and may also be required to file a publicly available annual report with state attorney generals. Many institutions will provide copies of their annual reports and audited financial statements on request. When an institution issues bonds, its financial statements are usually included in the bond prospectus.

FINANCIAL REPORTING STANDARDS

Accounting and financial reporting standards for colleges and universities in the United States have a relatively long and distinguished history. The financial reporting standards for colleges and universities apply to nonprofit organizations; they are not required to be used for proprietary institutions.

This is in contrast to the health care sector, in which both nonprofit and for-profit health care providers are covered by one audit guide. Meaningful financial analyses and good financial management depend on reliable financial data prepared according to GAAP, and on users who understand the reporting standards that guide their construction.

Evolution of Financial Reporting

College and university accounting has received more attention than accounting for other nonprofit organizations because of the interest in higher education of John D. Rockefeller, Sr. and Andrew Carnegie. In 1910, the Carnegie Foundation for the Advancement of Teaching published a survey of practices in financial reporting and far-reaching recommendations for standardization of accounting, *Standard Forms for Financial Reports of Colleges, Universities and Technical Schools*.[28] The Carnegie Foundation continues to play a major role in research on higher education.

Rockefeller was heavily involved in many aspects of the University of Chicago, from design of its Gothic architecture and interiors to review of its financial affairs. His financial focus on the sources, uses, and magnitude of resources was the precursor of present day budgeting and accounting practices. The University of Chicago employed one of the first university auditors, Trevor Arnett, who wrote the widely read *College and University Finance*. The Rockefeller Foundation sponsored the national committee that produced *College and University Business Administration* (CUBA), which was published by the American Council on Education (ACE) in the early 1950s.[29]

Codification of accounting practices proceeded with the 1968 publication of the well-regarded single volume second edition of CUBA by the National Association of College and University Business Officers (NACUBO).[30] The primary organization for financial managers of higher education institutions, NACUBO plays a key role in shaping and implementing accounting and financial reporting standards. Current financial reporting standards for private colleges and universities were set by the 1973 AICPA *Audits of Colleges and Universities* (hereafter referred to as the audit guide).[31] CUBA was revised again in 1974, in close cooperation with the AICPA, to adhere to the standards adopted in the audit guide. In August of 1974, the AICPA adopted *Statement of Position 74-8*, "Financial Accounting and Reporting by Colleges and

[28]*Standard Forms for Financial Reports of Colleges, Universities and Technical Schools* (New York, NY: Carnegie Foundation for the Advancement of Teaching, 1910).

[29]National Committee on the Preparation of a Manual on College and University Business Administration, *College and University Business Administration*, 1 and 2 (American Council on Education, 1952 and 1955).

[30]*College and University Business Administraiton* (National Association of College and University Business Officers, 1968, 1974, 1982).

[31]AICPA Committee on College and University Accounting and Auditing, *Audits of Colleges and Universities*, 2d ed. (New York, NY: AICPA, 1975).

Universities'' (hereafter SOP 74-8)[32] formally to incorporate the 1974 CUBA revenue and expense categories into the AICPA audit standards. These standards are to be used in auditing all private colleges and universities and were adopted by a number of public ones as well. NACUBO published the fourth edition of CUBA in 1982, without a comprehensive revision, pending action by the FASB and AICPA.

Until recently, the audit guide and SOP 74-8 generally were considered as the source of GAAP for both private and public universities. However, while FASB SFAS 93 and SFAS 99[33] required recognition of depreciation by private colleges and universities, effective with fiscal years beginning on or after January 1, 1990, the GASB, as standard setter for public universities, has not yet concluded its deliberations on the depreciation issue. As a result, the depreciation requirements of GAAP for public and private institutions of higher education differ. GASB Statement No. 15[34] explicitly requires state and local governmental reporting entities that include colleges and universities to follow either the AICPA audit guide or the amended governmental model developed by the National Council on Governmental Accounting (NCGA).

Current and Proposed Standards

This section will discuss those aspects of college and university accounting and financial reporting that differ from other nonprofits. It is based on the standards set by the AICPA college and university guide, except where otherwise noted. The NCGA governmental model is covered in Chapter 18. Refer to Part One for a discussion of the basic nature of nonprofit annual reports, audit opinions, financial statements (including notes), funds, and financial reporting standards. Our discussion will include unresolved controversial issues and the effects on colleges and universities of the proposed changes in standards currently being considered. Many of the financial reporting differences between higher education institutions and other types of nonprofits would be eliminated by the proposed standards. Exhibit A (pages 569-577) shows sample financial statements that illustrate the application of the current standards; refer to them throughout the following discussion.[35]

---

[32]AICPA, Accounting Standards Division, *Statement of Position 74-8*, "Financial Accounting and Reporting by Colleges and Universities" (New York, NY: AICPA, August 31, 1974).

[33]Financial Accounting Standards Board, *Statement of Financial Accounting Standards No. 93*, "Recognition of Depreciation by Not-for-Profit Organizations" (Norwalk, CT: FASB, August 1987); and Financial Accounting Standards Board, *Statement of Financial Accounting Standards No. 99*, "Deferral of the Effective Date of Recognition of Depreciation by Not-for-Profit Organizations" (Norwalk, CT: FASB, September 1988).

[34]Governmental Accounting Standards Board, *Statement No.15*, "Governmental College and University Accounting and Financial Reporting Models" (Norwalk, CT: GASB, 1991).

[35]AICPA, *Audits of Colleges and Universities*, pp. 108-121.

Many, if not most, colleges and universities prepare an *annual report*, of which the financial statements are a relatively small part. Data on enrollments, tuition levels, and other performance data (usually unaudited) may also be presented in the annual report. These data can be quite useful in analyzing the organization's status and performance. If the full financial statements are not presented in the annual report, a separate set of audited financial statements is generally available. The auditor's reports (opinions) for colleges and universities are the same as for other types of organizations.

Funds and Fund Groupings   Colleges and universities use the fund types discussed in Chapter 6. They most commonly employ current (restricted and unrestricted), plant, endowment and similar, life income, and loan funds. Endowment, life income, and loan funds are more important to higher education institutions than to many other types of nonprofits.

Colleges and universities group restricted and unrestricted funds into *current funds* on the primary activity statement and display them separately only in the Statement of Current Funds. Resources used as quasi-endowment are reported as part of *endowment and similar funds*, a single fund group in the financial statements, whereas other nonprofits report quasi-endowment funds as part of the appropriate current fund. This reporting convention has important repercussions for financial analysis of college and university statements, which will be discussed below. The amount of quasi-endowment must be clearly distinguished from true endowment, but determining true endowment may require careful reading of the footnotes. Proposed standards would change the reporting of quasi-endowments for colleges and universities to be consistent with other types of nonprofit organizations. They would require clear segregation of quasi-endowments from true endowment funds[36] and distinguish clearly the amount of investments that are legally available for use in current operations.

Only dividend, interest, and royalty (ordinary) income on endowment and similar funds is classified as *investment income*, which is reflected directly as revenue in the funds that may use it. *Gains or losses* on permanently restricted investments are reported as increases (additions) or decreases (deductions) in the fund balance of the appropriate fund group. Many educational institutions have adopted some variant of the total return concept, which allows them to spend part of both realized and unrealized gains on investments. Gains used by the current or other funds are reported as nonmandatory transfers from the endowment and similar funds, rather than as investment income. Investments may be valued at either cost or market. Investment pool allocations must be made using a market basis for unit valuation.

---

[36]Financial Accounting Standards Board, Invitation to Comment, *Financial Reporting by Not-for-Profit Organizations: Form and Content of Financial Statements* (Norwalk, CT: FASB, August 29, 1989).

Life income funds account for assets contributed to a college with the requirement that they will pay income to designated beneficiaries for a specified time period, or until a specified event occurs, usually the death of the beneficiary. They are similar to and often are combined with endowment funds for reporting purposes. When life income funds mature, the transition to another fund is shown as an addition to the recipient fund and a deduction from the life income fund. *Assets held in trust*, whose income is paid to the school, are usually not included in the balance sheet, but disclosed either parenthetically in the endowment funds or in the notes. However, the assets, properly described, may be included in the balance sheet if the institution has legally enforceable rights or claims.

Loan funds are more commonly found in educational institutions than in other types of nonprofits. They account for assets that can be loaned, usually to students and sometimes to faculty and staff. Their financing can originate from gifts, grants, endowment fund income, transfers or loans from other funds, or external borrowing. They are usually replenished by the repayment of loan principal and payment of interest. Loans are reflected as receivables, with a reserve for any loans expected to be uncollectible. Management is responsible for following good lending and collection procedures in awarding and collecting loans.

Higher education institutions recognize interest on loans only when it is received (cash basis), rather than as it is earned (accrual basis). Thus, an accrual for interest receivable from loans is not reflected on the financial statements. This is a rare instance where GAAP requires cash instead of accrual basis accounting. As a result, the loan fund assets may be understated by the amount of unrecorded accrued interest receivable. Some feel that the amount receivable is negligible because interest is billed in advance of its due date and those who have not paid by the due date are those who will not pay. Others argue that it is better to reflect the amounts earned and the related bad debts. Interest income from loans is strongly influenced by collection policy and procedures. The current cash basis standard also has operational implications. Unlike the tuition billing system, which records income in the accounting system when billed, the loan billing system for principal and accrued interest payments due would be separated from the accounting system, which would record income only as the cash is received.

The audit guide requires reporting fixed (plant) assets in the *plant fund*, and the usual limitations on the usefulness of historial plant values apply. There is some inconsistency in the kinds of assets included in fixed assets. Gifts in kind, books, low-cost equipment, and government-loaned equipment all may or may not be included in the plant asset balance. When coupled with the inconsistent use of depreciation and the wide variation in asset age, meaningful comparison of plant values among institutions is difficult.

Depreciation reporting has only recently become required for colleges and universities. Prior standards permitted, but did not require, educational institutions to report depreciation in the plant fund; it could not be reported in the current funds. Depreciation was required only for income producing real property investments in the endowment fund group and for auxiliary enterprises that were to be self-supporting. The rationale for not including depreciation in the current fund was that the primary purpose of accounting for colleges and universities was to disclose resources received and resources expended, not net income.

Effective for years beginning on or after January 1, 1990, SFAS 93 and SFAS 99 require all nonprofit organizations under FASB jurisdiction to report depreciation, without specifying the fund in which it should be disclosed.[37] Supporters claim that requirements to record depreciation and disclose depreciation methods in the notes will improve users' ability to understand the financial aspects of the institution's physical plant and to compare institutions. Others disagree, however, and the debate continues. The GASB standards do not currently require depreciation to be reported by public higher education institutions. GASB is undertaking a major project on whether to require depreciation. Whatever the GASB's decision, the inherent limitations of depreciation based on historical cost are likely to remain.

Financial Statements   Current standards require the basic financial statements of a higher education institution to include a *Balance Sheet*, a *Statement of Changes in Fund Balances*, a *Statement of Current Fund Revenues, Expenditures, and Other Changes*, and *Notes* that are much like the general statement of position, activity statements, and notes discussed in Part One.

The Statement of Changes in Fund Balances is the primary activity statement. It summarizes the activity within each group of funds during the period covered by the financial statements. The changes in this statement are categorized as *revenues and other additions*, *expenditures and other deductions*, and *transfers among funds*. It may contain summary totals for revenues and expenditures of current funds. Although its resource outflows are called expenditures, they are measured with the accrual basis of accounting.

The *Statement of Current Fund Revenues, Expenditures, and Other Changes* (hereafter *Current Funds Statement*) is an additional activity statement. The restricted and unrestricted current fund activities are presented in separate columns, with a total column for the current year. The prior year's total column often is provided to facilitate temporal comparisons. This statement is unique to higher education institutions because other nonprofits report unrestricted and restricted current funds separately in the primary activity statement. In lieu of presenting a separate current funds statement, details about restricted and unrestricted current funds may be provided in the Statement of Changes in Fund Balances and additions to fund balances in excess of expenditures may be disclosed in the Notes.

[37]Financial Accounting Standards Board, *Statement No. 93* and *Statement No. 99*.

The recommended revenue and expenditure categories for this statement are shown in Table 15-3. If a separate Current Fund Statement is presented, it often uses a classification of current fund activities that provides greater detail on the nature and magnitude of the operating revenues and expenses than does the Statement of Changes in Fund Balances. Although the details may be organized and classified differently, the net change in fund balances must be the same in both activity statements.

Revenues are categorized by source, such as tuition and fees, government appropriations, government grants, private gifts, endowment income, and the income earned from sales of various goods and services. Revenue sources differ in controllability and are subject to different environmental and internal pressures. Management must understand the underlying factors that influence each significant revenue source.

The full amount of tuition and fees is recognized as revenues; any related fee waivers, scholarships, fellowships, and uncollectible accounts are reported as expenditures rather than as deductions from revenues. This appears to be inconsistent with the treatment of charity care required by the new health care financial reporting standards (discussed in Chapter 17).

TABLE 15-3 **Recommended Revenue and Expenditure Categories**

Revenues	Expenditures
Tuition and fees	Educational and general
Federal appropriations	Expenditures
State appropriations	Instruction
Local appropriations	Research
Federal grants and contracts	Public service
State grants and contracts	Academic support
Local grants and contracts	Student services
Private gifts, grants, and contracts	Institutional support
Endowment income	Operation and maintenance of plant
Sales and services of educational activities	Scholarships and fellowships
	Mandatory transfers
Sales and services of auxiliary enterprises	Nonmandatory transfers
	Auxiliary enterprises
Sales and services of hospitals	Hospitals
Other sources	Independent operations
Independent operations	

Source: Adapted from AICPA *Statement of Position 74-8,* "Financial Accounting and Reporting by Colleges and Universities," American Institute of Certified Public Accountants, Accounting Standards Division, August 31, 1974, pp. 90, 100.

Treatment of uncollectible accounts is consistent with the new health care and other standards.

Tuition and fee revenue and the related expenditures for a term of instruction that spans two fiscal years is reported in the fiscal year in which the term is predominantly conducted. Although somewhat unusual, this practice does not cause financial analysis problems in most cases.

Under current standards, most colleges and universities do not recognize pledges as revenue. Revenue is recognized only when the donation is received. Proposed standards on accounting for contributions would require unconditional pledges to be recognized as revenue when the pledge is made, with an allowance for uncollectible pledges based on past collection experience and other relevant factors.[38] Conditional pledges would be recognized as revenue when the conditions are met. This controversial proposal has been widely resisted by colleges and universities, as well as other types of nonprofits, because of their concern that revenues may be inflated with pledges that may ultimately prove to be uncollectible. The proposed changes would recognize revenue earlier and would provide data on pledge collection experience. They would also require more careful tracking of pledges, classification of pledges as conditional or unconditional, and estimates of future pledge collections that are now common practice.

Expenditures are grouped by functions, such as instruction, research, and plant maintenance, rather than by the object of the expenditure, such as salary, fringe benefits, office supplies, and travel. This classification is intended to increase comparability among statements of similar institutions and to disclose the costs of the institution's program and support activities. In practice, the contents of these categories vary. Each institution should adopt those functional breakdowns that management considers meaningful and practical. For example, if it is difficult to separate research from instruction costs because both use common space and personnel, these two categories might be combined into one category, Instruction and Research. Although a functional classification is required for financial reporting and is useful for many internal management activities, a responsibility center and an object of expense classification also should be maintained in the accounting system because they are more relevant for many managerial control activities.

The two activity statements are organized somewhat differently. The Current Funds Statement groups mandatory transfers with expenditures; shows auxiliary enterprises in a separate section following expenditures and mandatory transfers; and combines other transfers with other additions and deductions in the final section. Restricted operating resources are not recognized as revenues in this statement until expenditures have been made for the

---

[38]Financial Accounting Standards Board, Exposure Draft, Proposed Statement of Financial Accounting Standards, *Accounting for Contributions Received and Contributions Made and Capitalization of Works of Art, Historical Treasures, and Similar Assets* (Norwalk, CT: FASB, October 31, 1990), pp. 4-5.

purpose to which they were restricted. They are classified as *other additions to fund balance*, rather than as revenues or deferred revenues, until that time. The account called *excess of restricted receipts over transfers to revenues* represents the amount of restricted resources received in excess of the amount earned by performing the activities to which their use was restricted. Thus, the restricted revenues and restricted expenditures in the Current Funds Statement are equal, by definition. For example, the resources granted to cover indirect costs are included in the current restricted fund balance as *additions* when received. When the criteria for recovering indirect costs are met, the amounts to be recovered are reported as an *other deduction* from the restricted fund balance, and as Revenue of the current unrestricted fund. (This treatment is complex. The important point is that all restricted amounts received are reflected in the fund balance and generally are not recorded as deferred revenues as they would be in a business or some other types of nonprofit organizations. However, amounts received but not yet earned may be classified differently on the two activity statements.)

Mandatory transfers by colleges and universities most frequently are required by debt instruments. Principal payments, interest expenditures, and reserves for renewal and replacement are transferred from the current fund to the plant fund, which accounts for their receipt and expenditure. Also, schools that participate in the National Direct Student Loan (NDSL) program sponsored by the U.S. government must contribute a fraction of the government's share to the loan fund. This mandatory transfer is usually made from unrestricted current funds to the loan fund.

Nonmandatory transfers commonly move money to and from the current funds and the endowment and similar fund group. Transfers to the endowment and similar funds are unique to colleges and universities because other types of nonprofits report the legally unrestricted investments functioning as endowment (quasi-endowment) as part of the current funds, whereas colleges and universities include such investments as part of the endowment and similar funds for financial reporting purposes. Transfers from the endowment fund reflect gains on investments that have been allocated for use in operations. Mandatory transfers should be clearly distinguished from nonmandatory transfers in the financial statements.

Current Reporting Practices An extensive, nationwide survey of higher education financial reporting practices, "Principles and Presentation: Higher Education," found that colleges and universities generally follow current accounting and financial reporting standards.[39] The most common criticisms of public reports were: the institution's mission is seldom stated clearly; the text is excessively long and presents too much information; information is presented in a confusing and overly complex manner; and interpretations

---

[39]Peat Marwick & Company, "Principles and Presentation: Higher Education" (National Association of College and University Business Officers, 1985).

are lacking or unclear. Most of the reported information relates to inputs rather than to results or performance efficiency. The areas of lowest compliance with clearly stated standards were: most institutions do not report pledges (70 percent) or annuity fund liabilities (77 percent); additions to quasi-endowment are not first reported as current fund revenues (30 percent); endowment fund gains are not first reported as additions to endowment principal (48 percent); book value is used for investment pools (42 percent); separate related entities are not reported correctly (30 percent); and non-mandatory transfers are not separately identified (17 percent).

Proposed Standards   Proposed report format and content standards[40] would enhance the consistency between financial reporting for colleges and universities and other types of private nonprofit organizations. They permit a single column balance sheet, thus eliminating the requirement for a separate balance sheet for each fund group. Net assets would be separated into three classes: unrestricted, temporarily restricted, and permanently restricted. The proposesd Statement(s) of Changes in Unrestricted Net Assets, to replace the Statement of Changes in Fund Balances and the Current Funds Statement, would present a separate column for each of the three classes. Multicolumn statements that distinguish operations, long-term investments, and plant within each asset class would be an allowable alternative. The total column in each multicolumn statement would be the same as would be found in a single column statement. A Statement of Cash Flows would be required.

AN EXAMPLE OF FINANCIAL STATEMENT PREPARATION[41]

Although general managers or directors prepare financial statements in only the smallest organizations, some participation in the preparation of simple statements enables better understanding. This practice should provide a better feel for the origin of numbers used in financial analysis, the judgments involved in their creation, what they mean, and the types of errors that can arise from an inadequate accounting system. For these reasons, we present the following simple organization, its summarized transactions, and the related journal entries, T-accounts, and financial statements. Each journal entry shows the fund followed by the account. Functional classifications are also provided where relevant. Unrestricted and restricted refer to the current funds. Transfers are posted directly to the fund balance account.

[40] Financial Accounting Standards Board, Invitation to Comment, *Form and Content of Financial Statements*.
[41] David Sherman, currently Professor of Accounting at Northeastern University, developed this example as a Research Assistant to Professor Herzlinger in 1979.

A school is established with a gift of a $1 million endowment for general purposes and a $2 million gift of capital funds. A building is purchased for $1.9 million. The beginning entries would be as follows:

Endowment—Cash	$1,000,000	
Endowment—Fund Balance		$1,000,000

To reflect the receipt of endowment gift.

Unexpended Plant—Cash	$2,000,000	
Unexpended Plant—Fund Balance		$2,000,000

To reflect receipt of capital funds to purchase plant facilities.

Investment in Plant—Plant and Equipment	$1,900,000	
Investment in Plant—Transfer (Nonmandatory)		$1,900,000
Unexpended Plant—Transfer (Nonmandatory)	1,900,000	
Unexpended Plant—Cash		1,900,000

To reflect purchase of plant for $1,900,000 and to transfer funds from unexpended plant fund to investment in plant.

The resulting balance sheet at the beginning of the first year of operations is shown in Table 15-4.

During the first year, the following activities take place and are reflected in the accounting records by the related journal entries. Figure 15-1 and Figure 15-2 show the posting of the entries to T-accounts. The numbers in parentheses indicate the journal entry, (BB) indicates the beginning balance in an account, (EB) indicates the ending balance in an account, and (C) indicates a closing entry.

TABLE 15-4   Sample College Balance Sheet, Beginning of Year 1

Balance Sheet As of the Beginning of Year 1			
Current Funds			
No Assets or Liabilities			
Plant Funds			
Cash	$ 100,000	Fund Balance:	
		Investment in plant	$1,900,000
Plant and equipment	1,900,000	Unexpended	100,000
Total Assets	$2,000,000	Total Liabilities and Fund Balance	$2,000,000
Endowment Funds			
Cash	$1,000,000	Fund Balance	$1,000,000
Total Assets	$1,000,000	Total Liabilities and Fund Balance	$1,000,000

FIGURE 15-1 T-Accounts for Current Funds

Unrestricted Current Fund

	Cash					Fund Balance		
(2)	$190,000	$220,000	(3)				$ 38,000	(C)
(7)	45,000						$ 38,000	(EB)
(EB)	$ 15,000							

	Tuition Receivable					Tuition Revenue		
(1)	$213,000	$190,000	(2)		(C)	$213,000	$213,000	(1)
(EB)	$ 23,000						$ 0	

	Institutional Support Expenditures					Operation and Maintenance Expenditures		
(3)	$ 30,000	$ 30,000	(C)		(3)	$ 40,000	$ 40,000	(C)
	$ 0					$ 0		

	Revenue, Investment Income					Instructional Expenditures		
(C)	$ 45,000	$ 45,000	(7)		(3)	$150,000	$150,000	(C)
		$ 0				$ 0		

Restricted Current Fund—Scholarships

	Cash					Fund Balance		
(4)	$300,000	$300,000	(5)				$ 5,000	(C)
(7)	15,000	10,000	(9)				$ 5,000	
(EB)	$ 5,000							

	Revenue—Investment Income					Additions—Investment Income		
(C)	$ 10,000	$ 10,000	(C)		(9)	$ 10,000	$ 15,000	(7)
		$ 0			(C)	5,000		
							$ 0	

	Student Aid Expense					Gifts		
(9)	$ 10,000	$ 10,000	(C)		(C)	$300,000	$300,000	(4)
	$ 0						$ 0	

	Nonmandatory Transfers			
(5)	$300,000	$300,000	(C)	
	$ 0			

Restricted Current Fund—Grants

	Cash					Fund Balance		
(10)	$ 40,000	$ 20,000	(11)				$ 20,000	(C)
(EB)	$ 20,000						$ 20,000	(EB)

	Research Expenditures					Grants		
(11)	$ 20,000	$ 20,000	(C)		(C)	$ 40,000	$ 40,000	(10)
	$ 0						$ 0	

FIGURE 15-2 **T-Accounts for Other Funds**

Endowment Fund

	Cash				Fund Balance	
(BB)	$1,000,000	$1,000,000	(6)		$1,000,000	(BB)
(EB)	$ 0				55,000	(C)
					$1,055,000	(EB)

	Investments at Cost			Unrealized Gain on Investments		
(6)	$1,000,000		(C)	$ 55,000	$ 55,000	(8)
(EB)	$1,000,000				$ 0	

	Investments—Adjustment to Market	
(8)	$ 55,000	
(EB)	$ 55,000	

Quasi-Endowment Scholarship Fund

	Cash				Fund Balance	
(5)	$ 300,000	$ 300,000	(6)		$ 310,000	(C)
(EB)	$ 0				$ 310,000	(EB)

	Investments at Cost			Unrealized Gain on Investments		
(6)	$ 300,000		(C)	$ 10,000	$ 10,000	(8)
(EB)	$ 300,000				$ 0	

	Investments—Adjustment to Market			Nonmandatory Transfer		
(8)	$ 10,000		(C)	$ 300,000	$ 300,000	(5)
(EB)	$ 10,000				$ 0	

Unexpended Plant Fund

	Cash			Fund Balance	
(BB)	$ 100,000			$ 100,000	(BB)
(EB)	$ 100,000			$ 100,000	(EB)

Investment in Plant Fund

	Plant				Fund Balance	
(BB)	$1,900,000		(C)	$ 60,000	$1,900,000	(BB)
(EB)	$1,900,000				$1,840,000	(EB)

	Allowance for Depreciation				Instructional Expense, Depreciation	
	$ 60,000	(12)	(12)	$ 60,000	$ 60,000	(C)
	$ 60,000	(EB)		$ 0		

Tuition income billed was $213,000, of which $190,000 was collected.

| (1) | Unrestricted—Tuition Receivable | $213,000 | |
| | Unrestricted—Tuition Revenue | | $213,000 |

To recognize revenues earned during the year.

| (2) | Unrestricted—Cash | $190,000 | |
| | Unrestricted—Tuition Receivable | | $190,000 |

To reflect tuition payments received during the year.

The school incurred the following expenditures: instructional of $150,000, operation and maintenance of $40,000, and institutional support of $30,000. Purchase orders for supplies outstanding at the end of the year amounted to $15,000. All expenditures were paid for in cash.

(3)	Unrestricted—Instructional Expenditure	$150,000	
	Unrestricted—Operation and Maintenance Expenditures	40,000	
	Unrestricted—Institutional Support Expenditures	30,000	
	Unrestricted—Cash		$220,000

To reflect expenditures incurred and paid during the year. Purchase commitments are not recorded until the materials are received in the subsequent year.

A $300,000 gift restricted for use in student aid was received. The trustees decided to invest the principal as a quasi-endowment and use the resulting income for scholarships.

| (4) | Restricted Scholarships—Cash | $300,000 | |
| | Restricted Scholarships—Gifts | | $300,000 |

To reflect receipt of gift.

(5)	Restricted Scholarships—Transfer (Nonmandatory)	$300,000	
	Restricted Scholarships—Cash		$300,000
	Quasi-Endowment Scholarships—Cash	300,000	
	Quasi-Endowment Scholarships—Transfer (Nonmandatory)		300,000

To reflect nonmandatory transfer from current restricted scholarship fund to quasi-endowment scholarship fund.

All endowment and quasi-endowment fund assets were invested. The endowment investments earned $45,000 of income that was received in cash and they also appreciated by $55,000. The quasi-endowment investments designated for scholarships earned $15,000 received in cash and appreciated in value by $10,000.

(6)	Quasi-Endowment Scholarships—Investments	$ 300,000	
	Quasi-Endowment Scholarships—Cash		$ 300,000
	Endowment—Investments	1,000,000	
	Endowment—Cash		1,000,000

To reflect investment of endowment and quasi-endowment fund cash.

(7) Unrestricted—Cash	$45,000	
Unrestricted—Revenue, Investment Income		$45,000
Restricted Scholarships—Cash	15,000	
Restricted Scholarships—Additions, Investment Income		15,000

To record investment income earned. (Income on endowment and similar investments is credited directly to the current or other funds which can use it.)

(8) Endowment—Investments, Adjustment to Market	$55,000	
Endowment—Addition, Unrealized Gain		$55,000
Quasi-Endowment—Investments, Adjustment to Market	10,000	
Quasi-Endowment—Addition, Unrealized Gain		10,000

To reflect appreciated market value of investments. (This entry is recorded only if investments are accounted for at market value rather than at book value.)

Scholarships for $10,000 were granted to students and paid in cash.

(9) Restricted Scholarships—Student Aid Expenditures	$10,000	
Restricted Scholarships—Cash		$10,000
Restricted Scholarships—Addition, Investment Income	10,000	
Restricted Scholarships—Revenue, Investment Income		10,000

To record the scholarship expenditure of $10,000 and the related revenue earned. This reflects the reclassification of the earned portion of investment income from additions to revenue.

The school received $40,000 for research grants.

| (10) Restricted Grants—Cash | $40,000 | |
| Restricted Grants—Revenue, Grants | | $40,000 |

To record receipt of grant money.

$20,000 in cash was expended for supplies related to the research grant.

| (11) Restricted Grants—Research Expenditures | $20,000 | |
| Restricted Grants—Cash | | $20,000 |

To recognize the grant expenses incurred this period.

Depreciation expense of $60,000 was recorded on the building, using a $100,000 estimated salvage value, 30 year life, and straight-line depreciation [$60,000 = ($1,900,000 − $100,000) ÷ 30 years].

| (12) Investment in Plant—Depreciation Expense—Instruction | $60,000 | |
| Investment in Plant—Allowance for Depreciation | | $60,000 |

To record depreciation, all of which is charged to instructional expense.

Closing entries are needed to bring the balances of each of the temporary revenue, expenditure, addition, and deduction accounts to a zero balance, and to adjust the fund balances to reflect the net activity in these accounts during the period.

(C)	Unrestricted—Tuition Revenue	$213,000	
	Unrestricted—Investment Income	45,000	
	Unrestricted—Instructional Expenditures		$150,000
	Unrestricted—Operations and Maintenance Expenditures		40,000
	Unrestricted—Institutional Support Expenditures		30,000
	Unrestricted—Fund Balance		38,000
	Restricted Scholarships—Gifts	300,000	
	Restricted Scholarships—Additions, Investment Income	5,000	
	Restricted Scholarships—Revenue, Investment Income	10,000	
	Restricted Scholarships—Scholarship Expenditure		10,000
	Restricted Scholarships—Transfer (Nonmandatory)		300,000
	Restricted Scholarships—Fund Balance		5,000
	Restricted Grants—Grants	40,000	
	Restricted Grants—Research Expenditures		20,000
	Restricted Grants—Fund Balance		20,000
	Endowment—Unrealized Gain on Investments	55,000	
	Endowment—Fund Balance		55,000
	Quasi-Endowment—Unrealized Gain on Investments	10,000	
	Quasi-Endowment—Transfer (Nonmandatory)	300,000	
	Quasi-Endowment—Fund Balance		310,000
	Investment in Plant—Fund Balance	60,000	
	Investment in Plant—Instructional Expense, Depreciation		60,000

To record closing entries.

The resulting Balance Sheet, Statement of Changes in Fund Balances, and Statement of Current Fund Revenues, Expenditures, and Other Changes are contained in Table 15-5, Table 15-6, and Table 15-7. In all these reports, the scholarship and grant restricted funds are combined in a single restricted fund column. In the reports prepared under current standards, the endowment and quasi-endowment funds are combined in a single endowment and similar funds column. In the columnar balance sheet prepared under the proposed standards, quasi-endowment is reported as part of temporarily restricted net assets.

Even this simple example highlights several issues critical to understanding the financial statements. Had the trustees not transferred $300,000 to quasi-endowment, the restricted current fund balance at year end would have been higher by that amount plus appreciation. This illustrates the importance of considering the effects of nonmandatory transfers to quasi-endowment and nonmandatory transfers from endowment under the total return concept to evaluate the financial position of an institution.

TABLE 15-5 **Balance Sheet at the End of Year 1**

**Layered Format Balance Sheet
At End of Year 1**

Unrestricted Current Fund

Cash	$ 15,000	Fund Balance		$ 38,000
Receivables	23,000			
Total	$ 38,000	Total		$ 38,000

Restricted Current Fund

Cash	$ 25,000	Fund Balances:		
		Scholarship		$ 5,000
		Research grant		20,000
Total	$ 25,000	Total		$ 25,000

Endowment and Similar Funds

Investments at book value	$1,300,000	Fund Balances:		
Unrealized gains (losses)	65,000	Endowment		$1,055,000
		Quasi-endowment		310,000
Total	$1,365,000	Total		$1,365,000

Plant Fund

Cash	$ 100,000	Fund Balances:		
Plant (net of $60,000		Investment in plant		$1,840,000
depreciation)	1,840,000	Unexpended		100,000
Total	$1,940,000	Total		$1,940,000

**Columnar Format Balance Sheet
Grouped per Proposed Standards
At End of Year 1**

	Unrestricted	Temporarily Restricted	Permanently Restricted	Total
Assets				
Cash	$15,000	$ 25,000	$ 100,000	$ 140,000
Receivables	23,000			23,000
Investments (at market)		310,000	1,055,000	1,365,000
Plant (net of $60,000 accumulated depreciation)			1,840,000	1,840,000
	$38,000	$335,000	$2,995,000	$3,368,000
Liabilities				
Net Assets:				
Unrestricted	$38,000			$ 38,000
Restricted—Scholarships		$315,000		315,000
Restricted—Research Grants		20,000		20,000
Investment in Plant			$1,840,000	1,840,000
Unexpended Plant			100,000	100,000
Endowment			1,055,000	1,055,000
Total Net Assets	38,000	335,000	2,995,000	3,368,000
Total Liabilities and Net Assets	$38,000	$335,000	$2,995,000	$3,368,000

TABLE 15-6 **Statement of Changes in Fund Balance, Year 1**

Statement of Changes in Fund Balances
For the First Year of Operation

| | Current Funds | | Endowment and Similar Funds | Plant Funds | |
	Unrestricted	Restricted		Invested in Plant	Unexpended Plant Funds
Revenues and other additions:					
Tuition	$213,000				
Gifts		$300,000			
Grants	45,000	40,000			
Endowment income		15,000			
Unrealized gains on investments			$ 65,000		
Total revenue and other additions	$258,000	$355,000	$ 65,000		
Expenditures:					
Education and general:					
Instruction	$150,000				
Research		$ 20,000			
Institutional support	30,000				
Operations and maintenance	40,000			$ 60,000	
Scholarships		10,000			
Total Expenditures	$220,000	$ 30,000		$ 60,000	
Transfers between funds:					
Nonmandatory:					
From restricted to quasi-endowment		(300,000)	300,000		
Total transfers		(300,000)	300,000		
Net increase (decrease)	$ 38,000	$ 25,000	$ 365,000	$ (60,000)	$100,000
Balance at beginning of year	0	0	1,000,000	1,900,000	
Fund balance at end of year	$ 38,000	$ 25,000	$1,365,000	$1,840,000	$100,000

TABLE 15-7   **Statement of Current Fund Revenues, Expenditures, and Other Changes**

Statement of Current Fund Revenues, Expenditures, and Other Changes
For Year 1

	Unrestricted	Restricted	Total
Revenues:			
Tuition	$213,000		$ 213,000
Gifts		$300,000	300,000
Grants		20,000	20,000
Endowment income	45,000	10,000	55,000
Total Revenues	$258,000	$ 330,000	$ 588,000
Expenditures:			
Education	$150,000	$ 20,000	$ 170,000
Institutional support	30,000		30,000
Operations and maintenance	40,000		40,000
Scholarships		10,000	10,000
Total Expenditures	$220,000	$ 30,000	$ 250,000
Nonmandatory Transfers:			
Restricted to quasi-endowment	$ 0	$(300,000)	$(300,000)
Other Additions:			
Endowment income		$ 5,000	$ 5,000
Grants		20,000	20,000
Total Other Additions	$ 0	$ 25,000	$ 25,000
Net Increase in Fund Balance	$ 38,000	$ 25,000	$ 63,000

At the end of the fiscal year, the investments could have been sold for $65,000 over cost. However, no such sale took place and the school did not receive the $65,000 in cash. The institution has the choice of reporting the investments at cost or at market. The method used and the value under the alternative method must be disclosed in the footnotes. Last, the older the fixed assets, the less likely book value is to approximate their market value.

A FRAMEWORK FOR ANALYSIS

External parties, directors, and management all need to evaluate the performance of individual institutions. The data and techniques available for evaluating higher education performance continue to improve as their importance is recognized. Prior performance as reported in the financial statements is the most commonly used internal financial performance standard because it is readily available. Planned or budgeted performance also is commonly used by directors and managers, as well as by external users who have access to such data.

Some *external* financial performance standards, such as those listed in Table 15-8, can be calculated on the basis of population totals or averages. For example, the data in Table 15-2 could be used to calculate ratios. However, the diversity among institutions limits the usefulness of averages based on the entire population. Data on *peer institutions* (those considered to be similar to the institution of interest) are usually more relevant but less readily available. Data segregated by public and private institutions are more useful, but there is still a tremendous amount of diversity within these categories. One study presents 25 measures, primarily ratios, for subgroups by type of institution (two-year or four-year, private or public) and operating size.[42]

[42]KPMG Peat Marwick, "Ratio Analysis in Higher Education," 2d ed., prepared by L. F. Rothschild, Towbin Unterberg, John Minter Associates, and Fredric Prager and Associates (KPMG Peat Marwick, 1982, 1987, 1988, 1990).

TABLE 15-8 **Financial Performance Measures**

Balance Sheet
- Current ratio
- Quick ratio
- Assets by fund as a percentage of total assets
- Debt to total capital ratio
- Amount of unrestricted current and quasi-endowment funds
- Amount of receivables and receivables turnover
- Reliance on interfund borrowing

Operating Statement
- Current fund expenditures to revenues
- Educational expenditures to education revenue
- Current fund gifts, grants, and contracts as a percentage of revenues
- Educational and general to total current fund expenditures
- Student services to total current fund expenditures
- Administrative and general to current fund expenditures
- Amount and percentage of unfunded student aid expenditures
- Student aid expenditures as a percentage of tuition and fees
- Current fund revenues to plant assets
- Ratio of expenditures to revenue of auxiliary operations
- Fixed operating costs to revenues

Financial statement and other data on individual peer institutions may be available from an annual report, a bond prospectus, or reports filed with state agencies. Higher education associations sometimes publish data for sets of peer institutions. The shortcoming of using data from specific institutions is that the differences in application of accounting standards may cause significant variation in the reported results. The effect of this can be minimized, although not eliminated, by selecting only peer institutions that use similar accounting practices, or by adjusting the financial statement data to a standard set of accounting procedures.

Higher education institutions refer to operating performance measures (such as those listed in Table 15-9) as *institutional data*. These are important, but may be difficult to acquire. NACUBO and AGB have been at the forefront of developing educational materials,[43] analytic techniques,[44] and data[45] on a combination of institutional and financial performance measures to support governing boards in strategic decision making. Table 15-10 lists the items addressed in *Strategic Analysis: Using Comparative Data to Understand Your Institution*, which also discusses analysis techniques using the data and provides examples of how the strategic analyses might be performed.

Any measure that differs significantly from external standards should be investigated to determine the causes of the differences. Although it may be possible to exchange institutional and financial information with similar institutions for comparison purposes, such sharing could possibly lead to charges of price-fixing or unfair competition by government attorneys.

Many colleges and universities have substantial long-term liabilities in the form of publicly sold and traded bonds. Public and private institutions differ in the types of bonds they issue and the collateral they pledge to secure them. Public institutions issue both general obligation and revenue bonds, while private institutions issue only revenue bonds, such as student fee, student loan, or enterprise bonds. Only the student fees actually pledged are used in calculating coverage ratios for student fee revenue bonds. Student loan bonds are used to provide financial aid to students. Enterprise (usually dormitory) bonds are for either free-standing or system issues. Repayment of a *free-standing* issue is formally secured only by revenues from the assets it finances, while revenues from the entire dormitory system are pledged to cover payment of the loan in a *system* issue. Some institutions use their

[43]*Financial Responsibilities of Governing Boards of Colleges and Universities*, 2d ed. (Association of Governing Boards of Universities and Colleges and National Association of College and University Business Officers, 1979, 1985).

[44]Carol Frances, George Huxel, Joel Meyerson, and Dabney Park, *Strategic Decision Making: Key Questions and Indicators for Trustees* (Association of Governing Boards of Universities and Colleges, 1987).

[45]Joel Meyerson, Lewis Morrell, Dabney Park, and Barbara Taylor, *Strategic Analysis: Using Comparative Data to Understand Your Institution* (Association of Governing Boards of Universities and Colleges, 1991).

TABLE 15-9 **Operating Performance Measures**

Admissions
- Number of inquiries
- Number of applications
- Proportion of applicants who meet academic entrance requirements

Registration and Student Quality
- Proportion of admitted students registering
- Full-time equivalent (FTE) enrollment
- Percentage of enrollment in high-cost programs
- Retention rates
- Student qualtiy (measured by board scores and prior GPA)

Research
- Number of grant applications made
- Number and percentage of grant applications funded
- Average grant size
- Number of articles, books, and other scholarly works published

Academic Administration
- Teaching loads
- Average number of students per section
- Student-faculty ratio
- Faculty salaries
- Percentage tenured faculty

Student Financial Aid and Charges
- Percentage of students requiring financial aid
- Loan defaults
- Tuition and fee levels

Academic Quality and Image
- Ranking in national or regional polls
- Media coverage
- Other awards or recognition
- Accreditations
- Faculty credentials

Mixed Measure
- Plant assets per FTE student
- Endowment per FTE student
- Educational and general expenditures per FTE student

TABLE 15-10 **Comparative Data for Strategic Analysis**

Students

Full-time-equivalent enrollment
First-year applications
Acceptances as a percent of applications
Matriculants as a percent of acceptances
Enrollment by racial/ethnic status
Maintenance of enrollment

Faculty and Administration

Full-time-equivalent faculty
Full-time-equivalent administrators
Full-time-equivalent faculty by racial/ethnic
    status
Tenured faculty by racial/ethnic status and
    gender
Percent of faculty who are tenured
Percent of full-time faculty 60 years or older
Percent of faculty who are part-time

Instruction

Number of degree programs
Instructional expenditures as a percent of
    total expenditures
Instructional expenditures per full-time-
    equivalent student

Research

Revenue for sponsored research
Institutionally funded research as a percent
    of total research expenditures
Externally funded research as a percent of
    total research expenditures

Plant

Estimated level of deferred maintenance as
    a percent of total replacement value of
    plant and per gross square foot of plant

Tuition and Financial Aid

Tuition and fees per full-time student
Financial aid per full-time-equivalent student
Institutionally funded financial aid as a
    percent of total financial aid
Externally funded financial aid as a percent
    of total financial aid
Percent of students with college-work-study
    jobs
Institutional student aid as a percent of
    tuition and fee revenue

Student Support

Full-time-equivalent student staff per full-
    time-equivalent student

Giving

Total contributions
Total number of gifts
Percent of alumni who contributed
Mean size of gifts
Percent of gifts less than $25,000
Percent of gifts less than $5,000
Percent of contribution from alumni, other
    individuals, corporations, foundations,
    and other sources

Finances

Excess (deficit) of operating revenue over
    expenditures
Outstanding plant debt as a percent of
    unrestricted quasi-endowment
Market value of endowment per full-time-
    equivalent student
Total return on endowment
Endowment utilization rate
Percent of current revenue represented by
    different sources

Source: Adapted from Joel Meyerson, Lewis Morrell, Dabney Park, and Barbara Taylor, *Strategic Analysis: Using Comparative Data to Understand Your Institution*, Association of Governing Board of Universities and Colleges, 1991.

endowments as collateral for bond issues. This provides another layer of security for the bonds, but the portfolios must be analyzed as to the quality of investments, the amount of collateral, the number of times a year it is priced, and the provisions for substitutions.

Like bonds of other organizations, most higher education bonds are rated by Moody's or Standard and Poor's (S&P). The bond's rating has a substantial effect on its interest cost. Bond ratings are based on three to five years of audited financial statements, projected cash flows through the maturity date along with the underlying assumptions, the issuer's business plan, the bond resolution, and a variety of other related documentation. Bond raters perform very thorough analyses that encompass a variety of operating and financial data. Investment portfolio managers and loan officers for local bank borrowings perform similar types of analysis.

As part of the rating process, S&P uses the financial ratios listed in Table 15-11. The financial factors most critical to lenders are those that indicate the likelihood that the organization will be able to meet its debt-related obligations. Thus, measures that focus on liquidity, solvency, and sustainability are very important.

The unrestricted current fund is analyzed carefully. The total unrestricted resources are compared to the annual budget to measure the financial cushion. Balance sheets of the unrestricted current fund and plant funds are also considered important in determining overall liquidity at fiscal year-end. Long-term debt is compared to endowment levels to help determine the relative debt burden. For project revenue bonds, it is necessary to assess all the various factors that will influence the net revenue streams of the specific enterprise involved. Revenue and expenditure composition is also examined, with a more diversified revenue base being viewed more favorably. Expenditures are assessed to determine if they can be readily reduced if revenues decline. State support is generally viewed positively, but a public university's rating depends on the state's credit strength, financial condition, and support of higher education. Adequacy of plant maintenance, student aid, faculty and staff salary levels, and the portion of funds retained for future years, and the endowment per student and endowment relation to unrestricted fund expenditures are also considered.

However, financial factors are but one part of the educational bond rating process. Legal and demand factors are evaluated by on-site visits, discussions with management, the proposed bond instrument, and other data from a wide variety of sources. The security pledges, rate covenants, and credit supports (guarantees by third parties or use of endowment fund assets as collateral) are all legal considerations related to a specific bond issue. They affect the bond rating because they influence the amount of risk associated with the specific issue.

Demand is critical and is analyzed using enrollment size and trends, including applications, acceptances, and matriculations. The institution's level

TABLE 15-11 **Standard & Poor's College Financial Ratios**

Ratio	Definition
Liquidity	Unrestricted Current Fund Balance + Quasi-Endowment + Unrestricted Plant and Other Unrestricted Fund Balances
	$$\frac{}{(UCF\ EXP + MT)^*}$$
Historical Debt Service Burden	$$\frac{Historical\ Debt\ Service}{Related\ Year's\ (UCF\ EXP + MT)}$$
Future Debt Service Burden	$$\frac{Future\ Maximum\ Annual\ Debt\ Service}{Last\ Full\ Year's\ (UCF\ EXP + MT)}$$
Debt Versus Endowment	$$\frac{Total\ Long\text{-}Term\ Debt}{Total\ Endowment}$$
Endowment per Student	$$\frac{Total\ Endowment}{FTE^{**}\ students}$$
Endowment Versus Operations	$$\frac{Total\ Endowment}{(UCF\ EXP + MT)}$$
Endowment Liquidity	$$\frac{Quasi\text{-}Endowment}{Total\ Endowment}$$
Financial Aid	$$\frac{University\ Generated\ Financial\ Aid}{Tuition\ Revenues}$$
Tuition Dependence	$$\frac{Tuition\ Revenues}{Total\ Educational\ and\ General\ Revenues}$$
Gift Income	$$\frac{Private\ Gifts}{Total\ Educational\ and\ General\ Revenues}$$
Unrestricted Fund Liquidity	$$\frac{Cash\ and\ Investments}{Accounts\ Payable}$$
Unrestricted Fund Operations	Surplus or Deficit as a Percentage of (UCF EXP + MT)
Unrestricted Fund Cumulative Position	$$\frac{Unrestricted\ Fund\ Balance,\ End\ of\ Year}{(UCF\ EXP + MT)}$$

*(UCF EXP + MT) = Unrestricted Current Fund Expenditures + Mandatory Transfers
**FTE = Full-Time Equivalent

Source: Adapted from Standard & Poor's Corporation, *S&P's Municipal Finance Criteria*, New York, NY: S&P, 1989, p. 70.

of flexibility is assessed based on geographic diversity, student quality, tenured faculty percentage, breadth of program offerings, and the institution's competitive position. Competitors are defined by factors such as comparable student quality; close proximity; program similarity; type of student attracted; tuition, fees, and student aid; and religious affiliation.

APPLYING THE FOUR KEY QUESTIONS TO EVERDASH

This section illustrates the financial analysis of a higher education institution, using the available financial statements, institutional data, and comparable data from peer institutions. We use the data and the ratios derived from it to address the four key questions introduced in Part One. You may wish to refer to the relevant sections of Chapter 5 for details on financial calculations.

Introduction to Everdash

Everdash College (our fictitious name) is a relatively small, selective liberal arts college located in the small town of Everdash, Michigan. This old, established institution has loyal alumni, most of whom remained in Michigan after graduation. Everdash offers a surprisingly broad selection of liberal arts courses and majors at the undergraduate level, has relatively small classes, and prides itself on the excellence of its art collection. All students are traditional, full-time students; relatively few work while attending college, and most graduate after four years of study. Everdash offers no graduate, professional, continuing education, or part-time programs. It is in the process of completing a successful $50 million fund drive for library renovations and a chair in agriculture.

The 19X8 Everdash College and Everdash College Student Loan Corporation (hereafter Everdash) audit report, consolidated financial statements, and notes are shown in Exhibit B (pages 578-586). Everdash College presented its Balance Sheet as of June 30, 19X8, in columnar format and included substantial detail on revenues and expenses in the Statement of Changes in Fund Balances. The unrestricted and restricted portions of the current funds are disclosed in Note 10, which contains a Balance Sheet, a Current Funds Statement, and a listing of the current restricted fund balances by source and purpose. The financial statements received an unqualified audit opinion, which indicates that they should provide a reliable basis for performing financial analysis.

To facilitate our internal analysis of Everdash, we reorganized the financial statement data as shown in Exhibit C (pages 587-588). The Current Funds

Statement data from Note 10 was incorporated into the main Balance Sheet and Statement of Changes in Fund Balances. Current assets and liabilities were classified as well as possible with the given information and subtotalled, and the absolute dollar and percentage change between 19X7 and 19X8 was calculated. In the following analysis, most of the absolute dollar amounts refer to Exhibit C, unless otherwise noted. Remember that all dollar amounts are in thousands. Exhibit D (pages 590-592) shows common size finanical statements, in which each line item is shown as a percentage of the relevant total (vertical analysis). Exhibit E (pages 593-595) shows the percentage that each fund constitutes of the 19X8 line-item total (horizontal analysis). Selected other relevant financial ratios are shown in Exhibit F (page 596). Once such an analysis is set up on an electronic spreadsheet, it is relatively easy to enter each new year's data from the audited financial statements and have the spreadsheet program calculate the differences and ratios.

The ERR messages displayed in Exhibit E and Exhibit F are messages from the spreadsheet that a calculation error has occurred in these locations, in this case because of an attempt to divide by zero. Some spreadsheets may allow you to print a blank space or a different message, such as DIVZERO, instead of the more generic ERR.

It is useful to compare Everdash's performance to that of similar institutions. Exhibit G (page 597) provides data on several measures that were available for Everdash and a set of peer institutions. Note that all of the measures in the first three sections are derived directly from the financial statements. To compare your school to peer institutions on such measures, get a copy of their financial statements directly from the schools or from the state Attorney General's office. While the first attempt to perform such analysis may seem like more trouble than it is worth, it quickly becomes both easier and more useful as you become familiar with the financial and other characeristics of the peer institutions.

Internal Analysis

This section highlights the major issues and findings that resulted from analysis of the Everdash financial data in Exhibits B, C, D, E, and F. Applying the four key questions to the Everdash College financial statements enables us to summarize and organize this welter of detail to assess the financial condition of the college. As is true of many colleges today, Everdash's financial analysis presents a mixed picture. Hereafter, all dollar amounts are in thousands, as displayed in the financial statements, unless otherwise indicated.

Consistency Between Goals and Resources With over $200 million [1] in assets, Everdash appears to have a relatively large, solid asset base, although its total assets at June 30, 19X8, were 1 percent [2] less than the prior year [Exhibit C]. Most of Everdash's assets are in short- and long-term investments (70 percent) [3] and plant (23 percent) [4] [Exhibit D]. Everdash College as a whole appears to be very liquid and solvent, with an overall current ratio of 4.0 [5] and a quick ratio of 2.5 [6] [Exhibit F]. It has plenty of debt capacity with debt-to-assets ratios of 0.10 [7] overall and 0.21 [8] in the plant fund and a hefty coverage (times interest earned) ratio of 4.29 [9]; Everdash could safely borrow more money. The Everdash current unrestricted fund, however, has dangerously low current and quick ratios (0.55 [10] and 0.09 [11]), and a dangerously high debt-to-total-assets ratio of 1.82 [12]. The overall asset turnover ratio is a low 0.22 [13], while the current unrestricted fund asset turnover ratio is a high 12.52 [14].

Everdash's current unrestricted fund is like a lean greyhound, burning all its resources as it runs, while the rest of Everdash is a contented cow, slowly ambling along with lots of resources to burn. Could the ample resources of the other funds be used to fuel the current fund? Perhaps. Quasi-endowment assets can be used to support current operations, although some may be restricted for only limited types of current expenses.

Endowment and similar funds are important to many private and some public higher education institutions. The true endowment principal must be maintained intact. Although this has traditionally been considered to mean only the nominal value of the principal, some have argued persuasively that the higher current or inflation-adjusted value of principal should be maintained. Boards that have adopted the total return concept must decide how much of the endowment earnings should be used for current operations, subject to the legal requirement to maintain nominal principal. Treating investment income differently from gains and losses in the financial statements is confusing, and makes analysis more difficult. A special problem in analyzing financial statements of higher education institutions occurs because quasi-endowment assets are reported as part of endowment and similar funds. True endowment must be distinguishable from quasi-endowment to accurately assess the overall performance and condition of the organization. A thorough analysis of an educational institution must consider all activities (gifts, transfers, and market value changes) affecting the funds functioning as endowment, both true and quasi.

The principal balance of true endowment contributed to Everdash over the years is only $47,086. The remaining $50,821 of the total $97,907 endowment fund balance came from investment income and transactions in excess of transfers out of endowment [Exhibit B, Note 2]. An additional $1,164 of unrestricted and $11,453 of restricted current assets are also being invested as quasi-endowments, at the discretion of the board of directors. Despite the $3,604 [15] net decline in the market value of endowment and similar fund investments during 19X8, the total market value of investments at July 31, 19X8, is $13,574 [16] above the value when acquired by purchase or donation. Thus, a substantial amount of the endowment and similar fund assets may be legally available to support current operations. If consumed, however, they would no longer be able to generate investment income to support future current operations.

In 19X8, the current unrestricted fund received $2,352 ($1,913 + $439) [17] from the endowment funds in investment income and transfers under the spending formula, but gave back $1,336 [18] in transfers to quasi-endowment [Exhibit C]. Thus, Everdash managed to support its current unrestricted fund operations with a net contribution of only $1,016 ($2,352 − $1,336) from the endowment and similar funds in 19X8. Although the unrestricted current fund 19X8 deficit of $850 [19] at first appears to be financed by the other funds, in fact, the unrestricted current fund deficit in 19X8 was caused by its transfer of resources to the other funds. It would, however, still have a cumulative negative fund balance of $630 ($1,996 [20] − $1,336) even without the transfer to quasi-endowment. Thus, if the negative cumulative fund balance has been caused by transfers to quasi-endowment each year, there is little cause for alarm. Careful analysis of prior period statements would normally disclose the cause of the negative current fund balance.

So Everdash's resources as a whole are consistent with its goals, but the unrestricted current fund resources may be only marginally sufficient, even after considering unrestricted quasi-endowment resources. The meager $1,164 in unrestricted quasi-endowment [Exhibit B, Note 2] is not much of a cushion against a $29,055 [21] unrestricted current operating budget. Also, any quasi-endowment resources used for current operations will no longer generate investment income and earnings to support current operations in future years, requiring new sources to be found to replace the foregone investment income. The availability of restricted fund support for unrestricted operating expenses should be investigated. Current standards leave management with substantial discretion to decide whether to charge qualifying expenditures to restricted funds; proposed standards would limit this discretion. However, if restricted funds cannot be more widely used, the current unrestricted fund is running under very tight constraints.

Intergenerational Equity Everdash's overall operating return on fund balance of only 2 percent [22] [Exhibit F], a rate substantially lower than inflation that year, means that it did not maintain its purchasing power. A primary reason for the poor return appears to be the performance of investments, which depreciated by $3,767 [23] in 19X8.

Everdash has increased the spending (total return) amount of its endowment funds in each of the past several years [Exhibit B, Note 1], which often signals the cannibalization of endowment to support operating deficits. While sometimes a viable short-term strategy in a severe crisis, this can be extremely dangerous, and should be carefully monitored and controlled. As the endowment decreases in value, it will generate less income to support operations, thus adding more fiscal stress. On the other hand, since

Everdash's endowment appears to have grown substantially since 19X4 as the result of a capital campaign [Exhibit B, Note 11], the spending amount should increase proportionately.

A spending policy stated as a percentage of endowment fund assets would better indicate whether cannibalization or an appropriate increase in spending has occurred. The 19X8 spending increase of $2,190 ($7,200 − $5,010) [Exhibit B, Note 1] is more than a third of the $6,226 [24] of endowment fund gifts received in the prior year, 19X7. An increase this large is likely to indicate cannibalization. On the other hand, a spending amount of $7,200 on an investment base of $127,123 [25] is a reasonably conservative 5.7 percent. The large increase in the 19X8 spending amount may reflect correction of an inappropriately conservative spending amount in the past. The 19X8 drop in endowment value also indicates a net consumption of resources. Everdash College appears to have subsidized 19X8 operations with resources donated by past generations, thus depriving future generations of the benefits that could have been derived from the investment earnings on those resources.

The low $4,396 total return on investments ($8,163 [26] of investment income less $3,767 [23] depreciation of investments) in 19X8 might lead one to question the ability of the endowment fund to support operations. Everdash achieved a relatively high total return of $18,734 [27] ($11,682 of appreciation plus $7,052 of investment income) on investments during 19X7. Using $140,000 as a rough but adequate approximation of the 19X7 and 19X8 investment portfolio values, Everdash's return on investments was over 13 percent in 19X7, and only about 3 percent in 19X8. Everdash's investment strategy should, in the long run, yield higher overall gains than a more conservative strategy. Total return was developed to deal with the fluctuations in return from year to year. The danger is that an organization will use too much of its gains in the good years, will become dependent on high distribution levels, and will severely impair the value of its investment portfolio when the inevitable bad years arrive. Since inflation was only about 5 percent in 19X7 and 19X8, it may be worth suffering an occasional bad year if the fluctuations do not jeopardize the college's viability.

Everdash's investment performance should be compared to the market (which suffered heavy losses overall in 19X8), and its willingness and ability to carry the risk of volatile investments should be reviewed. The 19X8 Everdash spending amount was $6,824 [28] ($6,729 current investment income + $1,431 transfer of gains under spending formula − $1,336 transfers from unrestricted to quasi-endowment), about 5 percent of the investment asset portfolio. Its trustees and management must assess whether Everdash can continue to spend this much and still maintain the current value of the investment assets on which it is so dependent.

As a matter of fiscal prudence, the spending amount should be set to preserve the value of the investment principal. It should not exceed the expected return rate on the endowment resources, unless a conscious decision has been made to shift resources from quasi-endowment to operating uses. The result of such a decision would be a future decrease in the amount of investment income available to support operations. Alternatively, investing current contributions as quasi-endowment, instead of using them for current operations, represents a decision to save resources donated by the current constituents to benefit future generations and may be counter to the intentions of donors. This is a matter for careful consideration by the board of directors. Adequate internal data should be provided to assist them in making these decisions wisely.

Match Between Sources and Uses of Resources Everdash's sources and uses of resources on the Balance Sheet appear to be well matched. Current assets exceed current liabilities, only about 20 percent of the investment in plant is financed with debt, and virtually all of the long-term but relatively liquid investments are offset by fund balance. From this perspective, Everdash could afford to invest in additional fixed assets, take on more borrowing, or weather lean years, if necessary.

From the perspective of the activity statement, sources and uses are less well matched; expenses are growing faster than revenues. From 19X7 to 19X8, the largest component of revenue, tuition and fees, grew by 7.3 percent [29] [Exhibit C]. All other sources of revenue and other additions also increased, except for private and endowment gifts. Total revenue and other additions declined by 1.6 percent [30], due primarily to the sharp 61.8 percent [31] decrease in endowment gifts. Total expenditures and other deductions grew by 8.9 percent [32], contributed to by the substantial growth of instruction and research (15.4 percent) [33], academic support (8.2 percent) [34], student services (11.4 percent) [35], and interest (117.7 percent) [36]. Although investment income increased by 15.8 percent [37], its growth was more than offset by the $3,767 depreciation in investment value. In fact, the total excess of revenues over expenditures of $3,677 [38] was completely wiped out by the $3,767 depreciation in investment value.

Educational expenses grew faster than the related tuition and fee revenues, private gifts decreased, and the endowment fund investments declined in value. The outflow of resources grew faster than the inflow of resources. In short, 19X8 was not a great financial year for Everdash. A continuation of these patterns could seriously erode the school's currently strong position. If endowment gifts and investment appreciation are removed from the 19X7 picture, Everdash's revenues barely covered its expenses in that year. This points to an operating squeeze that Everdash is attempting to alleviate by increasing endowment gifts and earnings.

Auxiliary and independent operations do not appear to be helping matters and should be monitored carefully. Intended to provide a service to the school community and be self-supporting, there is an ever-present danger that auxiliary operations will deteriorate to the point that they do neither. Although Everdash's auxiliary and independent revenues increased at higher rates than the related expenses, the bad news is that independent operations are still losing money, $108 ($1,683 − $1,791) [39] in 19X8. Since this loss appears not to include any depreciation expense on the fixed assets used in those operations (despite the GAAP requirement to do so), it is very likely that the auxiliary and independent operations are draining Everdash's resources instead of contributing to them. This is an inappropriate use of school resources.

Resource Sustainability   Everdash's assets are heavily concentrated in investments (70 percent in short- and long-term combined) and plant (23.4 percent). Its capital is concentrated in fund balance, which is the best place to have it if it's concentrated. Everdash's revenues are most heavily concentrated in tuition and fees (37.8 percent) [40], followed by investment income (18.6 percent) [41], auxiliary enterprises (14.1 percent) [42], and private gifts (12.7 percent) [43]. The reliance on tuition and fees increased slightly from 34.7 percent [44] in 19X7. Expenditures are less concentrated, with the largest being instruction and research (19.3 percent) [45]. Everdash is fairly heavily dependent on investment and tuition performance and is sensitive to pressures on educational expenses (the first six items listed under expenditures). Together, auxiliary and independent operations also exert a relatively large influence at 17 percent [42][46] of revenues.

Exhibit C summarizes Everdash's problems: while revenues decreased by 1.6 percent, expenses increased by 8.9 percent, and the endowment investments lost value. Reversing these trends requires increases in revenues or decreases in expenses. Improving endowment earnings is the responsibility of the investment manager and should probably be a high priority item. The auxiliary and independent operations should become self-supporting and, perhaps, contribute positively to Everdash's financial position. If this is not feasible, they should probably be abandoned or contracted out.

Can educational revenues be increased? Tuition revenues already account for 37.8 percent of the total, having grown by 7.3 percent. Tuition price increases are limited by those charged at similar colleges. If Everdash is already charging as much as its competitors, tuition revenues can be increased only if the college admits more students. Private gifts have decreased 4.9 percent [47], further exacerbating the current fund's fiscal woes. Perhaps they can be increased substantially, but this possibility seems unlikely if they have held at about the same level for two years. Thus, a review of revenue dispersion shows no obvious candidates for increases, other than expansion of the student body. This, too, may prove difficult in a period of declining enrollments, although it depends heavily on the reputation and selectivity of the school.

Why have education-related expenses increased, and can the trend be slowed or reversed? Most of Everdash's expenses are growing rapidly, as discussed above and illustrated in Exhibit C. The largest expense categories and those growing at the fastest rates are good candidates for initial investigation. Comparing expense levels to those of peer institutions is another way to determine which expenses may be susceptible to control. This requires the external data analyzed below. Everdash should perform a zero-based analysis on the internal operations and expense data of those categories that appear to be most out of line and most readily amenable to cost cutting. One way to cut educational expenses is to cut back on the number and variety of courses, programs, and amenities that the institution offers. Both market and internal data are needed to determine which components are the most costly and can be eliminated with the least negative impact on the school's reputation and ability to attract students.

External Comparisons

The data in Exhibit G show that Everdash's *expendable fund balances to plant debt* ratio is near zero [48]. This is far lower than the other institutions, which range from 0.5 [49] for College *C* to 3.7 [50] for College *D*. This ratio measures the amount of unrestricted resources available to repay plant debt. It is extremely low because Everdash has only limited unrestricted resources, rather than because of high plant debt. Everdash's *total plant equity to plant debt* ratio of 3.8 [51] is close to that of *A* and *E* and double that of *B* an *C*. (The ratio of College *D* is so large that it is clearly in an unusually strong position, unless an error was made in the source data calculations.) This ratio indicates that Everdash does not have excess debt and that its plant fund assets and liabilities are reasonably well matched.

Everdash's *tuition and fees to total education and general expense* ratio is the lowest of the group. Like many signals, this can be good news (Everdash may have other sources of support or room to raise its tuition rates if they are lower than other institutions) or bad (if its total education and general expense is excessively high). Everdash's total tuition and fees per student (near the bottom of the table) are virtually the same as their peer institutions, which rules out the hypothesis of low tuition and indicates little room for additional increases.

Everdash has a higher *private gifts and grants to total education and general expense* ratio than any of its peers, and is second highest on the *endowment income to total education and general expense* ratio. Although Everdash has relatively diversified sources of support, it is more dependent on private gifts and endowment income than its peers, which rekindles the concerns raised above about a decline in private gifts and the possible cannibalization of endowment to support operations.

Less peer data is available on the remaining ratios, which reduces the reliability of the conclusions to be drawn from them. Because ratio differences may result from differences in accounting practices, as well as differences in operating and economic performance, conclusions drawn from comparison with only one or two peer organizations should be used with caution.

Keeping in mind these considerations, it is worth noting that Everdash, at 27 percent [52], spends less of its educational and general revenue on instruction than do the other institutions, whose percentages range from 29 percent to 36 percent. It spends 13 percent [53] on operations and maintenance, whereas the others' ratios range from 8 percent to 12 percent. Its 15 percent [54] for scholarships and fellowships is in the middle of the 11 percent to 18 percent range spanned by its peers. Although there is data from only one other institution (College A) for the remaining expense ratios, it is worth noting that Everdash spends much more (21 percent versus 15 percent) on institutional support, slightly more (11 percent versus 8 percent) on academic support, and about the same (12 percent versus 13 percent) on student services as did College A in 19X8. Remember that some of the differences in expense distributions may be due to different organization structures and to different allocation procedures that are well within the realm of GAAP.

The last set of ratios uses one nonfinancial piece of data: the number of students. Enrollment and related figures are often available from the school bulletin and public relations materials. However, students are not always counted in quite the same way by different institutions. If an institution has only a four-year, full-time undergraduate student body, the student numbers are likely to be comparable. However, if graduate, two-year, part-time, or nontraditional students constitute a significant part of the student body, comparisons across institutions must insure that their students are counted in similar ways.

With that caveat, and the recognition that these schools are traditional, full-time, four-year institutions, the first thing we notice is that Everdash's *endowment per student* is $80 thousand [55]. This is much higher than the $55 thousand of its next competitor, College E, and about four times as large as the per-student endowments of Colleges A and D. Unfortunately, Everdash's rapidly growing expenses are also already the highest among its peer group. Its *total education and general expense per student* at $22 thousand [56] and its *total education and general revenue per student* at $23 thousand [57] are both substantially higher than the $15 to $17 thousand of Colleges A, D, and E. The key appears to be in the total students figures; at 1,388 students [58], Everdash simply has a much smaller student body than its peers, which range from 1,700 to 2,030 students in size. Everdash offers the same breadth, diversity, and quality, but it is supported by a much smaller student base, which leads to higher costs per student. Tuition and fees per student are the same as those of other peer institutions. The resulting larger difference between tuition and fees and total expenses must be made up from other sources, the larger per-student endowment earnings and private gifts.

Diagnosis

In summary, Everdash College is financially strong, but it has a few ailments: the very lean current unrestricted funds operations, the declining endowment fund values, and the apparently growing spending rate. Because they are related, these ailments will become chronic and worsen unless Everdash treats them appropriately. One or more of the following remedies may be applicable to the current fund operations: increasing the student body, reducing expenses, using restricted money to cover more current operating costs, or expanding the endowment. Growing seems difficult in a time of reducing enrollments and growing competition; cutting costs is painful and difficult; using restricted funds may not be feasible because of the nature of the restrictions on the resources; and expanding endowment is what nine out of ten colleges will try. Get ready for another Everdash College endowment campaign! Eventually, however, like many other colleges and universities, Everdash will be forced to control its expenses more stringently. The endowment fund asset management and total return spending level must be reviewed and adjusted in light of the current market and needs of the institution for stability as well as return.

SUMMARY

The great opportunities facing higher education today include the increased need for life-long learning and the recognition of the U.S. as a world leader in professional education. Nevertheless, managers and directors of colleges and universities are increasingly challenged to provide outstanding financial management. The daunting challenges include escalating costs, shrinking government funding and traditional undergraduate population, deteriorating plant, threats to the tax-exempt status of several activities, scandals involving improper indirect cost charges to grants, growing competition from businesses that provide education and training, and a widespread questioning of schools' ability and intention to teach students.

Each part of the Annual Report of a college or university conveys useful information about its financial condition. College and university general purpose financial statements include a Balance Sheet, a Statement of Changes in Fund Balances, and a Statement of Current Funds Revenues, Expenditures, and Other Changes. The Statement of Current Funds Revenues, Expenditures, and Other Changes documents the financial effect of operations on the current restricted and unrestricted funds. The Statement of Changes in Fund Balances documents the resource inflows and outflows that affect each fund, and the Balance Sheet states the financial position of each fund. The most common fund groups are the current unrestricted, current restricted, loan, plant, and endowment and similar funds. Most colleges and universities report several mandatory and nonmandatory transfers. The mandatory transfers result primarily from the requirements of bonds and grants. The auditor's opinion indicates the fairness of presentation of the financial statements.

Financial analysis of college and university statements is an important aspect of being a good manager or useful board member. The general purpose financial statements provide a wealth of information about the financial position and performance of the organization. The four questions provide a framework for the process, which we believe and hope will make it much easier to conduct a productive financial statement analysis.

Even the most skilled and experienced analysts must calculate the relevant ratios before the fun part of interpretation and sleuthing can begin. Although analysts prepare a set of standard ratios for their first cut of analysis, the process thereafter can take many different paths, as the results of that first cut suggest other areas to be investigated or different ways of looking at a particularly troublesome area. Thus, analysis seldom follows a simple linear process, and no two thorough analytic processes will be exactly alike. However, even with different approaches, two good analysts will identify the same financial problems, opportunities, strengths, and weaknesses.

The integration of financial and institutional data is an increasingly feasible and important component of higher education financial analysis. Admissions, registrations, student quality, retention, faculty salaries, teaching loads, and class size, along with the financial trends and ratios, are important in evaluating the status and performance of a college or university. National or private data sources, including data from peer institutions, can be used to provide standards of comparison in these areas. Managers and trustees must understand the higher education industry as well as their own institutions.

EXHIBIT A Sample Financial Statements

Sample Educational Institution
Balance Sheet
June 30, 19___, with Comparative Figures at June 30, 19___

Assets	Current Year	Prior Year
Current funds:		
Unrestricted:		
Cash	$ 210,000	$ 110,000
Investments	450,000	360,000
Accounts receivable, less allowance of $18,000 both years	228,000	175,000
Inventories, at lower of cost (first-in, first-out basis) or market	90,000	80,000
Prepaid expenses and deferred charges	28,000	20,000
Total unrestricted	1,006,000	745,000
Restricted:		
Cash	145,000	101,000
Investments	175,000	165,000
Accounts receivable, less allowance of $8,000 both years	68,000	160,000
Unbilled charges	72,000	-
Total restricted	460,000	426,000
Total current funds	$ 1,466,000	$ 1,171,000
Loan funds:		
Cash	$ 30,000	$ 20,000
Investments	100,000	100,000
Loans to students, faculty, and staff, less allowance of $10,000 current year and $9,000 prior year	550,000	382,000
Due from unrestricted funds	3,000	-
Total loan funds	$ 683,000	$ 502,000
Endowment and similar funds:		
Cash	$ 100,000	$ 101,000
Investments	13,900,000	11,800,000
Total endowment and similar funds	$14,000,000	$11,901,000

Liabilities and Fund Balances	Current Year	Prior Year
Current funds:		
Unrestricted:		
Accounts payable	$ 125,000	$ 100,000
Accrued liabilities	20,000	15,000
Students' deposits	30,000	35,000
Due to other funds	158,000	120,000
Deferred credits	30,000	20,000
Fund balance	643,000	455,000
Total unrestricted	1,006,000	745,000
Restricted		
Accounts payable	14,000	5,000
Fund balances	446,000	421,000
Total restricted	460,000	426,000
Total current funds	$ 1,466,000	$ 1,171,000
Loan funds:		
Fund balances:		
U.S. government grants refundable	$ 50,000	$ 33,000
University funds:		
Restricted	483,000	369,000
Unrestricted	150,000	100,000
Total loan funds	$ 683,000	$ 502,000
Endowment and similar funds:		
Fund balances:		
Endowment	$ 7,800,000	$ 6,740,000
Term endowment	3,840,000	3,420,000
Quasi-endowment—unrestricted	1,000,000	800,000
Quasi-endowment—restricted	1,360,000	941,000
Total endowment and similar funds	$14,000,000	$11,901,000

(Continued)

Adapted from *Audits of Colleges and Universities*, pp. 108-121. Reprinted with permission.

EXHIBIT A (Continued)

Sample Educational Institution
Balance Sheet (Continued)

Assets	Current Year	Prior Year
Annuity and life income funds:		
Annuity funds:		
Cash	$ 55,000	$ 45,000
Investments	3,260,000	3,010,000
Total annuity funds	3,315,000	3,055,000
Life income funds:		
Cash	15,000	15,000
Investments	2,045,000	1,740,000
Total life income funds	2,060,000	1,755,000
Total annuity and life income funds	$ 5,375,000	$ 4,810,000
Plant funds:		
Unexpended:		
Cash	$ 275,000	$ 410,000
Investments	1,285,000	1,590,000
Due from unrestricted current funds	150,000	120,000
Total unexpended	1,710,000	2,120,000
Renewals and replacements:		
Cash	5,000	4,000
Investments	150,000	286,000
Deposits with trustees	100,000	90,000
Due from unrestricted current funds	5,000	-
Total renewals and replacements	260,000	380,000
Retirement of indebtedness:		
Cash	50,000	40,000
Deposits with trustees	250,000	253,000
Total retirement of indebtedness	300,000	293,000

Liabilities and Fund Balances	Current Year	Prior Year
Annuity and life income funds:		
Annuity funds:		
Annuities payable	$ 2,150,000	$ 2,300,000
Fund balances	1,165,000	755,000
Total annuity funds	3,315,000	3,055,000
Life income funds:		
Income payable	5,000	5,000
Fund balances	2,055,000	1,750,000
Total life income funds	2,060,000	1,755,000
Total annuity and life income funds	$ 5,375,000	$ 4,810,000
Plant funds:		
Unexpended:		
Accounts payable	$ 10,000	$ -
Notes payable	100,000	-
Bonds payable	400,000	-
Fund balances:		
Restricted	1,000,000	1,860,000
Unrestricted	200,000	260,000
Total unexpended	1,710,000	2,120,000
Renewals and replacements:		
Fund balances:		
Restricted	25,000	180,000
Unrestricted	235,000	200,000
Total renewals and replacements	260,000	380,000
Retirement of indebtedness:		
Fund balances:		
Restricted	185,000	125,000
Unrestricted	115,000	168,000
Total retirement of indebtedness	300,000	293,000

(Continued)

EXHIBIT A (Continued)

Sample Educational Institution
Balance Sheet (Continued)

Assets	Current Year	Prior Year	Liabilities and Fund Balances	Current Year	Prior Year
Investment in plant:			Investment in plant:		
Land	$ 500,000	$ 500,000	Notes payable	$ 790,000	$ 810,000
Land improvements	1,000,000	1,110,0000	Bonds payable	2,200,000	2,400,000
Buildings	25,000,000	24,060,000	Mortgages payable	400,000	200,000
Equipment	15,000,000	14,200,000	Net investment in plant	38,210,000	36,540,000
Library books	100,000	80,000			
Total investment in plant	41,600,000	39,950,000	Total investment in plant	41,600,000	39,950,000
Total plant funds	$43,870,000	$42,743,000	Total plant funds	$43,870,000	$42,743,000
Agency funds:			Agency funds:		
Cash	$ 50,000	$ 70,000	Deposits held in custody for others	$ 110,000	$ 90,000
Investments	60,000	20,000			
Total agency funds	$ 110,000	$ 90,000	Total agency funds	$ 110,000	$ 90,000

See accompanying Summary of Significant Accounting Policies and Notes to Financial Statements.

EXHIBIT A (Continued)

Sample Educational Institution
Statement of Changes in Fund Balances For Year Ended June 30, 19___

	Current Funds		Loan Funds	Endowment and Similar Funds	Annuity and Life Income Funds	Plant Funds			
	Unrestricted	Restricted				Unexpended	Renewal and Replacements	Retirement of Indebtedness	Investment in Plant
Revenues and other additions:									
Unrestricted current fund revenues	$ 7,540,000								
Expired term endowment—restricted						$ 50,000			
State appropriations—restricted						50,000			
Federal grants and contracts—restricted		$ 500,000							
Private gifts, grants, and contracts— restricted		370,000	$100,000	$ 1,500,000	$ 800,000	115,000		$ 65,000	$ 15,000
Investment income—restricted		224,000	12,000	10,000		5,000	$ 5,000	5,000	
Realized gains on investments— unrestricted				109,000					
Realized gains on investments— restricted			4,000	50,000		10,000	5,000	5,000	
Interest on loans receivable			7,000						
U.S. government advances			18,000						
Expended for plant facilities (including $100,000 charged to current funds expenditures)									1,550,000
Retirement of indebtedness									220,000
Accrued interest on sale of bonds								3,000	
Matured annuity and life income restricted to endowment				10,000					
Total revenues and other additions	7,540,000	1,094,000	141,000	1,679,000	800,000	230,000	10,000	78,000	1,785,000
Expenditures and other deductions:									
Educational and general expenditures	4,400,000	1,014,000							
Auxiliary enterprises expenditures	1,830,000								
Indirect costs recovered		35,000							
Refunded to grantors		20,000							
Loan cancellations and write-offs			10,000						
Administrative and collection costs			1,000						1,000
Adjustment of actuarial liability for annuities payable					75,000				
Expended for plant facilities (including noncapitalized expenditures of $50,000)						1,200,000	300,000		
Retirement of indebtedness								220,000	
Interest on indebtedness								190,000	

(Continued)

EXHIBIT A (Continued)

Sample Education Institution
Statement of Changes in Fund Balances (Continued)

	Current Funds		Loan Funds	Endowment and Similar Funds	Annuity and Life Income Funds	Plant Funds			
	Unrestricted	Restricted				Unexpended	Renewal and Replacements	Retirement of Indebtedness	Investment in Plant
Expenditures and other deductions (Continued):									
Disposal of plant facilities									115,000
Expired term endowments ($40,000 unrestricted, $50,000 restricted to plant)				90,000					
Matured annuity and life income funds restricted to endowment					10,000				
Total expenditures and other deductions	6,230,000	1,069,000	12,000	90,000	85,000	1,200,000	300,000	411,000	115,000
Transfers among funds—additions/(deductions):									
Mandatory:									
Principal and interest	(340,000)							340,000	
Renewals and replacements	(170,000)						170,000		
Loan fund matching grant	(2,000)		2,000						
Unrestricted gifts allocated	(650,000)		50,000	550,000		50,000			
Portion of unrestricted quasi-endowment funds investment gains appropriated	40,000			(40,000)					
Total transfers	(1,122,000)		52,000	510,000		50,000	170,000	340,000	
Net increase/(decrease) for the year	188,000	25,000	181,000	2,099,000	715,000	(920,000)	(120,000)	7,000	1,670,000
Fund balance at beginning of year	455,000	421,000	502,000	11,901,000	2,505,000	2,120,000	380,000	293,000	36,540,000
Fund balance at end of year	$ 643,000	$ 446,000	$683,000	$14,000,000	$3,220,000	$1,200,000	$260,000	$300,000	$38,210,000

See accompanying Summary of Significant Accounting Policies and Notes to Financial Statements.

EXHIBIT A (Continued)

Sample Educational Institution
Statement of Current Funds Revenues, Expenditures, and Other Changes
Year Ended June 30, 19__

| | Current Year | | | Prior Year |
	Unrestricted	Restricted	Total	Total
Revenues:				
Tuition and fees	$2,600,000		$2,600,000	$2,300,000
Federal appropriations	500,000		500,000	500,000
State appropriations	700,000		700,000	700,000
Local appropriations	100,000		100,000	100,000
Federal grants and contracts	20,000	$ 375,000	395,000	350,000
State grants and contracts	10,000	25,000	35,000	200,000
Local grants and contracts	5,000	25,000	30,000	45,000
Private gifts, grants, and contracts	850,000	380,000	1,230,000	1,190,000
Endowment income	325,000	209,000	534,000	500,000
Sales and services of educational departments	190,000		190,000	195,000
Sales and services of auxiliary enterprises	2,200,000		2,200,000	2,100,000
Expired term endowment	40,000		40,000	
Other sources (if any)				
Total current revenues	7,540,000	1,014,000	8,554,000	8,180,000
Expenditures and mandatory transfers:				
Educational and general:				
Instruction	2,960,000	489,000	3,449,000	3,300,000
Research	100,000	400,000	500,000	650,000
Public service	130,000	25,000	155,000	175,000
Academic support	250,000		250,000	225,000
Student services	200,000		200,000	195,000
Institutional support	450,000		450,000	445,000
Operation and maintenance of plant	220,000		220,000	200,000
Scholarships and fellowships	90,000	100,000	190,000	180,000
Educational and general expenditures	4,400,000	1,014,000	5,414,000	5,370,000
Mandatory transfers for:				
Principal and interest	90,000		90,000	50,000
Renewals and replacements	100,000		100,000	80,000
Loan fund matching program	2,000		2,000	
Total educational and general	4,592,000	1,014,000	5,606,000	5,500,000
Auxiliary enterprises:				
Expenditures	1,830,000		1,830,000	1,730,000
Mandatory transfers for:				
Principal and interest	250,000		250,000	250,000
Renewals and replacements	70,000		70,000	70,000
Total auxiliary enterprises	2,150,000		2,150,000	2,050,000
Total expenditures and mandatory transfers	6,742,000	1,014,000	7,756,000	7,550,000
Other transfers and additions/(deductions):				
Excess of restricted receipts over transfers to revenues		45,000	45,000	40,000
Refunded to grantors		(20,000)	(20,000)	
Unrestricted gifts allocated to other funds	(650,000)		(650,000)	(510,000)
Portion of quasi-endowment gains appropriated	40,000		40,000	
Net increase in fund balances	$ 188,000	$ 25,000	$ 213,000	$ 160,000

See accompanying Summary of Significant Accounting Policies and Notes to Financial Statements.

EXHIBIT A (Continued)

Sample Educational Institution
Summary of Significant Accounting Policies
June 30, 19__

The significant accounting policies followed by Sample Educational Institution are described below to enhance the usefulness of the financial statements to the reader.

Accrual Basis

The financial statements of Sample Educational Institution have been prepared on the accrual basis except for depreciation accounting as explained in Notes 1 and 2 to the financial statements. The statement of current funds revenues, expenditures, and other changes is a statement of financial activities of current funds related to the current reporting period. It does not purport to present the results of operations or the net income or loss for the period as would a statement of income or a statement of revenues and expenses.

To the extent that current funds are used to finance plant assets, the amounts so provided are accounted for as (1) expenditures, in the case of normal replacement of movable equipment and library books; (2) mandatory transfers, in the case of required provisions for debt amortization and interest and equipment renewal and replacement; and (3) transfers of a nonmandatory nature for all other cases.

Fund Accounting

In order to ensure observance of limitations and restrictions placed on the use of the resources available to the Institution, the accounts of the Institution are maintained in accordance with the principles of "fund accounting." This is the procedure by which resources for various purposes are classified for accounting and reporting purposes into funds that are in accordance with activities or objectives specified. Separate accounts are maintained for each fund; however, in the accompanying financial statements, funds that have similar characteristics have been combined into fund groups. Accordingly, all financial transactions have been recorded and reported by fund group.

Within each fund group, fund balances restricted by outside sources are so indicated and are distinguished from unrestricted funds allocated to specific purposes by action of the governing board. Externally restricted funds may only be utilized in accordance with the purposes established by the source of such funds and are in contrast with unrestricted funds over which the governing board retains full control to use in achieving any of its institutional purposes.

Endowment funds are subject to the restrictions of gift instruments requiring in perpetuity that the principal be invested and the income only be utilized. Term endowment funds are similar to endowment funds except that upon the passage of a stated period of time or the occurrence of a particular event, all or part of the principal may be expended. While quasi-endowment funds have been established by the governing board for the same purposes as endowment funds, any portion of quasi-endowment funds may be expended.

All gains and losses arising from the sale, collection, or other disposition of investments and other noncash assets are accounted for in the fund which owned such assets. Ordinary income derived from investments, receivables, and the like is accounted for in the fund owning such assets, except for income derived from investments of endowment and similar funds, which income is accounted for in the fund to which it is restricted or, if unrestricted, as revenues in unrestricted current funds.

All other unrestricted revenue is accounted for in the unrestricted current fund. Restricted gifts, grants, appropriations, endowment income, and other restricted resources are accounted for in the appropriate restricted funds. Restricted current funds are reported as revenues and expenditures when expended for current operating purposes.

Other Significant Accounting Policies

Other significant accounting policies are set forth in the financial statements and the notes thereto.

EXHIBIT A (Continued)

Notes to Financial Statements
June 30, 19__

1. Investments exclusive of physical plant are recorded at cost; investments received by gift are carried at market value at the date of acquisition. Quoted market values of investments (all marketable securities) of the funds indicated were as follows:

	Current Year	Prior Year
Unrestricted current funds	$ 510,000	$ 390,000
Restricted current funds	180,000	165,000
Loan funds	105,000	105,000
Unexpended plant funds	1,287,000	1,600,000
Renewal and replacements funds	145,000	285,000
Agency funds	60,000	20,000

Investments of endowment and similar funds and annuity and life income funds are composed of the following:

	Carrying Value	
	Current Year	Prior Year
Endowment and similar funds:		
Corporate stocks and bonds (approximate market, current year $15,000,000, prior year $10,900,000)	$13,000,000	$10,901,000
Rental properties—less accumulated depreciation, current year $500,000, prior year $400,000	900,000	899,000
	$13,900,000	$11,800,000
Annuity funds:		
U.S. bonds (approximate market, current year $200,000, prior year $100,000)	$ 200,000	$ 110,000
Corporate stocks and bonds (approximate market, current year $3,070,000, prior year $2,905,000)	3,060,000	2,900,000
	$ 3,260,000	$ 3,010,000
Life income funds:		
Municipal bonds (approximate market, current year $1,400,000, prior year $1,340,000)	$ 1,500,000	$ 1,300,000
Corporate stocks and bonds (approximate market, current year $650,000, prior year $400,000)	545,000	440,000
	$ 2,045,000	$ 1,740,000

Assets of endowment funds, except nonmarketable investments of term endowment having a book value of $200,000 and quasi-endowment having a book value of $800,000, are pooled on a market basis, with each individual fund subscribing to or disposing of units on the basis of the value per unit at market value at the beginning of the calendar quarter within which the transaction takes place. Of the total units, each having a market value of $15.00, 600,000 units were owned by endowment, 280,000 units by term endowment, and 120,000 units by quasi-endowment at June 30, 19__.

EXHIBIT A (Continued)

Notes to Financial Statements (Continued)

The following tabulation summarizes changes in relationships between cost and market values of the pooled assets:

| | Pooled Assets | | Net Gains | Market Value |
	Market	Cost	(Losses)	per Unit
End of year	$15,000,000	$13,000,000	$2,000,000	$15.00
Beginning of year	10,900,000	10,901,000	(1,000)	12.70
Unrealized net gains for year			2,001,000	
Realized net gains for year			159,000	
Total net gains for year			$2,160,000	$ 2.30

The average annual earnings per unit, exclusive of net gains, were $0.56 for the year.

2. Physical plant and equipment are stated at cost at date of acquisition or fair value at date of donation in the case of gifts, except land acquired prior to 1940, which is valued at appraisal value in 1940 at $300,000. Depreciation on physical plant and equipment is not recorded.

3. Long-term debt includes: bonds payable due in annual installments varying from $45,000 to $55,000 with interest at 5 7/8 percent, the final installment being due in 19__, collateralized by trust indenture covering land, buildings, and equipment known as Smith dormitory carried in the accounts at $2,500,000, and pledged net revenue from the operations of said dormitory; and mortgages payable due in varying amounts to 19__ with interest at 6 percent, collateralized by property carried in the accounts at $800,000 and pledged revenue of the Student Union amounting to approximately $65,000 per year.

4. The Institution has certain contributory pension plans for academic and nonacademic personnel. Total pension expense for the year was $350,000, which includes amortization of prior service cost over a period of 20 years. The Institution's policy is to fund pension costs accrued, including periodic funding of prior years' accruals not previously funded. The actuarially computed value of vested benefits as of June 30, 19__ exceeded net assets of the pension fund by approximately $300,000.

5. Contracts have been let for the construction of additional classroom buildings in the amount of $3,000,000. Construction and equipment are estimated to aggregate $5,000,000, which will be financed by available resources and an issue of bonds payable over a period of 40 years amounting to $4,000,000.

6. All interfund borrowings have been made from unrestricted funds. The amounts due to plant funds from current unrestricted funds are payable within one year without interest. The amount due to loan funds from current unrestricted funds is payable currently.

7. Pledges totaling $260,000, restricted to plant fund uses, are due to be collected over the next three fiscal years in the amounts of $120,000, $80,000, and $60,000, respectively. It is not practicable to estimate the net realizable value of such pledges.

EXHIBIT B **Everdash Financial Statements**

INDEPENDENT AUDITOR'S REPORT

To the President and Trustees and the Board of Overseers of Everdash College:

We have audited the consolidated balance sheet of Everdash College and Everdash College Student Loan Corporation as of June 30, 19X8, and the related consolidated statement of changes in fund balances (including current fund revenues, expenditures, and other changes) for the year then ended. We previously audited and reported upon the consolidated financial statements of the College for the year ended June 30, 19X7, which condensed statements are presented for comparative purposes only. These financial statements are the responsibility of the College's management. Our responsibility is to express an opinion on these financial statements based on our audit.

We conducted our audit in accordance with generally accepted auditing standards. Those standards require that we plan and perform the audit to obtain reasonable assurance about whether the financial statements are free of material misstatement. An audit includes examining, on a test basis, evidence supporting the amounts and disclosures in the financial statements. An audit also includes assessing the accounting principles used and significant estimates made by management, as well as evaluating the overall financial statement presentation. We believe that our audit provides a reasonable basis for our opinion.

In our opinion, the financial statements referred to above present fairly, in all material respects, the consolidated financial position of Everdash College as of June 30, 19X8, and the changes in its fund balances for the year then ended in conformity with generally accepted accounting principles.

Klinger & Hawk
Certified Public Accountants

Everdash, MI
October 23, 19X8

EXHIBIT B (Continued)

Everdash College and Everdash College Student Loan Corporation
Consolidated Balance Sheet
As of June 30, 19X8, with Comparative Totals for 19X7
(in thousands)

	Current Funds (Note 10)	Loan Funds	Endowment and Similar Funds	Life Income Funds	Plant Funds	Total 19X8	Total 19X7
ASSETS							
Cash	$ 175	$ 119			$ 1,081	$ 294	$ 871
Short-term investments	3,801	1,707	$ 5,945	$2,342	1,405	14,876	14,312
Funds held by trustee		2,238				3,643	3,632
Student loans receivable (less allowance of $354)		5,718				5,718	5,086
Other loans and accounts receivable	750	117	713			1,580	1,392
Inventories	673					673	689
Prepaid expenses and deferred charges	908	2				910	631
Investments, at market			118,162	7,250		125,412	131,702
Unamortized bond issuance costs		150			234	384	416
Plant assets					46,991	46,991	43,690
Total assets	$6,307	$10,051	$124,820	$9,592	$49,711	$200,481	$202,421
LIABILITIES							
Accounts payable and accrued expenses	$3,923	$ 240	$ 722		$ 314	$ 5,199	$ 6,628
Deferred revenues	529	5				534	636
Notes payable					753	753	892
Bonds payable		4,770			9,220	13,990	14,170
Total liabilities	4,452	5,015	722	—	10,287	20,476	22,326
FUND BALANCES							
Unrestricted	(1,966)		1,164		503	(299)	66
Restricted	3,821	2,346	11,453	8,974	205	26,799	24,877
Endowment			97,907			97,907	86,638
U.S. government grants		2,690				2,690	2,497
Invested in plant					38,716	37,716	35,803
Unrealized appreciation of investments			13,574	618		14,192	30,214
Total fund balances	1,855	5,036	124,098	9,592	39,424	180,005	180,095
Total liabilities and fund balances	$6,307	$10,051	$124,820	$9,592	$49,711	$200,481	$202,421

The accompanying notes are an integral part of the financial statements.

EXHIBIT B (Continued)

Everdash College and Everdash College Student Loan Corporation
Consolidated Statement of Current Fund Revenues, Expenditures, and Other Changes in Fund Balances
For the Year Ended June 30, 19X8, with Comparative Totals for 19X7
(in thousands)

	Current Funds (Note 10)	Loan Funds	Endowment and Similar Funds	Life Income Funds	Plant Funds	Total 19X8	Total 19X7
Revenues and other additions:							
Tuition and fees	$16,579					$ 16,579	$ 15,454
Private gifts, grants, and contracts	5,579					5,579	5,867
Endowment and similar fund gifts		$ 7	$ 1,997	$ 373		2,377	6,226
Interest on student loans		333				333	308
Investment income	6,729	230	288	801	$ 115	8,163	7,052
Matured life income funds			187			187	63
Auxiliary enterprises	6,188					6,188	5,619
Independent operations	1,683					1,683	1,499
Government grants and contracts	1,378	211			23	1,612	1,397
Other sources	1,146					1,146	1,083
Total revenues and other additions	39,282	781	2,472	1,174	138	43,847	44,568
Expenditures and other deductions:							
Instruction and research	8,468					8,468	7,336
Academic support	3,306					3,306	3,055
Student services	3,688					3,688	3,312
Institutional support	6,575					6,575	6,235
Operation and maintenance of plant	4,237					4,237	4,142
Scholarships, fellowships, and prizes	4,773		21			4,794	4,424
Independent operations	1,791					1,791	1,664
Auxiliary enterprises	5,181					5,181	5,057
Payments to life income beneficiaries				758		758	662
Loss on disposal of plant facilities							296
Loan cancellation and write-offs		9				9	27
Interest on indebtedness		462			657	1,119	514
Amortization of bond issuance costs		15			16	31	30
Matured life income funds				187		187	63
Other	8	18				26	59
Total expenditures and other deductions	38,027	504	21	945	673	40,170	36,876

(Continued)

EXHIBIT B (Continued)

Everdash College and Everdash College Student Loan Corporation
Consolidated Statement of Current Fund Revenues, Expenditures, and Other Changes in Fund Balances (Continued)

	Current Funds (Note 10)	Loan Funds	Endowment and Similar Funds	Life Income Funds	Plant Funds	Total 19X8	Total 19X7
Appreciation (depreciation) of investments:							
Realized		(36)	12,131	161	(1)	12,255	19,248
Unrealized		25	(15,735)	(312)		(16,022)	(7,566)
Total appreciation (depreciation) of investments		(11)	(3,604)	(151)	(1)	(3,767)	11,682
Transfers among funds:							
Mandatory:							
Provision for debt service	(921)				921		
Loan fund matching grant	(23)	23					
Other:							
For plant assets	(949)		(1,700)		2,649		
Unrestricted bequests to quasi-endowment	(1,336)		1,336				
Transfer of realized gains under spending formula	1,431		(1,431)				
Amortization of bond issuance costs	(15)				15		
Other transfers	200	(60)	(77)	(25)	(38)		
Total transfers among funds	(1,613)	(37)	(1,872)	(25)	3,547		
Net increase (decrease)	(358)	229	(3,025)	53	3,011	(90)	19,374
Fund balances, beginning of year	2,213	4,807	127,123	9,539	36,413	180,095	160,721
Fund balances, end of year	$ 1,855	$5,036	$124,098	$9,592	$39,424	$180,005	$180,095

The accompanying notes are an integral part of the financial statements.

EXHIBIT B (Continued)

Everdash College and Everdash College Student Loan Corporation
Excerpts from Notes to Consolidated Financial Statements

1. **Summary of Significant Accounting Policies:**

The significant accounting policies followed by Everdash College are set forth below.

Basis of Consolidation   Everdash College (the College) is a private undergraduate institution of higher education that offers a Bachelor of Arts degree and is dedicated exclusively to a liberal arts program. The accompanying financial statements include the accounts of the College and the Everdash College Student Loan Corporation.

—NOTES OMITTED—

Endowment and Similar Funds   The following are combined and distributed pro rata to the appropriate funds: all realized gains (losses) from the sales of investments; any excess (deficiency) of market value over the book value of withdrawals from funds; and any excess (deficiency) of actual investment income over a formulated spending rate applied to operations provided, however, that at no time shall the value of any fund be reduced below the aggregate amount of all gifts and bequests to such fund.

Investments   Investments in securities are stated at market value. Market values denominated in foreign currencies are translated into U.S. dollars using exchange rates prevailing at the end of the year. Real estate investments are stated at appraised value. Mortgages and notes receivable are stated at amortized cost, since the College intends to retain such investments until their maturity. Venture capital investments are currently stated at cost, to be adjusted for changes as the investments are sold or in the event of permanent impairment in value. Certain of the College's investments in venture capital involve future cash commitments. Consistent with the College's investment strategy, the total current authorized limit to venture capital, including the cost of investments at June 30, 19X8, will not exceed $7 million.

Investment of the College's endowment and similar funds is based upon a total return policy. The Governing Boards established a spending amount of $3,500,000 for the year ended June 30, 19X3. The approved spending amount each year thereafter was equal to 108 percent of the prior year's amount through 19X6. In 19X7, the spending amount equaled 108 percent of the prior year's amount plus an additional authorized amount of $250,000 or a total spending amount in 19X7 of $5,010,000.

On May 22, 19X7, the Governing Boards elected to increase the spending amount to $7,200,000 for the fiscal year ending June 30, 19X8. The spending amount each year thereafter will be indexed by a factor to be approved by the Governing Boards. The resulting spending amount in each successive year

EXHIBIT B (Continued)

Everdash College and Everdash College Student Loan Corporation
Excerpts from Notes to Consolidated Financial Statements (Continued)

cannot, however, exceed a specified amount to be approved by the Governing Boards.

In the event that the total return requirement for a year is not fulfilled by interest, dividends, and rents of the regular investment pool, the College will utilize the appreciation of its endowment and similar funds. The deficiency of actual interest, dividends, and rental income and mandatory transfers over the spending amount was $1,431,000 and $123,000 in 19X8 and 19X7, respectively.

Revenue Recognition   Gifts of securities and other non-cash assets are recorded at fair market value at the date of donation.

Cash Equivalents   Cash equivalents consist principally of money market funds, United States Treasury Bills, and United States Treasury Notes.

Plant Assets   Land, building, fixtures, and equipment are stated at appraised value at June 21, 1920, plus subsequent additions at cost, or fair value at date of donation in the case of gifts. Fixed assets acquired with plant funds are capitalized; expenditures from current funds are generally expensed. Depreciation on physical plant and equipment has not been recorded.

Inexhaustible Collection   Since the value of the College's inexhaustible collections, primarily art objects, are not readily determinable, no value for such items has been reflected in the financial statements. The insured value of such collections at June 30, 19X8, was approximately $31,000,000.

Deferred Financing Costs   Certain costs related to the issuance of debt are deferred and amortized over the lives of the respective debt issues.

Inventories   Inventories are valued at the lower of cost or market with cost determined on the moving average method.

—NOTES OMITTED—

2. Fund Balances:

Unrestricted current fund balances consist of the excess of expenses and transfers for capital acquisitions and allocations to endowment and similar funds, over revenues and other additions, of $850,000 for the year ended June 30, 19X8, and $1,116,000 as of July 1, 19X7 (see Note 10).

As described in the Summary of Significant Accounting Policies, excesses or deficiencies of actual interest, dividends, and rental income and mandatory transfers over the "total return" spending rate have been allocated to the appropriate funds. Therefore, the fund balances in the endowment and similar and life income funds include principal balances of gifts and bequests received

EXHIBIT B (Continued)

Everdash College and Everdash College Student Loan Corporation
Excerpts from Notes to Consolidated Financial Statements (Continued)

by the College plus an allocation of net gains, withdrawals, and accumulated excesses (deficiencies) of actual investment income over the spending amount. As of June 30 19X8, the composition of the funds was as follows:

	Principal Balance of Gifts and Bequests	Allocation of Net Gains, Withdrawals, and Accumulated Excesses of Actual Investment Income Over the Spending Rate	June 30, 19X8 Fund Balance
Endowment and similar funds:			
Unrestricted quasi-endowment	$ 1,164	$ -	$ 1,164
Restricted quasi-endowment	6,508	4,945	11,453
Endowment	47,086	50,821	97,907
Life income funds	8,197	777	8,974

The allocation of gains, withdrawals, and accumulated excesses of actual investment income over the spending rate is available to offset losses from future investment transactions and/or excesses of the spending rate formula over actual investment income solely to the extent generated under the total return policy. In all cases, the original principal balance of restricted gifts and bequests will remain intact and not be used for expenses related to continuing unrestricted operations.

—NOTES OMITTED—

10. Current Funds:

The June 30, 19X8, balance sheet and statement of changes in fund balances of the current funds reflect unrestricted and restricted amounts as follows:

Balance Sheet	Unrestricted	Restricted	Total
Cash	$ 175		$ 175
Short-term investments	228	$3,573	3,801
Other loans and accounts receivable	410	340	750
Inventories	673		673
Prepaid expenses and deferred charges	908		908
	$2,394	$3,913	$6,307
Accounts payable and accrued expenses	$3,839	$ 84	$3,923
Deferred revenues	521	8	529
Fund balances:			
Unrestricted	(1,966)		(1,966)
Restricted		3,821	3,821
	$2,394	$3,913	$6,307

EXHIBIT B (Continued)

Everdash College and Everdash College Student Loan Corporation
Excerpts from Notes to Consolidated Financial Statements (Continued)

Consistent with the generally accepted accounting principles for colleges and universities, the statement of changes in fund balances includes all receipts, expenditures, and transfers of current unrestricted and restricted funds. In accordance with these principles, restricted receipts are recorded as increases in the respective fund balances when received, and recognized as revenues when expended for their restricted purpose. Net changes in current fund balances for the year ended June 30, 19X8, including $492,000 of receipts not recognized as revenues, were as follows:

Statement of Changes in Fund Balance	Unrestricted	Restricted	Total
Revenues and other additions:			
Tuition and fees	$16,285	$ 294	$16,579
Private gifts, grants, and contracts	4,375	1,204	5,579
Investment income	1,913	4,816	6,729
Auxiliary enterprises	5,304	884	6,188
Independent operations	1,513	170	1,683
Government grants and contracts	90	1,288	1,378
Other sources	490	656	1,146
Total revenues and other additions	29,970	9,312	39,282
Expenditures:			
Instruction and research	6,595	1,873	8,468
Academic support	2,105	1,201	3,306
Student services	3,279	409	3,688
Institutional support	6,144	431	6,575
Operation and maintenance of plant	4,001	236	4,237
Scholarships, fellowships, and prizes	382	4,391	4,773
Independent operations	1,411	380	1,791
Auxiliary enterprises	5,130	51	5,181
Other	8		8
Total expenditures	29,055	8,972	38,027
Transfers among funds:			
Mandatory:			
Provision for debt service	(332)	(589)	(921)
Loan fund matching grant	(23)		(23)
Other:			
For plant assets	(838)	(111)	(949)
Unrestricted bequests to quasi-endowment	(1,336)		(1,336)
Transfer of realized gains under spending formula	439	992	1,431
Amortization of bond issuance costs	(15)		(15)
Other transfers	340	(140)	200
Net transfers	(1,765)	152	(1,613)
Net increase (decrease)	(850)	492	(358)
Fund balance, June 30, 19X7	(1,116)	3,329	2,213
Fund balance, June 30, 19X8	$ (1,966)	$3,821	$1,855

EXHIBIT B (Continued)

Everdash College and Everdash College Student Loan Corporation
Excerpts from Notes to Consolidated Financial Statements (Continued)

The composition of current restricted funds is as follows (in thousands of dollars):

	June 30, 19X8	June 30, 19X7
Unexpended endowment income	$2,165	$1,638
Gifts and grants for current purposes	938	1,052
Research and special program grants	188	208
Reserves for special purposes	530	431
	$3,821	$3,329

11. Pledges:

—NOTES OMITTED—

The Capital Campaign for Everdash, which began in 19X4 and will end in 19X9, has a goal of raising $56 million for endowment and academic facilities. Through June 30, 19X8, approximately $38.6 million has been received on pledges of approximately $49.9 million. The realizable value and period of collection of outstanding pledges is not determinable for financial reporting purposes.

EXHIBIT C Everdash Restated Financial Statements

Everdash Consolidated Balance Sheet—June 30, 19X8 and 19X7
Absolute Dollars, Changes, and Percentage Increase (Decrease)
(in thousands)

	Unrestricted	Restricted	Current Funds (Note 10)	Loan Funds	Endowment and Similar Funds	Life Income Funds	Plant Funds	Total 19X8	Total 19X7	Absolute Increase (Decrease)	Percentage Increase (Decrease)
ASSETS											
Cash	$ 175		$ 175	$ 119				$ 294	$ 871	$ (577)	−66.2%
Short-term investments	228	$3,573	3,801	1,707	$ 5,945	$2,342	$ 1,081	14,876	14,312	564	3.9%
Students loans receivable (less $354 allowance)			0	5,718				5,718	5,086	632	12.4%
Other loans and accounts receivable	410	340	750	117	713			1,580	1,392	188	13.5%
Inventories	673		673					673	689	(16)	−2.3%
Prepaid expenses and deferred charges	908		908	2				910	631	279	44.2%
Current assets	2,394	3,913	6,307	7,663	6,658	2,342	1,081	24,051	22,981	1,070	4.7%
Unamortized bond issuance costs				150			234	384	416	(32)	−7.7%
Funds held by trustee				2,238			1,405	3,643	3,632	11	0.3%
Investments, at market					118,162	7,250		125,412	131,702	(6,290)	−4.8%
Plant assets							46,991	46,991	43,690	3,301	7.6%
Total assets	$2,394	$3,913	$6,307	$10,051	$124,820	$9,592	$49,711	$200,481[1]	$202,421	$(1,940)	−1.0%[2]
LIABILITIES											
Accounts payable and accrued expenses	$3,839	$ 84	$3,923	$ 240	$ 722		$ 314	$ 5,199	$ 6,628	$(1,429)	−21.6%
Deferred revenues	521	8	529	5				534	636	(102)	−16.0%
Notes payable—current			0				148	148	141	7	5.0%
Bonds payable—current			0				90	90	180	(90)	−50.0%
Current liabilities	4,360	92	4,452	245	722	0	552	5,971	7,585	(1,614)	−21.3%
Notes payable—long-term			0				605	605	751	(146)	−19.4%
Bonds payable—long-term			0	4,770			9,130	13,900	13,990	(90)	−0.6%
Total liabilities	4,360	92	4,452	5,015	722	0	10,287	20,476	22,326	(1,850)	−8.3%
FUND BALANCES											
Unrestricted	(1,966)		(1,966)		1,164		503	(299)	66	(365)	−553.0%
Temporarily restricted		3,821	3,821	2,346	11,453	8,974	205	26,799	24,877	1,922	7.7%
Endowment					97,907			97,907	86,638	11,269	13.0%
U.S. government grants				2,690				2,690	2,497	193	7.7%
Invested in plant							38,716	38,716	35,803	2,913	8.1%
Unrealized appreciation of investments			0		13,574[16]	618		14,192	30,214	(16,022)	−53.0%
Total fund balances	(1,966)	3,821	1,855	5,036	124,098	9,592	39,424	180,005	180,095	(90)	0.0%
Total liabilities and fund balances	$2,394	$3,913	$6,307	$10,051	$124,820	$9,592	$49,711	$200,481	$202,421	$(1,940)	−1.0%

EXHIBIT C (Continued)

Everdash Consolidated Statement of Changes in Fund Balances (Including Current Fund Statement)—June 30, 19X8 and 19X7 Restated Absolute Dollars, Changes, and Percentage Increase (Decrease) (in thousands)

	Unrestricted	Restricted	Current Funds (Note 10)	Loan Funds	Endowment and Similar Funds	Life Income Funds	Plant Funds	Total 19X8	Total 19X7	Absolute Increase (Decrease)	Percentage Increase (Decrease)
Revenues and other additions:											
Tuition and fees	$16,285		$16,579					$16,579	$15,454	$1,125	7.3%[29]
Private gifts, grants, and contracts	4,375	1,204	5,579					5,579	5,867	(288)	-4.9%[47]
Endowment and similar fund gifts			0	$7	$1,997	$373		2,377	6,226[24]	(3,849)	-61.8%[31]
Interest on student loans			0	333				333	308	25	8.1%
Investment income	1,913[17]	4,816	6,729[28]	230	288	801	115	8,163[26]	7,052[27]	1,111	15.8%[37]
Matured life income funds			0		187			187	63	124	196.8%
Auxiliary enterprises	5,304	884	6,188					6,188	5,619	569	10.1%
Independent operations	1,513	170	1,683					1,683[39]	1,499	184	12.3%
Government grants and contracts	90	1,288	1,378	211			23	1,612	1,397	215	15.4%
Other sources	490	656	1,146					1,146	1,083	63	5.8%
Total revenues and other additions	29,970	9,312	39,282	781	2,472	1,174	138	43,847	44,568	(721)	-1.6%[30]
Expenditures and other deductions:											
Instruction and research	6,595	1,873	8,468					8,468	7,336	1,132	15.4%[33]
Academic support	2,105	1,201	3,306					3,306	3,055	251	8.2%[34]
Student services	3,279	409	3,688					3,688	3,312	376	11.4%[35]
Institutional support	6,144	431	6,575					6,575	6,235	340	5.5%
Operation and maintenance of plant	4,001	236	4,237					4,237	4,142	95	2.3%
Scholarships, fellowships, and prizes	382	4,391	4,773		21			4,794	4,424	370	8.4%
Independent operations	1,411	380	1,791					1,791[39]	1,664	127	7.6%
Auxiliary enterprises	5,130	51	5,181					5,181	5,057	124	2.5%
Payments to life income beneficiaries			0			758		758	662	96	14.5%
Loss on disposal of plant facilities			0					0	296	(296)	-100.0%
Loan cancellation and write-offs			0	9				9	27	(18)	-66.7%
Interest on indebtedness			0	462			657	1,119	514	605	117.7%[36]
Amortization of bond issuance costs				15			16	31	30	1	3.3%
Matured life income funds			0			187		187	63	124	196.8%
Other	8		8	18				26	59	(33)	-55.9%
Total expenditures and other deductions	29,055[21]	8,972	38,027	504	21	945	673	40,170	36,876	3,294	8.9%[32]

(Continued)

EXHIBIT C (Continued)

Everdash Consolidated Statement of Changes in Fund Balances (Continued)

	Current Funds (Note 10)		Loan Funds	Endowment and Similar Funds	Life Income Funds	Plant Funds	Total 19X8	Total 19X7	Absolute Increase (Decrease)	Percentage Increase (Decrease)
	Unrestricted	Restricted								
Excess (deficit) of revenues over expenditures	915	340	277	2,451	229	(535)	3,677[38]	7,692	(4,015)	−52.2%
Appreciation (depreciation) of investments:										
Realized	—	—	(36)	12,131	161	(1)	12,255	19,248	(6,993)	−36.3%
Unrealized	—	—	25	(15,735)	(312)	—	(16,022)	(7,566)	(8,456)	111.8%
Total appreciation (depreciation)	0	0	(11)	(3,604)[15]	(151)	(1)	(3,767)[23]	11,682[27]	(15,449)	−132.2%
Transfers among funds:										
Mandatory:										
Provision for debt service	(332)	(589)				921	0			
Loan fund matching grant	(23)		23				0			
Other:										
For plant assets	(838)	(111)		(1,700)		2,649	0			
Unrestricted bequests to quasi-endowment	(1,336)[18]			1,336			0			
Transfer of realized gains under spending formula	439[17]	992		(1,431)			0			
Amortization of bond issuance costs	(15)					15	0			
Other transfers	340	(140)	(60)	(77)	(25)	(38)	0			
Total transfers among funds	(1,765)	152	(37)	(1,872)	(25)	3,547	0			
Net increase (decrease)	(850)[19]	492	229	(3,025)	53	3,011	(90)	19,374	(19,464)	−100.5%
Fund balances, beginning of year	(1,116)	3,329	4,807	127,123[25]	9,539	36,413	180,095	160,721	19,374	12.1%
Fund balances, end of year	$(1,966)[20]	$3,821	$5,036	$124,098	$9,592	$39,424	$180,005	$180,095	$ (90)	0.0%

Note: Current Funds column (Note 10) — Excess 1,255; Realized 0; Unrealized 0; Total appreciation 0; Provision for debt service (921); Loan fund matching grant (23); For plant assets (949); Unrestricted bequests to quasi-endowment (1,336)[28]; Transfer of realized gains under spending formula 1,431[28]; Amortization of bond issuance costs (15); Other transfers 200; Total transfers among funds (1,613); Net increase (decrease) (358); Fund balances, beginning of year 2,213; Fund balances, end of year $1,855.

EXHIBIT D   Everdash Common Size Statements

Everdash Consolidated Balance Sheet—June 30, 19X8 and 19X7
Common Size
Line Item as a Percentage of Total (Vertical Analysis)

	Unrestricted	Restricted	Current Funds (Note 10)	Loan Funds	Endowment and Similar Funds	Life Income Funds	Plant Funds	Total 19X8	Total 19X7
ASSETS									
Cash	7.3%	0.0%	2.8%	1.2%	0.0%	0.0%	0.0%	0.1%	0.4%
Short-term investments	9.5%	91.3%	60.3%	17.0%	4.8%	24.4%	2.2%	7.4%[3]	7.1%
Student loans receivable (less $354 allowance)	0.0%	0.0%	0.0%	56.9%	0.0%	0.0%	0.0%	2.9%	2.5%
Other loans and accounts receivable	17.1%	8.7%	11.9%	1.2%	0.6%	0.0%	0.0%	0.8%	0.7%
Inventories	28.1%	0.0%	10.7%	0.0%	0.0%	0.0%	0.0%	0.3%	0.3%
Prepaid expenses and deferred charges	37.9%	0.0%	14.4%	0.0%	0.0%	0.0%	0.0%	0.5%	0.3%
Current assets	100.0%	100.0%	100.0%	76.2%	5.3%	24.4%	2.2%	12.0%	11.4%
Unamortized bond issuance costs	0.0%	0.0%	0.0%	1.5%	0.0%	0.0%	0.5%	0.2%	0.2%
Funds held by trustee	0.0%	0.0%	0.0%	22.3%	0.0%	0.0%	2.8%	1.8%	1.8%
Investments, at market	0.0%	0.0%	0.0%	0.0%	94.7%	75.6%	0.0%	62.6%[3]	65.1%
Plant assets	0.0%	0.0%	0.0%	0.0%	0.0%	0.0%	94.5%	23.4%[4]	21.6%
Total assets	$2,394	$3,913	$6,307	$10,051	$124,820	$9,592	$49,711	$200,481	$202,421
LIABILITIES									
Accounts payable and accrued expenses	160.4%	2.1%	62.2%	2.4%	0.6%	0.0%	0.6%	2.6%	3.3%
Deferred revenues	21.8%	0.2%	8.4%	0.0%	0.0%	0.0%	0.0%	0.3%	0.3%
Notes payable—current	0.0%	0.0%	0.0%	0.0%	0.0%	0.0%	0.3%	0.1%	0.1%
Bonds payable—current	0.0%	0.0%	0.0%	0.0%	0.0%	0.0%	0.2%	0.0%	0.1%
Current liabilities	182.1%	2.4%	70.6%	2.4%	0.6%	0.0%	1.1%	3.0%	3.7%
Notes payable—long-term	0.0%	0.0%	0.0%	0.0%	0.0%	0.0%	1.2%	0.3%	0.4%
Bonds payable—long-term	0.0%	0.0%	0.0%	47.5%	0.0%	0.0%	18.4%	6.9%	6.9%
Total liabilities	182.1%	2.4%	70.6%	49.9%	0.6%	0.0%	20.7%	10.2%	11.0%
FUND BALANCES									
Unrestricted	-82.1%	0.0%	-31.2%	0.0%	0.9%	0.0%	1.0%	-0.1%	0.0%
Temporarily restricted	0.0%	97.6%	60.6%	23.3%	9.2%	93.6%	0.4%	13.4%	12.3%
Endowment	0.0%	0.0%	0.0%	0.0%	78.4%	0.0%	0.0%	48.8%	42.8%
U.S. government grants	0.0%	0.0%	0.0%	26.8%	0.0%	0.0%	0.0%	1.3%	1.2%
Invested in plant	0.0%	0.0%	0.0%	0.0%	0.0%	0.0%	77.9%	19.3%	17.7%
Unrealized appreciation of investments	0.0%	0.0%	0.0%	0.0%	10.9%	6.4%	0.0%	7.1%	14.9%
Total fund balances	-82.1%	97.6%	29.4%	50.1%	99.4%	100.0%	79.3%	89.8%	89.0%
Total liabilities and fund balances	100.0%	100.0%	100.0%	100.0%	100.0%	100.0%	100.0%	100.0%	100.0%

EXHIBIT D (Continued)

Everdash Consolidated Statement of Changes in Fund Balances (Including Current Fund Statement)—June 30, 19X8 and 19X7
Common Size
Line Item as a Percentage of Total (Vertical Analysis)

	Unrestricted	Restricted	Current Funds (Note 10)	Loan Funds	Endowment and Similar Funds	Life Income Funds	Plant Funds	Total 19X8	Total 19X7
Revenues and other additions:									
Tuition and fees	54.3%	3.2%	42.2%	0.0%	0.0%	0.0%	0.0%	37.8%[40]	34.7%[44]
Private gifts, grants, and contracts	14.6%	12.9%	14.2%	0.0%	0.0%	0.0%	0.0%	12.7%[43]	13.2%
Endowment and similar fund gifts	0.0%	0.0%	0.0%	0.9%	80.8%	31.8%	0.0%	5.4%	14.0%
Interest on student loans	0.0%	0.0%	0.0%	42.6%	0.0%	0.0%	0.0%	0.8%	0.7%
Investment income	6.4%	51.7%	17.1%	29.4%	11.7%	68.2%	83.3%	18.6%[41]	15.8%
Matured life income funds	0.0%	0.0%	0.0%	0.0%	7.6%	0.0%	0.0%	0.4%	0.1%
Auxiliary enterprises	17.7%	9.5%	15.8%	0.0%	0.0%	0.0%	0.0%	14.1%[42]	12.6%
Independent operations	5.0%	1.8%	4.3%	0.0%	0.0%	0.0%	0.0%	3.8%[46]	3.4%
Government grants and contracts	0.3%	13.8%	3.5%	27.0%	0.0%	0.0%	16.7%	3.7%	3.1%
Other sources	1.6%	7.0%	2.9%	0.0%	0.0%	0.0%	0.0%	2.6%	2.4%
Total revenues and other additions	$29,970	$9,312	$39,282	$781	$2,472	$1,174	$138	$43,847	$44,568
Expenditures and other deductions:									
Instruction and research	22.0%	20.1%	21.6%	0.0%	0.0%	0.0%	0.0%	19.3%[45]	16.5%
Academic support	7.0%	12.9%	8.4%	0.0%	0.0%	0.0%	0.0%	7.5%	6.9%
Student services	10.9%	4.4%	9.4%	0.0%	0.0%	0.0%	0.0%	8.4%	7.4%
Institutional support	20.5%	4.6%	16.7%	0.0%	0.0%	0.0%	0.0%	15.0%	14.0%
Operation and maintenance of plant	13.4%	2.5%	10.8%	0.0%	0.0%	0.0%	0.0%	9.7%	9.3%
Scholarships, fellowships, and prizes	1.3%	47.2%	12.2%	0.0%	0.8%	0.0%	0.0%	10.9%	9.9%
Independent operations	4.7%	4.1%	4.6%	0.0%	0.0%	0.0%	0.0%	4.1%	3.7%
Auxiliary enterprises	17.1%	0.5%	13.2%	0.0%	0.0%	0.0%	0.0%	11.8%	11.3%
Payments to life income beneficiaries	0.0%	0.0%	0.0%	0.0%	0.0%	64.6%	0.0%	1.7%	1.5%
Loss on disposal of plant facilities	0.0%	0.0%	0.0%	0.0%	0.0%	0.0%	0.0%	0.0%	0.7%
Loan cancellation and write-offs	0.0%	0.0%	0.0%	1.2%	0.0%	0.0%	0.0%	0.0%	0.1%
Interest on indebtedness	0.0%	0.0%	0.0%	59.2%	0.0%	0.0%	476.1%	2.6%	1.2%
Amortization of bond issuance costs	0.0%	0.0%	0.0%	1.9%	0.0%	0.0%	11.6%	0.1%	0.1%
Matured life income funds	0.0%	0.0%	0.0%	0.0%	0.0%	15.9%	0.0%	0.4%	0.1%
Other	0.0%	0.0%	0.0%	2.3%	0.0%	0.0%	0.0%	0.1%	0.1%
Total expenditures and other deductions	96.9%	96.3%	96.8%	64.5%	0.8%	80.5%	487.7%	91.6%	82.7%

(Continued)

EXHIBIT D (Continued)

Everdash Consolidated Statement of Changes in Fund Balances (Continued)

	Unrestricted	Restricted	Current Funds (Note 10)	Loan Funds	Endowment and Similar Funds	Life Income Funds	Plant Funds	Total 19X8	Total 19X7
Excess (deficit) of revenues over expenditures	3.1%	3.7%	3.2%	35.5%	99.2%	19.5%	−387.7%	8.4%	17.3%
Appreciation (depreciation) of investments:									
Realized	0.0%	0.0%	0.0%	−4.6%	490.7%	13.7%	−0.7%	27.9%	43.2%
Unrealized	0.0%	0.0%	0.0%	3.2%	−636.5%	−26.6%	0.0%	−36.5%	−17.0%
Total appreciation (depreciation)	0.0%	0.0%	0.0%	−1.4%	−145.8%	−12.9%	−0.7%	−8.6%	26.2%
Transfers among funds:									
Mandatory:									
Provision for debt service	−1.1%	−6.3%	−2.3%	0.0%	0.0%	0.0%	667.4%		
Loan fund matching grant	−0.1%	0.0%	−0.1%	2.9%	0.0%	0.0%	0.0%		
Other:									
For plant assets	−2.8%	−1.2%	−2.4%	0.0%	−68.8%	0.0%	1,919.6%		
Unrestricted bequests to quasi-endowment	−4.5%	0.0%	−3.4%	0.0%	54.0%	0.0%	0.0%		
Transfer of realized gains under spending formula	1.5%	10.7%	3.6%	0.0%	−57.9%	0.0%	0.0%		
Amortization of bond issuance costs	−0.1%	0.0%	0.0%	0.0%	0.0%	0.0%	10.9%		
Other transfers	1.1%	−1.5%	0.5%	−7.7%	−3.1%	−2.1%	−27.5%		
Total transfers among funds	−5.9%	1.6%	−4.1%	−4.7%	−75.7%	−2.1%	2,570.3%		
Net increase (decrease)	−2.8%	5.3%	−0.9%	29.3%	−122.4%	4.5%	2,181.9%	−0.2%	43.5%
Fund balances, beginning of year	−3.7%	35.7%	5.6%	615.5%	5,142.5%	812.5%	26,386.2%	410.7%	360.6%
Fund balances, end of year	−6.6%	41.0%	4.7%	644.8%	5,020.1%	817.0%	28,568.1%	410.5%	404.1%

EXHIBIT E   Everdash Fund Distribution Statements

Everdash Consolidated Balance Sheet—June 30, 19X8 and 19X7
Fund Amount as a Percentage of Total 19X8 (Horizontal Analysis)

	Unrestricted	Restricted	Current Funds (Note 10)	Loan Funds	Endowment and Similar Funds	Life Income Funds	Plant Funds	Total 19X8	Total 19X7
ASSETS									
Cash	59.5%	0.0%	59.5%	40.5%	0.0%	0.0%	0.0%	$294	296.3%
Short-term investments	1.5%	24.0%	25.6%	11.5%	40.0%	15.7%	7.3%	$14,876	96.2%
Student loans receivable (less $354 allowance)	0.0%	0.0%	0.0%	100.0%	0.0%	0.0%	0.0%	$5,718	88.9%
Other loans and accounts receivable	25.9%	21.5%	47.5%	7.4%	45.1%	0.0%	0.0%	$1,580	88.1%
Inventories	100.0%	0.0%	100.0%	0.0%	0.0%	0.0%	0.0%	$673	102.4%
Prepaid expenses and deferred charges	99.8%	0.0%	99.8%	0.2%	0.0%	0.0%	0.0%	$910	69.3%
Current assets									
Unamortized bond issuance costs	0.0%	0.0%	0.0%	39.1%	0.0%	0.0%	60.9%	$384	108.3%
Funds held by trustee	0.0%	0.0%	0.0%	61.4%	0.0%	0.0%	38.6%	$3,643	99.7%
Investments, at market	0.0%	0.0%	0.0%	0.0%	94.2%	5.8%	0.0%	$125,412	105.0%
Plant assets	0.0%	0.0%	0.0%	0.0%	0.0%	0.0%	100.0%	$46,991	93.0%
Total assets	1.2%	2.0%	3.1%	5.0%	62.3%	4.8%	24.8%	$200,481	101.0%
LIABILITIES									
Accounts payable and accrued expenses	73.8%	1.6%	75.5%	4.6%	13.9%	0.0%	6.0%	$5,199	127.5%
Deferred revenues	97.6%	1.5%	99.1%	0.9%	0.0%	0.0%	0.0%	$534	119.1%
Notes payable—current									
Bonds payable—current									
Current liabilities									
Notes payable—long-term	0.0%	0.0%	0.0%	0.0%	0.0%	0.0%	100.0%	$605	124.1%
Bonds payable—long-term	0.0%	0.0%	0.0%	34.3%	0.0%	0.0%	65.7%	$13,900	100.6%
Total liabilities	21.3%	0.4%	21.7%	24.5%	3.5%	0.0%	50.2%	$20,476	109.0%
FUND BALANCES									
Unrestricted	657.5%	0.0%	657.5%	0.0%	−389.3%	0.0%	−168.2%	$(299)	−22.1%
Temporarily restricted	0.0%	14.3%	14.3%	8.8%	42.7%	33.5%	0.8%	$26,799	92.8%
Endowment	0.0%	0.0%	0.0%	0.0%	100.0%	0.0%	0.0%	$97,907	88.5%
U.S. government grants	0.0%	0.0%	0.0%	100.0%	0.0%	0.0%	0.0%	$2,690	92.8%
Invested in plant	0.0%	0.0%	0.0%	0.0%	0.0%	0.0%	100.0%	$38,716	92.5%
Unrealized appreciation of investments	0.0%	0.0%	0.0%	0.0%	95.6%	4.4%	0.0%	$14,192	212.9%
Total fund balances	−1.1%	2.1%	1.0%	2.8%	68.9%	5.3%	21.9%	$180,005	100.0%
Total liabilities and fund balances	1.2%	2.0%	3.1%	5.0%	62.3%	4.8%	24.8%	$200,481	101.0%

EXHIBIT E (Continued)

Everdash Consolidated Statement of Changes in Fund Balances (Including Current Fund Statement)—June 30, 19X8 and 19X7
Fund Amount as a Percentage of Total 19X8 (Horizontal Analysis)

	Unrestricted	Restricted	Current Funds (Note 10)	Loan Funds	Endowment and Similar Funds	Life Income Funds	Plant Funds	Total 19X8	Total 19X7
Revenues and other additions:									
Tuition and fees	98.2%	1.8%	100.0%	0.0%	0.0%	0.0%	0.0%	$16,579	93.2%
Private gifts, grants, and contracts	78.4%	21.6%	100.0%	0.0%	0.0%	0.0%	0.0%	$5,579	105.2%
Endowment and similar fund gifts	0.0%	0.0%	0.0%	0.3%	84.0%	15.7%	0.0%	$2,377	261.9%
Interest on student loans	0.0%	0.0%	0.0%	100.0%	0.0%	0.0%	0.0%	$333	92.5%
Investment income	23.4%	59.0%	82.4%	2.8%	3.5%	9.8%	1.4%	$8,163	86.4%
Matured life income funds	0.0%	0.0%	0.0%	0.0%	100.0%	0.0%	0.0%	$187	33.7%
Auxiliary enterprises	85.7%	14.3%	100.0%	0.0%	0.0%	0.0%	0.0%	$6,188	90.8%
Independent operations	89.9%	10.1%	100.0%	0.0%	0.0%	0.0%	0.0%	$1,683	89.1%
Government grants and contracts	5.6%	79.9%	85.5%	13.1%	0.0%	0.0%	1.4%	$1,612	86.7%
Other sources	42.8%	57.2%	100.0%	0.0%	0.0%	0.0%	0.0%	$1,146	94.5%
Total revenues and other additions	68.4%	21.2%	89.6%	1.8%	5.6%	2.7%	0.3%	$43,847	101.6%
Expenditures and other deductions:									
Instruction and research	77.9%	22.1%	100.0%	0.0%	0.0%	0.0%	0.0%	$8,468	86.6%
Academic support	63.7%	36.3%	100.0%	0.0%	0.0%	0.0%	0.0%	$3,306	92.4%
Student services	88.9%	11.1%	100.0%	0.0%	0.0%	0.0%	0.0%	$3,688	89.8%
Institutional support	93.4%	6.6%	100.0%	0.0%	0.0%	0.0%	0.0%	$6,575	94.8%
Operation and maintenance of plant	94.4%	5.6%	100.0%	0.0%	0.0%	0.0%	0.0%	$4,237	97.8%
Scholarships, fellowships, and prizes	8.0%	91.6%	99.6%	0.0%	0.4%	0.0%	0.0%	$4,794	92.3%
Independent operations	78.8%	21.2%	100.0%	0.0%	0.0%	0.0%	0.0%	$1,791	92.9%
Auxiliary enterprises	99.0%	1.0%	100.0%	0.0%	0.0%	0.0%	0.0%	$5,181	97.6%
Payments to life income beneficiaries	0.0%	0.0%	0.0%	0.0%	0.0%	100.0%	0.0%	$758	87.3%
Loss on disposal of plant facilities	ERR	ERR	ERR	ERR	ERR	ERR	ERR	$0	ERR
Loan cancellation and write-offs	0.0%	0.0%	0.0%	100.0%	0.0%	0.0%	0.0%	$9	300.0%
Interest on indebtedness	0.0%	0.0%	0.0%	41.3%	0.0%	0.0%	58.7%	$1,119	45.9%
Amortization of bond issuance costs	0.0%	0.0%	0.0%	48.4%	0.0%	0.0%	51.6%	$31	96.8%
Matured life income funds	0.0%	0.0%	0.0%	0.0%	0.0%	100.0%	0.0%	$187	33.7%
Other	30.8%	0.0%	30.8%	69.2%	0.0%	0.0%	0.0%	$26	226.9%
Total expenditures and other deductions	72.3%	22.3%	94.7%	1.3%	0.1%	2.4%	1.7%	$40,170	91.8%

(Continued)

EXHIBIT E (Continued)

Everdash Consolidated Statement of Changes in Fund Balances (Continued)

	Unrestricted	Restricted	Current Funds (Note 10)	Loan Funds	Endowment and Similar Funds	Life Income Funds	Plant Funds	Total 19X8	Total 19X7
Excess (deficit) of revenues over expenditures	24.9%	9.2%	34.1%	7.5%	66.7%	6.2%	−14.5%	$3,677	209.2%
Appreciation (depreciation) of investments:									
Realized	0.0%	0.0%	0.0%	−0.3%	99.0%	1.3%	0.0%	$12,255	157.1%
Unrealized	0.0%	0.0%	0.0%	−0.2%	98.2%	1.9%	0.0%	$(16,022)	47.2%
Total appreciation (depreciation)	0.0%	0.0%	0.0%	0.3%	95.7%	4.0%	0.0%	$(3,767)	−310.1%
Transfers among funds:									
Mandatory:									
Provision for debt service									
Loan fund matching grant									
Other:									
For plant assets									
Unrestricted bequests to quasi-endowment									
Transfer of realized gains under spending formula									
Amortization of bond issuance costs									
Other transfers									
Total transfers among funds									
Net increase (decrease)	944.4%	−546.7%	397.8%	−254.4%	3,361.1%	−58.9%	−3,345.6%	$(90)	−21,526.7%
Fund balances, beginning of year	−0.6%	1.8%	1.2%	2.7%	70.6%	5.3%	20.2%	$180,095	89.2%
Fund balances, end of year	−1.1%	2.1%	1.0%	2.8%	68.9%	5.3%	21.9%	$180,005	100.0%

ERR = attempt to divide by zero.

EXHIBIT F **Everdash Selected Ratios**

Everdash College, July 31, 19X8 and 19X7

RATIOS	Unrestricted	Restricted	Current Funds (Note 10)	Loan Funds	Endowment and Similar Funds	Life Income Funds	Plant Funds	Total 19X8	Total 19X7
Current	0.55[10]	42.53	1.42	31.28	9.22	ERR	1.96	4.03[5]	3.03
Quick	0.09[11]	38.84	0.89	7.45	8.23	ERR	1.96	2.54[6]	2.00
Debt to Assets	1.82[12]	0.02	0.71	0.50	0.01	0.00	0.21[8]	0.10[7]	0.11
Long-Term Debt to Capitalization	0.00	0.00	0.00	0.49	0.00	0.00	0.20	0.08	0.08
Times Interest Earned	ERR	ERR	ERR	1.60	ERR	ERR	0.19	4.29[9]	15.97
Asset Turnover (using ending asset balance)	12.52[14]	2.38	6.23	0.08	0.02	0.12	0.00	0.22[13]	0.22
Fixed Asset Turnover	ERR	ERR	ERR	ERR	ERR	ERR	0.00	0.93	1.02
Receivables Turnover	73.10	27.39	52.38	0.13	3.47	ERR	ERR	6.01	6.88
Accounts Payable Turnover	7.57	106.81	9.69	2.10	0.03	ERR	2.14	7.73	5.56
Operating Return on Beginning Fund Balance	−0.82	0.10	0.57	0.06	0.02	0.02	−0.01	0.02[22]	0.05
Return on Fund Balance After Transfers	0.76	0.15	−0.16	0.05	−0.02	0.01	0.08	0.00	0.12

ERR = attempt to divide by zero.

FORMULAS

Cash Flow from Operations = Excess or Deficit of Revenues Over Expenses + Noncash Charges

Fixed Charges = Interest + Lease Payments + Other Fixed Expenses

Current Ratio = Current Assets ÷ Current Liabilities

Quick Ratio = (Current Assets − Nonliquid Current Assets) ÷ Current Liabilities

Debt to Assets = Total Liabilities ÷ Total Assets

Long-Term Debt to Capitalization = (Total Liabilities − Current Liabilities) ÷ (Total Liabilities and Fund Balance − Current Liabilities)

Times Interest Earned = (Cash Flow from Operations + Interest Expense) ÷ Interest Expense

Asset Turnover = Total Revenues and Other Additions ÷ Total Assets

Fixed Asset Turnover = Total Revenues and Other Additions ÷ Net Fixed Assets

Receivables Turnover = Total Revenues and Other Additions ÷ Receivables

Accounts Payable Turnover = Total Expenditures and Other Deductions ÷ (Accounts Payable + Accrued Liabilities)

Operating Return on Beginning Fund Balance = Excess or Deficit of Revenues Over Expenses ÷ Beginning Fund Balance

Return on Fund Balance After Transfers = Net Increase or Decrease in Fund Balance ÷ Beginning Fund Balance

EXHIBIT F Comparative Ratios for Peer Institutions

	Everdash		A		Peer Colleges B	C	D	E
	19X8	19X7	19X8	19X7	19X8	19X8	19X8	19X7
Balance Sheet Ratios								
Expendable fund balance to plant debt[a]	0.0[48]	0.0	1.6	1.6	1.9	0.5[49]	3.7[50]	1.2
Total plant equity to plant debt	3.8[51]	3.6	4.0	3.9	1.7	1.2	71.4	3.1
Revenue Ratios: to Total Educational and General Expense								
Tuition and fees	0.53	0.51	0.77	0.79	0.63	0.74	0.76	0.74
Private gifts and grants	0.18	0.19	0.08	0.07	0.13	0.04	0.09	0.08
Endowment income	0.22	0.20	0.08	0.07	0.37	0.19	0.05	0.16
Expense Ratios: to Educational and General Revenue								
Instruction	0.27[52]	0.22	0.36	0.34	0.36	0.31	0.31	0.29
Institutional support	0.21	0.21	0.15	0.14				
Operations and maintenance	0.13[53]	0.13	0.09	0.11	0.10	0.08	0.12	0.08
Academic support	0.11	0.10	0.08	0.09				
Student services	0.12	0.11	0.13	0.13				
Scholarships and fellowships	0.15[54]	0.14	0.17	0.17	0.11	0.12	0.18	0.15
Per Student Rates (in thousands)								
Endowment	80[55]	83	23	21			18	55
Total education and general expense	22[56]	22	16	15			15	15
Total education and general revenue	23[57]	23	17	15			15	16
Total tuition and fees	12	11	12	11			12	11
Total instruction expense	6	5	6	5				
Total scholarship and fellowship expense	3	3	3	3				
Total students	1,388[58]	1,380	1,700	1,700	2,030	1,990	1,900	1,750

[a]Includes unrestricted current, endowment, and plant fund balances.

DISCUSSION QUESTIONS

1. What are the purposes of the Balance Sheet, Statement of Changes in Fund Balances, and Statement of Current Funds?

2. Describe the kinds of economic events contained in the unrestricted current fund, restricted current fund, plant fund, loan fund, and endowment fund of a college or university.

3. What is the difference between a mandatory and a nonmandatory transfer?

4. What are the main areas of flexibility in accounting for colleges and universities?

5. Do you think depreciation should be recognized as required in SFAS 93 and 99? Does it matter if the depreciation requirements differ between public and private institutions?

6. What are the signals of impending financial distress for a college or university?

7. What nonfinancial measures do you think are important for assessing the condition of an institution?

8. Some people say a college or university should never borrow money. Do you agree or disagree with this statement, and why?

9. What are the main sources of financing for a college or a university? List the strengths and the weaknesses of each source.

10. What factors do the rating agencies use in assigning a grade to a bond? Why are these factors important?

11. What is the current status of higher education in the U.S.?

12. What are the major challenges and opportunities facing higher education, and how should they be met?

EXERCISES

Hart College did not report its financial statements by individual fund, as shown in the Balance Sheet of June 30, 19X1, and the Statement of Revenue and Expenses for the year ended on that date.

Additional information about the financial status of Hart College is presented below:

- The bank loan and accounts payable were all extended for current operating purposes.
- During the course of the year, $10,000 of current funds were spent to acquire additional plant and equipment, and the current fund paid the $30,000 mortgage principal payment and the interest due on the mortgage.
- Endowment fund revenues were unrestricted, but the endowment itself was a true endowment and was to be kept intact. Total cumulative endowment gifts were $690,000.

(Adapted from an AICPA problem.)

Hart College
Balance Sheet
June 30, 19X1

ASSETS

Current assets:

Cash	$ 86,000	
Tuition and fees receivable	48,000	
Inventory of supplies	2,000	$ 136,000
Investments		600,000
Plant and equipment, at cost		830,000
		$1,566,000

LIABILITIES AND FUND BALANCES

Current liabilities:

Bank loans	$125,000	
Accounts payable	9,000	$ 134,000
First-mortgage bonds, 5%, maturing at the rate of $30,000 annually on June 30		450,000
Equity:		
Balance at beginning of year	$975,000	
Excess of revenues over expenses	7,000	982,000
		$1,566,000

Hart College
Statement of Revenues and Expenses
For the Year Ended June 30, 19X1

Revenues:

Tuition	$430,000	
Endowment income	49,000	
Auxiliary enterprise revenue	65,000	
Unrestricted donations	33,000	
Miscellaneous	4,000	$581,000
Expenses:		
Instruction and research	$375,000	
Expenses of auxiliary enterprises	80,000	
Administration	59,625	
Operation and maintenance	35,375	
Bond interest	24,000	574,000
Excess of Revenues over Expenses		$ 7,000

Assignment

1. Convert the Balance Sheet into the fund accounting format recommended by current financial reporting standards for colleges and universities.
2. Convert the Statement of Revenues and Expenses into the fund accounting format recommended by current financial reporting standards for colleges and universities.
3. What, if any, additional information do the fund accounting statements convey about the financial condition of Hart College?
4. As a board member, which form of financial statement would you prefer, and why?

Cases

CASE STUDIES

Case 15.1, a fictitious case, enables you to practice assigning transactions to the appropriate funds in the college and university financial statements. Case 15.2, also a fictitious case, examines the impact of alternative financing options on the financial statements. Case 15.3 blends the financial characteristics of a number of large private universities in a typical set of financial statements. What is Concord University's financial condition?

CASE 15.1 Harriman Center for Communications

Adolph Harriman, a successful communications entrepreneur, was interested in creating a new school devoted to communications, film, and the arts. He located an ideal director for the school and decided to develop a business plan for an independent nonprofit institution. He planned to donate $40,000,000 in cash and a parcel of land with a market value of $1,000,000 to the school. Mr. Harriman planned to restrict some of these funds to insure that the school's activities were carried out in accordance with his intentions. Together, Mr. Harriman and the director developed the following plan for the school's activities during the first two years.

Plan for Year 1

The $40,000,000 cash and the land would be given to the school at the beginning of the first year, with the following stipulations.

(1) $10,000,000 of the cash was to be treated as endowment, but the principal could be expended for important purposes.
(2) $7,000,000 of it was to be restricted for use as scholarship endowment to provide financial aid to students. Mr. Harriman, himself a scholarship student,

David Sherman prepared this case under the supervision of Professor Regina E. Herzlinger. Copyright © 1977 by the President and Fellows of Harvard College. Harvard Business School case 177-1244. Revised January 1993.

wanted his school to attract high-quality students who could not afford to pay tuition.

(3) $23,000,000 would be used to construct a building to house the school and for general operating costs.

(4) The land, valued at $1,000,000, would be donated by Mr. Harriman.

During the first year, the director would develop the curriculum, recruit faculty, select students, and publicize the school and its objectives to the educational and communications community. Expenditures during this year would include:

(5) $18,000,000 for construction of the buildings and purchases of needed equipment and furnishings

(6) $200,000 for staff to develop the curriculum

(7) $100,000 of general administrative expenses, for travel, promotion, etc.

(8) $200,000 of supplies for general and administrative purposes were to be purchased; the end-of-year supply inventory was expected to be $50,000.

(9) Investments would earn 6 percent but not appreciate or depreciate.

(10) A purchase order for $50,000 of supplies would be put in just prior to the end of Year 1, but the supplies would be delivered in Year 2. No liabilities would be outstanding as of the end of the year.

Plan for Year 2

In Year 2, the first class would be enrolled and the school would begin operating. Proposed cash expenditures and other transactions are:

(11) $600,000 will be paid during the year for salaries and fringe benefits. $450,000 of the $600,000 would be for academic salaries, $150,000 for administrative.

(12) $30,000 for maintenance and grounds upkeep.

(13) $50,000 for supplies, teaching materials, etc. All of the supplies would be consumed by year end.

(14) $100,000 for research projects.

(15) $100,000 for library books.

(16) $50,000 in general administration expenses.

(17) Invested funds will earn 6 percent and will appreciate 2 percent. The gains will be realized in cash and distributed to the current fund.

(18) 100 students are expected to enroll in the one year program. Tuition would be $3,000 per student, which would all be received in cash during the year. A total of $90,000 would be granted to students as scholarships.

(19) A colleague of Mr. Harriman's, D. Trump, pledged a gift of $100,000 in Trump Inc. Securities. Mr. Trump was a real-estate investor. His company was currently in bankruptcy and the stock generally considered to be worthless. Mr. Trump, however, had been very successful in the past.

In addition:

(20) Although the building is expected to last for at least 18 years, Mr. Harriman thinks it will have an infinite life if it is well maintained.

(21)   The current fund operations would be financed by a $300,000 loan from the endowment fund at the beginning of the first year. As of the end of the second year, the loan would not yet be repaid. Interest rates for short-term financing were expected to be 9 percent at that time.

ASSIGNMENT

1.   Prepare a balance sheet as of the date Mr. Harriman's gifts were received.
2.   Prepare a Balance Sheet and a Statement of Changes in Fund Balances for the first year of operation.
3.   Prepare a Balance Sheet and a Statement of Changes in Fund Balances for the second year of operation.
4.   Mr. Harriman's financial advisor reviewed the plans and suggested that:
     a.   The school is over-endowed and some of the money could be more usefully donated to other causes without detriment to this project.
     b.   The proposed restrictions on the donated money will unduly restrict the school's ability to optimize its use; giving the funds to a responsible group of trustees without specific restriction would be a better approach.
     Do you agree?
5.   A growing number of organizations that provide post-secondary education programs are being structured as for-profit businesses. Should Mr. Harriman consider starting a for-profit school instead of a nonprofit one? What are the pros and cons of each type of organization?

CASE 15.2 Pepys College

Pepys College is a small liberal arts college that has been operating for 40 years. The past five years have been relatively difficult with rising costs, declining enrollments, continuing deficits, and fewer gifts than were received in the past. Tightened budgetary controls and improved development efforts have resulted in a more optimistic outlook; however, the recent deficits have resulted in cash shortages during the summer and winter periods before tuition revenue is received. The financial manager has generally just held back on paying bills, but she felt that some other means should

David Sherman prepared this case under the supervision of Professor Regina E. Herzlinger.

be found to help relieve these cash binds. Two interesting alternatives developed when she began exploring possibilities with various trustees and local banks.

Mortgage Financing Because the center city building the college occupied was much more valuable than the book value reported in the financial statements, one bank offered to give the college a ten-year mortgage of $500,000 at $9\frac{1}{2}$ percent annual interest with annual payments (of $50,000 principal plus the full year's interest) to begin after one year.

Line of Credit Secured by Endowment Income Another bank offered the college a one-year renewable line of credit against which it could draw up to $200,000 when needed, repaying the loan when funds became available. The bank would charge 10 percent on borrowed funds, would require an average $15,000 compensating cash balance, and would like to have the borrowing secured by the college's endowment. The endowment assets currently earn income at the rate of 6 percent of the market value. Although the restricted endowment assets themselves could not be pledged to repay such a loan, the unrestricted income earned on endowment could be pledged as collateral; however, it might require up to five years to generate $200,000 of unrestricted endowment income to repay such a loan.

Exhibit 1 shows the Balance Sheet at the end of the last fiscal year.

ASSIGNMENT

1. Adjust the Balance Sheet at June 30, 1991, to reflect the mortgage option. Would the interest payments on the mortgage be an expense of the current funds or the plant funds? Prepare the entries to set up the mortgage and record interest and principal payments.
2. Adjust the Balance Sheet at June 30, 1991, to reflect borrowing of only as much cash as is needed under the line of credit option. How would the $200,000 line of credit be disclosed on the financial statements? Prepare the entries to set up the loan and record interest and principal payments.
3. Which of these two alternatives presents a better financial picture?
4. What other alternatives exist, and what alternative would you recommend to the trustees?

EXHIBIT 1 **Pepys College**

Pepys College Balance Sheet
(dollars in thousands—June 30, 1991)

Assets		Liabilities and Fund Balance	
Current Funds			
Cash (overdraft)	$ (35)	Due to plant fund	$ 100
Accounts receivable	160	Accounts payable and accrued	
Other assets	30	liabilities	55
		Other liabilities	200
		Restricted current fund balances:	
		Investment income	230
		Unexpended gifts	270
		Unrestricted fund balance	(700)
Total	$ 155	Total	$ 155
Endowment Funds			
Uninvested cash	$ 22	Endowment funds:	
Investments at market value	5,600ª	For Unrestricted	$3,300
		For Other	2,212
		Quasi-endowment funds:	
		For Operations	-
		For Other	110
Total	$5,622	Total	$5,622
Plant Funds			
Due from current fund	$ 100	Unexpended plant funds	$ 100
Land	300	Funds expended for plant	4,300
Property, plant, and equipment	4,000		
Total	$4,400	Total	$4,400

ªThe cost of the investments is $1,000,000. The investments consist of 100,000 shares of stock in the Pepys Corporation, book publishers. The stock was donated 40 years ago by S. Pepys, president of the Pepys Corporation and founder of the college.

	Market	Cost
1991	$5,600,000	$1,000,000
1990	$5,550,000	$1,000,000

CASE 15.3 Concord University

"We have achieved four years of balanced budgets."

The chancellor's brief letter struck a cautiously optimistic note, stressing his longing for financial stability, his quest for financial integrity, and the university's steady progress toward these goals. He urged his readers to study the financial statements. But the message from the statements did not seem all that positive. For one, the auditors were changed from one Big Six firm to another and the new auditor's opinion noted a new policy of capitalizing library collections as part of the plant fund. And the excess of unrestricted revenues over expenditures and transfers was only $25,000. (See **Exhibits 1** through **4**.) Also, Concord was competing with the state university nearby, which was increasingly rated as one of the country's finest and which charged much lower tuition.

ASSIGNMENT

Analyze the financial condition of Concord University.

Professor Regina E. Herzlinger prepared this case.

EXHIBIT 1   Concord University—Current Funds, Revenues, Expenditures, and Other Charges

| | Year Ended | | | June 30, 1990 |
| | June 30, 1991 | | | |
	Unrestricted	Restricted	Total	Total
REVENUES:				
Educational and general:				
Student tuition and fees	$60,830,685		$ 60,830,685	$ 56,638,219
Governmental appropriations—state	4,108,200		4,108,200	4,137,600
Governmental grants and contracts:				
Federal	1,717,791	$ 9,456,708	11,174,499	11,413,844
State	429,448	798,078	1,227,526	860,372
Gifts and private grants	813,498	2,403,331	3,216,829	1,862,273
Gifts designated for plant funds	595,457	-	595,457	105,276
Endowment income	783,396	1,053,492	1,836,888	2,224,262
Endowment income—designated	161,264	-	161,264	162,989
Sales and services of educational departments	316,964	-	316,964	166,775
Other	1,295,718	9,525	1,305,243	1,728,175
Total educational and general	$71,052,421	$13,721,134	$ 84,773,555	$ 79,299,785
Auxiliary enterprises	22,629,657		22,629,657	21,848,214
Total revenues	$93,682,078	$13,721,134	$107,403,212	$101,147,999
EXPENDITURES AND MANDATORY TRANSFERS:				
Educational and general:				
Instruction and departmental research	$36,008,619	$ 5,371,142	$ 41,379,761	$ 38,137,935
Sponsored research	-	4,805,892	4,805,892	4,737,194
Academic support	7,774,805	351,768	8,126,573	7,555,583
Student services	4,551,047	328,096	4,879,143	4,287,070
Institutional support	10,780,806	183,623	10,964,429	11,522,969
Operation and maintenance of plant	6,741,577	46,796	6,788,373	5,108,423
Student aid	3,600,020	2,111,797	5,711,817	7,035,850
Educational and general expenditures	$69,456,874	$13,199,114	$ 82,655,988	$ 78,385,024
Mandatory transfers for:				
Principal and interest	289,710	36,910	326,620	254,939
Loan fund matching grant	247,144	-	247,144	270,616
Total educational and general	$69,993,728	$13,236,024	$ 83,229,752	$ 78,910,579
Auxiliary enterprises:				
Expenditures	$18,729,055	$ 485,110	$ 19,214,165	$ 18,282,820
Mandatory transfers for:				
Principal and interest	3,059,742	-	3,059,742	3,466,517
Renewals and replacements	314,948	-	314,948	185,747
Total auxiliary enterprises	$22,103,745	$ 485,110	$ 22,588,855	$ 21,935,084
Total expenditures and mandatory transfers	$92,097,473	$13,721,134	$105,818,607	$100,845,663
OTHER TRANSFERS AND ADDITIONS (DEDUCTIONS):				
Excess of restricted receipts over transfers to revenues	$ -	$ 442,799	$ 442,799	$ 380,098
Annuity and life income receipts over expenditures	55,035	-	55,035	5,955
Unrestricted gifts designated	(595,457)	-	(595,457)	112,046
Allocated from (to) quasi-endowment funds	(327,585)	-	(327,585)	89,428
Allocated to plant funds	(737,363)	-	(737,363)	(340,773)
Allocated from restricted funds	45,291	(65,291)	(20,000)	(20,000)
Total other transfers and additions (deductions)	$ (1,560,079)	$ 377,508	$ (1,182,571)	$ 226,754
Net increase in fund balance	$ 24,526	$ 377,508	$ 402,034	$ 529,090

The accompanying notes are an integral part of the financial statements.

EXHIBIT 2 **Concord University—Balance Sheet**

Assets	June 30, 1991	June 30, 1990
CURRENT FUNDS:		
Cash	$ 1,567,152	$ 1,756,707
Accounts receivable—contractual	1,628,909	1,632,946
Accounts receivable (less allowance for doubtful accounts—1991, 615,618; 1990, $332,594)	4,940,297	5,724,761
Due from other funds:		
Plant funds (Note 8)	7,611,488	7,190,780
Endowment funds	188,177	225,134
Inventories	1,542,009	1,552,718
Other assets	2,446,953	2,190,839
Total current funds	$ 19,924,985	$ 20,273,885
LOAN FUNDS:		
Cash	$ 578,472	$ 494,129
Investments—at cost (market value—1991, $62,000; 1990, $56,650)	65,012	65,012
Notes receivable (less allowance for doubtful accounts—1991, $71,626; 1990, $39,596)	13,023,957	10,708,671
Total loan funds	$ 13,667,441	$ 11,267,812
ENDOWMENT AND SIMILAR FUNDS:		
Cash, including time deposits of $190,000 in 1991 and 1990	$ 369,891	$ 328,556
Accounts receivable	1,499,178	1,430,706
Investments (Note 2)	47,167,641	47,551,767
Due from plant funds	176,746	205,114
Total endowment and similar funds	$ 49,213,456	$ 49,516,143
PLANT FUNDS:		
Cash and U.S. government securities on deposit with trustees	$ 9,327,992	$ 8,042,859
Construction funds retained by Belmont State Dormitory Authority	-	103,482
Investments—at cost (market value—1991, $2,029,564; 1990, $140,429)	2,026,415	140,429
	$ 11,354,407	$ 8,286,770
Land, buildings, equipment, and library collection		
Education	$113,242,568	$111,932,084
Library collection	46,362,978	-
Dormitories (less accumulated depreciation—1991, $13,061,608; 1990, $11,906,519)	53,179,970	54,424,086
Other real estate (less accumulated depreciation—1991, $176,149; 1990, $211,494)	1,302,195	2,243,323
	$214,087,711	$168,599,493
Total plant funds	$225,442,118	$176,886,263

The accompanying notes are an integral part of the financial statements.

EXHIBIT 2 (Continued) **Concord University—Balance Sheet (Continued)**

Liabilities and Fund Balances	June 30, 1991	June 30, 1990
CURRENT FUNDS:		
Notes payable	$ 3,509,021	$ 4,665,379
Accounts payable	2,848,999	2,928,937
Accrued liabilities	3,089,759	2,764,064
Deposits, primarily student advance payments	3,683,931	3,450,624
Deferred revenues	3,377,140	3,450,780
	$ 16,508,850	$ 17,259,784
Fund balances:		
Unrestricted deficit	$ (1,089,134)	$ (1,113,660)
Restricted	4,505,269	4,127,761
	$ 3,416,135	$ 3,014,101
Total current funds	$ 19,924,985	$ 20,273,885
LOAN FUNDS:		
Fund balances:		
National Direct Student Loan Funds	$ 12,450,079	$ 10,284,346
Other loan funds—restricted	1,217,362	983,466
Total loan funds	$ 13,667,441	$ 11,267,812
ENDOWMENT AND SIMILAR FUNDS:		
Endowment funds:		
Security deposits held on loaned investments	$ 225,500	$ 1,203,500
Other liabilities	11,250	-
Due to current funds	188,177	225,134
	$ 424,927	$ 1,428,634
Fund balances:		
Endowment	$ 21,140,908	$ 19,581,974
Term endowment	536,752	3,579,220
Quasi-endowment—restricted	2,673,334	2,605,336
Quasi-endowment—unrestricted	15,549,123	13,556,866
	$ 39,900,117	$ 39,323,396
Total endowment funds	$ 40,325,044	$ 40,752,030
Annuity and Life income funds:		
Annuities payable	$ 1,715,931	$ 1,779,919
Fund balances:		
Annuities	$ 2,020,592	$ 1,883,863
Life income	5,151,889	5,100,331
	$ 7,172,481	$ 6,984,194
Total annuity and life income funds	$ 8,888,412	$ 8,764,113
Total endowment and similar funds	$ 49,213,456	$ 49,516,143
PLANT FUNDS:		
Due to other funds:		
Current funds (Note 8)	$ 7,611,488	$ 7,190,780
Endowment and similar funds	176,746	205,114
Long-term debt (Note 3)	67,016,690	70,711,962
	$ 74,804,924	$ 78,107,856
Fund balances:		
Unexpended	$ 3,848,419	$ 1,702,086
Renewal and replacement	2,743,339	1,853,685
Retirement of indebtedness	6,991,127	6,228,814
Investment in plant	137,054,309	88,993,822
	$150,637,194	$ 98,778,407
Total plant funds	$225,442,118	$176,886,263

The accompanying notes are an integral part of the financial statements.

EXHIBIT 3   **Concord University—Changes in Fund Balances**

	Current Funds		Loan Funds	Endowment and Similar Funds		Plant Funds			
	Un-restricted	Restricted		Endow-ment	Annuity and Life Income	Unex-pended	Renewal and Replacement	Retirement of Indebtedness	Investment in Plant
Revenues and Other Additions:									
Educational and general revenues	$71,052,421	$ 11,804							
Auxiliary enterprises revenues	22,629,657								
Governmental grants and contracts		9,913,946							
Private gifts, grants, and contracts		2,813,373	$ 15,886	$ 2,393,445	$ 171,974	$ 20,000	$ 54,415	$ 411,221	$ 120,001
Investment income		1,424,810	29,927	192,140	539,724	12,552	111,542	161,662	
Disposal of plant facilities						1,020,911			
Additions to sinking funds									
Realized gain on investments					62,339				
Adjustment of liability for annuities payable					63,988				
Interest on loans receivable			95,382						
U.S. government advances			2,224,297						
Matured life income and annuity agreement to endowment				26,608					
Expended for plant facilities (including $847,112 charged to current funds expenditures)							191,072		2,532,490
Capitalization of library collection									45,400,000
Reduction of indebtedness									1,454,051
Total revenues and other additions	$93,682,078	$14,163,933	$ 2,365,492	$ 2,612,193	$ 838,025	$1,053,463	$ 357,029	$ 572,883	$ 49,506,542
Expenditures and Other Deductions:									
Educational and general expenditures	$69,456,874	$13,199,114							
Auxiliary enterprises expenditures	18,729,055	485,110							
Loan cancellations and write-offs			$ 121,713						
Loan administrative and collection costs			91,294						
Realized losses on investments				$ 164,781			$ 494		
Expended for plant facilities				176,690		$1,553,364	146,396		
Reduction of indebtedness								$1,224,000	
Interest								1,531,149	
Depreciation on dormitories and other real estate									$ 1,238,044
Payments to annuity and life income participants					$ 484,689				
Matured life income and annuity agreements					110,014				
Disposal of plant facilities									1,013,399
Total expenditures and other deductions	$88,185,929	$13,684,224	$ 213,007	$ 341,471	$ 594,703	$1,553,364	$ 146,890	$2,755,149	$ 2,251,443

(Continued)

EXHIBIT 3 (Continued)

| | Current Funds | | Loan Funds | Endowment and Similar Funds | | Plant Funds | | | |
	Un-restricted	Restricted		Endow-ment	Annuity and Life Income	Unex-pended	Renewal and Replacement	Retirement of Indebtedness	Investment in Plant
Transfers Among Funds—Additions (Deductions):									
Mandatory:									
Principal and interest	$(3,349,452)	$ (36,910)						$3,128,552	$ 257,810
Renewal and replacement	(314,948)					$ (98,209)	$ 597,130	(183,973)	
Loan fund matching grant	(247,144)		$ 247,144						
Allocated from restricted funds	45,291	(65,291)				20,000			
Unrestricted gifts designated	(595,457)			$ 595,457					
Annuity and life income receipts over expenditures	55,035				$ (55,035)				
Allocated from (to) quasi-endowment funds	(327,585)			(2,289,458)		2,617,043			
Allocated to plant funds	(737,363)					107,400	82,385		547,578
Total transfers	$(5,471,623)	$ (102,201)	$ 247,144	$(1,694,001)	$ (55,035)	$2,646,234	$ 679,515	$2,944,579	$ 805,388
Net increase for the year	$ 24,526	377,508	$ 2,399,629	576,721	188,287	$2,146,333	$ 889,654	$ 762,313	$ 48,060,487
Fund balance, July 1, 1990	(1,113,660)	4,127,761	11,267,812	39,323,396	6,984,194	1,702,086	1,853,685	6,228,814	88,993,822
Fund balance, June 30, 1991	$(1,089,134)	$ 4,505,269	$13,667,441	$39,900,117	$7,172,481	$3,848,419	$2,743,339	$6,991,127	$137,054,309

The accompanying notes are an integral part of the financial statements.

EXHIBIT 4 **Edited Notes to the Financial Statements**

Note 2   Endowment and Similar Funds Investments

Investments of the endowment and similar funds are summarized as follows:

	June 30, 1991		June 30, 1990	
	Book	Market	Book	Market
Bonds	$26,266,159	$25,384,387	$26,451,449	$24,869,062
Preferred stock	888,083	965,197	475,375	476,542
Common stock	16,597,660	19,566,359	16,519,060	16,661,272
	$43,751,902	$45,915,943	$43,445,884	$42,006,876
Notes and mortgages receivable	2,254,794		2,918,411	
Real estate (net of accumulated depreciation)	1,160,945		1,187,472	
Total	$47,167,641		$47,551,767	

Income earned on investments of the endowment and similar funds was $2,828,616 in fiscal 1991 and $2,701,574 in fiscal 1990.

Earnings on funds administered by others accrue to the benefit of the university and were approximately $150,000 and $141,000 in fiscal 1991 and 1990, respectively.

Note 3

The university had pledged 110 percent of marketable securities in its endowment fund against a new loan for dormitory construction issued in 1991 and due in 1993 for $14,500,000.

Note 7   Pledges Receivable

Pledges totaling approximately $1,100,000 are not recorded on the financial statements of the university because it is not practicable to estimate the net realizable value of such pledges. Some of the pledges are restricted for specific uses and some are unrestricted. They are due to be collected over the next three fiscal years.

Note 8   Plant Funds Borrowing from Current Funds

It is anticipated that the plant funds borrowing from current funds will be repaid with receipts from the Capital Fund drive, the sale of the university's Steam Station, and proceeds from the termination of several annuity and life income agreements.

Note 9   Contingencies

The university is guarantor of debt obligations aggregating approximately $4,308,162 for the loans of businesses wholly or partially owned by it.

16 Voluntary Health and Welfare and Certain Nonprofit Organizations

No society can be a satisfactory homeland for anyone unless the processes through which it operates work for the people they serve and offer hope and dignity to all. The quest for a better society is the legitimate concern of every individual.

North Americans share a unique tradition of voluntarily assuming responsibility for the conduct of community affairs. Concerned people have long banded together to cope with human problems.[1]

VOLUNTARY HEALTH AND WELFARE ORGANIZATIONS ARE today's Davids, standing up to the Goliaths of homelessness, domestic violence, environmental destruction, poverty, child abuse, natural disasters, and illiteracy. They form the front lines of combat against our worst social problems. Too often their resources are mere slingshots against giants, yet they sometimes work miracles. Some view the grass-roots, help-your-neighbor approaches of these charitable organizations as the salvation of today's society. To many, these organizations embody the cooperation and willingness to help those less fortunate that is an integral part of a democracy. Indeed, they are called *voluntary* because they rely heavily on volunteer donations of money, goods, and time for everything from licking stamps to staffing hotlines and providing legal services. Never have they faced greater challenges.

As voluntary health and welfare organizations care for the human body and mind, cultural, social, and religious nonprofit organizations minister to the human spirit. Accounting standards refer collectively to cultural, religious, affiliative, and all other nonprofit organizations that were not covered by an existing audit guide in 1978 as *certain nonprofit organizations*. The list (see Table 16-1) of nonprofit organization types included in this grouping is not all-inclusive and many of these organization types have little in common.

---

[1]United Way of America, *Standards of Excellence* (Alexandria, VA: United Way of America, September 1988), p. 1.

TABLE 16-1   **Certain Nonprofit Organizations**

Cemetery organizations
Civic organizations
Fraternal organizations
Labor unions
Libraries
Museums
Other cultural institutions
Performing arts organizations
Political parties
Private and community foundations
Private elementary and secondary schools
Professional associations
Public broadcasting stations
Religious organizations
Research and scientific organizations
Social and country clubs
Trade associations
Zoological and botanical societies

Source: Adapted from American Institute of Certified Public Accountants, *Audits of Certain Nonprofit Organizations* (New York, NY: AICPA, 1987), p. 1-2.

This chapter discusses both voluntary health and welfare organizations and certain nonprofit organizations.

SECTOR OVERVIEW

Sectorwide descriptions and statistics for voluntary health and welfare organizations are less meaningful than for the higher education, health care, and governmental sectors because voluntary organizations are more diverse and perform a wider variety of services. Organizations covered by the audit guide for certain nonprofit organizations are even more diverse than voluntary organizations. Nevertheless, the need to compare organizations of different types for some purposes and the fact that some organizations have characteristics of multiple types (such as voluntary, membership, and health care) often are advanced as reasons for common financial reporting standards. The concerns and issues of each type of nonprofit organization are addressed in depth by its trade associations.

History

Charitable organizations have existed almost from the beginning of civilized society. The Old Testament contains references to organizations whose purpose was to help the poor, the abused, and the wretched. The practice of tithing to religious organizations began in those early days. It continues in many religions today, and has a secular parallel in the United Way's plea for everyone give his or her fair share.

Voluntary organizations existed in America as early as the 1650s when several merchants made bequests to the town of Boston to provide an almshouse for care of the poor. Reflecting the early Americans' distaste for government, these voluntary organizations were informal and typically had no legal charter as a corporation.[2] They were followed by a number of small, local voluntary associations usually organized for recipients of a specific age, religion, nationality, or gender, such as the "Home for Little Wanderers" and the "Penitent Females' Refuge." During the nineteenth century, many local agencies *affiliated* with other similar organizations to form nationwide networks and national organizations. For example, the Pennsylvania Society for the Prevention of Tuberculosis, organized in 1892, soon grew to a nationwide organization. The names of large national organizations such as the YMCA, Girl Scouts, and American Red Cross have become household words. Some are single large organizations with local branches, and others are loose federations of individual entities that are related by common membership in a separate national headquarters organization.

The nature and regulation of the services provided by voluntary organizations mirror the changes in society. As the needs of society became more complex, voluntary organizations provided an increasingly larger range of services. For example, voluntary nonprofit organizations sprang into action to address AIDS and homelessness much more quickly than did government programs. Many of the *social services*, or *health and human services* provided by voluntary organizations are now highly regulated and professionalized, and are relied on by a much larger and more diverse segment of society than in earlier years. Voluntary organizations are now formally organized, incorporated, and operated as nonprofit organizations, which are exempt from federal income tax because they are organized to benefit the public rather than for private gain.

Initially, voluntary organizations were individually financed by citizens in the local geographic area. As they grew, some national organizations provided financing to their local branches, and others were financed by the local affiliates. As organizations became larger, their base of support shifted from philanthropic contributions from a few wealthy individuals to a broader and

[2]Peter Dobkin Hall, "A Historical Overview of the Private Nonprofit Sector," in *The Nonprofit Sector*, ed. Walter M. Powell (New Haven, CT: Yale University Press, 1987), pp. 4-5.

more diffuse base of support. Consolidated (or *federated*) fund-raising agencies, such as the United Way, began to raise funds and allocate them to individual member agencies, using agency financial statements to assist them in their allocation decisions. Passage of social legislation in the 1930s substantially increased the amount of governmental funding for voluntary health and welfare organizations. Today's voluntary organizations have a wide variety of funding sources, including direct donations of time, goods, and money from individuals; support from national organizations and consolidated fund raisers; grants from foundations, corporations, and governments; payment for services by both clients and third party payers; the ubiquitous bake or tee-shirt sales; and even income from unrelated businesses that is subject to federal income taxes.

Other types of nonprofit organizations also diversified their funding sources. Government and foundation support of cultural nonprofit organizations, such as museums and performing arts organizations, has grown. The sale of mission-related items has become an important source of revenue for many cultural organizations, as exemplified by the growth in museum shops. Although membership organizations, such as professional associations and fraternal organizations, continue to derive much of their revenues from membership fees, they are becoming more sales and service oriented by charging members and nonmembers for specific items, such as conferences, seminars, and publications.

As nonprofit organizations began to solicit donations from the general public, regulators moved to protect the public interest by requiring registration and filing of information on operations and financial activities. Charitable soliciting by nonprofit organizations is now monitored and regulated by several groups. At the federal level, most nonprofit organizations must file an informational tax return, Form 990, with the U.S. Internal Revenue Service (IRS). At the state government level, the Office of the Attorney General and the Secretary of State are the primary regulatory agencies, and they require nonprofit organizations soliciting funds to file a state informational return that usually differs somewhat from the IRS return.

The *National Charities Information Bureau (NCIB)* in New York City, a private nonprofit organization, analyzes charitable organizations' financial statements and other documents and makes the results of the analysis available to the public. It attempts both to help charities improve performance and to inform contributors about wise giving. The Council of Better Business Bureaus (BBB) Philanthropic Advisory Services (PAS) division in Washington, DC, also publishes standards for charitable solicitations and a report on selected organizations and their compliance with the BBB standards.

The unions that play a strong role in many performing arts organizations also use financial data to argue for a larger share of the financial resources. A large company, such as New York City's Metropolitan Opera, may have 20 or more unions representing its employees, and even small symphonies and ballet companies may have between 2 and 5 unions. If financial statements do not accurately reflect the financial condition of the organization, unions and management may be needlessly deadlocked on issues of compensation. Conflicts between unions and management over increasing compensation versus investment principal have led to bitter strikes and can significantly affect all aspects of a cultural organization's performance.

Sector Structure

The annual revenues of individual organizations range from minuscule to $1 billion for the American Red Cross. One study estimated that in 1984 the entire nonbusiness-nongovernment sector had $250 billion of revenues, $200 billion in current operating expenses, $325 billion in assets, 6.5 million employees, and 89 million volunteers who donated 16 billion hours, the dollar value of which was estimated at $110 billion. It is difficult even to know the exact number of charitable organizations. In 1987 the IRS reported 881,019 total exempt organizations in the 501(c) classification, 400,160 of which were 501(c)(3) organizations. (Tax-exempt organization classifications were described in Chapter 4.) This estimate is thought to be conservative because some organizations are not required to file a return, including those with less than $25,000 annual gross receipts. Another study estimated that in the mid-seventies there were as many as 6 million private nonprofit organizations in the United States. The recent growth in their number is clear; almost 100,000 new 501(c)(3) entities were added to the IRS rolls from 1983 through 1987. Because of its diversity, estimates of the size of the voluntary health and welfare and certain other nonprofits sector are difficult to interpret and of limited reliability. Estimates are very sensitive to differences in measurements and definitions.[3]

Although numerous unaffiliated local organizations exist, the health and human services sector includes many large charities such as those listed in Table 16-2. These organizations typically consist of relatively autonomous local *chapters* affiliated with a national organization. The *National Health Council* and the *National Assembly of National Voluntary Health and Social Welfare Organizations* are associations of major voluntary health organizations.

Voluntary organizations also work closely with the United Way of America, an association of more than 2,300 community-based United Way agencies. Local United Way agencies are best known for raising funds that they distribute to local voluntary agencies. However, they also act as community resources to local nonprofit agencies to assess needs, bring people and

[3]These studies are summarized by Russy D. Sumariwalla, ''Modern Management and the Nonprofit Sector,'' in Chapter 11 of *New Management in Human Services*, ed. Paul R. Keys and Leon H. Ginsberg (National Association of Social Workers, Inc., 1988), pp. 188-193.

TABLE 16-2 **Selected Large National Voluntary
Health and Welfare Agencies**

American Red Cross
Big Brothers/Big Sisters of America
Boys Clubs of America
Boy Scouts of America
Camp Fire, Inc.
Catholic Charities USA
Child Welfare League of America, Inc.
Council of Jewish Federations, Inc.
Family Service America
Girls Incorporated
Girl Scouts of the U.S.A.
Goodwill Industries of America, Inc.
National Mental Health Association, Inc.
National Urban League, Inc.
The Salvation Army
United Neighborhood Centers of America, Inc.
YMCA of the U.S.A.
YWCA of the U.S.A., National Board

Source: United Way of America, National Agencies Division, "Roster of 'Top 17' National Agencies" (Alexandria, VA: United Way of America, July 1990).

organizations together to address them, provide volunteer training, and offer management and technical help. In 1990, they raised $3.1 billion.[4] Charitable giving is big business.

Table 16-3 and Table 16-4 provide statistics on some of the types of organizations in these sectors. Because these data include only organizations with payrolls, they exclude all-volunteer organizations. With this caveat, however, they provide data on the number of establishments, revenues, annual payroll, number of employees, revenues per establishment, revenues per employee, expenses per establishment, expenses per employee, annual payroll per employee, and the number of employees per establishment of various categories of tax-exempt service organizations. (More detailed statistics on organizations of different sizes are also available from the same source.)

Health service organizations clearly represent the largest part of the private tax-exempt sector in terms of both total and average revenue, although not in terms of number of organizations. Excluding health services organizations, this source reported nearly 157,000 nonprofit organizations in 1987,

[4]United Way of America, "Fact Sheet" (Alexandria, VA: United Way of America, August 1990).

TABLE 16-3 **Summary Statistics for Selected Tax-Exempt Organizations**

Kind of Business or Operation, 1987	Establishments (number)	Revenue ($1,000)	Annual Payroll ($1,000)	Paid Employees[a] (number)
Total	**175,829**	**$267,489,778**	**$117,976,275**	**6,736,670**
Total health services	**19,106**	**191,795,083**	**91,588,425**	**4,648,435**
Total except health services	**156,723**	**75,694,695**	**26,387,850**	**2,088,235**
Camps and membership lodging	**3,533**	**604,250**	**155,972**	**16,957**
Selected amusement, recreation, and related services	**12,045**	**8,454,656**	**3,067,846**	**236,105**
Theatrical producers (except motion picture), bands, orchestras, and entertainers	2,132	1,780,521	728,467	56,494
Membership gymnasiums, sports and recreation clubs	6,706	3,807,636	1,510,590	121,423
Fairs	512	269,341	50,515	6,084
Museums, art galleries, botanical and zoological gardens	2,695	2,597,158	778,274	52,104
Legal aid societies and similar legal services	**1,439**	**665,366**	**372,733**	**16,191**
Selected educational services	**4,728**	**1,753,306**	**614,799**	**49,278**
Libraries	1,392	379,957	162,682	13,217
Vocational schools	846	361,231	131,051	10,202
School and educational services, n.e.c.	2,490	1,012,118	321,066	25,859
Social services	**63,002**	**31,551,965**	**11,616,832**	**1,109,536**
Child day-care services	13,822	2,233,489	1,239,094	155,402
Individual and family social services	21,862	8,585,174	3,629,417	312,711
Job training and vocational rehabilitation services	5,005	3,663,736	1,740,595	238,195
Residential care	10,474	6,125,174	2,767,787	240,530
Social services, n.e.c.	11,839	10,944,392	2,239,939	162,698
Selected membership organizations	**67,997**	**23,459,273**	**7,099,938**	**538,868**
Business associations	12,299	6,756,268	1,995,622	87,454
Civic, social, and fraternal associations	40,415	8,568,502	2,778,581	322,933
Other membership organizations	15,283	8,134,503	2,325,735	128,481
Research, testing, and consulting services, except facilities support management	**3,979**	**9,205,879**	**3,459,730**	**121,300**

Includes only establishments with payroll.
[a]For pay period including March 12.
n.e.c. = not elsewhere classified.

Source: Adapted from Bureau of the Census, *1987 Census of Service Industries*, Geographic Area Series, SC87-A-52, November 1989, Tables 1 and 2.

TABLE 16-4 **Averages for Selected Tax-Exempt Organizations**

Kind of Business or Corporation	Revenue per Establishment (dollars)	Revenue per Employee (dollars)	Expenses per Establishment (dollars)	Expenses per Employee (dollars)	Annual Payroll per Employee (dollars)	Employees per Establishment (number)
Total	$ 1,521,306	$39,707	$1,440,512	$37,598	$17,513	38
Selected health services	10,038,474	41,260	9,678,643	39,781	19,703	243
Camps and membership lodging	171,030	35,634	163,221	34,007	9,198	5
Selected amusement, recreation, and related	701,922	35,809	639,055	32,602	12,994	20
Legal aid societies and similar services	462,381	41,095	440,065	39,111	23,021	11
Selected educational services	370,835	35,580	360,972	34,634	12,476	10
Social services	500,809	28,437	426,716	24,230	10,470	18
Child day-care services	161,589	14,372	158,365	14,086	7,973	11
Individual and family social services	392,698	27,454	377,332	26,380	11,606	14
Job training and vocational rehabilitation	732,015	15,381	710,234	14,924	7,307	48
Residential care	584,798	25,465	562,428	24,491	11,507	23
Social services, n.e.c.	924,436	67,268	591,282	43,026	13,767	14
Selected membership organizations	345,005	43,534	323,962	40,879	13,176	8
Business associations	549,335	77,255	535,137	75,258	22,819	7
Civic, social, and fraternal organizations	212,013	26,533	197,972	24,776	8,604	8
Other membership organizations	532,258	63,313	487,191	57,592	18,102	8
Research, testing, and consulting services, except facilities support management	2,313,616	75,893	2,220,967	72,854	28,522	30

Includes only establishments with payroll.
n.e.c. = not elsewhere classified.

Source: Adapted from Bureau of the census, *1987 Census of Service Industries*, Geographic Area Series, SC87-A-52, November 1989, Tables 1 and 2.

with revenues of over $75 billion, nearly 2.1 million employees, and an annual payroll of $26 billion. At $2,313,616, research testing and consulting services had the highest average revenue per establishment. The other types of organizations averaged less than a million dollars per establishment in revenues, with a low of $161,589 for child day-care services. The average number of employees per establishment is less than 50 in all cases. These organizations clearly tend to be smaller than health care and higher education organizations. Excluding hospitals but including other tax-exempt health care organizations, their total expenses grew by 60 percent from 1982 to 1987.[5]

Data Sources

Government data, such as those cited in the tables in this text, are supplied and supplemented by associations for the various types of nonprofit organizations. For example, the American Symphony Orchestra League conducts surveys and reports statistical measures and trends of orchestra financial and program performance. It also provides training and publications related to orchestra management, including accounting and finance. Such trade associations are excellent sources of data and guidance for managers and boards of nonprofit organizations.

The NonProfit Times (Davis Information Group) and Nonprofit World (Society for Nonprofit Organization) are both monthly publications that provide current news and articles on issues relevant to leadership, management, and marketing for nonprofit organizations. Foundation News (The Council on Foundations), also a monthly publication, focuses primarily on issues of philanthropy and charitable giving. These publications provide important information and guidance to managers and board members of all types of nonprofit organizations.

The Support Centers of America (Washington, DC), the United Way of America (Alexandria, VA), and The Independent Sector (Washington, DC) are three organizations that are actively involved in providing support to and collecting data on nonprofit organizations. United Way focuses on organizations supported by local United Way agencies, and the other two cover all types of nonprofit organizations.

Data on individual nonprofit organizations can be acquired from several sources. Most nonprofit organizations must file an IRS Form 990 with the federal government and may also be required to file a publicly available annual report with state attorney generals. Many organizations will provide copies of their annual reports and audited financial statements on request. The NCIB and the Better Business Bureaus PAS division, discussed above, publish both guidelines and reports on selected individual organizations.

[5]Bureau of the Census, *1987 Census of Service Industries*, Geographic Area Series, SC87-A-52 (November 1989), Table 3b.

Opportunities and Challenges

Voluntary and certain nonprofit organizations share the challenges that confront nonprofit organizations in general. Threats to their nonprofit status are continuing. IRS scrutiny has intensified. The level of competition, both with other nonprofits and with for-profit organizations, is increasing. Changing social values and needs require frequent adaptation of program content and structure, as well as financing strategies. Reductions in government spending affect virtually all types of nonprofit organizations. Regulation of both financial and service activities is costly. Reporting to multiple resource providers, each with its own unique forms and formats, increases the complexity of the accounting and other information systems of nonprofit organizations relative to a business of similar size.

These organizations may have the worst of the common nonprofit human resource problems of low salary scales, high burn-out risk, limited career paths, and little management training relative to the private sector. But their greatest, and unique, human resource challenge may be motivating, mobilizing, and effectively directing the large numbers of volunteers who are so vital to their viability. The juxtaposition of volunteers with paid employees has led to strife in more than one organization. Considerable confusion can arise around issues of volunteer time versus compensatory time-off for paid employees. The challenge of recruiting volunteers has increased with women's greater presence in the work force. Indeed, some question whether women should be encouraged to continue selflessly to volunteer time for which they would otherwise be paid. This was made apparent by those Wellesley College students who questioned the choice of Barbara Bush as a speaker at their 1990 graduation ceremony because of her traditional volunteer orientation.[6]

To meet these challenges, nonprofit organizations borrow and adapt a growing number of management techniques, such as financial analysis and cost measurement, from the for-profit world. However, there is widespread recognition that nonprofit organizations differ from businesses in important ways that must be reflected in their management techniques in order to maintain their social orientations. A nonprofit organization cannot be totally driven by either mission or finances; its success depends on both. This requires judicious selection from and blending of the existing for-profit management tools with proven nonprofit management techniques. In addition, it requires the creation of new management tools that will be appropriate for managing the nonprofit organizations of the future.

[6]Abigail Trafford, "SECOND OPINION—Smart Women, Hard Choices," *The Washington Post*, 8 May 1990, Health, p. 6.

FINANCIAL REPORTING STANDARDS

General purpose financial statements provide the primary data available to the public for financial analysis of voluntary and certain nonprofit organizations. The financial statements should enable the reader to measure the resources acquired for and consumed by the provision of services and how well management has performed its stewardship responsibilities. The type and nature of the financial statements are determined by financial accounting and reporting standards, which differ between voluntary and certain nonprofit organizations.

Evolution of Financial Reporting

Accounting for charitable organizations is almost as old as the organizations themselves. Like for-profit accounting, it began with simple statements of cash inflows and outflows and evolved to the complex financial statements prepared today. The changes in accounting practices reflect the increasing complexity and other changes in both the organizations and in the nature of the accounting function.

Changes in the sources of financing since the 1950s increased the importance of the stewardship aspect of accounting for these organizations. The diverse financial supporters want to know whether their support was used prudently and for the intended purposes. The fund accounting used by these organizations enables supporters to monitor and evaluate management's stewardship of the organization's resources by distinguishing restricted from unrestricted resources. The functional basis of accounting, which reports the expenses of each of the organization's programs and of the supporting services required to implement them, was motivated by the need to accurately account for the increasingly complex services provided. Additional impetus toward formalized accounting came from the IRS and state attorney generals, which required charitable organizations to file financial statements that demonstrated their nonprofit nature for the purposes of tax exemption and charitable solicitation.

In 1961, operating under a grant from the Rockefeller Foundation, the Ad Hoc Citizen's Committee formally stated the need for accounting standards for voluntary organizations. A joint project of the National Social Work Assembly and the National Health Council resulted in the 1964 issuance of the first edition of the widely adopted study on uniform accounting, *Standards of Accounting and Financial Reporting for Voluntary Health and Welfare Organizations*. It provided the impetus for the accounting profession's first set of nonprofit standards, published in 1966 by the American Institute for Certified Public Accountants (AICPA) as *Audits of Voluntary Health and Welfare Organizations.*[7]

In 1974 the voluntary audit guide was revised by the Committee on Voluntary Health and Welfare Organizations of the AICPA, in consultation with the Joint Liaison Committee formed by the National Health Council, the National Assembly for Social Policy and Development, and the United Way of America. The revisions were intended to provide more comprehensive information, clarify issues, or inhibit potentially misleading accounting practices. For example, the 1974 guide required voluntary organizations to provide a more comprehensive statement of their financial resources by accounting for the historical cost of their fixed assets and accumulated depreciation on those assets. To curtail potentially misleading accounting practices, it prohibited the use of titles (such as board-designated restricted funds) that might give readers the unwarranted impression that those resources were legally restricted. The guide also clarified the difference between revenue and capital changes to articulate clearly the total amount of support received by the organization.

As of the mid-1970s, there were four nonprofit audit guides, one each for hospitals, colleges and universities, voluntary health and welfare organizations, and state and local governmental units. Each type of nonprofit organization was subject to a different set of reporting standards. Some members of the accounting profession were concerned by the diversity of standards and claimed that it made the statements difficult to use. Some argued that an intelligent lay user could probably not read the various statements. Also, there was little guidance on appropriate accounting principles for the many types of nonprofit organizations that do not fit into any of these categories.

The Accounting Advisory Committee issued a *Report to the Commission on Private Philanthropy and Public Needs*, recommending that a uniform set of accounting principles be adopted by all philanthropic organizations and that a uniform financial report be adopted by every government organization that required annual financial information from philanthropic organizations.[8] The intent was to simultaneously diminish the quantity of paperwork required and delineate a uniform set of accounting principles so that the financial statements of similar organizations could be readily compared. The report was greeted with something less than wild enthusiasm. Neither governmental oversight agencies nor representatives of the various organizations were pleased by the prospect of losing principles that they felt were uniquely tailored to their needs. Also, other members of the accounting profession raised a number of sound technical arguments against some of the specific recommendations. The report was placed on a cool back burner.

[7]American Institute of Certified Public Accountants, *Audits of Voluntary Health and Welfare Organizations* (New York, NY: AICPA, 1966).
[8]Accounting Advisory Committee, *Report to the Commission on Private Philanthropy and Public Need,* (1974).

In 1978, to address the lack of standards for a substantial portion of the private nonprofit sector, the AICPA issued Statement of Position (SOP) 78-10, *Accounting Principles and Reporting Practices for Certain Nonprofit Organizations*.[9] In 1981, the AICPA Nonprofit Organizations Subcommittee issued *Audits of Certain Nonprofit Organizations*, which incorporates SOP 78-10 as an appendix.[10] This guide provided accounting standards for all types of nonprofit organizations not covered by the already existing guides, except for types of entities that operate essentially as commercial businesses for the direct economic benefit of members or stockholders. Table 16-1 lists several, but not necessarily all, of the types of nonprofit organizations that are covered by this guide. Although each type of organization may use certain unique account and statement titles, all are required to present the same financial statements and to prepare them using the same accounting principles.

A subsequent addition to financial reporting standards for voluntary and certain nonprofit organizations governs reporting costs of activities that include a fund-raising appeal and also serve some other program or management and general purpose. In 1987, the AICPA issued Statement of *Position 87-2*, "Accounting for Joint Costs of Informational Materials and Activities of Not-for-Profit Organizations That Include a Fund-Raising Appeal."[11] The AICPA reissued both the voluntary and the certain nonprofit audit guides, incorporating *SOP 87-2* as an amendment thereto.

The AICPA has also produced what it calls a nonauthoritative technical practice aid, *Checklists and Illustrative Financial Statements for Nonprofit Organizations*.[12] It covers the same types of organizations and is otherwise consistent with the voluntary and certain nonprofit audit guides. It goes beyond the audit guides by providing more detailed checklists for audit steps, and by incorporating the effects of financial reporting and auditing standards that have been issued since the last publication of the audit guides. Although it has no official or authoritative status, it provides useful guidance on how subsequent pronouncements, such as FASB *Statement No. 87*[13] on pension reporting, affect standards promulgated in the audit guides.

[9]American Institute of Certified Public Accountants, Accounting Standards Division, *Statement of Position 78-10, Accounting Principles and Reporting Practices for Certain Nonprofit Organizations* (New York, NY: AICPA, 1978).

[10]American Institute of Certified Public Accountants, *Audits of Certain Nonprofit Organizations*, (New York, NY: AICPA, 1978, 1981, 1987).

[11]American Institute of Certified Public Accountants, *Statement of Position 87-2*, "Accounting for Joint Costs of Informational Materials and Activities of Not-for-Profit Organizations That Include a Fund-Raising Appeal" (New York, NY: AICPA, 1987).

[12]American Institute of Certified Public Accountants, Technical Information Division, *Checklists and Illustrative Financial Statements for Nonprofit Organizations: A Financial Reporting Practice Aid* (New York, NY: AICPA, November 1990).

[13]Financial Accounting Standards Board, *Statement of Financial Accounting Standards No. 87*, "Employers' Accounting for Pensions" (Norwalk, CT: FASB, December 1985).

Since the 1960s, the public accounting profession and voluntary health and welfare sector representatives have worked together very closely, presenting a united front in their agreement on accounting standards. The audit guide provides CPA's with direction on accounting issues and audit practices that they need to perform a financial audit. *Standards of Accounting and Financial Reporting for Voluntary Health and Welfare Organizations* (commonly known as the "Black Book") provides the greater level of detail needed by the managers and accountants of United Way affiliated and other nonprofit organizations.[14] It elaborates on the accounting standards of the audit guide. The United Way of America's *Accounting and Financial Reporting* is relatively readable yet detailed, extending beyond financial reporting standards to include a general introduction to nonprofit accounting and the operation of a financial system.[15] These publications are required reading for nonprofit accountants and useful references for nonprofit managers and directors. Many national social service and funding agencies provide additional guidance to local organizations about accounting, strategic planning, budgeting, evaluation, and other management systems.

Because nonprofits exist to improve the quality of life, it is important to measure their effects on individual or societal well-being in addition to measuring the financial results of their operations. To evaluate performance, managers and many external financial statement users need information on outcome and output quality and quantity, units of input other than dollars, and costs of outputs. Nevertheless, *performance measures*, or *service efforts and accomplishments* (SEAs), are not reported in the audited general purpose financial statements and are not expected to be in the foreseeable future. Although their importance is widely recognized, progress toward requiring audited statements that report outputs and outcomes has been slow.

In 1987 the Committee on Nonprofit Performance Measures undertook an assessment of the current state of performance measurement, as reported in *Measuring the Performance of Nonprofit Organizations: The State of the Art*.[16] It provides a general conceptual framework for performance measures and discusses sample measures for several specific types of nonprofit organizations. It concludes with suggestions for improving performance measurement and reporting, instruments and sample reports, an extensive annotated bibliography, and a discussion of the methodology, including a list of the

[14]National Health Council, Inc., National Assembly of National Voluntary Health and Social Welfare Organizations Inc., and United Way of America, *Standards of Accounting and Financial Reporting for Voluntary Health and Welfare Organizations*, 3d ed. (New York, NY: National Health Council, Inc., 1988).

[15]United Way of America, *Accounting and Financial Reporting: A Guide for United Ways and Not-for-Profit Human-Service Organizations*, 2d ed. (Alexandria, VA: United Way of America, 1989).

[16]American Accounting Association, Government and Nonprofit Section, Committee on Nonprofit Entities' Performance Measures, *Measuring the Performance of Nonprofit Organizations: The State of the Art* (Sarasota, FL: American Accounting Association, 1989).

persons and organizations contacted for the study. It provides an excellent review of the current state of performance evaluation, as well as guidance for improving performance measurement and reporting.

Some SEA performance data must be reported to the IRS in Form 990, Part III, "Statement of Program Service Accomplishments." The organization must describe what it achieved in carrying out its exempt purposes, the services provided, and the number of persons benefitted or other relevant information for each of its four largest programs. Related expense amounts for each program are also required to be provided by 501(c)(3) and (4) organizations. Interest in performance data is growing among government agencies and voluntary groups that review and evaluate charities.

Many organizations now include unaudited data about their accomplishments in internal statements, annual reports, and statements for federated fund raisers that support their requests for funding from major donors. For example, the 1989-90 Metropolitan Opera Association Annual Report discusses in detail the Met's mission-related accomplishments, including its re-entry into the recording field and receipt of a 1990 Grammy, its fiftieth anniversary broadcast, television broadcasts, and various performances and programs.[17] Performance measurement and reporting should continue to increase and improve.

Standards for Voluntary Health and Welfare Organizations

As with the audit guides for other sectors, the standards prescribe the funds to be used, the type and contents of the general purpose financial statements, and the accounting for specific items and transactions that may be treated differently by voluntary organizations than by other nonprofits. Many of these items deal with revenue recognition issues, an area of great diversity among nonprofit organizations. The illustrative financial statements and notes adapted from AICPA publications (Exhibit A) provide examples of financial statements that conform to the current standards, including relevant pronouncements issued subsequent to the audit guide.[18] Refer to Exhibit A for examples of how the items discussed in the following sections are displayed in the financial statements.

Fund Types   The fund definitions used by voluntary organizations are consistent with those of other nonprofits. The most commonly used fund

[17]*Metropolitan Opera Association Annual Report 1989-1990* (New York, NY: Metropolitan Opera Association, Inc., 1990).

[18]American Institute of Certified Public Accountants, *Audits of Voluntary Health and Welfare Organizations* (New York, NY: AICPA, 1988), pp. 42-50; and AICPA, *Checklists and Illustrative Financial Statements*, pp. 117-125.

types are current unrestricted, current restricted, plant, and endowment; life income and custodial funds also may be used. Investments other than true endowments are reported in the appropriate unrestricted or restricted fund, as with all other types of nonprofit organizations except higher education institutions.

Financial Statements   Voluntary organizations are required to present a *Balance Sheet* and a *Statement of Support, Revenue, and Expenses and Changes in Fund Balances* for each fund, a *Statement of Functional Expenses*, and *Notes* to those financial statements. The Statement of Functional Expenses, which is unique to voluntary organizations, reports expenditures by object class for each function. A total of all funds column is generally shown for the revenues and expenses in the activity statement but is not shown for the changes in fund balances. A total of all funds column is optional for the balance sheet and is typically shown only when a columnar balance sheet format is used. If significant subgroups exist within any fund type, supplemental schedules may be required for compliance reporting to grantors and may be included in the financial statements. For example, restricted funds may be required to show the activities related to each specific grant.

The Balance Sheet in Exhibit A (shown on page 663) presents the financial position of the organization. The assets most commonly owned by voluntary organizations are cash, investments, pledges receivable, grants receivable, accounts receivable, inventories, accrued interest, prepaid expenses, and fixed assets. Common liabilities are accounts payable, accrued salaries and related expenses, grants payable, deferred revenue (pledges, contributions, or grants explicitly designated for future periods), and notes or mortgages payable. Amounts representing interfund borrowing due from (assets) and due to (liabilities) other funds are also common in voluntary organizations.

At December 31, 19X2, the sample current unrestricted fund had cash of $2,207,000, the current restricted fund had only $3,000, the plant fund had $3,000, and the endowment funds had $4,000 in cash. The total cash held by the organization at December 31, 19X2, is not shown on this Balance Sheet, which is typical of the layered format. The user must calculate the total cash amount of $2,217,000 ($2,207,000 + $3,000 + $3,000 + $4,000). Although the audit guide shows a layered statement Balance Sheet, some other standard setting documents use a columnar statement format, with a total column for the current and prior years. A columnar format is acceptable under current standards and would be required under the recommended new standards.

The *designated* portions of fund balance in the current unrestricted fund are shown at the discretion of the reporting organization and indicate the programmatic or investment purposes for which the board intends to use the resources. The restricted current fund balances are distinguished by the purposes for which they must be used. This breakdown often is supplemented by a note that provides more detailed information. The fund balances and the detailed resource flows that caused the changes in them during the year are reflected in the activity statement.

In the plant (or land, building, and equipment) fund, the amount of mortgage principal owed to the mortgagor was $32,000 at December 31, 19X2, and $36,000 at December 31, 19X1. The mortgage might be classified into its current and long-term portions, and the mortgage payment schedule and terms should be disclosed in a note. The expended fund balance plus the mortgage payable equals the net book value of the land, buildings, and equipment. The expended and unexpended portions of the plant fund balance must be clearly reported.

The primary activity statement title used by the AICPA is the *Statement of Support, Revenue, and Expenses and Changes in Fund Balances*. The United Way standards omit the word "Support." The title is sometimes abbreviated to *Statement of Changes in Fund Balances* or varied in other ways. Alternatively, the same information may be presented in two separate statements, a *Statement of Revenue and Expenses* and a *Statement of Changes in Fund Balances*. The term "fund balances" would be replaced with the term "net assets" under the proposed standards; both mean exactly the same thing.

Whatever its title or structure, the primary activity statement tells the story of all the economic transactions that occurred during the period in each type of fund, and usually also provides comparative total amounts for the preceding year. It is divided into three major sections: revenue (or public support and revenue), expenses, and other changes in fund balance.

Public support includes all resources donated or granted to the organization by outside individuals or agencies, whether to current, endowment, or plant funds. During 19X2, the Sample Voluntary Health and Welfare Service received net contributions and pledges of $3,928,000 directly from the public. Gross contributions and pledges of $4,123,000 are calculated by adding the $195,000 estimated as uncollectible to the net amount reported in the statement. Of the net contributions, $3,764,000 were for current operating purposes with no restrictions on their use, $162,000 were restricted to use for only certain types of current operations, and $2,000 constituted an addition to the principal of the endowment fund. Additional contributions of $72,000 restricted for the building fund are shown as a separate line item in this example.

Special events proceeds are reported net of the direct costs of items furnished to donor-participants or their designees, with the direct costs disclosed parenthetically. For example, if a benefit dinner dance brings in $285,000 but costs $181,000 for food and entertainment, only the $104,000 of net revenues is reported as the proceeds of the special event, as shown in Exhibit A. Other indirect expenses of promoting and conducting special events, such as printing tickets or mailing invitations, are to be reported as fund-raising expenses. The distinction between direct costs and fund-raising expenses is subject to judgment. Essentially, the proceeds of special events are reported as net gains (inflows less outflows) rather than as total revenues, with expenses reported separately. This is consistent with the reporting of gains or losses recommended in the recent health care audit guide.

Legacies and bequests of $92,000 left to the organization on the donor's death are shown separately from other gifts. Distinguishing them helps the statement users to forecast future revenues and support more accurately because they tend to fluctuate more from year to year than other contributions.

The $275,000 of public support received from federated and nonfederated campaigns is the amount received indirectly from the public via organizations, such as the United Way, that primarily raise funds and transfer the proceeds to organizations that provide program services. Although the entire amount was unrestricted in 19X2, part or all of it is sometimes restricted or designated as additions to the plant fund for acquiring fixed assets. It is to be reported net of the related fund-raising expenses incurred by the campaign. The necessary information should be provided by the federated fund raiser.

Revenue accounts for all the earned income of the organization. It typically consists of membership dues, fees for services, sales of products, and investment earnings. Many organizations generate revenues by performing services and issuing memberships for which dues are paid. If the organization provides no services to its members, the dues are immediately accounted for as revenues. If membership includes a right to receive services, then membership receipts are initially recorded as deferred revenues (liabilities) and revenues are recognized only when the services are delivered.

As with other types of nonprofits, investment income is limited to such items as interest, dividends, royalties, and rental income and is generated by investments in income producing securities, accounts, or property. It is reflected directly as a revenue in the fund that has the right to use it and may be restricted or unrestricted.

The realized gain (or loss) on investment transactions reflects the net gain (or loss) on those investments actually traded or sold during the current year. Because this organization accounts for investments at cost, only· realized gains or losses are reported; a gain or loss is recognized only when the investment is sold or traded. If investments were accounted for at market value, this statement would also show unrealized gains or losses. An unrealized gain (or loss) on investments reflects the appreciation (gain) or decline (loss) in the market value of the unsold investments. Note 2 shows the effect of carrying investments at market instead of cost.

Gains and losses are reflected in the endowment or other fund that owned the investments. Gains on quasi-endowment investments are reflected directly in the funds that own the investments and are immediately available for use in the activities conducted by those funds without further board action. Gains on true endowment investments are reflected in the endowment fund. Under the total return concept, before gains can be made available to the current or other funds for any purpose other than reinvestment, they must be transferred to a current fund by board action and shown as transfers on the Statement of Changes in Fund Balances. The transfer is from the fund where the gains were earned to the fund in which they are to be used.

Miscellaneous revenue is a catch-all category for those relatively small items that do not fit any existing specific categories and that are not large enough to warrant separate specific categories. Common examples include occasional sales of literature, fees for speakers (although this could also be a fee for service, depending on the organization), rental of space for community group meetings, vending machine income, rental of films, etc. Any significant amounts should be separately identified instead of being included in miscellaneous. Total revenue plus total support yields the total support and revenue amount for each fund and for the total of all funds of $4,867,000.

Expenses are accounted for in voluntary organization activity statements by fund, object class, and function (the purpose of the expense). The object-of-expense (or natural) classification refers to the nature of the good or service for which the resources were expended, such as salaries, occupancy expenses, and depreciation of buildings and equipment. Other types of nonprofits are required to report expenses either by function or object, but not both.

Functional classifications are divided into program and supporting activities. *Program services* reflect the mission-oriented social service activities of the organization. Individual programs are often separately identified and accounted for in the financial statements as subgroups under the general program service classification. *Supporting services* reflect costs of activities that are only indirectly related to the organization's mission, but are necessary to its overall successful functioning. Activities undertaken to induce others to contribute resources for which the contributor receives no direct economic benefit are classified as *fund raising*. They are somewhat analogous to the sales and marketing classification found in the operating statements of businesses. Activities necessary to the operations of the organization as a whole, but not directly related to fund raising or to any specific program, are classified as *management and general*. This is the same term commonly used in business organizations. It commonly includes such items as general legal and accounting services and the executive director's salary and staff.

An organization has one or more classes of program services. Separate identifiable service functions should be reported as different programs. Program service subclasses are diverse and vary among organizations according to the purposes for which they are organized, the types of services they provide, and how management views the mission and operations. The resulting variety limits the comparability of different organizations. Examples of common program services include direct client services, community education, professional training, and research.

The United Way of America has developed a taxonomy of social goals and human service programs, called *UWASIS II* codes.[19] The program account codes are organized and numbered on the basis of the broad goals shown in Table 16-5. Detailed account descriptions and numbers for the chart of accounts and United Way of America Accounts Coding System (UWAACS) are provided by the United Way's *Accounting and Financial Reporting*.[20] At present, these publications provide primary guidance on program and object of expense classification for voluntary health and welfare organizations.

TABLE 16-5 **United Way Goals**

  I. Optimal income security and economic opportunity
 II. Optimal health
III. Optimal provision of basic material needs
 IV. Optimal opportunity for the acquisition of knowledge and skills
  V. Optimal environmental quality
 VI. Optimal individual and collective safety
VII. Optimal social functioning
VIII. Optimal assurance of the support and effectiveness of service through organized action

The Sample Voluntary Health and Welfare Service reported four distinct types of program services: research, public health education, professional education and training, and community services. These are summed to calculate total program services expense of $3,154,000, which was predominantly unrestricted. Research is the largest program in terms of expense dollars, with $1,257,000 of unrestricted current operating expenses and $155,000 of restricted current operating expenses. The only other research expense was $2,000 of depreciation in the land, building, and equipment fund, for a total research expense of $1,414,000 in 19X2, up $49,000 from $1,365,000 in 19X1. The other program service categories had only current unrestricted and depreciation in land, building, and equipment fund expenses. Thus, all current restricted funds that were used were required to be used for research.

In these statements, supporting expenses are charged only to the current unrestricted and plant funds. Fund-raising expenses typically are charged to current unrestricted. They also may be charged to plant or endowment if special fund-raising efforts are undertaken to generate revenues for either

[19]Russy D. Sumariwalla, *UWASIS II: A Taxonomy of Social Goals & Human Service Programs*, 2d ed. (Alexandria, VA: United Way of America, 1976).
[20]United Way, *A Guide for United Ways*, pp. 242-268.

either of those purposes and if fund-raising costs may legally be paid for with the proceeds. Some of the management and general expenses often are charged to current restricted.

Total supporting service expense and total program expense are added to calculate the total expenses of $4,382,000. Total expenses are subtracted from total support and revenue to compute the excess (or deficiency) of public support and revenue over expenses. The total excess of $485,000 can be calculated by summing the individual fund amounts or by subtracting total expenses from total revenue. This amount may be shown on the activity statement, although it is not shown in Exhibit A.

The *other changes* section accounts for interfund transfers and any return of funds to donors. Interfund transfers have no impact on the total organization; they merely reflect permanent movements of capital among funds within the organization. The most common transfers reflect decisions to purchase plant assets from current funds and to use endowment investment appreciation under the total return concept, causing a transfer from the endowment fund to current funds. Property and equipment acquisitions of $17,000 by the current unrestricted fund resulted in a transfer (deduction) from the current unrestricted fund balance and an equal transfer (addition) to the plant fund. The transfer of realized endowment fund appreciation represents the portion of the realized endowment fund appreciation ($100,000) that the board has made available for current operations, according to the endowing document, organization policy, and applicable state and local law. It reduces the endowment fund balance and increases the fund balance of the current unrestricted fund.

Returned to donor ($8,000) represents restricted funds that were returned to the donor because they were not expended in the manner or time period to which they were restricted. Such a return reduces the fund balance. The excess and other changes in fund balances are added to the beginning of year fund balances to calculate the ending fund balances.

The Statement of Functional Expenses is unique to voluntary organizations. It shows what objects of expense were charged to each program and supporting function. The amounts in the total expense row, the bottom row of the Statement of Functional Expenses, are equal to the amounts in the 19X2 total all funds column for expenses in the Statement of Support, Revenue and Expenses and Changes in Fund Balance. The proposed standards would eliminate the requirement to present this statement although it could be presented as a supplementary statement. Some funding agencies strongly support retaining it and probably would require its inclusion in financial statements submitted for their evaluation purposes. Because controllability of expenses is more strongly related to object than to function, the information provided by this statement is useful for sustainability analysis.

Of the total $1,414,000 research expense in 19X2, $45,000 was spent for salaries, $4,000 for employee health and retirement benefits, $2,000 for telephone and telegraph, and so on, for a total of $1,412,000 in expenses before depreciation. The $2,000 depreciation on fixed assets used for research is added to calculate the total research program expense of $1,414,000. This breakdown is shown for each separate program and for the total of all programs, for each type of supporting service and the total of all supporting services, and for total 19X2 expenses, with the comparative total expenses for 19X1.

Pledges and Cash Donations Promises (*pledges*) to make future contributions are both common and significant for many voluntary organizations. They should be recorded as assets valued at the amount the organization actually expects to collect (their *net realizable value*). As with other receivables, pledges should only be recorded if there is evidence of both their existence and likelihood of collection. In the past, pledges were seldom reflected in the financial statements, and many organizations are reluctant to include them. The proposed Statement of Financial Accounting Standards (SFAS), *Accounting for Contributions Received and Contributions Made and Capitalization of Works of Art, Historical Treasures, and Similar Assets*, would require pledges to be reported.[21]

The *write-down* of pledges for uncollectible amounts should be based on the organization's past experience with pledge collection and any other relevant information. The amount of pledges receivable on the Balance Sheet reflects all pledges made in the current and prior years and not yet received or written off as uncollectible. Pledges should be reviewed carefully at least once per year and should be written off when considered to be uncollectible. Allowances for uncollectible amounts should be adjusted as needed to reflect changing collection experience.

Pledges and cash donations should be recorded as revenue when a pledge is made or when a cash donation is made without a pledge, unless their use is restricted to a future period. If the donor states that a pledge or cash donation is intended for use in a future period, it should be recorded as *deferred revenue* when received and as revenue only in the period during which it becomes available for use. Pledges scheduled to be paid in installments are reflected as revenue in the period they are scheduled to be collected. In the absence of any evidence of donor intent on their timing, pledges should be assumed to be for the current period.

Restricted Revenue The proceeds of restricted gifts and grants are recorded as revenue when the organization has received them and they are available for use. They are thereby included in the excess (deficit) of revenue and support over expenses and in the end of period restricted fund balance

---

[21]Financial Accounting Standards Board, *Exposure Draft, Proposed Statement of Financial Accounting Standards, Accounting for Contributions Received and Contributions Made and Capitalization of Works of Art, Historical Treasures, and Similar Assets* (Norwalk, CT: FASB, October 31, 1990).

if they are available for use and not restricted to future periods. The logic is that restricted resources are available for current use whether spent or not, and full accountability requires them to be recognized by reflecting such amounts as revenue and support. Those who disagree express concern that recognizing such amounts as revenue and support overlooks the legal obligation to return such amounts if they are not expended for the restricted purpose. Also, large amounts received near the end of the period may significantly distort the financial statements of the organization. This accounting treatment differs from that of health care providers and colleges and universities.

Some resources, such as government grants, are not earned until the expenditures for which they are designated have been made, and they must be returned to the granting agency if they are not expended for the designated purpose within a specified time frame. Although some argue that they should be reported as deferred liabilities, they are reported as revenue if they are available for use. Other items, such as interest and dividends earned on quasi-endowments restricted for scholarships, are not likely to be returned to the donors under any foreseeable circumstances, and will remain in the hands of the organization until they are expended for the intended purpose. Recognition as revenue, and the resulting balance sheet classification as fund balance, seems most appropriate to such resources under these circumstances. Under current standards, voluntary organizations recognize virtually all restricted grants as revenue immediately. It would seem more appropriate to carefully consider the economic, legal, and practical realities of each activity and reflect them appropriately in the financial statements.

Voluntary organizations record donations restricted to nonoperating purposes as support in the receiving fund. This treatment stands in contrast to that of other types of nonprofit organizations, which call such donations *capital additions* and show them in a separate section of the activity statement to highlight the fact that they are increases in the permanent capital of the organization rather than for use in operations.

Donated Goods and Service   Just as individuals, corporations, foundations, and government agencies provide resources in the form of cash to voluntary organizations, they also frequently donate goods (materials) or services. At one time, most voluntary organizations used primarily volunteer labor although this is now less common. Omitting the value of significant donated materials and services from the financial statements would understate the cost of performing the organizations' activities. The audit guide for voluntary organizations requires that donated services, if significant, be recorded when all of the following circumstances exist:

(1) The services performed are a normal part of the program or supporting services and would otherwise be performed by salaried personnel.

(2) The organization exercises control over the employment and duties of the donors of the services.

(3) The organization has a clearly measurable basis for the amount.[22]

Traditionally, organizations staffed by personnel of a religious order have tended to have the largest reportable amounts of donated labor.

Types of services that are generally not recorded as contributions, even though they may be significant, include supplementary efforts of volunteer workers provided directly to beneficiaries of the organization (auxiliary activities or other services that would not otherwise be provided), periodic services of volunteers for fund drives, and professional personnel for research and training (which are not usually subject to a sufficient degree of operating supervision and control). However, the value of volunteers performing administrative functions that would otherwise be done by salaried personnel may be recorded. The financial statements should clearly disclose the methods used to evaluate, record, and value donated services and which donated services are and are not reflected.

Investments and Related Income and Earnings   *Investments* in securities and other items appear on the balance sheet of the fund to which they belong and may be valued at cost or market, according to the audit guide. On the other hand, SFAS 12 explicitly exempts nonprofit organizations from the requirement to use the lower of cost or market method for valuing securities.[23] Whatever basis of valuation is chosen, it must be used by all funds for all investments. The method used must be clearly explained in a footnote, and sufficient information must be provided to allow the statement user to convert the statements to another valuation method. Purchased investments are initially valued at the cost of acquiring them, including brokerage fees and other purchase-related payments. The cost of donated investments is determined by their fair market value at the date of the gift.

The market value of the total investment portfolio at the balance sheet date is compared to its cost. Valuation is done on the basis of the combined values of all investments, not individual ones. Under the cost basis, securities typically continue to be reported at cost until they are sold. Securities must be written down to market if their value has suffered a permanent impairment but not if a decline in market value is expected to be temporary. Thus, if the market value is significantly below cost and is expected to remain so, the investments must be written down to their current market value and a loss recorded to reflect the decline in market value. Investments may

[22]AICPA, *Audits of Voluntary Health and Welfare Organizations*, p. 21.
[23]Financial Accounting Standards Board, *Statement of Financial Accounting Standards, No. 12*, ''Accounting for Certain Marketable Securities,'' (Norwalk, CT: FASB, December 1975), paragraph 5.

not be written back up if the market value later increases. Gains are recognized under the cost basis only when the security is sold.

With *lower of cost or market* valuation, investments are written down to market (if it is lower than cost) even if the decline is expected to be temporary. They are written back up to (but not above) cost if their value subsequently increases. The market basis of valuation adjusts investments up or down to the market value at each balance sheet date, without regard to their cost. It can be argued that carrying investments at market value best reflects how well the organization has managed its invested resources. The effects of investments on the activity statement were discussed above.

Fixed Assets and Depreciation   The 1974 audit guide required voluntary organizations to capitalize and depreciate fixed assets, which are valued at original cost or at fair market value on the date they were donated. Consequently, capitalization and depreciation of fixed assets are fairly well accepted in voluntary organizations. Fixed assets used for program or supporting services are reported in a separate land, building, and equipment (plant) fund, along with any unexpended amounts contributed by donors specifically for the purchase of fixed assets. The valuation basis of fixed assets should be clearly described in the notes. If adequate cost records are not available, appraisals of historical cost or fair value at the date of a gift are acceptable. Depreciation is recorded as an expense in the plant fund.

Contributed fixed assets should be reported in a donor-restricted fund if the assets have donor-imposed restrictions that prevent their being disposed of currently or being used in normal program or supporting services. When the restrictions lapse or specified conditions have been met, the assets should be transferred to the plant fund if they are to be used in the organization's normal operations or to unrestricted fund investments if they are to be held for resale or other use as investments. Fixed assets donated without restrictions should be reported as support and investments in the unrestricted fund if they are being held for conversion to cash or the production of income.

Allocating Joint Costs of Informational Materials   One of the often quoted and closely monitored measures of voluntary performance is *fund raising as a percentage of expenses*, or closely related measures such as *fund raising as a percentage of revenues* or *fund raising as a percentage of contributions*. Essentially, these measure how much of the resources of the organization are spent on raising more money instead of on providing program services. For example, in "Charity Checklist," Jim Cook, *Forbes'* vigilant observer of nonprofit organizations, computed the ratio of fund-raising expenses to public support for many nonprofits. He noted that the American Heart Disease Prevention Foundation of Fairfax, Virginia, spent 40 percent for fund raising![24]

[24]Jim Cook, "Charity Checklist," *Forbes* (October 28, 1991): 180.

Nonprofit organizations traditionally have communicated with the public by direct mail, and are increasing their use of other media, such as billboards, radio, television, and newspaper advertisements. Such communications, which often serve both fund-raising and program functions, are referred to as informational materials. In 1987 the AICPA issued SOP 87-2, which stated the conditions under which costs of informational materials could be allocated and required footnote disclosure of the allocated amounts.[25] The prior practices varied widely because standards were ambiguous and conflicting. Various standards were interpreted to require either that all expenses of any communication that included a fund-raising appeal be charged to fund-raising expense, or that informational costs could be allocated at management discretion. These different interpretations led to wide variation in treatment and reporting practices.

SOP 87-2 clarifies GAAP for public communication costs, makes it consistent with other cost allocation standards, and provides criteria for determining whether a nonfund-raising function or purpose has been served. It states that joint costs of informational activities and materials should be allocated among the functions served if and only if it can be demonstrated that a bona fide management or program function has been served in conjunction with an appeal for funds. The three key indicators of the function served are the message content, the audience to whom it is directed, and any other available evidence of the intent of the communication. The actual content of the communication and the target audience also provide supporting or refuting evidence of whether the intentions stated in such documentation were followed and realized.

These standards became effective for years beginning after December 31, 1987. Managers and auditors of charitable organizations need to review informational materials and communications in light of the new standards to determine whether they meet the tests for allocation eligibility.[26] Financial statement users must be aware that such cost allocation is necessarily a matter of judgment and interpret the resulting financial statements accordingly.

Standards for Certain Nonprofit Organizations

The standards for certain nonprofit organizations are similar to those of voluntary organizations, with some notable differences. This section will discuss only the standards that differ from or are more detailed than those of voluntary organizations. Exhibit H shows illustrative financial statements adapted from *Audits of Certain Nonprofit Organizations* and *Checklists and Illustrative Financial Statements for Nonprofit Organizations: A Financial Reporting*

---

[25]*AICPA, Statement of Position 87-2.*
[26]Denise Nitterhouse and Florence C. Sharp, "Allocation of Joint Costs: Special Audit Problems for Nonprofits," *Today's CPA* (January-February 1988): 24-27.

Practice Aid.[27] Refer to them throughout the following discussion of certain nonprofit financial reporting standards.

Fund Types   Reporting by funds is suggested but not required of certain nonprofit organizations. This is similar to the reporting standards adopted in 1990 for health care providers. Even if an organization does not report assets and liabilities on a fund accounting basis, it must disclose all material restrictions in the fund balances section and the notes to the financial statements. Although certain nonprofits commonly use the same four fund types as voluntary organizations, they may combine funds into expendable and nonexpendable categories for financial reporting purposes. *Expendable* funds account for resources available to finance the organization's programs and include the current unrestricted and restricted funds. *Nonexpendable* funds account for resources that the donor specified cannot be used for operating purposes and include plant and endowment funds. It is recommended, but not required, that the financial statements include a *total of all funds* column. Permitting, indeed encouraging, such consolidation of the information in the funds was a major departure from the voluntary standards and indicated the direction that recommended standards have since taken. The proposed new standards would require consolidation in a total all funds column and would allow, but not require, balance sheet presentation by fund.

Financial Statements   Certain nonprofit organizations must present a Balance Sheet (columnar or layered), an activity statement (Statement of Support and Revenue, Expenses, Capital Additions, and Changes in Fund Balance), a Statement of Changes in Financial Position, and Notes to the financial statements. A Statement of Functional Expenses is not required. A Statement of Cash Flows may be used as an alternative to a Statement of Changes in Financial Position, although SFAS No. 95, which requires Statements of Cash Flows for businesses, does not apply to nonprofit organizations.[28] Both are presented in Exhibit H. The proposed standards are likely to require a Statement of Cash Flows.

Because of the diversity of organizations covered by the audit guide for certain nonprofit organizations, no single financial statement format is prescribed. The guide provides examples of acceptable statements for an independent school, a cemetery organization, a country club, a library, a museum, a performing arts organization, a private foundation, a public broadcasting station, a religious organization, a research and scientific organization, a trade association, a union, and a zoological and botanical society.

---

[27]American Institute of Certified Public Accountants, *Audits of Certain Nonprofit Organizations* (New York, NY: AICPA, 1987), pp. 101-108; and AICPA, *Checklists and Illustrative Financial Statements*, pp. 84-90.
[28]Financial Accounting Standards Board, *Statement of Financial Accounting Standards No. 95, Statement of Cash Flows*, (FASB, 1987).

The audit guide uses several different titles for the activity statements of these various organizations. Items are classified into four major categories: revenue and support, expenses, capital additions, and transfers.

Revenue and support accounts for only those inflows that are available for operations, including earned revenues, such as membership or program fees, and public support, such as contributions or gifts. *Capital additions* or *nonexpendable additions* include gifts of future interests and other gifts, grants, and bequests that are not expendable for current operating purposes because the donor restricted them to endowment, plant, or loan funds, either permanently or for extended periods of time. Requiring separation of capital additions from revenue and support highlights the fact that these resources are part of the permanent capital of the organization and cannot be consumed for current operations. The capital additions section of the activity statement is shown after expenses and before other changes in fund balances. Capital additions include any investment income, gains, and losses with legal restrictions that they be added to principal. Whereas voluntary organizations record these items as revenue, certain nonprofit organizations report them as *capital additions*.

Gifts of future interests include *life income* and *annuity* gifts. A life income gift arises from the donation to the organization of income-producing assets under an agreement providing for the payment to the donor of all or part of the earnings from the assets for a stipulated time period. An annuity gift creates an obligation on the part of the organization to pay specified amounts to the donor, whether or not earned from the gift. The principal amount of a life income gift (i.e., the fair value of the asset donated) should be recorded as a capital addition when the gift is made. An annuity gift should be reflected as a capital addition in an amount representing the excess of the value of the gift over the organization's liability to the donor. Amounts recorded in life income or annuity funds are transferred to the appropriate fund when the gift terms have been met.

Expenses are reported by function, subdivided into program and support expenses, so that the cost of each significant program and supporting activity is separately presented. Program expenses include all the resources devoted to program activities, including administrative and fund-raising activities undertaken for that program alone. Program activities are those directly related to the organization's purpose and include grants to affiliates and other organizations. Supporting expenses consist of those activities not traceable to any particular programs, including fund-raising, membership development, and unallocated management and general expenses. Support expenses are subdivided into general administrative and fund raising. Time studies may be required to obtain the data needed to allocate expenses. Allocating costs among programs and support categories is often difficult and involves substantial judgment.

Fund-raising expenses include personnel, occupancy, mailing list maintenance, printing, and mailing expenses incurred in soliciting contributions.

Generally, they should be expensed as incurred, although the cost of literature and other materials acquired in one period for use in a fund-raising drive in the succeeding period should be deferred. Specifically identifiable fund-raising costs related to contributions that are required to be deferred also may be deferred if the contributions may be used to cover them. SOP 87-2 governs allocation of informational costs for certain as well as voluntary nonprofit organizations.

Performing arts organizations often capitalize expenditures incurred and defer revenues received in advance of a performance. The resulting asset is expensed and revenue is recognized when the performance occurs, to match revenues and expenses. An anticipated loss on a production should be recognized as soon as the organization realizes that a loss is likely.

Organizations such as private foundations must record a multiyear grant as an expense and liability when they approve the grant and notify the recipient, if the grant does not require subsequent review and approval except for routine performance requirements. Other grants may be recognized when renewal is approved or when their terms are fulfilled, depending on the conditions of the grant. Remaining grant commitments should be disclosed in the notes to the financial statements.

Restricted Gifts, Grants, and Bequests[29] As noted earlier, standards for reporting restricted resources vary widely among the different types of nonprofit organizations. Two major issues are: (1) when restricted resources should be deemed to be expended and (2) whether to report restricted amounts as part of fund balance or as liabilities when they are received.

Audit guides before SOP 78-10 did not address the first issue, and management traditionally decided whether expenses should be charged to restricted or unrestricted funds. Expenses were typically charged to unrestricted funds unless management stated that restricted resources were used. The authors of SOP 78-10 considered it inappropriate for management to be able to choose for accounting purposes whether restricted or unrestricted dollars were used. It recommended that donor restrictions be assumed as met when expenditures are made that satisfy the conditions of the restrictions, unless the expenditures are attributable to other restricted funds.

If a donor restricted a contribution for a specific program service and the organization subsequently spent money for that program service, the obligation imposed by the restriction is met and restricted resources are accounted for as expended and earned. Absent donor language to the contrary, the donee organization should consider only expenditures made after the date the restricted contribution is received, unless expenditures were

[29]American Institute of Certified Public Accountants, *Audits of Certain Nonprofit Organizations*, Appendix A: Statement of Position 78-10, *Accounting Principles and Reporting Practices for Certain Nonprofit Organizations* (New York, NY: AICPA, 1987), pp. 67-69, 73-77, paragraphs 25-31, 51-62.

made in the contemplation of the receipt of the funds with the knowledge of the donor or grantor.

The issue of where to report the receipt of restricted resources was explicitly addressed in the other audit guides. Voluntary organizations must report the full amount of restricted resources received and available for use in current operations as revenue and support in the current restricted fund, whether or not the restrictions for their use were met. Unspent amounts are reflected in the excess (deficit) of revenue and support over expenses and included in the current restricted fund balance. Health care providers and colleges and universities recognize such amounts as additions to fund balance when received, and as revenue only when the restrictions are met and the revenues are earned. In these cases, the restricted resources are also included in the restricted fund balance, but their arrival is called an addition instead of revenue.

Those who disagreed with this treatment of restricted resources argued that recognition of such amounts as revenue or additions overlooks the legal obligation to return such amounts if they are not used for the restricted purpose and that large amounts received near the end of the period may significantly distort the financial statements. Accordingly, SOP 78-10 requires that restricted gifts and income be reported as deferred revenue or support (that is, outside the fund balance section in the Balance Sheet), until the organization makes expenditures that satisfy the terms of the restriction. At that time, such amounts should be reported as revenue and support in the activity statement.

Therefore, certain nonprofit organizations report current restricted resource inflows as revenue and support in the activity statement to the extent that the restrictions on them (including incurring expenses for the purposes specified by the donor or grantor) have been met. Any additional amounts, for which the restrictions have not yet been met, are reported as deferred revenue on the Balance Sheet until the restrictions on them are satisfied. Generally, restricted resources are to be reported in a manner that reflects the restrictions on them.

Nonexpendable resources are restricted to plant, endowment, or loan funds either permanently or for an extended period of time. They are reported as capital additions in a separate category, additions to fund balance, on the activity statement. Capital additions restricted for plant are to be classified on the Balance Sheet as deferred capital support until they are used for the specified purpose, at which time they are reported as capital additions on the activity statement.

Investments and Related Earnings[30]   Certain nonprofits also traditionally valued investments at cost, with fair market value as of the date of the gift used as the cost basis for donated investments. Current standards require that investments in securities and other assets appear on the Balance

---

[30]AICPA, *Audits of Certain Nonprofit Organizations*, pp. 81-82, paragraphs 77-83.

Sheet of the fund to which they belong and be valued either at market or at the lower of cost or market. Cost is not an acceptable method for valuing most marketable securities, with the exception of marketable debt securities that the organization expects and appears to be able to hold to maturity. Such debt securities may be valued at amortized cost. Investments for which quoted market values are not available must be reported at either fair value or the lower of cost or fair value. The basis of valuation chosen must be used by all funds for all investments. When investments are carried at market value, the unrealized gain or loss is accounted for in the same manner as the realized gain or loss.

If investments are pooled, the income, gains, and losses of individual funds are determined using the unit method, which attributes a certain number of shares to each fund. Additions to the investment pool are based on the market value of a unit when the money is received.

Donated Goods and Services   Individuals, corporations, foundations, and government agencies frequently provide *donated goods and services* to certain nonprofits, in addition to cash contributions. For example, museums rely heavily on donations of art for their collections. The criteria for recording amounts of donated goods and services in the financial statements of certain nonprofits are similar to but slightly more stringent than the criteria for voluntary organizations. Significant amounts of donated materials and facilities should be recorded at fair value only if there is a clearly measurable and objective basis for determining a value, and if they do not pass directly through the organization to its charitable beneficiaries.

Donated services should be recorded only if all of the following conditions are met: (1) The services performed are significant, are an integral part of the organization's efforts, would otherwise be performed by salaried personnel, and would be continued if the donated services were not available; (2) the organization controls the employment and duties of the donors as it would if they were employees; (3) it has a clearly measurable basis for valuing the services; and (4) the services are not intended principally for the benefits of members. If any amounts are reported for donated services, the types of services reported and the valuation bases should be disclosed in the notes. Compliance with the criteria should be clearly documented in the organization's information systems.

Fixed Assets   The authors of the guide considered the desirability of capitalizing (but not depreciating) the *inexhaustible collections* owned by museums, art galleries, botanical gardens, libraries, and similar entities. From the standpoint of accountability to the public, it is difficult to justify omission of the largest asset of the organization from its financial statements. However, current standards do not require such collections to be capitalized because of the cost of assigning values to existing collections. When art objects are purchased or donated, however, their cost or value must be reported in the financial statements or notes. Museum accounting practices usually follow the *Museum Accounting Guidelines*[31] except where they conflict with the SOP.

Proposed standards for capitalizing works of art, historical treasures, and similar assets as revenues and assets have met with a loud outcry by museums. The standards would require all long-lived purchased items and contributed items that are intended to be sold or have an existing market to be capitalized.[32] They should be capitalized at cost if purchased and at fair market value when donated. The nature and the cost, or contributed value, of current year accessions (acquisitions) and the nature of and proceeds from deaccessions (disposals) should be disclosed.

SFAS 93 requires that all long-lived tangible assets be depreciated, but it applies only to those assets required to be capitalized. Fixed assets used in operations should be depreciated. Exhaustible collections, such as exhibits with a limited display life, should be capitalized and amortized over their useful life. Not all assets will necessarily be depreciated: "depreciation need not be recognized on individual works of art or historical treasures whose economic benefit or service potential is used up so slowly that their estimated useful lives are extraordinarily long."[33] Accounting for long-lived assets and depreciation is hotly debated by certain types of nonprofit organizations, such as museums, which continue to resist capitalization and depreciation.[34]

Many private elementary and secondary schools follow the accounting guidelines of *Business Management for Independent Schools*.[35] It deviates from the SOP in several areas, most importantly in its prohibition of depreciation expense. The omission of depreciation understates the schools' expenses.

Controversies and Trends

The current accounting standards have been accepted fairly well by voluntary organizations, and the initial controversies over accounting requirements for depreciation, funds, total return, and revenues versus capital additions have generally died down. The UWASIS definitions of programs and supporting services, which were initially somewhat controversial, have led to greater uniformity in the reporting of program and supporting services

[31] Association of Science-Technology Centers, *Museum Accounting Guidelines* (Washington, DC: 1976).

[32] FASB, *Exposure Draft, Proposed Statement of Financial Accounting Standards, Accounting for Contributions Received and Contributions Made and Capitalization of Works of Art, Historical Treasures, and Similar Assets.*

[33] Financial Accounting Standards Board, *Statement of Financial Accounting Standards No. 93*, "Recognition of Depreciation by Not-for-Profit Organizations" (Norwalk, CT: FASB, August 1987), paragraph 6.

[34] Alison Leigh Cowan, "Pricing the Priceless: Museums Resist, Accountants Insist," *The New York Times*, 1 May 1990, section C, page 13.

[35] National Association of Independent Schools, *Business Management for Independent Schools* (Boston, MA: 1987).

by voluntary organizations. Nevertheless, because voluntary organizations differ substantially from each other, such uniform definitions remain difficult to use and interpret for the purpose of comparing one voluntary organization to others.

The requirement to allocate joint costs of informational materials has raised several concerns. Nonprofit organizations are trying to determine which, if any, of their communication costs are allocable to programs. Auditors are trying to figure out how to audit the appropriateness and accuracy of such allocations. And some regulators are arguing that the AICPA has opened a Pandora's box that will impair their ability to effectively monitor nonprofit agencies and protect the public from unscrupulous fund raisers. Nonprofit organizations, auditors and oversight agencies continue to adapt to these standards.

Reporting Entity   Nonprofit organizations affiliate with each other in many ways. Many local associations, professional societies, and voluntary and religious organizations are affiliated with a larger network. Determining the appropriate entity for financial reporting is a key issue for such organizations. Is it the local chapter, the local chapter in combination with its affiliated network, or some other combination? Articulation of the appropriate entity is important for assuring financial statement readers that they are informed about the major activities and resources of the organization. The FASB and GASB are both studying the concept of a reporting entity and appropriate reporting and disclosures for related entities.

Current standards for certain nonprofit organizations are consistent with and more explicit than those for voluntary organizations. SOP 78-10 states that one organization is considered to control another if it directly or indirectly can determine the direction of its management and policies through ownership, by contract, or otherwise. If one organization controls another, the financial statements should be combined if any of the following criteria are also met:

- Another organization solicits funds in the name of and with the approval of the reporting organization and substantially all of the funds solicited are to be used by the reporting organization.

- An organization's resources were obtained from and are to be used for the benefit of the reporting organization.

- An organization that derives its support primarily from sources other than public contributions is created primarily to fulfill a function of the reporting organization.

The Notes should disclose the basis for combining financial statements and the interrelationship of the combined organizations. The notes should also disclose the existence of any affiliated organizations that are not combined and their relationship to the reporting organization.

Financial Statement Form and Content The proposed standard for financial statement display, *Financial Reporting by Not-for-Profit Organizations: Form and Content of Financial Statements*,[36] has created some furor, partly because of the amounts and types of information that users believe they will lose. These proposed standards would eliminate the current requirement for voluntary organizations to present a Statement of Functional Expenses, and require a combined single-column Balance Sheet without requiring a separate Balance Sheet or column for each fund. The authors feel that, contrary to its stated goals, the proposed form and content would increase the difficulty of analyzing the organization's financial status and performance. The proposed addition of a Statement of Cash Flows is generally seen as useful and not especially difficult.

The proposed SFAS on accounting for contributions and capitalization of collections has proven to be very controversial, as discussed above. Museums are fighting against the new requirement to capitalize and depreciate or amortize long-lived assets. Several types of nonprofit organizations are arguing against the proposed requirement to report pledges as assets and revenues. It is unclear at this point when the final standards will be set and how different they will be from the exposure draft.

Recognition and reporting of restricted resources continues to be a confused and inherently complex area. Theoretically, unexpended restricted resources should be reported in a manner that reflects the restrictions on them and the underlying economic nature of the transaction. If resources are restricted as to purpose but will remain the property of the organization until expended, they should be reflected as revenue when pledged or received. On the other hand, resources that may have to be returned to the donor or grantor if not expended for the specified purposes within a certain time period should be reported as deferred revenue until the specified criteria are met and the revenues are earned. This is typically the situation with grants from governments and some foundations. The proposed financial statement display standards do not address revenue recognition issues. The AICPA is currently considering a revised audit guide for all types of private nonprofits except health care providers. It is likely to provide more consistent guidance on the treatment of restricted resources among voluntary, higher education, and other types of nonprofit organizations.

There is some question as to which (if any) organizations that have previously been subject to the voluntary audit guide are now covered under the new health care audit guide. For example, visiting nurse associations that provide home health care may be affected.

[36]Financial Accounting Standards Board, Invitation to Comment, *Financial Reporting by Not-for-Profit Organizations: Form and Content of Financial Statements* (Norwalk, CT: FASB, August 29, 1989).

Accounting changes are most likely in three areas: the requirement for fund accounting may soften, pledges may have to be reported, and functional reporting may become discretionary.

AN EXAMPLE OF FINANCIAL STATEMENT PREPARATION

Although managers and board members seldom prepare financial statements, understanding the preparation process can help one to conduct a financial analysis. The following example shows journal entries and statements for a simple organization, the Social Welfare Center, which has only one program (community education), has no restricted funds, and has collected only cash donations for current operations.

During the first year of operation, 19X7, the Social Welfare Center had the following activities:

(1) Was incorporated at a cost of $800 paid in cash.

(2) Received $37,000 in unrestricted cash contributions, which was put into a savings account, with transfers made to the checking account as necessary.

(3) Earned and received $900 interest from a savings account.

(4) Received $80 in miscellaneous income from vending machines.

(5) Purchased equipment to be used in community education for $500. The equipment is expected to have a five-year life and be depreciated on a straight-line method, with one-half year of depreciation taken in the first and last years of its life.

(6) Paid $18,000 in salaries and related fringe benefits for social workers and assistants who were engaged in the community education program. Accrued salary and fringe benefits earned but not paid as of December 31, 19X7, was $200.

(7) Paid $2,000 to a professional fund-raising organization to conduct the campaign that generated the contributions.

(8) Paid, in cash, the following operating expenses:
   —$1,200 rent (all for program purposes)
   —$280 telephone (all for program purposes)
   —$410 supplies and postage ($170 for program, $240 for management and general)
   —$400 professional fees to an accountant

(9) Purchased $600 of educational literature, of which $90 had been used at December 31, 19X7. The educational literature was received

on November 20, 19X7, on terms of net 60 days, and had not been paid for as of year end.

The following journal entries record the funds and accounts in which each transaction is entered. Expense entries also designate the program or supporting service to which they apply.

		DR	CR
(1)	Unrestricted—Incorporation Expense, M&G	$ 800	
	Unrestricted—Cash		$ 800
(2)	Unrestricted—Cash	37,000	
	Unrestricted—Contributions		37,000
(3)	Unrestricted—Cash	900	
	Unrestricted—Interest Income		900
(4)	Unrestricted—Cash	80	
	Unrestricted—Miscellaneous Revenue		80
(5)	Unrestricted—Transfer to Plant Fund Balance	500	
	Unrestricted—Cash		500
	Plant—Equipment	500	
	Plant—Transfer from Unrestricted Fund Balance		500
	Plant—Depreciation Expense, Community Education	50	
	Plant—Allowance for Depreciation		50
(6)	Unrestricted—Payroll Expense, Community Education	18,200	
	Unrestricted—Cash		18,000
	Unrestricted—Accrued Payroll and Related		200
(7)	Unrestricted—Contracted Services Expense, Fund Raising	2,000	
	Unrestricted—Cash		2,000
(8)	Unrestricted—Rent Expense, Community Education	1,200	
	Unrestricted—Telephone Expense, Community Education	280	
	Unrestricted—Supplies and Postage Expense, Community Education	170	
	Unrestricted—Supplies and Postage Expense, M&G	240	
	Unrestricted—Professional Fees Expense, M&G	400	
	Unrestricted—Cash		2,290
(9)	Unrestricted—Inventory	600	
	Unrestricted—Accounts Payable		600
	Unrestricted—Educational Materials, Community Education	90	
	Unrestricted—Inventory		90

These entries result in the statements shown in Table 16-6. The numbers in parentheses on the statements refer to the number of the accounting transaction above.

TABLE 16-6 Social Welfare Center Financial Statements

Social Welfare Center
Balance Sheet
As of December 31, 19X7

Assets			Liabilities and Fund Balances		
Current Fund Unrestricted					
Cash	(1)(2)(3)(4)(5)(6)(7)(8)	$14,390	Accounts payable	(9)	$ 600
Inventory of educational material	(9)	510	Accrued payroll and related	(6)	200
			Fund balance		14,100
Total assets		$14,900	Total liabilities and fund balance		$14,900
Land, Building, and Equipment Fund					
Equipment, at cost, less accumulated depreciation of $50	(5)	$ 450	Fund balance		$ 450

Social Welfare Center, Inc.
Statement of Support, Revenue, Expenses, and Changes in Fund Balance
For the Year Ended December 31, 19X7

		Current Fund Unrestricted		Plant Fund		Total All Funds
Public Support and Revenue:						
Public support contributions	(2)	$37,000			(2)	$37,000
Revenue—interest	(3)	900			(3)	900
Revenue—miscellaneous	(4)	80			(4)	80
Total public support revenue		$37,980		$ 0		$37,980
Expenses:						
Program—community education	(6)(8)(9)	$19,940	(5)	$ 50		$19,990
Support Services:						
Management and general	(8)(1)	1,440				1,440
Fund raising	(7)	2,000				2,000
Total expenses		$23,380		$ 50		$23,430
Excess of revenue over expenses		$14,600		$ (50)		$14,550
Other Changes in Fund Balance:						
Purchase of equipment	(5)	(500)	(5)	500		0
Fund balance, beginning of year		0		0		0
Fund balance, end of year		$14,100		$450		$14,550

Social Welfare Center
Statement of Functional Expense
For the Year Ended December 31, 19X7

		Community Education		Supporting Services Management and General		Fund Raising	Total Supporting Services	Total Expenses
Salaries and related benefits	(6)	$18,200						$18,200
Professional fees			(8)	$ 400	(7)	$2,000	$2,400	2,400
Incorporation expense			(1)	800			800	800
Rent	(8)	1,200						1,200
Education materials	(9)	90						90
Telephone	(8)	280						280
Supplies and postage	(8)	170	(8)	240			240	410
Total expenses before depreciation		19,940		1,440		2,000	3,440	23,380
Depreciation	(5)	50						50
Total expenses		$19,990		$1,440		$2,000	$3,440	$23,430

A FRAMEWORK FOR ANALYSIS: THE
UNITED WAY ALLOCATION PROCESS

For some purposes, it is reasonable and adequate to compare the performance of a single type of organization, such as shelters for the homeless or museums. For example, management and board members are most likely to compare their organization to other similar organizations, in terms of both financial and program performance. When the objective is to see how well an organization is doing, its peers provide the most relevant benchmark.

However, individual donors, funding agencies (such as the United Way), and government agencies (such as the National Endowment for the Arts) also need to compare the performance of very different types of organizations to decide how to allocate resources among them. This presents a tremendous challenge to those who are responsible for making resource allocation decisions. Financial statement analysis provides important support for both tasks.

Ideally, the evaluation of performance should include integrated financial statement and program data analysis using both internal and external performance standards. Internal standards might include both the planned and the historical performance of the organization being evaluated. External standards consist of comparable performance data for similar organizations. This is a tall order, given the great diversity in organization size and programs and the relative paucity of data.

The process a local United Way organization uses to determine annual allocations to member agencies incorporates both internal and external performance measures and integrates strategic planning as well. The process discussed below is a composite based on input from several local United Way organizations. Thus, it will differ somewhat from the process followed in any individual United Way. Local United Way organizations, with the help of the United Way of America, constantly refine and improve the way they evaluate organizations and community need to support their allocation decision process.

In general, each local United Way attempts to determine the highest priority service needs (by type of service, geographic area, and age group) and to allocate its money to those organizations expected to make the most effective and efficient use of the resources to meet those needs. The *service priorities* are determined and reviewed early in the annual cycle and then used as guidelines in the subsequent allocation process. Service priorities will shift with the advent or awareness of new problems (such as AIDS and homelessness), changing economic conditions (such as a large plant closing that increases the need for job placement and retraining), and changing needs of specific age groups (such as addicted newborns or indigent elderly).

The process of deciding how much to allocate to each organization is carried out by volunteer teams called *allocation committees, review committees,* or another descriptive title. Each United Way trains its volunteers to perform allocation reviews. There is strong competition among agencies for money, and the amounts requested usually far exceed the amounts available. The allocation task is to support needed services in the community to the fullest extent possible with the limited funds available.

The allocation process begins by sending applications and service priorities to *member agencies* (those that previously received United Way funding) and other agencies that wish to apply for funding. Each agency then sends a completed application and a copy of its most recent year's audited financial statements to the United Way. The United Way staff checks materials for completeness and distributes them to the allocation committee volunteers assigned to evaluate that agency. The committee evaluates whether the agency and program for which support is requested meet recognized community needs and carry out program services, agency management, and fiscal management effectively and efficiently.

The agency applications include a detailed narrative proposal that explains the agency and the programs for which it is requesting funding (*program proposal*), a *budget* for these programs, a copy of the annual audit report and management letter, and an explanation of the progress made on any recommendations of the prior year's United Way allocation committee. Once the committee has reviewed these materials, it undertakes a *site visit*, in which the committee members observe the agency operations and meet and question agency staff and board members. Table 16-7 lists examples of possible questions related to the three areas of *financial management, governance*, and *program* that are addressed during the site visit. The proposed budget is shown in detail by program and by United Way account codes. The total proposed budget is also compared to the prior year's actual performance, to the current year's budget, and to the current year-to-date actual expenses. The audited financial statements are analyzed to evaluate the agency's financial status and past performance.

Once the evaluation of submitted materials and the site visit are completed, the committee prepares a report that summarizes its evaluation, recommends any areas of service provision or management that need to be improved, and recommends the level of funding (if any) for the agency. Based on these reports, each committee chair then explains to the United Way board how the agency's programs meet community needs, its relationship to similar programs in the community, the cost-effectiveness of its service delivery, and the rationale for its recommendations of funding level. The United Way board considers the recommendations of all the allocation committees and allocates the available resources based on the needs priorities and the relative effectiveness and efficiency with which each agency provides services.

In addition to the processes and data discussed above, internal users need additional detail about the organization and its performance. The board has fiduciary and stewardship responsibilities to ensure that the organization

TABLE 16-7 **Typical Performance Evaluation Questions**

Financial

Is the agency meeting its budget projections?
Is the agency using all potential income sources?
What is the status of income sources other than United Way?
What results have fund-raising and grantsmanship efforts produced?
How are fees set, and what is their relation to costs?
Is there an appropriate relation between revenues and expenses?
How do the agency's costs compare to those of similar organizations?
Does the agency have enough working capital?
Is the overall financial structure of the agency sound?
Are supporting expenses reasonable and being contained?
Are increases in expenses justified by increase in service?
How does the agency determine staff compensation levels?
Are volunteers used where possible to contain costs?

Governance

Is the board an appropriate size?
Does the board have the skills needed to effectively govern the agency?
Is board membership stable without being stagnant?
How often does the board meet, and what is its average attendance?
Are complete accurate board minutes maintained?
What has the board identified as its primary responsibilities?
What level of participation is expected of board members? Is it achieved?
What board committees exist, what are their functions, and are they active?
How are new board members recruited?
What orientation and training do new board members receive?
What is the agency's long-range plan?

Program

What is the agency's mission?
Is there a clear, convincing, current statement of need for the program?
How many people have the need or problem that the program seeks to address?
Is the need for program services growing, stable, or decreasing?
Is there a waiting list for the service?
How does the agency collaborate with other service providers?
How does the agency develop its annual program service objectives?
How is program success evaluated? Does the process make sense?
Are clear, reasonable service objectives stated and monitored?
Do the objectives specify the expected impact or outcome of the program?
Is program capacity defined, and is it well utilized?
How successful was the program last year? Why?
How well is the program doing this year? Why?
Are the proposed objectives for next year attainable yet challenging?
Are service units and costs comparable to those of similar programs?
What has been the staff turnover rate?
What are staff qualifications and what training have they received?

Source: Based on and adapted from various local United Way documents.

carries out its mission, uses resources in compliance with any restrictions on them, maintains adequate records, has an annual audit, and complies with all relevant laws and regulations including the timely filing of federal tax and other forms. The treasurer and audit committee will be most heavily involved with such matters. Carrying out these duties requires substantial managerial accounting information in addition to the published financial statements.

APPLYING THE FOUR KEY QUESTIONS TO LYA

The internal and external analyses discussed in the following sections could be used by a United Way or other allocation committee to analyze the financial condition and relative effectiveness and efficiency of an agency that has applied for support. Program and governance primarily are evaluated with other analytic approaches, although financial performance is one factor used to indicate the quality of governance.

Introduction to Longwood Youngsters Association (LYA)

The Longwood Youngsters Association (LYA) is a voluntary health and welfare organization that provides services to youth from 1 to 18 years of age. It was founded 15 years ago to serve the town of Longwood and the surrounding rural areas of Longwood county, which include both relatively affluent and poor communities of the southwestern U.S. state in which it is located. Its programs include youth activities, camping, day care, and counseling services.

Financial Data and Calculations

Exhibit B contains the 19X7 and 19X8 LYA audited financial statements, which provide the basis for financial analysis. It includes a Balance Sheet, Statement of Changes in Fund Balances, Statement of Functional Expenses, Statement of Cash Flows, and Notes to the financial statements. These statements received an unqualified audit opinion, which indicates that the statements were prepared in accordance with GAAP and are reasonably reliable.

The calculation and display of data in Exhibits C, D, E, and F follow the general pattern introduced in Chapters 5 and 6. The calculations differ somewhat, due to sector-specific differences in report format and content and to variations in what is relevant for an individual organization. Other analysts might perform similar calculations in a different manner.

Exhibit C restates the financial statements, classifying assets and liabilities into current and noncurrent as well as possible with the available data. This is necessary because nonprofits are not required to classify assets and liabilities as current and noncurrent on the Balance Sheet. Cash, receivables, and prepayments are clearly current, and equipment is clearly not current. Investments and interfund loans are more difficult to classify and may significantly affect the outcomes of the analysis. The worst case assumption (which should be made only in the absence of information to the contrary) is to classify all interfund borrowings as current and all investments as noncurrent. We have classified them as such in Exhibit C. Ambiguous liabilities are classified in the same way as the assets to which they relate, if any. Thus, the interfund liability (due to) is classified as current and the bond discount as noncurrent.

The dollar change column in Exhibit C is calculated by subtracting the prior from the current year's figures. This could also be called the increase (decrease) column. For example, total cash increased by $23,513 [1] ($73,967 − $50,454) from 19X7 to 19X8. The corresponding percent change column is calculated by dividing the change by the prior year's figure for each line item. Thus, the $23,513 increase in cash was a 46.6 percent [2] increase ($23,513 ÷ $50,454) over its 19X7 level.

Note on the Statement of Changes in Fund Balances that the deficit of revenues over expenses in 19X7 and excess in 19X8 yield an arithmetically correct, but meaningless, −935.8 percent [3] change. This occurs because the 19X7 deficit is used as the denominator in calculating the percent change. If both numbers were either deficits or excesses, it would make sense to talk about the growth or shrinkage in the size of the annual excess or deficit in percentage (relative) terms. With an excess and a deficit, however, it only makes sense to consider the absolute value of the change. If there is a deficit in both years, and the deficit in the second year is smaller than the deficit in the first year, the sign of the percent change will be incorrect although the percent will be meaningful. The point of this discussion is that the implications of such calculations cannot be taken for granted. Carefully assess their underlying meaning before drawing conclusions.

Exhibit D shows *common size* financial statements (*vertical analysis*), where each line item on each statement is stated as a percentage of the relevant column total. For example, total assets is the denominator for the balance sheet calculations. The common size Balance Sheet shows that cash made up only 2.0 percent [4] ($10,177 ÷ $510,065) of the assets in the current unrestricted fund and 9.7 percent [5] ($73,967 ÷ $763,617) of the total assets in 19X8. These statements are useful for assessing the relative dispersion among the different sources and uses of resources.

Total revenues and total expenses are the denominators for the revenue and expense line items, respectively. Excess, transfers, and fund balances are shown as a percentage of revenues. Common size statements may also use slightly different calculations. On the common size Statement of Changes in Fund Balances, contributions made up 1.7 percent [6] ($14,656 ÷ $842,223) of the total public support and revenue of the current unrestricted fund. Counseling program expenses made up 0.4 percent [7] ($13 ÷ $3,121) of the total plant fund expenses. The functional expense percentages are based on the column total. On the common size Statement of Functional Expenses, transportation made up 7.9 percent [8] ($10,935 ÷ $137,936) of the total camping program expense.

The ERR messages displayed in the plant fund column of the Statement of Changes in Fund Balances are messages from the spreadsheet that a calculation error has occurred in these locations, in this case because of an attempt to divide by zero (the value of plant fund total revenues). Some spreadsheets may allow you to print a blank space or a different message, such as DIVZERO, instead of the more generic ERR.

The *fund distribution statements* (*horizontal analysis*) shown in Exhibit E highlight the distribution of resources among funds. The percentages show how much each fund constituted of the total for that row. For example, the current restricted fund held 66.8 percent [9] ($510,065 ÷ 763,617) of the total assets in 19X8.

Exhibit F contains various other difference measures and ratios that involve comparisons among, rather than within, categories. They have the same meanings and use the same calculations as those presented in Chapters 5 and 6.

The startup time in the first year of such an analysis is likely to be significant, but the current year's data can be entered and analyzed relatively quickly once data are in a spreadsheet. Historical data by fund are available from prior years' financial statements or may be summarized in the annual report.

Our analysis refers to the numbers in the relevant exhibits without further explanation of the calculations. Make sure you understand how the numbers on each of the exhibits were calculated before proceeding to the analysis.

Internal Analysis

The four key questions will provide the framework for analyzing the financial data in Exhibits B through F.

Consistency Between Goals and Financial Resources With $763,617 [10] in total assets, LYA is a medium-size voluntary agency. During 19X8, its most recent year of operations, LYA had a small positive growth in total assets; they increased by $14,128 [11], or 1.9 percent [12], from $749,489 to $763,617. Even with all investments considered to be long term (a rather stringent assumption), in 19X8 the current ratio is 5.7 [13] and the quick ratio is 5.5 [14]; in 19X7 they were 16.0 [15] and 16.2 [16], respectively. These very high liquidity ratios indicate that LYA's financial position is extremely strong.

Liabilities make up only 6.1 percent [17] of LYA's total assets in 19X8, down from an already low level of 8.2 percent [18] in 19X7. There are no liabilities in either the plant or endowment funds, indicating that all of the assets of those funds were financed internally. The high proportion of assets (66.8 percent [19]) in the current unrestricted fund indicates board discretion over the use of most of LYA's assets. The fixed assets (in the form of equipment) are so small as to have negligible impact on LYA's financial position and performance. LYA has no long term debt. The bond discount net of amortization relates to bonds LYA owns as investments.

The 19X8 end of the year total fund balance equals 81.7 percent [20] of the year's revenues, although 34.5 percent [21] of it is restricted for endowment and cannot be used for operating expenses. The 19X8 current unrestricted ending fund balance is equal to 55.0 percent [22] of its revenue, which is substantial. LYA clearly has adequate resources to support its goals, and probably to expand them.

The asset growth, high liquidity ratios, lack of debt, and large amount of unrestricted resources indicate that LYA has a very, perhaps overly, sound financial structure. The board policy of investing resources rather than using them to provide more services may warrant examination. From a societal perspective, an organization is granted nonprofit status to perform a social service, not to save and invest. Although institutions may want to build their quasi-endowment investments to ensure independence from fluctuations in the fee and contribution environment, it is also important to ask whether this a good bet for society. LYA is clearly capable of supporting higher program levels than it is currently executing. One hint that it may be considering increasing its service levels is the designation of $55,000 [23] of the 19X8 unrestricted fund balance (10.8 percent [24] of its total assets) for extended services.

Intergenerational Equity   In 19X8, the total excess of public support and revenues over expenses was $29,076 [25], composed of a current fund excess of $38,758 [26] and plant and endowment fund deficits of $3,121 [27] and $6,561 [28], respectively. In 19X7, LYA had a total deficit of $3,479 [29]. The 19X8 excess was 3.3 percent [30] and the 19X7 deficit was −0.5 percent [31] of revenues in the respective year. The return on fund balance was 4 percent [32] in 19X8, approximately equal to the inflation rate for the year. By this measure, LYA is not using resources acquired from past generations to fund services to present clients. However, a closer look at the effects of the accounting principles used and the separate effects of operations and investment activities is warranted.

The 19X8 endowment fund deficit was due to the $8,133 [33] loss on investment transactions. However, analysis of the information on market values (disclosed in Note 2 of Exhibit B) alleviates concern about investment performance. If LYA had used the market method of valuing investments, the financial statements would reflect the $17,450 by which the market value of the unsold endowment fund investments exceeded their cost, and would show an unrealized gain on investments in that amount. The endowment fund deficit for 19X8 would be turned into a healthy surplus merely by using a different accounting method. Note that an investment strategy of selling investments that decreased in value and holding those that increased in value results in poor performance indicators under any valuation method except market. Additional analysis of the investment values and returns could be performed, and the financial statements could be converted to the market basis if desired.

Unlike the endowment fund, the current unrestricted fund had a substantial realized gain of $38,534 [34] on investment transactions, in addition to a year end market value $19,770 above cost. Total investment performance is calculated by adding the investment income of $39,862 [35]; the net realized gain of $30,401 [36]; and the increase in total unrealized appreciation during the current year per Note 2 ($25,257 = $37,220 − $11,963). Thus, LYA's total investment return in 19X8 was $95,520. The total investment return rate of more than 16 percent ($95,520 ÷ $574,316) appears to be fairly strong, although it should be compared to the overall market performance or the investment performance of similar organizations to evaluate it more accurately. Resources earned on investments by the current generation have increased the purchasing power of the organization.

If fixed assets were a significant portion of LYA's assets, then they should also be adjusted, along with the related depreciation expense, to assess intergenerational equity. The lack of replacement of equipment would be an item of concern. At only 0.8 percent [37] of total assets, however, fixed assets do not play a significant role in this organization's financial position. An organization with relatively few fixed assets tends to purchase new ones infrequently, use and depreciate them until they are consumed, and then replace them. The resulting erratic patterns of fixed asset related costs is not necessarily a sign of problems.

Investment performance should be evaluated separately from operating performance, to the extent possible. Closer investigation of current fund performance shows that without the $38,534 gain on investment transactions, it would have had a very small positive difference of $224 ($38,758 − $38,534) between revenues and expenses in 19X8. With an inflation rate of 4 percent in 19X8, the 0 percent ($224 ÷ $424,736) operating return on beginning fund balance indicates that the operations of LYA did not contribute to maintaining its purchasing power. Although this initially raises a red flag about the relationship between revenues and expenses for LYA, a deliberate break-even operating strategy is not unreasonable in light of its strong financial position and investment performance. From an operating perspective, LYA used resources provided by the current constituents to provide services to the same generation of constituents. They did not use resources contributed by prior generations or borrow against future generations. Endowment fund income can be viewed as resources that prior generations explicitly designated for the use of current and future generations. Unrestricted investments, and the income from them, represents resources that prior constituencies intended for use by their own generations, but that the organization instead chose to save and invest to earn income and provide a reserve cushion for future generations.

Match Between Sources and Uses of Resources   LYA's resources are well matched, perhaps even overly conservative. Both long-term and current assets are safely covered with fund balance. This is additional evidence that the organization has more capacity than it is currently using. It is very safe, but may not be using resources to provide as much service as it could.

The Statement of Functional Expenses provides data on how resources were used. A large proportion (85.1 percent [38]) of LYA's 19X8 expenses were used for salaries and related expenses, which is common among voluntary organizations. If personnel costs are relatively fixed, as they are in many institutions, this indicates little short-term flexibility to reduce this expense. If, however, LYA uses a significant amount of part-time personnel on an hourly basis as needed, it may have the ability to adjust its personnel expenses to match the income generated by the services those personnel provide. The relation between personnel costs and government fees and grants, program service fees, and the sale of services to other agencies and towns indicates that sources and uses of resources are probably well matched. LYA has no other uncontrollable, long-term expenses, such as depreciation, maintenance, lease payments or interest payments.

Using an alternative approach, the 19X7 expenses of $705,624 [39] can be considered as the long-term base expenses and can be adjusted for the 19X8 4 percent rate of inflation to $733,849 ($705,624 × 1.04). Long-term revenue is estimated in the same way, by adjusting 19X7 revenue of $702,145 [40] by 4 percent to $730,230. Using this approach, the amount of long-term revenue does not cover the long-term expenses. However, the actual $877,975 [41] of public support and revenue was more than adequate to meet the estimated long-term expenses. This type of analysis has more validity if several years of data are used instead of a single year. It could also be performed on operating data only, after eliminating the effects of investments and any one-time occurrences of either revenue or expenses.

Resource Sustainability   Total revenue increased by 25.0 percent [42], while expenses grew at a much lower 20.3 percent [43] rate. While apparently desirable, this phenomenon also warrants further investigation. How did they do it? One possible cause is an increase in rates charged for services, of which the board and management would certainly be aware. Another is that improved efficiency allowed more services to be delivered with the same amount of resources. If this is so, and if the pace can be maintained, this is a good sign. However, short-term efficiency gained by applying extreme pressure and straining capacity can explode in higher costs, burnout, and other negative repercussions in the future. The ideal efficiency improvement lets employees provide more services with the same amount of resource consumption and effort, just as a winch can allow a laborer to lift more weight with a given amount of effort.

Note that LYA allocated no expenses to fund raising and that a relatively small and declining percentage of revenue is derived from contributions. A slightly larger, but still relatively small, percentage of revenue came from United Way. Instead of direct or indirect contributions, LYA relies primarily on grants and fees for service. LYA's limited fund-raising activities are probably performed by the volunteer board of directors. However, if items such as printing and mailing costs or time and materials used to prepare United Way applications are borne by LYA, they should be allocated to fund raising. While it is not strictly required to segregate such items unless they are material, it may be worthwhile to track them to prevent any suspicion of deliberate deception. It is also important to have account classifications and a processing system for even small fund-raising costs, so that increases in such costs will be captured and easily identifiable. Fund-raising costs are among the items most carefully monitored by regulators and funders.

The increases in expenses were caused primarily by increases in the youth activities and camping programs. Management and general expenses increased only 4.6 percent [44], and actually declined from 6.6 percent [45] to 5.7 percent [46] as a percent of total expenses. Although less significant financially, the decrease in counseling and increase in teen parenting (a new program) indicates a programmatic shift, for which the future financial and mission-related effects need to be assessed.

The largest increases in revenues were caused by increases of $74,374 [47], or 16.1 percent, in government fees and grants; increases of $76,850 [48], or 96.3 percent, in program fees (nearly doubling); and increases in sales of services of $18,782 [49], or 36.0 percent. This explains, and helps to justify, the increase in receivables of $60,637 [50].

Assuming that all three of these revenues generate accounts receivable, the 19X8 receivables turnover rate of 4.2 [51] is somewhat worse than the 4.9 [52] turnover of 19X7. That it takes nearly three months, on average, to collect receivables deserves attention. If the long receivables cycle is caused by a large amount of uncollectible accounts, they should be written off and a bad debt expense considered. If it is due to lax collection procedures, they should be improved. If it is a necessary condition of doing business with governments and insurers, then there may be no way to improve matters. In any case, management should be aware of the situation and its causes.

Relative reliance on government fees and grants decreased slightly, while the proportion of revenues contributed by program service fees and sales of service increased. In combination, these three accounted for 87.0 percent [53] and 84.6 percent [54] of the revenue in 19X8 and 19X7, respectively, indicating that LYA, already heavily dependent on service fees, is becoming even more so. However, it is a positive sign that the payors of the fees appear to be fairly well diversified among governments, clients, and other agencies. The drop in public support, from 8.6 percent [55] to 4.8 percent [56], may be cause for alarm. LYA appears to be shifting from a charitable voluntary agency to a business-like operation that primarily sells services. This is not necessarily a bad shift, but will affect the organization's perception of its mission and the way it operates.

The Statement of Functional Expenses shows substantial increases of $127,935 [57] in total salaries and related, and $9,251 [58] in transportation expenses in 19X8. The decrease in insurance expense of $1,981 [59] is potentially alarming if it indicates inadequate coverage. Many organizations will foolishly underinsure in times of financial stress to save money on insurance premiums. Although this explanation of the insurance expense decrease is unlikely in view of LYA's strong, highly liquid financial position, the adequacy of the insurance coverage and the currency of premium payments should be investigated. As is typical, depreciation expenses are exactly equal to the expenses of the plant fund.

The asset growth was not consistent among the various asset accounts, but was made up of large increases in some accounts offset by large decreases in others. The large increase in accounts receivable of $60,637 (49.9 percent) deserves investigation because it essentially means the organization is lending its customers more money. It appears to be justified in light of the increase in the revenues that generate receivables, as discussed previously.

Investments decreased by $69,474 [60], or 12.4 percent, from 75.0 percent [61] to 64.5 percent [62] of assets, which is a large decrease. Whether it is cause for alarm or an appropriate reduction (considering the very high percentage of assets in investments) is a relevant question. However, all assets should be invested wisely, which begs the question of why 25.8 percent [63] of the endowment fund assets are in cash. If cash includes short-term liquid securities, such as money market funds and Treasury bills that are viewed as cash equivalents, this may reflect an appropriately diversified investment strategy. Although reasonable and appropriate, the classification of such safe, highly liquid investments as cash complicates investment analysis, and would suggest modification of the investment analysis performed above to include the cash in the endowment fund in the investment base.

The Statement of Cash Flows (Exhibit B) indicates that cash inflow exceeded cash outflow by $23,513 [64], the amount of the change in cash. However, the cash flow from operations was a decrease in cash (net outflow) of $27,243 [65]. The primary operating use of cash was to finance the $60,637 [50] increase in accounts receivable. Increases of $22,227 [66] in payables and $13,561 [67] in accrued payroll provided a large part of this operating cash. The net cash outflow from operations was offset by a net cash inflow of $50,756 [68] from investing activities, primarily due to the sale of securities at a gain. Thus, the Statement of Cash Flows supports the conclusions drawn from the analysis of revenues and expenses. The $23,513 increase in cash was due to investing activities rather than to operations. The advisability of relying on investing activities to provide cash flows to support operations should be explicitly addressed by the board. It may be reasonable for LYA to do, but it should be done consciously.

External Comparisons

A regional association of youth organizations collected financial and operating statistics from member organizations and reported the average statistics shown in Exhibit G. They did not disclose data for individual entities. Because the youth organizations in this region are of relatively similar size and character, these averages provide a reasonable basis for comparison.

LYA compares very favorably to the other youth associations on the measures of financial strength: liquidity (current ratio), financial risk (debt ÷ total capital ratio), and profitability (expenses ÷ revenue). The average youth services organization in the group had a deficit in each of the past two years, whereas LYA had a slight deficit in the prior year and an excess in the current year. LYA has somewhat less diversified revenue sources and is more dependent on service fees and (apparently volatile) investment income. LYA gets a growing, and higher than average, percentage of its revenues from service fees and sales, leading to possible questions about whether it is serving less of a charitable mission and becoming more heavily focused on sales.

LYA unit costs were lower than average in the current year for camping days, but higher than average for all other programs. Counseling unit costs had the largest increase, due to an even larger drop in service than in expenses. LYA has a much lower, and declining, percentage of its program expenses (and, it is implied, its services) in counseling than the average. It would appear that LYA is either deliberately phasing out its counseling program, or that the program is in dire straits for unidentified reasons. LYA began a new teen parenting program, which has slightly higher than average unit costs. If this program serves clients previously served by the counseling program, the shift may reflect primarily a change in service delivery approach. It would be useful to have government revenues separated into grants and fees for services, as the two are earned in different ways and susceptible to somewhat different operational, political, and economic forces.

Diagnosis

LYA appears to be a financially healthy, stable organization that is undergoing fairly substantial changes in program emphasis. It is a service provider with relatively few fixed assets and very little debt. It has a relatively sizable pool of investments in both endowment and unrestricted funds. It has recently earned a good return on its investments and barely broken even on operations. While barely break-even operations are a cause for concern in less financially secure organizations, LYA's solid financial position makes this seem to be a reasonable operating philosophy for it.

The program mix of expenses and the comparison with other youth organizations leads one to question how much of a charitable or public service mission LYA is currently accomplishing, or if it has become essentially a business. A local federated fund raiser analyzing these statements would be likely to use site visits and operating data to answer these questions before allocating resources to LYA. Local for-profit businesses providing similar services, especially camping, may attempt to apply pressure to have LYA's nonprofit status revoked or to have that part of its revenues be subject to income tax.

SUMMARY

Voluntary health and welfare and certain other nonprofit organizations perform valuable social and cultural services in today's society. They consist of a wide variety of organizations. Some are large national organizations whose names are household words, such as the Red Cross, and many are small independent local organizations. Most people are involved with such organizations in some way, as service recipients, donors, or volunteers.

Voluntary and certain nonprofit organizations are subject to two sets of similar, but somewhat different, financial reporting standards. Both are required to present a Balance Sheet and Statement of Changes in Fund Balances. In addition, voluntary organizations are required to present a Statement of Functional Expenses, and certain nonprofit organizations are required to present a Statement of Changes in Financial Position or Statement of Cash Flows. Certain nonprofit organizations may aggregate their fund presentations into expendable and unexpendable, whereas voluntary organizations must show each fund type separately on all statements. Other significant differences include the treatment of restricted revenues and the use of a separate capital additions classification by certain nonprofits. More consistent and comprehensive financial reporting standards are being developed by standard setters.

Analysis of these organizations' performance is further complicated by differences in operating practices and services provided and the lack of definitions of the services and outputs to be measured. However, individual donors, federated fund raisers and government agencies are faced with the task of analyzing individual organizations and comparing them to others that may be similar or different in many ways. The financial analysis procedures presented here can help support the comparison process.

EXHIBIT A **Sample Voluntary Health and Welfare Financial Statements**

Sample Voluntary Health and Welfare Service
Balance Sheets
(December 31, 19X2 and 19X1)

Assets	19X2	19X1
CURRENT FUNDS		
Unrestricted		
Cash	$2,207,000	$2,530,000
Investments (Note 2)		
For long-term purposes	2,727,000	2,245,000
Other	1,075,000	950,000
Pledges receivable less allowance for uncollectibles of $105,000 and $92,000	475,000	363,000
Inventories of educational materials, at cost	70,000	61,000
Accrued interest, other receivables and prepaid expenses	286,000	186,000
Total	$6,840,000	$6,335,000
Restricted		
Cash	$ 3,000	$ 5,000
Investments (Note 2)	71,000	72,000
Grants receivable	58,000	46,000
Total	$ 132,000	$ 123,000
LAND, BUILDING, AND EQUIPMENT FUND		
Cash	$ 3,000	$ 2,000
Investments (Note 2)	177,000	145,000
Pledges receivable less allowance for uncollectibles of $7,500 and $5,000	32,000	25,000
Land, buildings, and equipment, at cost less accumulated depreciation of $296,000 and $262,000 (Note 5)	516,000	513,000
Total	$ 728,000	$ 685,000
ENDOWMENT FUNDS		
Cash	$ 4,000	$ 10,000
Investments (Note 2)	1,944,000	2,007,000
Total	$1,948,000	$2,017,000

Liabilities and Fund Balances	19X2	19X1
CURRENT FUNDS		
Unrestricted		
Accounts payable	$ 148,000	$ 139,000
Research grants payable	596,000	616,000
Contributions designated for future period	245,000	219,000
Total liabilities and deferred revenues	989,000	974,000
Fund balances		
Designated by governing board for		
Long-term investments	2,800,000	2,300,000
Purchases of new equipment	100,000	-
Research purposes (Note 3)	1,152,000	1,748,000
Undesignated, available for general activities (Note 4)	1,799,000	1,313,000
Total fund balance	5,851,000	5,361,000
Total	$6,840,000	$6,335,000
Restricted		
Fund balances		
Professional education	$ 84,000	$ -
Research grants	48,000	123,000
Total	$ 132,000	$ 123,000
LAND, BUILDING, AND EQUIPMENT FUND		
Mortgage payable, 8%, due 19XX (Note 7)	$ 32,000	$ 36,000
Fund balances		
Expended	484,000	477,000
Unexpended—restricted	212,000	172,000
Total fund balance	696,000	649,000
Total	$ 728,000	$ 685,000
ENDOWMENT FUNDS		
Fund balance	$1,948,000	$2,017,000
Total	$1,948,000	$2,017,000

(See accompanying notes to financial statements.)

Adapted from *Audits of Voluntary Health and Welfare Organizations*, AICPA, 1988, pp. 42-50; and *Checklists and Illustrative Financial Statements for Nonprofit Organizations*, AICPA, 1990, pp. 117-125.

EXHIBIT A (Continued)

Sample Voluntary Health and Welfare Service
Statement of Support, Revenue, and Expenses and Changes in Fund Balances
(Year ended December 31, 19X2 with comparative totals for 19X1)

	Current Funds		Land, Building, and Equipment Fund	Endowment Fund	Total All Funds	
	Unrestricted	Restricted			19X2	19X1
Public Support and Revenue						
Public support						
Contributions (net of estimated uncollectible pledges of $195,000 in 19X2 and $150,000 in 19X1)	$3,764,000	$162,000	$ -	$ 2,000	$3,928,000	$3,976,000
Contributions to building fund			72,000	-	72,000	150,000
Special events (net of direct costs of $181,000 in 19X2 and $163,000 in 19X1)	104,000	-	-		104,000	92,000
Legacies and bequests	92,000	-	-	4,000	96,000	129,000
Received from federated and nonfederated campaigns (which incurred related fund-raising expenses of $38,000 in 19X2 and $29,000 in 19X1)	275,000	-			275,000	308,000
Total public support	4,235,000	162,000	72,000	6,000	4,475,000	4,655,000
Revenue						
Membership dues	17,000		-		17,000	12,000
Investment income	98,000	10,000	-		108,000	94,000
Realized gain on investment transactions	200,000		-	25,000	225,000	275,000
Miscellaneous	42,000				42,000	47,000
Total revenue	357,000	10,000		25,000	392,000	428,000
Total support and revenue	4,592,000	172,000	72,000	31,000	4,867,000	5,083,000
Expenses						
Program services						
Research	1,257,000	155,000	2,000		1,414,000	1,365,000
Public health education	539,000		5,000		544,000	485,000
Professional education and training	612,000		6,000		618,000	516,000
Community services	568,000		10,000		578,000	486,000
Total program services	2,976,000	155,000	23,000		3,154,000	2,852,000
Supporting services						
Management and general	567,000		7,000		574,000	638,000
Fund raising	642,000		12,000		654,000	546,000
Total supporting services	1,209,000		19,000		1,228,000	1,184,000
Total expenses	4,185,000	155,000	42,000		4,382,000	$4,036,000
Excess (deficiency) of public support and revenue over expenses	407,000	17,000	30,000	31,000		
Other changes in fund balances						
Property and equipment acquisitions from unrestricted funds	(17,000)		17,000	-		
Transfer of realized endowment fund appreciation	100,000			(100,000)		
Returned to donor		(8,000)				
Fund balances, beginning of year	5,361,000	123,000	649,000	2,017,000		
Fund balances, end of year	$5,851,000	$132,000	$696,000	$1,948,000		

(See accompanying notes to financial statements.)

EXHIBIT A (Continued)

Sample Voluntary Health and Welfare Service
Statement of Functional Expenses
(Year ended December 31, 19X2 with comparative totals for 19X1)

	Program Services					Supporting Services			Total Expenses	
19X2	Research	Public Health Education	Professional Education and Training	Community Services	Total	Management and General	Fund Raising	Total	19X2	19X1
Salaries	$ 45,000	$291,000	$251,000	$269,000	$ 856,000	$331,000	$368,000	$ 699,000	$1,555,000	$1,433,000
Employee health and retirement benefits	4,000	14,000	14,000	14,000	46,000	22,000	15,000	37,000	83,000	75,000
Payroll taxes, etc.	2,000	16,000	13,000	14,000	45,000	18,000	18,000	36,000	81,000	75,000
Total salaries and related expenses	51,000	321,000	278,000	297,000	947,000	371,000	401,000	772,000	1,719,000	1,583,000
Professional fees and contract service payments	1,000	10,000	3,000	8,000	22,000	26,000	8,000	34,000	56,000	53,000
Supplies	2,000	13,000	13,000	13,000	41,000	18,000	17,000	35,000	76,000	71,000
Telephone and telegraph	2,000	13,000	10,000	11,000	36,000	15,000	23,000	38,000	74,000	68,000
Postage and shipping	2,000	17,000	13,000	9,000	41,000	13,000	30,000	43,000	84,000	80,000
Occupancy	5,000	26,000	22,000	25,000	78,000	30,000	27,000	57,000	135,000	126,000
Rental of equipment	1,000	24,000	14,000	4,000	43,000	3,000	16,000	19,000	62,000	58,000
Local transportation	3,000	22,000	20,000	22,000	67,000	23,000	30,000	53,000	120,000	113,000
Conferences, conventions, meetings	8,000	19,000	71,000	20,000	118,000	38,000	13,000	51,000	169,000	156,000
Printing and publications	4,000	56,000	43,000	11,000	114,000	14,000	64,000	78,000	192,000	184,000
Awards and grants	1,332,000	14,000	119,000	144,000	1,609,000	-			1,609,000	1,448,000
Miscellaneous	1,000	4,000	6,000	4,000	15,000	16,000	21,000	37,000	52,000	64,000
Total expenses before depreciation	1,412,000	539,000	612,000	568,000	3,131,000	567,000	650,000	1,217,000	4,348,000	4,004,000
Depreciation of buildings and equipment	2,000	5,000	6,000	10,000	23,000	7,000	4,000	11,000	34,000	32,000
Total expenses	$1,414,000	$544,000	$618,000	$578,000	$3,154,000	$574,000	$654,000	$1,228,000	$4,382,000	$4,036,000

(See accompanying notes to financial statements.)

EXHIBIT A (Continued)

Sample Voluntary Health and Welfare Service
Statement of Cash Flows*
Year Ended December 31, 19X2 with Comparative Totals for 19X1

| | Current Funds | | Land, Building, and | Endowment | Total All Funds | |
	Unrestricted	Restricted	Equipment Fund	Fund	19X2	19X1
Cash flows from operating activities						
Public support	$4,129,000	$150,000	$ -	$ -	$4,279,000	$4,407,000
Membership dues	17,000	-	-	-	17,000	18,000
Investment income	98,000	11,000	-	-	109,000	112,000
Other revenues	42,000	-	-	-	42,000	44,000
Cash paid to suppliers and employees	(2,831,000)	-	-	-	(2,831,000)	(2,916,000)
Cash paid for awards and grants	(1,454,000)	(155,000)	-	-	(1,609,000)	(1,657,000)
Net cash flow from operating activities	1,000	6,000	-	-	7,000	8,000
Capital cash flows						
Investment income	-	-	-	25,000	25,000	27,000
Public support	-	-	57,000	6,000	63,000	65,000
Net capital cash flow	-	-	57,000	31,000	88,000	92,000
Cash flows from investing activities						
Land, buildings, and equipment						
Purchases	-	-	(37,000)	-	(37,000)	(35,000)
Proceeds from sales	-	-	-	-	-	-
Investments						
Purchases	(1,107,000)	-	(32,000)	(100,000)	(1,239,000)	(1,202,000)
Proceeds	700,000	-	-	163,000	863,000	837,000
Net cash flow from investing activities	(407,000)	-	(69,000)	63,000	(413,000)	(400,000)
Cash flows from financing activities						
Proceeds from borrowing	-	-	(4,000)	-	(4,000)	(4,000)
Repayment of debt	-	-	(4,000)	-	(4,000)	(4,000)
Net cash flow from financing activities	(406,000)	6,000	(16,000)	94,000	(322,000)	(304,000)
Increase (decrease) in cash						
Transfers						
Property and equipment acquisitions from unrestricted funds	(17,000)	-	17,000	-	-	-
Realized endowment fund appreciation	100,000	-	-	(100,000)	-	-
Funds returned to donors	-	(8,000)	-	-	(8,000)	-
Net increase (decrease) in cash	(323,000)	(2,000)	1,000	(6,000)	(330,000)	(304,000)
Cash						
Beginning of year	2,530,000	5,000	2,000	10,000	2,547,000	2,851,000
End of year	$2,207,000	$ 3,000	$ 3,000	$ 4,000	$2,217,000	$2,547,000

*A voluntary health and welfare nonprofit entity may, but is not required to, present a Statement of Cash Flows. This Statement of Cash Flows is based on the commentary and advisory conclusions contained in "Display in the Financial Statements of Not-for-Profit Organizations," a report of the AICPA Task Force on Not-for-Profit Organizations (December 16, 1988).

EXHIBIT A (Continued)

Sample Voluntary Health and Welfare Service
Notes to Financial Statements
December 31, 19X2

Note 1—Summary of Significant Accounting Policies

The financial statements of Sample Voluntary Health and Welfare have been prepared on the accrual basis and include the accounts of the Service and its affiliated chapters.

Fund Accounting

To ensure observance of limitations and restrictions placed on the use of resources available to the service, the accounts of the service are maintained in accordance with the principles of fund accounting. This is the procedure by which resources for various purposes are classified for accounting and reporting purposes into funds established according to their nature and purposes. Separate accounts are maintained for each fund; however, in the accompanying financial statements, funds that have similar characteristics have been recorded and reported by fund group.

The assets, liabilities, and fund balances of the service are reported in three self-balancing fund groups as follows:

- Current funds, which include unrestricted and restricted resources, represent the portion of expendable funds that is available for support of operations.
- Land, building, and equipment funds represent resources restricted for plant acquisitions and funds expended for plant.
- Endowment funds represent funds that are subject to restrictions of gift instruments requiring in perpetuity that the principal be invested and the income only be used.

Expendable Restricted Resources

Operating and plant funds restricted by the donor, grantor, or other outside party for particular operating purposes or for plant acquisitions are deemed to be earned and reported as revenues of operating funds or as additions to plant funds, respectively, when the service has incurred expenditures in compliance with the specific restrictions. Such amounts received but not yet earned are reported as restricted deferred amounts.

Plant Assets and Depreciation

Uses of operating funds for plant acquisitions and principal debt service payments are accounted for as transfers to plant funds. Donated assets are capitalized at fair value. Proceeds from the sale of plant assets, if unrestricted, are transferred to operating fund balances, or, if restricted, to deferred amounts restricted for plant acquisitions. Depreciation of buildings and equipment is provided over the estimated useful lives of the respective assets on a straight-line basis.

Other Matters

All gains and losses arising from the sale, collection, or other disposition of investments and other noncash assets are accounted for in the fund that owned the assets. Ordinary income from investments, receivables, and the like is accounted for in the fund owning the assets, except for income derived from investments of endowment funds, which is accounted for, if unrestricted, as revenue of the current unrestricted fund or, if restricted, as deferred amounts until the terms of the restriction have been met.

Legally enforceable pledges less an allowance for uncollectible amounts are recorded as receivables in the year made. Pledges for support of current operations are recorded as operating fund support. Pledges for support of future operations and plant acquisitions

EXHIBIT A [Continued]

Notes to Financial Statements (Continued)

are recorded as deferred amounts in the respective funds to which they apply. Policies concerning donated materials and services are described in **Note 6**.

Note 2—Investments

Investments are stated at cost. Market values and unrealized appreciation (depreciation) at December 31, 19X2 and 19X1, are summarized as follows:

| | (Thousands of Dollars) | | | |
| | December 31, 19X2 | | December 31, 19X1 | |
	Quoted Market Value	Unrealized Appreciation	Quoted Market Value	Unrealized Appreciation (Depreciation)
Current unrestricted funds				
For long-term purposes	$2,735	$ 8	$2,230	$ (15)
Other	1,100	25	941	(9)
Current restricted funds	73	2	73	1
Endowment funds	2,125	181	2,183	176
Land, building, and equipment fund	184	7	153	8

Interfund transfers include $100,000 for 19X2, which represents the portion of the realized appreciation ($25,000 realized in the current year and $75,000 realized in prior years) in endowment funds that, under the laws of (a state), were designated by the governing board for unrestricted operations. At December 31, 19X2, $200,000 of realized appreciation was available in endowment funds, which the governing board may, if it deems prudent, also transfer to the unrestricted fund.

If the organization accounts for its investment on the market value basis, the first part of the above note might be worded as follows:

Cost and unrealized appreciation (depreciation) at December 31, 19X2 and 19X1 are summarized as follows:

| | (Thousands of Dollars) | | | |
| | December 31, 19X2 | | December 31, 19X1 | |
	Cost	Unrealized Appreciation	Cost	Unrealized Appreciation (Depreciation)
Current unrestricted funds				
For long-term purposes	$2,727	$ 8	$2,245	$ (15)
Other	1,075	25	950	(9)
Current restricted funds	71	2	72	1
Endowment funds	1,944	181	2,007	176
Land, building, and equipment fund	177	7	45	8

Note 3—Research Grants

The Service's awards for research grants-in-aid generally cover a period of one to three years, subject to annual renewals at the option of the governing board. At December 31, 19X2, $1,748,000 had been designated by the board for research grants, of which $596,000 had been awarded for research to be carried out within the next year.

EXHIBIT A (Continued)

Notes to Financial Statements (Continued)

Note 4—Proposed Research Center

The XYZ Foundation has contributed $50,000 to the Service with the stipulations that it be used for the construction of a research center and that construction of the facilities begin within four years. The Service is considering the construction of a research center, the cost of which would approximate $2,000,000. If the governing board approves the construction of these facilities, it is contemplated that its cost would be financed by a special fund drive.

Note 5—Land, Buildings, and Equipment and Depreciation

Depreciation of buildings and equipment is provided on a straight-line basis over the estimated useful lives of the assets. At December 31, 19X2 and 19X1, the costs of such assets were as follows:

	19X2	19X1
Land	$ 76,000	$ 76,000
Buildings	324,000	324,000
Medical research equipment	336,000	312,000
Office furniture and equipment	43,000	33,000
Automobiles and trucks	33,000	30,000
Total costs	812,000	775,000
Less accumulated depreciation	296,000	262,000
Net	$516,000	$513,000

Note 6—Donated Materials and Services

Donated materials and equipment are reflected as contributions in the accompanying statements at their estimated values at date of receipt. No amounts have been reflected in the statements for donated services inasmuch as no objective basis is available to measure the value of such services; however, a substantial number of volunteers have donated significant amounts of their time in the organization's program services and in its fund-raising campaigns.

Note 7—Long-Term Debt

Long-term debt at December 31, 19X2 and 19X1, consists of the following:

	19X2	19X1
8 percent mortgage note payable in semiannual installments of $5,400 (including principal and interest) to December 31, 19Y0, collateralized by equipment	$32,000	$36,000

Long-term debt maturing in the next five years consists of:

19X3	$ 4,000
19X4	4,000
19X5	4,000
19X6	4,000
19X7	4,000
Total	$20,000

EXHIBIT A (Continued)

<hr>

Notes to Financial Statements (Continued)

Note 8—Leased Facilities

The buildings used by the organization for its community services programs are leased under operating leases. At December 31, 19X2, fifteen such buildings were being leased for an annual cost of approximately $12,000.

Note 9—Pension Plan

Effective January 1, 19X0, Sample Voluntary Health and Welfare Organization adopted Statement of Financial Accounting Standards No. 87, Employers' Accounting for Pensions. Adoption of the statement is accounted for prospectively, without adjustment to prior years. The effect of this change in accounting principles on net pension expense for the year ended December 31, 19X2, was a reduction of $XX,XXX.

A summary of the components of income follows:

	December 31,	
	19X2	**19X1**
Service cost—benefits earned during the year	$ XX,XXX	$ XX,XXX
Interest cost on projected benefit obligation	XX,XXX	XX,XXX
Actual return on plan assets	(XX,XXX)	(XX,XXX)
Net asset gain (loss) deferred for later recognition	(XX,XXX)	(XX,XXX)
Amortization of unrecognized net asset	(XX,XXX)	(XX,XXX)
Net periodic pension income	$(XX,XXX)	$(XX,XXX)
Funded status of the plan:		
Actuarial present value of benefit obligation		
Accumulated benefit obligation, including vested		
benefits of $XX,XXX in 19X2 and $XX,XXX in 19X1	$(XX,XXX)	$(XX,XXX)
Projected benefit obligation for service rendered to		
date	(XX,XXX)	(XX,XXX)
Assets available for benefits		
Plan assets at fair value, primarily listed stocks and		
U.S. government securities	XXX,XXX	XXX,XXX
Plan assets in excess of benefit obligation	XX,XXX	XX,XXX
Unrecorded net (gain) loss from past experience		
different from that assumed and effects of changes		
in assumptions	XXX	XXX
Unrecognized net assets at January 1, 19X0, being		
recognized over XX years	(XX,XXX)	(XX,XXX)
Prepaid pension cost included in other assets	$ XX,XXX	$ XX,XXX

<hr>

The weighted average discount rate and rate of increase in future compensation levels in determining the actuarial present value of the projected benefit obligation was X percent. The expected long-term rate of return on assets was X percent.

In 19X2 and 19X1, $X,XXX and $XX,XXX, respectively, of the vested benefit portion of the projected benefit obligation were settled through the purchase of nonparticipating annuity contracts for certain retired participants and lump sum payments for certain terminated participants. As a result, the Service recognized gains of $X,XXX and $X,XXX in 19X2 and 19X1, respectively.

EXHIBIT A (Continued)

Notes to Financial Statements (Continued)

Note 10—Postretirement Health Care and Life Insurance Benefits

Sample Voluntary Health and Welfare Service offers postretirement health care and life insurance benefits to substantially all of its retired regular full-time employees. Sample Voluntary Health and Welfare Service shares the cost of providing these benefits with all affected retirees. Sample Health and Welfare Service's cost of providing such benefits is recognized by expensing the insurance programs' premiums as paid. The aggregate amount so expensed totaled $XX,XXX and $XX,XXX for the years ended December 31, 19X1 and 19X0, respectively. Sample Voluntary Health and Welfare Service has made no provision for recognizing the cost of postretirement benefits which may eventually be paid to employees who have not yet retired.

EXHIBIT B Longwood Youngsters Association Financial Statements

Longwood Youngsters Association, Inc.
Balance Sheets
As of December 31, 19X8 and 19X7

ASSETS	19X8	19X7	LIABILITIES AND FUND BALANCES	19X8	19X7
			CURRENT FUND		
			Unrestricted		
Cash	$ 10,177	$ 26,405	Accounts payable	$ 32,228	$ 10,001
Accounts receivable	182,064	121,427	Accrued payroll and payroll taxes	14,293	732
Prepayments	8,396	4,348	Due to endowment fund	-	412
Investments (Note 2)	309,428	283,701	Total liabilities	$ 46,521	$ 11,145
			Fund balance:		
			Designated by the governing board for:		
			Long-term investments	254,428	283,701
			Extended services	55,000	-
			Undesignated	154,116	141,035
			Total fund balance	463,544	424,736
Total	$510,065	$435,881	Total	$510,065	$435,881
			EQUIPMENT FUND		
Equipment, at cost, less accumulated depreciation of $10,351 and $7,230 (Notes 1 and 3)	$ 6,311	$ 8,807	Fund balance	$ 6,311	$ 8,807
			ENDOWMENT FUND		
Cash	$ 63,790	$ 24,049	Discount on bond purchased (net of amortization)	$ -	$ 50,324
Accrued interest receivable	-	1,688	Fund balance	247,241	254,477
Accounts receivable—current fund	-	412			
Investments (Note 2)	183,451	278,652			
Total	$247,241	$304,801	Total	$247,241	$304,801

(See accompanying notes to financial statements.)

EXHIBIT B (Continued)

Longwood Youngsters Association, Inc.
Statement of Changes in Fund Balances
For the Year Ended December 31, 19X8 with Comparative Totals for 19X7

	Current Fund Unrestricted	Current Fund Restricted	Equipment Fund	Endowment Fund	Total All Funds 19X8	Total All Funds 19X7
Public support and revenue:						
Public support:						
Contributions	$ 14,656	$ -	$ -	$ -	$ 14,656	$ 29,735
United Way allocation	27,134	-	-	-	27,134	31,000
Total public support	41,790				41,790	60,735
Fees and grants from governmental agencies	510,553	25,962			536,515	462,141
Other services:						
Program service fees (net of allowances of $115,180 and $48,350, respectively)	156,629	-	-	-	156,629	79,779
Sale of services to other agencies/towns	70,948	-	-	-	70,948	52,166
Investment income	23,769	16,093	-	-	39,862	35,625
Gain (loss) on investment transactions	38,534			(8,133)	30,401	9,112
Bond amortization				1,830	1,830	1,830
Miscellaneous revenue				-	-	757
Total other revenue	289,880	16,093		(6,303)	299,670	179,269
Total public support and revenue	842,223	42,055		(6,303)	877,975	702,145
Expenses:						
Program services:						
Counseling	6,674	-	13		6,687	15,831
Youth activities	598,471	42,055	2,163		642,689	564,163
Camping	137,118	-	818		137,936	79,377
Teen parenting	13,155		34		13,189	-
Total program services	755,418	42,055	3,028		800,501	659,371
Supporting services:						
Management and general	48,047	-	93	258	48,398	46,253
Total expenses	803,465	41,055	3,121	258	848,899	705,624
Excess (deficiency) of public support and revenue over expenses	38,758		(3,121)	(6,561)	$ 29,076	$ (3,479)
Other changes in fund balances:						
Equipment acquisitions from unrestricted funds	(625)		625	-		
Transfer under total return	675			(675)		
Fund balances, beginning of year	424,736	-	8,807	254,477		
Fund balances, end of year	$463,544	$ -	$6,311	$247,241		

(See accompanying notes to financial statements.)

EXHIBIT B (Continued)

Longwood Youngsters Association, Inc.
Statement of Functional Expenses
For the Year Ended December 31, 19X8 with Comparative Totals for 19X7

	Program Services					Supporting Services	Total Expenses	
	Counseling	Youth Activities	Camping	Teen Parenting	Total	Management and General	19X8	19X7
Salaries	$5,160	$492,154	$108,795	$10,714	$616,823	$28,893	$645,716	$535,514
Employee health and retirement:								
Benefits	435	31,107	2,741	281	34,564	1,142	35,706	23,196
Payroll taxes	345	31,456	6,469	683	38,953	1,894	40,847	35,624
Total salaries and related expenses	5,940	554,717	118,005	11,678	690,340	31,929	722,269	594,334
Professional fees and contract service payments	52	16,053	1,344	136	17,585	9,815	27,400	24,009
Supplies	140	8,421	697	10	9,268	434	9,702	7,928
Telephone	33	3,504	851	86	4,474	497	4,971	4,408
Postage and shipping	42	3,072	638	-	3,752	231	3,983	1,566
Space occupancy	160	17,197	4,174	424	21,955	1,209	23,164	22,517
Transportation	289	35,607	10,935	773	47,604	1,335	48,939	39,688
Subscriptions	-	-	-	-	-	-	-	533
Membership dues	-	-	-	-	-	2,678	2,678	2,161
Insurance	18	1,955	474	48	2,495	177	2,672	4,653
Interest	-	-	-	-	-	-	-	274
Miscellaneous	-	-	-	-	-	-	-	376
Total expenses before depreciation	6,674	640,526	137,118	13,155	797,473	48,305	845,778	702,447
Depreciation of equipment	13	2,163	818	34	3,028	93	3,121	3,177
Total expenses	$6,687	$642,689	$137,936	$13,189	$800,501	$48,398	$848,899	$705,624

(See accompanying notes to financial statements.)

EXHIBIT B (Continued)

Longwood Youngsters Association, Inc.
Statement of Cash Flows
For the Year Ended 19X8

		19X8
Operating cash flows:		
Excess of revenue over expenses		$29,076
Noncash items:		
Depreciation (not affecting cash)	$ 3,121	
Bond amortization	(1,830)	1,291
Nonoperating items:		
Gain on investment transactions		(30,401)
Changes in assets and liabilities:		
Accounts receivable	(60,637)	
Accrued interest receivable	1,688	
Prepayments	(4,048)	
Accounts payable	22,227	
Accrued payroll	13,561	(27,209)
Total operating cash flows		(27,243)[65]
Investing cash flows:		
Sale of investments	69,474	
Gain on investment transactions	30,401	
Bond discount net of amortization	(48,494)	
Purchase of fixed assets	(625)	
Total investing cash flows		50,756 [68]
Increase in cash		$23,513 [64]

(See accompanying notes to financial statements.)

EXHIBIT B (Continued)

Longwood Youngsters Association, Inc.
Notes to Financial Statements

Note 1—Summary of Significant Accounting Policies

Organization   The Association is a nonstock, nonprofit corporation organized in the United States. The Association is exempt from federal income taxes under the Internal Revenue Code 501(c)(3).

Equipment and Depreciation   Equipment is recorded at cost. Expenditures for maintenance and repairs are charged to space occupancy. When items are sold or otherwise disposed of, the cost and related accumulated depreciation are removed from the respective accounts and the resulting gain or loss is reflected in the equipment fund. Depreciation is computed on a straight-line method based on the estimated useful lives of the assets, primarily five years.

Note 2—Investments

| | December 31, 19X8 | | December 31, 19X7 | |
	Approximate Market Value	Unrealized Appreciation (Depreciation)	Approximate Market Value	Unrealized Appreciation (Depreciation)
Current unrestricted	$329,198	$19,770	$291,321	$ 7,620
Endowment fund	200,901	17,450	282,995	4,343
Total investment portfolio	$530,099	$37,220	$574,316	$11,963

Note 3—Equipment and Depreciation

Depreciation of equipment is provided on a straight-line basis over the estimated useful lives of the assets. At December 31, 19X8 and 19X7, the cost of such assets were as follows:

	19X8	19X7
Furniture and equipment	$11,585	$10,960
Automobiles	5,077	5,077
Total cost	16,662	16,037
Less, accumulated depreciation	10,351	7,230
Net	$ 6,311	$ 8,807

Note 4—Pension Plan

The Association has a defined contribution pension plan which covers substantially all eligible employees. Employee contributions are limited to a percentage of salary. The Association matches each employee's contribution to the plan. Contributions by the Association are fully vested to the employee on the contribution date. Total pension expense for the year amounted to $19,997.

EXHIBIT C LYA Restated Financial Statements

LYA Balance Sheet—June 30, 19X8 and 19X7
Restated Dollars, Changes, and Percentage Increase (Decrease)

	Current Unrestricted 19X8	Current Restricted 19X8	Plant 19X8	Endowment 19X8	Total 19X8	Total 19X7	Dollar Change	Percent Change
ASSETS								
Cash	$ 10,177	$-	$ -	$ 63,790	$ 73,967	$ 50,454	$ 23,513[1]	46.6%[2]
Accounts receivable	182,064				182,064	121,427	60,637[50]	49.9%
Accrued interest receivable					0	1,688	(1,688)	-100.0%
Prepayments	8,396				8,396	4,348	4,048	93.1%
Due from current fund					0	412	(412)	-100.0%
Current assets	200,637	0		63,790	264,427	178,329	86,098	48.3%
Equipment, at cost			16,662		16,662	16,037	625	3.9%
Less accumulated depreciation			(10,351)		(10,351)	(7,230)	(3,121)	43.2%
Equipment net of depreciation			6,311		6,311	8,807	(2,496)	-28.3%
Investments (Note 2)	309,428			183,451	492,879	562,353	(69,474)[60]	-12.4%
Total assets	$510,065	$0	$ 6,311	$247,241	$763,617[10]	$749,489	$ 14,128[11]	1.9%[12]
LIABILITIES AND FUND BALANCES								
Accounts payable	$ 32,228	$-	$ -	$	$ 32,228	$ 10,001	$ 22,227[66]	222.2%
Accrued payroll and payroll taxes	14,293				14,293	732	13,561[67]	1,852.6%
Due to endowment fund					0	412	(412)	-100.0%
Current liabilities	46,521	0	0	0	46,521	11,145	35,376	317.4%
Bond discount net of amortization (Note 2)					0	50,324	(50,324)	-100.0%
Total liabilities	46,521	0	0	0	46,521	61,469	(14,948)	-24.3%
Fund balances:								
Unrestricted, designated by the board for:								
Long-term investments	254,428				254,428	283,701	(29,273)	-10.3%
Extended services	55,000[23]				55,000	0	55,000	ERR
Unrestricted, undesignated	154,116				154,116	141,035	13,081	9.3%
Invested in plant			6,311		6,311	8,807	(2,496)	-28.3%
Invested for endowment				247,241	247,241	254,477	(7,236)	-2.8%
Total fund balances	463,544	0	6,311	247,241	717,096	688,020	29,076	4.2%
Total liabilities and fund balances	$510,065	$0	$6,311	$247,241	$763,617	$749,489	$ 14,128	1.9%

EXHIBIT C (Continued)

LYA Statement of Changes in Fund Balances—June 30, 19X8 and 19X7
Restated Dollars, Changes, and Percentage Increase (Decrease)

	Current Unrestricted	Current Restricted	Plant	Endowment	Total 19X8	Total 19X7	Dollar Change	Percent Change
REVENUE								
Public support:								
Contributions	$ 14,656	$ -	$ -	$ -	$ 14,656	$ 29,735	$(15,079)	-50.7%
United Way allocation	27,134				27,134	31,000	(3,866)	-12.5%
Total public support	41,790	0	0	0	41,790	60,735	(18,945)	-31.2%
Government fees and grants	510,553	25,962	0	0	536,515	462,141	74,374[47]	16.1%
Other services:								
Program service fees (gross)	271,809	0	0	0	271,809	128,129	143,680	112.1%
Less: allowances	115,180				115,180	48,350	66,830	138.2%
Net Program service fees	156,629	0	0	0	156,629	79,779	76,850[48]	96.3%
Sale of services to other agencies/towns	70,948				70,948	52,166	18,782[49]	36.0%
Investment income	23,769	16,093			39,862[35]	35,625	4,237	11.9%
Gain (loss) on investment transactions	38,534[34]			(8,133)[33]	30,401[36]	9,112	21,289	233.6%
Bond amortization				1,830	1,830	1,830	0	0.0%
Miscellaneous revenue					0	757	(757)	-100.0%
Total other revenue	289,880	16,093	0	(6,303)	299,670	179,269	120,401	67.2%
Total public support and revenue	842,223	42,055	0	(6,303)	877,975[41]	702,145[40]	175,830[42]	25.0%
EXPENSES								
Counseling	6,674		13		6,687	15,831	(9,144)	-57.8%
Youth activities	598,471	42,055	2,163		642,689	564,163	78,526	13.9%
Camping	137,118		818		137,936	79,377	58,559	73.8%
Teen parenting	13,155		34		13,189	-	13,189	ERR
Total program services	755,418	42,055	3,028	0	800,501	659,371	141,130	21.4%
Supporting services:								
Management and general	48,047		93	258	48,398	46,253	2,145	4.6%[44]
Total expenses	803,465	42,055	3,121	258	848,899	705,624[39]	143,275	20.3%[43]
Excess (deficit) of revenue over expenses	38,758[26]	0	(3,121)[27]	(6,561)[28]	29,076[25]	(3,479)[29]	32,555	-935.8%[3]
Transfers and other changes in fund balances:								
Equipment acquisitions	(625)		625		0			
Transfer under spending policy	675			(675)	0			
Total transfers and other changes	50	0	625	(675)	0			
Fund balances, beginning of year	424,736	0	8,807	254,477	688,020	691,499		
Fund balances, end of year	$463,544	$ 0	$ 6,311	$247,241	$717,096	$688,020		

EXHIBIT C (Continued)

LYA Statement of Functional Expenses—June 30, 19X8 and 19X7
Restated Dollars, Changes, and Percentage Increase (Decrease)

	Counseling	Youth Activities	Camping	Teen Parenting	Total	Management and General	Total Expense 19X8	19X7	Increase (Decrease)
Salaries	$5,160	$492,154	$108,795	$10,714	$616,823	$28,893	$645,716	$535,514	$110,202
Employee health and retirement:									
Benefits	435	31,107	2,741	281	34,564	1,142	35,706	23,196	12,510
Payroll taxes	345	31,456	6,469	683	38,953	1,894	40,847	35,624	5,223
Total salaries and related expenses	5,940	554,717	118,005	11,678	690,340	31,929	722,269	594,334	127,935[57]
Professional and contractor's fees	52	16,053	1,344	136	17,585	9,815	27,400	24,009	3,391
Supplies	140	8,421	697	10	9,268	434	9,702	7,928	1,774
Telephone	33	3,504	851	86	4,474	497	4,971	4,408	563
Postage and shipping	42	3,072	638		3,752	231	3,983	1,566	2,417
Space occupancy	160	17,197	4,174	424	21,955	1,209	23,164	22,517	647
Transportation	289	35,607	10,935	773	47,604	1,335	48,939	39,688	9,251[58]
Subscriptions					0		0	533	(533)
Membership dues					0	2,678	2,678	2,161	517
Insurance	18	1,955	474	48	2,495	177	2,672	4,653	(1,981)[59]
Interest					0		0	274	(274)
Miscellaneous					0		0	376	(376)
Total expenses before depreciation	6,674	640,526	137,118	13,155	797,473	48,305	845,778	702,447	143,331
Depreciation of equipment	13	2,163	818	34	3,028	93	3,121	3,177	(56)
Total expenses	$6,687	$642,689	$137,936	$13,189	$800,501	$48,398	$848,899	$705,624	$143,275

EXHIBIT D LYA Common Size Statements

LYA Balance Sheet—June 30, 19X8 and 19X7
Common Size
Line Item as a Percentage of Total (Vertical Analysis)

	Current Unrestricted 19X8	Current Restricted 19X8	Plant 19X8	Endowment 19X8	Total 19X8	Total 19X7
ASSETS						
Cash	2.0%[4]	ERR	0.0%	25.8%[63]	9.7%[5]	6.7%
Accounts receivable	35.7%	ERR	0.0%	0.0%	23.8%	16.2%
Accrued interest receivable	0.0%	ERR	0.0%	0.0%	0.0%	0.2%
Prepayments	1.6%	ERR	0.0%	0.0%	1.1%	0.6%
Due from current fund	0.0%	ERR	0.0%	0.0%	0.0%	0.1%
Current assets	39.3%	ERR	0.0%	25.8%	34.6%	23.8%
Equipment, at cost	0.0%	ERR	264.0%	0.0%	2.2%	2.1%
Less accumulated depreciation	0.0%	ERR	−164.0%	0.0%	−1.4%	−1.0%
Equipment net of depreciation	0.0%	ERR	100.0%	0.0%	0.8%[37]	1.2%
Investments (Note 2)	60.7%	ERR	0.0%	74.2%	64.5%[62]	75.0%[61]
Total assets	100.0%	ERR	100.0%	100.0%	100.0%	100.0%
LIABILITIES AND FUND BALANCES						
Accounts payable	6.3%	ERR	0.0%	0.0%	4.2%	1.3%
Accrued payroll and payroll taxes	2.8%	ERR	0.0%	0.0%	1.9%	0.1%
Due to endowment fund	0.0%	ERR	0.0%	0.0%	0.0%	0.1%
Current liabilities	9.1%	ERR	0.0%	0.0%	6.1%	1.5%
Bond discount net of amortization (Note 2)	0.0%	ERR	0.0%	0.0%	0.0%	6.7%
Total liabilities	9.1%	ERR	0.0%	0.0%	6.1%[17]	8.2%[18]
Fund balances:						
Unrestricted, designated by the board for:						
Long-term investments	49.9%	ERR	0.0%	0.0%	33.3%	37.9%
Extended services	10.8%[24]	ERR	0.0%	0.0%	7.2%	0.0%
Unrestricted, undesignated	30.2%	ERR	0.0%	0.0%	20.2%	18.8%
Invested in plant	0.0%	ERR	100.0%	0.0%	0.8%	1.2%
Invested for endowment	0.0%	ERR	0.0%	100.0%	32.4%	34.0%
Total fund balances	90.9%	ERR	100.0%	100.0%	93.9%	91.8%
Total liabilities and fund balances	100.0%	ERR	100.0%	100.0%	100.0%	100.0%

EXHIBIT D (Continued)

LYA Statement of Changes in Fund Balances—June 30, 19X8 and 19X7
Common Size
Line Item as a Percentage of Total (Vertical Analysis)

	Current Unrestricted	Current Restricted	Plant	Endowment	Total 19X8	Total 19X7
REVENUE						
Public support:						
Contributions	1.7%[6]	0.0%	ERR	0.0%	1.7%	4.2%
United Way allocation	3.2%	0.0%	ERR	0.0%	3.1%	4.4%
Total public support	5.0%	0.0%	ERR	0.0%	4.8%[56]	8.6%[55]
Government fees and grants	60.6%	61.7%	ERR	0.0%	61.1%[53]	65.8%[54]
Other services:						
Program service fees (gross)	32.3%	0.0%	ERR	0.0%	31.0%	18.2%
Less: allowances	13.7%	0.0%	ERR	0.0%	13.1%	6.9%
Net program service fees	18.6%	0.0%	ERR	0.0%	17.8%[53]	11.4%[54]
Sale of services to other agencies/towns	8.4%	0.0%	ERR	0.0%	8.1%[53]	7.4%[54]
Investment income	2.8%	38.3%	ERR	0.0%	4.5%	5.1%
Gain (loss) on investment transactions	4.6%	0.0%	ERR	129.0%	3.5%	1.3%
Bond amortization	0.0%	0.0%	ERR	−29.0%	0.2%	0.3%
Miscellaneous revenue	0.0%	0.0%	ERR	0.0%	0.0%	0.1%
Total other revenue	34.4%	38.3%	ERR	100.0%	34.1%	25.5%
Total public support and revenue	100.0%	100.0%	ERR	100.0%	100.0%	100.0%
EXPENSES						
Counseling	0.8%	0.0%	0.4%[7]	0.0%	0.8%	2.2%
Youth activities	74.5%	100.0%	69.3%	0.0%	75.7%	80.0%
Camping	17.1%	0.0%	26.2%	0.0%	16.2%	11.2%
Teen parenting	1.6%	0.0%	1.1%	0.0%	1.6%	0.0%
Total program services	94.0%	100.0%	97.0%	0.0%	94.3%	93.4%
Supporting services:						
Management and general	6.0%	0.0%	3.0%	100.0%	5.7%[46]	6.6%[45]
Total expenses	95.4%	100.0%	ERR	−4.1%	96.7%	100.5%
Excess (deficit) of revenue over expenses	4.6%	0.0%	ERR	104.1%	3.3%[30]	−0.5%[31]
Transfers and other changes in fund balances:						
Equipment acquisitions	−0.1%	0.0%	ERR	0.0%		
Transfer under spending policy	0.1%	0.0%	ERR	10.7%		
Total transfers and other changes	0.0%	0.0%	ERR	10.7%		
Fund balances, beginning of year	50.4%	0.0%	ERR	−4,037.4%	78.4%	98.5%
Fund balances, end of year	55.0%[22]	0.0%	ERR	−3,922.6%	81.7%[20]	98.0%

EXHIBIT D (Continued)

LYA Statement of Functional Expenses—June 30, 19X8 and 19X7
Common Size
Line Item as a Percentage of Total (Vertical Analysis)

	Counseling	Youth Activities	Camping	Teen Parenting	Total	Management and General	Total Expense 19X8	Total Expense 19X7	Increase (Decrease)
Salaries	77.2%	76.6%	78.9%	81.2%	77.1%	59.7%	76.1%	75.9%	20.6%
Employee health and retirement:									
Benefits	6.5%	4.8%	2.0%	2.1%	4.3%	2.4%	4.2%	3.3%	53.9%
Payroll taxes	5.2%	4.9%	4.7%	5.2%	4.9%	3.9%	4.8%	5.0%	14.7%
Total salaries and related expenses	88.8%	86.3%	85.6%	88.5%	86.2%	66.0%	85.1%[39]	84.2%	21.5%
Professional and contractor's fees	0.8%	2.5%	1.0%	1.0%	2.2%	20.3%	3.2%	3.4%	14.1%
Supplies	2.1%	1.3%	0.5%	0.1%	1.2%	0.9%	1.1%	1.1%	22.4%
Telephone	0.5%	0.5%	0.6%	0.7%	0.6%	1.0%	0.6%	0.6%	12.8%
Postage and shipping	0.6%	0.5%	0.5%	0.0%	0.5%	0.5%	0.5%	0.2%	154.3%
Space occupancy	2.4%	2.7%	3.0%	3.2%	2.7%	2.5%	2.7%	3.2%	2.9%
Transportation	4.3%	5.5%	7.9%[8]	5.9%	5.9%	2.8%	5.8%	5.6%	23.3%
Subscriptions	0.0%	0.0%	0.0%	0.0%	0.0%	0.0%	0.0%	0.1%	-100.0%
Membership dues	0.0%	0.0%	0.0%	0.0%	0.0%	5.5%	0.3%	0.3%	23.9%
Insurance	0.3%	0.3%	0.3%	0.4%	0.3%	0.4%	0.3%	0.7%	-42.6%
Interest	0.0%	0.0%	0.0%	0.0%	0.0%	0.0%	0.0%	0.0%	-100.0%
Miscellaneous	0.0%	0.0%	0.0%	0.0%	0.0%	0.0%	0.0%	0.1%	-100.0%
Total expenses before depreciation	99.8%	99.7%	99.4%	99.7%	99.6%	99.8%	99.6%	99.5%	20.4%
Depreciation of equipment	0.2%	0.3%	0.6%	0.3%	0.4%	0.2%	0.4%	0.5%	-1.8%
Total expenses	100.0%	100.0%	100.0%	100.0%	100.0%	100.0%	100.0%	100.0%	20.3%

EXHIBIT E **LYA Fund Distribution Statements**

LYA Balance Sheet—June 30, 19X8 and 19X7
Fund Amount as a Percentage of Total 19X8 (Horizontal Analysis)

	Current Unrestricted 19X8	Current Restricted 19X8	Plant 19X8	Endowment 19X8	Total 19X8	Total 19X7
ASSETS						
Cash	13.8%	0.0%	0.0%	86.2%	100.0%	68.2%
Accounts receivable	100.0%	0.0%	0.0%	0.0%	100.0%	66.7%
Accrued interest receivable	ERR	ERR	ERR	ERR	ERR	ERR
Prepayments	100.0%	0.0%	0.0%	0.0%	100.0%	51.8%
Due from current fund	ERR	ERR	ERR	ERR	ERR	ERR
Current assets	75.9%	0.0%	0.0%	24.1%	100.0%	67.4%
Equipment, at cost	0.0%	0.0%	100.0%	0.0%	100.0%	96.2%
Less accumulated depreciation	0.0%	0.0%	100.0%	0.0%	100.0%	69.8%
Equipment net of depreciation	0.0%	0.0%	100.0%	0.0%	100.0%	139.5%
Investments (Note 2)	62.8%	0.0%	0.0%	37.2%	100.0%	114.1%
Total assets	66.8%[9][19]	0.0%	0.8%	32.4%	100.0%	98.1%
LIABILITIES AND FUND BALANCES						
Accounts payable	100.0%	0.0%	0.0%	0.0%	100.0%	31.0%
Accrued payroll and payroll taxes	100.0%	0.0%	0.0%	0.0%	100.0%	5.1%
Due to endowment fund	ERR	ERR	ERR	ERR	ERR	ERR
Current liabilities	100.0%	0.0%	0.0%	0.0%	100.0%	24.0%
Bond discount net of amortization (Note 2)	ERR	ERR	ERR	ERR	ERR	ERR
Total liabilities	100.0%	0.0%	0.0%	0.0%	100.0%	132.1%
Fund balances:						
Unrestricted, designated by the board for:						
Long-term investments	100.0%	0.0%	0.0%	0.0%	100.0%	111.5%
Extended services	100.0%	0.0%	0.0%	0.0%	100.0%	0.0%
Unrestricted, undesignated	100.0%	0.0%	0.0%	0.0%	100.0%	91.5%
Invested in plant	0.0%	0.0%	100.0%	0.0%	100.0%	139.5%
Invested for endowment	0.0%	0.0%	0.0%	100.0%	100.0%	102.9%
Total fund balances	64.6%	0.0%	0.9%	34.5%	100.0%	95.9%
Total liabilities and fund balances	66.8%	0.0%	0.8%	32.4%	100.0%	98.1%

EXHIBIT E *(Continued)*

LYA Statement of Changes in Fund Balances—June 30, 19X8 and 19X7
Fund Amount as a Percentage of Total 19X8 (Horizontal Analysis)

	Current Unrestricted	Current Restricted	Plant	Endowment	Total 19X8	Total 19X7
REVENUE						
Public support:						
Contributions	100.0%	0.0%	0.0%	0.0%	100.0%	202.9%
United Way allocation	100.0%	0.0%	0.0%	0.0%	100.0%	114.2%
Total public support	100.0%	0.0%	0.0%	0.0%	100.0%	145.3%
Government fees and grants	95.2%	4.8%	0.0%	0.0%	100.0%	86.1%
Other services:						
Program service fees (gross)	100.0%	0.0%	0.0%	0.0%	100.0%	47.1%
Less: allowances	100.0%	0.0%	0.0%	0.0%	100.0%	42.0%
Net Program service fees	100.0%	0.0%	0.0%	0.0%	100.0%	50.9%
Sale of services to other agencies/towns	100.0%	0.0%	0.0%	0.0%	100.0%	73.5%
Investment income	59.6%	40.4%	0.0%	0.0%	100.0%	89.4%
Gain (loss) on investment transactions	126.8%	0.0%	0.0%	-26.8%	100.0%	30.0%
Bond amortization	0.0%	0.0%	0.0%	100.0%	100.0%	100.0%
Miscellaneous revenue	ERR	ERR	ERR	ERR	ERR	ERR
Total other revenue	96.7%	5.4%	0.0%	-2.1%	100.0%	59.8%
Total public support and revenue	95.9%	4.8%	0.0%	-0.7%	100.0%	80.0%
EXPENSES						
Counseling	99.8%	0.0%	0.2%	0.0%	100.0%	236.7%
Youth activities	93.1%	6.5%	0.3%	0.0%	100.0%	87.8%
Camping	99.4%	0.0%	0.6%	0.0%	100.0%	57.5%
Teen parenting	99.7%	0.0%	0.3%	0.0%	100.0%	0.0%
Total program services	94.4%	5.3%	0.4%	0.0%	100.0%	82.4%
Supporting services:						
Management and general	99.3%	0.0%	0.2%	0.5%	100.0%	95.6%
Total expenses	94.6%	5.0%	0.4%	0.0%	100.0%	83.1%
Excess (deficit) of revenue over expenses	133.3%	0.0%	-10.7%	-22.6%	100.0%	-12.0%
Transfers and other changes in fund balances:						
Equipment acquisitions						
Transfer under spending policy						
Total transfers and other changes						
Fund balance, beginning of year	61.7%	0.0%	1.3%	37.0%	100.0%	100.5%
Fund balance, end of year	64.6%	0.0%	0.9%	34.5%[21]	100.0%	95.9%

EXHIBIT E (Continued)

LYA Statement of Functional Expenses—June 30, 19X8 and 19X7
Fund Amount as a Percentage of Total 19X8 (Horizontal Analysis)

	Counseling	Youth Activities	Camping	Teen Parenting	Total	Management and General	Total Expense	
							19X8	19X7
Salaries	0.8%	76.2%	16.8%	1.7%	95.5%	4.5%	100.0%	82.9%
Employee health and retirement:								
Benefits	1.2%	87.1%	7.7%	0.8%	96.8%	3.2%	100.0%	65.0%
Payroll taxes	0.8%	77.0%	15.8%	1.7%	95.4%	4.6%	100.0%	87.2%
Total salaries and related expenses	0.8%	76.8%	16.3%	1.6%	95.6%	4.4%	100.0%	82.3%
Professional and contractor's fees	0.2%	58.6%	4.9%	0.5%	64.2%	35.8%	100.0%	87.6%
Supplies	1.4%	86.8%	7.2%	0.1%	95.5%	4.5%	100.0%	81.7%
Telephone	0.7%	70.5%	17.1%	1.7%	90.0%	10.0%	100.0%	88.7%
Postage and shipping	1.1%	77.1%	16.0%	0.0%	94.2%	5.8%	100.0%	39.3%
Space occupancy	0.7%	74.2%	18.0%	1.8%	94.8%	5.2%	100.0%	97.2%
Transportation	0.6%	72.8%	22.3%	1.6%	97.3%	2.7%	100.0%	81.1%
Subscriptions	ERR	ERR	ERR	ERR	ERR	ERR	ERR	ERR
Membership dues	0.0%	0.0%	0.0%	0.0%	0.0%	100.0%	100.0%	80.7%
Insurance	0.7%	73.2%	17.7%	1.8%	93.4%	6.6%	100.0%	174.1%
Interest	ERR	ERR	ERR	ERR	ERR	ERR	ERR	ERR
Miscellaneous	ERR	ERR	ERR	ERR	ERR	ERR	ERR	ERR
Total expenses before depreciation	0.8%	75.7%	16.2%	1.6%	94.3%	5.7%	100.0%	83.1%
Depreciation of equipment	0.4%	69.3%	26.2%	1.1%	97.0%	3.0%	100.0%	101.8%
Total expenses	0.8%	75.7%	16.2%	1.6%	94.3%	5.7%	100.0%	83.1%

EXHIBIT F **LYA Selected Ratios**

LYA—July 31, 19X8 and 19X7
Selected Ratios

	Current Unrestricted 19X8	Current Restricted 19X8	Plant 19X8	Endowment 19X8	Total 19X8	Total 19X7
RATIOS						
Current	4.31	ERR	ERR	ERR	5.68[13]	16.00[15]
Quick	4.13	ERR	ERR	ERR	5.50[14]	16.17[16]
Working Capital	$154,116	$0	$0	$63,790	$217,906	$167,184
Debt/Assets	0.09	ERR	0.00	0.00	0.06	0.08
Times Interest Earned	N/A	N/A	N/A	N/A	ERR	−11.70
Asset Turnover	1.65	ERR	0.00	−0.03	1.15	0.94
Receivables Turnover	4.05	ERR	ERR	ERR	4.20[51]	4.89[52]
Return on Fund Balance	0.09	ERR	−0.35	−0.03	0.04[32]	−0.01

N/A = data not available
ERR = attempt to divide by zero

FORMULAS

Current = Current Assets ÷ Current Liabilities

Quick = (Current Assets − Nonliquid Current Assets) ÷ Current Liabilities

Working Capital = Current Assets − Current Liabilities

Debt/Assets = Total Liabilities ÷ Total Assets

Times Interest Earned = Excess or Deficit Before Interest Expense ÷ Interest Expense

Asset Turnover = Total Revenues and Other Additions ÷ Total Assets

Receivables Turnover = Revenues and Other Additions that Generate Receivables ÷ Receivables

Return on Fund Balance = Excess or Deficit ÷ Beginning Fund Balance

EXHIBIT G **LYA Comparative Statistics**

LYA—July 31, 19X8 and 19X7
External Comparison Data for Longwood Youngsters Association

	LYA		Average	
	Total 19X8	*Total 19X7*	*Total 19X8*	*Total 19X7*
Percent Revenues from:				
Public Support	4.8%	8.6%	29.6%	28.3%
Governments	61.1%	65.8%	58.1%	58.5%
Service Fees and Sales	25.9%	18.8%	14.0%	11.6%
Investment Income and Earnings	8.2%	6.6%	1.2%	1.1%
Other	0.0%	0.1%	0.7%	0.5%
Percent Expenses by Function:				
Counseling (hours)	0.8%	2.2%	12.5%	12.7%
Youth Activities (hours)	75.7%	80.0%	40.9%	40.8%
Camping (days)	16.2%	11.2%	20.2%	21.1%
Teen Parenting (hours)	1.6%	0.0%	7.6%	5.4%
Other Program			8.2%	7.9%
Total Program	94.3%	93.4%	89.4%	87.9%
Management and General	5.7%	6.6%	10.6%	12.1%
Service Units/Program:				
Counseling (hours)	160	483	N/A	N/A
Youth Activities (hours)	69,725	67,246	N/A	N/A
Camping (days)	7,315	3,845	N/A	N/A
Teen Parenting (hours)	983	0	N/A	N/A
Cost/Service Hour by Program:				
Counseling (hours)	41.79	32.78	35.22	33.84
Youth Activities (hours)	9.22	8.39	7.85	7.89
Camping (days)	18.86	20.64	22.98	23.76
Teen Parenting (hours)	13.42	ERR	11.71	12.85
Current Ratio	5.68	16.00	1.34	1.52
Debt/Total Capital Ratio	0.06	0.08	0.85	0.73
Expenses/Revenue Ratio	96.7%	100.5%	103.2%	102.4%

EXHIBIT H   Sample Independent School Financial Statements

Sample Independent School
Balance Sheet
June 30, 19X1

	Operating Funds	Plant Funds	Endowment Funds	Total All Funds
Assets				
Cash	$ 87,000	$ 15,000	$ 19,000	$ 121,000
Accounts receivable, less allowance for doubtful receivables of $3,000	34,000	-	-	34,000
Pledges receivable, less allowance for doubtful pledges of $10,000	-	75,000	-	75,000
Inventories, at lower of cost (FIFO) or market (Note 3)	7,000	-	-	7,000
Investments (Note 2)	355,000	10,000	100,000	465,000
Land, buildings, equipment, and library books, at cost less accumulated depreciation of $980,000 (Note 4)	-	2,282,000	-	2,282,000
Other assets	17,000	-	-	17,000
Total assets	$500,000	$2,382,000	$119,000	$3,001,000
Liabilities and Fund Balances				
Accounts payable and accrued expenses	$ 13,000	$ -	$ -	$ 13,000
Deferred amounts (Note 8)				
Unrestricted	86,000	-	-	86,000
Restricted	27,000	100,000	-	127,000
Long-term debt (Note 5)	-	131,000	-	131,000
Total liabilities	126,000	231,000	-	357,000
Fund balances				
Unrestricted				
Designated by the governing board for long-term investment	355,000	-	-	355,000
Undesignated	19,000	-	-	19,000
	374,000	-	-	374,000
Restricted—nonexpendable	-	-	119,000	119,000
Net investment in plant	-	2,151,000	-	2,151,000
Total fund balances	374,000	2,151,000	119,000	2,644,000
Total liabilities and fund balances	$500,000	$2,382,000	$119,000	$3,001,000

Adapted from *Audits of Certain Nonprofit Organizations*, AICPA, 1987, pp. 101-108; and *Checklists and Illustrative Financial Statements for Nonprofit Organizations*, AICPA, 1990, pp. 1, 84-90.

EXHIBIT H (Continued)

Sample Independent School
Statement of Support and Revenue, Expenses, Capital Additions, and Changes in Fund Balances
For Year Ended June 30, 19X1

	Operating Funds			Plant Funds	Endowment Funds	Total All Funds
	Unrestricted	Restricted	Total			
Support and revenue						
Tuition and fees	$ 910,000	$ -	$ 910,000	$ -	$ -	$ 910,000
Contributions	104,000	80,500	184,500	-	-	184,500
Endowment and other investment income	23,000	1,500	24,500	-	-	24,500
Net loss on investment transactions	(8,000)	-	(8,000)	-	-	(8,000)
Auxiliary activities	25,000	-	25,000	-	-	25,000
Summer school and other programs	86,000	-	86,000	-	-	86,000
Other sources	26,000	-	26,000	-	-	26,000
Total support and revenue	1,166,000	82,000	1,248,000	-	-	1,248,000
Expenses						
Program services						
Instruction and student activities	798,000	43,000	841,000	69,000	-	910,000
Auxiliary activities	24,000	-	24,000	-	-	24,000
Summer school and other programs	91,000	-	91,000	7,000	-	98,000
Financial aid	-	37,000	37,000	3,000	-	40,000
Total program services	913,000	80,000	993,000	79,000	-	1,072,000
Supporting services						
General administration	147,000	2,000	149,000	13,000	-	162,000
Fund raising	12,000	-	12,000	1,000	-	13,000
Total supporting services	159,000	2,000	161,000	14,000	-	175,000
Total expenses	1,072,000	82,000	1,154,000	93,000	-	1,247,000
Excess (deficiency) of support and revenue over expenses before capital additions	94,000	-	94,000	(93,000)	-	1,000
Capital additions						
Contributions and bequests	-	-	-	80,000	30,000	110,000
Investment income	-	-	-	5,000	-	5,000
Net gain on investment transactions	-	-	-	1,000	2,000	3,000
Total capital additions	-	-	-	86,000	32,000	118,000
Excess (deficiency) of support and revenue over expenses after capital additions	94,000	-	94,000	(7,000)	32,000	119,000
Fund balances at beginning of year	387,000	-	387,000	2,047,000	91,000	2,525,000
Transfers						
Equipment acquisitions and principal debt service payments	(111,000)	-	(111,000)	111,000	-	-
Realized gains on endowment funds utilized	4,000	-	4,000	-	(4,000)	-
Fund balances at end of year	$ 374,000	$ -	$ 374,000	$2,151,000	$119,000	$2,644,000

EXHIBIT H (Continued)

Sample Independent School
Statement of Changes in Financial Position
For Year Ended June 30, 19X1

	Operating Funds	Plant Funds	Endowment Funds	Total All Funds
Resources provided				
Excess (deficiency) of support and revenue over expenses before capital additions	$ 94,000	$ (93,000)	$ -	$ 1,000
Capital additions				
Contributions and bequests	-	80,000	30,000	110,000
Investment income	-	5,000	-	5,000
Net gain on investments	-	1,000	2,000	3,000
Excess (deficiency) of support and revenue over expenses after capital additions	94,000	(7,000)	32,000	119,000
Items not using (providing) resources				
Provision for depreciation	-	93,000	-	93,000
Net (gain) loss on investment transactions	8,000	(1,000)	(2,000)	5,000
Decrease in inventories	2,000	-	-	2,000
Increase in deferred amounts	3,000	75,000	-	78,000
Proceeds from sale of investments	160,000	2,000	47,000	209,000
Total resources provided	267,000	162,000	77,000	506,000
Resources used				
Purchases of equipment	-	145,000	-	145,000
Reduction of long-term debt	-	52,000	-	52,000
Purchases of investments	210,000	6,000	136,000	352,000
Increase in other assets	1,000	-	-	1,000
Increase in accounts and pledges receivable	3,000	60,000	-	63,000
Decrease in accounts payable and accrued expenses	3,000	-	-	3,000
Total resources used	217,000	263,000	136,000	616,000
Transfers				
Equipment acquisitions and principal debt service payments	(111,000)	111,000	-	-
Realized gains on endowment funds utilized	4,000	-	(4,000)	-
Total transfers	(107,000)	111,000	(4,000)	-
Increase (decrease) in cash	$ (57,000)	$ 10,000	$ (63,000)	$(110,000)

EXHIBIT H (Continued)

Sample Independent School
Statement of Cash Flows*
Year Ended June 30, 19X1

	Operating Funds	Plant Funds	Endowment Funds	Total All Funds
Cash flows from operating activities				
Tuition, fees and auxiliary activities	$ 1,044,000	$ -	$ -	$ 1,044,000
Endowment and investment income	24,500	-	-	24,500
Contributions	187,500	-	-	187,500
Cash paid to suppliers and employees	(1,145,000)	-	-	(1,145,000)
Interest paid	(11,000)	-	-	(11,000)
Net cash flow from operating activities	100,000	-	-	100,000
Capital cash flows				
Contributions	-	95,000	30,000	125,000
Investment income	-	5,000	-	5,000
Net capital cash flows	-	100,000	30,000	130,000
Cash flows from financing activities				
Repayments of long-term debt	-	(52,000)	-	(52,000)
Net cash flow from financing activities	-	(52,000)	-	(52,000)
Cash flows from financing activities				
Land, buildings, equipment, and library books				
Purchases	-	(145,000)	-	(145,000)
Proceeds from sales	-	-	-	-
Investments				
Purchases	(210,000)	(6,000)	(136,000)	(352,000)
Proceeds	160,000	2,000	47,000	209,000
Net cash flow from investing activities	(50,000)	(149,000)	(89,000)	(288,000)
Increase (decrease) in cash	50,000	(101,000)	(59,000)	(110,000)
Transfers				
Equipment acquisitions and principal debt service payments	(111,000)	111,000	-	-
Realized gains on endowment funds utilized	4,000	-	(4,000)	-
Net increase (decrease) in cash	(57,000)	10,000	(63,000)	(110,000)
Cash				
Beginning of year	144,000	5,000	82,000	231,000
End of year	$ 87,000	$ 15,000	$ 19,000	$ 121,000

*A nonprofit independent school may, but is not required to, present a Statement of Cash Flows instead of a Statement of Changes in Financial Position. This sample Statement of Cash Flows is based on the commentary and advisory conclusions contained in "Display in the Financial Statements of Not-for-Profit Organizations," a report of the AICPA Task Force on Not-for-Profit Organizations (December 16, 1988).

EXHIBIT H (Continued)

Sample Independent School
Notes to Financial Statements
For Year Ended June 30, 19X1

Note 1—Summary of Significant Accounting Policies

The financial statements of Sample Independent School have been prepared on the accrual basis. The significant accounting policies followed are described below to enhance the usefulness of the financial statements to the reader.

Fund Accounting

To ensure observance of limitations and restrictions placed on the use of resources available to the school, the accounts of the school are maintained in accordance with the principles of fund accounting. This is the procedure by which resources for various purposes are classified for accounting and reporting purposes into funds established according to their nature and purposes. Separate accounts are maintained for each fund; however, in the accompanying financial statements, funds that have similar characteristics have been combined into fund groups. Accordingly, all financial transactions have been recorded and reported by fund group.

The assets, liabilities, and fund balances of the school are reported in three self-balancing fund groups as follows:

- Operating funds, which include unrestricted and restricted resources, represent the portion of expendable funds that is available for support of school operations.
- Plant funds represent resources restricted for plant acquisitions and funds expended for plant.
- Endowment funds represent funds that are subject to restrictions of gift instruments requiring in perpetuity that the principal be invested and the income only be used.

Expendable Restricted Resources

Operating and plant funds restricted by the donor, grantor, or other outside party for particular operating purposes or for plant acquisitions are deemed to be earned and reported as revenues of operating funds or as additions to plant funds, respectively, when the school has incurred expenditures in compliance with the specific restrictions. Such amounts received but not yet earned are reported as restricted deferred amounts.

Plant Assets and Depreciation

Uses of operating funds for plant acquisitions and principal debt service payments are accounted for as transfers to plant funds. Proceeds from the sale of plant assets, if unrestricted, are transferred to operating fund balances, or, if restricted, to deferred amounts restricted for plant acquisitions. Depreciation of buildings and equipment is provided over the estimated useful lives of the respective assets on a straight-line basis.

Other Matters

All gains and losses arising from the sale, collection, or other disposition of investments and other noncash assets are accounted for in the fund that owned the assets. Ordinary income from investments, receivables, and the like is accounted for in the fund owning the assets, except for income derived from investments of endowment funds, which is accounted for, if unrestricted, as revenue of the expendable operating fund or, if restricted, as deferred amounts until the terms of the restriction have been met.

Legally enforceable pledges less an allowance for uncollectible amounts are recorded as receivables in the year made. Pledges for support of current operations are recorded as operating fund support. Pledges for support of future operations and plant acquisitions are recorded as deferred amounts in the respective funds to which they apply.

EXHIBIT H (Continued)

Notes to Financial Statements (Continued)

Note 2—Investments

Investments are presented in the financial statements in the aggregate at the lower of cost (amortized, in the case of bonds) or fair market value.

	Cost	Market
Operating funds	$355,000	$365,000
Plant funds	10,000	11,000
Endowment funds	100,000	109,000
	$465,000	$485,000

Investments are composed of the following:

	Cost	Market
Corporate stocks and bonds	$318,000	$320,000
U.S. government obligations	141,000	159,000
Municipal bonds	6,000	6,000
	$465,000	$485,000

The following tabulation summarizes the relationship between carrying values and market values of investment assets.

	Carrying Value	Market Value	Excess of Market Over Cost
Balance at end of year	$465,000	$485,000	$20,000
Balance at beginning of year	$327,000	$335,000	8,000
Increase in unrealized appreciation			12,000
Realized net loss for year			(5,000)
Total net gain for year			$ 7,000

For the year ended June 30, 19X1, the average annual yield exclusive of net gains (losses) was 7 percent, and the annual total return based on market value was 9 percent.

Note 3—Inventories

Inventories at June 30, 19X1 consist of:

Paper and supply stock	$2,000
Textbooks	5,000
	$7,000

Note 4—Plant Assets and Depreciation

A summary of plant assets follows:

Land	$ 255,000
Buildings	2,552,000
Equipment	340,000
Library books	115,000
	3,262,000
Less accumulated depreciation	980,000
	$2,282,000

EXHIBIT H (Continued)

Notes to Financial Statements (Continued)

Note 5—Long-Term Debt

A summary of long-term debt follows:

$7\frac{1}{2}$ percent unsecured notes payable to bank due in quarterly installments of $2,500	$ 29,000
$8\frac{1}{2}$ percent mortgage payable in semiannual installments of $3,500 through 19X7	102,000
	$131,000

Long-term debt maturing in the next five years consists of:

19X2	$17,000
19X3	17,000
19X4	16,000
19X5	7,000
19X6	7,000
Total	$64,000

Note 6—Pension Plans

Effective July 1, 19X0, the school adopted Statement of Financial Accounting Standards No. 87, Employer's Accounting for Pensions. Adoption of the statement is accounted for prospectively, without adjustment to prior years. The effect of this change in accounting principles on net pension expense for the year ended June 30, 19X1, was a reduction of $XX,XXX.

A summary of the components of income follows:

Service cost-benefits earned during the year	$ XX,XXX
Interest cost on projected benefit obligation	XX,XXX
Actual return on plan assets	(XX,XXX)
Net asset gain (loss) deferred for later recognition	(XX,XXX)
Amortization of unrecognized net asset	(XX,XXX)
Net periodic pension income	$(XX,XXX)

Funded status of the plan:	
Actuarial present value of benefit obligation	
Accumulated benefit obligation, including vested benefits of $XX,XXX in 19X1	$(XX,XXX)
Projected benefit obligation for service rendered to date	(XX,XXX)
Assets available for benefits	
Plan assets at fair value, primarily listed stocks and U.S. government securities	XXX,XXX
Plan assets in excess of benefit obligation	XX,XXX
Unrecorded net (gain) loss from past experience different from that assumed and effects of changes in assumptions	XXX
Unrecognized net assets at July 1, 19X0, being recognized over XX years	(XX,XXX)
Prepaid pension cost included in other assets	$ XX,XXX

EXHIBIT H (Continued)

Notes to Financial Statements (Continued)

The weighted average discount rate and rate of increase in future compensation levels in determining the actuarial present value of the projected benefit obligation was X percent. The expected long-term rate of return on assets was X percent.

In 19X1, $X,XXX of the vested benefit portion of the projected benefit obligation was settled through the purchase of nonparticipating annuity contracts for certain retired participants and lump sum payments for certain terminated participants. As a result, the school recognized gains of $X,XXX in 19X1.

Note 7—Postretirement Health Care and Life Insurance Benefits

Sample Independent School offers postretirement health care and life insurance benefits to substantially all of its retired regular full-time employees. Sample Independent School shares the cost of providing these benefits with all affected retirees. Sample Independent School's cost of providing such benefits is recognized by expensing the insurance program's premiums as paid. The aggregate amount so expensed totaled $XX,XXX for the year ended June 30, 19X1. Sample Independent School has made no provision for recognizing the cost of postretirement benefits which may eventually be paid to employees who have not yet retired.

Note 8—Changes in Deferred Restricted Amounts

	Operating Funds	Plant Fund
Balances at beginning of year	$ 24,000	$ 25,000
Additions		
Contributions and bequests	79,000	158,000
Investment income	6,000	1,000
Net gain on investment transactions	-	2,000
	109,000	186,000
Deductions—funds expended during the year	82,000	86,000
Balances at end of year	$ 27,000	$100,000

Note 9—Functional Allocation of Expenses

The costs of providing the various programs and other activities have been summarized on a functional basis in the statement of support and revenue, expenses, capital additions, and changes in fund balances. Accordingly, certain costs have been allocated among the programs and supporting services benefited.

Note 10—Commitments

The school has entered into various agreements aggregating approximately $80,000 for the purchase of equipment to be received subsequent to June 30, 19X1.

DISCUSSION QUESTIONS

1. What are voluntary health and welfare organizations? Why are they called voluntary?

2. What characteristics of these organizations differ from those of other nonprofits?

3. What is the impact of these characteristics on the accounting requirements for voluntary health and welfare organizations?

4. What is a Statement of Functional Expenses?

5. Review the Statement of Functional Expenses in Exhibit A. List the five most important conclusions you have reached about the organization on the basis of this statement.

6. What are the accounting standards for the recognition of the following items in voluntary health and welfare organizations: pledges and cash donations, donated goods and services, restricted revenues, fund-raising expenses?

7. What kinds of organizations are included under "certain" nonprofit organizations?

8. What are the accounting standards for certain nonprofit organizations for the following items: funds, restricted revenues, functional expenses?

9. What are the key accounting issues for the following organizations: private foundations; clubs; museums and libraries; religious organizations and affiliated nonprofits; private elementary and secondary schools; performing arts organizations?

10. What are the nonprofit accounting items that the FASB and AICPA are considering? How do you think they will be resolved?

11. Summarize the process used by a United Way to evaluate whether a nonprofit organization should receive funds.

12. Apply the United Way's analytic process to a voluntary health and welfare or certain nonprofit organization with which you are familiar, such as the Girl or Boy Scouts or a local arts organization. List your conclusions about the likelihood of its receiving United Way funds, how much it is likely to receive, and your reasons for reaching these conclusions.

Cases

CASE STUDIES

The series of cases, Cases 16.1 and 16.2, enables you to practice the accounting transactions and fund accounts uniquely associated with voluntary health and welfare and other nonprofit organizations. Case 16.2 delves in greater detail into the accounting practices of a voluntary organization. It must be used along with Case 16.1. Case 16.3 raises some interesting accounting, financial analysis, and financial management issues in the context of a venerable voluntary agency.

CASE 16.1 Children's Center (A)

The Children's Center was incorporated in late 1991 as a Voluntary Health and Welfare Organization under Section 501(c)(3) of the Internal Revenue Code. It was formed by Dorothy Wilson in the Roxbury area of Boston, Massachusetts, to provide social services to parents and children in lower-income families and to inform these families about the health care services to which they were legally entitled. Dr. Wilson had grown up in Roxbury, continued to live there as an adult, and, as a practicing pediatrician, was well aware of the substantial health needs of the area's children and the lack of knowledge of the low-cost or free services and insurance available to their families. To eliminate this problem, she donated $25,000 of her own funds and convinced a large insurance firm to match her funds with another $25,000. These funds were to be used as seed money for the Children's Center—an organization whose purpose was to counsel and inform parents of medically indigent children.

In December of 1991, Rosanna Griff, an energetic and able social worker, was hired to staff the new organization. All general management functions were to be performed by the board of trustees until such time as the growth of the organization appeared to warrant hiring of administrative staff.

Denise Nitterhouse prepared this case under the supervision of Professor Regina E. Herzlinger. Copyright © 1977 by the President and Fellows of Harvard College. Harvard Business School case 177-216. Revised January 1993.

In 1991 the following activities took place:

(1) The center was incorporated, at a cost of $1,000, which was paid in cash.

(2) Rosanna Griff worked for one month at an annualized salary of $24,000 and related fringe benefits and payroll taxes of $3,600. All her time was spent in contacting community groups and health care providers to determine what services could be provided in the area. Net salary of $900 had been paid, and gross salary of $1,100 was not paid as of December 31. Payroll taxes and fringe benefits were unpaid on December 31. Rosanna used her own home as an office during this month.

(3) A used television and VCR were purchased on October 28, 1991, for $500, which had not been paid as of 12/31/91. Both were expected to have a five-year life, with minimal maintenance. Salvage value at the end of their lives was expected to be zero. The depreciation method chosen was straight line, with a full year's depreciation taken in the year of acquisition.

Dr. Wilson wanted proper accounting for the operations of the organization and its financial position. With the help of some notes borrowed from a friend who had attended a course for executives of nonprofit organizations, she proceeded to construct a Balance Sheet; a Statement of Revenue, Expenses, and Changes in Fund Balance; a Statement of Functional Expenses; and a Statement of Changes in Financial Position for the year ended December 31, 1991.

ASSIGNMENT

Construct the above statements for the year ended December 31, 1991.

CASE 16.2 Children's Center (B)

During 1992, the organization was established in the community, thanks to the unstinting efforts of Dr. Dorothy Wilson (chairperson of the board of trustees), the dedication of Rosanna Griff (social worker), and a small and carefully chosen board which had representatives from the local health care providers, the target community, and the business community. Various fund raising efforts proved highly productive.

(1) $20,000 of pledges were obtained by general solicitations, mostly via efforts of board members. As of 12/31/92, $18,000 of these pledges had been received in cash. It was expected that $1,500 more would be received early in 1993, and that the remaining $500 would never be collected. Related printing ($500) and postage ($1,000) costs were paid in cash.

Denise Nitterhouse prepared this case under the supervision of Professor Regina E. Herzlinger. Copyright © 1977 by the President and Fellows of Harvard College. Harvard Business School case 177-217. Revised January 1993.

(2) A federal grant of $6,000 was applied for and received; it was to be used in fiscal year 1992. The grant was for: $3,600 for the salary and related fringe benefits of an assistant social worker who would work part-time for nine months; $1,200 for purchase of educational films; $400 for supplies to produce outreach educational pamphlets; and $800 for administrative expenses. All were paid for in cash.

(3) The City of Boston provided a welfare worker (annual salary $8,000 and fringe $1,200) to the center one day per week for patient education about city-provided services and the procedures for acquiring them.

(4) A part-time assistant social worker was hired on 4/1/92 to do outreach work. Her salary was set at $6,300, fringe $900. It was completely paid for at the end of the year.

(5) In addition to the $400 of supplies and $1,200 of films paid for by the grant, the Children's Center bought and paid for $3,000 of educational materials and $800 of education films in April. By the end of 1992, $2,500 worth of the educational materials were used. All films were expected to last five years, and the straight-line depreciation policy of 1991 was continued.

(6) Expenses of $1,600 were incurred and paid for in cash, $1,400 for administrative expenses and $200 for Rosanna's travel expenses.

(7) A small storage space was provided at no rent by another local agency. It was estimated that the space would rent for $100 per month. The entire space was devoted to program services, but it could have been used for any purpose desired by the board.

(8) Rosanna worked half time for the entire year on her social work activities for the program. Her salary and fringe remained as in 1991. They were paid in full by the end of the year.

(9) In January of 1992, George Hart donated 1,000 shares of Hart Company stock to the center. Dr. Wilson had treated him when he was a boy for free and he felt his donation was one way to express his gratitude to her. At the time of his donation, the market value of the stock was $50,000.

By December 31, 1992, Hart Company stock was trading at $150 a share because George Hart had developed a successful monitoring device for patients undergoing surgery. The stock had been trading at this level for several months, and since projected earnings per share for the next year was $20, this seemed to be a fairly conservative valuation.

George Hart had stipulated that the stock be used as endowment and that the income from it be used for operating purposes. The dividends per share were $1.00, and because the company was expanding very rapidly, they weren't likely to increase substantially. The dividends for 1992 were received in November 1992.

Dr. Wilson had read about the total return policy and wondered whether to use it. She considered using 5 percent of the market value of the portfolio as income if she used total return.

(10) A desk, three chairs, and three filing cabinets were donated to the center by a local merchant on February 1, 1992. The furniture had cost $1,500 when purchased a decade earlier, could have been sold in 1992 for about $200, and was replaced by the merchant with similar furniture costing $2,500. The donated furniture was expected to have another five years of use.

(11) On March 30, 1992, the board of trustees decided to invest $1,000 of cash in more Hart Company stock. It bought 20 shares. On December 31, the stock was worth $3,000.

(12) All liabilities from the prior year (1991) were paid during 1992.

ASSIGNMENT

1. Prepare the financial statements for 1992, assuming that the total return approach was applied. Use the end of year market values to calculate the amount of the return.

2. Comment on the implications of the financial statements.

CASE 16.3 San Bernardino YWCA

On March 23, the executive director, the treasurer, and the finance chairman of the board of trustees of the YWCA of San Bernardino met to discuss the draft of the audit report for the year ended December 31 (see **Exhibit 1**). The YWCA had given increasing attention to matters of accounting, control, and financial reporting in the past few years. This was partially in response to United Way guidelines and influence and also to publication of the AICPA *Industry Audit Guide* for voluntary health and welfare organizations, and the National Board's publication, *YWCA Financial Manual*.

For the first time, this year's statements were reported on the accrual basis in accordance with the AICPA *Audit Guide* requirements. Board members and management alike were pleased to have taken this important step and were looking forward to having a clean opinion, viewed by many as a clean bill of health. The newly elected treasurer, a member of the local business community, was somewhat familiar with audit reports of private businesses. She was particularly interested to see how the statements would compare to those with which she was familiar.

There was some surprise when they read the draft and found that the auditor's opinion contained a "subject to" clause. Its relevant paragraphs read as follows:

> In August 1961, the fixed assets of the Association were recorded at the fair market values of the real property and at replacement costs for personal property. The recording of fixed assets at these values are not in accordance with generally accepted accounting principles (Note 2). Fixed asset additions subsequent to August 1961 have been recorded at cost.
>
> In our opinion, subject to the effects if any, on the financial statements of the recording of fixed assets at fair market values and replacement costs, the aforementioned

Professor Regina E. Herzlinger prepared this case.

financial statements present fairly the financial position of the Young Women's Christian Association of San Bernardino and the results of its operations and changes in fund balances for the year then ended, in conformity with generally accepted accounting principles applied on a basis consistent with that of the preceding year after giving retroactive effect to the change, with which we concur, to the accrual method of accounting as described in Note 1 to the financial statements.

The representative of the CPA firm who presented the draft explained that GAAP (generally accepted accounting principles) required recording fixed assets at historical cost. She said that the attestation of the lack of consistency was also required because of the change to the accrual basis. This would be the only time this qualification would need to be made. However, the qualification due to asset valuation had been a regular part of the opinion in the past and could be expected to be so in the future.

The treasurer wanted to have more time to examine the statements in view of these unexpected developments. She accordingly asked that another meeting be set for the following week to discuss the final report form again. That night she determinedly sat down with the *Audit Guide*.

ASSIGNMENT

1. How would you interpret the financial results for the year?
2. What should be done about the auditor's opinion?

EXHIBIT 1 **San Bernardino YMCA**

Young Women's Christian Association of San Bernardino
Statement of Support, Revenue and Expenses, and Changes in Fund Balances

	Current Funds		Land, Building, and	Total
	Unrestricted	*Restricted*	**Equipment Fund**	**All Funds**
Public support and revenue:				
Received directly:				
Contributions	$ 2,400	$ 102	$ -	$ 2,502
Special events (net of direct benefit				
costs of $1,823)	869	-	1,191	2,060
Legacies and bequests	-	-	500	500
Total received directly	3,269	102	1,691	5,062
Received indirectly:				
Allocated by United Way of San				
Bernardino	68,630	-	-	68,630
Total support from the public	71,899	102	1,691	73,692
Fees and grants from government agencies	508	-	-	508
Other revenues:				
Membership dues—individual	18,581	-	-	18,581
Program service fees	67,750	-	-	67,750
Investment income	2,355	-	1,359	3,714
Gain (or loss) on investment transactions	-	-	478	478
Gain on sale of land and building—Note 2	-	-	212,186	212,186
Miscellaneous revenue	72	-	-	72
Total other revenue	88,758	-	214,023	302,781
Total public support and revenue	$161,165	$ 102	$215,714	$376,981
Expenses:				
Program services:				
Employment, training, and assistance	$ 1,078	$ -	$ 31	$ 1,109
Health education	10,433	35	481	10,949
Adult social education	40,755	-	1,726	42,481
Personal development	69,612	273	2,858	72,743
Community development	6,968	-	298	7,266
Total program services	128,846	308	5,394	134,548
Supporting services—management and				
general	29,839	-	1,163	31,002
Total expenses	$158,685	$ 308	$ 6,557	$165,550
Excess of public support and revenue over				
expenses	$ 2,480	$(206)	$209,157	
Other changes in fund balances:				
Property and equipment acquisitions from				
unrestricted funds	(403)	-	403	
Fund balance, beginning of year	398	438	193,123	
Fund balance, end of year	$ 2,475	$ 232	$402,683	

See accompanying notes to financial statements.

EXHIBIT 1 (Continued)

Young Women's Christian Association of San Bernardino
Statement of Functional Expenses

	Goal I Employment Training and Assistance	Program Services						Supporting Services Management and General	Total Program and Supporting Services Expenses
		Goal III Health Education	Goal IV Adult Social Education	Goal V Personal Development	Goal VI Community Development	Total			
Salaries	$ 504	$ 7,873	$28,271	$46,810	$4,887	$ 88,345		$19,067	$107,412
Employee benefits	22	349	1,252	2,074	216	3,913		845	4,758
Payroll taxes, etc.	46	768	2,739	4,540	476	8,569		2,093	10,622
Total salaries and related expenses	572	8,990	32,262	53,424	5,579	100,827		22,005	122,832
Professional fees	36	93	1,356	2,459	144	4,088		510	4,598
Supplies	31	193	2,275	1,961	945	5,405		545	5,950
Telephone	97	242	652	995	92	2,078		230	2,308
Postage and shipping	38	93	253	386	35	805		89	894
Occupancy	220	527	2,787	8,836	94	12,464		1,219	13,683
Rental and maintenance of equipment	-	-	-	436	-	436		-	436
Printing and publications	34	119	472	449	31	1,105		299	1,404
Travel	33	115	458	436	31	1,073		290	1,363
Conferences, conventions, meetings	11	40	158	150	11	370		100	470
Specific assistance to individuals	-	35	-	273	-	308		-	308
Dues and subscriptions	6	21	82	78	5	192		51	243
Support to national headquarters	-	-	-	-	-	-		4,500	4,500
Miscellaneous	-	-	-	2	1	3		1	4
Total before depreciation	1,078	10,468	40,755	69,855	6,968	129,154		29,839	158,993
Depreciation of building and equipment	31	481	1,726	2,858	298	5,394		1,163	6,557
Total expenses	$1,109	$10,949	$42,481	$72,743	$7,266	$134,548		$31,002	$165,550

See accompanying notes to financial statements.

EXHIBIT 1 (Continued)

Young Women's Christian Association of San Bernardino

Balance Sheet

ASSETS		LIABILITIES AND FUND BALANCES	
CURRENT FUNDS—UNRESTRICTED		*CURRENT FUNDS—UNRESTRICTED*	
Cash in checking account and on hand	$ 2,713	Accounts payable	$ 648
Cash in savings account	1,679	Payroll and sales taxes payable	2,296
Deposits	15	Total liabilities	2,944
Prepaid expenses	1,012	Fund balance:	
		Undesignated, available for general activities	2,475
	$ 5,419		$ 5,419
CURRENT FUNDS—RESTRICTED		*CURRENT FUNDS—RESTRICTED*	
Cash in checking account	$ 423	Due to land, building, and equipment fund	$ 191
		Funds for designated purposes	232
	$ 423		$ 423
LAND, BUILDING, AND EQUIPMENT FUND			
Cash in savings account and savings certificates	$301,134	Fund balances:	
Investments in bonds—at cost, which is approximately market value	3,995	Expended	$ 97,363
Due from current funds—restricted	191	Unexpended—restricted	305,320
Land, building, and equipment, less accumulated depreciation of $52,874—Notes 1 and 2	97,363		$402,683
	$402,683		

See accompanying notes to financial statements.

EXHIBIT 1 (Continued)

Edited Notes to Financial Statements

Note 1: Summary of Significant Accounting Policies

(This year), the Association began following the standards of accounting and financial reporting developed by the National Health Council, Inc., the National Assembly of National Voluntary Health and Social Welfare Organizations, Inc., and United Way of America. These standards are in conformity with the recommendations of the American Institute of Certified Public Accountants. In accordance with these standards, all expenditures for land, building, and equipment in excess of $50 and the fair value of donated fixed assets are capitalized. Depreciation is recorded over the estimated useful lives of the assets (Note 2). Investments are stated at cost. All contributions are considered available for the general program of the Association, unless specifically restricted by the donor. Policies for valuing donated goods and services are discussed in Note 4.

Since the Association does not conduct a formal fund-raising campaign, no operating expenses have been allocated to "fund raising" in the *Statement of Functional Expenses*.

Note 2: Land, Buildings, Improvements, and Equipment

The land and building located at Fifth and Arrowhead Streets, San Bernardino, was sold (this year). This property was recorded at estimated fair market value of $62,250 as of August 1961. Subsequent building improvements cost $9,320, less accumulated depreciation of $2,861. Proceeds from the sale of property were $280,895.

Remaining land, building, improvements, and equipment are shown in the balance sheet at the following values:

	Cost and/or Appraisal Value	Accumulated Depreciation	Net Book Value
Equipment and furnishings—(An inventory was taken August 1961. The items acquired prior to August 1961 and original costs were not available. The inventory was valued at replacement costs, and it was estimated that the items had a salvage value of 15 percent.)			
August 1961 inventory	$ 15,036	$12,780	$ 2,256
Subsequent additions—at cost	30,375	21,426	8,949
Autos and trucks	5,176	2,589	2,587
Rialto property—at cost	43,500	-	43,500
Rialto property building improvements—at cost	56,150	16,079	40,071
Totals	$150,237	$52,874	$97,363

EXHIBIT 1 (Continued)

Edited Notes to Financial Statements (Continued)

Note 6: YWCA, in Concert With Other Organizations

The Young Women's Christian Association of San Bernardino and the Young Men's Christian Association of San Bernardino jointly raise capital funds for additions and improvements to the properties of both parties. All expenses from the fund-raising campaign were deducted from gross contributions. The remaining balance of contributions are to be distributed 72.67 percent to the YMCA and 27.33 percent to the YWCA. The YWCA has recognized as contributions only its share of contributions that it has received in cash from the capital fund. As of year end, the YWCA's allocable share of contributions not yet received was approximately $152,000. This amount will be recognized as a contribution when cash payment is received from the YMCA-YWCA Capital Fund.

17 Health Care Service Providers

FOR THE PAST THREE DECADES, THE U.S. health care industry has experienced rapid growth and drastic change. The rate of growth of the health care sector regularly outstripped that of the national economy in the U.S. and other developed countries. Growth was accompanied by increased costs per capita. Although the increased costs were caused partly by the growing intensity of care provided, some critics charged that inefficiency of health care providers was also a major contributing factor. This has created challenges and opportunities for nonprofit health care managers and board members who are concerned about maintaining financial viability while adhering to their organization's social mission. Health care organizations have responded with changes in organization structure, care delivery, and financial management.

Attitudes toward health care have also changed. Health care activism, including demands for patient rights and provider accountability, has grown. Access to adequate health care has come to be viewed as a basic right in much of the world, although there is disagreement about how best to deliver it and what constitutes adequacy. New medical technology can work miracles but is very expensive. The costs of treating a serious illness or accident today would impose great financial hardship on most families that are without insurance coverage. U.S. government officials, employers, and the general public are gravely concerned about the high and growing costs of health care and the number of people who are uninsured. Possible solutions continue to be hotly debated.

The growing elderly population, the AIDS crisis, and the medical results of drug abuse are straining parts of the health care system, especially urban hospitals, to the breaking point. Yet, other parts of the health care system are very profitable. The gap between the haves and the have-nots of health care is widening among both patients and providers. Some health care providers have financial conditions that are as poor as the medical status of their patients.

707

Their social mission, competition with for-profit providers, cost pressures, financing complexities, and rapid advances in medical technology enormously complicate the financial management of nonprofit health care organizations. This chapter will discuss the health care sector, the accounting standards it uses to express financial performance and resources, and how the resulting financial statements can be analyzed to answer the four key questions discussed in Chapter 5.

SECTOR OVERVIEW

Once composed primarily of physicians, nurses, and general acute-care hospitals, the sector now includes a wide and growing range of organizations that provide and finance health care. Health care is delivered and financed in a very different manner from a decade ago, and continued change seems to be the only constant. A complex mixture of for-profit, nonprofit, and government organizations makes balancing financial and social mission considerations all the more difficult for nonprofit organizations. With expenditures exceeding $660 billion and 12 percent of the GNP, U.S. health care in the 1990s is very big business whatever form the individual organizations take.

Sector History

The first recorded American health institution was an almshouse established in 1663 on Manhattan Island to take care of sick soldiers. In 1751, the Pennsylvania General Hospital was chartered as the first U.S. voluntary community hospital financed by public funds. During the nineteenth century, hospitals were established in larger cities, some organized and financed through communities. The development of antiseptics in the late 1880s created a demand for equipment and facilities to match the new technology.

Health *insurance* plans have played an important role in the financing and distribution of health care in the U.S. Insurance for disability caused by accident or disease became available during the late 1800s. Montgomery Wards is thought to have implemented the first group health insurance policy in 1910, and Baylor Hospital helped to establish the forerunner of the Blue Cross health insurance plans in 1929. The depression of the 1930s pressured doctors and hospitals to seek a reliable source of income, and the public to seek a way to avoid excessive debt because of illness. Blue Cross insurance plans were set up as nonprofit organizations, often sponsored by local hospitals. By the 1940s, commercial insurers had also entered the health insurance market. By the 1950s, health insurance to cover hospital costs was a common employee benefit, most frequently paid for by the employer.[1]

---

[1] Health Insurance Association of America, *Source Book of Health Insurance Data 1990* (Washington, DC: Health Insurance Association of America, 1990) pp. 103-105.

Hospital expansion was virtually halted by the depression and World War II. The Hill-Burton Act of 1946 provided federal funds that combined with pent-up demand to produce a post-war boom in hospital construction. Passage of Medicare and Medicaid health insurance legislation in the 1960s introduced the federal government as a large-scale payor for ongoing health care operating expenses and enabled the startling rate of growth of the industry.

Payments in the health care industry are commonly referred to as *reimbursements* because health care service providers were usually paid only after services were rendered and costs had been incurred. Private insurers typically pay hospitals negotiated fees for services provided. Medicare and Medicaid, however, initially paid the lower of charges or *allowable costs*, which were defined by contract or regulation and did not necessarily cover all the costs actually incurred by the hospital.

Health care expenditures grew alarmingly, from 4.4 percent of the GNP in 1950 to over 12 percent in 1990. The cost of a day of hospital care increased much faster than the consumer price index, and in the 1970s several controls were adopted to attempt to contain hospital costs. Several state regulatory agencies required hospitals or nursing homes to obtain a *certificate-of-need (CON)* before acquiring new equipment or facilities, to determine community need for the proposed acquisition and avoid unnecessary duplication. Insurers introduced *peer review organizations (PROs)* and *utilization reviews* to monitor whether patients are staying in the hospital for longer than necessary, quality of care, and various other aspects of provider performance.

In the early 1980s, the federal payment systems for hospital inpatient services were drastically restructured in another attempt to control costs. In 1983, a Social Security amendment incorporated a *prospective payment system (PPS)* for Medicare that established in advance a fixed price for each medical service provided on an inpatient basis, using *diagnostic related groups (DRGs)* to classify medical services. This system caused each health care provider to absorb the loss or keep the gain if its costs were more or less than the fixed price. The federal government continues to reimburse some health care services on the basis of costs or charges, although it is moving to PPS for more items. Despite the advent of PPS, hospital and health care expenditures continue to grow faster than inflation.

Sector Structure

Health care is continuously changing in terms of where and by whom services are provided, and the relationship between insurance and service provision. An increasing proportion and variety of procedures and services are performed on an outpatient or in-home basis, both by traditional providers and new organizations. Creative delivery mechanisms, such as mobile or shared health care units, are being developed to improve service in sparsely populated areas and provide health care in previously under-served communities. The growing elderly population and changing family structures have led to growth of long-term care facilities and home care.

Rapidly developing new medical technology is like the little girl with the curl in the middle of her forehead. When it is good, it is very, very good, such as the biotechnology product that now enables children who might otherwise have been dwarfs to grow to normal height. But, when it is bad, it is horrid, as unnecessary acquisitions and uses of expensive medical technology for diagnosis, treatment, and life sustainment fuel cost increases.

Legal Structure and Organization   Health care service providers are classified by sponsorship or legal structure as *private nonprofit*, *public* (operated by state or local governments), and *proprietary* (commercial) organizations. Private nonprofit health care providers are either independent organizations or parts of other nonprofit organizations, such as private universities. Some are related to religious organizations, such as St. Vincent's Hospital in Birmingham, Alabama, and Ohio Presbyterian Retirement Services in Ohio.

In response to criticisms of inefficiency and excessive costs, many health care service providers undertook major structural reorganizations. Organizations that provided similar health care services were *horizontally integrated* into a chain or group (either for-profit or nonprofit) that would enjoy economies of scale in such functions as purchasing. Organizations that provided different but related health care services were *vertically integrated* to produce a smooth continuum of care by transferring patients from expensive sites, such as hospitals, to cheaper sources of care, such as rehabilitation centers, as quickly as was medically appropriate. A growing number of health care entities are subsidiaries of other nonprofit organizations, own subsidiaries offering other services, or are affiliated with separate foundations for fundraising purposes.

Health care entities are also classified by the nature of their services or their delivery mechanisms. This classification includes clinics; long-term care facilities, including continuing care retirement communities (CCRCs) or nursing homes; rehabilitation centers; managed care organizations, including health maintenance organizations (HMOs) and preferred provider organizations (PPOs); home health agencies; and hospitals. Many of these organizations provide both health care services and an insurance function.

Hospitals   Hospitals typically charge fees for services, which are paid by private or public insurers or by the patient. Hospital care is the largest component (44 percent) of total U.S. health care costs (see Table 17-1), followed by physicians' services (23.2 percent) and nursing home care (9.2 percent). At the heart of the U.S. health care delivery system, hospitals also heavily influence physicians and other health care providers.

Hospitals are classified by their *teaching status*, *services offered*, and *market*. Most are *community* hospitals that provide short-term general acute care and serve well-defined and limited geographic areas, such as a county or town.

TABLE 17-1   **Personal Health Care Expenditures by Object and Source of Payment (dollars in billions)**

	Line Item Percent of Total	Total	Direct Patient Payments	Private Health Insurance	Government	Philanthropy
1970		$65.4	$26.6	$15.3	$22.4	$1.1
1980		$219.7	$63.0	$67.5	$86.5	$2.7
1987		$442.6	$123.0	$139.0	$175.3	$5.3
1987 by Object of Payment:						
Hospital	44.0%	$194.7	$18.5	$71.9	$102.2	$2.2
Physicians' services	23.2%	102.7	26.3	44.6	31.8	-
Nursing home care	9.2%	40.6	20.0	0.4	19.9	0.3
Dentists	7.4%	32.8	20.0	12.2	0.7	-
Other professional services	3.7%	16.2	6.4	4.3	5.4	0.1
Drugs and drug sundries	7.7%	34.0	25.5	4.7	3.9	-
Eyeglasses and appliances	2.1%	9.4	6.3	1.1	2.1	-
Other health services	2.7%	12.0	-	-	9.4	2.6
1970		$65.4	40.7%	23.4%	34.2%	1.7%
1980		$219.7	28.7	30.7	39.4	1.2
1987		$442.6	27.8	31.4	39.6	1.2
1987 Object of Payment as a Percent of Line Item:						
Hospital	44.0%	$194.7	9.5%	36.9%	52.5%	1.1%
Physicians' services	23.2	102.7	25.6	43.4	31.0	-
Nursing home care	9.2	40.6	49.3	1.0	49.0	0.7
Dentists	7.4	32.8	61.0	37.2	2.1	-
Other professional services	3.7	16.2	39.5	26.5	33.3	0.6
Drugs and drug sundries	7.7	34.0	75.0	13.8	11.5	-
Eyeglasses and appliances	2.1	9.4	67.0	11.7	22.3	-
Other health services	2.7	12.0	-	-	78.3	21.7

Personal health care expenditures excludes net cost of insurance and administration and government public health activities.

Source: Adapted from U.S. Depertment of Commerce, Bureau of the Census, *110th Edition, Statistical Abstract of the United States, The 1990 National Data Book*, January 1990, Table No. 139, "Personal Health Care Expenditures, by Object and Source of Payment: 1987," and Table No. 138, "Personal Health Care—Third Party Payments and Private Consumer Expenditures," p. 94.

They offer a fairly broad range of services to both *inpatients* who stay overnight and *outpatients* (*ambulatory* patients) who do not stay overnight in the hospital. Hospitals whose inpatients stay fewer than 30 days are termed *acute-care* institutions. *Long-term care* hospitals specialize in treating inpatients who have chronic diseases that require longer-term care; many are state or municipal hospitals. Some hospitals incorporate a separate extended care unit to provide services to long-term patients.

Teaching hospitals are affiliated with medical schools, such as Harvard University and Massachusetts General Hospital. They offer training for medical school students and intern and residency programs for medical doctors who need to complete on-the-job training to be certified in their medical specialty. Most teaching hospitals serve a relatively large geographic market in addition to the local community because they provide technologically sophisticated services, such as burn units and heart transplants. Because such services tend to require costly equipment and multidisciplinary medical teams, only a limited number of specialists and facilities can provide them.

Each *specialized hospital* provides a limited range of services. Some specialize in certain types of *rehabilitation*, including drug and alcohol detoxification, physical rehabilitation, or psychiatric treatment. Others specialize in treating certain types of diseases, such as cancer, or performing certain types of operations, such as Toronto's Shouldice Hospital which specializes in hernia operations. Traditionally, many specialized hospitals were run by governments and had primarily poor patients who had little chance of recovery. Recent decades have seen a growing number of specialized hospitals with very different operations, clientele, and financial performance.

The demand for hospital services has changed dramatically. Table 17-2 shows that 6,780 hospitals contained 1.2 million beds, admitted 34 million patients, and had 336 million outpatient visits in 1988. According to the data shown in Table 17-2, the number of hospitals, beds, and average daily census peaked in 1970 and have dropped steadily since then by 4.8 percent, 22.8 percent, and 33.5 percent, respectively. The decline in the number of hospitals was caused primarily by hospital closings, although it may also reflect mergers, acquisitions, and sales of facilities.

Hospital inpatient admissions increased by 22 percent from 1970 through 1980, and decreased 12 percent from 1980 to 1988. This resulted in a net increase of 7.4 percent, much less than the population growth from 1970 to 1988. *Average daily census* represents the average number of inpatients on any day during the year. *Average length of stay* (*ALOS*) is the average number of days a patient spent in the hospital. *Occupancy rate* measures utilization, defined as the percentage of time that the available beds are occupied (average daily census divided by number of beds). Despite increased admissions, a drastic decrease of the ALOS to around 7 days in 1988 is generally credited with causing the average daily census to decrease by 33.5 percent and occupancy to decrease from 80.3 percent to 69.2 percent, even though bed capacity also decreased.

PPS provides a motivation for hospitals to release patients as early as possible, and advances in medical technology have reduced the time that patients need to spend in the hospital or have allowed them to be treated on an outpatient basis. Because many surgical procedures that once required inpatient care are now being provided on an outpatient basis, remaining hospital procedures are the most complicated and intensive, which has caused ALOS to increase again. The 85.4 percent increase in outpatient visits reflects

TABLE 17-2 Selected Hospital Utilization Statistics

Classification	Year	Number of Hospitals	Number of Beds*	Admissions*	Average Daily Census	Occupancy	Average Length of Stay	Outpatient Visits*
Total United States	1950	6,788	1,456	18,483	1,253	86.0%	N/A	N/A
	1970	7,123	1,616	31,759	1,298	80.3%	N/A	181,370
	1980	6,965	1,365	38,892	1,060	77.7%	N/A	262,951
	1987	6,821	1,267	34,439	873	58.9%	N/A	310,707
	1988	6,780	1,248	34,107	863	69.2%	N/A	336,208
Absolute change, 1970 to 1988		(343)	(368)	2,348	(435)	11.1		154,838
Percent change, 1970 to 1988		−4.8%	−22.8%	7.4%	−33.5%	−13.8%		85.4%
By Type (1988):								
Federal		342	105	1,862	77	73.2%	N/A	57,353
Nonfederal psychiatric		726	166	688	140	84.6%	N/A	5,623
Nonfederal respiratory diseases		4	0	2	0	68.0%	N/A	15
Nonfederal long-term general and other special		129	27	75	24	87.3%	N/A	1,780
Hospital units of institutions		46	3	27	1	51.0%	18.8	2,307
Community hospitals (total):		5,533	947	31,453	621	65.5%	7.2	269,129
Nongovernment not-for-profit		3,242	668	22,939	456	68.2%	7.3	195,363
Investor owned (for profit)		790	104	3,090	53	50.9%	6.2	17,926
State and local government		1,501	175	5,424	112	63.9%	7.6	55,840
Percentage by Type (1988):								
Federal		5.0%	8.4%	5.5%	8.9%			17.1%
Nonfederal psychiatric		10.7%	13.3%	2.0%	16.2%			1.7%
Nonfederal respiratory diseases		0.1%	0.0%	0.0%	0.0%			0.0%
Nonfederal long-term general and other special		1.9%	2.2%	0.2%	2.8%			0.5%
Hospital units of institutions		0.7%	0.2%	0.1%	0.1%			0.7%
Community hospitals (total):		81.6%	75.9%	92.2%	72.0%			80.0%
Nongovernment not-for-profit		47.8%	53.5%	67.3%	52.8%			58.1%
Investor owned (for profit)		11.7%	8.3%	9.1%	6.1%			5.3%
State and local government		22.1%	14.0%	15.9%	13.0%			16.6%

*Numbers in thousands.

Source: Adapted from American Hospital Association, *Hospital Statistics: A hospital fact book, 1989-90 edition* (Chicago, IL: American Hospital Association, 1989), Table 1, pp. 2-7.

the shift toward delivering more services on an outpatient basis. Outpatient visits accounted for 20 percent of the gross patient revenue of community hospitals in 1988.[2]

In 1988, the 5,533 community hospitals had a total of 947,000 beds and constituted the majority (81.6 percent) of hospitals (Table 17-2). Nongovernment nonprofit community hospitals made up nearly half (47.8 percent) of the total hospital population and accounted for more than half of the beds, admissions, average daily census, and outpatient visits. State and local government-owned community hospitals made up 22.1 percent of the hospitals but only 14.0 percent of the beds, indicating that they are smaller than average. They also had relatively low utilization rates (63.9 percent). Investor-owned for-profit community hospitals made up 11.7 percent of all hospitals. With only 8.3 percent of the beds, they, too, are smaller than average, and they had the lowest occupancy rate (50.9 percent).

The federal government operated 342 hospitals with 105,000 beds to serve military personnel, veterans, and other special groups. These hospitals are larger than average and have higher than average occupancy rates. Nonfederal psychiatric and long-term general hospitals are also larger than average and have higher than average occupancy rates. Outpatients are served predominantly by federal hospitals and nonprofit and government community hospitals.

Managed Care Organizations   A growing number of health care service providers have joined forces with insurers in *managed care organizations*. These are designed to reduce costs by aligning the interests of providers and insurers. Generally, they organize providers and facilities in a network designed to efficiently provide a broad range of coordinated patient services. Typically, a *gate-keeper* physician must approve the patients' use of specialists, hospitals, and diagnostic tests. Most managed care organizations limit the providers and facilities for which they will pay.

A wide variety of structures exist, including *health maintenance organizations (HMOs)*, *preferred provider organizations (PPOs)*, *exclusive provider organizations (EPOs)*, *independent practice associations (IPAs)* and *point-of-service plans*. The distinctions among these organizations are blurred and new organization forms continue to evolve. Some managed care organizations, such as *staff model HMOs*, employ physicians and other health care professionals to provide services. Others resemble traditional health insurance companies that subcontract with independent physicians, hospitals, and other health care providers on a fee-for-service basis at negotiated rates.

Bolstered by federal legislation in the 1970s that required many employers to offer a managed care health insurance option, the number of persons enrolled in managed care plans grew from under 10 million in 1970

---

[2]American Hospital Association, *Hospital Statistics: A Hospital Fact Book, 1989-90 Edition* (Chicago, IL: American Hospital Association, 1989), p. 204, Table 11.

to over 50 million (more than 14 percent of the U.S. insured population) in 1990.[3] Managers of these organizations face the challenges of both health care service providers and insurance companies, which adds to the complexity of their accounting and financial management. It is not universally agreed that managed care organizations provide health care services more efficiently than traditional arrangements.

Continuing Care Retirement Communities (CCRCs) A rapidly growing part of the health care sector consists of organizations that provide long-term care, primarily for the elderly. Many are organized as nonprofit organizations, and some are affiliated with religious organizations. They supply their residents with a wide range of nursing care and residential services (such as housing, food, laundry, and recreation). There is a trend of increasing state regulation of CCRCs, primarily to ensure their financial stability.

A typical continuing-care contract includes both *advance* and *periodic fees*. The advance fee may be partially refundable under specified conditions. Periodic fees may be fixed or subject to adjustment. Contracts generally specify the services that will be provided, how residents will be charged, refund policies (if any), and the obligations of the CCRC and resident if the contract is terminated or the unit reoccupied.

CCRCs offer three basic types of contracts. *All-inclusive* contracts include all residential services and long-term nursing care for little or no increase in periodic fees. *Modified* contracts cover all residential services but only a limited amount of long-term nursing care; additional required nursing care is charged on a specified per-diem basis. *Fee-for-service* contracts include only residential and emergency nursing care, with all long-term nursing care provided at specified per-diem rates.

Finances

Each health insurer pays for services in a different way and may pay different rates for similar services, which poses a managerial challenge. The sources of both operating and capital financing have shifted, along with payment bases. The absence of health insurance for many poor people imposes an important but costly social mission on nonprofit health service providers. Managers and trustees must oversee this complex web so that the organization's social mission is fulfilled while financial viability is maintained.

Revenues Table 17-1 shows that health care is financed primarily by payments from private or government insurers and by direct payments from patients. Government (Medicare/Medicaid), private nonprofit (Blue Cross/ Blue Shield), and independent commercial insurers are called *third-party payors* because the first party (the patient) receives services from a second

[3]Health Insurance Association of America, *1990 Source Book*, p. 4.

party (the health care provider) who is then paid by a third party (the insurer). Since 1970, self-insured plans in large companies and managed care organizations have gained popularity.

The largest governmental insurance programs in the U.S. are Medicare and Medicaid, Titles 18 and 19 of the U.S. Social Security Act.[4] Medicare covers persons age 65 and older, disabled persons under age 65 who receive cash benefits under Social Security or Railroad Retirement programs, and people of all ages with chronic kidney disease. It pays for hospital care and related services (Part A) and for physician bills and related services (Part B). Medicare is administered on a national level by the U.S. *Department of Health and Human Services, Health Care Financing Administration (HCFA)*, which sets standards for payment levels and health care provider qualifications. Medicaid provides medical assistance to low-income individuals and families, primarily those who are eligible for cash assistance programs, such as Supplemental Security Income (SSI). It is financed by a combination of state and federal funds but is administered by state governments, with wide variations among states in the coverage of services.

Private insurers include traditional commercial and nonprofit insurance companies, managed care organizations, and self-insured employers. Premiums for most private insurance are paid by employers or individuals. Most traditional health insurance policies require the patient to pay some initial amount of expenses (*the deductible*) and co-pay with the insurance company the expenses above the amount of the deductible (*co-insurance*) up to a specified amount; insurance then pays all expenses in excess of the specified amount. Many also limit the amount of payment by the insurance company.

In the past half-century, health care has come to be considered a government-ensured basic right in the U.S., much like primary education. In 1940, only 12 million persons (less than 10 percent of the U.S. population) were insured for health care expenses, half of them by nonprofit Blue Cross and Blue Shield plans (BCBS or the Blues). Health care was considered to be an individual option and responsibility. By the early 1990s, there was widespread concern that more than 30 million persons in the U.S., nearly 13 percent of the population, remained uninsured or seriously underinsured. Most other industrialized nations provide government-financed universal health care coverage for all citizens.

By 1988, 212 million persons (87 percent of the population) were covered by either private or public health care insurance.[5] The Blues still insured an estimated 74 million persons, but commercial insurance companies have dominated the market since the early 1950s, insuring 93 million persons in 1988. Other plans, including self-insured plans and managed care organizations, insured an estimated 71 million persons, having gained substantial

---

[4]Social Security Amendments of 1965, (Public Law 89-97), Social Security Act (U.S. Code Title XVIII Medicare and XIX Medicaid).
[5]Health Insurance Association of America, *1990 Source Book*, pp. 22-23, 32.

market share in recent decades. Nearly half of these persons were enrolled in HMOs. Some individuals are covered by more than one plan.

Direct patient payments financed 34 percent of hospital expenditures in 1950, a ratio that declined dramatically to 9.5 percent by 1987. Government programs and private health insurance covered most of the difference. The scope of items covered by third-party payments is also increasing. In 1965, third parties paid 81 percent of the expenditures for hospital care, but only 38 percent of physician services and 34 percent of nursing home care. In 1987, third parties paid 89 percent of the expenditures for hospital care, 74 percent of physician services, and 50 percent of nursing home care (Table 17-1). Third parties cover a lower proportion of other health care items and services, such as drugs, eyeglasses, and dental services. Direct patient payments covered 27.8 percent, private health insurance covered 31.4 percent, government covered 39.6 percent, and philanthropy covered only 1.2 percent of total 1987 health care costs.

Most nonprofit hospitals also derive revenues from several nonpatient sources, including gifts, donations, grants, contracts, tuition, and operation of such auxiliary activities as cafeterias, parking lots, and gift shops. Many also operate physician office buildings in which hospital-affiliated physicians see their nonhospitalized private patients. These revenue sources may be subject to unrelated business income tax (UBIT) and are excluded from most statistical data.

In 1987, health care providers accounted for only 11 percent of the 175,829 reported tax-exempt service organizations, but for 72 percent of their $267 billion total revenue.[6] Table 17-3 shows that the average tax-exempt health care provider is larger than other tax-exempt organizations, and hospitals are the largest. Most hospitals, HMOs, and long-term care facilities are nonprofit organizations; other parts of the health care sector are dominated in number by 407,000 for-profit establishments.[7] (Yet, statistical anomalies abound. For example, this data source claims 1,400 for-profit hospitals, nearly double the 790 investor-owned community hospitals indicated in Table 17-2.) However, total health services revenue is about evenly split between nonprofit and for-profit.

Expenses Payroll and benefits (personnel) decreased from nearly 61 percent of total hospital expenses in 1970 to 55 percent by 1988 (Table 17-4), reflecting increased use of high-technology medical equipment and of contractual services, especially for nursing. (Contractual services are reported under supplies and other rather than under payroll expenses.) Most physician

[6]U.S. Department of Commerce, Bureau of the Census, *1987 Census of Service Industries*, Geographic Area Series, SC87-A-52, November 1989, Table 1b, "Summary Statistics for Firms Exempt from Federal Income Tax for the United States: 1987," p. US-13.

[7]U.S. Department of Commerce, Bureau of the Census, *110th Edition, Statistical Abstract of the United States, The 1990 National Data Book*, January 1990, Table No. 1380, "Service Industries— Summary of Establishments by Tax Status: 1987," p. 783.

TABLE 17-3   **Average Statistics, Tax-Exempt Health Care Organizations: 1987**

Kind of Business Operation	Revenue per Establishment (dollars)	Revenue per Employee (dollars)	Expenses per Establishment (dollars)	Expenses per Employee* (dollars)	Annual Payroll per Employee (dollars)	Employees per Establishment (number)
Total	$ 1,521,306	$39,707	$ 1,440,512	$37,598	$17,513	38
Other than health care	482,984	36,248			12,636	13
Selected health services	10,038,474	41,260	9,678,643	39,781	19,703	243
Clinics of doctors and dentists	2,380,062	65,481	2,228,023	61,298	22,611	36
Nursing and personal care facilities	1,995,485	22,077	1,954,662	21,625	11,479	90
Hospitals	29,137,875	43,390	28,093,503	41,834	20,772	672
Other health services	888,206	26,338	860,912	25,529	13,404	34

Includes only establishments with payroll.
*Based on number of employees for pay period including March 12.

Source: Adapted from U.S. Department of Commerce, Bureau of the Census, *1987 Census of Service Industries, Geographic Area Series,* SC87-A-52, November 1989, Table 2b, "Selected Ratios for Firms Exempt From Federal Income Tax for the United States: 1987," p. US-17.

TABLE 17-4 **Selected Personnel and Finance Statistics**

Classification	Year	FTE Personnel (thousands)	Payroll and Benefits Expense (millions)	Total Expense (millions)	Personnel as a Percentage of Expenses
Total United States	1950	1,058	$ 2,191	$ 3,651	60.0%
	1970	2,537	15,706	25,556	61.5%
	1980	3,492	54,191	91,886	59.0%
	1987	3,472	99,096	178,662	55.5%
	1988	3,839	108,831	196,704	55.3%
Absolute change, 1970 to 1988		1,302	$ 93,125	$171,148	−6.2%
Percent change, 1970 to 1988		51.3%	592.9%	669.7%	−10.0%
By Type:					
Federal	1988	295	9,867	14,601	67.6%
Nonfederal psychiatric	1988	281	7,957	10,855	73.3%
Nonfederal respiratory diseases	1988	1	23	35	65.7%
Nonfederal long-term general and other special	1988	54	1,552	2,271	68.3%
Hospital units of institutions	1988	4	131	219	59.8%
Community hospitals (total):	1988	3,205	89,302	168,722	52.9%
Nongovernment not-for-profit	1988	2,373	66,664	124,703	53.5%
Investor owned (for profit)	1988	249	6,655	15,545	42.8%
State and local government	1988	583	15,983	28,474	56.1%
Percentage by Type:					
Federal	1988	7.7%	9.1%	7.4%	
Nonfederal psychiatric	1988	7.3%	7.3%	5.5%	
Nonfederal respiratory diseases	1988	0.0%	0.0%	0.0%	
Nonfederal long-term general and other special	1988	1.4%	1.4%	1.2%	
Hospital units of institutions	1988	0.1%	0.1%	0.1%	
Community hospitals (total):	1988	83.5%	82.1%	85.8%	
Nongovernment not-for-profit	1988	61.8%	61.3%	63.4%	
Investor owned (for profit)	1988	6.5%	6.1%	7.9%	
State and local government	1988	15.2%	14.7%	14.5%	

Source: Adapted from American Hospital Association, *Hospital Statistics: A hospital fact book, 1989-90 edition* (Chicago, IL: American Hospital Association, 1989), Table 1, pp. 2-7.

fees are billed and paid separately from hospital charges, and neither their revenues nor any related expenses appear in hospital financial statements. The expenses of some organizations, for example, staff model HMOs, do include physician expenses. Personnel expenses represent a lower percentage of expenses in for-profit hospitals than other types.

Capital   Individual philanthropy was a major source of many hospitals' initial facilities. Later, community fund raising was used to finance new hospitals and attract more physicians. After World War II, under the Hill-Burton act, government grants provided a substantial amount of plant financing. Today, the major sources of plant financing for nonprofit health care providers are debt and internally generated funds. Debt appears to remain readily available despite some ill-founded loans, such as the one to Arizona's St. Luke's Health System. This once-successful hospital has been in difficult financial straits after years of highly leveraged expansion and ill-fated diversification.[8]

Tax-exempt revenue bonds and other obligations issued by public *health and education financing authorities (HEFAs)* are an important source of financing for 501(c)(3) hospitals and other nonprofit health care providers. HEFAs are government organizations that borrow money on a governmental, tax-exempt basis and then reloan it to private nonprofit organizations. These loans are liabilities of the health care provider for whose benefit they were issued, and are reported as such in the provider's financial statements. Initially, a fairly complex and long-term relationship between the provider and the HEFA was common. Now, the HEFA may merely ascertain the tax-exempt status of the issuer, the purpose of the loan, and the legal propriety of the issuing documents and process. Many bond issues are simply property mortgages, and some bonds are issued without even a mortgage contract. In rare cases, a nonprofit health care provider's bond issue is backed by taxpayers. Many nonprofit health care bond issues are now *credit-enhanced* (guaranteed by another organization through bond insurance or letters of credit). The financial statements of the enhancing organization may be included in the prospectus instead of or in addition to those of the issuing health care provider.

Data Sources

Health care industry financial statistics and ratios are compiled and published annually by a variety of governmental and private organizations. They are very useful for health care trustees and managers, as well as for others concerned with the health care industry. This section discusses a few of the major sources of these data; most are available in large public and medical school libraries.

The Health Care Financing Administration, which administers Medicare and the federal portion of Medicaid, collects and disseminates a substantial amount of health care statistical data. Its quarterly journal, *Health Care Financing Review*, reports data on health care as a percentage of GNP, sources

[8]Brad Patten, "St. Luke's Grapples with Debt," *The Phoenix Gazette*, 16 April 1990, pp. A1-A2.

of financing, and expenditures for various components of health care. It is a primary data source for the health care industry.

The American Hospital Association (AHA) is the primary industry association representing hospitals. It conducts an annual survey of hospitals and reports the results in its annual *Hospital Statistics: A Hospital Fact Book*, which provides both detailed data and a lucid summary of the events and trends relevant to hospital management. Its data include the number of different types of hospitals by geographic region and several measures of size and utilization, including beds, admissions, census, occupancy, outpatient visits, FTE personnel, and expenses. It also publishes health care related books and several journals aimed at different groups that are involved in hospital management, including *Hospitals*, *Trustee*, *Health Facilities Management*, *Medical Staff Leader*, and *Volunteer Leader*. The AHA is very active in shaping U.S. hospital and health care policy.

Another prominent, financially oriented, health care industry organization, the Healthcare Financial Management Association (HFMA), also collects, publishes, and sells a variety of financial and performance data, primarily based on an annual survey that it conducts. Its Financial Analysis Service (FAS) provides financial ratios that individual hospitals can use as a benchmark to evaluate their financial strengths and weaknesses. The Strategic Operating Indicators (SOI) service provides productivity ratios related to pricing, utilization, intensity, efficiency, and costs. It publishes two annual reports, *Financial Report of the Hospital Industry* and *Performance Report of the Hospital Industry*, based on these data. Other HFMA data services include receivables analysis and Medicare cost reports. The HFMA monthly journal, *Healthcare Financial Management*, is an excellent source of information on current events and trends in the health care industry. It also publishes newsletters, monographs, textbooks, accounting and financial reporting statements, and study guides.

The Health Insurance Association of America (HIAA) publishes an annual *Source Book of Health Insurance Data* that provides data for the major forms of health insurance coverage, medical care costs, and medical facilities utilization. It is an excellent basic reference tool.

Bond rating agencies also publish data on health care. Standard & Poor's Corporation (S&P) periodically publishes an industry survey on health care in its *Creditweek*. Moody's Investors Service periodically publishes a *Review of Hospital Bonds* by state.

Data for individual nonprofit health care providers can be acquired from several sources. Most nonprofit providers must file an IRS Form 990 with the federal government and a publicly available annual report with the attorney general of any state in which it solicits donations. When a provider issues bonds, its financial statements are usually included in the bond prospectus.

Opportunities and Challenges

U.S. health care is among the most expensive and technologically advanced in the world. Yet, despite its many great successes, the health of the average U.S. citizen is not better, and is in some ways worse, than the health of citizens of other countries that spend less on health care. The growing public concern about the effectiveness, cost, and accessibility of health care poses both opportunities and challenges for the industry, managers, and board members. They must be actively involved in the redesign of the health care system to preserve the good parts of the existing system and improve those that are currently deficient.[9] A wide variety of solutions have been proposed.

The redesign of the health care system poses difficult choices. How much and what type of health care should taxpayers be required to finance? As the case of one terminally and catastrophically ill patient points out,[10] the three fundamental questions are: "Who decides" how much and what kind of care should be provided? "Who gets" medical care? "Who pays" for it? At the other end of the spectrum from terminally ill patients are children unprotected from childhood diseases because their parents do not choose or have the ability to pay for health care. U.S. economic competitiveness and health depends on finding good answers and making good health care choices. The fact that health care policy is inextricably bound up with life and death issues makes it a particularly thorny problem in the religiously pluralistic U.S. society.

Some health care advocates suggest that inadequate policy setting for health care has put the burden of cost control on providers, while insurers and governments sidestep saying "no." The important question is how to provide, distribute, and finance health care: by pure markets, by government regulation, by the existing third-party insurance structure, by a judicious combination, or by an as yet unforeseen alternative? Trustees, managers, and policymakers must carefully assess the pros and cons of various approaches and their likely effects in the context of the U.S. economic, social, and political systems. The recent experiences of eastern Europe have demonstrated that the distribution mechanism has a profound effect on the production system.

Virtually everyone seems to be concerned about the growing cost and declining accessibility of U.S. health care. Employers are alarmed by the rising and seemingly uncontrollable costs of health insurance, and many small businesses and individuals find themselves entirely priced out of the health insurance market.

[9]Regina E. Herzlinger, "Healthy Competition," *The Atlantic Monthly* 268, no. 2 (August 1991): 69-81.
[10]John Dorschner, "Stayin' Alive: Ed Van Houten and America's Health-Care Dilemma," *The Chicago Tribune Magazine*, 27 October 1991, section 10, pp. 14-19.

In 1989, the state of Oregon passed legislation to implement a health care rationing system that expanded the number of persons but limited the types of medical problems covered by its medical programs. The intent is to focus on treatments that are expected to yield relatively high medical benefits at relatively low cost. Some European countries use similar rationing procedures in their health care systems, as well as less direct rationing methods, such as extended waiting times for medical treatment. The U.S. appears likely to adopt some form of national health insurance; it is less clear at this point what form it would take. Whatever system is adopted will have a significant effect on employers, governments, health care providers, and consumers.

At the same time, competition has grown within the U.S. health care industry. Hospitals bid up salaries as they compete for prized specialist physicians and invest heavily in the latest medical technology to attract both physicians and patients. New technology is expensive to acquire and is accompanied by the cost of educating medical technicians and other personnel to use it. A national nursing shortage, which appears to be chronic rather than short-lived, has applied additional pressures in a major cost area. Hospitals that provide charity care are often strained financially by it. Others are being slowly strangled by long payment cycles of insurers or their own inefficient billing procedures.

Hospitals appear to be taking a renewed interest in health care and community issues. This is in contrast to the 1980s, when "Hospital administrators regularly quoted a newly popular phrase, 'There is no mission without a [profit] margin.'"[11] The wide range of expert opinions on the right answer to "The Case of the Unhealthy Hospital"[12] shows that health care management professionals certainly do not have a uniform opinion on the roles or responsibilities of health care organizations or managers.

Regulators and the public have begun to question whether some nonprofit hospitals are providing sufficient charitable care to justify their tax-exempt status. For example, the Texas attorney general charged Houston's Methodist Hospital with violating its corporate charter and failing to provide enough free health care services to merit tax-exempt status.[13] Although the outcomes in this and similar suits have generally been unsuccessful under existing law, new laws have been proposed at federal, state, and local levels to tie nonprofit status to charitable care. A large part of the January 1991 issue of *Healthcare Financial Management* was devoted to the challenges to tax-exempt status of hospitals, and strategies for meeting those challenges.

[11]Michael L. Millenson, "Hospital Leader Seeks Return to Community Approach," *The Chicago Tribune*, 4 August 1991, section 7, p. 3.
[12]Anthony R. Kovner, "The Case of the Unhealthy Hospital," *Harvard Business Review*, Harvard Business School Publishing Division, 69, no. 5 (September-October 1991): 12-25, reprint no. 91506.
[13]"Update: Methodist Hospital's Tax-Exempt Status Challenged," *Trustee* 44, no. 1 (Chicago, IL: American Hospital Publishing, Inc., January 1991): 24.

In addition to the possible loss of tax-exempt status, Unrelated Business Income Tax (UBIT) is an important issue for nonprofit health care providers. For example, hospitals' outpatient pharmacy operations that sell to the general public compete with local and large chain drugstores. Their competitors claim that hospital pharmacies, which already have the advantage of low prices due to large purchase volumes, should not have a tax advantage as well. Local businesses have become very vocal in arguing that nonprofits have an unfair tax advantage in providing services that are also provided by for-profit businesses.

Due to the proliferation of related organizations, the appropriate reporting entity is an important and difficult issue for health care providers. If combined financial statements for related entities are not reported, users may find it difficult to assess the provider's financial performance. For example, when a well-endowed captive foundation is not consolidated with the provider because it is a separate legal entity, readers are unaware of a major financial resource. Separate (unconsolidated) financial statements could make it more difficult for trustees to recognize problems that potentially endanger their tax-exempt nonprofit status, such as benefits that inure to related parties.

Hospital advocates lament declining profitability and predict continuing negative trends in financial performance unless changes are made. The financial problems of some health care providers, particularly those in areas that are difficult to serve or with many poor people, have been serious enough to bankrupt them. However, the poor profitability of others may be an accounting illusion that obscures the reality of very large cash reserves.[14]

At this point, the only promise seems to be that the challenges to the U.S. health care system will continue. If these challenges are not met successfully, they may seriously jeopardize and undermine the health of both the U.S. economy and its citizens.

FINANCIAL REPORTING STANDARDS

Among nonprofit organizations, financial reporting for health care providers continues to be the most similar to financial reporting for businesses. Financial reporting standards for health care organizations were revised by the American Institute of Certified Public Accountants' (AICPA) *Audits of Providers of Health Care Services*, which is effective for fiscal years beginning on or after July 15, 1990. This new audit guide applies to all health care providers, in contrast to its predecessor which covered only hospitals. The most

[14]Richard A. Knox, ''Are Hospitals Crying Wolf?'' *Boston Sunday Globe, Business Section*, 3 February 1991, pp. 73, 75, 83.

significant changes for hospitals appear to relate to reporting revenues and related discounts, charity care, and bad debt expense, although many other changes were made.

Evolution of Financial Reporting

The development of accounting in health care institutions paralleled the major events in the industry's history. Until the 1930s, hospital accounting was relatively simple and focused on patient receivables. Reporting practices were diverse, and comparison among hospitals was difficult. Many hospitals refused to divulge the results of their operations, even safeguarding the information internally.

Interest in accounting issues grew along with the health care sector and third-party funding. In 1929, the United Hospital Fund of New York required uniform reporting for comparative purposes in distributing funds to its member hospitals. By 1950, the New Jersey Hospital Association had prepared a uniform accounting manual, including a complete chart of accounts and standardized financial reporting forms.

Since the early 1900s, such industry associations as the American Hospital Association have issued accounting and financial management manuals. In 1969 the AICPA published a Medicare audit guide, followed in 1972 by the *Hospital Audit Guide*.[15] Current health care accounting and financial reporting standards are set by the AICPA Audit and Accounting Guide, *Audits of Providers of Health Care Services*,[16] which includes SOP 89-5, *Financial Accounting and Reporting by Providers of Prepaid Health Care Services*,[17] and SOP 90-8, *Financial Accounting and Reporting by Continuing Care Retirement Communities*.[18]

The AICPA health care audit guide applies to all private health care service providers. Governmental providers are covered for all issues except those for which GASB has different standards, such as depreciation. Governmental health care providers that use enterprise fund accounting may follow all the provisions of the AICPA guide. Some of the nonprofit organizations that were previously subject to other audit guides, such as home care providers, may be covered by the health care audit guide. The appropriate audit guide is determined by the organization's mission and operations. Other entities now covered by the health care audit guide, such as CCRCs, were not previously covered by an industry audit guide. Hospitals are anticipated

[15]American Institute of Certified Public Accountants, *Hospital Audit Guide* (New York, NY: AICPA, 1972).

[16]American Institute of Certified Public Accountants, *Audits of Providers of Health Care Services*, as of December 31, 1990 (New York, NY: AICPA, 1991).

[17]AICPA, *Statement of Position 89-5*, "Financial Accounting and Reporting by Providers of Prepaid Health Care Services" (May 1989).

[18]AICPA, *Statement of Position 90-8*, "Financial Accounting and Reporting by Continuing Care Retirement Communities" (November 1990).

to have relatively little difficulty implementing the new standards; providers not previously covered by the hospital standards may experience more difficulty.

Industry association publications, such as the Healthcare Financial Management Association's (HFMA) *Principles and Practices Board Statements*[19] and the AHA's *Chart of Accounts for Hospitals*,[20] elaborate and extend the standards. In addition to suggesting financial statement accounts, the *Chart of Accounts* also deals with statistics needed for cost determination, budgeting, unit pricing, and external reporting. The AHA's *Uniform Hospital Definitions*[21] recommended and defined the uniform units of measurement for admissions, patient service, length of stay, and departmental service that form the basis for the measurement units in use today.

At one time, hospitals were required to report more cost data to external users than most other organizations except government contractors. In its effort to control the runaway growth of Medicare and Medicaid in the 1970s, Congress recommended cost-accounting systems and gave the government the authority to implement uniform reporting. However, its *System for Hospital Uniform Reporting*[22] (SHUR), designed to facilitate comparison of cost data among hospitals and enable cost control, was abandoned as unworkable. Instead Medicare turned to the DRG-based PPS. Although its implementation diminished the importance of cost accounting for external reporting purposes, most hospitals are still required to submit a Medicare Cost Report (MCR); and some items, such as outpatient services and fixed assets, are still reimbursed based on costs. (Medicare is charged with ultimately using prospective payments for all reimbursable items.)

Current efforts in health care cost accounting are motivated by internal rather than external pressures. Product and process cost data are needed for control and to determine the profitability of various procedures for financial decision making.

Funds and Fund Accounting

Nonprofit health care providers with restricted resources must adequately account for them. Fund accounting is the mechanism traditionally used to ensure and disclose that restrictions are met. Current standards allow either traditional presentation of financial statements for each fund type

---

[19]Healthcare Financial Management Association, *Principles and Practices Board Statements 1-12* (Westchester, IL: Healthcare Financial Management Association).

[20]American Hospital Association, *Chart of Accounts for Hospitals* (Chicago, IL: American Hospital Association, 1976).

[21]American Hospital Association, *Uniform Hospital Definitions* (Chicago, IL: American Hospital Association, 1960).

[22]Health Care Financing Administration, *System for Hospital Uniform Reporting* (Washington, DC: Government Printing Office, 1978).

or disclosure of only the fund balances for each fund type in a total entity Balance Sheet.

The *general fund* accounts for resources available for general operating purposes. These include resources generated internally by hospital operations, as well as unrestricted gifts, grants, endowment fund income, fixed assets used in operations (whether donated or purchased), and transfers from specific purpose funds when they are expended. The general fund includes resources for which the organization acts as an agent, holding them for other parties; assets whose use is limited by the board for specified purposes; and plant and equipment.

The inclusion of fixed assets in the general fund significantly differentiates accounting for health care service providers from accounting for other nonprofits. Even fixed assets with donor restrictions on the use of proceeds of asset disposition are accounted for as part of the general fund if their use within patient operations is not restricted. Any limitations on the use or proceeds of physical assets should be disclosed in the Notes. At times, hospitals have had to resort to legal remedies when major new construction plans required the destruction of a plant asset carrying donor limitations. If use of the assets is restricted, they may be accounted for in a restricted fund.

Nonprofit health care organizations frequently receive resources from private individuals, foundations, businesses, or government agencies that stipulate how the resources are to be spent. The *restricted fund* accounts enable outside users to evaluate the stewardship role of the health care board. Restricted fund balances are increased by donor-restricted gifts, bequests, or pledges, and by gains or income from restricted investments. Decreases in restricted fund balances are caused by transfers to other funds, investment losses, and investment expense (recognized in the fund that realizes related investment income).

Restricted funds are often limited to use for research, education, or charity care, or are invested to produce income restricted for such purposes and may be classified by purpose in the financial statements. They are classified as either *temporarily* or *permanently restricted funds*. Temporarily restricted funds include: *specific purpose funds*, which are temporarily donor restricted for special operating purposes; *term endowment funds*, which are temporarily donor restricted for investment until the time they are to be transferred to a current fund for use in operations; and *annuity* and *life income funds*. Specific purpose funds eventually lapse because they are used or because of donor required transfer to the unrestricted fund.

Although fixed assets are reported in the unrestricted fund, assets restricted by donors for the expansion and replacement of plant are accounted for in a separate temporarily restricted *plant replacement and expansion (PR&E) fund*, which contains primarily cash and securities. When expenditures are made for the designated purposes, the fixed assets and related fund balance are transferred from the PR&E fund directly to the plant assets and general fund balance. The most common sources of PR&E resources are building fund drives and investment income restricted to PR&E. The PR&E fund balance may be broken down by donor category, if desired. Board-designated resources for similar purposes appear in the general fund.

True endowment funds account for assets that donors have permanently restricted for investment and generate income that may be restricted or unrestricted. It has become common for hospitals to transfer at least some of these endowment assets to a separate foundation or other nonprofit entity.

Financial Statements

The audit guide requires the four financial statements shown in Exhibit A: a *Balance Sheet*, a *Statement of Revenues and Expenses of General Funds*, a *Statement of Changes in Fund Balances*, and a *Statement of Cash Flows of General Funds* (and restricted funds of governmental health care entities).

Balance Sheet   Nonprofit health care providers may choose to present either a traditional nonprofit multifund Balance Sheet that reports separate funds or an *aggregated*, single-column Balance Sheet in which fund balance amounts are disclosed by fund type but assets and liabilities are not identified by fund. The unrestricted, temporarily restricted, and permanently restricted fund balances in this presentation may also be labeled *net assets*. The aggregated presentation is consistent with the proposed financial statement display standards for all nonprofit organizations.[23] Exhibit A shows both a layered and an aggregate Balance Sheet.

Accounts receivable usually represent a significant portion of the current assets of health care providers and are important to good health care financial management. Accounts receivable are often classified by patient status (inpatients not discharged, inpatients discharged, outpatients) and by payor. *Electronic data interchange (EDI)*, which is used by a growing number of manufacturing firms for billing and remittance of payments, is expected to facilitate receivables management, improve accuracy, and speed collections for health care providers. Other receivables typically are classified by source, such as government appropriations, tuition, and donations.

Each fund may have investments in securities of varying terms, depending on the liquidity needed. Investments are carried at lower of cost or market, with disclosure of market values in the Notes. Thus, unrealized gains are not recognized. The exception is that debt securities are to be reported at amortized cost, rather than market, if there is both the intent and ability to hold them until maturity.

---

[23]Financial Accounting Standards Board, Invitation to Comment, *Financial Reporting by Not-for-Profit Organizations: Form and Content of Financial Statements* (Norwalk, CT: FASB, August 29, 1989).

Although health care provider inventories generally are not material to their financial position, purchases often are significant to operating results. Certain inventory items, such as drugs and supplies that are subject to rapid obsolescence or theft, must be carefully monitored. A perpetual inventory system, with periodic physical inventories to verify accuracy, may be used. Discrepancies of controlled substances may be investigated carefully even if the cost is relatively inconsequential. Some health care providers employ independent services to inventory drugs and other medical supplies. Large health care providers use a variety of inventory management methods similar to those of other businesses. *Just-in-time (JIT)* production processes are used to improve the inventory management of health care providers that deal with high-cost, short-shelf-life items, such as drugs used in specialized cancer treatments.

Health care providers use a classification called *assets whose use is limited*, or *reserves*, in the noncurrent assets section of the general fund. These assets actually consist of cash and other investments (usually fairly liquid securities) that have been set aside, either by contractual agreement or by board designation, such as some self-insurance reserves. This classification does not reflect the liquidity of the assets but, rather, their intended purpose. The classification of highly liquid assets as noncurrent may confuse financial statement users who are unfamiliar with health care standards.

A *bond fund account* may be used to hold the proceeds of a debt issue until it is expended for the construction or for the principal and interest payments to which it is typically restricted. Assets classified as *third-party revenues restricted to depreciation funding (funded depreciation)* are investments that the board has designated for use in preserving the physical plant base. They are not donor restricted. This unusual use of the term restricted to refer to board-designated items may also be confusing to new users.

Some bond issues require the establishment of *bond sinking funds* to ensure that bond principal and interest payments are met; occasionally, these resources must be placed in the control of a trustee. In general, the debt, the financed assets, and the resources related to debt retirement are all accounted for in the same fund. Health care providers usually report bond sinking fund assets in the unrestricted fund as assets whose use is limited. Governmental accounting requires such assets, if legally restricted as to use, to be reported in a restricted fund. A *bond covenant* (agreement) that merely requires certain cash or other asset balance or ratios to be maintained does not legally restrict the use of the assets. It should be disclosed in the footnotes, along with any implications for asset management and debt repayment.

Classifying liquid assets as noncurrent may make it difficult for financial statement users, including trustees, to assess their availability. Some argue that the likely eventual disposition of all assets that are not legally restricted should be reflected only on the liabilities and fund balance side of the Balance Sheet; the assets themselves should be classified by their nature as cash or investments, and as current or noncurrent according to their liquidity. The magnitude, nature, and liquidity of the assets is relatively objective and verifiable; the magnitude of the related needs for which the assets are designated is much more subjective. The current accounting standards do not clearly distinguish the two. The classification of such assets as current or noncurrent can significantly affect several important ratios.

The property, plant, and equipment in the unrestricted fund represents the historical cost of physical facilities used for operations. Fixed assets not used for operations are reported separately. The Notes also disclose whether fixed assets are owned, leased, donated, shared under affiliation programs, or provided by a governmental unit. The Notes may disclose current replacement values of fixed assets, if desired. Donated property or equipment is recorded at fair market value when contributed; the corresponding credit is classified as a direct addition to the fund balance. All plant assets are depreciated, usually on a straight-line basis. Accumulated depreciation and depreciation expense are reported in the same fund as the fixed assets, usually the unrestricted fund.

Health care organizations typically have the liabilities found in other organizations: accounts payable and personnel-related current liabilities and short-term and long-term debt. Most liabilities, including long-term mortgages, bonds payable, leases, and pension obligations, are in the unrestricted fund, although they may occasionally appear in restricted funds.

Health care providers encounter several difficult and unusual revenue recognition issues. *Deferred revenues* represent cash paid, primarily by patients and third-party payors, for services that have not yet been rendered but are likely to be rendered in the future. Deferred revenues may be current, long-term, or a combination. Many CCRCs charge a large fixed entrance fee in exchange for the promise to provide residents with care for the remainder of their lives, making deferred revenues and recognition issues significant for them. HMOs may also have deferred revenues for premiums paid but not yet earned.

Estimated settlements to (from) third-party payors are liabilities (or assets) commonly found in health care providers' financial statements, but seldom found in the statements of other industries. They arise because the preliminary rate paid by third parties when the service is rendered and billed is expected to differ from the actual settlement amount, which is determined after the service is provided and the revenue earned. For financial reporting purposes, providers should estimate and recognize revenue equal to the actual final amount to which they will be entitled. These estimates are subjective and difficult to make. When the final rate settlements are reached, health care providers recognize additional revenues or deductions from revenues related to services rendered in prior periods, referred to as *prior years' settlements*, in the activity statement.

Statement of Revenues and Expenses of the General Fund   A nonprofit health care organization usually calls its activity statement a *Statement of Revenues and Expenses of General Funds* (Exhibit A). For-profit and some nonprofit health care organizations call it an *Income Statement*. Whatever its title, the activity statement portrays both the revenues and expenses incurred by the unrestricted fund and the net excess (also referred to as surplus) or deficit of revenues and gains over expenses and losses that will increase or decrease the unrestricted fund balance.

Revenues are resource inflows that occur as a result of an entity's ongoing major or central operations. They are further classified as either *health care service* or *other* revenues. The nonoperating revenues classification allowed under prior standards is no longer used. Peripheral or incidental transactions result in *gains and losses* which may be classified as either operating or nonoperating, depending on their relation to the provider's major ongoing operations. Gains and losses may be reported net; revenues and expenses may not be netted. However, even if contributions are classified as gains, expenses incurred in soliciting contributions must be disclosed separately in the financial statements.[24]

The classification of nonpatient items, such as unrestricted contributions and investment income, as a revenue or gain depends on how the individual health care provider defines its mission. Thus, two providers may report the same transaction differently. The importance of an organization's mission definition to accounting treatments underscores the importance of defining this mission in the Notes to the Financial Statements.

Revenues are reported only in the general fund. *Patient service* or *health care service* revenue is recognized in the period in which it is earned (at point of sale or when a service is rendered) and is classified based on the type of service rendered. A major, and somewhat controversial, change from the prior standards for hospitals is that they must now report patient service revenues as a single line item, net of all related deductions and allowances, rather than at the gross charge rate. Other types of health care providers already reported revenues net of pricing adjustments. Hospitals' prior practices of reporting gross charges were considered to be misleading because they were rarely paid in full. Gross revenue and deductions may be disclosed in the Notes, if desired.

The deductions from gross revenues include *courtesy allowances* or *policy discounts*, which arise from charging lower rates to certain parties (such as doctors, clergymen, or employees) and are relatively insignificant. Much more significant are *contractual allowances*, which arise from the difference

---

[24]American Institute of Certified Public Accountants, *Audits of Providers of Health Care Services*, as of December 31, 1990 (New York, NY: AICPA, 1991), paragraph AAG-HCS 12.15-16, pp. 89-90.

between billings at established rates and the amounts actually paid by third-party payors under contractual agreements. Patient revenue accounting is straightforward under pure prospective payment systems: the amount the insurer agrees to pay is the amount recorded as revenue. However, determining revenue for the items that are not paid under prospective payment systems is complex and subjective. Third-party payors may have different contractual allowances, ways of determining the rates they will pay, audits, filing requirements, and settlement timing. Final rate settlements may not be reached until several years after the service provision, billing, and initial payment.

The new standards distinguish between charity care and bad debts and require that they be treated differently in the financial statements. Patients whose inability to pay is ascertained under board-approved policy and criteria are classified as *charity* or *free care*. Patients who are charged for services but are unwilling to pay are classified as *bad debt*. Health care providers must carefully consider, articulate, and document their admission and credit management policies and procedures, and some may need to develop new information systems to capture the necessary data.

The distinction between charity and bad debt is difficult to make in practice and has led to some consternation among health care providers. Bad debts, which occur among self-paying patients and for the uninsured portion of the expenses of third-party patients, are to be classified as an operating expense. Although this treatment essentially double counts the cost of providing the related care, it is consistent with how businesses treat bad debts.

The amount of charity care provided must be reported in the Notes, either at established rates, at cost, or in the form of care-related statistics. Charity care is not considered to generate revenue. There is some concern that relegating the information on charity care to the footnotes will obscure the amount of care provided, and that allowing several alternative valuation methods will reduce comparability among providers. (Charity care and bad debts were both treated as deductions from gross revenue under prior reporting standards.)

Governmental bodies and the general public have shown a growing interest in the amount of charity care provided by health care entities and have proposed making tax-exempt status contingent on providing some specified level of charitable care.[25] In some states, nonprofit hospitals already are no longer automatically exempt from property or sales taxes.

Other revenues arise from ongoing activities other than the delivery of health care services, and are recognized when earned. Examples include revenues from educational programs, research and other grants, space rental, and gift shop sales.

[25]"Inside the IRS: IRS Increases Its Compliance Efforts Toward Exempt Nonprofit Hospitals," *The Practical Accountant* (December 1990): 26.

Past reporting practices in the CCRC segment of the health care industry have been diverse, reducing comparability of statements among providers. Appendix C of the audit guide, AICPA SOP 90-8, *Financial Accounting and Reporting by Continuing Care Retirement Communities*, became effective for fiscal years beginning on or after December 15, 1990, with retroactive application and prior period restatements recommended. It provides CCRCs with guidance on applying generally accepted accounting principles to reporting of fees, obligations to provide future services, and costs of acquiring initial contracts.

Revenue recognition in CCRCs is the most complex issue addressed by the SOP. The basic questions are when and what portion of advance fees are revenues, deferred revenues, or liabilities. The amount of refundable advance fees that is expected to be refunded to current residents should be reported as a liability. The remainder of advance fees should be reported as deferred revenue and amortized (typically using the straight-line method) over the shorter of the remaining life of the resident or the contract period. Estimates of the remaining life of each resident should be based on the best available experience data from the individual facility, comparable facilities, and other relevant actuarial data sources. The Balance Sheet should disclose the refund policies and the gross amount of contractual refund obligations at the balance sheet date. Amounts refunded are reported in the Statement of Cash Flows as financing transactions.

If the advance fees are refundable only when the organization receives a new advance fee for the same unit from its next resident, then advance fees are accounted for as deferred revenue and amortized to income over the useful life of the facility. Law, management policy, and management practice should all be considered as evidence of whether refunds will actually be withheld under this condition. Nonrefundable advance fees are reported as deferred revenue and amortized over the shorter of the estimated remaining life of the resident or the contract period. The amortization period is to be adjusted annually, and the amortized amount should not exceed the amount actually available to the CCRC under regulation, the contract, or management policy. A liability to provide future services in excess of anticipated revenues should be reported when the unamortized value of deferred revenue is lower than the present value of future net cash outflows plus depreciation and any unamortized costs of acquiring the related contracts.

In the past, large amounts of services were donated to hospitals affiliated with religious groups whose members were either unpaid or paid less than the fair market value of their services. Although such relationships have become less common, many other types of volunteers remain active in the health care industry. Donated services should be reported if they are significant and an integral part of the efforts of the entity, if the entity controls the employment and duties of the donor, and if there is a clearly measurable basis for the amount to be recorded. Revenues equivalent to the fair market value of donated services are reported, with a corresponding amount of expense. Donated current assets that would normally be purchased, such as drugs, linens, and office supplies, are also reported as revenues and expenses and valued at their fair market value.

Unlike most other types of nonprofit organizations, health care providers may report expenses by either functional or natural (object of expense) classes. Responsibility center classifications were also used previously but are not mentioned in the current standards. The expense classifications recommended by the audit guide are shown in Table 17-5. Depreciation, interest, and bad debt expenses are usually reported as separate line items under either classification system because of their importance for financial analysis. Expenses of soliciting contributions must be disclosed separately in the financial statements.

Functional expenses often reflect organizational structure and include professional patient care, dietary, general service, and administrative service. *Professional* departments provide health care services, such as nursing, radiology, and anesthesiology. Hospitals may also have separate units, such as the outpatient department (OPD) and intensive care unit (ICU). *Ancillary* professional medical services include laboratory testing, radiology, electrocardiography, ambulances, and the emergency room. *General services* refer to the hotel functions, such as dietary, housekeeping, and maintenance; dietary is sometimes shown separately. *Administrative services* provide fiscal, personnel, admissions, medical records, and other business functions.

Health care providers must recognize expenses on the accrual basis. If expenses cannot be matched to revenues, they are treated as costs of the current period or recognized when assets have no future economic benefit.

TABLE 17-5 **Suggested Functional and Natural Expense Classifications**

Functional	Natural
Nursing services	Salaries and wages
Other professional services	Employee benefits
General services	Fees to individuals and organizations
Fiscal services	Supplies and other expenses
Administrative services	Purchased services
Bad debts	Bad debts
Depreciation	Depreciation
Interest	Interest

Source: Adapted from American Institute of Certified Public Accountants, *Audits of Providers of Health Care Services*, as of December 31, 1990 (New York, NY: AICPA, 1991), paragraph AG-HCS 12.15, p. 90.

Expense recognition is problematic for prepaid health care providers, especially HMOs, many of which are nonprofit organizations. Appendix B of the audit guide is SOP 89-5, *Financial Accounting and Reporting by Providers of Prepaid Health Care Services*, which is effective for fiscal years beginning on or after June 15, 1989. Prior accounting practices in this area varied greatly, and the SOP is designed to provide guidance that will increase uniformity across providers.

Current standards require health care costs to be accrued as services are rendered, including estimates of the costs of rendering services for claims *incurred but not reported (IBNR)*. Two other types of costs must also be accrued, net of any related anticipated revenues. These are costs due to future obligations to render services to specific members beyond the premium period or the term of the contract (due to contract provisions or regulatory requirements) and costs of guaranteed salaries, rent, or depreciation that will be incurred after a contract is terminated. Such costs can be substantial for prepaid health care providers, and estimating them is among the most challenging of health care accounting problems. Expert estimates can vary widely.

Losses are to be recognized when it is probable that expected future health care and maintenance costs under a group of existing contracts will exceed expected future premiums and *stop-loss insurance (reinsurance)* recoveries on those contracts. Many prepaid health care providers limit their financial risk by purchasing stop-loss coverage from insurance companies for costs in excess of a stated amount. Stop-loss premiums are included in health care costs, with recoveries reported as reductions of health care costs.

Prepaid health care providers' contract acquisition costs are expensed as incurred, consistent with the treatment of marketing costs in other industries. The exception is that some costs of acquiring initial CCRC contracts (up to one year after completion of construction) may be capitalized and amortized over the expected term of the related services.

Prior period adjustments are excluded from excess or deficit determination and are charged directly to the fund balance; they are relatively rare. Extraordinary items are unusual and occur infrequently. For nonprofit health care providers, the most likely prior period adjustment is the correction of errors in the financial statements of a prior period. The most common extraordinary item is a gain or loss on advance refunding of debt, which is required to be treated as extraordinary by SFAS 4. Retroactive third-party payor settlements, changes in the useful lives of depreciable assets, adjustments to malpractice liabilities, and adjustments related to realization of assets are neither prior period adjustments nor extraordinary items. They are elements of activity for the period in which the uncertainty was resolved.

Statement of Changes in Fund Balances The Statement of Changes in Fund Balances (Exhibit A) shows the beginning fund balances, all additions to and deductions from each fund balance, and transfers among funds.

Additions to the unrestricted fund include the net effect of revenues, expenses, gains, and losses (the bottom line) from the activity statement. Only one unrestricted fund column may be shown to avoid giving a reader the impression that plant or board-designated funds are donor restricted and legally unavailable for general purposes.

Permanent capital additions, such as endowment principal, are also additions to fund balance when received. They are never recognized as revenues because they are never transferred to the unrestricted fund. Donated property, plant, or equipment that is placed in service immediately is not reported as revenue. It is recognized and reported as an addition to the unrestricted fund balance. If donated property is held before being placed in service, it is reported as an addition to the appropriate restricted fund balance when received. When placed in service, it is reported as a transfer (deduction) from the plant replacement and expansion or other restricted fund balance and a transfer (addition) to the general fund balance.

Temporarily restricted resource inflows of contributions, bequests, investment income, and grants are classified as *additions* to the temporarily restricted fund balance when received or receivable from the donor. Resources for restricted purposes are recognized as revenues in the general fund only when the provider performs the donor-specified activity, or the donor-specified amount of time elapses. When the restrictions are met and the resources become available for operating purposes, they are reflected as other operating revenues on the Statement of Revenues and Expenses of the General Fund and as a transfer out of (deduction from) the restricted fund balance on the Statement of Changes in Fund Balances.

For example, consider a term-endowment gift received now that has a donor restriction that it and all proceeds be invested in securities for ten years, at which time all resources are to be transferred to the unrestricted fund. The gift is recognized as an addition to term endowment fund balance when received; investment income, gains, and losses will be reported as additions to the restricted fund each year; and revenue equal to the total amount of the accumulated resources will be recognized in the general fund ten years from now.

An organization should report only necessary transfers, and they should be clearly identified, particularly when one half is displayed as revenue on the Statement of Revenues and Expenses and the other half appears only in the Statement of Changes in Fund Balances. Only one half of a transfer to a related entity is reported in the financial statements of each organization.

Statement of Cash Flows of General Funds   A Statement of Cash Flows of General Funds is required for all health care providers. For-profit and private nonprofit health care providers should apply the provisions of FASB Statement No. 95, "Statement of Cash Flows." Governmental health care providers should apply the provisions of GASB Statement No. 9,

"Reporting Cash Flows of Proprietary and Nonexpendable Trust Funds and Governmental Entities that Use Proprietary Fund Accounting." Either the direct or indirect method may be used; Exhibit A illustrates both methods. Note that if there are substantial transactions in other funds, the Statement of Cash Flows of General Funds may omit important information about the organization's overall cash flows and position.

Commitments and Contingencies

Commitments and contingencies of health care providers arise from many sources, including *malpractice claims, risk contracting* (related to insurance contracts), *third-party payment programs, construction contracts, obligations to provide uncompensated care,* contractual agreements with physicians, pension plans, operating leases, purchase commitments, and loan guarantees. Standards require that the estimated contingencies resulting from such sources be accrued and disclosed in conformity with the provisions of FASB Statement No. 5, "Accounting for Contingencies," and FASB Interpretation No. 14, "Reasonable Estimation of the Amount of a Loss."

Basically, these accounting standards require a loss contingency to be accrued if an incident has occurred that resulted in a probable loss that can be reasonably estimated. If a probable loss cannot be reasonably estimated, it must be fully disclosed in the Notes, and may require an additional paragraph in the audit opinion if the effect on the financial statements is material. If the potential effects of the uncertainty surrounding the eventual loss is so pervasive that it compromises the meaning of the financial statements, the auditor may issue a disclaimer of opinion.

It can be very difficult to accurately estimate the amount of a loss or the total cost of contingencies and commitments that have been incurred. Specialists, such as actuaries, are often used to help make or audit loss estimates and quantify the uncertainties inherent in such estimates.

The number of medical malpractice suits and the cost of medical malpractice insurance have grown tremendously in recent decades. Successful plaintiffs often receive large settlements. Insurers have reacted by reducing the limits of their liability (for example, lowering policy limits and increasing deductibles), by raising premiums, by insuring only for claims made during the period the policy is in effect, by refusing to renew policies, and even by withdrawing from this line of the insurance business.

Health care providers have also attempted to control the cost of malpractice insurance. Some became partially *self-insured* by increasing their deductibles or fully self-insured (*uninsured*) by canceling all malpractice coverage. Several hospital groups have formed captive insurance companies, which often adjust premiums retrospectively to reflect actual experience. The health care provider's malpractice insurance coverage program and the basis for any related loss accrual should be disclosed in the Notes. Disclosure should include any exposure to material malpractice contingencies in excess of accruable amounts, retrospective determination of premiums, and discounting policy and rates.

Malpractice costs include the costs of litigating and settling claims of incidents that occurred during the period, and adjustments to estimates of the ultimate cost of claims for incidents that occurred in prior periods. For reported malpractice incidents (*asserted claims*), the most likely amount of the loss should be accrued. If no amount within an estimated range is more likely than any other amount within that range, the minimum amount should be accrued and the potential additional loss disclosed in the Notes. Estimated losses can be accrued either individually or on a group basis. Losses resulting from incidents that have occurred but not yet been reported should be accrued based on the best available estimate of ultimate costs. To the extent that they are relevant, both industry and individual provider experience should be used in constructing estimates. Chapter 10 of the audit guide provides additional detail on accounting for malpractice costs.

Reporting Entity and Related Organizations

Other nonprofit organizations (such as *foundations, auxiliaries*, or *guilds*) frequently assist nonprofit health care providers, especially hospitals, with fund raising. A nonprofit health care provider may be owned by another nonprofit organization, may itself own for-profit or other nonprofit organizations, and may have very close relationships to other nonprofit organizations. The relationships may be extremely complex and can be difficult for financial statements readers to identify. Although the health care audit guide excludes reporting entities from its scope because of the FASB's and GASB's current reporting entity projects, it does provide some guidance on reporting for related organizations.

A separate organization is considered to be *related* to a health care entity if one of the following conditions is met:

> Contracts or other legal documents give the health care entity the authority to direct the activities, management, and policies of the separate organization.
>
> For all practical purposes, the health care entity is the sole beneficiary of the separate organization, as when one of the following three circumstances exists:
>
>> The separate organization solicits funds in the name of the health care entity to be used by the health care entity.
>>
>> The health care entity transferred some of its resources to the separate organization, and substantially all of the separate organization's resources are held for the benefit of the health care entity.
>>
>> The separate organization operates primarily for the benefit of the health care entity and carries out certain functions for the health care entity.[26]

---

[26]AICPA, *Audits of Providers of Health Care Services*, paragraph AAG-HCS 13.03, p. 103.

For reporting entity matters not addressed by the current standards, health care entities, especially hospitals, seem likely to continue to follow the recommendations of the prior guide until new standards are issued.

In short, consolidated statements are appropriate if the health care entity can control the separate organization, is under common control with it, or is the sole beneficiary of it. If consolidated statements are not provided under such circumstances, the current standards require that the Notes to the health care organization's financial statements describe the relationships with the separate organization and disclose summarized information about the assets, liabilities, results of operations, and changes in fund balances of the separate organization. If material transactions between the health care organization and the related organization exist, the Notes should also contain a summary description of the transactions, their dollar volume, and amounts due from and to the related organization.

Reporting for related organizations is currently a very complex accounting issue that requires careful, informed consideration and expert advice. The forthcoming standards should clarify the rules but cannot eliminate the inherent complexity.

Trends in Health Care Accounting

The recent issuance of the health care audit guide is likely to mean that little new health care specific guidance will emerge in the near future, except to clarify and elaborate the existing standards. Implementing the standards may be difficult for those health care providers, such as some CCRCs, that were not subject to the hospital audit guide and previously used accounting methods substantially different from the current standards. Both providers and analysts have expressed concern over the new requirements for reporting patient revenues and charity care, arguing that important information provided by the old disclosure methods will now be unavailable.

The upcoming FASB pronouncements on contributions, financial statement display, and reporting entities are likely to affect the health care standards. It also remains to be seen how many governmental hospitals adopt the AICPA standards and how the reporting standard changes will affect comparability among governmental and nongovernmental hospitals.

Adoption of a national health care plan would be likely to have a significant impact on health care accounting and information systems. Even under the current system, demands are increasing for accountability to the public and regulators on financial and nonfinancial matters. Consumers are demanding access to controversial nonfinancial data, such as success rates of providers for various procedures, other measures of quality, and the prevalence of AIDS among the medical staff. They are concerned about hospital efficiency, rating hospitals last among common consumer items in terms of value received for money spent. Policymakers and politicians are concerned that the U.S. spends more on health care than other countries yet does not have better health. Governments wish to ascertain whether nonprofit health care providers are providing enough charity care to justify their nonprofit status. The focus on health care costs, availability, and quality ensures that challenges to accounting and other reporting requirements will grow rather than diminish.

A FRAMEWORK FOR ANALYSIS: RATING HEALTH CARE BONDS[27]

Bond rating agencies, such as Moody's Investors Service and Standard and Poor's Corporation (S&P), analyze the credit-worthiness of health care providers that issue bonds. The analysis considers both credit-related factors and the legal structure of the proposed bond issue to assess the provider's ability to repay the debt. Based on this analysis, the agency assigns a credit rating that indicates the bond quality. Investment houses, institutional investors, trustees, management, and regulators perform similar analyses for their own purposes. The unusually high incidence of defaults and rating downgrades in the 1980s and the unsettled economics of health care providers have led to increased caution and more sophisticated analytic approaches.

Similar analytic techniques, focused on averages and aggregates rather than individual providers, may also be used by the government and private organizations that set reimbursement rates. Rate setters have a goal of setting payment rates sufficiently high to maintain the service quality and financial viability of health care providers, but not so high as to allow excessive profitability or extravagant spending.

The *credit factors* considered in these analyses include financial, utilization, hospital type, medical staff, market, competition, environment, management, and economic factors. Past performance over at least a three-year period, recent trends, and current status are combined with statistical factors and long-term risk predictions to forecast future performance and ability to repay the debt.

Liquidity, leverage, profitability, cash flow, and stability are important indicators of a health care provider's financial condition. The HFMA FAS data are valuable for performing comparative analyses. Cash, marketable securities, board-designated assets, and funded depreciation are treated as current assets if the Notes to the Financial Statements disclose that they are liquid. Trustee-held assets usually are not included in liquidity ratios, except for currently available funded depreciation. Significant restricted or endowment funds may be analyzed separately. The excess before (rather than after) extraordinary items is generally used.

---

[27]The authors are grateful to Laura Ann Ryan of Prudential-Bache for her insights on the financial analysis of health care organizations.

Accounts receivable (net of an adequate allowance for doubtful accounts) are important in their own right and also reflect management quality. Reimbursement terms can significantly affect financial performance. For example, Medicare has paid higher rates to rural hospitals designated as sole providers or rural referral centers. Although each state's unique situation must be examined, a high Medicaid load may indicate vulnerability because Medicaid often pays rates below full costs. Although receivables turnover is heavily dependent on third-party practices, management is responsible for timely, accurate billings and credit management.

The provider's market share and competitive environment are also evaluated. The highly competitive market for health care services differs from the relative monopolies of traditional tax-exempt bond issuers, such as governments, utilities, or water authorities. Utilization factors and trends to be examined vary with type of provider and may include bed size, occupancy rate, admissions, emergency room visits, outpatient visits, and ALOS. An individual health care provider is compared to national, regional, and peer group averages for these factors, as possible. If a provider's percent of admissions is lower than its percent of beds in the market area, it would be investigated. The number and reimbursement rates of HMO contracts and PPO arrangements with area businesses for services to employees are also important. Other factors to be considered include pooling of resources, shared services, shared staff, provision of unique services, trends opposite those of competitors, and regional dispersion of providers.

The medical staff is a primary determinant of hospital admissions, revenue, and expenses. A wide distribution among admitters is preferred to heavy reliance on a few. For example, a high proportion of admissions generated by physicians near retirement age could signal impending problems. High loyalty to one facility, measured by the percentage of doctors admitting solely to the facility, is a positive sign. Malpractice insurance is assessed for adequacy and the reasonableness of its costs relative to the industry. The likely effects of any outstanding malpractice suits or other pending litigation, commitments, or contingencies are carefully considered.

The community's dependence on a provider is important, and the local economy will affect operations. Trends in the population, unemployment, employment sectors, state Medicaid policy, and the top ten employers are relevant. High concentration in a particular industry makes the local economy, and the provider, more vulnerable to a downturn in that industry.

The need for proposed new equipment, additional programs, or changes in services must be assessed. An institution may want to undertake a project for competitive reasons even though the community need is adequately met by existing facilities. As CONs are being phased out in many states, an independent assessment of community need may be more difficult to acquire.

Management quality can best be assessed by meeting the management team. However, the audited financial statements and other financial documents also reflect management's track record and management biographies indicate tenure and past experience. Dramatic fluctuations in financial indicators are discussed with management. The chief financial officer should be able to answer any questions about the provider's performance, competition, future plans, and strategy, including additional debt needs and anticipated projects. The provider's labor relations record is important, especially past or predicted labor problems, unionization efforts, or staffing problems, such as nursing or technician shortages. A management contract with a proprietary chain may be a positive credit factor for a small provider.

Several *legal factors* also influence the evaluation of a health care provider's public bond issue. A *security interest* in receivables, a revenue pledge, or a mortgage on fixed assets will increase the security of the lender. *Restrictions on the issuance of additional debt* also protect current bondholders. At one time, many borrowers were required to maintain a trustee-held *debt service reserve fund* containing the amount of *maximum annual debt service*, the largest amount of principal plus interest plus debt service on any other debt paid in any one year during the life of the bonds. This requirement has been relaxed but not entirely eliminated; it is now most common for bonds with lower ratings. A minimum debt service coverage level *covenant* is often stated as a percentage of the new maximum annual debt service for a specified number of fiscal years following completion of the project being financed. Bond issuers are responsible for maintaining compliance with the bond covenants.

Gone are the days when a few financial ratios were considered sufficient for credit analysis; it is now a complex multidisciplinary endeavor. Bond rating agencies continue to refine their analytic procedures. They readily share their general analysis approach with bond issuers because a well-prepared management team with honest, considered answers to difficult questions makes the bond analyst's job easier and has a positive impact on the assessment of management quality.

APPLYING THE FOUR KEY QUESTIONS TO ABC

Creditors, employees, regulators, insurers, and patients are concerned about the financial condition of health care providers. In the 1980s, a growing number of nonprofit health care providers defaulted on debt, ceased operations, or narrowly skirted the abyss by merging with other institutions. Financial analysis can help interested parties diagnose a provider's financial condition and assess the cause of observed problems or the potential to safely serve larger social goals. We use the four financial analysis questions to organize our analysis of the 1984 audited financial statements of ABC Medical Center and to illustrate the financial analysis process.[28]

[28]We are grateful to Nancy Kane, Associate Professor, Harvard School of Public Health, for providing us with these financial statements and related data, as well as parts of the analysis.

Introduction to ABC

ABC Medical Center is an adapted and disguised version of an acute-care teaching institution that provides a broad spectrum of care to a 13-county area in a U.S. state. A large community hospital, it had 934 beds and total assets of $139 million in 1984. ABC states that its policy is to not deny care because of a patient's inability to pay, to implement state of the art technology, and to attempt to control costs. In 1985, it requested a 7.4 percent rate increase from the state for fiscal year 1986. The analysis of past financial performance, as reflected in the most recent (1984) audited financial statements, is an important part of the rate-setting process.

Internal Analysis

Exhibit B contains the 1984 ABC financial statements (including comparative data for 1983), which received an unqualified audit opinion. It includes a Balance Sheet, a Statement of Revenues and Expenses and Changes in Accumulated Equity, a Statement of Changes in Financial Position, and excerpts from the Notes to the Financial Statements. These statements were prepared under the standards set forth by the AICPA hospital audit guide in effect when they were prepared. ABC presents a single column for each statement for each year. If it had restricted funds, the statement of changes in fund balances would have multiple columns.

To facilitate analysis, we prepared the statements shown in Exhibit C. They consist of a rearranged balance sheet and activity statement, the absolute dollar changes (1984 amounts minus 1983 amounts), percent changes (the absolute dollar change of an item divided by the 1983 amount for that item), and common size statements for 1984 and 1983 (each line item divided by the relevant total of assets, revenue, or expenses). Hereafter, all dollar amounts are in thousands, as displayed on the financial statements, unless otherwise indicated.

The ERR messages displayed in Exhibit C are messages from the spreadsheet that a calculation error has occurred in these locations, in this case because of an attempt to divide by zero. Some spreadsheets may allow you to print a blank space or a different message, such as DIVZERO, instead of the more generic ERR.

Consistency Between Goals and Resources   In 1984, ABC's total assets of $139,238 [1] were 2.7 percent [2] higher than their 1983 level. They were relatively evenly split among current (25.4 percent [3]), other (36.0 percent [4]), and net fixed (38.6 percent [5]) asset classifications.

Both current and other assets increased (by 15.3 percent [6] and 58.4 percent [7], respectively) and fixed assets decreased by 26.7 percent [8] from 1983 levels. The current ratio improved from an already healthy 1.5 [9] in 1983 to 2.0 [10] in 1984, although the 1984 cash balance is very low. Net patient receivables grew by $2,934 [11], or 14.6 percent, which was somewhat higher than the 9.1 percent [12] by which net patient revenues grew. This indicates a slowing of receivables collections, which is also reflected in the three-day increase (from 61 [13] to 64 [14] days) in days receivables outstanding. Prepaid expenses also grew significantly; its composition and the reason for the change should be investigated. In short, the current assets grew and their composition shifted; the low cash balance and receivables collection slowdown bear watching.

The two largest and fastest growing other assets, bond and self-insurance funds, consist of cash and investments held for construction or debt retirement and for payment of claims against which ABC self-insures. Its bond funds equal half of the total long-term capital lease and debt liability. As bonds were just issued in 1984, the assets will probably soon be used for plant expansion. The $4,000 [15] decrease in board-designated assets for funded depreciation may be due to retirement of related debt, purchase of fixed assets, or the transfer of assets to another entity (discussed below).

Self-insured funds exactly match the liabilities for self-insured claims, which are based on estimates. Such assets may be in a separate, legally unavailable trust fund or may be held by the hospital itself. If the liabilities are overstated, the organization appears to be in worse shape than it actually is. If understated, the reverse is true. As discussed above, determining the amount of expense and liability for such items is difficult and subjective. ABC indicates its financial security by setting aside the full amount of the estimated liability in other assets.

The substantial (26.7 percent) decrease in net property plant and equipment raises a red flag. It would often indicate that an organization is either shrinking voluntarily or cannibalizing its plant to keep afloat. That is emphatically not the case with ABC, which transferred its plant to other entities that are closely related to it. Effective July 1984, a newly created holding company, ABC Inc., became the parent of ABC and of three other subsidiaries, DEF, GHI, and ABC Foundation. All of the organizations are nonprofit, except GHI, which is for-profit. If any material restrictions, charters, or bond covenants were violated by this reorganization, the audit opinion would have been qualified.

The Statement of Revenues and Expenses and Changes in Accumulated Equity shows that ABC transferred $36,182 [16] of assets to affiliated entities as a result of the reorganization. Note 9 shows that ABC transferred net plant of $21,090 ($27,357 cost − $6,267 accumulated depreciation) to DEF and assets of $750 to GHI. Additional assets of $14,342 ($36,182 − $21,090 − $750), probably cash and investments, were transferred to ABC Foundation or ABC Inc. All debt was retained by ABC, although Note 5 indicates that at least $10 million of the long-term lease obligations remaining in ABC's financial statements is related to assets that were transferred to an affiliate.

Transferring assets while keeping the debt caused ABC's financial position to appear to deteriorate. Had the assets been sold to an unrelated entity,

ABC would have received an amount equal to their market value, and the related debt would have been eliminated. ABC's financial statements now paint an incomplete picture of the resulting status. Consolidated statements for ABC Inc. plus individual financial statements for each related organization would present more clearly the net effect of such inter-entity transactions. Both before and after a reorganization, trustees need to carefully consider the ethics, legality, and financial and control repercussions of reorganizations, relationships, and transfers among related entities. It is likely that ABC Inc. would be required to present consolidated financial statements under the reporting standards for related entities currently under consideration by the FASB.

On the liability side, the $1,911 [17] increase in accounts payable and $814 [18] increase in accrued expenses, in conjunction with the drastic cash decline and low cash balance, would typically signal a problem. Under the existing circumstances, however, there seems to be no cause for alarm. The growth in settlement amounts due to third parties indicates that ABC has recently been reimbursed at preliminary rates higher than the final rates it expects to receive and that it anticipates returning some of the money already received. The decrease in the asset, settlement amounts due from third parties, indicates that ABC has been paid part of the amounts to make up for earlier under-reimbursement by third-party payors.

The bond anticipation notes (short-term notes issued while a bond issue is being finalized) caused high current debt maturities in 1983. The long-term debt increase of $23,939 [19] is partially offset by the $6,274 [20] decrease in current maturities of long-term debt. The $21,850 [21], or 32 percent, decrease in accumulated equity (fund balance) would have been a $14,332 ($36,182 − $21,850) increase if assets had not been transferred to related parties. The transfer of assets without related debt is responsible for the decline from a 50 percent to a 33 percent equity to capital ratio. Had the debt been transferred to ABC Inc. along with the assets, the equity to capital ratio would not have declined so drastically.

ABC appears to have decreased its charity care in 1984. Its charity allowances declined by $517 [22], or 6 percent, from 1983 to 1984. If gross charges per procedure increased during the same period, which is likely, then actual charity care decreased by even more than 6 percent. Charity allowances decreased from 5.6 percent to 5.0 percent of total patient revenues. However, net expenses for education programs increased by $503 [23], or nearly 10 percent. This may be viewed as an alternative social goal that ABC has chosen to pursue instead of charity care.

ABC presents a situation where many of the financial ratios and trends initially and individually look bad, but a different picture emerges when one looks more carefully at the financial statement details and Notes. ABC's remaining resources appear to be adequate to meet its goals. Had ABC not transferred resources to other entities, it would be even more financially comfortable and able to pursue an even higher level of social goals.

Intergenerational Equity   ABC had an excess of revenues over expenses of $6,386 [24] before the $7,844 [25] extraordinary gain on debt extinguishment. This is a 4.7 percent [26] return on revenues and a nearly 10 percent [27] return on equity. The return on equity exceeded inflation; thus, current constituents are providing resources to ABC for the benefit of future generations. (There is no evidence that resources are needed to pay the debts of past beneficiaries.) Thus, ABC generated more than enough revenue to cover its expenses and added to its already sizable equity. It chose to save, rather than to provide more services.

Because settlements due to third parties and liabilities for self-insurance claims are estimates, they may be either overstated or understated. If understated, then future generations will have to pay more to cover them. If overstated, then the current generation is saving even more money than shown by the excess for the benefit of future generations. The large amounts of assets set aside indicates that ABC can easily repay the liabilities when they fall due, unless they are badly underestimated.

Match Between Sources and Uses of Resources   Net revenue from operations grew by 8.2 percent [28], faster than the 7.4 percent [29] growth in total operating expenses. Although 1984 long-term debt is larger than net plant assets, which is usually cause for alarm, this occurred because recent bond proceeds in bond funds have not yet been used to acquire fixed assets. Current liabilities are certainly not being used to finance long-term assets, which is the primary concern when comparing asset and capital lives.

Total current assets can cover three months of expenses. The sources appear more than adequate to cover ABC's uses, and they appear to be conservatively well matched. GAAP requires ABC to disclose any commitments it had made to support ABC Inc. or other affiliates.

Resource Sustainability   As a hospital, most of ABC's revenue (96 percent [30] in 1984) derives from patient care. As the primary provider in a 13-county area, it seems to have a fairly broad captive market. This somewhat alleviates concerns about overdependence on a single revenue source, even though its home state has had chronic economic problems. Knowledge of the dispersion of revenue sources among Medicare, Medicaid, private insurance, and self-pay by patients would be useful, but is not provided in these financial statements.

At 54 percent [31], personnel is the largest component of expenses, followed by supplies and other expenses at 29.5 percent [32]. The latter category usually contains many diverse items, including the cost of any nurses and others who are paid on a contractual basis rather than as employees. Salaries and wages were nearly flat from 1983 to 1984, but benefits rose by 17.46 percent [33], probably due to the return to the Social Security system (Note 4) and to estimates of other payroll-related expenses for which ABC self-insures (Note 3).

External Comparisons

Exhibit D contains formulas and median values of several useful ratios from hospitals in the region, derived from the HFMA FAS service data for each year. ABC ratios are calculated from the financial statements shown in Exhibit C.

ABC's 0.15 [34] deductible ratio, well below the 0.20 [35] median, indicates that ABC had some combination of better debt collection experience, lower discounts to third parties, and less charity care than others in the region. The ABC operating margin was near the median in both years.

The ABC current ratio of 2.0 [10] in 1984 is near the 2.17 [37] median, although its 1.5 [9] ratio in 1983 was well below the median. ABC collects its receivables a few days sooner than most others.

ABC dropped from being slightly above the 1983 equity financing median of 0.496 [39]. Its transfer of assets to other organizations left ABC, at 0.33 [40], more highly leveraged than most hospitals in the region. Whereas the median cash flow to total debt ratio increased from 0.176 [41] to 0.232 [42], ABC's ratio dropped from slightly below the median at 0.17 [43] to 0.14 [44], due primarily to the increase in debt in 1984. The ABC return on total assets at 0.05 [45] is below the median in 1984. This indicates that ABC has relatively more than average assets because its operating margin was at the median.

ABC's 1984 return on equity is up slightly and its fixed asset financing is high. This resulted primarily from the transfer of assets and equity out of ABC, the retention of all debt in ABC, and the issuance of more debt without yet acquiring related fixed assets. ABC's average plant age of 6.3 [46] years is stable and slightly newer than the median, which does not indicate a need for plant replacement and might lead one to question the need for the recent debt issue. The financial statement analysis indicates that ABC is in fairly good shape relative to the hospitals in the region.

Diagnosis

ABC appears to be financially healthy and solid. It generated cash from operations and long-term debt and remains liquid and not overburdened with debt, even after investing heavily in other assets and transferring assets to other entities. If the other entities have preserved the transferred assets, the combined financial position of the parent organization, ABC Inc., should be even better than that of the Medical Center alone. Unless there was a decrease in the health care needs of the poor and uninsured from 1983 to 1984, ABC chose to decrease its charitable care in order to pursue other social objectives, such as increasing medical education, or to improve its financial health (and that of related entities). The difficult task of making such trade-offs is the responsibility of the trustees and management of the organization. Thorough financial analysis and planning can assist them to make such decisions and to maintain both the financial health of the organization and the health of the human population it serves, without straining the financial health of the governments, businesses, and individuals that finance health care.

SUMMARY

The health care industry is one of the fastest growing, most rapidly changing, and most controversial nonprofit sectors. Because good health and health care affect the quality of life and the economic success of a nation, health care providers play a crucial role in the success of our economy and society. Escalating costs and rapid advances in medical technology promise to bring continued change.

Because nonprofit health care providers derive most of their revenues from patient services and because for-profit health care providers are relatively common, the health care sector competitive environment, operations, and accounting are more similar to for-profit businesses than to other types of nonprofit organizations. Nonprofit providers find it increasingly difficult to provide expensive charitable care. Indeed, many U.S. hospitals have reorganized into complex entities that contain for-profit businesses within them.

As a result, the requirement for fund accounting is less marked in the health care sector, although special purpose, plant replacement and expansion, and endowment restricted funds and an unrestricted (general) fund are used. Only the Statement of Changes in Fund Balances must show separate funds. The Balance Sheet may aggregate the assets and liabilities of the separate funds, and the Statement of Revenues and Expenses and the Statement of Cash Flows apply only to the general fund. Health care provider revenues are often classified by source, and expenses may be classified by natural or functional categories. Revenue recognition for CCRCs and expense recognition for some managed care organizations are complex because the timing of revenues and expenses requires the need for significant, complex, and subjective estimates.

Increased competition and cost-containment pressures and the related increase in failures and defaults of health care providers lend added importance to careful analysis. Important financial indicators include revenue and expense magnitude and trends, liquidity, leverage, coverage, asset management, and utilization ratios. Several industry and government sources of health care data facilitate comparisons to relevant peer groups and individual competitors. It is also important, although difficult, to assess and predict management quality, economic stability, and government reimbursement and other policies. This requires additional data to that provided in financial statements. Health care management continues to become increasingly sophisticated and challenging.

EXHIBIT A Sample Hospital Financial Statements

Sample Hospital
Balance Sheets (Layered Approach)
December 31, 19X7 and 19X6

GENERAL FUNDS

Assets	19X7	19X6
Current assets:		
Cash and cash equivalents	$ 3,103,000	$ 4,525,000
Assets whose use is limited—required for current liabilities (Notes 5, 7, 8)	970,000	1,300,000
Patient accounts receivable, net of estimated uncollectibles of $2,500,000 in 19X7 and $2,400,000 in 19X6	15,100,000	14,194,000
Estimated third-party payor settlements—Medicare (Note 3)	441,000	600,000
Supplies at lower of cost (first-in, first-out) or market	1,163,000	938,000
Other current assets	321,000	403,000
Due from donor-restricted funds, net	-	500,000
Total current assets	21,098,000	22,460,000
Assets whose use is limited: (Notes 5, 7, 8)		
By board for capital improvements	11,000,000	10,000,000
By agreements with third-party payors for funded depreciation	9,234,000	6,151,000
Under malpractice funding arrangement—held by trustee	3,007,000	2,682,000
Under indenture agreement—held by trustee	11,708,000	11,008,000
Total assets whose use is limited	34,949,000	29,841,000
Less assets whose use is limited and that are required for current liabilities	970,000	1,300,000
Noncurrent assets whose use is limited	33,979,000	28,541,000
Property and equipment, net (Notes 6, 7)	51,038,000	50,492,000
Other assets:		
Prepaid pension cost (Note 12)	85,000	35,000
Deferred financing costs	693,000	759,000
Investment in affiliated company (Note 4)	917,000	576,000
Total other assets	1,695,000	1,370,000
	$107,810,000	$102,863,000

Liabilities and Fund Balances	19X7	19X6
Current liabilities:		
Current installments of long-term debt (Note 7)	$ 970,000	$ 1,200,000
Current portion of capital lease obligations (Note 7)	500,000	550,000
Accounts payable	2,217,000	2,085,000
Accrued expenses	3,396,000	3,225,000
Estimated third-party payor settlements—Medicaid (Note 2)	2,143,000	1,942,000
Deferred third-party reimbursement	200,000	210,000
Advances from third-party payors	122,000	632,000
Current portion of estimated malpractice costs (Note 8)	600,000	500,000
Retainage and construction accounts payable	955,000	772,000
Due to donor-restricted funds	300,000	-
Total current liabilities	11,403,000	11,116,000
Deferred third-party reimbursement	746,000	984,000
Estimated malpractice costs, net of current portion (Note 8)	3,207,000	2,182,000
Long-term debt, excluding current installments (Note 7)	22,644,000	23,614,000
Capital lease obligations, excluding current portion (Note 7)	500,000	400,000
Fund balance	69,310,000	64,567,000
Commitments and contingent liabilities (Notes 3, 6, 8, 12, 13)		
	$107,810,000	$102,863,000

See accompanying notes to financial statements.

Adapted from *Audits of Providers of Health Care Services*, Appendix A, pp. 123-143.

EXHIBIT A (Continued)

Sample Hospital
Balance Sheets (Layered Approach—Continued)
December 31, 19X7 and 19X6

DONOR-RESTRICTED FUNDS

Assets

Assets	19X7	19X6
Specific-purpose funds:		
Cash	$ 378,000	$ 378,000
Investments, at cost that approximates market	728,000	455,000
Grants receivable	613,000	535,000
	$1,719,000	$1,368,000
Plant replacement and expansion funds:		
Cash	$ 24,000	$ 321,000
Investments, at cost that approximates market	252,000	165,000
Pledges receivable, net of estimated uncollectibles of $60,000 in 19X7 and $120,000 in 19X6	132,000	380,000
Due from general funds	150,000	-
	$ 558,000	$ 866,000
Endowment funds:		
Cash	$1,253,000	$ 653,000
Investments, net of $175,000 valuation allowance in 19X7, market value $3,798,000 in 19X7 and $5,013,000 in 19X6 (Note 9)	3,856,000	5,320,000
Due from general funds	150,000	100,000
	$5,259,000	$6,073,000

Liabilities and Fund Balances

Liabilities and Fund Balances	19X7	19X6
Specific-purpose funds:		
Accounts payable	$ 205,000	$ 72,000
Deferred grant revenue	92,000	225,000
Due to general funds	-	-
Fund balance	1,422,000	1,041,000
	$1,719,000	$1,368,000
Plant replacement and expansion funds:		
Due to general funds	$ -	$ 345,000
Fund balance	558,000	521,000
	$ 558,000	$ 866,000
Endowment funds:		
Fund balance	$5,259,000	$6,073,000
	$5,259,000	$6,073,000

See accompanying notes to financial statements.

EXHIBIT A (Continued)

Sample Hospital
Balance Sheets* (Aggregate Approach)
December 31, 19X7 and 19X6

Assets	19X7	19X6
Current assets:		
Cash and cash equivalents	$ 2,803,000	$ 5,025,000
Assets whose use is limited—required for current liabilities	1,267,000	1,372,000
Patient accounts receivable, net of estimated uncollectibles of $2,500,000 in 19X7 and $2,400,000 in 19X6	15,100,000	14,194,000
Estimated third-party payor settlements—Medicare	441,000	600,000
Supplies at lower of cost (first-in, first-out) or market	1,163,000	938,000
Other current assets	321,000	403,000
Total current assets	21,095,000	22,532,000
Assets whose use is limited or restricted		
By board for capital improvements	11,000,000	10,000,000
By agreements with third-party payors for funded depreciation	9,234,000	6,151,000
Under malpractice funding arrangement—held by trustee	3,007,000	2,682,000
Under indenture agreement—held by trustee	11,708,000	11,008,000
By donors or grantors for specific purposes	2,277,000	1,634,000
By donors for permanent endowment funds	5,259,000	6,073,000
Total assets whose use is limited or restricted	42,485,000	37,548,000
Less assets whose use is limited and that are required for current liabilities	1,267,000	1,372,000
Noncurrent assets whose use is limited or restricted	41,218,000	36,176,000
Property and equipment, net	51,038,000	50,492,000
Other assets:		
Prepaid pension cost	85,000	35,000
Deferred financing costs	693,000	759,000
Investment in affiliated company	917,000	576,000
Total other assets	1,695,000	1,370,000
	$115,046,000	$110,570,000

Liabilities and Fund Balances	19X7	19X6
Current liabilities:		
Current installments of long-term debt	$ 970,000	$ 1,200,000
Current portion of capital lease obligations	500,000	550,000
Accounts payable	2,422,000	2,157,000
Accrued expenses	3,396,000	3,225,000
Estimated third-party payor settlements—Medicaid	2,143,000	1,942,000
Deferred third-party reimbursement	200,000	210,000
Advances from third-party payors	122,000	632,000
Current portion of estimated malpractice costs	600,000	500,000
Retainage and construction accounts payable	955,000	772,000
Advances and deferred revenue	92,000	-
Total current liabilities	11,400,000	11,188,000
Deferred third-party reimbursement	746,000	984,000
Estimated malpractice costs, net of current portion	3,207,000	2,182,000
Long-term debt, excluding current installments	22,644,000	23,614,000
Capital lease obligations, excluding current installments	500,000	400,000
Total liabilities	38,497,000	38,368,000
Net assets:		
Unrestricted	69,310,000	64,567,000
Temporarily restricted by donors/grantors	1,980,000	1,562,000
Permanently restricted by donors	5,259,000	6,073,000
Total net assets	76,549,000	72,202,000
	$115,046,000	$110,570,000

*This aggregated Balance Sheet format is an alternative to the layered fund Balance Sheet format. The approach used to prepare this aggregated balance sheet is discussed following the notes to financial statements.

EXHIBIT A (Continued)

Sample Hospital
Statement of Revenues and Expenses of General Funds
Years Ended December 31, 19X7 and 19X6

	19X7	19X6
Net patient service revenue (Notes 3, 7)	$92,656,000	$88,942,000
Other revenue	6,010,000	5,380,000
Total revenues	98,666,000	94,322,000
Expenses: (Notes 7, 8, 12, 13)		
Professional care of patients	53,016,000	48,342,000
Dietary services	4,407,000	4,087,000
General services	10,888,000	9,973,000
Administrative services	11,075,000	10,145,000
Employee health and welfare	10,000,000	9,335,000
Medical malpractice costs	1,125,000	200,000
Depreciation and amortization	4,782,000	4,280,000
Interest	1,752,000	1,825,000
Provision for bad debts	1,010,000	1,103,000
Total expenses	98,055,000	89,290,000
Income from operations	611,000	5,032,000
Nonoperating gains (losses):		
Unrestricted gifts and bequests (Note 11)	822,000	926,000
Loss on investment in affiliated company (Note 4)	(37,000)	(16,000)
Income on investments of endowment funds	750,000	650,000
Income on investments whose use is limited:		
By board for capital improvements	1,120,000	1,050,000
By agreements with third-party payors for funded		
depreciation	850,000	675,000
Under indenture agreement	100,000	90,000
Other investment income	284,000	226,000
Nonoperating gains, net	3,889,000	3,601,000
Revenue and gains in excess of expenses and losses	$ 4,500,000	$ 8,633,000

See accompanying notes to financial statements.

EXHIBIT A (Continued)

Sample Hospital
Statement of Changes in Fund Balances
Years Ended December 31, 19X7 and 19X6

	19X7				19X6			
		Donor-Restricted Funds				Donor-Restricted Funds		
	General Funds	Specific-Purpose Funds	Plant Replacement and Expansion Funds	Endowment Funds	General Funds	Specific-Purpose Funds	Plant Replacement and Expansion Funds	Endowment Funds
Balances at beginning of year	$64,567,000	$1,041,000	$521,000	$6,073,000	$56,679,000	$ 933,000	$501,000	$5,973,000
Additions:								
Excess of revenues over expenses	4,500,000	-	-	-	8,633,000	-	-	-
Gifts, grants, and bequests (Notes 10, 11)	-	869,000	220,000	-		558,000	290,000	-
Investment income	-	62,000	20,000	-		50,000	15,000	-
Net realized gain on sale of investments	-		100,000	-			20,000	-
Transfer to finance property and equipment additions	243,000		(243,000)	-	255,000		(255,000)	100,000
	4,743,000	931,000	97,000	-	8,888,000	608,000	70,000	100,000
Deductions:								
Provision for uncollectible pledges			(60,000)				(50,000)	
Capital contributions to Sample Health Systems (Note 11)					(1,000,000)			
Net realized loss on sale of investments				(639,000)				
Unrealized loss on marketable equity securities (Note 9)				(175,000)				
Transfer to other revenue		(550,000)				(500,000)		
	-	(550,000)	(60,000)	(814,000)	(1,000,000)	(500,000)	(50,000)	-
Balances at end of year	$69,310,000	$1,422,000	$558,000	$5,259,000	$64,567,000	$1,041,000	$521,000	$6,073,000

See accompanying notes to financial statements.

EXHIBIT A *(Continued)*

Sample Hospital
Statement of Cash Flows of General Funds (Direct Method)*
Years Ended December 31, 19X7 and 19X6

	19X7	19X6
Cash flows from operating activities and gains and losses:		
Cash received from patients and third-party payors	$ 90,342,000	$ 85,619,000
Cash paid to employees and suppliers	(89,214,000)	(81,510,000)
Other receipts from operations	6,042,000	5,563,000
Receipts from unrestricted gifts and bequests	1,122,000	905,000
Interest and dividends received	2,510,000	2,330,000
Interest paid (net of amount capitalized)	(1,780,000)	(1,856,000)
Net cash provided by operating activities and gains and losses	9,022,000	11,051,000
Cash flows from investing activities:		
Purchase of property and equipment	(4,728,000)	(5,012,000)
Transfer from donor-restricted fund for purchase of property and equipment	243,000	255,000
Investment in affiliated company	(394,000)	(425,000)
Capital contribution to Sample Health System	-	(1,000,000)
Cash invested in assets whose use is limited	(4,798,000)	(855,000)
Net cash used by investing activities	(9,677,000)	(7,037,000)
Cash flows from financing activities:		
Increase in retainage and construction accounts payable	183,000	175,000
Repayments of long-term debt	(1,200,000)	(1,630,000)
Payments from donor-restricted funds related to temporary loans	500,000	-
Payments on capital lease obligations	(550,000)	(600,000)
Temporary loans from (to) donor-restricted funds	300,000	(193,000)
Net cash used by financing activities	(767,000)	(2,248,00)
Net increase (decrease) in cash and cash equivalents	(1,422,000)	1,766,000
Cash and cash equivalents at beginning of year	4,525,000	2,759,000
Cash and cash equivalents at end of year	$ 3,103,000	$ 4,525,000

Reconciliation of Revenue and Gains in Excess of Expenses and Losses to Net Cash Provided by Operating Activities and Gains and Losses:

	19X7	19X6
Revenue and gains in excess of expenses and losses	$ 4,500,000	$ 8,633,000
Adjustments to reconcile revenue and gains in excess of expenses and losses to net cash provided by operating activities and gains and losses:		
Depreciation and amortization	4,782,000	4,280,000
Provision for bad debts	1,010,000	1,103,000
Amortization of deferred financing costs	66,000	45,000
Loss on investment in affiliated company	53,000	-
Noncash gifts and bequests	-	(175,000)
Decrease in amounts due to third-party payors	(398,000)	(77,000)
Increase in liability for estimated malpractice cost	1,125,000	200,000
Increase in patient accounts receivable	(1,916,000)	(3,141,000)
Increase in supplies and other current assets	(193,000)	(118,000)
Increase in accounts payable and accrued expenses	303,000	301,000
Increase in interest earned but not received on assets whose use is limited	(310,000)	-
Net cash provided by operating activities and gains and losses	$ 9,022,000	$ 11,051,000

Supplemental Disclosures of Cash Flow Information
Sample Hospital entered into capital lease obligations of $600,000 for new equipment in 19X7.

See accompanying notes to financial statements.

*The direct and indirect methods of reporting cash flows by hospitals are presented for illustrative purposes.

EXHIBIT A (Continued)

Sample Hospital
Statement of Cash Flows of General Funds (Indirect Method)*
Years Ended December 31, 19X7 and 19X6

	19X7	19X6
Cash flows from operating activities and gains and losses:		
Revenue and gains in excess of expenses and losses	$ 4,500,000	$ 8,633,000
Adjustments to reconcile revenue and gains in excess of expenses and losses		
to net cash provided by operating activities and gains and losses:		
Depreciation and amortization	4,782,000	4,280,000
Provision for bad debts	1,010,000	1,103,000
Amortization of deferred financing costs	66,000	45,000
Loss on investments in affiliated company	53,000	-
Noncash gifts and bequests	-	(175,000)
Decrease in net amounts due to third-party payors	(398,000)	(77,000)
Increase in liability for estimated malpractice costs	1,125,000	200,000
Increase in patient accounts receivable	(1,916,000)	(3,141,000)
Increase in supplies and other current assets	(193,000)	(118,000)
Increase in accounts payable and accrued expenses	303,000	301,000
Increase in interest earned but not received on assets whose use is limited	(310,000)	-
Net cash provided by operating activities and gains and losses	9,022,000	11,051,000
Cash flows from investing activities:		
Purchase of property and equipment	(4,728,000)	(5,012,000)
Transfer from donor-restricted fund for purchase of property and equipment	243,000	255,000
Investment in affiliated company	(394,000)	(425,000)
Transfer to Sample Health System	-	(1,000,000)
Cash invested in assets whose use is limited	(4,798,000)	(855,000)
Net cash used by investing activities	(9,677,000)	(7,037,000)
Cash flows from financing activities:		
Increase in retainage and construction accounts payable	183,000	175,000
Repayments of long-term debt	(1,200,000)	(1,630,000)
Payments from donor-restricted funds related to temporary loans to donor-		
restricted funds	500,000	-
Payments on capital lease obligation	(550,000)	(600,000)
Temporary loans from (to) donor-restricted funds	300,000	(193,000)
Net cash used by financing activities	(767,000)	(2,248,000)
Net increase (decrease) in cash and cash equivalents	(1,422,000)	1,766,000
Cash and cash equivalents at beginning of year	4,525,000	2,759,000
Cash and cash equivalents at end of year	$ 3,103,000	$ 4,525,000

Supplemental Disclosures of Cash Flow Information

Sample Hospital entered into capital lease obligations of $600,000 for new equipment in 19X7.

Cash paid for interest (net of amount capitalized) in 19X7 and 19X6 was $1,780,000 and $1,856,000, respectively.

See accompanying notes to financial statements.

*The direct and indirect methods of reporting cash flows by hospitals are presented for illustrative purposes.

EXHIBIT A (Continued)

Sample Hospital
Notes to Financial Statements
December 31, 19X7 and 19X6

1. **Summary of Significant Accounting Policies**

Organization. Sample Hospital (Hospital) is a nonprofit acute-care hospital. Effective June 30, 19X6, under a plan of reorganization, Sample Health System was formed as the parent holding company of the Hospital. In its capacity as sole member of the Hospital, Sample Health System has the right to appoint Hospital trustees, approve major Hospital expenditures, and approve long-term Hospital borrowings.

Charity Care. The Hospital provides care to patients who meet certain criteria under its charity care policy without charge or at amounts less than its established rates. Because the Hospital does not pursue collection of amounts determined to qualify as charity care, they are not reported as revenue.

Income Taxes. The Hospital is a nonprofit corporation as described in Section 501(c)(3) of the Internal Revenue Code and is exempt from federal income taxes on related income pursuant to Section 501(a) of the Code.

Net Patient Service Revenue. Net patient service revenue is reported at the estimated net realizable amounts from patients, third-party payors, and others for services rendered, including estimated retroactive adjustments under reimbursement agreements with third-party payors. Retroactive adjustments are accrued on an estimated basis in the period the related services are rendered and adjusted in future periods as final settlements are determined.

Investments and Investment Income. Donated investments are reported at fair value at the date of receipt, which is then treated as cost. Marketable equity securities included in investment portfolios are carried at the lower of aggregate cost (determined on an average-cost basis) or market at the balance sheet date. Other marketable securities are stated at cost, adjusted for impairments in value that are deemed to be other than temporary. Sample Hospital's investment in Affiliated Company is reported on the equity method of accounting that approximates Sample Hospital's equity in the underlying net book value of Affiliated Company.

Investment income on proceeds of borrowings that are held by a trustee, to the extent not capitalized, and investment income on assets deposited in the malpractice trust are reported as other revenue. Investment income from all other general fund investments and investment income of endowment funds are reported as nonoperating gains. Investment income and gains (losses) on investments of donor-restricted funds are added to (deducted from) the appropriate restricted fund balance.

Pledges. Pledges, less an allowance for uncollectible amounts, are recorded as receivables in the year made. Unrestricted pledges are reported in the statement of revenues and expenses of general funds; restricted pledges are reported as additions to the appropriate restricted fund balance.

Statement of Revenues and Expenses of General Funds. For purposes of display, transactions deemed by management to be ongoing, major, or central to the provision of health care services are reported as revenues and expenses. Peripheral or incidental transactions are reported as gains and losses.

Costs of Borrowing. Interest cost incurred on borrowed funds during the period of construction of capital assets is capitalized as a component of the cost of acquiring those assets.

EXHIBIT A (Continued)

Notes to Financial Statements (Continued)

Deferred financing costs are amortized over the period the obligation is outstanding using the interest method.

Amortization of deferred financing costs is capitalized during the period of construction of capital assets.

Donor-Restricted Funds.   Donor-restricted funds are used to differentiate resources, the use of which is restricted by donors or grantors, from resources of general funds on which donors or grantors place no restriction or that arise as a result of the operations of the Hospital for its stated purposes. Restricted gifts and other restricted resources are recorded as additions to the appropriate restricted fund.

Resources restricted by donors for plant replacement and expansion are added to the general fund balance to the extent expended within the period.

Resources restricted by donors or grantors for specific operating purposes are reported in other revenue to the extent used within the period.

Assets Whose Use Is Limited.   Assets whose use is limited include assets set aside by the Board of Trustees for future capital improvements, over which the Board retains control and may at its discretion subsequently use for other purposes; assets set aside in accordance with agreements with third-party payors; assets held by trustees under indenture agreements and self-insurance trust arrangements.

Property and Equipment.   Property and equipment acquisitions are recorded at cost. Property and equipment donated for hospital operations are recorded as additions to the donor-restricted plant replacement and expansion funds at fair value at the date of receipt and as a transfer to the general fund balance when the assets are placed in service.

Depreciation is provided over the estimated useful life of each class of depreciable asset and is computed on the straight-line method. Equipment under capital leases is amortized on the straight-line method over the shorter period of the lease term or the estimated useful life of the equipment. Such amortization is included in depreciation and amortization in the financial statements.

An accelerated method for depreciating certain operating equipment acquired before 1970 has been elected for third-party reimbursement purposes. Third-party reimbursement is deferred to the extent of the effect of the difference between accelerated depreciation used for reimbursement reporting and straight-line depreciation used for financial reporting.

Cash and Cash Equivalents.   Cash and cash equivalents include investments in highly liquid debt instruments with a maturity of three months or less, excluding amounts whose use is limited by board designation or other arrangements under trust agreements or with third-party payors.

Estimated Malpractice Costs.   The provision for estimated self-insured medical malpractice claims includes estimates of the ultimate costs for both reported claims and claims incurred but not reported.

2.   Charity Care

The Hospital maintains records to identify and monitor the level of charity care it provides. These records include the amount of charges foregone for services and supplies furnished under its charity care policy, the estimated cost of those services and supplies, and equivalent service statistics. The following information measures the level of charity care provided during the years ended December 31, 19X7 and 19X6.

EXHIBIT A (Continued)

Notes to Financial Statements (Continued)

	19X7	19X6
Charges foregone, based on established rates	$6,000,000	$5,700,000
Estimated costs and expenses incurred to provide charity care	$5,600,000	$5,000,000
Equivalent percentage of charity care patients to all patients served	5.7%	5.6%

---

3. **Net Patient Service Revenue**

The Hospital has agreements with third-party payors that provide for payments to the Hospital at amounts different from its established rates. A summary of the payment arrangements with major third-party payors follows.

- *Medicare.* Inpatient acute-care services rendered to Medicare program beneficiaries are paid at prospectively determined rates per discharge. These rates vary according to a patient classification system that is based on clinical, diagnostic, and other factors. Inpatient nonacute services, certain outpatient services, and defined capital and medical education costs related to Medicare beneficiaries are paid based on a cost reimbursement methodology. The Hospital is reimbursed for cost reimbursable items at a tentative rate with final settlement determined after submission of annual cost reports by the Hospital and audits thereof by the Medicare fiscal intermediary. The Hospital's classification of patients under the Medicare program and the appropriateness of their admission are subject to an independent review by a peer review organization under contract with the Hospital. The Hospital's Medicare cost reports have been audited by the Medicare fiscal intermediary through December 31, 19X6.
- *Medicaid.* Inpatient and outpatient services rendered to Medicaid program beneficiaries are reimbursed under a cost reimbursement methodology. The Hospital is reimbursed at a tentative rate with final settlement determined after submission of annual cost reports by the Hospital and audits thereof by the Medicaid fiscal intermediary. The Hospital's Medicaid cost reports have been audited by the Medicaid fiscal intermediary through December 31, 19X6.
- *Blue Cross.* Inpatient services rendered to Blue Cross subscribers are reimbursed at prospectively determined rates per day of hospitalization. The prospectively determined per-diem rates are not subject to retroactive adjustment. The Hospital has also entered into payment agreements with certain commercial insurance carriers, health maintenance organizations, and preferred provider organizations. The basis for payment to the Hospital under these agreements includes prospectively determined rates per discharge, discounts from established charges, and prospectively determined daily rates.

4. **Investment in Affiliated Company**

In 19X2 the Hospital entered into an agreement with two unrelated hospitals to establish and operate an ambulatory care center. In accordance with this agreement, each hospital invested $970,000 for a $33\frac{1}{3}$-percent equity interest in the common stock of the center. The investment was made in installments during the years 19X5 through 19X7, and in

EXHIBIT A (Continued)

Notes to Financial Statements (Continued)

May 19X7 the ambulatory care center began operations. The investment is recorded on the equity method.

Summarized financial information from the unaudited financial statements of Affiliated Company follows:

	December 31, 19X7	December 31, 19X6
Current assets	$1,779,000	$1,835,000
Noncurrent assets	4,052,000	4,007,000
Current liabilities	1,566,000	1,325,000
Noncurrent liabilities	1,514,000	2,789,000
Shareholders' equity	2,751,000	1,728,000

	Year Ended	
	December 31, 19X7	December 31, 19X6
Revenue	$3,220,000	$2,899,000
Net loss	(111,000)	(48,000)

5.   Assets Whose Use Is Limited

Assets whose use is limited that are required for obligations classified as current liabilities are reported in current assets. The composition of assets whose use is limited at December 31, 19X7 and 19X6, is set forth in the following table. Investments are stated at cost that approximates market.

	19X7	19X6
By board for capital improvements:		
Cash and short-term investments	$11,000,000	$10,000,000
By agreements with third-party payors for funded depreciation:		
Cash and short-term investments	$ 8,503,000	$ 5,712,000
U.S. Treasury obligations	316,000	316,000
Interest receivable	415,000	123,000
	$ 9,234,000	$ 6,151,000
Under malpractice funding arrangement—held by trustee:		
Cash and short-term investments	$ 1,058,000	$ 857,000
U.S. Treasury obligations	1,949,000	1,825,000
	$ 3,007,000	$ 2,682,000
Under indenture agreement—held by trustee:		
Cash and short-term investments	$ 592,000	$ 1,260,000
U.S. Treasury obligations	11,024,000	9,674,000
Interest receivable	92,000	74,000
	$11,708,000	$11,008,000

EXHIBIT A (Continued)

Notes to Financial Statements (Continued)

6. **Property and Equipment**

A summary of property and equipment at December 31, 19X7 and 19X6, follows:

	19X7	19X6
Land	$ 3,000,000	$ 3,000,000
Land improvements	472,000	472,000
Buildings and improvements	46,852,000	46,636,000
Equipment	29,190,000	26,260,000
Equipment under capital leases	2,851,000	2,752,000
	82,365,000	79,120,000
Less accumulated depreciation and amortization	34,928,000	30,661,000
	47,437,000	48,459,000
Construction in progress	3,601,000	2,033,000
Property and equipment, net	$51,038,000	$50,492,000

Construction contracts of approximately $7,885,000 exist for the remodeling of Hospital facilities. At December 31, 19X7, the remaining commitment on these contracts approximated $4,625,000.

7. **Long-Term Debt and Capital Leases**

A summary of long-term debt and capital leases at December 31, 19X7 and 19X6, follows:

	19X7	19X6
9.25% Revenue Notes, due November 1, 19XX, collateralized by a pledge of the Hospital's gross receipts	$21,479,000	$22,016,000
9.25% mortgage loan, due January 19XX, collateralized by a mortgage on property and equipment with a depreciated cost of $1,800,000 at December 31, 19X7	2,010,000	2,127,000
9.75% note payable, due March 19XX, unsecured	125,000	671,000
Total long-term debt	23,614,000	24,814,000
Less current installments of long-term debt	970,000	1,200,000
Long-term debt excluding current installments	$22,644,000	$23,614,000
Capital lease obligations, at varying rates of imputed interest from 9.8% to 12.3% collateralized by leased equipment with an amortized cost of $1,500,000 at December 31, 19X7	$ 1,000,000	$ 950,000
Less current portion of capital lease obligations	500,000	550,000
Capital lease obligations, excluding current portion	$ 500,000	$ 400,000

Under the terms of the Revenue Note Indenture, the Hospital is required to maintain certain deposits with a trustee. Such deposits are included with assets whose use is limited in the financial statements. The Revenue Note Indenture also places limits on the

EXHIBIT A (Continued)

Notes to Financial Statements (Continued)

incurrence of additional borrowings and requires that the Hospital satisfy certain measures of financial performances as long as the notes are outstanding.

Scheduled principal repayments on long-term debt and payments on capital lease obligations for the next five years are as follows:

	Long-Term Debt	Obligations Under Capital Leases
19X8	$ 970,000	$ 500,000
19X9	912,000	260,000
19Y0	983,000	260,000
19Y1	1,060,000	95,000
19Y2	1,143,000	-
	$5,068,000	1,115,000
Less amount representing interest on obligations under capital leases		115,000
Total		$1,000,000

A summary of interest cost and investment income on borrowed funds held by the trustee under the Revenue Note Indenture during the years ended 19X7 and 19X6 follows:

	19X7	19X6
Interest cost:		
Capitalized	$ 740,000	$ 740,000
Charged to operations	1,752,000	1,825,000
Total	$2,492,000	$2,565,000
Investment income:		
Capitalized	$ 505,000	$ 663,000
Credited to other revenue	330,000	386,000
Total	$ 835,000	$1,049,000

8.   Medical Malpractice Claims

The Hospital is uninsured with respect to medical malpractice risks. Losses from asserted claims and from unasserted claims identified under the Hospital's incident reporting system are accrued based on estimates that incorporate the Hospital's past experience, as well as other considerations including the nature of each claim or incident and relevant trend factors. Accrued malpractice losses have been discounted at rates ranging from 7 percent to 9 percent. No accrual for possible losses attributable to incidents that may have occurred but that have not been identified under the incident reporting system has been made because the amount is not reasonably estimable.

The Hospital has established an irrevocable trust fund for the payment of medical malpractice claim settlements. Professional insurance consultants have been retained to assist the Hospital with determining amounts to be deposited in the trust fund.

EXHIBIT A (Continued)

<hr>

Notes to Financial Statements (Continued)

9. Endowment Funds—Investments

Donor-restricted endowment fund investment portfolios include marketable equity securities that are carried at the lower of cost or market. Marketable equity securities of endowment funds at December 31, 19X7 and 19X6, are summarized as follows:

	Cost	Quoted Market Value	Gross Unrealized Gains	Gross Unrealized Losses
19X7	$1,476,000	$1,301,000	$ 8,000	$183,000
19X6	1,620,000	1,832,000	228,000	16,000

Realized gains on marketable equity securities of the endowment funds amounted to $10,000 in 19X7 and $50,000 in 19X6.

10. Funds Held in Trust

The Hospital is an income beneficiary of the Thomas A. Smith trust. Because the assets of the trust are not controlled by the Hospital, they are not included in the Hospital's financial statements. At December 31, 19X7, the market value of the assets totaled approximately $2,652,000. Distributions of income are made at the discretion of the trustees. Income distributed to the Hospital by the trust is restricted for construction or equipment additions and amounted to $150,000 in 19X7 and $140,000 in 19X6.

11. Related Party Transactions

Because of the existence of common trustees and other factors, Sample Hospital and Sample Health Foundation (Foundation) are related parties. The Foundation is authorized by the Hospital to solicit contributions on its behalf. In its general appeal for contributions to support the community's providers of health care services, the Foundation also solicits contributions for certain other health care institutions. In the absence of donor restrictions, the Foundation has discretionary control over the amounts, timing, and use of its distributions.

Contributions made by the Foundation to the Hospital during the years ended December 31, 19X7 and 19X6, are reported in the Hospital's financial statements as follows:

	19X7	19X6
Unrestricted gifts and bequests	$375,000	$525,000
Restricted contributions for:		
Specific purposes	300,000	200,000
Plant replacement and expansion	70,000	85,000

In addition, the Hospital made a capital contribution of $1,000,000 to Sample Health Systems during 19X6.

12. Pension Plan

The Hospital has a defined benefit pension plan covering substantially all its employees. The plan benefits are based on years of service and the employees' compensation during the last five years of covered employment. The Hospital makes annual contributions to the plan equal to the amounts of net periodic pension cost. Contributions are intended to provide not only for benefits attributed to service to date but also for those expected to be earned in the future.

EXHIBIT A (Continued)

━━━━━━━━

Notes to Financial Statements (Continued)

The actuarially computed net periodic pension cost for 19X7 and 19X6 includes the following components:

	19X7	19X6
Service-cost benefits earned during the period	$ 905,000	$ 770,000
Interest cost on projected benefit obligation	700,000	650,000
Actual return on plan assets	(950,000)	(800,000)
Net amortization and deferral	70,000	80,000
Net periodic pension costs	$ 725,000	$ 700,000

Assumptions used in the accounting for net periodic pension costs were as follows:

	As of December 31	
	19X7	19X6
Discount rates	7.0%	7.0%
Rates of increase in compensation levels	6.0	6.0
Expected long-term rate of return on assets	8.0	8.0

The following table sets forth the plan's funded status and amounts recognized in the Hospital's financial statements at December 31, 19X7 and 19X6:

	19X7	19X6
Actuarial present value of benefit obligations:		
Vested benefit obligation	$ 8,020,000	$6,800,000
Nonvested benefit obligation	1,900,000	1,930,000
Accumulated benefit obligation	9,920,000	8,730,000
Effect of projected future compensation levels	1,000,000	980,000
Projected benefit obligation	10,920,000	9,710,00
Plan assets at fair value (primarily listed stocks and		
U.S. bonds)	11,050,000	9,800,000
Plan assets in excess of projected benefit		
obligation	130,000	90,000
Unrecognized net gain from past experience different		
from that assumed	(30,000)	(40,000)
Prior service cost not yet recognized in net periodic		
pension cost	50,000	55,000
Unrecognized net asset at January 1, 19X6, being		
recognized over 15 years	(65,000)	(70,000)
Prepaid pension cost, included in other assets in the		
balance sheets	$ 85,000	$ 35,000

13. Commitments

Leases that do not meet the criteria for capitalization are classified as operating leases with related rentals charged to operations as incurred.

EXHIBIT A (Continued)

Notes to Financial Statements (Continued)

The following is a schedule by year of future minimum lease payments under operating leases as of December 31, 19X7, that have initial or remaining lease terms in excess of one year.

Year Ending December 31	Minimum Lease Payments
19X8	$ 517,000
19X9	506,000
19Y0	459,000
19Y1	375,000
19Y2	343,000
Total minimum lease payments	$2,200,000

Total rental expense in 19X7 and 19X6 for all operating leases was approximately $859,000 and $770,000, respectively.

14. Subsequent Event

On February 9, 19X8, the Hospital signed a contract in the amount of $1,050,000 for the purchase of certain real estate.

EXHIBIT A (Continued)

Sample Hospital
Approach Used to Prepare Aggregated Balance Sheets
Years Ended December 31, 19X7 and 19X6

A. Assets

Assets of the restricted funds (excluding due-to/due-from accounts—see Note C) are included with assets whose use is limited, with amounts required for restricted fund current liabilities classified as current assets.

B. Liabilities

Liabilities of the restricted funds (excluding due-to/due-from accounts) are deemed to be current and therefore are reported with current liabilities.

C. Due-to/Due-from Accounts

There are two reasons why due-to/due-form accounts may exist:

- Cash of one fund is deposited with the cash account of another fund at the reporting date.
- A loan between funds has occurred.

If an aggregated balance sheet is prepared, due-to/due-from accounts generally are not reported on the balance sheet. In either situation above, cash may be reported at different amounts depending on the situation.

The due-to/due-from accounts in this illustrative statement were deemed to exist because of the first situation described above. Therefore, the due-to/due-from accounts were eliminated and the corresponding amounts of cash balances were adjusted as if the cash was actually exchanged.

Additional Disclosures

1. The amount of the assets, including details of their composition and the nature of the restrictions imposed by donors for specific purposes and permanent endowment funds
2. The details of interfund borrowing arrangements

EXHIBIT B ABC Financial Statements

ABC Medical Center
Balance Sheet
December 31, 1984 and 1983
(000's omitted)

	1984	1983
ASSETS		
CURRENT ASSETS:		
Cash and short-term investments	$ 3	$ 1,366
Patient receivables (net of allowances for uncollectible accounts of $3,557 and $2,810 in 1984 and 1983, respectively, and contractual allowances of $7,787 and $4,653 in 1984 and 1983, respectively)	23,068	20,134
Other receivables	3,996	2,640
Settlement amounts due from third-party reimbursement programs	3,312	4,184
Supplies inventory at cost (last-in-first-out)	1,996	1,999
Prepaid expenses and other	3,015	366
Total current assets	35,390	30,689
OTHER ASSETS:		
Bond funds	31,564	13,699
Self-insurance funds	13,060	8,634
Board-designated assets for funded depreciation	2,100	6,100
Unamortized debt expense and other	2,349	2,162
Notes receivable	1,022	1,024
Total other assets	50,095	31,619
PROPERTY, PLANT, AND EQUIPMENT:		
Land	1,430	3,235
Buildings and improvements	39,886	60,013
Equipment	50,115	49,533
Construction in progress	2,315	1,215
	93,746	113,996
Less: Accumulated depreciation	(39,993)	(40,696)
Net property, plant, and equipment	53,753	73,300
Total Assets	$139,238	$135,608
LIABILITIES AND ACCUMULATED EQUITY		
CURRENT LIABILITIES:		
Accounts payable and other	$ 7,866	$ 5,955
Settlement amounts to third-party reimbursement programs	640	40
Accrued expenses and other	7,440	6,626
Current maturities of capital lease obligations, long-term debt, and notes payable	1,194	7,468
Deferred income	359	295
Total current liabilities	17,499	20,384
CONTINGENT LIABILITIES (Notes 3 and 9)		
LIABILITIES FOR SELF-INSURED CLAIMS	13,060	8,634
CAPITAL LEASE OBLIGATIONS AND LONG-TERM DEBT, less current maturities	62,278	38,339
ACCUMULATED EQUITY	46,401	68,251
Total Liabilities and Accumulated Equity	$139,238	$135,608

The accompanying notes are an integral part of these statements.

EXHIBIT B (Continued)

ABC Medical Center
Statement of Revenues and Expenses and Changes in Accumulated Equity
For the Years Ended December 31, 1984 and 1983
(000's omitted)

	1984	1983
REVENUES FROM PATIENT SERVICES:		
Daily patient service revenues	$ 52,778	$ 54,124
Ancillary services—inpatient	83,531	77,255
Ancillary services—outpatient	17,780	16,438
Total patient revenues	154,089	147,817
OTHER OPERATING REVENUES	5,498	6,074
Total revenues from operations	159,587	153,891
CHARITY ALLOWANCES	7,752	8,269
Net revenues from operations	151,835	145,622
OPERATING EXPENSES:		
Salaries and wages	59,554	59,666
Employee benefits	12,228	10,410
Professional compensation and fees	4,005	3,165
Supplies and other expenses	39,019	33,810
Energy	2,421	2,425
Depreciation	5,978	5,920
Interest and debt expense	3,275	2,432
Provision for uncollectible accounts	5,490	4,197
Total operating expenses	131,970	122,025
Income from operations before contractual allowances	19,865	23,597
Less: Contractual allowances	9,206	14,664
NET INCOME FROM OPERATIONS	10,659	8,933
NONOPERATING REVENUES (EXPENSES):		
Other nonoperating revenues	1,496	1,769
Net expenses for medical staff office building	(93)	(226)
Net expenses for education programs	(5,676)	(5,173)
EXCESS OF REVENUES OVER EXPENSES BEFORE EXTRAORDINARY ITEMS	6,386	5,303
EXTRAORDINARY ITEM, gain on extinguishment of debt (Note 5)	7,844	
EXCESS OF REVENUES OVER EXPENSES	14,230	5,303
TRANSFERS:		
Additions to property, plant, and equipment from restricted contributions	102	116
Transfers of assets to affiliated entities as a result of corporate reorganization (Notes 1 and 9)	(36,182)	
Balance, beginning of year	68,251	62,832
Balance, end of year	$ 46,401	$ 68,251

The accompanying notes are an integral part of these statements.

EXHIBIT B (Continued)

ABC Medical Center
Statement of Changes in Financial Position
For the Years Ended December 31, 1984 and 1983
(000's omitted)

	1984	1983
SOURCES OF FUNDS:		
From operations and nonoperating revenue:		
Excess of revenues over expenses before extraordinary items	$ 6,386	$ 5,303
Items not requiring funds during the current year:		
Depreciation	6,308	6,410
Amortization of debt expense	644	51
Funds provided by operations and nonoperating revenue	13,338	11,764
Extraordinary item, gain on extinguishment of debt	7,844	0
Proceeds from long-term debt	54,830	8,230
Restricted contributions for fixed assets	102	116
Total sources of funds	76,114	20,110
USES OF FUNDS:		
Board-designated funded depreciation, net of transfers	2,700	4,625
Self-insurance and bond funds held by trustees, net of estimated liabilities	22,896	3,695
Expenditures for fixed assets—bond funds	3,461	1,803
Expenditures for fixed assets—operations	4,500	3,835
Current portion of capital lease obligations and long-term debt	(6,274)	7,468
Retirement of capital lease obligations and long-term debt	37,235	3,176
Other	1,258	947
Total uses of funds	65,776	25,549
TRANSFER OF ASSETS:		
Reduction of accumulated equity	(36,182)	
Transfer of assets to other entities:		
Cash and short-term investments	2,002	
Other receivables	750	
Bond funds	5,031	
Board-designated assets for funded depreciation	6,700	
Unamortized debt expense and other	499	
Property, plant, and equipment	27,467	
Accumulated depreciation	(6,267)	
Increase (decrease) in working capital	$ 10,338	$ (5,439)

The accompanying notes are an integral part of these statements.

EXHIBIT B (Continued)

ABC Medical Center
Notes to Financial Statements
December 31, 1984 and 1983

1. ORGANIZATION

ABC Medical Center, Inc. (Medical Center) is a corporation exempt from federal income tax under Section 501(c)(3) of the Internal Revenue Code. The Medical Center was established on January 1, 1972, through the merger of two previously independent hospitals. The accumulated equity of the Medical Center does not inure to the benefit of any member, trustee, or officer of the Medical Center or any private individual; but is Board designated for growth and development, including replacement and renovation of obsolete buildings, acquisition of new equipment, replacement of old equipment, and development of new patient services.

The Board of Trustees of the Medical Center completed a corporate reorganization during 1984 with an effective date of July 1, 1984. The reorganization created a holding company, ABC Inc., which is now the parent of the Medical Center. The Board of Trustees further modified the Articles of Incorporation and Bylaws of the Medical Center to provide for appointment of the Medical Center Board by the holding company. The holding company now provides general guidance and management for the following additional subsidiaries:

- —DEF—A nonprofit organization offering health care related services. This corporation assumed certain capital assets which are leased by the Medical Center.
- —GHI—A for-profit organization providing services to health care organizations and others.
- —ABC Foundation—A nonprofit organization established for the purpose of raising funds for the Medical Center and other area health care organizations.

As a result of the reorganization, the Medical Center transferred certain assets summarized in Note 9 to affiliated entities.

2. SIGNIFICANT ACCOUNTING POLICIES

Medicare, Medicaid, and Other Government Programs

The Medical Center provides care to patients covered by Medicare, Medicaid, and other government programs. During 1984, Medicare reimbursed inpatient services by payment for each discharge using diagnosis-related groups (DRGs), increased for Medicare's pro-rata share of capital and medical education costs. During 1983, Medicare reimbursed the reasonable cost of providing care to Medicare patients. Medicare reimburses the reasonable cost of providing outpatient services. Reimbursement under Medicaid and other government programs is based on cost, as defined, of providing service to program beneficiaries.

EXHIBIT B (Continued)

ABC Medical Center
Notes to Financial Statements (Continued)

Normal billings for services to these patients are included in patient service revenue, and contractual allowances are recorded to reduce these billings, as necessary, to the amount to be paid by these government agencies. Final determination of amounts earned under cost-reimbursement programs is subject to review and audit by the appropriate agencies. Management believes that adequate provisions have been made for any adjustments that may result from such reviews.

—NOTES OMITTED—

Reclassifications

Certain reclassifications have been made to amounts reported in 1983 to conform to the presentation used in 1984.

3.   **LIABILITIES FOR SELF-INSURED CLAIMS**

Effective February 1, 1978, the Medical Center commenced a partially self-insured program for professional malpractice and general liability claims and established a self-insurance trust for claims arising from events occurring after January 31, 1978. Malpractice liability from incidents occurring prior to entering the self-insurance program are covered by commercial insurance policies. The trust is administered by a bank trust department. The contributions to the trust are made as determined by an actuarial study. The trust funds are used for payment of any professional malpractice losses, certain general liability claims, expenses relating thereto, costs of administering the trust, and insurance premiums for coverage in excess of the self-insured limits.

There are several lawsuits and claims pending and incidents that occurred in the past whereby claims may be asserted against the Medical Center for which the ultimate liability, if any, has not been determined. The Medical Center's management believes that the ultimate settlement of these claims will not have a material adverse effect upon the financial position of the Medical Center.

The Medical Center is also self-insured for worker's compensation, employee hospitalization and dental expense, employee income protection, unemployment compensation, retirement benefits, and dependent death benefits. These plans are also administered by a bank trust department and funded in accordance with actuarial studies. The trust funds are used for payment of employee claims. The results of the most recent actuarial evaluations indicate that the trust funds are adequate to provide for anticipated employee claims.

4.   **SUPPLEMENTAL RETIREMENT PLAN**

Effective July 1982, the Medical Center ceased participation in the Social Security program and became self-insured for the benefits offered by this program.

EXHIBIT B (Continued)

ABC Medical Center
Notes to Financial Statements (Continued)

Under this plan, the Medical Center contributed 6.7 percent of employee's wages to an irrevocable Master Trust fund. Effective January 1, 1984, the Medical Center was required by law to re-enter the Social Security program. Based upon an actuarial evaluation of the Plan, the available assets are adequate to fund projected future benefits.

5.   1977 BOND EXTINGUISHMENT

—NOTES OMITTED—

During May 1984, the County Building Commission (the Commission) issued Hospital Revenue Refunding Bonds, Series 1984 A, in the aggregate principal amount of $22,880,000 to refund, prior to the respective dates of maturity, the Series 1977 bonds. The difference between the reacquisition price and the net carrying amount of the extinguished debt ($7,844,000) is recognized as an extraordinary gain in the current period. This gain did not generate any funds for the Medical Center at the time of refunding.

6.   BOND FUNDS HELD BY TRUSTEE

In 1982, the Commission authorized the issuance of approximately $6,800,000 of Hospital Revenue Bond Anticipation Notes. In 1983, the Commission authorized additional financing of $8,200,000 for current renovation projects and equipment purchases at the Medical Center.

In 1984, the Commission authorized the issuance of the Series 1984 A bonds described in Note 5 above. In July 1984, the Commission also issued Annual Tender Hospital Revenue Bonds, Series 1984 B, in the aggregate principal amount of $33,100,000. The proceeds of the issuance are to be used for the following purposes: (i) the renovation of operating rooms, intensive care and cardiac care units, and the Radiology Department of the Medical Center; (ii) the construction of new space for a 40-bed rehabilitation unit and the renovation of related areas for rehabilitation services; (iii) the reimbursement of the Medical Center for certain prior expenditures for capital equipment; and (iv) the refinancing of the Commission's Hospital Revenue Bond Anticipation Notes, Series 1982, and certain other debt of the Medical Center.

The terms of associated lease agreements and bond indentures require that certain funds be maintained with the Trustee during the life of the bonds. These funds consist principally of cash and investments held by the Trustee and are designated for various debt service requirements and expansion purposes.

EXHIBIT B (Continued)

ABC Medical Center
Notes to Financial Statements (Continued)

The balance of the funds held by the Trustee at December 31 include:

—All bonds combined, condensed from original notes.—

	(000's Omitted)	
	1984	1983
Revenue fund	$ -	$ 277
Debt Service Reserve fund	6,805	2,220
Reserve Requirement fund	-	255
Depreciation fund	-	4,622
Acquisition fund	16,803	6,325
Bond fund	7,507	-
Contingency fund	449	-
Total	$31,564	$13,699

7. LEASES

The Medical Center leases a major portion of its facilities from the Commission. Assets totaling $10,446,241 that were transferred to various entities due to the corporate reorganization and that fall under the provision of the previous lease agreement are also subject to certain provisions in the existing lease agreements. The leases under the Series 1983, 1984 A, and 1984 B Bonds are treated as capital leases. These agreements, which expire on dates through November 1, 2013, the mandatory retirement date of the Series 1984 B Bonds, provide that title to the original land, existing facilities, and planned projects described in the lease agreements rests with the Commission. The amounts of the annual rentals to be paid by the Medical Center over the terms of the leases are sufficient to cover principal and interest requirements of all related bonds. In addition, the rental payments are secured by a security interest in the Medical Center's gross revenues and certain assets as specified in the Master Trust Indenture. Terms of the leases grant to the Medical Center an option to purchase the facilities for the sum of $100 for a period of 120 days after the expiration of the lease period.

The Medical Center assets that are related to these agreements are as follows as of December 31:

	(000's Omitted)	
	1984	1983
Land	$ 1,399	$ 1,200
Buildings and improvements	39,272	59,708
Equipment	36,655	27,421
Construction in progress	2,315	1,215
	79,641	89,544
Accumulated depreciation	(32,558)	(33,236)
	$ 47,083	$ 56,308

EXHIBIT B (Continued)

<hr>

ABC Medical Center
Notes to Financial Statements (Continued)

—NOTES OMITTED—

[Annual lease payments will be about $8 million per year through 1989.]

8.   CAPITAL LEASE OBLIGATIONS AND LONG-TERM DEBT

Obligations under capitalized leases and long-term debt outstanding are as follows as of December 31:

—NOTES OMITTED AND SUMMARIZED—

	(000's Omitted)	
	1984	1983
Current portion	$ 1,194	$ 7,468
Long-term portion	62,278	38,339
Total liability	$63,472	$45,807

[Average interest was approximately 7 percent in 1983 and 8.25 percent in 1984.]

9.   RELATED PARTIES AND OTHER TRANSACTIONS

The Medical Center receives contributions from an affiliated entity, the ABC Foundation, Inc. (the Foundation), which is a tax-exempt organization. The Foundation receives various gifts, grants, contributions, devises, and bequests (holding the same primarily as endowment funds) and makes distributions of such funds, and the investment thereof, to or for the benefit of the Medical Center and other area health care organizations. The funded depreciation transfers from the Medical Center will remain designated for capital improvements of the Medical Center.

The Medical Center is also related to the ABC Housing Corporation (the Housing Corporation), which is a tax-exempt organization. The purpose of the Housing Corporation is to provide housing for students, interns, residents, and staff personnel of the Medical Center and the local division of the state's University Medical Center. To accomplish this purpose, the Housing Corporation has constructed apartments for rental to such persons and their families. The Medical Center had receivables from the Housing Corporation of $972,000 and $1,167,000 at December 31, 1984 and 1983, respectively, for construction funds advanced to the Housing Corporation.

The Medical Center conducts various transactions with DEF, an affiliated entity. DEF was formed in 1982 to serve as the general partner in an entity formed to construct a physicians office building. The Medical Center has unconditionally guaranteed the payment of principal and interest on $5,000,000 of Commercial Development Bonds used to finance the construction. The Medical Center also

EXHIBIT B (Continued)

ABC Medical Center
Notes to Financial Statements (Continued)

rents parking and storage space from DEF and provides services to DEF for various programs. As of December 31, 1984 and 1983, and Medical Center had accounts payable to DEF of $813,000 and $-0-, respectively, and accounts receivable from DEF of $1,019,000 and $275,000, respectively.

The Medical Center conducts various transactions with GHI and subsidiaries which were formed and commenced operations in late 1983. Through its operative divisions and subsidiaries, GHI provides the following services: laboratory, landscaping and grounds maintenance, laundry, contract management, physical therapy, respiratory analysis, outpatient surgery, collections agency, and other miscellaneous services. As of December 31, 1984 and 1983, the Medical Center had accounts payable to GHI of $84,000 and $-0-, respectively, and accounts receivable from GHI of $365,000 and $330,000, respectively.

Following is a summary of transactions between the Medical Center and affiliated entities.

	(000's Omitted)	
	1984	**1983**
Revenues Earned From:		
DEF: Substance abuse program and other	$ 40	$ -
GHI: Laundry services	183	45
Laboratory and nuclear medicine services	162	31
Management fee and other	40	27
Foundation: Nursing and education program	100	86
Total revenues	$ 525	$189
Expenditures Paid To:		
DEF: Fees for parking and storage space	$ 898	$ -
GHI: Grounds maintenance	87	-
Physician recruitment and other	20	-
Total expenditures	$ 1,005	$ -
Assets Transferred To:		
DEF: Land, buildings and improvements, and equipment	$27,357	-
Accumulated depreciation	(6,267)	-
	$21,090	-
GHI: Capital investment	$ 750	-

EXHIBIT C ABC Percent Change and Common Size Statements

	Restated Balance Sheet				Common Size	
	1984	1983	Dollar Change	Percent Change	*1984*	*1983*
ASSETS						
Cash and short-term investments	$ 3	$ 1,366	$ (1,363)	− 99.78%	0.0%	1.0%
Patient receivables (gross)	34,412	27,597	6,815	24.69%	24.7%	20.4%
Less: Allowance for uncollectible accounts	3,557	2,810	747	26.58%	2.6%	2.1%
Contractual allowances	7,787	4,653	3,134	67.35%	5.6%	3.4%
Net patient receivables	23,068	20,134	2,934[11]	14.57%	16.6%	14.8%
Other receivables	3,996	2,640	1,356	51.36%	2.9%	1.9%
Settlement amounts due from third parties	3,312	4,184	(872)	− 20.84%	2.4%	3.1%
Supplies inventory at cost (LIFO)	1,996	1,999	(3)	− 0.15%	1.4%	1.5%
Prepaid expenses and other	3,015	366	2,649	723.77%	2.2%	0.3%
Total current assets	35,390	30,689	4,701	15.32%[6]	25.4%[3]	22.6%
Bond funds	31,564	13,699	17,865	130.41%	22.7%	10.1%
Self-insured funds	13,060	8,634	4,426	51.26%	9.4%	6.4%
Board-designated assets for funded depreciation	2,100	6,100	(4,000)[15]	− 65.57%	1.5%	4.5%
Unamortized debt expense and other	2,349	2,162	187	8.65%	1.7%	1.6%
Notes receivable	1,022	1,024	(2)	− 0.20%	0.7%	0.8%
Total other assets	50,095	31,619	18,476	58.43%[7]	36.0%[4]	23.3%
Land	1,430	3,235	(1,805)	− 55.80%	1.0%	2.4%
Buildings and improvements	39,886	60,013	(20,127)	− 33.54%	28.6%	44.3%
Equipment	50,115	49,533	582	1.17%	36.0%	36.5%
Construction in progress	2,315	1,215	1,100	90.53%	1.7%	0.9%
Total fixed assets at cost	93,746	113,996	(20,250)	− 17.76%	67.3%	84.1%
Less: Accumulated depreciation	(39,993)	(40,696)	703	− 1.73%	− 28.7%	− 30.0%
Net property, plant, and equipment	53,753	73,300	(19,547)	− 26.67%[8]	38.6%[5]	54.1%
Total Assets	$139,238[1]	$135,608	$ 3,630	2.68%[2]	100.0%	100.0%
LIABILITIES AND ACCUMULATED EQUITY						
Accounts payable and other	$ 7,866	$ 5,955	$ 1,911[17]	32.09%	5.6%	4.4%
Settlement amounts due to third parties	640	40	600	1,500.00%	0.5%	0.0%
Accrued expenses and other	7,440	6,626	814[18]	12.28%	5.3%	4.9%
Current maturities of long-term leases and debt	1,194	7,468	(6,274)[20]	− 84.01%	0.9%	5.5%
Deferred income	359	295	64	21.69%	0.3%	0.2%
Total current liabilities	17,499	20,384	(2,885)	− 14.15%	12.6%	15.0%
Contingent liabilities			0	ERR	0.0%	0.0%
Liabilities for self-insured claims	13,060	8,634	4,426	51.26%	9.4%	6.4%
Capital lease and long-term debt	62,278	38,339	23,939[19]	62.44%	44.7%	28.3%
Total liabilities and deferred revenues	92,837	67,357	25,480	37.83%	66.7%	49.7%
Accumulated equity	46,401	68,251	(21,850)[21]	− 32.01%	33.3%	50.3%
Total liabilities and accumulated equity	$139,238	$135,608	$ 3,630	2.68%	100.0%	100.0%

ERR = attempt to divide by zero.

EXHIBIT C (Continued)

Restated Statement of Revenues and Expenses and Changes in Accumulated Equity

	1984	1983	Dollar Change	Percent Change	Common Size 1984	Common Size 1983
REVENUES:						
Daily patient service revenues	$ 52,778	$ 54,124	$ (1,346)	−2.49%	38.5%	42.7%
Ancillary services—inpatient	83,531	77,255	6,276	8.12%	60.9%	60.9%
Ancillary services—outpatient	17,780	16,438	1,342	8.16%	13.0%	13.0%
Total patient revenues	154,089	147,817	6,272	4.24%	112.4%	116.6%
Charity allowances	7,752	8,269	(517)[22]	−6.25%	5.7%	6.5%
Contractual allowances	9,206	14,664	(5,458)	−37.22%	6.7%	11.6%
Provision for uncollectible accounts	5,490	4,197	1,293	30.81%	4.0%	3.3%
Total Deductions from Revenues	22,448	27,130	(4,682)	−17.26%	16.4%	21.4%
Net Patient Revenues	131,641	120,687	10,954	9.08%[12]	96.0%[30]	95.2%
Other operating revenues	5,498	6,074	(576)	−9.48%	4.0%	4.8%
Net revenues from operations	137,139	126,761	10,378	8.19%[28]	100.0%	100.0%
OPERATING EXPENSES:						
Salaries and wages	59,554	59,666	(112)	−0.19%	45.1%[31]	48.5%
Employee benefits	12,228	10,410	1,818	17.46%[33]	9.3%[31]	8.5%
Professional compensation and fees	4,005	3,165	840	26.54%	3.0%	2.6%
Supplies and other expenses	39,019	33,810	5,209	15.41%	29.5%[32]	27.5%
Energy	2,421	2,425	(4)	−0.16%	1.8%	2.0%
Depreciation on operating plant	5,978	5,920	58	0.98%	4.5%	4.8%
Interest and debt expense	3,275	2,432	843	34.66%	2.5%	2.0%
Total patient care operating expenses	126,480	117,828	8,652	7.34%	95.7%	95.8%
Net expenses for education programs, except depreciation	5,346	4,683	663[23]	14.16%		
Depreciation expense for education programs	330	490	(160)[23]	−32.65%	0.2%	0.4%
Total operating expenses	132,156	123,001	9,155	7.44%[29]	100.0%	100.0%
NET INCOME FROM OPERATIONS	4,983	3,760	1,223	32.53%	3.6%	3.0%
Net expenses for medical staff office building	(93)	(226)	133	−58.85%	−0.1%	−0.2%
Nonoperating revenues	1,496	1,769	(273)	−15.43%	1.1%	1.4%
EXCESS OF REVENUES OVER EXPENSES BEFORE EXTRAORDINARY ITEMS	6,386[24]	5,303	1,083	20.42%	4.7%[26]	4.2%
EXTRAORDINARY ITEM, gain on extinguishment of debt	7,844[25]	0	7,844	ERR		
EXCESS OF REVENUES OVER EXPENSES	14,230	5,303	8,927	168.34%		
TRANSFERS						
Additions to plant property and equipment	102	116	(14)	−12.07%		
Transfers to affiliated entities	(36,182)[16]	0	(36,182)	ERR		
Balance, beginning of year	68,251	62,832	5,419	8.62%		
Balance, end of year	$ 46,401	$ 68,251	$(21,850)	−32.01%		

ERR = attempt to divide by zero.

EXHIBIT D **ABC Comparative Statistics**

| | Regional Median Values | | ABC | |
	1984	1983	1984	1983
RATIOS				
Deductible	0.201[35]	0.208	0.15[34]	0.18
Operating Margin	0.045	0.028	0.04	0.03
Return on Total Assets	0.060	0.045	0.05[45]	0.04
Return on Equity	0.119	0.090	0.09[27]	0.08
Current	2.170[37]	2.110	2.02[10]	1.51[9]
Days in Accounts Receivable	67.500	63.200	64.00[14]	61.00[13]
Equity Financing	0.527	0.496[39]	0.33[40]	0.50
Cash Flow to Total Debt	0.232[42]	0.176[41]	0.14[44]	0.17[43]
Fixed Asset Financing	0.600	0.634	1.16	0.52
Average Age of Plant	6.760	6.560	6.34[46]	6.35

FORMULAS

Deductible = Deductions ÷ Gross Patient Service Revenue

Operating Margin = (Total Operating Revenue − Operating Expenses) ÷ Total Operating Revenue

Return on Total Assets = Excess of Revenues Over Expenses ÷ Total Assets

Return on Equity = Excess of Revenues Over Expenses ÷ Fund Balance

Current = Current Assets ÷ Current Liabilities

Days in Accounts Receivable = Net Patient Accounts Receivable ÷ (Net Patient Service Revenue ÷ 365)

Equity Financing = Fund Balance ÷ Total Assets

Cash Flow to Total Debt = (Excess of Revenues Over Expenses + Depreciation) ÷ Total Debt

Fixed Asset Financing = Long-Term Liabilities ÷ Net Fixed Assets

Average Age of Plant = Accumulated Depreciation ÷ Depreciation Expense

DISCUSSION QUESTIONS

1. What is the role of the third parties in the health care industry?

2. Explain how each of the following items would be accounted for by a health care organization, and why:
   Donations of services
   Donations of equipment
   Payment of a loan
   Receipt of a gift restricted for research
   Receipt of a gift for plant replacement purposes
   Expenses incurred on a research grant
   Purchase of new plant
   Revenues from the gift shop
   Endowment fund earnings
   A nonrefundable client prepayment for residence in a long-term care facility

3. What are the differences among the following items: bad debts, courtesy allowances, charity or free care, and contractual adjustments?

4. Discuss the accounting issues surrounding malpractice loss and other contingencies.

5. How do deferred revenues arise? When are they reduced?

6. Why might it be difficult to define a health care entity? What sorts of entity definition problems could arise and how should they be handled for financial reporting purpose under the current standards? What do you think the standards should require?

7. What are the key signs of financial difficulties in health care providers?

8. What is the difference between uniform accounting and uniform reporting?

EXERCISES

1. Bamf Hospital provides you with the following account balances at September 30, 19XX:

	($ in thousands)
Notes payable to banks	$ 45
Receivables—patients	157
Investments—specific purpose fund	290
Bonds payable	200
Prepaid expenses	20
Investments—unrestricted fund (current)	90
Accrued expenses payable	100
Cash—board-designated	50
Investments—endowment fund	310
Accounts payable	140
Allowance for uncollectible accounts	57
Mortgage payable	160

	($ in thousands)
Equipment	$560
Cash—plant replacement and expansion fund	30
Cash—unrestricted fund (current)	150
Current portion of long-term debt	25
Investments—plant replacement and expansion fund	180
Cash—specific purpose fund	35
Investments—board-designated	70
Accumulated depreciation	260
Deferred revenue (current)	120
Inventories	40
Cash—endowment fund	50

Assignment

Prepare an all-funds (aggregated) and a traditional Balance Sheet for Bamf Hospital at September 30, 19XX.

2. Fordlan Hospital provides you with the following information taken from its accounting records at June 30, 19XX, the end of its fiscal year:

	($ in thousands)
Nursing services expense	$ 400
Deductions from revenues	364
Income and gains from board-designated investments	14
General services expense	280
Depreciation	160
Unrestricted gifts and bequests	72
Gross patient service revenues	1,900
Fiscal services expense	120
Unrestricted income from endowment fund	42
Other professional services expense	300
Other operating revenues	100
Administrative services expense	130
Unrestricted fund balance—beginning of year	358
Interest expense	190
Transfer from specific purpose fund for free service	14
Transfer from PR&E fund for purchase of fixed assets	54

Assignment

Prepare (1) an activity statement, and (2) a statement of changes in unrestricted fund balances for the year ended June 30, 19XX.

Case

CASE 17.1 Beverly Hospital

On a mild April weekend, Northeast Health Systems Inc./Beverly Hospital was about to hold its board retreat. In its CEO's view, attendees should "come away from our retreat with a clear vision of the strategic initiatives that must be pursued to preserve our provision of high-quality patient care services and financial integrity." In his opinion, the following were the key to the hospital's survival:

(1) The need to anticipate and preempt any loss of patient volume resulting from the increasingly competitive health care environment
(2) The plan for expansion of services to outlying north suburban areas
(3) The development of closer relationships with nearby hospitals

BACKGROUND OF BEVERLY HOSPITAL

Founded in 1888, Beverly Hospital was a 238-bed acute care nonprofit community institution, serving primarily the North Shore area of metropolitan Boston, including the city of Beverly and eleven other municipalities (**Exhibit 1**). The hospital was located on a 38-acre site in the city of Beverly, a coastal community approximately 20 miles northeast of Boston. Route 128, the major circumferential highway serving the greater Boston area, was a quarter-mile to the north of the hospital, and the hospital owned a licensed heliport on its property. The service area had a good employer base, with 123 firms employing over 100 people each.

The four most significant demographic factors affecting the Beverly Hospital/NHSI were:

(1) A stable, no-growth total population
(2) An increase in the elderly population, especially in the over-75 age group. The North Shore had a greater proportion of elderly than the nation as a whole (14 percent vs. 11.5 percent).
(3) Low growth in the number of children in the area
(4) Higher-than-average income and asset levels in Beverly's primary and secondary service areas, particularly for the older age groups

Professor Regina E. Herzlinger prepared this case as the basis for class discussion rather than to illustrate either effective or ineffective handling of an administrative situation.

Modern facilities were available in the hospital's maternity and pediatric floor and the emergency, physical, speech and occupational therapy, surgery, renal dialysis, audiology, ancillary, and outpatient departments. But in 1986, 116 of its medical-surgical beds were still in outmoded four-room suites and the psychiatric beds were on the third floor of a building constructed in 1927. To renovate these areas, add 3 maternity beds, and buy a full-body scanner to replace the head scanner, the hospital filed CON applications.

The hospital's occupancy and lengths of stay had remained stable since 1981, unlike some of its competitors (see **Table 1**). (The hospital's description of its competitors is in **Exhibit 2**.)

The number of physicians affiliated with the hospital had grown by 44 from 1980 to 205 MDs and 20 dentists by 1985. Twenty practiced full time with the hospital; all others were in private practice, mostly in the primary service area. The 10 MDs who accounted for 27 percent of the hospital's 1984 discharges all had their principal offices in one of the hospital's two condominium medical office buildings. Total discharges by department and physician, by age, are in **Table 2**.

THE CHANGING HEALTH CARE ENVIRONMENT

The changes detailed below in the 1980s health care system affected all hospitals, including Beverly.

Reimbursement Changes

Hospital finances were dramatically affected because both government and private insurance companies focused on cost savings. Medicare destroyed the cost-plus mentality of hospital management when it initiated prospective pricing schedules in the fall of 1983. The private insurance industry, prodded by corporate America, was also forcing hospitals to be competitive and reviewing their utilization. In 1981, Massachusetts Blue Cross began to set the prospective annual level of allowable costs on the basis of 1981 costs adjusted forward for inflation, changes in volume and case mix, and exceptions for costs associated with a CON. For 1985, Beverly Hospital's Blue Cross reimbursement was 9.1 percent below the amount it would have received prior to the prospective payment system.

These changes caused reductions in hospital occupancy, as the lengths of patient stays and admission rates declined sharply.

New Entrants Competing for a Hospital's Patient Base

New competitors in Massachusetts' health care delivery sector included HMOs and PPOs, free-standing urgi- and surgi-centers, and home health care.

The HMOs' and PPOs' growth affected hospital utilization in two ways: (1) they had an economic incentive to minimize inpatient hospitalization and to encourage alternative outpatient health care for members, and (2) utilization for certain hospitals was increased because members could use only those hospitals with which they had an affiliation agreement. Free-standing urgi-centers and surgi-centers also provided a challenge. They were operated by private physicians who banded together to raise the capital outlay needed and, increasingly, by for-profit chains such as Health Stop. Those

TABLE 1 **Beverly Hospital—Summary of Historical Operating Statistics for Service Area Hospitals, 1980 and 1984**

	Discharges	Patient Days[a]	Length of Stay (days)	Occupancy (%)	Beds					
					MED/SURG	ICU/CCU	Obstetric	Pediatric	Psychiatric	Total
Beverly Hospital										
1980	7,965	68,334	8.6	78.50	173	19	14	16	16	238
1984	7,895	69,028	8.7	80.90	173	19	14	11	16	238
Hunt Memorial Hospital										
1980	5,590	42,027	7.5	83.00	107	8	10	13	0	138
1984	5,217	40,461	7.8	76.00	115	8	10	11	0	144
Addison Gilbert Hospital										
1980	4,694	37,941	8.1	80.80	97	10	8	14	0	129
1984	4,560	39,754	8.7	80.50	102	8	8	5	12	135
Lynn Hospital										
1980	11,273	103,008	9.1	93.20	232	14	31	28	0	305
1984	8,649	74,431	8.6	67.60	232	14	30	25	0	301
Union Hospital										
1980	2,425	21,843	9.0	51.50	84	5	0	0	27	116
1984	6,509	54,567	8.4	72.70	174	12	0	0	24	210
Salem Hospital										
1980	10,902	118,106	10.8	85.10	304	23	17	0	35	379
1984	12,097	108,143	8.9	78.00	304	23	17	0	35	379

[a]Patient days are not precisely equal to the product of discharges and length of stay because of rounding errors.

TABLE 2 **Beverly Hospital—Analysis of Physician Age and Discharges by Speciality, Fiscal Year Ended September 30, 1984[a]**

Active Staff	Number of Physicians	Total Discharges 1984	Age 30-44 Physician	Age 30-44 Discharge	Age 45-54 Physician	Age 45-54 Discharge	Age 55-64 Physician	Age 55-64 Discharge	Age Over 65 Physician	Age Over 65 Discharge
Anesthesia	4	0	2	0	1	0	0	0	1	0
Emergency and Outpatient	5	5	2	0	2	0	1	5	0	0
Family Practice	11	1,055	7	865	1	89	1	65	2	36
Internal Medicine	38	3,145	23	1,348	14	1,517	1	280	0	0
Obstetrics and Gynecology	9	1,278	4	420	3	526	2	332	0	0
Pathology	2	0	0	0	1	0	1	0	0	0
Pediatrics	15	969	8	480	3	170	3	258	1	61
Psychiatry	8	178	5	178	1	0	1	0	1	0
Radiology	5	0	1	0	3	0	1	0	0	0
Surgery	29	1,888	8	268	15	1,296	4	100	2	224
Total Active Staff	126	8,518	60	3,559	44	3,598	15	1,040	7	321
Cumulative Active Staff Discharges by Age Group		8,518		3,559		3,598		1,040		321
Cumulative Active Staff Discharges as a % of Total Discharges		96.65%		40.38%		40.83%		11.80%		3.64%
Total Associate, Courtesy, and Consulting Staff	86	295								
Total All Physicians	212	8,813								

Note: Active staff includes provisional physicians.

[a]Total number of discharges accounts separately for each physician involved with a discharge.

institutions, run on a high-volume, low-overhead basis, had begun to make inroads into hospital emergency rooms (which account for 15-30 percent of inpatient admissions) and surgical visits.

The large home health care market was considered both a benefit and problem for hospitals. On the one hand, with the availability of home care, hospitals could more easily reduce the length of stay. On the other, the home health market was becoming more sophisticated and some routine hospital procedures, such as kidney dialysis, could shift completely to the home.

PRODUCT LINE MANAGEMENT

In 1984, Beverly Hospital established 16 product lines. These "centers of excellence" were structured into four groups, each independently responsible to a strategy review board of senior management representatives. The product line groups, for example, included one comprising Emergency Room, Respiratory/Pulmonary, Psychiatry, and General Surgery services.

The product line process began with intensive training of all managers in marketing and strategic problem-solving. The product line team leader presented the product strategies for the coming year to the review board, which then set priorities for each product line for the coming year. Although only one product line for each team was reviewed per year, the planning process was thought to be beneficial for those more comfortable with operations.

Beverly Hospital's current marketing slogans resulted from the first year of product line management. To reposition itself and communicate its new role in the North Shore community, Beverly adopted as a marketing logo, "More than a Hospital . . . a Family Centered Health Care System." This concept provided the basis for advertising several of the product lines with "high-tech" ads stressing medical qualities and "high-touch" ads stressing warmth.

One product, women's health, resulted from a number of focus groups, marketing studies, surveys, and brainstorming sessions. Marketing data indicated that although most health care services were purchased by women, services were not geared to fulfill their need for a place with a "comfort zone" and for providers who delivered specialized care. The studies also found that North Shore women wanted "someone to talk with who will listen to my needs." As a result, Beverly's Women's Health Connection was established as a referral line staffed by volunteers and specialized professionals. The project team described the connection as a place "where your search for information ends." Additional plans for the Women's Health Connection include a women's library, an off-site mammography unit, and specialized women's health care services.

Another product line resulted from the nurse manager of the general surgery group observing the problems the surgical staff and patients experienced in admission time and surgical scheduling. In the past, surgical patients were admitted the day before their operations to give the nursing staff ample time to make the patients comfortable, order and receive results for all appropriate tests, and answer questions. As HMO admissions began to represent a more significant percentage of Beverly's patient load, this comfortable process changed and patients came to the hospital the day of surgery as "am admits." Tests performed outside the hospital (usually at the HMO) caused problems in record keeping. At times, patients did not receive adequate preparation for their operations.

As day surgery increased, Beverly Hospital found alternative ways to educate patients before admission. A videotape was produced and shown in the hospital and community. A volunteer program enabled patients to come into the hospital a few days prior to their procedures, have their tests performed, ask questions, and tour the facility. Comfortable "living rooms" were set aside for patients and their families to use. Patients were to be treated as guests in a hotel rather than as admits in a hospital. For example, where once patients who entered the outpatient area were given a dressing room and a garbage bag for their clothing, they were now assigned a locker.

The current product line strategy was to create a pre-admission testing center for central control of all testing and information, so that physicians and their staff could retrieve test information from one point.

HMO AFFILIATIONS

In 1986, HMOs accounted for 15 percent of admissions in medical/surgical, 32.4 percent in obstetrical, 38.4 percent in pediatric, and 12.7 percent in pychiatric. By 1987, Beverly Hospital's affiliations with seven major HMOs and PPOs were critical to its future (see **Exhibit 3**).

In 1982, a hospital Subcommittee on Alternative Delivery Systems was established to educate the hospital staff about HMO affiliations and to review opportunities. Its original members were six physicians, the CEO, six board members, and two management representatives. The first meeting consisted of a presentation of the benefits of HMO affiliations to physicians, as well as the hospital.

One significant proposal emerged when the committee learned that the largest Massachusetts HMO was negotiating with a competitor, Salem Hospital, for services to the HMO's North Shore health center. Beverly made an aggressive attempt to capture the HMO's interest before it had an opportunity to solidify this relationship. After reviewing a lengthy document stressing Beverly's lower length of stay, the HMO chose Beverly Hospital as its primary acute care facility for North Shore members.

ORGANIZATIONAL CHARACTERISTICS

In 1983, Beverly Hospital established Northeast Health Systems Inc./Beverly Hospital, a vertically integrated system providing all levels of health care services, including acute, long-term, and home care; medically assisted housing; and ambulatory care. Its principal assets were 12 acres of prime land in the city of Peabody, five miles to the south of Beverly. The land was to house (1) a magnetic resonance imaging center in cooperation with Beverly Hospital and four other area hospitals, (2) a free-standing ambulatory surgical center, (3) a 142-bed nursing home, and (4) a medical office building. Its principal subsidiaries were as follows:

MedQuest Corporation was to arrange for services provided by new health care organizations. MedQuest was constructing and operating a 122-bed long-term care facility on the grounds of Beverly Hospital, as an equal partner with a subsidiary of National Medical Enterprises, a for-profit California-based health services firm. It also filed CON applications to construct and operate a Peabody nursing home and a free-standing kidney dialysis center with nine stations in Lynn, Massachusetts, as a jointly owned venture between MedQuest and Massachusetts General

Hospital, a large Harvard University teaching hospital. Its subsidiary, Northeast Medical Management Services, Inc., was a for-profit company that provided management services to ambulatory medical providers.

NHS Properties, Inc. was a nonprofit real estate holding company.

Cable Housing and Health Services Corporation was established to develop the hospital's Ipswich property. The hospital also owned another 10-acre site in Ipswich on which it ran an emergency room and medical office building.

SurgiQuest was established to construct and operate an ambulatory surgical center on the Peabody property along with Medical Care International (a publicly traded corporation). A CON application for construction of a surgery center had been approved.

PHYSICIAN RELATIONS

Dr. William Otto was the elected president of the medical staff. Dr. Otto recalled the "tremendous rupture" occurring between the primary care physicians (Internal Medicine, Pediatrics, Family Practice, and Ob/Gyn) and the specialists when HMOs came in. "Capitated" HMOs placed the primary care physician in control of all fees so as to serve as the patient's care manager or "gatekeeper." Under the old system, the specialists were in the catbird seat, with few checks on their cost and/or reimbursement structures.

About 50 of Beverly's physicians incorporated as the Beverly Doctors' Association so that they could respond to financial opportunities that might not be obtainable without a formal structure. The primary care physicians controlled this organization. Dr. Otto stated that one of the most significant issues facing Beverly's physician group was "who will be in control? If it is not the primary care physician, the primary care physicians will not join the alternative delivery system model. Without the primary care physicians, the capitated plans cannot survive."

EMPLOYEES

For fiscal year 1984, Beverly Hospital employed an average of 881 full-time equivalent employees or approximately 3.2 full-time equivalent employees per adjusted occupied bed. Of this staff, 269 were nurses, 112 were administrative and supervisory personnel, and 159 were professionals, including laboratory, pharmacy, radiology, therapy, and social workers. The hospital was eager to preserve its non-union status.

FINANCIAL DATA

See **Tables 3** to **9** and **Exhibit 4** for Beverly Hospital's financial performance during the early 1980s.

ASSIGNMENT

1. Assess the hospital's competitive position in the North Shore area. What opportunity is the Beverly Hospital seeking to fulfill with its product line management, joint ventures with other hospitals, reorganization, and HMO initiatives?
2. Will the hospital be successful in these ventures and why?

TABLE 3 Beverly Hospital Hospital—Income Statement

	Years Ended September 30,					Ten-Month Period Ended July 31,	
	1980	1981	1982	1983	1984	1984	1985
Patient service revenue	$26,144,960	$30,486,975	$35,865,886	$37,577,571	$41,705,412	$35,281,500	$36,550,923
Deductions from revenue	3,396,581	3,962,713	5,280,612	4,444,378	6,255,825	5,704,200	4,621,818
Net patient service revenue	$22,748,379	$26,524,262	$30,585,274	$33,133,193	$35,449,587	$29,577,300	$31,929,105
Other operating revenue	304,760	314,074	385,572	383,723	612,596	568,813	468,281
Total operating revenue	$23,053,139	$26,838,336	$30,970,846	$33,516,916	$36,062,183	$30,146,113	$32,397,386
Total operating expenses	22,575,908	26,825,438	31,808,511	33,191,214	35,698,984	29,861,063	31,364,788
Income (loss) from operations	$ 477,231	$ 12,898	$ (837,665)	$ 325,702	$ 363,139	$ 285,050	$ 1,032,598
Total nonoperating revenue—net	1,072,909	3,010,577	1,837,865	1,691,757	1,845,444	1,434,993	1,560,886
Excess of revenues over expenses	$ 1,550,140	$ 3,023,475	$ 1,000,200	$ 2,017,459	$ 2,208,573	$ 1,720,043	$ 2,593,484

TABLE 4 Beverly Hospital—Comparative Charges

	Beverly Hospital	Salem Hospital	Hunt Hospital	Addison Gilbert Hospital	Lynn Hospital	Union Hospital
Average Semi-Private Room Rates						
Medical/Surgical	$195	$260	$220	$260	$192	$395
Maternity	170	200	200	260	250	NA
Psychiatric	235	260	NA	325	NA	395
Pediatric	170	NA	201	254	247	NA
ICU/CCU	340	700	450	550	480	699
Newborn	130	185	140	164	225	NA

TABLE 5 **Beverly Hospital—Balance Sheets**

| | September 30, | |
	1984	1983
ASSETS		
Unrestricted Funds		
Current		
Cash	$ 1,173,888	$ 1,396,585
Patient receivables, less allowance for uncollectible accounts		
of $475,000 in 1984 and $450,000 in 1983	5,406,542	4,551,940
Other receivables	873,212	703,038
Due from third-party payers	-	278,160
Funds held by trustees	434,488	449,307
Inventories	787,310	784,723
Prepaid expenses	190,857	130,307
Accounts receivable—affiliate	275,307	69,680
Total current assets	$ 9,141,604	$ 8,363,740
Other		
Cash and cash equivalents	231,072	793,921
Investments	11,876,563	9,354,285
Funds held by trustees	1,854,314	1,981,190
Unamortized financing costs and bond discounts	594,429	626,004
Other assets	27,716	4,206
Total other assets	$14,584,094	$12,759,606
Property, plant, and equipment—net	23,995,340	23,795,416
Total unrestricted funds	$47,721,038	$44,918,762
Restricted Funds		
Specific-Purpose Funds		
Investments	$ 104,519	$ 96,358
Due from unrestricted funds	338,266	265,208
Total specific-purpose funds	$ 442,785	$ 361,566
Plant Expansion Funds		
Pledges receivable, less allowance for uncollectible pledges		
of $48,000 in 1984 and $87,000 in 1983	$ 238,013	$ 436,441
Total plant expansion funds	$ 238,013	$ 436,441
Endowment Funds		
Cash	$ -	$ 1,817
Investments	3,723,529	3,536,678
Total endowment funds	$ 3,723,529	$ 3,538,495

Note: See notes to financial statements (**Exhibit 4**).

TABLE 5 (Continued

| | September 30, | |
	1984	1983
LIABILITIES AND FUND BALANCE		
Unrestricted Funds		
Current		
Notes payable to bank	$ 167,977	$ 407,907
Accounts payable	876,743	999,282
Construction costs payable	-	52,150
Accrued vacation pay	886,619	781,518
Accrued expenses	822,530	454,673
Accrued interest expense	352,561	354,943
Advances from third-party payers	128,767	227,110
Due to third-party payers	1,062,146	-
Current installments on long-term debt	327,783	316,916
Due to restricted funds	304,163	246,437
Total current liabilities	$ 4,929,289	$ 3,840,936
Long-term Debt		
Bonds payable—Series A	2,780,000	3,000,000
—Series B	10,485,000	10,545,000
Mortgage notes payable	-	-
Capital lease obligation	7,202	31,290
Installment loan payable	347,267	311,750
Total long-term debt	$13,619,469	$13,888,040
Fund Balances		
Operating	29,172,280	27,189,786
Total unrestricted funds	$47,721,038	$44,918,762
Restricted Funds		
Specific-Purpose Funds		
Fund balance	$ 442,785	$ 361,566
Total specific-purpose funds	$ 442,785	$ 361,566
Plant Expansion Funds		
Due to unrestricted funds	$ 22,993	$ 7,661
Fund balance	215,020	428,780
Total plant expansion funds	$ 238,013	$ 436,441
Endowment Funds		
Due to unrestricted funds	$ 11,110	$ 11,110
Fund balance	3,712,419	3,527,385
Total endowment funds	$ 3,723,529	$ 3,538,495

TABLE 6   **Beverly Hospital—Statements of Revenues and Expenses—Unrestricted Funds**

	Years Ended September 30,	
	1984	*1983*
Patient Service Revenue	$41,705,412	$37,557,571
Less allowances and uncollectible accounts	6,255,825	4,444,378
Net Patient Service Revenue	$35,449,587	$33,133,193
Other Operating Revenue	612,596	383,723
Total Operating Revenue	$36,062,183	$33,516,916
Operating Expenses		
Salaries and wages	17,825,650	16,776,648
Physician salaries and fees	1,645,066	1,573,566
Fringe benefits	2,941,074	2,546,863
Supplies and contracted services	10,123,782	9,412,659
Depreciation	1,701,716	1,495,460
Interest	1,461,696	1,385,918
Total Operating Expenses	$35,698,984	$33,191,214
Income from Operations	$ 363,199	$ 325,702
Nonoperating Revenue (Expense)		
Unrestricted gifts and bequests	186,617	218,235
Unrestricted income from endowment and board-designated funds	1,610,074	1,449,180
Gain on sale of securities	144,962	75,668
Net loss from rental properties	(87,417)	(87,873)
Other nonoperating revenues (expenses)—net	(8,802)	36,547
Total Nonoperating Revenue—Net	$ 1,845,444	$ 1,691,757
Excess of Revenues Over Expenses	$ 2,208,573	$ 2,017,459

Note: See notes to financial statements (**Exhibit 4**).

TABLE 7 **Beverly Hospital—Statements of Changes in Fund Balances**

	Unrestricted Funds	Restricted Funds		
		Specific Purpose	Plant Expansion	Endowment
Balances—October 1, 1982	$24,694,932	$301,899	$ 833,335	$3,347,777
Excess of revenues over expenses	2,017,459	-	-	-
Contributions	-	43,082	70,480	-
Restricted investment income and gains	-	29,084	-	179,608
Transfers to:				
Unrestricted funds included in revenues and expenses	-	(4,080)	(6,059)	-
Finance property, plant, and equipment	477,395	(8,419)	(468,976)	-
Balances—September 30, 1983	$27,189,786	$361,566	$ 428,780	$3,527,385
Excess of revenues over expenses	2,208,573	-	-	-
Contributions	-	63,248	8,788	-
Restricted investment income and gains	-	31,655	-	-
Decrease in allowance for uncollectible pledges	-	-	39,000	-
Transfer of net assets to Northeast Health Systems, Inc.	(483,973)	-	-	-
Transfers to:				
Unrestricted funds included in revenues and expenses	-	(2,006)	(15,332)	-
Finance property, plant, and equipment	257,894	(11,678)	(246,216)	-
Balances—September 30, 1984	$29,172,280	$442,785	$ 215,020	$3,712,419

Note: See notes to financial statements (**Exhibit 4**).

TABLE 8 **Beverly Hospital—Gross Patient Service Revenue, by Service, Year Ending September 30, 1984**

Service	Routine	Ancillary	Total
Inpatient			
Medical-Surgical	$ 9,304,837	$10,616,861	$19,921,698
Pediatric	468,892	559,616	1,028,508
Obstetrics	740,807	859,332	1,600,139
Psychiatry	1,194,313	149,504	1,343,817
ICU	1,772,976	3,021,428	4,794,404
Newborn	493,950	65,240	559,190
Subtotal inpatient	$13,975,775	$15,271,981	$29,247,756
Outpatient			
Emergency	$ 1,947,755	$ 1,039,674	$ 2,987,429
Clinic	539,742	2,930,415	3,470,157
Satellite clinic	0	2,786,660	2,786,660
Surgery	219,976	1,148,021	1,367,997
Ambulatory dialysis	0	1,845,407	1,845,407
Subtotal outpatient	$ 2,707,473	$ 9,750,177	$12,457,650
Total patient care	$16,683,248	$25,022,158	$41,705,406

TABLE 9 **Beverly Hospital—Ancillary Expenses, by Service (dollars in thousands)**

Service	Total	Direct	Allocated
Inpatient			
Medical-Surgical	$ 6,593	$ 4,256	$2,337
Pediatric	367	239	128
Obstetrics	869	565	304
Psychiatry	90	59	31
ICU	1,740	1,131	609
Newborn	187	122	65
Subtotal inpatient	$ 9,846	$ 6,372	$3,474
Outpatient			
Emergency	$ 874	$ 568	$ 306
Clinic	2,277	1,480	797
Satellite clinic	2,315	1,505	810
Surgery	658	428	230
Ambulatory dialysis	1,642	1,067	575
Subtotal outpatient	$ 7,766	$ 5,048	$2,718
Total expenses	$17,612	$11,420	$6,192

EXHIBIT 1   **Beverly Hospital's Service Area**

	Population			Percent of Beverly Hospital's Discharges	
	1970	*1985*	*1990*	*1982*	*1984*
Beverly	38,348	37,880	38,380	42.9	43.0
Hamilton	6,373	6,900	6,850	5.2	5.5
Manchester	5,151	5,390	5,370	4.2	4.8
Salem	40,556	37,300	35,980	3.5	3.6
Danvers	26,151	23,320	22,590	4.4	4.0
Gloucester	27,941	28,200	28,540	4.9	5.7
Ipswich	10,750	11,300	11,370	10.6	8.5
Wenham	3,849	3,870	3,840	2.5	2.9
Topsfield	5,225	5,780	5,840	1.7	1.7
Essex	2,670	3,040	2,110	2.7	2.4
Boxford	4,032	5,610	5,840	0.8	0.8
Rowley	3,040	4,100	4,380	0.9	1.1
Total primary service area	174,086	172,690	171,090	84.3	84.0
Total secondary service area	NA	NA	NA	15.7	16.0

Massachusetts Health Service Area VI

EXHIBIT 2   Beverly Hospital—Competitive Hospitals

The other short-term acute care hospitals providing health care services to residents of Beverly Hospital's primary and secondary service areas include Hunt Memorial Hospital, Addison Gilbert Hospital, Salem Hospital, North Shore Children's Hospital, and AtlantiCare Corporation. A summary of management's information regarding these organizations follows.

Hunt Memorial Hospital

The hospital is owned by the Town of Danvers and is the only hospital that shares the primary service area of Beverly Hospital. Hunt has recently renovated its ICU, increased its bed complement by eight, and obtained a head computerized tomography scanner. Recently, Hunt supported the establishment of a physician in the Town of Middletown and opened a walk-in urgent care center adjacent to a shopping mall in Danvers. A proprietary urgent care chain has also opened a facility across from the same shopping mall. Hunt has announced plans to extensively renovate its labor, delivery, and day surgery areas. Hunt has also discussed a possible management contract with Hospital Corporation of America officials. Hunt is unaffiliated with most HMOs in the area, with some small exceptions.

Addison Gilbert Hospital

The hospital is a 135-bed acute care general hospital located in Gloucester, approximately 12 miles northeast of Beverly. A recent renovation project improved several ancillary departments and established the psychiatric service. Addison Gilbert has limited HMO affiliations to one IPA. Addison Gilbert plans to construct a skilled nursing facility. No long-term care beds are available in the current bed need formula, published by the Massachusetts Department of Public Health, for the Gloucester area.

Salem Hospital

The hospital is located in Salem, approximately 5 miles from Beverly Hospital. Salem provides several specialized services, including radiation therapy and cardiac catherization. Salem plans to modernize its emergency and ambulatory care departments and its maternity suites and to replace its power plant at a total cost of about $26,000,000. Salem is affiliated with many HMOs. It has also indicated an interest in long-term care with possible plans for a home and/or durable medical equipment venture. Salem and Beverly Hospital are currently discussing the feasibility of a joint venture. Salem now has a management contract for a 35-bed hospital in Marblehead, 6 miles from Beverly, and a contract for selected services for a 99-bed municipal hospital in Peabody, 6 miles from Beverly.

North Shore Children's Hospital

The hospital is a 50-bed pediatric hospital adjacent to Salem Hospital. It has a teaching affiliation with Tufts/New England Medical Center, Boston, and a number of shared service arrangements with Salem Hospital. North Shore Children's

EXHIBIT 2 (Continued)

maintains an 8-bed inpatient pediatric physiatric service and operates a number of specialized outpatient clinics and human service counseling programs. It opened a satellite outpatient facility in Peabody that provides a range of therapeutic day care and counseling services, along with some preventive medical services. Other satellites are planned. North Shore Children's is discussing with Beverly Hospital a psychiatric outpatient joint venture in Beverly. North Shore Children's is the only pediatric hospital north of Boston and provides most of its inpatient services to patients who reside in Lynn, Salem, and Peabody.

AtlantiCare Corporation

This is the corporate holding company for Lynn Hospital and Union Hospital, both located in Lynn, about 15 miles southwest of Beverly. Lynn Hospital, a 301-bed acute care facility, is located in the center of the city. Union Hospital, with 210 beds, is located in the north suburban area. In September 1985, AtlantiCare submitted a $59 millon Determination of Need application to consolidate Lynn Hospital operations at the Union Hospital site with a reduction of 130 beds from a total bed complement of 511. Although both Lynn and Union Hospitals are in the secondary service area of the hospital, they are considered competitors because of the growing importance of HMOs on the North Shore.

EXHIBIT 3   **Beverly Hospital—HMO/PPO Affiliations**

Beverly has hospital service agreements with five area HMOs. In 1985, approximately 13 percent of all hospital admissions were members of an HMO, a percentage expected to increase in the future.

In May 1984, the hospital entered into a five-year hospital service agreement with a 213,000-member closed-panel HMO. Beverly Hospital is currently its sole provider for its Peabody Center for all hospital services, except for psychiatric services and tertiary-level services not provided at the hospital. It also has a three-year hospital service agreement with a group practice HMO with 57,863 members. Beverly and Hunt Hospitals are currently its only providers of hospital services on the North Shore. The hospital has an agreement with an IPA whose enrollment is currently 120,000 members, the second largest HMO in Massachusetts. The IPA currently has agreements with all of the hospitals within Beverly Hospital's competitive area.

In May 1985, the hospital entered into an agreement with a Blue Cross IPA. Each subscriber elects a primary care physician and a primary hospital upon enrollment. Both hospital and physician are then paid a fixed sum per enrollee each month for providing all services to patients. The hospital's limited experience with this plan precludes prediction of its eventual impact. However, there are risk-sharing arrangements between primary care physician providers, the hospital, and specialist providers. As of August 1, 1985, 500 of the plan's 1,055 members chose Beverly Hospital as their primary hospital.

EXHIBIT 3 (Continued)

In 1984, the hospital entered into an agreement with a closed panel HMO sponsored by Blue Cross which operates a medical center located in Peabody, a five-minute drive from the hospital. The HMO has an enrollment of 3,602 as of August 11, 1985, and also has agreements with Salem Hospital and the two AtlantiCare Corporation hospitals to provide similar services.

In 1984, the hospital entered in an agreement with John Hancock Mutual Life Insurance Company to participate as a network hospital in John Hancock's SelectCare, a preferred provider organization (PPO) which began operations in the fall of 1984 and had an enrollment of approximately 20,000 members as of January 1, 1985.

EXHIBIT 4   **Beverly Hospital—Edited Notes to Financial Statements, Years Ended September 30, 1984 and 1983**

A.   Summary of Significant Accounting Policies: Investments

Investments are recorded at cost or quoted market on the date of the gift. Allowances are provided for permanent declines in value. Investment income and net gains and losses on security sales of unrestricted funds, as well as unrestricted investment income on endowment funds, are included in nonoperating revenue in the statements of revenues and expenses. Investment income on specific-purpose funds, restricted investment income on endowment funds, and the net gains and losses on security sales of specific-purpose funds and endowment funds are included in the statements of changes in fund balances of the restricted funds.

B.   Corporate Restructuring

Effective January 1983, the Beverly Hospital Corporation's Board of Trustees approved certain resolutions in connection with a corporate restructuring of the Hospital. The restructuring provided, among other things, the establishment of a new corporation, Northeast Health Systems, Inc., which will function as a parent holding company for Beverly Hospital Corporation and several other newly formed organizations. As part of the restructuring, the Hospital transferred $483,973 of unrestricted cash to Northeast Health Systems, Inc. during 1984. This transfer was accounted for as a reduction in unrestricted fund balance and is included in the statement of changes in fund balances.

18 Governmental Entities

GOVERNMENTS PLAY SIGNIFICANT, OFTEN DOMINANT, ROLES in the economies and societies of most countries. Known collectively as the *public sector*, governmental entities heavily influence health care, education, social services, transportation, trade, communication, finance, energy, and defense. They play multiple roles, directly providing some services and financing others through payments to businesses and private nonprofit organizations. They influence virtually every part of the society and economy through laws and regulations. They are unique in their power to make and enforce laws and to generate revenue by taxing citizens. These and other special characteristics of governments, and the related requirements for accountability to the citizens of countries with elected governmental representatives, pose unique and massive challenges to accounting and reporting for governments.

The difficulties of managing governments regularly make front page news in the U.S. In the early 1990s the federal deficit, the HUD scandal, tax caps, the savings and loan bailout, and state and city financial crises reflect the shortcomings, or outright failures, of existing governments. Governments around the world are in a state of transition. Most of the formerly communist countries of Eastern Europe are embracing capitalism. Managing governments effectively and efficiently is a massive and important undertaking.

Although governments are distinct from both businesses and private nonprofit organizations, they are included in this book because they share with private nonprofit organizations many objectives and accounting and management problems that U.S. businesses do not face. Also, government and nonprofit accounting were closely related until the 1980s, and both use fund accounting. Many nonprofit sectors contain a substantial number of organizations operated by or as governmental entities.

THE PUBLIC SECTOR

Most countries have multiple levels of government, and each level has certain structures, functions, and activities. All three levels of U.S. government directly provide goods or services, make transfer payments to individuals and other governments, and perform the basic governmental legislative, judicial, regulatory, oversight, and administrative functions. U.S. governmental organizations are accountable to the elected representatives charged with operating them and, ultimately, to the citizens.

U.S. Government Activities, Revenues, and Expenses

Governments are among the oldest forms of organizations, and the accounting records of ancient rulers are among the earliest known written records. Accountability of governments to their constituencies dates back to early Greek and Roman societies, as do many of the problems grappled with by today's citizens and government officials. However, the scope and magnitude of government activities, organizations, and problems are now much greater and more complex.

Citizens' rights to elect representatives and control governments are meaningless without adequate information on which to base choices. A public track record of important economic and other performance indicators is an integral part of the premise of public accountability on which the U.S. is founded. Good financial accounting and reporting contributes significantly to the effective and efficient operation of governments. Without it, the lack of accountability effectively denies citizens the control over government operations to which they are entitled.

In the U.S. hierarchy of a single federal, 50 state, and more than 80,000 local governmental units, each level performs the legislative, executive, and judicial functions of making and enforcing laws and collecting and expending resources to provide services. The scope of U.S. *general government* operations has grown like Topsy throughout the two centuries of its existence. It has expanded far beyond the initial focus on defense, foreign trade, and public safety to include education, transportation, sanitation, communication, health, income maintenance, finance, labor, welfare, housing, culture, and recreation. With government expenditures accounting for more than a third of its GNP, the U.S. clearly is not a purely capitalist economy.

Total U.S. government revenue in 1987 was $1.68 trillion and expenditures were $1.81 trillion. The difference represents deficit spending financed by borrowing. More than half of the revenue was federal (57 percent), a quarter was state (25 percent), and the remainder was local (19 percent), primarily from various sorts of taxes.[1] Of direct expenditures, 57 percent were federal, 17 percent were state, and 25 percent were local. The difference between state and local revenue and expenditures percentages reflects the large transfers from state to local governments. The 1987 total outstanding debt of $3 trillion is equal to nearly three years of general government revenue. Outstanding debt was $12,624 per capita: $9,672 federal and $2,953 state and local.

Although governments' activities vary among and within states, each level of government has several common functions and revenue sources. Variations in organization form and responsibilities make it difficult to compare the financial costs and performance of state and local governments and have important implications for financial reporting standards. The expenditures of a municipality that includes primary and secondary education in general government will not be directly comparable to one that uses a separate school district to provide these services.

Federal Government Since 1862, U.S. federal government financing has shifted from foreign sources through customs to domestic sources through income taxes. Until 1862, over 90 percent of U.S. federal government receipts were from customs, with the remainder primarily from sales of public lands. In 1863, Pandora's box was opened with internal revenue receipts of $37 million, or 33 percent of total receipts for that year. For the next five decades, customs made up less than 50 percent of federal receipts. Internal revenue receipts ballooned from $321 million (46 percent of total federal receipts) in 1912 to over $3 billion (87 percent) in 1918. Together with social insurance taxes, they have dominated federal receipts since then.

In 1989, over half of federal government revenue came from income taxes, 44 percent individual and 10 percent corporate. Reliance on these taxes had decreased from 47 percent and 12 percent, respectively, in 1980. Social insurance, essentially another form of income tax that is paid about equally by employees and employers, grew from 31 percent of federal receipts in 1980 to 37 percent in 1989. Simply stated, it has been politically easier to raise Social Security taxes than other types of income-based federal taxes. Essentially, 80 percent of federal revenue comes from taxes that are based on the amount of individual earnings, and another 10 percent from taxes based on corporate earnings. The remainder comes from excise taxes (4 percent), estate and gift taxes (1 percent), federal reserve deposits (2 percent), and customs duties (2 percent).

Initially, military defense was the primary, nearly exclusive, activity of the U.S. federal government, constituting over 90 percent of the federal

---

[1]U.S. Department of Commerce, Bureau of the Census, *110th Edition, Statistical Abstract of the United States, The 1990 National Data Book* (January 1990), p. 274, Table No. 456.

government outlays in the late 1700s. By the late 1800s, nondefense-related spending had risen to over a quarter of federal outlays in times of peace. Federal government outlays by function for *domestic* items are identified in detail only after 1940.[2]

In 1989, 29 percent of federal government outlays were for national defense and veterans benefits, up slightly as a percentage of outlays from 1980 to 1989. Income security, Social Security, and Medicare constituted about 40 percent, the same percentage of outlays in both 1980 and 1989. Other federal outlays—for international affairs, health (other than Medicare, which is included in Social Security), education, commerce, transportation, national resources, energy, community and regional development, agriculture, science, general government, fiscal assistance, and justice administration—each represent less than 4 percent of total federal outlays, and their percentage of the total has declined since 1980.[3]

Interest in 1988 is shown as 14.3 percent of total federal outlays in one table, but as 20.1 percent in another.[4] This significant difference illustrates the difficulty in using such data and the importance of ensuring consistency and comparability. Both do show that interest consumes an alarming 6 percent more of federal expenditures in 1989 than it did in 1980. Clearly, the only places to significantly affect the total federal budget are in the big three: defense, social security, and interest.

The advent of Medicare and Medicaid in the mid-1960s made the federal government a major player in health care financing. Popular sentiment in the early 1990s holds government responsible for improving the U.S. health care system. Governments provide virtually all health care in many western countries, and similar plans are intermittently proposed for the U.S. As discussed in Chapter 17, health care costs are among the fastest growing costs in the U.S. economy, and U.S. health care costs are among the highest in the developed countries as a percentage of GNP, without comparably better health for the U.S. population. AIDS, drug abuse, and an aging population are straining the U.S. health care system. Results to date bode ill for our ability to curb future cost growth.

Education expenditures decreased from 5.4 percent to 3.2 percent of federal outlays between 1980 and 1989. Although the magnitude is small relative to the total budget, since the 1960s the federal government has been an important source of tuition grants, research grants, and student loans for higher education. Widespread functional illiteracy has recently led to recognition of a national primary and secondary education crisis. Although increased

[2]U.S. Department of Commerce, Bureau of the Census, *Historical Statistics of the United States, Colonial Times to 1970, Bicentennial Edition, Part 2* (Washington, DC: 1975), pp. 1114-1116, Series Y 457-471.
[3]Bureau of the Census, *110th Edition, Statistical Abstract*, pp. 310-311, Table No. 499.
[4]Ibid., pp. 310-311, Table No. 499, and p. 309, Table No. 497.

federal spending is a common response to such crises, business involvement, volunteerism, and voucher payment systems are among the alternatives being applied to primary and secondary education.

The federal government provides a significant amount of *subsidies* or *transfer payments* to state and local governments. Federal aid to state and local governments more than quadrupled, from $24 billion in 1970 to $115 in 1988. Federal aid for education, employment, training, and social services grew more slowly than other types of aid, dropping from 27 percent of federal aid in 1970 to only 17 percent in 1988. By far the largest growth was in health, which jumped from 16 percent to 28 percent in the same time period. Income security, another large component, grew only slightly in relative emphasis, from 24 percent to 27 percent of total federal aid. Aid for transportation also dropped slightly from 19 percent of 1970 aid to 16 percent of 1988 aid. These four largest categories accounted for 88 percent of all federal aid to state and local governments in 1988.[5]

The federal government is the single largest employer in the U.S., with more than 3.1 million civilian employees in 1988. Over 1 million (34 percent) are in the defense department, and another 0.8 million (27 percent) are employed by the U.S. Postal Service. The next largest agency is Veterans Affairs, with 0.2 million (8 percent), and all the other agencies are considerably smaller.

State Government State revenue is reasonably well diversified over sales and income taxes, intergovernmental transfers, charges, and insurance trust revenue. In 1987, taxes made up 45 percent of state revenues, 22 percent from sales and gross receipts taxes and 14 percent from individual income taxes. Intergovernmental revenue, primarily from the federal government, made up 19 percent of state revenue in 1987, down from 22 percent in 1980. Insurance trust revenue was 16.6 percent and charges and miscellaneous were 12.7 percent of 1987 state revenue.

In addition to performing state legislative, executive, judicial, regulatory, and police functions, most state governments finance and operate higher education, highway, public welfare, hospital, correction, natural resource, liquor control, economic development, and unemployment compensation systems. State expenditures have more than doubled fairly consistently every ten years since 1902.[6] About a third of state expenditures are *intergovernmental* transfers to local governments, primarily for education, highways, and public welfare.

Total state expenditures grew by 80 percent between 1980 and 1987, from $263 to $476 billion. State expenditures per capita grew by 68 percent over that period. Both total and per capita outstanding state debt more than

---

[5]Ibid., p. 276, Table No. 460.
[6]Bureau of the Census, *Historical Statistics*, pp. 1130-1131, Series Y 736-782.

doubled, indicating that part of the expenditure growth was financed by borrowing. Outstanding state debt in 1987 was $1,094 per capita.[7]

State university systems enroll the majority of the students in U.S. higher education institutions. States also provide significant amounts of financing to local governments for primary and secondary education. Education accounted for 31.5 percent of state direct and indirect expenditures in 1987, down slightly from 33 percent in 1980. Public welfare, the next largest expenditure, was slightly under 17 percent in both 1987 and 1980. Highway expenditures dropped from 9.5 percent in 1980 to 8.0 percent in 1987. This decrease may be appropriate if it reflects completion of the state highway system. However, if it reflects inadequate highway maintenance, it may signal impending trouble. Corrections grew from 1.7 percent to 2.5 percent of state expenditures, yet jails remain overcrowded and undermaintained.

From 1946 to 1970, total state employment more than tripled, from 0.8 to 2.8 million employees.[8] By 1987 it had grown to 4.1 million, higher than federal civilian employment and a 49 percent increase over 1970 levels.[9] State government employment grew faster than either federal or local government employment between 1970 and 1987.

Local Governments   Local governments are classified as either *county*, *municipal*, *township* (including towns), or *special district*. Each county typically contains several municipalities or towns, although there are some combined county and township governments. A special district provides a certain type of service, such as water or education, and usually serves the residents of several other local government units. For example, a water district may serve several counties and the cities and towns within them.

The number of local governments decreased by about half between 1942 and 1972, from 155,116 to 78,269 governmental units.[10] The number of county, municipal, town, and township governments during this period were relatively stable, with a slight growth in municipal governments being offset by a comparable decline in the number of town and township forms. However, the number of school districts shrank drastically, from 108,579 to 15,781, while the number of other types of special districts grew from 8,299 to 23,885. Between 1972 and 1987, the total number of local governments grew to 83,186, primarily due to continued growth in the number of special districts.

County, municipal, and township governments perform local legislative, executive, and judicial activities, referred to as *governmental administration*. They also perform many other activities, such as primary and secondary

[7]Bureau of the Census, *110th Edition, Statistical Abstract*, p. 284, Table No. 468.
[8]Bureau of the Census, *Historical Statistics*, p. 1100, Series Y 272-289.
[9]Bureau of the Census, *110th Edition, Statistical Abstract*, p. 300, Table No. 488.
[10]Ibid., p. 272, Table No. 454.

education, public safety (police and fire), public works (streets, sewers, and sanitation), public welfare, public transportation, airports, utilities (water and power), colleges, hospitals, corrections, community development, and parks and recreation facilities.

These activities may be performed directly by a local general government unit as part of the general government operations or by a self-supporting enterprise fund. Alternatively, they may be subcontracted to independent nonprofit or for-profit organizations or carried out by separate special districts. In some cases, they may be financed and operated by the private sector, subject only to government regulation. The distinction depends on the legal structure and organization choices of the individual unit, which may also be dictated or constrained by state law. Local governments operate many of the community hospitals and colleges that serve their citizens.

Intergovernmental revenues are the largest source of revenue (33 percent) for local governments, followed by property taxes (25 percent), charges for various services (12 percent), and utility revenues (9 percent).

Local governments provide most primary and secondary education, which constituted 34 percent of total 1987 local government expenditures. Much of it is financed by intergovernmental revenues from the states.[11] Utilities were the next largest at 13 percent, interest on general debt followed at 7 percent, and the remainder was spread fairly evenly among the other functions.

From 1946 to 1970, local government employment nearly tripled, from 2.8 to 7.4 million employees.[12] By 1987, it had grown to 10 million, a 36 percent increase over 1970 levels and more than both state and federal civilian employment combined.[13]

Government Debt

Throughout most of U.S. history, federal government borrowing skyrocketed to finance deficit spending during wars, financial victories in the form of federal government surpluses followed military victories, and debts were repaid. Until 1930, the federal government ran a surplus in most years; since 1931, there has been a deficit in all except a very few years.[14] The federal debt was $2.85 per capita in 1851, dropped to $0.93 by 1857, grew to $75.42 by 1866, and declined gradually but consistently to $11.85 in 1915.[15] Citizens trusted elected officials to borrow large amounts and repay them

---

[11]Ibid., p. 274, Table No. 456.
[12]Bureau of the Census, *Historical Statistics*, p. 1100, Series Y 272-289.
[13]Bureau of the Census, *110th Edition, Statistical Abstract*, p. 300, Table No. 488.
[14]Bureau of the Census, *Historical Statistics*, pp. 1104-1105, Series Y 335-342; and *110th Edition, Statistical Abstract*, p. 309, Table No. 497.
[15]Bureau of the Census, *Historical Statistics*, pp. 1117-1118, Series Y 493-504.

as soon as the military threat was repelled. Elected representatives earned that trust with responsible fiscal management.

Since the 1930s, debt increases have been fueled by domestic as well as military spending, and the growth has been inexorable. In 1988, outstanding federal public debt was $10,556 per capita, nearly 1,000 times its 1915 level, and was 54.4 percent of the GNP. Interest on the federal debt grew alarmingly during the 1980s, from around the fairly stable 10 percent of the GNP that it had constituted since the 1950s to 20 percent of the 1988 GNP.[16] The most alarming aspect of the rapid and continuous growth in annual deficits, outstanding debt, and related interest in the 1980s is that it occurred during a time of peace. This is not emergency borrowing that the citizenry will rally to repay. It is a long-term, serious blight on the U.S. financial infrastructure, a cost that taxpayers are reluctant to bear. The U.S. is unable even to stem the annual deficit growth rate; reducing the outstanding federal debt level seems impossible. This is a new problem, unique in U.S. history, and, so far, unsolvable.

Federal debt outstanding remained below $1.3 billion until 1916. It jumped to $25 billion in 1919, and was reduced to $16 billion in 1930.[17] Since then it climbed in all but a very few years to $914 billion in 1980. The 1980s saw the fastest debt growth ever in the U.S. during peacetime. In 1987, the debt outstanding was $2.4 trillion, nearly $10,000 per capita.[18]

Most state and local government fixed assets are financed by selling short- or long-term *municipal bonds* (*munis*). The bond interest and principal payment schedule is usually linked to asset life, distributing the burden of costs across the future beneficiaries of the assets through taxes. *General obligation* (*GO*) *bonds* are backed by the *full faith and credit* of the issuer, its taxing power. *Revenue bonds* are not backed by the general tax base of the borrower, but are secured by a specific revenue stream. Revenue bonds are typically used for utilities, hospitals, sewage lines, and other such projects that generate revenues by assessments on the beneficiaries or fees for services rendered to users. This is considered to be more equitable than having all taxpayers pay for them, and may circumvent legal GO debt limits of the governmental entity.

Bond anticipation notes (*BANs*) are short-term debt instruments issued in advance of bonds. They are often used to avoid making long-term commitments when interest rates are unusually high, and are replaced with long-term bonds when interest rates drop. Government use of short-term debt to finance working capital has also increased. *Tax anticipation notes* (*TANs*) and *revenue anticipation notes* (*RANs*) are repaid when the tax or other revenue is received.

---

[16]Bureau of the Census, *110th Edition, Statistical Abstract*, p. 309, Table No. 497.
[17]Bureau of the Census, *Historical Statistics*, pp. 1104-1105, Series Y 335-338.
[18]Bureau of the Census, *110th Edition, Statistical Abstract*, p. 273, Table No. 455.

Government debt instruments constitute a significant part of the debt markets. Because the interest on municipal debt is exempt from federal income tax, individual investors in high income tax brackets accept lower yields than they would demand from taxable bonds. Municipal bonds are less interesting investments to tax-exempt institutional investors, such as endowment and pension funds.

A wave of heavy municipal borrowing in the 1820s and 1830s ended when the 1837 depression caused nine states and one territory to default; four of the states repudiated some of their debt. The next heavy wave of borrowing occurred during the Civil War, and the weak postwar economy again led to substantial default and repudiation.[19] The economic depression of the 1930s had similar effects. In 1934, the cost of municipal debt exceeded the cost of corporate bonds, and by 1935, 3,251 municipal bonds were in default.[20]

The municipal market picked up in the 1940s and remained calm until the 1960s when volume rose to $70 billion. That level of borrowing was tripled by the late 1970s. There were few defaults during this period, and all but three defaults were revenue bonds.[21] This stability was interrupted in 1975, when the New York Urban Development Corporation (UDC) was unable to pay a $100 million short-term note to the Chase Manhattan Bank. While not directly liable to make up the default, the state of New York had given its *moral obligation* pledge on the notes. New York State's moral obligation long-term debt totaled about $6 billion at this time, including $1.1 billion UDC long-term debt, and its finances and the value of its pledge became questionable. The default and resulting uncertainty caused apprehension among some potential purchasers of other New York bonds[22] and caused some governmental organizations to be crowded out of the market or to incur higher interest costs. One expert estimated that New York City's default added from 30 to 60 basis points (a basis point is 0.01 percent) to the interest cost of other large municipal borrowings.[23]

New York City's collapse had been brought on by an unsustainable increase in its short-term debt from $747 million to $4.5 billion in six years. The New York State Charter Revision Commission attributed this increase to

> ... the City's refusal to soundly finance its expense budget. Since 1970-71, every expense budget has been balanced with an array of gimmicks—revenue accruals, capitalization of expenses, raiding reserves, appropriation of illusory

[19]B. U. Ratchford, *American State Debts* (Durham, NC: Duke University Press, 1941), pp. 191-196.
[20]A. M. Hillhouse, *Municipal Bonds: A Century of Experience* (New York, NY: Prentice-Hall, 1936), pp. 17-21.
[21]Lennox Moak and Albert Hillhouse, *Local Government Finance* (Chicago, IL: Municipal Finance Officers Association, 1978), p. 273.
[22]John H. Winders, "The Editor's Corner," *The Weekly Bond Buyer* (February 18, 1975): 1, 4.
[23]David L. Hoffland, "The New York City Effect in the Municipal Bond Market," *Financial Analysts Journal* (March/April 1977): 36-39.

fund balances, suspension of payments, carry-forward of deficits and questionable receivables and finally, the creation of a public benefit corporation whose purpose is to borrow funds to bail out the expense budget.

For example, as much as $408 million of the City's $500 million of real estate tax receivables were subsequently estimated to be uncollectible. The problems of New York City and state were soon echoed by a number of other state and local governments, leading to grave concerns about the municipal market. The close correlation between bond ratings and interest expense caused concern that political pressures on bond rating agencies could have an undesirable influence on the municipal market.[24]

Prior to the New York City crisis of 1975, government debt was widely treated as virtually risk free. Since that disruptive event, government debt issues have been subjected to much closer scrutiny. Since 1975, new municipal financing techniques and intricately structured borrowing instruments have flourished. Municipal bond analysis has kept pace by becoming increasingly sophisticated. Use of revenue bonds has grown rapidly; they constituted two-thirds of the bonds issued in 1987, up from about half in 1976. The use of short-term notes has also increased, as has third-party financial support, such as bond insurance and letters of credit. The development of municipal bond mutual funds has made municipal debt ownership even more attractive to individuals.

State government debt grew from $230 million in 1902 to $42 billion outstanding in 1970.[25] By 1987, it was $266 billion.[26] With the exception of the late 1930s and early 1940s, state debt grew continuously throughout the century. Local government debt also grew fairly consistently, but more slowly than state debt, from $1.9 billion in 1902 to $102 billion outstanding in 1970.[27] By 1987, it was $453 billion,[28] still about double the state debt level. In 1987, combined state and local debt per capita was $2,953. In 1988, $103.8 billion of municipal bonds were issued.[29]

Data Sources

Many data on financial and economic statistics for governments are readily available. The U.S. Bureau of the Census provides a wealth of current and historical information about the governments and other aspects of the U.S. economy and society.[30]

---

[24]John E. Petersen, *The Rating Game* (New York, NY: Twientieth Century Fund, 1974).
[25]Bureau of the Census, *Historical Statistics*, p. 1130, Series Y 736-782.
[26]Bureau of the Census, *110th Edition, Statistical Abstract*, p. 273, Table No. 455.
[27]Bureau of the Census, *Historical Statistics*, p. 1132, Series Y 783-795.
[28]Bureau of the Census, *110th Edition, Statistical Abstract*, p. 273, Table No. 455.
[29]Standard and Poor's Corporation, *S&P's Municipal Finance Criteria* (New York, NY: Standard and Poor's Corporation, 1989), p. 19.
[30]Bureau of the Census, *Historical Statistics* and *110th Edition, Statistical Abstract*.

Two major debt rating agencies, Moody's Investors Service (Moody's) and Standard & Poor's Corporation (S&P), publish data on state and local government performance and debt. Moody's *Selected Indicators of Municipal Performance* (*Moody's Medians*), published annually, includes debt-related per capita statistics for the 50 states, and for cities, counties, school districts, and several types of enterprises.[31] S&P also publishes ratios periodically in *CreditWeek*.

The Government Finance Officers Association (GFOA) is developing a municipal financial database that will provide additional external benchmarks to which municipalities can compare themselves. International City Managers Association (ICMA), the professional and educational association of appointed administrators in local governments in the U.S. and other countries, also provides information on city performance.

Opportunities and Challenges

There are federal and state government offices in virtually every county in the country. The managerial challenge of controlling such a large, complex, dispersed organization is substantial. The now well-worn statement, "A billion here, a billion there—pretty soon you're talking about real money,"[32] reflects the magnitude of federal fiscal management. The separation of executive, legislative, and judicial functions and the fact that many important players are elected officials further complicates the management task.

All levels of government face significant challenges. Exacerbated by recession, savings and loan failures, and U.S. involvement in the 1991 Middle East war, the federal deficit in the 1990s threatens the U.S. economy. Since the 1970s, taxpayers in several states have voted to limit state and local government spending by enacting *tax caps* that force administrators to decide how to maintain services with less resources or to decide which services to cut. After a decade of growth dubbed the Massachusetts miracle, a drastic economic and financial reversal plunged that state's bond rating to the lowest in the country in the spring of 1990. Bridgeport, Connecticut, and Philadelphia, Pennsylvania, joined the list of urban crises begun spectacularly by New York City in the 1970s. Perhaps most importantly, public faith in the ability of elected, appointed, and hired government officials to manage our governments well and honestly is badly shaken.

The distinctions between the roles and responsibilities of government, businesses, and private nonprofit organizations are changing and blurring, and each sector is increasingly dependent on the actions or inactions of the others. Businesses are voluntarily grappling with improving the educational systems to ensure that they will have a sufficiently well trained labor force

[31]Moody's Investors Service, *1990 Medians, Selected Indicators of Municipal Performance* (New York, NY: Moody's Investors Service, 1990).

[32]Senator Everett Dirksen, as quoted in *The Great Business Quotations*, comp. Rolf B. White (Lyle Stuart, Inc., 1986), p. 69.

in the future. Both long-time capitalist and erstwhile communist countries are turning to privatization.

Businesses are being required to bear more of the cost of limiting or cleaning up pollution. These costs were previously borne by others or accumulated a large environmental debt that many believe is due for immediate payment. The effectiveness of government regulation and the ability of an inherently slow moving and unwieldy government bureaucracy to adapt to today's constantly and rapidly changing environment are questionable. The challenge is to design and establish an appropriate mix of roles and relationships among the government, business, and private nonprofit sectors to preserve the public due process fundamental to democratic governments and provide the flexibility and innovativeness to solve difficult problems in a rapidly changing environment.

The traditional value trade-offs between guns and butter (defense and social services) still must be made. The various constituencies in the U.S. melting pot have diverse opinions on what goals should be pursued. And in the rare case when there is general agreement on a goal, such as the current need to improve primary education, there are violent disagreements about the best way to accomplish it. Managing governments to achieve their goals is more difficult than ever before. Financial reporting should be reliable, should allow comparisons to be made among government units and between government plans and actual performance, and should help elected officials, managers, and citizens to determine whether government is working well.

STATE AND LOCAL GOVERNMENT FINANCIAL REPORTING STANDARDS

In terms of accounting and financial reporting, governments differ even more from business than do private nonprofit organizations. Creation of the Governmental Accounting Standards Board (GASB) in 1984 significantly increased the attention that the accounting profession and other interested parties devoted to governmental accounting and facilitated the divergence of governmental from nongovernmental accounting. The GASB standards apply only to state and local governments. Separate federal government reporting standards, which are set by federal agencies and are not subject to either GASB or FASB jurisdiction, are discussed in a later section. Illustrative government financial statements from the GASB codification[33] are shown in Exhibit A.

---

[33]Governmental Accounting Standards Board, *Codification of Governmental Accounting and Financial Reporting Standards*, as of May 31, 1990, 3d ed. (Norwalk, CT: GASB, 1990), pp. 151-171, 210-216.

Evolution of Governmental Accounting Standards

Accountants have consistently reacted to periodic government financial crises with academic and technical critiques and a blizzard of recommendations for governmental accounting. The New York City fiscal crisis associated with the corrupt government officials in the "Tweed Ring" in 1871 sparked a flurry of interest in accounting and accountability for local government. In the early twentieth century, publication of the document known as the *Metz Fund Handbook* established the first municipal accounting principles.[34] The financial crises of state and local governments during the depression of the 1930s led to another round of efforts, including formation of the National Committee on Municipal Accounting in 1934 by the Municipal Finance Officers Association (MFOA). Its publications came to be accepted as standards for local government accounting and financial reporting.

Having been renamed the National Committee on Governmental Accounting (NCGA) to reflect its interest in state as well as municipal accounting, in 1951 the committee consolidated its standards in one publication, *Municipal Accounting and Auditing*.[35] In 1968, this publication was succeeded by *Governmental Accounting, Auditing, and Financial Reporting* (GAAFR 68), which then constituted governmental accounting and financial reporting standards.[36] In 1973, MFOA replaced the temporary committee with an ongoing body called the National Council on Governmental Accounting (still NCGA), which issued authoritative statements until the formation of the GASB in 1984.

In 1974, the AICPA issued *Audits of State and Local Governmental Units*, which provided auditing standards, sample audit opinions, and some additional guidance on financial reporting standards and presentation.[37] It recognized as authoritative the standards established by the NCGA in GAAFR 68, except as modified by the audit guide.

Task forces, new organizations (such as New York City's Municipal Assistance Corporation), accountants, and consultants blossomed forth on the shell-shocked landscape that followed the mid-1970s municipal financial crises of Cleveland, New York City, and numerous smaller governmental units. In its wake, Brenton Harries, president of Standard and Poor's, commented:

> The City did disclose to us and did publish a great deal of information. It wasn't the volume of information disclosed but that people didn't read it. . . . For the most part, the facts were there to be known, to be seen, and to be read. . . . the

[34]Bureau of Municipal Research Metz Fund, *Handbook of Municipal Accounting* (New York, NY: D. Appleton and Company, 1913).

[35]National Council on Governmental Accounting, *Municipal Accounting and Auditing* (Chicago, IL: Municipal Finance Officers Association, 1951).

[36]National Council on Governmental Accounting, *Governmental Accounting, Auditing, and Financial Reporting* (Chicago, IL: Municipal Finance Officers Association, 1968).

[37]American Institute of Certified Public Accountants, Committee on Governmental Accounting and Auditing, *Audits of State and Local Governmental Units* (New York, NY: AICPA, 1974).

City's current prospectus . . . is over 600 pages long. I defy you to find me a hundred people who buy New York City's securities who would read it. The problem of disclosure today is now terribly, terribly serious.[38]

His observations were echoed by many others who felt that governmental accounting should become more businesslike. One publication recommended that state and local governments adopt reporting on a consolidated basis and produce a Balance Sheet for restricted and unrestricted funds, a Statement of Changes in Financial Position, and a Statement of Changes in Municipal Equity.[39] These recommendations differed from GAAFR by consolidating the funds into restricted and unrestricted, reporting a total all funds column, and excluding the traditional governmental budgetary reporting. Others proposed to leave the fund format intact but to remedy major deficiencies in governmental accounting for the billions of dollars in governmental pension obligations, debt instruments, and overlapping debt.

Suggestions to adopt businesslike accounting for governments did not win out, as many recognized the importance of financial reporting standards that met the special needs of governmental financial statement users. Although governmental accounting is an integral part of accounting and shares many basic concepts and conventions with business accounting, it exists in a sufficiently different environment to require its own accounting standards. In 1984, the NCGA was disbanded and the Governmental Accounting Standards Board (GASB) was established to set accounting standards for state and local governments. The first GASB statement recognized the existing effective NCGA pronouncements and the AICPA audit guide as authoritative until superseded by explicit GASB pronouncements. The GASB Codification, as it is known, now provides authoritative standards for state and local government financial reporting.[40] The revised *Audits of State and Local Governmental Units*, published by the AICPA in 1989, provides additional guidance on financial reporting and auditing standards.[41]

Renamed in 1984, the Government Finance Officers Association (GFOA, previously MFOA) remains the leading industry organization providing significant research, education, and technical direction for accounting and financial reporting by state and local governmental units. Its latest *Governmental Accounting, Auditing and Financial Reporting (GAAFR '88)* is consistent with and elaborates on the GASB Codification and AICPA state and local audit

---

[38]Brenton W. Harries, "Some Recent Trends in Municipal and Corporate Securities Markets," in an interview by John J. Clark, *Financial Management* (Spring 1976): 12.

[39]S. Davidson, D. Green, W. Hellerstein, A. Madansky, and R. Weil, *Financial Reporting by State and Local Government Units* (Chicago, IL: The Center for Management of Public and Nonprofit Enterprise, University of Chicago, 1977).

[40]GASB, *Codification*.

[41]American Institute of Certified Public Accountants, State and Local Government Committee, *Audits of State and Local Governmental Units* (New York, NY: AICPA, 1989).

guide, as they existed when it was published.[42] Since 1945, it has annually awarded certificates (currently called *Certificates of Achievement for Excellence in Financial Reporting*) to governments whose published financial statements meet governmental financial reporting standards.

The current hierarchy of GAAP for U.S. state and local governments begins with GASB, followed by FASB, pronouncements of other bodies composed of expert accountants, widely recognized practices, and other accounting literature, in that order. A proposed hierarchy would lower to the status of other accounting literature any standards not explicitly made applicable to state and local governments by a GASB pronouncement.[43] The test of its force may come with the FASB requirement that all private nonprofit organizations record and depreciate fixed assets, whereas similar government-operated organizations are not required to do so.

Historically, government financial reporting was determined by state governments and varied widely among them. Because state laws governing debt limits and financial reporting requirements continue in force, supplemental schedules are frequently presented to reconcile GAAP-based and legal-based statements. An AICPA study documenting the various types of disclosure used in governmental unit single-audit reports provides useful guidance for government accounts, auditors, and audit committees.[44] An historical perspective can be gained by comparing current disclosure practices to those observed in earlier studies.[45]

Objectives of Governmental Financial Reporting

GASB Concepts Statement 1 establishes objectives and provides a framework within which the GASB develops financial reporting standards for governmental entities. It broadly describes the governmental environment and the nature of the information needed by users of external governmental financial reports. This section draws heavily from it.

Financial reporting encompasses all reports that contain information generally found in financial statements. It is intended to help fulfill governments' duty to be *publicly accountable*, to provide needed information to the many users who rely on these reports because they have limited authority, ability, or resources to obtain information by other means. *Financial statements* form the core of financial reporting and the principal means of communicating financial information to external users.

---

[42]Government Finance Officers Association, *Governmental Accounting, Auditing, and Financial Reporting* (Chicago, IL: GFOA, 1988).

[43]GASB, *Codification*, p. xiv.

[44]American Institute of Certified Public Accounts, *Local Governmental Accounting Trends & Techniques*, 3d ed., ed. Susan Cornwall (New York, NY: AICPA, 1990).

[45]Cornelius E. Tierney and Philip T. Calder, *Governmental Accounting Procedures and Practices* (New York, NY: Elsevier Science Publishing Co., Inc., 1983 and 1985).

General purpose external financial reporting includes both the detailed and often voluminous *comprehensive annual financial reports* (*CAFR*) and more condensed *popular reports*. Both usually contain financial statements, or data extracted from them, and a wide variety of nonfinancial data. The CAFR must contain the *general purpose financial statements* (*GPFS*), which may also be published separately. *Special purpose* financial reporting satisfies the needs of specific users who have the legal authority or other ability to require governments to issue reports that meet legal or contractual requirements, are prepared on a basis different from GAAP, use prescribed formats, or report on specified elements, accounts, or items. The GASB can establish standards for nonfinancial statistical data it considers important in fulfilling governmental accountability although standards set to date have focused on financial data.

Businesses, private nonprofit organizations, and governments are all accountable to various constituencies for their financial position and performance, but the legal structure and relationship of each type of organization to its constituencies are very different. The primary business constituents are voluntary investors or creditors in a market where alternative investments exist. Private nonprofit organizations are accountable primarily to donors and regulators.

Citizens are the ultimate government constituents, and financial reporting must enable them to assess whether the government has met their needs. They are involuntary resource providers, lacking the choice of whether to pay taxes. There is not an exchange relationship between the resources a citizen provides and the services received, and the amount of taxes paid seldom bears a proportional relationship to the cost or value of the services a taxpayer receives. Government-provided services are often monopolistic and at least partially public goods, making it very difficult to determine optimal quantity, quality, or pricing. These measurement problems are compounded by the lack of a market mechanism and by involuntary resource provision through taxation. Public accountability should allow users to evaluate performance through a variety of measures because there is no adequate single overall performance measure.

The separation of powers among the legislative, executive, and judicial branches of government, designed to provide checks and balances that prevent the abuse of power by any branch, requires accountability relationships among the branches. The substantial intergovernmental resource flows among the federal, state, and local levels of government also require the government that receives resources to be accountable to those that provide them.

In contrast to the business goal of maximizing investor wealth, the primary goal of government is to promote the general welfare of its citizens. Governments try to balance limited available resources with virtually unlimited demands for services. Short-term horizons of elected representatives can lead to such practices as satisfying the needs of some constituents while deferring others; paying for increased service levels with nonrecurring revenue; and deferring the cash effects of current period events (for example, by conceding future pension benefits in lieu of present wage increases in labor negotiations).

These structural, political, and legal aspects of governments have led budgetary and fund accounting control mechanisms to assume special importance. Typically, an annual government operating budget is proposed by the executive branch and modified during budget negotiations between the legislative and executive branches. The modified budget, formally approved by the legislature, constitutes the legal *appropriation* of the amounts the executive branch can spend for each purpose. The executive branch is responsible and accountable to the legislative branch, and both are responsible and accountable to the citizenry.

Governmental budgets are an expression of both *public policy* and *financial intent*. The legislative branch can pass laws that embody their policies, but resources are needed to carry them out. The budget provides or denies resources, formally expressing the entity's objectives and priorities and how financial resources will be provided to meet them. As a form of control, the governmental budget has the force of law, both authorizing and limiting the amounts that may be spent for particular purposes.

The budget also provides another form of control, a benchmark for evaluating performance. Comparing actual results to the legally adopted budget helps users assess whether resources were obtained and expended as anticipated. Legal requirements can cause the budget to be prepared on an accounting basis different from GAAP. If this occurs, the entity needs to maintain only one accounting system, usually on the legal budgetary basis, that includes the additional information needed to prepare financial statements in conformity with GAAP at year end. Fund accounting is also commonly used by governments for control purposes, to reflect financial and legal requirements and restrictions, and to ensure that resources are used only in compliance with those limitations. Funds may be created by law (local ordinance), covenant (bond indentures), or management decision.

Because of these characteristics, NCGA Statement 1, "Governmental Accounting and Financial Reporting Principles," states that:

> A governmental accounting system must make it possible both: (a) to present fairly and with full disclosure the financial position and results of financial operations of the funds and account groups of the governmental unit in conformity with generally accepted accounting principles, and (b) to determine and demonstrate compliance with finance-related legal and contractual provisions.
>
> Generally accepted accounting principles (GAAP) are uniform minimum standards of and guidelines to financial accounting and reporting[46]

[46]NCGA Statement 1, "Governmental Accounting and Financial Reporting Principles," *GASB Codification*, p. 39, paragraphs 2-3.

Legal compliance reporting is deemed essential:

> Where financial statements prepared in conformity with GAAP do not demonstrate finance-related legal and contractual compliance, the governmental unit should present such additional schedules and narrative explanations in the comprehensive annual financial report as may be necessary to report its legal compliance responsibilities and accountabilities. . . . In extreme cases, preparation of a separate legal-based special report may be necessary.[47]

Governmental accounting thus fulfills not only the traditional financial decision-making role but also enables assurance of compliance with finance-related legal provisions. This requires that governmental accounting terminology, fund structure, and procedures incorporate finance-related legal requirements.

An important objective of governmental financial reporting is to reflect the *interperiod equity*, or resource flows among current and past or future periods. GASB uses this term despite the prevalence of the term *intergenerational equity* because of the length of a generation and because, it claims, "intergenerational equity has implications that go beyond financial reporting."[GASB Concepts Statement 1, PR 60]

Reporting Entity

Under current standards, effective for periods beginning after December 15, 1992, *financial accountability* is the primary determinant of the reporting entity. A governmental *financial reporting entity* consists of ". . . (a) the *primary government*, (b) organizations for which the primary government is financially accountable, and (c) other organizations for which the nature and significance of their relationship with the primary government are such that exclusion would cause the reporting entity's financial statements to be misleading or incomplete."[48] The new standards clarify how to determine the reporting entity and the appropriate form and content of disclosures.

In addition to the organizations that make up its legal entity, a primary government is also financially accountable for legally separate organizations that it closely controls or with which it has close financial relationships. The first consideration is whether primary government officials appoint a voting majority of the separate organization's governing body. If so, the separate organization is included in the financial reporting entity if the primary government can impose its will on the separate organization or the separate organization has the potential to provide financial benefits to or impose financial burdens on the primary government.

[47]Ibid., p. 42, paragraph 12.
[48]Governmental Accounting Standards Board, *Statement No. 14 of the Governmental Accounting Standards Board*, "The Financial Reporting Entity" (Norwalk, CT: GASB, June 1991), p. 4.

Most *component units* of the reporting entity should be included by *discrete presentation*, reporting data in a column separate from the primary government. *Blending*, which reports the component unit as part of the primary government, is used only when the operations of a legally separate component unit are so closely intertwined that they are essentially part of the primary government.

The Notes to the financial statements should distinguish information related to the primary government from that related to discretely presented component units. The Notes should also describe the relationship between component units and the primary government, and provide information on how to obtain the separate financial statements of individual component units. Relationships with organizations other than component units should also be disclosed.

Fund Types and Account Groups

Governments are required to use fund accounting systems. A *fund* is defined as

> a fiscal and accounting entity with a self-balancing set of accounts recording cash and other financial resources, together with all related liabilities and residual equities or balances, and changes therein, which are segregated for the purpose of carrying on specific activities or attaining certain objectives in accordance with special regulation, restrictions or limitations.[49]

There are seven types of funds plus two fund-like entities called *account groups*. A government should use as many funds as required by law and sound financial administration, but no more than the minimum number required to meet those needs. Funds are classified as *governmental*, *proprietary*, or *fiduciary*.

Many major government capital projects, such as sidewalks or sewer systems, are financed by separate appropriations, taxes, or *special assessments* that are levied against the individual property owners who will benefit from the project and are restricted for the purpose of financing that project. Prior standards used a separate *special assessment fund* to account for such construction projects and resources. However, GASB Statement 6 eliminated their use and requires such projects to be accounted for in the appropriate general, special revenue, agency, or enterprise fund, as determined by the physical and legal nature of the project and its financing.

Governmental Funds There are four types of governmental funds. As in nonprofit organizations, the *general fund* accounts for all financial resources except those required to be accounted for in another fund. Like restricted

[49]GASB, *Codification*, p. 33, Section 1100.101.

operating funds, *special revenue funds* account for the proceeds of revenue sources that are restricted to expenditures for specific purposes other than expendable trusts or resources for major capital projects. *Capital projects funds* account for financial resources to be used for acquiring or constructing major capital facilities, other than those financed by proprietary and fiduciary funds. *Debt service funds* account for the accumulation of resources for and the payment of general long-term debt principal and interest. The latter two fund types account for items that are included in the plant fund in most private nonprofit organizations.

Proprietary Funds   Proprietary funds account for activities that are intended to be operated like a business. They must follow the financial reporting standards of business entities engaged in similar operations.

Enterprise funds account for operations of entities that provide goods and services directly to outside parties and are intended to be self-supporting, such as most airports and utilities. The costs (expenses, including depreciation) of providing goods or services to the general public on a continuing basis are intended to be recovered primarily through user charges. The use of enterprise funds helps to distinguish general government operations that are intended to be supported by taxes from activities that are intended to be self-supported by service fees and sales. An enterprise fund may also be used to account for any activity for which the governing body decides that periodic determination of revenues earned, expenses incurred, and/or net income is appropriate for capital maintenance, public policy, management control, accountability, or other purposes.

Internal service funds account for operations that provide goods or services to other parts of the governmental organization, usually on a cost reimbursement basis. Vehicle maintenance, purchasing functions, and information systems services are examples of activities that are often provided by internal service funds.

Fiduciary Funds   *Fiduciary (trust and agency) funds* account for assets held by a governmental unit in a trustee capacity or as an agent for individuals, private organizations, other governmental units, or other funds. They include *expendable trust funds*, *nonexpendable trust funds*, *pension trust funds*, and *agency funds*. These funds are equivalent to the endowment and trust and agency funds used by other types of nonprofits.

Fixed Asset and Long-Term Debt Account Groups   Fixed asset purchases and debt payments of both principal and interest are reported as current period governmental fund expenditures. Prior standards did not require the fixed assets or the long-term debt payable in future periods to be reported because they did not affect current period operations. General fixed assets and long-term debt must now be reported in separate account groups, rather than in funds. This distinction preserves the fund focus on current operations.

In addition to the usual types of fixed assets (land, buildings, equipment, furniture, and fixtures) used in operations, governments typically own large amounts of relatively long-lived *public domain* or *infrastructure* assets that are immovable and of value only to the governmental unit. These include items such as bridges, roads, sidewalks, and drainage and lighting systems.

The general government fixed assets and long-term debt must be clearly distinguished from those of proprietary or trust funds. Fixed assets, depreciation, and long-term debt must be reported in the proprietary and trust funds that measure the expenses, net income, or capital maintenance. All other general fixed assets and long-term debt are to be reported in the two account groups, the *General Fixed Assets Account Group* (*GFAAG*) and the *General Long-Term Debt Account Group* (*GLTDAG*). Fixed asset accounts in GFAAG and proprietary and trust funds should include the cost of capitalized fixed assets acquired from grants, entitlements, and shared revenues. As with other nonprofit organizations, fixed assets are accounted for at cost or, if donated, at their fair market value on the date received. Reporting infrastructure fixed assets is optional. Depreciation of general fixed assets should not be recorded in governmental funds but may optionally be recorded in the GFAAG. The chosen accounting policies should be consistently applied and disclosed in the Notes.

The GASB is considering whether to require reporting of infrastructure assets and depreciation of general fixed assets in order to reconcile a major difference between financial reporting requirements for governments and other types of organizations. Because of these projects, GASB Statement 8 allows governmental colleges and universities that follow the AICPA standards to optionally report depreciation, but does not require them to change their practices on the basis of FASB 93 (which requires depreciation of fixed assets).

Financial Reports and Statements

A CAFR (comprehensive annual financial report) covering all funds and account groups of the reporting entity should include: an introductory section; appropriate combined, combining, and individual fund statements; notes to the financial statements; required supplementary information; schedules; narrative explanations; and statistical tables. The *combined statements* show the data for all fund types and account groups on a single statement. *Combining statements* show the data for each fund of a given type.

General purpose financial statements (*GPFS*) are part of the CAFR and may also be published separately. They include the basic combined financial statements essential to fair presentation of financial position and results of operations. Proprietary and nonexpendable trust fund types must also include statements of cash flows. Table 18-1 lists the combined statements to be included in the GPFS. *Component unit financial reports* (*CUFR*) and *component unit financial statements* (*CUFS*) may also be published separately, if necessary. These

TABLE 18-1 **GPFS—Combined Statements—Overview**

Combined Balance Sheet—All Fund Types and Account Groups

Combined Statement of Revenues, Expenditures, and Changes in Fund Balances—All Governmental Fund Types

Combined Statement of Revenues, Expenditures, and Changes in Fund Balances—Budget and Actual—General and Special Revenue Fund Types (and similar governmental fund types for which annual budgets have been legally adopted)

Combined Statement of Revenues, Expenses, and Changes in Retained Earnings (or Equity)—All Proprietary Fund Types

Combined Statement of Cash Flows—All Proprietary Fund Types and Nonexpendable Trust Funds

Trust fund operations may be reported with governmental or proprietary fund types, as appropriate, or separately.

Notes to the Financial Statements

Required Supplementary Information

Source: Adapted from Governmental Accounting Standards Board, *Codification of Governmental Accounting and Financial Reporting Standards as of May 31, 1990,* Third Edition (GASB, 1990), p. 137.

would contain the same types of data as presented in the CAFR and GPFS for each individual component governmental unit. Appropriate interim financial statements and reports are to be prepared for purposes of management control, legislative oversight, and external reporting, as needed.

In governmental funds, *revenues* are increases in current financial resources from sources other than interfund transfers and debt issue proceeds. Governmental fund revenues are classified by fund and source: taxes, licenses and permits, intergovernmental revenues, charges for services, fines and forfeits, and miscellaneous. Governmental fund *expenditures* are decreases in (uses of) current financial resources that occur for purposes other than interfund transfers. They are classified by fund, function (or program), organization unit, activity, character, and object class. Interfund transfers and proceeds of general long-term debt issues are classified separately from fund revenues and expenditures or expenses. Proprietary fund revenues and expenses are to be classified like those of similar businesses, trusts, or activities.

Basis of Accounting

Governments use two different bases of accounting. The *modified accrual basis* recognizes revenues in the period that they become available and measurable and recognizes expenditures in the accounting period that the fund liability is incurred, if measurable (except for unmatured interest on general long-term debt, which is recognized when due). The *accrual basis* recognizes revenues when earned and measurable and expenses when incurred, if measurable. Thus, the modified accrual basis requires revenue to be available as well as measurable and does not recognize unmatured interest on long-term debt until it is due. *Available* means collectible soon enough to pay liabilities of the current period.

Governmental fund types must use the modified accrual basis of accounting whereas proprietary fund types use the accrual basis. Fiduciary funds use the basis that is consistent with their measurement objectives: nonexpendable and pension trust funds use accrual; expendable trust and agency funds use modified accrual. Transfers are recognized when the interfund receivable and payable arise.

Budgetary and Encumbrance Reporting

The GASB Codification Section 1700 states that every governmental unit should adopt an annual budget and that the accounting system should provide the basis for appropriate budgetary control. Common terminology and classification should be used consistently throughout the budget, the accounts, and the financial reports of each fund.

A statement comparing budget and actual results for governmental funds that have adopted an annual budget is included in the financial statements and schedules. The accounting basis of the budget and the accounting system should be consistent, and the budget should be prepared on the modified accrual basis, if possible. If legal or other restrictions require the budget to be prepared on a different accounting basis, the actual data in the budget-to-actual statements should be prepared on the budgetary basis, and any differences between GAAP and the budgetary basis should be explained in the Notes.[50]

Because of its legal force, the budget is a very important control mechanism in accounting for governmental funds. Proprietary and fiduciary fund budgets may not have the same legal status and force. If *budgetary accounting* is used, the budget is formally recorded in the accounting records of governmental funds so that the accounting system continually reflects the remaining balance of the budget that is available for expenditures or expected to be generated by revenues.

The term *budgetary accounting* is also commonly used to include *encumbrance accounting*. An *encumbrance* is a commitment to purchase goods or services that have not yet been received. Such commitments are typically represented by a formal contract or *purchase order* that authorizes and commits the organization to make the purchase. Under an encumbrance accounting system, an encumbrance is recorded when goods or services are ordered,

---

[50]AICPA, *Local Governmental Accounting*, pp. 4-9.

to indicate how much of the budget has been committed (*encumbered*) and, thus, is no longer available for other purposes. When the items and an invoice for them are received, the entry to record the encumbrance is reversed (eliminated), and the actual amount of the expenditure is recorded. Encumbrance accounting is intended to prevent overspending by showing how much of the budget has been committed, as well as how much has actually been spent. It is useful for budgetary control. The budgetary and encumbrance accounting cycle generally proceeds as shown in Table 18-2.

Traditionally, government financial statements reported encumbrances as well as actual expenditures. Current GAAP presents only expenditures. Encumbrances outstanding at year end may be presented in notes or supplementary schedules if desired or required by law. Where encumbered appropriations do not lapse at year end, or where appropriations lapse but the government intends to honor outstanding encumbrances, outstanding encumbrances are disclosed by designating part of the fund balance as a *reserve for encumbrances*. The method of accounting for encumbrances should be consistently applied and disclosed.

Audits

The three levels of compliance audits and audit reports currently required for governmental units are shown in Table 18-3. This hierarchy of reports is designed to meet the needs of all three sets of auditing standards. The AICPA Statement on Auditing Standards 63, *Compliance Auditing Applicable to Governmental Entities and other Recipients of Governmental Assistance*, provides auditors with guidance for meeting the needs of the three sets of audit requirements.

The oldest, narrowest, best known, and most commonly performed audit is a *financial audit*. It is conducted either by independent Certified Public

TABLE 18-2 **Budgetary Accounting Cycle**

Activity	Accounting Treatment
Adopt budget	Debit estimated revenues and credit fund balance for the budgeted amount of revenue.
	Credit appropriations and debit fund balance for the budgeted amount of appropriations.
Earn revenue	Credit revenues and debit cash or receivables.
Issue purchase order	Debit encumbrances and credit reserve for encumbrances.
Receive goods	Reverse entry made when PO was issued. Debit expenditures and credit cash or payables for the actual amount owed.

TABLE 18-3 **Hierarchy of Governmental Audit Reports**

(1)   Generally accepted auditing standards (GAAS):
      Opinion on financial statements

(2)   Generally accepted *government* auditing standards (GAGAS):
      Report on internal controls
      Report on compliance
      Supplementary schedule for federal assistance programs

(3)   Single Audit Act of 1984:
      Internal control report for federal assistance programs
      Opinion on compliance for major federal assistance programs with respect
          to *specific* compliance criteria
      Report on compliance for major federal assistance programs with respect
          to *general* compliance criteria
      Schedule of findings and questioned costs
      Report on compliance for nonmajor federal assistance programs
      Report on fraud or illegal acts (when appropriate)

Each level requires the reports required by the level(s) above it in addition to
its own unique reports.

Source: Adapted from AICPA, *Local Governmental Accounting Trends & Techniques*, Third Edition, Susan Cornwall, Ed., p. 1-2.

Accountants (CPAs) under *generally accepted auditing standards* (GAAS) established by the AICPA or by *state auditors* under either GAAS or state law.

To address federal government concerns, the General Accounting Office (GAO) set forth *generally accepted government auditing standards* (*GAGAS*) and requires that federal programs and activities carried out by state and local governments be audited in accordance with both GAAS and GAGAS. GAGAS are not intended to require any additional audit work beyond that required under GAAS. However, they require additional audit reports stating (1) that the audit was performed in accordance with GAGAS, (2) that the audited governmental entity complied with laws and regulations that may have a material effect on the financial statements, and (3) the results of evaluating internal accounting controls as part of the audit.

The *Single Audit Act of 1984* imposed the third level of audit requirements on governmental units receiving $100,000 or more of federal assistance for fiscal years beginning after December 31, 1984. It is implemented by the federal regulations contained in *OMB Circular A-128*,[51] and may represent a significant expansion of audit scope and requirements in many situations.

[51]U.S. Office of Management and Budget, *Circular No. A-128*, "Audits of State and Local Governments" (Washington, DC: Office of Management and Budget, April 12, 1985).

In contrast to audits that monitor financial and legal compliance, a *performance audit* evaluates and analyzes an organization's success in meeting its goals. It may focus on effectiveness or efficiency or both, or it may assess whether goals are appropriate. Performance audits are typically conducted by an internal audit staff or consultants. They are valuable but difficult to implement. The results of many performance audits are reported only internally although the results of audits performed by the GAO are publicly available.

Challenges and Trends in Financial Reporting

The early 1990s saw the U.S. in a recession, large and growing deficits at all levels of government, and citizens resisting both additional taxes and cuts in existing service. Several states and municipalities were in jeopardy of bond defaults and the city of Bridgeport, Connecticut, attempted to file for bankruptcy. Improved accounting and financial reporting cannot cure these ills, but it can assist with decisions about appropriate courses of action.

The sheer size and complexity of state and large local government organizations pose a formidable challenge to accounting and financial reporting, one exacerbated by the political process and the nonfinancial aspects of government mission and accountability. But the viability of the U.S. political and economic system rests on accountability to its citizens; without it, a democracy is an empty shell. Although the quality of governmental accounting improved in the 1980s, much remains to be done.

GASB Standard Setting   In May 1990, the GASB issued Statement No. 11, *Measurement Focus and Basis of Accounting—Governmental Fund Operating Statements*, which changes the basis of accounting for governmental funds. It is scheduled to become effective only for periods beginning after June 15, 1994. Earlier application is not permitted because it must be implemented simultaneously with other GASB pronouncements that have not yet been made. The GASB's agenda includes setting standards for financial reporting, capital reporting, pension accounting, risk financing and insurance, and nonrecurring projects with long-term economic benefit. Standards governing all these areas are intended be set and implemented simultaneously with the provisions of Statement 11.

Measuring Interperiod Equity   Interperiod equity, the measure of whether current-year revenues are sufficient to pay for current year services, is an important component of GASB Statement 11. Interperiod equity deals only with financial flows; it does not attempt to assess nonfinancial measures. Even with this limitation, measuring interperiod equity is very difficult.

Self-insurance and pension and other post-retirement benefits are among the most difficult items due to inherent measurement problems. For example, it is often difficult to estimate the eventual cost of post-retirement benefits earned by employees in the current period. Until recently, even estimates of many such future commitments were not required to be reflected in the financial statements, making it very difficult to determine the resources consumed during the current period. The current trend is toward standards that require reporting all costs incurred in the current period in the financial statements.

It is also difficult to measure whether fixed assets are adequately maintained to ensure that their potential useful lives are realized. Under current governmental accounting standards, and under GASB Statement 11, financial statements do not reflect whether fixed assets were maintained or consumed. If fixed assets are not adequately maintained, there is unobservable consumption of resources during the current period that was not paid for by the citizens during that period.

Additional interperiod equity issues are raised by some expenditures, such as those for research and education, that are expected to benefit future periods. The cost of such items does not appear on a balance sheet because their future value to the organization is difficult to measure and the organization does not own future rights to their results. Only items that have objectively determinable and measurable future financial benefits are assets for financial reporting purposes. All other expenditures are reflected in the financial statements as consumption. Whether or how GASB will address these issues remains to be seen.

Although it is important to measure interperiod equity, maintaining financial interperiod equity may not always be appropriate. The amounts an organization invests today may be consumption appropriately foregone in the current period to provide for needs of future periods, or they may be inappropriate denial of current benefits to people in need. Government borrowing or use of equity acquired in prior periods may finance either irresponsible consumption or valuable current investments that will be repaid many times over in the future. Neither saving nor borrowing is inherently good or bad. Information is needed to assess the effects and appropriateness of the chosen strategies.

Measuring and Reporting Outcomes   Although financial budgets provide a critical form of control, financial data alone are not sufficient to measure government performance. After all, the purpose of government is not primarily financial. Budget and actual data on *service efforts and accomplishments (SEA)* that measure changes in social welfare are also needed to evaluate government performance.

Performance can be measured using inputs, outputs, or outcomes. *Inputs*, which are the easiest to measure, represent the resources used to provide a service. They are often measured in dollars, such as $100,000 of expenditures for the police department, or in units of input, such as number of police officers. *Outputs* are measures that represent activities accomplished, such as 56 arrests or an average time of 17 minutes to arrive at the scene of a reported crime. Outputs are less likely to be measurable in dollar terms and typically draw their data from other information systems. *Outcomes*, which are the most difficult to assess, measure the degree to which the organization accomplished the intended goal of public safety, including crime prevention. The AAA project on performance measurement[52] and GASB projects on service efforts and accomplishment[53] offer encouragement and direction for improving outcome measurement and reporting.

Measurement difficulties also arise because the condition of a governmental organization is not the same as the condition of the geographic area over which it has jurisdiction although they are inextricably intertwined. For example, the closing of a small town's major business will have a profound effect on the local government, economy, and society. It may cause demand for some government services to increase and others to decrease and cause the amount of tax revenue to decrease. Ideally, financial reports will eventually reflect both the operations and position of the government organization and the performance and position of the economy, health, education, public infrastructure, social welfare, and physical environment of the geographic area and citizenry. This would allow more accurate assessments of the performance of the governmental unit and of the area, which is affected by many factors in addition to the performance of the governmental organization.

Popular Reporting Unused information is wasted, and citizens cannot be empowered unless they are able to use the available information. The news media has become active in reporting on government finances and attempting to assess their effects on programs and outcomes. Imaginative efforts are needed both to improve citizens' ability to use financial information in its existing form and to provide better *popular* reports that are readable and widely used by the average citizen, who does not have a college degree or accounting experience. A GASB research report on Popular Reporting: *Local Government Financial Reports to the Citizenry* provides many useful insights and an example of a popular report.[54]

FEDERAL FINANCIAL REPORTING STANDARDS

As the largest government organization and largest employer in the U.S., with disbursements that exceed $1 trillion per year, the federal government may present today's greatest management and accounting challenge. In spite

[52]American Accounting Association, Government and Nonprofit Section, Committee on Nonprofit Entities' Performance Measures, *Measuring the Performance of Nonprofit Organizations: The State of the Art* (Sarasota, FL: American Accounting Association, August 1989).
[53]Governmental Accounting Standards Board, *Service Efforts and Accomplishments Reporting: Its Time Has Come*, a series of research reports (Norwalk, CT: GASB, 1990).
[54]Frances H. Carpenter and Florence C. Sharp, *Popular Reporting: Local Government Financial Reports to the Citizenry*, research report (Norwalk, CT: GASB, 1992).

of consistent efforts, federal accounting is not meeting that challenge very well. It is difficult to determine either the costs or the effects of federal programs, and the GAO continues to find inadequate internal controls in many of the federal agencies that it audits.

Responsibility for Federal Accounting and Financial Reporting

The federal government has the same separation of powers found in lower levels of U.S. governments. The legislative branch, the Congress, provides authority and financing for all programs. The budget is proposed by the president and is usually modified and then passed as an appropriation bill by Congress. The president cannot modify an appropriation bill but can veto it in its entirety; overriding a presidential veto requires a two-thirds vote by both houses of Congress. The Congressional Budget and Impoundment Control Act of 1974 established that appropriations are not only authorizations but orders to obligate. This act prevents the president from refusing to spend the resources that Congress has authorized.

The GAO, which is headed by the Comptroller General of the United States, performs a variety of functions. Its primary purpose is to support the Congress in oversight of the executive branch. It does this by conducting and reporting the results of audits of federal agencies; performing special studies and investigations for Congress; setting federal government accounting, financial reporting, internal control, and auditing standards; and assisting agencies with systems design.

The *Congressional Budget Office (CBO)*, established in 1974, supports the Congress in its consideration of the budget. Its activities, which revolve around the budgetary process, include providing cost and economic forecasts, analyzing fiscal policy, preparing an annual report on the budget, and performing special studies as needed.

The president has ultimate responsibility for managing the executive branch and being accountable to Congress and the citizens. The *Office of Management and Budget (OMB)*, an agency within the Executive Office of the President, is responsible for preparing the executive budget and developing financial management systems and techniques for the executive branch. It periodically issues bulletins, circulars, and directives on federal budgeting, accounting, and reporting.

The *Secretary of the Treasury*, head of the *Department of the Treasury*, is chief accountant and treasurer of the federal government. Treasury functions include managing cash receipts, cash disbursements, public debt, and trust funds, as well as accounting and reporting for the federal government as a whole. The treasury has issued many directives on federal accounting and financial reporting.

The federal agencies and departments conduct the day-to-day operations of the government. Their accounting and financial reporting related duties include preparing agency budgets; establishing and maintaining effective accounting and internal control systems that conform to the standards prescribed by the GAO; and reporting on reviews of systems and other matters required by the GAO, treasury, and OMB. Most agencies have an *inspector general*, appointed by the president, who conducts and reports to Congress and the president the results of audits and investigations of the agency's activities.

The comptroller general's *1990 Annual Report* provides an excellent model for a federal agency or other governmental or nonprofit organization. It includes financial statements audited by independent CPAs, a narrative discussion of the performance and accomplishments of the agency during the past year, and plans for the future. The 1990 message from the comptroller general focuses first on the federal budget deficit and then briefly reviews the agency's accomplishments for the year. It concludes with a discussion of the importance of financial management and information.

The Chief Financial Officers Act of 1990 established several important financial management related positions, required long-range planning to guide financial management improvement, and established a set of pilot financial statements and audits for ten departments and major component agencies. This is an important step toward much-needed financial management reform in the federal government. The report states:

> Financial management reform holds the promise of real progress in the way the federal government operates. But it also has special significance in light of the weakening of public confidence in government that the budget problem has provoked. The whole budget crisis, after all, is about money. Over the long haul, regaining the taxpayers' confidence in the way their money is being handled can be achieved only by putting reliable financial systems in place throughout the government. Only then, when policymakers can see exactly where we are and how we are doing, will they be able to decide responsibly where we ought to go and how we can get there.[55]

For over 40 years, the *Joint Financial Management Improvement Program* (*JFMIP*) has promoted the improvement of financial management policies and practices in the federal government through cooperative efforts. Early efforts focused on the improvement of accounting operations; current emphasis is on employing information technology to better manage government resources, enhance public accountability, and improve government services and financial management.[56] Much remains to be accomplished. Most federal agencies lack managerial accounting systems that are adequate to protect against fraud and abuse, enable evaluation, and support planning.

[55]U.S. General Accounting Office, *Comptroller General's 1990 Annual Report* (Washington, DC: U.S. General Accounting Office, 1990), p. 7.
[56]Joint Financial Management Improvement Program, *40 Years of Progress and the Challenges Ahead* (Washington, DC: Joint Financial Management Improvement Program, 1989).

Federal Accounting and Financial Reporting Standards

Federal government accounting is similar in many respects to accounting for state and local governments. Funds used by the federal government are classified as *government-owned* (*federal*) *funds* or *trust* (*custodian*) *funds*. Government-owned funds include the *general fund*, *special funds* (parallel to special revenue funds), *revolving funds* (parallel to enterprise and internal service funds), and *management funds*, which facilitate accounting for transactions that will ultimately be charged to multiple appropriations (they have no clear parallel in other government or nonprofit accounting). Custodian funds are classified as either *trust funds* (as in state and local governments) or *deposit funds* (parallel to agency funds).

Accounting standards for federal agencies are set by the comptroller general in *Accounting Principles and Standards for Federal Agencies*.[57] The primary objectives of federal accounting and financial reporting are to provide information that is useful for allocating resources and assessing management's performance and stewardship. Federal agencies must report on an accrual basis. However, the accounting system must also record an encumbrance (obligation) when the order is placed, an expenditure (expended appropriation) and asset when the materials are delivered, an expense (applied cost) when the materials are used, and a cash disbursement when the payment is made. A key difference between federal and other governmental accounting is that the federal accounting standards require reporting depreciation in some instances and encourage it for all fixed assets. The *equity of the U.S. government* account is the federal equivalent of net assets (fund balance) in other governments.

William Simon, then secretary of the treasury, endorsed a prototype report on the financial condition of the U.S. government. It contained a Balance Sheet, a Statement of Operations, and a Reconciliation of Accrued Operating Results to the Budget Deficit, prepared on a consolidated basis for the federal government using full accrual accounting.[58] Simon explained that the report was an attempt to apply the principles of business accounting to government, with the express purpose of facilitating judgments about the financial health of the government. The statements revealed a liability for Social Security of $499.5 billion, an excess of liabilities over assets of nearly $1 trillion, and a deficit that was $95 billion higher than the government's own figures. A footnote on Social Security indicated that as of June 30, 1975, the present value of the projected excess of benefits over contributions for present participants over the next 75 years was $2.7 trillion.

---

[57]U.S. General Accounting Office, *Accounting Principles and Standards for Federal Agencies* (Washington, DC: U.S. General Accounting Office, 1984).
[58]U.S. Government, *Consolidated Financial Statements: Prototype Report* (Washington, DC: Government Printing Office, 1977).

This report unleashed a storm of controversy. Charles Schultze, a nominal member of the committee that produced the report and subsequently chairman of the Council of Economic Advisors, disagreed with the inclusion of Social Security liabilities and labeled the statement as "absolute nonsense."[59] (Social Security is legally a fund separate from direct U.S. obligations.) There was concern that revelation of the liability in the retirement funds would lead to demands for full funding. Others objected to reporting on a commercial basis for the government, maintaining a need for fund and budgetary accounting in its statements.

Despite the initial controversy, all agencies are now required to prepare an annual Balance Sheet, Statement of Operations, Statement of Changes in Financial Position (Cash Basis), and Statement of Reconciliation of Budget Reports. These statements must also be prepared annually on a consolidated basis for the entire federal government, including federally owned government corporations and legislative and judicial branches. All interdepartmental and interagency transactions and balances should be eliminated to properly report the statements from the perspective of the federal government as a single reporting entity.

A FRAMEWORK FOR ANALYSIS

Government financial statements are used by several different constituencies, including citizens, taxpayers, unions, higher government levels, funders, regulatory agencies, and creditors. Bond underwriters, rating agencies, and many investors are financially sophisticated users of state and local government financial statements. These analytic approaches provide a useful model for analyzing the financial position and performance of governmental units. Approaches used by creditors, management, and citizens consider economic, management, and financial factors. In addition, the credit community considers the legal structure of the debt issue in performing a credit analysis to assign a rating.

The International City Managers Association publication, *Evaluating Financial Condition, A Handbook for Local Government* (ICMA Handbook) follows a similar general framework to the credit rating agencies.[60] It provides detailed procedures for calculating 36 specific indicators that are related to a set of 12 financial, economic, and organizational factors. A formula, a warning trend, a description, a commentary, suggestions for analysis, and suggestions for policy statements are given for each indicator. Worksheets are also

---

[59]As quoted in "Simon's Plan for Businesslike Bookkeeping," *Business Week* (November 22, 1976): 92.
[60]Sanford M. Groves and Maureen Godsey Calente, *Evaluating Financial Condition: A Handbook for Local Government*, 2d ed. (International City Managers Association, 1986), p. v.

included for collecting data from the financial statements and census publications and for calculating each ratio. This structured approach can be especially helpful to financially unsophisticated communities. Popular reporting to citizens also uses similar data and analysis techniques although the language and presentation may be quite different.

Both Moody's and S&P's debt rating agencies publish documents explaining their bond rating analysis processes. *Moody's on Municipals*, a general introduction to the process of issuing public debt, explains their credit analysis process, the role of ratings, types of debt, and the way to bring the debt issue to market. It succinctly summarizes the fundamental purpose of its credit analysis as "evaluating the borrower's ability and willingness to pay." Moody's has rated tax-exempt debt since 1918 and currently maintains more than 33,000 ratings on the long- and short-term debt of some 18,000 municipalities.[61] *S&P's Municipal Finance Criteria* provides an overview of their rating criteria and discusses in more detail the various types of local and state borrowings for different purposes.[62] Together, the two publications provide a comprehensive overview of the debt issuance and rating process. Although they do not describe their procedures exactly, bond raters freely disclose the factors they consider important in rating an issue. The rating agencies would prefer that management perform regular in-depth financial and economic analyses, be aware of any problems, and formulate plans to deal with the identified problems before the actual credit rating is performed.

Economy

The economy is an important factor that is difficult to predict and is not controllable by the government. Both the vulnerability of the local economy to downturns and the relation between the economy and the government's financial performance and debt repayment are assessed. Economic data are available from U.S. census statistics on population, housing, employment, unemployment, and production. If an individual company or industry exerts a major influence on a local economy, relevant data from other sources, such as the company's corporate annual report or industry trade associations, may be analyzed.

The sensitivity of government revenues and expenditures to economic fluctuations is also considered. An economic downturn typically causes government revenues to decline because of lower personal and business income tax collections, deterioration of the property tax base, and increased property tax and fee delinquencies. At the same time, the demand for many government services does not decline; the cost of others is relatively fixed even if

---

[61]Moody's Investors Service, *Moody's on Municipals* (New York, NY: Moody's Investors Service, 1989), preface and p. 40.
[62]Standard and Poor's, *Municipal Finance Criteria*.

the demand does decline; and the demand for housing, health, and welfare related services may increase. This combination can lead to a squeeze on the financial performance of the government in times of economic decline. Bond raters are concerned with the likelihood that such a squeeze will occur and lead to defaults on debt obligations. It is important to assess the relationships between various aspects of the economy and government performance.

Financial

At least three years of audited financial statements should be used for trend analysis. Statements prepared in conformance with GAAP and statements that are awarded the GFOA Certificate of Achievement are the most reliable and comparable. Analysis should include both examination of the trends within the unit and comparisons with averages and trends for similar units.

Governmental fund revenues are examined for composition, with diversity considered to be a strength. Shifts in proportion or decreases in revenue sources are analyzed carefully for indications of future financial difficulties. Expenditure patterns, in total and per capita, are analyzed for fluctuations and in relation to revenue sources. Large or fixed expenditure items are examined carefully, as are changes in expenditure classifications.

Deficits, especially as a continuing trend, are viewed negatively. Debt service is analyzed in relation to total expenditures and revenue streams. Liquidity, fund balance, cash flows, reserves, and the composition of assets and liabilities are assessed. Growing or excessive reliance on short-term borrowing is generally viewed as a sign of financial distress.

Pensions, other long-term liabilities, and contingent liabilities are receiving more attention. Pension funding and the conservative or liberal nature of underlying actuarial and investment assumptions are carefully considered. Unfunded accrued liabilities are generally a negative indicator although they must be evaluated in light of the assumptions and funding methods used. Long-term contingent liabilities indicate exposure to financial pressures. The complexity of risk management for government units requires careful evaluation of self-insurance assumptions and funding.

Management

Management of the borrowing unit includes the government organization and legal structure, the internal management control systems, and the quality and continuity of managers and elected officials. The U.S. has many different forms of local government, with almost limitless variety in the forms of separate districts and joint ventures. The government unit's structure heavily influences management's ability to control revenues, expenditures, and debt repayment. Structure is determined by the *municipal charter* and related state laws that govern the incorporation of the unit. Some forms of government give substantial fiscal power to appointed or elected officials while others do not.

Management quality is crucial but is difficult to quantify and predict. Managers must be able to effectively exercise the available control to implement plans and fulfill legal requirements. Quantitative indicators of management quality include turnover and past financial performance. Actual performance that is consistent with budgets indicates effective budgeting processes, plans, and forecasts. Management that can make and implement plans effectively is viewed positively. Labor negotiation documents provide insight on labor relations. Bond raters usually conduct a site visit and interview with management as part of the process of evaluating management.

Effective management is supported by good internal management control systems. The audit report and management letter should disclose any significant management and internal control weaknesses. Effective long-range planning for capital improvements, debt needs, and debt retirement is an important indicator of good management. Management should understand the nature and implications of a proposed debt issue. According to S&P,

> Updated accounting and financial reporting systems are an integral part of management teams' readiness to meet the challenges of hard decision-making. Only with current and reliable data can financial managers provide a solid framework for intelligent executive and legislative decisions.[63]

Legal Structure of Debt

The legal structure of a debt issue is also important to debt rating although it seldom affects the assessment of overall government performance. It includes the type of security, the size of the issue, the interest rate structure, the covenants by which the issuer agrees to abide, the call provisions, and any reserve requirements. A fully funded debt service reserve means that the government unit sets aside (reserves) sufficient cash and liquid assets to cover the maximum annual debt service (combined principal and interest payment), or has an insurance policy or letter of credit for the amount of debt service. Positive terms support the borrower's willingness and ability to repay while negative factors may indicate excessive risk or vulnerability related to the specific issue.

APPLYING THE FOUR KEY QUESTIONS

Because of the size and complexity of government financial statements, it is infeasible to reproduce and analyze an entire CAFR in this chapter. Interested readers are referred to the CAFR displayed in the *GAAFR 88*[64] and

---

[63]Ibid., pp. 13-14.
[64]GFOA, *Governmental Accounting*, Appendix D, pp. 217-365.

the popular report that is based on it contained in *Popular Reporting: Local Government Financial Reports to the Citizenry*.[65] Instead, the four key questions are applied to the sample financial statements shown in Exhibit A. Although some overall statistics are mentioned, the analysis focuses primarily on individual funds because the total column in governmental financial statements does not accurately reflect the consolidated position of the governmental entity.

This analysis is not intended to be as comprehensive as those in the preceding three chapters. Instead, it uses only a few ratios and statistics to illustrate the application of each of the four key questions to a governmental entity. No external comparisons are performed because of the lack of external comparison data for these statements. Also keep in mind that the Notes to the Financial Statements, if available, would provide additional valuable information.

Consistency Between Goals and Resources

Because assets and liabilities are not identified as current or noncurrent, calculating current ratios requires several assumptions. Considering all assets preceding the land account and all liabilities preceding general obligation bonds payable to be current yields 19X2 total current assets of $5,703,961 and current liabilities of $2,230,492 (Exhibit B). The corresponding overall current ratio is a healthy 2.6 for 19X2, up from 1.9 in 19X2. Under this assumption, all the assets and liabilities in the general, special revenue, debt service, and capital projects funds are current; all those in the GFAAG and GLTDAG are noncurrent; and only the proprietary enterprise and internal service funds have both current and noncurrent.

The current ratios of the individual funds are all above 1.0, with most of them over 2.0. The lower ratios of 1.02 in the internal service fund and 1.39 in the debt service fund are acceptable because it is not necessary for these types of funds to carry many more resources than are needed to meet current obligations. The $65,000 advance from the general fund appears to be a noncurrent liability in substance if not in form. If so, then both the general fund asset and the internal service fund liability should be treated as noncurrent. This exclusion would decrease the general fund current ratio slightly, to 2.0 [($494,350 − $65,000) ÷ $215,050], but improve the internal service fund ratio significantly, to 5.4 ($81,700 ÷ $15,000).

It appears that the $1,239,260 of investments in the trust and agency funds may be reserved for long-term purposes. Excluding them from current asset drops that fund's 19X2 current assets to $845,552 and its current ratio to 1.2. The overall current assets and current ratio decline to $4,464,701 and 2.0.

[65]Carpenter and Sharp, *Popular Reporting*.

Because government receivables and inventory may not be quickly convertible to cash, the relationship between current liabilities and liquid resources (cash plus near-cash investments) is often considered. There are sufficient liquid resources in the general, special revenue, capital projects, enterprise, and trust and agency funds to cover all current liabilities. The internal service fund has sufficient liquid resources to cover all current liabilities to external parties. The debt service fund has sufficient liquid resources to cover the matured bonds and interest payable, which are the only current liabilities that are likely to require cash outlays. (Deferred revenue typically represents cash or other assets already received but not yet earned, and is converted to revenue rather than liquidated by a cash payment.)

This government has an overall debt to assets ratio of 0.34 in 19X2, down from 0.39 in 19X1. Excluding from assets the GLTDAG amounts to be provided ($2,398,720 = $1,939,790 + $458,930 in 19X2) increases the ratios to 0.39 in 19X2 and to 0.43 in 19X1. More than half of the total assets are financed with equity, which indicates some unused debt capacity. However, it is difficult to assess this accurately because the governmental fund assets are valued at undepreciated historical cost. The enterprise and internal service funds also have a reasonably conservative proportion of debt at 0.44 and 0.43, respectively.

Interperiod Equity

An assessment of interperiod equity based on these financial statements is necessarily limited by the nature of the information they contain. The change in fixed assets from 19X1 to 19X2 and the $1,939,100 capital outlay indicate significant additions to the fixed assets during the year. The capital outlay was 64-percent financed ($1,250,000 ÷ $1,939,100) by intergovernmental revenues. If the outlay was for a needed addition or replacement or maintenance of important capital assets, it may reflect investment in the current period that will allow future consumption. On the other hand, if this project is ill-conceived or unnecessary or has high maintenance or operating costs, in future periods it may impose a burden that outweighs the benefits it provides. Governments sometimes undertake new construction and related debt because intergovernmental grants are available to support them, while deferring needed maintenance of existing infrastructure or construction of other new facilities that would have to be financed solely by the reporting entity. When the basic fixed assets eventually must be maintained or replaced, the entity's debt capacity may have been exhausted by the less vital projects.

The $216,135 negative undesignated fund balance in trust and agency funds may indicate that the employee retirement system is not fully funded. If so, this represents resource consumption in current and prior periods that will have to be paid for in future periods.

The general, special revenue, debt service, enterprise, and internal service funds all had revenues in excess of expenditures, or a positive net income. This is an indication that resources of the current period were sufficient to finance operations of the current period. The 50-percent increase ($602,927 ÷ $1,213,328) in fund balance from 19X1 to 19X2 indicates that operations of the current period contributed more resources than they used, assuming all resource consumption is reflected in the financial statements.

Match Between Sources and Uses of Resources

The sources and uses of resources in the governmental and expendable trust funds seem to be fairly well matched although the lack of natural expense classifications makes this difficult to assess. Total revenues exceeded total expenditures in all except the capital projects and expendable trust funds. The shortfall of revenues in both these funds was made up by transfers and, in the capital projects fund, by the proceeds of issuing debt, which is the most common way of financing capital projects. The $602,927 total excess of revenues and other sources over expenditures and other uses was 15 percent ($602,927 ÷ $3,951,987) of the total revenue in these funds, and led to a 50-percent increase in their fund balances.

All proprietary and similar trust funds also had positive net income. Although the $92,988 of interest expense and fiscal charges in the enterprise fund is a relatively high fixed charge, the times interest earned coverage ratio is 1.85 [($78,812 + $92,988) ÷ $92,988)]. It is 3.4 [($78,812 + $144,100 + $92,988) ÷ $92,988)] if depreciation is added back to approximate cash flow instead of operating income. Although personal services are the largest proportion of expenses in both the proprietary funds, they are less than half in both cases. Comparison statistics for comparable types of proprietary funds or businesses would be useful to assess the management of these fund types. The low 0.105 ($672,150 ÷ $6,375,514) total asset turnover rate in the enterprise fund may indicate low asset efficiency and should be further investigated.

Resource Sustainability

The availability of budgetary figures for general and special revenue funds aids in the evaluation of resource sustainability. It shows, for example, that government managers were able to counter the unexpected revenue shortfall (unfavorable revenue variances) with reductions of expenditures below their budgeted amounts (favorable expenditure variances) to end the year with an excess of revenues over expenditures and other uses that was even slightly larger than budgeted. Similarly, the special revenue funds went from a budgeted deficit to an actual surplus. This type of performance picture is a favorable indicator of resource sustainability and management quality.

SUMMARY

Governments play extremely important roles in the economy and in society. In a democracy, government accounting is an important mechanism by which citizens are informed so that they can exercise their voting rights wisely. Accounting is also crucial for effective and efficient management of even nondemocratic governments.

Accounting for governmental organizations has been heavily criticized. Government financial reporting standards have become much clearer and more consistent in the past decade, due largely to the GASB and other standard setters. The federal government has provided a strong impetus toward having a single audit replace inefficient multiple audits. Yet, the prevalence of differing state laws governing state and local accounting and financial reporting impedes movement to consistent financial reporting for all such governmental entities.

Current financial and other reporting standards are set by the GASB and embodied in the GASB Codification. They are supplemented by the AICPA audit guide and industry publications and practices. Although the focus to date has been primarily on financial reporting, the GASB also has responsibility for standard setting in the statistical reporting that is crucial to evaluating government performance. Recent standards intended to improve government reporting included a move toward accrual (instead of cash basis) accounting; combined funds statements; clarification of the appropriate reporting entity; and better disclosure for pensions, overlapping debt, and debt instruments. Difficult issues in government accounting include capitalization and depreciation of fixed assets (especially infrastructure), accounting for post-retirement benefits, risk financing, measuring and reporting outcomes, and measuring interperiod equity. Governmental financial reporting is substantially more complex than reporting for other types of entities.

Evaluating the financial condition and predicting the financial future of governments are important to citizens, prospective citizens, businesses, other governmental units, and creditors, as well as to those directly responsible for managing the governmental unit. Government fiscal health depends jointly on the general and local economic environments, the actions of other higher and lower government levels, the constituent populations, and the actions of elected and appointed governmental decision-makers and managers. Thus, all these factors need to be considered in assessing and predicting the financial performance of a government. The financial community, government associations, and the GASB have all contributed to development of practical financial and economic analysis procedures. Government financial and other performance analysis methods will continue to evolve and improve as more constituencies recognize their importance to economic prosperity, social welfare, and effective government.

EXHIBIT A   Sample Financial Statements

Example 1
Name of Governmental Unit
Combined Balance Sheet—All Fund Types and Account Groups, December 31, 19X2

Assets	Governmental Fund Types				Proprietary Fund Types		Fiduciary Fund Types	Account Groups		Totals (Memorandum Only)	
	General	Special Revenue	Debt Service	Capital Projects	Enterprise	Internal Service	Trust and Agency	General Fixed Assets	General Long-Term Debt	December 31, 19X2	December 31, 19X1
Cash	$258,500	$101,385	$185,624	$659,100	$257,036	$29,700	$216,701	-	$ -	$1,708,046	$1,300,944
Cash with fiscal agent	-	-	102,000	-	-	-	-	-	-	102,000	-
Investments, at cost or amortized cost	65,000	37,200	160,990	-	-	-	1,239,260	-	-	1,502,450	1,974,354
Receivables (net of allowances for uncollectibles):											
Taxes	58,300	2,500	3,829	-	-	-	580,000	-	-	644,629	255,400
Accounts	8,300	3,300	-	100	29,130	-	-	-	-	40,830	32,600
Special assessments	-	-	458,930	-	-	-	-	-	-	458,930	420,000
Notes	-	-	-	-	2,350	-	-	-	-	2,350	1,250
Loans	-	-	-	-	-	-	35,000	-	-	35,000	40,000
Accrued interest	50	25	1,907	-	650	-	2,666	-	-	5,298	3,340
Due from other funds	2,000	-	-	-	2,000	12,000	11,189	-	-	27,189	17,499
Due from other governments	30,000	75,260	-	640,000	-	-	-	-	-	745,260	101,400
Advances to internal service funds	65,000	-	-	-	-	-	-	-	-	65,000	75,000
Inventory of supplies, at cost	7,200	5,190	-	-	23,030	40,000	-	-	-	75,420	70,900
Prepaid expenses	-	-	-	-	1,200	-	-	-	-	1,200	900
Restricted assets:											
Cash	-	-	-	-	113,559	-	-	-	-	113,559	272,968
Investments, at cost or amortized cost	-	-	-	-	176,800	-	-	-	-	176,800	143,800
Land	-	-	-	-	211,100	20,000	-	1,259,500	-	1,490,600	1,456,100
Buildings	-	-	-	-	447,700	60,000	-	2,855,500	-	3,363,200	2,836,700
Accumulated depreciation	-	-	-	-	(90,718)	(4,500)	-	-	-	(95,218)	(83,500)
Improvements other than buildings	-	-	-	-	3,887,901	15,000	-	1,036,750	-	4,939,651	3,922,200
Accumulated depreciation	-	-	-	-	(348,944)	(3,000)	-	-	-	(351,944)	(283,750)
Machinery and equipment	-	-	-	-	1,841,145	25,000	-	452,500	-	2,318,645	1,924,100
Accumulated depreciation	-	-	-	-	(201,138)	(9,400)	-	-	-	(210,538)	(141,900)
Construction in progress	-	-	-	-	22,713	-	-	1,722,250	-	1,744,963	1,359,606
Amount available in debt service funds	-	-	-	-	-	-	-	-	256,280	256,280	284,813
Amount to be provided for retirement of general long-term debt	-	-	-	-	-	-	-	-	1,939,790	1,939,790	1,075,187
Amount to be provided from special assessments	-	-	-	-	-	-	-	-	458,930	458,930	420,000
Total Assets	$494,350	$224,860	$913,280	$1,299,200	$6,375,514	$184,800	$2,084,816	$7,326,500	$2,655,000	$21,558,320	$17,479,911

The notes to the financial statements are an integral part of this statement.

Adapted from *GASB Codification*, Section 2200.

EXHIBIT A (Continued)

Example 1 (Continued)

Liabilities and Fund Equity	Governmental Fund Types				Proprietary Fund Types		Fiduciary Fund Types	Account Groups		Totals (Memorandum Only)	
	General	Special Revenue	Debt Service	Capital Projects	Enterprise	Internal Service	Trust and Agency	General Fixed Assets	General Long-Term Debt	December 31, 19X2	December 31, 19X1
Liabilities:											
Vouchers payable	$118,261	$ 33,850	$ -	$ 49,600	$ 131,071	$ 15,000	$ 3,350	$ -	$ -	$ 351,132	$ 223,412
Contracts payable	57,600	18,300	-	119,000	8,347	-	-	-	-	203,247	1,326,511
Judgments payable	-	2,000	-	33,800	-	-	-	-	-	35,800	32,400
Accrued liabilities	-	-	-	10,700	16,870	-	4,700	-	-	32,270	27,417
Payable from restricted assets:											
Construction contracts					17,760					17,760	-
Fiscal agent					139					139	-
Accrued interest					32,305					32,305	67,150
Revenue bonds					48,000					48,000	52,000
Deposits					63,000					63,000	55,000
Due to other taxing units							680,800			680,800	200,000
Due to other funds	24,189	2,000		1,000						27,189	17,499
Due to student groups							1,850			1,850	1,600
Deferred revenue	15,000		555,000							570,000	423,000
Advance from general fund						65,000				65,000	75,000
Matured bonds payable			100,000							100,000	-
Matured interest payable			2,000							2,000	-
General obligation bonds payable					700,000				2,100,000	2,800,000	2,110,000
Special assessment debt with governmental commitment									555,000	555,000	420,000
Revenue bonds payable					1,798,000					1,798,000	1,846,000
Total Liabilities	215,050	56,150	657,000	214,100	2,815,492	80,000	690,700		2,655,000	7,383,492	6,876,989
Fund Equity:											
Contributed capital					1,392,666	95,000				1,487,666	815,000
Investment in general fixed assets								7,326,500		7,326,500	5,299,600
Retained earnings:											
Reserved for revenue bond retirement					129,155					129,155	96,975
Unreserved					2,038,201	9,800				2,048,001	1,998,119

(Continued)

EXHIBIT A (Continued)

Example 1 (Continued)

Liabilities and Fund Equity	Governmental Fund Types				Proprietary Fund Types		Fiduciary Fund Types	Account Groups		Totals (Memorandum Only)	
	General	Special Revenue	Debt Service	Capital Projects	Enterprise	Internal Service	Trust and Agency	General Fixed Assets	General Long-Term Debt	December 31, 19X2	December 31, 19X1
Fund Balances:											
Reserved for encumbrances	$ 38,000	$ 46,500	$ -	$1,076,500	$ -	$ -	$ -	$ -	$ -	$ 1,161,000	$ 410,050
Reserved for inventory of supplies	7,200	5,190	-	-	-	-	-	-	-	12,390	10,890
Reserved for advance to internal service funds	65,000	-	-	-	-	-	-	-	-	65,000	75,000
Reserved for loans	-	-	-	-	-	-	50,050	-	-	50,050	45,100
Reserved for endowments	-	-	-	-	-	-	134,000	-	-	134,000	94,000
Reserved for employees' retirement system	-	-	-	-	-	-	1,426,201	-	-	1,426,201	1,276,150
Unreserved:											
Designated for debt service	-	-	256,280	-	-	-	-	-	-	256,280	325,888
Designated for subsequent years' expenditures	50,000	-	-	-	-	-	-	-	-	50,000	50,000
Undesignated	119,100	117,020	-	8,600	-	-	(216,135)	-	-	28,585	106,150
Total Fund Equity	279,300	168,710	256,280	1,085,100	3,560,022	104,800	1,394,116	7,326,500	-	14,224,828	10,602,922
Total Liabilities and Fund Equity	$494,350	$224,860	$913,280	$1,299,200	$6,375,514	$184,800	$2,084,816	$7,326,500	$2,655,000	$21,558,320	$17,479,911

The notes to the financial statements are an integral part of this statement.

EXHIBIT A (Continued)

Example 2
Name of Governmental Unit
Combined Statement of Revenues, Expenditures, and Changes in Fund Balances—All Governmental Fund Types and Expendable Trust Funds
For the Fiscal Year Ended December 31, 19X2

	Governmental Fund Types				Fiduciary Fund Type	Totals (Memorandum Only) Year Ended	
	General	Special Revenue	Debt Service	Capital Projects	Expendable Trust	December 31, 19X2	December 31, 19X1
Revenues:							
Taxes	$ 881,300	$ 189,300	$ 79,177	$	$	$1,149,777	$1,137,900
Special assessments			55,500			55,500	250,400
Licenses and permits	103,000					103,000	96,500
Intergovernmental revenues	186,500	831,100	41,500	1,250,000		2,309,100	1,258,800
Charges for services	91,000	79,100				170,100	160,400
Fines and forfeits	33,200					33,200	26,300
Miscellaneous revenues	19,500	71,625	36,235	3,750	200	131,310	111,500
Total Revenues	1,314,500	1,171,125	212,412	1,253,750	200	3,951,987	3,041,800
Expenditures:							
Current:							
General government	121,805					121,805	134,200
Public safety	258,395	480,000				738,395	671,300
Highways and streets	85,400	417,000				502,400	408,700
Sanitation	56,250					56,250	44,100
Health	44,500					44,500	36,600
Welfare	46,800					46,800	41,400
Culture and recreation	40,900	256,450				297,350	286,400
Education	509,150				2,420	511,570	512,000
Capital outlay				1,939,100		1,939,100	803,000
Debt service:							
Principal retirement			115,500			115,500	52,100
Interest and fiscal charges			68,420			68,420	50,000
Total Expenditures	1,163,200	1,153,450	183,920	1,939,100	2,420	4,442,090	3,039,800
Excess of Revenues over (under) Expenditures	151,300	17,675	28,492	(685,350)	(2,220)	(490,103)	2,000
Other Financing Sources (Uses):							
Proceeds of general obligation bonds				900,000		900,000	-
Proceeds of special assessment debt				190,500		190,500	-
Operating transfers in				74,500	2,530	77,030	89,120
Operating transfers out	(74,500)					(74,500)	(87,000)
Total Other Financing Sources (Uses)	(74,500)			1,165,000	2,530	1,093,030	2,120
Excess of Revenues and Other Sources over (under) Expenditures and Other Uses	76,800	17,675	28,492	479,650	310	602,927	4,120
Fund Balances—January 1	202,500	151,035	227,788	605,450	26,555	1,213,328	1,209,208
Fund Balances—December 31	$ 279,300	$ 168,710	$ 256,280	$1,085,100	$ 26,865	$1,816,255	$1,213,328

The notes to the financial statements are an integral part of this statement.

EXHIBIT A (Continued)

Example 3
Name of Governmental Unit
Combined Statement of Revenues, Expenditures, and Changes in Fund Balances—Budget and Actual—General and Special Revenue Fund Types
For the Fiscal Year Ended December 31, 19X2

	General Fund			Special Revenue Funds			Totals (Memorandum Only)		
	Budget	Actual	Variance— Favorable (Unfavorable)	Budget	Actual	Variance— Favorable (Unfavorable)	Budget	Actual	Variance— Favorable (Unfavorable)
Revenues:									
Taxes	$ 882,500	$ 881,300	$ (1,200)	$ 189,500	$ 189,300	$ (200)	$1,072,000	$1,070,600	$ (1,400)
Licenses and permits	125,500	103,000	(22,500)	-	-	-	125,500	103,000	(22,500)
Intergovernmental revenues	200,000	186,500	(13,500)	837,600	831,100	(6,500)	1,037,600	1,017,600	(20,000)
Charges for services	90,000	91,000	1,000	78,000	79,100	1,100	168,000	170,100	2,100
Fines and forfeits	32,500	33,200	700	-	-	-	32,500	33,200	700
Miscellaneous revenues	19,500	19,500	-	81,475	71,625	(9,850)	100,975	91,125	(9,850)
Total Revenues	1,350,000	1,314,500	(35,500)	1,186,575	1,171,125	(15,450)	2,536,575	2,485,625	(50,950)
Expenditures:									
Current:									
General government	129,000	121,805	7,195	-	-	-	129,000	121,805	7,195
Public safety	277,300	258,395	18,905	494,500	480,000	14,500	771,800	738,395	33,405
Highways and streets	84,500	85,400	(900)	436,000	417,000	19,000	520,500	502,400	18,100
Sanitation	50,000	56,250	(6,250)	-	-	-	50,000	56,250	(6,250)
Health	47,750	44,500	3,250	-	-	-	47,750	44,500	3,250
Welfare	51,000	46,800	4,200	-	-	-	51,000	46,800	4,200
Culture and recreation	44,500	40,900	3,600	272,000	256,450	15,550	316,500	297,350	19,150
Education	541,450	509,150	32,300	-	-	-	541,450	509,150	32,300
Total Expenditures	1,225,500	1,163,200	62,300	1,202,500	1,153,450	49,050	2,428,000	2,316,650	111,350
Excess of Revenues over (under) Expenditures	124,500	151,300	26,800	(15,925)	17,675	33,600	108,575	168,975	60,400
Other Financing Sources (Uses):									
Operating transfers out	(74,500)	(74,500)	-	-	-	-	(74,500)	(74,500)	-
Excess of Revenues over (under) Expenditures and Other Uses	50,000	76,800	26,800	(15,925)	17,675	33,600	34,075	94,475	60,400
Fund Balances—January 1	202,500	202,500	-	151,035	151,035	-	353,535	353,535	-
Fund Balances—December 31	$ 252,500	$ 279,300	$ 26,800	$ 135,110	$ 168,710	$ 33,600	$ 387,610	$ 448,010	$ 60,400

The notes to the financial statements are an integral part of this statement.

EXHIBIT A (Continued)

Example 4
Name of Governmental Unit
Combined Statement of Revenues, Expenditures, and Changes in Retained Earnings/Fund Balances—All Proprietary Fund Types and Similar Trust Funds
For the Fiscal Year Ended December 31, 19X2

	Proprietary Fund Types		Fiduciary Fund Types		Totals (Memorandum Only) Year Ended	
	Enterprise	Internal Service	Nonexpendable Trust	Pension Trust	December 31, 19X2	December 31, 19X1
Operating Revenues:						
Charges for services	$ 672,150	$88,000	$ -	$ -	$ 760,150	$ 686,563
Interest	-	-	2,480	28,460	30,940	26,118
Contributions	-	-	-	160,686	160,686	144,670
Gifts	-	-	45,000	-	45,000	-
Total Operating Revenues	672,150	88,000	47,480	189,146	996,776	857,351
Operating Expenses:						
Personal services	247,450	32,500			279,950	250,418
Contractual services	75,330	400			75,730	68,214
Supplies	20,310	1,900			22,210	17,329
Materials	50,940	44,000			94,940	87,644
Heat, light, and power	26,050	1,500			27,550	22,975
Depreciation	144,100	4,450			148,550	133,210
Benefit payments				21,000	21,000	12,000
Refunds				25,745	25,745	13,243
Total Operating Expenses	564,180	84,750		46,745	695,675	605,033
Operating Income	107,970	3,250	47,480	142,401	301,101	252,318
Nonoperating Revenues (Expenses):						
Operating grants	55,000	-	-		55,000	50,000
Interest revenue	3,830	-	-		3,830	3,200
Rent	5,000	-	-		5,000	5,000
Interest expense and fiscal charges	(92,988)	-	-		(92,988)	(102,408)
Total Nonoperating Revenues (Expenses)	(29,158)	-	-		(29,158)	(44,208)
Income before Operating Transfers	78,812	3,250	47,480	142,401	271,943	208,110
Operating Transfers In (Out)			(2,530)		(2,530)	(2,120)
Net Income	78,812	3,250	44,950	142,401	269,413	205,990
Retained Earnings/Fund Balances—January 1	2,088,544	6,550	139,100	1,040,800	3,274,994	3,069,004
Retained Earnings/Fund Balances—December 31	$2,167,356	$ 9,800	$184,050	$1,183,201	$3,544,407	$3,274,994

The notes to the financial statements are an integral part of this statement.

EXHIBIT A (Continued)

Example 6
Name of Governmental Unit
Combining Balance Sheet—All Special Revenue Funds
December 31, 19X2

	Parks	State Gasoline Tax	Motor Vehicle License	Parking Meter	Juvenile Rehabilitation	Totals Year Ended December 31, 19X2	December 31, 19X1
ASSETS							
Cash	$39,525	$22,460	$ 5,420	$16,260	$17,720	$101,385	$ 91,459
Investments, at cost	16,200	-	-	15,000	6,000	37,200	25,000
Receivables:							
Taxes receivable—delinquent (net of allowance for uncollectibles of $500)	2,500	-	-	-	-	2,500	-
Accounts receivable (net of allowance for uncollectibles of $800)	3,300	-	-	-	-	3,300	2,700
Accrued interest	25	-	-	-	-	25	-
Due from state government	-	47,250	28,010	-	-	75,260	62,400
Inventory of supplies, at cost	1,100	990	702	1,066	1,332	5,190	5,190
Total Assets	$62,650	$70,700	$34,132	$32,326	$25,052	$224,860	$186,749
LIABILITIES AND FUND BALANCES							
Liabilities:							
Vouchers payable	$10,000	$11,220	$ 4,260	$ 3,220	$ 5,150	$ 33,850	$ 23,414
Contracts payable	12,500	4,000	-	1,800	-	18,300	12,300
Judgments payable	2,000	-	-	-	-	2,000	-
Due to general fund	2,000	-	-	-	-	2,000	-
Total Liabilities	26,500	15,220	4,260	5,020	5,150	56,150	35,714
Fund Balances:							
Reserved for encumbrances	14,000	16,500	10,000	500	5,500	46,500	12,550
Reserved for inventory of supplies	1,100	990	702	1,066	1,332	5,190	5,190
Unreserved	21,050	37,990	19,170	25,740	13,070	117,020	133,295
Total Fund Balances	36,150	55,480	29,872	27,306	19,902	168,710	151,035
Total Liabilities and Fund Balances	$62,650	$70,700	$34,132	$32,326	$25,052	$224,860	$186,749

EXHIBIT A (Continued)

Example 7
Name of Governmental Unit
Combining Statement of Revenues, Expenditures, and Changes in Fund Balances—All Special Revenue Funds
For the Fiscal Year Ended December 31, 19X2

	Parks	State Gasoline Tax	Motor Vehicle License	Parking Meter	Juvenile Rehabilitation	Totals Year Ended December 31, 19X2	December 31, 19X1
Revenues:							
Taxes	$189,300	$ -	$ -	$ -	$ -	$ 189,300	$ 168,400
Intergovernmental revenues	-	422,500	201,000	-	207,600	831,100	749,990
Charges for services	-	-	-	79,100	-	79,100	71,420
Miscellaneous revenues	70,700	-	-	600	325	71,625	63,614
Total Revenues	260,000	422,500	201,000	79,700	207,925	1,171,125	1,053,424
Expenditures:							
Public safety	-	-	199,400	80,900	199,700	480,000	414,040
Highways and streets	-	417,000	-	-	-	417,000	346,414
Culture and recreation	256,450	-	-	-	-	256,450	238,873
Total Expenditures	256,450	417,000	199,400	80,900	199,700	1,153,450	998,873
Excess of Revenues over (under) Expenditures	3,550	5,500	1,600	(1,200)	8,225	17,675	54,551
Fund Balances—January 1	32,600	49,980	28,272	28,506	11,677	151,035	96,484
Fund Balances—December 31	$ 36,150	$ 55,480	$ 29,872	$27,306	$ 19,902	$ 168,710	$ 151,035

EXHIBIT A (Continued)

Example 8
Name of Governmental Unit
Statement of Revenues, Expenditures, and Changes in Fund Balance—Budget and Actual—Parks Fund
For the Fiscal Years Ended December 31, 19X2 and 19X1

	19X2			19X1		
	Budget	*Actual*	*Variance—* *Favorable* *(Unfavorable)*	*Budget*	*Actual*	*Variance—* *Favorable* *(Unfavorable)*
Revenues:						
Taxes:						
Current	$189,000	$188,700	$ (300)	$170,000	$168,000	$(2,000)
Penalties and interest on						
delinquent taxes	500	600	100	500	400	(100)
Total Taxes	189,500	189,300	(200)	170,500	168,400	(2,100)
Miscellaneous Revenues:						
Rents and royalties	80,000	70,100	(9,900)	60,000	62,414	2,414
Interest and revenue	500	600	100	500	500	-
Total Miscellaneous						
Revenues	80,500	70,700	(9,800)	60,500	62,914	2,414
Total Revenues	270,000	260,000	(10,000)	231,000	231,314	314
Expenditures:						
Culture and Recreation:						
Supervision of parks	20,000	19,300	700	16,500	17,200	(700)
Parkways and boulevards	32,500	30,000	2,500	26,000	28,842	(2,842)
Park areas	129,050	122,850	6,200	120,000	122,432	(2,432)
Park lighting	33,300	29,850	3,450	28,000	26,414	1,586
Park policing	20,700	20,220	480	10,000	14,219	(4,219)
Forestry and nursery	36,450	34,230	2,220	30,500	29,312	1,188
Total Expenditures	272,000	256,450	15,550	231,000	238,419	(7,419)
Excess of Revenues over						
(under) Expenditures	(2,000)	3,550	5,550	-	(7,105)	(7,105)
Fund Balance—January 1	32,600	32,600	-	39,705	39,705	-
Fund Balance—December 31	$ 30,600	$ 36,150	$ 5,550	$ 39,705	$ 32,600	$(7,105)

EXHIBIT A (Continued)

Example 9
Name of Governmental Unit
Combining Statement of Changes in Assets and Liabilities—All Agency Funds
For the Fiscal Year Ended December 31, 19X2

	Balance January 1, 19X2	Additions	Deductions	Balance December 31, 19X2
Special Payroll Fund				
Assets				
Cash	$ 6,000	$ 40,900	$ 43,550	$ 3,350
Liabilities				
Vouchers payable	$ 6,000	$ 40,900	$ 43,550	$ 3,350
Property Tax Fund				
Assets				
Cash	$ 25,800	$ 800,000	$ 725,000	$100,800
Taxes receivable (net of allowance for uncollectibles)	174,200	1,205,800	800,000	580,000
Total Assets	$200,000	$2,005,800	$1,525,000	$680,800
Liabilities				
Due to Other Taxing Units:				
County	$180,000	$1,085,220	$ 652,500	$612,720
Special district	20,000	120,580	72,500	68,080
Total Liabilities	$200,000	$1,205,800	$725,000	$680,800
Student Activity Fund				
Assets				
Cash	$ 1,600	$ 1,900	$ 1,650	$ 1,850
Liabilities				
Due to student groups	$ 1,600	$ 1,900	$ 1,650	$ 1,850
Totals—All Agency Funds				
Assets				
Cash	$ 33,400	$ 842,800	$ 770,200	$106,000
Taxes receivable (net of allowance for uncollectibles)	174,200	1,205,800	800,000	580,000
Total Assets	$207,600	$2,048,600	$1,570,200	$686,000
Liabilities				
Vouchers payable	$ 6,000	$ 40,900	$ 43,550	$ 3,350
Due to other taxing units	200,000	1,205,800	725,000	680,800
Due to student groups	1,600	1,900	1,650	1,850
Total Liabilities	$207,600	$1,248,600	$ 770,200	$686,000

EXHIBIT B **Selected Statistics and Ratios**

	General	Special Revenue	Debt Service	Capital Projects	Enterprise	Interest Service	Trust and Agency	General Fixed Assets Account Group	General Long-Term Debt Account Group	19X2	19X1	Change
Current Assets	494,350	224,860	913,280	1,299,200	605,755	81,700	2,084,816	0	0	5,703,961	4,710,355	993,606
Current Liabilities	215,050	56,150	657,000	214,100	317,492	80,000	690,700	0	0	2,230,492	2,500,989	(270,497)
Current Ratio	2.30	4.00	1.39	6.07	1.91	1.02	3.02	ERR	ERR	2.56	1.88	0.67
Debt to Assets	0.44	0.25	0.72	0.16	0.44	0.43	0.33	0.00	1.00	0.34	0.39	−0.05

DISCUSSION QUESTIONS

1. How do governments differ from businesses and private nonprofit organizations? What are the relationships between these three types of organizations?

2. Who are the users and what are the uses of financial reports of governments?

3. To what extent do different users need different types of information? Different types of reports?

4. What is the current status of government accounting and financial reporting in the U.S.?

5. How does standard setting for governments differ from that of businesses and private nonprofit organizations?

6. Discuss the relationship between a government and the economy of the area it governs. Should there be separate financial reporting for each, and, if so, how and why should they differ?

7. How do effective accounting systems and financial reporting contribute to managing government?

8. Explain the nature and purpose of budgetary and encumbrance accounting. Should governments be required to use them?

9. How is the governmental reporting entity determined? What are the implications of an incorrectly defined governmental reporting entity?

10. What funds and account groups do governments use? How do they differ from those used by private nonprofit organizations?

11. Discuss the differences between the three levels of audits, and the likely effects of the single audit act on financial and compliance auditing.

12. Why is it important to measure government performance? Why is it difficult?

13. Discuss the difference between output and outcome measures.

14. How does federal government accounting and financial reporting differ from that of state and local governments?

Cases

CASE STUDIES

Case 18.1 is a disguised version of the financial statements of a typical U.S. city. Review it and the text to analyze Wabash's financial condition. (Please note that the data for cities other than Wabash are also disguised.) Case 18.2, a fictitious case, enables you to practice assigning transactions to the appropriate funds or account groups for government organizations.

CASE 18.1 Wabash

Bob Carleton, mayor of Wabash, raised his eyes from his notes and looked wearily across the conference table at the three city council members. It was past midnight and the council had been in session all day trying to grapple with what appeared to be an inordinate shortfall in revenues for the 1988 budget. From Mayor Carleton's calculations, a 15 percent to 25 percent budget cut could be in order. He doubted whether taxes could be raised because there had been a recall attempt two years ago when the council proposed the last property tax increase. Budget cutting would also be difficult because the council members were also elected heads of the city departments.

BACKGROUND

Wabash, situated in coastal Georgia on the Savannah River, is a major manufacturing center in the South. Until recently, it had enjoyed a diversified manufacturing base and strong government employment by a major regional authority's headquarters.

In the past decade, employment had been below the state and national averages. In 1987 it rose from 7.6 percent to 12.3 percent because the recession had taken a

Research Assistant James E. Hass and Professor Regina E. Herzlinger prepared this case.

Copyright © 1991 by the President and Fellows of Harvard College. Harvard Business School case 182-248. Revised January 1993.

severe toll on the auto-related manufacturing and other heavy industry that were a major presence in Wabash. The virtual closing down of the nuclear power plant industry, which was a major source of skilled employment in Wabash, exacerbated the unemployment problem. Finally, the reduction in federal aid to counties and cities had reduced government employment (see **Table 1**).

TABLE 1   **Employment Data for Wabash, Georgia**

Unemployment

Year	Wabash SMSA	State of Georgia	U.S.
1987	12.2%	7.8%	9.7%
1985 (January-July)	7.6	7.2	7.1
1984	5.8	5.8	5.8
1983	5.5	5.8	6.0
1982	6.1	6.3	7.0
1981	5.5	6.0	7.7

Estimated Nonagricultural Employment (July 1985) Wabash SMSA

	Number		Percentage	
Total	**168,300**		**100.0%**	
Manufacturing	50,000		30.0	
Durable goods		21,200		12.6
Nondurable goods		29,200		17.4
Nonmanufacturing	47,300		28.1	
Mining		1,400		0.8
Construction		6,600		3.9
Transportation, community, and public utilities		7,200		4.3
Trade	32,100		19.1	
Wholesale trade		8,600		5.1
Retail trade		23,500		14.0
Finance, insurance, and real estate	9,800		5.8	
Service	29,000		17.2	
Government	31,800		18.9	
Federal		9,600		5.7
State and local		22,200		13.2

Population

Year	Count
1955	131,041
1965	130,009
1975	169,000
1980	241,000
1985	235,000

The stagnant economy was reflected in decreasing retail sales, per-family income, property values, property tax bases (if plants closed and land was vacant), the ability of households to pay taxes on their property, and revenues from sales taxes. Moreover, the recession made it difficult for the city council to justify adding user charges or other fees to compensate for the revenue shortfall.

CITY GOVERNMENT

Although many other medium-sized cities had a city manager type of organization, Wabash continued to have city councilors who were elected at large to operate specific departments (see **Table 2**).

As with many cities that adopted the populist initiatives at the turn of the century, Wabash had incorporated recall, a referendum, and initiative into its city charter. Because its city council could not meet privately, developing strategies for dealing with the current budget situation became more difficult.

In some governments, the mayor independently develops the budget and is responsible for its execution through a chief administrator. In these, the city council votes primarily as an advisory body to approve the budget. In Wabash, the mayor has much less power because the other city commissioners manage their own departments, prepare the budget, and administer its implementation. Wabash's weak mayoral system of government gave Bob Carleton no independent power to approve and initiate budget or legislative acts, or to control spending in individual departments.

The county in which Wabash was located was governed by nine commissioners. The elected county executive was the chief administrative officer. The county government was charged with health services, human services, public works, and finance responsibilities. There was some overlap of services between the city and the county, particularly in the elementary and secondary education systems. The city's school board was autonomous from the city government, although nearly half the city budget was devoted to education. Its funding came from the state government and directly

TABLE 2 **City Council**

Commissioner Crockett	Commissioner Boone	Mayor Carleton	Commissioner Rhenquist
Department of Public Works	Department of Public Safety	Department of Finance and Administration	Department of Human Services and Economic Development
—Sewers	—Fire department	—Attorney	—Welfare
—Garbage collection	—Police department	—Clerk	—Employment and
—Highway department	—Crossing guards	—Treasurer	social services
—Recreation department	—Maintenance shop		—Economic developments
—Airport			• grants
—Golf course			• planning
—Docks			

transferred from the city to the school board upon receipt. The school enrollment was 40,159 and declining in the city, and 31,253 in the county school system. The county had a population of 650,000, including the population of Wabash. Its assessed property value was $518 million, while Wabash's topped $1 billion.

BUDGETARY TRENDS

Fiscal 1987's budget of $176,250,000 was only slightly increased from the previous year's expenditures, reflecting the zero-growth approach the city council had been taking toward increases in government expenditures. In 1986, users were charged for the municipal golf course and a few police officers were removed in order to keep expenditures in line with revenues.

Between 1970 and 1979 the budget's annual growth rate was 10 percent. Although some of the growth reflected increases in the city's population, on a per-capita basis, the budget still increased (see **Table 3**).

Tax Structure

The city had increased taxes to compensate for lost federal funds and maintain a constant level of services. Property taxes increased substantially in the early 1970s, remained level until 1984, then, in 1985, increased to $43 million from $31 million the year before. This raise prompted the recall effort that year.

In 1972, total revenues were 4.7 percent of family income. By 1985, with cuts in federal aid to cities and the high unemployment in Wabash, total revenues were a slightly lower 4.4 percent of family income, with locally raised funds 2.4 percent of family income. The national average is 10 percent taxes to income (see **Table 4**).

TABLE 3 **City of Wabash: Revenues by Source 1970-1987 ($ in millions)**

	1970-71	1979-80	1986-87	Per Capita 1985 National Average, Cities with 150,000-250,000 Population[a]
Total Revenue	$62.3	$155.2	$159.6	NA
Intergovernmental	31.6	96.3	92.3	NA
State	14.8	31.7	41.0	$ 53.19
Federal	4.9	36.6	20.1	37.50
Local	4.8	27.8	31.1	NA
Own Source	30.6	58.8	67.0	268.00
Property Tax	9.7	29.0	42.0	125.99
Sales Tax	2.8	11.8	8.0	77.94
User Charges	16.2	12.4	12.0	17.12
Miscellaneous	1.8	5.9	3.0	46.96

[a]*Trends in the Fiscal Condition of Cities*, Joint Economic Committee, 97th Congress (Washington GPO).

TABLE 4 **Property Tax**

	Rate per $100 of Valuation
Wabash	$2.56
Tyler County (within Wabash)	2.42
Combined rate	4.98
Byran County	2.90
Chatham County	1.07
Liberty County	2.08
McIntosh County	0.57

Property tax was levied on property at 50 percent of appraised value for utilities, 40 percent for commercial and industrial sites, and 25 percent for residential housing and farms. There was a 1.75 percent local sales tax and a 4.5 percent state sales tax. There was no income tax in the state.

Expenditures

Over the past decade, the allocation of city funds to various departments had changed substantially. While in 1970 public works expenditures were 28 percent of the city budget, by 1987 they had declined to 18 percent. Administrative activities gradually increased their share of the budget, from 11 percent of the budget to 15 percent, accounted for by increases in the number of administrative personnel, in pension and fringe benefit accounts, and in interest payments on the city's debt.

Social service and economic development spending was about 1.5 percent of the budget, rose to 7 percent, and recently had declined to 1970 levels. It was expected to drop even lower in the next few years. Police and fire expenditures grew from 11 percent of the budget to 15 percent. They then went through a period of decline to about 13 percent of the budget in 1980, but recently had increased faster than any other component of the budget. The Department of Public Safety represented about 21 percent of the city's budget.

Capital outlays had been on a roller coaster in Wabash for the past two decades. Outlays for maintaining and improving the capital stock of the sewers, streets, utilities, housing, and educational facilities in Wabash were $6.3 million in 1970, $10 million in 1974, rose to $23 million in 1979, and dropped to $10 million in 1984. Some of the increase in the early seventies corresponded to the increase in the city's population: per-capita capital outlays were $48 in 1976, $84 in 1978, $142 in 1979, and in 1984 were $60 per person. As in many other cities, Wabash had been able to maintain a balanced operating budget by delaying some capital outlays.

Comparison to Other Cities

Mayor Carleton asked his aide to compile statistics on cities with characteristics similar to Wabash in population sizes, manufacturing bases, and average incomes. He identified four cities that fell into the same general range as Wabash on all of these measures and compared the trends in their revenues and program expenditures over the last decade.

	Population	Rank in: Manufacturing	Income
1. Wilmington, DE	72	87	52
2. Wichita, KS	93	121	43
3. Springfield, MA	69	72	158
4. Richmond, VA	61	166	226
5. Wabash, GA	92	57	210

As shown in **Table 5**, Wabash is consistently in the middle of the group during the early part of the decade, then decreases the rate of growth in spending in the latter part of the decade. Wabash and Springfield, Massachusetts, have similar spending patterns, with 1974 per-capita revenues of $404 and $385 respectively. By 1984, Springfield was leading Wabash with $837 per person, compared to $728 per person.

Revenues raised from their own sources do not show such close correlation among these cities (see **Table 6**). By 1984 Wabash raised the least funds per capita from its own sources of all the cities. While Wabash raised its $189 per capita in 1974 to $250 per capita in 1984, the national average had increased from $172 per capita to $352 per capita. Richmond, Virginia, increased its per-capita local taxation from $353 in 1974 to $695 in 1984.

TABLE 5 **Per-Capita General Revenues**

	1974-75	1979-80	1983-84	1985-86
National averages, cities 200,000-300,000 population	$246	$432	$ 589	
Wilmington, DE	775	907	766	
Wichita, KS	190	325	538	
Springfield, MA	385	646	837	
Wabash, GA	404	679	728	$737
Richmond, VA	542	938	1,136	

TABLE 6 **Per-Capita, Own-Source Revenues**

	1974-75	1979-80	1983-84
National average	$172	$256	$352
Wilmington, DE	510	580	537
Wichita, KS	114	215	372
Springfield, MA	265	328	468
Wabash, GA	189	257	250
Richmond, VA	353	569	695

Comparisons of expenditures for specific functions showed no consistent patterns. For example, Wabash was lowest for the five cities in urban development and housing expenditures per capita, spending only $2 per person in 1984 compared to an average of $25 per capita in the other cities. Police and fire outlays per capita ranged from Wilmington's high of $118 to Wichita's low of $31. Wabash was near the lower end with per-capita police and fire protection budgets in the $40 range (see **Table 7**).

An important difference between the cities was the amount of debt per capita. Three of the cities—Wilmington, Wichita, and Richmond—had debt levels of over $1,100 per person, while Springfield and Wabash had debt levels of $300 to $400 per capita.

The Budget Development Process

Wabash's budget development process began in March with the budget office sending each department a form showing current expenditures by line item and requesting that the department heads (commissioners) estimate the funds needed for the next fiscal year. Because the department heads were also the city commissioners, they were aware of the budget strains in the city and had in recent years requested only nominal increases in their departmental budgets.

The budget officer received the request forms back in mid-April, and compiled them into an initial budget request. At about the same time he received estimates of property, income, and sales tax revenues from the county tax assessor and the state finance department. He also attempted to estimate the amount of federal funding that the city would receive.

In early May, the officer presented the estimate of revenues and requests for funds to the city council. In previous years the discrepancy between revenues and expenditures had been small, and the council members had made the adjustment by allocating the budget cuts proportionally to each department.

TABLE 7 **Per-Capita Expenditures for Various Functions**

1984	U.S.	Wilmington	Wichita	Springfield	Wabash	Richmond	1985 National Average, Cities Between 150K-250K Population
1. Police	$58	$ 116	$ 31	$ 71	$ 45	$ 56	$ 78
2. Fire	32	100	25	76	38	43	51
3. Parks and recreation	24	31	25	30	18	37	NA
4. Sewers and highway	80	68	118	46	75	188	NA
5. Urban renewal	25	85	8	10	2	51	NA
6. Debt	NA	1,348	1,989	300	361	1,428	352[a]

[a]Data for general purposes. Enterprise fund debt is excluded.

Current Situation

This year, however, the fall in revenues was the largest ever incurred. In addition, several considerable increases in expenditures had been requested. A deficit of $25 to $40 million would result unless serious measures were considered. The magnitude of the conflict had forced the city to consider alternative ways of allocating the cuts, and the budget officer had already requested that department heads resubmit lower budget estimates. These changes are reflected in the current estimates (**Table 8**).

Revenues were to decrease $17 million when compared to the prior year's budget, caused by the $11 million decrease in federal aid; a $5 million reduction in state aid to education because of the declining school enrollment ($4 million); and lower sales tax collections caused by the recession ($1 million). Property taxes were also decreasing from declining housing prices and the shrinking tax base caused by several plant closings.

The major increases in expenditures, totaling $21 million, were accounted for by a $7 million increase in the public works budget to increase maintenance and rebuild major sewer connections in the city. The previous year the city engineer's office found major deterioration on three key sewer arteries and recommended that repairs and rebuilding begin immediately. In addition, $5 million additional funds were needed by the school district to meet increased teacher salaries. Six million dollars in additional funds were requested by the police and fire departments to meet cost-of-living increases. Finally, $3 million in additional funds were requested by the city administrative department to meet pension obligations, to increase interest payments, and to allow for fringe benefits increases.

TABLE 8 **Budgets**

	1986-87	1987-88
Revenues	176	159
Intergovernmental:	108	92
State	46	41
Federal	31	20
County	31	31
Own Source:	68	67
Property	43	42
Sales	8	8
User charges	12	12
Miscellaneous	3	3
Expenditures	176	197
Education	81	86
Public safety	33	39
Public works	38	45
Human services and economic development	4	4
Finance and administration	20	23
Revenue shortfall	0	38

THE MAYOR'S ALTERNATIVES

Mayor Carleton was considering what instructions to give the city council to help them decide which departments should absorb the $33 million budget cut. This year it seemed that a new procedure for balancing the budget would be needed.

Mayor Carleton also knew that similar strains would be put on the city's budget in future years. He felt that the process that the council used to develop the lower budget requests in the next few weeks should be the foundation for a better method of spending public funds in the future. He was considering two alternative budgeting processes.

One alternative was to have the department heads each develop zero-based budgets for their departments, and the city council would then rank the decision package to set priorities for the various activities of the government. He would suggest that each department prepare ten decision packages based on what programs the departments would cut for each 10 percent cut in the budget. His second alternative was to have the department heads structure their departments into cost and profit centers and submit proposals to reduce costs and to produce revenues through user fees.

Finally, he wanted the council members' ideas for how the council would decide on specific revenue and expenditure items. He asked that they recess until the morning and then present their opinions. If the council could not decide on a viable process for allocating the cuts, Mayor Carleton had decided to support an initiative (proposed by the local Chamber of Commerce, the Wabash Bar Association, and several other civic groups) to change the form of government from the commission-mayor structure to a city council-city manager organization. He was convinced that the problems facing the city were so serious that the current form of government might not be effective to meet the challenge. But he would wait until the morning before telling the other commissioners about his decision.

ASSIGNMENT

1. Use the data in the case and the financial statements in **Exhibits 1** through **9** to assess the severity of the financial crisis in Wabash. Cold, flu, or pneumonia?
2. How should Mayor Carleton deal with the revenue shortfall? Be specific in your recommendations and develop a short-run and long-run action plan.

EXHIBIT 1 **Combined Statement of Revenues—General and Special Revenue Funds for the Fiscal Year Ended June 30, 1987**

	Estimated	Actual	Surplus (deficit)
Taxes:			
General fund	$ 40,887	$ 41,963	$ 1,074
Licenses and permits:			
General fund	2,723	2,797	73
Special fund	162	178	89
Total	$ 2,885	$ 2,975	$ 37
Receipts for use of facilities:			
General fund	30	34	4
Special fund	722	755	33
Total	$ 752	$ 789	$ 37
Intergovernmental revenues:			
General fund	80,503	81,331	767
Special fund	17,951	35,182	15,230
Total	$100,514	$116,513	$15,997
Interest revenues:			
General fund	1,230	3,314	2,083
Special fund	0	818	818
Total	$ 1,230	$ 4,132	$ 2,648
Miscallaneous:			
General fund	3,585	4,090	505
Special fund	2,878	3,583	705
Total	$ 6,463	$ 7,673	$ 1,210
Total Revenues	$152,739	$174,056	$21,721

EXHIBIT 2   **Combined Statement of Governmental Expenditures and Encumbrances Compared with Appropriation General and Special Revenue Funds for the Fiscal Year Ending June 30, 1987**

	Budget Appropriation	Actual Expenditures	Encumbrances June 30, 1987	Total
General Government:				
General fund	$ 23,783	$ 23,376	$ 107	$ 23,483
Special fund	3,230	1,472	81	1,553
Total	$ 27,013	$ 24,848	$ 188	$ 25,036
Public Safety:				
General fund	22,371	22,270	99	22,369
Special fund	923	1,382	393	1,775
Total	$ 23,294	$ 23,652	$ 492	$ 24,144
Public Works:				
General fund	17,221	17,028	99	17,127
Special fund	4,021	10,253	393	10,646
Total	$ 21,242	$ 27,281	$ 492	$ 27,773
Public Welfare				
General fund	4,193	3,902	2	3,903
Special fund	3,712	10,854	85	16,941
Total	$ 7,905	$ 20,756	$ 87	$ 20,844
Education:				
General fund	65,307	65,307	-	65,307
Special fund	11,124	11,075	299	11,374
Total	$ 76,431	$ 76,382	$ 299	$ 76,681
Total Expenditures and Encumbrances:	$155,891	$172,931	$4,045	$176,978

EXHIBIT 3 **Internal Service Funds Combined Balance Sheet, June 30, 1987**

	Total All Funds	Municipal Service Station	Public Works Garage
Assets			
Current Assets:			
Cash (overdrafts)	$(384,788)	$(296,151)	$ (88,227)
Due from other funds	273,344	108,875	164,469
Accounts receivable	1,622	1,622	-
Inventories of materials and supplies	425,697	55,250	370,447
Total Current Assets	$ 316,285	$(130,404)	$446,689
Fixed Assets:			
Buildings	$ 422,208	$ 7,500	$414,708
Machinery and equipment	83,342	48,216	35,126
	$ 505,550	$ 55,716	$449,834
Less—accumulated depreciation	23,404	12,313	11,091
Net fixed assets	$ 482,146	$ 43,404	$438,743
Total Assets	$ 798,431	$ (87,001)	$885,432
Liabilities and Retained Earnings			
Current Liabilities:			
Due to other funds	$ 1,151	$ 147	$ 1,004
Accounts payable and accrued liabilities	27,993	10,353	17,640
Total Current Liabilities	$ 29,144	$ 10,500	$ 18,644
Contribution from general fund	717,512	-	717,512
Retained earnings (deficit)	41,738	(98,169)	139,907
Reserve for encumbrances	10,037	668	9,369
Total Liabilities and Retained Earnings	$ 798,431	$ (87,001)	$885,432

EXHIBIT 4 **Internal Service Funds—Municipal Service Station Fund Statement of Operations and Retained Earnings for the Fiscal Year Ended June 30, 1987**

Revenues	
Billings to departments	$1,166,089
Other	32,720
Total Revenues	$1,198,809
Less: Costs of Services Rendered	
Cost of Materials Used	
Inventory—July 1, 1979	$ 44,705
Purchases—gasoline, oil, kerosene, lubricants, etc.	1,270,879
	$1,315,584
Inventory—June 30, 1980	55,250
Total Cost of Materials Used	$1,260,334
Other Operating Costs	
Salaries and wages	$ 112,564
Other services, rentals, and allowances	1,378
Office and administrative expenses	840
Vehicle repairs, operations, and maintenance	15,355
Buildings and grounds repairs and maintenance	67
Insurance and bonds	132
Materials and supplies	2,282
Depreciation	5,197
Total Other Operating Costs	$ 137,815
Total Cost of Services Rendered	$1,398,149
Excess of Expenses over Revenues	$ 199,340
Retained Earnings—July 1, 1986	115,328
Prior Period Adjustments:	
Fixed assets purchased in prior years	7,500
Errors on prior year's encumbrances and payables	(13,368)
Errors on prior year's accounts receivable	(1,173)
Depreciation recorded on prior year's fixed asset purchases	(7,116)
Retained Earnings (deficit)—June 30, 1987	$ (98,169)

EXHIBIT 5   **Internal Service Funds—Public Works Garage Fund Statement of Operations and Retained Earnings for the Fiscal Year Ended June 30, 1987**

Revenues	
Billings to departments	$1,856,470
Other	591
Total Revenues	$1,857,061
Less: Costs of Services Rendered	
Cost of Materials Used	
Inventory—July 1, 1986	$ 508,053
Purchases	749,761
	$1,257,814
Inventory—June 30, 1987	370,447
Total Cost of Materials Used	$ 887,367
Other Operating Costs	
Salaries and wages	$ 717,591
Services, rentals, and allowances	107,195
Office and administrative expenses	4,863
Buildings and grounds repairs and maintenance	15,548
Materials and supplies	32,609
Insurance and bonds	1,098
Depreciation	8,339
Total Other Operating Costs	$ 887,243
Total Cost of Services Rendered	$1,774,610
Excess of Revenues over Costs	$ 82,451
Retained Earnings—July 1, 1986	59,813
Prior Period Adjustments:	
Depreciation recorded on prior year's fixed asset purchases	(2,752)
Cancellation of prior year's encumbrances	8
Errors on prior year's encumbrances and payables	387
Retained Earnings—June 30, 1987	$ 139,907

EXHIBIT 6 **Combined Balance Sheet—All Funds, June 30, 1987**

	General Fund	Debt-Service Fund	Special Funds	Internal Service Funds	Bond Funds	Trust and Other Funds	Electric Power Board	General Pension Plan	General Long-Term Debt	General Fixed Assets
Assets										
Cash on hand and in bank	$ 1,168,802	$ 471,444	$ 760,348	$(384,378)	$1,245,120	$390,579	$ 590,000	$ 63,474	-	$ -
Investments	7,355,000	3,075,000	12,883,527	-	1,172,000	8,150	20,540,000	10,551,613		
Dividends and interest receivable							10,238,000	147,155		
Receivables—customer service										
Accounts receivable	284,209	1,632	1,958,984	1,622		16,100	846,000	897,994		
Notes receivable								30,899		
Taxes receivable	1,855,361									
Due from other funds	3,077,805		7,571,165	273,344		58,183				
Due from other governments	3,110,255									
Inventories	483,145		686,541	425,697			1,607,000			
Fixed assets—net after depreciation				482,146			85,512,000			
Land										23,041,279
Buildings										124,451,089
Vehicles and machinery										24,052,392
Improvements										942,963
Work in progress										8,354,476
Amount provided for retirement of bonds and interest									3,548,076	
Amount provided for retirement of bonds and interest									49,946,924	
Other										
	$17,334,547	$3,548,076	$23,860,565	$ 798,431	$2,417,120	$473,012	$119,651,000	$11,691,135	$53,495,000	$180,842,199

(Continued)

EXHIBIT 6 (Continued)

	General Fund	Debt-Service Fund	Special Funds	Internal Service Funds	Bond Funds	Trust and Other Funds	Electric Power Board	General Pension Plan	General Long-Term Debt	General Fixed Assets
Liabilities, Reserves, and Fund Balances										
Liabilities:										
Accounts payable and accrued liabilities	$ 371,978	$ -	$ 3,835,032	$ 27,993	$ 11,010	$270,837	$ 23,702,000	$ 9,724	$ -	$ -
Due to custodian for trustees of pension plans	781,259	-	-	-	-	-	-	-	-	-
Due to other funds	5,149,929	-	4,952,538	1,151	584,324	292,255	1,607,000	-	-	-
Customers' deposits	-	-	-	-	-	-	3,999,000	-	-	-
Long-term debt	-	-	-	-	-	-	-	-	-	-
Bonded indebtedness—future maturities	-	-	-	-	-	-	-	-	53,495,000	-
	$ 6,303,166	$ -	$ 8,787,870	$ 29,144	$ 595,334	$563,092	$ 29,308,000	$ 9,724	$53,495,000	$ -
Reserves and Balances:										
Reserve for encumbrances	$ 215,263	$ -	$ 4,248,193	$ 10,037	$ 135,442	$ 190	$ -	$ -	$ -	$ -
Reserve for taxes receivable	1,855,361	-	-	-	-	-	-	-	-	-
Reserve for inventories	483,145	-	686,541	-	-	-	-	-	-	-
Reserve for unemployment compensation	-	-	310,139	-	-	-	-	-	-	-
Reserve for accounts receivable	-	-	-	717,512	-	-	-	-	-	-
Contribution from General Fund	-	-	-	-	-	-	439,000	-	-	-
Net assets available for benefits	-	-	-	-	-	-	-	11,681,411	-	-
Retained earnings	-	-	-	41,738	-	-	89,904,000	-	-	-
Investment in general fixed assets	-	-	-	-	-	-	-	-	-	180,842,199
Fund balances	9,477,612	3,548,076	9,827,822	-	1,686,344	(90,270)	-	-	-	-
	$11,031,381	$3,548,076	$15,072,695	$ 769,287	$1,821,786	$ (90,080)	$ 90,343,000	$11,681,411	$ -	$180,842,199
	$17,334,547	$3,548,076	$23,860,565	$ 798,431	$2,417,120	$473,012	$119,651,000	$11,691,135	$53,495,000	$180,842,199

Note: The accompanying notes are an integral part of this statement.

EXHIBIT 7 **Statement of Changes in General Fixed Assets—By Source for the Fiscal Year Ended June 30, 1987**

	Total	Land and Buildings	Vehicle and Machinery	Improvements	Work-in-Progress
General Fixed Assets—July 1, 1986	$174,216,457	$146,754,939	$22,746,070	$937,928	$3,777,520
Additions					
Expenditures from:					
General fund	$ 57,963	$ -	$ 52,927	$ 5,036	$ -
Special funds:					
Education	2,325,253	1,044,865	277,428	-	1,003,060
Capital projects	3,894,365	230,615	765,122	-	2,898,628
Other	563,464	4,656	558,808	-	-
Bond funds	815,659	136,002	4,389	-	675,268
Total Additions	$ 7,656,804	$ 1,416,138	$ 1,658,674	$ 5,036	$4,576,956
Deductions					
Fixed assets abandoned, sold, and traded in	$ 1,031,062	$ 678,710	$ 352,352	$ -	$ -
General Fixed Assets—June 30, 1987	$180,842,199	$147,492,367	$24,052,392	$942,964	$8,354,476

The Notes to Financial Statements are an integral part of this statement.

EXHIBIT 8 **Statements of Changes in Net Assets Available for Benefits Years Ended June 30, 1987 and 1986**

Balance—Beginning	$ 9,810,738	$7,909,141
Additions:		
Investment income		
Investments sold during year	$ 41,112	$ 44,172
Investments held at year end	(73,688)	134,377
Interest	517,469	322,435
Dividends	281,573	248,177
	$ 766,466	$ 749,161
Contributions:		
Employer	$ 1,527,043	$1,556,921
Employees	298,062	225,180
Refunds to terminated employees	(56,497)	(38,148)
Reinstatement of prior service (Note 3)	20,777	117,936
Other income:		
Interest on notes receivable from employees	2,821	982
Total Additions	$ 2,558,672	$2,612,032
Deductions:		
Benefits paid	$ 664,621	$ 687,590
Administrative expenses	23,378	22,845
Total Deductions	$ 687,999	$ 710,435
Net Additions	1,870,673	1,901,597
Balance—End of Year	$11,681,411	$9,810,738

The Notes to Financial Statements are an integral part of this statement.

EXHIBIT 9 **General Pension Plan Notes to Financial Statements—June 30, 1987**

Note 1—Description of the Plan

The Pension Plan is a defined benefit plan which provides for a normal retirement benefit payable for life of 60 percent average earnings during the highest three years before retirement minus 50 percent of the primary Social Security benefit, all of which is reduced pro rata for each year of credited service less than twenty-five (25) years.

Special provisions cover early retirement, disability retirement, and death before and after retirement.

Employee contributions are 2 percent of earnings subject to Social Security and 5 percent of earnings not subject to Social Security tax. The balance of the cost of benefits is borne by the City.

On November 7, 1978, the voters of the City approved a resolution which significantly amended the Plan, the principal changes being:

1. Effective February 1, 1979, all permanent employees who were previously excluded (hourly employees and those hired over age 55) may join the Plan. All permanent employees hired after that date must join the Plan as a condition of employment.
2. Any permanent employee as of February 1, 1979, who elected to participate could also choose to deposit to the Pension Fund an amount determined to be sufficient to obtain credit for prior service.
3. Monthly benefits for pensioners who reached age 65 will increase each year beginning in 1980 reflecting the annual change in the cost-of-living index, subject to a maximum increase in any year of 3 percent of the benefits paid in the previous year.
4. The period for amortizing the unfunded past service liability was extended to thirty (30) years from December 31, 1978.

Note 2—Acturial Valuation

An actuarial valuation of the Plan was prepared as of January 1, 1987. The actuarial method used in the valuation of liabilities for all benefits is the entry age normal method. The present value of vested benefits as of the valuation date is as follows:

Present value of vested benefits for:

Terminated vested employees	$ 64,278
Retired employees	6,957,859
Active vested employees	11,283,211
Total	$18,305,348

In accordance with Section 3 of the Plan, the City is required to contribute 9 percent of payroll plus additional amounts necessary to finance the unfunded

EXHIBIT 9 (Continued)

past service liability over thirty (30) years from December 31, 1978. The past service liability as of January 1, 1987, was as follows:

Total past service liability	$18,654,581
Less—Trust fund assets (20 percent of market value, plus 80 percent of book value)	10,272,366
Unfunded past service liability	$ 8,382,215

The changes since the last valuation (January 1, 1986) in actuarial assumptions for valuation of liabilities are as follow:

(1)   Interest rate changed from 4 percent to 6 percent
(2)   Salary scale changed from 3 percent to 6 percent
(3)   Mortality table changed from 1960 Group Annuity to 1970 Group Annuity

Note 3—Reinstatement of Prior Service

In accordance with amendments to the Plan (Note 1), various employees elected to deposit to the Fund amounts sufficient to obtain credit for prior service. The employees were given the option of paying the past costs in cash or to make notes for periods up to a five-year maximum, the employees to become vested in the Plan upon the full payment of the notes and interests thereon.

CASE 18.2 The Mayfair School System

(1) In the beginning of the year, the Mayfair School District budgeted estimated revenues of $1,007,000 and appropriations of $850,000 for operating expenses and $150,000 for other expenditures.

(2) At the end of the year, the actual revenues were $1,008,200; actual expenses were:

Operating expenses:	
Administration	$ 24,950
Instruction	601,800
Other	221,450
Debt service from current funds (principal and interest)	130,000
Capital outlays (equipment)	22,000

(3) At the end of the year, the general fund's cash account consisted of $47,250; the taxes receivable were $31,800, with an estimated loss of $1,800; the inventory of supplies was $11,450; and there were temporary investments of $11,300.

(4) At the end of the year, the general fund owed the intragovernmental fund $950 for the services of the machine shop.

(5) The local government unit gave the school district 20 acres of land to be used for a new grade school and a community playground. The estimated value of the land donated was $50,000. In addition, a state grant of $300,000 was received, and the full amount was used to pay for the construction of the grade school. Purchases of classroom and playground equipment costing $22,000 were paid from general funds. The building was worth $1,300,000.

(6) Five years ago a 4 percent ten-year bond was issued in the amount of $1,000,000 for constructing school buildings. Interest on the issue is payable at maturity. Budgetary requirements of an annual contribution of $90,000 and accumulated earnings to date aggregating $15,000 were accounted for in separate Debt Service Fund accounts. The total amount available to repay the debt at the beginning of the year was $420,000.

(7) Outstanding purchase orders for operating expenses not recorded in the accounts at year end were:

Administration	$1,000
Instruction	1,200
Other	600
Total	$2,800

ASSIGNMENT

Prepare Balance Sheets for the General Fund and the Long-Term Debt and Fixed Asset Groups as of the end of the year.

Professor Regina E. Herzlinger adapted this case from an AICPA examination.

Index